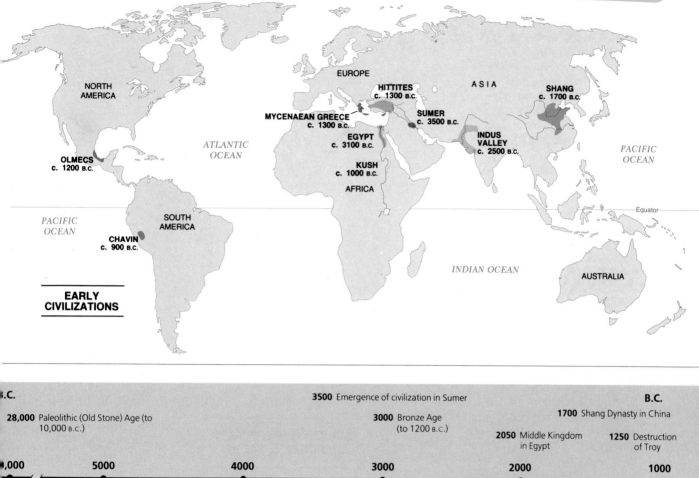

EUROPE

ASIA

NORTH
AMERICA

HITTITES
c. 1300 B.C.

SHANG
c. 1700 B.C.

MYCENAEAN GREECE
c. 1300 B.C.

SUMER
c. 3500 B.C.

ATLANTIC
OCEAN

EGYPT
c. 3100 B.C.

INDUS
VALLEY
c. 2500 B.C.

PACIFIC
OCEAN

OLMECS
c. 1200 B.C.

KUSH
c. 1000 B.C.

AFRICA

Equator

PACIFIC
OCEAN

SOUTH
AMERICA

CHAVIN
c. 900 B.C.

INDIAN OCEAN

AUSTRALIA

**EARLY
CIVILIZATIONS**

B.C.		**3500** Emergence of civilization in Sumer		**B.C.**
28,000 Paleolithic (Old Stone) Age (to 10,000 B.C.)		**3000** Bronze Age (to 1200 B.C.)		**1700** Shang Dynasty in China
			2050 Middle Kingdom in Egypt	**1250** Destruction of Troy
,000	**5000**	**4000**	**3000**	**2000**	**1000**

7000 Neolithic (New Stone) Age (to 3000 B.C.)

2370 Akkadian Empire in Sumer

1122 Chou Dynasty in China

2500 Rise of civilization in Indus valley

10,000 Mesolithic Age (to 7000 B.C.)

2700 Old Kingdom in Egypt— Pyramid Age

1760 Babylonian Empire

This map, like the others that follow, is designed to show historical relationships from a global perspective. More precisely, it delineates the major societies that coexisted within a specific time frame and engaged in cultural exchanges.

As the Time Line above makes clear, societal evolution has been *accelerating*. After hundreds of thousands of years, the food-gathering Paleolithic Age yields to the Mesolithic, followed relatively quickly by the food-producing Neolithic Age. Next comes the first of four riverine civilizations, which evolved independently. Great urban societies on the Tigris-Euphrates and Nile were linked by the Fertile Crescent, and cultural exchanges also took place with the Indus Valley civilization. Developing along the Huang Ho, China was geographically most distant from the other civilizations, so that cultural exchanges with civilizations to the west were minimal.

During the second millenium B.C. Indo-European tribes migrated into India (Indo-Aryans), Anatolia (Hittites), and the Mediterranean (Greeks, Romans). Civilizations also evolved in the Americas, but much later and independently. A similar evolutionary sequence—food gathering, food producing, and urban civilizations—occurred, it too marked by increasing societal complexity.

What has happened to the four riverbank civilizations shown in the preceding map? Chinese society has expanded to the Yangtse River. The Indus Valley civilization has disappeared, but numerous Indo-Aryan states have now arisen in the Ganges plain. Land in the Tigris-Euphrates valleys have been annexed by the Persians, who also control a declining Egyptian civilization.

The Mediterranean lands have become much more significant. Phoenician cities flourish on the east coast and Carthage in North Africa. Especially important are Athens and other city-states in Greece, about to enter into a deadly struggle with expansionist Persia. In Italy are two more Indo-European peoples: the Etruscans and a still small but virile city-state, the newly created Republic of Rome.

Iron-making techniques have spread into sub-Sahara Africa. An iron-age culture existed at Nok, while in the upper Nile valley flourished the kingdom of Kush. Stone-age peoples still inhabit most of the New World. During the Formative period of Mesoamerican culture (to A.D. 150) the Olmecs are prominent in the Gulf Coast plain of Mexico, while early Mayan villages are developing in the lowlands.

NORTH AMERICA

ATLANTIC OCEAN

OLMECS   MAYAS

Equator

PACIFIC OCEAN

SOUTH AMERICA

MAJOR STATES AND EMPIRES, c. 500 B.C.

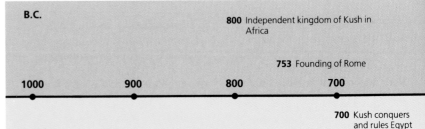

B.C.				
			800 Independent kingdom of Kush in Africa	
				753 Founding of Rome
1000	**900**	**800**	**700**	
				700 Kush conquers and rules Egypt

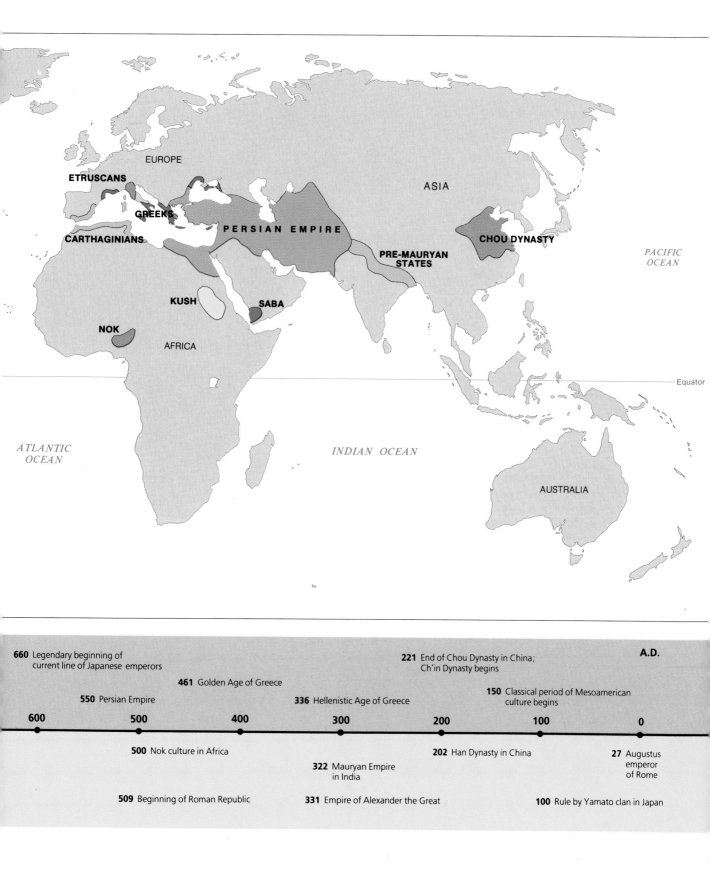

EUROPE

ETRUSCANS

GREEKS

CARTHAGINIANS

PERSIAN EMPIRE

ASIA

CHOU DYNASTY

PACIFIC OCEAN

PRE-MAURYAN STATES

KUSH

SABA

NOK

AFRICA

ATLANTIC OCEAN

Equator

INDIAN OCEAN

AUSTRALIA

660 Legendary beginning of current line of Japanese emperors

221 End of Chou Dynasty in China; Ch'in Dynasty begins

A.D.

461 Golden Age of Greece

550 Persian Empire

336 Hellenistic Age of Greece

150 Classical period of Mesoamerican culture begins

| 600 | 500 | 400 | 300 | 200 | 100 | 0 |

500 Nok culture in Africa

202 Han Dynasty in China

27 Augustus emperor of Rome

322 Mauryan Empire in India

509 Beginning of Roman Republic

331 Empire of Alexander the Great

100 Rule by Yamato clan in Japan

The most prominent development in this era is the growth of the Roman world-state, by A.D. 200 at the height of its power and prosperity. Its diverse lands and peoples surround the entire Mediterranean Sea, extending from Britain to Mesopotamia and from the Baltic Sea well into Africa. Rome's most dangerous rival, the Parthian Empire, lies immediately to Rome's east. Parthian nomads had wrested a large portion of the old Persian Empire and for several hundred years managed to withstand Roman power. East of Parthia is the Kushan Empire, which stretches to the Indus River. To the east of the Kushan Empire lie the far-flung territories of the Han Dynasty in China. The suzerainty and dynamic economy of the Han stretch southward well into Southeast Asia. Tenuous trade routes commercially unite the vast Eurasian landmass. The silk route stretches overland across Parthian and Kushan territory, while sea routes link the Roman world with India, Ceylon, Southeast Asia, and China. In Africa Axum has supplanted the kingdom of Kush, while in the New World Mesoamerican civilizations are now well established in Central America and in the Central Andes of South America.

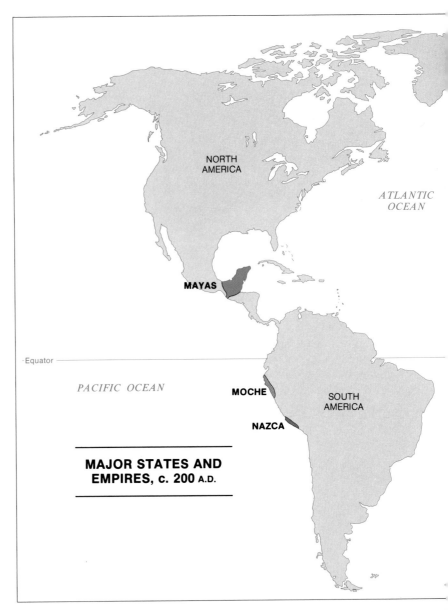

MAJOR STATES AND EMPIRES, c. 200 A.D.

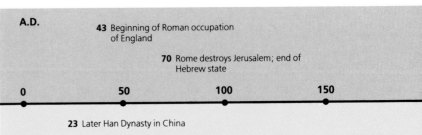

A.D.

43 Beginning of Roman occupation of England

70 Rome destroys Jerusalem; end of Hebrew state

0   50   100   150

23 Later Han Dynasty in China

96 Beginning of reigns of Five Good Emperors of Rome

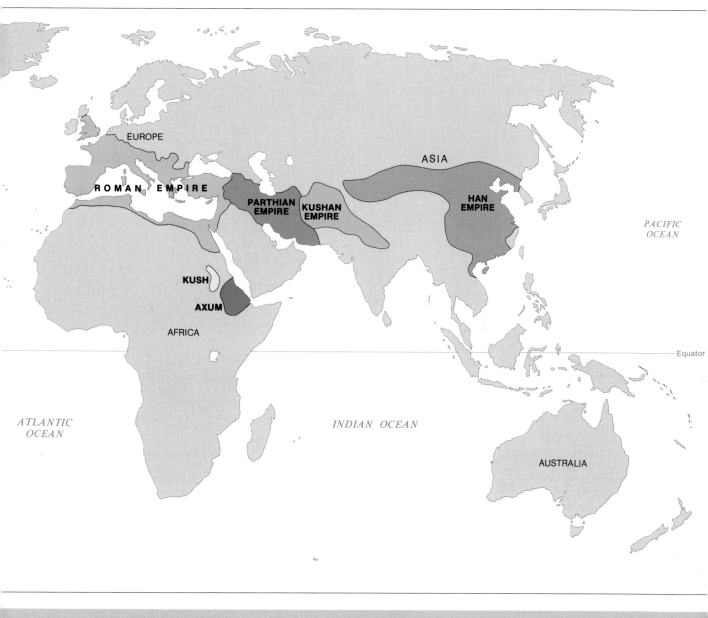

EUROPE

ASIA

ROMAN EMPIRE

PARTHIAN
EMPIRE

KUSHAN
EMPIRE

HAN
EMPIRE

PACIFIC
OCEAN

KUSH

AXUM

AFRICA

Equator

ATLANTIC
OCEAN

INDIAN OCEAN

AUSTRALIA

A.D.

200 Funan dominates border states of
Southeast Asia

330 Founding of Constantinople

476 Traditional date of
fall of Roman Empire

220 Fall of Later Han Dynasty in China
Collapse of Kushan state in India

378 Visigoths defeat Romans at Battle
of Adrianople

| 200 | 250 | 300 | 350 | 400 | 450 | 500 |

320 Chandra Gupta I establishes
Gupta Empire in India

481 Clovis I becomes
ruler of small
Frankish kingdom

300 Rise of Ghana in Africa

395 Theodosius I divides Roman
Empire between his two sons

The global map has altered markedly during the past 600 years. The western portion of the Roman world-state has disappeared, while the eastern part is now the Byzantine Empire. In what was Roman Gaul, Charlemagne has just created the new but unstable Carolingian Empire. Flanking the Byzantine Empire to the north is another unstable coalition, one formed by Bulgarian warbands. The area between the Black and Caspian seas is the domain of the Khazars, a steppe people notable for facilitating trade between East and West.

The most spectacular changes in the world map have been wrought by the triumph of Islam. The Abbasid Caliphate dominates the Middle East, and new Muslim kingdoms have appeared in North Africa and Spain. The most notable state in Africa is Ghana on the upper Niger. In the New World, Mayan civilization has reached its apogee, while in the Peruvian highlands have arisen the kingdoms of Huari and Tiahuanaco.

In northern India are numerous states, including the Rashtrakuta, Pratihara, and Pala kingdoms. China is now ruled by the T'ang, one of the greatest dynasties in its history. Chinese influence has extended eastward to the flourishing independent states in Korea and Japan.

MAJOR STATES AND EMPIRES, c. 800 A.D.

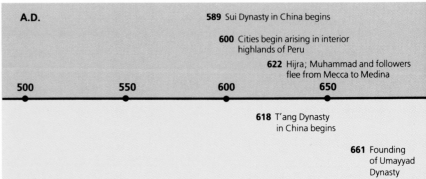

A.D.

589 Sui Dynasty in China begins

600 Cities begin arising in interior highlands of Peru

622 Hijra; Muhammad and followers flee from Mecca to Medina

500   550   600   650

618 T'ang Dynasty in China begins

661 Founding of Umayyad Dynasty

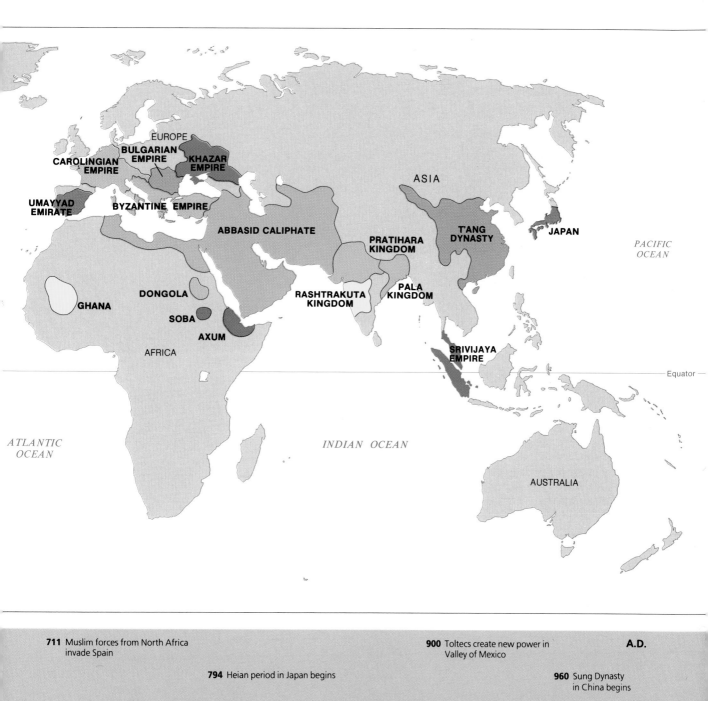

EUROPE

BULGARIAN
EMPIRE

CAROLINGIAN
EMPIRE

KHAZAR
EMPIRE

ASIA

UMAYYAD
EMIRATE

BYZANTINE EMPIRE

ABBASID CALIPHATE

T'ANG
DYNASTY

JAPAN

PACIFIC
OCEAN

PRATIHARA
KINGDOM

GHANA

DONGOLA

RASHTRAKUTA
KINGDOM

PALA
KINGDOM

SOBA

AXUM

AFRICA

SRIVIJAYA
EMPIRE

Equator

ATLANTIC
OCEAN

INDIAN OCEAN

AUSTRALIA

711 Muslim forces from North Africa
invade Spain

900 Toltecs create new power in
Valley of Mexico

A.D.

794 Heian period in Japan begins

960 Sung Dynasty
in China begins

700   750   800   850   900   950   1000

800 Charlemagne crowned emperor;
peak of power of Frankish state
and Carolingian Empire

910 *Reconquista*; Christians begin
reclaiming Spain from Muslims

750 Beginning of Abbasid
Dynasty; high tide of Islamic
power and civilization

907 Last T'ang emperor deposed

The Islamic world now straddles North Africa while its grasp of Eurasian territory reaches from the Iberian Peninsula eastward into India, where in 1206 Muslim forces penetrated the Punjab and established the Delhi Sultanate. In Southeast Asia the Khmer Empire is the dominant state and the kingdom of Srivijaya is the chief power in the Indonesian archipelago.

The central and northern portions of Eurasia are about to be engulfed by the Mongols, a warlike, nomadic people from the Asian interior. The Mongols eventually conquered China, overwhelmed the Muslim states in central Asia, invaded Europe, and for a time threatened the West.

The European powers of this era included the Holy Roman Empire and the new nation-states of France and England, which will come to dominate Western politics. At the beginning of the thirteenth century, Ghana fell to Mali, a new African Islamic kingdom that reached from the Atlantic to the upper Niger. The Aztecs of Mesoamerica migrated to the valley of Mexico, where they will create a powerful empire, as will the Incas, who by 1250 had conquered Tiahuanaco and other mountain tribes in the Peruvian Andes.

MAJOR STATES AND EMPIRES, c. 1200

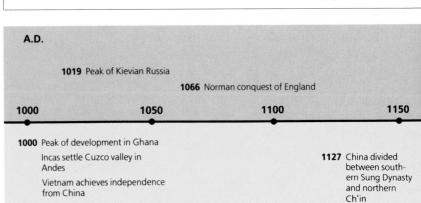

A.D.

1019 Peak of Kievian Russia

1066 Norman conquest of England

| 1000 | 1050 | 1100 | 1150 |

1000 Peak of development in Ghana

Incas settle Cuzco valley in Andes

Vietnam achieves independence from China

Kingdom of Kanem in Africa

1127 China divided between southern Sung Dynasty and northern Ch'in

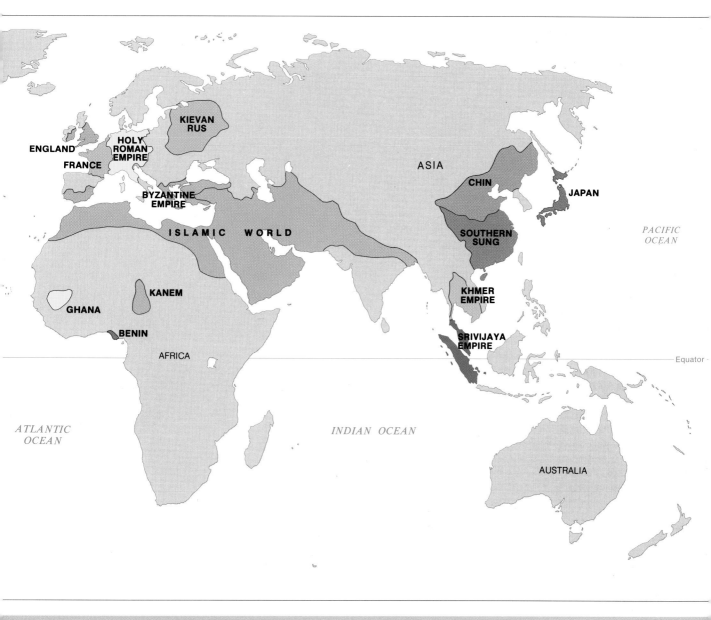

ENGLAND

HOLY ROMAN EMPIRE

FRANCE

KIEVAN RUS

BYZANTINE EMPIRE

ISLAMIC WORLD

ASIA

CHIN

JAPAN

SOUTHERN SUNG

KHMER EMPIRE

KANEM

GHANA

BENIN

AFRICA

SRIVIJAYA EMPIRE

ATLANTIC OCEAN

INDIAN OCEAN

PACIFIC OCEAN

Equator

AUSTRALIA

1185 Kamakura shogunate in Japan

1281 Japan stops Mongol invasion

A.D.

1200 Peak of Khmer Empire in Southeast Asia
Kingdom of Benin in Africa

1392 Yi Song-gye founds Yi Dynasty in Korea

1336 Ashikaga shogunate in Japan

1200   **1250**   **1300**   **1350**   **1400**

1206 Delhi Sultanate established
Mongol leader Temujin recognized as Genghis Khan

1300 Aztec confederacy in Mexico

1368 Ming Dynasty established in China

1348 Black Death sweeps Europe

1275 Marco Polo at court of Kublai Khan

1215 Magna Carta

Between the fourteenth and seventeenth centuries, Asian superiority gradually waned before the rising technical and commercial strength of the West. This shift was largely due to the European's discovery of the New World and their opening of sea lanes to all continents. But in 1500 Europe was far from dominant.

China has been reunited under the Ming and will expand into Mongolia and Annam (Vietnam). Torn by civil war, Japan will be reunited and also invade Korea. The weak Delhi Sultanate is about to be invaded by Babur, who will lay the foundation for the luxurious Mughul Empire in India.

Important new actors on the political stage include the Ottomans, whose empire will eventually touch three continents. The expanding Duchy of Moscow is paving the way for Russia's vast Eurasian empire. Explorers from Spain and Portugal are creating overseas colonial empires for the Iberian powers.

The African kingdoms of the era are the Bantu states of Zimbabwe in the southern highlands, Kongo near the Congo estuary, Benin in what is now Nigeria, and Songhai in the western Sudan. In the New World, the Aztecs in Mexico and the Incas in South America are flourishing, unaware of their impending destruction at the hands of the Spanish *conquistadores*.

MAJOR STATES AND EMPIRES, c. 1500

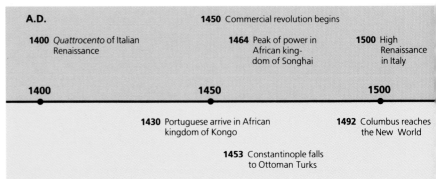

A.D.			
		1450 Commercial revolution begins	
1400 *Quattrocento* of Italian Renaissance		**1464** Peak of power in African kingdom of Songhai	**1500** High Renaissance in Italy
1400	**1450**		**1500**
	1430 Portuguese arrive in African kingdom of Kongo		**1492** Columbus reaches the New World
		1453 Constantinople falls to Ottoman Turks	

RUSSIA

POLAND-
LITHUANIA

HOLY
ROMAN
EMPIRE

ENGLAND

FRANCE

PORTUGAL SPAIN

OTTOMAN
EMPIRE

ASIA

JAPAN

PACIFIC
OCEAN

MAMLUKS

DELHI
SULTANATE

MING
DYNASTY

SONGHAI

KANEM-
BORNU

ETHIOPIA

BENIN

AFRICA

Equator

KONGO

ATLANTIC
OCEAN

ZIMBABWE

INDIAN OCEAN

AUSTRALIA

1527 Beginning of Mughul Empire in
India

1531 Pizzaro conquers Peru

1588 Spanish Armada defeated

1603 Tokugawa shogunate in Japan

A.D.

1644 Manchus invade Ming China;
establish Ch'ing Dynasty

1550   1600   1650   1700

1517 Luther issues ninety-five theses

1519 Cortés arrives in Mexico

1520 Ottoman power peaks under
Suleiman the Magnificent
(1520-66)

1613 Michael Romanov establishes
Romanov Dynasty in Russia

1628 Mughul Empire reaches height
under Shah Jahan (1628–58)

1637 Japan expels all Europeans

1688 Glorious Revolution
in England

When we contrast this map with its predecessors, we see a marked expansion of "civilized" areas at the expense of vestigial primitive societies. This map further demonstrates cartographically European dominance at the beginning of the nineteenth century. The economic dynamics set in motion by the Industrial Revolution created in Europe an insatiable appetite for raw materials and opened vast new markets for finished good.

The British Empire now stretches over five continents with British colonial settlements in northern North America, Africa (Cape Colony), Asia (India), and Australia. In 1800 Napoleon's victories establish French rule over Egypt, and in 1830 France will invade Algeria in northern Africa. The Netherlands is spreading its control in Southeast Asia, and Spain rules the Philippines. Meanwhile, Russia has consolidated its control over northern Eurasia.

Isolated by choice from the West are Japan under the Tokugawa Shogunate and China ruled by the Ch'ing (Manchu) Dynasty. A number of independent states still dot Africa, but unexplored lands remain in much of the African interior as well as in Australia, in the northern latitudes of North America, and in South America, including the Amazon basin.

MAJOR WORLD STATES AND COLONIAL POSSESSIONS, 1800

- France
- Great Britain
- Batavian Republic (The Netherlands)
- Portugal
- Spain
- Other independent states

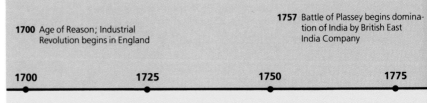

1700 Age of Reason; Industrial Revolution begins in England

1757 Battle of Plassey begins domination of India by British East India Company

1700　　　1725　　　1750　　　1775

1775 American Revolution begins

ICELAND
(DENMARK)

NORWAY
(DENMARK)

SWEDEN

BATAVIAN
REPUBLIC

DENMARK

RUSSIAN EMPIRE

GREAT
BRITAIN

PRUSSIA

AUSTRIAN
EMPIRE

FRANCE

OTTOMAN EMPIRE

BLACK SEA

CASPIAN SEA

CHINA
(CH'ING DYNASTY)

JAPAN
(Tokugawa
Shogunate)

PORTUGAL   SPAIN

MEDITERRANEAN SEA

MOROCCO   ALGIERS   TUNIS

PERSIA

PACIFIC
OCEAN

TRIPOLI

EGYPT
(FRANCE)

RED SEA

MARATHA
CONFEDERACY

NEPAL

BURMA

FULANI
STATES

KANEM-
BORNU

ARABIAN
SEA

SIAM

PHILIPPINE
ISLANDS

SEGU

HAUSA
STATES

Bay of
Bengal

SOUTH
CHINA
SEA

ASANTE   OYO

ETHIOPIA

BUGANDA

Equator

DUTCH EAST INDIES

OMANI
SUPREMACY

ATLANTIC
OCEAN

KINGDOM OF
IMERINA

NEW
SOUTH
WALES

INDIAN OCEAN

CAPE
COLONY

1788 First English colony
in Australia

1829 Greece achieves independence
from Turkey

1898 Spanish-American
War

1789 French Revolution begins;
U.S. Constitution adopted

1822 Brazil achieves
independence

1859 Darwin publishes
Origin of Species

1894 Sino-Japanese
War begins

1800   **1825**   **1850**   **1875**   **1900**

1804 Napoleon declares
himself emperor

1830 July Revolution in Paris
enthrones Louis Philippe

1885 French gain control over
Indochina

1848 *Communist Manifesto*
published

1815 Napoleon defeated,
exiled to St. Helena

1899 Boer War
begins

1854 Japan opens ports to the West

Events of the nineteenth century further increased European hegemony over the world. The map of Africa shows the most notable effects. In 1870 only 10 percent of the continent was under direct European control. By 1900 most independent African states have disappeared, and the major European nations have divided the continent among themselves as they go about expanding their colonial empires.

In the Western Hemisphere, Canada has confederated and Latin America has thrown off Spanish and Portuguese rule to evolve into a collection of independent states. The United States, on the verge of becoming a great power, has begun acquiring a colonial empire, annexing both Alaska and the Philippines.

An emergent Eastern power is Japan, which annexed Formosa in 1895 and Korea in 1910. The Western powers and Japan have taken advantage of China's internal weakness to wrest both trading ports and economic concessions. Elsewhere in Asia, the Dutch, German, French, and British still claim colonial possessions.

Several important geopolitical coalitions exist among the nations of Europe; these are the military alliances that will precipitate World War I.

MAJOR WORLD STATES AND COLONIAL POSSESSIONS, 1900

- Belgium
- France
- German Empire
- Great Britain
- Italy
- The Netherlands
- Portugal
- Spain
- United States
- Other independent states

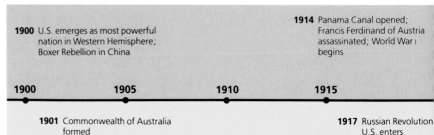

1900 U.S. emerges as most powerful nation in Western Hemisphere; Boxer Rebellion in China

1914 Panama Canal opened; Francis Ferdinand of Austria assassinated; World War I begins

1900 — 1905 — 1910 — 1915

1901 Commonwealth of Australia formed

1917 Russian Revolution U.S. enters World War I

1909 Union of South Africa formed

1918 Armistice ends World War I

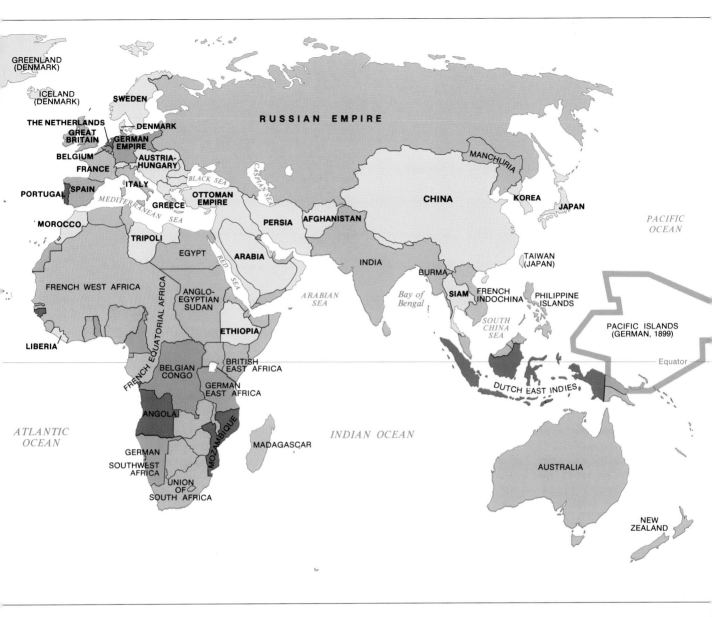

GREENLAND (DENMARK)

ICELAND (DENMARK)

SWEDEN

THE NETHERLANDS
GREAT BRITAIN
DENMARK
GERMAN EMPIRE
BELGIUM
AUSTRIA-HUNGARY
FRANCE
ITALY
PORTUGAL SPAIN
MOROCCO
GREECE
OTTOMAN EMPIRE
PERSIA
AFGHANISTAN

RUSSIAN EMPIRE

MANCHURIA

CHINA

KOREA

JAPAN

TAIWAN (JAPAN)

PACIFIC OCEAN

BLACK SEA
CASPIAN SEA
MEDITERRANEAN SEA

TRIPOLI
EGYPT
ARABIA
RED SEA

INDIA

BURMA

FRENCH INDOCHINA
SIAM
PHILIPPINE ISLANDS

FRENCH WEST AFRICA
ANGLO-EGYPTIAN SUDAN
ARABIAN SEA
Bay of Bengal
SOUTH CHINA SEA

PACIFIC ISLANDS (GERMAN, 1899)

LIBERIA
ETHIOPIA

FRENCH EQUATORIAL AFRICA
BELGIAN CONGO
BRITISH EAST AFRICA
GERMAN EAST AFRICA

Equator

DUTCH EAST INDIES

ATLANTIC OCEAN

ANGOLA
MOZAMBIQUE

INDIAN OCEAN

MADAGASCAR

GERMAN SOUTHWEST AFRICA
UNION OF SOUTH AFRICA

AUSTRALIA

NEW ZEALAND

1922 Union of Soviet Socialist Republics established; Mussolini marches on Rome

1933 Hitler becomes dictator of Germany

1929 Stock market crash in U.S.; worldwide depression

1939 Germany invades Poland; World War II begins

| 1920 | 1925 | 1930 | 1935 | 1940 | 1945 | 1950 |

1919 Paris Peace Conference; League of Nations created; Third Communist International (Comintern) formed

1927 Stalin takes power in Russia; Chiang Kai-shek purges Communists from China

1931 Spain becomes republic; Japan invades Manchuria

1936 Mussolini conquers Ethiopia; Spanish civil war begins

1941 Japanese attack Pearl Harbor; U.S. enters World War II

1945 Germany surrenders; Hiroshima, Nagasaki bombed, Japan surrenders; World War II ends

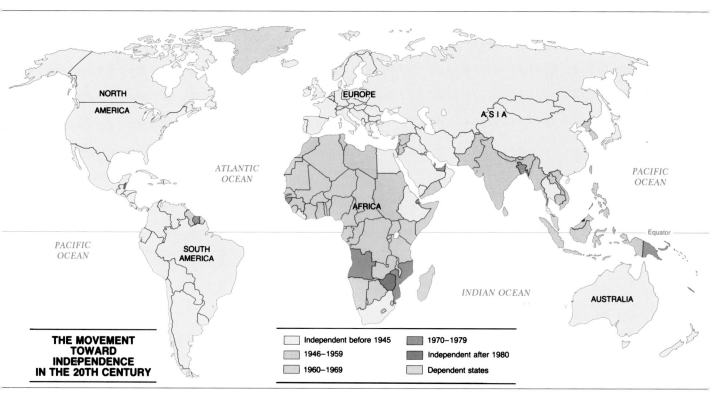

NORTH AMERICA

EUROPE

ASIA

ATLANTIC OCEAN

PACIFIC OCEAN

AFRICA

PACIFIC OCEAN

SOUTH AMERICA

Equator

INDIAN OCEAN

AUSTRALIA

THE MOVEMENT TOWARD INDEPENDENCE IN THE 20TH CENTURY

- Independent before 1945
- 1946–1959
- 1960–1969
- 1970–1979
- Independent after 1980
- Dependent states

The twentieth century has been called "The Age of Global Civilization"—a characterization compatible with the astronauts' pictures showing an indivisible sphere swimming in space. A global economy links the nations of the world, and daily we are made aware of shared dangers to our planetary environment.

The most striking geopolitical development of the twentieth century has been the liquidation of empires, replaced by scores of new independent nation-states. This occurrence is most evident in Africa, but the twentieth century has also seen the emergence of new nations in Asia, India, the Far East, and South America. Today there are more states—about 180—than ever before in history.

In the bipolar world of the twentieth century, competing ideologies, racial tensions, and disparities between rich and poor lands are some of the conditions bedeviling international relations. As the twenty-first century nears, humankind is slowly acquiring a new self-awareness: of interrelatedness among all its members, and no less with other forms of life compromising the ecology of the planet.

Civilization
Past & Present

Seventh Edition

Civilization
Past & Present

Seventh Edition

Volume II Since 1648

T. WALTER WALLBANK
Emeritus, University of Southern California

ALASTAIR M. TAYLOR
Emeritus, Queen's University

NELS M. BAILKEY
Emeritus, Tulane University

GEORGE F. JEWSBURY
Oklahoma State University

CLYDE J. LEWIS
Emeritus, Eastern Kentucky University

NEIL J. HACKETT
Director, Oklahoma State University—Kyoto, Japan

HarperCollins*Publishers*

Executive Editor: Bruce Borland
Development Editor: Betty Slack
Project Coordination, Text and Cover Design: PC&F, Inc.
Cover/Photo: Blaeu Wall Map, The British Library
Photo Researcher: Sandy Schneider
Production Manager: Michael Weinstein
Compositor: PC&F, Inc.
Printer and Binder: Von Hoffmann Press
Cover Printer: The Lehigh Press, Inc.

For permission to use copyrighted material, grateful acknowledgment is made to the copyright holders on pp. C1–C3, which are hereby made part of this copyright page.

Civilization Past & Present, Seventh Edition
Copyright © 1992 by HarperCollins Publishers Inc.

Library of Congress Cataloging-in-Publication Data

Civilization, past & present / T. Walter Wallbank . . . [et al.]. — 7th
  ed.
       p.   cm.
    Includes bibliographical references and indexes.
    ISBN 0-673-38868-9 (v. I)
    ISBN 0-673-38869-7 (v. II)
    1. Civilization.   I. Wallbank, T. Walter (Thomas Walter), 1901–
.   II. Title: Civilization, past & present.
  CB69.C564   1991
  909—dc20   91-25406
                                                          CIP

93 94 9 8 7 6 5 4

Brief Contents

*Each chapter ends with a Conclusion, Suggestions for Reading, and notes.

Epilogue

Toward the Twenty-First Century *E1*

Chronological Tables *T1*

Credits *C1*

Index *I1*

Reference Maps *M1*

Retrospective/Prospective, 1942–1992

> *Of making many books there is no end; and much study is a weariness of the flesh.*
>
> *Ecclesiastes 12:12*

Authors and publishers can attest to the truth of the first part of this maxim; students will wholeheartedly endorse the second part! But this essay is about the making of only one book and how it came to chronicle historical events on a global scale. *Civilization Past & Present* was the first American college text to undertake the challenge to record the evolution of humanity from earliest times to the present. Today, half a century and seven editions later, its mission continues.

Genesis

A half century ago, when the book was conceived, the world was at war. The year 1940 witnessed the Nazi conquest of Western Europe and the Battle of Britain, while 1941 was marked by Hitler's invasion of Soviet Russia and Japan's attack on Pearl Harbor, immediately followed by the spread of war throughout the Pacific. By 1942, millions of Americans were in uniform, and shipyards and factories were turning out a vast armada of ships, planes, and tanks. Hollywood continued to produce movies, many with war themes; radio brought Jack Benny's jokes and Bing Crosby's songs into city apartments and country farmhouses; and college students across the country danced to the music of Glenn Miller and Artie Shaw. Television was still in the experimental stage, and the electronic computer had yet to be invented.

Conflict and carnage continued until, by 1945, the United States and its allies had destroyed Hitler's Berlin bunker, annihilated Hiroshima, and marked the end of history's most lethal war by creating the United Nations. On every continent people longed and worked for a new era of peace and prosperity in a world which would never again be the same.

This book grew out of a survey course offered at the University of Southern California. That course's purpose was to offer all students, whether in arts or commerce or engineering, a clearer idea of how the world in which they lived came to be. The textbook was planned when the totalitarian governments in Europe and Asia were bent on conquest, yet the majority of Americans still endeavored to insulate themselves from participating in, or accepting the consequences of, world events. Many believed it possible to rely on the geographical protection of oceans, on the Monroe Doctrine, and the tradition of "no foreign entanglements." This widespread attitude was reflected in the limitation of most college survey courses to Western culture.

In the face of such historical egocentrism, the authors believed that the United States was about to embark on a new role of world leadership, one which would require having an informed citizenry for its successful execution. To become so informed, students needed to learn about the great culture systems of the world, their historical antecedents, and those current trends and problems which were shaping the course of contemporary world affairs. To meet this need, the authors of *Civilization Past & Present* undertook to describe the significant factors in the evolution not only of Western civilization but also of the Middle East, Africa, South Asia, China, Japan, and Latin America. It was a large challenge, and the result proved to be innovative and unique.

Basic Approach and Structure

It has been said that the most difficult task in writing any book is conceiving and structuring the table of contents. What should be included? What must be left out? How should the parts be arranged so that they are coherent and make sense and also move logically from the beginning to the conclusion of the book? If these questions confront every author, then how daunting—if not madly presumptuous—the challenge becomes when authors attempt to cope with global history from Stone Age to contemporary times, and to do so within the confines of a single volume.

From the beginning, a holistic approach was applied to the structure and contents of *Civilization Past & Present*. More particularly, in order to minimize the authors' inevitable cultural bias (from having been born into and conditioned by the knowledge, values, and behavior of a Western society), they adopted from social anthropologists the concept of the "universal culture pattern." According to this principle (discussed in more detail in the Prologue), all members of the human species in every generation and every society share a fundamental commonality: to satisfy certain basic needs. How a given society responds to these needs determines its individual culture pattern. The universal culture pattern offers a useful analytical device for studying the interconnected components of societies and for understanding and appreciating the unique contributions of each. Throughout seven editions of *Civilization Past & Present*, the authors have utilized this approach, with excellent results.

The evolution of humankind has followed a particular sequence in historical geography. Stone Age peoples lived in small and scattered communities. Next arose archaic civilizations along the banks of major rivers, whose waters were utilized for irrigation and farming. Move-ment and activities in these riverine systems occurred in essentially one-dimensional space. Classical civilizations, such as those of Greece and Rome, grew up along the shores of seas and expanded into the hinterland. This conquest of two-dimensional space was expanded in early modern times across oceans and then to the exploration and control of entire continental regions. In this century, our species' geographical reach has soared vertically into space, linking all peoples in a "global village" and enabling humans to set foot on the moon. The authors of *Civilization Past & Present* used this anthropogeographical sequence as another guiding principle in structuring a logical and coherent format for the text.

From the beginning, a comprehensive map program has been an integral part of the text's focus on historical geography. The first edition included nearly 150 maps prepared by R. M. Chapin, Jr., who had developed at *Time* magazine his skill in dramatizing historical movements in spatial perspective. Later editions featured two-color maps distributed throughout the text; an atlas of full-color reference maps, accompanied by explanatory notes; and a series of full-color maps on the development of civilization, with timelines and explanatory text.

Special features have long been noteworthy additions to *Civilization Past & Present*. For example, the fourth edition included a series of Frontier Essays, written by eminent scholars to supplement the narrative with discussions of revolutionary discoveries of past events and to show the nature and trends of historical scholarship. In later editions appeared Historical Critiques, a second series of essays, also written by noted specialists. These Critiques dealt with such topics as the birth of history in the West, the historical method in China and India, the question of whether there had been an "Industrial Revolution," and a review of reinterpretations of history and society throughout the twentieth century.

Three kinds of Profiles have appeared in various editions of *Civilization Past & Present*. The first set of Profiles provided an in-depth focus on the human side of history. For example, one of these essays, which described the unraveling of the hoax concerning Piltdown Man as the evolutionary "missing link," demonstrated the age-old danger of attempting to fit "facts" into preconceived theories. In an account of the fate of Native Americans, another Profile dealt with the origins and consequences of the most massive uprooting of one population by another in modern times.

The fifth edition introduced Family Profiles, each one describing living conditions in different historical eras. The Family Profiles offered insights into the lives of a working-class Roman family, an upper-class family in Sung China, an Aztec family, English families in the 16th and 17th centuries, a Parisian family in 1815 and its descendants in 1914, a Jewish family in Nazi Germany, two generations of an Indian family in the 1930s and in the present, and an upper-middle class family in contemporary Venezuela.

To focus attention on the unique role played by human actors on the world stage, the sixth edition offered biographical Profiles of fascinating men and women. Hatshepsut, Diogenes, Saint Augustine, Empress Wu, Babur the Tiger, Petrarch, Catherine the Great, Sir Isaac Newton, Beethoven, Emmeline Pankhurst, Shaka the Zulu, Charlie Chaplin, and Anwar el-Sadat were some of the subjects of these Profiles. The current edition of the text features excerpts from primary source documents, allowing students to experience at first hand the voices and records of the past.

Integral to the book's format are the suggestions for reading at the end of each chapter; the chronological tables, which show the sequence of events discussed in the text and their relationship across a global spectrum; and the general index, which also provides a pronunciation guide to the names and places referred to throughout the text. Last but far from least, the authors and editors have always taken special interest—and pride—in the text's illustration program. The first edition included more than 350 photographs, drawings, and diagrams, placed directly in relation to the textual discussions they reinforced visually. In later editions, inserts of full-color art reproductions appeared throughout the text. These works of art were carefully selected to illustrate some facet of the universal culture pattern and, together with the accompanying commentary, constituted a capsule history of world art.

Focusing on the Past

Why should we give thought to focusing on the past which, after all, can never return? The answer can be simply put: because history provides a means for profiting from human experience. As the philosopher George Santayana reminds us: "Those who cannot remember the past are condemned to repeat it." To remain ignorant of our antecedents is akin to opening a novel at random, say to page 199, and then attempting to make sense of the plot without having any idea of what has gone before.

Civilization Past & Present approaches the study of history from a dual perspective: the past as past, and the past as prologue. In terms of the first perspective, it seeks to understand humanity's previous experiences—failures and triumphs alike—in their own right and to be enriched by that knowledge. It is like vacationing in Rome. The experience of walking through the ruins of the Forum and the Colosseum or looking in awe upon Michelangelo's frescoes in the Sistine Chapel is immeasurably enhanced by some understanding of how and why Rome came to be called the "Eternal City."

According to the Greek philosopher Heraclitus, change is the one constant in life. Hence, like other historians, the authors of this book recognize that although the past is indeed past, our knowledge and understanding of it can never be static. From one edition to the next, *Civilization Past & Present* has taken account of new discoveries as well as of fresh interpretations of the past. In this regard, the book brought a new global focus to bear on the interactions of the major civilizations of India, China, and Rome to show that a meaningful exchange of commerce and ideas between East and West took place for centuries in classical times and again a thousand years later. Moreover, history needs to be reviewed at frequent intervals, not only to reflect new knowledge but also to relate it to the needs and aspirations of the present. For example, in the third edition, the intense interest of the newly independent African history. This coverage has been revised and expanded again in subsequent editions in the light of new research.

Focusing on the Present

The perspective of past as prologue has meant that the text has focused as needed on contemporary concerns. This book's half century of exisitence coincides with the occurrence of many of the most momentous events in world history. Just as the nature and tempo of these events underwent change, so successive editions kept pace with the shifts and assessed their significance. For example, the first edition, published in 1942, allocated some 40 pages to the events leading up to World War II and the conflagration itself, while the second edition, appearing in 1949, shortened the treatment of that conflict to focus more attention on postwar domestic conditions and international issues.

Editions of *Civilization Past & Present* published in the 1950s and 1960s reflected the outbreak and evolution of the Cold War, as the world became polarized into two ideological blocs and alliances, directed by two superpowers, each armed with the most lethal weapons in history. As a direct consequence of the Cold War, thousands of people died in two "hot" wars in Korea and Vietnam. The editions published in the 1960s and 1970s attested that the Cold War with its ever-constant threat of a nuclear holocaust remained uppermost in the minds of people everywhere. President Kennedy was echoing the thoughts of many Americans when he stated: "This is a dangerous and uncertain world . . . . No one expects our lives to be easy—not in this decade, not in this century." Nor, he might have added, should we expect our times to be devoid of surprises and sudden changes in world events. As this latest edition makes abundantly clear, the political and economical upheavals of 1989–1990 sent shock waves through the Soviet Union and Eastern Europe, and in their wake collapsed decades-old ideological structures and military alliances. The Cold War that had polarized entire continents and cost trillions of dollars in wasted resources and lost economic opportunities had come to an end, and the world was moving into a new era—one that would still be uncertain but militarily, perhaps, less dangerous.

Focusing on the Golden Anniversary Edition

In its continuing concern about contemporary issues, *Civilization Past & Present* has undertaken to identify and analyze what its authors consider the major problems confronting humanity for both today and tomorrow. Currently, one of these problems, the widespread and accelerating deterioration of the global environment, has become a matter of concern for many Americans. Yet it is interesting to note that when the second edition appeared in 1949—more than four decades ago—the text had already drawn attention to the "ecological dilemma." The text opened its discussion by pointing out that

> *statistics portend the swift approach of a problem so vast in its complexity as to be potentially more tragic than any existing political or ideological conflict. For an understanding of this problem we must leave the tense conference room of foreign ministers and the semicircular table of the Security Council, and visit the quiet office of the ecologist—a scientist who studies the relations between organisms, including human beings, and their environment.*

This scientist warned that the population is increasing by leaps and bounds at the very time natural resources are dwindling at an ever-accelerating speed. The fate of every human being depends on the use or misuse of four major elements: water, soil, plants, and animals. There is a natural balance among these elements; should it be destroyed nature can swiftly wreak destruction on all forms of life—and turn wheat lands into dust bowls. Back in 1949, the ecologist was already describing the earth as a "plundered planet." In the 1990s, the ecologist's concerns have become even more pressing.

In 1949 the text suggested that at its current rate of growth, "the world's population may well exceed the 3,000,000,000 mark by the end of the century." This demographic projection underestimated the prospect by virtually 100 percent. After some three million years, the planet's human population amounted to about 1.7 billion in A.D.

1900. Within one century, it will have increased almost fourfold—and the end is not yet in sight. Furthermore, the overwhelming proportion of that increase is occurring in developing nations, which are struggling to obtain the technology and resources to support their burgeoning populations. What can—what will—the rich nations do to assist them?

The ecological dilemma and unchecked population growth were but two problems identified in the text back in 1949. Others included mass illiteracy, hunger, and disease in the developing nations; atomic energy and its promise of abundant peacetime power coupled with its perils of destruction and radiation (as the disaster at Chernobyl would demonstrate decades later); the dynamics of nationalism and the politics of new nations, all too often accompanied by the erosion or outright destruction of individual rights; and the struggle over those rights, manifested in the strife caused by racial bondage in South Africa. Technology's promises and problems have long been a focus of the text, in discussions of the revolution in communications, the impact of automation on the economy, and the individual in mass society.

Focusing on the Future

The world's problems will not disappear of their own accord but will continue, and in many cases intensify, to the end of the century and beyond. As a result of the end of the Cold War, today's students can be reasonably certain they will not be consumed in a nuclear holocaust. Given the exciting prospects suggested by science and technology, they will have little cause to be bored to death. But humanity's sojourn on this planet will be undoubtedly very different. All peoples and all nations are becoming progressively interdependent; rich and poor, Western and non-Western, societies can expect to find themselves in mutual win-win, or perhaps lose-lose, situations. In short, we are fast becoming a "global village" and in so becoming are attesting as well to the validity of the underlying thesis which motivated the authors of *Civilization Past & Present* in the late 1930s to accept the challenge to write a world history.

It should be refreshing to learn that even in an age which by our standards seems calm and contented, that valiant old warrior, the Duke of Wellington, viewed the future with such foreboding that when he lay on his deathbed in 1854, he declared, "I thank God that I am spared the ruin that is gathering around us." History teaches us that men and women have never yet given up their struggle not only to survive but also to improve human existence. All through the killing days of World War II and the wrenching upheavals of the succeeding decades, the authors and editors of *Civilization Past & Present* remained optimistic about the outcome, their optimism tempered with realism. Now as American society moves toward a new century, with its myriad promises and perils alike, they continue to remain realistically optimistic.

Alastair M. Taylor
Emeritus, Queen's University

Originally published in 1942, *Civilization Past & Present* was the first text of its kind. Its objective was to present a survey of world cultural history, treating the development and growth of civilization not as a unique European experience but as a global one through which all the great culture systems have interacted to produce the present-day world. It attempted to include all the elements of history—social, economic, political, religious, aesthetic, legal, and technological.

The purposes of *Civilization Past & Present*, as envisaged in the first edition five decades ago, have even more relevance today. A knowledge of Western civilization is an essential aim of education, but this alone is no longer adequate. With the accelerating tempo of developments in communication and technology, every day each part of the world is brought into closer contact with the other parts; the world is now truly a "global village." Perhaps the most significant happening in our time is the political and cultural reemergence of the world's non-Western peoples. They have played an important role in world affairs, and in the future their role will be even more important. Hence, these people, their cultures, and their civilizations must be known and understood.

New to the Seventh Edition

The Seventh Edition maintains the various strengths that have made *Civilization Past & Present* a widely popular introductory textbook. The authors have sought to profit from the many helpful suggestions that have come from users and reviewers, to utilize the latest historical scholarship, and to extend the historical narrative to the present day. While the seventh edition retains the basic organization and approach of its predecessors, all chapters have been reviewed and revised in the light of new developments. The number of chapters has been reduced from 39 to 37 as several chapters have been condensed and combined. Many chapters have been completely rewritten, and there are some new chapters. Chapter 6, new to this edition, describes the beginning, spread, and zenith of Islamic civilization and culture. Chapter 7, another new chapter, examines the Byzantine Empire and the early history of Eastern Europe and Russia.

Chapters 9, 10, and 11 have been thoroughly revised to integrate better the social, political, economic, cultural, and intellectual history of the European Middle Ages. Better integration of topics was also the goal for revision of chapters 23, 24, and 25, which examine the Napoleonic and Industrial Revolutions; the revolutions of the mid-nineteenth century, their ideological underpinnings, and the cultural responses to them; and European domestic politics of the late nineteenth century to the brink of World War I. Chapters 35, 36, and 37, which cover the period since the end of World War II, have also been thoroughly revised to reflect the shift from a world of East and West—Soviet and American—spheres to a new bipolarism of North and South, the spheres of the industrialized and the industrializing nations. Finally, the Epilogue uses the recent Persian Gulf War to examine the past both as past and as prologue to the future.

Features

This text has been developed with the dual purpose of helping students acquire a solid knowledge of past events and, equally important, of helping them think more constructively about the significance of those events for the difficult times in which we now live. Several features assist students toward achievement of those goals.

The Maps

Two-color maps are distributed liberally throughout the text. Some are designed to make clear the nature of a single distinctive event or discussed in the text; others illustrate larger trends. Thirty-two new maps have been added throughout the text to provide a geographical framework for the material presented. The series of full-color maps (including timelines and narrative) at the front of the text presents a comparative view of major world states and empires over the centuries from the Stone Age to the present. The narrative provides brief descriptions of the various empires, while the accompanying timeline highlights significant events of the era. The fourteen full-color maps at the back of the text constitute an atlas of historical reference maps. The notes preceding the Historical Atlas describe the principal features and significance of each of the reference maps.

The Color Plates

Nine inserts of full-color art reproductions appear throughout the text. The works of art have been carefully selected to illustrate some facet of a cultural pattern discussed in the text. These reproductions, with the accompanying commentary, constitute a capsule history of world art.

The Document Excerpts

Each chapter includes one or more excerpts from documents of the era under discussion. The excerpts have been selected from a variety of documents—political, economic, legal, intellectual, popular—to show students the kinds of materials historians use to understand and interpret the past. Reading the excerpts will permit students to experience at first hand the voices and records of the past.

Suggestions for Reading

Each chapter ends with an annotated bibiliography listing special historical studies, biographies, reputable historical fiction, and some collections of source materials. The works listed are intended to provide students with ample sources from which to prepare special reports or with which to improve their understanding of a particular subject.

The Chronological Tables

At the end of the book are chronological tables showing the sequence of events discussed in the text. These tables are intended to show the relationship among events in various parts of the world over periods of time.

The Pronunciation Key

In the general index, the correct pronunciation is given for most proper names. Thus, students will find it easy, as well as helpful, to look up the correct pronunciation of the names and places referred to in the text. The index also provides pronunciation guides for many unusual, difficult, or foreign words.

The pedagogical features of the Seventh Edition, along with the text narrative, are intended to provide the reader with an understanding of the contribution of past eras to the shaping of subsequent events and to illuminate the manner in which the study of global history affords insights into the genesis, nature, and direction of our civilization. As we approach the end of the twentieth century, the need for this kind of historical perspective has never been greater.

Supplements

The following supplements are available for use in conjunction with this book:

For the Student

Studying Civilization, in two volumes, prepared by David G. Egler, Sterling J. Kernek, and Charles O'Brien, of Western Illinois University. Volume I covers chapters 1 through 18. Volume II covers chapters 17 through 37. The study guides include chapter overviews, lists of chapter themes and concepts, and many varied exercises, including multiple-choice questions and map quizzes.

Mapping World Civilization: Student Activities is a free map workbook for students by Gerald Danzer, University of Illinois, Chicago. It features numerous map skill exercises written to enhance students' basic geographical literacy. The exercises provide ample opportunities for interpreting maps and analyzing cartographic materials as historical documents. The instructor is entitled to one free copy of *Mapping World Civilization: Student Activities* for each copy of the text purchased from HarperCollins.

SuperShell II Computerized Tutorial is an interactive program for computer-assisted learning, prepared by Paul A. Bishoff, Oklahoma State University. It features multiple-choice, true-false, and completion quizzes, comprehensive chapter outlines, flash cards for key terms and concepts, and diagnostic feedback capabilities. This tutorial is available for IBM computers.

Timelink: World History Computerized Atlas by William Hamblin, Brigham Young University. This is a highly graphic, Hypercard-based computerized atlas and historical geography tutorial for the Macintosh.

For the Instructor

Instructor's Resource Manual by George Jewsbury, Oklahoma State University. This unique instructor's manual offers a multi-resource presentation for each chapter, including chapter outlines and suggestions for integrating a variety of conceptual hooks into class lectures, including art, music, literature, quotations, and media resouces. The manual is shrinkwrapped with a free music cassette.

Experiencing World Music is a 60-minute audio cassette containing over 20 selections of important music from a wide range of times and cultures. Selections range between 1 and 4 minutes in length. Commentaries about the pieces and suggestions for using them in lectures, prepared by Evan Tonsing, Oklahoma State University, and Jane Adas, Rutgers, are included in the *Instructor's Resource Manual*. Western pieces include short selections from the medieval period to the present. Non-western pieces include short selections from China, India, Japan, Iran, Africa, Turkey, and other countries. The audiocassette comes shrinkwrapped with the *Instructor's Resource Manual*.

Test Bank by George Jewsbury, Oklahoma State University. A total of 2000 questions, including 50 multiple-choice questions and 5 essay questions per text chapter. Each test item is referenced by topic, type, and text page number. *Test Bank* is available in print and computerized format.

TestMaster Computerized Testing System is a test-generation software package available for the IBM and Macintosh. It allows users to add, delete, edit, and print test items. The system is available free to adopters.

World History Through Maps and Views prepared by Gerald Danzer, University of Illinois, Chicago, winner of the AHA's James Harvey Robinson Award for his work in the development of map transparencies. This set of 100 four-color transparencies from selected sources is bound in a three-ring binder and is available free to adopters. It also contains an introduction on teaching history with maps and a detailed commentary on each transparency. The collection includes cartographic and pictorial maps, views and photos, urban plans, building diagrams, classic maps, and works of art.

Map transparencies is a set of 48 two- and four-color transparencies of basic maps designed to be used in teaching world civilization courses.

The HarperCollins World Civilization Media Program offers a wide variety of media enhancements, including videos and historical newsreels. This program is useful for teaching world civilization courses. It is offered to qualified adopters of HarperCollins world civilization texts.

Grades is a grade-keeping and classroom-management software program that maintains data for up to 200 students.

___

Acknowledgments

To the following reviewers who gave generously of their time and knowledge to provide thoughtful evaluations and many helpful suggestions for the revision of the text, the authors express their gratitude.

Jay Pascal Anglin
University of Southern Mississippi

Joel Berlatsky
Wilkes College

Jackie R. Booker
Kent State University

Darwin F. Bostwick
Old Dominion University

Robert F. Brinson, Jr.
Santa Fe Community College

Robert H. Buchanan
Adams State College

James O. Catron, Jr.
North Florida Junior College

William H. Cobb
East Carolina University

J. L. Collins
Allan Hancock College

Lawrence J. Daly
Bowling Green State University

John D. Fair
Auburn University at Montgomery

Nels W. Forde
University of Nebraska

Joseph T. Fuhrmann
Murray State University

Jeffrey S. Hamilton
Old Dominion University

J. Drew Harrington
Western Kentucky University

Conrad C. Holcomb, Jr.
Surry Community College

Michael L. Krenn
University of Miami

Caroline T. Marshall
James Madison University

Norman Pollock
Old Dominion University

J. Graham Provan
Millikin University

George B. Pruden, Jr.
Armstrong State College

John D. Ramsbottom
Northeast Missouri State University

Ruth Richard
College of Lake County

Hugh I. Rodgers
Columbus College

Patrick J. Rollins
Old Dominion University

Barry T. Ryan
Westmont College

Louis E. Schmier
Valdosta State College

Barbara G. Sniffen
University of Wisconsin-Oshkosh

Lawrence Squeri
East Stroudsburg University

Gordon L. Teffeteller
Valdosta State College

Malcolm R. Thorp
Brigham Young University

Helen M. Tierney
University of Wisconsin-Platteville

David L. White
Appalachian State University

John R. Willertz
Saginaw Valley State University

Perspective on Humanity

If the time span of our planet—now estimated at some 5 billion years—were telescoped into a single year, the first eight months would be devoid of any life. The next two months would be taken up with plant and very primitive animal forms, and not until well into December would any mammals appear. In this "year," members of *Homo erectus,* our ancient predecessors, would mount the global stage only between 10 and 11 p.m. on December 31. And how has the human species spent that brief allotment? Most of it— the equivalent of more than half a million years—has been given over to making tools out of stone. The revolutionary changeover from food-hunting nomads to farmers who raised grain and domesticated animals would occur in the last sixty seconds. And into that final minute would be crowded all of humanity's other accomplishments: the use of metal; the creation of civilizations; the mastery of the oceans; and the harnessing of steam, then gas, electricity, oil, and, finally, in our lifetime, nuclear energy. Brief though it has been, humanity's time on the globe reveals a rich tapestry of science, industry, religion, and art. This accumulated experience of the human species is available for study. We call it *history.*

Past and Present

As we read and learn about early societies and their members, we discover them to be very different from us and the world in which we live. And yet, we are linked by more than curiosity to our ancient predecessors. Why? Because we are of the same species, and we share a fundamental commonality that connects present with past: the human-environment nexus. It is the dynamic interplay of environmental factors and human activities that accounts for the terrestrial process known as history. The biological continuity of our species, coupled with humanity's unflagging inventiveness, have enabled each generation to build on the experiences and contributions of its forebears—so that continuity and change in human affairs proceed together.

The Universal Culture Pattern

In the interplay of men and women with their environment and fellow beings, certain fundamental needs are always present. Six needs, common to people at all times and in all places, form the basis of a "universal culture pattern" and deserve to be enumerated.

1. *The need to make a living.* Men and women must have food, shelter, clothing, and the means to provide for their offsprings' survival.

2. *The need for law and order.* From earliest times, communities have had to keep peace among their members, defend themselves against external attack, and protect community assets.

3. *The need for social organization.* For people to make a living, raise families, and maintain law and order, a social structure is essential. Views about the relative importance of the group and the individual within it may vary with any such social structure.

4. *The need for knowledge and learning.* Since earliest times, humankind has transmitted knowledge acquired through experience, first orally and then by means of writing systems. As societies grow more complex, there is increasing need to preserve knowledge and transmit it through education to as many people as possible.

5. *The need for self-expression.* People have responded creatively to their environment even before the days when they decorated the walls of Paleolithic caves with paintings of the animals they hunted. The arts appear to have a lineage as old as human experience.

6. *The need for religious expression.* Equally old is humanity's attempt to answer the "why" of its existence. What primitive peoples considered supernatural in their environment could often, at a later time, be explained by science in terms of natural phenomena. Yet today, no less than in archaic times, men and women continue to search for answers to the ultimate questions of existence.

Culture Change and Culture Lag

When people in a group behave similarly and share the same institutions and ways of life, they can be said to have a common *culture*. Throughout this text we shall be looking at a number of different cultures, some of which are designated as *civilizations*. (If all tribes or societies have culture, then civilization is a particular *kind* of culture.) "A culture is the way of life of a human group; it includes all the learned and standardized forms of behavior which one uses and others in one's group expect and recognize. . . . Civilization is that kind of culture which includes the use of writing, the presence of cities and of wide political organization, and the development of occupational specialization."[1]

Cultures are never wholly static or wholly isolated. A particular culture may have an individuality that sets it off sharply from other cultures, but invariably it has been influenced by external contacts. Such contacts may be either peaceful or warlike, and they meet with varying degrees of acceptance. Through these contacts occurs the process of culture *diffusion*. Geography, too, has profoundly influenced the development of cultures, although we should not exaggerate its importance. Environmental influences tend to become less marked as people gain technological skill and mastery over the land. The domestication of animals and cereals, for example, took place in both the old and new worlds, but the animals and grains were different because of dissimilar ecological factors. Invention is another important source of culture change, although it is not clear to what extent external physical contact is required in the process of invention. Perhaps it may be possible for men and women in different times and places to hit on similar solutions to the challenges posed by their respective environments—resulting in the phenomenon known as *parallel invention*.

Some parts of a culture pattern change more rapidly than others, so that one institution sometimes becomes outmoded in relation to others in a society. When different parts of a society fail to mesh harmoniously, the condition is often called *culture lag*. Numerous examples of this lag could be cited: the exploitation of child laborers during the nineteenth century, the failure to allow women to vote until this century, and the tragedy of hunger in the midst of plenty.

Past and Present as Prologue

What can the past and present—as history—suggest to us for tomorrow's world? In the first place, changes in the physical and social environments will probably accelerate as a result of continued technological innovation. These changes can result in increased disequilibrium and tensions among the various segments comprising the universal culture pattern—in other words, in increased culture lag.

Has the past anything to tell the future about the consequences of cultural disequilibrium—anything that we might profitably utilize in present-day planning for the decades ahead? Because our planet and its resources are finite, at some point our society must expect to shift progressively from exponential growth toward an overall global equilibrium. By that term, we mean the setting of maximal levels on the number of humans who can inhabit this planet with an assured minimal standard of life and on the exploitation of the earth's resources required to provide that standard. Otherwise, environmental disaster on an unprecedented scale could result in the decades ahead. Past and present conjoin to alert us to the need to engage in new forms of planning for the years ahead and also to the need to rethink our existing social goals and value systems. We need as long and as accurate a perspective as possible to make realistic analyses and to take the proper actions to improve our quality of life.

The "How" of History

History is the record of the past actions of humankind, based on surviving evidence. History shows that all patterns and problems in human affairs are the products of a complex process of growth. By throwing light on that process, history provides a means for profiting from human experience.

History as a Science

There is more than one way to treat the past. In dealing with the American Revolution, for example, the historian may describe its events in narrative form or, instead, analyze its general causes and compare its stages with the patterns of revolutions in other countries. Unlike the scientist who attempts to verify hypotheses by repeating experiments under controlled conditions in the laboratory and to classify phenomena in a general group or category, the historian has to pay special attention to the *uniqueness* of data, because each event takes place at a particular time and in a particular place. And since that time is now past, conclusions cannot be verified by duplicating the circumstances in which the event occurred.

Nevertheless, historians insist that history be written as scientifically as possible and that evidence be analyzed with the same objective attitude employed by the scientist examining natural phenomena. This scientific spirit requires historians to handle evidence according to established rules of historical analysis, to recognize biases and attempt to eliminate their effects, and to draw only such conclusions as the evidence seems to warrant.

The Historical Method

To meet these requirements, historians have evolved the "historical method." The first step is the search for *sources*, which may be material remains, oral traditions, pictorial data, or written records. From the source the historian must infer the facts. This process has two parts. *External criticism* tests the genuineness of the source.

In *internal criticism* the historian evaluates the source to ascertain the author's meaning and the accuracy of the work.

The final step in the historical method is *synthesis*. Here the historian must determine which factors in a given situation are most relevant to the purpose at hand, since obviously not everything that occurred can be included. This delicate process of selection underscores the role that subjectivity plays in the writing of history. Furthermore, the more complex the events involved, the more crucial becomes the historian's judgment.[2]

Periodization

Can we really categorize history as "ancient," "medieval," or "modern"? Clearly, what is "modern" in the twentieth century could conceivably be considered "medieval" in the twenty-fifth century, and eventually "ancient" in the thirty-fifth century A.D. Yet not to break up the account would be akin to reading this book without the benefit of parts, chapters, paragraphs, or even separate sentences. Like time itself, history would then become a ceaseless flow of consciousness and events. To simplify the task and to manage materials more easily, the historian divides time into periods. The divisions chosen and the lines drawn reveal the distinctive way in which the historian regards the past—namely, in terms of patterns that seem logical and meaningful.

The "Why" of History

The historian seeks to describe not only *what* has happened and *how* it happened, but also *why* society undergoes change. Any search of this kind raises a number of fundamental questions: the roles of Providence, the individual, and the group in history; the extent to which events are unique or, conversely, can fit into patterns; and the problem of progress in human affairs. The answers vary with different philosophical views of the universe and the human role therein.

Those who hold the teleological view see in history the guidance of a Divine Will, directing human destinies according to a cosmic purpose. Other thinkers have exalted the role of the individual in the historical process—such as Thomas Carlyle, who contended that major figures chiefly determined the course of human events. Opponents of Carlyle's thesis often contend that history is determined by "forces" and "laws" and by the actions of entire societies. Sociologists approach history primarily by analyzing the origins, institutions, and functions of groups. Economists tend to look at the historical record from the standpoint of group action and especially the impact of economic forces.

To Karl Marx irresistible economic forces governed human beings and determined the trend of events. Marx contended that the shift from one economic stage to another—such as the shift from feudalism to capitalism—is attained by upheavals, or revolutions, which occur because the class controlling the methods of production eventually resists further progress in order to maintain its vested interests.

Numerous other attempts have been made to explain societal processes according to a set of principles. Oswald Spengler maintained that civilizations were like organisms; each grew with the "superb aimlessness" of a flower and passed through a cycle of spring, summer, autumn, and winter. Charles Darwin's evolutionary hypothesis made a strong impact on nineteenth-century thought and gave rise to the concept that the principle of "survival of the fittest" must also apply to human societies. This line of thought—known as Social Darwinism—raises social and ethical questions of major importance.

Does history obey impersonal laws and forces so that its course is inevitable? Or, at the other extreme, since every event is a unique act, is history simply the record of unforeseen and unrelated episodes? Can this apparent dilemma be avoided? We believe it can. Although all events are, in various respects, unique, they also contain elements that invite comparison. The comparitive approach permits us to seek relationships between historical phenomena and to group them into movements or patterns or civilizations. We eschew any "theory" of history, preferring to see merit in a number of basic concepts. These include the effects of physical environment on social organization and institutions; the roles played by economic, political, and religious factors; and the impact exerted by men and women occupying key positions in various societies.

The Challenge of History

Progress and growth is a continuous factor. It depends on, and contributes to, the maintenance of peace and security, the peaceful settlement of international disputes, and worldwide improvement in economic and social standards. Surely an indispensable step toward solving contemporary humanity's dilemma—technology without the requisite control and power without commensurate wisdom—must be a better understanding of how the world and its people came to be what they are today. Only by understanding the past can we assess both the perils and the opportunities of the present—and move courageously and compassionately into the future.

Notes

1. David G. Mandelbaum, "Concepts of Civilization and Culture," *Encyclopaedia Britannica*, 1967 ed., vol. 5, p. 831A.
2. See P. Gardiner, *The Nature of Historical Explanation* (London: Oxford University Press, 1952), p. 98.

Civilization
Past & Present

Seventh Edition

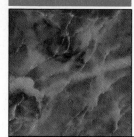

Chapter 17

The Strife of States and Kings

European Religion, Politics, and Art in a Century of Strife, 1560–1660

On a dark misty day in November 1632, two great armies, one Protestant and one Catholic, met in the German Saxon countryside near Lutzen. The Protestants won a decisive victory that day but lost their general, King Gustavus Adolphus (1594–1632) of Sweden, known as the "Lion of the North." According to a familiar story, the dying king was discovered on the battlefield and asked his name by enemy soldiers. "I am the King of Sweden," he replied, "who so seal the religion and liberty of the German nation with my blood."[1]

The fate of Sweden's warrior-king reflected the tragedy and the ambiguity of the age. This second phase of the Reformation was marked by bloody religious wars, economic depression, and rampant disease. It was also a time when religious fanaticism interacted with pragmatic politics, contributing, in the process, to the development of modern states. Sometimes religious conflict caused the reshaping of feudal values to justify movements against royal authority; more often, it promoted centralized monarchies, whose rulers promised to restore order by wielding absolute power. Despite pious declarations, kings and generals often conducted war with little regard for moral principles; indeed, as time passed, they steadily subordinated religious concerns to dynastic ambitions or assumed national interests. This change, however, came slowly and was completed only after Europe had been ravaged by the human suffering and material destruction of religious conflict.

A specific political result of the long religious conflict was a shift in the European balance of power. At the opening of the period, the Habsburg dynasty sought to maintain its dominant position in alliance with the Catholic Church. It failed in its struggle against opposing coalitions, which were often allied with Protestantism. The long-term beneficiary of this political struggle was France, a leading Catholic state.

Baroque art and literature somewhat ambiguously expressed the values of its period. The baroque style emphasized the heroic, the bizarre, and the powerful, in keeping with strong rulers and warring states. Despite its masculine values, the Baroque glorified women in the abstract at a time when ordinary women were losing social status. This apparent contradiction might be explained by the dominant contemporary roles of famous queens, powerful female regents, and the aristocratic women who acted as hostesses of the salons.

Internal Religious and Political Developments

Although it ended a short war in Germany, the Peace of Augsburg (1555) failed to end religious contention. Even before John Calvin died in 1564, his movement was spreading rapidly in France, Germany, Poland, Bohemia, and Hungary. The Council of Trent launched a formidable counteroffensive, led by the Jesuits and supported by Spain, against all Protestants. England narrowly avoided the religious civil wars that ended the Valois line in France; the Spanish Netherlands exploded in religious rebellion; and the militant counter-Reformation suppressed Protestantism in eastern Europe. For decades, problems of religion dominated politics within every European state.

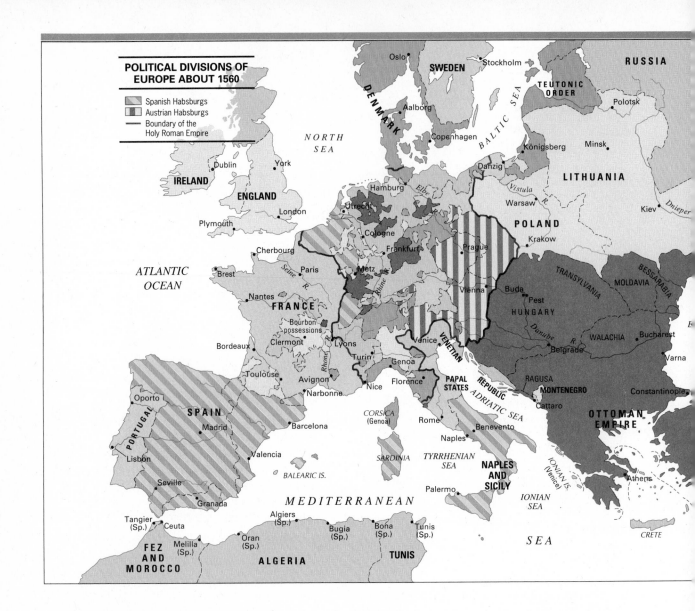

POLITICAL DIVISIONS OF EUROPE ABOUT 1560

Spanish Habsburgs
Austrian Habsburgs
Boundary of the
Holy Roman Empire

Spain as the Model for Catholic Absolutism

Under Philip II (1556–1598), Spain was recognized as the strongest military power in Europe and the major defender of the Catholic faith. This reputation arose from the rigidly disciplined Spanish infantry, silver that seemed to flow in unlimited quantities from America, and the record of the famed Spanish Inquisition, which had dealt effectively earlier with the Jews and Moors and was now being used to snuff out Spanish Protestantism. Philip accepted this interpretation, deliberately projecting an image of himself as the iron-willed champion of Catholic orthodoxy.

This responsibility was part of Philip's inheritance from his father, Charles V, whose long reign ended in 1556 when he abdicated his imperial throne and entered a monastery. As Charles stepped down from the throne, he split his holdings between his brother, Ferdinand, who received Austria, Bohemia, and Hungary; and his son, Philip, who received Naples, Sicily, Milan, the Netherlands, and Spain. Philip also gained control of a vast overseas empire, which was much more lucrative than had been his father's imperial crown in the Germanies.

indeed, the division of Habsburg lands appeared to be a blessing for Philip, allowing him to shed his father's worrisome "German problem" and concentrate more effectively upon his Spanish realm (see map, p. 450). There were, however, less favorable aspects of the legacy—Charles left his son the Turkish menace in the Mediterranean as well as the expensive task of leading the Catholic crusade against Protestantism.

Philip was an obedient son and took very seriously his father's admonitions. A slight, somber, and unemotional man, he was almost completely absorbed by his awesome official obligations. Charles had warned him about becoming too intimate with subordinates and, particularly, against trusting or depending upon women. Philip heeded this advice. Although he was involved briefly with mistresses, none of them influenced his judgment or policies. The same could be said about his four wives, Maria of Portugal, Mary of England, Elizabeth of France, and his niece, Anne of Austria, all of whom he married for political reasons. They bore his children, but did not eat at his table, except at official banquets. Elizabeth was his favorite and Philip doted on her daughters, to whom he wrote notes of tender and loving concern; but such revelations of his inner feelings were very rare.

The standard historical portrait of Philip, depicting him as a single-minded idealogue and lackey of the pope, is largely false. By using the Inquisition to destroy Islamic and Protestant heresies, Philip sought to enforce Spanish traditions, arouse patriotism, increase his popularity, and strengthen the state. But he was no tool of the papacy; indeed, like his father, he defied more than one pope, carefully weighing the costs of papal military proposals against the benefits and using the church for his own political purposes. He denied the pope jurisdiction over Spanish church courts, ignored objectionable papal decrees, defied the Council of Trent on church appointments in Spanish territories, and fought the Jesuits when they challenged his authority. Although a dedicated Catholic, Philip saw the church as an arm of his government, expecting its cooperation in return for his support.

Throughout his long reign, Philip tried with only moderate success to be an absolute monarch. His councilors, appointed as advisors more than as administrators, submitted most decisions for his resolution. In the *Escorial*, the cold and somber palace which he had built north of Madrid, he labored endlessly, reading and annotating their documents. His concerns were directed mainly towards Castile, where Philip furthered the process of developing absolutism, issuing royal edicts as law and using the *Cortes*, the traditional assembly of estates, as a device for measuring public opinion rather than as a legislative body. But such pretensions of centralized government were without much meaning in other parts of Spain. There, as well as in the Netherlands and Italy, proud noble families dominated the assemblies, jealously guarding their privileges and often opposing royal viceroys. They were aided by the weight of tradition, by poor communications, and—in the eastern

The lives of Europe's monarchs were interwoven through ties of marriage and kinship; these bonds were utilized to further the monarchs' nationalistic aims. While Philip II of Spain was married to Mary Tudor of England, it seemed that England might come under Spanish domination.

The Venetian Ambassador's Portrait of Philip II

This sketch of Philip II was written in a dispatch by Ambassador Paolo Tiepolo in 1563. Notice the king's characteristic physical weakness, hypochondria, languidness, religiosity, and penchant for privacy, even from his queen.

The king was born of the Empress Isabella, daughter of the king of Portugal, on May 21, 1527. He is slight of stature and round-faced, with very pale blue eyes, somewhat prominent lips, and pink skin, but his overall appearance is very attractive. His temperament is very phlegmatic and his condition weak and delicate; he often takes to his bed, sometimes with chest pains and shortness of breath and sometimes, others say, with more serious illnesses. I have heard doctors say that it is unlikely he will live for long. Like other Spaniards he sleeps a great deal; not only does he take a long siesta after dinner, but he does not get out of bed in the morning in any season of the year until two and a half hours before noon. As soon as he rises he hears mass, and then he has little time for anything else before dinner. Sometimes he dines with his court and sometimes privately—in fact, usually alone, since he rarely eats with his wife, child, and sister, and others are not considered worthy to be at his table. . . .

He appears to be extremely religious, since he goes to church very often and takes communion four times a year. When he assigns bishoprics and benefices what concerns him most about the candidates is their Christian learning and morality. He accepted the Council against the wishes and advice of the Spanish bishops, who enjoyed a very comfortable position and had no desire to endanger it. He maintains nearly perpetual hostilities with the infidels, persecutes heretics more than any other ruler, and claims to be the readiest and loyalest defender of the pope and the apostolic see. In everything he does he seeks to appear as a true Catholic king, guided by his conscience. But what religious zeal inspires always seems to coincide with his own purposes. . . .

From this anyone can see that his natural inclination is to avoid difficulties; he showed this trait during the fighting in the Netherlands when he got angry and frustrated over the way things were going. Anyone who ponders this king's way of life—how he enjoys staying in Spain and how unwillingly he wrestles with problems—is sure to conclude that when he can the king will stay at peace with everyone and keep far from the noise of battle. If he does start a fight with anyone, it will be with the infidels [Turks], because he could attack them without having to go in person; his soldiers would run all the dangers. . . .

The queen is little more than seventeen years old, and she has a lively personality but is not very pretty. So far she has shown no symptoms of pregnancy, but the truth is that she is still very young. The indications of maturity as a woman only appeared about ten months ago, as her own doctor told me. In public the king treats her as if he loves and respects her very much, but actually he does little to make her happy. He frequently stays away from her for long periods, and when he is at court he purposely visits her late at night; if he finds her sleeping he goes away, as if he does not want to awaken her, satisfied with having made this gesture. So the queen, in order not to miss having his company, many times has stayed up most of the night. She knows that the king has many affairs with other ladies, but she has learned from her mother to put up with this, and she patiently endures it without a murmur of complaint.

Source: James C. Davis, ed., *Pursuit of Power: Venetian Ambassadors' Reports on Spain, Turkey, and France in the Age of Philip II, 1560–1600* (New York: Harper & Row, 1970), pp. 81–84.

Spanish kingdoms of Aragon and Catalonia—by revenue potentials below the cost of subjecting them.

The backward Spanish sociopolitical system caused Philip many economic problems. Tax-exempt nobilities, comprising under 2 percent of the people, owned 95 percent of the land; the middle classes, overtaxed and depleted by purges of Jews and *Moriscos* (Spanish Muslims), were almost eliminated; and the peasants were so exploited that agricultural production, particularly grains, was insufficient to feed the population. The use of arable lands for the nobles' sheep runs worsened the situation. State regulation of industry and trade further limited revenues and forced primary reliance on specie from America, which ultimately brought ruinous inflation. When his income failed to meet expenses, Philip borrowed at rising interest rates. In 1557 and 1575, he had to suspend payments, effectively declaring national bankruptcy.

The Revolt of the Netherlands

Philip's Catholic absolutism encouraged some unity in Spain; in the Netherlands, which he also controlled, his policies promoted disaster. The seventeen provinces, each with its own feudal tradition, were originally suspicious of their Spanish king. When Philip confirmed their fears by attempting to enforce Catholic conformity, he generated resistance which soon grew into open rebellion.

This outcome could have been expected. The Netherlands then included much of modern Holland, Belgium, Luxembourg, and a few petty fiefs, located along 200 miles of marshy coast between France and Germany, an area not open to easy conquest. The geography promoted strong local nobilities but also relatively independent peasants and townsfolk. Even in medieval times, cities were centers of rapidly expanding commerce; of the 300 walled towns in 1560, nineteen had populations over 10,000 (England had only three or four); and Antwerp was the leading commercial and banking center of northern Europe. This combination of localism, feudalism, and commerce found a truly appropriate religious expression in the Reformation, first with Anabaptism and then with Calvinism after the 1550s.

Philip first appointed his illegitimate half-sister, Margaret of Parma, as regent of the Netherlands. An able administrator and like her father, a native of the region, this thick-set, hard-riding matron was at first popular because she understood her subjects. Philip wasted this asset by ordering her to combat heresy with the Inquisition, a policy which drove the leading nobles from her council and brought increasingly threatening popular protests. For years, Philip ignored Margaret's frantic appeals for leniency before permitting her to dismiss the hated Cardinal Granville from her government. Margaret also authorized Protestant preaching. Despite these belated concessions, Calvinist mobs began desecrating churches and terrorizing Catholics.

To meet this challenge, Philip dispatched the Duke of Alva, with 10,000 Spanish troops, a great baggage train, and 2000 prostitutes, to the Netherlands. Alva relieved Margaret of her regency and clamped a brutal military dictatorship on the country. By decree, he centralized church administration, imposed new taxes, and established a special tribunal—soon dubbed "The Council of Blood"—to stamp out treason and heresy. During Alva's regime, between 1567 and 1573, at least 8,000 people were killed, including the powerful Counts of Egmont and Horne. Women and children were often victims. In 1568, one woman was executed because she had refused to eat pork; an eighty-four-old woman whose son-in-law had given hospitality to a heretic, was condemned at Utrecht. In addition to such atrocities, the Catholic terror deprived 30,000 people of their property and forced 100,000 to flee the country.

By 1568, Alva's excesses had provoked open rebellion, led by William of Orange (1533–1584), nicknamed the silent. Born of Lutheran parents, William had been raised a Catholic at the court of Charles V, where he became a favorite, known for his practical statecraft. Alienated by Spanish violation of traditional rights, he reluctantly became a rebel. His gradual ideological transformation is illustrated by his four marriages. The first two, before 1561, were for status and convenience; the last two, after 1577, were to Charlotte de Bourbon and Louise de Coligny, both sincere French Huguenots, who served him as committed partners in a religious cause.

Until 1579, William persevered. Constant early defeats left him impoverished and nearly disgraced, but in 1572, the port of Brill fell to his notorious privateers, "the sea beggars," an event which triggered revolts throughout the north. Soon after, William cut the dikes, mired down a weary Spanish army, and forced Alva's recall to Spain. The continuing war was marked by savage ferocity, such as the sack of Antwerp by mutinous Spanish soldiers (1576). At the Spanish siege of Maestricht (1579), women fought beside their men on the walls, and soldiers massacred the population, raping the women before tearing some limb from limb in the streets. That same year, in the Pacification of Ghent, Catholics and Protestants from the seventeen provinces united to defy Philip, demand the recall of his army, and proclaim the authority of their traditional assembly, the States General.

Unfortunately for the rebel cause, this unity was soon destroyed by religious differences between militant northern Calvinists and Catholic southerners, particularly the many powerful nobles. The Spanish commander, Alexander Farnese, exploited these differences by restoring lands and privileges to the southern nobles. He was then able to win victories which induced the ten southern provinces to make peace with Spain in 1579. The Dutch, now alone, proclaimed their continued resistance to Spanish persecution and in 1581 declared their independence of Spain. They persisted after William was assissinated in 1584, while the Spanish continued their war on heresy, hanging, butchering, burning, and burying alive Protestants who would not renounce their faith. This cruelty lasted until a truce was negotiated in 1609.

Religious Wars in France

Although frustrated in the Netherlands, Philip did not face his father's French problem. By the Treaty of Cateau-Cambrésis in 1559, France gave up claims in Italy and the Netherlands. This humiliating surrender to the Habsburgs marked a definite hiatus in French history. Over the next four decades, France gradually lost its leverage in foreign affairs as the country was torn by internal dissension.

By the 1560s Calvinism had become a major source of that contention. Although outlawed and persecuted earlier, the movement appealed to the urban middle classes, particularly to women, who were among its most active promoters. It also attracted nobles through the influential friends of Jeanne d'Albret, the Calvinist Queen of Navarre and wife of Antoine de Bourbon, a Prince of the blood. In 1559, the Huguenots held a secret synod in Paris which drew representatives from seventy-two congregations and a million members. Although still a minority, the Calvinists were well organized, with articulate leaders and the promise of military support from an increasing number of converts from among the nobility.

The growing interest among nobles was largely political. When Henry II died in 1559, the throne passed to his sickly fifteen-year-old son, Francis II. Francis' queen was Mary Stuart (later Mary, Queen of Scots), whose uncles, the brothers Guise, assumed control of the government. The Guises championed the Catholic cause and were opposed, although not always openly, by the Bourbons, who were turning Protestant, and by the Montmorency family, some of whose members were Protestants.

Francis died in 1560 and was succeeded by his nine-year-old brother, Charles IX. The real power behind the throne, however, was his mother, Catherine de Médicis, the neglected wife of Henry II. She was a most able woman, single-minded, crafty, ready to take any advantage but also open to compromise, and determined to save the throne for one of her three sons, none of whom had produced a male heir. Exploiting the split between the Guises and their enemies, she assumed the regency for Charles. She then attempted, through reforms of the church, to reconcile the differences between Catholics and Protestants. In this endeavor she was unsuccessful, but she retained a tenuous control by using every political strategy, including a squadron of highborn ladies who solicited information by seducing powerful nobles.

Religious wars erupted in 1561, lasting through eight uneasy truces until 1593. Religious fanaticism evoked the most violent and inhumane acts on both sides. Assassinations, raids, and atrocities became commonplace. Catherine maneuvered through war and uneasy peace, first favoring the Guises and then the Bourbons. In 1572, when she feared the Huguenots were gaining supremacy over Charles, she joined a Guise plot which resulted in the murder of some 10,000 Huguenots in Paris. This "massacre of Saint Bartholomew's Eve" was a turning point in decisively dividing the country. The final "war of the three Henries" in the 1580s involved Catherine's third son, Henry III, who became king on the death of Charles IX in 1574, Henry of Guise, and the Protestant Henry of Navarre. When the first two were assassinated, Henry of Navarre proclaimed himself king of France in 1589.

Elizabethan England

England, like France in the late sixteenth century, was threatened with civil war and governed by a woman who sought stability in compromise. But unlike Catherine de Médicis, Elizabeth I of England had learned earlier to separate personal attachments from Tudor politics, where she almost lost her head as well as her chance for the crown. England became her family and her primary interest. She was skilled at judging people, projected charisma in public speeches, and dealt with foreign diplomats in their own languages. These talents were especially valuable at her succession in 1558, when the country's religious divisions invited foreign invasion.

The immediate danger was Scotland, where Mary of Guise, a stalwart proponent of Catholicism, was regent for her daughter, Mary Stuart, queen of both France and Scotland. French troops in Scotland supported this Catholic regime. Because Mary Stuart was also a direct descendent of Henry VII of England, she was a leading claimant for the English throne and a potential rallying symbol for Catholic interests, who hoped to reestablish their religion in England. These expectations were diminished in 1559 when a zealous Calvinist named John Knox (1505–1572), fresh from Geneva, led a revolt of Scottish nobles. Aided by English naval forces, they broke religious ties with Rome, established a Presbyterian (Calvinist) state church, and drove the French soldiers out of Scotland. Temporarily, Elizabeth had averted disaster.

She furthered her escape from the sectarian strife which was destroying France by a compromise policy more effective than that of Catherine de Médicis. Moving firmly but slowly, Elizabeth recreated an Anglican Church similar to her father's. It confirmed the monarch as its head, recognized only baptism and communion as sacraments, rejected the veneration of relics, conducted services in English, and avoided other controversial Protestant tenets. It also retained the old organization, under bishops and archbishops, along with much of the Catholic ritual.

This policy avoided open rebellion but failed to end the opposition of both Protestants and Catholics to the state church. Nonconformists attacked the establishment in sermons and pamphlets; some, like the Presbyterian minister Thomas Cartwright, were jailed by church courts. Catholics faced more severe persecution and were therefore even more determined and daring. A network of Jesuit priests operated throughout the country, particularly in the north and west, secretly performing masses and working with a Catholic political underground. Women played prominent roles on both sides. The Duchess of Suffolk and Lady Russell were two of the Protestant women who steadily pressured the queen; others organized meetings and distributed literature. Catholic women were most effective allies of the Jesuits; one of them, Margaret Clitherow, died under torture in 1586 rather than deny her faith.

While dealing with this internal dissension, Elizabeth faced a serious danger from abroad. In 1568, Mary Stuart was forced into exile by her Protestant subjects and received in England by her royal cousin. Although kept a virtual prisoner, Mary became involved in a series of Catholic plots, which appeared even more dangerous after the pope excommunicated Elizabeth in 1570. Philip of Spain aided the plotters but still hoped to enlist Elizabeth's cooperation in helping him create a Catholic hegemony in Europe.

Religious Conflict in the International Arena, 1571–1609

By 1580, the European religious conflict had burst beyond national boundaries and entered the international arena. Philip of Spain was the prime mover in this process. In his efforts to maintain leadership in the Counter-Reformation and achieve a Spanish hegemony in Europe, he shifted from a policy of diplomacy to one of direct military action. In the process, he succeeded only in weakening his country and strengthening its enemies, the Dutch, the English, and the French.

The Futile Spanish Bid for Supremacy

A number of factors combined to encourage Philip in his bid for supremacy. His diplomatic efforts, particularly his marriage to Mary Tudor in 1558, his next marriage to Elizabeth of Valois in 1560, and his clumsy efforts to court Elizabeth I of England had brought no lasting influence over English or French policies. Indeed, English captains were preying on Spanish shipping in the Atlantic and Dutch privateers, with English and Huguenot support, were interrupting the flow of vital supplies from northern Europe. Finally, after 1571, Spain was more free of the Turkish menace in the Mediterranean and therefore more able to move against Protestant enemies in northern Europe.

Philip's policies toward Turkey promoted his reputation as the champion of Catholicism, boosted Spanish morale, and revived the traditional national pride in defending the faith. When Cyprus, the last Christian stronghold in the eastern Mediterranean, fell to the Turks in 1570, Philp responded to the pope's pleas and formed a Holy League to destroy Turkish naval power. Spanish and Venetian warships, together with smaller squadrons from Genoa and the Papal States, made up a fleet of over two hundred vessels, which drew recruits from all over Europe. In 1571, the League's fleet and the Turkish navy clashed at Lepanto, off the western coast of Greece. The outcome was a decisive victory for Christian Europe; Ottoman sea power was never again to be a major threat to Christendom.

In 1580, after nine years of frustration in the Netherlands, Philip launched the first phase of his new offensive policy, enforcing his claim to the Portuguese throne by military force. As king of Portugal, he gained control of the Portuguese navy and Atlantic ports, where he began collecting an ocean-going fleet capable of operations against the Dutch and English in their home waters. International tensions increased in 1585, when Philip openly signed an alliance with the

Guise faction and sent troops into France. Elizabeth, who had been engaging Philip in a game of duplicity, allowing him to think that she might turn Catholic and perhaps even marry him, was especially fearful of invasion from the Netherlands. To thwart such an invasion, she sent token military forces, in addition to the financial aid she was already providing, to the Dutch and French Protestants. By 1586, Philip's policies were about to precipitate a major war.

Philip's last hope for an easy solution to his problem was dashed in 1587. Pressed by the pope and the English Catholic exiles, he had tried for years to use Mary Stuart to overthrow Elizabeth, thereby regaining England for Catholicism and taking control of the country; but Mary's complicity in a plot against Elizabeth's life was discovered; and Elizabeth, reluctantly convinced that Mary alive was more dangerous than Philip frustrated, ordered Mary's execution. Mary's death confirmed Philip's earlier decision that England could only be conquered with powder and steel.

In pursuing this end, Philip planned a "great enterprise," an invasion of England, blessed by the pope. The Spanish strategy depended upon a massive fleet, known as the "Invincible Armada." It was ordered to meet a large Spanish army in the southern Netherlands and land this force on the English coast. But in 1588, when the Armada sailed for Flanders, Dutch ships blocked the main ports, preventing the convoying of troops to the Spanish galleons, which could not come into shallow waters. Philip's project was completely ruined when the smaller and more maneuverable English ships, commanded by Sir Francis Drake, defeated the Armada in the English Channel. A severe storm, the famed "Protestant wind," completed the debacle. After a long voyage around Scotland, the Armada limped back to Spain, having lost a third of its ships.

The Post-Armada Stalemate

Contrary to English expectations, defeat of the Armada brought no immediate shift of international power. While Spain built new ships and successfully defended its sea lanes, neither side gained dramatic victories. All the major combatants were exhausted, a factor which largely

An English view of the Spanish Armada shows the pope and the devil plotting the Spanish invasion of England. The engraving is dated 1620.

explains the Bourbons' acquisition of the French crown and continued Dutch independence through the 1590s. Lingering war brought new opportunities for France and the Netherlands but only a strength-draining stalemate for England and Spain.

During the last decade of Philip's life, his developing failure foreshadowed the decline of his country. He encountered rebellion in Aragon, quarreled with Pope Clement VIII over recognizing the Bourbons, and sent two more naval expeditions against England, both of which were scattered by storms. In 1598, he handed over the southern Netherlands to his favorite daughter Isabel and her husband, Archduke Albert, an Austrian Habsburg. Then, before he died in 1598, Philip had to make peace with France. He left Spain bankrupt for the third time during his reign, having wasted the country's considerable resources and sacrificed its future to his dynastic pride. The same poor judgment was even more pronounced in his successor, Philip III

(1598–1621), who was also lazy, extravagant, and frivolous and whose henchmen increased an already prevalent graft and inefficiency.

Elizabeth experienced similar difficulties. Sea raids on Spanish shipping continued and returned some profits; yet all the grand projects failed, including a fiasco in 1596, when the English, commanded by the Earl of Essex, plundered Cadiz but missed the Spanish treasure fleet. Land campaigns in France and the Netherlands, plus a continuing rebellion in Ireland, depleted Elizabeth's carefully husbanded resources. When asked for grants, Parliament insisted on debating constitutional questions and hearing Puritan demands for reform of the Church. While the old queen grew crotchety, muttering about cutting off heads, the country needed peace. It didn't come until the year after her death in 1603.

The Dutch, meanwhile, were stumbling toward independence, fearing the advancing Spanish tide in the South and pleading for English or French Protestant aid, but stubbornly persevering. Their declaration of 1581, while displaying what could be interpreted later as democratic rhetoric, reflected more concern for aristocratic privilege and national survival. After failing to find a suitable French or English monarch, the Dutch created a republic in 1587 and held on to sign a truce with Spain in 1609. As time passed, their growing maritime trade and naval power guaranteed their security.

The post-Armada stalemate was most beneficial to war-torn France. With the death of the last Valois claimant in 1589, the Bourbon Protestant Henry of Navarre was proclaimed Henry IV, king of France. This provoked the Catholic Holy League to fanatic anti-royalist frenzy and caused Philip's military intervention in France to support his daughter's claim to the throne. But English aid and Henry's willingness to turn Catholic led to Philip's withdrawal and the Peace of Vervins in 1598. To pacify the Huguenot minority, Henry then issued the Edict of Nantes, which guaranteed the Huguenots some civil and religious rights while permitting them to continue holding more than a hundred fortified towns. Henry thus achieved peace, but the French economy was prostrated, and powerful Protestant armed forces within the country challenged royal authority.

The Thirty Years' War

Spain's golden age had ended, but the religious and political strife of dynasties continued with even greater intensity. Despite the weakening of Spain, other nations still feared a Habsburg resurgence and other dynasties sought to win more territories and power. Moreover, the increasing number of Calvinists and proponents of the counter-Reformation were still hoping for complete victory in the struggle over "true religion." These issues ultimately produced the Thirty Years' War, which began in 1618. At enormous cost in lives and wealth, this war finally completed the political transition from medievalism by burning out old religious obsessions and clearly revealing the secular rivalries of European states.

Background and Setting of the Conflict

During the sixteenth century, Europeans had looked out upon the world with pride in their vitality and superiority. Now in the early 1600s, they faced severe economic depression, along with intensified conflict in every sphere of human relations. It was a time of disruption and frustration, quite in contrast with earlier optimism. A deepening sense of crisis gripped the continent.

The first few decades of the seventeenth century brought a marked decline to the European economy, even before the advent of open warfare. Prices fell until about 1660, reversing the inflation of the 1500s. International trade declined, as did Spanish bullion imports from America. Heavy risks on a falling market caused failures among many foreign trading companies; only the larger houses, organized as joint stock companies, were able to survive. European industry and agriculture also fell on hard times; urban craftsmen saw their wages drop, and peasants faced increasing exploitation.

Tensions accompanying economic depression added to those arising from religious differences. Calvinism was becoming a more formidable force, having become official in Scotland and Holland and achieving an uneasy toleration in France. It was also spreading in eastern Europe and Germany. In England, soon after James of Scotland succeeded Elizabeth, both the Anglicans and the more radical sects feared the southward march of Scottish Presbyterianism. A similar tension prevailed in the Dutch Republic, where a militant movement for Calvinist uniformity strove to wipe out all other churches. But the most dangerous area was Germany, which had directly experienced an increasingly militant Counter-Reformation since the Peace of Augsburg.

Although absolute monarchy was already a recognized ideal and a dominant trend in the early seventeenth century, every royal house from England to Russia was somewhat insecure. The usual threat was posed by nobles defending their traditional privileges. In England and Holland, however, where commercial development was most advanced, nobles tended to support central authority against the urban commercial classes. Theoretical opposition to absolutism, based on a monarch's contractural responsibilities to his subjects, had gained some popularity everywhere during the early religious wars. It was particularly common among radical Protestants; but the same theme had even been expressed among extreme royalists, such as the French Guises who opposed Henry IV.

France best illustrates developing absolutism during the period. Henry IV and his hard-headed chief minister, the Duke of Sully (1560–1641), produced a balanced budget and a treasury surplus in little more than a decade. At the same time, Henry ended the nobility's control of hereditary offices and council seats. This royalist centralization was temporarily disrupted in 1610, when Henry was assassinated; but his queen Marie de Médicis (1573–1642), served as regent for her son Louis XIII until 1617. Like her distant relative Catherine, Marie had survived a tragic marriage to play a dominant role in French affairs. Her peace policy toward Spain and her successful defenses, both military and diplomatic, kept the Huguenots and the great nobles in check, thus securing the succession. Meanwhile, she negotiated a marriage between her son and the Habsburg princess Anne of Austria.

When he was fifteen, the new king seized power from his mother. For the next thirteen years, mother and son vied for power. Marie favored a pro-Spanish and Catholic policy; Louis, following the advice of his famous minister, Cardinal Richelieu (1585–1642) saw the Habsburgs and the papacy as the main threats to French interests. Richelieu finally prevailed, and Marie was banished in 1631, after which she continued to conspire with Spain and the French Catholic party. Inside France, Richelieu relentlessly worked to increase the king's power. He organized a royal civil service, restricted the traditional courts, brought local government under royal agents (*intendants*), outlawed dueling, prohibited fortified castles, stripped the Huguenots of their military defenses, and developed strong military and naval forces.

Absolutism elsewhere in Europe was moving in the same general direction but with less success. The Vasa dynasty of Sweden, supported by a strong national church and an efficient army, was building an empire involving Finland, the Baltic states, parts of Poland, and Denmark. In Germany, many of the princes, particularly the Hohenzollerns of Brandenberg, hoped to become independent absolute monarchs. As was true of earlier Habsburgs, the Holy Roman Emperor, Ferdinand II (1619–1637), struggled to concentrate his control over Austria, Hungary, and Bohemia, while extending his limited authority in Germany at the expense of the princes. Other rulers, including those in England, Spain, Russia, and Poland, faced determined local opposition as they sought to centralize power.

This political contention within states was accompanied by rising internationl apprehensions. Although the European power balance in 1618 resembled that of the 1500s, it was much less fixed. The Habsburgs still evoked counteralliances, but their vulnerability was now greater, not only because Spain was weakening but also because other states—France, the Netherlands, and Sweden—were growing more powerful. Under these circumstances, European revolt against Habsburg dominance was almost inevitable. A general awareness of the coming conflagration was perhaps the most important source of European insecurity.

The Thirty Years' War, fought between 1618 and 1648, was a culmination of all these related religious and political dissensions. Almost all of western Europe, except England, was involved and suffered accordingly. Wasted resources and manpower, along with disease, further checked economic development and curtailed population expansion. Germany was particularly hard hit, suffering great population loss in many areas. Despite the terrible devastation, neither Protestantism nor Catholicism won decisive victory. What began as a religious war in the German principalities turned into a complex political struggle, involving the ambitions of north German rulers, the expansionist ambitions of Sweden, and the efforts of Catholic France to break the "Habsburg ring."

Reviving Habsburg Prospects, 1618–1630

Despite the general decline of Habsburg supremacy, the early years of the war before 1629, usually cited as the Bohemian and Danish phases, brought a last brief revival of Habsburg prospects. The new Habsburg emperor, Ferdinand II, who had been raised by his mother as a fanatic Catholic, was determined to intensify the Counter-Reformation, set aside the Peace of

Cardinal Richelieu. The power behind the throne of Louis XIII, Richelieu was chiefly responsible for the direction of the government, including France's involvement in the Thirty Years' War.

Augsburg, and wipe out Protestantism in central Europe. For a time, he almost succeeded.

Ferdinand's succession came amid severe political tension. Spreading Calvinism, plus the aggressive crusading of the Jesuits, had led to the formation of a Protestant league of German princes in 1608 and a Catholic counter-league the next year. The two had almost clashed in 1610 over a territorial dispute in northwest Germany. Meanwhile, the Bohemian Protestants had extracted a promise of toleration from their Catholic king, the Holy Roman Emperor, Rudolf II (1576–1612). In 1618, the Bohemian leader, fearing that Ferdinand would not honor the promise, threw two of his officials out of a window—an incident which became known as the "defenestration of Prague." When Ferdinand mobilized troops, the Bohemians deposed him and offered their throne to Frederick, the Protestant Elector of the Palatinate, in western Germany.

In the short Bohemian war which followed, Frederick was quickly overwhelmed. At the urging of his wife, Elizabeth, the daughter of James I of England, Frederick reluctantly accepted the Bohemian crown. But while he and Elizabeth held court in Prague, no practical military support came from England, the Netherlands, or the Protestant German princes. Ferdinand, in contrast, deployed two superb armies, one from Spain and the other from Catholic Bavaria. In 1620 Frederick's meager forces were scattered at the Battle of the White Mountain, near Prague. Afterward, the hapless Bohemian monarch and his queen fled the country, ultimately settling at the Hague, in the Netherlands, where they continued to pursue their lost cause. Ferdinand gave their lands to Maximillian of Bavaria, distributed the holdings of Bohemian Protestant nobles among Catholic aristocrats, and proceeded to stamp out Protestantism in Bohemia.

War began again in 1625 when Christian IV (1588–1648), the Lutheran king of Denmark, invaded Germany. As Duke of Holstein and thus a prince of the Empire, he hoped to revive Protestantism and win a kingdom in Germany for his youngest son. Christian was luckier than Frederick had been in attracting support. The Dutch reopened their naval war with Spain; England provided subsidies; and the remaining independent German Protestant princes, now thoroughly alarmed, rose up against the Catholics and the

Emperor. All of these renewed efforts were in vain. Ferdinand's new general, Albert von Wallenstein, defeated the Protestants in a series of brilliant campaigns. By 1629, Christian had to admit defeat and withdraw his forces, thus ending the Danish conflict with another Protestant debacle.

Their successful campaigns of the 1620s gave the Habsburgs almost complete domination in Germany. Using the army Wallenstein raised in Bohemia, Ferdinand reconquered the north. In 1629, he issued the Edict of Restitution, restoring to the Catholics all properties lost since 1552. This seemed to be only a first step toward eliminating Protestantism completely and creating a centralized Habsburg empire in Germany.

The End of Habsburg Supremacy, 1630–1648

Fearing the Counter-Reformation and the growing Habsburg power behind it, the threatened European states resumed the war again in 1630. As the conflict rapidly spread and intensified, religious issues were steadily subordinated to power politics. This was evidenced by the phases of the conflict, usually designated as the Swedish (1630–1635) and the French (1635–1648), because these two countries led successive anti-Habsburg coalitions. Utlimately, their efforts were successful. By 1648, the Dutch Republic had replaced Spain as the leading maritime state and Bourbon France had become the dominant European land power.

Protestant Swedes and French Catholics challenged Ferdinand's imperial ambitions for similar political reasons. Gustavus Adolphus, the Swedish king, wanted to save German Lutheranism, but he was also determined to prevent a strong Habsburg state on the Baltic from restricting his own expansion and interfering with Swedish trade. A similar desire to liberate France from Habsburg encirclement motivated Cardinal Richelieu. He offered Gustavus French subsidies, for which the Swedish monarch promised to invade Germany and permit Catholic worship in any lands he might conquer. Thus the Catholic cardinal and the Protestant king compromised their religious differences in the hope of achieving mutual political benefits.

Gustavus invaded Germany in 1630 while the Dutch attacked the Spanish Netherlands. With

Hardships in a German Town During the Thirty Years' War

This account of disaster and suffering by a refugee from Calw, who returned to find his "beloved town" in "ashes and rubble," illustrates the terrible havoc experienced by ordinary German people during the conflict.

During the pillage of Calw by Croat Imperial troops in September 1634] I never totally forsook my flock and only sought to escape from falling into the hands of the enemy. I joined a band of women and children soon amounting to more than 200 people. Like ants we scurried over hills and rocks. The beneficial influence of Heaven helped up continuously throughout this time. If we had bad weather we would have fared even worse than we did.

After it became known that the town [Calw in Württemberg] had been burnt down, we escaped to Aichelberg, a rough place. We had agreed among ourselves where each of us should hide but since our presence had been betrayed to the enemy, we were barely able to escape a quarter of an hour before we would have been totally ruined. At this the enemy became angry and vented his wrath upon the richest peasant in the place, who after hideous torture was burnt along with his house. . . .

Since the enemy was also active in these parts, . . . we decided to make an attempt to ask the victor for mercy. But to our further consternation we had to flee once again into the hills where no one could readily follow us. From there we wandered around, divided into smaller bands, and on the 15 September alone with my nephew John Joshua and son Gottlieb I hid in the deep Lauterback valley near the stream in a barn on the fields. We spent the night calmly and also the next one.

Since our lodging was moved to another barn where a certain Peter Schill, whom I must praise for his great honesty among the wood-folk, provided us with food and drink, our lack of caution led us back to Gernsbach where we scarcely avoided falling into the net of the enemy. As we lived scattered about all the secret places on Obertsrot, Hilpertsau, Reichtal, Weissenbach, Langenbrand and elsewhere, the hue and cry was raised after us and huntsmen were hired who knew the forests to track us down with their dogs. We saw them in the distance and became heartily dispirited, but also took a serious warning from the event.

I finally arrived at a peasant's place where the wife was nearing her childbirth, and I had a sleepless night since three hours before dawn I had climbed over the peaks of the hills, gone through hill and dale and eventually arrived back at my own vineyard where I had placed my little son Ehrenreich [aged ten], and in which farm we now spent our exile [*exilierte*]. I found my little son much weakened and unable to stand cold and hunger. The Lord took him and released his spirit into the freedom of Heaven on the 20 September. But shortly before this I had already left. We were called back in a letter from our friends, since everything, as far as the times allowed, was back in order, which accorded with the enemy's own best interest.

When I saw my beloved town of Calw in ashes and rubble—it was however not the first time that I had seen a town in ruins—I felt a cold shudder and I brooded repeatedly on that which I neither can nor wish to repeat now. What struck me most deeply was that long ago I had already prophesied the calamity, and that my prophecy had now come true in as much as it had also included me.

Source: Gerhard Benecke, ed., *Germany in the Thirty Years' War* (London: Edward Arnold, 1978), pp. 85–87.

his mobile cannon and his hymm-singing Swedish veterans, Gustavus and his German allies won a series of smashing victories, climaxed in November 1632 at Lutzen, near Leipzig, where Wallenstein was decisively defeated. Unfortunately for the Protestant cause, Gustavus died in battle. Meanwhile, a Dutch army in Flanders advanced toward Brussels, where Philip II's aging daughter, Isabella, was still governing. Aware of her subjects' desperate need for peace, Isabella began negotiations, but the news from Lutzen raised Habsburg hopes in Vienna and Madrid. Subsequently, Isabella was removed, a Spanish army was dispatched to Germany, and Wallenstein was mysteriously murdered. This Habsburg flurry brought no significant victories but led to the compromise Peace of Prague in 1635 between the emperor and the German Protestant states.

The situation now demanded that France act directly to further its dynastic interests. The final, French phase of the war began in 1635 when Richelieu and Louis XIII declared war on the Habsburgs, sending French troops into Germany and toward the Spanish borders. They also subsidized the Dutch and Swedes, while recruiting an army of German Protestant mercenaries. France continued limiting Protestantism within its borders but gladly allied with Protestant states against Catholic Spain, Austria, Bavaria, and their Catholic allies. The war which had begun in religious controversy had now become pure power politics, completing the long political transition from medieval to modern times.

For thirteen more years the conflict wore on. France's allies, the Swedes and north Germans, kept Habsburg armies engaged in Germany, while French armies and the Dutch navy concentrated on Spain. In 1643, the French won a decisive battle at Rocroi in the southern Netherlands. Next, they moved into Germany, defeating the imperial forces and, with the aid of the Swedes, ravaging Bavaria. When Richelieu died in 1642, he had already unleased forces which would make the Bourbon dynasty supreme in Europe.

For all practical purposes the war was over, but years of indecisive campaigning and tortuous negotiations delayed the peace. The French held to rigid demands, despite the deaths of both Richelieu and Louis XIII in 1642 and 1643.

Richelieu's protege, Cardinal Mazarin, directed diplomacy, although he was technically responsible to Queen Anne, ruling as regent for her son, the future Louis XIV. Anne consistently supported her minister through budget crises and popular unrest. The Swedes took a more conciliatory approach after Queen Christiana, the daughter of Gustavus Adolphus, succeeded to the throne in 1644. A horde of emissaries from nearly every capital in Europe met that year at Westphalia to negotiate the peace. Although Spain and France could reach no agreement, a settlement for the Empire was finally completed in 1648.

The Peace of Westphalia

The Peace of Westphalia is among the most significant pacts in modern European history. It ended Europe's emergence from medievalism and prepared a way for the modern state system. Even so, it did not establish universal peace; the war between France and Spain lasted another eleven years, ending finally with the Peace of the Pyrenees in 1659.

The peace agreement at Westphalia signaled a victory for Protestantism and the German princes while dooming Habsburg imperial ambitions. France moved closer to the Rhine by acquiring Alsatian territory, Sweden and Brandenburg acquired lands on the Baltic, and Holland and Switzerland gained recognition of their independence (see map, p. 463). The German states won undisputed rights to self-government and the conduct of their foreign relations. The emperor was required to receive approval from the Imperial diet for any laws, taxes, military levies, or foreign agreements—provisions which practically nullified imperial power. The religious autonomy of the German states, as decreed at Augsburg, was reconfirmed, with Calvinism now permitted along with Lutheranism. In addition, Protestant states were conceded all Catholic properties taken before 1624.

In its religious implications, the Peace of Westphalia ended the dream of reuniting Christendom. Catholics and Protestants now realized that major faiths could not be destroyed; moreover, Europeans had finally tired of religious controversy, tending to think it dangerous. From such intuitions a spirit of toleration gradually

emerged. Although religious uniformity would be imposed within states for another century, it would not again be a serious issue in European foreign affairs.

The Peace confirmed the new European state system. Henceforth, states would customarily shape their policies in accord with the power of their neighbors, seeking to expand at the expense of the weaker and to protect themselves—not by religion, law, or morality—but by alliances against their stronger adversaries. The treaty also instituted the internationl conference as a means for negotiating power relationships among contending states.

Aside from its general implications, the peace left specific political legacies for Europe. Both Spain and Austria were weakened, and the Austrian Habsburgs shifted their primary attention from Germany to southeastern Europe. German disunity was perpetuated by the autonomy of many petty states. France, in contrast, emerged as the potential master of the continent and the model of successful absolute monarchy. The war also helped both Holland and England, although

This commemorative painting, *Signing of the Peace of Münster, May 15, 1648,* by the Dutch artist Gerard Ter Borch shows the scene in the Rathaus of Münster when the delegates swore the oath of ratification to the treaty, one of the agreements of the Peace of Westphalia ending the Thirty Years' War.

this was not evident for England in 1648 at the climax of its revolution (see pp. 466–467).

Perhaps the most significant legacy of Westphalia was a universal yearning for order and stability. The war disrupted trade, destroyed industries, undermined monetary systems, and caused the deaths of more than five million people. It perpetuated an economic depresssion in central Europe so severe that killing famines became commonplace. Armies on both sides lived from the land. Brutalized and half-starved mercenary soldiers looted, burned, tortured, and raped. Even in unoccupied areas, general disorder and crime prevailed among rural and urban populations, both of which declined drastically. In some places, law enforcement was virtually abandoned. For all who experienced these conditions directly, and for thousands of others who only heard the terrible rumors, restoration of order seemed a goal surpassing all others.

Emergence of Constitutional Governments

A notable development during the war was the emergence of constitutional governments in the Netherlands and England. The prolonged conflict affected the two countries in different ways. Holland prospered from developing trade and colonies, made possible by the weakening of Spain. Because other states were tied down in continental wars, England was free to experiment with its political structure. In both countries, rapidly developing commerce and rising middle classes encouraged a direct transition from feudalism to constitutional government, without a prolonged intermediate stage of absolute monarchy.

The Dutch Republic

The Thirty Years' War brought official independence to the Dutch Republic but its actual independence had long since been an established fact. Defeat of the Spanish Armada had bought the Dutch time in which to accumulate resources, create an efficient army, and drive out the Spaniards. After Spanish troops had sacked and then effectively blockaded Antwerp, most industry and banking moved north to Amsterdam, which became the leading port and financial center for northern Europe. The Dutch meanwhile developed a peculiar federal government, combining urban and feudal councils to limit executive power. The system was identified, in the Dutch independence declaration of 1581, with

The arts of Mughul India reflect the splendor and luxury of the great seventeenth-century empire. In the miniature painting *Jahangir's Dream* (c. 1618), left, the mighty emperor Jahangir embraces the frail Shah Abbas of Persia. In 1632 Jahangir's son, Shah Jahan, commissioned the building of the resplendent Taj Mahal, below, as a memorial to his late wife.

The outstanding artwork of Ming China is its porcelains, such as the mei p'ing vase, left. The vase is of the fa-hua type in which ridges of clay outline the design, then are filled with pale yellow and blue, in imitation of cloisonné enamel. The elegant simplicity of the late Ashikaga period in Japan is seen in the *Excursion to Takao*, below, of Kano Hideyori (d. 1557), which dates from the mid-sixteenth century.

Government officials of the Ashanti kingdom of Africa wore gold badges like the
turtle, right, or the double lizard, below,
to identify their rank and role in the state
system. The Ashanti state, a powerful
kingdom of the eighteenth and nineteenth centuries, extended into the Gold
Coast and present-day Ghana, Togo, and
the Ivory Coast.

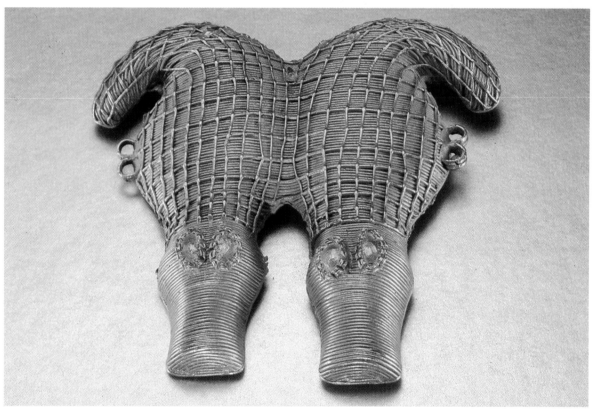

To the Aztecs, turquoise symbolized the preciousness of life, and turquoise mosaic was used to make ritual objects, such as masks, for statues of the gods. The turquoise mosaic on the mask, left, is placed on a backing of cedar wood, and the teeth and eyes are inlaid of white shell.

the abstract ideal of popular sovereignty, but this aristocratic polity of burghers and nobles only baguely resembed modern democracy. The Dutch system was, however, the first successful major challenge to absolute monarchy in western Europe, and it did provide a traditional base for many later democratic institutions.

Perhaps the most striking feature of the Dutch system was its internal pluralism. The Republic was literally a union of sovereign states, each empowered to veto any act of the States General (federal assembly). Theoretically, the *stadtholder,* as official chief of state, was merely a military commander, dependent upon the assembly for men and supplies. The provinces made public decisions in their own assemblies, which represented the nobles and the cities in varying proportions. Within the cities, policies were made by councils, whose members sat by inherited rights and usually represented the wealthy merchant-bankers. Local government, however, was a practical partnership between rich burghers and less affluent craftsmen. The latter held minor administrative posts and maintained peace through their service in the militias.

Concentration of power in any one office or individual was limited by this interaction of classes. Their differences were accented by their separate interests and by their indirect exercise of power, outside of government and often outside of the law itself. Wealthy urban merchants dominated the town councils, but their power was balanced against that of the nobles in the provincial assemblies. The merchants were also checked by differences within their own class and by dependence upon the urban militias. All three classes needed each other to maintain industry and commerce, upon which their prosperity depended. Because no one of the three major blocs could achieve absolute control, all regulations were lax, and individuals enjoyed more freedom than citizens anywhere else in Europe.

The internal Dutch power balance shifted during the early seventeenth century. Republicans, representing the great urban merchants, favored religious toleration, limited central authority, and peace. The monarchists, representing a majority of the urban lower classes, the nobles, and the House of Orange, wanted a Calvinist state church, a strong stadtholder, a large army, and an aggressive foreign policy against the Habsburgs. Until 1619, the republicans held power, but their leader, John Oldenbarnveldt (1547–1619), was ultimately overthrown and executed after a royalist uprising. Between 1619 and the Peace of Westphalia, the country was ruled by domineering stadtholders, who conducted the war against Spain and acquired a status similar to that of European kings.

At the end of the war the Dutch Republic enjoyed prosperity and power far beyond its natural potential. During the interval between the collapse of Spain and the maturation of England and France the Dutch Republic enjoyed naval, commerical, and colonial supremacy. The Dutch predominance, of course, could only be transitory. The country was so small and so divided that it could not afford open competition with France in Europe or with England overseas. But even as a secondary power, which it was destined to become after 1650, it remained economically progressive, culturally advanced, and a pioneer in developing constitutional government.

The English Constitutional Crisis

While the Dutch prospered and mainland Europe experienced near-anarchy in the Thirty Years' War, England faced its most dangerous internal crisis. Peace with Spain in 1604 left a debt of £100,000 and the end of privateering, which had netted handsome profits for many London financiers. The English, like the Dutch earlier, also resented a foreign king, his "popish" religion, and his taxes. Despite these similarities, the English struggle against absolutism brought different results. Because it came later and was better protected, it was more extreme, more secular, and more precise than the Dutch had been. Consequently, the English experience became the main historical precedent for western constitutional government.

Contention began shortly after James I (1603–1625) succeeded to the English throne. He was the son of Mary Stuart, a cousin of Elizabeth, and king of Scotland, where he had reigned as James VI since 1567. Understandably, he was a committed proponent of absolute monarchy, having written a book expounding his views on the subject.

James faced an English Parliament that had recently become aggressive in its demands for church reform, lower taxes, and security for its members. Most elected members were from the landed gentry, who also controlled local government. They naturally opposed a foreign king and the courtiers who served him. Therefore, a wide gap soon opened between the "country party" and those inside the royal circle.

The resulting political struggle was fought mainly in Parliament. James dismissed his first Parliament in 1611. The second sat for only two months in 1614. James then ruled by decree, without Parliament, until 1621, when he quickly ended another session by personally attending the House of Commons and angrily rejecting its proposals against his policies.

James' son, Charles I (1625–1649), fared even worse. After enduring many stormy debates with Parliament, he accepted the famous "Petition of Right" in 1628. Theoretically, this document affirmed ancient English rights by securing parliamentary approval of taxes, abolishing arbitrary imprisonment, ending the quartering of soldiers on citizens, and prohibiting martial law in peacetime. But Charles' cooperation was only temporary. From 1629 to 1640, he ruled without Parliament, alienating much of English society, particularly the Puritan church reformers and the gentry. When the Scots rebelled against his religious policies and invaded England in 1640, he was forced to conclude a humiliating peace and pay the invaders to withdraw.

In this age of religious strife, the early Stuart kings consistently provoked resentment from Protestant subjects. Although he was not a Catholic, James made peace with Spain, abandoned his Protestant son-in-law during the Thirty Years' War, and married Charles to a French princess, Henrietta Marie, who brought her Catholic confessor to England. Both James and Charles regarded Calvinism, with its independent clergy and elected synods, as threatening to monarchy. James resolutely fought reform of the Anglican Church, threatening to expel Calvinists from the country. Charles went further. Archbishop Laud, his Anglican advisor, forced absolute conformity; he whipped, mutilated, and jailed Protestant dissidents. As a result, thousands of religious refugees left the country. The Scottish invasion, which led directly to civil war, was a Calvinist reaction to Charles' religious policies.

The English crisis was nevertheless as much political as religious. The nation's governing class was divided; the economy was depressed; government expenses were rising; and the common people were suffering hard times. The struggle pitted the King's supporters, who advocated the king's divine right to rule, levy taxes, and control the economy, against the opposition who represented property owners and who wanted to govern in partnership with the king, control expenditures, and be free from government regulation of business affairs, particularly from royal monopolies. But the freedom that they advocated usually meant protection of a minority's profits. These aspirations reflected the country's commercial potential and the increasing self-awareness of the urban middle classes.

The English Civil War and Interregnum

After Charles agreed to buy off the Scots in 1640, he called Parliament to raise the money and secure his future finances. Known later as the "Long Parliament," because it sat through twenty years of constitutional debate and civil war, this Parliament immediately began limiting the king's powers. Led by the dauntless Puritan, John Pym, Parliament imprisoned Laud, executed Charles' hated chief minister, the Earl of Strafford, provided for its own regular meetings, abolished the royal courts of Star Chamber and High Commission, and eliminated taxes levied without parliamentary consent. The struggle with Charles would last another nine years; the monarchy would be replaced by a republic for a decade; and then the monarch would be restored, but absolutism was gone forever.

Increasingly intense contention between Charles and Parliament polarized public opinion and led to civil war, beginning in 1642. Charles left London in January of that year, raising his standard at Nottingham in August. London expected attack, but fighting began at South Molton, in Devonshire, where a mob of men and women, armed with rocks, clubs, and muskets, resisted royalist troops in the town square. During the ensuing civil war the royalists, or "cavaliers," were largely countrymen, led by noblemen, such as the dashing Prince Rupert, Charles' nephew and son of Elizabeth, the dethroned queen of Bohemia. The parliamentary forces included many townsmen, although some commanders, like the incompetent Earl of Essex, were aristocrats. English women were active on both sides, petitioning Parliament, handling business affairs while their men were fighting, and sometimes, as in the cases of the royalist Countess of Derby or the Parliamentarian Lady Harley, supervising defense of their homes against enemy soldiers.

At first, the royalist forces were successful, until the rebels turned to extreme measures. They made alliance with the Scots, reorganized their armies, enlisted popular support, and raised their morale by appeals to radical Protestantism. In 1646, they defeated Charles and took him prisoner. He escaped and renewed the war as dissension arose between the conservative Parliament and its more radical army. When Charles was defeated a second time, the army officers defied parliament and their own soldiers who wanted a democratic government. Led by the Puritan general, Oliver Cromwell (1599–1658), they executed the king in 1649 and proclaimed a republic.

Although their efforts were largely premature, some English rebels in this period first conceived of democracy. Their most striking pronouncements came from a group led by "honest John Lilburne" and known as "Levellers," because they advocated reforms to favor the common people. Many were active among the soldiers in Cromwell's army. Between 1646 and 1649, Levellers and the near-mutinous troops produced a series of documents, each known as an "Agreement of the People." These first written democratic constitutions proposed that the English government be organized as a republic, with a one-house legislature elected by universal manhood suffrage. They did not propose that women vote, but women were active in the movement, writing, speaking, and organizing. The program did, however, list civil and religious liberties, to be held as rights by all citizens. Thus the Levellers and their "Agreements" anticipated modern democratic theory.

The Leveller movement was suppressed when the officers regained control of the army and established a military regime. Their government, known as "the Commonwealth," was a republic dominated by property holders. It was never popular enough to be maintained without military force. After Cromwell's death in 1658, the system gave way almost immediately to a restored Stuart monarchy.

Despite these failures, the period of the civil war and the interregnum brought significant changes to England. Constitutionally, it confirmed Parliament's necessary role in the English system, thereby decisively checking the trend toward absolutism. At the same time, the royalist defeat opened opportunities for capitalisic development and imperial expansion under Cromwell. England effectively challenged the naval and maritime supremacy of the Dutch in the 1650s, while beginning to develop into the world's leading empire.

Cultural Expressions of the Age

European cultural expression during the century before 1650 reflected a strange ambiguity, combining reflections of the insecurity, violence, and general pessimism of the era with a great creative energy. For a time, artists and writers abandoned the confidence and enthusiasm of the Renaissance, seeking new forms of escape or becoming preoccupied with bizarre distortions of reality. Later, in the early seventeenth century, artistic works lacked balance and discipline but displayed a fresh vitality in symbolizing the power of religious upheaval and developing national states.

The Post-Renaissance Transition

Cultural ambiguity was most evident in the latter part of the sixteenth century. By then the Renaissance spirit was beginning to be transformed in Italy but was reaching a climax elsewhere in Europe (see pp. 327–328). The Counter-Reformation, stimulated by the Council of Trent, was also polarizing European thought and producing unique cultural developments. Sometimes, reviving religious sensitivities were accompanied by perplexing uncertainties. In other instances, lingering Renaissance values coexisted with Protestant Puritanism. Such incongruities were indications of a cultural transition, like those in political and social affairs, between medieval and early modern times.

John Lilburne, "The Agreement of the People"

John Lilburne, the nearly forgotten hero of the Puritan revolution, wrote this demand for popular sovereignty in 1647, when the common soldiers were near mutiny in the parliamentary army and before Cromwell and the army officers crushed the movement. This was the first among a number of such documents, which have been called the earliest appeals for democracy in the Western world.

Having by our late labors and hazards made it appear to the world at how high a rate we value our just freedom, . . . we do now hold ourselves bound in mutual duty to each other to take the best care we can for the future . . . so may we safely promise to ourselves that, when our common rights and liberties shall be cleared, their endeavors will be disappointed that seek to make themselves our masters. Since, therefore, our former oppressions and scarce-yet ended troubles have been occasioned, either by want of frequent national meetings in Council, or by rendering those meetings ineffectual, we are fully agreed and resolved to provide that hereafter our representatives be neither left to an uncertainty for the time nor made useless to the ends for which they are intended. In order whereunto we declare:

I. That, the people of England, being at this day very unequally distributed by Counties, Cities, and Boroughs for the election of their deputies in Parliament, ought to be more indifferently proportioned according to the number of the inhabitants. . . .

II. That, to prevent the many incoveniences apparently arising from the long continuance of the same persons in authority, this present Parliament be dissolved upon the last day of September which shall be in the year of our Lord 1648.

III. That the people do, of course, choose themselves a Parliament once in two years. . . .

IV. That the power of this, and all future Representatives of this Nation, is infereior only to theirs who choose them, and does extend, without the consent or concurrence of any other person or persons, to the enacting, altering, and repealing of laws, to the erecting abolishing of offices and courts, to the appointing, removing, and calling to account magistrates and officers of all degrees, to the making of war and peace, to the treating with foreign states, and, generally, to whatsoever is not expressly or impliedly reserved by the represented to the themselves:

Which are as follows:

1. That matters of religion and the ways of God's worship are not at all entrusted by us to any human power, because therein we cannot remit or exceed a tittle of what our consciences dictate to be the mind of God without wilful sin: nevertheless the public way of instructing the nation (so it be not compulsive) is referred to their discretion.

2. That the matter of impressing and constraining any of us to serve in the wars is against our freedom; and therefore we do not allow it in our Representatives. . . .

3. That after the dissolution of the present Parliament, no person be at any time questioned for anything said or done in reference to the late public differences. . . .

4. That in all laws made or to be made every person may be bound alike, and that no tenure, estate, charter, degree, birth, or place do confer any exemption from the ordinary course of legal proceedings whereunto others are subjected.

5. That as the laws ought to be equal, so they must be good, and not evidently destructive to the safety and well-being of the people.

These things we declare to be our native rights, and therefore are agreed and resolved to maintain them with our utmost possibilities against all opposition whatsoever.

Source: Lowell H. Zuck, ed., *Christianity and Revolution* (Philadelphia: Temple University Press, 1975), pp. 236–37.

In art and architecture, the post-Renaissance transition was reflected in a new style called mannerism (see p. 322). Perhaps the greatest of the "mannerists" was El Greco (1547–1614), who was born in Crete, studied in Italy, and settled in Spain. He is known for his imaginative but morbidly ascetic treatment of religious themes, using *chiaroscuro* (strong contrasts of light and shade). Andrea Palladio (1518–1580) exemplified the style in architecture with his Villa Rotunda, near Venice, which displays an exaggerated magnificence in its grouping of four identical temple facades on the sides of a square-domed building.

Like art and architecture, trends in music reflected the transition of the era, but in different ways. Both in Italy and in the northern Renaissance, music developed new complexities in keeping with a spirit of gaiety and respect for aesthetic beauty. This was evident in the increase of chordal writing, in great expansion of tonal ranges, and in the emergence of new secular forms, such as the chanson and the madrigal, which often had poetic lyrics. At the other extreme, church music also became very popular. Protestant hymn-writing and singing were given priorities by the reformers. Luther's "A Mighty Fortress is Our God" is only one example; many hymns were composed by women, who turned to this form of expression when they were prohibited from preaching. Catholic church music was also revolutionized after the Council of Trent ruled that it be simpler and more appealing. The new spirit, simple but emotionally powerful, was well expressed in the masses of Giovanni Palestrina (1525–1594), who has been called the "first Catholic Church musician."

The Baroque Era in the Arts

After 1600, European culture generated a new artisitic style, known as the Baroque. Taken literally, the term means "irregular" and is applied generally to the dynamic and undisciplined artistic creativity of the seventeenth century. At first, the Baroque style grew out of the Catholic pomp and confidence accompanying the Counter-Reformation. Later, as the style spread north, it became popular at royal courts, where it symbolized the emerging power of the new monarchies. Wherever it showed itself, the Baroque approach was likely to exhibit some combination of power, massiveness, or dramatic intensity, embellished with pageantry, color, and theatrical adventure. Without the restraints of the High Renaissance or the subjectiveness of Manneristic painting, the Baroque sought to overawe by its grandeur.

Baroque painting originated in Italy and spread north. One of its Italian creators was Michelangelo da Caravaggio (1565–1609), whose bold and light-bathed naturalism impressed many northern artists. The Italian influence was evident in the works of Peter Paul Rubens (1557–1640), a well-known Flemish artist who chose themes from pagan and Christian literature, illustrating them with human figures involved in dramatic physical action. Ruben also did portraits of Marie de Médicis and Queen Anne, at the French court of Louis XIII. Another famous Baroque court painter was Diego Velasquez (1599–1660), whose canvases depict the haughty formality and opulence of the Spanish royal household. A number of Italian women were successful Baroque painters, including Livonia Fontana (1552–1614), who produced pictures of monumental buildings, and Artemesia Gentileschi (1593–1652), a follower of Caravaggio.

While the Baroque style profoundly affected the rest of Europe, the Dutch perfected their own characteristic style, which grew directly from their pride in political and commerical accomplishments and emphasized the beauty of local nature and the solidity of middle class life. Dutch painting was sober, detailed, and warmly soft in the use of colors, particularly yellows and browns. Almost every town in Holland supported its own school of painters who helped perpetuate local traditions. Consequently a horde of competent artists arose to meet the demand for this republican art.

Only a few among hundreds can be cited here. The robust Frans Hals (1580–1666) employed a vigorous style that enabled him to catch the spontaneous and fleeting expression of his portrait subjects. He left posterity a gallery of types—from cavaliers to fishwives and tavern loungers. His most successful follower, whose works have often been confused with those of Hals, was Judith Leyster (1609–1660), a member of the Haarlem painter's guild with pupils of her own. Somewhat in contrast, Jan Vermeer (1632–1675) exhibited a subtle delicacy. His way of treating the fall of subdued sunlight upon interior scenes has never been equaled.

Towering above all the Dutch artists—and ranking with the outstanding painters of all time—was Rembrandt van Rijn (1606–1669). While reflecting the common characteristics of his school, he produced works so universally human that they not only expressed Dutch cultural values but also transcended them. His canvasses show tremendous sensitivity, depicting almost every human emotion except pure joy. This omission arose partially from his own troubled consciousness and partially from his republican, Calvinist environment. Nevertheless, his work furnished profound insights into the human enigma. He has been called the "Dutch Baroque version of da Vinci."

Baroque architecture, like painting, was centered in Italy, from whence it permeated western Europe. The most renowned architect of the school in the seventeenth century was Giovanni Bernini (1598–1660). He designed the colonnades outside St. Peter's Basilica, where his plan illustrates the Baroque style in the use of vast spaces and curving lines. Hundreds of churches and public buildings all over Europe displayed the elaborate Baroque decorativeness in colored marble, intricate designs, twisted columns, scattered cupolas, imposing facades, and unbalanced extensions or bulges. Stone and mortar were often blended with statuary and painting; indeed it was difficult to see where one art left off and the other began.

The seventeenth century also brought Baroque innovations in music. New forms of expression moved away from the exalted calmness of Palestrina and emphasized melody supported by harmony. Instrumental music—particularly for organ and violin—gained equal popularity, for the first time, with song. Outstanding among Baroque innovations was opera, which originated in Italy at the beginning of the century and quickly conquered Europe. The new form utilized many arts, integrating literature, drama, music and painting of the elaborate stage settings.

The literature of the Baroque age before 1650 showed a marked decline from the exalted heights of the northern Renaissance (see p. 327).

Even before 1600, however, Puritanism and the Counter-Reformation inclined many writers toward religious subjects. In England, this trend continued in the next century and was augmented by a flood of political tracts during the civil war. Religious concerns were typical of the two most prominent English poets, John Donne (1573–1631) and John Milton (1608–1674). Milton's magnificent poetic epic, *Paradise Lost* was planned in his youth but not completed until 1667. French literature during the early 1600s was much less memorable. The major advance came in heroic adventure novels, pioneered by Madeleine Scudery (1608–1701). Most other French writers, influenced by the newly formed French Academy, were increasingly active in salon discussions but more concerned with form than with substance.

Conclusion

The century after the Peace of Augsburg was an era of wrenching transition for Europe. At the opening of the period, most people were still imbued with the medieval concern for salvation, which gave meaning to the religious issues of both Reformations, Protestant and Catholic. Long and exhaustive religious wars burned out this obsession. As the wars continued, secular political concerns became increasingly evident, and at the end of the Thirty Years' War, in 1648, the Peace of Westphalia registered the existence of secular nation-states.

A major question raised by such states involved internal organization and sources of power. One answer, as provided by the Dutch and the English, called for representative political institutions, with power divided and balanced among a number of social groups or governmental offices. The idea of popular sovereignty, justified and maintained under law, developed from both feudal and religious precedents in this period. It caught on in Holland and England where developing commerce had already produced strong middle classes. These maritime states laid foundations for later constitutional governments.

Such precedents, however, exerted little influence in this era or in the half century that followed. A revolution in military tactics, the rise of professional militarism, and the disorders accompanying a century of warfare all contributed to the growth of centralized authority, as demonstrated in the emerging system of absolute monarchy. The trend was illustrated most obviously by the Bourbon dynasty in France. By the time of the Peace of Westphalia, the Bourbon monarchy had become a model for European absolutism, and the way was prepared for Louis XIV (1673–1715), who would soon be hailed as "the Grand Monarch."

A second innovation accompanying the emergence of secular sovereign states was the turn toward power politics in international relations. Although not entirely new, the practice had been obscured in Europe during the Middle Ages by the moral and religious claims of the Church. As the religious wars continued and religious diversities were intensified, rulers sought to realize national interests by looking to their own power, buttressed by alliances. Because each state tended to expand until checked by another, weaker states were forced to form alliances among themselves, no matter what their traditions or religions. The dominant state would thus be curtailed by a "balance of power." Wars to secure this balance ultimately elevated France above Habsburg Spain to dominance on the Continent. At the same time, Holland temporarily replaced Spain as the major maritime state.

The principle of unlimited sovereignty in conducting national affairs was questioned, even before 1648. In the 1620s, as the Thirty Years' War was beginning its terrible devastation, a few European thinkers called for European union to keep the peace. They included Emeric Cruce, an obscure French monk, the Duke of Sully, Louis XIII's chief minister and Hugo Grotius, the famous Dutch political authority. Their proposals were set aside but not forgotten. Since Westphalia, unlimited state sovereignty has generally prevailed, but much study has been devoted to averting international conflicts by subordinating international disputes to the rule of law.

Suggestions For Reading

Two excellent recent overall surveys of this period are Robert Bireley, *Religion and Politics in the Age of the Counter-Reformation* (Univ. of North Carolina, 1981) and

H. G. Koenigsberger, *Early Modern Europe, 1500–1789* (Longman, 1987). The classic treatment of the early seventeenth century, still worth reading, is Carl J. Friedrich, *The Age of the Baroque* (Torchbooks, 1961). For interesting special interpretations, see Trevor Henry Aston, ed., *Crisis in Europe, 1560–1660* (Torchbooks, 1974) and Perez Zagoren, *Rebels and Rulers, 1500–1660* (Cambridge Univ., 1982). Roland Bainton has produced two solid general works on the roles of women: *Women of the Reformation in France and England* (Augsburg Pub. House, 1973) and *Women of the Reformation: From Spain to Scandinavia* (Augsburg Pub. House, 1977). Helga Mobiusm *Women of the Baroque Age* (Abner Schram, 1984) provides good detail, particularly for women painters, but is less scholarly and more superficial in its generalizations.

Four sound studies of Spain during the period are John Lynch, *Spain Under the Habsburgs,* Vol. I, *Empire and Absolutism, 1516–1598* (New York Univ., 1984); Reginald Trevor-Davis, *The Golden Century of Spain, 1501–1621* (Greenwood Press, 1984); R. J. W. Evans, *The Making of the Habsburg Monarchy, 1550–1700* (Oxford Univ., 1984); and H. A. F. Kamen, *The Golden Age of Spain* (Humanities Press, Int., 1988). John H. Elliott, *Spain and Its World* (Yale Univ., 1989) is a collection of excellent previously published essays. A. W. Lovett, *Early Habsburg Spain* (Oxford Univ., 1986) is a readable teachers' manual but is weak on relevant developments in non-Spanish areas. The classic treatment of the Armada, appearing in a recent edition, is Garrett Mattingly, *The Armada* (Houghton Mifflin, 1988). Among a spate of books celebrating the four hundredth anniversary of the legendary battle, Peter Kemp, *The Campaign of the Spanish Armada* (Facts on File, 1988) is perhaps the most readable but, like the others, breaks no new ground. Felipe Fernóudez-Armesto, *The Spanish Armada* (Oxford Univ., 1988) presents the Spanish contention that defeat was caused by the elements rather than English naval guns. Peter Pierson, *Commander of the Armada* (Yale Univ., 1989) is a biography of the ill-fated Spanish admiral Median Sidonia. For a good analysis of Spanish decline after 1588, see Edward Grierson, *The Fatal Inheritance* (Doubleday, 1969).

The best-known account of the Dutch rebellion is Peter Geyl, *The Revolt of the Netherlands* (Barnes and Noble, 1958). Noel G. Parker, *The Dutch Revolt* (Cornell Univ., 1977) and John C. Cadoux, *Philip of Spain and the Netherlands* (Archon Books, 1969) are two excellent later studies, J. I. Israel, *The Dutch Republic and the Hispanic World, 1606–1661* (Oxford Univ., 1986) S. Schama, *The Embarrassment of Riches,* (Knopf, 1987); and C. R. Boxer, *The Dutch Sea-Borne Empire* (Penguin Books, 1989) depict the Republic's problems at the apex of its struggle for power and wealth. The social backgrounds are treated in S. Marshall, *The Dutch Gentry, 1500–1650* (Greenwood Press, 1987). See also K. H. Halley, *The Dutch in the Seventeenth Century* (Harcourt Brace Jovanovich, 1972); J. L. Price, *Culture and Society in the Dutch Republic During the Seventeenth Century* (Columbia Univ., 1974); and Charles H. Wilson, *The Dutch Republic* (McGraw-Hill, 1968). Cicely V. Wedgewood, *William the Silent* (Norton, 1968) is a superb biography.

French society and politics during the whole era are ably surveyed in Robert Briggs, *Early Modern France, 1560–1715* (Oxford Univ., 1977) and Natalie Davis, *Society and Culture in Early Modern France* (Stanford Univ., 1975). George D. Balsama, *The Politics of National Despair*

(Washington, 1978) describes the catastrophic religious wars. See also John E. Neale, *The Age of Catherine de Medici* (Harper Torchbooks, 1962). This tragic time is also reflected in Frederick J. Baumgartner's recent readable biography, *Henry II, King of France* (Duke Univ., 1988). Robert M. Kingdon, presents a Catholic view in *Myths About the Saint Bartholomew's Day Massacres 1572–1576* (Harvard Univ., 1988). For the early seventeenth century, see V. L. Tapie, *France in the Age of Louis XIII and Richelieu* (Cambridge Univ., 1984). The best biographies for this later period are A. Lloyd Moote, *Louis XIII* (Univ. of California, 1989); J. Bergin, *Richelieu* (Yale Univ., 1985); and Ruth Kleinman, *Ann of Austria* (Ohio State Univ., 1985). Elizabeth Warwick has produced two controversial but interesting studies in *Louis XIII, the Making of a King* (Yale Univ., 1986) and *The Young Richelieu* (Univ. of Chicago, 1983). The role of French Protestantism in both eras is clearly depicted in George A. Rothrock, *The Huguenots: a Biography of a Minority* (Nelson Hall, 1979).

A soundly researched coverage of economic, social, and political trends during the period in England by two New Zealanders is Michael A. R. Graves and Robin Silcock, *Revolution, Reaction, and the Triumph of Conservatism, 1558–1700* (Auckland, N. Z.: Longman Paul, 1984). Another outstanding survey of English social history is J. A. Sharpe, *Early Modern England: A Social History, 1550–1760* (E. Arnold, 1987). For the growing social and political awareness of English women in both the sixteenth and seventeenth centuries, see Katherine A. Henderson and Barbara McManus, *Half Humankind: Contexts and Texts of the Controversy About Women in England, 1540–1640* (Univ. of Illinois, 1985) and Mary Prior, ed., *Women in English Society, 1500–1800* (Methuen, 1985).

Excellent general interpretations of Elizabethan England are presented in Arthur Bryant, *The Elizabethan Deliverance* (St. Martin's, 1982) and David B. Quinn and A. N. Ryan, *England's Sea Empire, 1550–1642* (Allen and Unwin, 1983). A creditable but less creative work which supplies broad coverage of Elizabethan experience is S. White-Thomson, *Elizabeth I and Tudor England* (Bookwright Press, 1985). John E. Neale, *Queen Elizabeth I* (Cape, 1967) is still respected as an authoritative study, but a number of more recent biographies are worth consulting: Jasper G. Ridley, *Elizabeth: the Shrewdness of Virtue* (Viking, 1988); Allison Plowden, *Elizabeth Tudor and Mary Stuart* (Barnes and Noble, 1984); J. Mary Wormald, *Mary, Queen of Scots* (George Philip & Son, 1988); and Carolly Erickson, *The First Elizabeth* (Summit Books, 1983). For studies of Elizabethan politics and diplomacy, see Joel Hurstfield, *Elizabeth I and the Unity of England* (Torchbooks, 1967); Charles Wilson, *Queen Elizabeth and the Revolt of the Netherlands* (Univ. of Calif., 1970); and a pair of companion volumes by Richard B. Wernham. These are *Before the Armada: The Emergence of the English Nation, 1485–1588* (Norton, 1972) and *After the Armada: Elizabethan England and the Struggle for Western Europe*, revised ed. (Oxford Univ., 1984). Noteworthy special works on Elizabethan women include Pearl Hogrefe, *Women of Action in Tudor England* (Iowa State Univ., 1977); Retha M. Warnick, *Women of the English Renaissance and Reformation* (Greenwood Press, 1983); and Susan Cahn, *The Transformation of Women's Work in England, 1500–1600* (Col. Univ., 1987)

For the reigns of the first two Stuart monarchs and the civil war, see J. P. Kenyon, *Stuart England* (Penguin Books, 2nd. ed., 1986); Derek Hirst, *Authority and Conflict in England, 1603–1658* (Harvard Univ., 1986); David Underdown, *Revel, Riot, and Rebellion: Politics and Culture in England 1603–1660* (Oxford Univ., 1985); and Christopher Hill, *The Century of Revolution* (Norton, 1980). For political backgrounds of the civil war, see Perez Zagoren, *The Court and the Country* (Atheneum, 1970); Graham Perry, *The Golden Age Restored: the Culture of the Stuart Court* (St. Martin's, 1981); R. Malcolm Smuts, *Court Culture and the Origin of a Royalist Tradition in Early Stuart England* (Univ. of Pennsylvania, 1987); and Thomas Cogswell, *The Blessed Revolution: English Politics and the Coming of the War* (Cambridge Univ., 1989). Two recent relatively light biographies of Charles I are C. Carlton, *Charles I, the Personal Monarch* (Routledge & Kegan Paul, 1983) and Pauline Gregg, *King Charles I* (Univ. of California, 1984). For special studies on the civil war, see Christopher Hill, *The World Turned Upside Down* (Viking, 1972); G. E. Aylmer, *Rebellion or Revolution: England, 1640–1660* (Oxford Univ., 1986); and John P. Kenyon, *The Civil Wars of England* (Knopf, 1988). Among interesting studies of radicalism are Jerome Friedman, *Blasphemy, Immortality, and Anarchy: The Ranters and the English Revolution* (Ohio Univ., 1987); F. D. Dow, *Radicalism in the English Revolution* (Blackwell, 1985); Henry Noel Brailsford, *The Levellers and the English Revolution* (Stanford Univ., 1961); and Joseph Frank, *The Levellers* (Harvard Univ., 1955). For conditions facing women in Stuart England, see Alice Clark, *The Working Life of Women in the Seventeenth Century* (Routledge, Chapman, and Hall, 1982) and Margaret George, *Women in the First Capitalistic Society* (Univ. of Illinois, 1988).

Cicely V. Wedgewood, *The Thirty Years' War* (Anchor Books, 1961) is still reliable. Two other excellent treatments are Georges Pages, *The Thirty Years' War* (Torchbooks, 1970) and Josef V. Polisensky, *War and Society in Europe, 1618–1648* (Cambridge Univ., 1978). Michael Roberts, *Sweden's Age of Greatness* (St. Martin's, 1973) gives good coverage of both political background and military events of the conflict.

For the baroque artistic style in its historical setting, see Michael Kitson, *The Age of Baroque* (London: Paul Haslyn, 1966) and Victor L. Tapie, *The Age of Grandeur: Baroque Art and Architecture* (Praeger, 1961). Three excellent relevant biographies are Henry Bonnier, *Rembrandt* (G. Braziller, 1968); Christopher White, *Rembrandt and His World* (Viking, 1964); and Andrew M. Jaffe, *Rubens and Italy* (Cornell Univ., 1977).

Notes

1. Quoted in C. R. L. Fletcher, *Gustavus Adolphus and the Struggle of Protestantism in Europe* (New York: G. P. Putnam's Sons, 1923) p. 284.

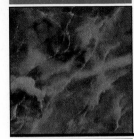

Chapter 18

L'Etat, C'Est Moi

European Absolutism and Power Politics

Louis XIV (1643–1715) of France is remembered best as a strong-willed monarch who reportedly once exclaimed to his fawning courtiers, "L'état, c'est moi" (I am the state). Whether or not he really said these words, Louis has been regarded by historians as the typical absolute monarch—a symbol of his era. Similarly, historians have often referred to this period, when kings dominated their states and waged frequent dynastic wars against one another as an age of absolutism.

Absolute monarchy, admittedly, was not exactly new in Europe. Since the late medieval period, rulers had been attempting to centralize their authority at the expense of feudal nobles and the church. In the sixteenth and early seventeenth centuries, however, religious strife blurred political issues and somewhat restricted developing monarchies. After the Peace of Westphalia, which ended the era of disastrous religious wars, absolutism rapidly gained popularity because it promised to restore order and security.

Parallel economic developments encouraged the maturing of absolutism. As the Spanish and Portuguese overseas empires declined, the Dutch, English, and French assumed commercial and colonial leadership, bringing the European economy to a second stage of expansion. The commercial revolution, centered in northern Europe, generated great wealth and brought increasingly complex capitalistic institutions, both of which furthered the process of state-building.

When the Peace of Westphalia ended the Thirty Years' War in 1648, it marked a significant turning point in European history. Peace, after such prolonged religious conflict and political chaos, renewed possibilities for centralizing royal authority within European states.

The Shift in Fundamental European Values

The era after Westphalia also saw a fundamental shift in European values. Although many Europeans—both Protestant and Catholic—were still concerned about personal salvation, they were now also apprehensive about prospects in this world. Like their Renaissance predecessors, they enjoyed sensual as well as aesthetic pleasures; but they put more emphasis on profits, power, and the need for security. With the memory of war and social upheaval still fresh, they were inclined toward a belief in order, which shaped their other values.

Secularism and Classicism

Although often subtle, the new secular outlook after 1650 was revealed in many ways. Despite their many expressed religious concerns, kings now routinely used religion for secular political ends. The prevailing secularism was also evident in the elegance, frivolity, intrigue, and sexual license that characterized royal courts and the private lives of the nobility. In educated circles, secularism was demonstrated in the growing popularity of science, with its avowed materialism and its implied refutation of scripture. But even unlearned common people shared a universal boredom with religious contention, along with the prevailing desire for stable social conditions.

This yearning for stability and order was clearly demonstrated in the arts. Earlier, during Europe's era of transitional turbulence, the baroque style had symbolized flamboyant power and restless frustration. Although the forms of baroque art and architecture remained popular, they were overshadowed in this era by a return to traditional classicism. Retaining the baroque deference to power, the revived classical mode emphasized order in its discipline, formality, and balance. Classicism owed much to the aristocratic world where it flourished. It reflected the growing scientific faith in an ordered universe, and it also expressed the political values of absolute monarchs, such as Louis XIV, who sponsored many artistic endeavors. Indeed, the French court led Europe's classical revival.

Classical literature was perhaps best exemplified in the polished and elegant French dramas of Pierre Corneille (1606–1684), Jean Racine (1639–1699), and Jean-Baptiste Molière (1622–1673). The first two were the great tragedians of the seventeenth century. They followed Aristotle's traditional rules of dramatic unity but produced works noted for psychological insights and beauty of language. Usually borrowing their plots from Greek and Roman antiquity, they often depicted heroes and heroines as idealized portraits of contemporary courtiers. Molière, an author of witty comedies, contrasted the artificiality of his society with the dictates of moderation and good sense. All three writers were sometimes mildly critical of established institutions, although their criticism was not direct enough to offend patrons.

A similar deference for patronage and authority was revealed in classical architecture and painting. In these areas, France also led the way. A state-sponsored culture, begun by Richelieu and Louis XIII in the French Academy, was continued by Louis XIV in academies of architecture, painting, dance, and music. The latter's palace at Versailles, with its horizontal lines, ninety-degree angles, and formal gardens, was copied all over Europe. So was the work of French court painters, such as Charles Le Brun (1619–1690), who glorified the Grand Monarch and his society in colorful portraits and panoramic scenes, emphasizing the common values of elegance and order.

The Capitalistic Ethic

The worlds of art and business, apparently so far removed from each other, shared common perspectives in this era. Traders and bankers, like most Europeans after Westphalia, felt a sense of relief and some hope for more tranquil times in the future. They could now more freely follow their own capitalistic ethic, which usually placed acquisition of profit over humane or religious concerns. This commercial secularism was also oriented toward securing order. Social upheavals obviously hurt business, and a strong state could promote prosperity in an increasingly interdependent world economy.

By the seventeenth century, particularly after mid-century, this economy depended upon the exchange of bulk commodities, rather than imported gold and silver. Eastern Europe and the Baltic supplied grains, timber, fish, and naval stores. Western Europe supplied manufactures for its outlying regions and for overseas trade. Dutch, English, and French merchant-bankers controlled shipping and credit. Plantation agriculture in the tropics, particularly the cultivation of Caribbean sugar, produced the greatest profits from overseas commerce. The African slave trade, along with its many supporting industries, also became an integral part of the intercontinental system.

The New World economy widened European horizons while contributing to European wealth. New foods, such as potatoes, yams, lima beans, tapioca, and peanuts became part of the European diet. Tropical plantation crops, such as rice, coffee, tea, cocoa, and sugar ceased to be luxuries. Production from European industries, particularly metals, coal, and textiles, also increased noticeably. Although the European economy slowed considerably in the seventeenth century, some profits remained enormous, particularly in eastern Europe and on tropical plantations, where production depended on serfs and slave labor. Lagging wages in western Europe produced similar advantages for capitalists, who remained in a most favorable economic position.

Such conditions contributed directly to the development of capitalistic institutions. As the volume of business rose, great public banks, chartered by governments, replaced earlier family banks like the Fuggers of Augsburg. The Bank of Amsterdam (1609) and the Bank of England (1694) are typical examples. Such banks, holding public revenues and creating credit by issuing notes, made large amounts of capital available for favored enterprises. Another method of concentrating capital came with joint-stock companies, such as the Dutch and English East India Companies, which could pool the resources of many investors. In the late seventeenth century, exchanges for buying and selling stock were becoming common, as were maritime insurance companies. Lloyd's of London, the most famous of these, began operations about 1688 and is still in business. Such capitalistic institutions regularized business and helped justify materialistic values in the popular mind.

They also fitted into the emerging state systems. The new capitalism depended upon overseas trade, which, in turn, required government protection or subsidy. Government policies affected money, credit, and capital accumulation. If capitalists needed government, governments also needed them. Powerful states were increasingly expensive, and overseas trade was a vital source of revenue. Capitalists could often help monarchs acquire foreign credit. Military force and bureaucratic organization, so important to rising states, often depended on capitalistic support. This tacit partnership between kings and capitalists produced a system known as mercantilism (see p. 476). It was most typical of France, but all absolute regimes were conditioned by the integrated European economy. Consequently, both profit and power were compatible subordinates to order in the European value system.

Philosophical Justifications for Absolutism

The prevailing respect for power was most clearly revealed in theoretical justifications for absolute monarchy. In the past, defenders of royal authority had employed the idea of "divine right" in claiming that kings were agents of God's will. This religious argument for absolutism was still quite common during the period, but it was supplemented by new secular appeals to scientific principles.

Bishop Jacques Bossuet (1627–1704), a prominent French churchman and the tutor of Louis XIV's son, produced a classic statement of divine right theory. In *Politics Drawn from Scriptures*, Bossuet declared:

> the person of the king is sacred, and to attack him in any way is sacrilege . . . the royal throne is not the throne of a man, but the throne of God himself. . . . Kings should be guarded as holy things, and whosoever neglects to protect them is worthy of death. . . . the royal power is absolute . . . the prince need render accounts of his acts to no one . . . Where the word of a king is, there is power . . . Without this absolute authority the king could neither do good or repress evil[1]

The most penetrating and influential secular justification for absolutism came from the English philosopher, Thomas Hobbes (1588–1679), whose famous political treatise, *Leviathan*, appeared in 1651. The French religious wars, the Thirty Years' War, and the English civil war of the 1640s inclined Hobbes to view order as the primary social good and anarchy as the greatest social disaster. Unlike Bossuet, he did not see God as the source of political authority. According to Hobbes, people created governments as protection against themselves, because they were naturally "brutish," "nasty," "selfish," and as cruel as wolves. Having been forced by human nature to surrender their freedoms to the state, people had no rights under government except obedience. The resulting sovereign state could take any form, but according to Hobbes, monarchy was the most effective in maintaining order and security. Any ruler, no matter how bad, was preferable to anarchy. Monarchs were therefore legitimately entitled to absolute authority, limited only by their own deficiencies and by the power of other states.[2]

Absolutism as a System

Unlimited royal authority, as advocated by Bossuet and Hobbes, was the main characteristic of absolutism. It was demonstrated most obviously in political organization but also served to integrate into government most economic, religious, and social institutions. In this section, we will preview this general pattern of absolutism before assessing its development within specific European states.

Government and Religion Under Absolutism

Theoretically, the ruler made all major decisions in a typical absolute state. Although this was not actually possible, chief ministers were responsible directly to the monarch, and all of their actions were taken in the sovereign's name. The monarch was officially the supreme lawgiver, the chief judge, the commander of all military forces, and the head of all administration. Central councils and committees discussed policy, but these bodies were strictly advisory and concerned primarily with administrative matter. All authority originated in orders coming down from the top and going out to the provinces from the royal capital.

In conducting foreign policy, monarchs identified their personal dynastic interests with those of their countries. They usually considered the acquisition of foreign territory to be legitimate and pursued their objectives in a competitive game of power politics with other monarchs. This competition required a large military establishment, sometimes involving naval forces. Rulers sought to form alliances against the most dominant foreign state, giving little consideration to moral or religious principles. A concern for the "balance of power" exemplified the new secular spirit in foreign relations.

Local government was a concern to all aspiring absolute monarchs. Wherever possible, they replaced traditional local authorities, usually feudal nobles, with royal governors from other places. Where that could not be done, local nobles were rewarded so they would support the crown. Sometimes, new nobles were created and old land grants reassigned. Town governments were often brought under royal authority through contacts between urban guildsmen and the king's middle-class servants. Using such means as monopoly grants, political favors, or bribery, monarchs extended their control over local law and revenues.

Organized religion remained important under absolutism but lost its independence of government. Instead of dominating politics, as they had done earlier, churches—Protestant and Catholic alike—now tended to become government agencies. Even in Catholic countries, such as France, the king exerted more political control over the church than did the pope. Although this had been true of earlier secular rulers, they had faced much more religious opposition. After Westphalia, monarchs could deliberately use their clergies as government servants, to enlist and hold popular support. Such controlled churches exerted tremendous influence in support of absolute monarchies, not only in the formal services but also in their social and educational functions.

Mercantilism in the Structure of Absolutism

In typical absolute monarchies, the regulation of state churches was accompanied by a system of national economic regulations known as *mercantilism*. Although it had originated earlier, with the emergence of modern states, mercantilism was not adopted generally by European governments until the late seventeenth century. The expansion of overseas trade, expenses incurred in religious and dynastic wars, and the depression of the middle 1600s accentuated the trend toward mercantilism as states hoped to promote prosperity and increase their revenues.

The system attempted to apply the capitalistic principle of profit-seeking in the management of national economies. "Bullionism" was the fundamental maxim of mercantilist theory. Proponents of bullionism sought to increase precious metals within a country by achieving a "favorable balance of trade," in which the monetary value of exports exceeded the value of imports. The result, in a sense, was a national profit. This became purchasing power in the world market, an advantage shared most directly by the government and favored merchants.

Mercantilists believed state regulation of the economy to be absolutely necessary for effecting a favorable balance. Absolute monarchies used subsidies, chartered monopolies, taxes, tariffs, harbor tolls, and direct legal prohibitions in order to encourage exports and limit imports. For the same purpose, state enterprises were given advantages over private competitors. Governments standardized industrial production, regulated wages, set prices, and otherwise encouraged or restricted consumer purchases.

Governments also built roads, canals, and docks to facilitate commerce.

Because mercantilists viewed the world market in terms of competing states, they emphasized the importance of colonial expansion. They regarded colonies as favored markets for home products and as sources of cheap raw materials. Colonial foreign trade and industries were controlled to prevent competition with the parent countries. In pursuing such policies, absolute states needed strong military and naval forces to acquire colonies, police them, and protect them from foreign rivals. Thus mercantilist policies often extended beyond commercial competition to international conflict.

Class Structure Under Absolutism

The class structures of absolute monarchies were marked by clear distinctions, precisely defined by law. Hereditary feudal aristocrats lost status unless they acquired an official appointment from the monarch. Such state nobles owed their privileges to their political service rather than birth. They often came from merchant families; indeed, the state often sold titles to wealthy commoners to provide income for the monarch. State nobles served in public administration, in the army, the church, or as attendants at court, where they accented the royal magnificence. They usually received tax exemptions, pensions, titles, and honors. Their legal rights, dress, and way of life differed markedly from even wealthy non-nobles.

In contrast, commoners, including middle-class townspeople, paid most of the taxes required by frequent wars and extravagant royal courts. Peasant landholders usually owed fees and labor dues to local aristocrats. The poorest peasants in western Europe were hired laborers or vagabonds; in eastern Europe, they were serfs. Slavery was rare in western Europe, but provided a major labor force on overseas plantations.

While tightening legal class distinctions, absolute monarchies also further downgraded the status of women. The Reformation had offered some opportunities for self-expression among women, and before 1650 many women had assumed temporary positions of leadership. The situation changed after Westphalia. Although a number of queens and regents were able to rule

The oppression of the peasantry is the subject of this engraving, which compares the noble and the peasant to the spider and the fly. The poor peasant brings all he has to the rich noble, who sits ready to receive all the produce.

as absolute monarchs, most aristocratic women could find recognition only as Catholic nuns, writers, artists, salon hostesses, court gossips, or royal mistresses, the latter gaining official status in this era. The status of commoner women did not fall as much or as quickly, but the advent of early capitalism and the decline of domestic economies was already excluding them from many industries and enterprises in the latter seventeenth century.

French Absolutism as the Model Under Louis XIV

Although absolutism was not a French invention, it appeared in a typically French form in the later seventeenth century. French armies had recently humbled the Habsburgs, bringing the Bourbon dynasty to predominance, and Louis XIV continued these military successes, at least for a while. Wealth poured into France from abroad, particularly from sugar islands in the

Louis XIV to His Son

This memoir, designed to instruct a young prince who never became king, nevertheless provides revealing insights into Louis' personal rationalizations for his one-dimensional view of government.

I laid a rule on myself to work regularly twice every day, and for two or three hours each time with different persons, without counting the hours which I passed privately and alone, nor the time which I was able to give on particular occasions to any special affairs that might arise. There was no moment when I did not permit people to talk to me about them, provided that they were urgent; with the exception of foreign ministers who sometimes find too favourable moments in the familiarity allowed to them, either to obtain or to discover something, and whom one should not hear without being previously prepared.

I cannot tell you what fruit I gathered immediately I had taken this resolution. I felt myself, as it were, uplifted in thought and courage; I found myself quite another man, and with joy reproached myself for having been too long unaware of it. This first timidity, which a little self-judgment always produces and which at the beginning gave me pain, especially on occasions when I had to speak in public, disappeared in less than no time. The only thing I felt then was that I was King, and born to be one. I experienced next a delicious feeling, hard to express, and which you will not know yourself except by tasting it as I have done. . . .

All that is most necessary to this work is at the same time agreeable: for, in a word, my son, it is to have one's eyes open to the whole earth; to learn each hour the news concerning every province and every nation, the secrets of every court, the mood and the weaknesses of each Prince and of every foreign minister; to be well-informed on an infinite number of matters about which we are supposed to know nothing; to elicit from our subjects what they hide from us with the greatest care; to discover the most remote opinions of our own courtiers and the most hidden interests of those who come to us with quite contrary professions. I do not know of any other pleasure we would not renounce for that, even if curiosity alone gave us the opportunity. . . .

I gave orders to the four Secretaries of State no longer to sign anything whatsoever without speaking to me; likewise to the Controller, and that he should authorise nothing as regards finance without its being registered in a book which must remain with me, and being noted down in a very abridged abstract form in which at any moment, and at a glance, I could see the state of the funds, and past and future expenditure.

The Chancellor received a like order, that is to say, to sign nothing with the seal except by my command, with the exception only of letters of justice, so called because it would be an injustice to refuse them, a procedure required more as a matter of form than of principle. . . . I let it be understood that whatever the nature of the matter might be, direct application must be made to me when it was not a question that depended only on my favour; and to all my subjects without distinction I gave liberty to present their case to me at all hours, either verbally or by petitions. . . .

Regarding the persons whose duty it was to second my labours, I resolved at all costs to have no prime minister; and if you will believe me, my son, and all your successors after you, the name shall be banished for ever from France, for there is nothing more undignified than to see all the administration on one side, and on the other, the mere title of King. . . .

From *A King's Lesson in Statecraft: Louis XIV: Letters to His Heirs* in Harry J. Carroll et al., eds., *The Development of Civilization*, 2 vols. (Glenview, IL: Scott, Foresman, 1970), Vol. 2, pp. 120–121.

Caribbean. The magnificent royal palace at Versailles, the luxury of the French court, and the brilliance of French cultural expression dazzled the rest of Europe. It is no wonder that Louis was considered the ultimate in political wisdom or that his arbitrary methods were widely copied. Like the solar system, then being emphasized in Newtonian physics, France appeared in the European state system as a central star, surrounded by its orbiting satellites.

The Grand Monarch

The strong absolutism of Louis XIV followed a long monarchical tradition. Francis I in the early sixteenth century had subordinated the feudal nobility, created a centralized administration, and waged continuous warfare against his Habsburg enemy, Charles V. Religious conflicts of the late 1500s ended the Valois dynasty but only temporarily disrupted the development of French absolutism. Henry IV, the first Bourbon, restored peace and royal authority. Cardinal

Louis XIV in Robes of State by court painter Hyacinthe Rigaud. The portrait captures the splendor of the Grand Monarch, known as the Sun King, who believed himself to be the center of France as the sun was the center of the solar system.

Richelieu, as minister in the next reign, broke the power of the nobility and the independent Protestant cities.

Yet for a while in the 1650s, the country appeared to be entering another time of troubles. It was nearly bankrupted by the Thirty Years' War, further drained of blood and treasure by continued conflict with Spain until 1659, and racked by the civil war of the Fronde between 1649 and 1653. More than once, Louis, as a boy, narrowly escaped capture by rebel forces. As a result he was deeply suspicious of the nobility, because many Fronde leaders had come from that class. He was particularly alienated by court ladies, such as Madame de Longueville, who organized rebel forces, and his cousin, Mademoiselle de Montpensier, who turned the guns of the Bastille on royalist troops. Louis' other nemesis was Cardinal Mazarin (1602–1661), his frantic mother's Italian lover and chief minister, who neglected Louis and ran the government. When Mazarin died in 1661, the twenty-three-year-old Louis took personal control of the state; he never appointed another chief minister.

During the remainder of his long reign, Louis worked at projecting an image of the "Grand Monarch." His personal political convictions were clearly revealed in a characteristic statement:

> All power, all authority resides in the hands of the king, and there can be no other in his kingdom than that which he establishes. The nation does not form a body in France. It resides entire in the person of the king.[3]

To symbolize his life-giving presence in the council chamber, Louis had a rising sun painted on his official chair. Today such overbearing egotism might appear as ridiculous as Louis' red-heeled shoes and enormous wig, but it was all taken seriously in his time. Louis, particularly, took his responsibilities very seriously. His lingering childhood insecurities produced in him an enormous capacity for work and an absolute dedication to the art of ruling, which he accomplished with remarkable shrewdness.

Louis constantly strove to inspire awe of the monarchy, as was evidenced by his great palace at Versailles, a short distance from Paris. It was set in 17,000 beautifully landscaped acres. The parks and buildings, surrounded by a 40-mile wall, contained 1400 fountains, 2000 standing statues, and innumerable rooms, decorated with marble columns, painted ceilings, costly draperies, mirrored walls, and hand-crafted furniture.

In this fairyland at Versailles, Louis lived amid studied elegance, formal manners, extravagant expressions of courtesy, and witty but shallow conversation. It was an artificial and carefully-ordered society, exemplified by the graceful minuet, with manners more important than either morals or religion. By requiring the nobles to attend his glittering court, Louis retained them in an elegant prison where they could be more easily controlled. Unfortunately, Louis was also imprisoned. Preoccupied with etiquette and protocol, he sacrificed his private life to hundreds of noble courtiers, who followed him about, observing the elaborate ceremonies associated with his every move, from the time he arose and was dressed in the morning, until he was disrobed and assisted into bed at night.

A marked characteristic of the court was its loose sexual morality. Here, again, Louis set the example. Before and after his marriage in 1659 to the Spanish Infanta, whom he formally honored but consistently neglected, Louis shared his bed with numerous women, each of whom was designated, in her time, as "head mistress." The best known among the early ones were the child-like Louise de la Vallière and the sensuous Madame de Montespan. Louis shared none of his problems with them and was extremely wary of their efforts to extract political favors. After his experience with the ladies of the Fronde, he made a conscious effort to limit female participation in government. He may have changed later in life; after his wife died, Louis secretly married Madame de Maintenon, the governess of his illegitimate children. This level-headed matron offered the companionship he had never known, but even she could provoke his ire. The grand monarch left his stamp upon an era when women's limited influence was mainly confined to the boudoir.

This point is well illustrated by seventeenth-century French cultural expression. During the early decades many aristocratic women became involved in amateur efforts as writers, artists, and critics. Their main milieu was the salons of Paris, where aristocratic women hosted regular meetings devoted to discussion of high culture, mostly literature. Ladies of the Fronde had frequented the salons, as did the well-known novelists Madame de Scudéry and Madame de Lafayette. But the collapse of the Fronde and Louis' accession depressed the salons until the eighteenth century. Competition from the carefully regimented art and literature sponsored by the French royal academies diminished their influence. Louis XIV's age of classicism was largely a reflection of state patronage.

The French Social and Political Structure

Court attendance was vitally important to the nobility, because honor and income depended on royal favor. Louis virtually eliminated independent feudal aristocrats from public service outside the church and the military. He gave or sold titles to his working middle-class officials known as "nobles of the robe," in contrast to the old landed "nobles of the sword." Those of the latter who remained away from court were suspect and subject to investigation. The nobility, thus divided, was a privileged class under law, along with the clergy. A third class, or estate, of taxpaying commoners, included merchants, craftsmen, and peasants. Most peasants owed manorial dues and services to their landlords, although they were no longer bound to the soil as serfs.

This aristocratic social structure was integrated with the administrative system developed earlier by Richelieu. Without a chief minister, Louis worked closely with his appointed council and the secretaries who headed major agencies. Subordinate councils supervised ministries and their large supporting corps of officials. One such body, the Council of Dispatches, received reports from the intendants, who were responsible for finance, police, and justice in the provinces. Louis professionalized this body of royal agents, increasing their powers, standardizing their salaries, and assigning them outside of their home areas. They supervised some 40,000 lesser officials. Within this vast organization, the king's government issued laws, censored litereature and art, conducted widespread spying, imprisoned its enemies, and dominated the courts. Within the limits imposed by space and technology, royal agents regulated everything.

Louis also claimed authority over the French church and the religious lives of his subjects, enforcing that authority against both Protestants and the papacy. The king was involved in a long struggle with the pope over revenues. Ultimately, after Bishop Bossuet and a convocation of the French clergy had upheld him, Louis won Rome's approval to collect the income from vacant bishoprics, although he abandoned the idea of heading an independent French church. In 1685, he revoked the Edict of Nantes, by which Henry IV had granted freedom of worship to the Protestant Huguenots almost a century before. The new law subjected practicing Protestants to torture or imprisonment. Luckily for them but not for France, some 200,000 of the most industrious French Huguenots escaped to other lands, taking with them valuable skills and knowledge.

This disastrous policy has been attributed to the influence of Madam de Maintenon. The charge has not been proved, although it is known that Louis was becoming increasingly concerned about his soul and that de Maintenon was an ardent Catholic with a missionary obsession. If she did not cause him to revoke the edict, there can be no doubt that she thoroughly agreed with the action.

French Mercantilism, Militarism, and Colonialism

State control of religion in France was paralleled by an all-embracing mercantilist system, deployed by Louis' comptroller of finance, Jean Baptiste Colbert (1619–1683). Colbert sought French economic self-sufficiency at the expense of Dutch overseas commerce. He created a comprehensive system of tariffs and trade prohibitions levied against foreign imports. French luxury industries—silks, laces, fine woolens, and glass—were subsidized or produced in government shops. The state imported skilled workers and prescribed the most minute regulations for each industry. Colbert also improved internal transportation by building some roads and canals. He chartered overseas trading companies, granting them monopolies on commerce with North America, the West Indies, India, Southeast Asia, and the Middle East. The system, called Colbertism, came to be identified with thoroughness.

French foreign and imperial policy under Louis XIV required a highly efficient war machine. To achieve it, the king's brutal but able minister of war, the Marquis de Louvois (1641–1691), revolutionized the French army. In addition to infantry and cavalry, he organized special units of supply, ordnance, artillery, engineers, and inspectors. Command ranks, combat units, drills, uniforms, and weapons were standarized for the first time in Europe. Louvois also improved weaponry by such innovations as the bayonet, which permitted a musket to be fired while the blade was attached. By raising military pay, providing benefits, and improving conditions of service, the war minister increased the size of the army from 72,000 to 400,000, a force larger than all belligerents put together at any one time during the Thirty Years' War. Louvois also improved and expanded the navy. In addition to a Mediterranean galley fleet based at Toulon, the overseas forces by 1683 consisted of 217 men-of-war, operating from Atlantic ports and served by numerous shipyards.

Jean Baptiste Colbert. His financial reforms were so successful that within six years a debt of 22 million French pounds had been transformed into a surplus of 29 million pounds.

The new navy was part of Colbert's grand strategy for building an enormous overseas dominion. In the last decades of the seventeenth century, the French Empire took shape on three continents. In North America, fur trappers and missionaries pushed south down the Mississippi. In 1683, when the Marquis de La Salle reached the Gulf of Mexico, he claimed the continental interior for his king, naming it Louisiana. A second important area was the West Indies, where a number of French sugar islands, particularly Martinique and Guadeloupe, experienced a booming prosperity. Across the Atlantic, French West African trading posts on the Senegal River supplied slaves for the West Indian plantations.

The other areas of interest were in East Africa and southern Asia, where the French had acquired footholds in Madagascar, the Isle of Bourbon in the Indian Ocean, and trading centers at Pondicherry and Chandernagore on the east coast of India.

The Gravitational Pull of French Absolutism

The popular image of Louis XIV as the Sun King symbolized his position in France but also implied that French absolutism exerted a magnetic influence upon other European states. Like all such symbolism, the idea was only partially true. As much as it was a response to French example, absolutism was accepted because it promised efficiency and security, the greatest political needs of the time. Yet French wealth and power certainly generated European admiration and imitation of the French example.

Typical Satellites of France

Among the most obvious satellites of the French sun were numerous German principalities of the Holy Roman Empire. By the Treaty of Westphalia, more than 300 were recognized as sovereign states. Without serious responsibilities to the emperor and with treasuries filled by confiscated church properties, their petty rulers struggled to increase their personal powers and play the exciting game of international diplomacy.

Many sought French alliances against the Habsburg emperor; those who could traveled in France and attended Louis' court. Subsequently, many a German palace became a miniature Versailles. Even the tiniest states were likely to have standing armies, state churches, court officials, and economic regulations. The ultimate deference to the French model was shown by the Elector of Brandenburg; although sincerely loyal to his wife, he copied Louis XIV by taking an official mistress, displaying her at court functions without requiring her to perform other duties usually associated with the position.

The era of the Sun King also witnessed an upsurge of absolutism in Scandinavia. After an earlier aristocratic reaction against both monarchies, Frederick III (1648–1670) in Denmark and Charles XI (1660–1697) in Sweden broke the power of the nobles and created structures similar to the French model. In 1661 Frederick forced the assembled high nobility to accept him as their hereditary king. Four years later, he proclaimed his exclusive right to issue laws. A similar upheaval in Sweden in 1680 allowed Charles to achieve financial independence by seizing the nobles' lands. These beginnings were followed by the development of thoroughly centralized administrations in both kingdoms. Sweden, particularly, resembled France with its standing army, navy, national church, and mercantilist economy. Although Swedish royal absolutism was overthrown by the nobles in 1718, the Danish system remained into the nineteenth century.

States in Irregular Orbits

Unlike the Sandinavian and German states, most European governments resembled Louis' system more in the way they developed rather than in their specific institutions. As agricultural economies became commercialized, restricting the developing interests of monarchs and commoners, rulers sought to ignore their feudal councils and exercise unlimited authority. Some states in this period had not yet developed as far in this direction as had France; others were already finding absolutism at least partially outmoded. All felt the magnetic pull of French absolutism, but their responses varied according to their traditions and local conditions.

The process is well illustrated by a time lag in the Spanish and Portuguese monarchies. United by Spanish force in 1580 and divided again by a Portuguese revolt in 1640, the two kingdoms were first weakened by economic decay and then nearly destroyed by the Thirty Years' War and their own mutual conflicts, which lasted until Spain accepted Portuguese independence in 1668. Conditions deteriorated further under the half-mad Alfonso VI (1656–1668) in Portugal and the feeble-minded Charles II (1665–1700) in Spain.

The nobilities, having exploited these misfortunes to regain their dominant position in both countries, could not be easily dislodged. Not until the 1680s in Portugal did Pedro II (1683–1706) successfully eliminate the Cortes (assembly of feudal estates) and restore royal authority. With new wealth from Brazilian gold and diamond strikes, John V (1706–1750) centralized the administration, perfected mercantilism, and extended control over the church. In Spain, similar developments accompanied the War of the Spanish Succession and the grant to Louis XIV's Bourbon grandson, Philip V (1700–1746), of the Spanish crown. Philip brought to Spain a corps of French advisors, including the Princess des Ursins, a friend of de Maintenon's and a spy for Louis XIV. Philip then followed French precedents by imposing centralized ministries, local intendants, and economic regulations upon the country.

Aristocratic limits on absolutism, so evident in the declining kingdoms of Portugal and Spain, were even more typical of the Habsburg monarchy in eastern Europe. The Thirty Years' War had diverted Habsburg attention from the Holy Roman Empire to lands under the family's direct control. By 1700, they held the Archduchy of Austria, a few adjacent German areas, the Kingdom of Bohemia, and the Kingdom of Hungary, recently conquered from the Turks. This was a very large domain, stretching from Saxony in the north to the Ottoman Empire in the southeast. It was strong enough to play a leading role in the continental wars against Louis XIV after the 1670s.

Leopold I (1657–1705) was primarily responsible for strengthening the Austrian imperial monarchy during this period. In long wars with the French and the Turks, Leopold modernized the army, not only increasing its numbers but also instilling professionalism and loyalty in its officers. He created central administrative councils, giving each responsibility for an arm of the imperial government or a local area. He staffed these high administrative positions with court nobles, rewarded and honored like those in France. Other new nobles, given lands in the home provinces, became political tools for subordinating the local estates. Leopold suppressed Protestantism in Bohemia and Austria and kept his own Catholic church under firm control. In 1687, the Habsburgs were accepted as hereditary monarchs in Hungary, a status they had already achieved in Austria and Bohemia.

In the eighteenth century, Maria Theresia (1740–1780) faced Leopold's problems all over again. When she inherited her throne at the age of twenty-two, her realm was threatened by Prussia and lacking both money and military forces. In the years after Leopold's time, the nobles had regained much of their former power and were again building their own dominions at the expense of the monarchy. Maria was a religious and compassionate woman, known as "Her Motherly Majesty," but she put aside this gentle image to hasten much needed internal reforms. Count Haugwitz, her reforming minister, rigidly enforced new laws which brought provincial areas under more effective royal control.

Despite its glitter and outward trappings, the Austrian Habsburg monarchy was not a truly absolute monarchy. The economy was almost entirely agricultural and therefore dependent upon serf labor. This perpetuated the power of the nobles and diminished revenues available to the state. In addition, subjects of the monarchy comprised a mixture of nationalities and languages—German, Czech, Magyar, Croatian, and Italian, to name only a few. Without real unity, the various Habsburg areas stubbornly persisted in their localism. Even the reforms of Leopold and Maria Theresia left royal authority existing more in name than in fact. Imposed on still functioning medieval institutions, it resulted in a strange combination of absolutism and feudalism.

While Habsburg absolutism wavered in an irregular orbit, Poland was in no orbit at all. Local trade and industry were even more insignificant in its economy; the peasants were more depressed; and land-controlling lesser nobles—

some 8 percent of the population—grew wealthy in supplying grain for western merchants. Nobles avoided military service and most taxes; they were lords and masters of their serfs. More than fifty local assemblies dominated their areas, admitting no outside jurisdiction. The national Diet (council), which was elected by the local bodies, chose a king without real authority. In effect, Poland was fifty small, independent feudal estates.

Western Maritime States

Although impressed by French absolutism, the agricultural states of eastern Europe were not yet capable of applying it. At the other extreme, England and Holland rejected the system, partially beause they had outgrown it. Yet both states felt the pull toward absolutism in their internal politics.

The Dutch Republic, in the seventeenth century, was a confusing mixture of medievalism and modernity. Its central government was a federation of seven nearly independent states. The stadtholder, as chief executive, led the military forces but had no control of budget or revenues. Neither did the States General, the legislative body, which could act only as a council of ambassadors from the provinces. These were governed by local estates, which limited the authority of their own executives. The main difference between this system and Poland's was the political weakness of the aristocracy. Although rural nobles were strong in some provincial assemblies, the cities, particularly those in the province of Holland, provided revenues that maintained the government. Thus wealthy bankers and merchants, who dominated the major town councils, held the real power.

Even in this political environment, absolutism was a political force. As successful military leaders, the Dutch stadtholders appealed to popular loyalties. The House of Orange supplied so many successive stadtholders that the office became virtually hereditary in the family. By the 1640s, stadtholders were addressed as "your highness" and intermarried with European royalty, including the English Stuarts. They created a political machine that controlled some provincial systems. Arguing for efficiency, they gained the right to name their councilors as working

ministers. From 1618 to 1647 and again from 1672 to 1703, monarchists controlled the state. In the latter period, William III built a highly efficient army and centralized administration.

The Dutch state outdistanced contemporary monarchies in creating the first northern European empire overseas. Between 1609 and 1630, while at war with Spain and Portugal, the Dutch navy broke Spanish sea power, drove the Portuguese from the Spice Islands of Southeast Asia, and dominated the carrying trade of Europe. In this same period, the republic acquired Java, western Sumatra, the spice-producing Moluccas of Indonesia, and part of Ceylon. The Dutch East India Company took over most European commerce with ports between the Cape of Good Hope and Japan. Elsewhere, the Dutch acquired the Portuguese West African slaving stations, conquered most of Brazil, and established New Amsterdam (present-day New York City and the Hudson River valley) in North America. Dutch commercial and colonial predominance ended after 1650, but the Dutch Asian empire lasted into the twentieth century.

As Dutch commercial and imperial fortunes declined, England became the main rival of France for colonial supremacy. The two nations were already traditional enemies and different in many respects. While France was perfecting a model absolute monarchy, England was subordinating

A 1665 painting of the Dutch East India Company's trading station on the Hooghly River in Bengal. The station was a key link in the network of bases that made up the eastern trading empire of the Dutch Republic.

its kings to Parliament. Before 1688, however, England also felt the strong attraction of French absolutism.

The period from 1660 to 1688 was marked by increasingly severe struggles between English kings and Parliament. England had earlier been torn by fanatic religious controversy, political revolution, bloody civil war, the beheading of a king, and rigid military dictatorship (see ch. 17). Almost everyone welcomed the new ruler, Charles II (1660–1685), called back from exile in France and restored to the throne, with his lavish court and his mistresses. But Charles, the cleverest politician of the Stuart line, exploited this common desire for normality to violate the terms of his restoration, which bound him to rule in cooperation with Parliament.

Charles almost succeeded in becoming an absolute monarch. With the help of his favorite sister, Henrietta Anne, who had married Louis XIV's brother, Charles negotiated the secret Treaty of Dover, which bound him to further English Catholicism and aid France in war against Holland. In return, Charles received subsidies from France that made him independent of Parliament. He then used all of his deceit and cunning to create a political machine. This precipitated a political crisis, forcing him to back down. Ultimately, he dismissed four Parliaments. After 1681, Charles governed without Parliament, taking advantage of a strong desire among the propertied classes to avoid another civil war.

Charles' brother James II (1685–1688) proved to be a more determined absolutist. Like Charles, he was an admirer of Louis XIV and a known Catholic. His wife, Mary of Modena, had been persuaded by the pope to marry James as a holy commitment to save England for Rome. Having been repeatedly insulted by Protestants at Charles' court, she was now determined to accomplish her mission. James was quite willing to cooperate. Early in his reign, he suppressed an anti-Catholic rebellion in southwest England. With his confidence thus buttressed, he attempted to dominate the courts, maintain a standing army, take over local government, and turn the English church back to Catholicism. Most of this was done in defiance of the law while Parliament was not in session.

In 1688, after James had unsuccessfully tried to control parliamentary elections, the country was roused to near revolt by the birth of a royal prince, who might perpetuate a Catholic dynasty. A group of aristocrats met and offered the crown to the former heir, Mary Stuart, the Protestant daughter of James by an earlier marriage. Mary accepted the offer with the provision that her husband, William of Orange, be co-ruler. William landed with an efficient Dutch army, defeated James, and forced him into exile. This "Glorious Revolution" pushed England in the direction of limited monarchy (see p. 547).

After 1688, England turned away from French-styled absolutism but continued to follow mercantilist principles in building a worldwide empire. By enforcing the Navigation Act of 1651 and other similar laws passed under Charles, England sought to regulate foreign trade and exploit colonial economies.

Rising Absolute Monarchies in Eastern Europe

Following the Age of Louis XIV, strong absolute monarchies rose in eastern Europe. The area had formerly been an agricultural dependency of western European capitalism, retarded by its isolation and reliance upon serf labor. In time, the ideas and economic prosperity of western Europe spread slowly eastward, furthered by great wars and colonial contentions, which diverted western states from suspicion of eastern rulers and opened opportunities for two new despotisms. One was Prussia, under its Hohenzollern dynasty, and the other was Slavic Russia, under the Romanovs.

Prussia: The Typical Military State

The rise of the Hohenzollerns was among the most striking political development of the era. Once relatively unimportant nobles occupying a castle on Mount Zollern in southern Germany, they pursued their ambitious policies through marriage, intrigue, religious factionalism, and war. By the early seventeenth century, they held lands scattered across north Germany (see map. p. 486). The Thirty Years' War was almost disastrous for the Hohenzollerns but conditioned them to austerity, perseverence, and iron discipline.

Two reigns laid permanent foundations for the later monarchy. Frederick William (1640–1688), called "the Great Elector," used his small but well-trained army to win eastern Pomerania at the end of the Thirty Years' War. In the near anarchy which prevailed in Germany immediately after Westphalia, he reformed the administration in Brandenburg, crushed the nobles in Prussia and Cleves, created a tough army of 30,000 soldiers, and brought all three areas under his direct control. His son, Frederick I (1688–1713), exploited Russia's victory over Sweden to annex western Pomerania. As a reward for fighting France in the War of the Spanish Succession (see p. 492), Frederick was recognized as "King in Prussia" by the states which signed the Peace of Utrecht in 1713.

After Utrecht, Prussia was generally regarded as a drill yard, with the king as drillmaster. This reputation was largely created by Frederick William I (1713–1740), a crusty soldier-king, whose maxims were order, discipline, work, and loyalty. Demanding absolute obedience, he once told a group of subjects: "No reasoning! Obey orders." His conception of royal authority was simple. "Salvation belongs to the Lord," he once exclaimed and added, "Everything else is my business." With such unabashed absolutism, he reorganized the government under a General Directory, established a civil service for local administration, created a royal supreme court, taxed the nobles, required them to train for professional military careers, and built an army of 80,000, considered to be the best trained and equipped in Europe. At the end of his reign, the Hohenzollern monarchy was ready for military expansion.

Frederick William I held high hopes for his son, Frederick II (1740–1786). The young prince,

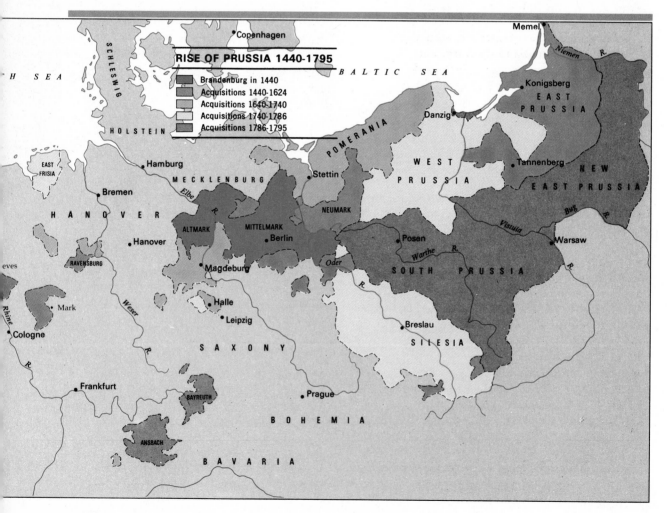

Frederick the Great, Political Testament

In 1752 Frederick published his thoughts on government in *A Political Testament*. This excerpt is taken from that essay.

Politics is the science of always using the most convenient means in accord with one's own interests. In order to act in conformity with one's interests one must know what these interests are, and in order to gain this knowledge one must study their history and application. . . . One must attempt, above all, to know the special genius of the people which one wants to govern in order to know if one must treat them leniently or severely, if they are inclined to revolt . . . to intrigue. . . .

A well conducted government must have an underlying concept so well integrated that it could be likened to a system of philosophy. All actions taken must be well reasoned, and all financial, political and military matters must flow towards one goal: which is the strengthening of the state and the furthering of its power. However, such a system can flow but from a single brain, and this must be that of the sovereign. Laziness, hedonism and imbecility, these are the causes which restrain princes in working at the noble task of bringing happiness to their subjects . . . a sovereign is not elevated to his high position, supreme power has not been confined to him in order that he may live in lazy luxury, enriching himself by the labor of the people, being happy while everyone else suffers. The sovereign is the first servant of the state. He is well paid in order that he may sustain the dignity of his office, but one demands that he work efficiently for the good of the state, and that he, at the very least, pay personal attention to the most important problems. . . .

You can see, without doubt, how important it is that the King of Prussia govern personally. Just as it would have been impossible for Newton to arrive at his system of attractions if he had worked in harness with Leibniz and Descartes, so a system of politics cannot be arrived at and continued if it has not sprung from a single brain. . . . All parts of the government are inexorably linked with each other. Finance, politics and military affairs are inseparable; it does not suffice that one be well administered; the must all be . . . a Prince who governs personally, who has formed his [own] political system, will not be handicapped when occasions arise where he has to act swiftly; for he can guide all matters towards the end which he has set for himself. . . .

Catholics, Lutherans, Reformed, Jews and other Christian sects live in this state, and live together in peace; if the sovereign, actuated by a mistaken zeal, declares himself for one religion or another, parties will spring up, heated disputes ensue, little by little persecutions will commence and, in the end, the religion persecuted will leave the fatherland and millions of subjects will enrich our neighbors by their skill and industry.

It is of no concern in politics whether the ruler has a religion or whether he has none. All religions, if one examines them, are founded on superstitious systems, more or less absurd. It is impossible for a man of good sense, who dissects their contents, not to see their error; but these prejudices, these errors and mysteries were made for men, and one must know enough to respect the public and not to outrage its faith, whatever religion be involved.

From *A Political Testament* in George L. Mosse et al., comp. and eds., *Europe in Review* (Chicago: Rand McNally, 1962), pp. 110–112.

however, reacted against his Spartan training, secretly seeking escape in music, art, and philosophy. When caught after attempting flight to France, he was forced to witness the beheading of his accomplice and best friend. More years of severe training and discipline brought him into line with his father's wishes but robbed the future king of capacity for feeling. In later years, while retaining his cultural interests and mingling freely with writers and artists, he developed no lasting relationships, particularly not with women. He married early to escape his father's household, then ignored his wife, Elizabeth, subjecting her to a courteous but cold formality. Neither she nor any of his frequent but temporary mistresses could influence his judgment. This was also true of his family, after the old king died. Wilhelmina, the sister who had shared his youthful emnity against their father, lost his confidence as they both matured. Such was the price he paid to become a superb administrator, a master of Machiavellian diplomacy, and the greatest soldier of his day.

In 1780, the Prussia of Frederick II, called "the Great," was regarded as a perfectly functioning absolute monarchy. Stretching some 500 miles across northern Germany between the Elbe and Niemen rivers, its flourishing population had grown from three quarters of a million in 1648 to five million. For twenty-three years from 1740 to 1763, it had waged nearly continuous war. See pp. 492–494 in this chapter. The government ran as precisely as an efficient army. Like any good commander, Frederick claimed all ultimate authority. He required rigid discipline and deference to superiors from civilian officials as well as from military officers. Prussian nobles were honored over merchants or non-noble officials and were permitted complete mastery over their serfs. Frederick's mercantilism stressed tariff protection for agriculture, encouraged industry with government subsidies, imported artisans, and sought economic self-sufficiency as a means of achieving military superiority.

The Rise of Russia

Russia, the other eastern monarchy that rose to prominence in the eighteenth century, was even farther from the European economic hub than Poland and therefore even more backward

(see map, p. 489). The country had experienced a "time of troubles" in the latter sixteenth century, when the nobles engaged in civil war against the monarchy. Later, between 1613 and 1676, the first two Romanov tsars, Michael and Alexis, integrated most aristocrats into the state nobility and achieved some degree of stability. As in Prussia, the nobles and the government were united in their common exploitation of the serfs, and the primitive agricultural economy encouraged aristocratic independence. Russian ignorance and technical deficiencies, along with a conservative-minded nobility, made the country stagnant and retarded in comparison with western states.

A new era in Russian history began with Peter I (1682–1725). When he was ten years old, in 1682, Peter's half-sister, Sophia, effected a palace coup, in which her troops looted the palace, killing many of Peter's maternal uncles. For seven years, while Sophia ruled as regent for Peter and his demented half-brother, Ivan, the young co-tsar lived in fear and insecurity, without discipline or much formal education. He recruited and drilled his own guard regiments and roamed Moscow's foreign quarter, learning about boats and western ways. When he was sixteen, his mother arranged his marriage to a young noblewoman, Evdokia Lopukhina. From the first, this was a mismatch; after impregnating his wife, Peter abandoned her within three months. He was by now a young giant, weighing 230 pounds and standing six feet eight inches tall, with a temper to match his size. Fortunately, he also possessed a sharp mind and boundless energy.

After 1689, Peter took control of the country and his own life. When Sophia failed in an attempt to become sole ruler, he forced her into a convent, although Ivan remained co-tsar to his death in 1696. Peter amused himself with a mistress and wild drinking parties but continued his pursuit of western ways. His difficulties in wars with the Turks convinced him that he must modernize his army and build a navy. In 1697, he went incognito as a member of a great embassy to Poland, Germany, Holland, and England. He worked as a common ship's carpenter in Holland, learning Dutch methods at first hand. Back in Moscow, Peter crushed a rebellion of his palace guards with savage cruelty. This was followed by extensive reforms and wars against the

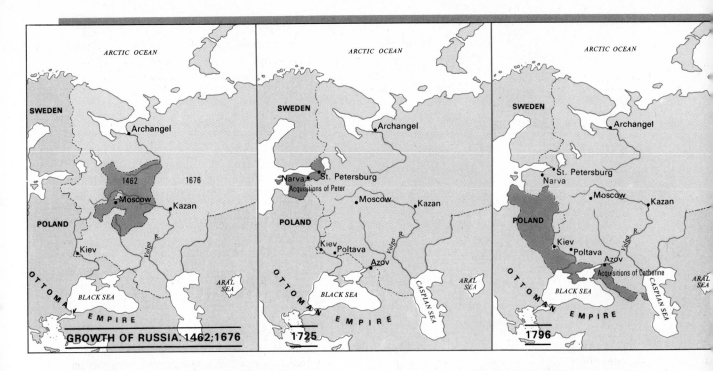

GROWTH OF RUSSIA: 1462; 1676

1725

1796

Turks and Swedes, as Peter sought "a window on the sea." He achieved this goal in 1703, when he founded St. Petersburg, as his future capital on the Baltic. That same year, Peter met Marfa Skavronska, a Lithuanian peasant girl, who became his mistress, friend, campaign companion, and after Evdokia's death in a convent, his wife.

Peter's reforms made Russian absolutism functional, in fact as well as in theory. He completely centralized government, replacing all representative bodies with an appointed council and appointed ministries. Royal military governors assumed local authority. A Chancery of Police maintained order and collected information from an elaborate spy network. By forcing his nobles to shave their beards and don European clothes, he conditioned them to accept change and become living symbols of his power over them. They were now required to serve in the army, the government, or industry. Peter also officially abolished the office of Patriarch, as head of the state church, substituting a Holy Synod of bishops, dominated by a secular official, the procurator, who represented the Tsar. In copying European mercantilism, Peter established factories, mines, and shipyards, importing technical experts, along with thousands of laborers. He levied tariffs to protect native industries and taxed almost everything, including births, marriages, and caskets. As revenues increased, he improved the army and navy, both of which were expanded, professionalized, and equipped with efficient western weapons.

Before and after Peter's time Russian absolutism also created its own empire in the forested wastes of Siberia. Russian cossacks and fur traders explored this enormous territory between 1580 and 1651. During the seventeenth century, it remained a vast game preserve, exploited by the Russian government for its fur. Agents responsible to the Siberian Bureau in Moscow or St. Petersburg governed the relatively peaceful native people, collecting tribute from them in furs and a percentage from the profits of chartered companies. With the tightly regulated fur trade so lucrative, the government discouraged settlement in Siberia. In the eighteenth century, however, restrictions were eased and western Siberia, between the Ob and Yenesei rivers, began attracting colonists, as well as convicts and political prisoners. Some 400,000 had come by 1763, but Siberia was largely undeveloped until the late nineteenth century.

Even after his death in 1725, Peter's policies continued to drive Russian politics through the eighteenth century. The main struggle was between "old believers," most prominent among the nobles and the clergy, who reacted strongly against the new ways and foreign influences Peter had sponsored. Another striking characteristic of the period was the prevalence of female rulers. Of the eight Russian monarchs in the eighteenth century, only three were tsars, who ruled a total of only three and a half disastrous years. The five tsarinas of the period were Catherine I (1725–1727), Peter's camp-following second wife and the first Russian empress; Anna Ivanovna (1730–1740), daughter of Peter's half-brother, Ivan; Elizabeth (1741–1762), daughter of Peter and Catherine I; and Catherine II (1762–1796), known as "the Great." All tried to continue Peter's policies, but Catherine I and Anna Ivanovna allowed foreigners too much power, thus alienating their Russian subjects. Elizabeth avoided this mistake. She was particularly successful in consolidating the central government and again winning respect in western Europe for Russian military power. She laid the foundations for the long and successful reign of Catherine the Great, whose role as an "enlightened despot" will be discussed in the next chapter.

Diplomacy and War in the Age of Absolutism

Because of dynastic and colonial rivalries, Europeans were constantly involved in conflicts in the Age of Absolutism. Fighting took place in America, Africa, and Asia—not only against non-Europeans but also in global wars among European colonial powers. At the same time, major wars battered Europe as dynastic states competed for dominance. While Spain, Sweden, and Poland were declining, Prussia, Russia, and even Austria were becoming first-class powers. Along with England's weight overseas, the last three exerted major influences on the European balance of power.

From Westphalia to Utrecht: The Dominance of France

France was the strongest and most threatening military power in Europe from the Peace of Westphalia (1648) to the Treaty of Utrecht (1713). Louis XIV first dreamed of expanding French frontiers to the Rhine; later he coveted the Spanish crown. Colbert also helped him plan the conquest of a large overseas empire in America, Africa, and Asia. The diplomacy of other European states in the era can largely be explained by their common efforts to unite against this French expansion.

One important exception to this general trend was the Russian policy. In early wars with the Turks Peter the Great took Azov on the Black Sea, but his main target in the Great Northern War (1709–1721) was Sweden. Peter's allies, Denmark and Poland, quickly fell to the Swedish warrior-king Charles XII (1697–1718). When the Swedes invaded Russia, they were first met with a "scorched earth" withdrawal, then annihilated at Poltavia (1709). The war ended in 1721 with Sweden exhausted and Peter gaining a section of the Baltic coast, where he had already begun building his new capital at St. Petersburg.

The three Anglo-Dutch naval wars between 1652 and 1674 provide an example of the intricate balance of power principle in action. Conflicting commercial and colonial interests of the two maritime states were the immediate issues. At the same time, both belligerents were increasingly aware of danger from a powerful and aggressive France. The Dutch were most directly affected because French expansion toward the northern Rhine threatened the survival of Holland as a nation. In order to deal with this problem, the Dutch came to terms, tacitly accepting English maritime supremacy while preparing the way for Anglo-Dutch alignment against Louis XIV. Ultimately the French menace was more decisive than naval actions in bringing an end to the Anglo-Dutch hostilities.

After 1670, Louis was the prime mover in European diplomacy. He fought four major wars, each with overseas campaigns. In the first, Louis claimed the Spanish Netherlands (Belgium). Thwarted by the Dutch and their allies, he next bought off Charles II of England and attacked the Dutch directly. Frustrated again by a combination of enemies, he tried in the 1690s to annex certain Rhineland districts. This time, almost all of Europe allied against him and forced him to back down. The climax to these repeated French efforts came between 1701 and 1713, in the War

Catherine the Great Assumes Power in Russia

Catherine became empress in 1762 in a coup which overthrew her estranged husband, Peter III. This selection is from her own written account of the episode.

The Hetman [Razumovsky,] Volkonsky and Panin were in the secret. I was sleeping calmly at Peterhof at 6 o'clock in the morning of the 28th [July Old Style] The day had been a very disturbing one for me as I knew all that was going on. [Suddenly] Alexius Orlov enters my room and says quite gently: "It is time to get up; all is ready for your proclamation. . . ." I dressed myself quickly without making my toilet and got into the carriage which he had brought with him. . . .

Five versts from the town I met the elder Orlov with the younger Prince Bariatinsky. Orlov gave up his carriage to me, for my horses were done up, and we got out at the barracks of the Ismailovsky Regiment. [At the gates] were only twelve men, and a drummer, who began sounding an alarm, when the soldiers came running out, kissing me, embracing my hands and feet and clothes, and calling me their deliverer. Then they began swearing allegiance to me. When this had been done, they begged me to get into the carriage, and the priest, cross in hand, walked on in front. We went [first] to the [barracks of the] Semenovsky Regiment, but the regiment came marching out to meet us, crying, Vivat! Then we went to the church of Kazan, where I got out. Then the Preobrazhensky Regiment arrived, crying, Vivat! "We beg your pardon," they said to me, for being the last. Our officers stopped us, but here are four of them whom we have arrested to shew you our zeal. We want what our brothers want." Then the horse-guards arrived frantic with joy, I never saw anything like it, weeping and crying at the deliverance of their country. . . . I went to the new Winter Palace where the Synod and the Senate were assembled. A manifesto and a form of oath were hastily drawn up. Then I went down and received the troops on foot. There were more than 14,000 men, guards and country regiments. As soon as they saw me they uttered cries of joy which were taken up by an innumerable crowd. I went on to the old Winter Palace to take [my] measures and finish [the business,] there we took counsel together, and it was resolved to go to Peterhof, where Peter III was to have dined with me, at their head. All the great roads had been occupied and rumours came in every moment. . . .

Peter III abdicated, at Oranienbaum, in full liberty, surrounded by 5000 Holsteiners, and came with Elizabeth Vorontsov, Gudovich and Ismailov to Perterhof, where, to protect his person, I gave him five officers and some soldiers. . . . Thereupon I sent the deposed Emperor to a remote and very agreeable place called Ropsha, 25 versts from Peterhof, under the command of Alexius Orlov, with four officers and a detachment of picked, good-natured men, whilst decent and convenient rooms were being prepared for him at Schlusselburg. But God disposed otherwise. Fear had given him a diarrhoea which lasted three days and passed away on the fourth; in this [fourth] day he drank excessively, for he had all he wanted except liberty. Nevertheless, the only things he asked me for were his mistress, his dog, his Negro and his violin; but for fear of scandal [sic] and increasing the agitation of the persons who guarded him, I only sent him the last three things. . . .

Source: Warren B. Walsh, comp. and ed., *Readings in Russian History* (Syracuse, NY: Syracuse University Press, 1948), pp. 185–187.

of the Spanish Succession, when Louis sought, upon the advice of Madame de Maintenon and with the later help of his spy, the Princess des Ursins, to secure the Spanish throne for his grandson, Philip. Although he finally succeeded in this project, the victory was a hollow one, bought at tremendous cost in lives and resources.

In this most destructive of Louis' wars, women played a major part behind the scenes. In England, during the early years, Sarah Churchill, wife of the English supreme commander, the Duke of Marlborough, consistently pressured the Queen and members of Parliament for vigorous prosecution of the war. On the other side, at the Spanish court and elsewhere on the continent, Mary of Modena, in exile with her husband, the deposed James I of England, exerted all of her influence to bolster support for France. Other women were most instrumental in bringing peace. Among them were Madame Maintenon and the Princess des Ursins, who helped persuade Louis to drop the idea of uniting the French and Spanish Bourbon monarchies. In England, after about 1709, Queen Anne, a patient and plodding monarch but at least one with some common sense, freed herself from Sarah Churchill's influence and guided her ministers toward the Peace of Utrecht.

Louis could not overcome all the power balanced against him. As France became stronger it invariably provoked more formidable counteralliances. At first, Louis faced Spain, Holland, Sweden and some German states. In the last two wars, England led a combination that included almost all of western Europe. In this anti-French alignment, the old Anglo-Dutch commercial rivalry and other traditional prejudices, such as Anglo-Dutch hatred of Spain, were subordinated to the balance of power principle.

The Treaty of Utrecht (1713) ushered in a period of general peace, lasting some thirty years. Philip V, Louis' grandson, was confirmed as king of Spain, with the provision that the two thrones would never be united. Since Spain had been declining for a century and France was drained financially, the Bourbon succession promised little for French ambitions in Europe. This was particularly true because Spain surrendered the southern Netherlands (Belgium) and its Italian holdings (Naples, Milan, and Sardinia) to the Austrian Habsburgs. In addition, Savoy was ceded to Sicily, which was subsequently traded (1720) to Austria for Sardinia. The Duke of Savoy was also recognized as a king, as was Frederick I of Prussia. In the nineteenth century, the House of Savoy would unify Italy and the Hohenzollerns would accomplish the same for Germany.

Almost all the participants except England lost more in the wars than they gained by the treaty. Holland had borne the cost of most land fighting against the French; France had been demoralized by a three-front war and a Huguenot uprising, for which it received no tangible compensation except the retention of Alsace; and Spain lost heavily to the Austrian Habsburgs. England, on the other hand, received both Newfoundland and Nova Scotia from France, plus French acceptance of English claims to the Hudson Bay area. England also retained the Mediterranean naval bases at Gilbraltar and Minorca, taken from Spain. Even more important commercially were the concessions permitting England to supply Spanish America with slaves and land one shipload of goods each year at Porto Bello in Panama. These stipulations helped England become the leading colonial power.

From Utrecht to Paris: The Duel for Empire and the Wavering Balance

The balance of European power wavered dangerously in the eighteenth century. Prussia and Russia—and even Habsburg Austria—attained great military potential, and each was tempted by power vacuums in Poland and Turkey. The situation was complicated by the difficulty in determining which of the eastern states was the most serious threat and therefore the logical object of counteralliances. To confuse matters more, both England and France were absorbed in their growing colonial rivalry, in which England was the obvious front runner. Major conflicts were on the way, although Europe was able to avoid them for some thirty years after Utrecht.

By 1730, it was apparent that France and England must soon clash over their conflicting colonial ambitions. Both empires were rapidly increasing their wealth and populations. In the Caribbean, French sugar production had surpassed the British, while French slavers were not only supplying their own islands but challenging

British trading privileges in Spanish America, as defined at Utrecht. On the other side of the world, the English and French were also scrambling to obtain influence among the petty rulers of southern India. The two powers, with their American Indian allies, were also fighting sporadic little wars in North America. In the preliminary diplomatic testing, French size and military force in Europe were balanced against British financial resources, naval power, and a larger American colonial population.

Conflict began in 1739 over British trade in Spanish America. An English captain testified before Parliament that Spanish authorities had boarded his vessel and cut off his ear, which he displayed, wrapped in cotton. The "War of Jenkins' Ear" soon spread, as France immediately supported Spain. Frederick II of Prussia, meanwhile, seized Silesia, part of the family holdings

of the Habsburg heiress, Maria Theresia, who had just succeeded to the Austrian throne. France and Spain now threw in with Frederick, along with the German states of Saxony and Bavaria. Fearful of France, England and Holland, allied with Hanover, joined Austria in 1742. By 1745, Prussia had almost knocked Austria out of the war, but fighting dragged on overseas in North America and India until 1748. The resulting Peace of Aix-la-Chapelle left Frederick with Silesia and the colonial positions of England and France about the same as they had been in 1739.

The agreements at Aix-la-Chapelle brought no peace but only a short truce of eight years. During the cessation of hostilities, France and England prepared to renew their global conflict. At the same time, Maria Theresia, having learned some lessons in international politics and effected some necessary internal reforms, joined with

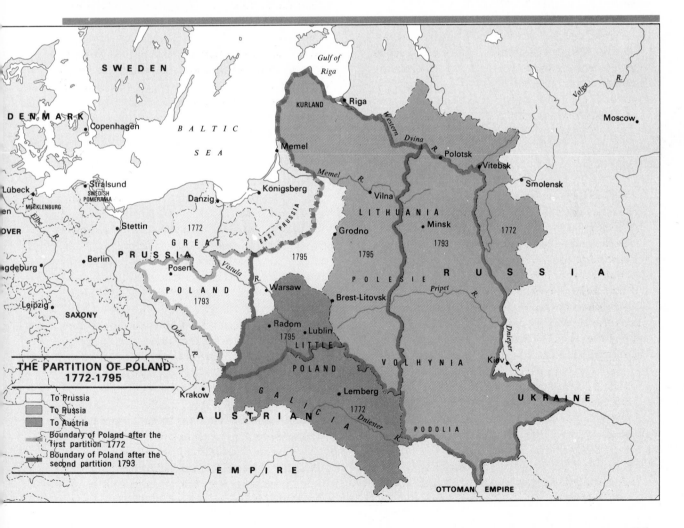

THE PARTITION OF POLAND
1772-1795

To Prussia
To Russia
To Austria
Boundary of Poland after the first partition 1772
Boundary of Poland after the second partition 1793

Tsarina Elizabeth of Russia to negotiate an alliance against Frederick, which also included Sweden and some German states. Her greatest coup, however, was recruiting France, the old Habsburg enemy, possibly with help from Madame Pompadour, Louis XV's mistress, who despised Frederick. Prussia was now effectively isolated but so was England, which was more concerned about colonial issues than agression on the continent. England therefore formed a new alliance with Prussia against France, Russia, and Austria. This shift in alliances is known as the diplomatic revolution of the 1750s.

Beginning in 1756, war was waged relentlessly on three continents—Europe, North America, and Asia (India). It is known in American history as the French and Indian War and in Europe as the Seven Years' War. Attacked on all sides by three major powers, Frederick marched and wheeled his limited forces, winning battles but seeing little prospect for ultimate victory. He even tried, with no success, to buy Madame Pompadour's influence for peace. Later he described the nearly hopeless predicament, comparing himself to a man assaulted by flies:

When one flies off my cheek, another comes and sits on my nose, and scarcely has it been brushed off than another flies up and sits on my forehead, on my eyes, and everywhere else.[4]

Frederick was saved and the war won by the narrowest of margins when a new pro-French tsar, Peter III, recalled the Russian armies from the gates of Berlin and withdrew from the war. Austria then sued for peace, leaving Frederick with Silesia.

The Seven Years' War confirmed the emergence of Prussia and Russia as great powers and prepared the way for a new diplomatic order in eastern Europe. Despite its tremendous losses, Prussia gained enormously in prestige; its internal damage would not be revealed until the nineteenth century. Russia regained the military reputation it had achieved under Peter without winning any striking victories. Austria lost prestige and was further weakened militarily but managed to retain its respectability. Turkey and Poland were the real losers in the postwar decades. In 1772, Poland lost most of its territory to the eastern powers in a three-way partition, despite Maria Theresia's protestations of remorse (see map, p. 493). In the 1790s, Poland was eliminated entirely in two partitions carried out by Prussia and Russia. Turkey, meanwhile, lost the Crimea and most of the Ukraine to the aggressive expansionist policies of Catherine the Great of Russia.

Much more significant than the war's effects on eastern Europe was its impact on Anglo-French colonial rivalry. Britain gained even more than it had at Utrecht while French colonial hopes were all but destroyed. By the Peace of Paris (1763), France lost to England the St. Lawrence Valley and the trans-Appalachian area east of the Mississippi. Spain also ceded Florida to England, receiving Louisiana west of the Mississippi from France as compensation. In the West Indies, France gave up Granada, Dominica, and St. Lucia. The French kept their main trading stations in India but were not permitted to fortify them or continue their political ties with local rulers. On the other hand, the British East India Company not only extended its political influence but acquired Bengal outright. The Peace of Paris made England the largest, wealthiest, and most powerful empire in the world.

Conclusion

The Peace of Westphalia marked a very significant turning point in European history. Following a century of destructive religious wars, it brought a new age, when Europeans longed for stability and order. This main concern was modified by the general attachment to worldly values associated with power, profit, and pleasure. Life became more frivolous as it became more secular, particularly among the wealthy. Acquiring money and credit became major objectives of businessmen looking for capital. Kings also sought money, not only for their personal enjoyment, but as the means to power. Even in the arts, there was much flamboyant display and luxurious elegance, along with a classical emphasis on order and formality.

Absolutism as a political system reached its European zenith in this era. With its control of the economy and the church, its large military establishments, and its rigid class distinctions, it met the psychological needs of its time and also supplied the force to effect necessary reforms. France under Louis XIV was a nearly perfect example of the system. Yet virtually all European states in this era were affected somewhat by absolutism in theory or fact.

The age produced its own approach to international relations. Absolute monarchy was a system for conducting war according to secular principles. Rulers felt compelled to follow their national interests, without reference to higher morality or religious maxims. Under these circumstances, it seemed that peace and international order could be achieved only by a balance of power, in which aggressive states would be checked by the counteralliances formed against them. The nearly continuous wars in this process between 1650 and 1763 brought varying fortunes to European states. Sweden, Turkey, Spain, and Poland slipped into decline or extinction. France and Austria achieved stability without establishing mastery. Prussia and Russia became major military powers, and England established its supremacy as a world empire.

Suggestions for Reading

Among the best general surveys of Europe in the period are H. O. Koenigsberger, *Early Modern Europe* (Longman, 1987); G. R. R. Treasure, *The Making of Modern Europe* (Methuen, 1985); Robert Zeller, *Europe in Transition, 1660–1815* (Univ. Press of America, 1988); and Maurice Ashley, *A History of Europe, 1648–1815* (Prentice Hall, 1973).

Special emphases on absolutism and its milieu may be found in Maurice Ashley, *The Age of Absolutism* (Merriam, 1974); William Doyle, *The Old European Order* (Oxford Univ., 1978), and Ragnhild Hatton, *Europe in the Age of Louis XIV*. The political side of absolutism is treated in J. Miller, *Bourbon and Stuart Kings and Kingship in France and England* (Duke Univ., 1988); and J. H. Shennan, *Liberty and Order in Early Modern Europe* (Longman, 1986). For economic aspects of the era and the system, see Michael Beaud, *A History of Capitalism* (Monthly Rev. Press, 1983); Philip W. Buck, *The Politics of Mercantilism* (Octagon, 1964); and Andre G. Frank, *World Accumulation, 1492–1789* (Monthly Rev. Press, 1978). Mary Fulbrook deals with religion and absolutism in *Piety and Politics: Religion and the Rise of Absolutism in England, Wurtemberg, and Prussia* (Cambridge Univ., 1984). For the burdens and accomplishments of women during the late seventeenth century, see Helga Mobius, *Women of the Baroque Age* (Abner Schram, 1984).

Excellent general overviews of the era in France are provided in Robin Briggs, *Early Modern France, 1560–1775* (Oxford Univ., 1977); V. Mallia-Milanes, *Louis XIV and France* (Macmillan, 1986); and Paul Sonnino, ed., *The Reign of Louis XIV* (Humanities Press, 1990).

Joseph Barry, *Passions and Politics: A Biography of Versailles* (Doubleday, 1972) is a highly personalized account of Louis XIV's glittering world at Versailles. See also Dianna De Marly, *Louis XIV and Versailles* (Holmes and Meier, 1987); Ragnhild Hatton, *Louis XIV and His World* (Putnam, 1972); and G. Walton, *Louis XIV's Versailles* (Univ. of Chicago, 1985). French political and social affairs are effectively depicted in Roger Mettam, *Power and Faction in Louis XIV's France* (Blackwell, 1987); W. Beik, *Absolutism and Society in Seventeenth-Century France* (Cambridge Univ., 1989); and Raymond F. Kersted, ed. *State and Society in Seventeenth-Century France* (Watts, 1975).

Three sound biographies of Louis XIV are John B. Wolf, *Louis XIV* (Hill and Wang, 1972); O. Bernier, *Louis XIV* Doubleday, 1987); and L. Marin, *Portrait of the King* (Univ. of Minnesota, 1988). For French women of the court, the salons, the markets, and the streets, see Louis Auchincloss, *False Dawn: Women in the Age of the Sun King* (Doubleday, 1984); Carolyn C. Lougee, *Le Paradis de Femmes* (Princeton Univ., 1976); Elborg Forster, ed., *A Woman's Life in the Court of the Sun King* (Johns Hopkins Univ., 1984); and the memoir of Madame de Maintenon, *The King's Way* (Penquin, 1985). See also Charlotte Haldane, *Madame de Maintenon* (Bobbs-Merrill, 1970).

For French-style absolutism in other countries, see Hajo Holburn, *A History of Modern Germany*, 3 vols., vol. I, (Knopf, 1964); T. K. Derry, *A History of Scandinavia* (Univ. of Minnesota, 1979); Eric Elstob, *Sweden, A Political and Cultural History* (Rowman and Littlefield, 1979); Michael Roberts, *Sweden's Age of Greatness* (St. Martin's, 1973); Samuel S. Franklin, *Sweden, the Nation's History* (Univ. of Minnesota, 1977); Stuart Oakley, *A Short History of Denmark* (Praeger, 1972); W. G. Jones, *Denmark* (Croom Helm, 1986); Henry A. Kamen, *Spain in the Latter Seventeenth Century* (Longman, 1980) and *Spain, 1469–1714: A Society in Conflict* (Longman, 1983); John Lynch, *Spain Under the Habsburgs*, vol. I: *Spain and America, 1598–1700* (New York Univ., 1984); R. A. Stradling, *Philip IV and the Government of Spain, 1621–1665* (Cambridge Univ., 1988); John Lynch, *Bourbon Spain* (Blackwell, 1989); and Harold V. Livermore, *A New History of Portugal* (Cambridge Univ., 1976).

For less developed absolutism in eastern Europe, see R. J. W. Evans, *The Making of the Habsburg Monarchy* (Oxford, 1984); the first volume of Norman Davies, *A History of Poland*, 2 vols. (Columbia Univ., 1981) and, by the same author, *Heart of Europe: A Short History of Poland* (Oxford, 1986). See also Robert N. Bain, *Slavonic Europe* (Arno Press, 1971).

An informative study of the Dutch maritime state is J. L. Price, *Culture and Society in the Dutch Republic During the Seventeenth Century* (Scribners, 1974). See also Pieter Geyl, *The Netherlands in the Seventeenth Century* (Barnes and Noble, 1961); Kenneth Haley, *The Dutch in the Seventeenth Century* (Harcourt Brace Jovanovich, 1972); and Charles Wilson, *The Dutch Republic and the*

Civilization of the Seventeenth Century (McGraw-Hill, 1968). Bernard H. Viekke, *The Evolution of the Dutch Nation* (Roy, 1945) is still useful.

Among the best general treatments of the whole Stuart period in England are Barry Coward, *The Stuart Age* (Longman, 1984); J. P. Kenyon, *Stuart England*, 2nd ed. (Penguin, 1986); and Blair Worden, *Stuart England* (Salem House, 1987). See also Antonia Fraser's study of English "women's lot" in the seventeenth century: *The Weaker Vessel* (Knopf, 1984) and James R. Jones, *Country and Court* (Harvard Univ., 1978).

D. Ogg, *England in the Reign of Charles II*, 2nd ed. (Oxford Univ., 1984) still provides solid coverage. For the Restoration, see R. Hutton, *The Restoration* (Oxford Univ., 1987); James R. Jones, *The Restored Monarchy* (Rowman and Littlefield, 1979); J. Miller, *Restoration England* (Longman, 1985); and H. Weber, *The Restoration Rake-Hero* (Univ. of Wisconsin, 1986). Political and social aspects of the reign are ably described in Kenneth H. Haley, *Politics in the Reign of Charles II* (Blackwell, 1985); James R. Jones, *Country and Court, 1658–1714* (Harvard Univ., 1978); and Tim Harris, *London Crowds in the Reign of Charles II* (Cambridge Univ., 1987). Among the best relevant biographies are Antonia Fraser, *Royal Charles* (Knopf, 1979); James R. Jones, *Charles II* (Allen and Unwin, 1987); and Bryan Bevan *Nell Gwyn* (Roy, 1970).

For the Glorious Revolution, see James R. Jones, *The Revolution of 1688 in England* (Weidenfield and Nicholson, 1984); K. M. Chacksfield, *The Glorious Revolution* (Winecanton Press, 1988); W. A. Speck, *Reluctant Revolutionaries: Englishmen and the Revolution of 1688* (Oxford Univ., 1989); and Stuart E. Prall, *The Bloodless Revolution* (Univ. of Wisconsin, 1985). D. Ogg, *England in the Reigns of James II and William III* (Oxford, 1984) and J. R. Weston, *Monarchy and Revolution* (Macmillian, 1985) are new editions of standard incisive works on the English political scene after the late 1680s. Among the best biographies of later English monarchs are Maurice Ashley, *James II* (Univ. of Minnesota, 1977) and Edward Gregg, *Queen Anne* (Routledge, Kegan Paul, 1980).

Two excellent short surveys of Prussian history in this period are H. W. Koch, *A History of Prussia* (Longman, 1978) and Otis Mitchell, *A Concise History of Brandenburg-Prussia to 1786* (Univ. Press of America, 1980). For revealing special studies of the Prussian political structure, see Hans Rosenberg, *Bureaucracy, Aristocracy, and Authority: The Prussian Experiment, 1660–1815* (Beacon, 1966) and Hubert C. Johnson, *Frederick the Great and His Officials* (Yale Univ., 1975). Robert R. Ergang, *The Potsdam Führer* (Octagon, 1972) is a colorful and stimulating portrait of Frederick William I, the founder of Prussian absolutism and militarism. Among the many biographies of Frederick the Great are three excellent recent ones: C. Duffy, *Frederick the Great* (Routledge, Kegan Paul, 1985); Robert

B. Asprey, *Frederick the Great* (Ticknor and Fields, 1986); and Mary Kittridge, *Frederick the Great* (Chelsea House, 1987).

The rise of the Romanov state is ably described in Otto Hoetzsch, *The Evolution of Russia* (Harcourt Brace and World, 1966) and W. Bruce Lincoln, *The Romanovs* (Dial, 1981). Sound historical studies of Peter the Great and his impact are Peter B. Putnam, *Peter, the Revolutionary Tsar* (Harper and Row, 1973); V. O. Kliuchevski, *Peter the Great* (Beacon, 1984); A. Tolstoy, *Peter the Great*, 2 vols, (Raduga, 1985); Robert K. Massie, *Peter the Great: His Life and World* (Ballantine, 1986); and H. Troyat, *Peter the Great* (Dutton, 1987).

For interesting studies of the great eighteenth-century Russian empresses who followed Peter, see Talbot T. Rice, *Elizabeth, Empress of Russia* (Praeger, 1970) and Robert Coughlan, *Elizabeth and Catherine* (New Amer. Lib., 1975). Among excellent biographies of Catherine are Vincent Cronin, *Catherine, Empress of All the Russias* (Morrow, 1978); Leslie Max-Mcguire, *Catherine the Great* (Chelsea House, 1986); and John T. Alexander, *Catherine the Great* (Oxford Univ., 1989). Perspectives on Catherine's impact are provided in Isabel De Madarlaga, *Russia in the Age of Catherine the Great* (Yale Univ., 1981) and G. S. Thomson, *Catherine the Great and the Expansion of Russia* (Greenwood, 1985).

For good general analyses of international relations in this age of developing power politics, see John B. Wolf, *Toward a European Balance of Power, 1620–1715* (Rand McNally, 1970); Geoffrey Symcox, *War, Diplomacy, and Imperialism, 1618–1763* (Walker, 1974); Theodore K. Rabb, *The Struggle for Stability in Early Modern Europe* (Oxford Univ., 1975); and Derek McKay and H. M. Scott, *The Rise of the Great Powers and the European State System* (Longman, 1983). For more specialized studies, see Carl J. Ekberg, *The Failure of Louis XIV's Dutch War* (Univ. of North Carolina Press, 1979); Michael Roberts, *The Swedish Imperial Experience, 1560–1718* (Cambridge Univ., 1984); and Paul Sonnino, *Louis XIV and the Origins of the Dutch War* (Cambridge Univ., 1989).

Notes

1. Quoted in James Harvey Robinson, *Readings in European History*, 2 vols. (Boston: Ginn and Co., 1906), vol. 1, pp. 273–275.
2. Thomas Hobbes, *Leviathan* (New York: Liberal Arts Press, 1958), pp. 106–170.
3. Quoted in F. Tyler, *The Modern World* (Farrar and Rinehart, 1939), p. 186.
4. Quoted in P. Gaxotte, *Frederick the Great* (London: G. Bell and Sons, 1941), p 357.

Chapter 19

The Crisis of the Old Regime 1714–1774

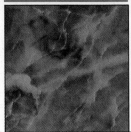

When Louis XIV died in 1715, he was succeeded by his five-year-old great-grandson, who later became Louis XV. This new Louis, however, was never capable of ruling as a "sun king." Although he retained all of his royal prerogatives, by the time he reached middle age he was so openly pessimistic about the future that he hoped only that the monarchy would last through his reign. He easily might have delivered the famous prophecy so often attributed to him: "Après moi, le déluge" (After me, the deluge).

Like his great-grandfather, Louis XV (1715–1774) was a symbol of European monarchy, but the monarchical system had changed significantly by the middle of the eighteenth century. It had lost prestige and was now often associated with the waste arising from costly wars and royal extravagances. An aristocratic revival, common all over Europe in the eighteenth century, also contributed to its decline. In a time which demanded reform, most European monarchies were mired down in tradition and vested interests.

While established regimes became more static, European society in the eighteenth century was increasingly dynamic. Foreign expansion entered a new phase after the seventeenth century, unleashing social and ecomomic forces that weakened monarchies and their social orders. The rising volume of colonial trade and the flood of information from the non-European world stimulated warfare and commercial rivalry among European powers. At the same time, increasing wealth further propelled the rising middle class, encouraged freedom in capitalistic endeavor, and escalated revolutionary changes almost beyond human control.

Inadequacies of the Old Regime

Absolute monarchy during the eighteenth century had developed a characteristic social structure and aristocratic way of life known as the Old Regime. By midcentury, it had acquired the sanctity of tradition, the confidence of long experience, the gentleness of maturity, and the infirmities of old age. Although no longer purposefully violent or vulgar, the Old Regime was marked by privileges, injustices, and political deficiencies.

A Social Order Based on Privilege

Perhaps the most striking feature of the Old Regime was its legalized privilege, conferring exclusive political power and fabulous wealth on a small elite, while dooming the masses to grinding poverty. The system cut across class lines. Most of the clergy and nobles were as poor as some peasants, and the great majority of the urban middle classes were denied the leisured comfort of the great bankers and merchants.

The aristocratic nature of the Old Regime derived partly from a successful counteroffensive by European nobilities after the Peace of Westphalia. Temporarily checked by such strong monarchs as Louis XIV and Peter the Great, the nobles retained or regained political power in the Habsburg domain, in Germany, and in Poland. Early in the eighteenth century, they recovered their supremacy in Sweden, in Spain, in Russia after Peter' death, and particularly in France under Louis XV.

A comparable development came in eighteenth-century England. After James II was

497

The ornate staircase and lavishly decorated ceiling of the Bishop's Palace in Würzburg, Germany, suggests the splendor and luxury enjoyed by the high clergy.

immunities, and numerous honors, they contributed almost nothing beyond decoration to church or state.

France provides a good illustration of the system. There, the church owned 20 percent of the land and collected returns equal to half those of the royal estates. The clergy included 130,000 churchmen and nuns. Although it supported some education, social work, and charities, most of its income went to 11,000 members of the higher clergy, particularly to 123 bishops and 28 archbishops. Some of their annual incomes exceeded the equivalent of $1 million, but many of the overworked lower clergy existed on $100 a year. Among the 400,000 nobles, only a thousand families were represented among the court nobility. Each aristocrat at Versailles held many honorific appointments in court service, inactive military commissions, honorary wardships of royal palaces, or obsolete provincial offices, requiring no work. Titled nobles held 20 percent of the land, most by feudal tenures, which permitted them to collect numerous customary fees from their peasants. From all such sources, high French nobles probably averaged the equivalent of well over $100,000 in annual income.

Throughout Europe, conspicuous consumption was typical of the high nobility, such as the Fitzwilliams in Ireland, the Newcastles in England, the Schönborns in Bohemia, the Radziwills in Poland, and the Esterhazys in Hungary. Prince Esterhazy owned about 10,000 acres in 29 estates. His lands included 160 market towns and 414 villages, while his revenues exceeded 700,000 florins annually, or the equivalent of $400,000. With such wealth, the magnates built elaborate town dwellings and sumptuous country retreats, filling them with priceless handcrafted furniture, rich tapestries, and fine works of art. While most people scratched for food, the high nobles enjoyed delicacies, meats, and rare fruits, which were almost unknown among common people. The nobles lived lavishly in a fantasy world, marred only by the dull ceremonies accompanying their brilliant but busy social activities.

Viewed from the top, the Old Regime appeared aristocratic, but it presented quite a different picture when viewed from the side. Most people in Europe were peasants, who constituted more than 80 percent of the total population; of these, 75 percent were landless, and

dethroned in 1688, the landed gentry—functionally a lower landed aristocracy—gained almost complete control of the House of Commons. From this base, they greatly influenced state policy through a prime minister and a cabinet that became responsible to Parliament. The gentry made government a closed system, putting members of their class into most public offices, most of the lucrative positions in the Anglican church, and most commissioned ranks in the army and navy. These privileges were shared only with a few remaining nobles, who sat in the House of Lords.

Europe's Old Regimes were topped by official ruling classes of high clergy and nobles. Combined, these two privileged orders accounted for less than 2 percent of the total European population; but the great magnates, who enjoyed real wealth and power, were concentrated in only 5000 families, among some four million titled aristocrats. Most of the true elite lived in city mansions and palaces, far away from their broad acres in the country. For their high incomes, tax

many were serfs, bound to their villages, not only in Russia, Poland, and Prussia, but also in Denmark. Among city dwellers, only a tiny minority were wealthy bankers and overseas merchants. A larger number, some 10 percent of the population, were shopkeepers, artisans, and professional people. This proportion was higher in Holland, England, and northern Italy, but generally lower elsewhere, particularly in eastern Europe, where it dropped sharply. At the bottom of urban society was the mass of indigent poor, barely able to survive. Commoners of all economic levels paid most taxes. They were subject to legal discrimination in favor of the nobility, from whom they were also separated by differences in education, speech, manners, dress, and social customs.

This general pattern was evident in the French third estate. Consisting of some 26 million people, it was more varied in its extremes than the first two estates of clergy and nobles. At the top were about 75,000 wealthy bankers and merchants who had not bothered to buy titles. Another 3 million urban dwellers consisted largely of lesser merchants, shopkeepers, lawyers,

In *The Oyster Luncheon* (1731), the self-indulgent French nobles are more concerned with their own sensual pleasures than with the plight of the peasants or the well-being of the country as a whole.

doctors, craftsmen, and people of the streets, the latter being especially prevalent in Paris and the ports. The great mass of commoners in France, as in Europe generally, were the 23 million peasants who tilled the soil. Most held some property rights to their lands, but many were tenants or sharecroppers. As late as 1789 about a million were still serfs. Almost all peasants, serf or free, paid fees to their local nobles. Government taxes were irregular but heavy everywhere; the *taille*, or main land tax, fell heaviest on the class least able to pay. French peasants lived better than serfs in eastern Europe or the starving farm laborers of England, but life in a French village was a constant struggle for survival.

Malfunctioning Government

While the Old Regime favored the nobility and clergy at the expense of other citizens, its governmental system displayed major defects. Absolute monarchies had promised to bring order out of feudal chaos, correct the abuses of organized religion, and provide national economic security. By the eighteenth century, however, absolutism was failing. Nobilities were back in power, taxes were rising, economic enterprise was restricted, and most European monarchies were extravagant, corrupt, and inefficient.

Political inefficiency took many forms. Laws were a perlexing mix of variable local customs, feudal presumptions, and royal decrees. Provincial tolls were imposed on trade within states. Coinages, as well as weights and measures, were sometimes different in adjoining provinces. Because of overlapping authorities, courts and officials were not sure of their jurisdictions. Public servants avoided responsibilities, fearing they would be blamed for error, a situation which produced bureaucratic delay and elaborate red tape. Every form of bribery, fraud, and distortion characterized governments at every level. Such evils were difficult to combat, because legalized privilege was so common.

Again, France exemplifies the general situation. Despite all efforts at centalization, Louis XIV had left a chaotic jumble of councils and committees, each with its expanding network of officials and clerks, whose conflicting claims to authority were barely less perplexing than their fussy procedures. The French had no body comparable to the English Parliament for registering public opinion; the Estates General had not convened since 1614. Government was most deficient in handling revenues, which it attempted to do without budgets, regularized accounting, or uniform assessments. If possible, French local government was even more chaotic. Late medieval districts, with their bailiffs and seneschals, coexisted with ornamental provincial governors and royal intendants, who assumed most control of local affairs after the seventeenth century. Some 360 different legal codes and 200 customs schedules applied in different parts of the country. Attempts to achieve uniformity invariably provoked vested local interests, who sponsored exceptions and compromises, further complicating the situation.

French government, like some others, was severely damaged by the indolence of its monarch, Louis XV, who hated the tedium of governing. Until the 1740s, he turned his government over to an able minister, Cardinal Fleury, who maintained peace and reasonable stability. Even then, however, policy and appointments were affected by court intrigues. These endeavors often involved noblewomen, who traded their favors for political influence. Such indirect but effective "mistress power," not only flourished among the court nobility but also with the king himself. His Polish wife, Maria Leczinska, endured a series of Louis' chief mistresses, who were installed in the palace near the king's bedchamber, granted titles, showered with costly gifts, and paraded by Louis in public. They earned France a reputation for petticoat governance, but their influence was negligible during Fleury's tenure.

Mistress government came into full flower in France after 1745, the era of Madame Pompadour (1721–1764). Born Jeanne-Antoinette Poisson to middle-class parents and married later to a royal tax collector, as Madame d'Etioles, she contrived to meet and bewitch Louis at a public ball in 1745. For the next few years, as the newly titled Marquise de Pompadour and the king's favorite, she dominated court life at Versailles. She was also the recipient of 17 estates, had a personal staff of more than 50 attendants, and enjoyed unlimited access to the royal treasury. After 1749, she left Louis' bed but remained a trusted advisor, monitoring all of his appointments and sharing many of his conferences with officials and diplomats. She used her influence against the Jesuits and was an ardent advocate of the Austrian alliance, which led to French defeat in the Seven Years' War. She was a strong and determined woman, truly devoted to the king and to France, but the methods which she rose to power reflect the weakness of the system.

Four years after Pompadour's death, Louis took another mistress. Jeanne Bécu (1743–1793), the illegitimate daughter of a seamstress, was trained for her life's mission while living with Jean Du Barry, a notorious rake and minor noble on the fringe of the French court. He arranged for her to meet the king, who was immediately stricken by her beauty and took her into the palace. A contrived marriage with the brother of her former lover made her a countess. As Madame Du Barry, she was now qualified to enter the ruthless competition of the court arena. Lacking Pompadour's drive and political instincts, she nevertheless became a tool for the conservative nobles, who helped her overcome her rivals in a series of backbiting struggles for royal favor. Until Louis died in 1774, she revelled in her power, her jewels, and her luxurious houses. As if in expiation for these years of glory, she died nineteen years later on a Paris guillotine crying, "please do not hurt me."[1]

Like Louis, many European kings squandered fortunes on mistresses, palaces, courts, and idle aristocrats, thus contributing to the common problem of rising public debt. This was also partially encouraged by developing capitalism, which made borrowing possible. Another significant cause was the maintenance of military and naval forces strong enough to protect colonial possessions and play power politics in Europe. By the late eighteenth century, each of the major continental powers, France, Russia, and Austria, kept standing armies of 250,000 men.

European rulers might have borne these expenses if they had been able to govern by brute force, as former emperors had done. They were prevented from doing so by their dependence on an international market, which supplied their needs only in exchange for goods, bullion, or credit. Ultimately, they were forced to borrow, putting their states at the mercy of bankers and their own credit ratings. Such financial accountability, almost unknown in the ancient world, placed a serious restriction on European monarchies.

Public finance was even a serious problem for England, the most commercially advanced state in Europe. In 1700, after war with France, the state debt reached £13 million sterling and was secured by the bank of England. The public debt continued to rise, despite the government's efforts in the 1720s to eliminate it with profits from the South Sea Company, an overseas trading monopoly. This venture failed following a wild stock speculation (the "South Sea" bubble). Colonial wars with France drove the debt still higher. Between 1763 and 1783, it rose from £140 million to £238 million. England was very wealthy and could carry this tremendous burden relatively easily, but the debt nevertheless contributed to internal political unrest.

For France, where the economy was less expansive and commanded less foreign credit, the problem was more serious. Badly weakened by Louis XIV's wars, France averted financial disaster in the 1720s and 1730s only by Fleury's peaceful foreign policy and reduced military spending. After 1742, however, deficits mounted steadily while France fought three major wars. In 1780 the French debt amounted to an equivalent of $600 million; interest payments absorbed half the annual income of approximately $33,750,000; and total government expenditures were $40 million. Admittedly, the French debt was not excessive, in comparison with England's. What the French lacked, however, was the Dutch capital that poured into England. Without adequate foreign credit, France was thrown back on its own resources, which caused a tripling of taxes between 1715 and 1785. The ensuing tax burden, plus the growing anxiety of wealthy government creditors, created the most serious threat to the Old Regime in France.

Dynamic Forces in European Society

Economic and social forces challenged European absolutism as it was becoming more static and inefficient. Society had been changing steadily since the late medieval period, but the rate of change was so rapid in this era that the process itself seemed unique. Every part of Europe, from Holland past the Russian borders, and every social class, from peasants to the most tradition-bound nobles, felt the insecurity and restlessness inherent in a general social transformation.

Expanding Commercial Capitalism

The primary cause for change was a vibrant capitalistic economy, developing so rapidly that it could hardly be controlled or even predicted. Absolutism had risen on a steady wave of economic expansion, but the wave was now so strong that it tossed the political vessel about and determined the craft's direction, no matter how the tiller might be set. Capitalism generated new economic pursuits, developing almost spontaneously outside of established institutions. It also brought unprecedented increases in the volume of trade.

Four new conditions produced the commercial boom of the eighteenth century. First, government demand for goods reached astronomical heights, as huge standing armies required mountains of food, clothing, arms, and ammunition. The French army, varying between 140,000 and 250,000, was still the largest, but even Britain had a military establishment of some 80,000, including a strong navy. Rising European population created another expanding market, demanding bulk commodities. Developing plantation agriculture in the tropical colonies provided another decided stimulus to foreign trade. Finally, Brazilian gold and diamond strikes raised prices and encouraged all European business after the 1730s.

Inflation brought mixed economic results. Wages, for example, increased far less than food prices, thus depressing the condition of workers. French nobles, who received fixed money fees from their peasants, or English landlords who had let their fields on long-term leases, were also hurt badly. On the other hand, those landowners who rented to casual tenants or received payment in kind gained appreciably. The former were likely to be capitalistic investors of the same class who profited from the general increase in the cost of goods. At times their profits soared in a wildly speculative market.

The rapidly expanding volume of foreign commerce was a clear indicator of eighteenth-century business properity. Although the Dutch imperial decline brought a decrease, English and French foreign trade increased 500 percent during the period. In 1789, imports from the French West Indies, an index of profits in sugar and slaves, were ten times higher than in 1716. At Liverpool, the major English port for sugar and slaves, annual imports jumped from 27,000 to 140,000 tons between 1700 and 1770.

The Growth of Free Enterprise

Such prosperity created serious problems for mercantilist systems. As opportunities for profit increased, capitalists sought gains outside traditional enterprises and even the legal limits set by governments. Some of these endeavors were deliberate efforts to evade the law; others—perhaps most—were responses to new, unanticipated economic conditions. This rising free-enterprise capitalism, as distinct from mercantilist state capitalism, was evident in every phase of the eighteenth-century economy.

A rising demand for food encouraged the trend in agriculture. As food prices soared, investors poured their surplus capital into land. This was most typical of England, but the agricultural boom, on somewhat smaller scales, touched France, Holland, the Austrian Netherlands, and even the vine cultures of Italy and Spanish Catalonia. Wherever it developed, capitalistic agriculture emphasized efficiency and profits, which usually required procedures that were inconsistent with the traditional cooperative methods of rural villages.

Three English commercial landowners pioneered in concentrating capital investments to improve agricultural techniques. Jethro Tull (1674–1741) carefully plowed the land, planted in neat rows, using a drill he invented, and kept the plants well cultivated as they grew to maturity. Viscount Charles Townshend (1674–1738), nicknamed "turnip Townshend," specialized in restoring soil fertility by such methods as applying clay-lime mixtures and planting turnips in crop rotation. Robert Bakewell (1725–1795) attacked the problem of scrawny cattle. Through his select breeding of choice animals, he was able to increase the size of meat animals and also the milk yields from dairy cows.

Another Englishman, Arthur Young (1741–1820), an ardent publicist for the new agriculture, lectured throughout Europe and edited a farm journal. Translated into many foreign languages his writings popularized the advantages of well-equipped farm and economical agricultural techniques. He did much to free European agriculture from the unproductive methods of the past.

New agricultural techniques required heavy capital investment and complete control of the land. The new methods could not be used on common fields, where villagers shared customary rights. Selective stockbreeding could not be practiced with animals in a community herd. Capitalistic landlords thus sought to fence, or enclose, their acres. By outright purchase, foreclosure, suit, fraud, or even legislation, they tried to free their lands from lingering manorial restrictions, particularly from traditional rights to community use of the commons.

The enclosure movement, which began in the sixteenth century, reached its peak after 1750. Most prevalent in England, it was also typical of the continent. Because French peasants were so important as taxpayers, the government could not allow many to be driven from the land. Consequently, French capitalistic landlords were still complaining about manorial restrictions in the late 1780s. In England, where the lower aristocracy (gentry) had already become capitalists and were also powerful in government, they were able to push 2000 enclosure laws through Parliament between 1760 and 1800 (see map, p. 503).

In industry, the movement toward free enterprise produced the "domestic system," which involved contractual arrangements between capitalists and handworkers. Capitalists supplied materials to the workers in their homes and later collected the products, to be sent through another stage of finishing or sold directly on the market. The system became common in industries where demand was high, returns attractive, and capital available. Domestic manufacturing moved early to the country, away from the regulations imposed by city guilds. The advantages and disadvantages were those associated with

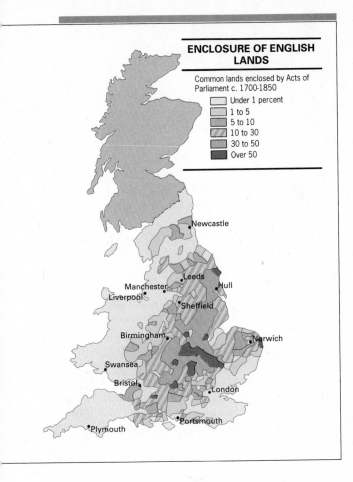

ENCLOSURE OF ENGLISH LANDS

Common lands enclosed by Acts of Parliament c. 1700-1850

- Under 1 percent
- 1 to 5
- 5 to 10
- 10 to 30
- 30 to 50
- Over 50

The career of Ambrose Crowley illustrates the domestic system in the infant English iron industry. Crowley started as a blacksmith who worked as a guildsman in Greenwich, where he accumulated a little capital. Around 1680, he moved to a small Durham village and built a domestic organization for the large-scale production of hardware. By 1700, the village had become a thriving town of 1500 workers. Most of them were employed by Crowley, who rented them their houses and supplied some of their tools as well as ore and fuel. The village produced nails, locks, bolts, hammers, spades, and other tools, which Crowley marketed elsewhere. As a wealthy and respected citizen, he was knighted in 1706.

In chapter 18 we described the rise of banks, stock exchanges, and insurance companies as part of the developing cooperation between capitalists and governments. Such cooperation does not fully explain the rise of these institutions. Although the great public banks usually operated under government charters and the new financial institutions affected government policies, all functioned within the opportunities and limitations of the free market. To this extent, they demonstrated the characteristics of free-enterprise capitalism.

Joint stock companies were drastically reoriented during the late 1600s. Originally they were exclusive monopolies, both in their areas of operation and in their limited number of stockholders. Prospective investors were denied stock or charged excessive fees. The companies were generally criticized and their trading rights were regularly violated by competitors and smugglers. Under pressure, the English East India Company and similar firms steadily liberalized their policies until eventually most stocks were sold on the open market. Free sale of stock greatly increased opportunities for investment and multiplied the number of joint stock companies. By 1715, more than 140 existed in England. This situation also encouraged a mushroom growth of stock exchanges, which sprang up in taverns and coffeehouses all over western Europe. In the early eighteenth century they had become necessary institutions in the private sector of Europe's economy.

Banking performed a similar necessary role. In a sense, the banks of Sweden, Amsterdam, and London were examples of state operation; their

unregulated industry. Contracts were freely negotiated and prices were usually low, but capitalists, workers, and consumers faced considerable risks.

Domestic industry was common all over western Europe after 1500, but it developed most in the eighteenth century, particularly in England. It was typical of all essential processes in the woolen industries, notably spinning, weaving, fulling, and dyeing. The system also spread among other textile industries, such as linens and cottons, which provided a decided stimulus to the trend in the 1700s. Other industries affected were lace, leather, silk, paper, glass, pottery, and the metal trades. A high proportion of those employed in all these industries were woman, because they were readily available for part-time work at home and because they could be paid less than men. Children were also often employed. By 1750, English domestic manufacturing involved more than four million workers.

Daniel Defoe, The Cloth Market at Leeds

The author of *Robinson Crusoe* also wrote on other subjects. This is a revealing picture of preindustrial capitalism in England.

Early in the Morning, Tressels are placed in two Rows in the Street, sometimes two Rows on a Side, cross which Boards are laid, which make a kind of temporary Counter on either Side, from one End of the Street to the other.

The Clothiers come early in the Morning with their Cloth; and, as few bring more than one Piece, the Market-days being so frequent, they go into the Inns and Public-houses with it, and there set it down.

At about Six o'Clock in the Summer, and about Seven in the Winter, the Clothiers being all come by that Time, the Market Bell at the Old Chapel by the Bridge rings; upon which it would surprise a Stranger, to see in how few Minutes, without Hurry, Noise, or the least Disorder, the whole Market is filled. . . .

As soon as the Bell has ceased ringing, the Factors and Buyers of all Sorts enter the Market, and walk up and down between the Rows, as their Occasions direct. Some of them have their foreign Letters of Orders, with Patterns sealed on them, in their Hands; the Colours of which they match, by holding them to the Cloths they think they agree to. When they have pitched upon their Cloth, they lean over to the Clothier, and, by a Whisper, in the fewest Words imaginable, the Price is stated; one asks, the other bids; and they agree or disagree in a Moment. . . .

If a Merchant has bidden a Clothier a Price, and he will not take it, he may go after him to his House, and tell him he has considered of it, and is willing to let him have it; but they are not to make any new Agreement for it, so as to remove the Market from the Street to the Merchant's House.

The Buyers generally walk up and down twice on each Side of the Rows, and in little more than an Hour all the Business is done. In less than half an Hour you will perceive the Cloth begin to move off, the Clothier taking it up upon his Shoulder to carry it to the Merchant's House. At about half an Hour after Eight the Market Bell rings again, upon which the Buyers immediately disappear, the Cloth is all sold; or if any remains, it is carried back into the Inn. . . .

Thus you see £10,000 or 20,000 worth of Cloth, and sometimes much more, bought and sold in little more than an Hour, the Laws of the Market being the most strictly observed that I ever saw in any Market in *England*.

If it be asked, How all these Goods at this Place, at *Wakefield*, and at *Halifax*, are vended and disposed of? I would observe,

First, That there is an Home-consumption; to supply which, several considerable Traders in *Leeds* go with Droves of Pack-horses, loaden with those Goods, to all the Fairs and Market-towns almost over the whole Island, not to sell by Retail, but to the Shops by Wholesale. . . .

There are others, who have Commissions from *London* to buy, or who give Commissions to Factors and Warehousekeepers in *London* to sell for them, who not only supply all the Shop-keepers and Wholesale Men in London, but sell also very great Quantities to the Merchants, as well for Exportation to the *English* Colonies in *America*, which take off great Quantities of the coarse Goods, especially *New England, New York, Virginia*, &c. as also to the *Russia Merchants*. . . .

The third Sorts are such as receive Commissions from abroad, to buy Cloth for the Merchants chiefly in *Hamburg*, and in *Holland*, &c. These are not only many in Number, but some of them very considerable in their Dealings, and correspond with the farthest Provinces in *Germany*.

From Daniel Defoe, *Tour Through Great Britain, 1724–1725* in Elizabeth K. Kendell, ed., *Source-Book of English History* (New York: Macmillan, 1912), pp. 321–24.

directors were often government advisors, authorized to perform semiofficial functions, such as issuing notes and financing public debts. In another sense, however, these institutions became integral parts of the free market economy, providing the necessary credit for business enterprise while creating their own nonofficial commercial methods and institutions. Moreover, smaller banks developed within the private monetary and credit systems. The first English country bank was founded as a private enterprise in 1716 at Bristol; by 1780, there were 300 in the country.

Major insurance companies, banks, and stock exchanges formed an integrated institutional system, functioning within a free international market. Their standardized procedures became so complicated that they could not be understood by ordinary people. That strange new world of business enterprise, unlike the political world, was not controlled directly by anyone, not even by the power of concentrated capital. Goods and credit, commodity prices and wages, monetary values and stock quotations, all interacted according to their own laws, which could be studied but only partially predicted.

A Turbulent European Society

This second stage of capitalist revolution was both cause and result of powerful social turbulence, marked by urbanism, migration, and an unprecedented population explosion. The number of people in Europe increased 68 percent, from about 110 million in 1700 to 185 million in 1800; some 50 million of the increase came after 1750. European population growth during the era was much higher than in Asia or Africa and also above that of any earlier comparable period; it has not been exceeded since, not even in the post-World War II era of the twentieth century.

This tremendous expansion was common to most of Europe between 1650 and 1800. The English population rose from 5 to over 9 million; that of Russia went up from 17 to 36 million; and the French population rose more moderately, from 21 to 28 million. The gain from 275,000 to 4 million in the English American colonies was by far the most striking. Other areas, which had earlier seen declines, posted gains.

Spanish population rose from 7.5 million to 11 million people, while that of Italy expanded from 11 to 19 million.[2]

Such statistics go far toward explaining the eighteenth-century social world. The incredible population increase may have been partially caused, for example, by the insecurity of impoverished rural families, who regarded children as sources of support or excuses for state aid. It is equally obvious that it was a product and a reflection of such varying social conditions as rising agricultural production; cleaner underclothes and dishes, made possible by the new textile and pottery industries; cheaper transportation of food supplies; better water and sewage facilities, resulting from wider use or iron piping; and improved medical techniques, which both combatted infant mortality and increased life expectancy. There can be little doubt that surging population contributed to the growth of cities, an increasing surplus of labor, vagabondage, and rising economic demand. It was thus an integral part of the universal social change.

As the population increased, people moved in all directions. Some, like the Swiss and Irish, became foreign mercenaries. Others, like the French Huguenots, were victims of religious persecution; of the original 300,000 refugees, 40,000 settled in England and some 20,000 of the most skilled went to Prussia. Both the Prussians and Russian governments regularly imported specialized craftsmen. German peasants by the thousands also went east to acquire land in the Hungarian or Russian Ukraines. In the eighteenth century, more than 750,000 English and 100,000 Irish settlers arrived in America. These were the largest national contigents of a European migration which numbered some 2 million people.

Life in the New World varied widely among the Spanish, Portuguese, French, and English colonists, but in all the colonies, the frontier atmosphere encouraged self-reliance and optimism. Upward mobility was everywhere much more possible overseas than in Europe at that time. This was particularly true in the English American colonies, where Benjamin Franklin could become rich after begininng life penniless or Thomas Jefferson, the son of a poor backcountry farmer, could marry into a wealthy family.

The adventurous spirit that had developed overseas returned to Europe in the eighteenth century. Europeans were fascinated by the cultures of foreigners, whether Chinese, Africans, or Native Americans. Everything American excited great curiosity, particularly after mid-century, when regular mail service brought Europe into closer contact with the colonies. Americans and British merchants developed strong ties based on common profits. Americans frequented certain London coffeehouses, and some former Americans won election to Parliament. Tremendous interest was aroused by retiring employees of the East India Company, many of whom had risked everything on making their fortunes in India and had succeeded beyond their wildest dreams. Their country estates excited widespread wonder and envy.

Migration overseas was accompanied by rising urban populations. This occured to some extent in eastern Europe, notably in Prussia and Austria, but the trend was especially pronounced in the west, where commerce and finance were centered. England was most affected. The populations of English towns and cities generally grew faster than those of rural areas, although migration from the country was a relatively insignificant factor. In England, as on the continent, population increased most decisively in those commercial centers which were involved in foreign trade.

The scope and significance of the trend may be quickly illustrated by a few figures. London's population rose from 400,000 to 900,000 between the Peace of Utrecht (1713) and the French Revolution (1789). Other English cities, such as Bristol, Norwich, Liverpool, Leeds, Halifax, and Birmingham, which had been country towns in the 1600s, became medium-sized cities, ranging in size between 20,000 and 50,000 inhabitants (see map below). On the continent, the population of Paris reached 800,00 by 1789, and the number of residents in Bordeaux, Nantes, Le Havre, and Marseilles all increased appreciably. Amsterdam, the nucleus of the Dutch urban cluster, increased from 200,000 residents in 1670 to 250,000 in 1800. Farther east were other expanding cities such as Hamburg, Frankfurt, Geneva, Vienna, and Berlin; populations of the latter two exceeded 100,000 in the eighteenth century.[3]

Cities, of course, were the breeding grounds of ideas and contention. There were the books and newspapers, coffeehouses, sailors from

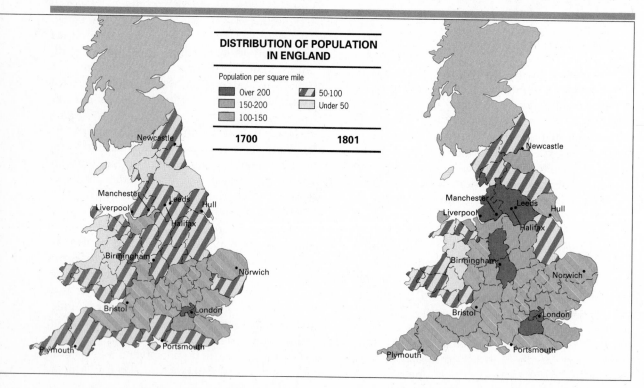

DISTRIBUTION OF POPULATION IN ENGLAND

Population per square mile

- Over 200
- 150-200
- 100-150
- 50-100
- Under 50

1700   1801

English artist William Hogarth used his engravings as "morality plays" to preach virtue and campaign against vice. *Gin Lane* depicts the London poor in alcoholic delirium, their escape from the misery of their lives.

foreign lands, and varied populations, exchanging views and challenging prejudices. Urban life was not only exciting, it was also more impersonal, dangerous, and frustrating. Using every kind of trick and deceit, a large criminal element flourished in the streets. Mobs were easily formed and more easily aroused, particularly in London and Paris, which regularly faced riots in the eighteenth century. Unlike the relatively placid inhabitants of rural villages, city dwellers thrived on such change and diversity.

Rising Expectations

New wealth and new ideas brought higher living standards to the middle classes, opening opportunities for social display and hopes for advancement. Even ordinary people could acquire the muslins and calicoes that permitted them to dress better and thus imitate their social superiors. More products stimulated appetites for even more goods, accenting the acquisitiveness already so common [in ur]- an society.

The conspicuous display of wealth, more [than] birth, came to be associated with social statu[s.] Bewigged merchants as well as nobles were resplendent in white silk coats, knee breeches, silk stockings, and gold-braided hats. Young English fops, on their way up, might spend the equivalent of $2000 for a single outfit and lose that much more of borrowed money at the gaming tables. Well-to-do women decked themselves out in imported brocades, ostrich feathers, fans, furs, parasols, and silver lace. Home decor featured Persian rugs and imported draperies of chintzes and chiffons. There was also a passion for objects from China and Japan—china, screens, lacquered trays, and gilded tables. With their appetite for ostentation and uncultivated tastes, the newly rich, particularly low-born East India Company men, scandalized old English aristocrats.

Although sanitation and the quality of life among the poor remained terrible, there were some improvements for those above poverty level. In a few of the most progressive urban areas, some streets were paved and sewers constructed. Water was piped to some private mansions, and public baths were increasing. At the same time, social graces were becoming more refined. Manners, for example, improved somewhat, as middle-class Europeans set their tables with beautiful china and silver, provided napkins, and lifted food with forks rather than fingers. No longer did they throw bones on the floor or use pocket knives to pick their teeth. Eating, therefore, became more of an art than a simple necessity or a purely sensual satisfaction.

Such refinements suggested that the comforts of the nobility were being shared by the upwardly mobile middle classes. Some 250,000 European families had acquired this status by the middle of the eighteenth century. In France the middle class constituted about 8 percent of the population and had acquired about 25 percent of the land. Like their counterparts among the English landed gentry, they enjoyed privileges formerly confined largely to the aristocracy. Meanwhile, an increasingly large number of individuals entered the middle class from below. Shopkeepers, lawyers, and professionals improved their conditions and raised

Caffure nouvelle ?
ditte le Caprice ?
des jolies femmes.

Fantastic hair styles, like that shown in this engraving, were one of the ways in which the French upper classes displayed their extravagance.

their expectations. For the first time, they became truly conscious of individual interests, apart from those of a caste or a dynasty.

The rising middle class enjoyed luxuries but valued respectablility, rejecting the flamboyant display so typical of nobilities. Most accented the importance of private family life and religion. Indeed many shopkeepers and merchants had reinterpreted Calvinism as it spread among them, identifying usury and profit seeking with diligent stewardship in God's service and translating Calvin's original idea of a "calling" to mean profession or business. This integration of Calvinism and capitalism was also reflected in the similarity between elected church deacons and the representative boards of joint stock companies. Whether they were Calvinists or not—and many were not—members of the middle class were ambitious, aggressive, cunning, and, above all, competitive. They prided themselves on being

"self-made." A perfect example was William Miles of Bristol, who started with almost nothing, amassed a fortune in the sugar trade, and ended by controlling the largest refining operation in his city.

Although largely denied government posts at the higher levels, many members of the new middle class possessed great potential for leadership. They were determined, confident, and often well educated. Many were members of the medical and legal professions, which were striving to earn respect. Physicians and lawyers often became very concerned about public issues. Lawyers, particularly, were familiar with parliamentary procedures and were trained to express themselves clearly. Middle-class leaders were also closer than the nobles to urban workers, with whom they could still share some common experiences and values.

Improving conditions among the middle classes brought some moderate gains for women. The refinement of manners, the growing concern for fads and fashions, along with the emphases upon family ties and religious morality, were all reflections of growing feminine influence. The same family emphasis and the middle class penchant for individualism encouraged women to demand more voice in choosing their husbands; fewer middle-class marriages were negotiated by parents without consulting their offspring. More wealth and leisure afforded increased opportunities for women's education, as indicated in the large number of new schools for girls, particularly in France and England. As a result, women became more prominent in literary and artistic fields. Educated and fashionable middle-class women often attended or hosted salons, which were centers for intellectual discussion, open to anyone with recognized talents. The salons originated in France but were copied all over Europe, a most notable example was the "bluestocking" gathering at the homes of wealthy English ladies.

Problems Facing Old Regimes

Despite its great promise, Europe's dynamic society generated countless ambitions, frustrations, and resentments associated with the rising middle classes, crowded cities, dispossessed peasants, rising populations, contrasting cultures, and an expanding world economy. Standing directly in the way of these forces were most absolute monarchies and their Old Regimes. Because of their vested interests and their rigidity, they were peculiarly incapable of dealing with social problems threatening from every side.

The Prevalence of Human Misery

Terrible human misery among the poor was typical of Europe in the eighteenth century. Like the conflicts that preceded it, the Seven Years' War had destroyed crops, ruined cities, created hordes of starving refugees, and depopulated whole provinces. Armies contributed to prevailing diseases, such as smallpox, typhus, and malaria. Flies swarmed about the sanitary waste and horse manure that filled roads and streets, encouraging the spread of typhoid and infantile diarrhea, which killed thousands of children.

Beggar Feeding a Child by Giacomo Ceruti. When they could not work, the poor turned to begging. When they could no longer beg, they died.

While epidemics of plague spread through central Europe, rickets and tuberculosis reflected the malnutrition preventing half the workers from achieving marginal proficiency. The mortality was appalling: half of the children died before they were six; 20 percent of fertile women died in childbirth; and life expectancy was only about 28 years. For a large proportion of Europeans, unemployment, homelessness, grinding poverty, and hunger was inevitable. Indeed, horrible reality could only be escaped, on rare affordable occasions, in alcohol.

Life in the cities may have been exciting, but it was also miserable for many. The urban poor made up some 20 to 25 percent of city populations; most had come in from the country seeking survival. Without homes, friends, or steady work, they lived, as best they could, working at transitory menial jobs, begging, stealing or selling themselves as prostitutes. Only a social notch higher were the apprentices and journeymen of the decaying craft guilds, who also faced real hardships. The discipline, particularly for apprentices, was hard, hours were long, and wages were barely enough to buy their food. Crowded into filthy quarters, without adequate light, air, or bathing facilities, they lived dull lives fraught with ignorance, disease, crime, and squalor. Bad as these conditions were, they might always get worse, for as the guilds faced competition, many shops were forced to close, forcing their journeymen to become wandering artisans among the vagabonds on the roads.

Most of these pitiful derelicts were products of the century's most serious social challenge: the problem of rural poverty. Despite a general prosperity, lasting until about 1770, European peasants suffered severely from rising food prices amid increasing agricultural specialization. The resulting seller's market turned aristocrats into aspiring capitalists, willing to gouge their peasants in order to realize greater profits. Some nobles, particularly on the continent, revived and enforced their old manorial rights to fees and services. Others moved in an opposite direction by eliminating the peasants' medieval rights and using hired labor to work their lands. Either way, the peasants lost a substantial amount of their livelihood and were likely to become criminals, vagrants, or part of an alienated subculture. They ceased to be assets

Arthur Young, Conditions Among Eighteenth-Century French Peasants

Young made these observations just before the French Revolution. He saw better conditions elsewhere but was appalled at the backward state of French agriculture and the great gap in living standards between the nobility and the lower classes in the country.

SEPTEMBER 1ST. To Combourg. The country has a savage aspect; husbandry not much further advanced, at least in skill, than among the Hurons, which appears incredible amidst enclosures; the people almost as wild as their country, and their town of Combourg one of the most brutal filthy places that can be seen; mud houses, no windows, and a pavement so broken, as to impede all passengers, but ease none; yet here is a château, and inhabited. Who is this Mons. de Chateaubriand, the owner, that has nerves strung for a residence amidst such filth and poverty? Below this hideous heap of wretchedness is a fine lake, surrounded by well-wooded enclosures. Coming out of Hédé, there is a beautiful lake belonging to Mons. de Blossac, Intendant of Poitiers, with a fine accompaniment of wood. A very little cleaning would make here a delicious scenery. There is a château [Château de Blossac], with four rows of trees, and nothing else to be seen from the windows in the true French style. Forbid it, taste, that this should be the house of the owner of that beautiful water; and yet this Mons. de Blossac has made at Poitiers the finest promenade in France! . . .

SEPT. 5TH. To Montauban. The poor people seem poor indeed; the children terribly ragged, if possible worse clad than if with no clothes at all; as to shoes and stockings they are luxuries. A beautiful girl of six or seven years playing with a stick, and smiling under such a bundle of rags as made my heart ache to see her. They did not beg, and when I gave them anything seemed more surprised than obliged. One-third of what I have seen of this province seems uncultivated, and nearly all of it in misery. . . .

JULY 11TH. Pass [Les] Islettes, a town (or rather collection of dirt and dung) of new features, that seem to mark, with the faces of the people, a country not French.

JULY 12TH. Walking up a long hill, to ease my mare, I was joined by a poor woman, who complained of the times, and that it was a sad country. Demanding her reasons, she said her husband had but a morsel of land, one cow, and a poor little horse, yet they had a *franchar* (42 lb.) of wheat, and three chickens, to pay as a quit-rent to one seigneur; and four *franchar* of oats, one chicken and 1 *sou* to pay to another, besides very heavy tailles and other taxes. She had seven children, and the cow's milk helped to make the soup. But why, instead of a horse, do not you keep another cow? Oh, her husband could not carry his produce so well without a horse; and asses are little used in the country. It was said, at present, that *something was to be done by some great folks for such poor ones, but she did not know who nor how*, but God send us better, *car les tailles et les droits nous écrasent*. This woman, at no great distance, might have been taken for sixty or seventy, her figure was so bent, and her face so furrowed and hardened by labour; but she said she was only twenty-eight. An Englishman who had not travelled cannot imagine the figure made by infinitely the greater part of the countrywomen in France; it speaks, at the first sight, hard and severe labour. I am inclined to think, that they work harder than the men, and this, united with the more miserable labour of bringing a new race of slaves into the world, destroys absolutely all symmetry of person and every feminine appearance. . . .

From Arthur Young, *Travels in France*, edited by Constantia Maxwell. (Cambridge: Cambridge University Press, 1929), pp. 107ff.

to the state—as either taxpayer or soldiers—and instead became potentially dangerous and expensive liabilities.

Although faring better than the serfs of eastern Europe, western peasants faced serious difficulties. Some in France were reduced from tenants to laborers when merchants bought up land to profit from rising food prices. Under Louis XV, some 30,000 rural vagrants thronged French roads. Some 35 percent of the peasants who had managed to acquire land were still paying manorial fees and services to local lords, in accordance with feudal law. Earlier these exactions had hurt the peasants' pride more than their chances for survival, but when the practice was stepped up during the depression of the 1780s, many lost their land.

In England, the situation was quite different. Although English manorial fees and services were abolished in the seventeenth century, many villages had retained their medieval rights to pasturage and fuel-gathering on the commons. These rights were lost to enclosures. From 1750 until the end of the century, 40,000 to 50,000 small farms disappeared into large capitalistic estates. Some of those forced from the land went to the cities, some because agricultural laborers at pitifully poor wages, and some went into parish poor houses, which were soon filled to overflowing.

Relief for the poor was one of the most persistent and perplexing problems facing England in the eighteenth century. Rural unemployment became a way of life, encouraged by the large landowners, who wanted cheap labor. More than a million unemployed people were languishing in 4000 parish work houses at the end of the century. Local taxpayers used every means to prevent vagrants from settling in their parishes, thus prohibiting the unemployed from finding work. Even a pregnant woman, or one with a sick child, might be given a few pennies and turned away. Ultimately the government built larger workhouses for fewer parishes, attempting to spread the cost of poor relief. Such policies destroyed the initiative of the poor, who turned to public welfare as their source for relief.

Oppressive Conditions for Women

Such conditions were especially oppressive to women, whose general prospects grew worse in the eighteenth century, despite some slight gains among those in the upper classes. Rising capitalism diminished work opportunities for all women, but poor widows were hit hardest, as suggested by the number starving in English workhouses. Women's life expectancy was five years less than men's. This fact is explained partially by the large proportion of mothers who

In some mining regions, women miners were common. In this engraving from an 18th-century French work, women work at the pit head of a primitive coal mine.

died in childbirth; a significant factor here was malnutrition. Poor women lacked calcium in their diets and were therefore subject to hemorrhaging. For women among the rural and urban poor, life was a nightmare of deprivation, suffering, and struggling to survive.

This was particularly true of poor country women, as noted by Arthur Young, who described a French peasant woman of 28 years but appearing to be 60 or 70. Capitalistic agriculture and the accompanying aristocratic encroachments depressed farm wages, forcing farm laborers to leave the villages in search of work. Women had to stay with the children and eke out support for the family in domestic spinning or weaving. Some worked in the fields for lower wages than men. As work opportunities declined, thousands of women took to the roads, carrying their babies and begging for food. Many died with their children by the roadsides. Others joined gangs of robbers or smugglers. The hardiest and the most determined reached the cities, where the best hope for a displaced peasant woman was employment as a cook or maid with a well-to-do family.

Among the urban poor, a woman's life was not much better than in the villages. The lucky few who were hired as household servants were paid much less than men, housed in cramped quarters, fed scraps, and frequently exploited sexually by their masters. Employment outside domestic service was extremely limited, because women were denied membership in most craft guilds. A few could find work in nonguild industries, spinning, weaving, sewing, or working leather for long hours at starvation wages in sweatshops. They were often employed at dirtier and heavier jobs in the metal trades and in the coal fields, both above and below ground. Another option, and one chosen by many women who could not easily find other work, was prostitution, which was growing rapidly in every large city, with 50,000 known prostitutes plying their trade in London and more than 40,000 in Paris at about the same time. Their lives were marked by social degradation, venereal disease, and continuous harassment by civil authorities, who allowed them to operate but subjected them to periodic imprisonment.

A vast social chasm separated poor women from those of the wealthy classes; yet at the top social levels another broad gulf divided the sexes. Royal and noble women, as we have seen, exercised considerable political power in this era, but except for the numerous ruling monarchs, women operated as satellites of the men they manipulated. Among both aristocratic women and those of the wealthy middle class, many were withdrawn from meaningful work as mothers and managers to become social drones, advertising, in an ornamental way, the positions of their husbands. Legally, upper-class wives remained subordinated to their husbands in the disposition of property and rights to divorce; the double standard concerning marital fidelity was still supreme, both socially and legally. Indeed, despite their improving education and their activities in literature and the arts, eminent eighteenth-century men, including Rousseau, Frederick the Great, and Lord Chesterfield, characterized women as childlike, irresponsible, and ruled by passion. In the council chambers and the counting houses, it was still a man's world.

Social Discontent

Even a quick survey of privileges, exploitation, and living conditions under the Old Regime reveals obvious sources of social discontent, which arose not only because of human misery and injustice—both conditions had been equally prevalent in earlier times. But now the spirit of change and improvement, coupled with the hopeless confusion and inefficiency of most monarchies, aroused general feelings of dissatisfaction. Peasants and city workers were certainly not pleased with their lot, although they lacked the confidence, education, and opportunities to register direct protest. The middle class, particularly the lawyers, were much better equipped to voice their grievances, which they did often. For monarchs, however, the most frightening development should have been the critical attitude of many nobles. The nobles' casual indifference proved that privilege no longer worked among the ruling class to ensure loyalty and leadership.

Because essential records are not available, no one can say for sure what were the attitudes of peasants on the continent. They surely varied from place to place, as did the conditions. Generally, peasants lacked long-range political objectives but were easily aroused by immediate threats to their well-being. Seventy-three peasant rebellions occurred in eighteenth-century Europe, including ones in Poland (1730s), Bohemia (1775), and Russia (1773–1775). The suffering English farm laborers rioted six times between 1710 and 1772. French peasants were generally docile, but nevertheless precipitated violent upheavals in 1709, 1725, 1740, 1749, and 1772. Arthur Young recognized the surly attitudes and contempt for authority among French peasants. In 1789, when they could express grievances to delegates headed for the Estates-General, they were universally bitter against feudal exactions and government taxes.

Workers, in general, were more aggressive and perhaps better informed than peasants but more confused by the complexities of their problems. While their numbers were increasing with the size of cities, they were becoming alienated from the upper classes by periodic unemployment and inflation. Rioting among workers and the idle poor of the cities was thus quite common, particularly in London and Paris. Such outbreaks, however, were usually more violent than politically significant. Workers did recognize two potential enemies. One was the capitalist who contracted for labor and used political influence to eliminate government welfare. The other enemy was the guild, which exploited the journeyman in favor of the master. To combat these enemies, workers formed some weak organizations in England and France. Their efforts, however, usually failed for want of leadership.

That leadership was available in the middle class, whose members were most conscious of defects in the Old Regime and most aggressive in their attitudes. Although they lent money or paid the taxes that supported governments, they were everywhere excluded from political participation. In England, the House of Commons was dominated by the gentry and the House of Lords by the nobles. Local government in England and France was monopolized by self-perpetuating cliques. In both France and England the middle class had wealth without responsibility, intelligence without authority, and ability without recognition. Small merchants and shopkeepers, in particular, were suspicious of government favors, lucrative offices, and monopolies. They wanted, as one merchant told Colbert, to be left alone so they could mind their businesses. Their wants were in direct opposition to the absolutist political ideal.

Middle-class discontent, like some discontent of the peasants, arose more from thwarted expectations than from terrible suffering. Upward mobility, from middle class to aristocracy, was a by-product of economic prosperity all over Europe, particularly in England and France. Such upward movement took many forms—purchase of land and titles, marriage, even reward for personal services of lawyers, doctors, tutors, or governesses. This middle-class struggle for respectability was individualistic and competitive so long as opportunities were open. Unfortunately, room at the top was limited; as the middle class increased, more of its members sought to ascend the social ladder. They met with repeated frustrations as the Old Regime became stable. At this point, ambitious middle-class outsiders became dangerously hostile to the system.

Most dissenting action, whether physically violent or merely vocal, came from men, but women were also represented among the malcontents. They were regularly involved in local uprising against the high cost of bread, the introduction of machines to depress labor, and rising taxes. A striking case of female activism occurred in 1770, when a mob of Parisian women left their work places and protested the deporting of their vagrant children to the colonies; their endeavor succeeded temporarily but did not end the practice. Such actions were not yet directed against the Old Regime itself. Nor were the writings and agitations of middle-class women among the English humanitarians. One of these was Hannah More, who supported the English Evangelical movement against slavery. Other English women, led by the Countess of Huntingdon, helped popularize Methodism among the English working classes. Later in the century, as we shall see in chapter 21, other French and English women would go further, championing women's rights, along with "the rights of man."

The main voices of opposition from outside the Old Regime in this era came from middle-class men, but aristocratic insiders were also discontented. Gains achieved by the nobles in Sweden, Spain, Austria, and even France increased their confidence and whetted their appetites for more power. Nobles at the top were frantically determined to maintain their positions; indeed, they professed to believe that they were more legitimate rulers than were the kings. This was partially an effort to combat middle-class influence, for nobles were often heavily in debt and feared legal reforms that might require them to pay. Only a few lesser nobles, resenting the court cliques, dreamed of making common cause with the middle classes to change the system. Aristocratic criticism was indeed varied, but none of it promised cooperation with the kings in curtailing special privileges. On this point nearly all aristocrats were in rebellious agreement.

Difficulties in Enforcing Mercantilism

Perhaps the most serious problems facing monarchs were those related to enforcing mercantilism. In the sixteenth century, merchant-bankers had accepted the system because they shared common interests with kings in combatting the Catholic Church and the feudal nobilities. As time passed, however, monarchical states became increasingly paternalistic and ordered while capitalism developed spontaneously in the direction of more freedom.

In eighteenth-century Europe, the success of mercantilism varied widely between East and West. In Prussia and Russia, reforms were effected through state control and worked well, compared with what had gone before; state-imported craftsmen and tools from western Europe continued to improve the economies of both monarchies. Habsburg efforts met with less success, because the Empire was unable to impose regulations effectively on the aristocracy. Meanwhile, most states in western Europe could not easily keep their controlled maufactures competitive in the world market.

This was particularly true of France. Government regulations favored luxury goods over bulk commodities, which limited French participation in world trade. Reliance on urban guilds created another limitation. These medieval monopolies were given the responsibility for enforcing thousands of minute regulations in every aspect of industry. Government inspectors then sought to monitor the regulatory actions of the guilds. The system, which suffered from

vested interests, local politics, corruption, and bureaucratic confusion, provoked periodic confrontations, particularly when it was extended into the countryside. In 1770, the guilds and the French government attempted to stop the domestic production of printed calicoes. More than 16,000 people died in the violent conflicts and subsequent executions. On one day in Valence, 631 offenders were sentenced to the galleys, 58 were put to torture on the wheel, and 77 were hanged. Yet despite all such efforts, printed calicoes continued to be printed and sold illegally in France.

England experienced another kind of industrial problem. Because most guild monopolies had passed with the seventeenth century, domestic industry faced few legal obstacles; but it did experience frequent functional crises. Despite widespread business prosperity, wages failed to keep up with the steady inflation. Between 1756 and 1786 wages rose by 35 percent, while food prices increased by more than 60 percent. Workers also had to accept periodic unemployment even in good times. They were thus inclined to resist the wage system and agitate for state intervention against low wages and high prices. Their bitter discontent was expressed in violent riots, most notably in 1765 and 1780.

Difficulties in industry were mild compared with those in foreign trade. All mercantilist economies attempted the careful control of external commerce, but the increased volume and consequent promise of rich profits from such enterprise encouraged widespread smuggling. No government of a coastal state was sufficiently wealthy to police a long and irregular coastline. Moreover, the coast guards, port authorities, and customs officials charged with enforcing trade restrictions were usually so corrupt that they were ineffective. Thus, despite feeble efforts to stop it, illegal trade flowed with growing pressure through rotten and fragile mercantilists sieves, violating increasingly complicated commercial laws. To meet this problem, governments resorted to private contractors, often granting immunity from the laws as payment for enforcing the regulations. The resulting monopolies assumed and usually abused government authority.

English controls were probably more successful than the French or the Spanish, but they were extremely costly in the long run. A great body of officials—more than 1250 in London alone—cost the government more than the amounts they were supposed to save in revenues. In the second half of the century, government imposed stricter controls over the trade of the American colonies. As the result of this mercantilist revival, smugglers almost took over the English coasts and the colonies were pushed toward armed rebellion.

Smuggling was big business in the New World, where it exceeded legal trade in the 1700s. West Indian planters of all nationalities conducted illicit commerce with English colonial merchants. New England timber and manufactures were regularly exchanged for French molasses, which was then made into rum and smuggled into Europe. Half the trade of Boston in 1750 violated English laws; Rhode Island and Pennsylvania merchants grew rich supplying the French during the Seven Years' War; and 80 percent of all teas used in the English colonies before 1770 came in free of duties. In addition, large quantities of tobacco were landed illegally in England with the connivance of Virginia and Carolina planters.

Smuggling was just as common in Europe, where every seacoast teemed with illegal traders. Families grew wealthy in the business, and fathers trained their sons to continue their enterprises. Contraband runners and government agents engaged in continual civil war, using intelligence operations, pitched battles, and prepared sieges. Systematic enforcement was almost impossible, because officials were bribed or personally involved, witnesses refused to testify, and juries often acquitted offenders caught in the act. During their classic era, after the Seven Years' War, English smugglers operated openly in almost all west country ports, including Bristol and Liverpool. On the other side of the country, desperate smuggling cliques roamed Kent, Sussex, and East Anglia. One of these, the notorious Hawkhurst gang of 500 armed men, forced farmers to store smuggled goods. The goods were then moved, under armed convoys, from depot to depot and ultimately to waiting London merchants. During the American Revolution, when the government attempted to stop this traffic, civil war nearly resulted, and smuggling was not appreciably curtailed.

Ordinary people accepted smuggling but tried to avoid entanglement in its dangerous web. One night in 1752, Horace Walpole found one inn filled with smugglers and moved on to the next, which was occupied by excise men. Walpole expressed relief in his diary for having passed safely as a "neutral" through "both armies." Another illuminating commentary was provided in 1765 by a Norfolk parson, who made the following entry in his journal:

Andrews, the smuggler brought me this night about 11 o'clock a bag of Hyson tea of 6 lb. weight. He frightened us a little by whistling under the parlor window just as we were going to bed. I . . . paid him for the tea at 10s., 6d. per pound.[4]

Another illegal enterprise, closely related to smuggling, was piracy. It too was encouraged by the mercantilist policies of European states and by the fortunes to be made in foreign goods. In the seventeenth century, groups of freebooting adventurers operated out of the West Indies. By 1700 they were working with smugglers in western England, who refitted their ships and marketed their goods. They also did a thriving business with the colonies, where pirate ships were built to order in New England shipyards. Merchants in Carolina, Virginia, Rhode Island, Pennsylvania, and New York regularly took pirate cargoes after the English Navigation Acts prohibited foreign ships from entering colonial ports. Piracy, like smuggling, was considered a trade, and pirate crews were dedicated profit-seekers, organized to share their booty according to written contracts. Until the English navy cleared the Caribbean in the early eighteenth century, piracy ranked with slaving and smuggling as among the most profitable maritime enterprises.

The Failure of Monarchical Reform

At any time after the middle of the eighteenth century, an urgent need for reform challenged every major European state. Neither the nobles nor the clergy could provide the necessary leadership. Although they had acquired social status and power everywhere, they were committed to exercise that power, according to the code of their class, in protecting their privileges. Yet those privileges, particularly immunity from taxation, had to be limited if the states were to avoid collapse. Action by the monarchs, who symbolized their nations' well-being and supposedly wielded absolute power, seemed the best hope for solution of the problem.

The French Debacle: Enlightenment and Despotism

The necessity for monarchical leadership was well understood in France, where philosophers expressed it in the theory of "benevolent" or "enlightened" despotism. The proponents were mostly French middle-class intellectuals, such as Voltaire and Diderot (see ch. 20). Their writings were widely read in many European courts, a continued deference to French ideas, which were considered to be the latest in intellectual fashion. Their appeal, however, was more than a literary fad. European kings were easily influenced, because the need for forceful royal action was so pressing that it could hardly be ignored.

The last Bourbon kings in France were affected by these reforming ideas of the Enlightenment. Tax and budgetary reform, if not "enlightened despotism," was attempted half-heartedly in France under Louis XV and his grandson, Louis XVI (1774–1792). Although he was almost indifferent to affairs of state and dozed through his council meetings, Louis XV tried twice to tax the nobles and once to curtail the special privileges of the traditional courts, particularly the most prestigious, privileged, and aristocratic *Parlement* (court) of Paris. Each attempt led to years of controversy between the government and the nobles; in each instance, Louis ultimately gave up the fight.

Louis XVI was well meaning put poorly educated, indolent, and shy. Shirking government business, he spent his happiest hours in a workshop, tinkering with locks. His child-bride, the frivolous Habsburg princess, Marie Antoinette, furnished him with no wisdom or practical support. Although dimly aware of problems, Louis was no more successful than his grandfather. The clamor of the nobles forced him to abandon proposals for eliminating the more undeserved pensions and levying a very modest tax on all landed property.

Enlightened Despotism Outside France

Unlike the later Bourbons, some eighteenth-century kings were known as "enlightened despots." Perhaps the major figure in this "monarch's age of repentance" was Frederick II, the Great, of Prussia, who won a reputation as a model ruler during the last half of his reign. As an avowed admirer of Voltaire, his writings popularized the ideal monarch as "the first servant of the state," "the father of his people", and "the last refuge of the unfortunate."[5] "Old Fritz," as his subjects called him, was slavishly committed to his principles. He left his bed at five each morning and worked until dark, reading reports, supervising, traveling, listening to complaints, and watching over every aspect of government.

Under Frederick, Prussia was known as the best-governed state in Europe. Within only a few years, it had recovered economically from the terrible ravages of war, largely through the state's aid in distributing seed, livestock, and tools. Frederick imported new crops, attracted skilled immigrants, opened new lands, and tried to promote new industries, such as silk and other textiles. He codified the law and reorganized the courts, along with the civil service. Following the ideas of the French Enlightenment, he established civil equality for Catholics, abolished torture in obtaining confessions from criminals, decreed national compulsory education, and took control of the schools away from the church. Until he died in 1786, Frederick worked diligently at improving Prussia.

His achievements, nevertheless, were more despotic than enlightened, and his successes were matched by failures. Although Frederick played the flute, wrote French poetry, and corresponded with Voltaire, his reforms were continuations of his father's mercantilism rather than adjustments to changes in his time. His monetary policy caused inflation, and this, along with his penchant for state monopolies, seriously hurt many Prussian merchants. Frederick's agricultural program did not touch serfdom. His use of French tax collectors precipitated civil disorders, and his consistent appointment of aristocrats as officials helped exclude the middle class from government. Even his religious and educational reforms were marred by official discrimination against Jews and failure to provide necessary funds for schools. Frederick's approach succeeded so well because it came at a time when mercantilism still worked in Prussia. It left much to be done later, when social change would require quite different policies.

Frederick's contemporary, Catherine II of Russia was also known in her time as an enlightened despot. Having learned the politics of survival at the Russian court, she and her lover had conspired with palace guards to put aside her erratic husband, Peter, and have herself declared Czarina in 1762. Although a ruthless Machiavellian in foreign affairs and a libertine, Catherine was a sensitive woman who appreciated the arts, literature, and the advantages of being considered enlightened. She corresponded with Voltaire and gave Diderot a pension. The latter even stayed at her court for a year, meeting with her daily for private discussions on intellectual subjects, including improvements for her empire.

Catherine's reign brought considerable enlightenment and social progress. She subsidized artists and writers, permitted publication of controversial works, established libraries, patronized galleries, and transformed St. Petersburg with beautiful architecture. Catherine also founded hospitals and orphanages, notably those providing foundling children with improved education, one of her main interests. After many years of study, she launched a national system of elementary and secondary schools during the decade after 1775. In that same year, she began a reorganization of local government, including the cities, one of many administrative reforms which literally demilitarized the empire. She secularized church land, secured some rights for serfs, and restricted the use of torture; but her early, much publicized efforts to modernize and codify Russian laws were sabotaged by the aristocracy.

Catherine's program, however, like that of Frederick, was limited in scope and significance. Almost every reform had been attempted or suggested earlier and enhanced royal authority. For example, rigid state control and political indoctrination of the curriculum was fixed in the new educational system. Local government, after 1775, was controlled by aristocratic landowners. Such deference to the aristocracy was typical of Catherine's later internal policies after Pugachev's revolt, when the nobles' alarm forced

Catherine the Great of Russia. Although she is usually regarded as an enlightened despot, her liberalism was more eloquent theory than actual practice.

her to issue a charter giving them freedom from taxes, release from compulsory government service, and guaranteed ownership of their serfs. The reaction thus begun was continued during the French Revolution, when Catherine reversed most of her earlier stated libral opinions and imposed severe censorship. Her political legacy was a rigid autocracy, based on support from an aristocratic elite.

The most sincere of the would-be benevolent despots was Joseph II (1780–1790), the son of Maria Theresia and her successor as Habsburg ruler of Austria. He was a true product of the Enlightenment, intelligent and well educated; Catherine the Great called him "the most solid, profound, and best-informed mind I have ever met."[6] He was also completely converted to the principles of the philosophers. "I have made philosophy the legislator of my empire," he wrote to a friend in 1781, shortly after his succession.[7] During his whole reign, he fancied himself a royal voice of reason, fighting for human progress against ignorance, superstition, and vice.

Joseph II, Two Letters

Joseph's brand of "enlightened despotism," as well as his inflexibility and his jealousy of more renowned monarchs, are revealed in these private letters, written in the 1780s.

To Count Kollowrat, Grand Chancellor of Bohemia, and First Chancellor of Austria [October 1784].

Sir,—For the encouragement of home productions, and in order to check the progress of luxury and fashion, my commands respecting a general prohibition of foreign merchandise have been made known.

The Austrian commerce has become more passive in consequence of the increasing consumption of foreign productions, and the funds of the state, which has thereby lost more than twenty-four millions annually, would be this time have been nearly exhausted, but for the produce of our excellent mines.

It has been hitherto, one would almost think, the particular object of the Austrian government to benefit the manufacturers and merchants of the French, English, and Chinese, and to deprive itself of all the advantages the state must necessarily enjoy, when it provides for the national wants by national industry.

I know what sensations the prohibition caused among the merchants . . . and I have conversed with Prince Kaunitz on this subject, but I granted them nothing, except that I prolonged the term for their disposing of the foreign merchandise; and more they do not deserve; they are merely the commissioners of the other European merchants.

As to the rest, Prince Kaunitz will give the necessary instructions to the officers of the Custom-houses, that inventories may be made of the stock; that depots may be established; and in general, that such dispositions may be made as will ensure the execution of my orders.

To Tobias Philip, Baron von Gebler, Bohemian and Austrian Vice-Chancellor [March 1785].

Mr. Vice-Chancellor,—The present system of taxation in my dominions, and the inequality of the taxes which are imposed on the nation, form a subject too important to escape my attention. I have discovered that the principles on which it is founded are unsound, and have become injurious to the industry of the peasant; that there is neither equality, nor equity, between the hereditary provinces with each other, nor between individual proprietors, and therefore it can no longer continue.

With this view I give you the necessary orders to introduce a new system of taxation, by which the contribution, requisite for the wants of the state, may be effected without augmenting the present taxes, and the industry of the peasant, at the same time, be freed from all impediments.

Make these arrangements the principal object of your care, and let them be made conformably to the plan which I have proposed, particularly as I have nominated you President of the Aulic Commission, appointed for that purpose.

Adieu, Gebler! Hasten every thing that brings me nearer to the accomplishment of my plans for the happiness of my people, and, by your zeal, justify the respect which they have always had for your services.

Source: Harry J. Carroll et al., eds., *The Development of Civilization*, 2 vols. (Glenview, IL: Scott, Foresman, 1970), vol. 2, pp. 142–43.

Joseph's reign was an explosion of reform effort which threatened to topple much of the old aristocratic Habsburg structure. He proposed to simplify Catholic services, abolish the monasteries, take over church lands, remove religion from education, and grant civil equality to Protestants and Jews. Attacking the ancient landed establishment head-on, he planned to tax the nobles and free the serfs. With increasing revenues, he hoped to pay for a national education system, balance the budget, and improve opportunities for industry and trade. The whole undertaking would be consolidated and regulated under a comprehensive code of laws.

Despite their theoretical benefits, Joseph's endeavors aroused a storm of protest, which lasted throughout the reign and brought him practical failure. For all of his interest in progress, Joseph was a hard-headed and narrow-minded autocrat, incapable of flexibility, who was determined to build a centralized state on the Prussian model. His administrative reforms were aimed not only at higher efficiency but also at centralized government over all the many-cultured Habsburg territories. His attempted unification of administration alienated the Hungarians and caused revolts in Belgium, Bohemia, and the Tyrol. Peasants were angry because he subjected them to compulsory military service; the clergy harangued against him; and the nobles conspired to hinder the conduct of government at every level. He died in 1790, painfully aware of his failed policies and unfulfilled ideals.

Other less well known rulers of the period were probably more successful. One was Joseph's brother, Leopold of Tuscany, who was not only enlightened but also flexible and practical. Without throwing his little country into turmoil, he abolished the Inquisition and reformed the penal code, according to the principles of the well-known Italian humanist philosopher, Cesare Bonesana Beccaria (1735–1794). Another successful enlightened despot was Charles Frederick of Baden, who freed the serfs, promoted agrarian development, and achieved the fiscal regularity to make his little country a most prosperous German state. Gustavus III of Sweden seized power from the nobles by force. He then reorganized the justice system, abolished torture, reformed agriculture, made taxes more equitable, improved education, decreed religious toleration, and established freedom of the press. Unfortunately, he was assassinated. Charles III of Spain crushed the Jesuits, simplified the legal system, improved education, and balanced the budget, but his regime was a cruel dictatorship.

Even with all their good intentions and achievements, benevolent despots proved incapable of rooting out the deep-seated evils of the Old

Lithograph of Austrian emperor Joseph II working in the field. His abolition of serfdom was the most revolutionary decree of this enlightened despot, but his most lasting reform was his reorganization of the legal system.

Regime. Most of them underestimated the need for change and overestimated the durability of absolutist systems. All were dependent upon, and therefore prisoners of, outmoded aristocratic orders. Finally, they were often limited by chaotic administrative systems and mounting public debts. They were caught between a static past and a dynamic future.

Conclusion

Western European society in the eighteenth century was struggling hard against itself. The established regimes were becoming more fixed, while at the same time forces of change were growing with such intensity that they could not be permanently resisted.

These forces generated countless frustrations in conflicts arising from new middle-class interests, urbanism, expanding population, and tremendously widening opportunities for profit. Overseas expansion contributed, in one way or another, to the whole process. Free-enterprise capitalism was also common to all the forces of change. It substituted social incentives—mainly profit incentives—for the force and fear that drove the engines of absolutism. This new fuel could not fire safely in the old cylinders.

The situation called for radical adjustment, a complete retooling rather than a little tinkering. European monarchies were heavily in debt; their revenues could not meet expenses; they wasted vast sums on an upper class that gave little service; they openly perpetuated injustices; and their administrations were not only hopelessly inefficient but flagrantly corrupt. Even more dangerous was the growing alienation among nobles, as well as among the middle and lower classes.

Attempted reforms by kings produced too little and came too late. The policies of benevolent despots, for the most part, touched only the surface of the problems. Other monarchs, particularly the later Bourbons in France, were so lazy, bored, or naïve that they could not face realities. The nobles were in position to act decisively, but their efforts were naturally directed toward resisting necessary reforms.

Suggestions for Reading

Excellent general European surveys include Maurice Ashley, *A History of Europe, 1648–1815 (Prentice-Hall, 1973) and Matthew Smith Anderson, Europe in the Eighteenth Century*, 3rd ed. (Longman, 1987). For more interpretive coverage, see Vincent J. Knapp, *Europe in the Era of Social Transformation, 1700–Present* (Prentice-Hall, 1976); and Robert Zeller, *Europe in Transition, 1660–1815* (Univ. Press of America, 1988). Narrower national concentrations are provided in Louis R. Gottschalk, *Toward the French Revolution* (Scribner's, 1973); Dorothy Marshall, *Eighteenth-Century England* (Longman, 1974); and D. Jarrett, *England in the Age of Hogarth* (Yale Univ., 1986). *Britain in the Age of Walpole* (St. Martin's, 1985), edited by Jeremy Black, is a collection of interesting special studies.

William Doyle, *The Old European Order 1660–1800* (Oxford, Univ. 1978) is a superb study, covering all aspects of the Old Regime. In addition, see E. Neville Williams, *The Ancien Régime in Europe* (Harper and Row, 1970) and Catherine B. Behrens, *The Ancien Régime* (Norton, 1989). For France, see G. Chaussinand-Nogoret, *The French Nobility in the Eighteenth Century* (Cambridge Univ., 1985); Catherine B. Behrens, *Society, Government, and the Enlightenment* (Harper and Row, 1985); and J. C. Riley, *The Seven Years War and the Old Regime in France* (Princeton Univ., 1986). Intimate biographical insights into the French royal court are presented in O. Bernier, *Louis the Beloved* (Doubleday, 1984); Nancy Mitford, *Madame Pompadour* (Harper and Row, 1968); and Stanley Loomis, *Du Barry* (Lippincott, 1959). For similar analyses of the English system, see W. B. Willcox, *The Age of Aristocracy*, 4th ed. (Heath, 1983); John V. Beckett, *The Aristocracy in England*, (Blackwell, 1986); and T. H. White, *The Age of Scandal* (Oxford. Univ., 1986).

Michel Beaud, *A History of Capitalism* (Monthly Review, 1983) gives a brief but sound account of the major trend. The last two volumes of Immanuel Wallenstein's *The Modern World System* (3 vols.): vol. 2, *Mercantilism and the Consolidation of the World Economy* (Academic, 1980) and vol. 3, *The Second Era of Great Expansion of the Capitalist World Economy* (Academic, 1988) are excellent for fine details but hard going for beginners. See also Carlo M. Cipolla, *Before the Industrial Revolution* (Norton, 1980).

Dynamic European economic growth is strongly emphasized in Fernand Braudel, *Civilization and Capitalism* (2 vols.): vol. 2, *The Wheels of Commerce* (Harper and Row, 1986); N. Rosenberg, *How the West Grew Rich* (Basic Books, 1986); and Andre G. Frank, *World Accumulation, 1492–1789* (Monthly Review, 1978). See also Ralph Davis, *The Rise of the Atlantic Economies* (Cornell Univ., 1973); Herman Kellenberg, *The Rise of the European Economy* (Gerharde Benecke, 1976); and Gunnar Persson, *Economic Growth in Pre-industrial Europe* (Blackwell, 1988). For capitalistic development in England, see Ralph Davis, *The Rise of English Shipping in the Seventeenth and Eighteenth Centuries* (David and Charles, 1972); James A. Yelling, *Common Field and Enclosure in England, 1450–1750* (Archon, 1977); J. J. McCusker, *The Economy of British America, 1607–1789* (Univ. of North Carolina, 1986); and I. K. Steele, *The English Atlantic* (Oxford Univ., 1986).

For economic problems facing the old regimes, see, in addition to the above, Jan de Vries. *The Economy of Europe in an Age of Crisis, 1600–1750* (Cambridge Univ., 1976). Difficulties in regulating the import trade are ably treated in Frederick F. Nicholls, *Honest Thieves; the Violent Heyday of English Smuggling* (Heinemann, 1973); and R. Guttridge, *Smugglers* (Dorset, 1987). The following works depict the adventurous business of piracy: Philip Grosse, *The History of Piracy* (Rio Grande, 1988); Frank Sherry, *Raiders and Rebels: The Golden Age of Piracy* (Morrow, 1987); John F. Jameson, *Privateering and Piracy in the Colonial Period* (Kelley, 1970); John Esquemiling, *Buccaneers of America* (Dorset, 1988); and Robert R. Ritchie, *Captain Kidd and the War Against the Pirates* (Harvard Univ., 1989).

Numerous informative works treat the dynamic social trends of the period. Colin McEvedy and Richard Jones, *Atlas of World Population History* (Penguin, 1978) is a handy reference for monitoring population growth; and Herbert Moller, *Population Movements in Modern European History* (Macmillan, 1964) is still useful. For urban growth, see Jan de Vries, *European Urbanization, 1500–1800* (Harvard Univ., 1984) and Paul M. Hohenberg, *The Making of Urban Europe, 1000–1950* (Harvard Univ., 1987). Changes in the European class structure are treated in George Rude, *Europe in the Eighteenth Century: Aristocracy and the Bourgeois Challenge* (Harvard Univ., 1985) and Jerome Blum, *The End of the Old Order in Rural Europe* (Princeton Univ., 1978). Some obvious social threats to European monarchies are described in Jerome Blum, *The European Peasantry From the Fifteenth to the Nineteenth Century* (Prentice-Hall, 1978; M. S. Anderson, *War and Society in Europe of the Old Regime* (St. Martin's, 1988); and Frederick Krantz, *History from Below: French and English Popular Protest, 1600–1800* (Blackwell, 1988). For negative conditions affecting European women, see Helga Mobius, *Women of the Baroque Age* (Abner Schram, 1984).

For the French class structure and its discontents, see Isser Woloch, *The Peasantry in the Old Regime* (R. E. Kreiger, 1977); and Elinor G. Barber, *The Bourgeoisie in Eighteenth-century France* (Princeton Univ., 1975). Government bad judgment and oppression is convincingly established by Warren C. Scoville's *The Persecution of the French Huguenots and French Economic Development* (Univ. of California, 1960). See also R. D. Gwynn, *The Huguenot Heritage* (Routledge, Kegan Paul, 1985). For the role of eighteenth-century French women, see Sania Spencer, ed., *French Women of the Age of the Enlightenment* (Indiana Univ., 1984) and Joan Landes, *Women and Public Sphere in the Age of the French Revolution* (Cornell Univ., 1988).

Roy Porter, *English Society in the Eighteenth Century* (Penguin, 1983) and J. C. D. Clark, *English Society, 1688–1832* (Cambridge Univ., 1985) provide excellent accounts of the social scene in England. Robert W. Malcolmson focuses on life among the working classes in his *Life and Labor in England, 1700–1780* (St. Martin's, 1981). For conditions in the country, see L. M. Cantor, *The Changing English Country-side, 1400–1700* (Routledge, Kegan Paul, 1987) and P. Horn, *Life and Labor in Rural England, 1760–1850* (Macmillan, 1987). Some indication of English social problems may be gained from Leslie A. Clarksin, *Death, Disease, and Famine in Pre-industrial England* (St. Martin's, 1975); and J. C. Clark, *Revolution and Rebellion: State and Society in England in the Seventeenth and Eighteenth Centuries* (Cambridge Univ., 1986). Problems facing English women are defined in Barbara Kanner, *Women of England* (Archon, 1979); Alice Clark, *Working Life of Women in the Seventeenth Century* (Routledge, Chapman, and Hall, 1982); and Bridget Hill, *Eighteenth-Century Women* (Unwin Hyman, 1987).

For the pros and cons of monarchical reform, see Geoffrey Bruun, *The Enlightened Despots* (Holt, Rinehart and Winston, 1967); John G. Gagliardo, *Enlightened Despotism* (Crowell, 1967); and J. F. Brennen, *Enlightened Despotism in Russia*, (P. Lang, 1987). Excellent biographies of Frederick the Great and Catherine the Great are included in Suggested Readings at the end of chapter 18.

Notes

1. Stanley Loomis, *Du Barry* (New York: J. B. Lippincott, 1959), p. 303.
2. Colin McEvedy and Richard Jones, *Atlas of World Population History* (New York: Penguin, 1978), pp. 18. 43, 57, 79, 101, 107, and 286.
3. For rising urbanization, see Jan de Vries, *The Economy of Europe in an Age of Crisis, 1600–1700* (New York: Cambridge University Press, 1976), pp. 87–88; William Doyle, *The Old European Order* (Oxford: Oxford University Press, 1978), pp. 28–33; and J. D. Chambers, *Population, Economy, and Society in Pre-industrial England* (New York: Oxford University Press, 1972), pp. 115–121.
4. Quoted in Neville Williams, *Contraband Cargoes* (Hampden, CT: Shoe String Press, 1961), p. 98. See also p. 128 for Walpole's entry.
5. Quoted in James Harvey Robinson and Charles A. Beard, *Readings in European History*, 2 vols. (Boston: Ginn and Co., 1908), vol. I, pp. 202–205.
6. E. Neville William, *The Ancien Régime in Europe* (New York: Harper and Row, 1970), p. 424.
7. Ibid.

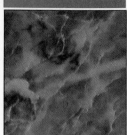

Chapter 20

The European Dream of Progress and Enlightenment

Science, Art, and Philosophy in the Eighteenth Century

In the eighteenth century, while royal absolutism faced serious problems, many learned and thoughtful Europeans held a shining vision of the future. They saw civilization advancing toward a future of diminished ignorance, brutality, and exploitation. Most believed that human reason, having finally reached its true potential, would bring the downfall of Old Regimes, which were being recognized as violating recently discovered laws of nature. Unlike Saint Augustine, who had described a City of God in the next world, many eighteenth-century thinkers confidently anticipated a happy earthly community. In the words of American historian Carl Becker they dreamed of a beautiful but terrestrial "heavenly city."[1]

Such ideas arose partially from social experience. European wealth was expanding rapidly, in comparison with all other societies. In fashionable European salons, philosophers and artists rubbed elbows with bored nobles and sons of enterprising bankers, who indulged in clever criticism of the Old Regime as a form of recreation. But a new popular philosophy appealed directly to the vested interests of the middle classes. By emphasizing the systematic regularity of nature, it automatically denied justification for most royal authority. The laws of nature promised to replace the laws of monarchs, along with their state churches, idle nobles, arbitrary courts, high taxes, and mercantilist control of business.

The concern for special interests was one source of the new vision, but it also rose from an intellectual stimulus. In the late seventeenth century, Europeans yearned for order, which scientists were finding throughout the universe. New discoveries in astronomy, physics, chemistry, and even biology strongly suggested that nature, from the smallest particle to the most distant stars, was an interlocking mechanism of harmoniously working parts. Here, apparently, was the simple answer to an everlasting search for certainty and the immediate origin of optimistic hopes for humanity.

Impact of the Scientific Revolution

By the later seventeenth century, science had won general acceptance and was beginning to dominate the European mind. The victory had been hard won. When during the late Renaissance the Italian universities and a few northern Europeans made advances in anatomy, medicine, and astronomy, their work was considered inconsequential or irreligious. Later scientists who persisted in taking their own conclusions seriously were either ignored or persecuted. Even the work of Copernicus was regarded more as mathematical exercise than a description of reality. This situation changed drastically after Sir Isaac Newton (1641–1727) expressed his universal law in mathematical terms and supported its validity by empirical results.

The Early Pioneering Era of Modern Science

The most notable of the scientific pioneers were astronomers, whose field of study was peculiarly suited to the new scientific method. As it was developed in the sixteenth century, this methodology involved a combination of two approaches, each depending upon human reason, with differing applications. The deductive approach started with self-evident truths and moved toward complex propositions, which might be applied to practical problems. It emphasized logic and mathematical relationships. The inductive approach started with objective facts, that is, knowledge of the material world. From facts, proponents of induction sought to draw valid general conclusions. In the past, the two procedures had often been considered contradictory. Early European astronomers were uniquely dependent on both kinds of reasoning.

The French scholar-mathematician René Descartes (1596–1650) initiated a new and critical mode of deduction. In his famous *Discourse on Method* (1627), Descartes rejected every accepted idea that could be doubted. He concluded that he could be certain of nothing except the facts that he was thinking and that he must therefore exist. From the basic proposition, "I think, therefore I am," Descartes proceeded in logical steps to deduce the existence of God and the reality of both the spiritual and material worlds.[2] He ultimately conceived a unified and mathematically ordered universe, which operated as a perfect mechanism. In the Cartesian physical universe, supernatural processes were impossible; everything could be explained rationally, and preferably in mathematical terms.

Descartes' method was furthered by discoveries in mathematics, and the method, in turn, popularized the study of the subject. Descartes' work coincided with the first use of decimals and the compilation of logarithmic tables. The latter advance, by halving the time required to solve intricate problems, may have doubled the effective influence of mathematics in the early 1600s. Descartes himself was successful in developing analytical geometry, which permitted relationships in space to be expressed in algebraic equations. Using such equations, astronomers could represent the movements of celestial bodies in

mathematical symbols. Astronomers received further aid later in the century when Sir Isaac Newton in England and Gottfried von Leibniz (1646–1716) in Germany independently perfected differential calculus, or the mathematics of infinity, variables, and probabilities.

The other great contributor to the theory of scientific methodology in this era was the Englishman Sir Francis Bacon (1561–1626). At a time when traditional systems of thought were crumbling, Bacon set forth a program extolling human reason, as applied to human sensory experiences. He advocated an inductive approach, using systematically recorded facts derived from experiments. These facts, he believed, would lead toward tentative hypotheses, which could then be tested by fresh experiments under new conditions. Ultimately, the method would reveal fundamental laws of nature. Bacon's ideas, outlined in his *Novum Organum* (1626), were the first definitive European statement of inductive principles.[3]

The inductive approach became even more practical with the remarkable improvement of scientific instruments. Both the telescope and the microscope came into use at the opening of the seventeenth century. Other important inventions included the thermometer (1597), the barometer (1644), the air pump (1650), and the pendulum clock (1657). With such devices, scientists were better able to study the physical universe.

Using both mathematics and observation, early astronomers before 1600 prepared the way for a scientific revolution. This was certainly true after 1543, the year of Copernicus' death and the publication of his famous book, *On the Revolutions of the Heavenly Spheres*. In the book, Copernicus posited a theory directly opposed to the traditional Ptolemaic explanation for passing days and the apparent movement of heavenly bodies. The old geocentric theory had assumed that the sun, the planets, and the stars all circled the earth. The new heliocentric theory postulated the sun as the center, around which the sun and planets moved.

Copernicus offered his idea as merely mathematical theory. By the end of the century, However, Tycho Brahe (1546–1601), a Danish astronomer, aided by his accomplished sister, Sophia (1556–1643), had recorded hundreds of observations that pointed to difficulties in the Ptolemaic explanation. Brahe even attempted, without much success, to find a compromise between the Ptolemaic and Copernican systems by postulating that the planets moved about the sun while the latter orbited the earth. This proposition raised even more problems and therefore met with little acceptance.

Brahe's data were used by his former assistant, the brilliant German mathematician, Johannes Kepler (1571–1630), to support the Copernican theory. While working mathematically with Brahe's records on the movements of Mars, Kepler was ultimately able to prove that the planet did not move in a circular orbit but in an ellipse. He also discovered that the paces of the planets accelerated when they approached the sun. From this he concluded that the sun might emit a magnetic force that directed the planets in their courses. The idea was not yet confirmed by a mathematical formula, but that would soon be achieved by Newton, using Kepler's hypothesis. Even in their own time, however, Kepler's laws of planetary motion almost completely undermined the Ptolemaic theory.

In 1596 Kepler created a model of the solar system with reference to five regular polyhedrons that fit between the spheres of the six known planets—Mercury, Venus, Earth, Mars, Jupiter, and Saturn.

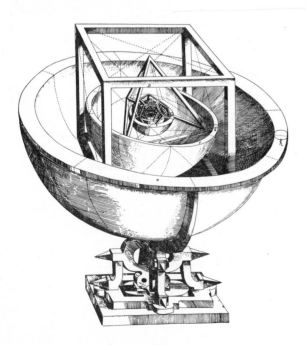

During the early seventeenth century, growing acceptance of the heliocentric theory precipitated an intellectual crisis affecting organized religion, particularly the Catholic church. Medieval Catholicism had accepted Aristotle on physics and Ptolemy on astronomy. The church now felt its authority and reputation challenged by the new ideas. Copernicus and Brahe had both evaded the issue by purporting to deal only in mathematical speculations. Kepler and others of his time became increasingly impatient with this subterfuge. The most persistent of these scientific rebels was the Italian mathematician-physicist, Galileo Galilei (1564–1642).

Galileo discovered more facts to verify the Copernican theory, but as he wrote to Kepler,

> . . . up to now I have preferred not to publish, intimidated by the fortune of our teacher Copernicus, who though he will be of immortal fame to some, is yet by an infinite number (for such is the multitude of fools) laughed at and rejected.[4]

In 1609, Galileo made a telescope, and with it he discovered mountains on the moon, sunspots, the satellites of Jupiter, and the rings of Saturn. Having published his findings and beliefs, he was constrained by the Church in 1616 to promise that he would "not hold, teach, or defend" the heretical Copernican doctrines. After another publication, he was again hauled before a church court in 1633. This time, he was forced to make a public denial of his doctrines. Galileo was defeated, but by the end of the century the heliocentric theory had won common acceptance.

Newton and the Law of Gravitation

Great as were the contributions of Galileo and Kepler, their individual discoveries had not been synthesized into one all-embracing principle that would describe the universe as a unity. When Sir Isaac Newton achieved this goal, the opponents of science, such as Galileo's persecutors, were effectively silenced.

The notion of gravitation occurred to Newton in 1666, when he was only twenty-four. According to his own later account, he hit on the idea while sitting in thought under an apple tree. A falling apple roused him to wonder why it, and

Newton, Rule III of Reasoning

This selection, from Book III of the *Principia,* illustrates Newton's conception of universal gravity.

RULE III

The qualities of bodies, which admit neither intensification nor remission of degrees, and which are found to belong to all bodies within the reach of our experiments, are to be esteemed the universal qualities of all bodies whatsoever.

For since the qualities of bodies are only known to us by experiments, we are to hold for univeral all such as universally agree with experiments, and such as are not liable to diminution can never be quite taken away. We are certainly not to relinquish the evidence of experiments for the sake of dreams and vain fictions of our own devising; nor are we to recede from the analogy of Nature, which is wont to be simple and always consonant to itself. We in no other way know the extension of bodies than by our senses, nor do these reach it in all bodies; but because we perceive extension in all that are sensible, therefore we ascribe it universally to all others also. That abundance of bodies are hard we learn by experience; and because the hardness of the whole arises from the hardness of the parts, we therefore justly infer the hardness of the undivided particles, not only of the boides we feel, but of all others. That all bodies are impenetrable, we gather not from reason, but from sensation. The bodies which we handle we find impenetrable, and thence conclude impenetrability to be a universal property of all bodies whatsoever. That all bodies are movable and endowed with certain powers (which we call the inertia) of persevering in their motion, or in their rest, we only infer from the like properties observed in the bodies which we have seen. The extension, hardness, impenetrability, mobility, and inertia of the whole result from the extension, hardness, impenetrability, mobility and inertia of the parts; and hence we conclude the least particles of all bodies to be also all extended, and hard and impenetrable, and movable, and endowed with their proper inertia. And this is the foundation of all philosophy. Moreover, that the divided but contiguous particles of bodies may be separated from one another is a matter of observation; and, in the particles that remain undivided, our minds are able to distinguish yet lesser parts, as is mathematically demonstrated. But whether the parts so distinguished and not yet divided may, by the powers of Nature, be actually divided and separated from one another we cannot certainly determine. Yet had we the proof of but one experiment that any undivided particle, in breaking a hard and solid body, suffered a division, we might by virtue of this rule conclude that the undivided as well as the divided particles may be divided and actually separated to infinity.

Lastly, if it universally appears, by experiments and astronomical observations, that all bodies about the earth gravitate toward the earth, and that in proportion to the quantity of matter which they severally contain; that the moon likewise, according to the quantity of its matter, gravitates toward the earth; that, on the other hand, our sea gravitates toward the moon; and all the planets one toward another; and the comets in like manner toward the sun: we must, in consequence of this rule, universally allow that all bodies whatsoever are endowed with a principle of mutual gravitation. For the argument from the appearances concludes with more force for the universal gravitation of all bodies than for their impenetrability, of which, among those in the celestial regions, we have no experiments nor any manner of observation. Not that I affirm gravity to be essential to bodies; by their *vis insita* I mean nothing but their inertia. This is immutable. Their gravity is diminished as they recede from the earth.

Source: H. S. Thayer and John H. Randall, eds., *Newton's Philosophy of Nature* (New York: Hafner Publishing Co., 1953), pp. 3–5.

other objects, fell toward the center of the earth and not sideways or upward. There must be, he thought in a flash of insight, some drawing power associated with matter. If this were true, he reasoned, the drawing power was proportionate to quantity, which would explain why the smaller apple, despite its own attracting force, was pulled to earth. In his *Principia* (1687), Newton expressed this idea precisely in a mathematical formula. The resulting law of gravitation states that all material objects attract other bodies inversely according to the square of their distances and directly in proportion to the products of their masses. Hundreds of observations soon verified this principle, firmly establishing the validity of scientific methods.

Not only had Newton solved astronomical problems defined by Kepler and Galileo he had also confirmed the necessity of combining methods advocated by Descartes and Bacon. In the *Principia*, Newton stressed the importance of supplementing mathematical analysis with observation. Final conclusions, he insisted, must rest on solid facts; on the other hand, any hypothesis, no matter how mathematically plausible, must be abandoned if not borne out by obsevation or experimentation.

Newton had also confirmed the basic premise of modern science that all nature is governed by laws. Indeed, his own major law was applicable to the whole universe, from a speck of dust on earth to the largest star in outer space. The magnitude of this idea—that is, the concept of universal laws—was almost infinitely exciting and contagious. Within decades it had spread throughout the Western world and had been applied in every area, including human relations.

The Widening Scope of Scientific Study

The impressive achievements of astronomers, climaxed by Newton's amazing revelations, encouraged scientific interest and endeavors in all related fields. As science widened its scope, the first advances outside of astronomy came in physics and physiology. Both fields owed much to earlier influences from Italian universities; both also reflected the new mechanistic ideas so prevalent in astronomy. Chemistry, long affected by medieval alchemy, did not reach maturity until the eighteenth century. By that time, in general biology, apart from human anatomy and physiology, cellular studies and classification systems had begun to develop, although there was as yet no comprehensive evolutionary theory. Late in the century, however, geologists were suggesting such a scheme.

In astronomy the period after Newton was a time of elaboration and "filling in" the main outline, rather than one of new beginnings. A possible exception was the brilliant French astronomer-mathematician, Pierre Laplace (1749–1827), who has been called the Newton of France. Although a leading disciple of Newton, Laplace went beyond his master. Newton believed that God tended the universal machine to compensate for irregularities, but Laplace demonstrated that apparent inconsistencies, such as comets, were also governed by mathematical laws. Laplace is best known for his nebular hypothesis, which maintained that our sun, once a gaseous mass, threw off the planets as it solidified and contracted. Until recently, this hypothesis was widely accepted.

Despite their lack of opportunities for scientific education, a number of women became involved in astronomical studies during the eighteenth century. In France, Emilie du Châtelet (1706–1749), the sometime mistress and lifelong friend of Voltaire, translated the *Principia*, helping introduce Newton among the French *philosophes*. Maria Kirch (1670–1720), while assisting her husband, Gottfried, the royal astronomer in Berlin, discovered the comet of 1702. After her husband's death, she published their observations, which were widely read. Caroline Herschel (1750–1848), a native of Hanover working with her brother William in England, helped build huge telescopes, shared the discovery of 2500 new nebulae, and by herself found a number of new comets. The Herschels' work demonstrated that Newtonian principles applied to distant stars, outside the solar system.

In physics, the field most closely related to astronomy, Galileo was the pioneer. He defined the law of falling bodies, demonstrating that their acceleration is constant, no matter what their weight or size. His experiments also revealed the law of inertia: a body at rest or in motion will remain at rest or continue moving (in a straight line at constant speed) unless affected by an external force. In addition, he showed that the path of a fired projectile follows a parabolic curve to earth, an inclination explained later by the law of gravitation. Galileo made additional notable discoveries through his studies of the pendulum, hydrostatics, and optics. His work was clarified by two famous professors at the University of Bologna, Maria Agnesi (1718–1799), in mathematics, and Laura Bassi (1700–1778), in physics.

Other physicists made significant contributions. For example, Newton and the Dutch scientist, Christian Huygens (1629–1695) developed a wave theory to explain light. A more prosaic discovery, and one that promised more immediate practical results, demonstrated the material composition of air. The German physicist, Otto von Guericke (1602–1668), pumped air from two joined steel hemispheres, creating a vaccum so complete that the two sections could not be pulled apart by teams of horses. Ultimately, Guericke and other scientists proved that air could be weighed and that it could exert pressure, both properties in accord with Newton's law.

Although electricity remained a challenging mystery to physicists during this era, magnetic properties were recognized early. In 1600, the Englishman William Gilbert (1540–1603) published a book that described magnetic force and the possibilities of generating it by friction. Gilbert's suggestion of a similarity between magnetism and gravity exerted some influence on Newton. Electricity, generated by friction, was conducted short distances to produce sound and light in various experiments during the seventeenth century. The first crude storage battery— the Leyden Jar—was invented in 1745 at the Dutch University of Leyden. A last important achievement during the period came in 1752, when Benjamin Franklin (1706–1790), with his famous kite-and-key experiment, proved that lightning is natural electricity.

While physics and astronomy flourished, chemistry advanced more slowly. Robert Boyle (1627–1691), the son of an Irish nobleman and the father of modern chemistry, was the first to emphasize the difference between compounds (unified by chemical action) and mixtures. From his many experiments, he conceived a crude atomic theory, superseding the "four elements" and "four humors" of medieval alchemists and physicians. Boyle also investigated fire, respiration, fermentation, evaporation, and the rusting of metals. Joseph Priestley (1733–1804), an English dissenting minister and a famous eighteenth-century chemist, isolated ammonia, discovered oxygen, and generated carbon monoxide. Another Englishman, Henry Cavendish (1731–1810), discovered hydrogen (1766). His experiments, along with Priestley's, furnished an explanation for combustion.

More definitive studies of combustion were completed by the French scientist Antoine Lavoisier (1743–1794), who is generally considered the leading chemist of the eighteenth century. Lavoisier proved that burning is a chemical process involving the uniting of oxygen with the substances consumed. He also showed that respiration is another form of oxidation. Such discoveries led him to define the law of conservation: "matter cannot be created or destroyed." With this law, he laid a foundation for the discipline of quantitative analysis, which makes possible the precise measurement of substances in any compound. Much of the credit for Lavoisier's scientific success should go to his wife, Marie-Anne (1758–1836), whom he married when she was fourteen and educated in his laboratory. She assisted with all his major experiments, took notes, kept records, illustrated his books, and published her own papers. After he died on the guillotine during the French Revolution, she edited and published a compilation of his works.

Robert Boyle's seventeenth-century counterpart in the life-sciences was William Harvey (1578–1657). Born in England and educated at the University of Padua in Italy, Harvey continued in the tradition that had earlier produced Vesalius (see p. 313). Harvey's major contribution was a description of the human circulatory system: He traced the flow of blood from the heart, through the arteries, capillaries, and veins, and back to the heart. He also studied embryology in animals and put forth the theory of "epigenesis," which maintains that embryos develop progressively, through definite stages, prior to birth. Harvey provided medical science with many practical keys to understanding the human body. He also applied to biology the mechanistic interpretation developed by Galileo, Newton, and other modern scientists.

Biologists in the seventeenth century also achieved notable results. Jan Swammerdam (1637–1680) in Holland and Marcello Malpighi (1628–1694) in Italy studied circulation and added details to Harvey's general description. Anton van Leeuwenhoek (1627–1723), a Dutch biologist, discovered protozoa, bacteria, and human spermatozoa; Swammerdam studied the anatomies and life cycles of frogs and insects; and Robert Hooke (1635–1703), an Englishman, first described the cellular structure of plants. These studies, as did those of William Harvey, also furthered the idea of bodies as machines.

Biology in the eighteenth century was characterized by classification rather than the formulation of theory. An early example was Maria Sibylla Merian (1647–1717), a German entomologist who settled in Holland. She was a specialist on insects, and in 1705 published a well-known treatise dealing with those of Surinam, where she had studied for two years. Her work was just one approach to thousands of new species, discovered as a result of overseas expansion and collected in Europe, where they were classified and described. The most successful classifiers were John Ray (1627–1705) in England, Karl von Linné (1707–1778)—perhaps better known by his Latin name as Linnaeus—in Sweden, and Georges Buffon (1707–1788) in France. They established the basic terminology and categories still used in the twentieth century.

Three women deserve mention for their contributions to eighteenth-century anatomy and medicine. A recognized expert in anatomy was Anna Manzolini (1716–1774), professor at the University of Bologna, a lecturer at the Court of Catherine the Great, and a member of the Russian Royal Scientific Society. The French anatomist Genevieve d'Arionville (1720–1805), wrote treatises on chemistry, medicine, anatomy, and physiology. In addition to her self-illustrated textbooks on anatomy, she published a study on putrefaction and introduced bichloride of mercury as an antiseptic. Mary Motley Montague (1689–1762) was not a research scientist or a medical doctor, but she advocated innoculation against smallpox in England, a treatment she had observed in Turkey as the wife of the English ambassador there. Her efforts aided the English physician Edward Jenner (1749–1823), who published his famous defense of vaccination in 1798.

The most revolutionary thesis in modern biology, the evolutionary theory that all life has evolved from simpler organisms, was not yet widely accepted in the eighteenth century, although some classifiers, such as Buffon, were already speculating along these lines. A stronger case was argued by the Scottish gentleman farmer, James Hutton (1726–1797). In his *Theory of the Earth* (1795), Hutton described the earth as constantly wearing away and rebuilding itself through natural results of wind, water, and chemical reactions. This thesis contradicted traditional religious theories of creation and supported the concept of natural law.

Science as Popular Culture

The achievements of science, particularly its practical applications in such fields as medicine and navigation, completely transformed its social role. After long being suspect among the leaders of society, it now became respectable. By the beginning of the eighteenth century, scientists frequented the best salons, and scientific academies gained public support as they sprang up all over Europe. The most famous were the Royal Society of London, chartered in 1662, and the French Academy of Science, founded in 1664. Most academies published journals that circulated widely. Scientists and would-be scientists carried on voluminous correspondence, developing a cosmopolitan community with its own language, values, and common beliefs.

Rising enthusiasm on the public fringes of the scientific community was matched by a popular mania. Frederick the Great dabbled in scientific experiments, as did hundreds of other ordinary craftsmen, wealthy merchants, and bored nobles. Support for academies was merely one form of public endorsement. Kings endowed observatories; cities founded museums; and well-to-do women helped establish botanical gardens. Scientists became popular heroes. Giordano Bruno, an Italian philosopher-scientist, had been burned for heresy by the Holy Inquisition in 1600; Galileo was hounded by persecutors through his most productive years; but Newton received a well-paying government position. He was lionized and knighted during his lifetime, and after he died in 1727, he was buried in a state funeral at Westminster Abbey.

In sharp contrast to the robust exuberance and emotionalism of the Baroque style was the dainty elegance and delicate decoration of the Rococo, the characteristic style of the eighteenth century. The Rococo at its best is seen in the works of Antoine Watteau (1683–1721), who often painted scenes of aristocratic society in parklike settings. With the graceful gallantry and gay frivolity of its figures, *Les Plaisirs du Bal* (1719), above, is a typical example of the Rococo.

A popular English portraitist of the eighteenth century was Sir Joshua Reynolds (1723–92), first president of England's Royal Academy of Arts. In his portraits, such as *Lady Elizabeth Delmé and Her Children* (1777–80), right, Reynolds sought to show his subjects as models of nobility, grace, and elegance.

The leader of the Neoclassic style, a reaction against Baroque and Rococo excesses, was Jacques Louis David (1748–1825), who became the semiofficial artist of the French Revolution. *The Death of Socrates* (1787), below, was regarded as a political allegory and protest against the injustices of the Old Regime.

Thomas Jefferson (1743–1826), third president of the United States as well as a talented amateur architect, built his own home, Monticello, in Charlottesville, Virginia, in the Neoclassic style. The building, constructed of brick with wood trim, features a central dome on an octagonal base, a pedimented porch, and severely simple ornament to achieve the single-story effect of a Roman temple.

By 1700, science had surpassed the Reformation in affecting Western thought. Unlike the Reformation, science revolutionized people's view of their own purposes. No longer could they consider the universe as stage equipment, created by God expressly for the human drama of sin and salvation. People now looked up toward an unknown number of stars, each moving silently but regularly through infinite space. On one planet, orbiting one of the smaller stars, were human creatures, among other forms of life. Their obvious similarity was material composition, which also obeyed Newtonian principles. Matter and motion, the fundamental realities of this strange new universe, everywhere acted impersonally, without discernible human purpose. In all of this, the individual was apparently rendered insignificant, but some thinkers sensed more human potential than had been promised formerly by Christian free will. For if God were not directly determining human affairs, human reason might learn the natural laws and effect unlimited human progress.

Reflections of the Age in Cultural Expression

The eighteenth century, when Newtonian science exerted its greatest impact, was exceptionally noteworthy for European cultural expression. This was most evident in philosophy, which sought to find in human affairs natural laws similar to those science had discovered in the physical universe. This approach, with its optimistic utopianism, found some expression in literature, but it was much more obscured in the visual arts and barely noticeable in music. Because they were largely affected by tradition, individual feeling, and patronage, the arts were less responsive to scientific influence. They were, nevertheless, quite rich and varied, reflecting the increasing wealth, widening perspectives, and rising technical proficiency of European life.

Developments in the Arts

The quantity and diversity of artistic works during the period do not fit easily into categories for interpretation, but some loose generalizations may be drawn. At the opening of the century, baroque forms were still popular, as they would be at the end. They were partially supplanted, however, by a general lightening in the rococo motifs of the early 1700s. This was followed, after the middle of the century, by the formalism and balance of neoclassicism, with its resurrection of Greek and Roman models. Although the end of the century saw a slight romantic turn, the era's characteristic accent on reason found its best expression in neoclassicism.

In painting, rococo emphasized the airy grace and refined pleasures of the salon and the boudoir, of delicate jewelry and porcelains, of wooded scenes, artful dances, and women, particularly women in the nude. Rococo painters also specialized in portraiture, showing

Fragonard, *The Lover Crowned*. Fragonard's paintings contain the sensual subject matter, soft colors, and delicate curves typical of the Rococo style, which was a reaction against the heavy formal style characteristic of Louis XIV's court.

aristocratic subjects in their finery, idealized and beautified on canvas. The rococo painting of Antoine Watteau (1684-1721) blended fantasy with acute observations of nature, conveying the ease and luxury of French court life. Watteau's successors in France included François Boucher (1703–1770) and Jean Fragonard (1732–1806). Italian painters, such a Giovanni Tiepolo (1696–1730), also displayed rococo influences. English painting lacked the characteristic rococo frivolity, but the style affected works by Sir Joshua Reynolds (1723–1792) and Thomas Gainsborough (1727–1788), whose portraits tended to flatter their aristocratic subjects.

Eighteenth-century neoclassicism in painting is difficult to separate from some works in the era of Louis XIV. Both Charles Le Brun (1619–1690) and Nicolas Poussin (1594–1665) had earlier projected order and balance, often in grandiose scenes from antiquity or mythology. Jean Chardin (1699–1779) carried some of this over into the 1700s. The neoclassic approach, however, often expressed powerful dissatisfaction and criticism of the existing order, sometimes in stark realism and sometimes in colossal allegory. The most typical representative of this approach was Jacques Louis David (1748–1825), whose most famous work, *Death of Socrates* illustrates his respect for Greco-Roman tradition. His sketch of Marie Antoinette enroute to the guillotine clearly represents his revolutionary sympathies. The best examples of pure realism and social criticism are the London street scenes by the English painter William Hogarth (1697–1764) and the Spanish court portraits of Francisco Goya (1746–1828).

The number of women painters increased during the eighteenth century, but they were so limited by traditions and so dependent upon public favor that they could hardly maintain consistent styles. Very few were admitted to academies, where their work might be shown; in France, they were not permitted to work with nude models. The result was their practical restriction to still-life and portraiture. Among rococo painters, the two best-known were Rachel Ruysch (1664–1750), a court painter of flowers in Düsseldorf, and Rosalba Carriera (1675–1757), a follower of Watteau, who was admitted to the French Academy in 1720. Two very famous French portrait painters and members of the

Academy, were Vigee Le Brun (1755–1842) and Adelaide Labille-Guiard (1749–1803). If possible, they were overshadowed by Angelica Kaufmann (1741–1807), a Swiss-born artist who painted in England and Italy. All three were celebrated in their time. Each produced grand scenes in the neoclassical style, but their market limited them to flattering portraits, at which they excelled.

Neoclassicism also found expression in architecture and sculpture. Architecture was marked by a return to the intrinsic dignity of what a contemporary called "the noble simplicity and tranquil loftiness of the ancients." The Madeleine of Paris is a faithful copy of a still-standing Roman temple, and the Brandenburg Gate in Berlin was modeled after the monumental entrance to the Acropolis in Athens. In England, where the classical style had resisted baroque influences, the great country houses of the nobility now exhibited a purity of design, which often included a portico with Corinthian columns. Mount Vernon is an outstanding example of neoclassicism in colonial America. The trend in sculpture often revived classical themes from Greek and Roman mythology; statues of Venus became increasingly popular. Claude Michel (1738–1814) and Jean Houdon (1741–1828) were

Francisco Goya, *Ni Por Esas*. In his series of engravings, *The Disasters of War,* Goya vividly depicted the brutality of war and the horrors of human suffering.

two French neoclassical sculptors who also achieved notable success with contemporary portraits. Houdon's *Portrait of Voltaire* is a well-known example.

At the opening of the eighteenth century, music demonstrated typical baroque characteristics. These were evident in instrumental music, especially that of the organ and the strings. The most typical baroque medium was opera, with its opulence and highly emotional content. The era culminated in the sumptuous religious music of Johann Sebastian Bach (1685–1750), a prolific German organ master and choir director. Bach's equally great contemporary, the German-born naturalized Englishman, George Frideric Handel (1685–1759), is known for his grand and dramatic operas, oratorios, and cantatas; he is best known today for his religious oratorio, *Messiah* (1742).

Composers of the late eighteenth century turned from the heavy and complex baroque styles to classical music of greater clarity, simpler structures, and more formal models. Plain, often folklike melodies also became common. With the appearance of symphonies, sonatas, concertos, and chamber music, less interest was shown in mere accompaniment for religious services or operatic performances. The general emphasis on technical perfection, melody, and orchestration is summed up in the work of the Austrian composers Franz Joseph Haydn (1732–1809) and Wolfgang Amadeus Mozart (1756–1791). Haydn wrote over 100 symphonies, along with numerous other works. Mozart wrote more than 600 works, including 41 symphonies, 22 operas, and 23 string quartets, climaxing his career with his three most famous operas: *The Marriage of Figaro* (1786) *Don Giovanni* (1787), and *The Magic Flute* (1791).

Musical expression at the turn of the century was touched by the genius of the immortal German composer Ludwig van Beethoven (1770–1827). The passion of his sonatas and symphonies expressed a revolutionary romanticism, which challenged the sedate classicism of his time.

Reflections of the Age in Literature

More than in art, neoclassicism in literature came closer to voicing the eighteenth century's fascination with reason and scientific law. Indeed, the verbal media of poetry, drama, prose, and exposition were commonly used to convey the new philosophic principles.

A typical poetic voice of the Age of Reason in England was Alexander Pope (1688–1744). In his most famous work, *An Essay on Man* (1733), Pope expressed the optimism and respect for reason that marked the era. He described a Newtonian universe in the following often quoted lines:

> All are but parts of one stupendous whole,
> Whose body nature is, and God the soul ...
> All nature is but art, unknown to thee;
> All chance, direction, which thou cannot see.
> All discord, harmony not understood;
> All partial evil, universal good
> And, spite of pride, in erring reason's spite,
> One truth is clear: Whatever is, is right.[5]

Two other poetic voices deserve mention here. One belonged to the English Countess of Winchelsea (1661–1720), who extolled reason and feminine equality in her verse. The other was that of a Massachusetts slave girl, Phyllis Wheatley (1753–1784), whose rhyming couplets, in the style of Pope, pleaded the cause of freedom for the American colonies and for her race.

Reflecting the common disdain for irrational customs and outworn institutions were such masterpieces of satire as *Candide* (1759), by the French man of letters, François-Marie Arouet, better known as Voltaire (1694–1778). Another famous satirist, England's Jonathan Swift (1667–1745), ridiculed the pettiness of human concerns in *Gulliver's Travels* (1726), wherein Captain Gulliver, in visiting the fictitious land of Lilliput, found two opposing factions: the Big-endians, who passionately advocated opening eggs at the big end, and the Little-endians, who vehemently proposed an opposite procedure.

The novel became a major literary vehicle in this period. It caught on first in France during the preceding century and was then popularized in England. *Robinson Crusoe* (1719), by Daniel Defoe (1659–1731), is often called the first modern English novel. The straight prose of the novel satisfied a prevailing demand for clarity and simplicity; but the tendency in this period to focus on middle-class values, heroic struggle, and sentimental love foreshadowed the coming romantic movement. Writing along these lines,

Samuel Richardson (1689–1761) produced *Pamela* (1740–1741), the story of a virtuous servant-girl, and Henry Fielding (1707–1754) wrote the equally famous *Tom Jones* (1749), the rollicking tale of a young man's deep pleasures and superficial regrets. Each novel, in its own way, defined a natural human morality.

In both France and England women found a uniquely promising outlet for their long-ignored talents in the romantic novel, with its accent on personal feminine concerns and domestic problems. Two among the multitude of able French women novelists were Madame de Graffigny (1695–1758), whose *Lettres D'Une Peruvienne* (1730) became a best-seller, and Madame de Tencin (1682–1749), who wrote *The Siege of Calais*, a historical novel of love and danger. In England, Fanny Burney (1753–1840) was universally acclaimed after publication of her first novel, *Eveline* (1778), about "a young lady's entrance into the world." Aphra Behn (1640–1689) was an early playwright whose novel, *Oroonoko* (1688), was a plea for the natural person, long before the works of Defoe and Rousseau.

The Enlightenment and the Age of Reason in Philosophy

Western Europe's worship of reason, reflected only vaguely in art and literature, was precisely expressed in a set of philosophic ideas known collectively as the Enlightenment. It was not originally a popular movement. Catching on first among scientists, philosophers, and some theologians, it was then taken up by literary figures, who spread its message among the middle classes. Ultimately, it reached the common people in simplified terms associated with popular grievances.

The most fundamental concept of the Enlightenment were faith in nature and belief in human progress. Nature was seen as a complex of interacting laws governing the universe. The individual human being, as part of that system, was designed to act rationally. If free to exercise their reason, people were naturally good and would act to further the happiness of others. Accordingly, both human righteousness and happiness required freedom from needless restraints, such as many of those imposed by the state or the church. The Enlightenment's uncompromising hostility towards organized religion and established monarchy reflected a disdain for the past and an inclination to favor utopian reform schemes. Most of its thinkers believed passionately in human progress through education. They thought society would become perfect if people were free to use their reason.

Before the eighteenth century, the Enlightenment was confined to Holland and England. Its earlier Dutch spokesmen were religious refugees, like the French Huguenot Pierre Bayle (1674–1706), whose skepticism and pleas for religious toleration were widely known in France. Baruch Spinoza (1632–1687), a Jewish intellectual and Holland's greatest philosopher, was a spokesman for pantheism, the belief that God exists in all of nature. Spinoza's influence, along with Newton's, profoundly affected English thinkers. Mary Astell (1666–1731), perhaps the earliest influential English feminist, lauded rational thinking and cited Newton as proof of an ordered universe. Such ideas were given more credibility by John Locke (1632–1704), the famous English philosopher. Back home from exile in Holland after the Glorious Revolution of the 1680s, Locke applied Newton's recently published principles to psychology, economics, and political theory. With Locke, the Enlightenment came to maturity and began to spread abroad.

After the Peace of Utrecht (1713), the Enlightenment was largely a French Phenomenon. Its leading proponents were known as the *philosophes*, although the term cannot in this instance be translated literally as "philosophers." The *philosophes* were mostly writers and intellectuals who analyzed the evils of society and sought reforms in accord with the principles of reason. Their most supportive allies were the *salonnières*, that is, the socially conscious and sometimes learned women who regularly entertained them, at the same time sponsoring their discussion of literary works, artistic creations, and new political ideas. By 1750, the *salonnières*, their salons, and the *philosophes* had made France once again the intellectual center of Europe.

A leading light among the *philosophes* was the Marquis de Montesquieu (1688–1755), a judicial official as well as a titled nobleman. He was among the earliest critics of absolute monarchy. From his extensive foreign travel and wide reading he developed a great respect for English liberty and a sense of objectivity in viewing European institutions, particularly those of France. Montesquieu's *Persian Letters* (1721), which purported to contain reports of an Oriental traveler in Europe, describing the irrational behavior and ridiculous customs of Europeans, delighted a large reading audience. His other great work, *The Spirit of Laws* (1748), expressed his main political principles. It is noted for its practical common sense, its objective recognition of geographic influences on political systems, its advocacy of checks and balances in government, and its uncompromising defense of liberty against tyranny.

More than any of the *philosophes*, Voltaire personified the skepticism of his century toward traditional religion and the injustices of the Old Regimes. His caustic pen brought him two imprisonments in the Bastille and even banishment to England for three years. On returning to France, Voltaire continued to champion toleration. He popularized Newtonian science, fought for freedom of the press, and actively crusaded against the church. In such endeavors, he turned out hundreds of histories, plays, pamphlets, essays, and novels. His estimated correspondence of 10,000 letters, including many to Frederick the Great and Catherine the Great, employed his wry wit in spreading the gospel of rationalism and reform of abuses. Even in his own time, his reputation became a legend, among kings as well as literate commoners.

Voltaire had many disciples and imitators, but his only rival in spreading the Enlightenment was a set of books—the famous French *Encyclopédie*, edited by Denis Diderot (1713–1784). The *Encyclopédie*, the chief monument of the *philosophes*, declared the supremacy of the new science, denounced superstition, and expounded the merits of human freedom. Its pages contained critical articles, by tradesmen as well as scientists, on unfair taxes, the evils of the slave trade, and the cruelty of criminal laws.

More than has been widely understood, the *Encyclopédie*, and many other achievements of the *philosophes* were joint efforts with their female colleagues among the *salonnières*. Madame de Geoffrin (1699–1777) contributed 200,000 livres (roughly $280,000 equivalent) to the *Encyclopédie* and made her salon the headquarters for planning and managing it. Mademoiselle de Lespinasse (1732–1776), the friend and confidential advisor of Jean d'Alembert (1717–1783), who assisted Diderot in editing the work, turned her salon into a forum for criticizing prospective articles. Most of the *philosophes* relied upon such assistance. Voltaire was coached in science by Madame du Châtelet; and the Marquis de Condorcet (1742–1794), the prophet of progress and women's rights among the *philosophes*, was intellectually partnered by his wife, Sophie (1764–1812), who popularized their ideas in her own salon. Even Madame de Pompadour aided the *philosophes* in 1759, when she presuaded Louis XV to allow sale of the *Encyclopédie*.

Perhaps the best-known of all the *philosophes* was that eccentric Swiss-born proponent of romantic rationalism, Jean-Jacques Rousseau (1712–1778). Although believing in the general objectives of the Enlightenment, Rousseau distrusted reason and science. He gloried in human impulse and intuition, trusting emotions rather than thought, the heart rather than the mind. His early rebuffs from polite society encouraged his hatred for the Old Regime. He also professed admiration for "noble savages," who lived completely free of law, courts, priests, and officials. In his numerous writings, he spoke as a rebel against all established institutions. The most famous of these works, *The Social Contract* (1762), was Rousseau's indictment of absolute monarchy. It began with the stirring manifesto: "Man is born free, but today he is everywhere in chains."[6]

The French Enlightenment exerted a powerful influence on English thought. Many young upper-class Englishmen visited France to complete their education. Among them were three leading English thinkers: Adam Smith (1723–1790), the Scottish father of modern economics; David Hume (1711–1766), the best-known English skeptic; and Jeremy Bentham (1748–1832), the founder of utilitarian philosophy. Another famous English rationalist was the historian, Edward Gibbon (1737–1794), whose *Decline and Fall of the Roman Empire* markedly criticized early Christianity. Among English political radicals after 1770, Joseph Priestley, Richard Price (1723–1791) and Thomas Paine (1737–1809) were also very much affected by French thought. Paine, who figured prominently in the American and French revolutions, was also a leader in English radical politics.

The Enlightenment also affected English women. Hannah Moore and a coterie of lady intellectuals, known as "bluestockings," maintained a conservative imitation of the French salons after the 1770s. One atypical "bluestocking" was Catherine Macaulay (1731–1791), a leading historian who published eight widely acclaimed volumes on the Stuart period. A republican defender of the American and French Revolutions, Macaulay exerted a decided influence on Mary Wollstonecraft (1759–1797), whose life symbolized the Enlightenment and the emerging English feminist movement. Born in poverty and burdened by a dependent family, Wollstonecraft became a teacher and a successful professional writer. She was personally acquainted with leading English radicals, including Richard Price, Thomas Paine, and William Godwin (1756–1836), whom she later married. Her *Vindication of the Rights of Man* (1790) was the first serious answer to Edmund Burke's diatribe against the French Revolution, which Wollstonecraft personally observed and ardently supported.

The reforming rationalism of the Enlightenment spread over Europe and also reached the New World. A leading spokesman in Germany was Moses Mendelssohn (1729–1786), who wrote against dogmatism and in favor of natural religion. In Italy, the Marquis of Beccaria (1738–1794) pleaded for humanitarian legal reforms. The Enlightenment was popular among the upper classes in such absolutist strongholds as Prussia, Russia, Austria, Portugal, and Spain. French ideas were read widely in Spanish America and Portuguese Brazil. In the English colonies, Locke and the *philosophes* influenced such leading thinkers as Benjamin Franklin, Thomas Jefferson (1743–1826), Mercy Otis Warren (1728–1814), and Abigail Adams (1744–1818).

The Case Against Absolutism

The Enlightenment's highest achievement was the development of a tightly organized philosophy, purportedly based on scientific principles and contradicting every argument for absolute monarchy as it generally existed in the eighteenth century. The case against absolutism, as presented by the *philosophes* and their foreign sympathizers, condemned divine-right monarchy, aristocracy by birth, state churches, and mercantilism. Each was found to be irrational, unnatural, and therefore basically evil.

Basic Arguments in the Case

One fundamental indictment against absolutism was its lack of human concern. Critics argued that maintaining order by forcing or frightening people into conformity, destroyed the innate human potential for moral judgment. The social environment was responsible for corrupting people, who were naturally good. Human beings could be perfected by removing the corrupting influences. For example, Beccaria insisted that unjust and irrational laws should be changed, so that they would teach morality and not just punish those who were caught. Prisons, argued the English reformer John Howard (1726–1790) should rehabilitate criminals, not brutalize them. These and other eighteenth-century rationalists believed that humanitarian reforms, in conformity with nature's laws, would lead toward unlimited human progress. Their message was voiced effectively by Condorcet, the most idealistic of the *philosophes*, in his *Progress of the Human Mind* (1794).

Behind Condorcet's humanitarianism was a passionate faith in human freedom. Enlightenment thinkers saw the arbitrary policies of absolute monarchs as violations of innate rights, required by human nature. The most fundamental part of this nature was human reason, the means by which people learned and realized their potential. Learning, as described by Locke in his *Essay Concerning Human Understanding* (1690), consisted entirely of knowledge gained through the senses, interpreted by reason, and stored in memory. There were no internal sources of knowledge; indeed, the mind at birth was like blank pieces of paper, upon which experience would write. The individual, in short, was primarily a thinking and judging mechanism, which required maximum freedom to operate effectively. The best government, therefore, was the government that ruled least. This argument for human freedom was the heart of the anti-absolutist case.

Religious Arguments in the Case

By the late eighteenth century, organized religion in Europe faced serious problems. The preceding century of religious wars had produced many contending sects and shaken the unquestioning faith of medieval times. Overseas expansion and the resulting contacts with non-Christian religions contributed to the same result. State churches, often used by kings to support corrupt regimes, also undermined respect for traditional Christianity. Added to all of this was the impact of the Newtonian revolution as well as earlier religious persecution of scientists. Between the orderly universe described by scientists and the relative chaos of human society, the contrast was indeed shocking. It led to serious reconsideration of religious ideas and institutions.

For such early thinkers as Descartes, the major theoretical problem was reconciling the mechanistic, self-regulating universe with the traditional belief in an all-powerful God. Descartes solved this problem, for himself, by dividing all realities between the realms of mind and matter. According to Descartes, both realms were governed by a divine will, but they appeared disconnected to human beings. Through science, human reason could accurately comprehend the material world; through faith and theology, the mind might know, directly from God, those truths beyond the material world of science. Thus, Descartes, a loyal Catholic, sought to reconcile the old and the new. In contrast, his Dutch pupil, Baruch Spinoza, saw mind and matter as dual parts of nature, which was one with God. This pantheistic theory identified God with every natural process, leaving few mysteries to be revealed by theology or supernatural revelation.

John Locke's religious ideas were similar to Spinoza's, but a little more orthodox. In his *Reasonableness of Christianity* (1695), Locke confirmed the existence of God by the regularities and apparent purposes of nature. He then attempted to prove that Christianity was consistent with natural law. This effort was somewhat self-defeating because it required natural explanations of religious miracles, thus nullifying their traditional religious significance. Nevertheless, arguments for such rational Christianity were quite common, particularly among "enlightened" clergymen in the eighteenth century.

The most popular religious belief of the later Enlightenment was deism. It was held by such well-known figures as Thomas Paine in England, Thomas Jefferson and Benjamin Franklin in the English American colonies, and Voltaire in France. To deists, God was an impersonal force—the master "clockwinder" of the universe. Generally, they rejected religious miracles and Christ's divinity. People, according to their view, were totally responsible for their actions. This "natural religion" required that individuals act morally without churches, clergy, ritual, or prayers. Although accepting the idea of an afterlife, deists attached no significance to emotional faith as a means to salvation. They placed all reliance on the individual reason and conscience.

Deism was popular but somewhat logically inconsistent. If the universe operated automatically, how could people possess free will and assume moral responsibility? What material evidence indicated an afterlife? Such questions led some thinkers to religious skepticism and even to atheism. Joseph Priestley, who was trained as an English minister and considered himself a Christian theologian, insisted that the soul did not exist independent of the body. David Hume (1711–1776), the famous English skeptic, questioned the existence both of God and of heaven. The most extreme views were professed in France, particularly in the circle of Paul Henri, Baron d'Holbach (1723–1789). In *The System of Nature* (1770), d'Holbach denied the existence of God or any human purpose in the universe. Such ideas, however, were held only by a minority of Enlightenment thinkers.

Despite some differences on the details of their beliefs, eighteenth-century rationalists were in almost perfect agreement on one point. They championed religious freedom of conscience. In addition, most were participants in a continuing struggle against the alleged fallacies of organized religion. Hundreds of their writings, especially those of Voltaire and the *philosophes*, depicted churches and priests as part of a vast conspiracy aimed at perpetuating injustice and tyranny. State churches were special targets for their attacks. Their crusade for religious liberty was particularly threatening to absolutism.

The Economic Argument

Natural law, a basic concept of the Enlightenment, was applied most consistently and effectively in economic arguments against absolutism. Contradictions that natural law raised in religious theory were not nearly so typical in economics. In addition, by the eighteenth century, developing capitalism clearly indicated the stimulus of profit to individual incentive. This realization, coming with the scientific revolution, strongly suggested that capitalism had outgrown mercantilism, with its state assistance and accompanying controls. The new economic philosophy contended that the free play of economic forces would ensure the greatest prosperity.

Such ideas were promoted by the physiocrats, a group of economic thinkers in eighteenth-century France. Their leading spokesman was François Quesnay (1694–1774), the personal physician to Louis XV but also a contributor to the *Encyclopédie*. Originally, Quesnay and his followers opposed Colbert's policy of subordinating agriculture to government-controlled industry. This narrow emphasis later developed into a comprehensive theory based on natural law. Quesnay, for example, compared the circulation of money to the circulation of blood. He likened mercantilist controls to tourniquets, which shut off a life-giving flow. Quesnay also denounced the mercantilist theory of bullionism, arguing that prosperity depended on production, not gold and silver in the royal treasury. According to another physiocrat, Robert Turgot (1720–1781), selfish profit-seeking in a free market would necessarily result in the best service and the most goods for society.

The most influential advocate of the new economic theory was Adam Smith, a Scottish professor of moral philosophy at Glasgow University, who had visited France and exchanged ideas with the physiocrats. In 1776, Smith published *An Inquiry into the Nature and Causes of the Wealth of Nations*, in which he set forth his systematic formulation of ideas. The work has since become the bible of classical economic liberalism, the doctrine of free enterprise, or *laissez-faire* economics.

Smith was indebted to the physiocrats for his views on personal liberty, natural law, and the role of the state as a mere "passive policeman." He argued that increased production depended largely on division of labor and specialization. Because trade increased specialization, it also increased production. The volume of trade, in turn, depended on every person being free to persue individual self-interest. In seeking private gain, each individual was also guided by an "invisible hand" (the law of supply and demand) in meeting society's needs:

> It is not from the benevolence of the butcher, the brewer, or the baker, that we expect our dinner, but from their reward to their own interests. We address ourselves, not to their humanity, but to their self-love . . . [7]

Smith regarded all economic controls, whether by the state or by guilds and trade unions, as injurious to trade. He scoffed at the mercantilist idea that the wealth of a nation depended on achieving a surplus of exports, amassing bullion, and crippling the economies of other countries. In Smith's view, trade should work to the benefit of all nations, which would follow if the trade were free. In such a natural and free economic world, the prosperity of each nation would depend on the prosperity of all.

A number of other thinkers in the late eighteenth century combined or elaborated the ideas of Smith and the physiocrats. In France, d'Holbach repudiated mercantilism, arguing that free trade would permit one nation to supply the deficiencies of another. Jeremy Bentham, in England, followed Smith in developing his idea of utilitarianism "as the greatest good for the greatest number" but denied that economic equality would promote happiness, because it would destroy incentive and limit production. Other commentators, such as Richard Price and Benjamin Franklin, suggested that rising wealth naturally increased the population, except in new lands, where resources were almost unlimited. In one way or another, such propositions supported the basic idea that economic controls were futile or damaging the society.

A few radical thinkers of the Enlightenment, such as Richard Price and Mary Wollstonecraft, toyed with the idea of redistributing property, but the dominant creed was the laissez-faire philosophy, which sanctified capitalism and the

Adam Smith, On the Division of Labor Self-interest

The last section of this excerpt is perhaps the most often quoted. It is based on Mandeville's *Fable of the Bees* (1729).

This division of labor, from which so many advantages are derived, is not originally the effect of any human wisdom which foresees and intends that general opulence to which it gives occasion. It is the necessary, though very slow and gradual, consequence of a certain propensity in human nature which has in view no such extensive utility: the propensity to truck, barter, and exchange one thing for another.

Whether this propensity be one of those original principles in human nature, of which no further account can be given; or whether, as seems more probable, it be the necessary consequence of the faculties of reason and speech, it belongs not to our present subject to inquire. It is common to all men, and to be found in no other race of animals, which seem to know neither this nor any other species of contracts. Two greyhounds, in running down the same hare, have sometimes the appearance of acting in some sort of concert. Each turns her toward his companion, or endeavors to intercept her when his companion turns her toward himself. This, however, is not the effect of any contract, but of the accidental concurrence of their passions in the same object at that particular time. . . . When an animal wants to obtain something either of a man or of another animal, it has no other means of persuasion but to gain the favor of those whose service it requires. A puppy fawns upon its dam, and a spaniel endeavors by a thousand attractions to engage the attention of its master who is at dinner, when it wants to be fed by him. Man sometimes uses the same arts with his brethren, and when he has no other means of engaging them to act according to his inclinations, endeavors by every servile and fawning attention to obtain their good will. He has not time, however, to do this upon every occasion. In civilized society he stands at all times in need of the co-operation and assistance of great multitudes, while his whole life is scarcely sufficient to gain the friendship of a few persons. In almost every other race of animals each individual, when it is grown up to maturity, is entirely independent, and in its natural state has occasion for the assistance of no other living creature. But man has almost constant occasion for the help of his brethren, and it is in vain for him to expect it from their benevolence only. He will be more likely to prevail if he can interest their self-love in his favor, and show them that it is for their own advantage to do for him what he requires of them. Whoever offers to another a bargain of any kind proposes to do this. Give me that which I want, and you shall have this which you want, is the meaning of every such offer; and it is in this manner that we obtain from one another the far greater part of those good offices which we stand in need of. It is not from the benevolence of the butcher, the brewer, or the baker that we expect our dinner, but from their regard to their own interest. We address ourselves not to their humanity, but to their self-love, and never talk to them of our own necessities, but of their advantages. Nobody but a beggar chooses to depend chiefly upon the benevolence of his fellow citizens. Even a beggar does not depend upon it entirely. The charity of well-disposed people, indeed, supplies him with the whole fund of his subsistence. But though this principle ultimately provides him with all the necessities of life for which he has occasion, it neither does nor can provide him with them as he has occasion for them. . . .

From Adam Smith, *An Inquiry into the Nature and Causes of the Wealth of Nations*, edited by Bruce Mazlish. (New York: Bobbs-Merrill, 1961), pp. 13–15.

freely operating profit motive. The so-called economic laws seemed to parallel mathematically proven laws of science. Indeed, the middle classes came to consider free enterprise as practically equivalent in validity to the law of gravitation. In an age of high taxes, contradictory commercial regulations, and expanding opportunities for profit, the new principles seemed to provide practical solutions for all economic problems. They certainly went a long way toward discrediting mercantilism and the Old Regimes built upon it.

The Political Argument

Economic freedom, like religious freedom, depended ultimately on government, the source of most restrictions or coercion. For this reason, political principles in the case against absolutism were fundamental to all others. They were developed in two main categories: ideas concerning individual rights, and ideas concerning the organization of government. Both categories of thought were directed toward securing individual freedom against unnatural abuses of authority.

According to Locke and most political theorists of the Enlightenment, government existed to maintain the rights of its people. This idea ran directly counter to the divine-right theory, which was held by most reigning monarchs in the seventeenth and eighteenth centuries.

Locke at the opening of the period and Rousseau at its end answered the divine-right doctrine with the opposing theory of a "social contract." Thomas Hobbes had used the contract idea to justify royal authority; Locke turned Hobbes' argument around. In his famous *Second Treatise on Government* (1690), Locke contended that political systems were originally formed by individuals for defense of their natural rights to life, freedom, and property, against local or foreign enemies. They voluntarily ceded to government their individual right of protecting their liberties. In this transaction, government's authority was derived from the governed. It was not absolute but limited to maintaining the people's rights, for which it was constituted. When its authority was used for other purposes, the contract was broken and the people were justified in forming another government.

As insurance against abuses of political authority, political theorists of the Enlightenment generally advocated the separation of powers. Locke, for example, proposed that kings, magistrates, legislatures, and judges should share authority and check on one another. Spinoza also stressed the need for local autonomy and a locally based militia to guard against power concentrated in a central government. Montesquieu, although somewhat skeptical about natural laws or Locke's version of the social contract, developed a theory of separation of powers in his *Spirit of Laws;* most of the *philosophes* subscribed to this idea.[8]

Political freedom and guarantees for human rights were common goals, but ideas concerning the ideal form of government varied considerably. The majority of the *philosophes* were not opposed to monarchy, despite their rejection of the divine-right principle. Voltaire believed that the most likely way to attain desirable reforms was through the rule of an "enlightened despot." In a sense, this theory of government was akin to the Platonic ideal of the philosopher-king. A few monarchs professed to accept this role, although their policies did not always match their principles (see ch. 19).

Perhaps the most popular form of government among natural law theorists was constitutional monarchy on the English model. Locke, of course, was the recognized spokesman for the Glorious Revolution and the limited English monarchy established by Parliament. Both Voltaire and Montesquieu were very much impressed with the English system as they understood it. For Montesquieu, it appeared to be a practical balance of traditional forces, which secured liberty without sacrificing order.

Concern for internal order was typical of most political thought in the Enlightenment. Both Locke and Voltaire, to name only two well-known examples, advocated that political power be confined to property owners. This, they believed, would secure sound government against the ignorant masses, at the same time holding open opportunities to intelligent and industrious citizens. Presumably, those with most to lose from anarchy could best be trusted with political rights. Such ideas also squared with the English parliamentary system, dominated as it was by the propertied classes.

John Locke, On the Origin of Government

In this passage, Locke presents his well-known assumptions about human adversities in "a state of nature," which led to the cooperative forming of states and which made all governments logically responsible to their citizens.

Men being, as has been said, by nature all free, equal, and independent, no one can be put out of this estate, and subjected to the political power of another, without his own consent. The only way by which any one divests himself of his natural liberty and puts on the bonds of civil society is by agreeing with other men to join and unite into a community for their comfortable, safe, and peaceable living one amongst another, in a secure enjoyment of their properties, and a greater security against any that are not of it. This any number of men may do, because it injures not the freedom of the rest; they are left as they were in the liberty of the state of nature. When any number of men have so consented to make one community or government, they are thereby presently incorporated, and make one body politic, wherein the majority have a right to act and conclude the rest.

For when any number of men have, by the consent of every individual, made a community, they have thereby made that community one body, with a power to act as one body, which is only by the will and determination of the majority. For that which acts any community being only the consent of the individuals of it, and it being necessary to that which is one body to move one way, it is necessary the body should move that way whither the greater force carries it, which is the consent of the majority. . . . And therefore we see that in assemblies empowered to act by positive laws, where no number is set by that positive law which empowers them, the act of the majority passes for the act of the whole, and of course determines, as having by the law of nature and reason the power of the whole.

And thus every man, by consenting with others to make one body politic under one government, puts himself under an obligation to every one of that society, to submit to the determination of the majority, and to be concluded by it; or else this original compact, whereby he with others incorporates into one society, would signify nothing, and be no compact, if he be left free and under no other ties than he was in before in the state of nature. For what appearance would there be of any compact? What new engagement if he were no farther tied by any decrees of the society, than he himself thought fit, and did actually consent to? This would be still as great a liberty as he himself had before his compact, or any one else in the state of nature hath, who may submit himself and consent to any acts of it if he thinks fit. . . .

Whosoever therefore out of a state of nature unite into a community must be understood to give up all the power necessary to the ends for which they unite into society, to the majority of the community, unless they expressly agreed in any number greater than the majority. And this is done by barely agreeing to unite into one political society, which is all the compact that is, or needs be, between the individuals that enter into make up a commonwealth. And thus that which begins and actually constitutes any political society is nothing but the consent of any number of freemen capable of a majority to unite and incorporate into such a society. And this is that, and that only, which did or could give beginning to any lawful government in the world. . . .

From John Locke, *Second Treatise on Government* in *Sources of British Political Thought*, edited by Wilfrid Harrison. (New York: Macmillan, 1965), pp. 55–57.

Only a few eighteenth-century rationalists believed in democracy as a form of government. Like their more conservative colleagues, they were afraid of mob action but even more so of monarchs, aristocrats, and large centralized polities. They saw the ballot box as another check on arbitrary government and regarded political rights, particularly the franchise, as the ultimate security for personal liberty.

Because democratic ideas were so uncommon, they were often qualified in their expression. Thomas Jefferson suggested that common men should be represented in government, but he also accepted the property-based franchise. He harmonized the apparent contradiction by advocating that most land should be owned by small farmers. Other vague democratic references, sometimes contradictory, appeared in the political writings of Jeremy Bentham, Joseph Priestley, Richard Price, Thomas Paine, Mary Wollstonecraft, and William Godwin.

Since the late eighteenth century, Rousseau has been somewhat mistakenly considered the greatest democrat among the French *philosophes*. Admittedly, he respected the republican institutions of his native Geneva, but he did not think them appropriate for a large state such as France. He also exalted the "General Will" as representing the interests of the community or nation over the selfish interests of individuals. By "General Will," however, Rousseau meant the social contract as expressed in generally accepted law. This law secured each individual's freedom, up to the point where it threatened the freedom of others. Rousseau did not clearly oppose democracy, but he was more interested in the abstract ideas of popular sovereignty and equal rights under law. His so-called democracy was most evident in his general opposition to monarchy, aristocracy, and polite society.[9]

Such minor differences over forms of government were inconsequential, compared with the points of political agreement among Enlightenment thinkers. All of them rejected the idea of divine-right monarchy, considering kings as the public servants of their peoples and obligated to maintain natural rights for all. These rights to life, liberty, and property, as construed by the *philosophes* and their rationalist friends abroad, ran directly counter to absolutism.

The Argument for Women's Rights

The Enlightenment's case against absolutism brought the first clearly stated arguments for women's rights. Although such ideas were not implemented when they were most evident—during the French Revolution—and had largely been ignored when they were expressed earlier, this era saw them entered into the public consciousness.

Although a monarchist and a follower of Descartes rather than Locke, Mary Astell claimed legal equality for women on the basis of their natural rationality in her *Serious Proposal to the Ladies* (1694). This call for women's rights was not repeated for decades, but it was echoed in the writings of English women, such as Mary Montague, during the eighteenth century. In France, a number of *salonnières*, including Madame de Puisseux (1720–1798) and Madame Gacon-Dufour (1753–1835), authored books defending their sex. Outside the salons, between 1759 and 1758, the *Journal des Dames*, a magazine edited by women, preached freedom, progress, and women's rights. At about the same time, in the new United States, Abigail Adams chided her husband because the new American constitution ignored women.

Before the French Revolution, the "woman subject" did not concern many leading philosophers. Rousseau represented most of them when he described the ideal woman's proper role as housekeeper, mother, and quiet comforter of her husband, who was responsible for her protection and moral instruction. A few thinkers disagreed. Both Hobbes and Locke mildly questioned the idea that women were naturally subordinate to men. D'Alembert thought female limitations resulted from women's degradation by society, and Montesquieu saw absolute monarchy as the cause for women's lack of status. But Condorcet was the only *philosophe* who made a special plea for female equality. In his *Letters from a Bourgeois of New Haven* (1787), he claimed that women's rationality entitled them to full citizenship, including the right to vote and hold public office. Later, during the Revolution, he advocated full equality for women in public education. For the most part, however, his voice went unheard.

The fall of the Bastille and the subsequent *Declaration of the Rights of Man and Citizen* by the French National Constituent Assembly generated a wave of female intellectual agitation. Catherine Macaulay led the way in England, denouncing the prevailing "harem mentality" and advocating a liberal education for women in her *Letters on Education* (1790). In France, the first challenge came from a butcher's daughter and self-educated playwright, Olympe de Gouges (1748–1793). Her *Declaration of the Rights of Women* (1791) called for a social contract, which would give women equal rights in divorce, as well as free speech and assembly. The climax came with Mary Wollstonecraft's *Vindication of the Rights of Women* (1792). Like Condorcet, Macaulay, and de Gouges, Wollstonecraft used natural law arguments in justifying full civil rights and equal education for women, but she more effectively emphasized her demands with a withering attack upon the prejudice of Rousseau and his supporters. Her passionate appeal would become a future feminist tradition.

For a while during the 1790s, the flurry of concern continued. In England, Wollstonecraft's friend, Mary Hayes (1760–1843) took up the crusade, as did Mary Anne Radcliff (1764–1823), who stressed the lack of economic opportunities for women in *An Attempt to Recover the Rights of Women from Male Usurpation* (1799). Patricia Wakefield (1751–1832) also used an economic approach. Her book, *Reflections on the Present Condition of the Female Sex* (1798), followed Adam Smith in arguing that the exploitation of women would limit prosperity. Other voices were raised in Germany and America. In 1792, Theodore Hippel (1742–1796) rebuked the French for ignoring women in their new constitution. The American reaction came in the writings of Judith Sargent Murray (1751–1820) and Charles Brockden Brown (1771–1810), both of whom were influenced by Wollstonecraft.

The Reaction Against Reason

The eighteenth century was primarily an "Age of Reason," but in the latter decades there was a general reaction against rationalism. One form of the reaction came in philosophy with a new idealism, in opposition to the materialism of the early Enlightenment. Another form was an emotional religious revival, which won back many wavering Protestants and Catholics. A third form of reaction replaced reason with religion as the justification for humanitarian reforms. These movements stressed emotion over reason but continued the Enlightenment's accent upon individual liberty.

Idealistic Philosophy

Immanuel Kant (1724–1804), a kindly and contemplative professor of philosophy at the German University of Königsberg, was thoroughly aroused by the skeptical and materialistic extremes of the Enlightenment. While appreciating science and dedicated to reason, he determined to shift philosophy back to a more sensible position without giving up much of its newly discovered "rational" basis. His ideas, contained primarily in the *Critique of Pure Reason* (1781), ushered in a new age of philosophic idealism.

Kant agreed with Locke on the role of the senses in acquiring knowledge but insisted that sensory experience had to be interpreted by the mind's internal patterns. This meant that certain ideas—the mind's categories for sorting and recording experience—were *a priori*, that is, they existed before the sensory experience occurred. Typical innate ideas of this sort were width, depth, beauty, cause, and God; all were understood yet none were learned directly through the senses. Kant concluded, as had Descartes, that some truths were not derived from material objects through scientific study. Beyond the material world was a realm unapproachable by science. Moral and religious truths, such as God's existence, could not be proved by science yet were known to human beings as rational creatures. Reason, according to Kant, went beyond the mere interpretation of physical realities.

In Kant's philosophic system, pure reason, the highest form of human endeavor, was as close to intuition as it was to sensory experience. It proceeded from certain subjective senses, built into human nature. The idea of God was derived logically from the mind's penchant for harmony. The human conscience, according to Kant, might be developed or be crippled by experience, but it originated in the person's thinking nature. Abstract reason, apart from science and its laws, was a valid source of moral judgment and religious interpretation. Thus Kant used reason to give a philosophic base back to mystical religion.[10]

The Religious Reaction

Religious rationalism, despite its appeal to intellectuals, provoked considerable religious reaction. Part of this came from theologians such as Bishop Joseph Butler (1692–1752) and William Paley (1743–1805) in England, both of whom defended Christianity and challenged deism on its own rational grounds. Even more significant was a widespread emotional revival, stressing religion of the heart rather than the mind.

The new movement, known as pietism, began in England after 1738, when the brothers John (1703–1791) and Charles (1708–1788) Wesley began a crusade of popular preaching in the Church of England. The Anglican pietists discarded traditional formalism and stilted sermons in favor of a glowing religious fervor, producing a vast upsurge of emotional faith among the English lower classes. "Methodist," at first a term of derision, came to be the respected and official name for the new movement. After John Wesley's death in 1791, the Methodists officially left the Anglican church to become a most important independent religious force in England.

On the continent, Lutheran pietism, led by Philipp J. Spener (1635–1705) and Emanuel Swedenborg (1688–1772), followed a pattern similar to Methodism. Swedenborg's movement in Sweden began as an effort to reconcile science and revelation; after Swedenborg's death it became increasingly emotional and mystical. Spener, in Germany, stressed Bible study, hymn singing, and powerful preaching. The Moravian movement sprang from his background. Under the sponsorship of Count Nicholaus von Zinzendorf (1700–1760), it spread to the frontiers of Europe and to the English colonies in America.

The "Great Awakening," a tremendous emotional revival sustained by Moravians, Methodsts, Baptists, and Quakers, swept the colonial frontier areas from Georgia to New England in the late eighteenth century. Women played prominent roles in this activity, organizing meetings and providing auxiliary services, such as charities and religious instruction. Among the Quakers, women were often ministers and itinerant preachers. One was Jemima Wilkinson (1752–1819), leader of the Universal Friends; another was Ann Lee (1736–1784), who founded Shaker colonies in New York and New England.

By the 1780s, religious rationalism and pietism stood in opposition to each other. Proponents of each disagreed passionately on religious principles though they agreed on the issue of religious freedom. Both rationalists and pietists were outside the state churches, both feared persecution, and both recognized the flagrant abuses of religious establishments. The two movements were therefore almost equally threatening to state churches and the old regimes.

The New Humanitarianism

One dominant characteristic of the early Enlightenment—the concern for individual human worth—received new impetus from religion in the reaction against reason. The demand for reform and the belief in human progress were now equated with traditional Christian principles, such as human communality and God's concern for all people. Religious humanitarianism shunned radical politics and ignored the issue of women's rights, despite the movement's strong support among women. It did, however, seek actively to relieve human suffering and ignorance among children, the urban poor, prisoners, and slaves. This combination of humanitarian objectives and Christian faith was similar in some ways to the Enlightenment but markedly different in its emotional tone and religious justifications.

Notable among manifestations of the new humanitarianism was the antislavery movement in England. A court case in 1774 ended slavery within the country. From then until 1807, a determined movement sought abolition of the slave trade. It was led by William Wilberforce (1759–1833), aided by Hannah Moore and other Anglican Evangelicals, along with many Methodists and Quakers. Wilberforce repeatedly introduced bills into the House of Commons that would have eliminated the traffic in humans. His efforts were rewarded in 1807 when the trade was ended, although he and his allies had to continue to struggle for twenty-six more years, before they could achieve abolition in the British colonies.

Religious humanitarians enforced other movements that originated in the Enlightenment. For example, the movements for legal reform and prison reform were both supported by religious groups before 1800. Education, extolled by rationalist thinkers, also aroused interest among the denominations. The Sunday School movement, particularly in England, was a forerunner of many private and quasi-public church schools. Finally, concern for the plight of slaves, coupled with rising missionary zeal, brought popular efforts to improve conditions for native peoples in European possessions overseas.

While it was not as openly political as other aspects of the Enlightenment, the new humanitarianism played a significant part in weakening absolutism. In general, it contributed to a spirit of restlessness and discontent and encouraged independent thought, particularly as it improved education. Its successful campaign against the slave trade also struck a direct blow at the old mercantilist economies, which depended heavily on plantation agriculture overseas. In time, the missionaries would also prove to be the most consistent enemies of colonialism.

Conclusion

The Enlightenment brought a new vision of the future, which forecast the end of absolute monarchy. Philosophers of the Enlightenment thought they had discovered a simple formula for perpetual human happiness. They sought to deliver individuals from restraints so that they could act freely in accordance with their natures. On the one hand, the formula promised that pursuit of self-interest would benefit society; on the other, it promised that a free human reason would produce sound moral judgments. In other words, individual freedom permitted the operation of natural laws. Believing they had learned these laws, eighteenth-century rationalists thought they had found the secret of never-ending progress.

Rational philosophy undermined absolutism in all of its phases. Deism questioned the necessity of state churches and clergies. The physiocrats, Adam Smith, and other early economic liberals demonstrated the futility of mercantilism. Political theory in the Enlightenment substituted the social contract for divine right and emphasized natural human rights of political freedom and justice. Each of these ideas denied the absolute authority of monarchs.

Respect for rational philosophy was largely derived from the successes and popularity of science. The surprising discoveries of astronomers produced a new view of the individual's place in the universe; in his law of gravitation, Newton supplied mathematical evidence for their perspective. His laws, along with the other laws of science, suggested that human reason operated effectively only when it was interpreting sensory experience. Material reality was accepted as the only reality. Therefore, the natural laws affecting human society were also considered as basically materialistic.

Toward the end of the eighteenth century, a reaction against reason countered this materialism without affecting the fundamental objectives of the Enlightenment. Idealistic philosophy and pietism both challenged the scientific view of the individual, emphasizing that intuition and faith are human qualities as essential as reason. These new movements merged with the humane concerns of rational philosophy to produce a new humanitarianism, which accented both reason and sentimentality but also continued the eighteenth-century concern for human freedom. Together with the rationalism of the Enlightenment, the reaction against reason before 1800 also challenged absolutism's domination of the human body, mind, and spirit.

Suggestions for Reading

Good general surveys of intellectual developments during the early modern period in Europe may be found in two standard works that are still worth consulting: Jacob Bronowski and Bruce Mazlish, *The Western Intellectual Tradition from Leonardo to Hegel* (Torchbooks, 1962) and Crane Brinton, *The Shaping of Modern Thought* (P. Smith, 1968). Excellent coverage of general background is provided in William Doyle, *The Old Order in Europe* (Oxford, 1978).

Colin A. Ronan, *Science: Its History and Development Among the World's Cultures* (Facts on File, 1982) treats comprehensively the revolutionary developments of the seventeenth and eighteenth centuries. Two other useful general surveys of scientific achievements during the period are I. Bernard Cohen, *From Leonardo to Lavoisier* (Scribner, 1980) and Robert B. Downs, *Landmarks in Science* (Libraries Unlimited, 1982). For the changing place of science in society, Leonard M. Marsak, ed., *The Rise of Science in Reference to Society* (Macmillan, 1964) is still reliable. See also J. Weinberger, *Science, Faith and Society* (Cornell Univ., 1985). Mary Ornstein, *The Role of Scientific Societies in the Seventeenth Century* (Arno, 1975) is the classic study of this important subject. Overdue recognition of early women scientists is provdied in Margaret Alic, *Hypatia's Heritage: A History of Women in Science* (Beacon, 1986) and Marilyn B. Ogilive, *Women in Science* (M.I.T., 1986).

For the origins of scientific theory, see N. Jardine, *The Birth of the History and the Philosophy of Science* (Cambridge Univ., 1988). A flood of recent books deals with the special contributions of Descartes and Bacon. For Descartes, see T. Sorrel, *Descartes* (Oxford Univ., 1987); J. F. Scott, *The Scientific Work of René Descartes* (Garland, 1987); L. J. Beck, *The Method of Descartes* (Garland, 1987); and Desmond Clarke, *Descartes' Philosophy of Science* (Pennsylvania Sate Univ., 1982). For Bacon, see C. Whitney, *Francis Bacon and Modernity* (Yale Univ., 1986); P. Urbach, *Francis Bacon's Philosophy of Science* (Open Court, 1987); and Antonio Perez-Ramos, *Francis Bacon's Idea of Science and the Maker's Knowledge of Tradition* (Oxford Univ., 1989).

Alexander Koyre, *The Astronomical Revolution* (Cornell Univ., 1973) is a concise synthesis. Among the best interpretive biographies of the great astronomers are John Louis Emil Dreyer, *Tycho Brahe* (Dover, 1963); Arthur Koestler's study of Kepler, *The Watershed* (Univ. Press of America, 1984); Stillman Drake, *Galileo* (Hill and Wang, 1980); Ernan McMullin, *Galileo, Man of Science* (Scholar's Bookshelf, 1988). For Newton, see Gale E. Christianson, *In the Presence of the Creator* (Free Press, 1984) and Richard S. Westfall, *Never at Rest* (Cambridge Univ., 1983).

Achievements in biology and chemistry are covered in the following biographical works: Robert G. Frank, *Harvey and the Oxford Physiologists* (Univ. of California, 1980); Peter Alexander, *Qualities and Corpuscles: Locke and Boyle on the External World* (Cambridge Univ., 1985). For Lavoisier, see W. C. Anderson, *Between the Library and the Laboratory* (Johns Hopkins Univ., 1984); Vivian Grey, *The Chemist Who Lost His Head* (Coward Putnam, 1982); and Kenneth Sydney Davis' dual study of Lavoisier and Priestly, *The Cautionary Scientists* (Putnam's, 1966).

Hugh Honeur, *Neo-Classicism* (Penguin, 1987) is a well-balanced brief summary of the major artistic trend. Other sound treatments of art in this era are Halldor Soehner, *The Rococo Age: Art and Civilization in the Eighteenth Century* (McGraw-Hill, 1960); S. Jones, *The Eighteenth Century* (Cambridge Univ., 1985); Jean Starobinsky, *1789: The Emblems of Reason* (M.I.T., 1988); A. Boime, *Art in an Age of Revolution, 1750–1800* (Univ. of Chicago, 1987); and R. Paulson, *Representations of Revolution* (Yale Univ., 1987). For architecture, see Allan Braham, *The Architecture of the French Enlightenment* (Univ. of California, 1980);

Joseph Rykwert, *The First Moderns* (Harvard Univ., 1980); and J. L. Varriano, *Italian Baroque and Rococo Architecture* (Oxford Univ., 1986). Contributions of women artists are described in Helga Mobius, *Women of the Baroque Age* (Abner Schram, 1984); Karen Peterson, *Women Artists* (New York Univ., 1976); and Elsa H. Fine, *Women and Art* (Allenheld, Schram, and Prior, 1978).

Frederick Keener, *The Chain of Becoming* (Columbia Univ., 1983) is a thoughtful study of Enlightenment literature. It complements such other scholarly literary studies as J. Sambrook, *The Eighteenth Century — the Intellectual and Cultural Context of English Literature* (Longman, 1986) and P. Rogers, *Literature and Popular Culture in Eighteenth-Century England* (Barnes and Noble, 1985), for the intellectual and aesthetic atmosphere of early Georgian England, see Clive T. Probyn, *Jonathan Swift, the Contemporary Background* (Barnes and Noble, 1979). See also David Nokes, *Jonathan Swift* (Oxford Univ., 1985) and A. Ingram, *Intricate Laughter in the Satire of Swift and Pope* (Macmillan, 1986). Pope and his influence are covered in R. A. Brower, *Alexander Pope and the Arts of Georgian England*, 2nd ed. (Oxford, 1986); G. F. Plowden, *Pope on Classic Ground* (Ohio Univ., 1983); and M. Mack, *Alexander Pope* (Yale Univ., 1986). For a look at the French literary world at the end of the century, see Renée Winegarten, *Mme. de Staël* (St. Martin's, 1987) and C. Hogsett, *The Literary Existance of Germaine de Staël*.

Inclusive and coherent surveys of the Enlightenment are presented in Louis B. Snyder, *The Age of Reason* (Krieger, 1979) and Robert Anchor, *The Enlightenment Tradition* (Univ. of Pennsylvania, 1987). For intellectual origins of the movement, see Alan Kors and Paul J. Korshin, eds., *Anticipation of the Enlightenment in England, France, and Germany* (Univ. of Pennsylvania, 1987). Some common themes are treated in Henry Vyerberg, *Human Nature, Cultural Diversity, and the French Enlightenment* (Oxford Univ., 1989); Thomas J. Schlereth, *The Cosmopolitan Ideal in the Enlightenment* (Univ. of Notre Dame, 1977); and Donald C. Mell, et al, eds., *Man, God, and Nature in the Enlightenment* (Colleagues Press, 1989). For nationalistic variations, see Frederick Artz, *The Enlightenment in France* (Kent State Univ., 1968); John Redwood, *Reason, Ridicule, and Religion: The Age of the Enlightenment in England* (Harvard Univ., 1976); Henri Brunschwig, *Enlightenment and Romanticism in Eighteenth-Century Prussia* (Univ. of Chicago, 1974); Henry S. Commager, *The Empire of Reason: How Europe Imagined and America Realized the Enlightenment* (Peter Smith, 1984); and Ernest Cassirer, *The Enlightenment in America* (Univ. Press of Amer., 1988).

French and American colonial women who played roles in the Enlightenment are ably credited in Joan B. Lander, *Women and the Public Sphere in the Age of the French Revolution* (Cornell Univ., 1988); Samia I. Spender, *French Women and the Age of Enlightenment* (Indiana Univ., 1984); Margaret Hunt and Margaret Jacob, *Women and the Enlightenment* (Haworth Press, 1984); Linda K. Kerber, *Women of the Republic* (Univ. of North Carolina, 1980); and Mary Beth Norton, *Liberty's Daughters* (Little, Brown, 1980).

The following biographical studies are recommended for major participants in the Enlightenment: L. S. Feuer, *Spinoza and the Rise of Liberalism* (Transaction Books,

1987); Thomas L. Hankin, *Jean d'Alembert* (Oxford, 1970); Keith M. Baker, *Condorcet* (Univ. of Chicago, 1982); Otis E. Fellows, *Diderot* (Twayne, 1977); Alan C. Kors, *D'Holbach's Coterie* (Princetown Univ., 1976); Anthony Flew, *David Hume: Philosophy of Moral Science* (Blackwell, 1986); J. Y. Grieg, *The Philosophy of David Hume* (Garland, 1983); Maurice Cranston, *John Locke* (Oxford Univ., 1985); J. W. Yolton, *John Locke* (Blackwell, 1985); Norman Hampson, *Montesquieu, Rousseau, and the French Revolution* (Univ. of Oklahoma, 1983); J. N. Shklar, *Montesquieu* (Oxford Univ., 1987); A. J. Ayer, *Voltaire* (Random House, 1986); Maurice Cranston, *Jean-Jacques* (Penguin, 1987); J. Starobinski, *Jean-Jacques Rousseau* (Univ. of Chicago, 1988); and James J. Hoecher, *Joseph Priestley and the Idea of Progress* (Garland, 1987).

Religious issues in the Enlightenment are discussed in Edwin M. Curley, *Descartes Against the Skeptics* (Harvard Univ. 1978). The opposite orientation is revealed in Joseph P. Wright, *The Skeptical Philosophy of David Hume* (Univ. of Minnesota, 1983) and in T. A. Mitchell, *David Hume's Anti-theistic Views* (Univ. Press of America, 1986). Margaret C. Jacob, *The Radical Enlightenment* (Allen and Unwin, 1981) also deals with religion, along with republicanism and the prevailing radical influence of Free Masonry in the eighteenth century.

For the French economic assault upon absolutism, see Elizabeth Fox-Genovese, *The Origins of Physiocracy* (Cornell Univ., 1976) and Henry Higgs, *The Physiocrats* (Kelley, 1989). Adam Smith's significance is analyzed in R. H. Campbell, *Adam Smith* (St. Martin's, 1985); R. Lamb, *Property, Markets, and the State in Adam Smith's System* (Garland, 1987); and Maurice Brown, *Adam Smith's Economics: Its Place in the Development of Economic Thought* (Routledge Chapman and Hall, 1988). See also Michael Perelman, *Classical Political Economy* (Rowman and Allanhild, 1983) and Karl Pribram, *A History of Economic Reasoning* (Johns Hopkins Univ., 1983).

For Locke's political theory, see John Dunn, *The Political Thought of John Locke* (Cambridge Univ., 1983); Ruth W. Grant, *John Locke's Liberalism* (Univ. of Chicago., 1987); and James Tully, *A Discourse on Property: John Locke and His Adversaries* (Cambridge Univ., 1980). Other examples of conservative liberalism may be seen in Thomas L. Pangle, *Montesquieu's Philosophy of Liberalism* (Univ. of Chicago, 1989) and Peter Gay, *Voltaire's Politics*, 2nd ed. (Yale Univ., 1988). For the radical liberal movement, see Donald Harvey Meyer, *The Democratic Enlightenment* (Putnam's, 1975); Jack Fruchtman, *The Apacalyptic Politics of Richard Price and Joseph Priestley* (American Philosophical Society, 1983); and Nancy L. Rosenblum, *Bentham's Theory of the Modern State* (Harvard Univ., 1978).

On Rousseau as a political thinker, see Ramon M. Lemos, *Rousseau's Political Philosophy* (Cornell Univ., 1976) and R. Wokler, *Social Thought of J. J. Rousseau* (Garland, 1987). Rousseau's ambiguous views on democracy are given special attention in James Miller, *Rousseau, Dreamer of Democracy* (Yale Univ., 1984); John B. Noone, *Rousseau's Social Contract* (Univ. of Georgia, 1980); and P. Coleman, *Rousseau's Political Imagination* (Droz, 1984).

The radical Enlightenment produced a trickle of feminism, which is described in the following works: Ruth Perry, *The Celebrated Mary Astell* (Univ. of Chicago, 1986); Alice Browne, *The Eighteenth-Century Feminist Mind* (Wayne State Univ., 1987); and Moira Fergusun and Janet Todd, *Mary Wollstonecraft* (Twayne, 1984).

Kant's reinterpretation of the Enlightenment is thoroughly covered in Ernest Cassirer, *Kant's Life and Thought* (Yale Univ., 1981). See also A. V. Gulyga, *Immanuel Kant* (Kirkhauser, 1988). For special emphases on aspects of Kant's thought, see Robert Hahn, *Kant's Newtonian Revolution in Philosophy* (St. Martin's, 1988); H. E. Allison, *Kant's Transcendental Idealism* (Yale Univ., 1986); Gordon C. Brittan, *Kant's Theory of Science* (Princeton Univ., 1978); James Booth, *Interpreting the World: Kant's Philosophy of History and Politics* (Univ. of Toronto, 1987); and H. L. Williams, *Kant's Political Philosophy* (St. Martin's, 1986).

David Sherman Lovejoy, *Religious Enthusiasm and the Great Awakening* (Prentice-Hall, 1969) captures the spirit of pietism and religious humanitarianism. Among recent works on Methodism, two excellent ones are V. H. Green, *John Wesley* (Univ. Press of America, 1987) and T. E. Dowley, *Through Wesley's England* (Abingdon, 1988). See also Samuel J. Rogal, *John and Charles Wesley* (Twayne, 1983) Stanley E. Ayling, *John Wesley* (Collins, 1979); and Frank Baker, *John Wesley and the Church of England* (Abingdon, 1970). John Charles Pollock, *Wilberforce* (St. Martin's, 1978) is an excellent recent biography of the great English emancipator.

Notes

1. Carl L. Becker, *The Heavenly City of the Eighteenth-Century Philosophers* (New Haven: Yale University Press, 1932), pp. 49, 129.
2. René Descartes, *Discourse on Method* (New York: Liberal Arts Press, 1956), pp. 20–26.
3. Francis Bacon, *Novum Organum* (London: William Pickering, 1844), pp. 13–17, 84–89.
4. Quoted in Stillman Drake, *Galileo at Work* (Chicago: University of Chicago Press, 1978), p. 41.
5. Quoted in G. K. Anderson and W. E. Buckler, eds., *The Literature of England*, 2 vols. (Glenview, IL: Scott, Foresman, 1958), vol. 1, p. 1568.
6. Jean Jacques Rousseau, *The Social Contract*, trans. by W. Kendall, (Chicago: Henry Regnery Co., 1954), p. 2.
7. Adam Smith, *Selections From the Wealth of Nations* (Chicago: Henry Regnery Co., 1953), p. 12.
8. See John Locke, *Second Essay on Civil Government* (Chicago: Henry Regnery, 1955), pp. 2, 63–65, 71, 127–128, 154–170; Baron de Montesquieu, *The Spirit of Laws* (New York: Hafner Publishing, 1949), pp. 151–158.
9. Jean-Jacqes Rousseau, *A Discourse on Political Economy* (Chicago: Henry Regnery, 1949), pp. 118–119; and Jean-Jacques Rousseau, *The Social Contract* (Chicago: Henry Regnery, 1954), pp. 19–20, 24–25, 39.
10. See Immanuel Kant, *The Critique of Pure Reason* (New York: Collier, 1902.)

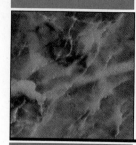

Chapter 21

The Rights of Man

Revolution in the Western World

The last four decades of the eighteenth century marked a decisive turning point in the history of Western Civilization. Before 1760, divine-right monarchy and aristocratic society were accepted as normal; after 1800, ever-stronger voices would speak for civil liberties and constitutions—political concepts that are basic to modern societies. The intervening era had seen a fundamental revolution in thought and political life.

This age of revolution was nevertheless a culmination of earlier trends. As we have seen, developing European capitalism, expanding population, growing cities, and a rising middle class had partially undermined traditional monarchies by 1750. The Enlightenment, particularly its more radical variation, was also approaching maturity. Each of these trends—economic, social, and intellectual—converged when colonial conflicts were plaguing the Western maritime states. The American Revolution, resulting from one such conflict, was first. It encouraged a much more comprehensive French upheaval, which had been brewing for more than a century. These were but the two most dramatic examples of the resulting revolutionary wave that rolled over much of western Europe and America during the late 1700s.

The American and French revolutions provided later generations with a new set of values. The two heroic struggles critically weakened the Old Regime, identifying freedom with progress in the popular mind and projecting democracy, as well as emotional nationalism, into the nineteenth century. For most Western societies before World War I, the revolutions provided a special heritage. This was particularly true for Americans, whose liberal ideals were deeply rooted in the developing traditions of a new land and assimilated in the folklore of a popular culture. Even in Europe and the rest of the world, however, the revolutionary dream of human liberty has lingered into the twentieth century, notably among the emerging nations of Asia and Africa.

Unfortunately, the revolutionary ideals were not all realized in their own time. The rights of "all men," proclaimed with such solemn dignity in 1776 and repeated with ringing appeal in 1789, were denied to women and most black people, many of whom had fought and died for liberty. This omission would have to be corrected later, at the price of great strife and hardship.

The Background of Revolution

Eighteenth-century revolutions can be explained by two sets of circumstances in their past. One of these was the momentous social change that outmoded institutions, disrupted traditional ways of life, and brought hardships or injustices. Such conditions became especially prevalent after the Seven Years' War in the 1760s. A second source of revolution can be found in ideas, some recently generated by the Enlightenment, and others, even older, derived from English precedents.

English Precedents

Eighteenth-century revolutionaries looked back with respect to the 1640s, when the English Parliament, after struggling to maintain its rights through two reigns, fought a civil war, executed a king, and established a republic. For one brief period, revolutionary soldiers had even proclaimed a democratic system, guaranteed by a written constitution. Although this effort failed and the republic ultimately produced an unpopular dictatorship, it could never destroy the traditional popular ideal of limited monarchy, functioning in cooperation with a representative Parliament.

After the monarchy was restored in 1660, Parliament continued its struggle against the last two Stuart kings. The Whig opposition party in Parliament forced the resignation of Charles II's first minister, imprisoned the second, excluded the king's Catholic supporters from public office, and provided individuals with legal security against arbitrary arrest and imprisonment. Such actions forced Charles to dismiss four Parliaments and face a serious political crisis during the last years of his reign. James II, who succeeded his brother in 1685, dismissed Parliament and attempted to rule as a despot, using a standing army, largely commanded by Catholics. His actions caused such universal opposition that James was forced to call a new Parliament, which he tried to pack with his supporters, but local officials would not cooperate. Finally, when his wife gave birth to a prince, who was widely regarded as a potential Catholic king, parliamentary leaders offered the English crown to William of Orange, the Protestant stadtholder of the Netherlands and husband of Mary, one of James' Protestant daughters by an earlier marriage.

William and his Dutch army, welcomed as deliverers, soon effected the so-called Glorious Revolution of 1688, and James fled to exile in France. Because he needed English support for his war with France, William was ready to accept Parliament's conditions, enacted as the famous "Bill of Rights." This declaration provided that

1. the king could not suspend laws.

2. no taxes would be levied or standing army maintained in peacetime without the consent of Parliament.

3. sessions of Parliament would be held frequently.

4. freedom of speech in Parliament would be assured.

5. subjects would have the right of petition and be free of excessive fines, bail, or cruel punishments.

6. the king would be a Protestant.

This document has exerted tremendous influence on developing constitutional governments, an influence that is seen in the first ten amendments to the U.S. Constitution.

Other parliamentary acts supplemented the Bill of Rights and consolidated the Revolution. In 1689, the Mutiny Act required parliamentary approval for extending martial law more than one year. Although Catholics were subjected to harsh new restrictions and non-Anglican Protestants were still excluded from public office, the Toleration Act (1689) gave all Protestants freedom of worship. In 1693, when Parliament failed to renew the customary Licensing Act, the country achieved practical freedom of the press. Finally, in the Act of Settlement in 1701, Parliament prescribed a Protestant succession to the throne and barred the monarch from declaring war, removing judges, or even leaving the country without parliamentary consent.

The Glorious Revolution permanently limited the English monarchy, guaranteed important legal rights, and helped popularize the ideal, if not the practice, of popular sovereignty. For these reasons it provided a model for Locke and hope for Voltaire and Montesquieu. In many respects, however, it was neither glorious nor revolutionary; it certainly did not establish democracy, for the country after 1688 continued to be governed by a minority of merchants and landowners.

Their control during the eighteenth century was exercised through the developing cabinet system. The first two Hanoverian kings, George I (1714–1727) and George II (1727–1760) were so ignorant of the English language and politics that they had to rely on chief advisors (prime ministers), who could maintain support in Parliament. Sir Robert Walpole (1676–1745) first held this post, managing a Whig political machine. Walpole insisted that the entire ministry (cabinet) should act as a body; single members who could not agree were expected to resign. Later, he learned the practicality of resigning with his whole cabinet, when he could not command a parliamentary majority. This pragmatically developed system of cabinet government and ministerial responsibility provided the constitutional machinery needed to apply the principles of 1689, permitting Parliament to assert its supremacy and still avoid awkward conflicts with royal authority.

Behind the cabinet was Parliament and behind Parliament was a tight aristocratic organization. Membership in the House of Commons after 1711 was confined to those with high incomes from land. It represented an electorate of about 6000 voters. Two representatives were elected from each county by the lesser freeholders, but most of these seats were filled by arrangements among the great land-owning families. Of more than 400 members from the boroughs, or towns, most were named by prominent political bosses. The Duke of Newcastle, for example, held estates in twelve counties, was Lord Lieutenant of three, and literally owned seven other seats in Commons. The system that filled the seats also determined votes in Parliament. Here the bases of loyalty were public offices, army commissions, and appointments in the church. Local magnates extracted all manner of concessions from the king's ministers, who framed policies in accordance with the system. English politics, which had been so dynamic in the 1600s, thus became stagnant by the end of George II's reign.

Conditions Favoring Revolution After 1760

While the English parliamentary system became increasingly conservative in the eighteenth century, converging economic, social, and intellectual forces pointed in an opposite direction. Sugar and slavery were transforming the European and American economies, encouraging the growth of cities and expanding populations. At the same time, the Enlightenment, with its emphasis upon reason and utopian expectations of progress, was reaching full maturity. Finally, and most importantly for the immediate future, the costs of imperial competition created serious problems for European maritime states. The most obvious source of such problems was the great Anglo-French colonial war, which ended with the Peace of Paris in 1763. The war left both France and Britain burdened with unprecedented debts. Since the international financial system was centered in the Netherlands, Dutch neutrality aroused more tensions. In addition, the elimination of a common French enemy in Canada generated new frictions between Britain and the American colonies. As the greatest world empire, Britain was suspicious of all its neighbors, particularly France. The fear was justified, because France, recently stripped of possessions in Canada and India, was determined on humbling Britain, not only to satisfy French pride but also to accommodate an expanding economy. Large objectives but limited resources encouraged the French and British governments, as well as other states such as Austria, to tighten administration and raise taxes. These policies naturally encouraged popular unrest.

Alignment with Britain after 1689 caused difficulties for the Dutch, whose trade in the eighteenth century declined while that of Britain increased. This ultimately forced the Dutch economy to specialize in financing foreign state debts, a policy which tied the Netherlands closer to Britain and increased the threat of French invasion. When this conflict actually occurred in the 1740s, the Dutch lower middle classes demanded better relations with France; in 1747, they even attempted revolution. The situation not only caused agitation in the Netherlands but also encouraged British and French meddling in Dutch internal politics.

A continuing French aggressive foreign policy against Britain after 1763 was a flagrant refusal to face fiscal realities and therefore a direct contribution to impending revolution. The steadily mounting French debt after 1740 reached a point in the 1760s when taxes failed to meet even the interest payments. Dutch bankers were reluctant to provide new loans because of declining French credit and the close official ties between the Netherlands and Britain. In 1769, following a struggle with the nobles in the provincial courts, Louis XV abandoned tax reform, which might have shifted more revenue burdens to the French upper classes. The country was thus almost bankrupt when it entered war against England on the side of the American colonies, a venture that led to the complete breakdown of French finances in the 1780s.

Britain faced similar problems. With a debt in 1763 roughly double that of 1756, the government had to manage an empire that had tripled

Purchasing a Seat in the Unreformed English Parliament

These selections are from the letters of Lord Chesterfield (1767) and the *Memoirs* of Sir Samuel Romilly (1807).

Bath, December 19, 1767.

My Dear Friend,

. . . In one of our conversations here, this time twelvemonth, I desired him to secure you a seat in the new Parliament; he assured me he would; and, I am convinced, very sincerely; he said even that he would make it his own affair; and desired I would give myself no more trouble about it. Since that, I have heard no more of it; which made me look out for some venal borough: and I spoke to a borough-jobber, and offered five-and-twenty hundred pounds for a secure seat in Parliament; but he laughed at my offer, and said, that there was no such thing as a borough to be had now; for that the rich East and West Indians had secured them all, at the rate of three thousand pounds at least; but many at four thousand; and two or three, that he knew, at five thousand. This, I confess, has vexed me a good deal; and made me the more impatient to know whether Lord Chatham had done anything in it; which I shall know when I go to town, as I propose to do in about a fortnight; and, as soon as I know it, you shall. To tell you truly what I think—I doubt, from all these *nervous disorders*, that Lord Chatham is *hors de combat*, as a Minister; but do not even hint this to anybody. God bless you!

(Signed) Chesterfield.

[June 27th, 1807.] I shall procure myself a seat in the new Parliament, unless I find that it will cost so large a sum, as, in the state of my family, it would be very imprudent for me to devote to such an object, which I find is very likely to be the case. Tierney, who manages this business for the friends of the late administration, assures me that he can hear of no seats to be disposed of. After a Parliament which has lived little more than four months, one would naturally suppose, that those seats which are regularly sold by the proprietors of them would be very cheap; they are, however, in fact, sold now at a higher price than was ever given for them before. Tierney tells me that he has offered £10,000 for the two seats of Westbury, the property of the late Lord Abingdon, and which are to be made the most of by trustees for creditors, and has met with a refusal. £6000 and £5500 have been given for seats with no stipulation as to time, or against the event of a speedy dissolution by the King's death, or by any change of administration. The truth is, that the new Ministers have bought up all the seats that were to be disposed of, and at any prices. . . .

This buying of seats is detestable; and yet it is almost the way in which one in my situation, who is resolved to be an independent man, can get into Parliament. To come in by a popular election, in the present state of the representation, is quite impossible; to be placed there by some great lord, and to vote as he shall direct, is to be in a state of complete dependence; and nothing hardly remains but to owe a seat to the sacrifice of a part of one's fortune. It is true that many men who buy seats, do it as a matter of pecuniary speculation, as a profitable way of employing their money: they carry on a political trade; they buy their seats, and sell their votes. For myself, I can truly say that, by giving money for a seat, I shall make a sacrifice of my private property, merely that I may be enabled to serve the public. I know what danger there is of men's disguising from themselves the real motives of their actions; but it really does appear to me that it is from this motive alone that I act. . . .

Source: Elizabeth K. Kendall, ed., *A Source-Book of English History* (London: The Macmillan Company, 1912), pp. 302–305.

in size during those same years. The cost of administering the North American colonies alone rose to £135,000 a year in 1763—five times what it had cost in 1756. Colonials were determined to resist new taxation and were intent on occupying western lands held by former Indian allies of the French. The tribes were restless and difficult to pacify since many had fought on both sides and did not know what to expect from British rule; Pontiac's rebellion, between 1763 and 1766, kept the northwestern colonial frontier in a state of near-anarchy. Restoring order to this vast land promised to be a long and expensive process, involving many differences between the crown and its colonial subjects.

At the same time, the new king, George III (1760–1820), was causing a stir in English politics. He alienated many commercial and colonial interests by opposing an aggressive policy toward France. Moreover, he demonstrated a determined intention of wielding constitutional powers never claimed by his Hanoverian predecessors, who had been virtual captives of Whig politicians. It took George only a few years to destroy the power of the Whigs and gain control of Parliament. His ministers accomplished this by means of lavish bribery and patronage, using methods developed earlier by Walpole. By 1770, they had filled the House of Commons with their supporters, known as "the King's Friends." For twelve years, George was the effective head of government, but his policies made enemies and produced a determined opposition party.

Parliamentary opposition merged with popular agitation in the person of John Wilkes (1725–1797), a wealthy member of the Commons and publisher of a newspaper, *The North Briton.* Wilkes became an outspoken critic of the king's policies. When he was imprisoned by the government, Wilkes posed as the champion of civil liberties, becoming overnight the darling of the London populace; but despite preliminary victories in court, he was ultimately forced into exile. Returning from France in 1768, he was again elected to the Commons, again thrown into jail, and again became the center of a great public clamor. For a while, in the early 1770s, England experienced a mild threat of revolution, as people were killed in clashes between protestors and government troops.

This trouble at home was less serious, in the long run, than that provoked in the American colonies. George Grenville (1712–1770), the king's chief minister after 1763, devised a comprehensive plan to settle problems in North America. He forbade colonial settlement beyond the Appalachians, put Indian affairs under English superintendents, established permanent garrisons of English troops for maintenance of order on the frontiers, issued orders against smuggling, sent an English fleet to American waters, assigned English customs officials to American ports, and had Parliament impose new taxes on the colonies. The Sugar Act of 1764 increased duties on sugar, wines, coffee, silk, and linens. The Stamp Act of 1765 required that government stamps be placed on practically every kind of American document, from college diplomas to newspapers. Grenville's program aroused an almost universal colonial protest, immediately allied in spirit with Wilkes' movement in England.

In response to the Stamp Act, colonial assemblies passed resolutions and sent petitions to the king and Parliament protesting the new measure. In the streets the reaction was one of violent protests, riots, and mob actions.

The American Revolution

Within a decade after passage of the Stamp Act, Britain faced open rebellion in its American colonies. The resulting conflict was also a civil war, with many colonists remaining loyal to the crown. Indeed, one of Benjamin Franklin's sons was a Loyalist leader and the last royal governor of New Jersey. But a majority of the colonists, whether New England merchants, Pennsylvania farmers, or Virginia planters, formed a united opposition. Their outlook, combining Locke's political ideas with a spirit of rough frontier independence, was also nationalistic in its dawning awareness tht many English ways were foreign to American needs and values.

A Revolution in Minds and Hearts

John Adams (1735–1826), looking back on the Revolution, was well aware of this developing American nationalism when he wrote in 1818:

> But what do we mean by the American Revolution? Do we mean the American war? The Revolution was effected before the war commenced . . . in the minds and hearts of the people . . . This . . . was the real American Revolution.[1]

From almost the beginning, the American colonies had developed in a direction different from England's. Most Puritan settlers in New England opposed the Stuart kings; hundreds went to fight against Charles I in the 1640s. At the restoration of Charles II, rebels fled again to America. Catholics, who had been favored by the later Stuarts, were persecuted at home after the Glorious Revolution, and many came to the colonies, particularly to Maryland. By 1775, 40 percent of the colonial population had descended from non-English stock, mostly from Ireland and southern Germany. The resulting cultural mix fostered more toleration for differences than was typical of any place in Europe.

Experience in self-government conditioned colonial development. Except for an unsuccessful attempt under James II, England had allowed the colonies relative freedom in conducting their own affairs. This was particularly true during the early eighteenth century, under the corrupt and static Whig oligarchy. Radical political opinion, driven deep underground in England after 1649, ran much nearer the surface in America. Educated colonists remembered Locke's emphasis on the social contract and the right of revolution. These ideas appealed to people who had created their own governments in the wilderness and who were somewhat suspicious of a distant king. In contrast, the ruling Whig politicians forgot Locke's revolutionary implications as they gained power and became proponents of stability.

Colonial political thought was shaped as much by growth as by circumstances, as over 2 million discontented Europeans arrived in the eighteenth century. The Irish and Scotch-Irish, who pushed the frontier to the Appalachians, settled on free or cheap western land. Its easy availability popularized the idea that property was each individual's birthright. Grenville's restriction on westward migration after 1763 therefore aroused much colonial resentment. His policy was generally interpreted as an English effort to monopolize land for a privileged aristocracy. Land speculators, in condemning the English land policy by appealing to free enterprise, found common interests with craftsmen, merchants, and planters, who felt themselves exploited by trade restrictions and credit controls. Expanding American enterprises and profits could not be easily accommodated within British mercantilism.

The peace of 1763, followed by the Grenville program, brought all the major differences between Britain and the colonies into focus. With the French and Spanish out of Canada and Florida, colonists felt little need for British protection while yearning to settle the new lands. They were naturally angered by new taxes and controls over trade, which were required by the rising costs of the new stabilization program. British troops, under these circumstances, were regarded as oppressors rather than defenders or peacekeepers. The changes in British imperial policy came at just the time when they were least likely to be successful.

Confrontation, War, and Independence

Between 1763 and 1775, relations between England and the colonies grew steadily worse, eventually erupting into open hostilities. Neither the king's government nor the colonists had foreseen or planned this result. The few American radicals who may have dreamed of a new political order did not advocate such ideas in this period, when most Americans wanted reforms to restore rights and redress grievances within the British system. The idea of an open break—of war and revolution—became acceptable only as reform efforts failed.

The first colonial protests came with the Grenville program, when the Sugar Act sparked outcries against "taxation without representation" in colonial newspapers and pamphlets. These reactions were mild, however, in comparison with those following the Stamp Act. Colonial assemblies in Massachusetts and New York denounced the law as "tyranny," and a "Stamp Act Congress" meeting in New York petitioned the king to repeal the law. Mob actions occurred in a number of places, but they were less effective than boycotts of English goods, imposed by a thousand colonial merchants. Soon hundreds of British tradesmen were petitioning Parliament, pleading that the taxes be rescinded. This was done in 1766, although Parliament issued a declaration affirming its absolute right to legislate for the colonies.

Having repealed the Stamp Act, Parliament almost immediately enacted other revenue measures. Charles Townshend (1725–1767), chancellor of the exchequer in the next cabinet, had Parliament levy duties on paint, paper, lead, wine, and tea imported into the colonies from Britain. The returns were to pay colonial governors and maintain troops garrisoned in America. Other laws established admiralty courts at Halifax, Boston, Philadelphia, and Charleston, to sit without juries and enforce trade regulations. The decisions of these courts soon generated popular agitation. In Boston, this culminated on March 5, 1770, when soldiers fired into an unruly crowd, killing five people. Meanwhile, American merchants had entered nonimportation agreements that cut British imports by 50 percent. Again, commercial losses induced Parliament to repeal most of the duties, on the very day of the Boston massacre.

For a while, the colonies appeared angry but pacified, until Lord North (1732–1792), the king's new chief minister, blundered into another

Outrage over the Boston Massacre was fanned by propaganda like this etching by Paul Revere, which shows British redcoats firing on unarmed colonial citizens. Revere's view of the incident strayed from the truth.

crisis. He persuaded Parliament to grant a two-thirds cut in duties on East India Company tea delivered to American ports. Because the Company could thus undersell smugglers and legitimate traders, both of these groups quickly converted to political radicalism. The tea was turned away from most American ports. In Boston, at the famous tea party, townsmen in Indian garb dumped the tea into the harbor. The English government retaliated in the "Intolerable Acts," by closing the port of Boston, revoking the Massachusetts Charter, and providing that political offenders be tried in England.

By September 1794, the crisis in Boston had created a revolutionary climate. Representatives of twelve colonies, meeting in the First Continental Congress at Philadelphia, denounced British tyranny, proclaimed political representation to be a natural right, and made plans for armed resistance. By the next April, the explosive situation around Boston had led to a conflict between British regulars and the Massachusetts militia. In battles at Lexington and Concord, near Boston, 8 Americans and 293 British soldiers were killed. Those shots "heard 'round the world" marked the beginning of the American Revolution.

The war begun at Lexington and Concord lasted eight years. At first, the American cause appeared almost hopeless, because the king's government was not inclined to compromise, wishing to make an example of the rebels. The prospect encouraged radical colonial leaders to fight on desperately. It was a time, as Thomas Paine wrote, "to try men's souls,"[2] but it was also a time for dreams of new liberties, new opportunities, and a new social justice that might come with independence.

The turning point of the war came in October 1777. Already occupying New York and Philadelphia, the British attempted to split the colonies by moving an army south from Canada. This army was forced to surrender after suffering a crushing defeat at Saratoga in upper New York. France, which had been cautiously helping the Americans, then signed an alliance guaranteeing American independence. Ultimately, the French persuaded their Spanish ally to enter the war. The Dutch also joined the alliance in a desperate effort to save their American trade. With their sea power effectively countered, the British pulled their two main armies back to defensive positions in New York and on the Virginia coast. In the final campaigns of 1781, French and American troops, aided by the French fleet, forced the surrender of British commander Lord Cornwallis (1738–1805) to George Washington (1732–1799) at Yorktown in Virginia.

While the war continued, American radicals were creating a new nation. Thomas Paine's *Common Sense*, published early in 1776 as a spirited plea for liberty, heavily influenced popular opinion and helped convince the American Congress to break with England. In June, a special Congressional Committee drafted a formal statement of principles. The resulting Declaration of Independence, written by Thomas Jefferson, first announced the creation of the United States. In claiming for every individual "certain inalienable rights . . . to life, liberty, and the pursuit of happiness,"[3] it embodied typical radical appeals to natural law and the social contract.

Similar radical political principles, drawn from the Enlightenment, were espoused in the Articles of Confederation. This document, completed by the Congress in 1778 and ratified by the states three years later, established the new government as a loose league, much like the Dutch Republic. Taxation, control of trade, and issuance of money were all left to the sovereign states, each represented by one vote in Congress. Major decisions required the assent of nine states; amendments to the Articles had to be accepted by the states unanimously. Although Congress could make war and peace, maintain armies, and conduct Indian affairs, it was financially dependent on the states for these functions. The system was designed to protect liberties against a distant central government, dominated by the wealthy.

More obvious demonstrations of radical principles were provided by the new states, which were the real centers of political power. Their constitutions, often ratified in town meetings, manifested Locke's and Montesquieu's ideas concerning the separation of executive, judicial, and legislative function. "Bills of rights" typically guaranteed freedom of speech, press, and religion. Eleven of the thirteen states provided for separation of church and state. Many great loyalist estates were divided into small holdings, and property qualifications for voting were considerably lowered. These were but a few indications of applied radicalism during the war years.

The Conservative Reaction and the American Constitution

After the war ended in 1783, the Articles of Confederation provoked a strong conservative reaction. Some merchants wanted to send their goods to English ports. Others wanted a common stable currency and tariff protection against foreign goods. Wealthy people were frightened by popular uprisings, such as Shays' Rebellion in Massachusetts, and by inflation, caused by state issues of cheap paper currency. Moved by such concerns, prominent conservatives urged a reconsideration of the Articles. Their efforts led to the Constitutional Convention, which met at Philadelphia from May to September 1787. Since radicals, such as Patrick Henry (1736–1799), refused to attend the convention, delegates were united by their concerns for protecting property and maintaining order. Led by George Washington, Alexander Hamilton (1757–1804), Benjamin Franklin (1706–1790), James Madison (1751–1836), and Charles Pinckney (1746–1825), they successfully compromised differences between large and small states, as well as those between mercantile New England and the plantation south. In the end, they succeeded in producing a document that strengthened the national government.

Despite the conservative views of its drafters, the Constitution affirmed some popular principles. It limited the autonomy of public officials, delegated specific powers to the states, and provided for state participation in the amending process. It thus retained some of the states' rights which were so important to the radicals.

The separation of powers was another fundamental principle of the Constitution. It was also revealed in the Constitution's careful definition of the functions ascribed to the legislative, judicial, and executive brances of government. Congress was to make the laws, the president was to apply and enforce them, and the courts were to interpret them. Other provisions prevented any one of the branches from becoming too independent and powerful. The president, for example, could veto laws passed by Congress, but the legislature, by a two-thirds vote, could override a presidential veto. The Supreme Court later expanded its original charge of interpreting laws to interpreting the Constitution itself, thus acquiring the right to declare any law void as unconstitutional.

In recognizing the principle of popular sovereignty, the Constitution was similar to the Articles; it differed in its centralization of government and in its securities against disorder. Proclaiming itself as the supreme law of the land, it specifically prohibited the states from coining money, levying customs, or conducting foreign diplomacy. The president, as chief executive, commanded national military forces, an arrangement meant to protect against popular unrest and disorder. Most of the delegates at Philadelphia feared democracy and favored property qualifications on the franchise, a policy they abandoned only because it was politically impractical. They indicated their distrust of democracy, however, by avoiding the direct election of senators and presidents.

The process of ratifying the Constitution precipitated a great political debate. Congress, dominated by conservatives, ignored the amending provisions of the Articles and appealed directly to the states. Radicals everywhere were alarmed but were generally overwhelmed by arguments from the wealthier, more articulate, and better educated Federalists, who supported the Constitution. By promising written guarantees of individual liberties, the Federalists ultimately won the required nine states and the Constitution was formally adopted on July 2, 1788. Three years later, the first ten amendments guaranteed freedom of religion, speech, and the press, along with security against arbitrary government. Thus the radicals left a lasting legacy, despite the Federalist triumph.

After winning their greatest victory, the Federalists dominated American politics for more than a decade. George Washington was elected as the first president in 1789. His two administrations imposed a high tariff, chartered a national bank, paid public debts at face value, negotiated a commercial treaty with England, and opposed the French Revolution, which began in the year of Washington's election. Ironically, some French revolutionaries, such as Lafayette, who had helped win American independence, were bitterly denounced by American leaders a decade later.

Unfinished Business of the American Revolution

The war for American rights and liberties left much unfinished business. The right to vote did not extend to all male citizens for decades, until changes were made in state constitutions, particularly in the developing western states. An even more flagrant omission involved blacks and women, who were denied freedom and full civil equality after the Revolution, despite their many contributions to the American cause.

Many women helped promote the Revolution. A few, like Mercy Warren, wrote anti-British plays and pamphlets; some published newspapers; and others organized boycotts against British goods. Female patriots in Philadelphia, including Benjamin Franklin's daughter, raised funds to buy shirts for Washington's troops. Women were often involved in dangerous exploits as spies and couriers. Seventeen-year-old Emily Geiger of South Carolina ate the message she was carrying to General Nathanael Green when she was captured by the British. She later delivered it verbally, after riding a hundred miles.

The Franchise Issue in the American Constitutional Convention

Excerpts from the debate here reported arose from a motion to place a property qualification on voting in the Constitution. The proposal failed, leaving authority to decide this question with the states.

Mr. GOUVENEUR MORRIS. He had long learned not to be the dupe of words. The sound of aristocracy, therefore, had no effect on him. It was the thing, not the name, to which he was opposed, and one of his principal objections to the Constitution as it is now before us, is that it threatens this country with an aristocracy. The aristocracy will grow out of the House of Representatives. Give the votes to people who have no property, and they will sell them to the rich who will be able to buy them. We should not confine our attention to the present moment. The time is not distant when this country will abound with mechanics and manufacturers who will receive their bread from their employers. Will such men be the secure and faithful guardians of liberty? Will they be the impregnable barrier against aristocracy? He was as little duped by the association of the words 'taxation and representation'. The man who does not give his vote freely is not represented. It is the man who dictates the vote. . . .

Col. MASON. . . . The true idea in his opinion was that every man having evidence of attachment to and permanent common interest with the society ought to share in all its rights and privileges. . . .

Mr. MADISON. The right of suffrage is certainly one of the fundamental articles of republican government, and ought not to be left to be regulated by the Legislature. A gradual abridgement of this right has been the mode in which aristocracies have been built on the ruins of popular forms. . . . In future times a great majority of the people will not only be without landed, but any other sort of, property. These will either combine under the influence of their common situation; in which case, the rights of property and the public liberty will not be secure in their hands: or what is more probable, they will become the tools of opulence and ambition, in which case there will be equal danger on another side. . . .

Dr. FRANKLIN. It is of great consequence that we should not depress the virtue and public spirit of our common people; of which they displayed a great deal during the war, and which contributed principally to the favorable issue of it. . . . He did not think that the elected had any right in any case to narrow the privileges of the electors. He quoted as arbitrary the British statute setting forth the danger of tumultuous meetings, and under that pretext narrowing the right of suffrage to persons having freeholds of a certain value. . . .

Mr. MERCER [Md.]. . . . He objected to the footing on which the qualification was put, but particularly to the mode of election by the people. The people can not know and judge of the characters of candidates. The worse possible choice will be made.

Source: Samuel E. Morison, ed., *Sources and Documents Illustrating the American Revolution* (Oxford, England: Clarendon Press, 1929), pp. 276–278.

In addition to those who stayed home, some 20,000 women moved with the armies. Many were wives of Continental common soldiers, who marched on foot behind the troops, carrying their baggage and their children. In camp, they cooked, washed, and cared for their men, sometimes foraging after battles among enemy dead for clothing and ammunition. A few saw combat, like the legendary Mary Hayes (Molly Pitcher) and Margaret Corbin, who continued to fire their husbands' artillery pieces after the men fell in battles at Fort Washington (1776) and Monmouth

(1778). Corbin's husband was killed, and she was severely wounded in the arm and chest. The most famous female fighter in the Revolution was Deborah Sampson, an orphaned Connecticut schoolteacher, who donned men's clothes and served for more than a year in Washington's army, before she was discovered and honorably discharged.

Despite their sacrifices, American women gained few immediate improvements. They remained legally subordinated to their husbands in the disposition of property and practically denied the possibility of divorce. Reacting against these conditions, Abigail Adams and Mercy Warren both urged their husbands to promote legal and political equality for women during the Revolution. For a while, a mild feminism was publicly expressed. The New Jersey constitution of 1776 gave women the vote, and the same state's election law of 1790 permitted local boards to enfranchise women. But general indifference to the nascent women's movement led the New Jersey legislature to end female suffrage in 1807.

The conservative reaction was even stronger against blacks, who provided a major problem to leaders of the Revolution. Although slavery was already losing its practical value, it was still important in the southern plantation economy. Moreover, free northern blacks, including several hundred around Boston, were already becoming politically conscious. To many slaveholders, the situation promised violent black rebellion.

In response to this fear, blacks were at first banned from military service, despite the embarrassing facts that many free blacks had supported the Stamp Act protest. But when the British promised freedom to slave recruits and the supply of white American volunteers dwindled, Congress began enlisting blacks, promising slaves their freedom. Even before they could be legally recruited, black soldiers fought at Lexington, Concord, and Bunker Hill, and they participated in every major battle afterward. They also served at sea, even on Virginia ships; but they were never admitted to the Virginia militia or to any military forces of Georgia and the Carolinas, although a contingent of Santo Domingo blacks under French command fought the British at Savannah. The southern adherence to slavery divided the new country, providing a major controversial issue at the Constitutional Convention.

Outside of the Deep South, a strong black emancipation movement developed during and immediately after the Revolutionary era. While more than 100,000 former slaves escaped to Canada, to the Indians, or to British sanctuary ships, many blacks, both free and slave, exploited the rhetoric of the Revolution to petition for their freedom and equality. Such petitions were supported by a growing number of white dissidents among Quakers and political activists, such as James Otis (1724–1783), Thomas Paine, Benjamin Rush (1745–1813), and Benjamin Franklin. In response, every state limited or abolished the slave trade; many owners, even in the south, freed their slaves; six state constitutions (Vermont, Connecticut, Rhode Island, Pennsylvania, New York, and New Jersey) abolished slavery; and practical legal emancipation was achieved in New Hampshire and Massachusetts. Free Massachusetts blacks won the vote in 1783, a precedent slowly adopted by other free states.

Such gains, however, were offset by losses. Many blacks who had been promised their freedom were enslaved by their former masters and even by their new British friends. Laws against slavery were not always enforced. Even in the northern states, emancipation was often legally delayed for decades, so that in 1810 there were more than 35,000 slaves in New York, New Jersey, and Pennsylvania. The conservative reaction of the 1790s, stimulated by debates in the Constitutional Convention, and the invention of the cotton gin, which gave a new impetus to cotton planting, confirmed the south in its economic and emotional commitments to slavery. American slaves after the 1790s were further from "the rights of all men" than they had been before the Revolution. This injustice was the ultimate cause for a subsequent bloody and tragic civil war.

Impact of the American Revolution Abroad

Even with its shortcomings, the American Revolution exerted a tremendous influence elsewhere in the world. Americans were generally regarded as having returned to a "state of nature" and then established a new government by a written social contract. As their republic promised freedom, maintained order, and achieved moderate prosperity, it seemed to validate the principles of the Enlightenment for literate peoples of western Europe, generating a wave of revolutionary sentiment, from Ireland to Hungary.

The trend was evident, even in England. Before the Revolution, a number of influential Englishmen, notably Edmund Burke (1729–1797), championed the American cause in Parliament and English radical reformers, like Major John Cartwright (1740–1824), welcomed American independence. Pro-American enthusiasm languished after the war began, but it revived when American fortunes improved after Saratoga. In 1779, reform societies sprang up in London and in rural Yorkshire. The more radical London society grew into a National Association, with delegates drawn from county organizations, imitating the American town meetings, state conventions, and Congress. The Association welcomed American independence while calling for parliamentary reform.

Even more drastic changes occurred in Ireland. During the war, after centuries of religious persecution and economic exploitation under English rule, Henry Gratton (1746–1820) and Henry Flood (1732–1791), two leaders of the Irish Protestant gentry, exploited British weakness to obtain concessions. Having created an Irish militia, supposedly to protect the coasts against American or French attacks, they then followed American precedents. In February 1782 a convention at Dublin, representing 80,000 militiamen, demanded legislative independence. After the British Parliament subsequently agreed, a new Irish legislature could make its own laws, subject only to a veto by the British king. Ireland thus acquired a status denied the American colonies in 1774.

Ireland's response to the Revolution was almost matched in the Netherlands, where a popular movement, in sympathy with the Americans and the French, nearly ruined the Dutch economy. William V, the stadtholder and a relative of the English royal family, was unjustly blamed for the nation's misfortunes. Radical propaganda during the 1780s subjected his government to the most violent abuse, followed by uprisings in 1785 and 1787, which forced William to leave his capital. For a brief period, in the ensuing civil war, "patriots" held most of the country. The revolt was suppressed only when William's brother-in-law, the king of Prussia, sent 20,000 troops.

In France, revolutionary refugees from Holland found a congenial atmosphere, decisively affected by American ideas. To French philosophical radicals, the American Revolution proved their principles; to Frenchmen in the establishment, it promised a new and favorable diplomatic alignment against Britain. Consequently, radical ideas were no longer confined to learned treatises but appeared everywhere in pamphlets, newspapers, and even in the theater. Aristocractic vanities and even royal formalities suddenly became subjects for humorous comment; but, as one French noble observed, no one "stopped to consider the dangers of the example which the new world set to the old."

The French Revolution

Beginning in 1789, France produced the most significant of the eighteenth-century revolutions. In some ways it was remarkably similar to the American movement that had preceded it. Both revolutions applied principles of the Enlightenment; both swept away traditional systems; both followed similar three-stage courses, moving from moderate to radical before a final conservative swing; and both helped set in motion modern constitutional government, along with democracy and nationalism. There were, however, striking differences. Unlike the American colonies, France had a classic Old Regime, with aristocratic privilege and monarchy. Instead of being far removed from the centers of civilization, it was the most populous and cultured state of western Europe. Its revolution, therefore, was more violent and more decisive.

The Explosive Summer of 1789

During the summer of 1789, France faced a financial crisis, caused primarily by military expenditures and a parasitic aristocracy, which resisted any cuts in its returns from the treasury and any taxes on its wealth. Louis XVI had succeeded his grandfather in 1774. The young king was intelligent but indolent and dominated by his frivolous wife, Marie Antoinette, whose limited political vision and influence over her husband increased his problems. The result of this lapse of leadership was a political near-breakdown, followed by a sudden explosion of popular unrest and agitation.

Between Louis' succession and 1789, his finance ministers continuously struggled with a rapidly rising debt. It had increased by 400 million livres during French participation in the American Revolution and had reached a total of 4 billion livres in 1789 (equivalent to $5.6 billion in 1980 dollars), when interest payments absorbed half of the national revenues. Robert Turgot (1727–1781), controller-general of finance, had proposed deep cuts in expenditure, but he was forced out by the nobles. His successor, Swiss banker Jacques Necker (1732–1804), after resorting to more exhaustive borrowing, was dismissed in 1781, and two succeeding ministers failed to deal with the problem. In 1788, Louis called an assembly of nobles, hoping that they might accept taxation and economy measures. They flatly rejected his requests, insisting that he call the Estates-General, which had not met since 1614. In this body, where the clergy and nobility traditionally voted separately, they hoped to dominate the Third Estate, including the middle-class majority of taxpayers.

Ultimately, Louis summoned the Estates-General, with more than 600 elected delegates representing the Third Estate. They were chosen during the spring of 1789, amid feverish excitement, and supplied by their constituents with lists of grievances, the famous *cahiers*, which involved a diverse mixture of reform proposals, including demands for a national legislature, a jury system, freedom of the press, and equitable taxes. Once the Estates-General had convened, the Third Estate insisted that voting should be by head rather than by chamber, because it had more members than the other two estates (clergy and nobles) combined. Six weeks of wrangling over this issue brought delegates from the Third Estate along with lesser numbers from the other two orders, to a meeting at an indoor tennis court. There, on June 20, 1789, they solemnly swore the historic tennis-court oath, agreeing not to disband until they had produced a French constitution. Later, after defying a royal order to reconvene separately, they declared themselves to be the National Constituent Assembly of France.

Within weeks, the king had completely lost control of the situation. Although grudgingly accepting the National Assembly, he had 18,000 troops moved to the vicinity of Versailles. Middle-class members of the Assembly, in near panic at the threat of military intervention, appealed for popular support. On July 14, an estimated 100,000 Parisian shopkeepers, workers, and women demolished the Bastille, liberating the prisoners. It had served as the most visible symbol of the Old Regime, and its fall clearly demonstrated the rapily growing popular defiance. The event also destroyed Louis' courage and his municipal Parisian government, which was replaced by a middle-class council, with its own "national guard." Meanwhile, other urban uprisings and peasant violence in the country consolidated the Assemby's position.

As emotional tensions ran high throughout the country, the government faced a serious problem involving blacks. Although illegal in France, slavery was a legal foundation of the economy in the French West Indies, that remaining valuable gem of the French empire. Many wealthy French aristocrats and businessmen who owned plantations in Santo Domingo and Martinique feared that revolutionary rhetoric would promote slave rebellion. Another complication was provided by mulattoes, many of whom were wealthy planters themselves, who supported the slave system but complained about infringement of their civil rights, both in France and in the islands. Their petitions were enforced and carried further by an organization known as the *Amis des Noirs* ("Friends of the Blacks"), which capitalized upon the revolutionary atmosphere during the summer of 1789 to spread abroad antiracist ideas from the Enlightenment.

Another unique aspect of the summer upheaval was the aggressive roles played by women. In the *cahiers* they had presented demands for legal equality, improved education, and better conditions in the markets. They were present in large numbers at the fall of the Bastille. Later, as bread prices rose, they organized street marches and protests. On August 7, hundreds went to Versailles and praised the king for accepting the Assembly. A climax in this drama came on October 5, when some 6000 women, many of them armed, marched to Versailles, accompanied by the National Guard. There a deputation of six women, led by a seventeen-year-old flower seller, Louison Chabray, met the king, who promised more bread for the city. Other women entered the hall where the Assembly was sitting, disrupted proceedings and forced an adjournment. The next day, after a mob stormed the palace and killed some guards, the king and his family returned to Paris as virtual prisoners, their carriage surrounded by women carrying pikes, upon which were impaled the heads of the murdered bodyguards.

The First Phase of Middle-Class Revolution

Shortly after the march on Versailles, the Assembly achieved some political stability by declaring martial law, to be enforced by the National Guard. During the next two years, its leaders followed the Enlightenment in attempting to reorganize the whole French political system. Because most came from the middle class, with a preponderance of lawyers and a sprinkling of nobles, they were committed to change but also determined to keep order, protect property, and further their special interests. Thus, as they achieved their goals, they became increasingly satisfied and conservative.

The most dramatic action of the Assembly occurred on the night of August 4, 1789. By then, order had been restored in the cities, but peasants all over France were still rising against their lords—burning, pillaging, and sometimes murdering—in desperate efforts to destroy records of their manorial obligations. Faced with this violence and at first undecided between force and concessions, the Assembly ultimately chose concessions. Consequently, on that fateful night, nobles and clergy rose in the Assembly to denounce tithes, serfdom, manorial dues, feudal privileges, unequal taxes, and the sale of offices. In a few hours between sunset and dawn, the Old Regime, which had evolved over a thousand years, was completely transformed.

To define its political principles and set its course, on August 26 the Assembly issued the *Declaration of the Rights of Man and the Citizen*. Intended as a preamble to a new constitution, it proclaimed human "inalienable rights" to liberty, property, security, and resistance to oppression. It also promised free speech, press, and religion, consistent with public order. Property was declared inviolate unless required for "public safety," in which case the owner was to receive "just compensation." All (male) citizens were to be equal before the law and eligible for public office on their qualifications. Taxes were to be levied only by common consent. With its emphases upon civil equality and property rights, the declaration was a typical middle-class statement.[4]

Understandably, the Assembly aimed its economic policies at freeing capitalistic enterprise. It assured payment to middle-class bondholders of government issues and financed this policy by sale of lands, confiscated from the church and from nobles who had fled the country. It sold to middle-class speculators much of this new public land; very little was ever acquired by peasants. The Assembly also abolished all internal tolls,

A contemporary print of Parisian women advancing on Versailles on October 5, 1789, shows the determined marchers carrying pikes and dragging an artillery piece. The following day the king and the royal family were returned to Paris, and the women were hailed as heroines of the Revolution.

The Declaration of the Rights of Man and Citizen

This moderate middle-class document of the French Revolution was inspired by the American Declaration of Independence. Notice, however, that it differs slightly in its precise mention of property rights.

The National Assembly recognizes and declares, in the presence and under the auspices of the Supreme Being, the following rights of man and citizen.

1. Men are born and remain free and equal in rights. Social distinctions can be based only upon the common good.

2. The aim of every political association is the preservation of the natural and imprescriptible rights of man. These rights are liberty, property, security, and resistance to oppression.

4. Liberty consists in the power to do anything that does not injure others; accordingly, the exercise of the natural rights of each man has no limits except those that assure to the other members of society the enjoyment of these same rights. These limits can be determined only by law.

5. The law can forbid only such actions as are injurious to society. Nothing can be forbidden that is not forbidden by the law, and no one can be constrained to do that which it does not decree.

6. Law is the expression of the general will. All citizens have the right to take part personally, or by their representatives, in its enactment. It must be the same for all, whether it protects or punishes.

7. No man can be accused, arrested, or detained, except in the cases determined by the law and according to the forms which it has prescribed. Those who call for, expedite, execute, or cause to be executed arbitrary orders should be punished; but every citizen summoned or seized by virtue of the law ought to obey instantly. . . .

8. The law ought to establish only punishments that are strictly and obviously necessary, and no one should be punished except by virtue of a law established and promulgated prior to the offence and legally applied.

9. Every man being presumed innocent until he has been declared guilty, if it is judged indispensable to arrest him, all severity that may not be necessary to secure his person ought to be severely suppressed by law.

10. No one should be disturbed on account of his opinions, even religious, provided their manifestation does not trouble the public order as established by law.

11. The free communication of thoughts and opinions is one of the most precious of the rights of man; every citizen can then speak, write, and print freely, save for the responsibility for the abuse of this liberty in the cases determined by law.

12. The guarantee of the rights of man and citizen necessitates a public force; this force is then instituted for the advantage of all and not for the particular use of those to whom it is entrusted.

13. For the maintenance of the public force and for the expenses of administration a general tax is indispensable; it should be equally apportioned among all the citizens according to their means.

14. All citizens have the right to ascertain, by themselves or through their representatives, the necessary amount of public taxation, to consent to it freely, to follow the use of it, and to determine the quota, the assessment, the collection, and the duration of it.

16. Any society in which the guarantee of the rights is not assured, or the separation of powers not determined, has no constitution.

17. Property being a sacred and inviolable right, no one can be deprived of it, unless a legally established public necessity evidently requires it, under the condition of a just and prior indemnity.

Source: George L. Mosse et al., eds., *Europe in Review* (Chicago: Rand McNally, 1962), pp. 162–164.

industrial regulations, and guilds, thus throwing open all arts and crafts. It banned trade unions, decreeing that wages be set by individual bargaining. Except for a few remaining controls on foreign trade, the Assembly applied the doctrines of Adam Smith and the physiocrats, substituting free competition for economic regulation.

The Assembly's land policies conditioned its approach to organized religion. Having taken church property and eliminated tithes, many members were reluctant to abolish the state church completely, believing the church, if controlled, would help to defend property. Consequently, the Assembly passed the Civil Constitution of the Clergy, which made the clergy salaried public servants but abolished all archbishoprics and reduced the number of bishoprics. Monastic orders were simply dissolved. Incumbent churchmen were required to swear first loyalty to the nation, but only seven bishops and half the clergy conformed. The remainder became bitterly hostile to the government, exerting great influence, particularly among the peasants.

Another serious problem involved the West Indian colonies, blacks, and free mulattoes. News from France in 1789 brought quick and sometimes violent political reactions in Santo Domingo and Martinique, as planters, merchants, poor whites, mulattoes, and slaves hoped that the Revolution would further their diverse interests. French absentee planters and island delegates in the Assembly differed on trade policies and local colonial autonomy, but they concurred in their fanatic defense of slavery and their opposition to civil rights for free mulattoes. Meanwhile, mulattoes in France spread their pamphlets and petitioned the Assembly, supported by the *Amis des Noirs*, whose spokesmen also angrily attacked slavery in the Assembly hall. The chamber was left divided and nearly powerless. It first gave the island governments complete control over their blacks and mulattoes. Then, yielding to the radicals, it granted political rights to mulattoes born of free parents. Finally, as civil war racked the islands, it bowed to the planters and repealed its last measure in September 1791.

The Assembly also dashed some high hopes for French women. The early Revolution enlisted many, not only from the poor rioting Parisians of the shops and markets, but also women of the middle class, whose salons were political centers. These hostesses included Theroigne de Méricourt (1762–1817), a Belgian courtesan who became a revolutionary street orator, Madame de Staël (1766–1817), Necker's daughter and a popular novelist, and Madame Roland (1754–1793), a successful party stategist. Women were already prominent in the political clubs of this era. Etta Palm d'Aelders, a Dutch activist, formed a woman's patriotic society, and even proposed a female militia. In addition, some women were involved in a strong feminist movement. Olympe de Gouges (see ch. 20), charged the Assembly with securing the "inalienable rights" of women. The cause was taken up by the *Amis de la Verité*, a women's organization which regularly lobbied the Assembly for free divorce, women's education, and women's civil rights. Its pleas, however, were ignored.

After two years of controversy, the Assembly produced the Constitution of 1791, which made France a limited monarchy. It assigned the law-making function to a single-chambered Legislative Assembly, which was to meet every two years. The king could select ministers and temporarily veto laws but could not dismiss the legislature. The Constitution also created an independent and elected judiciary. Local government was completely reorganized on three levels—departments, districts, and communes—with elected officials relatively free of supervision from Paris. Despite rights guaranteed in the Declaration, only those male citizens who paid a specified minimum of direct taxes acquired the vote. Property qualifications were even higher for deputies to the Assembly and national officials. Women were made "passive citizens," without the vote, but marriage became a civil contract, with divorce open to both parties. Other individual rights under a new law code were guaranteed according to the principles of the Declaration.

These provisions, and other acts of the Assembly involving the colonies, blacks, and women, indicated the conserative orientation of the early Revolution, before September 1791. This was particularly true of the property qualifications on voting and office-holding, which guaranteed that the new monarchy would be largely controlled by the upper middle classes. Their concern now was to retain their supremacy by blocking further changes.

The Drift Toward Radicalism

After June 1791, when the king and his family attempted to flee the country, the Revolution drifted steadily toward radicalism. Although the attempt failed, Louis' action as well as the suspicion that he was conspiring with enemies of the Revolution turned many French people into republicans.

When the Legislative Assembly met in September 1791, it was plagued with troubles. The lower classes distrusted the Assembly because they were not represented. Peasants, angry because their priests had been dispossessed, and urban workers, worried about inflation and unemployment, petitioned the Assembly with their grievances. Mulattoes on Santo Domingo denounced the recent denial of their civil rights and launched revolts against the governor. The Assembly also learned that many foreign governments were displeased with its treatment of the French royal family and the nobles.

Factionalism within the Assembly reflected divisions and differences of opinion in the country. About a third of the deputies supported the constitutional monarchy. Another large group wavered from issue to issue, and a vocal minority wanted to scrap the monarchy and establish a republic. These radical deputies generally expressed sentiments originating with the Jacobin Club, a highly vocal organization of political extremists who met regularly at a former Dominican monastery. Although most members were from the middle class, they ultimately depended upon support from Parisian artisans and workers.

Sterile debate gave way to enthusiasm as the country slipped into foreign war during the spring of 1792. Leopold of Austria, brother of the French queen, joined the king of Prussia in declaring publicly that restoration of French absolutism was "of common interest to all sovereigns."[5] In response, Theroigne Mérincourt, just released from Austrian custody, addressed the Jacobin Club, eloquently pleading for overthrow of the monarchy and war against the Habsburg enemy. Her call echoed all over France. At the same time, raging civil war in the West Indies, which drove up sugar prices and encouraged speculative hoarding, turned popular opinion against the planters. Angry mobs of men and women stormed the warehouses, seized the sugar, and sold it at reasonable prices. The Assembly responded to both challenges by restoring civil liberties to free black and mulatto citizens and declaring war on Austria. French citizens went mad with fanatic patriotism. Thousands of recruits enlisted, and Mérincourt organized a company of "Amazons," armed with pikes and muskets.

Despite their enthusiasm and dedication, French armies suffered early defeats when Prussia allied with Austria against France. These misfortunes aroused further suspicion of Louis, which intensified when the Prussian Duke of Brunswick, commanding the invading army, threatened in June to destroy Paris if the French royal family were harmed. The faction of the radicals known as the Girondists, who mainly represented the middle class outside of Paris, used the proclamation as propaganda. They relied on the support of paramilitary organizations of men and women in the provinces and used a mulatto legion in the army to arouse popular support.

The French nation, particularly Paris, responded to Brunswick's manifesto with fury maintained by the Jacobin leaders' impassioned oratory against the king and the moderates. The most effective of the Jacobins was Georges-Jacques Danton (1759–1794), the deputy prosecutor for the Paris Commune, an enormous brute of a man with a voice of commanding power, who mesmerized angry audiences as he denounced the king as a traitor. Supported by Paris mobs, the Commune seized power from the Legislative Assembly, deposed the king, and executed some 2000 suspected royalists in the notorious "September massacres." It then called for a national convention, with members elected by universal male suffrage, to draw up a new constitution. Jacobin hysteria spread throughout France, even after September 22 when the newly assembled National Convention declared France a republic.

Debate over the fate of the king and the nature of the new constitution intensified the contention between moderates and radicals. Danton shared leadership of the radicals in the Convention with Maximilien Robespierre (1758–1794), an idealistic and fanatic follower of Rousseau, and Jean-Paul Marat (1743–1793), publisher of *Ami du Peuple*, a newspaper which violently and consistently denounced traitors and counter-revolutionaries. Opposing Danton, Robespierre, and Marat were the Girondists, who also favored war but feared mob violence and democratic reforms. Most of them wanted to postpone the king's trial, but they lost ground during the fall. The Jacobins finally triumphed in the crucial debates that led to the king's execution in January 1793.

Imbued now with a new fighting spirit, French armies defeated the foreign invaders and went on the offensive, occupying the Rhineland, Belgium, Nice, and Savoy. These French victories so fired the hopes and imaginations of the Jacobins that they insisted on exporting the Revolution by force. The National Convention, which the Jacobins now controlled, announced that France would "grant fraternity to all peoples who wish to recover their liberty."[6] It then declared war on all tyrants and ordered the inhabitants of all countries to accept the principles of the Revolution. Alarmed by the execution of the king and this proclamation, England, Holland, Spain, and Sardinia joined Austria and Prussia in a general coalition against France. In the spring of 1793, four armies of the coalition crossed the French frontiers.

Louis' execution plus worsening conditions among the Paris poor widened the breach between Jacobins and Girondists and brought matters to a desperate crisis. When Girondists staged uprisings in Marseilles, Lyons, Bordeaux, and Toulon, Jacobins in the Paris Commune called a howling mob into the Convention hall on May 31, 1793 and purged the National Convention of any remaining Girondists. Other Girondists throughout France were placed under surveillance.

The Jacobin Republic

The Convention was now a council of the most extreme Jacobins, but the transition of power was not completed until after July 12, 1793, when Charlotte Corday, a young Girondist sympathizer, came to Paris from Caen and murdered Marat. He had been the revered leader of the extreme left, known as the *Enragés*, and his death

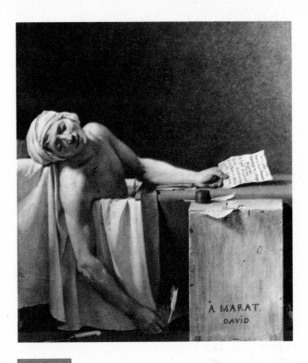

Jacques-Louis David, *The Death of Marat* (1793). David's painting extols the murdered Marat as a martyr of the Revolution.

infuriated the street people. The resulting wave of anti-Girondist hysteria brought the Convention under the domination of Robespierre, who remained in power until the late spring of 1794. During that time, revolutionary France reorganized itself, suppressed internal strife, and drove out foreign invaders, thus bringing to climax the success of the radical Jacobin party.

The regime achieved its success largely through rigid dictatorship and terror. The Convention created a twelve-member Committee of Public Safety, headed first by Danton and after July by Robespierre. Subordinate committees were established for the departments, districts, and communes. These bodies deliberately forced conformity by fear, using neighbors to inform on neighbors and children to testify against their parents. Suspects, once identified, were brought to trial before revolutionary tribunals, with most receiving quick death sentences. Between September 1793, and July 1794, some 25,000 victims were dragged to public squares in carts—the famous tumbrels—and delivered to the guillotine. Ultimately, the Terror swallowed most of the revolutionaries, including Danton in April 1794 and Robespierre himself in July 1794.

While it lasted, the Jacobin dictatorship was remarkably successful in its war efforts, mobilizing all of France to fight. The convention made all males between eighteen and forty eligible for military service, a policy which ultimately produced a force of 800,000, the largest standing army ever assembled in France. Officers were promoted on merit and encouraged to exercise initiative. The government also took over industries and directed them to produce large quantities of uniforms, arms, medical supplies, and equipment. In Paris alone, 258 forges made 1000 gun barrels a day. Between 1793 and 1795, the French citizen armies carried out a series of remarkably sucessful campaigns. They regained all French territory, annexed Belgium, and occupied other areas extending to the Rhine, the Alps, and the Pyrenees, thus gaining, in two years, the "natural frontiers" that Louis XIV had dreamed about. By 1794, Prussia and Spain had left the coalition and Holland had become a French ally. Only England, Austria, and Sardinia remained at war with France.

Flushed with their victories, the Jacobins enacted domestic reforms reflecting a peculiar combination of hysteria and reason. They abolished all symbols of status, such as knee breeches, powdered wigs, and jewelry. Titles were discarded, and people were addressed as "citizen" or "citizeness." Streets were renamed to commemorate revolutionary events or heroes. The calendar was reformed by dividing each month into three weeks of ten days each and giving the months new names; July, for example, became Thermidor (hot) to eliminate reference to the tyrant Julius Caesar. The Revolution took on a semireligious character in ceremonies and fêtes, which featured young attractive women as living symbols for reason, virtue, and duty. Along with these changes came a strong reaction against Christianity: churches were closed and religious images destroyed. For a while a "Worship of the Supreme Being" was substituted for Roman Catholicism, but finally in 1794 religion became a private matter.

Despite their stated beliefs in free enterprise as an ideal, the Jacobins imposed a number of economic controls. The government enacted emergency war measures such as rationing, fixed wages and prices, and currency controls. It also punished profiteers, used the property of emigrés to relieve poverty, sold land directly to peasants, and freed the peasants from all compensatory payments to their old lords.

Colonial problems, which had confounded the National and Legislative Assemblies, were met head-on by the Jacobin Convention. The grant of citizenship to free blacks and mulattoes of the islands in 1792 had drawn the mulattoes to the government side, but colonial armies, enlisted by the governors, faced determined insurrection from royalists and resentful escaped slaves. Sometimes the two forces were united, with support from Spain or the British. In the late spring of 1793, the harried governor of Santo Domingo issued a decree freeing all former slaves and calling upon them to join against foreign enemies. His strategy narrowly averted a British conquest. Subsequently, the Convention received a delegation from Santo Domingo and heard a plea for liberty from a 101-year-old former slave woman. The chamber responded by freeing all slaves in French territories, giving them full citizenship rights.

Unfortunately, the revolutionary women in France were not so successful. At first, the radicals welcomed women as supporters, but after the Jacobins gained power they regarded revolutionary women as troublemakers. By the spring of 1794, the Convention had suppressed all women's societies and imprisoned many, including Olympe de Gouges. She was soon sent to the guillotine for her alleged royalist sympathies. The Jacobin legislature continued to deny women the vote, although it did improve education, available medical care, and property rights for women.

Because they regulated the economy and showed concern for the lower classes, the Jacobins have often been considered socialists. The Constitution of 1793, which was developed by the Convention but suspended almost immediately because of the war, does not support this interpretation. The new constitution guaranteed private property, included a charter of individual liberties, confirmed the Constitution of 1791's accent on local autonomy, and provided for a Central Committee, appointed by the departments. The greatest difference, in comparison with the earlier constitution, was the franchise, which was now granted to all adult males. Although the Jacobin constitution indicated a concern for equality of opportunity, it also revealed its authors to be eighteenth-century radical liberals, who followed Rousseau rather than Locke.

End of the Terror and the Conservative Reaction

The summer of 1794 brought a conservative reaction against radical revolution. With French arms victorious everywhere, rigid discipline no longer seemed necessary, but Robespierre, still committed to Rousseau's "republic of virtue," was determined to continue the Terror. When he demanded voluntary submission to the "General Will" as necessary for achieving social equality, justice, and brotherly love, many practical politicians among his colleagues doubted his sanity. Others wondered if they would be among those next eliminated to purify society. They

In this satirical print, Robespierre, having executed all others during the Terror, guillotines the executioner. Robespierre himself was guillotined in the summer of 1794.

therefore cooperated to condemn him in the Convention. In July 1794 he was sent, with twenty of his supporters, to the guillotine, amid great celebration by his enemies.

Robespierre's fall ended the Terror and initiated a revival of the pre-Jacobin past. In 1794, the Convention eliminated the Committee of Public Safety; the next year it abolished the Revolutionary Tribunal and the radical political clubs, while freeing thousands of political prisoners. It also banned women from attendance in the Convention hall, an act which symbolized the return to a time when women's political influence was confined to the ballroom, the bedroom, or the salon. Indeed, as the formerly exiled Girondists, emigré royalists, and nonconforming priests returned to France, Parisian politics moved from the streets to private domiciles of the elite. Outside of Paris, by the summer of 1795, armed vigilantes roamed the countryside, seeking out and murdering former Jacobins. Everywhere, the earlier reforming zeal and patriotic fervor gave way to conservative cynicism.

There was to be one last gasp of idealism, although it was outside the revolutionary mainstream. Francois-Noël Babeuf (1760–1797) was a radical journalist and true believer in the spirit of the Enlightenment, who expected utopia from the Revolution. To its success, he sacrificed his worldly goods and his family; his wife and children went hungry while he moved into and out of jails before 1795. An earlier follower of Robespierre, he later condemned his former mentor as a traitor to the principle of equality. According to Babeuf, liberty was not possible while the rich exploited the poor; the solution had to be a "society of equals," where the republic would guarantee efficient production and equitable distribution of goods. Babeuf's nascent socialism, so out of tune with his times, was suppressed in May 1796, along with his attempted uprising against the government. At his trial, despite his heroic oratory, the support of his long-suffering wife, and his self-inflicted stab wound, he was condemned and sent to the guillotine.

Before it dissolved itself in 1795, the Convention proclaimed still another constitution and established a new political system known as the Directory, which governed France until 1799. Heading the new government was an executive council of five members (directors) appointed by the upper house of a bicameral (two-house) legislature. Deputies to the two chambers were selected by assemblies of electors in each department. These electors were chosen by adult male taxpayers, but the electors themselves had to be substantial property owners. Indeed, they numbered only some 20,000 in a total population of more than 25 million. Government was thus securely controlled by the upper middle classes, a condition also evident by the return to free trade.

The Directory was conspicuously conservative and antidemocratic, but it was also antiroyalist. A Bourbon restoration would have also restored church and royalist lands, which had been largely acquired by wealthy capitalists during the Revolution. Politicians who had participated in the Revolution or voted for the execution of Louis XVI had even greater reason to fear restoration of the monarchy.

In pursuing this antiroyalist path at a time when royalist principles were regaining popularity, the Directory had to depend on the recently developed professional military establishment. In 1797, for example, the army was used to prevent the seating of royalist deputies. The Directory encouraged further military expansion, hoping to revive the patriotic revolutionary fervor. Of three armies it sent into Austrian territory, two failed, but the one led by Napoleon Bonaparte (1769–1821) crossed the Alps in 1796 to crush the Austrians and Sardinians. After 1797, only England, protected by its fleet, remained at war with France. The French Revolution was over, but its momentous Napoleonic aftermath of military dictatorship was just beginning.

Significance of the French Revolution

The French Revolution, as evidenced by the Napoleonic dictatorship which it produced, was an immediate failure; for France at the turn of the nineteenth century, had secured neither liberty, nor equality, nor fraternity. Except for certain prosperous members of the middle classes, the French economy promised less for most people in 1796 than it had two decades earlier. Most discouraging was the realization that the Revolution had betrayed its own ideals, leaving the French people cynical and disillusioned.

The Revolution, nevertheless, had brought great changes. It had abolished serfdom and feudal privileges, created a uniform system of local government, laid the groundwork for a national education system, started legal reforms that would culminate in the great Napoleonic Code, abolished slavery in the colonies, and established the standardized metric system. The ideal, if not the practice, of constitutional government had been rooted in the French mind. Moreover, French armies, even before 1800, had scattered abroad the seeds of liberalism, constitutionalism, and even democracy. The most striking result of the Revolution in its own time was its violent disturbance of old orders; from Ireland to Poland, nothing would ever be the same again.

Long-term results of the Revolution may be evaluated much more positively than its immediate effects. During the first decade of the nineteenth century, many former idealists saw dark curtains drawn over windows through which the Enlightenment had once shone so brightly. This blackout, however, was only temporary. Even before Napoleon experienced his first major defeat at Leipzig in 1813, his enemies had adopted that philosophy of liberation which had fired French imagination in the early 1790s. The spirit of radicalism was revived again among English working-class rioters in 1817. Every other European liberal movement of the nineteenth century borrowed something from the French Revolution.

Another result was equally significant but less promising. The Jacobin republic spawned a fanatic and infectious patriotism, most effectively exploited by Napoleon. When this was combined with the self-righteous idealism of the Enlightenment, it produced a mass hysteria that seems common to most modern peoples as they first become aware of their national identities. A parallel development was French militarism, symbolized later by Napoleon. The concept of the nation in arms—military conscription and the marshalling of an economy for war—appears familiar today. This modern note was a forerunner of industrial society, with its complexities, interdependence, and mass conformity. France in 1800 was not yet industrialized, but it was ripe to be and was already populous enough to experience some tensions evident in modern industrial societies.

Conclusion

In the latter part of the eighteenth century, traditional governments in Europe were challenged by a wave of political revolutions, the most significant of which were the American and the French. These movements resulted from dynamic economies and drastically changing societies, but they were also products of the Enlightenment. In addition, they owed much to the English limited monarchy, with its cabinet system, which was initiated by the Glorious Revolution of the seventeenth century.

The American and French revolutions were similar to the earlier Dutch and English upheavals but they were conditioned more directly by an expanding capitalistic economy which gave them more of a middle-class orientation. They were also more secular in tone. Their impacts upon other societies were naturally more forceful; indeed, they nearly completely destroyed the credibility of absolutism and aristocracy by popularizing and applying the principles of the Enlightenment.

Despite their obvious similarities, the two revolutions also were significantly different. The American movement was more limited in scope and in direct political effects. It was unique in its own time as a demonstrable proof of the "return to nature" and the practicality of the "social contract." Its foreign influence was primarily indirect, through the emotional and intellectual appeal of its example. The French Revolution, on the other hand, was much broader in its economic, social, religious, and political results. It brought the violent overthrow of a social order that had lasted for centuries. Moreover, it launched military conquests that brought the same general upheaval to the whole of western Europe.

Both revolutions merit serious study today. They left a legacy of liberal and constitutional ideas for all peoples, as evidenced by the Latin American movements of the early nineteenth century and by many more recent ones in Asia and Africa. This heritage of the French Revolution has been partially obscured by another legacy of nationalism and war. In contrast, the American liberal heritage has been maintained, almost completely intact, into the twentieth century. Rural people in a vast land which continually beckoned the pioneer, stayed closer to the simple individualistic assumptions of the eighteenth century. That is why American individualism is dying so hard and with such contortions in our time.

Suggestions for Reading

Maurice Ashley, *A History of Europe, 1648–1815* (Prentice-Hall, 1973) is still among the best general surveys. See also G. R. Treasure, *The Making of Modern Europe, 1648–1780* (Methuen, 1985) and Michael S. Anderson, *Europe in the Eighteenth Century* (Longman, 1987). For internal political backgrounds in the revolutionary era, see William Doyle's comprehensive *The Old European Order* (Oxford Univ., 1978). Derek McKay and H. M. Scott, *The Rise of the Great Powers, 1648–1815* (Longman, 1983) provides excellent coverage of the international scene. Crane Brinton's classic *Anatomy of Revolution* (Vintage, 1957) is an interesting comparative study of the English, American, French, and Russian revolutions. An overview of a major social malaise of the era may be found in David B. Davis, *The Problem of Slavery in the Age of Revolution, 1770–1823* (Cornell Univ., 1975).

For English political developments under the later Stuarts, see Maurice Ashley, *England in the Seventeenth Century* (Penguin, 1975). Among the best treatments of Charles II and his problems are David Ogg, *England in the Reign of Charles II*, 2nd ed. (Oxford Univ., 1984); Kenneth H. D. Haley, *Politics in the Reign of Charles II* (Blackwell, 1985); and James R. Jones, *Charles II: Royal Politician* (Unwin Hyman, 1987). For James II and the Glorious Revolution, see Maurice Ashley, *James II* (Univ. of Minn., 1977); John Childs, *The Army, James II, and the Glorious Revolution* (St. Martin's, 1981); and K. M. Chacksfield, *The Glorious Revolution* (Wincanton Press, 1988). See also David Ogg, *England in the Reigns of James II and William III* (Oxford Univ., 1984) and D. S. Lovejoy, *The Glorious Revolution in America* (Wesleyan Univ., 1987).

Dorothy Marshall, *Eighteenth Century England* (Longman, 1974) presents excellent general background for the workings of the aristocratic parliamentary system. A sound biography of the first Hanoverian monarch is Ragnhild Hatton, *George I* (Harvard Univ., 1978). See also the following works dealing with Hanoverian society and politics: John Cannon, ed., *The Whig Ascendancy* (St. Martin's, 1981); Michael A. Reed, *The Georgian Triumph* (Routledge and Kegan Paul, 1983); Paul Langford, *Walpole and the Robinocracy* (Chadwyck-Healey, 1986); and S. Hopewell, *Walpole and the Georges* (Wayland, 1987).

The mid-eighteenth-century background for revolution is described in a number of pertinent studies. For England, see Peggy Liss, *Atlantic Empires: The Network of Trade and Revolution, 1713–1826* (Johns Hopkins Univ., 1983) and Alan Rogers, *Empire and Liberty* (Univ. of California, 1974). For biographical insights into both extremes of the English political spectrum see Reginald James White, *The Age of George III* (Walker, 1968); Richard Pares, *King George*

III and the Politicians (Oxford Univ., 1988); Louis Kronenberger, *The Extraordinary Mr. Wilkes* (Doubleday, 1974); and Audrey Williamson, *Wilkes, A Friend to Liberty* (Readers' Digest Press, 1974). Good perspectives on Dutch involvement are presented in M. C. Rady, *The Netherlands* (Arnold, 1987); in Alice Clare Carter, *Neutrality or Commitment: The Evolution of Dutch Foreign Policy, 1667–1795* (Arnold, 1975); and, by the same author, *The Dutch Republic in Europe in the Seven Years' War* (Univ. of Miami, 1971). For France, see Louis R. Gottschalk and Donald Lach, *Toward the French Revolution* (Scribner, 1973); Jacques Godechot, *France and the Atlantic Revolution of the Eighteenth Century* (Free Press, 1965); and Timothy Tacket, *Religion, Revolution, and Regional Culture in Eighteenth-century France* (Princeton Univ., 1986).

Page Smith, *A New Age Now Begins: A People's History of the American Revolution*, 2 vols. (Penguin, 1989) is a detailed and exciting narrative. Other good general histories of the American Revolution include Richard Ernest Dupoy, *The American Revolution: A Global War* (McKay, 1977); B. Lancaster, *The American Revolution* (Hill and Wang, 1985); E. Countryman, *The American Revolution* (Penguin, 1987); and John R. Alden, *A History of the American Revolution* (Da Capo Quality Paperbacks, 1989). For contrasting views on the nobility of the American struggle, see Robert Middlekauff, *The Glorious Cause* (Oxford Univ., 1985) and Norman Gelb, *Less Than Glory* (Putnam's, 1984). The revolution is evaluated in British terms by Robert W. Tucker and David C. Hendrickson in their *Fall of the First British Empire* (Johns Hopkins Univ., 1982).

Thomas Ladenburg, *The Causes of the American Revolution* (Social Sc. Education, 1989) is a useful study aid. Among the best other studies on the genesis of the Revolution are Cass Canfield, *Samuel Adams' Revolution, 1775–1776* (Harper and Row, 1976); Pauline Maier, *From Resistance to Revolution* (Knopf, 1972); R. B. Morris, *Founding of the Republic* (Lerner, 1985); D. E. Leach, *Roots of Conflict* (Univ. of North Carolina, 1986); and J. A. Henriatta, *Evolution and Revolution* (Heath, 1987).

The following works include the best studies on specific aspects of the Revolution. On economics and class interests, see T. H. Breen, *Tobacco Culture: The Mentality of the Great Tidewater Planters on the Eve of the Revolution* (Princeton Univ., 1985); Jack M. Sosin, *Agents and Merchants* (Univ. of Nebraska, 1965); John W. Tyler, *Smugglers and Patriots* (Northeastern Univ., 1986); and C. K. Wilbur, *Pirates and Patriots of the Revolution* (Globe Pequot Press, 1984). Ideological issues are probed in Thomas L. Pangle, *The Spirit of Modern Republicanism: The Moral Vision of American Founders and the Philosophy of John Locke* (Univ. of Chicago, 1988); J. P. Reid, *The Concept of Liberty in the Age of the American Revolution* (Univ. of Chicago, 1988); and Gordon S. Wood, *Social Radicalism and the Idea of Equality in the American Revolution* (Univ. of St. Thomas, 1976). Financial problems are given detailed attention in William G. Anderson, *The Price of Liberty, the Public Debt of the American Revolution* (Univ. of Virginia, 1982). For the very relevant constitutional results of the Revolution, see Charles A. Beard, *An Economic Interpretation of the Constitution of the United States* (Free Press, 1986) and Clinton L. Rossiter, *The Grand Convention* (Norton, 1987). James B. Perkins, *France in the American Revolution* (Corner House, 1970) throws light on revolutionary foreign policy.

For the hardships and heroics of women in the Revolution, see Anne Voth, *Women in the New Eden* (Univ. Press of America, 1983); Joseph J. Kelley and Sol Feinstone, *Courage and Candle Light* (Stackpole, 1974); Elizabeth Evans, *Weathering the Storm: Women of the American Revolution* (Scribners, 1975); Walter Hart Blumenthal, *(Women Camp Followers of the American Revolution* (Ayer, 1974); Robert Middlekauff, *The Glorious Cause* (Oxford Univ., 1985); Elizabeth Ellet, *The Women of the American Revolution*, 3 vols. (rev. ed., Corner House, 1980); Linda K. Kerber, *Women of the Republic* (Univ. of North Carolina, 1980); and Mary Beth Norton, *Liberty's Daughters* (Little, Brown, 1980).

For the roles played by blacks in the Revolution, see D. J. MacLeod, *Slavery, Race, and the American Revolution* (Gordon, 1975); Ira Berlin and Ronald Hoffman, *Slavery and Freedom in the Age of the American Revolution* (Univ. of Illinois, 1986); Philip S. Foner, *Blacks in the American Revolution* (Greenwood, 1976); John Hope Franklin, *From Freedom to Slavery*, 5th ed. (Knopf, 1980); Benjamin Quarles, *The Negro in the American Revolution* (Norton, 1973); and Sidney Kaplan and Emma Nogrady, *The Black Presence in the Era of the American Revolution*, rev. ed. (Univ. of Mass., 1989).

On effects of the American Revolution abroad, for Ireland, see Maurice R. O'Connell, *Irish Politics and Social Conflict in the Age of the American Revolution* (Greenwood, 1976); Robert B. McDowell, *Ireland in the Age of Imperialism and Revolution* (Oxford Univ., 1979); and Nicholas Canny, *Kingdom and Colony: Ireland in the Atlantic World, 1560–1800* (Johns Hopkins Univ., 1987). For England, see Colin Bonwick, *English Radicals and the American Revolution* (Univ. of North Carolina, 1977); Robert Toohey, *Liberty and Empire: British Radical Solutions to the American Problem* (Univ. of Kentucky, 1978); Bernard Peach, ed., *Richard Price and the Ethical Foundation of the American Revolution* (Duke Univ., 1979); Charles R. Ritcheson, *British Politics and the American Revolution* (Greenwood, 1981); and James E. Bradley, *Popular Politics and the American Revolution in England* (Mercer Univ., 1986). For the Netherlands, see Simon Schama, *Patriots and Liberators: Revolution in the Netherlands* (Knopf, 1977) and J. W. Schulte Nordhelt, *The Dutch Republic and American Independence* (Univ. of North Carolina, 1982). See also Horst Dippel, *Germany and the American Revolution* (Univ. of North Carolina, 1977) and Gwyn A. Williams, *The Search for Beulah Land: the Welsh and the Atlantic Revolution* (Holmes and Meier, 1980).

The following biographical studies of American revolutionary leaders are recommended: H. J. Merry, *The Founding Fathers* (McFarland, 1987); Pauline Maier, *The Old Revolutionaries* (Knopf, 1980); Richard R. Beeman, *Patrick Henry* (McGraw-Hill, 1974); Burke Davis, *George Washington and the American Revolution* (Random House, 1975); G. W. Nordham, *George Washington* (Adams Press, 1987); Forest McDonald, *Alexander Hamilton* (Norton, 1979); Henry Steele Commager, *Jefferson, Nationalist, and the Enlightenment* (Braziller, 1975); and Page Smith, *Jefferson* (American Heritage, 1976). Otto Vossler, *Jefferson and the Revolutionary Ideal* (Univ. Press of America, 1980) is a reinterpretation by a foreign scholar who sees Jefferson's revolutionary idealism as the result of a late conversion in France.

Robert Rosswell Palmer's classic *The World of the French Revolution* (Harper and Row, 1971) examines French eighteenth-century developments in broad perspective. The coming of the Revolution is described in a number of other thoughtful works: William Doyle, *Origins of the French Revolution* (Oxford Univ., 1980); Jean Egret, *The French Pre-Revolution* (Univ. of Chicago, 1977); Michel Vovelle, *The Fall of the French Monarchy* (Cambridge Univ., 1984); and Georges Lefebvre, *The Coming of the French Revolution* (Princeton Univ., 1989). The first three volumes of Claude Manceron's massive study of the French Revolution deal with the pre-Revolutionary period: *Twilight of the Old Order, 1774–1778* (Knopf, 1977); *The Wind from America, 1779–1781* (Knopf, 1978); and *Their Gracious Pleasure, 1782–1785* (Knopf, 1980). These presentations, however, are so highly detailed and personalized that they blur the big picture for anyone not very familiar with the era.

Among the best recent general surveys of the French Revolution are William Doyle, *The Oxford History of the French Revolution* (Oxford Univ., 1989); J. F. Bosher, *The French Revolution* (Norton, 1988); T. C. W. Blanning, *The French Revolution* (Macmillan, 1987); M. J. Sydenham, *The French Revolution* (Greenwood, 1985); and J. M. Thompson, *The French Revolution* (Blackwell, 1985). See also R. J. Caldwell, *The Era of the French Revolution* (Garland, 1975); and Leo Gershoy, *The Era of the French Revolution* (Krieger, 1984). Christopher Hibbert, *The Days of the French Revolution* (Morrow, 1981) complements any survey with its colorful accounts of selected major events.

L. A. Hunt, *Politics, Culture, and Class in the French Revolution* (Methuen, 1986) focuses on the total dynamics of the great upheaval. For the significance of class hostilities and mob psychology, see Peter Jones, *The Peasantry in the French Revolution* (Cambridge Univ., 1988); Allan I. Forrest, *The French Revolution and the Poor* (St. Martin's, 1981); and G. F. E. Rude, *The Crowd in the French Revolution* (Greenwood, 1986). Lynn Avery Hunt turns attention to the cities in *Revolution and Urban Politics in Provincial France, 1786–1790* (Stanford Univ., 1978). For the marshalling of public opinion, see Hugh Gough, *The Newspaper Press in the French Revolution* (Lyceum, 1988) and M. L. Kennedy, *The Jacobin Clubs in the French Revolution* (Princeton Univ., 1988). The role of the revolutionary army is ably depicted in Samuel Scott, *The Response of the Royal Army to the French Revolution* (Clarendon, 1978); Jean-Paul Bertaud, *The Army of the French Revolution: From Citizen Soldiers to Instrument of Power* (Princeton Univ., 1989); and Alan Forrest, *Conscripts and Deserters: The Army and French Society During the Revolution and Empire* (Oxford Univ., 1989). For glimpses of the chronological development of the Revolution, see Georges Lefebvre, *The Great Fear* (Vintage, 1973); Marc Bouloiseau, *The Jacobin Republic, 1791–1794* (Cambridge Univ., 1984); C. Blum, *Rousseau and the Republic of Virtue* (Cornell Univ., 1986); S. Loomis, *Paris in the Terror* (Richardson and Slierman, 1986); and Martyn Lyons, *France Under the Directory* (Cambridge Univ., 1975).

On the part played by women in the Revolution, see Linda Kelley, *Women of the French Revolution* (David and Charles, 1988); Joan B. Landes, *Women and the Public Sphere in the Age of the French Revolution* (Cornell Univ., 1988); Samia I. Spencer, *French Women and the Age of the Enlightenment* (Indiana Univ., 1984); and Winifred Stephens, *Women of the French Revolution* (Dutton, 1922).

For issues relating to blacks, see Edward S. Seebes, *Antislavery Opinion in France During the Second Half of the Eighteenth Century* (Greenwood, 1969); Shelby McCloy, *The Negro in France* (Univ. of Kentucky, 1961): Mitchell Ganett, *The French Colonial Question, 1789–1791* (Negro Universities, 1970); and Anna J. Cooper, *Slavery and the French Revolutionists* (Edwin Milleau Press, 1988).

The following biographical studies of French personalities in the revolutionary era are recommended: Robert R. Palmer, *Twelve Who Ruled* (Princeton Univ., 1970); James M. Thompson, *Leaders of the French Revolution* (Blackwell, 1988); John Mills Whitham, *Men and Women of the French Revolution* (Ayer, 1982); Vincent Cronin, *Louis and Antoinette* (Morrow, 1975); Bernard Fay, *Louis XVI* (Regnery, 1968); Olivier Bernier, *Lafayette, Hero of Two Worlds* (Dutton, 1983); Norman Hampson, *Danton* (Holmes and Meier, 1978); Louis R. Gottschalk, *Jean Paul Marat* (Univ. of Chicago, 1967); D. P. Jordan, *The Revolutionary Career of Maximilen Robespierre* (Free Press, 1985); and James M. Thompson, *Robespierre and the French Revolution* (English Universities, 1970).

For short-term impacts of the Revolution, see Robert R. Dozier, *For King, Constitution, and Country* (Univ. of Kentucky, 1983), which shows the reaction of British conservatives. The radical reaction is revealed in H. T. Dickenson, *British Radicalism and the French Revolution, 1789–1814* (Blackwell, 1985) and S. Deane, *The French Revolution and Enlightenment in England, 1789–1832* (Harvard Univ., 1988). The long-term effects are recognized in Geoffrey Best, *The Permanent Revolution: the French Revolution and Its Legacy, 1789–1989* (Univ. of Chicago, 1989).

Notes

1. Quoted in Clinton Rossiter, *The First American Revolution* (New York: Harcourt, Brace, 1956), prefatory note.
2. Thomas Paine, *The Crisis*, first published in the *Pennsylvania Journal*, Dec. 19, 1776, and reprinted in Moncure D. Conway, ed., *The Writings of Thomas Paine* (New York: Ames Press, 1967), p. 168.
3. William Macdonald, ed., *Select Documents Illustrative of the History of the United States* (New York: Bart Franklin, 1968), p. 2.
4. For the text of the Declaration, see J. N. Larned, ed., *The New Larned History*, 12 vols. (Springfield, MA, 1923), vol. 4, pp. 3301–3302.
5. For the text of Leopold's Declaration of Pilnitz (August 27, 1791), see John Hall Stewart, *A Documentary Survey of the French Revolution* (New York: Macmillan, 1951), pp. 223–224.
6. *Ibid.*, p. 181. Quotation is from the Convention's decree of November 19, 1792.

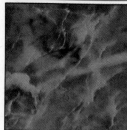

Chapter 22

The European Shadow over Africa and Asia

Developments in the Non-Western World, 1650–1815

Napoleon's occupation of Egypt (see ch. 23, p. 595) in 1798 was only one indication of a new European aggressiveness against Asia and Africa. Taking advantage of Iberian decline in the 1600s, northern Europeans eagerly sought to exploit the markets and influence the political affairs of people on other continents. This north European expansion was furthered by the Enlightenment, which encouraged interest in foreign lands; by European capitalism, which revolutionized native economies; and by increasing European, notably British, naval power.

Africans and Asians responded in various ways to these insistent challenges to their traditions and ways of life. The Japanese, fearful of contamination, attempted complete isolation of their country. Burma, Thailand, and Ethiopia tried similar policies, in defense against presumptuous Jesuit missionaries or unprincipled European soldiers of fortune. China cooperated with the Jesuits but cautiously kept them under strict controls. In other places, such as Vietnam, Persia, the Ottoman Empire, and parts of Africa and the Pacific, opinion and even official policy fluctuated between outraged rejection and enthusiastic acceptance of Western culture. Such divisiveness was most evident by 1800 in some regions of Indonesia and India, where Europeans were courted, and imitated, and treated as a new ruling class. Although some Asians and Africans were still openly scornful of European culture, all were now forced to take Europeans seriously.

At the end of the 18th century, large areas of the world were still free of European political domination, but their continued independence was becoming more doubtful. Even in East Asia, where China and Japan were strong states, with deep-rooted traditions and magnificent cultural achievements, changes brought by Europeans caused serious internal problems. Across southern Asia and along the African coasts, steady European penetration brought social disintegration while furthering civil and regional strife, results perhaps best illustrated by the African slave trade. Elsewhere, Europeans were already conquering and exploring less politically organized societies. The Russian movement across Siberia, the English and French forays into Polynesia, and Dutch advances in Indonesia and South Africa continued a process similar, if not identical, to earlier Spanish exploits in the Western hemisphere. The way was thus prepared for European mastery over Asia and Africa in the nineteenth century.

Sub-Sahara Africa

By 1800, the population of sub-Sahara Africa stood at more than forty million people, almost a third more than in 1650. Such expansion helps explain the continuing Bantu migrations, which reached the vicinity of the Cape of Good Hope by the late eighteenth century. Increasing population also contributed to great social and political changes, including the rise of new kingdoms, both in the interior and along the coasts. New inland states developed largely from native traditions, but along the West coast, from the Senegal beyond the Niger delta, European influences were growing rapidly with the rising Atlantic slave trade. For the most part, these European contacts did not yet threaten native authority; but farther south, the process of North European colonialism had already begun, with the Portuguese and the Dutch playing major roles.

The Dutch in South Africa

Established in 1652 as a supply post for Dutch East India Company ships, Cape Colony in South Africa developed very slowly at first but later grew rapidly, producing a dynamic society almost completely isolated from the outside world. The colony's white settlers, constantly at odds with the company and the home government, were even more antagonistic towards black Africans, some of whom made up a depressed majority of the Cape's population while others presented an imposing foreign obstacle to the colony's expansion.

During the first half century of its existence, the colony acquired its distinguishing characteristics. Although the first governor, Jan van Riebeeck, was given strict instructions to seek cooperation and avoid friction with Africans, the native Khoisans (Hottentots) and Bushmen were cattleherders and hunters who did not want to work for the Dutch or respect their property. After 1659, when nine company agents were permitted to occupy adjacent lands, the new settlers clashed with Hottentots over land rights and cattle raids. Such problems multiplied with the arrival of more settlers, including three hundred French Huguenots. Reluctantly, the company extended its lands, organizing the outlying provinces under appointed officials. By 1700, the colony had extended its domain a hundred miles beyond Cape Town, and the white population had expanded to more than sixteen hundred people.

This growth continued while the colony's distinctive culture developed to full maturity. Whites in Cape Town made up one distinct class among the elite; a second included the farmers within the colony's boundaries, which extended 300 miles north and 500 miles east by 1800. Twenty thousand whites lived there. Beyond the boundaries were more whites, already moving their families, wagons, and herds toward new pasturelands. Most free Hottentots and Bushmen had now been eliminated by wars or smallpox; some remained as servants and laborers, particularly at Cape Town, along with a large number of mixed-breed "colored peoples." Blacks from other parts of Africa and Malays from Southeast Asia made up a slave majority of the population. The typical colonist (*Afrikaner*) was an uneducated and narrow God-fearing Calvinist, who felt superior to all non-whites. Among ranchers on the frontier, these characteristics were augmented by fierce individualism, bravery, and aggressiveness.

While Afrikaners (also called Boers) were migrating toward the interior, a similar process was in progress among the Nguni, a Bantu people, ranging along the southeast coast. Like the Boers, the Nguni were cattle herders, looking for land as their population expanded. One of their numerous kinship groups, the Xosa, had reached the Fish River by 1700. Other Nguni groups were soon involved in wars leading toward political amalgamations. One of these groups, the Zulu, was a recognized formidable power among the Nguni. Around 1800, a Zulu chief named Dingiswayo developed mass infantry tactics and new weapons, such as the short stabbing spear, which were to be so effective in subsequent Zulu wars.

Although the major clash of cultures was yet to come, Boer and Bantu began a long series of wars when they first met along the Fish River. At first, the two sides traded cattle, horses, and even guns, but major violence erupted in 1779, when raiding blacks were driven back across the river. After another war ten years later, the provincial governor (*landrost*) prevented the white settlers from sending a punitive expedition into Xosa territory. The farmers, however, raised their own hard-riding commando forces and conducted their own campaigns. This was only one in a series of disagreements between the frontier farmers and the Cape government.

Discontent and political agitation increased markedly during the Napoleonic era. At first, the three major issues were the dictatorial policies of the government, the parent company's monopolistic trade policies, and the authorities' unwillingness to deal forcefully with the Xosa. In 1795, after another Xosa war, the provinces of Graaff Reinet and Swellendam rose against the Cape government and set up new republics.

These movements collapsed with British occupation of the Cape, which began in 1795 and was interrupted briefly between 1803 and 1806. The new regime restored order, affirmed the legal dependency of the Hottentots, freed trade, and erected garrisons on the eastern frontier; but it also forbade the importing of slaves and took legal action against those who abused their Hottentot servants. Moreover, the firm but essentially conciliatory British policy toward the Xosa continued to frustrate backcountry Boers. With the eastern frontier seething and recently-arrived English missionaries demanding human rights for slaves and Hottentots, the country faced a serious crisis in 1815.

Impact of the Atlantic Slave Trade

While Afrikaners were moving toward the Fish River, other Europeans were becoming increasingly active in the Atlantic slave trade, a great international complex of enterprises involving the economies of four continents. It had begun earlier with the Portuguese but reached its peak in the eighteenth century. Because it was conducted in parternerships between Africans and Europeans, the trade was a less obvious short-term danger to African interests than the migrating Dutch settlers, but it posed a more serious long-term threat.

The full historical significance of the trade can best be understood if it is viewed in its broader setting. Europe's economy at the time derived large profits from bulk plantation commodities like sugar, tobacco, and coffee. The most productive European plantations, in the West Indies, depended primarily upon slave labor from West Africa. Thus slaving ports like Liverpool in England and Bordeaux in France became thriving centers of a new prosperity. Other related industries, such as shipbuilding, sugar refining, distilling, textiles, and hardware also flourished. All contributed much to the development of European capitalism and ultimately to the Industrial Revolution.

Northern Europe's commercial impetus reached West Africa in the middle of the seventeenth century. The Portuguese, after losing the whole Atlantic coast to the Dutch, won back only Angola. For a while, the Dutch nearly monopolized the trade, operating from Elmina on the Gold Coast. The British subsequently established footholds there at Cormantin and Cape Castle; by 1700, they had seven other posts in the area. The French, meanwhile, acquired St. Louis on the Senegal, in the north, controlling most trade as far south as the Gambia River. In the resulting triangular competition, the Dutch faced constant pressure from their two rivals but maintained their dominance from a dozen strong Gold Coast forts.

By 1700, Britain was challenging this Dutch predominance. Having defeated the Dutch at sea in the late 1600s, England next defeated France in the War of the Spanish Succession. At the ensuing Peace of Utrecht in 1713, Britain obtained the right to sell 4800 slaves each year in Spanish ports. Another advantage after 1751 was the British shift from a monopolistic chartered company to an association of merchants, which increased incentives by opening opportunities for individual traders. Finally, in the continuing Anglo-French colonial wars of the eighteenth century, the British fleet consistently hampered French operations. For these reasons, the British by 1780 were transporting twice as many slaves from West Africa as all of their competitors.

Despite this regional competition among Europeans, they conducted the trade locally as a black-white partnership, largely on black terms. Native rulers, like Queen Auguina, a British ally on the Gold Coast in the eighteenth century, were not only able to enforce their authority but eagerly took profits from regular port fees, rents on the slave stockades, called *barracoons*, and a contracted percentage on the sale of slaves. Ordinary subjects also participated as partners in the slave trade. Some free native blacks conducted trading expeditions to the interior, while others found work as guides, clerks, or translators. Thus arose a middle class of semi-Europeanized blacks and mulattoes. Many adopted European dress, and a few were lionized in Europe or became Christian missionaries. For example, Betsy Heard, the mulatto daughter of a Liverpool slave factor on the Guinea Coast, was educated in England before returning to manage her father's post. She became wealthy, powerful, and respected, but most white traders were not so fortunate. Plagued by an unhealthy climate and surrounded by suspicious foreigners, they led short, dreary lives in their remote exiles.

Mungo Park, with a Slave Caravan to the Coast

This account of personal experiences is from the journal of Mungo Park, a great English pioneer of African exploration, who discovered the headwaters of the Niger. He died on the return journey down the river in 1805.

April 19th. The long wished-for day of our departure was at length arrived; and the Slatees [black slave traders] having taken the irons from their slaves, assembled with them at the door of Karfa's house, where the bundles were all tied up, and every one had his load assigned him. The coffle [caravan] on its departure from Kamalia, consisted of twenty-seven slaves for sale but we were afterwards joined by five at Maraboo and three at Bala, making in all thirty-five slaves.

When we depared from Kamalia, we were followed for about half a mile by most of the inhabitants of the town, some of them crying and other shaking hands with their relations, who were now about to leave them; and when we had gained a piece of rising ground, from which we had a view of Kamalia, all the people belonging to the coffle were ordered to sit down with their faces towards Kamalia. The schoolmaster, with two of the principal Slatees, pronounced a long and solemn prayer; after which they walked three times round the coffle, making an impression in the ground with the ends of their spears and muttering something by way of charm. When this ceremony was ended, all the people belonging to the coffle sprang up, and without taking a formal farewell of their friends set forward. As many of the slaves had remained for years in irons, the sudden exertion of walking quick with heavy loads upon their heads occasioned spasmodic contractions of their legs; and we had not proceeded above a mile before it was found necessary to take two of them from the rope, and allow them to walk more slowly until we reached a walled village, where some people were waiting to join the coffle.

. . . On the morning of the 21st we entered the woods. During this day's travel, two slaves, a woman and a girl, were so much fatigued that they could not keep up with the coffle; they were severely whipped, and dragged along until about three in the afternoon when they were both affected with vomiting, by which it was discovered that they had *eaten clay.* This practice is by no means uncommon amongst the Negroes; but whether it arises from a vitiated appetite, or from a settled intention to destroy themslves, I cannot affirm. They were permitted to lie down in the woods and three people remained with them until they had rested themselves; but they did not arrive at the town [where we were camping] until past midnight, and were then so much exhausted that the Slatees gave up all thought of taking them across the woods in their present condition. . . .

On the 30th we reached Jallacotta, a considerable town. Here one of the slaves belonging to the coffle, who had traveled with great difficulty for the last three days, was found unable to proceed any further: his master proposed therefore to exchange him for a young slave girl, belonging to one of the townspeople. The poor girl was ignorant of her fate until the bundles were all tied up in the morning, and the coffle ready to depart, when, coming with the other young women to see the coffle set out, her master took her by the hand, and delivered her to her new owner. Never was a face of serenity more suddenly changed into one of the deepest distress; the terror she manifested on having the load put upon her head, and the rope fastened around her neck, and the sorrow with which she bade adieu to her companions were truly affecting.

Source: Rhoda Hoff, ed., *Africa: Adventures in Eyewitness History* (New York: Henry Z. Walck, 1963), pp. 39–40, 42–44.

Most slaves awaiting shipment in West African *barracoons* had been taken in war, but some had been kidnapped or bought from their own people by profit-seeking black middlemen. Only a very few had been seized by white raiders. Slaves were usually forcibly marched to the coast in gangs, chained or roped together, and worn down by poor food, lack of water, unattended illnesses, and brutal beatings. Once in the *barracoons*, where they might stay for months, they were examined for physical defects by ship doctors and then displayed before captains, looking to buy their cargoes. The bargaining was hard and complex, as slaves were exchanged for trinkets, rum, cloth, and particularly firearms. Because the overseas demand was for plantation laborers, males brought the highest prices. Women were less valuable abroad and more desired for work in African villages, so they were less than half as frequently traded as men. Late in the eighteenth century, when slave prices rose, some efforts were made to use female slaves for breeding. Generally, however, such efforts failed, because most slave women regarded children as burdens and resisted pregnancy by every means possible to them.

Although relatively few African women were transported in the Atlantic trade, it hurt them in other ways. Slavery, as practiced earlier in African societies had been more humane than under white tutelage, but women had been customarily enslaved as concubines and used to produce offspring for rulers and wealthy men. As more black males were shipped abroad, this process was further encouraged. Thus more women lost the protection of their families, which they would have enjoyed as legal wives. But for females in the slaving ports, conditions were much worse. African rulers furnished women as favors to their European business partners, along with fresh fruit and flowers. Every white man had free access to black slave women, who could be used, abused, and discarded at will.

After the *barracoons*, slaves met a worse nightmare on the ships. Women were usually huddled together on an open deck; male slaves were packed together, side by side in lower decks, each being allotted a space sixteen inches wide by two and a half feet high. When some refused to eat, a special device, the "mouth opener" was used to force-feed them. Some slaves jumped into the sea while being exercised, and those who contracted diseases were frequently thrown overboard. Mutinies were common and were punished with savage brutality. One woman mutineer on a British ship in the early 1800s was hoisted by her thumbs, whipped, and slashed with knives, in view of other slaves, until she died. Understandably, the mortality rate on slave ships exceeded 12 percent, not counting those who died after landings. Yet these conditions did not shake the Christian faith of some captains. "This day," one confided to his journal in 1752, "I have reason . . . to beg a public blessing from Almighty God upon our voyage. . . ."[1]

The era after the Peace of Utrecht has been termed the slave century. Between 1600 and 1700, when the slave trading companies were mostly state-chartered monopolies, some 1.5 million slaves were carried across the Atlantic. In the next eleven decades, until 1810, when much more trade was being conducted by individual captains outside the forts, over 6 million slaves were actually landed in the Americas. In the decade after 1780, during which 750,000 blacks were taken from West Africa, the trade reached its peak.

In 1807, Britain outlawed the slave trade. The Enlightenment, plus the strong humanitarian movement in England, had prepared the way for this act, but even more decisive factors were Britains rapidly declining Caribbean plantations and pressure from British industrialists, whose primary concern was free foreign markets. With the British fleet patrolling the Atlantic after 1807, looking for slavers, many West Africans were confused by an economic future for which they were unprepared by two centuries of commerce with Europeans.

While it lasted, the Atlantic slave trade hurt emerging black states, but the results were not in themselves decisive. Even with the loss of ten to fifteen million people over three centuries, the population still expanded. Indeed, new foods bought from the West, such as cassava and sweet potatoes, may have increased population more than slaving diminished it. Other direct European influences failed to penetrate very far inland before 1800, but indirect influences were very significant. A native trend in the direction of political centralization was reoriented towards war, tyranny, and brutality. While concentrating upon European weapons and trinkets, West Africans failed to acquire the knowledge or capital for stimulating local productivity. Finally, the trade divided Africans and promoted racism, both in West Africa and abroad.

Native African States

While West Africa developed, under the influence of the slave trade, new states in the remote interior of the continent were forming and making contact with the outside world. In the process, royal powers, militarism, and male authority were all increasing. These trends, which were common among new inland states, were magnified in West Africa, where slave trading and war became the main activities.

The most Europeanized states of West Africa were the independent slave-market cities of the marshy Niger delta tributaries. Originally fishing villages under clan leaders, they developed with the trade after 1650 into wealthy republics like Brass and Calabar or autocratic monarchies, like Bonny, under Queen Kanbasa. Their old kinship wards became commercial "houses," each comprising a family, with an extended organization, including multiple laboring wives, servants, slaves, and sometimes, adopted white traders. These business organizations and secret societies combined African rites with European capitalism in conducting their slave trading. Using fleets of war canoes, armed with cannon and manned by musket-bearing paddlers, they acquired slaves from contacts in the interior. The most dependable source was a native religious order, which collected religious fines in slaves, using armed mercenaries to enforce its exactions.

West of the Niger and the declining empire of Benin, the period brought a political transition, as inland states were forced into slaving competition. The first of these was Oyo, inland on the savanna. It became a great military state, conquering an area along the coast near Bagdari and dominating the trade there. The *Alafins* (kings) of Oyo were autocrats, whose mothers were executed when their sons were crowned. A new official queen mother was given absolute authority over the king's conjugal wives and hundreds of other women who conducted palace business. But all were humble royal servants.

Of all the West African states, Dahomey, located west of Oyo, was perhaps most decisively affected by the slave trade. Constantly at war with Oyo and once nearly destroyed, it reoriented its whole culture toward discipline and military prowess, becoming an absolute monarchy, with every subject's life at the ruler's command. The slave trade and every aspect of the economy were rigidly controlled as royal business. Everyone was required to do military service, even women, who served in the famous "Amazon" contingents, fighting in major wars and providing an élite palace guard. Women comprised the inner government, centered in the palace. The king's first wife often shared real power in what was perhaps a carryover from an earlier day; but the appointed queen mother, her staff, which conducted all public affairs for the king, the royal harem, and a horde of female servants, were usually slaves. Despite such dangerous insecurity, they were considered safer than male subjects. This was all part of a ruthless, brutal realm, where human sacrifice was regularly performed and piles of freshly severed human heads adorned the royal chambers.

More successful in war than Dahomey was Assante (Ashanti), a state still farther west behind the Gold Coast, which was forced about 1680 to unite its clans and fight for its independence against a slave-seeking neighbor, Denkyra. This occurred under an *asantehene* (king) named Osei Tutu (1680–1717), who established control around his capital at Kumasi. His successor, Opoku Ware (1720–1750), extended Assante dominion into the Savannah. By 1800, Assante kings controlled most inland trade through European posts on the Gold Coast.

Although not a rigid military dictatorship like Dahomey, the Assante Empire was the most formidable military power in West Africa before 1815. It profited largely from the slave trade but also exported kola nuts, cloth, metalwork and gold to the Muslim north. This economic diversity allowed Assante to avoid complete dependence upon slave trading and preserve many of its rich traditions. Assante confidence, pride, and courage were also maintained without the brutal repression of Dahomey. Royal authority was shared locally by semiautonomous subkings; in the central government, the king was assisted by the official queen mother, who advised him on public decisions, sat in the council, presided over her own court, supervised affairs directly involving women, and, upon occasion, might participate in deposing a king. Such safeguards against absolutism did not prevent Assante from successfully opposing European imperialism into the nineteenth century.

The southwest coast, from the Bight of Biafra to the Cunene River, presented a contrasting picture, as it remained under disastrous Portuguese domination. In 1665, after years of friction, the Portuguese invaded Kongo, leaving the central government in a shambles and the country ruled by local nobles. By 1800, European influences there were hardly discernible, and the once-proud kingdom was only a distant memory. Angola suffered an even worse fate. Despite heroic efforts at defense by Queen Anna Nzinga (1623–1663), the Portuguese conquered the land and turned it into a vast slave-hunting preserve. In the eighteenth century a governing élite lived in luxury at the ports of Luanda and Benguela, while Portuguese captains ruled over native chiefs in outlying districts. The nearby kingdoms of Kasanje, Matamba, and Ovimbundu, having become Portuguese allies, acquired slaves for the coast by trading or raiding in remote inland areas.

Equally calamitous events followed Portuguese endeavors in southeast Africa. Soon after 1629, rebellion and wars ended Portuguese influence in the Rhodesian highlands. Portuguese puppet rulers, the Monomotapas, held only nominal control over the Zambezi hinterlands between Tete and Sena. In this unhappy country, the only effective authority was held by half-caste Portuguese, who occupied large estates (prazos), led armies, raised taxes, and took slaves where they could. Most of their slaves were laborers, but a few, including some women, became overseers or low-level managers on plantations. More ruthless and cruel than native African chiefs, prazo adventurers contributed most to the continuing turmoil of the region.

During the eighteenth century, strong new kingdoms arose in south central and eastern Africa. They included the Lunda Empire, east of Angola; Kazembe, one of Lunda's vassals and the strongest central African state just before 1800; the Shona state of Changamire, which drove out the Portuguese and ruled the upper Zambezi from the ancient capital of Great Zimbabwe; and finally Buganda, after the late 1600s a new empire of banana-growing farmers in the north, between Lakes Albert and Victoria. Each of these states, while unique in its own traditions, created a large territorial monarchy, complete with military forces and provincial administrations. They were especially similar in their still-functioning matriarchial institutions, with queen mothers (sometimes actually king's sisters) exercising real political power, often in their own palaces or commanding their own armies. Such institutions began to change, however, as each kingdom developed trade with the east coast in the eighteenth century.

While new states were rising in East Africa, the oldest African polity, Ethiopia, was near collapse in the same region. Trouble began when the political intrigues of resident Jesuits caused Emperor Fasilidas (1632–1667) to expel them and sever all relations with Europeans. This nationalistic reaction brought temporary unity and cultural advance, but isolation from the Christian world, along with traditional Muslim hostility, soon led to new wars and internal rebellions. In their permanent capital at Gondar, most eighteenth-century Ethiopian monarchs lost touch with their people, although an eccentric folk hero, Emperor Asma Giorgis, with the counsel of this queen, Burgan Mugassa, restored order between 1719 and 1729. After her husband's death, Mugassa provided relative stability during her son's reign and into the 1750s, but her era was followed by harem intrigues, palace murders, army mutinies, and foreign invasions. By 1790 the country was a strange synthesis of savagery and decaying grandeur.

The Muslim World in Decline

Political problems facing black African states after the middle of the seventeenth century were minor compared with those of the Muslim world. From North Africa to Indonesia, Muslim polities were verging on collapse after 1700. Even in the great Islamic empires, vested interests, traditional orthodoxy, and overconfidence continually prevented necessary adjustments. Only in parts of Africa, where Islam was still beginning to put down roots, could Muslim societies generate new energies.

Muslim Africa

The Swahili city-states of East Africa almost had been destroyed by the Portuguese, and the black states of the western Sudan languished after the Moroccan conquest. In this era, however, conditions were changing. Omani Arabs first drove the Portuguese from the East African coast. Then a wave of Muslim religious zeal, rising on the Senegal, spread past the Niger and Hausaland to the borders of Guinea. By the nineteenth century, Muslim Africa was beginning to recover.

In East Africa this revival was more symbolic than real. Two centuries of Portuguese domination and Portuguese-Omani wars had conditioned the area to ruthless brutality and treachery. Once free of the Portuguese, the Swahili cities fought among themselves and, except for Zanzibar, against their new Muslim masters. Although confusion prevailed, population did grow, and commerce prospered sporadically. Most trade was in slaves, particularly with the French, who were developing plantations on their Indian Ocean islands of Mauritius and Bourbon. But increasing wealth brought no cultural or religious renaissance. Although the maturing Swahili language produced some excellent literature, the strikingly beautiful architecture, so evident in earlier mosques and palaces, was generally missing in this period.

A similar evaluation might be made about another African Muslim state, Morocco under the Alawite dynasty. Sultan Mulay Ismail (1672–1727), the most colorful Alawite ruler, corresponded with Louis XIV and sent an ambassador to the court of Charles II in England. His uncontested power was based upon a standing army of black slaves, recruited or captured in the Sudan as children and trained for specialized tasks. The sultan proved himself to be an exceptionally competent administrator, a wily military commander, and a patron of the arts. Yet Morocco was a pirate state, similar to Algeria or Tunis; its values were symbolized when Mulay received the French ambassador with his royal hands bloodied by his personal participation in a recent execution.[2] Under Mulay's successors, the country achieved stability but remained isolated and economically backward.

Even more isolated were the Muslim states of the Sudan, as the overland gold trade declined after 1650. The Moroccan conquest of 1590 had broken the Songhai Empire into a number of small kingdoms, which fought among themselves while resisting the degenerating regimes of Moroccan *pashas* in the commerical cities. For awhile, Kanem-Bornu exerted a stabilizing force in the region around Lake Chad, but its power steadily weakened during the eighteenth century. By that time, the Hausa city states, notably Kano, Katsina, and Gobir, were rising to prominence as they profited from the expanding trade now moving across the central Sahara to the Mediterranean coast. Meanwhile, new Muslim states were rising at the eastern and western extremities of the region; Fulani-Tukulor kingdoms along the Senegal in the west and the sultanates of Tonjur, Fur, and Funj in the Egyptian Sudan.

In these areas, so remote from the complex Middle Eastern world, Islam launched its one effective crusade during the period. Supporting the movement were Fulani religious leaders, who criticized the lax morality, heretical policies, and the religious subordination of women by West African Muslims, particularly the rulers. The Fulani, a seminomadic people, having established a number of theocratic regimes on the Senegal, spread their communities and their religious societies throughout the western Sudan. Between 1786 and 1809, an eloquent Fulani holy man named Usman dan Fodio (1754–1817) led a holy war (*jihad*), which overthrew the native governments and united most Hausa lands into a highly centralized state, with a capital at Sokoto on the lower Niger. Although failing to conquer Bornu, Sokoto did expand considerably while evoking Muslim enthusiasm as far as the eastern Sudan. This fervor continued through much of the nineteenth century, although its concern for female piety did little to check the decline of women's rights in the region.

Delayed Disintegration of the Ottoman Empire

The African Islamic revival encouraged already rising unrest throughout the Ottoman Empire, which, in its glory days, had stretched across North Africa, around the Red Sea, and through the Middle East (see map, p. 366). Now many of these areas were breaking away, while internal revenues dropped and civil turmoil spread. Ottoman collapse was generally anticipated, but this catastrophe was somehow mysteriously delayed. While the sultan's government broke down, local authorities still functioned, imperial pretenses remained in court formalities, and, at times, some intellectual vigor flourished. Even in this dream world, however, it was readily apparent that what had once been the fighting empire of the Ghazis could no longer defend its boundaries and existed only as a pawn for European nations. Only the competitive distrust among these foreign powers delayed the Ottoman demise.

Toward the middle of the seventeenth century, the empire experienced an abortive revival. For nearly a decade after the deposition of Sultan Ibrahim in 1648, the state was nearly destroyed by palace intrigues and general rebellion, reaching a climax when mutinous janissaries hanged thirty officials before a mosque in Istanbul. The *vizier*, a seventy-nine-year-old Albanian bureaucrat named Mehmet Köprülü (1656–1661), restored order by executing more than 35,000 dissidents within his five year term. His son, Ahmed, who served effectively from 1661 to 1676, could afford to be more humane than his father. Under the two Köprülüs, taxes were reformed, a cultural renaissance encouraged, and Ottoman forces defeated Poland and Austria. It was the last significant period of Ottoman expansion and achievement.

After this brief revival, the Ottoman polity weakened steadily, as special interests multiplied. The central bureaucracy and the janissary contingents, no longer consisting of trained slaves, became self-perpetuating elites, consistently pursuing their selfish objectives while opposing reforms. Another grasping hereditary aristocracy arose among tax-farmers in the country. Their selfishness was matched by the narrow Muslim prejudices of the *ulema*, a religious guild that stubbornly controlled the courts and education. Non-Turkish minorities, who conducted most industry and internal trade, felt increasingly alienated from a government without respect for commerce. Yet representatives of French and English companies, while often subject to public indignities, had to be granted special trade concessions so they would supply necessary goods, such as military weapons and supplies. All of these problems reflected the Ottomans' inability to make necessary adjustments.

The most convincing evidence of the need for change was provided by continuing territorial losses. The Turks lost Hungary, part of Romania, and much of Serbia to Austria by the Peace of Carolowitz in 1699 and the Treaty of Passarowitz in 1718. In three wars with Russia, culminating in the Treaty of Kuchuk Kainarja (1774), they had to give up the Crimea, the right to protect Christians in Istanbul, and commercial access to the Black Sea. In the next two decades, as the Turks were pushed westward along the Black Sea coast, Russian plans for dismembering Turkey were abandoned only because of British and Prussian opposition. Meanwhile, the Ottomans were also losing territories to independence movements. Near home in European Rumelia and eastern Anatolia, native governors with popular backing established semi-independent dynasties, as did other nominal agents of the sultans in Kurdistan, Lebanon, and Arabia. In Iraq, Egypt, Tunis, Tripoli, and Algeria, *mamluk* or *janissary* garrisons created foreign military regimes amid native populations. A puritanical religious reaction against the Turkish caliphate, led by Abdul Wahhabi (1703–1792), laid foundations for the later Kingdom of Saudi Arabia. These new states sometimes nominally recognized Ottoman authority, but they were all practically independent by 1815.

Faced with so many serious problems, Ottoman policymakers alternated for more than a century between reform and reaction, as crises rose and abated. In the eighteenth century, two notable reform attempts occurred between 1713 and 1730 and again between 1774 and 1779. Each time, hopeful *viziers* attempted to reform the military along French lines and import new ideas from the West. Both efforts created mild initial enthusiasm, followed by violent reactions from the *ulema* and the janissaries. The classic example of such futility came during the reign of Selim III (1789–1807), who launched the most ambitious reform program yet attempted. He first conducted extensive investigations and then instituted sweeping changes in the whole Ottoman system, including administration, finance, and education. Most of his efforts and resources went to modernizing the navy and training a

Selim III's efforts to reform the Ottoman state were thwarted by the janissaries who deposed the sultan, imprisoned and later assassinated him.

"new model" army of 25,000 men, for which he used an enlarged corps of French officers. Unfortunately, Napoleon's invasion of Egypt in 1798 ruined everything. Caught in a squeeze between two sets of great European powers and accused at home of favoring the hated foreigners, Selim was deposed by a violent janissary uprising in 1807. His policies were all subsequently reversed or abandoned.

During the last years of the Napoleonic era, the Ottoman Empire endured still another serious crisis, barely surviving into the nineteenth century. The new sultan, Mahmud II (1807–1839), influenced by a strong-willed queen mother, was a progressive youth who was forced to hide his true intentions from the cabal of reactionary zealots surrounding him. Throughout the empire, local notables controlled the provinces; the Serbs were in revolt; the Wahhabi movement was sweeping through Arabia; and Egypt, under the Albanian strongman, Mehmet Ali, was rapidly becoming a new military power, capable of overthrowing Mahmud, despite Ali's assertions

of loyalty. Mahmud also faced a continuing war with Russia, which brought the loss of Bessarabia when the war finally ended in 1812. Under these circumstances, the only favorable prospect for the Muslim state was the British determination to exclude other great powers from the eastern Mediterranean.

Decline in Muslim Middle Eurasia

East of the weakening Ottoman realm, Muslim Middle Eurasia experienced its own dreary decadence. Central Asia, the earlier saviour of Islam, was now caught between the Russians and the Chinese, its nomad armies scattered and its bazaar cities languishing. Iran and Afghanistan, so prominent during the golden era of the Safavids and the Mughuls, now comprised a commercial and cultural backwater. Despite temporary military revivals and destructive forays into India, the area produced no lasting powerful states. Subject to rising pressure from Russia and increasing dependence upon Britain for protection and vital world trade, Iranians and Afghans had lost control of their destinies by 1815.

Much of Iran's degeneration resulted from a decree of 'Abbās I (1588–1629) stipulating that future princes be raised within the harem, isolated from affairs. Consequently, the four last Safavid shahs all lacked experience and leadership. The best of them, 'Abbās II (1642–1667), managed to take back Kandahar from the Mughuls and patronize the arts. Sulayman (1667–1694) left affairs to his vizier while pursuing his sensual pleasures. His son, Sultan Husayn (1694–1772), a meek man who let the *mullahs* make most decisions, finally abdicated his throne to a marauding Afghan chieftain, and for nearly a decade, the land was given over to civil war, massacre, and plunder. When the Turks and Russians attacked, the country survived only because the two invaders restrained each other.

Iran raised itself from such chaos twice during the eighteenth century, but in neither case was the recovery lasting. The first revival was effected by Nader Shah (1736–1747), an army officer of Turkish descent, who drove out the Afghans, reformed the government, reorganized the army, and assumed the imperial title. By 1747, he had regained territories lost to the Russians and the Turks, conquered western

Afghanistan, plundered the Mughul capital at Delhi, and extended Iranian hegemony over the Uzbegs to the north. But his plans for uniting Shi'ite and Sunni Muslims failed, and he ended his reign as a frustrated tyrant, struck down by his own officers. The second revival, a milder one, came under Karim Khan Zand, who ruled justly over a much smaller state in western Iran between 1750 and 1779. At his death the country lapsed again into savage feudal contention.

In the third quarter of the eighteenth century, a new Muslim empire arose between the faltering Iranian and Mughul states. It was created by a contingent of Nader Shah's Afghan cavalrymen, who chose Ahmad Shah Durrani to be their commander in 1747, thus establishing an Afghan dynasty that would last into the twentieth century. In twenty years, Ahmad united the Afghans and conquered a vast empire, which took in eastern Iran, present-day Afghanistan, the major part of Uzbeg Turkestan, and much of northwestern India, including Kashmir and the Punjab. During one campaign in India, Ahmad sacked Delhi, decisively defeating the Marathas, and opening the country to the British. Although brutal to his enemies, the Afghan monarch was very able, but his sprawling tribal-feudal state lapsed into continuous civil wars after he died in 1772.

As these states weakened, they faced increasing European pressures. Russia and Britain, particularly, had long competed for Iranian trade; in addition, the Russians continued to seek territories around the Caspian and actually forced substantial concessions from Iran after a long war, terminating in 1813. The British, fully occupied in India after Nader Shah's death, had about abandoned their commercial ventures in Iran, but their interests were aroused again by French designs on India during the Napoleonic period. An Anglo-Persian defense and commercial treaty of 1880 encouraged the Shah to expect aid against Afghanistan and Russia; when this was not forthcoming, he accepted a French military mission to train his troops. This entente collapsed when the French and Russians signed a temporary truce. The British now negotiated a military alliance, took over Iranian military tutelage, and agreed to pay the Shah an annual subsidy. Subsequently, the Persian Gulf became a British sphere of influence.

Collapse of the Mughul Empire

The decline of Muslim civilization in India was even more pronounced than in the Middle East. European advances had long been a problem in western Asia and the Persian Gulf, but the Mughul Empire had been one of the world's wealthiest and most powerful states, with rich traditions, art, and literature, affecting the whole subcontinent. Its sudden collapse in the eighteenth century was a major catastrophe.

This tragedy resulted largely from the empire's internal contradictions, but the speed of decline must be mainly attributed to the last emperor. Aurangzeb (1659–1707) defeated and eliminated his brothers before seizing the throne from his father, Shah Jahan. The old ruler died in captivity, attended by his daughter, Johanara. Later, Aurangzeb exiled or imprisoned all but one of his sons and confined his eldest daughter, the poetess Zeb-un-Nisa, for life, because she had aided a rebellious brother. Aurangzeb clamped the same ruthless tyranny upon the country. He was an effective military commander and an able administrator but utterly without humane concerns in pursuing his objectives. This rigid determination, arising from the most narrow-minded confidence, was both his greatest strength and weakness.

Aurangzeb's policies directly undermined the imperial order established by the great Akbar (see ch. 14, pp. 372–372). The new emperor destroyed Hindu temples and schools, reimposed the ancient poll tax on Hindus, and dismissed Hindus from government service. Until about 1679, while occupied in securing his northern frontiers, he did not push these policies vigorously; but his later reign brought unyielding persecution, along with a holy war against "infidels" and Muslim heretics in southern India. For the rest of his life, Aurangzeb stayed in the field, heading an unwieldy host of 500,000 servants, 50,000 camels, and 30,000 elephants, in addition to the fighting men. By 1690, after terrible losses, he had overcome most resistance, but the area could not be permanently pacified. Time and again the aging ruler, ailing and afraid of death because of his sins, was forced to undertake new campaigns. He died amid his failures in 1707.

Even during Aurangzeb's reign the empire showed unmistakable signs of degeneration.

Obsessed as he was by fanatic Muslim orthodoxy and determined to suppress all opposition, the grim ruler neglected architecture, ceased patronizing the arts, and discouraged literary activities, although he did sponsor various projects in law and theology. Hindus suffered terribly, particularly the women. Unlike their Muslim counterparts, many had been educated and active in public life; some among the Marathas even led armies. Most of this ended with Aurangzeb's wars. And as revenues declined, tax-farming raised quick government income but also enriched corrupt officials at the expense of both Hindu and Muslim peasants. When Aurangzeb died, the once flourishing empire faced a serious economic crisis.

For another half century, the system lingered on the verge of collapse. After a series of civil wars, Muhammad Shah (1719–1748) succeeded to the imperial throne. Described by one contemporary as "never without a mistress in his arms and a glass in his hand," this indolent monarch made some effort to placate Hindus, with little practical result. Local Muslim dynasties sprang up in the south and in Bengal; the Sikhs, a Hindu-Muslim sect, became autonomous in the northwest; the Hindu Rajputs, once Mughul allies, began to break away; and the fierce Hindu Marathas, whom Aurangzeb had fought thirty years to subdue, extended their sway over much of central India. The impotence of the empire was most effectively demonstrated in 1739, when an invading Persian army burned and looted the Mughul capital at Delhi, carrying away the imperial peacock throne.

The Persian invasion was but a prelude to a nearly complete anarchy known as the "Time of Troubles," which prevailed after Muhammad Shah's death in 1748. His two successors during the next ten years became prisoners of their ministers, who fought each other in alliance with any supporters available. The Maratha Confederacy soon emerged as the most powerful force. It was effectively opposed, however, by the Afghan ruler Ahmad Shah (see p. 580) who declared his independence of Persia and invaded Hindustan. He sacked Delhi for the first time in 1756 and returned two years later. At Panipat, in 1761, his Afghans crushed a huge Maratha army, with their north Indian Muslim allies. This disaster settled nothing because the Afghans soon left India, and the country became a nearly lawless land of tyrants, greedy brigands, deserted cities, and famine-stricken villagers.

As the Mughul Empire disintegrated, the French and British were drawn into Indian politics as they competed against each other. Both spread their influence by using native troops, the famous *sepoys*, to protect native rulers, with whom they had negotiated trade agreements and alliances. For a time, France gained the advantage in this game, but British sea power during the Seven Years' War forced the French to abandon their political position in India. The British, meanwhile, at the battle of Plassy in 1757, had won outright control of Bengal from the local lord. Between 1806 and 1812 governors of the East India Company succeeded in forcing the emperor to accept British supremacy. With the Mughul emperors subsisting on British pensions, many Muslim rulers protected by garrisons under British officers, and the wealth of Bengal flowing through British hands, Mughul India was no longer a center of power in the Muslim world.

European Encroachments Around East Asia

The destructive European impact upon Africa and Muslim lands was matched by a similar process in the outlying areas of East Asia. On the mainland and among the islands of Southeast Asia, Europeans continued to intervene, with varying degrees of success, in the chaotic internal affairs of perpetually contending established states. Farther east, on hundreds of Pacific islands, European discovery and exploration resulted in quick revolutions, which tended to demoralize and destroy native cultures.

European Influences in Southeast Asia

The islands and the mainland in Southeast Asia showed contrasting reactions to European influences. The more flexible culture of the archipelago largely succumbed or remained inertly traditional. The stronger mainland states, aware of their vulnerability to China or their immediate neighbors, were sometimes compromised in seeking European aid. A more decisive factor, however, was their relatively sterile wars for survival and supremacy, in which Thailand and Vietnam were more successful than Burma, Cambodia, and Laos.

The late seventeenth century was a chaotic time for all the mainland states, with the possible exception of tiny Laos. Burma struggled under weak kings, corrupt ministers, local uprisings, Thai invasions, and Chinese-European competition for advantage. Thailand, meanwhile, faced internal turmoil, complicated by Dutch commercial and political pressure, which led first to British and then to French efforts to take over the country. Vietnam emerged from savage civil wars as two separate states, north and south. Both became tributaries of Ming China while trying to avoid granting special concessions to Europeans. These efforts were mainly successful, except in the case of French missionaries, who gained a strong foothold in the southern kingdom. Only Laos, during the long reign of Souligna-Vongsa (1637–1692) enjoyed sustained peace and good relations with its neighbors.

This situation changed drastically during the eighteenth century. Burma enjoyed a brief revival between 1752 and 1776, when two strong monarchs, Alaungpaya (1752–1759) and his son, Hsinbyushin (1763–1776), defeated the Thai, French, British, and Chinese. But this was the apex of Burmese power. In Thailand, after all Europeans were expelled in the early 1700s, a half-Chinese military commander, Paya Taksin, drove out the Burmese invaders, made himself king, and extended Thai influence over Laos, Cambodia, and Malaya. South Vietnam, meanwhile, doubled its territory by expanding into the Mekong Valley at the expense of Cambodia. Between 1786 and 1801, it united the country and began eliminating French control of affairs. On the surface, Southeast Asia seemed to be consolidating political power, buttressing traditional institutions, and ending foreign domination. But the stage was nevertheless set for the British conquest of Burma and French moves into Indochina, later in the nineteenth century.

Farther south, in Indonesia, the European presence was much more compelling and the native resistance much weaker. Of all Muslim societies, those in the Malay archipelago were less imbued with Islamic values and loyalties. Muslim and Malay traditions had been transformed by thousands of migrating Chinese. Most important of all, the Dutch, by the end of the period, had subordinated native dynasties in Malaya, Java, Sumatra, and the islands. Dutch plantation agriculture had brought an economic revolution that conditioned much of life and labor in the whole area within the limits set by European commercial capitalism.

For a time a Muslim Malay people known in history as the Bugis challenged Dutch supremacy. Originating on the island of Celebes, the Bugis first won fame as searovers and mercenary warriors, serving all sides in the competitive spice trade through the city of Macassar. When the Dutch took Macassar in 1667, the Bugis scattered from Borneo to the Malay Peninsula, where they concentrated at Selangor. Through conquest, intermarriage, and intrigue, they gained control of Jahore, Perak, and Kedah on the mainland, while extending their influence to Borneo and Sumatra. The Bugis fought two wars against Dutch Malacca in 1756 and 1784 but were ultimately forced to accept Dutch overlordship. In the end, they accomplished little beyond a further weakening of Malay power.

At the same time, the Dutch were losing ground to the British. With their East India Company facing internal corruption, increasing costs, and mounting competition, the Dutch could no longer maintain their independence amid the rising Anglo-French colonial rivalry. In Asia, this rivalry was centered primarily in India, but the British were also expanding their trade through the Malacca Straits and seeking a naval port to counter the French in the Bay of Bengal. In 1786, the British obtained Penang on the Malay coast. Later, when France dominated Holland during the Revolution and the Napoleonic era, the British temporarily took Malacca and Java. Penang then became a rapidly expanding center of British influence in Malaya.

Europeans on New Pacific Frontiers

Before 1650, the Pacific area was almost unknown to Europeans, but during the next century, they moved much closer. Some of this contact involved Russian ships cruising southward toward Japan from Kamchatka and French and

British penetration of the North Pacific from Polynesia. By the late eighteenth century, Western ships at Canton often operated from Hawaii or other Polynesian islands, as they conducted the developing maritime trade of the Pacific. For the first time, East Asians felt the Western world crowding in upon them.

Russians moved out toward the Pacific in 1632, when they established Yakutsk in eastern Siberia. From there, adventurers drifted down the Lena, first reaching the Arctic, and later sailing east to the open Pacific. Their discoveries were largely ignored until 1728, when Vitus Bering (1680–1741), a Danish navigator sailing for Peter the Great, charted the Bering Strait, which links the Arctic and Pacific Oceans. This opened the North Pacific to Russia during the eighteenth century. Meanwhile, the Russians founded Okhotsk on the Pacific coast opposite the Kamchatka peninsula. At Okhotsk and at other timbered forts in Siberia, Russian governors and their Cossack soldiers exacted tribute in furs from a society of nomadic hunters. Relations between the conquerers and their subjects were not particularly friendly; indeed local native populations around the forts were often wiped out by direct violence or European diseases.

Shortly after Bering's expeditions, French and English navigators began their own extensive explorations. The most significant were those of the French noble, Louis de Bougainville (1729–1811), and the English captain, James Cook (1729–1779). Bougainville visited much of southern Polynesia, the Sandwich (Hawaiian) Islands, Australia, New Guinea, and New Britain. Cook's three voyages between 1768 and 1779 went beyond the known waters of the South Pacific to Antarctica and north of Alaska to the Arctic coasts, where Cook made contact with the Russians. Although Cook was killed by natives in Hawaii on his last voyage, his journals fired European imaginations and encouraged European migration across the Pacific. Botany Bay in eastern Australia, established by the English as a penal colony in 1788, soon became a colony of settlement. Meanwhile a swarm of Western traders, whalers, missionaries, and beachcombers descended upon the South Pacific islands and the North Pacific coasts.

Perhaps the most typical feature of relations between Europeans and Pacific natives was the

Captain James Cook charted the coasts of New Zealand, Australia, and New Guinea, the Pacific coast of North America, and mapped nearly every island in the Pacific.

contrast in sexual roles and mores, which French and British sailors callously exploited. Male islanders, unlike European men, were used to female leadership, if not absolute domination; men were less ambitious and possessive; and sexual gratification was considered by both men and women as pleasurable but not immoral or even very significant. No wonder that Polynesian women in Tahiti or Hawaii, when they learned that their charms could be traded for European goods, swarmed over the ships at every anchoring. Their preference for iron nails almost caused the ships to be taken apart. In time, the crews became so conditioned that they initiated similar transactions in North America, where the Indian women were less interested but more subservient to their greedy husbands and fathers.

In Polynesia, after Cook's time, original cultures rapidly declined, as trade goods, rum, and guns stimulated avarice, status seeking, competition for power, violence, and war. With European help, native rulers, male and female, fought to dominate their islands. Such conflict was particularly true of Hawaii in the decade after 1790, where a Hawaiian chief, Kamehameha, used European ships and cannons to unite the three main islands. Sexual commerce with European also brought syphilis to the islands, blame for which was long disputed by the French and the English.

Captain James Cook, Departure from Tahiti

This selection is from Cook's journal on his second voyage into the South Pacific (1772–1775) in a major effort to explore Antarctica.

Thursday 16th. This Morning the Natives came off to the Sloops in their Canoes as usual, after breakfast Captain Furneaux and I paid the Chief a Viset, we found him at his house perfectly easy and satisfied in so much that he and some of his friends came a board and dined with us. . . . Having got a board a large supply of refreshments I determined to put to Sea in the morning and made the same known to the chief who promised to come and take leave of me on board the Ship.

‡Whilest I was with him [Oreo] yesterday, my Otaheite young man Porio took a sudden resolution to leave me, I have mentioned before that he was with me when I followed Oreo, and of his advising me not to go out of the boat, and was so much affraid at this time that he remaned in the boat till he heard all matters were reconciled, then he came out and presently after met with a young woman for whom he had contracted a friendship, he having my powder horn in keeping came and gave it to one of my people who was by me and then went away; I, who knew that he had found his female friend, took no notice thinking that he was only going to retire with her on some private buisness of their own, probably at this time he had no other intention, she however had prevailed upon him to remain with her for I saw him no more and to day I was told, that he was married. . . . In the after noon our boats returned from Otaha . . . they made the Circuit of the isle, conducted by one of the Aree's whose name was Boba, and were hospitably entertained by the people who provided them with victuals lodgeing and bed fellows according to the custom of the Country; the first night they were entertained with a Play, the second night their repast was disturbed by the Natives stealing their military Chest, which put them upon making reprisals by which means they recovered the most of what they had lost.

Friday 17th. At 4 o'Clock in Morning we began to unmoor and as soon as it was light Oreo and some of his friends came to take leave, many Canoes also came off with Hogs and fruit, the former they even beged of us to take from them, calling out, Tyu Boa Atoi which was as much as to say, I am your friend take my Hog and give me an ax, but our decks were already so full of them that we could hardly move, having on board the Resolution about 230 and on board the Adventure about 150. . . .

The Chief and his friends did not leave us till the Anchor was a weigh. At parting I made him a present of a Broad Ax and several other things with which he went away well satisfied. He was extremely desirous to know if, and when I would return, these were the last questions he asked me. After we were out of the Harbour and had made sail we discovered a Canoe conducted by two men following us, upon which I brought to and they presently came a long side with a present of fruit from Oreo, I made them some return for their trouble, dismissed them and made sail to the Westward with the Adventure in company. The young man I got at Otahiete left me at Ulietea two days before we saild being inticed away by a young Woman for whom he had contracted a friendship. I took no methods to recover him as there were Volanteers enough out of whome I took one, a youth about [17 or 18] years of age who says he is a relation of the great Opoony and . . . may be of use to us if we should fall in with and touch at any isles in our rout to the west. . . .

From *The Voyage of the* Resolution *and* Adventure, *1772–1755*, edited by J. G. Beaglehole. (Cambridge: Cambridge University Press, 1961), pp. 228–30.

Other European imports included cattle, small-pox, and missionaries. Amid sensual competition and Christian condemnation, the old religion was largely abandoned; whole communities became alcoholic; other evidences of psychological malaise, such as suicide, became prevalent; and population declined drastically.

European expansion in the Pacific brought significant changes for civilized East Asia, particularly in maritime commerce. After the middle of the eighteenth century, the British began replacing the Dutch as the major European traders, a trend climaxed by the collapse of the Dutch East India Company in 1794. At Canton, the number of British and American ships increased dramatically after 1790. Seeking a product which might be exchanged profitably for Chinese silk and tea, the British first concentrated on opium from India. When the opium trade created friction with Chinese officials, British merchants began seeking furs, particularly sea otter skins, which were obtained in the North Pacific. Hawaiian ports soon became busy centers for fitting ships and recruiting sailors. By 1815, European expansion into the Pacific had generated a dynamic commercial revolution.

East Asia on the Defensive

Among the great states of the East Asian mainland, the European impact was felt less than elsewhere, but it still figured largely in a strange composite of contradictions, typical of the area. Although China and Japan remained strongly attached to traditional values and were the most prosperous and stable of all non-European states, each felt forceful changes that conflicted with their ancient heritages. While struggling against these changes, both nations saw their problems magnified by the increasing European presence around the western Pacific.

The Rise and Decline of Manchu China

After 1644, when the Manchu armies took Peking, China was the most populous country on earth. Its society was more refined than most in Europe; and its literature, art, and philosophy evoked great admiration from European intellectuals. The Manchu emperors were generally efficient and conscientious; but, like many barbarian rulers of the past, they were so awed by Chinese institutions that they were incapable of promoting necessary change. The main problem was not that China was backward—it developed and prospered under the Manchus—but its progress was much slower than that of the West.

The Manchu system was a unique and highly successful modification of the traditional Chinese institutional structure. Although the conquerors sought to maintain their identity by avoiding intermarriage with Chinese, they retained the Chinese examination system and the privileged scholar-bureaucracy. Manchu and Chinese, working in pairs, conducted government above the provincial level. The most significant innovation was the "banner" system, comprising elite military units, both Manchu and Chinese. Because they were kept distinct from family, tribal, or even geographic identities, the banner companies proved reliable imperial troops. Augmented by Chinese conscripts and foreign tributaries, they extended China's control farther than ever before. Manchu armies subdued Sinkiang, Taiwan, Mongolia, Turkestan, and Tibet (see map, p. 379). The emperors also established tributary control over Korea, North Vietnam, and Burma.

One reason for the stability of Manchu China was the strength and durability of the rulers, particularly the K'ang-hsi emperor, who reigned longer (1661–1722) than any predecessor. Intelligent, hardworking, and devoted to duty, he was a brave soldier, an inquisitive scholar, and an able administrator. In six grand tours of the country, he sought to improve local government and promote justice. Always fascinated by learning, he encouraged scholarship by sponsoring great research projects. As a commander, he defeated the remaining Ming forces, then directed the long and arduous campaigns that ultimately conquered Mongolia. At the end of his reign, having experienced the bitter disappointment of having to disinherit his only legitimate son, the old monarch, in a final testament, revealed his human weaknesses and concerns.[3] Of all the world's rulers, K'ang-hsi was among the wisest, the most efficient, and the most respected.

The Manchu regime reached its climax during the next two reigns. Between 1723 and 1735, the Yung-cheng emperor, one of K'ang-shi's nineteen illegitimate sons, ruthlessly eliminated opposition groups formed around his brothers. His dictatorial methods set dangerous precedents but also lessened corruption and prepared the way for the reign of the Ch'ien-lung emperor (1735–1796), the fourth son of Yung-cheng. At first the new ruler was sincere, frugal, and industrious, like his famous grandfather. His early reign was marked by peace at home, victories abroad, expanding wealth, and noteworthy achievements in scholarship and the arts. Unfortunately, these conditions did not last. After about 1770, the expensive military campaigns began depleting the treasury. The emperor also instituted a rigorous policy of censorship and book burning. Ultimately, government fell into the hands of a royal favorite, whose corruption and inefficiency brought widespread rebellions as the eighteenth century ended.

The weakening of the Manchu regime was accompanied by increasing foreign problems. After years of fighting along the Manchurian and Mongolian frontiers, K'ang-hsi negotiated the treaty of Nerchinsk in 1689, which set the Siberian-Manchurian border and permitted limited Russian trade in Peking. The Chinese-Russian accord was made more specific by the Treaty of Kiakhta in 1727, when the Russians recognized Chinese sovereignty over Mongolia. As advisors to the Manchu emperors, Jesuits helped negotiate both of these treaties. They enjoyed considerable status at Kang-hsi's court, where they preached a version of Christianity consistent with traditional Chinese beliefs, such as ancestor worship. But at the opening of the eighteenth century the pope required Chinese Christians to renounce such paganism. The new policy brought disfavor to Catholics and to western Europeans generally. In 1757, the Chinese government confined all trade to Canton, where Europeans were forced to deal through a merchant monopoly and corrupt officials. Because of these conditions, Europeans, particularly the British, continually pressed for free trade and regular diplomatic relations.

China during Ch'ien-lung's reign was rapidly approaching the limits of its traditional system. Although Europeans were impressed by the country's order, wealth, and expanding population, which doubled between 1700 and 1800, they saw a façade rather than actual conditions. Chinese agriculture increased its productivity but not enough to provide for three hundred million people. Consequently, migrating Chinese moved into the southwestern provinces, into North Vietnam, and even across the seas to the Philippines and Java. At home, famine became prevalent as the soil wore out. Peasant uprisings were matched by growing unrest in the southern cities, which were also swelling in size, without increased economic resources. While a few Cantonese merchants, Yangtse salt monopolists, and favored government officials amassed great wealth, Chinese below the élite classes suffered great hardships and injustices.

Despite these problems, the late Manchu emperors held fast to their faith in China's ancient values. K'ang-hsi had been curious about Western medicine, astronomy, and mathematics, without conceding the validity of Western Science. After his time, European material advances were noted without awe or envy. Both K'ang-hsi and Ch'ien-lung fostered massive scholarly projects in history and philosophy, as their predecessors had done. Thousands of Chinese scholars, supported by the state, labored at these compilations while others, less favored, taught the Confucian classics in government schools or private academies. Their conservatism was demonstrated in a movement that, like its Japanese counterpart, opposed Ming neo-Confucianism in favor of Confucian principles expounded in the Han period. Thus, while China slipped inevitably toward the future, its intellectuals remained preoccupied with the distant past.

Such paralyzing conservatism is perhaps best illustrated by the Manchu espousal of classic Confucian doctrine on the social status of women. Early Manchu emperors forbade footbinding among their own females, but the practice was so fashionable and the Manchu women so eager to prove their acceptability that the prohibition was soon forgotten. In the eighteenth century, Chinese women suffered more than ever under a stifling Confucian double standard for female chastity and self-denial, in comparison with men. A famous heroine of the time, accused along with some companions of having sexual relations with

Father Ripa, Family Relations in Manchu China

Father Ripa, an Italian Jesuit missionary, was at the court of the great Manchu emperor, K'ang-Hsi, from 1711 to 1723.

One day as I was talking in my own house with a mandarin who had come to pay me a visit, his son arrived from a distant part of the empire upon some business relating to the family. When he came in we were seated, but he immediately went down on one knee before his father, and in this position continued to speak for about a quarter of an hour. I did not move from my chair till, by the course of the conversation, I discovered who the person was, when I suddenly arose, protesting to the mandarin that I would stand unless he allowed his son to sit down also. A lengthy contest ensued, the father saying that he would quit his seat if I continued to stand; I myself declaring that it was impossible for me to sit while his son was kneeling; and the son protesting that before his father he must remain on his knees. At last, however, I overcame every scruple, and the mandarin signified to his son by a sign that he might be seated. He instantly obeyed, but he retreated to a corner of the room, where he timidly seated himself upon the edge of a chest. . . .

Chinese women live entirely shut up by themselves in a remote apartment of their houses. Among persons of rank they are seldom allowed to go out, unless it be during the rejoicings of the new year, and even then they are shut up in sedans. They are indeed kept so strictly that they are not allowed to speak even with the father or the brother of their husbands, much less with their uncles, or any other man, however close may be the relationship. . . . And here I will not omit the description of a practice which, while it proves the excellent social order of the Chinese, caused me to smile when I heard of it. If a man, for careless conduct or any other fault, considers it his duty to correct his daughter-in-law, as he cannot, according to the custom of the country either enter her room or speak to her, and much less beat her, he summons his son before him, and after reproaching him with the faults of his wife, he bids him prostrate himself, and inflicts a severe flogging upon him. The son then rises upon his knees, and, touching the ground with his forehead, thanks his father for the castigation; after which he goes to his wife, and repeats the correction exactly, giving her the same number of blows that he received from his father.

From their inordinate jealousy arose the custom of crippling the feet of the women, in order to render walking a torment, and induce them to remain at home. I was informed by Chinese that the first who discovered this stratagem was one of their ancient emperors, who purposely hinted that nothing was more beautiful in a woman than to have the smallest feet possible. This imperial opinion being made public throughout China, every husband desired that his wife should be in the fashion, and mothers sought to secure to their daughters an imaginary beauty which it was found could be procured by art. Accordingly, at the tender age of three months, female infants have their feet bound so tightly that the growth of this part of their body is entirely stopped, and they cannot walk without hobbling and limping; and if upon any occasion they endeavour to quicken their pace, they are in danger of falling at every step. . . . In cases of marriage, the parties not being able to see each other, it is customary to send the exact dimensions of the lady's foot to her intended, instead of sending him her portrait as we do in Europe.

Source: Rhoda Hoff, ed., *China: Adventures in Eyewitness History* (New York: Henry Z. Walck, 1965), pp. 63–66.

a lecherous monk, saved the other girls by showing a mole on her body that the monk could not describe. Having thus dishonored her family by revealing her nakedness, she committed suicide and was praised as a model. Mao Ch'i-ling, a rare Chinese champion of women's rights in the eighteenth century, condemned unreasonable contemporary customs, which required engaged women to remain single, commit suicide, or be buried alive if their fiancés died.

This conservative myopia was typical but not quite universal among writers and artists. Most creative endeavors aimed to please the aristocratic urban classes, who lived artificial lives in their gardens, amid their books and paintings. Painters usually followed the classical Sung schools. Traditional drama, having emerged in the Yuan period, remained popular into the nineteenth century. There were, however, some links between Chinese art and the contemporary world. Lacquer and porcelain wares attained such popularity in Europe that they were produced in great quantities to suit foreign tastes. The same was true of some Chinese painting, which came to utilize European techniques in achieving perspective. Finally, Chinese literature showed some social concern and attempted realism. *The Dream of the Red Chamber*, an eighteenth-century depiction of a declining aristocratic family, has been widely acclaimed as China's greatest novel.

Korea, the reluctant Manchu vassal state, experienced more serious problems but came closer to devising solutions. Japanese and Chinese invasions in the early seventeenth century so weakened the scholarly bureaucracy and central government that they could barely function. In the resulting disorder and confusion, the economy developed rapidly when controls were not enforced, but population increased by 50 percent and many suffered, particularly the peasants. Such conditions encouraged new thinking, and by the eighteenth century, a movement among intellectuals, known as "practical learning," was advocating reforms in government, while showing some sympathy for Western Christianity and science. Some of this reform spirit was revealed in the policies of King Yung-jo (1724–1776) and his grandson, Chongjo (1776–1800), who gradually restored some order and efficiency.

Tensions in Japan Under the Mature Tokugawa Shogunate

While the rest of Asia and Africa felt European influences, the Tokugawa regime in Japan seemed unaffected, in an immunity that was somewhat illusory. At first, after outlawing Christianity and expelling Europeans, the Japanese perfected an efficient bureaucratic system on the old feudal foundations. The economy flourished, cities grew, population stabilized, and the standard of living rose. But these favorable results also brought changes and great social tensions, which threatened the political order. At the same time, external stimuli caused some Japanese to advocate foreign ideas, while others reacted emotionally in defense of their sacred traditions.

The Tokugawa system, originally a rigid feudal order, became highly centralized during this era. Without the disruption of foreign wars, the shoguns consolidated their power by turning the *daimyo* into dependent courtiers and changing the *samurai* from vassals of their lords into state employees. This was largely accomplished by educating the warrior class in the Confucian classics, which emphasized civic duties over personal loyalties, as taught in the old *Bushido* code. Reorientation of the *samurai* was furthered by paying them fixed stipends and restricting some of their traditional violent practices, such as feuding or committing honorable suicide (*seppuku*). With its loyal *samurai* corps of soldiers, scholars, and bureaucrats, the shogunate became a highly efficient political organization.

Such bureaucratic order naturally lessened flexibility. Confucianism looked to the past, suspected the future, and resisted most proposed improvements. It was also narrowly male-oriented. This meant that female influence, particularly in politics, was often significant but limited largely to domination over shoguns by their mothers, plus other attendant intrigues and extravagances of court women. Among this elite group, practical affairs were hidden behind an artificial etiquette and old *samurai* standards, which demanded humble service and sacrifice, even unto death, by a wife for her husband and his family. Such principles, often ignored within families of the noble classes, were espoused by male *samurai* writers for public consumption.

Their efforts were at least partially successful in popularizing Confucian conservatism.

The official disciplinary tone was reflected in an outpouring of cultural expression during this era. While Buddhism declined generally, its temple schools fostered a rapid expansion of education. The intellectual climate was further improved by a phenomenal increase in book publishing. *Samurai* scholars produced national histories and Confucian philosophical works to honor Tokugawa accomplishments and provide a basic rationale for state and society. *Samurai* architects perpetuated traditional baroque grandeur in castles and public buildings. In painting, the *samurai* influence was represented by the Kano school's synthesis of classical Japanese and Chinese traditions, such as the literal pictoral essays of the "literati" (*nanga*) painters.

Although the Tokugawa government and society were supposedly prescribed within official limits, the economy underwent dynamic development and change. In agriculture, land reclamation, improved seeds, better fertilizers, and new tools brought a doubling of grain production between 1600 and 1730. Rising wealth in the villages was reflected in many new small industries and generally increased industrial output. A complex monetary and financial system gave rise to large capitalistic enterprises centered in the cities, which were rapidly expanding in number and size. With a population of nearly a million, Edo, capital of the shogunate, was among the largest cities of the world by 1750. The total Japanese population, meanwhile, peaked at approximately twenty-nine million, declining only slightly in the 1700s. This combination of increasing productivity and stable population, unmatched elsewhere in the world, produced a spirit of enterprise and optimism, most evident among the urban classes, especially among women, many of whom were actively involved in hand manufacturing or business.

Increasing wealth, rising expectations, and other changes subjected Japanese society to dangerous tensions after the late seventeenth century. Many peasants were alienated from the land and from the upper classes as they became hired laborers or free tenants. The new money economy, while stimulating a desire for luxuries among the *samurai*, diminished their economic independence and encouraged them to borrow heavily from merchant bankers. Even the *daimyo* were forced to engage in business enterprise to pay for their many social obligations at court. At the same time, their creditors among the urban middle classes were dissatisfied by numerous frivolous demands and penalties imposed by the government upon commerce and banking. As such dissatisfaction grew, frequent disorders in both the towns and villages had to be forcefully repressed.

Government met these problems with alternations between reform and inertia. The first four shoguns ruled wisely and forcefully, but later ones allowed their ministers to make policies, which brought increasing rigidity as often happens in bureaucracies. While revenues dropped, inflation increased, and respect for authority declined. Some partially successful efforts at reform were attempted by the scholar-minister, Arai Hakuseki (1709–1716). An even more determined reformer was the eighth shogun, Yoshimune (1716–1745). An honest, sincere, and just statesman, Yoshimune tried to restore traditional morality with the famous Kyoho reforms, which cut expenses, encouraged agriculture, regularized taxes, standardized the diverse feudal laws, and relaxed the ban on foreign technial books. He also ordered the dismissal of nearly half of the court women, a measure designed to save money and promote stability. With such policies, Yoshimune hoped to restore the efficiency of the past, but they were only temporary remedies rather than permanent solutions to his problems.

Yoshimune's successors pursued no consistent policies. His son, Ieshige (1745–1760), was a semi-invalid with a speech defect, who ushered in an era of definite political decline. The next shogun yielded to his chamberlain, an unscrupulous adventurer who courted the merchant-bankers, attempting to increase revenues and strengthen the regime. His extravagance and corrupt practices brought economic depression and frequent rice riots. This commercial policy was reversed by Matsudaira Sadanobu, who served as chief minister until 1793. A stern traditionalist, he tried to cut expenses and restore the *samurai* values. But after he retired, the government drifted aimlessly during the long reign of Shogun Ienari (1787–1837).

While the government floundered, a new urban subculture challenged official Confucian values. Prosperous urbanites, disillusioned with old-fashioned morality, idealized "the floating world" of irrational sensuality, featuring fine food, alcohol, gambling houses and brothels. Free love and sexual independence, illustrated by the lifestyles of adventurers, entertainers, and prostitutes, became subjects of a new literature, produced in the revolt against *samurai* morality. Other writings, rejecting artificial themes, evoked appreciation for the realistic or the esoteric. For example, *haiku* poetry, which won great popularity, used seventeen syllables in three lines and expressed pithy microcosmic observations on universal themes. A new pictoral art for the masses used woodblock printing and vivid colors to portray nature, street scenes, pretty women, and mild erotica. With or without conscious intent, such works weakened established values.

More threatening to the shogunate than the new urban alienation was the criticism from intellectuals. By the end of the eighteenth century, a growing number were questioning the shogun's authority and emphasizing loyalty to the emperor. Many of these "nationalists" were prejudiced militarists, who thought that the shogunate had betrayed Japanese traditions. A shade further to the left, Confucian proponents of "ancient learning" blamed all troubles on neo-Confucianists, who had strayed from the old texts. Others turned to practical subjects, such as economics, while rejecting the highly moralistic perspectives of official scholars. After Yoshimune relaxed the ban on foreign non-Christian writings in 1720, "Dutch studies" were pursued widely in medicine, astronomy, and various technical fields. The movement gained momentum as the century passed, indicating that Japanese society was torn by dissension and that European ideas were significantly involved.

Conclusion

Despite the near destruction of local cultures around the Cape, many African and Asian civilizations remained highly functional in 1815. Assante, Buganda, and Omani Zanzibar were all rising south of the Sahara without having yet reached their peaks. Sokoto was spreading its

Muslim orthodoxy throughout the Sudan; Morocco and the Barbary states continued to prey upon Mediterranean commerce; and the Egyptian ruler, Mehemet Ali, was apparently building a new Muslim empire. Along with the recently formed Sikh state, the Marathas posed serious military problems for British India. France had recently lost influence in a united Vietnam, which was now acutely aware of a revived Thailand. To the north, in East Asia, China persisted in rejecting regular diplomatic relations with European nations; Korea's "practical learning" was producing reforms; and Japan was a convincing example of prosperity and independence.

The non-European areas of Asia and Africa had nevertheless slipped considerably, in comparison with the West, since 1650. China and Japan were both seriously disturbed by internal tensions. Burma faced a military threat from the British in Bengal. A similar insecurity was felt by the tottering Muslim states of the Middle East and the slave-trading states of West Africa. In addition to South Africa, much of India, Indonesia, Polynesia, and Siberia had felt the direct shock of foreign conquest. One may conclude that much of sub-Sahara Africa had arrested its own development by accepting foreign ways, and that East Asia was so locked into its past that it could not effectively pursue its future.

All these cultures demonstrated a common connection between their misfortunes and the European presence. Indeed, the true significance of the period lies in the opportunities provided for European, particularly British, expansion. The Peace of Vienna in 1815 not only brought a decisive British victory over France in Europe, it also unofficialy ratified the recent rise in British power and influence around the globe—in China, Southeast Asia, India, the Persian Gulf, the eastern Mediterranean, and Africa. With other advantages derived from their phenomenal industrial development, the British were well prepared to lead the great European scramble for empire in the nineteenth century.

Suggestions for Reading

From the many good surveys of early South Africa, the following are recommended: Kevin Shillington, *A History of South Africa* (Longman, 1988); Christopher Saunders,

The Making of the South African Past (Barnes and Noble, 1988); T. R. Davanport, South Africa: A Modern History (Macmillan, 1987); and J.D. Omer-Cooper, A History of South Africa (Heinemann, 1987). For the beginning of the Xosa wars, see Donald R. Morris, The Washing of the Spears: The Rise and Fall of the Zulu Nation (Touchstone, 1986) and E. A. Ritter, Shaka Zulu (Penguin, 1985).

The best background treatments of black sub-Sahara Africa include Robert W. July, A History of the African People (Scribner 1980); Paul Bohannan and Philip Curtin, Africa and Africans, 3rd ed. (Waveland Press, 1988); Roland Oliver and J. D. Fage, A Short History of Africa, 6th rev. ed. (Penguin, 1989). See also Frank Willet, African Art (Thames and Hudson, 1985).

Philip Curtin, The Atlantic Slave Trade (Univ. of Wisconsin, 1972) is the classic work on the subject. See also James A. Rawley, The Trans-Atlantic Slave Trade (Norton, 1981); James Walvin, Slavery and the Slave Trade (Univ. of Minnesota, 1983); Edward Reynolds, Stand the Storm (Allison and Busby, 1985); Basil Davidson, The African Slave Trade (Little, Brown, 1988); and D. W. Galenson, Traders, Planters, and Slavers (Cambridge Univ., 1986). For the participation of Europeans, see Norman R. Bennet, Africa and Europe, 2nd ed. (Univ. of Calif., 1985); John C. Hatch, The History of the British in Africa (Praeger, 1969); Robert Stein, The French Slave Trade in the Eighteenth Century (Univ. of Wisconsin, 1980); Johannes M. Postma, The Dutch in the Atlantic Slave Trade (Cambridge Univ., 1989); and David Eltis, Economic Growth and the Ending of the Trans-Atlantic Slave Trade (Oxford Univ., 1987). For the effects of the trade on Africans, see J. E. Inikori, Forced Migration: The Impact of the Export Slave Trade on African Societies (Holmes and Meier, 1983); Paul E. Lovejoy, Transformations in Slavery (Cambridge Univ., 1983); and Paul E. Lovejoy, ed., Africans in Bondage: Studies in Slavery and the Slave Trade (Univ. of Wisconsin, 1987). The tragedy of African women in slavery is recounted in Claire C. Robertson and Martin A. Klein, eds., Women and Slavery in Africa (Univ. of Wisconsin, 1983); Marietta Morrissey, Slave Women in the New World (Kansas Univ., 1989); and Barbara Bush, Slave Women in Caribbean Society, 1650–1832 (Indiana University, 1989).

Black African regions and states in the era are overviewed in John Stewart, African States and Rulers (McFarland, 1989) and David Sweetmen, Women Leaders in African History (Heinemann, 1984). For West Africa, see Basil Davidson, A History of West Africa (Longman, 1987); C. W. Newbury, The Western Slave Coast and its Rulers (Greenwood, 1983); Robin Law, The Oyo Empire (Oxford, 1977); Karl Polyani and Abraham Rotstein, Dahomey and the Slave Trade (AMS, 1988); Patrick Manning, Slavery, Colonialism, and Economic Growth in Dahomey, 1640–1960 (Cambridge Univ., 1982); and J. K. Flynn, Asante and Its Neighbors, 1700–1807 (Northwestern Univ., 1971). For Central Africa, see David Birmingham and Phyllis Martin, eds., A History of Central Africa, 2 vols. (Longman, 1983); John Thornton, The Kingdom of Kongo, 1641–1718 (Univ. of Wisconsin, 1983); Anne Hilton, The Kingdom of Kongo (Oxford Univ., 1985); K. Somerville, Angola (Pinter, Rienner, 1986). For East Africa, see Gideon S. Were and Derek A. Wilson, East Africa Through a Thousand Years (Africana, 1970); Arnold H. Jones and Elizabeth Monroe, A History of Ethiopia (Oxford, 1966); and E. A. Budge, A History of Ethiopia (Methuen, 1966).

John S. Trimmingham, The Influence of Islam Upon Africa (Longman, 1980) is a well-researched treatment of a broad topic. For more limited studies, see the same author's History of Islam in West Africa (Oxford, 1959) and Islam in East Africa (Oxford, 1964). North Africa is covered in Jamil M. Abun-Nasir, A History of the Maghrib (Cambridge Univ., 1975) and Charles A. Julien, A History of North Africa (Praeger, 1970). The ambiguous role of women is described in Barbara Calloway, Muslim Hausa Women in Nigeria (Syracuse Univ., 1987).

The standard suvey of the declining Ottoman Empire is Lord Kinross, The Ottoman Centuries (Morrow, 1977). Useful special studies of Ottoman government and society are D. Nicolle, Armies of the Ottoman Turks (Osprey, 1985); Bruce McGowan, Economic Life in the Ottoman Empire, 1600–1800 (Cambridge Univ., 1982); and H. Inalcik, Studies in Ottoman Social and Economic History (Variorum Reproductions, 1985). For interesting biographical sketches, see Noel Barber, The Sultans (Simon and Schuster, 1973). Ottoman relations with Europe are treated in Charles A. Frazee, Catholics and Sultans (Cambridge Univ., 1983); P. F. Sugar, Southeastern Europe Under Ottoman Rule, 1354–1804 (Univ. of Washington, 1984); and Fatma M. Gocek, East Encounters West (Oxford Univ., 1987). A personalized look at English-Ottoman relations is provided in Sonia Anderson, An English Consul in Turkey: Paul Rycaut at Smyrna, 1667–1678 (Oxford Univ., 1989).

For backgrounds on Muslim Middle-Eurasia in this period, see Arthur Goldschmidt, A Concise History of the Middle East (Westview, 1979) and E. H. Parker, A Thousand Years of the Tartars (Dorset, 1988). The classical work on Iran, still indispensable, is Percy M. Sykes, A History of Persia (Gordon, 1976). See also D. Morgan, Medieval Persia, 1040–1797 (Longman, 1988) and Roger Savory, Iran Under the Safavids (Cambridge Univ., 1980). For eighteenth-century Iran, see L. Beck, The Qashqu'i of Iran (Yale Univ., 1986) and, for a readable biography, as well as a history of the period, see John R. Perry, Harim Kahn Zand (Univ. of Chicago, 1979). Yu. Gankovsky, The History of Afghanistan (Progress Pubs. [U.S.S.R.], 1985) throws welcome light on that obscure corner of Asia.

Stanley Wolpert's A New History of India, 3rd ed. (Oxford Univ., 1989) is a sound survey which puts the Mughul era in clear perspective. More concentrated attention is provided in Waldemar Hausen, Peacock Throne: The Drama of Mughul India (Orient Book Dist., 1986) and Stanley Lane-Poole, The Triumph and Fall of the Mughul Empire, 2 vols. (Found Class Reprints, 1987). Percival Spear, Twilight of the Mughuls (Cambridge Univ., 1951) is still valuable for its clear focus on Mughul decline. The following works present more specialized studies on varied aspects of the Mughul state and society: Neelan Chaudgary, Socio-economic History of Mughal India (South Asia Books, 1987); S. C. Dutta, The North-east and the Mughuls, 1661–1714 (D. K. Pubs., 1984); Robert C. Hallissey, The Rajput Rebellion Against Auranqzeb (Univ. of Missouri, 1977) and O. Prakash, The Dutch East India Company and the Economy of Bengal, 1630–1720 (Princeton Univ., 1985). For good biographical presentations, see Bamber Gascoigne, The Great Mughuls, rev. ed. (Cape, 1987); L. K. Agarwal, Biographical Account of the Mughal Nobility, 1556–1707 (Coronet Books, 1985); and Muni Lal, Aurangzeb (Advent, 1988).

Among the best general surveys of Southeast Asia in this period are Steven Warshaw, *Southeast Asia Emerges*, rev. ed. (Diablo, 1987) and G. Coedes, *The Making of Southeast Asia*, 2nd ed. (Allen and Unwin, 1983). The Beginning of European encroachment is discussed in A. Reid, *Southeast Asia in the Age of Commerce, 1450–1680* (Yale Univ., 1988). Good special studies of individual states include, for Burma, M. Aung-Thwin, *Pagan, the Origins of Modern Burma* (Univ. of Hawaii, 1985); for Vietnam, Joseph Buttinger, *A Dragon Defiant* (Praeger, 1972); for Cambodia, Martin F. Herz. *A Short History of Cambodia* (Praeger, 1958); and for Indonesia, John D. Legge, *Indonesia* (Prentice Hall, 1965) and Joseph Kennedy, *A History of Malaya* (St. Martin's, 1962).

European expansion into the Pacific, in its Russian phases, is traced in John A. Harrison, *Founding of the Russian Empire in Asia and America* (Univ. of Miami, 1971) and Gerhard F. Muller, *Bering's Voyages: The Reports From Russia* (Univ. of Alaska, 1988). See also G. W. Steller, *Journal of a Voyage With Bering, 1741–1742* (Stanford Univ., 1988). For English exploration, see Lynne Withen, *Captain Cook and the Exploration of the Pacific* (Univ. of California, 1989) and D. Hoobler, *The Voyages of Captain Cook* (Putnam, 1983). More detailed accounts are presented in J. Elliott, *Captain Cook's Second Voyage* (Caliban, 1985) and S. A. Parkinson, *A Journal of a Voyage to the South Seas* (Caliban, 1984). A recent biography of the great English navigator is Alan Blackwood, *Captain Cook* (Watts, 1987). See also W. G. McClymount, *The Exploration of New Zealand* (Greenwood, 1986).

Traditional native Pacific cultures are ably depicted in the following works: Peter S. Brentwood, *The Polynesians* (Thames and Hudson, 1978); K. Sinclair, *A History of New Zealand*, rev. ed. (Penguin, 1985); David A. Howarth, *Tahiti* (Penguin, 1985); Edwin N. Ferdon, *Early Tahiti as the Explorers Saw it* (Univ. of Arizona, 1981); and Elizabeth Bott, *Tongan Society at the Time of Captian Cook's Visits* (Univ. of Hawaii, 1983).

Alan Moorehead, *The Fatal Impact* (Harper and Row, 1987) registers the disasters to native cultures which came with European "invasion of the South Pacific." See also O. H. Spate, *Paradise Found and Lost* (Univ. of Minnesota, 1988) and Ernest S. Dodge, *Islands and Empires* (Univ. of Minnesota, 1976). For specific results on one island, see David A. Howarth, *Tahiti, a Paradise Lost* (Viking, 1984) and E. H. Dodd, *The Rape of Tahiti* (Dodd, Mead, 1983). The Hawaiian reaction is evident in Richard Tregeskis's *The Warrior King: Hawaii's Kamehameha the Great* (C. E. Tuttle, 1973).

A general perspective on China under the Manchus can be gained from Wolfrom Eberhard, *A History of China* (Univ. of California, 1977); Charles O. Hucker, *China to 1850* (Stanford Uiv., 1978); and William S. Morton, *China, Its History and Its Culture* (McGraw Hill, 1982). Lynn Struve, *The Southern Ming, 1644–1662* (Yale Univ., 1984) records the pathetic last years of the old dynasty. J. D. Spence, *Ts'ao yin and the K'ang-hsi Emperor* (Yale Univ., 1988) provides an intimate glimpse of the greatest Manchu ruler. Social conditions under the Manchu are carefully examined in Susan Naquin and Evelyn S. Rawski, *Chinese Society in the Eighteenth Century* (Yale Univ., 1989) and in Esther Yao, *Chinese Women, Past and Present* (Idle House, 1983). The deterioration arising from economic sources is evident in S. Arasaratram, *Merchants, Companies, and Commerce on the Coromandel Coast, 1650–1740* (Oxford Univ., 1987); Dean Murray, *Pirates of the South China Coast, 1790–1810* (Stanford Univ., 1987); and G. B. Souza, *The Survival of Empire: Portuguese Trade and Society in China and the South China Sea, 1630–1754* (Cambridge Univ., 1986).

Andrew C. Nahm, *Tradition and Transformation: A History of the Korean People* (Hollym International, 1988) gives a good account of major Korean developments during the period. See also Isabella Bird, *Korea and Its Neighbors* (Charles C. Tuttle, 1986); Ki-baik Lee, *A New History of Korea* (Harvard Univ., 1984); and William E. Griffis, *Korea* (AMS, 1971). For the roles of Korean women, see Yung-Chung Kim, *Women of Korea* (Ewha Women's Univ. [Seoul], 1979) and Laurel Kendall and Mark Peterson, eds. *Korean Women* (East Rock Press, 1983).

The mature Tokugawa era in Japan is given excellent coverage in Edwin O. Reischauer and Alfred M. Craig, *Japan, Story of a Nation*, 4th ed. (McGraw-Hill, 1989); Albert C. Danley, *Japan: A Short History* (Wayside, 1989); R. H. Mason, *A History of Japan* (Charles C. Tuttle, 1987); Mikiso Hane, *Modern Japan* (Westview, 1986); W. Scott Morton, *Japan, Its History and Culture* (McGraw-Hill, 1984); and Conrad Totman, *Japan Before Pery* (Univ. of California, 1981). John H. Wigmore, *Law and Justice in Tokugawa Japan* (Colorado Univ., 1986) reflects the lingering Japanese penchant for authority and discipline. Japanese social turmoil during the period is treated in Anne Walthall, *Social Protest and Popular Culture in Eighteenth-Century Japan* (Univ. of Arizona, 1986); S. Vlasos, *Peasant Protests and Uprisings in Tokugawa Japan* (Univ. of California, 1986); and H. P. Bix, *Peasant Revolt in Japan, 1590–1884* (Yale Univ., 1986). For Japanese intellectual developments, see R. N. Bellah, *Tokugawa Religion*, rev. ed. (Free Press, 1985); Herman Ooms, *Tokugawa Religion* (Princeton Univ., 1985); T. Najita, *Visions of Virtue in Tokugawa Japan* (Univ. of Chicago, 1987); and B. T. Wakaboyashi, *Anti-Foreignism and Western Learning in Early Modern Japan* (Harvard Univ., 1986).

Notes

1. Quoted in John Newton, *Journal of a Slave Trader*, edited by Catherine M. Bull (London: Epworth Press, 1962), p. 63.
2. This incident is cited in Charles André Julien, *A History of North Africa* (New York: Frederick A. Praeger, 1970), p. 79.
3. For the full text of this valedictory statement, see Jonathan Spence, *Emperor of China, a Self-Portrait of K'ang-hsi* (New York: Alfred A. Knopf, 1974), pp. 143–151.

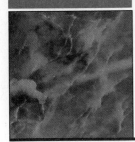

Chapter 23

Europe Transformed

The Napoleonic and Industrial Revolutions

N apoleon spread the values of the French Revolution throughout the continent, even as he stifled them in France, thus setting in motion the major social and political developments that dominated the century. By his military and foreign policies he inaugurated modern Latin American history and enabled the United States to double in size. Through rearranging the Holy Roman Empire he set in motion the development of "modern Germany." The breadth and nature of his conquests sparked the growth of modern nationalism throughout the continent (see map, p. 594). His economic policies changed the flow of capital and stimulated industrialization in Britian and economic reform throughout Europe.

Industrialization continued to bring new tools and power sources to do jobs formerly done by humans and animals. It brought about the biggest transformation of human life since the Neolithic Revolution. The economic strength generated by industrialization brought Europe global dominance during the nineteenth century.

Napoleon and the industrial inventors transformed Europe. The French leader broadcast the immense transformation that had occurred in his country to the world and made necessary a wholesale redrawing of political boundaries. The people who devised new tools and new ways to do old jobs set in process the transition from an agrarian to a modern, urbanized society. The monumental changes of this era engendered a new political vocabulary and a wide range of cultural responses.

Napoleon and France

Revolutions favor the bright, the ambitious, and the lucky. Napoleon Bonaparte (1769–1821) had all three qualities in abundance. He was born in Corsica to a lower-ranking Florentine or minor noble family in 1769—the year after control of that island passed from Genoa to France. At the age of ten his father placed him in the military academy at Brienne. Six years later he received his officer's commission. At the beginning of the French Revolution he was a twenty-year-old officer doomed by his family's modest standing and the restrictions of the Old Regime to a mediocre future. Ten years later, he ruled France. The revolution gave him the opportunity to use his brains, ability, charm, and daring to rise rapidly.

A potent mixture of eighteenth-century rationalism, romanticism, and revolutionary politics dominated his thought. He learned constantly, reading the classics, absorbing Enlightenment tracts, and constantly talking to people who could teach him. As an outsider from Corsica, he was tied to no particular faction in France and pursued his own interests with a fresh point of view. He drew close first to the men of 1789, then to the Jacobins, and later to the Directory (see ch. 21). Never did he allow control of his fate to escape from his own hands, pragmatically choosing whatever political, social, or religious option that could serve his goals.[1]

He never doubted that fate had chosen him to accomplish great things. Equipped with a vast

NAPOLEONIC EUROPE

- France in 1789
- Acquisitions of Napoleon to 1810
- Dependent States of Napoleon
- Allies of Napoleon
- → Napoleon's Campaigns

reserve of energy to match his enormous ego, Napoleon worked and studied ceaselessly, running on very little sleep. He was disciplined in his use of time and gifted in public relations skills. He pitched his messages and dreams to all levels of society, and had the ability to inspire and gain the maximum sacrifice from his nation and his armies.

The Opportunist

Napoleon came at the right time—a generation earlier or later and the situation would not have allowed him to gain power. He took advantage of the gutting of the old officer class by the revolutionary wars and the Jacobins to rise quickly to a prominent position from which he could appeal to the Directory. That self-interested group of survivors asked the Corsican to break up a right-wing uprising in October 1795. The following year the Directory gave Napoleon command of the smallest of the three armies sent to do battle with the Austrians.

The two larger forces crossed the Rhine on their way to attack the Habsburgs while Napoleon's corps went over the Alps into Italy as a diversionary move. Contrary to plan, the main forces did little while Napoleon, who was supposed to be little more than bait, crushed the Sardinians and then the Austrians in a brilliant series of campaigns. As he marched across northern Italy he picked off Venice and was well on the road to Vienna where the Austrians approached him to make peace. Without instructions from his government, Napoleon negotiated the Treaty of Campo Formio (1797) and returned home a hero.

After considering an invasion of Britain in the first part of 1798—a cross-Channel task he deemed impossible—Napoleon set out with the Directory's blessing to strike at Britain's economy by attacking its colonial structure. He would invade Egypt, expose the weakness of the Ottoman Empire, and from there launch an attack on India. The politicians were as much impressed by this grand plan as they were relieved to get the increasingly popular Napoleon out of town. He successfully evaded the British fleet in the Mediterranean, landed in Egypt and took Alexandria and Cairo in July. The British Admiral Horatio Nelson (1758–1805) found the French fleet and sank it at Aboukir on August 1, 1798. Even though their supply lines and access to France were cut off, Napoleon's forces fought a number of successful battles against the Turks in Syria and Egypt.[2]

However, the fact remained that the French armies were stranded in Egypt and would be forced to remain there until 1801 when a truce allowed them to come home. This development would normally be regarded as a defeat, yet when Napoleon abandoned his army in August

This heroic portrait by Antoine Jean Gros shows the 27-year-old Napoleon leading his troops at the Battle of Arcola in northern Italy in November 1796.

1799, slipped by the British fleet, and returned to Paris, he was given a frenzied, triumphant homecoming. In public appearances, he adopted a modest pose and gave addresses on the scientific accomplishments of the expedition, such as the discovery of the Rosetta stone, a development that led to deciphering hieroglyphics (see ch. 1).

Napoleon, his brothers, and the Abbé Sieyès sought to take advantage of the political crisis surrounding the Directory. A coalition including Russia, Great Britain, Austria, Naples, Portugal, and the Ottoman Empire threatened France from the outside, while a feverlike inflation ravaged the economy internally. Various political factions courted Napoleon, whose charisma made him appear to be the likely savior of the country. In the meantime, he and his confederates planned their course. They launched a clumsy, though successful, coup in November 1799 and replaced the Directory with the Consulate. The plotters shared the cynical belief that "constitutions should be short and obscure" and that the nature of democracy consisted of the fact that the rulers rule and the people obey.

The takeover ended the revolutionary decade. France remained, in theory, a republic, but nearly all power rested with the thirty-one-year-old Napoleon, who ruled as first Consul. Still another constitution was written and submitted to a vote of the people. Only half of the eligible voters went to the polls, but an overwhelming majority voted in favor of the new constitution: 3,011,007 in favor versus 1,526 against.[3]

France to 1804: New Foundations

Ten years of radical change made France ready for one-man rule—but of a type much different from that exercised by the Bourbon monarchy. The events of 1789 had overturned the source of political power. It no longer came from God, but from the people. The social structure of the Old Regime was gone and with it the privileges of hereditary and created nobility. The Church no longer had financial or overt political power. The old struggles between kings and nobles, nobles and bourgeoisie, peasants and landlords, and Catholics and Protestants were replaced by the rather more universal confrontation between rich and poor.

Ten years of revolution had seen three attempts to rebuild the French system: the bourgeois-constitutional efforts to 1791; the radical programs to 1794; and the rule to 1799 by survivors who feared both the right and the left. Although each attempt had failed, each left valuable legacies to the new France. The first attempt established the power of the upper middle classes; the second showed the great power of the state to mobilize the population; and the third demonstrated the usefulness of employing former enemies in day-to-day politics.

Being the pragmatic tactician that he was, Napoleon used elements from the Old Regime and the various phases of the revolution to reconstruct France. He built an autocracy far more powerful than Louis XVI's government and took advantage of the absence of old forms of competition to central power from the nobility and the feudal structure, which were destroyed in the name of liberty, equality, and fraternity. He used the mercantile policies, military theories, and foreign policy goals of the *Old Regime*, the ambitions of the middle class, and the mobilization policies of the Jacobins. All he asked from those who wished to serve him was loyalty. Defrocked priests, renegade former nobles, reformed Jacobins, small businessmen, and ambitious soldiers all played a role. His acceptance of the ambitious brought him popularity because ten years of constant change had compromised most politically active people in some form of unprincipled, immoral, or illegal behavior.

Napoleon built his state on the *philosophes'* conception of a system in which all French men would be equal before the law. The revolution destroyed the sense of personal power of a sovereign and substituted what the British historian Lord Acton would later in the century call the "tyranny of the majority." The French state accordingly could intervene more effectively than ever before, limited only by distance and communications problems.[4]

The mass democratic army created by the total mobilization of both people and resources was one of the best examples of the new state system. A revolutionary society had fought a mass ideological war, and the experience changed the nature of combat forever. Because advancement and success were based on valor and victory, rather than bloodlines or privilege, the army

profited from the new social structure and sought to preserve and extend it. The army best symbolized the great power of the French nation unleashed by the Revolution. Many of the economic and diplomatic problems that preceded the Revolution remained, but Napoleon's new state structure provided inspired solutions.

Taking advantage of his military supremacy, Napoleon gained a breathing space for his domestic reforms by making peace with the Second Coalition by March 1802. He then set about erecting the governing structure of France that remains with few changes to this day. He developed an administration that was effective in raising money, assembling an army, and exploiting the country's resources. His centralized government ruled through prefects, powerful agents in the provinces who had almost complete control of local affairs and were supported by a large police force. He then established a stable monetary policy based on an honest tax-collecting system, backed by up-to-date accounting procedures. The Bank of France that he created remains an institution regarded as a model of sound finance.

Napoleon knew that the country he ruled was overwhelmingly Catholic and that national interest dictated that he come to terms with the papacy. Through the Concordat of 1801 with Pope Pius VII the pope gained the right to approve the bishops whom the First Consul appointed to the re-established Catholic Church. The state permitted seminaries to be reopened and paid priests' salaries. Pius regained control of the Papal States and saw his church recognized as the "religion of the majority of Frenchmen." The Church thus resumed its position of prominence, but without its former power and wealth.

Napoleon viewed education as a way to train useful citizens to become good soldiers and bureaucrats, and he pursued the development of mass education by trying to increase the number of elementary schools, *lycées* (secondary schools), and special institutes for technical training. The schools were to be used to propagandize the young to serve the state through "directing political and moral opinion." Overarching the entire system was the University of France, more an administrative body to control education than a teaching institution.

Napoleon had neither the time nor the resources to put mass education in place during his lifetime, although he did gain immediate success in training the sons of the newly arrived middle classes to become state functionaries.[5]

Perhaps Napoleon's greatest accomplishment came in the field of law. Building on reforms begun ten years earlier, he put a talented team of lawyers to work to bring order to the chaotic state of French jurisprudence. At the time he took power the country was caught in the transition from the old legal system of 366 separate local systems to a uniform code. His staff compiled a comprehensive Civil Law Code by 1804 (called the Code Napoléon after 1807) that was a model of precision and equality, when compared to the old system. The Code ensured the continuation of the gains made by the middle classes in the previous decade and emphasized religious toleration and the abolition of the privileges held under the old order. Unfortunately, the Code perpetuated the inferior status of women in the areas of civil rights, financial activities, and divorce. Nonetheless it has influenced lawmaking in many other countries.

The price France paid for all of this was rule by police state that featured censorship, secret police, spies, and political trials that sent hundreds to their deaths and thousands into exile. Order did prevail, however, and for the first time in ten years it was safe to travel the country's roads. Napoleon also reduced the "representative assemblies" to meaningless rubber stamps. Liberty, equality, and fraternity meant little in a land where the First Consul and his police could deny a person's freedom and right of association because of a perceived intellectual or political conflict.

To consolidate all of the changes, Napoleon proclaimed himself emperor in December 1804. Fifteen years after the outbreak of the revolution, France had a new monarch. The nation approved the change in a plebiscite by 3,572,329 to 2,579. As Napoleon took the crown from Pope Pius VII, who had come from Rome for the occasion, and crowned himself, the First French Republic came to an end.

The artist Jacques Louis David, an ardent admirer of Napoleon, painted several pictures glorifying him. This is a preliminary sketch for David's coronation painting of the emperor.

Napoleon and the World

Since 1792, war had been France's primary occupation, and on the whole it had been a profitable one. The French had gained much land and money, as well as the opportunity to export the revolution. Napoleon's reforms helped make his country even stronger in battle. At the end of 1804 Napoleon embarked on a series of compaigns designed to show France's invincibility. A key to French success was the emperor himself, who brought his own remarkable genius to lead his strong and wealthy country.

Military Superiority

Napoleon brought equal parts of intellectual strength, sensitivity to mood and opportunity, and undoubted bravery to the task of making war. He had been trained in the most advanced methods of his day, and he had better, more mobile artillery and more potent powder to blow holes through the enemy's lines. He worked well with a talented command staff to which he gave much responsibility to wield their divisions as conditions dictated. Finally, he was the ultimate leader. Whether as lieutenant, general, first consul, or emperor, Napoleon inspired masses of soldiers in a dramatic way. At the same time he mobilized the home front through the use of the press and skillfully written despatches.

Beneath this image making, the supreme commander was extremely flexible in his use of resources, always changing his tactics. He was pragmatic, moved rapidly, and lived off the land—until the Russian campaign. He won the loyalty of his men by incentives and rewards, not brutal discipline. He set many military precedents, among them the use of ideological and economic warfare, and rapid simultaneous movement of a large number of columns which could quickly converse on a given point with devastating results, breaking the will of the enemy. Finally, he personally led his troops into battle, exposing himself to incredible dangers, with little regard for his own safety.[6]

His nemesis was Great Britain, and during 1803 and 1804 he prepared a cross-Channel invasion, but the inability of the French navy to control the Channel and the formation of the Third Coalition (Great Britain, Russia, Austria, and Sweden) forced him to march eastward. In October 1805 Admiral Nelson and the British ended Napoleon's hopes of dominating the seas by destroying the joint French-Spanish fleet at the Battle of Trafalgar.

France did far better on land, gaining mastery over the continent by the end of 1807. Napoleon totally demoralized the Third Coalition in the battles at Ulm (October 1805) and Austerlitz (December 1805). He then annihilated the Prussians who had entered the conflict in the battles at Jena and Auerstadt (October 1806). He occupied Berlin, where he established the Continental System, a blockade of the continent that was an effort to defeat Britain by depriving it of trade with the rest of Europe. Finally in June 1807 he defeated the Russians at the battle of Friedland, and forced Tsar Alexander I to sign the Tilsit Treaty in July. This treaty, signed on a raft anchored in the middle of the Nieman River, brought the two major land powers of Europe together in an alliance against Britain.

At the beginning of 1808 Napoleon stood supreme in Europe, leading France to dominance it had never experienced before or since. Several of his relatives occupied the thrones of nearby countries. The rest of the continent appeared to be mere satellites revolving around the Napoleonic sun.[7]

France's Revolution in Europe

In achieving his military goals, Napoleon set in motion a chain reaction of minirevolutions that had a profound impact on the rest of the century. British sea power stood in the way of France's total mastery of the continent. Safe behind its wall of ships, the British turned out increasing quantities of goods. Even though their economy suffered under the impact of the Continental System (exports dropped by 20 percent with a resultant cutback in production and rise in unemployment), the damage was not permanent. At the same time, Great Britain was in the midst of the early phases of industrialization (see p. 606), and in 1815 Britain stood generations ahead of the continent in economic development. Napoleon inadvertently contributed to Britain's development by forcing it to industrialize quickly as it sought new markets and methods.

Napoleon's armies carried French ideological baggage and institutional reforms with them as they fought across the continent. Even though the emperor consolidated the Revolution in a conservative way in France, he broke apart the old regime's fragile social and governmental structures when he marched across the Rhine. Napoleon consciously spread the messages of liberty, fraternity, and equality with all of the antifeudal, antiprivilege, and antirepressive themes inherent in the revolutionary triad. Where the French governed directly (see map, p. 594), they used the Code Napoléon and the reformed administrative practices. Although initially the changes were not always obvious, they became quite evident throughout most of Europe by 1848.

The French presence triggered a hostile wave. Many Europeans saw Napoleon as an imperialist, and the people he had "emancipated" began to realize that they had exchanged an old for a new form of despotism. By posing as the champion of the Revolution, Napoleon sowed the seeds of the opposition that would work against him later, especially in Prussia. With the exception of the Poles, who had labored under Russian dominance and now served Napoleon well, the rest of Europe reacted against the French yoke.

The most significant rebellion took place in Portugal and Spain. His entry into the countries to topple the passive Bourbons and strengthen the leaky Continental System was uncharacteristically shortsighted. Napoleon had a serious fight on his hands in the Peninsular War that followed. Guerrilla uprisings soon broke out, supported by a British expeditionary force and supplies. These bloody wars tied down from 200,000 to 300,000 French troops over a period of five years and drained the French treasury. The invasion of Spain also prompted a series of uprisings in the New World that gave birth to modern Latin American history (see p. 602).

The social and political changes the French triggered in Germany were equally profound. When he redrew the map of Europe after his victories, Napoleon destroyed the remnants of the Holy Roman Empire, and in so doing erased 112 states of that ancient league. Only six of the former fifty free cities retained their status. Further, by changing the territorial arrangements of other areas, he reduced the number of German political units from more than 300 to 39. The historial Hajo Holborn wrote that "it was the French invasion and the rule of Napoleon that finally led German intellectuals to the problem of the state." All over Germany a wave of nationalism stirred the politically conscious population and prepared the way for the liberation movement. Prussia in particular underwent a rebirth after 1806 to enable it to compete with France, and many German nationalists thereafter began to look to Berlin for strength and leadership.

Prussian Reform politicians such as Baron Heinrich vom und zum Stein (1757–1831) and Prince Karl von Hardenberg (1750–1822) initiated a program of social change that included abolition of serfdom—without turning land over to the peasants—a degree of self-government in the cities, and emancipation of the Jews. Although Napoleon had limited the Prussian army to 42,000 men, the Berlin authorities undermined this restriction by a subterfuge—as soon as one army was trained it was placed on reserve and a new army was called up for training. In this way Prussia managed to build a force of 270,000 men. These efforts gained the support of Prussian

intellectuals who used education as a means of nationalistic propaganda. The University of Berlin, founded in 1810, became a strong center for national movements.[8]

The Invasion of Russia

Opposition to Napoleon grew in both Austria and Russia. After the valiant but unsuccessful campaigns against the French in 1809, culminating in the bloody battle of Wagram, Vienna became a docile though not a dependable ally. Napoleon's marriage to Marie Louise, the daughter of Francis I of Austria, proved to be only a tenuous tie between the French emperor and the Habsburgs. In Russia, the Tilsit Treaty had never been popular, and the economic hardships brought on by the Continental System made a break in the alliance virtually inevitable. By the end of 1810 both France and Russia were preparing to go to war with each other.

Napoleon understood the shaky base on which his dominance rested. Involvement in Spain had drained France. The Continental System was not working against Britain. Alexander I proved to be an increasingly undependable ally. Finally, after two years of preparations, Napoleon launched a massive invasion of Russia in 1812 to put an end to at least one of his problems.

The emperor prepared carefully for his attack on Russia. Food supply would be a major problem for the 611,000 troops in the first and second lines of the invasion because his forces would be too large to live off the land. Furthermore the French troops took with them over 200,000 animals which required forage and water. The invasion force delayed its march until late June to ensure that the Russian plains would furnish sufficient grass to feed the animals. The well-thought-out, massive preparations for the invasion proved inadequate to the problems posed by the six-hundred-mile march from the Nieman River to Moscow.

Although Napoleon's twelve-nation army made almost constant headway, the Russian forces remained intact. Because they were outnumbered nearly three to one, the tsar's armies under the leadership of General Barclay de Tolly (1761–1818) and later General Mikhail Kutuzov (1745–1813) continually retreated into the vastness of their land, rather than face almost certain defeat in the hands of the invaders. The Russians destroyed everything of possible use to Napoleon's forces—the so-called scorched earth policy—continually harassed the advancing columns, and threatened the French supply lines. When the Russians finally stood their ground at Borodino (September 7, 1812), the effects of distance and disease had taken their toll among the French, and the numbers of the opposing forces were nearly equal. After a brutal conflict in which 75,000 of the total 200,000 combatants were left dead or wounded, the road to Moscow was open to the victorious French.

The Russian campaign was both a success and a failure for Napoleon. The French did gain their objective—the former capital city of Moscow—but the Russians refused to surrender. Shortly after the French occupied the city, fires broke out, destroying three-fourths of the ancient capital. After spending thirty-three days in the burned shell of the city waiting in vain for the tsar, who was 400 miles north in St. Petersburg, to agree to peace, Napoleon gave orders to retreat. He left the city on October 19. To remain would have meant having his lines cut by winter and being trapped with no supplies. His isolation in Moscow would have encouraged his enemies in Paris. Leaving the Russian capital, as it turned out, condemned most of his men to death.[9]

As the remnant of Napoleon's forces marched west in October and November, they were forced to retrace virtually the same route they had used in the summer. They suffered the attacks of the roving bands of partisans, starvation, and the continual pressure of Kutuzov's forces. Thousands perished daily, and by the end of November only about 100,000 of the original force had made their escape from Russia. Napoleon had thirteen years earlier abandoned an army in Egypt to return to Paris. In November 1812 he abandoned another army, this time in Russia, and returned to pursue his fortunes.

Napoleon's Defeat

Russia, which had stood alone against the French at the beginning of 1812, was soon joined by Prussia, Austria, and Britain in 1813 and 1814 in what came to be known as the "War of Liberation." While British armies under the Duke of Wellington (1769–1852) helped clear the French forces out of Spain, the allied troops pushed Napoleon's forces westward. A combination of Napoleon's genius and the difficulties in coordinating the allied efforts prolonged the war, but in October 1813 the French suffered a decisive defeat at Leipzig in the Battle of the Nations, one year to the day after Napoleon had fled Moscow.

The allies sent peace offers to Napoleon, but he refused them, pointing out that " . . . you sovereigns who were born to the throne may get beaten twenty times, and yet return to your capitals. I cannot. For I rose to power through the camp."[10] After Leipzig the Napoleonic empire rapidly disintegrated, and by the beginning of 1814 the allies had crossed the Rhine and invaded France. At the end of March the Russians, Austrians, and Prussians took Paris. Two weeks later Napoleon abdicated his throne, receiving in return sovereignty over Elba, a small island between Corsica and Italy.

Napoleon arrived in Elba in May and established his rule over his 85-square-mile kingdom. He set up a mini-state, complete with an army, navy, and court. Boredom soon set in and in February 1815 he eluded the British fleet and returned to France. His former subjects, disillusioned with the restored Bourbon, Louis XVIII, gave him a tumultuous welcome. Napoleon entered Paris and raised an army of 300,000 men and sent a message to the allies gathered to make peace at Vienna (see ch. 24) that he desired to rule France and only France. The allies, who were on the verge of breaking up their alliance, united, condemned Napoleon as an enemy of peace, and sent forces to France to put him down once and for all.

At the Battle of Waterloo on June 18, 1815, the Duke of Wellington, supported by Prussian troops under Field Marshall Gebhard von Blücher (1749–1819), narrowly defeated Napoleon. The vanquished leader sought asylum with the British, hoping to live in exile either in England or the United States. But the allies, taking no chances, shipped him off to the bleak south Atlantic island of St. Helena, five thousand miles from Paris. Here he set about writing his autobiography. He died of cancer in 1821 at the age of 51.

Even with the brief flurry of the One Hundred Days, Napoleon had no hope of recreating the grandeur of his empire as it was in 1808. The reasons for this are not hard to find. Quite simply,

Napoleon on His Place in History

In his conversations with the Count de Las Cases, Napoleon clearly expressed *his* notion of his place in history.

"I closed the gulf of anarchy and cleared the chaos. I purified the Revolution, dignified Nations and established Kings. I excited every kind of emulation, rewarded every kind of merit, and extended the limits of glory! This is at least something! And on what point can I be assailed on which an historian could not defend me? Can it be for my intentions? But even here I can find absolution. Can it be for my despotism? It may be demonstrated that the Dictatorship was absolutely necessary. Will it be said that I restrained liberty? It can be proved that licentiousness, anarchy, and the greatest irregularities, still haunted the threshold of freedom. Shall I be accused of having been too fond of war? It can be shown that I always received the first attack. Will it be said that I aimed at universal monarchy? It can be proved that this was merely the result of fortuitous circumstances, and that our enemies themselves led me step by step to this determination. Lastly, shall I be blamed for my ambition? This passion I must doubtless be allowed to have possessed, and that in no small degree; but at the same time, my ambition was of the highest and noblest kind that ever, perhaps, existed—that of establishing and of consecrating the empire of reason, and the full exercise and complete enjoyment of all the human faculties! And here the historian will probably feel compelled to regret that such ambition should not have been fulfilled and gratified!" Then after a few moments of silent reflection: "This," said the Emperor, "is my whole history in a few words."

From the Count de Las Cases, *Memoirs of the Life, Exile, and Conversations of the Emperor Napoleon,* new ed. (New York: Eckler, 1900).

Napoleon was the heart and soul of the empire, and after 1808 his physical and intellectual vigor began to weaken. Administrative and military developments reflected this deterioration, as Napoleon began to appoint sycophants to positions of responsibility. Further, by 1812 the middle classes on whom he depended began suffering the economic consequences of his policies. The Continental System and continual warfare made their effects deeply felt through decreased trade and increased taxes. Even though some war contractors profited, the costs of Napoleon's ambitions began to make Frenchmen long for peace.

Outside of France, the growth of national resistance on the continent worked against the dictator who first stimulated it by exporting the call for liberty, equality, and fraternity. Equally important, the twenty-five years of French military superiority disappeared as other nations adopted and improved on the new methods of fighting. Finally, the balance of power principle made itself felt. France could not eternally take on the whole world.

Napoleon and the Americas

The forces generated by the French Revolution and Napoleon deeply affected the Americas in the fifty years after 1776. The former English colonies south of Canada had gained their independence with French assistance and the new government had close relations with Paris until the outbreak of the revolutionary wars, when President George Washington proclaimed neutrality. When relations with the British began to improve during the 1790s, the French waged a virtual war on American shipping, taking over 800 ships in the last three years of the century. The United States benefited from one aspect of Napoleon's activities. In 1803, the emperor sold the region known as Louisiana for $15 million;

this Louisiana Purchase increased the land area of the new country by 200 percent. Unfortunately, the United States suffered considerable commercial losses as it became caught up in the French-British conflict.

The French overthrow of the Spanish Bourbons in 1808 encouraged the revolts that created thirteen republics in Spanish America by 1824 (see map, p. 603). The charismatic leader who stepped into the void was Simon Bolívar (1783–1830), hailed as "the Liberator " of South America. After completing his rationalist education in Paris during the last years of the Directory, he returned to his native Venezuela to exploit colonial resistance to the Napoleonic takeover of Spain in 1808. Convinced after the disaster at Trafalgar that transatlantic ambitions were pointless, Napoleon left the Spanish colonial empire to its own complex fate.[11]

Loyal at first to the deposed Spanish Bourbons and newly filled with refugees from the parent country, Spain's colonies soon began to entertain the idea that they had their own destinies to fulfill as new nations. The American-born elite of European blood, the creoles, were especially attracted to the prospect of expelling the controlling *peninsulares*, Spaniards of European birth who usually returned to Spain after a profitable term of colonial service.[12]

Bolívar stepped into this situation by issuing a series of inflammatory and visionary messages calling for the liberation of Venezuela and then of a larger unit called Gran Colombia (modern-day Colombia, Panama, Ecuador, and Venezuela) which he hoped would expand to include all of Spanish South America. He was frequently defeated by Spanish loyalist forces, yet he kept fighting, making use of skills as an orator and as a tactician. He eventually forced the remnants of the Spanish military and administrative personnel to go home. He proposed a constitution that favored the élite of the new nations, a document that was much like the one written by the Directory. He ran afoul of liberal critics and regional loyalties, and eventually died in exile in British Jamaica. He dreamed of continental state split into the nation-states of Venezuela, Colombia, Ecuador, Peru, and Bolivia.

Argentina, Uruguay, and Chile were liberated in comparable fashion by the stoic, Spanish-educated creole officer José de San Martín (1778–1850) who was as austere and reserved as Bolívar was flashy and outgoing. The two could never forge an alliance, partly because of personality differences and partly because of San Martín's preference for a constitutional monarchy like that of Britain or the French Constitution of 1791. His wishes were rejected by the Spanish

Simon Bolívar and his army battle the Spanish at Araure in Venezuela. Although the Spanish were better trained and equipped, Bolívar led his soldiers with such personal valor that he managed to liberate four countries.

colonies he had freed but were followed by the Portuguese in Brazil. King John VI of Portugal had fled his country in 1807 and ruled the Portuguese empire from Rio de Janeiro for the next fourteen years. Returning to Lisbon in 1821, the king left his son Dom Pedro as regent of Brazil. Impatient with the reactionary behavior of the Lisbon government, Pedro declared himself emperor of an independent Brazil, which he and his son Pedro II ruled as a constitutional monarchy for nearly seventy years.

The Mexican revolution began earlier and produced more extreme consequences than its South American counterpart. The Mexican middle class was even smaller than that of the rest of Spanish America and far more conservative. Between 1808 and 1810 anti-Bonapartist sentiment shifted to a general rejection of the European monarchy in creole circles throughout the vice-royalty of New Spain.

The revolution was actually begun by an enlightened provincial creole priest, Miguel Hidalgo (1753–1811), who issued a call for universal freedom on September 16, 1810 (the date is celebrated in Mexico today as the *Dia del Grito*, the Day of the Call). Hidalgo led his ragged army of Indians and idealists to the gates of Mexico City, but hesitated to take the city fearing the bloodbath that would follow. Although Hidalgo was condemned by the colonial bishops and executed for treason six months after his uprising began, his cause was taken up by others, including José Maria Morelos (1765–1815), a radical mestizo (mixed blood) parish priest who became an effective guerrilla leader. Finally, in August 1821, the last Spanish viceroy recognized the independence of Mexico, whose ruling classes promptly fell to squabbling over the constitution.

While men of ideas argued, military opportunists took power. Two would-be Napoleons, Augustín de Iturbide (1783–1824) and Antonio López de Santa Anna (1794–1876), dominated politics for the next quarter-century, at the end of which Mexico lost the northern half of its territory to the United States. Iturbide, a creole landowner and officer who had fought as a Spanish loyalist until 1816, became emperor of Mexico for a turbulent ten month reign in 1822–1823. Santa Anna, who emulated Napoleon's opportunism more successfully than many of his other qualities, became president or dictator of the

LATIN AMERICA 1826

European Colony

Mexican republic eleven times between 1833 and 1855. His career as a military leader included several disastrous incidents, notably his humiliating defeat and capture by Texan rebels at San Jacinto in April 1836—six weeks after he had exterminated their comrades at the secularized Franciscan mission in San Antonio known as the Alamo and a month after he had mercilessly massacred Texan prisoners at Goliad (see p. 713).[13]

The social and economic consequences of the Latin American revolutions were far different from those in North America and Europe. The area was much poorer and more divided. The new nations of Latin America quickly fell to the commercial dominance of the British Empire. Their economies, exploited by speculators in North America and Europe, have been subject to drastic fluctuations ever since, based as they are on exportation of raw materials. The conditions of the Indian population declined as the new liberal regimes confiscated the large landholdings of the religious orders which had served to insulate the surviving Indians from direct confrontations with the Europeans' economic and technological dominance. As in every country since the Reformation where Church property was bought up by the monied classes, the local population was reorganized into a new labor force more profitable to the new owners. In this case, the owners simply reorganized the Indian communities into a labor force and drove those who were not productive and the mestizos off the land. This movement in some countries has continued in one form or another to the present day.

The Latin American Church, staffed largely by *peninsulares,* was shattered by the national revolution. When reconstituted with greatly reduced property and clerical personnel, the Church desperately sought to win the protection of the more conservative elements in the creole elite by opposing liberalism in any form. Since the Church had been the exclusive instrument of education and social welfare before liberation and since the ruling classes showed little interest in providing for the continuation of schools, orphanages, and relief for the lower classes, the misery of the Latin American poor grew more acute throughout the nineteenth century.

The position of women rose momentarily and then fell, as in France. Individual creole women such as Bolívar's astute mistress Manuela Sanches, made major contributions to the revolution, but the adoption of the Napoleonic Code in the 1820s had the same impact on women's legal status as in Europe at the same time.

It can be argued that in the wake of Napoleon's deposing the Spanish Bourbons Latin America suffered a decline in political stability and internal economic health. The peasants and urban laborers of Indian and mixed blood descent, the culture-shaping Church, and women of all classes paid a heavy price for liberation from the Spanish and Portuguese overlords. The single group that gained was the secular, male Creole leadership. Nevertheless, what Napoleon had destroyed was gone, and no serious attempt was made to restore the old colonial regime. The political independence of the new nations of Latin America was guaranteed, at least in theory, by the United States in the proclamation of the Monroe Doctrine in 1823 (see p. 710).

Industrialization: The First Phase

While Europe's "great men" plotted grand schemes to pursue their political and intellectual ambitions during the crisis of the Old Regime, French Revolution, and Napoleonic wars, obscure British inventors designed machines whose impact would dwarf their efforts. They industrialized textile making by using machines and new power sources to accomplish a task formerly done by human and animal power. They began what has been called by some the Industrial Revolution.

The huge increase in productivity made possible by using machines can be shown in the amount of raw cotton Britain imported in 1760 and 1850. In 1760 the British imported a bit over 1000 tons; in 1850 the number had risen to over 222,000 tons. The story behind the growth of the textile industry is one of a continual "catch-up" game between the spinners and weavers to respond to a growing market. After the 1707 Act of Union with Scotland, Britain possessed an expanding population with a larger per capita income than that of any other European state. The population growth stemmed from a gradual decline in death rates and an increase in the birth rate.[14] It provided more customers and workers.

The Revolution in Making Cloth

Practical people seeing the need for greater output solved the practical problems of production. In the many steps from the raw cotton to the finished cloth, there were bottlenecks—primarily in making yarn and weaving the strands together. In 1733, John Kay (1704–1764), a spinner and mechanic, patented the first of the great machines—the flying shuttle. This device made it possible for one person to weave wide bolts of cloth by using a spring mechanism that sent the shuttle across the loom. This invention upset the balance between the weavers of cloth and the spinners of yarn: ten spinners were required to produce enough yarn needed by one weaver. James Hargreaves (d. 1778), a weaver

Power looms in operation in an English mill in the 1820s.

and carpenter, eliminated that problem in 1764 with his spinning jenny, a mechanical spinning wheel that allowed the spinners to keep up with the weavers.

Five years later, a barber named Richard Arkwright (1732–1792) built the water frame that made it possible to spin many threads into yarn at the same time. Ten years after that Samuel Crompton (1753–1827), a spinner, combined the spinning jenny and water frame into the water mule, which, with some variations, is used today. By this time the makers of yarn were outpacing the weavers, but in 1785 Edmund Cartwright (1743–1823) invented the power loom that mechanized the weaving process. In two generations what had once been a home-based craft became an industry.

The appetite of the new machines outran the supply of cotton. Since most of the material came from the United States, the demand exceeded the capability of the slave-based southern economy to fill the supply. The best worker could not prepare more than five or six pounds of cotton a day because of the problems of the seeds. American inventor Eli Whitney (1765–1825), among others, devised the cotton gin, a machine that enabled a worker to clean more than fifty times as much cotton a day. This device coincidentally played a major role in the perpetuation of slavery in the United States.

Finally, the textile industry became so large that it outgrew the possibilities of its power source: water power. Steam came to drive the machines of industrializing Britain. In the first part of the eighteenth century a mechanic, Thomas Newcomen (1663–1729), made an "atmospheric engine" in which a piston was raised by injected steam. As the steam condensed, the piston returned to its original position. Newcomen's unwieldy and inefficient device was put to use pumping water out of mines. James Watt (1736–1819), a builder of scientific instruments at the University of Glasgow, perfected Newcomen's invention. Watt's steam engine also was first used to pump water out of mines. It saved the large amounts of energy lost by the Newcomen engine and led to an increase in coal productivity. After 1785 it was also used to make cloth and drive ships and locomotives. The application of steam to weaving made it possible to expand the use of cloth-making machines to new areas, and after 1815 hand looms began to disappear from commercial textile making, replaced by the undoubted superiority of the cloth-making machines.

These inventors made their contributions in response to the need to solve a particular problem. Their machines and the new power sources expanded productivity and transformed society in ways never before dreamed of. The transition from a rural agrarian to an urban lifestyle merits applying the term *revolutionary* to the process of industrialization. The steps in increasing textile production were repeated and continue to be repeated in other goods as well. The liberation from the productive limitation of human and animal power to satisfy essentially unlimited demand is the great gift of industrialization.

Britain's Dominance

Industrialization began in Britain in the eighteenth century for a number of reasons. Neither the richest nor the most populous country in western Europe, it did, nevertheless, possess at virtually all levels of society a hard-working, inventive, risk-taking private sector that received strong support from the government. Industrialization could not begin and grow without individual business owners who took a chance on something new. The British kept this close tie between private initiative and creative governmental support throughout the eighteenth and nineteenth centuries.

Thanks to early governmental support of road improvements and canal construction, Britain had a better transportation network than any other country in Europe (see map at right). The British also had mastery of the seas, excellent ports, and a large merchant fleet. They enjoyed the advantage of living safely on their island, away from the carnage of war, even during the Napoleonic wars. The chance to industrialize in stable conditions gave them the opportunity to profit from war contracts between 1792 and 1815. They developed their industrial capacity without fear of battle damage or loss of life.

Probably the most important factor was the relative flexibility of the British social and political systems. Members of the élite, unlike their colleagues on the continent, pursued their wealth in the new industrial framework with great energy. They worked closely with the middle classes and workers, even to the point during the nineteenth century of sponsoring gradual reform efforts to stifle any chance of revolution from below.

The combination of inventiveness, growing markets, governmental support, and social flexibility made Britain the world's dominant economic power until the end of the nineteenth century. Napoleon's interference had hurt economic growth, but had also spurred the British to look for new manufacturing methods and markets. Once the wars were over, Britain flooded the continent and the Americas with high-quality, inexpensive goods. No nation could compete against British efficiency. When Britain began industrializing before 1789, there were isolated areas on the continent such as the French Le Creusot works that could have served as the base for a similar growth. Twenty-six years of revolution and mercantile policies made that competition impossible.[15]

Cotton production continued to increase and was supplemented by the arrival of the modern Iron Age. In 1800 Russia and Sweden had exported iron to Britain. By 1815 Britain exported more than five times as much iron as it imported. By 1848 the British produced more iron than the rest of the world combined. As in textile production, in ironmaking a number of inventions

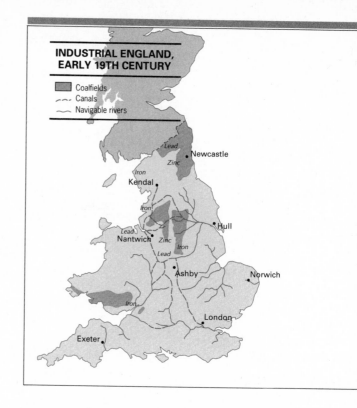

INDUSTRIAL ENGLAND,
EARLY 19TH CENTURY

☐ Coalfields
--- Canals
~ Navigable rivers

appeared to respond to problems. Refining of the brittle cast iron was improved to make it more malleable and tougher. At the same time more efficient mining processes for both coal and iron ore were used to ensure a constant supply of raw materials.

To further dominate the metals market, in the 1850s Henry Bessemer (1813–1898) developed a process to make steel, a harder and more malleable metal, quickly and cheaply. So effective was the process that between 1856 and 1870 the price of British steel fell to one half the amount formerly charged for the best grade of iron. The drastic reduction in price, a mark of industrialization, had a positive impact on all areas of the economy.

In the period after midcentury Britain produced more than two-thirds of the world's coal and more than half of the world's iron and cloth. Industrial development encouraged urbanization and by 1850 more than half of the population lived in cities and worked in industries. The British continued to enjoy the highest per capita income in the world, and the island nation stood head and shoulders above the world in terms of economic and material strength.

Industrialization: The Second Phase

The second phase of industrialization brought new products and power sources to the continent. Increased food production and improved health standards and diet led to a population explosion that promised both economic gains and bureaucratic burdens. The rapid and massive growth of cities brought with it the social problems of urbanization. Workers united to fight for their interests, while the middle classes extended their wealth and influence. Both groups changed the nature of social and political life.

Food and Population Increases

Liberated from many of the restraints of the past by the French, Napoleonic, and Industrial revolutions, most Europeans made the transition from a society based on agriculture to a modern urban society. The spectacular growth of the industrial sector makes it easy to overlook the great strides in food production during the nineteenth century. Because of the improved global transportation network and better farming methods, the expanding number of city dwellers had more and better food to eat in 1914 than they had had in 1815.

It is estimated that in 1815 around 60 percent of the money and 85 percent of the Europeans were tied to farming. These large quantities of capital and labor were not effectively used, because the advances made in Holland and Britain in the seventeenth and eighteenth centuries had not spread to the continent. However, progressive landowners gradually introduced these improved methods when they saw the money to be made feeding the growing population of the cities.

By the end of the nineteenth century farmers on the continent were plowing new lands and using higher yielding crop varieties to survive in the worldwide agricultural competition. Industrial nations such as Britain, in which only 10 percent of the population was engaged in farming, imported more than a fourth of their food. Farmers in the Americas, Australia, and New Zealand competed with each other in the cutthroat export market. The peasants of Ireland and southern and eastern Europe were unable to produce efficiently enough to prosper in this new setting. Russia, where the peasantry comprised 70 percent of the population, had to export to bring in foreign capital to finance industrialization. When the country had to compete with efficient foreign farmers, the tsarist minister of finance stated, "we may go hungry, but we will export."[16]

The expanded food supply supported the growth in European population from 175 million to 435 million.[17] This 130 percent increase between 1800 and 1910 partially disproved the views the British clergyman Thomas Robert Malthus (1766–1834) set forth in his *Essay on Population*. Malthus asserted that human reproduction could easily outrun the earth's ability to produce food.[18] In his own day he could point to the limited food supply and rapidly increasing population. From this evidence he concluded that the inevitable fate of humanity was misery and ruin, since the number of people would rise geometrically while food supply would grow only arithmetically. The experience of the next two centuries has at least temporarily disproved Malthus' thesis.

A gradual decline in mortality rates, slightly better medical care, more food, earlier marriages, and better sanitary conditions contributed to the population increase. The number of people grew so rapidly in Europe that although 40 million Europeans emigrated throughout the world, the continent still showed a population increase in one century that was greater than that of the previous two thousand years. Where the economies were advanced, such as in northern and western Europe, the population growth could be absorbed. But in the poorer countries of southern and eastern Europe, the masses faced the choices of overcrowding and starvation or emigration.

The Ties That Bind: New Networks

To bring the increased food supply to the growing population, to distribute new resources to larger markets, and to connect augmented capital with essential information, Europeans built the most complete and far-reaching transportation and communication networks ever known. Without rapid and dependable transport and contact the Industrial Revolution could not have occurred, cities would not have grown, factories could not have functioned, and the new millions of Europeans would not have been fed. The new networks became the arteries and nervous system of Europe.

The Duke of Bridgewater made a major step forward in water transportation in 1759 when he built a seven and one-half mile long canal from his mines to Manchester. Water transport cut the price of his coal in half and gave Britain a vivid lesson in the benefits of canals. Nearly four thousand miles of improved rivers and canals were built, with strong governmental support by the 1830s, making it possible to ship most of the country's products by water. Following the British example, canal building spread through Europe and North America and then to Egypt with the Suez Canal in 1869 and Latin America with the Panama Canal in 1914. The first project cut the sailing time between London and Bombay India by nearly half, while the second did away with the need to sail around South America to reach the Pacific Ocean.

Until 1815 most roads were muddy, rutted paths that were impassable during spring thaws and autumn rains. In that year a Scotsman, John McAdam, created the all-weather road by placing small stones in compact layers directly on the road bed. The pressure of the traffic moving over the highway packed the stones together to give a fairly smooth surface. This practical solution cut the stagecoach time for the 160 miles from London to Sheffield from four days in the 1750s to 28 hours.

Steam-powered vessels replaced the graceful though less dependable sailing ships in ocean commerce. Clipper ships are among the most beautiful objects ever built, but they could not move without wind. Sturdy, awkward-looking steamships carried larger cargo with greater regularity and revolutionized world trade. The price of American wheat on the European market dropped by three-fourths in the last part of the century, thanks to a considerable degree to the savings made possible by the large, reliable steam ships. Transatlantic passenger and mail services were also improved by the use of steam to power seagoing vessels.

The most important element in the European arterial network was the railroad. Between 1830 and 1860 rails linked every major market in Europe, and the United States. By 1903 the Russians had pushed the Trans-Siberian railroad to the Pacific Ocean. Railroads cheaply and efficiently carried large amounts of material and people long distances and knit countries and continents closer together. Within cities, urban rail lines and trolleys were widespread by the end of the century; these had an impressive effect on

Lavish ceremony celebrated the opening of the Suez Canal in 1869.

This English royal train was built in the early 1840s for the special use of Queen Victoria in her travels over the nation's rapidly expanding railway system.

housing and business patterns by permitting a wider diffusion of workers. London established subways first in the 1860s, followed by Budapest in 1896 and Paris in 1900.

Connected with the growth of the transportation networks and technological innovation, major improvements came in the area of communications. Postal agreements among the various countries made cheap and dependable mail service possible. The modern postage stamp and improved transportation brought astronomical increases in the amount of letters and packages mailed after 1850.[19] Starting in the 1840s the electric telegraph, undersea cable, telephone, wireless telegraph, and typewriter expanded humanity's ability to exchange ideas and information. No longer would distance be a critical obstacle after the transportation and communications revolutions. The world became a smaller, if not more unified, place.

The Continent Industrializes

The continent faced many hurdles to economic growth after 1815. Obstacles to mobility, communication, and cooperation among the classes prevented the social structures there from adapting as easily to change as had the British. The farther south and east the social system, the more repressive was the structure. In many parts of the continent, the restored nobilities reclaimed their power, and they were neither intellectually nor financially prepared to support industrial development. Fragmented political boundaries, geographical obstacles, and toll-takers along primary river and road systems hampered growth, especially in central Europe. In eastern Europe, the middle classes were weaker and more isolated than in the west.

At the end of the Napoleonic wars, the initial stages of industrialization could be found in Belgium, France, and Germany. In Sweden, Russia, and Switzerland there were pockets of potential mechanized production, but the total of all of these activities was tiny compared to Britain's economy. In 1850 only Belgium could compete with British products in its own markets. There a combination of favorable governmental policies, good transportation, and stability brought some success.

Governments and businesses sent officials and representatives to Britain to try to discover the secrets of industrialization. The British tried to protect their advantage by banning the export of machines and processes and limiting foreign access to their factories. Industrial espionage existed then as now, and continental competitors did uncover some secrets. Britain's success could be studied, components of it stolen, and its experts hired, but no country on the continent could combine all the factors that permitted Britain to dominate.

After midcentury, a long period of peace, improved transportation, and strategic government assistance encouraged rapid economic growth in France and the German states. Population increased 25 percent in France and nearly 40 percent in the Germanies, providing a larger market and labor supply. Two generations of borrowed British technology began to be applied and improved upon; but the two most important developments came in banking and customs and toll reforms.

After 1815, aggressive new banking houses appeared across Europe, strengthened by the profits they had made extending loans to governments during the Napoleonic wars. They saw the money to be made investing in new industries such as railroads and worked with both governments and major capitalists. Firms such as Hope and Baring in London, the Rothschilds in Frankfurt, Paris, Vienna, and London, and numerous Swiss bankers were representative of the private financiers who had well-placed sources and contacts throughout the state and business communities.[20]

Banking changed radically during this period to satisfy the growing demands for money. Long-range capital needs were met by the formation of investment banks, while new institutions were created to fill the need for short-term credit. The ultimate source of financial liquidity was the middle classes—the thousand of little people who put their money in banks to make their own profits on interest earned. More money could be gained from the many small investors than from the few rich families who used to dominate banking.

The Germans led the way in the other major development, the *Zollverein* (customs union), that began under Prussian leadership in 1819. This arrangement helped break down the trade barriers erected by state boundaries and in the next twenty-three years came to include most of central and northern Germany. Instead of the more than 300 divisions fragmenting the Germans in 1800, there was a virtual free trade market, something Britain had enjoyed since the union of Scotland and England in 1707—and which the European Economic Community will create after 1992. The significance of the *Zollverein* was that it allowed goods to circulate free of tolls and tariffs, thus reducing prices and stimulating trade.

In the second half of the century, industrialization grew rapidly, aided by the increased flow of credit and elimination of many internal barriers. Tariff walls throughout the area fell to a degree not matched until after World War II. Major firms such as the German Krupp works and the French silk industries controlled portions of the European market and competed effectively with Britain throughout the world.

Technological Growth and Advances

Another reason for the continent's economic emergence was a wide range of new technologies using new materials, processes, and transportation. New competitors began with state-of-the-art factories that allowed them to outproduce Britain, whose older factories were less productive.

The basic change in the second phase of industrialization was the use of electricity in all aspects of life. Scientists had discovered electricity's basic principles a century earlier, but it was difficult to generate and transmit power across long distances. When the first dependable dynamo, a device that changed energy from mechanical into electrical form, was perfected in 1876, it became possible to generate electricity almost anywhere. Inventors such as the American Thomas A. Edison began to use the new resource in industry, transportation, entertainment, and the home. Humanity had finally found a source of power that could be easily transported and used. The British took the lead in bringing electricity to home use. The Germans made the most advanced application of electric technology to industry.

Another fundamental change came in the use of gas and oil in the newly devised internal combustion engine. Steam power's use was limited by its appetite for huge amounts of fuel and its sheer bulk. Gottlieb Daimler perfected the internal combustion engine used in most automobiles today. In 1892 Rudolf Diesel invented the engine that bears his name. It burned fuel instead of harnessing the explosions that drove the Daimler engine.

These new developments led directly to the search for and use of petroleum and the beginning of the passenger car industry. By 1914 the making of cars was a key part of the Italian, Russian, German, French, and American economies. Automobile manufacturing called for a number of "spinoff" industries such as tires, ball bearings, windshields—the list extends to hundreds of items. Leaving aside the passenger car's economic contribution, the world's cities and people felt the complex impact of this new form of transportation, with consequences extending from the range of an individual's world to the increased noise level and pollution that changed the character of urban areas.

Other new machines changed life. Bicycles became commonplace in the 1890s, as did sewing machines, cameras, and typewriters, to name a few. Never had people had the ability to transform ideas almost instantly into products accessible to the average person. This was another dividend of industrialization and a symbol of a rapidly changing Europe.

The Human Costs of Industrialization

Industrialization drove society from an agricultural to an urban way of life. The old system, in which peasants worked the fields during the summer and did their cottage industry work in the winter to their own standards and at their own pace, slowly disappeared. In its place came urban life tied to the factory system. The factory was a place where people did repetitive tasks using machines over long hours to process large amounts of raw materials. This was an efficient way to make a lot of high-quality goods at cheap cost. But the factories were often dangerous places and the lifestyle connected to them had a terrible effect on the human condition.

In the factory system the workers worked and the owners made profits. The owners wanted to make the most they could from their investment and to get the most work they could from their employees. The workers, in turn, felt that they deserved more of the profits because their labor made production possible. This was a situation guaranteed to produce conflict, especially given the wretched conditions the workers faced in the first stages of industrialization.

The early factories were miserable places, featuring bad lighting, lack of ventilation, dangerous machines, and frequent breakdowns. Safety standards were practically nonexistent and workers in various industries could expect to contract serious diseases—workers with lead paint suffered lung problems, pewter workers fell ill to palsy, miners suffered black lung disease, and primitive machines claimed many fingers, hands, and even lives. Not until late in the century did health and disability insurance come into effect. In some factories workers who suffered accidents were deemed to be at fault, and since there was little job security, a worker could be fired for virtually any reason.

The demand for plentiful and cheap labor led to the widespread employment of women and children. Girls as young as six years old were used to haul carts of coal in Lancashire mines, and boys and girls of four and five years of age worked in textile mills—their nimble little fingers could easily untangle jammed machines. When they were not laboring, the working families lived in horrid conditions in such wretched industrial cities as Lille, France, and Manchester, England. There were no sanitary, water, or medical services for the workers and working families were crammed twelve and fifteen to a room in damp, dark cellars. Bad diet, alcoholism, cholera, and typhus led to a reduction of life span in the industrial cities. Simultaneous with, and perhaps part of, the industrialization process was the vast increase in illegitimate births. Up to midcentury, corresponding to the time of

Industrialization and Children

Early industrialization demanded huge sacrifices, especially from children.

Sarah Gooder, Aged 8 years

I'm a trapper in the Gawber pit. It does not tire me, but I have to trap without a light and I'm scared. I go at four and sometimes half past three in the morning, and come out at five and half past. I never go to sleep. Sometimes I sing when I've light, but not in the dark; I dare not sing then. I don't like being in the pit. I am very sleepy when I go sometimes in the morning. I go to Sunday-schools and read *Reading made Easy*. She knows her letters and can read little words. They teach me to pray. She repeated the Lord's Prayer, not very perfectly, and ran on with the following addition:—"God bless my father and mother, and sister and brother, uncles and aunts and cousins, and everybody else, and God bless me and make me a good servant. Amen. I have heard tell of Jesus many a time. I don't know why he came on earth, I'm sure, and I don't know why he died, but he had stones for his head to rest on. I would like to be at school far better than in the pit."

From *Parliamentary Papers* (London, 1842).

maximum upheaval, continent-wide figures indicate that at least one-third of all births were out of wedlock.[21]

Later generations profited from the sacrifices made by the first workers in the industrialization, and factory owners came to understand that they could make more profit from an efficient factory staffed by contented workers.

Urban Crises

Huge population increases and industrialization prompted a massive growth of European cities in the nineteenth century, as can be seen in the following table.[22]

CITY	1800	1910
London	831,000	4,521,000
Paris	547,000	2,888,000
Berlin	173,000	2,071,000
Vienna	247,000	2,030,000
St. Petersburg	220,000	1,907,000

In addition, new towns sprang up throughout the continent and soon reached the level of over 100,000 inhabitants. Even in agrarian Russia, where 70 percent of the population worked on the land, there were seventeen cities of more than 100,000 by the end of the century.

Political leaders faced serious problems dealing with mushrooming city growth. The factory system initially forced families to live and work in squalor, danger, and disease, a condition to be found today in countries undergoing the first stages of industrialization. City leaders had to maintain a clean environment, provide social and sanitation services, enforce the law, furnish transportation, and—most serious of all—build housing. They uniformly failed to meet the radical challenges of growth.

Until midcentury human waste disposal in some parts of Paris was taken care of by dumping excrement in the gutters or the Seine or through street-corner manure collections. Not until Haussman's urban renewal in the 1850s and 1860s did the city get an adequate garbage, water, and sewage system. Police protection remained inadequate or corrupt. Other cities shared Paris' problems to a greater or lesser degree. The new industrial towns were in even worse condition than the older centers.

The terrible life in the industrial towns touched observers like novelist Charles Dickens, who in his book *Hard Times* described a typical British factory town:

It was a town of red brick, or of brick that would have been red if the smoke and ashes had allowed it; but as matters stood, it was a town of unnatural red and black, like the painted face of a savage. It was a town of machinery and tall chimneys, out of which interminable serpents of smoke trailed themselves for ever and ever, and never got uncoiled. It had a black canal in it, and a river that ran purple with ill-smelling dye, and vast piles of building full of windows where there was a rattling and trembling all day long, and where the piston of the steam engine worked monotonously up and down, like the head of an elephant in a state of melancholy madness. It contained several large streets all very like one another, and many small streets still more like one another, inhabited by people equally like one another,

This illustration, *Over London—By Rail,* vividly depicts the problems that accompanied urbanization—cramped living spaces, crime, and air and water pollution.

who all went in and out at the same hours, with the same sound upon the same pavement, to do the same work, and to whom every day was the same as yesterday and tomorrow, and every year the counterpart of the last and the next.[23]

By the end of the century, however, governments began to deal effectively with urban problems. By 1914, most major European cities began to make clean running water, central heat, adequate street lighting, mass public education, dependable sewage systems, and minimal medical care available for their people.

Ideological Responses to an Age of Change

The terms that describe most of the world's political choices—nationalism, liberalism, conservatism, socialism, and communism—all came into common use in the first half of the nineteenth century. These "isms" describe European political theorists' responses to the great changes through which they were living. They built on the legacy of the Western tradition, especially the Enlightenment's exaltation of the power of reason to define "how man should live" in the wake of the French, Napoleonic, and Industrial revolutions.

In the half century after 1789 romantics made the first steps to define their relationship to the new world. As the world changed around them, they found little solace in socially approved standards. They preferred to look far to the past, to long-forgotten civilizations imprecisely recalled, and commemorated them in simulated ruins. They also paid serious attention to the hazy examples of the medieval world, especially myths and folklore. They rejected eighteenth century classicism and the cold logic of the Enlightenment. On the continent, romantics reacted against the French and Napoleonic dominance while their colleagues lashed out against the ugliness and de-humanization of industrialization.

Romantics wanted to break out of the rational, measured patterns, and rules of the classicists to respond to the emotional needs of the soul. They argued that one could not rationally define

beauty, love, friendship, or anger. Jean-Jacques Rousseau (1712–1778), for example, pointed out that a people must live more by their instincts and feelings than by society's scaffold of intellect and rationalization. He argued that the "noble savage" was to be admired because he was close to nature, uncontaminated by the false constraints of society. Lutheran Pietists also responded to this view and tried to replace the austerity and abstraction of their theology with the warmth, fervor, and emotion of religious sentiment.

By stressing an individual's past, uniqueness, emotions, and creativity, the romantics had a critical effect on the arts (see p. 618) and politics. The romantic movement opened the way for the rise of the modern age's most potent, enduring, and least-defined force—nationalism. By emphasizing the right of individuals to define their own standards instead of adhering to universal principles, the romantics contributed to the emergence of the one "ism" that cuts across class lines and intellectual divides, nationalism.

Nationalism

By emphasizing research into the past and the picturesque to find their own roots, the romantics helped give birth to nationalism. They investigated their own history, folklore, linguistic background, and myths to define their own uniqueness. They saw the world not as a cosmopolitan and rational unit, but as a place of natural variety. Scholars investigated myths and folklore ranging from the Scandinavian sagas to the French *Chanson de Roland* to the *Nibelungen* stories in Germany. During a time of uncertainty, change, and stress, looking to the past, even an imagined one, was both comforting and uplifting.

The persistence of nations and nationalities is not the same as nationalism, which involves pride in a common identity as well as loyalty to a state. After the events in France after 1789, this new ideological force dominated the cultural and political activities of the nation. The spirit of fraternity projected by the French Revolution united the French nation. Napoleon's domination over the continent had a similarly strong effect, bringing people together in opposition to him, especially in Germany, and this led to the belief in

The brothers Grimm are perhaps best known as collectors and publishers of German folk tales, known in English as *Grimm's Fairy Tales.*

the uniqueness and superiority of Germany that had such drastic consequences in the twentieth century.

The research and writings of the Germans Johann Gottfried von Herder (1744–1803) and Jakob (1785–1863) and Wilhelm Grimm (1786–1859) provided historical support and linguistic bases for the Slavic nationalist movements. Herder conceived of a world spirit *(Weltgeist)* made up of component parts of the various national spirits *(Volksgeist)*. Each of these national spirits was seen as playing an essential role in the world process, and Herder believed that the Slavs were soon to make an important contribution. The Grimm brothers' philological work aided the literary and linguistic revivals of many Slavic groups. Romantic nationalism was also found in the writings of history by Leopold von Ranke in Germany, Jules Michelet in France, František Palacky in Bohemia-Moravia, and George Bancroft in the United States.

George Wilhelm Friedrich Hegel (1770–1831), although not a romantic, built on the movement's contributions in his lectures and writings at the University of Berlin. For Hegel, history was a process of evolution in which the supremacy of primitive instincts would give way to the reign of clear reason and freedom—the "world spirit"—that would be manifested in the state. Hegel believed that the Prussia of his day offered the best example of the state as a spiritual organism, because in Prussia the individual had the greatest "freedom"—defined not as the individual escaping from society but as a condition in which there is no conflict between the individual and society. The Prussian state, in Hegel's eyes, blended the proper proportions of national identity and structure to enable its individuals to gain their greatest growth. His high regard for the state was not shared by most romantics, but his exaltation of the Prussian state at a time when Germany was still fragmented had a powerful unifying influence.

Romantic nationalism in Britain reacted strongly against the human costs of industrialization and the pretensions of the new merchant classes. It focused on the medieval roots of Britain, as well as on movements such as philhellenism (the love of ancient Greece). In France, Spain, Italy, Russia, and other parts of the continent the romantic movement made important contributions to the growth of national identity. In Italy, for example, Giuseppe Mazzini (1805–1872) and Alessandro Manzoni (1785–1873) played important roles in the unification struggle of the country (see ch. 24).[24]

Unique conditions in different parts of Europe produced different variants of nationalism. However, common to them all was a nation consciously embracing a common land, language, folklore, history, enemies, and religion. These elements are the ingredients of the nation's and the individual's identity and pull the members into an indivisible unity. Nationalism can exist where there is no state structure and can thrive in a state where the nation is repressed. Nationalism, unlike patriotism, does not need flags and uniforms. All that is needed is a historical and emotional unity around which the members of the nation can gather, a unity that entails the cultural and political loyalty to the nation and the prime element of each individual's identity.

Conservatism

The reaction to the French Revolution, especially as expressed by Edmund Burke, provided the basis of nineteenth-century European conservatism. There were many thinkers who did not believe in the revolutionary slogan of liberty, equality, and fraternity. They did not believe that liberation could be gained by destroying the historically evolved traditions of the Old Regime. Freedom could be found only in order and maintained solely by continual reference to precedents. A legitimate political and social life needed the framework of tradition to survive.

The conservatives did not have faith in the individual nor did they share the romantics' love of pure emotion and spontaneity. Beginning with Burke and continuing through the first part of the nineteenth century to the Frenchman Joseph de Maistre (1753–1821), the Russian Nicholas Karamzin (1766–1826), and the Spaniard Juan Donoso-Cortés (1809–1853) there was a body of intellectuals who found strength, not weakness, in the church and monarchy of the Old Regime; danger, not liberation, in the nationalistic movements; and degradation, not exaltation, in the new romantic art forms.

Conservatism took many forms during the nineteenth century, ranging from the romantic to the patriotic to the religious to the secular. Whatever their approach, conservatives stressed the need to maintain order through a constant reference to history. They believed that the welfare and happiness of humanity resided in the slowly evolving institutions of the past. Industrialization and the consequences of the French Revolution severed the connection with the past and were therefore dangerous. The conservatives were backward-looking, finding their standards and values in the proven events of the past, not in the untried reforms of the present.

Liberalism

The rising middle and commercial classes found their interests and ideals best expressed in the doctrine of liberalism. Liberalism affirmed the dignity of the individual and the "pursuit of happiness" as an inherent right. The ideology's roots were set firmly in the eighteenth-century soil of constitutionalism, laissez-faire economics, and representative government. Liberals thought in terms of individuals who shared basic rights, were equal before the law, and used parliament to gain power and carry out gradual reform. In addition, liberals believed that individuals should use their power to ensure that each person would be given the maximum amount of freedom from the state, or any other external authority.

In economics, liberals believed in the fair competition among individuals responding to the laws of supply and demand with a minimum of governmental regulation or interference. Scottish economist Adam Smith (1723–1790) best expressed this view in his *Wealth of Nations*. Liberals agreed with Smith that society benefitted more from competition among individuals motivated by their self-interest than from governmental regulation. The most intelligent and efficient individuals would gain the greatest rewards, society would prosper, and the state would be kept in its proper place—that of protecting life and property.[25]

Liberals fought foes from above and below as they translated their ideas into public policy. Nobles and the landed gentry still controlled most countries in Europe, so throughout the century the middle classes fought to gain political power commensurate with their economic strength. While they were trying to increase their own influence, they sought to limit the political base of the emerging working classes. By the end of the century the middle classes had consolidated their control over the industrialized world. This was perhaps the major political achievement of the century.

Liberals were sufficiently liberated from the demands of manual labor and possessed enough wealth to spend their spare time in public pursuits. They had the time and leisure to work in government to control state policy to protect their own interests. They gained sufficient security that they undertook the enactment of social reform to head off revolution. They became the dominant voices in the press and universities and gained a commanding authority over public opinion. The liberals' most important contributions came in the areas of civil rights, promotion of the rule of law, government reform, and humanitarian enterprises.

Not surprisingly, the main interpreters of liberalism came from Britain, and during the

Adam Smith, The Wealth of Nations

The ideological mainstream of industrialization was Adam Smith's *Wealth of Nations*.

Every individual is continually exerting himself to find out the most advantageous employment for whatever capital he can command. It is his own advantage, indeed, and not that of the society, which he has in view. But the study of his own advantage naturally, or rather necessarily, leads him to prefer that employment which is most advantageous to the society.

. . . As every individual, therefore, endeavours as much as he can both to employ his capital in the support of domestic industry and so to direct that industry that its produce may be of the greatest value, every individual necessarily labours to render the annual revenue of the society as great as he can. He generally, indeed, neither intends to promote the public interest nor knows how much he is promoting it. By preferring the support of domestic to that of foreign industry, he intends only his own security; and by directing that industry in such a manner as its produce may be of the greatest value, he intends only his own gain, and he is in this, as in many other cases, led by an invisible hand to promote an end which was no part of his intention. Nor is it always the worse for the society that it was no part of it. By pursuing his own interest he frequently promotes that of the society more effectually than when he really intends to promote it. I have never known much good done by those who affected to trade for the public good. It is an affectation, indeed, not very common among merchants, and very few words need be employed in dissuading them from it.

From Adam Smith, *The Wealth of Nations* (Oxford: Clarendon Press, 1880).

---

first half of the century Jeremy Bentham (1748–1832) and John Stuart Mill (1806–1873) adapted some liberal theories to modern reality. Bentham devised the concept of utilitarianism, or philosophical radicalism, based on the two concepts of utility and happiness. He connected these two by noting that each individual knows what is best for himself or herself and that all human institutions should be measured according to the amount of happiness they give. Bentham built on these two eighteenth-century concepts to form the pain-and-pleasure principle. He believed that government's function was to gain as great a degree of individual freedom as possible, for freedom was the essential precondition of happiness. Utilitarianism in government was thus the securing of the "greatest happiness for the greatest number." If society could provide as much happiness and as little pain as possible it would be working at maximum efficiency. Bentham recognized what later liberals would

eventually espouse—that the government would have to work at all levels—but he left no precise prescription as to how to proceed.

Mill spoke more to this issue. He began by noting that in industry the interests of the owners and workers did not necessarily coincide. He proposed the theory that government should, if necessary, pass legislation to remedy injustice, pointing out that when the actions of business owners harm the people, the state must step in to protect the citizenry. He challenged the liberal theory of minimal government interference in the economic life of the nation and pointed out that humanitarianism is more important than profit margin. He accepted that maximum freedom should be permitted in business and that natural law should dictate insofar as possible the relationship of citizens.

He also pointed out that the distribution of wealth depends on the laws and customs of society and that these can be changed by human will. The rights of property and free competition, therefore, should be upheld but within reasonable limits. Mill pointed out that the liberty of the individual is not absolute—it has to be placed under the wider interests of society. His ideas had within them the germ of the welfare state, but he had little effect on affairs in his own day.

In the late twentieth century the word *liberalism* has undergone some change in meaning. The term still implies reform, but liberals today advocate an active governmental role in minimizing the extremes of wealth, in balancing the great power enjoyed by business and labor, and in conserving natural resources. Today's liberals also advocate the state's intervention to help the individual by providing social security and in opposing racial, sexual, and age discrimination.

Socialism

The working classes of Europe, heartened by the French Revolution's call for equality and afflicted by the hardships inherent in the first phase of industrialization found that socialism best expressed their values and goals. Socialists attacked the system of laissez-faire capitalism as unplanned and unjust. They condemned the increasing concentration of wealth and called for public or worker ownership of business. The nature of the industrial system, dividing worker and owner, also raised serious problems, and socialists insisted that harmony and cooperation, not competition, should prevail.

Socialists believed that human beings are essentially good, and with the proper organization of society there would be a happy future with no wars, crimes, administration of justice, or government. In this perfectly balanced world there would also be perfect health and happiness. As one prophet foretold, "every man with ineffable ardor, will seek the good of all."[26] Karl Marx (see ch. 25) later derisively labeled socialists who sought such a world as "Utopians."

The first prominent Utopian socialist was the French noble Claude Henri de Rouvroy, Count de Saint-Simon (1760–1825). He defined a nation as "nothing but a great industrial society" and politics as "the science of production." He advocated that humanity should voluntarily place itself under the rule of the paternalistic despotism of scientists, technicians, and industrialists who would "undertake the most rapid amelioration possible of the lot of the poorest and most numerous class."[27]

Francois Marie Charles Fourier (1772–1837), another French utopian, believed that the future society must be cooperative and free. He worked out a communal living unit of 1620 people called a "phalanstery." The members of the group chose voluntarily those tasks that appealed to them to do the work needed to ensure the phalanstery's survival. Although his plan was endorsed by many prominent people, attempts made to found cooperative Fourierist communities were unsuccessful.

Plan for a model prison, called the Pantopicon, designed by Jeremy Bentham. The circular arrangement allowed a centrally located guard to monitor all outside cells. The Pantopicon was never built, but the plan influenced the design of later prisons.

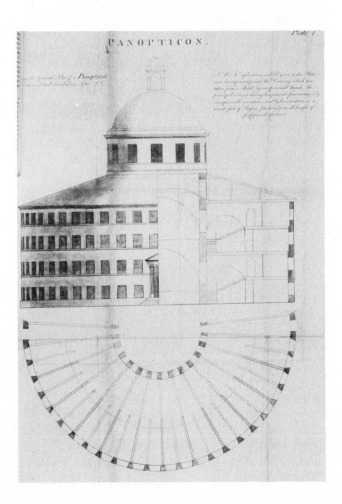

Artist's rendering of Robert Owen's utopian community at New Harmony, Indiana. Square, fortresslike buildings surround the community's interior gardens and exercise grounds. The community was established in 1825, but internal dissension forced its dissolution three years later.

The famous Brook Farm colony in Massachusetts was one such short-lived experiment.

Robert Owen (1771–1858), a successful mill owner in Scotland, was a more practical utopian socialist. His New Lanark, the site of his textile mills, was a model community. Here, between 1815 and 1825, thousands of visitors saw rows of neat, well-kept workers' home, a garbage collection system, schools for workers' children, and clean factories where workers were treated kindly and no children under eleven were employed. In 1825 Owen moved to the vicinity of Evansville, Indiana, where he established the short-lived community at New Harmony.

Their optimism blinded the utopians to the nature of humanity and the world in which they lived. Brook Farm and New Harmony were based on the notion that human beings naturally love one another or could be brought to that level. The basic impracticality of the experiments doomed them to failure. However, the notion that capitalism was inherently corrupt and that it was essential to remove the system remained an article of faith for subsequent socialists,

including Karl Marx, who had a far more comprehensive and hard-headed plan that will be examined in chapter 25.

Cultural Responses to an Age of Change

The romantic movement unleashed sensitivities that played a major role in forming the literary, artistic, and musical changes of the nineteenth century. The romantics' emphasis on the individual is apparent in the novels of Friedrich von Schiller (1759–1805) and Wolfgang von Goethe (1749–1832). Goethe's *The Sorrows of Young Werther* (1774) tells the story of a sensitive, feeling, outcast young man who kills himself with the pistol of his rival after failing to gain his true love. Schiller's *Wilhelm Tell* (1804) describes the heroic struggle of the Swiss patriots in their drive for independence against tyranny. Unlike the brittle wit and irony of

Enlightenment authors such as Voltaire, these stories were sentimental and emotional descriptions of people acting in response to that which their hearts told them was right. It was better to experience a moving young death or to rise up against impossible odds than to look dispassionately and rationally at life.

The romantic movement's emphasis on the individual created among some of its participants a truly picturesque lifestyle. For every Victor Hugo (1802–1885) who lived a long, full, and respectable life there were artists, writers, and musicians from London to Moscow who were deeply affected by the romanticism. To most romantics it was better to live briefly and intensely according to the commandments of the heart than to die old, fat, rich, bored, and bourgeois.

In Gustave Doré's illustration for Coleridge's *Rime of the Ancient Mariner,* the seaman bears the terrible burden of the albatross, hung around his neck as a curse for killing the bird of good luck.

Eugène Delacroix's illustration for the Prologue of Goethe's *Faust* portrays the archfiend Mephistopheles as a winged devil.

Literature

The novel form came into prominence in the eighteenth century, but it became the dominant literary form of the nineteenth. Writers such as Victor Hugo and Sir Walter Scott mined the myths and legends of France and Britain respectively to write vastly successful works for the ever-expanding middle-class audiences. Hugo's *Notre Dame de Paris* (1831) and Scott's *Ivanhoe* (1819) detailed their nations' past so effectively that both books were imitated and sequels and imitations appeared into the twentieth century. By midcentury a variety of social and psychological themes challenged the historical novel along with the gently critical works of William Makepeace Thackeray (1811–1863) who in works such as *Vanity Fair* (1848) poked deft characterizations at the *noveau riche* social climbers that dominated society.

Poets responded far more pointedly to the challenges thrown down by the Napoleonic and Industrial revolutions. The French poet Alphonse de Lamartine (1790–1869) led the way in making the transition from classicism to romanticism and had an impact across the continent.

In 1798, two young British poets, William Wordsworth (1770–1850) and Samuel Taylor Coleridge (1772–1834), published a volume of verse called *Lyrical Ballads.* Wordsworth wrote in the preface that poetry was "the spontaneous overflow of powerful feelings recollected in tranquility." Wordsworth sought to express "universal passions" and the "entire world of nature" through simple, unladen vocabulary. He stressed the intuitive and emotional contemplation of nature as a path to creativity. In an 1802 sonnet he expressed his love of nature and country.

... Oft have I looked round
With joy in Kent's green vales; but never found
Myself so satisfied in heart before.
Europe is yet in bonds; but let that pass
Thought for another moment. Thou are free,
My Country! and 'tis joy enough and pride
For one hour's perfect bliss, to tread the grass
Of England once again. . . .

In his *Rime of the Ancient Mariner* (1798) and *Kubla Khan* (1816) Coleridge pursued the supernatural and exotic facets of life. His vivid descriptions of distant subjects and nonrational elements of human life served as the precedent for later artists as they examined the areas of fantasy, symbolism, dream states, and the supernatural.

The British poets George Gordon (Lord Byron) (1788–1824) and Percy Bysshe Shelley (1792–

Lord Byron in Greek dress. One of the leading romantic poets, Byron lived the life of the romantic hero he created in his writing. He lived passionately and died tragically of fever in 1824 while he was in Greece fighting with Greek insurgents.

1822) rebelled against the constraints of their society and expressed their contempt for the standards of their time through their lives and works. Byron gloried in the cult of freedom, and when the Greeks rose up against the Turks in 1821 he joined their cause, dying of fever soon after his arrival. Shelley believed passionately that human perfectibility was possible only through complete freedom of thought and action. On the continent, Heinrich Heine (1797–1856), who was like Byron a cutting satirist and like Shelley a splendid lyricist, shared their romantic ideals. Heine is best remembered today for his *lieder*, which were put to music by Franz Schubert (1797–1828) and Felix Mendelssohn (1809–1847).

John Keats (1795–1821) was neither social critic nor rebel; for him, the worship and pursuit of beauty were of prime importance. In *Ode on a Grecian Urn* (1821) he states:

Beauty is truth, truth beauty—that is all
Ye know on earth, and all ye need to know.

Keats advocated for art's sake and beauty in itself, instead of the classical formulas of an earlier age or the socialist realism of the latter part of the century.

Alexander Pushkin (1799–1837), Russia's greatest poet, liberated his nation's language from the foreign molds and traditions forced upon it in the eighteenth century. While serving as the transition between the classical and romantic ages, Pushkin helped create a truly Russian literature, one that expressed the profound depth of his love for his country.

Art and Architecture

The age of change brought new tendencies to painting as well as to other art forms. There is a great contrast between the precise draftsmanship and formal poses of the classical painters and the unrestrained use of color and new effects of the romantic artists. Some artists such as the French master Eugène Delacroix (1798–1863) received major critical resistance. Conservative critics panned his *Massacre of Chios*, a flamboyant work painted in 1824 under the direct impact of receiving the news of the Turks' slaying of Christians on Chios, as the "Massacre of painting."

This watercolor by the romantic artist Joseph M. W. Turner is of Tintern Abbey, a famous 12th-century Gothic ruin in Wales. In his later work, Turner was chiefly concerned with the painting of light, and the subject matter became almost incidental.

Less flashy but equally part of the romantic transition are the works of the British painter John Constable (1776–1837). Deeply influenced by romanticism's emphasis on nature, Constable was in some respects the originator of the modern school of landscape painting. His choice of colors was revolutionary, as he used greens freely in his landscape, an innovation considered radical by critics who favored brown tones. Constable's countryman, J. M. W. Turner (1775–1851), sparked controversy with his use of vivid colors and dramatic perspectives, which gave him the ability to portray powerful atmospheric effects.

In the hands of Beethoven, formal music, which had previously reflected the polished and artificial manners of the salon, became a vehicle for expressing deep human emotions.

Around 1830 romanticism's fascination with the medieval period led to a shift from Greek and Roman models to a Gothic revival, in which towers and arches became the chief architectural characteristics. Sir Walter Scott's romances played a major role in this development, and his house at Abbotsford was a model, designed as it was along Scottish baronial lines. In France Eugène Viollet-le-Duc (1814–1879) spearheaded the movement by writing, teaching, and restoring properties under the aegis of the Commission on Historical Monuments. Victor Hugo's *Notre Dame de Paris* popularized the revival with its discussion of fifteenth-century life. For the next few decades, architecture was dominated by styles that looked back especially to the Gothic and Rococo styles, which were sometimes combined in esthetically disastrous presentations.

Music

Ludwig van Beethoven (1770–1827) served as a bridge between the classical and romantic periods. The regularity of the minuet, the precision of the sonata, and the elegant but limited small chamber orchestra—all forms he mastered—were not sufficient to express the powerful forces of the age. A comparison of his relatively measured and restrained First Symphony with the compelling and driven Fifth or the lyrical, nature-dominated Sixth Symphonies dramatically reveals the changes that he underwent. Beethoven was the ultimate romantic—a lover of nature, passionate champion of human rights, and fighter for freedom. Beethoven spoke to the heart of humanity through his music.

The momentum of the forces that Beethoven set in motion carried through the entire century. Carl Maria von Weber (1786–1826), Hector Berlioz (1803–1869), Robert Schumann (1810–1856), and Felix Mendelssohn and Franz Schubert made major contributions in developing the musical repertoire of Europe by midcentury.

Conclusion

The French Revolution had a bulldozerlike effect on traditional French institutions. Napoleon's impact had a similar, if delayed, result. Whether through the force of his arms or his ideas, his actions or reactions to him, the old structures of Europe and the new nations of the Americas were deeply affected.

In Britain, artisans bringing practical solutions to bottlenecks in the making of cotton cloth successfully escaped the bounds of animal and human power to increase output. The island nation possessed the proper balance of population, money, governmental support, internal markets, and a risk-taking entrepreneurial class to accomplish the first revolution in industrialization. The results achieved in textiles were reproduced in iron and steel, as Britain came to dominate the world economically by midcentury.

The second phase of industrialization brought new wealth and a whole new range of products to the continent and carried the urban problems already experienced in Britain across the Channel. The rapid growth of cities strained the capabilities of local and national authorities to respond to the challenges of providing utilities, education, law enforcement, and social services.

Both the Napoleonic and the Industrial revolutions brought with them heavy prices to be paid. Napoleon changed the nature of warfare and increased state power. Industrialization drew great sacrifices from the first generation of workers caught up in it.

Europe's political theorists and artists gave graphic testimony through their works to the reality of change brought about by the Napoleonic and Industrial revolutions. They devised modern ideologies and created diverse cultural expressions to define the new world that they faced.

Suggestions for Reading

Napoleon has attracted the attention of a broad range of historians. See, for example, P. Geyl, *Napoleon: For and Against* (Humanities Press, 1974). F. Markham, *Napoleon and the Awakening of Europe* (Collier, 1965) is a convenient introduction to the period. The best surveys dealing with Napoleon's activities are R. B. Holtman, *The Napoleonic Revolution* (Lippincott, 1967) and Owen Connelly, *French Revolution/Napoleonic Era* (Holt, Rinehart & Winston, 1979). See also Jean Tulard, *Napoleon: The Myth of the Saviour* (Weidenfeld and Nicholson, 1984).

The military art of the era is well described in Gunther Rothenberg, *The Art of Warfare in the Age of Napoleon* (Indiana, 1978). David G. Chandler's *The Campaigns of Napoleon* (Macmillan, 1966) is comprehensive and well written. One of Napoleon's opponent's receives excellent coverage in E. Longford, *Wellington, the Years of the Sword* (Harper, 1969). Leo Tolstoy's *War and Peace* gives an incomparably vivid coverage of the 1812 campaign. For those wanting complete bibliographic reference, see Donald D. Howard, ed., *Napoleonic Military History* (Garland, 1986).

G. Brunn's *Europe and the French Imperium* (Harper, 1938) is a classic. See also essays in Hajo Holborn's *Germany and Europe: Historical Essays* (Doubleday, 1971) for insights into the French emperor's impact in central Europe. Hans Kohn's *Prelude to Nation-States: The French and the German Experience, 1789–1815* (Van Nostrand, 1967) is useful.

The French influence on the Americas is reviewed in Alexander de Conde, *The Quasi-War: The Politics and Diplomacy of the Undeclared War with France 1797–1801* (Scribner, 1966). R. A. Humphreys and John Lynch edited a useful series of essays and primary documents in *The Origins of the Latin American Revolutions, 1806–1826* (Knopf, 1967). See also Irene Nicholson, *The Liberators: A Study of Independence Movements in Spanish America* (Praeger, 1969) for an essential volume in understanding the revolutionary period. The first chapters of David Bushnell and Neill Macaulay, *The Emergence of Latin America in the Nineteenth Century* (Oxford, 1988) provide essential social, economic, and political background.

David Landes' *The Unbound Prometheus: Technological Change and Industrial Development in Western Europe* from 1750 to the Present (Cambridge, 1969) is a well-written and excellent survey of the entire sweep of industrialization. For Britain specifically see T. Ashton, *The Industrial Revolution: 1760–1830* (Oxford, 1949). Also recommended is S. B. Clough, *Economic History of Europe* (Walker, 1968). C. Singer et al., eds., *The Late Nineteenth Century, 1850–1900*, vol. 5, in the series *A History of Technology* (Oxford, 1958) is lavishly illustrated and clearly written. See also W. O. Henderson, *The Industrialization of Europe: 1780–1914* (London, 1969) and J. C. Chambers and G. E. Mingay, *The Agricultural Revolution* (Schocken, 1966). Rondo E. Cameron's *France and the Economic Development of Europe: 1800–1914* (Octagon, 1961) gives another perspective along with A. S. Milward and S. B. Saul, *The Economic Development of Continental Europe 1780–1870* (Allen & Unwin, 1973). For a useful survey of German developments, see T. Hammerow, *Restoration, Revolution, Reaction: Economics and Politics in Germany* (Princeton, 1958). William Blackwell provides useful background on tsarist developments in his *Industrialization of Russia* (Crowell, 1970). A useful volume on international economic growth is Sidney Pollard, *European Economic Integration* (Harcourt Brace Jovanovich, 1974). Francis Sheppard's *London 1808–1970: The Internal War* (University of California, 1971) is a fine account of a city experiencing the challenge of growth.

The social impact of industrialization can be seen in the novels of Charles Dickens such as *Hard Times*. T. K. Rabb and R. I. Rotberg include several selections on the social impact of industrialization in *The Family in History* (Harper & Row, 1973). Asa Brigg's *Victorian Cities* (Harper & Row, 1968) and *Victorian People* (University of Chicago, 1959) are vivid portrayals. Peter Stearns, *European Society in Upheaval* (Macmillan, 1967), and W. L. Langer, *Political and Social Upheaval, 1832–1852* (Harper & Row, 1969) are valuable surveys.

H. D. Aiken, ed., *The Age of Ideology: The Nineteenth Century Philosophers* (Mentor, 1962) explores selections from the works of Hegel, Mill, and others. For a lively survey of the economic thinkers, see Robert L. Heilbroner's *The Worldly Philosophers* (Touchstone, 1970). One of the best surveys of nineteenth century European thought is G. L. Mosse, *The Culture of Western Europe: the Nineteenth and Twentieth Centuries* (Rand McNally, 1974).

Notes

1. Herbert Butterfield, *Napoleon* (New York: Collier Books, 1977), pp. 20–25.
2. Gunther E. Rothenberg, *The Art of Warfare in the Age of Napoleon* (Bloomington: Indiana University Press, 1980), pp. 31–45.
3. Alfred Cobban, *A History of Modern France*, vol. II (Harmondsworth: Penguin, 1970), pp. 9–13.
4. George LeFebvre, *The French Revolution: from 1793 to 1799*, vol. II, trans. by J. H. Steward and J. Friguglietti (New York: Columbia University Press, 1964), pp. 259–317.
5. Owen Connelly, *French Revolution/Napoleonic Era* (New York: Holt, Rinehart and Winston, 1979), pp. 236–237.

6. Robert B. Holtman, *The Napoleonic Revolution* (New York: J. B. Lippincott, 1967), pp 38–40.
7. Rothenberg, pp. 42–52.
8. Hajo Holborn, *Germany and Europe: Historical Essays* (New York: Doubleday, 1971), p. 9.
9. For a view from the Russian side, see Michael and Diana Josselson, *The Commander: A Life of Barclay de Tolly* (Oxford: Oxford Univ. Press, 1980).
10. H. A. L. Fisher, *A History of Europe*, vol. III (Boston: Houghton Mifflin, 1936), p. 891.
11. C. K. Webster, "British, French, and American Influences," in R. A. Humphreys and J. Lynch, eds., *The Origins of the Latin American Revolution, 1800–1826* (New York: Alfred A. Knopf, 1967), p. 78.
12. David Bushnell and Neill Macaulay, *The Emergence of Latin America in the Nineteenth Century* (New York: Oxford Univ. Press, 1988), pp. 3–9.
13. Bushnell and Macaulay, pp. 55–82.
14. J. D. Chambers, "Enclosures and the Labour Supply in the Industrial Revolution," *Economic History Review,* 2nd series, V, 1953, pp. 318–343, as cited in David Landes, *The Unbound Prometheus: Technological Change and Industrial Development in Western Europe from 1750 to the Present* (Cambridge: Cambridge University Press, 1969), p. 115.
15. E. J. Hobsbawm, *The Age of Revolution, 1789–1848* (New York: New American Library, 1964), pp. 44–73.
16. I. Vyshnegradsky, quoted in William L. Blackwell, *The Industrialization of Russia: An Historical Perspective* (New York: Thomas Y. Crowell, 1970), p. 24.
17. Fernand Braudel, *Capitalism and Material Life: 1400–1800* (New York: Harper & Row, 1975), p. 11; William Langer, "Checks on Population Growth: 1750–1850," *Scientific American* 226 (1972), pp. 92–99.
18. Thomas R. Malthus, "An Essay on Population," in *Introduction to Contemporary Civilization in the West,* vol. II (New York: Columbia University Press, 1955), p. 196.
19. Eugen Weber, *A Modern History of Europe* (New York: W. W. Norton, 1971), p. 988.
20. Sidney Pollard, *European Economic Integration: 1815–1970* (New York: Harcourt Brace Jovanovich, 1974), pp. 56–62.
21. Edward Shorter, "Illegitimacy, Sexual Revolution, and Social Change in Modern Europe," in Theodore K. Rabb and Robert I. Rotber, eds., *The Family in History* (New York: Harper & Row, 1973), pp. 48–84.
22. Heinz Gollwitzer, *Europe in the Age of Imperialism: 1880–1914* (New York: Harcourt Brace Jovanovich, 1969), p. 20.
23. Charles Dickens, *Hard Times* (London: Thomas Nelson and Sons, n.d.), p. 26.
24. Peter F. Sugar, "External and Domestic Roots of Eastern European Nationalism," in Peter F. Sugar and Ivo J. Lederer, eds., *Nationalism in Eastern Europe* (Seattle: University of Washington Press, 1969), pp. 3–21.
25. Robert L. Heilbroner, *The Worldly Philosophers* (New York: Simon and Schuster, 1972), pp. 40–72.
26. W. Godwin, "Political Justice," in Sidney Hook, *Marx and the Marxists: The Ambiguous Legacy* (Princeton: Van Nostrand, 1955), p. 28.
27. Quoted in E. R. A. Seligman, ed., *Encyclopedia of the Social Sciences*, vol. XIII (New York: The Macmillan Company, 1935), p. 510a.

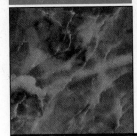

Chapter 24

Revolution, Reaction, and Reform

Political Change, 1815–1871

I n the half century after Waterloo, many changes took place in the political boundaries and population distribution of Europe. The French and Napoleonic revolutions created new conditions that challenged the leaders of Europe gathered at the Congress of Vienna in 1814–1815. Delegates had to construct a peace settlement that digested the political and social transformations that had taken place in the previous quarter century and anticipate the new demands created by those changes. They redrew the state borders and redefined the spheres of influence. The geopolitical structure they created and the surface order that resulted endured until 1848.

A wave of revolutions spread across the continent in that year and put an end to the structure created at Vienna. The revolutionaries, because of their conflicting goals, failed to turn their ideals into state policy. After 1848, continental politics would be built on the basis of *realpolitik*, that is, realism in politics. *Realpolitik* disregards theory or idealism and emphasizes the practical application of power to gain state goals, no matter the damage to ethics or morality. The European map changed once again as Cavour consolidated Italy and Bismarck united Germany.

The Vienna Settlement: 1815

Once Napoleon was "safely" exiled to Elba, representatives of all the European powers, except the Ottoman Empire, gathered in September at Vienna. They had the imposing task of building a new political and diplomatic structure for Europe after a quarter century of wars and revolutions. The factor that had brought the British, Prussians, Austrians, and Russians together —Napoleon—was gone, and wartime unity dissolved into peacetime pursuit of self-interest.

Work went slowly during the ten-month span of the Congress of Vienna. The leaders who gathered at Vienna—Lord Castlereagh of Great Britain, Count von Hardenberg of Prussia, Prince Klemens von Metternich of Austria, Tsar Alexander I of Russia, and Prince Charles Maurice de Talleyrand of France—met in small secret conferences to decide the future of Europe. Metternich came to dominate the conference, as much by his diplomatic skills as by his ability to impress on the participants the need for stability.

The Congress dealt with numerous issues: the status of France, the new political boundaries, the response to liberal and national attitudes sweeping the continent, the fate of those powers who had lost territory during the previous twenty-five years, and the future of dispossessed dynasties. The solutions proposed were moderate ones. France was allowed to return to its 1792 boundaries; however, after Napoleon's return and the One Hundred Days, the allies cut back the boundaries and imposed penalties. They virtually ignored the democratic, liberal, and nationalistic forces in favor of a more traditional solution to the upheavals of the past twenty-five years.[1]

Allied Dilemmas

The events since 1789 had drastically altered the map of Europe. For example, the thousand-year-old Holy Roman Empire had disappeared. In an attempt to restore some balance, the

Congress followed four principles: legitimacy, encirclement of France, compensation, and balance of power. The Congress ruled that royal houses that had been expelled, such as the Bourbons in France, Spain, and Naples, the House of Savoy in Sardinia-Piedmont, and the House of Orange in Holland, would be replaced on their thrones. The redrawn map of Europe resembled the 1789 configuration, except that the Holy Roman Empire remained dissolved (see map below). In its place were the thirty-nine states of the German Confederation, dominated by Austria. The redrawing of boundaries created a protective belt of states around France to make future aggression more difficult. The principle of compensation assured that no important power suffered a loss as the result of the Congress' work. Austria was compensated for the loss of the Austrian Netherlands by gaining territory in Italy and along the Adriatic. Sweden received Norway in return for permitting Russia to keep Finland.

The desire to construct an effective balance of power remained at the center of the Congress' attention. Each power, however, had its own idea of what constituted a proper balance. Russia's ambitions in Poland almost broke up the conference: Britain believed that an enlarged Russia threatened peace. Prussia wanted all of Saxony: Austria feared a growing Prussia. While the four wartime allies split, the clever French

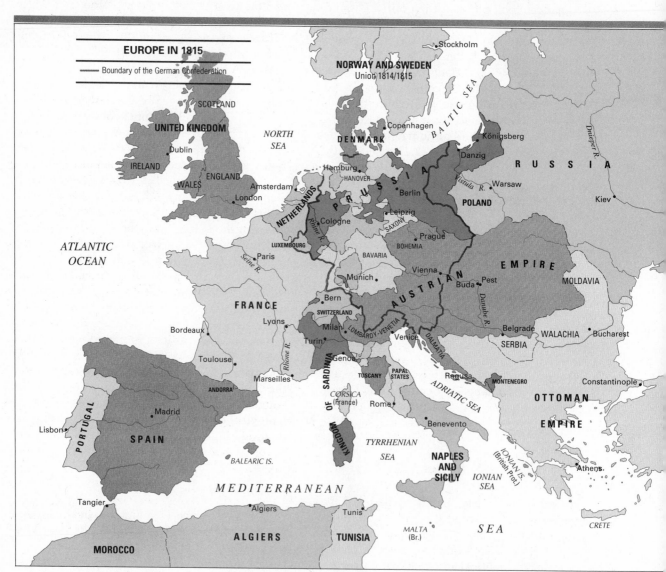

This cartoon, *La Balance Politique*, lampoons the balance of power politics played out at the Congress of Vienna. Here, Wellington places money on the scales opposite the king of Prussia and Metternich. At right, Tsar Alexander I confers with Talleyrand.

representative, Talleyrand, negotiated a secret treaty among the French, Austrians, and British that pledged mutual assistance to restrain the Russians and Prussians. Russia and Prussia eventually reduced their demands for land in Poland and Saxony, and the sought-after balance of power was achieved.

Although the Congress has received criticism for ignoring the growth of liberty, equality, and fraternity in Europe, it has received praise for finding a general settlement of a complex series of problems, especially from scholars who favorably compare its work to that of the victorious allies at Versailles after World War I (see p. 781).[2] The representatives were not totally, blindly reactionary: many of the changes of the previous twenty-five years were retained. The forty years of general peace that followed, flawed though they may have been, are testimony to the success of Metternich and his colleagues in gaining stability. But, by ignoring the forces of change, the representatives at Veinna ensured the ultimate failure of the system they created.

The Congress System and Revolution

The Vienna negotiators set out to coordinate their policies to maintain stability. The first proposal for postwar consultation was symbolic and quixotic. In the fall of 1815, Tsar Alexander I proposed the formation of a Holy Alliance to be based on "the precepts of justice, Christian charity, and peace." No one was quite sure what the tsar meant by this pact, but every ruler in Europe signed it, except the British king, the Turkish sultan, and the pope. Castlereagh dismissed the Holy Alliance as "a piece of sublime mysticism and nonsense." In November 1815 Austria, Prussia, Russia, and Britain signed the Quadruple Alliance—to become the Quintuple Alliance when France joined in 1818. Under this agreement the powers pursued their goals through what came to be known as the Congress System, a Europe-wide network to maintain order, peace, and stability. This was the first truly functional experiment in collective security.

The Congress System's dedication to the 1815 status quo was challenged in 1820 and 1821 by nationalistic and liberal revolts in the Germanies, Greece, Spain, Italy, and Latin America. The most violent revolutions occurred in Spain and Italy. Spanish liberals rebelled against the misgovernment of the restored Bourbon King Ferdinand VII, and their insurrection spread to the army, which mutinied. The general uprising that followed forced the king to give into the liberals' demands for a constitution and representative government. The Spaniards' success sparked rebellions in Naples and Sicily, governed by the Neapolitan Bourbon King Ferdinand I. The

Metternich on His Political Principles

In the aftermath of the Napoleonic age, waves of change threatened the structure erected at the Congress of Vienna. Metternich had a precise notion of what was happening.

Kings have to calculate the chances of their very existence in the immediate future; passions are let loose, and league together to overthrow everything which society respects as the basis of its existence; religion, public morality, laws, customs, rights, and duties, all are attacked, confounded, overthrown, or called in question. The great mass of the people are tranquil spectators of these attacks and revolutions, and of the absolute want of all means of defense. A few are carried off by the torrent, but the wishes of the immense majority are to maintain a repose which exists no longer, and of which even the first elements seem to be lost . . .

Having now thrown a rapid glance over the first causes of the present state of society, it is necessary to point out in a more particular manner the evil which threatens to deprive it, at one blow, of the real blessings, the fruits of genuine civilisation, and to disturb it in the midst of its enjoyments. This evil may be described in one word—presumption; the natural effect of the rapid progression of the human mind towards the perfecting of so many things. This it is which at the present day leads so many individuals astray, for it has become an almost universal sentiment.

Religion, morality, legislation, economy, politics, administration, all have become common and accessible to everyone. Knowledge seems to come by inspiration; experience has no value for the presumptuous man; faith is nothing to him; he substitutes for it a pretended individual conviction, and to arrive at this conviction dispenses with all inquiry and with all study; for these means appear too trivial to a mind which believes itself strong enough to embrace at one glance all questions and all facts. Laws have no value for him, because he has not contributed to make them, and it would be beneath a man of his parts to recognise the limits traced by rude and ignorant generations. Power resides in himself; why should he submit himself to that which was only useful for the man deprived of light and knowledge? That which, according to him, was required in an age of weakness cannot be suitable in an age of reason and vigour amounting to universal perfection, which the German innovators designate by the idea, absurd in itself, of the Emancipation of the People! Morality itself he does not attack openly, for without it he could not be sure for a single instant of his own existence; but he interprets its essence after his own fashion, and allows every other person to do so likewise, provided that other person neither kills nor robs him.

From Prince Richard Metternich, ed., *Memoirs of Prince Metternich, 1815–1829*, vol. III, Mrs. Alexander Napier, trans. (New York: Charles Scribner's Sons, 1881).

Italian revolt ran much the same path as that in Spain, and with much the same result—a constitution based on the Spanish model.

Metternich arranged for the Congress allies to meet at Troppau in 1820, Laibach in 1821, and Verona in 1822 to deal with the uprisings. Ferdinand I came to Laibach, supported Congress System intervention, and reneged on granting a constitution; Austrian troops invaded Italy and placed him back on his throne. In 1822 the Congress allies met to consider the Spanish problem, and the French volunteered to restore the status quo. They sent their armies in to crush the liberals. The repression of the revolts in Spain and Italy marked the high point of the Congress System's success.

Britain began its withdrawal from the continent into "splendid isolation" in 1820, and the ardent support of British liberals for the 1821 Greek revolt against the Turks further weakened London's interest in cooperating with its former allies. When the Congress System discussed restoring the Spanish king's authority in Latin America, the British objected. Further, U.S. President James Monroe in 1823 warned the Europeans that their intervention into the western hemisphere would be regarded as an unfriendly act. By the middle of the decade the Congress system had withered to an Austrian-Russian alliance in which Metternich set the agenda and the Russians acted as the "gendarme of Europe."

Restoration and Revolution: 1815–1848

The restored Bourbon monarch, Louis XVIII (1814, 1815–1824), was an unhappy choice for the French throne. The new king, a brother of the guillotined Louis XVI, was ill-equipped to lead France out of a quarter century of revolution and Napoleonic charisma. Dull and unpopular, he had been the target of a Talleyrand epigram that "the Bourbons have learned nothing and forgotten nothing." Nonetheless, he tried to hold the country together by blending elements of the revolutionary period with remnants of the old regime. Unfortunately, the mixture helped create the instability that plagued the country throughout the century.

Louis began by "granting" his subjects a charter that established a form of constitutional monarchy in which he kept all executive power, controlled lawmaking, and influenced the makeup of the legislature. The restored Bourbon made little attempt to return to the institutions of the old regime and accepted Napoleon's Civil Code, the Concordat with the papacy, and the governmental reforms. For nine years he suffered the fate of moderates trying to navigate between two extremes—he was attacked by both sides. The right wing assailed the charter for giving too much to the middle classes while the liberals and radicals said that he had not gone far enough in his policies. Louis was succeeded by his brother, Charles X (1824–1830), who cared nothing about maintaining political balance.

In the July Revolution of 1830, Parisians took to the streets to protest the restrictive laws of Charles X.

Charles did not accept any of the changes of the age. In 1829 he announced that he "would rather saw wood than be a king of the English type." So out of tune was he to the times that in July 1830 he drove the usually submissive legislature to the point that it refused to support his proposed ultraroyalist ministry. When elections went badly for him, he issued a set of laws censoring the press and further limiting the already heavily restricted right to vote. These repressive acts drove liberals, radicals, and their journalist allies to revolt. They barricaded the narrow streets of Paris with overturned carts, boxes, tables, and paving stones. Fighting behind these obstacles and from rooftops, they held off the army. Three days later a less reactionary faction took power after Charles fled across the Channel to exile in Great Britain.

The new government represented the upper middle classes and landed gentry, and represented a compromise between the French republicans—led by the aging Marquis de Lafayette, hero of the American Revolution—and the relatively liberal monarchist supporters of the Orléans branch of the Bourbons. The new king, Louis Philippe (1830–1848), who claimed the title of "the citizen king," resolutely supported the interests of the wealthy.

Louis Philippe took great pains to portray a "bourgeois" image. He received the crown from "the people" and replaced the white Bourbon flag with the revolutionary tricolor. However, Louis Philippe's policies consistently favored the upper bourgeoisie and gentry and shut the workers and middle classes out of the political arena. Of the 32 million French citizens, only 200,000 wealthy male property owners were allowed to vote.

Workers protested that the government was ignoring their interests. Louis Philippe and his advisers were more interested in pursuing a policy of divide-and-conquer and ignored most suggestions for reform. Restrictive legislation such as the "September Laws" were passed in 1835 to control the growing radical movement. The government kept control, but under the surface calm serious pressures were building. By 1848 France faced a serious crisis.

The French Influence in Belgium and Poland

Liberals across the continent were encouraged by the Paris uprising of 1830, but only in Belgium were there any lasting results. The Vienna Congress had placed the Belgians under the Dutch crown, but this settlement ignored the cultural, economic, religious, and linguistic differences between the two people. The Belgians were primarily French-speaking Catholic farmers and workers while the people of Holland were Dutch-speaking Protestant seafarers and traders.

Belgian liberals asked the Dutch King William I of Orange to grant them their own administration in August 1830. When he refused, rioting broke out in Brussels, which the Dutch troops were unable to put down. After expelling the

The citizen king, Louis Philippe, shown here strolling through Paris, attempted some reform, but it was not enough to stop the revolution of 1848.

troops, the Belgians declared their independence and drew up a liberal constitution. William asked in vain for help from Tsar Nichoas I. The principle of legitimacy as a pretext for intervention was dead. Stalemate ensued until the summer of 1831 when the Belgian national assembly met in Brussels and chose Prince Leopold of Saxe-Coburg-Gotha as king. Eight years later the international status of the new state was settled. Belgium was recognized to be a "perpetually neutral state."

The French rebellion had an impact in Poland, where Poles in and around Warsaw rose up in the name of liberal and national principles. After the Congress of Vienna, Poles in this region gained a special status. The area known as Congress Poland had its own constituion and substantial local autonomy. The winds of change and the repressive tendencies of Tsar Nicholas I combined to push the Poles into rebellion in the winter of 1830–1831. The rebels suffered from internal division and the numerically and militarily superior Russians crushed them. Their major accomplishment was to tie down the Russian troops, whom Nicholas wanted to send to help the Dutch king, for six months and perhaps save the Belgian revolution.[3]

German and Italian Nationalism

The forces of nationalism influenced central Europe from the tip of Italy through the Habsburg lands to the Baltic Sea. Napoleon had performed a great, though unwitting, service for the Germans and Italians through his direct governing in the area and also by his revising the European map. After 1815, the region knew the positive effects of a different style of governing and was divided into a much more rational set of political units.

Metternich had ensured that the Vienna Congress made Austria the dominant partner in the German Confederation. To preserve his country's dominance both in the Confederation and throughout the Habsburg monarchy he knew that he had to fight continually against nationalism. The currents of romanticism found forceful expression in the works of German poets and philosophers and in lectures in German classrooms. Nationalism and liberalism found many followers among the young. For example, in the great patriotic student festival that took place in Octber 1817 (the tercentenary of the Reformation) at Wartburg where Luther had taken refuge, liberal students burned reactionary books on the great bonfire to protest their discontent with the status quo. Protests spread both openly and secretly in the *Burschenschaften* (liberal societies). Metternich moved harshly against the students. He pushed through the Diet of the German Confederation the Carlsbad Decrees (1819). These acts dissolved student associations, censored the press, and restricted academic freedom. These decrees failed to stop the forces of liberalism and nationalism, and these forces grew during the next twenty years.

Italy, which Metternich saw as being only a "geographic expression" and not a nation, also posed special problems. The Congress of Vienna, in accord with the principles of legitimacy and compensation, had returned Italy to its geographic status of 1789, divided into areas dominated by the Bourbons, the Papal States, and the Austrians. This settlement ignored the fact that in the interim the Italians had experienced more liberty and better government than ever before. The return to the old systems was also a return to high taxes, corruption, favoritism, and banditry.

It was perhaps ironic that this fragmented, individualistic land should produce the most notable romantic nationalist in Europe, Giuseppe Mazzini (see p. 000). After the Austrians put down the Italian revolutionary movements in 1820 and 1821, Mazzini began to work actively for independence. In 1830 he was implicated in an unsuccessful revolution against the Sardinian royal government and thrown into jail for six months. Once released, he went to London and started a

Mazzini on the Duties of the Individual

Giuseppe Mazzini saw the individual's obligation to the human family to be transcendent.

Your first duties—first as regards importance—are, as I have already told you, towards Humanity. You are men before you are either citizens or fathers. If you do not embrace the whole human family in your affection, if you do not bear witness to your belief in the Unity of that family, consequent upon the Unity of God, and in the fraternity among the peoples which is destined to reduce that unit to action; if, wheresoever a fellow-creature suffers, or the dignity of human nature is violated by falsehood or tyranny—you are not ready, if able, to aid the unhappy, and do not feel called upon to combat, if able, for the redemption of the betrayed or oppressed—you violate your law of life, you comprehend not that Religion which will be the guide and blessing of the future.

From Emilie A. Venturi, *Joseph Mazzini: A Memoir* (London, 1875).

patriotic society that he called "Young Italy." This organization sent appeals to students and intellectuals to form an Italian nationalist movement. In the meantime, the reactionary forces weathered nationalist pressures.

Metternich also feared nationalism in the Habsburg realm, a mosaic composed of many different nationalities, languages, and religions. If nationalism and the desire for self-rule became strong among the Magyars, Czechs, southern Slavs, and Italians, the Habsburg Empire would fall apart. Nationalism threatened the Germans who controlled the Empire yet constituted only 20 percent of its population.

By understanding the complex and combustible nature of the region in which Metternich exercised his power, we can begin to appreciate his dread of democratic government and nationalism and his obsession with maintaining the status quo. Liberalism and nationalism would destroy his power. In a world that was rapidly industrializing, Metternich's power rested on a backward system. Except for Bohemia and the areas immediately around Vienna, there was no middle class. A great majority of the inhabitants were peasants, either powerless serfs, as in Hungary, or impoverished tenant farmers who owed one-half of their time and two-thirds of their crop to the landlord. Government was autocratic and the regional assemblies had little power and represented mainly the nobility. The social, political, and economic structures were extremely vulnerable to the winds of change that came in 1848.[4]

This painting, *24 Février 1848,* celebrates the revolutionary spirit of the mid-19th century. A young French hero encourages his fellow citizens to fight for liberty.

The Revolutionary Year of 1848

As it had before, France once again opened a revolutionary era, and the events there set a model for what was to occur throughout Europe in 1848. The overthrow of the old order came first in Paris in February and then spread to Berlin, Vienna, Prague, and Budapest in March. Never before had France—or Europe—seen such a fragmented variety of political and social pressures at work at the same time (see map at left). Romantics, socialists, nationalists, middle classes, peasants, and students could all agree that the old structure had to be abandoned, but each group had a different path to that goal and a separate view of what the new world should be Louis Philippe fled Paris, Metternich abandoned Vienna, and the Prussian King Frederick William IV gave in. But the movements in France and elsewhere fell apart as soon as they had won because of their diversity, lack of experience, and conflicting goals.

France and the Second Republic

The pressures building since 1830 and strengthened by economic depression in 1846 and 1847 erupted in Paris in February 1848 in a series of banquets. In this seemingly harmless arena, liberals and socialists pushed for an end to corruption and reforms of the electoral system. The government tried to block the banquet scheduled for February 22, and in response the opposition threw up more than 1500 barricades to block the streets of Paris. When violence broke out, republican leaders took the opportunity to set up a provisional revolutionary government and proclaimed the introduction of universal manhood suffrage. Louis Philippe fled to exile in England.

The new government, the Second Republic, had a brief (1848–1851) and dreary existence. Neither the new leaders nor the voters had any experience with representative government. The forces that united to overthrow the king soon split into moderate and radical wings. The first group wanted middle-class control within the existing social order, while the latter faction desired a social and economic revolution. By the summer the new government faced a major crisis over the issue of national workshops sponsored by the socialist Louis Blanc (1811–1882). The workshops were to be the state's means to guarantee every laborer's "right to work." The moderate-dominated government voiced its belief in Blanc's principle of full employment, but the leaders gave the plan's administration to men who wanted to ridicule it. As a result, the workshops became a national joke. Laborers were assigned "make-work" jobs such as carrying dirt from one end of a park to the other on one day, and then carrying it back the next.

The disbanding of the workshops incited a violent insurrection known as the "June Days." The unemployed workers raised a red flag as a sign of revolution—the first time that the red flag had been used as a symbol of the proletariat. With the cry of "bread or lead," the demonstrators rebuilt the barricades and tried to overthrow the government. The most bloody fighting Paris had seen since the Reign of Terror gave the insurgents far more lead than bread, and the movement was crushed. After that, the bourgeoisie and the workers would be on the opposite sides of political strife, and moderates would look elsewhere for their future.

Germany and the Frankfurt Assembly

The example of the French February revolution quickly crossed the Rhine River and spread to central Europe. At public assemblies throughout Germany patriotic liberals demanded unification. Rapid changes came with minimal casualties, thanks largely to the humane response of the Prussian king Frederick William IV. When his subjects erected barricades in Berlin on March 15, he decided to make concessions rather than unleash further violence and bloodshed. He ordered the regular army troops out of Berlin and tried to make peace with his "dear Berliners" by promising a parliament, a constitution, and a united Germany. Upon learning of this development, the rulers of the other German states agreed to establish constitutional governments and guarantee basic civil rights.

The Frankfurt Assembly opened its first session on May 18. Over 500 delegates attended, coming from the various German states, Austria, and Bohemia. The primarily middle-class membership of the assembly included about 200 lawyers, 100 professors, and many doctors and judges. Popular enthusiasm reached a peak when the assembly's president announced that "We are to create a constitution for Germany, for the whole Empire." The assembly deliberated at length over the issues of just what was meant by Germany and what form of government would be best for the new empire. Some debaters wanted a united Germany to include all Germans in central Europe, even Austria and Bohemia. Others did not want the Austrians included, for

a variety of religious and political reasons. Another issue of contention was whether the new imperial crown should be given to the Habsburgs in Vienna or the Hohenzollerns in Berlin.

Germany's history changed tragically when the Assembly failed to unite and bring a liberal solution to political problems. From May to December the Assembly wasted time in splendid debates over nonessential topics. As the participants talked they contributed to the failed dreams of 1848. Gradually, the conservatives recovered from the shocks of the spring revolts and began to rally around their rulers, exhorting them to undo the reformers' work. In Prussia, the king regained his confidence, as the army remained loyal and the peasants showed little interest in political affairs. The Berlin liberals soon found themselves isolated and the king was able to regain control.

Even though the anti-liberal forces were at full tide, the Frankfurt Assembly continued its work. It approved the Declaration of the Rights of the German People, an inspiring document that articulated the progressive political and social ideals of 1848. In April 1849, the Assembly approved a constitution for a united Germany that included an emperor advised by a ministry and a legislature elected by secret ballot. Austria was excluded when it refused to join the new union.

When the leadership of the new German Reich (nation) was offered to Frederick William, he refused to accept it, later declaring that he could not "pick up a crown from the gutter." After this contemptuous refusal, most of the Assembly's members returned home. Outbreaks against the conservative domination continued, but the Prussian army effectively put them down. Thousands of prominent middle-class liberals fled, many emigrating to the United States.

Italy

The news of the revolutions in Paris and Vienna triggered a rash of uprisings on the Italian peninsula. In Sicily, Venice, and Milan revolutionaries demanded an end to foreign domination and despotic rule. In response, King Charles Albert of Sardinia voluntarily granted a new liberal constitution. Other states such as Tuscany also issued constitutions. Absolute government

The artillery attempts to demolish a barricade in the scene of the street fighting during the Frankfurt insurrection of 1848.

The Habsburg Monarchy

The events of 1848 took a tragic toll in the Habsburg territories. When the news of the February uprising reached Vienna, Prague, and Budapest, reformers immediately called for change. In Budapest, the nationalist liberal Louis Kossuth (1802–1894) attacked the Habsburg ruler's "stagnant bureaucratic system" and spoke of the "pestilential air blowing from the Vienna charnel house and its deadening effect upon all phases of Hungarian life." He demanded parliamentary government for the whole of the empire.

In Vienna, Kossuth's speech inspired some Austrian students and workers to demonstrate in the streets. The movement soon gained the force of a rebellion and the frightened Austrian emperor forced Metternich, the symbol of European reaction, to resign. Meanwhile, the Hungarian

In this satiric cartoon, Pope Pius IX removes his liberal "saviour's" mask to reveal his true nature after his refusal to support the revolution in Italy.

in Italy almost disappeared. In the Papal States, meanwhile, reform had begun as early as 1846.

As in the rest of Europe, the liberal and nationalist triumphs and reforms were quickly swept away by the reactionary tide. The Austrians regained their mastery in the north of Italy in July when they defeated Charles Albert at the decisive battle of Custozza. Another defeat a year later forced him to abdicate in favor of his oldest son, Victor Emmanuel II. Austria helped restore the old rulers and systems of government in Italy to their pre-1848 conditions.

The final blow to the Italian movements came in November 1848 when Pope Pius IX, who had begun a program of reform, refused to join in the struggle against Catholic Austria for a united Italy. His subjects forced him to flee from Rome, and the papal lands were declared a republic, with Mazzini as the head. The pope's flight prompted a hostile reaction from conservative Europe, and the French sent in an army to crush the republic in July 1849. When the pope returned to Rome, he remained bitterly hostile to all liberal causes and ideas until his death in 1878.

Diet advocated a liberal, parliamentary government under a limited Habsburg monarchy. The Vienna-controlled Danubian region, that mosaic of nationalities, appeared to be on the verge of being transformed into a federation.

The empire's diversity soon became a characteristic of the revolutionary movements, as the various nationalities divided among themselves. The Hungarians wrote a new constitution that was quite liberal, calling for a guarantee of civil rights, an end to serfdom, and the destruction of special privileges. In theory, all political benefits guaranteed in the constitution were to extend to all citizens of Hungary, including non-Magyar minorities. The emperor accepted these reforms and promised, in addition, a constitution for Austria. He also promised the Czechs in Bohemia the same reforms granted the Hungarians.

By summer the mood suddenly shifted. German and Czech nationalists began to quarrel and the Magyars began to oppress the Slavic nationalities and Romanians after they, in their turn, demanded their own political independence. Divisions among the liberal and nationalistic forces gave the conservatives in Vienna time to regroup and suggested to them the obvious tactic to follow to regain their former dominance: divide and conquer the subject nationalities. In June demonstrations broke out in the streets of Prague, barricades were thrown up, and fighting began. The

Austrians lobbed a few shells, Prague surrendered, and any hope for an autonomous kingdom of Bohemia ended.

In Hungary, Kossuth announced that he would offer civil rights, but not national independence, to the minority nationalities under his control. In protest, the South Slavs under the Croat leader Joseph Jellachich (1801–1859) attacked the Magyars, and civil war broke out. The Austrians took advantage of the situation and made Jellachich an imperial general. Following his attack against the Magyars, he was ordered to Vienna where in October he forced the surrender of the liberals who controlled the capital.

By the end of the year the weak and incapable emperor Ferdinand I abdicated in favor of his nephew, Franz Joseph. The Austrians began to repeal their concessions to the Hungarians, arguing that their new emperor was not bound by the acts of his predecessor. The Magyars, outraged by this maneuver, declared complete independence for their country. The Austrians, aided by 100,000 Russian troops sent by Tsar Nicholas I, defeated the Hungarians in a bloody and one-sided struggle. By the summer 1849 Kossuth fled the country and the Hungarian revolution reached its tragic conclusion.[5]

New Political Forms in France, Italy, and Germany

In France, the violence of the June Days moved the conservatives in the countryside and the moderates in the cities to elect Louis Napoleon (1808–1873), nephew of Napoleon I, to the presidency of the Second Republic. Although he had failed miserably in his attempts to overthrow the king in 1836 and 1840, he was sure that destiny intended great things for him. When he came back to Paris after the revolution he was untainted by any involvement in the June Days and appeared to be a unifying force.

France's Second Empire

The republic's constitution gave strong powers to the president, but limited the office to only one term. Louis Napoleon took advantage of the

A French satirist's view of Jellachich, Radetzky, and Windischgrätz, the military leaders who crushed the 1848 revolts in the Austrian Empire.

One of the most outstanding achievements of Napoleon III's beautification program was the Operá in Paris. The baroque style of the building demonstrated the emphasis on recreating the grandeur of the past.

authority given him and his strong majority to fortify his position. He and his conservative allies dominated France for the next two years, becoming strong enough to overthrow the constitution in a coup d'état in December 1851. Louis Napoleon and his allies brutally put down the workers and peasants who opposed the coup and engineered a plebiscite that gave him virtually unanimous support. In 1852 he proclaimed himself Emperor Napoleon III, and the Second Empire replaced the Second Republic.

During its eighteen-year span the Second Empire accomplished a great deal. Industrialization brought prosperity to France. Production doubled. France supported the building of the Suez Canal and increased railway mileage by 500 percent. The partial legalization of labor unions and guarantee of the right to strike improved workers' conditions. Baron Georges Haussmann (1809–1891) transformed Paris in an ambitious urban renewal that featured broad boulevards, unified architecture, modern utilities, and improved traffic flow.

The price for the order and stability needed to build this prosperity came in the form of political control. The government remained, in theory, a parliamentary regime. The emperor's agents rigged the elections to ensure a majority in the powerless legislature for the emperor. The secret police hounded opponents—both real and potential—and the state censored the press, which accordingly rarely reported bad news.

At first the emperor brought glory to France through an interventionist and imperialist foreign policy. He continually claimed to be a man of peace, but he allied with Britain in the Crimean War (see ch. 26), supported Cavour—briefly—in Italy, expanded French influence to assure a foothold in Indochina, raised the French flag over Tahiti, and penetrated West Africa along the Senegal River. Foreign affairs soured for him in the 1860s when he made an ill-advised attempt to take advantage of the confusion caused by the U.S. Civil War to establish a foothold in the Americas. He placed Maximilian, a Habsburg prince, on the Mexican throne and sent 40,000 troops to support him. Mexican patriots expelled the forces and executed the prince. After 1866 Louis Napoleon met his match in the Prussian chancellor Otto von Bismarck (1815–1898), when his blundering ambition contributed to a quick Prussian victory over Austria. Finally, in 1870 he gambled on a successful war against Prussia and lost. With this defeat the Second Empire ended.[6]

Cavour Unites Italy

After 1848, the Italian unification movement came to be centered in the Kingdom of Sardinia,

Count Camillo Benso di Cavour, the leader of the movement for Italian unification.

declaring war. The French and Sardinians defeated them at Magenta and Solferino and drove them out of Lombardy. At the same time, revolts broke out in Tuscany, Modena, Parma, and Romagna. Napoleon received praise and was proclaimed the savior and liberator of Italy.

Upon receiving his share of the agreement, Napoleon III reversed himself and made peace with Austria, before the allies could invade Venetia. The massing of Prussian troops on French borders and second thoughts about the implications of a united Italy drove him to this move. The Sardinians were outraged, but there was little they could do but agree to a peace settlement. The agreement added Lombard to Sardinia; restored the exiled rulers of Parma, Modena, Tuscany, and Romagna; and set up an Italian confederation in which Austria was included.

where the young monarch Victor Emmanuel II refused to withdraw the liberal constitution granted by his father. The prime minister, Count Camillo Benso di Cavour (1810–1861), a liberal influenced by what he had seen in Switzerland, France, and Britain, assumed leadership of the drive to unify the peninsula.

From 1852, when he became prime minister, Cavour concentrated on freeing his country from Austrian domination. He knew, however, that Sardinia needed allies to take on the Habsburgs. To that end, in 1855 Sardinia joined Britain and France in their fight against Russia in the Crimean War (see p. 688). This step enabled Cavour to speak at the peace conference after the war, where he stated Italy's desire for unification.

Cavour's presentation won Napoleon III's support, and the two opportunists found that they could both make gains if they could draw the Austrians into war. They agreed that if Cavour could entice the Vienna government into war, France would come to Sardinia's aid and help eject the Austrians from Lombardy and Venetia. In return, France would receive Nice and Savoy from Sardinia. The plan worked to perfection. In April 1859, Cavour lured the Austrians into

THE UNIFICATION OF ITALY 1859–1870

Kingdom of Sardinia to 1859
To Kingdom of Sardinia 1860
Annexed to Kingdom of Sardinia 1861; establishes Kingdom of Italy
To Kingdom of Italy 1866
To Kingdom of Italy 1870

France's duplicity did not stop Cavour. A year later, appealing to the British, he made major changes in the peace settlement. Plebiscites were held in Tuscany, Modena, and Parma, and they voted to join Sardinia. Even with the loss of Nice and Savoy to France, the addition of the three areas made Sardinia the dominant power in the peninsula (see map at left).

With the consolidation of power in the north, Giuseppe Garibaldi (1807–1882) became the major figure in the unification struggle. This follower of Mazzini, secretly financed by Cavour, led his 1000 tough adventurers—the Red Shirts—to conquer Sicily and Naples. He then prepared to take the Papal States. This move prompted Cavour, who feared that a march on the pope's holdings might provoke French intervention, to rush troops to Naples. He convinced Garibaldi to surrender his power to Victor Emmanuel II, thus ensuring Sardinian domination of the unification movement. By November 1860, Sardinia had annexed the former kingdom of Naples and Sicily, and all the papal lands, except Rome and its environs.

A meeting at Turin in March 1861 formally proclaimed the existence of the Kingdom of Italy, a new nation of 22 million people. But Austrian control of Venetia and the pope's jurisdiction over Rome, were problems that did not find solution before Cavour's death in 1861. In the decade that followed Italy gained Venetia in 1866, acting as Prussia's ally in the Austro-Prussian war. When the Franco-Prussian war broke out in 1870, the French could do little to help the pope. Italian forces took control of Rome, and in 1871 it became the capital of a unified Italy.

The opportunistic methods used by the Sardinians have been criticized. Cavour made no attempt to hide the true nature of his policies. He once said "if we did for ourselves what we do for our country, what rascals we should be."[7] He fully understood the rules of the *realpolitik* game in the post-1848 state system. His skill in playing that game and in gaining Italian unification cannot be doubted.

Germanic Competition

Conservative forces regained control in Vienna and Berlin after 1848, but the Austrian Habsburgs operated from a much weaker position

"Right Leg in the Boot at Last" was the caption on the British cartoon of 1860. Garibaldi is surrendering his power to Victor Emmanuel II, king of Sardinia and later king of the united Italy.

than did the Prussian Hohenzollerns. The Habsburg victory over the Hungarians brought only temporary comfort. The collapse of the liberal and nationalistic movements in the Habsburg empire was followed by a harsh repression that did little to address the basic political problems facing Vienna. Centralizing and Germanizing tendencies stimulated nationalist sentiments in the empire. After their losses to the French and Sardinians in 1859, the Austrians considered moving toward a federal system for their lands. The Hungarians, however, demanded equality with Vienna.

Prussia, on the other hand, went from strength to strength. Facing a different range of problems in a much more unified state, King Frederick William issued a constitution in 1850 that paid lip service to parliamentary democracy but kept real power in the hands of the king and upper classes. The Berlin court wanted to form a confederation of north German states, without Austria. This plan frightened the Austrians and made the Russians uneasy. A conference of the three powers meeting at Olmütz in 1850 forced the

Prussians to withdraw their plan. Instead, the 1815 German Confederation was affirmed, with Vienna recognized as the major German power (see map below). The embittered Prussians returned to Berlin, pledging revenge for the "humiliation of Olmütz."

Despite this diplomatic setback, Prussia gained success in other areas. Berlin kept the Austrians out of the *Zollverein*, the customs union of German states, and fought off their efforts to weaken it. The noble-dominated government was modern and efficient, especially when compared with that in Vienna. The Prussians extended public education to more of their citizenry than in any other European state. At the end of the 1850s, a new ruler, William I (1861–1888), came to power. He had a more permissive interpretation of the 1850 constitution and allowed

liberals and moderates the chance to make their voices heard.

Bismarck and German Unification

A stalemate occurred in 1862 when the king wanted to strengthen his army, but the Chamber of Deputies would not vote the necessary funds. The liberals asserted the constitutional right to approve taxes, while the king equally strongly expressed his right to build up his forces. As the king struggled with this constitutional crisis, he called Otto von Bismarck (1815–1898) home from his post as Prussian ambassador in France and made him prime minister.

Bismarck advised the king to ignore the legislature and collect the needed taxes without the Chamber's approval. Bismarck knew the

THE UNIFICATION OF GERMANY 1815–1871

- Prussia 1815-1866
- Annexed by Prussia 1866
- Joined Prussia in forming the North German Confederation 1867
- Joined with Prussia to form the German Empire 1871
- Alsace-Lorraine ceded to German Empire by France 1871
- German Confederation 1815-1866

Otto von Bismarck, the "Iron Chancellor," was the shrewd and masterful prime minister of Prussia from 1862 and the first chancellor of the united Germany from 1871 to 1890.

accurately the actual state of conditions, the insight to gauge the character and goals of his opponents, and the talent to move skillfully and quickly.

Unlike most of his colleagues, he was a master image maker, so effective that historians have used his self-applied epithet "blood and iron" to describe his career. But in addition, few statesmen have ever accomplished so much change with such a comparatively small loss of life and controlled use of war. Bismarck was a master politician who knew that force was the final card to be played, to be used as the servant of diplomacy and not its master.[9]

Some historians have attributed his successes to mere luck, whereas others have deemed them products of genius. An example is his approach to Russia. Bismarck knew that he would have to solidify relations with Russia, and he achieved this in 1863 by promising the Russians that he would aid them in all Polish-related problems. Giving up virtually nothing, he gained a secure eastern flank and thus set up his three wars that brought about German unification.

The Danish and Austrian Wars

In 1864 Bismarck invited Austria to join Prussia and wage war on Denmark. The cause of the conflict was the disputed status of two duchies bordering on Prussia and Denmark. These two duchies of Schleswig and Holstein were claimed by both the Germans and the Danes. The two Germanic powers overwhelmed the modest Danish forces and split the duchies: Austria took Holstein, and Schleswig went to Prussia. With his eastern and northern flanks stabilized, Bismarck set out to isolate Austria.

Italy was already hostile to the Austrians and remained so when Bismarck promised it Venetia in return for its assistance in the future war. He encouraged the French to be neutral by intimating that Prussia might support France should it seek to widen its borders. Severe domestic crises with the Hungarians absorbed Austria, which soon found itself isolated. The Prussian leader provoked war with Vienna by piously expressing alarm at the manner in which the Austrians were ruling Holstein and sending troops into the province. Austria took the bait, entered the war, and was devastated by the

necessity of armed strength in order to gain Prussia's diplomatic goals. Ironically, his later military victories would gain him the support of many of the liberals whom he had encouraged the king to defy.

Bismarck's arrival in Berlin strengthened not only the king but also the hopes of those who wanted a united German state. Unification appealed to virtually all segments of German society, from the liberals to the conservatives such as the historian Heinrich von Treitschke who stated "There is only one salvation! One state, one monarchic Germany under the Hohenzollern dynasty."[8] The Berlin government through its leadership of the *Zollverein*, sponsorship of the confederation of north German states, and efficient bureaucracy was the obvious choice for the capital of a unified German state. With the arrival of Bismarck, the Prussians gained the necessary leadership for unification.

The prime minister was a master of the art of *realpolitik*. He had the intelligence to assess

Prussians at the battle of Sadowa. In this Seven Weeks' War, the Prussians avenged the "humiliation of Olmütz."

Prussia offered a moderate peace settlement that ended the old German Confederation. In its place Bismarck formed the North German Confederation, with Austria and the south German states excluded. Prussia annexed several territories such as Hanover, Mecklenberg, and other states north of the Main River in this penultimate stage in the unification of Germany (see map, p. 640).

The War with France

After 1867 Bismarck turned his attention westward to France and Napoleon III. The French leader had allowed himself to be talked into neutrality in 1866 because he anticipated a long war between his German neighbors that would weaken both of them and because he hoped to expand into the neutral state of Belgium. In August 1866 he approached Bismarck for his share of the fruits of victory, but the German leader refused to agree to French demands. Frustrated and offended, Napoleon III insisted that Prussia approve France's annexation of Luxembourg and Belgium. In a crafty move Bismarck

asked the French envoy to Berlin to put these demands into writing but still avoided giving a definite response. Four years later Bismarck sent the document to the British in order to gain their sympathy for the upcoming war with the French. After France's active participation in the Crimean War, there was no chance that Russia would come to Napoleon's aid. Bismarck let the Austrians know about France's cooperation with the Prussians during the 1866 war, and Italy was not about to help Napoleon III after his activities in 1859. By 1870 France was isolated. It was simply a question now of Bismarck maneuvering the French into war.

The immediate controversy centered on the succession to the Spanish throne left vacant after a revolution had overthrown the reactionary queen Isabella. The Spaniards asked Leopold, a Hohenzollern prince, to become the constitutional king of their country. France saw this as an unacceptable extension of Prussian influence, and Leopold withdrew his candidacy. But this was not enough for Paris. The French sent their ambassador to Ems, where the Prussian king was vacationing, to gain from him a pledge that he would not again permit Leopold to seek the Spanish throne. This was not a reasonable request, and the king refused to agree to it. After

German troops march down the Champs-Elysées in Paris during the Franco-Prussian War. The better prepared German troops, outnumbering the French nearly two to one, quickly overwhelmed the French during the short-lived war of 1870–1871.

Bismarck and the Ems Despatch

Bismarck knew how to manipulate public opinion through press leaks and doctored documents. See how he altered the Ems despatch to achieve his goals vis-a-vis France.

I made use of the royal authorization communicated to me through Abeken, to publish the contents of the telegram; and in the presence of my two guests I reduced the telegram by striking out words, but without adding or altering, to the following form: "After the news of the renunciation of the hereditary Prince of Hohenzollern had been officially communicated to the imperial government of France by the royal government of Spain, the French ambassador at Ems further demanded of his Majesty the King that he would authorize him to telegraph to Paris that his Majesty the King bound himself for all future time never again to give his consent if the Hohenzollerns should renew their candidature. His Majesty the King thereupon decided not to receive the French ambassador again, and sent to tell him through the aide-de-camp on duty that his Majesty had nothing further to communicate to the ambassador." The difference in the effect of the abbreviated text of the Ems telegram as compared with that produced by the original was not the result of stronger words but of the form, which made this announcement appear decisive, while Abeken's version only would have been regarded as a fragment of a negotiation still pending, and to be continued at Berlin.

After I had read out the concentrated edition to my two guests, Moltke remarked: "Now it has a different ring; it sounded before like a parley; now it is like a flourish in answer to a challenge."

From *Bismarck, The Man and the Statement*, tr. A. J. Butler, 2 vol. (New York, 1899).

---

the interview he directed that a message be sent to Bismarck, describing the incident. Bismarck altered the message of this "Ems dispatch" to give the impression that the French ambassador had insulted the Prussian king and that the king had returned the insult. The rumor was leaked to the press and infuriated both the Germans and the French.

France declared war in July. The two countries' forces appeared to be evenly matched in equipment, but the Germans had a better trained and more experienced army. In two months the Prussians overwhelmed the French, delivering the crowning blow at the battle of Sedan, where the emperor and his army were surrounded and forced to surrender. Forces of the north and south German states besieged France for four months before the final French capitulation. By the Treaty of Frankfurt, France lost Alsace and a part of Lorraine to Germany and was required to pay a large indemnity. In the Hall of Mirrors at Versailles, the Second Reich was proclaimed and William I was crowned German emperor.

The call for revenge for France's defeat and humiliation became a major issue in French politics.

Russia and Britain: The Extremes of Europe

Russia avoided the revolutionary currents after 1815, but unlike Britain, Russia had neither the economic strength nor the social and political flexibility to change. Tsar Alexander I (1801–1825) understood the major problems facing his empire, especially those of serfdom and the need to reform the autocratic system. His grandmother, Catherine II, had educated him in the traditions and assumptions of the Enlightenment, and for the first four years of his reign he attempted major reforms in the areas of education, government, and social welfare.

Russia, however, possessed neither the inventive and flexible ruling classes nor the economic wealth of Britain. Its problems were far more harsh. Serfdom, a system that held millions of Russians in its grip, was socially repressive and economically inefficient. The autocratic system simply was inadequate to govern efficiently the world's largest state.

Obstacles to Reform in Russia

Alexander's experiments with limited serf emancipation, constitutionalism, and federalism proved his desire for change. The tsar was all-powerful in theory, but in reality he depended on the nobles who, in turn, gained their wealth from serfdom. Carrying out the necessary reforms would destroy the foundations of Alexander's power. The fact that his father and grandfather had been killed by nobles made him cautious. Further, it was his misfortune to rule during the Napoleonic wars, and for the first fifteen years of his reign he had to devote immense amounts of money and time to foreign affairs. His reform plans were never carried through to completion, and not until the 1850s, when it was almost too late, would there be another tsar willing to make the fundamental social and political reforms needed to make Russia competitive in the industrializing world.[10]

In the reactionary decade after 1815 reformers fell from favor. However, the open discussion of the need for change in the first part of Alexander's reign, the experiences of the soldiers returning from western Europe and the activities of the expanding number of secret societies kept the dream of change alive. When Alexander failed to respond, the intensity of the reformers' discussions increased. Alexander died in December 1825, and there was confusion over which of his two brothers would succeed to the throne. The days between his death and the confirmation of his younger brother Nicholas I (1825–1855) gave a small circle of liberal nobles and army officers the chance to advance their ill-defined demands for a constitution. The officers who led this revolt had been infected with liberal French thought. They sought to end serfdom and establish representative government and civil liberties in Russia. On December 26 these liberals led a small uprising in St. Petersburg. This Decembrist revolt, as it was called, lasted less than a day and could have been put down even earlier had Nicholas been more decisive. This abortive, ill-planned attempt doomed any chance of liberal or democratic reform in Russia for thirty years.

Nicholas I and Reaction

The Decembrist incident shook Nicholas badly, and throughout his reign he remained opposed to liberal and revolutionary movements. He sponsored "Official Nationalism," whose foundations were "Autocracy, Orthodoxy, and Nationalism"—the Romanov dynasty, the Orthodox

This 1854 engraving by Gustave Doré satirizes the callous indifference of Russian serf owners. Masters hard-pressed for cash were occasionally known to bet their serfs as stakes in card games.

church, and a glorification of a putative Russian spirit. He carried out a thorough censorship that included the screening of foreign visitors, publications, even musical compositions. The government closely monitored both students' activities and curricula in schools and universities. Finally, some 150,000 "dangerous" people were exiled to Siberia. Millions of non-Russians in the empire began to experience a limitation of their identity through a forced adherence to Russian customs called "Russification." These activities strengthened Nicholas' immediate control and stopped potential upheaval, but he failed to address adequately the important social and political reforms Russia so badly needed.

Despite his efforts to control intellectual and political currents, Nicholas failed. Reformist activity may have been repressed, but the Russian intellectual was fruitful, tuned as it was to the works of the German philosophers and poets. In the 1840s and 1850s a new breed of intellectuals appeared, thinkers devoted to achieving political goals. Although they would not make their strength felt until after the 1860s, these thinkers, known as the *intelligentsia*, established strong roots during Nicholas' reign. Alexander Herzen (1812–1870) and Michael Bakunin (1814–1876) were the pioneers of this peculiarly Russian movement. Herzen was a moderate socialist who advocated freeing the serfs, liberalizing the government, and freeing the press. In 1847 he went into exile in London where he founded his famous paper, the *Kolokol* (the *Bell*) ten years later. It was widely read in Russia, supposedly appearing mysteriously on the tsar's table. Bakunin, the father of Russian anarchism, was more radical. He felt reform of Russia was useless and advocated terrorism. He preached that anarchy—complete freedom—was the only cure for society's ills. He too went into exile in the west.

The Russian intellectuals debated many questions, most important of which was whether Russia should imitate Europe or pursue its own tradition. The question had been posed since the reign of Peter the Great. The Westerners argued that if Russia wished to survive it had to imitate basic aspects of the west and renounce much of its own past. The Slavophiles, on the other side of the dialogue, renounced Europe and the west, regarding it as materialistic, pagan, and anarchic.

Michael Bakunin, the leading spokesman for anarchism, advocated destruction of the state through acts of violence and terrorism to achieve liberation.

Nicholas was able to maintain control to the extent that the 1830 and 1848 revolutions had little influence or impact on Russia. Some aspects of industrialization were introduced, as the first Moscow-to-St. Petersburg rail line was put into operation. The government appointed commissions to examine the questions of serfdom and reform, but these were extremely secret considerations.[11] Still basic doubts about Russia's future remained. Dissident intellectuals, economic and social weakness, and autocratic stagnation were indicators that difficult times were in store for the country.

Alexander II and the Great Reforms

Russia's inept performance in the Crimean war (see p. 687) spotlighted the country's weaknesses and the need for reform. When Alexander II (1855–1881) came to the throne, even the conservatives among his subjects acknowledged the need for major change. The new tsar moved quickly to transform the basis of the autocratic structure—the institution of serfdom—but ran into delay from the nobility. After five years of deliberation a committee appointed by Alexander drew up the Emancipation Proclamations, issued in March 1861. By this reform, 32 million state peasants and 20 million serfs who had no civil rights and could not own property and who owed heavy dues and services began the transition to landownership and citizenship.

The government paid the landlords a handsome price for the land that was to be turned over to the peasants. In return, the peasants had to pay the government for the land over a period of forty-nine years by making payments through their village commune, the *mir*. The drawn-out nature of the land transfer disappointed the former serfs, who had expected a portion of the lords' lands to be turned over to them without charge. Instead, the peasants were trapped in their village community, which received and allocated all of the land—much of it poor—and divided it among the various families and paid taxes. Even though they were granted ownership of their cottages, farm buildings, garden plots, domestic animals, and implements, the restrictions placed on the peasants by confining them to their villages constituted a serious problem. New generations of peasants would bring a large population increase, with no corresponding increase in their amount of land.

The emancipation of the serfs was the single most important event in the domestic history of nineteenth-century Russia. In its wake it brought about thoroughgoing reforms of the army, judiciary, municipal government, and system of local self-government. One of the most important reforms came in 1864 when local government was transformed by the *Zemstvo* Law. In the countryside the gentry, middle classes, and peasants elected representatives to local boards *(zemstvos)*. These boards collected taxes for and maintained roads, asylums, hospitals, and schools. The *zemstvos* became one of the most successful governmental organizations in Russia.[12]

British Flexibility

Like Russia, Britain did not directly experience the revolutionary upheaval that afflicted the continent, even though the island nation felt many of the same pressures as did France during the same period. The postwar period was the most difficult time for Britain, as the transition back to a peacetime economy and the wrenching changes caused by industrialization made their effects felt. Some handskilled workers lost their jobs due to the increasing use of machines, and in response, workers smashed the machines and destroyed some factories. Violence broke out when some working-class groups and radicals pushed for rapid reforms. The worst incident took place in August 1819 in what became known as the Peterloo Massacre. In Manchester, a crowd of 60,000 gathered at St. Peter's Fields to push for parliamentary reforms. When the army was sent to disband the meeting, several people were killed and hundreds injured.

Britain's ruling class, in power since the 1770s, were conservatives who were blind to the hardships of their workers. They continued to respond to the long-departed excesses of the French Revolution. Instead of dealing with the misfortunes of the poor and unemployed, they declared that the doctrine of "peace, law, order, and discipline" should be their guide. To that end, they pushed through a series of repressive acts after 1815 that suspended the Habeas Corpus Act, restricted public meetings, repressed liberal newspapers, and placed heavy fines on literature considered to be dangerous. Massive conflict between the rich and poor appeared inevitable.

The Duke of Wellington's failure to acknowledge the need for reforms in the 1830s so aroused the public that the "Iron Duke" and the Tories (Conservatives) were forced to resign. They were replaced by a more liberal group, the Whigs. The drive toward self-interested reform by the upper classes had begun in the 1820s, led by Robert Peel (1788–1850) and George Canning (1770–1827), who started the modern British reform tradition that continued to 1914. When Wellington was voted out of office, Lord Charles Grey (1764–1845), leader of the Whig party, became head of government. In 1832 Grey pushed immediately to reform Parliament.[13]

Britain's political abuses were plain for all to see. Representation in the House of Commons had no relation to the population. Three percent of the people dictated the election of members. The rapidly growing industrial towns such as Manchester and Birmingham—each with over

100,000 citizens—had no representatives, while other areas, virtually without population, had delegates. After being blocked by aristocratic interests, first in the House of Commons and then in the House of Lords, reform bills responding to these electoral abuses were finally passed. But this occurred only because King William IV threatened to create enough new members of the House of Lords who would vote for the bills in order to pass them. Grey's reform bills did not bring absolute democracy, but they pointed the way toward a more equitable political system.

The Reformist Tide

Beginning in the 1820s reformers pushed through laws that ended capital punishment for over one hundred offenses, created a modern police force for London, recognized labor unions, and repealed old laws that kept non-Anglican Protestants from sitting in Parliament. They also passed the Catholic Emancipation Act that gave Roman Catholics voting rights and the right to serve in Parliament and most public offices. The reform tide increased in the 1830s and 1840s. Abolitionist pressures brought about the ending of slavery in the British empire in 1833. Parliament passed laws initiating regulation of working conditions and hours. In 1835 the Municipal Corporations Bill introduced a uniform system of town government by popular elections.

Britain's government was far from being a democracy, and in the 1830s and 1840s a strong, popular movement known as Chartism developed. Its leaders summarized the country's needs in six demands: universal manhood suffrage, secret voting, no property qualifications for members of Parliament, payment of Parliament members so that the poor could seek election, annual elections, and equal districts. In 1839, 1842, and 1848 the Chartists presented their demands, backed by over a million signatures on their petitions. But, each time they failed to gain their goals, and the movement declined after 1848. By the end of the century, however, all of their demands, exept that for annual parliamentary elections, had been put into law.

Mirroring the ascendancy of the middle classes, economic liberalism became dominant. A policy of free trade came to be favored because, given Britain's overwhelming economic superiority,

the country could best profit from that approach. The Corn Laws' protective duties on imported grain, which had favored the gentry since 1815, no longer suited the industrializing British economy. These laws had been designed to encourage exports`and to protect the British landowners from foreign competition. By the middle of the century the population had grown to such an extent that British farmers could no longer feed the country and the price of bread rose alarmingly. The potato crop famine in Ireland in 1845 that led to the death of perhaps one-half million people spotlighted the situation and the need for low-priced food from abroad. Repeal of the Corn Laws made possible the import of cheaper food for the masses. Soon Britain abandoned customs duties of every kind. The economy boomed under the stimulus of cheap imports of raw materials and food.

For the next twenty years an alliance of the landed gentry and the middle classes worked together to dominate the government and to keep the lower classes "in their stations." The newly ascendant middle classes believed that political reforms had gone far enough, and the Whig government of Lord Palmerston who served as prime minister from 1855 to 1865 reflected this view.

Conclusion

The French seeds of individualism, freedom of thought, pride in nation, and equality under the law that had appeared after 1789 and were spread by Napoleon began to take root across the map of Europe. The middle classes and underprivileged throughout the continent demanded change and pursued rights and liberties inherent in these ideals. The Congress of Vienna failed to stop these currents and revolutions broke out in the 1820s, 1830s, and 1840s.

The 1848 outbreaks dealt a deadly blow to the idealistic liberals, nationalists, and romantics who failed to achieve their goals. In France, some moderates learned that a revolution in the name of liberal principles could unleash forces that would threaten the middle classes. They turned to Louis Napoleon, who destroyed the Second Republic and, as Napoleon III, installed a new empire. In the Habsburg realm the various nationalities who tried to free themselves from Vienna's control found that the nationalism that motivated each of them also doomed their struggle for freedom by making a unified attack impossible. The Habsburgs took advantage of this lack of unity and imposed twenty years of sterile repression, before they were defeated by the Prussians. By the end of 1848, the leaders of Germany and Italy discarded most of the liberal demands of the revolutionaries, but they retained the potent nationalistic forces that would eventually lead to unification.

Russia and Britain avoided the revolutionary upheavals: the first through a policy of repression that failed to respond effectively to its overwhelming problems and the second because of an improving standard of living and a flexible, self-interested political leadership. Throughout the half century after Waterloo, however, the advanced nations of Europe underwent the traumas of industrialization, which had as devastating an effect on the old idealism as had the political upheavals of 1848.

Suggestions for Reading

H. Nicolson, *The Congress of Vienna: A Study of Allied Unity, 1812–1822* (Compass, 1961) is a civilized analysis of diplomatic interaction and a good companion to Henry A. Kissinger, *A World Restored: Metternich, Castlereagh, and the Problems of Peace, 1812–1822* (Sentry, 1957). The following are excellent on the general background to the period: A. J. May, *The Age of Metternich, 1814–1848* (Holt, Rinehart, and Winston, 1967), E. Hobsbawm, *The Age of Revolution, Europe 1789–1848* (Mentor, 1969), J. Talmon, *Romanticism and Revolt: Europe 1815–1948* (Harcourt Brace Jovanovich, 1967), P. Stearns, *European Society in Upheaval* (Macmillan, 1967), R. C. Binkley, *Realism and Nationalism: 1852–1871* (Torchbooks, 1935), W. E. Mosse, *Liberal Europe* (Harcourt Brace Jovanovich, 1974), John Weiss, *Conservatism in Europe* (Harcourt Brace Jovanovich, 1977).

Vol. 4 of A. Cobban's *A History of Modern France* (Penguin, 1970) is a useful survey. For greater detail see F. Artz *France Under the Bourbon Restoration, 1814–1830* (Russell, 1931); T. Howarth, *Citizen King: The Life of Louis-Philippe, King of the French* (Verry, 1961); G. Duveau, *1848: The Making of a Revolution* (Vintage, 1967), and F. A. Simpson, *Louis Napoleon and the Recovery of France* (Greenwood, 1975).

Two valuable surveys on Britain are Asa Briggs, *The Making of Modern England, 1783–1867: The Age of Improvement* (Torchbooks, 1959) and E. L. Woodward, *The Age of Reform, 1815–1870* (Oxford, 1962).

A. J. P. Taylor, *The Course of German History* (Capricorn, 1962) is a short, controversial essay on German national history since the French Revolution. T. Hamerow, *Restoration, Revolution, Reaction: Economics and Politics in Germany, 1815–1871* (Princeton, 1966) is highly praised. L. Namier's *1848: The Revolution of the Intellectuals* (Anchor, 1946) is critical of the liberals at Frankfurt. E. Eyck's balanced *Bismarck and the German Empire* (Norton, 1964) is offset by Taylor's hostile *Bismarck: The Man and the Statesman* (Alfred A. Knopf, 1955). O. Pflanze's *Bismarck and the Development of Germany: The Period of Unification, 1815–1871* (Princeton, 1963) is first-rate. Barbara Jelavich's *The Habsburg Empire in European Affairs* (Rand McNally, 1969) is an excellent, brief history. C. A. Macartney's *The Habsburg Empire: 1790–1918* (Weidenfeld and Nicholson, 1968) is thorough, but pro-Hungarian.

J. N. Westwood's *Endurance and Endeavour: Russian History 1812–1986* (Oxford, 1988) is the best new survey, replacing Hugh Seton-Watson's *The Russian Empire 1801–1917* (Oxford, 1967). Allen McConnell's *Tsar Alexander I* (Crowell, 1970) remains the best short biography. W. Bruce Lincoln's *In the Vanguard of Reform* (Northern Illinois, 1982) sets the standard for scholarship on Nicholas I. Deep insights into Russian intellectual development are to be found in N. Berdyaev's *The Russian Idea* (Beacon, 1962). The best introductory book on nineteenth-century Russia is Marc Raeff's *Understanding Imperial Russia* (Columbia, 1984).

Notes

1. Geoffrey Bruun, *Europe and the French Imperium* (New York: Harper & Row, 1938), p. 38.
2. L. C. B. Seaman, *From Vienna to Versailles* (New York: Harper and Row, 1963), p. 8.
3. Norman Davies, *Heart of Europe: A Short History of Poland* (Oxford: Oxford University Press, 1987), pp. 166–167.
4. Barbara Jelavich, *The Habsburg Empire in European Affairs: 1814–1918* (Chicago: Rand McNally & Co., 1969), pp. 21–39.
5. Jorg K. Hoensch, *A History of Modern Hungary: 1867–1986* (London: Longman, 1988), pp. 4–10.
6. For vivid characterizations of this period see Roger L. Williams, *The World Of Napoleon III: 1851–1870* (New York: Collier Books, 1962).
7. Quoted in J. S. Schapiro, *Modern and Contemporary European History: 1815–1940* (Boston: Houghton Mifflin Co., 1940), p. 222.
8. Quoted in K. S. Pinson, *Modern Germany* (New York: The Macmillan Company, 1954), p. 116.
9. Seaman, pp. 96–129.
10. See Allen McConnell's biography *Tsar Alexander I: Paternalistic Reformer* (New York: Crowell, 1970), for a clear treatment of this most complex personality.
11. W. Bruce Lincoln, *In the Vanguard of Reform* (DeKalb: Northern Illinois University Press, 1982), pp. 139–167.
12. J. N. Westwood, *Endurance and Endeavour: Russian History 1812–1986* (Oxford: Oxford University Press, 1987), pp. 79–103.
13. G. Bingham Powell, Jr., "Incremental Democratization: The British Reform Act of 1832," in G. A. Almond, S. C. Flanagan, and R. J. Mundt, eds., *Crisis, Choice, and Change* (Boston: Little, Brown, 1973), p. 149.

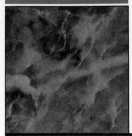

Chapter 25

Society, Politics, and Culture, 1871–1914

Since 1500 the European state system had been going through a process of competition and concentration; in the four centuries after 1500 the number of political units declined from around 500 to roughly 25.[1] The six largest survivors—Britain, Germany, France, Rusia, Italy, and the Austro-Hungarian monarchy—took advantage of their new material and economic power and adjusted more or less successfully to the challenges and opportunities presented by the times.

Industrialization gave some of these states immense material strength, economic power, and technology to affect the every day lives of their citizens. The states vastly expanded their activities in building up their armed forces, controlling the food supply, overseeing the economy, training technical personnel, increasing the police functions, and compiling statistical records.

During the second half of the nineteenth century, major European states turned their full attention to education. The increase in literacy and the corresponding growth of the mass circulation press during the latter part of the era brought politics to the common people and changed the nature of political life.

In the cultural realm, as in the areas of politics and economic growth, Europe experienced revolutionary changes by the end of the nineteenth century. "High culture" became more and more specialized, while increasing literacy created a wide market for popular novels and the sensationalist press among the lower middle class. Technology introduced new forms of popular entertainment, such as home photography, the cinema, and recorded music.

Modern, mass participation Europe came into existence between 1871 and 1914, built on the foundations of economic and demographic growth and dominated by astute politicians. By the end of the period, those states that had demonstrated the greatest flexibility in adapting to the new conditions—Britain, France, and Germany—would stand as Europe's most powerful countries.

Economic and Social Challenges: Political Responses

The Marxian Analysis

The middle of the nineteenth century did not in any way mark the arrival of workers as a major political force in Europe, but it was then that Karl Marx (1818–1883) made a major contribution to their cause through his ideological work. Marx and his colleague, Friedrich Engels (1820–1895) wrote the *Communist Manifesto* in late 1847. In it they outlined the theory of scientific socialism, sketched a wide-ranging program that advocated violent revolution, preached the inevitable conflict of the classes, rejected traditional morality and religion, and condemned contemporary governments. In so doing, they made the transition from a philosophical approach to social problems to a basis for modern socialist and communist movements. In the next three decades Marx conceptualized the framework he and Engels erected in the *Manifesto*.

Marx was born in Trier to middle-class Jewish parents who had converted to Protestantism.

Karl Marx and Friedrich Engels, Manifesto of the Communist Party

The Manifesto by Marx and Engels had little impact on 1848 Europe. However, it became one of the most widely read tracts in world history in the twentieth century.

A spectre is haunting Europe—the spectre of Communism. All the Powers of old Europe have entered into a holy alliance to exorcise this spectre; Pope and Czar, Metternich and Guizot, French Radicals and German police-spies.

. . . The first step in the revolution by the working class is to raise the proletariat to the position of ruling class, to win the battle of democracy.

The proletariat will use its political supremacy to wrest, by degrees, all capital from the bourgeoisie, to centralise all instruments of production in the hands of the State, i.e., of the proletariat organized by the ruling class; and to increase the total of productive forces as rapidly as possible.

. . . In the most advanced countries the following will be pretty generally applicable:

1. Abolition of property in land and application of all rents of land to public purposes.
2. A heavy progressive or graduated income tax.
3. Abolition of all right of inheritance.
4. Confiscation of the property of all emigrants and rebels.
5. Centralisation of credit in the hands of the State, by means of a national bank with State capital and an exclusive monopoly.
6. Centralisation of the means of communication and transport in the hands of the State.
7. Extension of factories and instruments of production owned by the State; the bringing into cultivation of waste lands, and the improvement of the soil generally in accordance with a common plan.
8. Equal liability of all to labour. Establishment of industrial armies, especially for agriculture.
9. Combination of agriculture with manufacturing industries; gradual abolition of the distinction between town and country, by a more equable distribution of the population over the country.
10. Free education for all children in public schools. Abolition of children's factory labour in its present form. Combination of education with industrial production, etc., etc.

When, in the course of development, class distinctions have disappeared, and all production has been concentrated in the hands of a vast association of the whole nation, the public power will lose its political character. Political power, properly so called, is merely the organised power of one class for oppressing another. If the proletariat during its contest with the bourgeoisie is compelled, by the force of circumstances, to organise itself as a class, if, by means of a revolution, it makes itself the ruling class, and, as such, sweeps away by force the old conditions of production, then it will, along with these conditions, have swept away the conditions for the existence of class antagonisms, and of classes generally, and will thereby have abolished its own supremacy as a class.

In place of the old bourgeois society, with its classes and class antagonisms, we shall have an association in which the free development of each is the condition for the free development of all.

From Karl Marx and Friedrich Engels, *Manifesto of the Communist Party* (International Press, 1911).

He attended the University of Berlin as a doctoral candidate in philosophy, instead of law as his father desired, and there joined a circle that followed some aspects of Hegel's thought. After finishing his degree, he could not find a university position, so he returned to the Rhineland where he began writing for a local liberal newspaper. The injustices he saw around him and his reading of the French Socialists Henri de Saint-Simon and Pierre Joseph Proudhon led him to concentrate on the economic factors in history. He went to Paris to continue his studies, met Engels, and was expelled by the authorities in 1845. From there he went first to Belgium and finally to England where, after 1848, he spent most of the rest of his life.

Marx was uncompromising in his hostility to capitalism, stating in the *Manifesto* that communists "openly declare that their ends can be attained only by the forcible overthrow of all existing social conditions." Virtually every day he made his way to the British Museum where he waged intellectual war on capitalism by doing research for his major works, especially *Das Kapital.*

At night he returned home to write, enduring difficult living conditions and the death of three of his children in the 1850s. He wrote prolifically, although suffering from boils, asthma, spleen and liver problems, and eye strain. His constant inability to handle money drove him into fits of rage against his creditors. He was increasingly intolerant of those who disagreed with him and became an embittered recluse; yet his vision and theories inspired reformers for the next century. Marx gave the oppressed an explanation for their difficult position and a hope for their future.

Marx held a materialistic view of history, stating that economic forces drove history. He did not deny the existence or importance of spiritual or philosophical values; nor did he doubt that the occasional genius could alter the flow of events. However, the material aspects of life were much more important. Marx believed that "it is not the consciousness of men which determines their existence, but on the contrary, it is the existence which determines their consciousness." As an economic determinist he believed that when the means of production of a given era changed, the whole social and ideological structure was transformed.

Karl Marx with his daughter. After being expelled from several European countries, Marx settled in England where he devoted himself to the development of his theory of scientific socialism.

Marx saw the productive forces of society as the key factor in history. The world was driven by class conflict between those who controlled the means of production and those who did not, whether master against slave in ancient Greece, patrician against plebeian in Rome, lord against serf in the middle ages, noble against bourgeois in the early modern times, or capitalist against the proletarian in the modern world. The world's history moved in this zigzag pattern through class struggle, a reflection of the Hegelian dialectic.

Hegel had written that history is made up of a number of cultural periods, each one the expression of a dominant spirit or idea. After fulfilling its purpose, a given period is replaced by a period of contradictory ideas or set of values. The original thesis is negated, and that negation in turn is also negated after it has run its course. Where Hegel saw history driven through a historical dialectic in cultural terms to a final phase, Marx saw history moving to its conclusion of the workers controlling the means of production.

The bourgeoisie, which had erected the new capitalist society by gaining control of the means of production through organizing trade and industry, created its opposition in the proletariat, the class-conscious workers. This group would be according to Marx, "the seeds of the bourgeoisie's own destruction." According to the dialectic, when the workers recognized their true power, they would overthrow the bourgeoisie. Out of this conflict would come the final act of the dialectical process, the classless society in which "each person would work according to his ability and receive according to his need." An interim dictatorship might have to occur, because a number of features of the old order would remain and the proletariat would have to be protected. However, as the classless society evolved, the state would wither away.

Through his research, Marx identified a number of defects that foretold the inevitable overthrow of the bourgeoisie, among them alienation and surplus value. The factory system turned workers into cogs in the larger machine, and deprived them of satisfaction in their work. In addition, Marx charged that owners did not pay workers for the value they created. A worker could, for example, produce in seven hours the necessary economic value to supply one individual's needs, but the owner would keep the worker laboring for twelve hours. The owner thereby took the "surplus value" of five working hours stolen from workers, thus robbing them of the fruits of their work.

Finally, Marx noted that in the capitalist system the rich got richer and fewer and the poor got poorer and more numerous. This produced huge discontent and increased the chance of revolution. Further, the masses would be unable to buy all of the goods they produced and economic crises of overproduction and unemployment would become the rule. In time, once the bourgeois phase of dominance had run its course, the contradictions between the classes would become so great that the proletariat would rise up and take over the means of production.

Marx was the last of the great universal theorists. As is the case with other ideologists in the rationalist eighteenth-century tradition he built on the foundations erected by others, making a creative synthesis that has had worldwide appeal. As was also the case with other major thinkers, his thoughts, which were often hypotheses, have been frozen in dogma or revised in various countries to take forms he would have trouble recognizing. It is not surprising that the rapidly changing age in which he lived would outrun many of his projections, especially those concerning the rigidity of the capitalists.

Labor Movements

Well before Marx conceived his theories, the British economy suffered through a difficult time after the end of the Napoleonic wars. High unemployment struck skilled workers, especially hand loom weavers. In frustration, some of them fought back and destroyed textile machines, the symbol of the forces oppressing them. Strikes, demonstrations, and incidents such as the tragedy at St. Peter's Fields (see p. 646) vividly expressed the workers' rage. Not until the British reformers came forward in the 1820s did the laborers begin to gain some relief.

Their efforts to form labor unions received an important boost in 1825 when the Combination Acts, passed in 1799 against the formation of workers' associations, were repealed. The first unions, such as the half-million strong Grand National Consolidated Trades Union, were weak

This plate commemorates a protest meeting of the Trades Union Congress held April 21, 1834, to present a petition to the king.

In this workers' demonstration in London, the banners of trade unions follow the standard of the Social Democratic party. Workers banded together to protect themselves from powerful business corporations.

Socialist parties in the second half of the century helped the workers' movements by providing a theoretical basis and an agressive public statement of their case. Karl Marx, who spent his life researching and writing in the defense of the proletariat—even though he had precious little contact with them, organized the International Organization of Workers, the First International, in London in 1864. The First International included labor activists ranging from English trades unions to East European refugees to anarchists to German theorists.

Not much came of the First International's efforts because of constant arguments among the factions and Marx's vindictiveness towards other major figures such as the Russian anarchist Bakunin. Defeat of the Paris Commune in 1871 (see p. 660) delivered a devastating blow to the French socialist movement. However, the Social Democrats—Marxian socialists—made important gains in Germany, forcing Bismarck to make concessions (see p. 662). It became the largest party in the country and the strongest socialist

This 1848 lithograph by Honoré Daumier contrasts the gluttonous bourgeois in his frock coat and top hat with the shabbily dressed workingman.

and disorganized, split by the gulf between skilled workers and common laborers. Nonetheless, the workers laid the foundations for the powerful unions that defended them by the end of the century.

As industry became more sophisticated and centralized, so too did the labor movement. Across Europe the workers could choose anarchist, socialist, or conservative paths to follow. Some unions centered on a particular occupation—the trade or the craft unions. Others found their focus in the various productive stages of an industry, while still others, such as the English Trade Unions Congress, were nationwide and all-encompassing, wielding great power. Whatever the choice, by 1900 unions had made important advances through their solidarity in launching paralyzing strikes.

party in Europe under the leadership of its founder, Ferdinand Lassalle. In 1871 there were two socialists in the *Reichstag;* by 1912 the number had risen to 110.

In the three decades after Marx's death in 1883 his theories dominated the European workers' movements, even if those movements themselves were not united. The French split into three distinct socialist groups. Some British socialists were greatly influenced by the maxims of Christianity, while the Fabian Society—among whose members were George Bernard Shaw, H. G. Wells, and Sidney and Beatrice Webb—pursued a more prosaic political path. With the spread of industrialization, workers and their leaders found important support in Marx's work even in places such as Russia, where Marx had never foreseen his thoughts having any influence. Because of the widespread impact of Marx's ideas in the social sciences and the labor movement, "the period of the Second International (1889–1914) may be called without any exaggeration the golden age of Marxism."[2] A broad spectrum of thinkers among the twelve million members of the Second International claimed Marx as their inspiration, even though they might differ on the role of the state, the functions of unions, the crisis of capitalism, or the role of the proletariat. There was not a single, monolithic Marxist movement in Europe. Yet despite their philosophical difference, the Social Democrats in all countries could agree on essential needs for the workers: an eight-hour day, the need to replace standing armies with militias, and the welfare state buttressed by universal suffrage.

The socialist movement strengthened labor unions, and the workers achieved substantial progress by 1914. Whether by working within the various states' legislatures or by raising the specter of revolution, the unions and their socialist allies helped bring about substantial reforms in the economy, labor practices, civil rights, the courts, and education. They pushed the capitalists to reform, thus avoiding the apocalyptic revolution forecast by Marx.

By 1914, although the workers could not negotiate on an equal basis with the owners, they had vastly improved their position over that endured by their grandparents. The British movement had four million members and was a powerful force, while German unions benefited members in a broad number of areas from life insurance to travel. The income gap between rich and poor began to narrow by 1914. Working hours were shortened and living conditions improved. The real wages of workers, that is, the amount of goods that their income could actually buy, increased by 50 perecent in the industrial nations in the last thirty years of the nineteenth century.

The Middle Classes

The greatest beneficiaries of industrialization were the *bourgeoisie,* the middle classes. They profited directly from the new industrial economy. Their newfound wealth, harnessed to the social and legal changes that resulted from the French Revolution on the continent and the reform movement in Britain, allowed them to dominate all aspects of European life.

While it is difficult to give a strict definition of the bourgeoisie, it is easier to say who was *not* middle class. Neither factory workers and peasants nor the aristocracy were included. Those closer to the laboring classes were called the lower middle classes, or the *petite bourgeoisie* while those near the élite were the upper middle classes, or the *haute bourgeoisie.* Included in the lower middle classes were skilled artisans, bureaucrats, clerks, teachers, shopkeepers, and the clergy. They realized how little separated them from the laboring masses and were constantly trying to climb socially. Later in the century they benefitted most from the compulsory education laws and were avid consumers of the books written by the new wave of authors, the penny-press newspapers, and state propaganda. Both literate and numerous, they played a key role in political affairs.

The *haute bourgeoisie* controlled most of the wealth created by industrialization. In fact, they were often much richer than the nobles. It was not easy to gain admittance to this level of society, but money, taste, and aggressiveness could open the doors for the bankers, factory owners, lawyers, architects, occasional professors, doctors, or high governmental officials who tried. Once admitted, they gained access to many of the benefits of the aritocracy such as the best

Queen Victoria's sitting room at Osborne House, her personal residence. The room, with its clutter of photographs, sentimental paintings, and heavy furniture, epitomizes the Victorian style.

schools, shops, restaurants, and cultural life. Because of their wealth and leisure time they dominated politics, the press, and the universities.

The British upper middle class was a group riddled with contradictions. The age in which they lived has come to be labeled the Victorian period, after Victoria (1837–1901), the long-reigning English queen. On the surface the Victorians had little doubt about what was right and wrong, moral and immoral, and most importantly, proper and improper. Underneath this surface propriety the middle classes pursued—as recent research indicates—a life marked by sexuality, perverted passion, and drug addiction. The prime minister of the era, William Gladstone, devoted considerable attention to reforming prostitutes. The Victorian literary establishment concentrated on "cleaning up" Shakespeare's plays and toning down some parts of Gibbon's *Decline and Fall of the Roman Empire.*

The British upper middle class employed more than two and a half million servants at century's end—nearly a million people more than farmed the land—and led crusades against slavery, alcohol, pornography, and child labor. Their efforts led to the passage of a series of reforms limiting the employment of young children, setting maximum working hours for teenagers, and regulating working conditions for women—even when the factory owners argued that such changes were bad for the country because they violated the freedom of contract between the worker and the employer. The British upper middle class set the tone to be imitated by their peers across the continent.[3]

The Leninist Critique

Western Europe responded successfully to the changes brought on by industrialization during the nineteenth century, but Russia presented an entirely different picture. The Russians did not experience the most demanding parts of industrialization until the end of the century and then on a different basis from that of the western European countries. Russia remained an overwhelmingly agrarian society in which the state paid for building factories by using grain produced by the peasants for export on the depressed world market. The government did little to aid the transition from an agrarian to an industrial society and crushed opposition political movements. In 1900 Russia lacked a tradition of gradual reform and the habits of compromise such as existed in England. The government controlled its populace through the use of force.

In this troubled environment, the solutions proposed by Karl Marx attracted a number of supporters. Marx himself did not believe that Russia would be a favorable laboratory for his theories, and he expressed surprise when *Das*

Lenin, the main force of the Russian Revolution from which emerged the Soviet Union, spent years studying Marx's theories and adapting them to conditions in Russia.

which Russia found itself. He overcame major obstacles from tsarist officials and passed his law exams at St. Petersburg University without formally attending classes.

After 1893 he began to compile his theories of tactics and strategy that continue to form the bulk of twentieth-century dogma. In 1895 a court sentenced him to exile in Siberia for his political activities. Although in exile, he enjoyed complete liberty of movement in the district and could hunt, fish, swim, study, read, and keep up a large correspondence. His comrade, Nadezhda Krupskaia, joined him and they were married. Later they translated Sidney and Beatrice Webb's *The History of Trade Unionism*. Lenin's exile ended in 1900 when he and Krupskaia went to Switzerland where they joined other Russian Social Democrats in exile in founding the newspaper *Iskra* ("Spark," whose motto was "From the Spark—the conflagration").

In applying Marx to Russian conditions, Lenin found it necessary to sketch in several blank spots. Lenin's methods differed greatly from those of western European Marxists, as did his theories. Lenin advocated the formation of a small élite of professional revolutionaries, the vanguard of the proletariat. These professionals, subject to strict party discipline, would anticipate the proletariat's needs and best interests and lead them . . . to the oxymoronic theory of "democratic centralism." After 1903 Lenin had little success in changing the political conditions of Russia, beyond affecting the most sophisticated part of the workers' movement. However, he continued to make significant doctrinal contributions. Lenin recommended a socialism whose weapon was violence and whose tactics allowed little long-range compromise with the bourgeoisie. However, he also saw the advantages of flexibility and encouraged temporary deviations that might serve the goals of the working class. He took little for granted and reasoned that the development of class unity to destroy the capitalists among the Russian workers might require some assistance. To that end he refined his notion of the way in which the élite party would function. In revolution the élite party would infiltrate the government, police, and army while participating in legal workers' movements; in government the party would enforce its dictates on the populace with iron discipline.

Kapital was translated into Russian in 1872 and pleasure when he learned of the broad impact of his theories there. Not until 1898, however, was there an attempt to establish a Russian Social Democratic party.

The nature of Marx's theories sparked debate over the way in which they applied to Russia. The thinker and actor who would eventually apply and implement Marxist theory was Vladimir Ilich Ulyanov (1870–1924), who later took the name of Lenin. Born in Ulyanovsk, formerly Simbirsk, a small city along the Volga river, Lenin grew up in the moderate and respectable circumstances provided by his father, a school administrator and teacher. In 1887, the government arrested and executed Lenin's brother, Alexander, in St. Petersburg for plotting against the life of the tsar.

Shortly thereafter Lenin began to master the writings of Marx and to study the situation in

The Romantic spirit often expressed itself in architecture in Gothic revival, a style best represented by London's Houses of Parliament, designed by Sir Charles Barry (1795–1860), with details designed by A. W. N. Pugin (1812–52). The horizontal symmetry of the buildings is broken by tall, irregularly spaced towers. At the west end is the elaborate Victoria tower and at the east, the smaller clock tower, probably designed by Pugin.

Two leading Romantic painters were the English landscape painter John Constable and the French artist Eugène Delacroix. In *Salisbury Cathedral from the Bishop's Garden* (c. 1826), left, Constable is less concerned with details of the scene than with conditions of light, atmosphere, and sky, which he regarded as ''the chief organ of sentiment.'' Delacroix' sensuous use of color and his love of exotic settings are evident in *Women of Algiers* (1834), below, inspired by the artist's 1832 trip to Morocco.

Rejecting the historical, religious, and mythological themes of the painters who preceded him, Gustave Courbet chose to portray what he saw—the contemporary life of the world around him. For this he was soundly criticized by his contemporaries. Critics attacked *Young Ladies from the Village Giving Alms to a Cowherd* (1851–52) for its "ugliness," vulgarity, lack of perspective, and violation of tradition. Yet it is these same attributes that made Courbet a revolutionary figure in the history of art.

Portfolio Seven

A concern for the effects of light and color united the impressionists, yet each also developed a personal style. Often regarded as the boldest innovator was Claude Monet, who did series of paintings of the same subject, such as *Water Lilies* (1906), opposite page. Mary Cassatt specialized in paintings of mothers and children, as in *The Bath* (1891–92), above left. With its vibrant color and shimmering light, *On the Terrace* (1881), above right, is a typical work of Auguste Renoir. Careful control of line, calculated design, and off-center composition are hallmarks of Edgar Degas, evident in *A Woman with Chrysanthemums* (completed in 1865), left.

Portfolio Seven

Originally associated with the impressionists, Paul Cézanne became dissatisfied with the limitations of impressionist style and began a relentless search for the structure and form beneath the color. *Montagne Sainte-Victoire* (1904) is one of a long series Cézanne painted of a mountain scene near his home in Aix-en-Provence. It was works like this that had such a profound influence on the cubists and expressionists who followed Cézanne.

Vincent van Gogh was less interested in the photographic reproduction of nature than in the recreation of his vision of what he saw, expressed through his use of brilliant, intense, unmodulated color and dynamic brush strokes. The swirling, exploding stars in *The Starry Night* (1889), painted at the sanatorium at St.-Rémy during one of van Gogh's lucid periods, seem to express the artist's turbulent emotions.

A growing disenchantment with the values and traditions of Western civilization led Paul Gauguin (1848–1903) to Tahiti, where he spent a number of years living in accord with the local life-style. In its carved look, bold pattern, tropical colors, and subject matter drawn from primitive life, *The Red Dog* (1892) is typical of Gauguin's later works in which the origins of modern primitivism can be found.

Lenin looked out at the undoubted strength of the advanced technological nation state and marveled at its extension of power. In his *Imperialism, the Highest Stage of Capitalism* (1916) he forecast that the modern capitalist states would destroy themselves. He argued that the wages of the workers did not represent enough purchasing power to absorb the output of the capitalists' factories, and that the vast amounts of capital that were accumulated could not be invested profitably in the home country. Therefore, the states would engage in an inevitable competition for markets, resources, and capitals that would drive them from cutthroat competition to outright war and their ultimate destruction. At that point, he reasoned his élite party would be ready to pick up the pieces from the blindly selfish powers.

The Modern State

By the end of the 19th century the major European states had transformed themselves to head off "inevitable" class conflict and to tap into the forces that raised the general level of prosperity. The states became unprecedentedly richer, more powerful, and more effective. New technology enabled them to touch the everyday lives of their citizens. They formed huge conscript armies, increased taxation, established universal education, improved medical and social support services, and installed communications networks. The states generated so much energy that they fueled Europe's imperialist expansion across the globe (see ch. 26) while improving the material lives of citizens at home.

The Committee of Public Safety during the French Revolution and then Napoleon Bonaparte had recognized the essential need for mass public education.[4] The state could not use illiterates for their jobs or as citizens. By 1900 all of the major states had invested heavily in education, and the evolution of the popular press to accommodate mass literacy helped change the nature of political life. Politics went from the reasoned discourse of the drawing rooms of the élite to the crude rhetoric of mass movements that reflected working class and middle class values.

With the increased effectiveness of communications brought by the railroads, the telephone, and the telegraph, nations became much more unified and governments intervened directly in each individual's life. The kept statistics and records of each citizen's life and exercised control over such matters as food supply and public order. As wealth and population grew, so did the number of bureaucracies. In two areas in Germany, the postal service and railroads, the number of employees soared from 245,000 in 1880 to nearly 700,000 in 1910.[5] Further, military conscription touched the lives of most young men, except in Britain. By 1897 France and Germany each had nearly 3,500,000 men in the field or on reserve, and these soldiers were better and more expensively armed than ever before.

The states tapped an increasing tax base to finance their augmented functions. The German empire's income grew from 263 million marks in 1873 to over 1200 million marks in 1909.[6] Other governments, even the poorest, registered comparable increases. By 1914, the states that were the most flexible—Britain, Germany, and France—were the most powerful. Russia, Italy, and the Austro-Hungarian monarchy struggled to remain great powers.

Britain and Democracy

Blessed by its wealth and adaptability, Britain built a truly democratic political structure by 1914. The state continued to support business even as it became more intimately involved in matters affecting the welfare of its citizens. Two great statesmen, William Ewart Gladstone (1809–1898), a Liberal, and Benjamin Disraeli (1804–1881), a Conservative, dominated the first part of this period with their policies of gradual reform. They alternated as prime minister from 1867 to 1880. After Disraeli's death, Gladstone prevailed until he retired in 1894.

Gladstone and Disraeli

The two leaders came from sharply contrasting backgrounds. The son of a rich Liverpool merchant, Gladstone had every advantage that wealth and good social position could give him. He entered Parliament in 1833 and quickly became one of the greatest orators of his day. He began as a Conservative, working in the tradition

In this *Punch* cartoon, political rivals William Gladstone (left) and Benjamin Disraeli (right) are ready to sling mud at each other. The cartoon's caption reads, "A Bad Example."

of the Tory reformer, Robert Peel. Gradually he shifted his alliance to the newly formed Liberal party in the 1850s and became a strong supporter of laissez-faire economics and worked to keep government from interfering in business. He was a far more effective political than social or economic reformer.

Disraeli had few of Gladstone's advantages. The son of a Jew who became a naturalized British subject in 1801, Disraeli was baptized an Anglican. He first made a name for himself as the author of the novel *Vivian Grey* (1826). In contrast to Gladstone, Disraeli went from liberalism to conservatism in his philosophy. He stood for office as a Conservative throughout his career and became the leader of the party.

Both Liberals and Conservatives had to face the fact that the complacency of government during the "Victorian Compromise" from 1850 to 1865 could not continue. The alliance of landed gentry and middle classes may have successfully kept the lower classes "in their stations" but serious problems plagued the country. Only one adult male in six was entitled to vote. Both parties felt the pressure to make the political

system more representative. Both parties also knew that reform must come, and each hoped to gain the credit and resultant strength for extending the vote.

The Liberals' turn came first. In 1866 they introduced a moderate reform bill enfranchising city workers. Some conservatives opposed it, fearful that increasing the franchise would bring the day of revolution closer. When the proposal failed to pass, political agitation and riots rocked the country. The outbreaks evidently impressed the members of Parliament and when the Conservatives came to power in 1867, Disraeli successfully sponsored the Second Reform Bill that added more than a million city workers to the voting rolls. The measure increased the electorate by 88 percent, although women and farm laborers were still denied the vote.

Even though the Conservatives passed the voter reform, the new elections in 1868 brought the Liberals back to power and Gladstone began his so-called Glorious Ministry, which lasted until 1874. With the granting of the vote to the urban masses it became imperative to educate their children. The Education Act of 1870 promoted the establishment of local school boards to build and maintain state schools. Private schools received governmental subsidies if they could meet certain minimal standards. Elementary school attendance, which was compulsory between the ages of five and fourteen, jumped from 1 to 4 million in ten years.

Other reforms included a complete overhaul of the civil service system. Previously, in both the government and military, appointments and promotions depended on patronage and favoritism. But in 1870, this method was replaced by open examinations. The government also improved the military by shortening enlistment terms, abolishing flogging, and stopping the sale of officers' rank. Gladstone's government successfully revamped the justice system and introduced the secret ballot. Finally, some restrictions on labor unions' activities were removed. By 1872 the Glorious Ministry had exhausted itself, and Disraeli referred to Gladstone and his colleagues in the House of Commons as a "range of exhausted volcanoes."

Disraeli's government succeeded the Glorious Ministry in 1874, and he stated that he was going to "give the country a rest." He was no stand-pat conservative, however. He supported an approach known as Tory democracy that attempted to weld an alliance between the landed gentry and the workers against the middle class. Even during this "time of rest" Disraeli's government pushed through important reforms in public housing, food and drug legislation, and union rights to strike and picket peacefully.

Gladstone returned to power in 1880 and continued the stream of reforms with the Third Reform Bill that extended the vote to agricultural workers. This act brought Britain to the verge of universal male suffrage. Gladstone also secured passage of the Employers' Liability Act, which gave workers rights of compensation in case of accidents on the job.

The Irish Problem

One dilemma escaped and continues to escape the solutions of well-meaning reformers in Britain, that of British rule in Ireland. The present-day crisis in Northern Ireland originated in the seventeenth century. The British placed large numbers of Scottish emigrants in the province of Ulster, in northern Ireland, building a strong colony of Protestants—the so-called Orangemen, or Scotch-Irish. In the eighteenth century the British passed a number of oppressive laws against the Irish Catholics, restricting their political, economic, and religious freedom and effectively taking their lands. Passage of the Act

of Union in 1801 forced the Irish to send their representatives to the Parliament in London. A large part of the Irish farmland passed into the hands of parasitic landlords who leased their newly gained lands in increasingly smaller plots to more and more people. Many peasants could not pay their rent and were evicted from the land. The Irish lost both their representation and their livelihood.

In 1845 the potato crop, the main staple of diet, failed and a terrible famine ensued, which led to a tremendous decline in population. Hundreds of thousands emigrated to the United States; perhaps as many as 500,000 people died. Between 1841 and 1891 the population fell by more than 40 percent, from 8,770,000 to less than 5,000,000.

The Irish gained a few concessions from the British during the century in the form of the Catholic Emancipation Act (1829) and protection from arbitrary eviction for tenants, during the Glorious Ministry. The Irish Anglican Church lost its favored position when Roman Catholics were freed of the obligation to pay tax support to a church they did not attend. In 1881 Gladstone pushed through an act that allowed the Irish peasants the chance gradually to regain land that had once been theirs.

None of these concessions made up for the lack of home rule and in 1874 the Irish patriot Charles Stewart Parnell (1846–1891) began to work actively to force the issue through Parliament.

Wracked by poverty and famine, Ireland was further tormented during the 1840s by the mass eviction of tenant farmers. After the evictions, cottages were burned down at once to prevent other homeless farmers from occupying them.

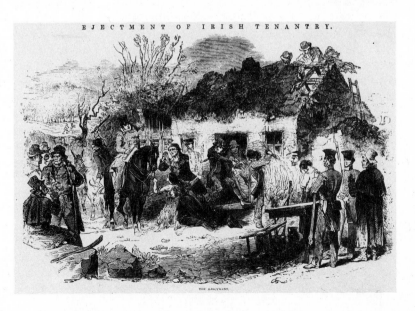

EJECTMENT OF IRISH TENANTRY.

THE EJECTMENT.

Gladstone introduced home rule bills in 1886 and 1893, but both were defeated. A home rule bill was finally passed in 1914, but by this time the Ulsterites strongly opposed the measure and prepared to resist by force incorporation into Catholic Ireland. The outbreak of war with Germany postponed civil strife, but this was only a two-year delay until the Easter Uprising of 1916. Not until 1921 did southern Ireland finally gain the status of a British dominion. The home rule bill never went into effect.

The New Liberals

Gladstone's fight for Irish home rule split his party and paved the way for a decade of Conservative rule in Britain (1895–1905). Partly because of foreign and imperial affairs, the Conservatives departed from the reformist traditions of Tory democracy. By 1905 the need for social and political reform again claimed the attention of the parties.

Over 30 percent of the adult male laborers made the unacceptably low wage of less than seven dollars a week. It was impossible to save for periods of unemployment and emergencies. Workers demonstrated their discontent in a number of strikes. Partially in response to the workers' needs and at the prompting of the Fabian Socialists the Labour party was founded in 1900, under the leadership of J. Ramsay MacDonald (1866–1937), a self-made intellectual who had risen from humble status, and the Scottish miner Keir Hardie (1856–1915). The liberals found themselves threatened on both their left and right flanks. They decided to abandon their laissez-faire economic concepts and embrace a bold program of social legislation. The radical Welsh lawyer Lloyd George portrayed their program. "Four spectres haunt the poor: Old Age, Accident, Sickness, and Unemployment. We are going to exorcise them."[7]

Led by prime minister Herbert Asquith, Lloyd George, and the young Winston Churchill who had defected from the Conservatives, the Liberal party—with the aid of the Labour bloc—put through a broad program. It provided for old-age pensions, national employment bureaus, workers' compensation protection, and sickness, accident, and unemployment insurance. In addition, labor unions were relieved of financial responsibility for losses caused by strikes. Members of the House of Commons, until that time unpaid, were granted a moderate salary. This last act allowed an individual without independent wealth to pursue a political career.

The House of Lords tried to block the Liberal reform plan by not passing the 1909–1910 budget, which laid new tax burdens, including an income tax, on the richer classes in order to pay for the new programs. The Liberals and Labour fought back by directly attacking the rationale for the Lords' existence. They argued that a hereditary, irresponsible upper house was an anachronism in a democracy. The result was the Parliament Bill of 1911 that took away the Lords' power of absolute veto. Asquith announced that the king had promised to create enough new peers to pass the bill if needed (a tactic used with the 1832 Reform Bill). The Lords had to approve and thereafter could only delay and force reconsideration of legislation.

By 1914 the evolutionary path to democracy and a modern democratic state structure had been largely completed, except for women's suffrage. In the previous generation some effort had been put in to gain the vote for women, but by and large the effort had been unsuccessful. Women's suffrage was not a major concern for the major parties, most of whom felt that women's proper place was in the home. At the turn of the century the most effective group to work for women's rights was the Women's Social and Political Union (WSPU), whose members were the first to be known as suffragettes. Its founder, Emmeline Pankhurst (1858–1928), first agitated, then disturbed, and then challenged the order and stability of England in the decade before World War I. Pankhurst and her colleagues traveled and worked constantly to make the case for the vote for women, and to 1910 the WPSU abandoned traditional rhetoric in favor of mass marches, hunger strikes, and property damage. In 1913 a young suffragette martyred herself by running in front of the king's horse at the Derby.[8] With the outbreak of the war, the WPSU backed the national effort against the Germans, and finally in 1918 women age thirty and over were granted the vote. Ten years later, they gained equal voting rights with men.

Emmeline Pankhurst, in white scarf, at a rally protesting a government unresponsive to women's issues. After 1910, the women's suffrage movement turned increasingly militant.

The Second Reich to 1914

Within the brief span of one lifetime, the fragmented German areas of central Europe successfully united under Prussian, that is, Hohenzollern, leadership to challenge Britain for world leadership. Bismarck provided the initial genius to bring about unification, but the source of German strength was found in its rapid economic growth, population increase, and efficient political structure. Prussia's success drew the enthusiastic support of prominent businessmen, intellectuals, and artists and the increasing concern of its neighbors.

The Second Reich came into existence at a ceremony in January 1871 in the Hall of Mirrors at the Palace of Versailles. There King William I became emperor of a federal union of twenty-six states with a population of 41 million. The bicameral (two-house) legislature of the new empire consisted of a *Bundesrat*, representing the ruling houses of the various states, and a *Reichstag*, representing the people through its 397 members elected by male suffrage. The dominant power rested with the emperor, who controlled military and foreign affairs and the seventeen votes in the *Bundesrat* needed to veto any constitutional change.

Bismarck as Chancellor

The actual head of government was the chancellor who was appointed by the kaiser and responsible to him only. This arrangement allowed the chancellor to defy or ignore the legislature if it served his purpose. However, he had to operate within the constraints of the federal state structure in which large powers of local government were given to the member states. Bismarck was more constrained in domestic than in foreign affairs. It is not surprising, therefore, that he fared better in foreign matters. As chancellor, Bismarck built modern Germany on his belief in the inherent efficiency of a state based on one faith, one law, and one ruler. He distrusted those institutions that did not fit that tripartite formula: specifically the Catholic church and the Socialist party.

The Catholic political party had sent a large bloc of representatives to the *Reichstag* in 1871, and these members supported the complete independence of the church from state control, denounced divorce, objected to secular education, and questioned freedom of conscience. Many Catholics strongly supported the new dogma of papal infallibility (see p. 682). Within the Protestant Prussian part of Germany Bismarck introduced anti-Catholic policies that triggered a conflict known as the *Kulturkampf* (the struggle for civilization). These so-called May laws made it an offense for the clergy to criticize the government, regulated the educational activities of the religious orders, and expelled the Jesuits from the country. The state also required civil marriages and dictated that all priests study theology at state universities. Pope Pius IX declared these acts null and void and told loyal Catholics to refuse to obey them. Many of the chancellor's laws applied equally to Protestants, who actively protested them.

As opposition spread, Bismarck struck hard at the Catholics, imprisoning priests, confiscating church property, and closing down pulpits. When the tide did not turn in his favor, he realized that he could not afford to create millions of martyrs. Showing his shrewd sense of power, he cut his losses, retreated, and repealed most of the anti-Catholic laws.

The Social Democratic (Marxist) movement posed a greater challenge to Bismarck's rule. The party's founder, Ferdinand Lassalle (1825–1864) rejected violence as a means to gain power and instead advocated working within the existing political structure. After his death the movement retained its nonviolent nature. The party's popularity soared when it was officially established in 1875 and its leaders pushed for true parliamentary democracy and wideranging social programs.

In 1878 Bismarck used two attempts on the emperor's life as an excuse to launch an all-out campaign to weaken the Social Democrats, even though they had no connection with the acts. He dissolved extralegal socialist organizations, suppressed their publications, and threw their leaders in jail. Despite these measures the socialists continued to gain support.

When he failed to weaken the socialists by direct confrontation, the chancellor changed tactics. He decided to undercut them by taking over their program. Through the 1880s he implemented important social legislation that provided wage earners with sickness, accident, and old-age insurance. He sponsored other laws that responded to many of the abuses workers encountered. The Social Democrats continued to grow in size and influence. However, by creating the first welfare state, the pragmatic Prussian chancellor defused a potential revolution.

Kaiser William II

In 1888 William II, the grandson of the emperor, became head of the Reich. Just as Bismarck had dominated European affairs since 1862, the new emperor would play a key role until 1918. Here was a person who, without Bismarck's finesse, advocated a policy of "blood and iron." Where Bismarck knew the limits and uses of force and appreciated the nuances of public statements, William was a militarist and a bully. Serving in a modern age, the new emperor still believed in the divine right of kings and constantly reminded his entourage that "he and God" worked together for the good of the state. With such a contrast in styles, it is not surprising that William saw Bismarck not as a guide but as a threat. He once stated that "it was a question of whether the Bismarck dynasty or the Hohenzollern dynasty should rule."[9] Finally, in March 1890 Bismarck resigned.

At the beginning of the twentieth century Germany presented a puzzling picture to the world. On the one hand the blustering kaiser made fiery and warlike statements. He encouraged militarism and the belief that *Alles kommt von oben* ("Everything comes down from above"). On the other hand his thoroughly advanced country made great scientific and cultural strides. Observers of German affairs noted that one-third of the voters supported the Social Democrats, an indication of a healthy parliamentary system. A commonly held pride in Germany's accomplishments knit the country together.

More important than William's behavior was the fact that by the beginning of the new century the Germans competed actively in all areas with the British. Although Germany did not

Kaiser William II's Naval Ambitions

Kaiser William knew Germany had a grand future, an expanding future. He wanted Germans to travel on the high seas, to the dismay of the British.

In spite of the fact that we have no such fleet as we should have, we have conquered for ourselves a place in the sun. It will now be my task to see to it that this place in the sun shall remain our undisputed possession, in order that the sun's rays may fall fruitfully upon our activity and trade in foreign parts, that our industry and agriculture may develop within the state and our sailing sports upon the water, for our future lies upon the water. The more Germans go out upon the waters, whether it be in the races of regattas, whether it be in journeys across the ocean, or in the service of the battle-flag, so much the better will it be for us. For when the German has once learned to direct his glance upon what is distant and great, the pettiness which surrounds him in daily life on all sides will disappear.

From C. Gauss, *The German Kaiser as Shown in His Public Utterances* (New York: Charles Scribner's Sons, 1915).

outproduce Britain, long-term projections showed that the island nation's growth had leveled out and that in the next generation the Reich would surpass it. The Germans dominated the world market in the chemical and electrical industries and were making strides in other areas. They boasted a more efficient organization of their industries, a higher literacy rate for their workers, better vocational training, and a more aggressive corps of businessmen. German labor unions were less combative than the British, while the government gave more support to industry than did Parliament.

The French Third Republic to 1914

The defeat of France's Second Empire at the battle of Sedan in 1870 gave birth to the Third Republic. The humiliating peace terms that stripped France of a part of Lorraine and all of Alsace and imposed a huge indemnity on the country created a desire for revenge. The spectacle of the Germans crowning their emperor and proclaiming the Second Reich at Versailles, the symbol of French greatness, left a bitter taste.

Persistent class conflicts, covered over during Louis Napoleon's reign, also contributed to many years of shaky existence before the republic gained a firm footing. A new, overwhelmingly royalist national assembly was elected to construct a new, conservative government after the signing of the peace. This added to the shock of the defeat touched off a revolutionary outburst that led to the Paris Commune (1871).

Shaky Beginnings

Parisians had suffered such severe food shortages during the seige of the city that some had been forced to eat rats and zoo animals. When it turned out that their sacrifices had been in vain, republican and radical Parisians joined forces in part of the city to form a commune, in the tradition of the 1792 Paris Commune (see p. 562), to save the republic. The Communards advocated government control of prices, wages, and working conditions (including stopping night work in the bakeries). After several weeks of civil strife, the commune was savagely put down. Class hatred split France further yet.

Because the two monarchist factions that constituted a majority could not agree on an acceptable candidate for the monarchy, they finally settled on a republic as the least disagreeable form of government. The national assembly approved the new republican constitution in 1875. Unde the new system, members of the influential lower house—the Chamber of Deputies—was elected by direct suffrage. There was also a

Senate, whose members were elected indirectly by electoral colleges in the departments. The constitution established a weak executive, elected by the legislature. The ministry exercised real power, but its authority depended on whatever coalition of parties could be assembled to form a tenuous majority in the legislature.

The Boulanger and Dreyfus Affairs

The stormy tenure of the Third Republic was marked by a series of crises such as increased anarchist violence leading up to a series of bombings in 1893, financial scandals such as the notorious Panama Canal venture that implicated a wide range of leading figures, and lesser scandals. The two most serious threats were the Boulanger and Dreyfus affairs.

The weak and traumatized republic was both threatened and embarrassed by the public cries for vengeance uttered in 1886 by General Georges Boulanger (1837–1891), the minister of war. This charismatic, warmongering figure made a series of speeches which he ended by emotionally proclaiming: "Remember, they are waiting for us in Alsace." The considerable number of anti-republicans saw him as a man on horseback who would sweep away the republic in a *coup d'état,* much as Louis Napoleon had done in 1851 and bring back French grandeur. The government finally ordered Boulanger's arrest on a charge of conspiracy, and he fled the country. Later, he committed suicide.

The Dreyfus case was far more serious because it polarized the entire country, divided and embittered French opinion by the anti-Semitic fervor it unleashed and challenged the fundamental ideals of French democracy. Captain Alfred Dreyfus (1859–1935), the first Jewish officer on the French general staff, was accused in 1894 of selling military secrets to Germany. His fellow officers tried him, found him guilty, stripped him of his commission, and condemned him to solitary confinement on Devil's Island, a dreadful convict settlement off the northeast coast of South America. Even with the case supposedly settled, military secrets continued to leak to the Germans, and subsequently a royalist, spendthrift officer named Major Esterhazy was accused, tried, and acquitted.

Captain Alfred Dreyfus had to pass through this "Guard of Dishonor" each day on his way to the courtroom during his second trial in 1899.

The case became a *cause célèbre* in 1898 when the French writer Emile Zola (1840–1902) wrote his famous letter *J'accuse* ("I accuse"), in which he attacked the judge for knowingly allowing the guilty party to go free while Dreyfus remained in jail. The next year Esterhazy admitted his guilt, but by that time the entire country had split into two camps. On the one side were the anti-Dreyfusards—the army, church, and royalists; on the other side were the pro-Dreyfusards—the intellectuals, socialists, and republicans. The case was once again placed under review in the military courts, and even though Esterhazy had confessed, the court continued to find Dreyfus guilty. Finally, the French president pardoned him and in 1906 the highest civil court in France found him innocent.

The case had greater significance than just the fate of one man. Those who had worked against Dreyfus, especially the church, would pay dearly for their stand. Many republicans believed that the church, a consistent ally of the monarchists, was the natural enemy of democratic government. They demanded an end to the church's official ties to the state. In 1904 and 1905 the government closed all church schools and repudiated the Napoleonic Concordat. All ties between church and state were formally ended.

After weathering forty difficult years, by 1914 the Third Republic had gained prosperity and stability. Workers had gained their voice in the country as the various trade and local union groups came together in the *Confédération Générale du Travail*, the General Confederation of Labor. Monarchists and other right-wing parties still had considerable influence, although the Dreyfus affair had weakened them.

French republicanism had wide support across the political spectrum. Most French citizens had basic democratic rights which were pursued through the extremely complex multiparty political system of the republic. The various ministries that were constructed from the fragile coalitions came and went with bewildering rapidity. Yet France was strong, prosperous, and one of only two republics among the world's great powers.

Russia: Reformers, Reactionaries, Revolutionaries

While Alexander II pushed through the "Great Reforms," the revolutionary movement grew stronger. In the 1850s the nihilist movement developed, questioning all old values, championing the freedom of the individual, and shocking the older generation. At first the nihilists tried to convert the aristocracy to the cause of reform. Failing there, they turned to the peasants in an almost missionary frenzy. Some of the idealistic young men and women joined the movement to work in the fields with the peasants, while others went to the villages as doctors and teachers to preach the message of reform. This "go to the people" campaign was known as the populist, or *narodnik*, movement. Not surprisingly, the peasants largely ignored the outsiders' message.

Revolutionary Response

Frustrated by this rejection, the idealistic young people turned more and more to terrorism. The radical branch of the nihilists, under the influence of Bakunin's protege Sergei Nechaev (1847–1882), pursued a program of the total destruction of the status quo, to be accomplished by the revolutionary élite. In his *Revolutionary Catechism* Nechaev stated that "everything that promotes the success of the revolution is moral and everything that hinders it is immoral." The soldiers in the battle, the revolutionaries, were "doomed men," having "no interests, no affairs, no feelings, no habits, no property, not even a name."[10] The revolution dominated all thoughts and actions of these individuals.

For the twenty years after his emancipation of the serfs, Alexander suffered under increasing revolutionary attack. It was as though the opposition saw each reform not as an improvement but as a weakness to be exploited. In Poland the tsar had tried to reverse the Russification program of his father and in return saw the Polish revolt of 1863. Would-be assassins made a number of attempts on him, and the violence expanded throughout the 1870s as a number of his officials were attacked by young terrorists such as Vera Zasulich (1851–1919). Finally Alexander was assassinated in 1881, on the very day he had approved a proposal to call a representative assembly to consider new reforms.

Reaction: 1881–1905

The slain tsar's son, Alexander III (1881–1894) could see only that his father's reforms had resulted in increased opposition and, eventually, death. During his reign he tried to turn the clock back and reinstate the policy of "Autocracy, Orthodoxy, and Nationalism." Under the guidance of his chief adviser, Constantine Pobedonostsev (1827–1907), Alexander pursued a policy of censorship, regulation of schools and universities, and increased secret police activities. Along with renewing Russification among the minorities, he permitted the persecution of Jews, who were bullied and sometimes massacred in attacks called pogroms. Alexander may have been successful in driving the revolutionaries underground or executing them and the nationalities may have been kept in their place, but under Alexander III Russia lost thirteen valuable years in its attempt to become competitive with western Europe.

Alexander was succeeded by his son, Nicholas II (1894–1917), a decent but weak man. He inherited and retained both his father's advisers and policies. Larger forces overwhelmed him. Industrialization and rural overpopulation spawned a wide range of political pressures that the autocratic structure could not deal with.

To fill the vacuum, different political movements, all illegal, developed. The Liberal party (Constitutional Democrats, or *Kadets*) wanted a constitutional monarchy and peaceful reform on the British model. The Social Revolutionaries combined non-Marxian socialism with the narodnik tradition and simplistically called for "the whole land for the whole people." These agrarian socialists wanted to give the land to the peasants. The Social Democrats, Marxian socialists in a Russian framework, attracted radical intellectuals and politically active city workers. They advocated complete social, economic, and political revolution.

The Social Democrats met in 1903 in London and split into two wings—the Bolsheviks and the Mensheviks—over the questions of the timing of the revolution and the nature of the party. (In Russian, Bolshevik means "majority" and Menshevik means "minority," the names stemming from a vote on party policies in 1903 when the Bolsheviks did prevail. On most occasions, however, the Bolsheviks were in fact in the minority.)

The two factions differed sharply on strategy and tactics. The Bolsheviks, led by Vladimir Ilich Lenin (see p. 656) were prepared to move the pace of history along through "democratic centralism" (see p. 656). The Mensheviks believed that Russian socialism should grow gradually and peacefully in accord with Marxist principles of development and historical evolution, and they were prepared to work within a framework dominated by bourgeois political parties. They knew that their victory was inevitable, given the historical dialectic, and that the proletariat would play the lead role, assisted by the party.

The tsarist regime worked energetically to eliminate the opposition by placing secret agents among them to act as spies. The government continued to launch violent assaults on opponents and to carry on the diversionary anti-Semitic activities with bands of thugs called the Black Hundreds. By attacking the opposition, Nicholas' government concentrated on a symptom of Russia's problems, rather than their causes—the repeated failures to carry out effective reform.

The Revolution of 1905 and Its Aftermath

Once again, a failure in war—this time a "splendid little war" against Japan—exposed the weaknesses of the autocratic tsarist regime. Strikes and protests spread throughout the land in response to the military failure in the last days of 1904. On January 22, 1905, the Cossacks opened fire on a peaceful crowd of workers who had advanced on the Winter Palace in St. Petersburg carrying a petition asking for the tsar's help. In response, a general strike broke out with the strikers demanding a democratic republic, freedom for political prisoners, and the disarming of the police. Soviets—councils of workers—appeared in the cities to direct revolutionary activities. Most business and government offices closed and the whole machinery of Russian economic life creaked to a halt. The country was virtually paralyzed.

After a series of half-measures and stalling in response to strikes and revolutionary activities, the tsar found himself pushed to the wall. Unable to find a dictator to impose order, he was forced to issue the October Manifesto of 1905 which promised "freedom of person, conscience, assembly, and union." A national Duma (legislature) was to be called without delay. The right to vote would be extended, and once in session, no law could be enacted without the Duma's approval. The Manifesto split the moderate from the socialist opposition and kept Nicholas on the throne, although he was heartbroken for having made the compromise. The socialists tried to start new strikes, but the opposition was now totally split apart.

Most radical forces boycotted the first Duma meeting in the spring of 1906. As a result, the *Kadets* became the dominant force. Even with this watered-down representation, the tsar was upset by the criticism of the government's handling of the Russo-Japanese war, treatment of minorities, handling of political prisoners, and economic policies. Claiming that the representatives "would not cooperate" with the government, Nicholas dissolved the first Duma. The Russian

On January 22, 1905, Russian imperial troops opened fire on the crowd of peaceful demonstrators outside the Winter Palace in St. Petersburg. The day is known in history as Bloody Sunday.

people turned a cold shoulder to the Kadets' appeals for support. Sensing the decline of political fervor, Nicholas appointed a law-and-order conservative, Peter Stolypin (1862–1911) as prime minister. He cracked down on a number of the radicals, ruling under the emergency article #87.

Unlike previous tsarist appointees, Stolypin knew that changes had to be made, especially in the area of agriculture. Stolypin created the process to develop a class of small farmers, even without Nicholas' full support. He pushed through reforms that abolished all payments still owed by the peasants under the emancipation law and permitted peasants to withdraw from the commune and claim their shares of the land and other wealth as private property. He also opened lands east of the Urals to the peasants and extended financial aid from the state. He was well on the way to finding a solution to that most enduring of Russian problems, the peasant problem, before he was assassinated in 1911 by a Social Revolutionary, who was also an agent of the secret police.[11]

In spite of a reactionary tsar and unprogressive nobility, Russia made major gains in the nine years after 1905 toward becoming a constitutional monarchy. The nation made great economic and social progress in that time. Industrialization increased and generated new wealth. Increased political and civil rights spawned an active public life. Stolypin's death, however, deprived the country of needed leadership. The coming First World War gave Russia a test it could not pass.

The Lesser Great Powers

Italy, united in 1861 and territorially completed by 1870, and the Austro-Hungarian monarchy, set in motion by the 1867 *Ausgleich*, faced overwhelming problems. The Italians had to deal with north-south differences, relations with the papacy, a lack of natural resources, and a politically inexperienced population. The Austro-Hungarian monarchy had to work through a cumbersome structure to govern a mosaic of nationalities.

Italy

This newly unified country faced serious problems. It had few natural resources and too many people. The political goals of the industrialized north and impoverished south rarely coincided. Most troubling was the question of the papacy, which seriously weakened the state. The pope, the spiritual father of most Italians, refused to accept the incorporation of Rome into the new nation. He called himself the "prisoner of the Vatican," and encouraged—with little effect—his Italian flock not to vote. In an attempt to satisfy the pope, the government passed the Law of Papal Guarantees (1871) that created the Vatican as a sovereign state and allocated the pope an annual sum of $600,000 (roughly the amount of money he had received from his previously held lands). Pius IX rejected the offer, but the state refused to repeal the law.

Despite conflicting and unstable political parties, the new state carried on an impressive program of railroad building, naval construction, and attempts at social and welfare legislation. But major problems remained, especially with the peasantry in the south. Radical political parties made their presence felt after the turn of the century in the form of widespread strikes. In 1900 an anarchist assassin killed King Umberto, who had taken the throne in 1878. Change proceeded slowly after that, and not until 1912 did the country gain universal manhood suffrage, a time when there was still widespread illiteracy.

The Italian leaders' ambition to make Italy a world power placed a great burden on the nation. Money spent on the army came at the expense of needed investments in education and social services. National resources were squandered in an unsuccessful attempt to build an empire in Africa.

Up to the beginning of World War I, Italy faced severe economic crises and labor unrest. In June 1914 a general strike spread through the central part of the peninsula. Benito Mussolini, editor of a socialist journal, played a key role in this movement. Attempts to achieve compulsory education, freedom of the press, and better working conditions did little to improve the economic hardships and high taxes that had driven thousands to emigrate to the United States. The south especially suffered, because it had not shared in the industrial gains of the northern part of the country.

The Austro-Hungarian Monarchy

After the Austrians' disastrous defeat by Prussia, Franz Joseph was forced to offer the Hungarians an equal partnership with Vienna in ruling the empire. The offer was accepted and in 1867 the constitution known as the *Ausgleich*

(compromise) was enacted. Under this document the Dual Monarchy came into existence in which the Habsburg ruler was both the king of Hungary and the emperor of Austria—that is, the area that was not a part of Hungary. Each country had its own constitution, language, flag, and parliament. Ministers common to both countries handled finance, defense, and foreign affairs, but they were supervised by "Delegations" which consisted of sixty members from each parliament who did not meet together, except in emergency circumstances. The *Ausgleich* was to be renegotiated every ten years.

The Dual Monarchy contained 12 million Germans, 10 million Hungarians, over 24 million Slavs, and 4 million Romanians, among other nationalities (see map, p. 669). Although the Germans of Austria had recognized the equality of the Hungarians, the rest of the nationalities continued to live under alien rule. Now, instead of having to deal with one dominant national group, they had to cope with two. In some cases, such as in the prospering, cosmopolitan, and sophisticated area of Bohemia-Moravia, the people wanted an independent state or, at the very least, more rights within the Habsburg realm. Others, such as the Serbs, sought the goal of joining their countrymen living in adjacent national states. The nationalities question remained an explosive problem for the authorities in Vienna and Budapest.

The functioning of the Dual Monarchy was best symbolized by the official bank notes which were printed in eight languages on one side and in Hungarian on the other. In the Hungarian part of the Dual Monarchy the aristocracy governed under the Kossuth constitution of 1848 (see p. 635). The Magyars refused to share rule with the minorities in their kingdom. A small, powerful landed oligarchy dominated the mass of backward, landless peasants. The conservative leadership carried out a virtual process of Magyarization with their minorities, while they continually squabbled with the Austrians.

In the Austrian portion, wealthy German businessmen and the landed aristocracy dominated political life. But even with this concentration of power, the government was much more democratic, especially after 1907 when the two-house legislature was elected by universal manhood suffrage. Here, too, nationalism was a

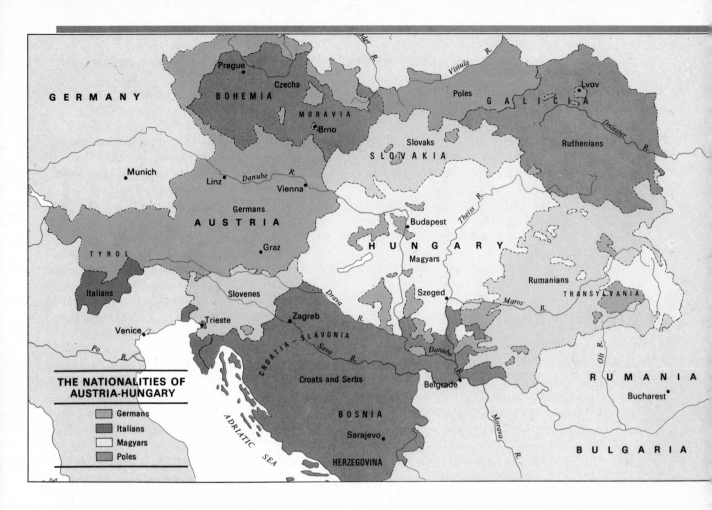

THE NATIONALITIES OF
AUSTRIA-HUNGARY

- Germans
- Italians
- Magyars
- Poles

serious problem, and political parties came to be based not on principle but on nationality. Each nationality had to work with the Germans, even though it might detest them. The nationalities frequently disliked one another, and this prevented the formation of any coalitions among them. By 1914 the Austrians had extended their subject nationalities substantial local self-government, but this concession did little to quiet discontent.

The *Ausgleich* functioned poorly, yet its defenders could still tell themselves that they were, after all, citizens of a "great" empire. The Dual Monarchy occupied a strategic geographical location and had enough military strength to be very influential in the Balkans. In addition, the area had great economic potential with Hungarian wheat, Croatian and Slovenian livestock, Prague banks and industry, and Vienna commerce. But Franz Joseph ruled over a disjointed conglomeration of peoples whose economic and political strength could not compare with that of Germany or even France.

Modern Cultural Responses

After the middle of the nineteenth century, artists and writers reponded to the new age in the realist movement. Artists, especially the French, who were among the most notable early proponents of realism, focused on the concrete aspects of life. From the end of the century until and beyond 1914 the artistic community experimented with a range of new forms and structures in the modernist movement. At the same time that these movements were developing, a huge new group of consumers, the lower and middle classes, were becoming participants in the new mass culture. They might find little to admire in the fine arts, but through their buying power and their numbers, they would come to have a great effect on some parts of the creative community.

Realism

In literature and art as in politics, realism replaced romanticism after midcentury. To the realists it was no longer enough to be true to one's instincts and emotions. Now they must faithfully observe and graphically report all aspects of life in a dispassionate, precise manner in order to depict individuals in their proper setting. In this age of change, there was much for writers and artists to portray, and a much larger public now had the leisure time and political interests to respond to their works.

The trend towards the realistic novel had been foreshadowed in the work of Honoré de Balzac (1799–1850), the author of the ninety-volume *La Comédie Humaine (The Human Comedy)*, which depicts French life in the first half of the nineteenth century. Balzac, a master of characterization, described life in such detail that his work is a valuable reference on social history for twentieth-century scholars. Gustave Flaubert (1821–1880) was the first French realist writer. His masterpiece, *Madame Bovary* (1856), exhaustively described how the boredom of a young romantic provincial wife led her into adultery, excess, and ultimately, suicide.

British novelist Charles Dickens (1812–1870) protested social conditions in his works characterizing the everyday life of the middle classes and poor. In such works as *Oliver Twist* (1838), *Dombey and Son* (1847–1848), and *Hard Times* (1854), he describes some of the worst excesses of industrial expansion and social injustice. Later, in novels such as *Far from the Madding Crowd* (1874) Thomas Hardy (1840–1928) dealt with the struggle—almost always a losing one—of the individual against the impersonal, pitiless forces of the natural and social environment.

American writers such as Henry James (1843–1916), Samuel Clemens (1835–1910), and Harriet Beecher Stowe (1811–1896) made important contributions to the realist tradition. James tried to catch the "atmosphere of the mind" through an almost clinical examination of the most subtle details. Clemens, perhaps better known as Mark Twain, used humor and accurate descriptions of the midwest and far west to underscore social injustice. Stowe, through her detailed work in *Uncle Tom's Cabin* (1852), captured the American public's attention and strongly influenced the antislavery movement.

The Russian novelists Leo Tolstoy (1828–1910) and Feodor Dostoevski (1821–1881) produced the most developed presentation of the realistic novel. Tolstoy stripped every shred of glory and glamor from war in his *War and Peace* (1869) and gave an analytical description of the different levels of society. Dostoevski devised a chilling, detailed view of life in St. Petersburg in *Crime and Punishment* (1866), and his *Brothers Karamazov* (1880) offered a painstaking analysis of Russian life during a period of change.

Drama was deeply influenced by realism, as could be seen in the works of the Norwegian Henrik Isben (1828–1906), the Irishman George Bernard Shaw (1856–1950), and the Russian Anton Chekhov (1860–1904). In his *Doll's House* (1879) Ibsen through his exhausting, quiet, tension-filled work assailed marriage without love as being immoral. Though his characters are not heroic in their dimensions, Ibsen captures the quiet desperation of normal life. Shaw used satire and nuance to shock the British public into reassessing their conventional attitudes. Finally, Chekhov's *Cherry Orchard* (1904) showed the changes wrought by emancipation of the serfs on the lives of a gentry family. Lacking obvious plot and action, the play depends on portrayal of detail to build a subtle, exhausting tension.

Modernism

Romanticism broke the classical forms and opened the way for diversity in forms, styles, and themes. Romantics followed their emotions, while realists advocated a more objective way of portraying the world by stressing accuracy and precision. By the end of the century a new movement—modernism—fragmented, disorganized, and united only in its reaction to the past came to dominate Europe's writers, artists, and musicians.

Modernism freed the writer from all rules of composition and form and obligations to communicate to a large audience. Poetry was especially affected by this new tendency. Toward the end of the century, in reaction to the demands of realism, French poets Stéphane Mallarmé (1842–1898) and Paul Verlaine (1844–1896) inaugurated the symbolist movement. Poetry rather than prose best fit the symbolists' goal of conveying ideas by suggestion rather than by precise, photographic word-pictures.

In a sense, all modern literature stems from the symbolist movement. By increasing the power of the poet to reach the readers' imagination through expanded combinations of allusions, symbols, and double meanings, symbolism gave new life to the written word. But in exploring new poetic realms and possibilities, the symbolists left behind the majority of readers who had been trained to see clarity, precision, simplicity, and definition as positive aspects of literature.

Modernism freed painters from the need to communicate surface, photographic reality. Gustave Courbet (1819–1877) consciously dropped all useless adornments and instead boldly painted the life of the world in which he lived. He was soon surpassed by his countrymen who became preoccupied with problems of color, light, and atmosphere. Artists such as Claude Monet (1840–1926), Edouard Manet (1832–1882), Edgar Degas (1834–1917), Mary Cassatt (1845–1926), and Pierre Auguste Renoir (1841–1919) tried to catch the first impression made by a scene or an object on the eye, undistorted by intellect or any subjective attitude. They were called impressionists and worked in terms of light and color rather than solidity of form.

The impressionists found that they could achieve a more striking effect of light by placing one bright area of color next to another without any transitional tones. The also found that shadows could be shown not as gray but as colors complementary to those of the objects casting the shadow. At close range an impressionist painting may seem little more than a splotch of unmixed colors, but at a proper distance the eye mixes the colors and allows a vibrating effect of light and emotion to emerge. The impresssionists' techniques helped revolutionize art.

One of the weaknesses of the impressionists' work was that they sacrificed much of the clarity of the classical tradition to gain their effects. Paul Cezanne (1839–1903) addressed that problem. He tried to simplify all natural objects by stressing their essential geometric structure. He believed that everything in nature corresponded to the shape of a cone, cylinder, or sphere. Proceeding from this theory, he was able to get below the surface and give his objects the solidity that had eluded the impressionists, yet he kept the impressionists' striking use of color.

The Dutch artist Vincent van Gogh (1853–1890) pursued his own style of using short strokes of heavy pigment, which accentuated the underlying forms and rhythms of his subjects. He achieved intensely emotional results, as he was willing to distort what he saw to communicate the sensations he felt. His short life of poverty and loneliness was climaxed by insanity and suicide.

Before 1914 other modernist inspired forms emerged. French artist Henri Matisse (1869–1954) painted what he felt about an object, rather than just the object itself. He had learned to simplify form partly from his study of African primitive art and the color schemes of oriental carpets. The Spanish artist Pablo Picasso (1881–1974) and others helped develop the school called cubism. Cubists would choose an object, then construct an abstract pattern from it, giving the opportunity to view it simultaneously from several points. Such a pattern is evident in Picasso's *Three Musicians* (1921).

Pablo Picasso painted *Three Musicians* in the summer of 1921.

Music

After midcentury, Johannes Brahms (1833–1897), Anton Bruckner (1824–1896), and Gustav Mahler (1860–1911) built on the momentum of forces that Beethoven had set in motion and made lyrical advances in composition and presentation. Each made unique use of the large symphony orchestra, and Brahms also composed three exquisite string quartets.

In addition, many composers turned to their native folk music and dances for inspiration. Beethoven had used native themes as had Schubert and Schumann in Austria and Germany. Frederick Chopin (1810–1849), even though he did most of his work in France, drew heavily on Polish folk themes for his mazurkas and polonaises. Jean Sibelius (1865–1957) in Finland, Anton Dvořák (1841–1904) and Bedrich Smetana (1824–1884) in Bohemia-Moravia, and Russians Peter Ilich Tchaikovsky (1840–1893), Modest Moussorgsky (1835–1881), and Sergei Rachmaninov (1873–1943) all incorporated folk music in their work. This use of folk themes was aesthetically satisfying and pleasing to the audiences.

Romanticism and nationalism, plus the increasing number of enthusiasts, sparked developments in operas during the century. In his fervid Germanic works, Richard Wagner (1813–1883) infused old Teutonic myths and German folklore with typically romantic characteristics such as emphasis on the supernatural and the mystical. Wagner's *Ring* cycle was the culmination of a long and productive career. His descendants still manage the *Festspielhaus*, a theater in Bayreuth, Germany, that he designed and his admirers financed.

The greatest operatic composer of the century was Giuseppi Verdi (1813–1901) who composed such masterpieces as *Aida, Rigoletto, Il Trovatore, La Forza del Destino*, and many others. His operas, along with those of Wagner, form the core of most of today's major opera house repertoires.

Modernism affected music, such as it had affected poetry and art. The French composer Claude Debussy (1862–1918) tried in his music to imitate what he read in poetry and saw in impressionist paintings. He engaged in "tone painting" to achieve a special mood or atmosphere. This device can be seen in his *Prélude à l'aprés-midi d'un faune (Prelude to the Afternoon of a Faun)*, which shocked the musical world when it was first performed in 1892. The impressionist painters had gained their effects by juxtaposing widely different colors. The composers juxtaposed widely separate chords to create similarly brilliant, shimmering effects.

The music world rarely dealt with social problems or harsh realism. Its supporters were by and large the newly ascendant middle classes who had benefitted from the economic growth triggered by industrialization. They used the wealth derived from their commercial prosperity to finace the building of new opera and symphony halls and maintain the composers and orchestras. Major soloists were the idols of their day, as they showed their virtuosity in compositions that made use of romantic subject matter infused with sentiment and, not infrequently, showmanship. The drew capacity audiences of contented listeners.

Popular Culture

The urban working and lower middle classes began to be important consumers of the popular cultural products of their countries. With increasing literacy these classes provided a huge audience for publishers. More leisure time and money enabled them to fill the music halls and public sporting arenas. They would rarely be found in the concert halls, art galleries, or in serious bookstores. Rather they read the penny press and the "dime novel," both of which featured simple vocabulary and easy to follow information and plots. The penny press served many functions: to inform, entertain, and sell goods. Sensationalism, whether the confessions of a "fallen woman" or the account of some adventurer, was the main attraction of the "dime novel." Comic strips first appeared in central Europe in the 1890s.

There was a level of literature between "great" novels and the penny press, and that was the comforting literature such as the works of Scottish author Samuel Smiles (1812–1904). Smiles' *Self Help* (1859) sold 20,000 copies its first year and 130,000 in the following thirty years. Titles of Smiles' other works—*Thrift, Character*, and *Duty*—form a catalog of Victorian virtues. In the

United States, Horatio Alger (1834–1899) wrote over a hundred novels following similar themes: virtue is rewarded, the good life will win out in the struggle with temptation, and the heroes—usually poor but purehearted youths—will come to enjoy wealth and high honor.

A number of technological advances—coated celluloid film, improved shutter mechanisms, reliable projectors, and a safe source of illumination—were combined to introduce the cinema, or the movies, to the world. These developments seem to have come together almost simultaneously in France, Britain, and the United States. The first public moving picture performances took place in Paris in 1895 and soon after in London and New York. Even though another twenty years passed before feature-length films were produced, movies proved to be an immediate success, attracting an infinitely larger audience than live performances could ever reach.

Sports, including football—in its North American and European forms—bicycle racing, cricket, baseball, and boxing, captured the popular imagination. Pierre de Coubertin (1863–1937) revived the Olympic games of ancient Greece in 1896 in Athens. Thirteen nations took part in an event that instantly caught the international public's imagination.[12]

In the new society of early twentieth-century Europe, the popular culture of mass literature, movies, and sports played as important a role as did high culture. In a simpler way, purveyors of popular culture communicated values and lessons that bound a nation together much more than did the serious writers and artists of the age. The gulf between "high" and "popular" culture has yet to be bridged.

Conclusion

In the latter half of the nineteenth century, workers and the middle classes entered the public arena, the first group struggling, with the help of the socialist parties, for just treatment in the modern, industrial world and the second profiting from their advantaged positions in society. Both groups pressed the state structures to respond to their demands. Strengthened by increased tax revenues and improved technology, the governments of Europe expanded their scope and influence, while providing an outlet for public opinion.

By the beginning of the twentieth century, Britain and Germany were the most powerful states in Europe. Both countries made the necessary adjustments to the new economic and social forces generated by industrialization to build state structures based on mass democratic participation. France and Russia recovered from defeats in wars in 1871 and 1856 to reform and rebuild their state structures. Emerging from the ruins of the Franco-Prussian War, the French Third Republic endured serious class conflict and the Boulanger and Dreyfus affairs to become the strongest republic in Europe. Russia tried reform, but after the assassination of Alexander II reverted to its traditional reactionary stance until the 1905 Revolution. Despite the unfortunate Nicholas II, the country made considerable strides by 1914. Both Italy and Austria-Hungary faced overwhelming problems, and neither state could compete with the four largest powers.

At all levels of European society, life-styles, aesthetic standards, and the means for self-expression changed dramatically by the end of the nineteenth century. Cultural activities were no longer the sole preserve of the élite and elect, all of whom shared a common classical conception of "good" and "bad." At the end of the century, cultural activities were as fragmented and diverse as was the European world. The classicism of the eighteenth century at least had the advantage of unifying the participants in cultural activities. By 1900, in art, music, poetry, prose, and architecture it would have been difficult to gain a consensus between the artist and the audience on what was "good" and "bad."

Never before had the creators of poetry, art, prose, music, and architecture had a greater opportunity to communicate to such a large audience. The cinema and vastly increased publishing facilities held out great opportunity to artists and writers. Unfortunately, by the end of the century the modernist writers, artists, and musicians were seemingly able to communicate only with a finely trained élite. In a sense, what was needed was a new series of classical definitions, forms, and functions upon which all could agree. But the romantic drive to individualism, which came to full flower in the century, made that impossible. Even today, the vast gulf between "mass culture" and the "fine arts" continues to grow.

Suggestions for Reading

In the immense number of works dealing with Karl Marx, the following are clear and valuable introductions for the student: I. Berlin, *Karl Marx: His Life and Environment* (Oxford, 1963); George Lichtheim, *Marxism* (Praeger, 1961); and Alexander Balinky, *Marx's Economics* (Heath, 1970). A well-written and penetrating biography of Lenin is L. Fischer, *The Life of Lenin* (Harper & Row, 1965).

D. Thomson, *England in the Nineteenth Century, 1815–1914* (Penguin, 1964) and J. Conacher, ed., *The Emergence of Parliamentary Democracy in Britain in the Nineteenth Century* (Wiley, 1971) are valuable brief accounts. See also F. Ensor, *England, 1870–1914* (Oxford, 1936); G. Kitson Clark, *The Making of Victorian England* (Atheneum, 1967); George M. Young, *Victorian England, Portrait of an Age* (Galaxy, 1954); P. Magnus, *Gladstone* (Dutton, 1954); and Robert Blake *Disraeli* (Anchor, 1969). G. Dangerfield's *The Strange Death of Liberal England 1910–1914* (Capricorn, 1935) describes the inability of the Liberals to deal with major problems.

D. W. Brogan, *The French Nation: From Napoleon to Pétain* (Colophon, 1957) is a good survey. See also B. Gooch, *The Reign of Napoleon III* (Rand McNally, 1970); D. Thomson, *Democracy in France Since 1870* (Oxford, 1946); Stewart Edwards, *The Paris Commune, 1871* (Quadrangle, 1970); and Douglas Johnson, *France and the Dreyfus Affair* (Walker). See also John McManners, *Church and State in France, 1870–1914* (Harper & Row, 1972). Eugen Weber, *Peasants into Frenchmen* (Univ. of California, 1976) and T. Zeldin, *France: 1848–1945* (Oxford, 1973–1975) are two brilliant, conflicting social surveys.

Michael Balfour, *The Kaiser and His Times* (Houghton Mifflin, 1964) describes the impact of William II on Germany and Europe. See also A. Rosenberg, *Imperial Germany: The Birth of the German Republic, 1871–1918* (Oxford, 1970). F. Stern's *Gold and Iron* (Vintage, 1979) is a fascinating study of the interaction of capital and politics.

Events in Russia have been thoroughly studied in L. H. Haimson, ed., *The Politics of Rural Russia: 1905–1914* (Indiana, 1979); Philip Pomper, *Sergei Nechaev* (Rutgers, 1979); D. W. Treadgold, *The Great Siberian Migration* (Princeton, 1957); Paul Avrich, *The Russian Anarchists* (Norton, 1978); A. Yarmolinsko, *The Road to Revolution* (Collier, 1962); and B. D. Wolfe, *Three Who Made a Revolution* (Beacon, 1974). A fine collection of translation documents giving a first-hand view of the huge changes Russia underwent at this time is G. L. Freeze, *From Supplication to Revolution* (Oxford, 1988).

A notion of the complexity of the nationalities question in the Habsburg realm can be found in the chapters of P.

F. Sugar and I. Lederer, eds., *Nationalism in Eastern Europe* (Univ. of Washington, 1969). C. E.Shorske's *Fin de Siècle Vienna: Politics and Culture* (Vintage, 1981) is a classical intellectual history of the Dual Monarchy in its decline. Jorg K. Hoensch discusses Hungary's motivations and programs in chapter 2 of *A History of Modern Hungary* (Longman, 1988). Christopher Seton-Watson's *Italy from Liberalism to Fascism: 1870–1925* (Methuen, 1967) is clear and concise.

Useful guides to nineteenth-century cultural developments are D. S. Mirsky, *A History of Russian Literature* (Vintage, 1958); H. L. C. Jaffe, *The Nineteenth and Twentieth Centuries*, Vol. 5, *The Dolphin History of Painting* (Thames and Hudson, 1969); C. Edward Gauss, *The Aesthetic Theories of French Artists: From Realism to Surrealism* (Johns Hopkins, 1949); and H. C. Colles, *Ideals of the Nineteenth and Twentieth Century*, Vol. 3, *The Growth of Music* (Oxford, 1956).

Notes

1. Charles Tilly, "Reflections on the History of European State-Making," in Charles Tilly, ed., *The Formation of National States in Western Europe* (Princeton: Princeton Univ. Press, 1975), p. 15.
2. Leszek Kolakowski, *Main Currents of Marxism*, Vol. 2., P. S. Falla, trans. (Oxford: Oxford Univ. Press, 1978), p. 1.
3. J. H. Plumb, "The Victorians Unbuttoned," *Horizon*, XI, n. 4, 1969, pp. 16–25. See also S. Marcus, *The Other Victorians: A Study of Sexuality and Pornography in Mid-Nineteenth Century England*, (New York: Basic Books, 1966.)
4. Edward H. Reisner, *Nationalism and Education Since 1789* (New York: Macmillan, 1923), pp. 35, 145, 211.
5. Robert Schnerb, "Le XIXe Siècle: L'Apogée de L'Expansion Européene (1815–1914)," *Histoire Générale des Civilisations*, Vol. 6 (Paris: Presses Universitaires de France, 1955), p. 235.
6. Gabriel Ardant, "Financial Policy and Economic Infrastructure of Modern States and Nations," in Charles Tilly, ed., *The Formation of National States in Western Europe* (Princeton: Princeton Univ. Press, 1975), pp. 219–222.
7. Quoted in F. Owen, *Tempestuous Journey: Lloyd George, His Life and Times* (London: Hutchinson, 1954), p. 186.
8. Emmeline Pankhurst, *My Own Story* (New York: Source Book Press, 1970), *passim*.
9. Quoted in C. G. Robinson, *Bismarck* (London: Constable, 1918), p. 472.
10. Quoted in Basil Dmystryshyn, ed., *Imperial Russia: A Source Book, 1700–1917* (New York: Holt, Rinehart, & Winston, 1967), p. 241.
11. Hans Rogger, *Russia in the Age of Modernisation and Revolution: 1881–1917* (London: Longman, 1988), pp. 243–247.
12. Schnerb, pp. 468–469.

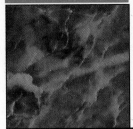

Chapter 26

The Foundations of European Global Dominance

The word *imperialism* has come to mean many things to many people. Broadly speaking, the term refers to the extension of authority or control, whether direct or indirect, of one nation over another. But we use the term *imperialism* in a more restricted sense to refer to the period from 1870 to 1914 when western Europe, which controlled much of the world's finance, commerce, military power, and intellectual life, extended its power over many of the peoples of the world.

As we will see in the next three chapters, Europeans gained control over most of Asia, Africa, and the Americas in the nineteenth century. They achieved their domination by sending their people to settle, their armies to conquer, or their merchants to trade.

Scientific and economic superiority harnessed to efficient state structures provided the strength for the European expansion and domination. The nations of western Europe justified their imperialism with a number of rationalizations. Imperialism was variously defended as an attempt to spread civilization, to bring Christianity to the "heathen," and to introduce progress to the "less fortunate." Some inventive thinkers distorted scientific discoveries and theories to devise self-serving arguments for the supposed inevitability and eternal nature of their dominance.

Not all Europeans approved. Some observers saw in Europe's inability to deal with the rivalry surrounding the exploitation of the Ottoman empire a portent of approaching disaster. Some critics warned that the imperialistic rush was the prelude to the capitalist world's death struggle.

Scientific Superiority

Europe's world dominance in basic scientific research began with Copernicus in the 1500s and extended through the nineteenth century. The major difference between sixteenth-century work and modern discoveries was that the effects of the latter research had almost immediate and widespread economic and intellectual implications.

Darwin and Evolution

In the mid-nineteenth century Charles Darwin (1809–1892) formulated a major scientific theory in *On the Origin of Species by Means of Natural Selection* (1859). This theory of evolution, stating that all complex organisms developed from simple forms through the operation of natural causes, challenged traditionalist Christian beliefs on creation and altered views on life on earth. The theory contended that no species is fixed and changeless. Classical thinkers first stated this view, and contemporary philosophers such as Hegel had used the concept of evolutionary change. In the century before Darwin, other research supported the concept of change, both biological and social.

Darwin built on the work of Sir Charles Lyell (1797–1875) and Jean Baptiste Lamarck (1744–1829) when he began his investigations. Lyell's three-volume *Principles of Geology* (1830–1833) confirmed the views of the Scottish geologist James Hutton (1726–1797), who stated that the earth developed through natural rather than supernatural causes. Lyell helped popularize the notion of geological time operating over a vast span of years. This understanding is essential to the acceptance of any theory of biological evolution, based as it is on changes in species over many thousands of generations. Lamarck, a naturalist, argued that every organism tends to develop new organs to adapt to the changing conditions of its environment. He theorized that these changes are transmitted by heredity to the descendants, which are thereafter changed in structural form.

Though he had originally studied medicine at Edinburgh and prepared for the ministry at Cambridge University, Darwin lost interest in both professions and became a naturalist in his twenties. From 1831 to 1836 he studied the specimens he had collected while on a five-year surveying expedition aboard the ship *Beagle*, which had sailed along the coast of South America and among the Galapagos Islands. The works of his predecessors, plus questions that he had about the theories of Thomas Robert Malthus, as presented in Malthus' *Essay on Population*, helped him define the problem he studied. When Darwin's book finally appeared, it changed many basic scientific and social assumptions.

In his revolutionary work, Darwin constructed an explanantion of how life evolves that upset the literal interpretation of the Bible taught in most Christian churches.

> *... Species have been modified, during a long course of descent ... chiefly through the natural selection of numerous successive, slight, favorable variations; aided in an important manner ... by the direct action of external conditions, and by variations which seem to us in our ignorance to arise spontaneously.*[1]

His explanation radically affected the views of the scientific community about the origin and

THE MODERN THEORY OF THE DESCENT OF MAN.

In *The Descent of Man* (1871), Charles Darwin theorized that humans evolved from lower life forms. Using Darwin's theory, Ernst Haeckel prepared this schematic history of the process of evolution showing the progression from the simplest single-cell organisms to present-day human beings.

Gregor Johann Mendel. Mendel's experiments on the formation and development of hybrids laid the foundation for modern biological research.

evolution of life on the planet. The hypothesis, in its simplified form, states that all existing plant and animal species are descended from earlier and, generally speaking, more primitive forms. The direct effects of the environment causes species to develop through the inheritance of minute differences in individual structures. As the centuries passed, the more adaptable, stronger species lived on, while the weaker, less flexible species died out. Additionally, a species may also be changed by the cumulative working of sexual selection, which Darwin saw to be the "most powerful means of changing the races of man."

After the announcement of Darwin's theories, others, such as the German biologist August Weismann (1834–1914) and the Austrian priest Gregor Mendel (1822–1884), worked along similar lines to explore the genetic relationships among living organisms. Weismann proved that acquired characteristics cannot be inherited. Mendel's investigations into the laws of heredity, based on his experiments with the crossing of garden peas, proved to be invaluable in the

scientific breeding of plants and animals and demonstrated that the evolution of different species was more complex than Darwin had concluded. Based on their work, biologists hypothesized that there are chromosomes that carry the characteristics of an organism. Darwin had hinted at and now further research supported the mutation theory, which states that sudden and un-predictable changes within a chromosome can be transmitted by heredity to produce new species. Scientists began to work with the very fundamental building blocks of life, establishing the groundwork of contemporary biotechnical research.

Darwin and his colleagues carefully researched and cautiously stated their findings. Unlike earlier discoveries however, their work came to be widely reported in popular journals and applied by commentators and politicians. The newly ascendant middle classes responded enthusiastically to their understanding of evolutionary theory, finding in it a comfortable reassurance of their own upward mobility and Europe's dominance in the world.

Medicine, Chemistry, and Physics

Important advances in medicine, chemistry, and physics contributed to a population explosion on the continent and had significant economic implications, further strengthening the bases of Europe's dominance. At the beginning of the nineteenth century, medical practices were making the slow transition from the use of leeches and bleeding. By 1900, fairly sophisticated and much safer surgical procedures were available. In the 1840's, physicians began to use ether and chloroform to reduce pain during operations. The Scottish surgeon Joseph Lister (1827–1912) developed new antiseptic practices that made major advances against the spread of infection. Probably the most important single advance came with the substantiation of the germ theory of disease by Louis Pasteur (1822–1895) and Robert Koch (1843–1910). During his search for a cure to anthrax—a disease that in the late 1870s destroyed over 20 percent of the sheep in France—pasteur established the principle that the injection of a mild form of disease bacterium will cause the body to form antibodies that will prevent the vaccinated individual from

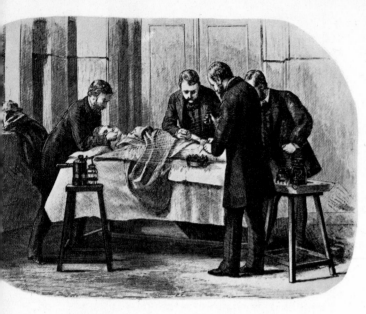

This 1882 engraving shows the Lister carbolic spray being used as an antiseptic as the surgeons perform an operation.

getting the severe form of the particular disease. Koch discovered the specific organisms that caused eleven diseases, including tuberculosis. The work of Pasteur and Koch placed the sciences of bacteriology and immunology on a firm footing and gave promise that the end of such deadly diseases as typhoid and smallpox might be in sight.

Modern chemistry gained its foundations during the ninteenth century, founded on the atomic theory advanced by an English Quaker schoolmaster, John Dalton (1766–1844). In 1869 the Russian chemist Dmitri Mendeleev (1834–1907) drew up a periodic table in which all known elements were classified according to their weights and properties. From gaps in this table, chemists were able to deduce the existence of undiscovered elements. Other researchers made advances in the field of nutrition, discovering significance of vitamins. Biochemical research threw light on the presence and function of the ductless glands. Chemotherapy advanced with the discovery of a chemical that could destroy the syphilis bacteria and of procedures that woud lead to the discovery of sulfa drugs, penicillin, and other antibiotics.

Revolutionary strides in physics came in the areas of electricity and thermodynamics, of which the First Law was formulated in 1847. Michael Farady (1791–1867) prepared the way for the dynamo, a device that made possible changes in communications, the transmission of current over long distances, and the development of the electric motor. The Scottish scientist James Clerk Maxwell (1831–1879) and the German Heinrich Hertz (1857–1894) conducted basic research into the nature of electromagnetic phenomena such as light, radiant heat, and ultraviolet radiation.

Pierre (1859–1906) and Marie (1867–1934) Curie made major strides toward the discovery of the X-ray and radioactivity. When they extracted radium from uranium ore in 1896 the scientific world became aware of the strength of radioactivity. Marie Curie was the first person to be awarded two Nobel prizes, one in physics and one in chemistry.

At the beginning of the twentieth century, the British physicist Ernest Rutherford (1871–1937) helped develop the electron theory. It had been postulated that the atom contains particles known as electrons. Rutherford contributed the idea that each atom has a central particle, or nucleus, that is positively charged and separate from the negatively charged electrons. These discoveries destroyed one of the foundations of traditional physics—that matter is indivisible and continuous.

New Certainties

The territory opened up by the scientists seemed to complement the global claims of the imperialists. The optimism generated by science in the laboratory and Europe's advance across the globe supported the commonly-held belief in inevitable progress. It also buttressed the theories of a new breed of social scientists known as the positivists. Positivism is a mechanistic way of though that uses the methods and principles of science to define the laws of a strictly material world that presumably may be scientifically verified.

Auguste Comte (1798–1857), an engineer who was formerly secretary to Saint-Simon (see p. 651), established the foundations for the philosophical approach known as positivism in a series of lectures and publications in the 1830s and 1840s. He stated that one could find and verify the laws that controlled society in the same way that a scientist discovered physical laws. For Comte humanity was a part of a machine, possessing neither free will nor a divinely infused spark of life. Comte's goal was to understand the machine and to devise a science to discover the laws of history and society. He developed the social science of sociology and stated that once humanity could base itself on science, and not on opinion, harmony would arise.

Darwin's hypotheses were very attractive to the positivists, who, along with their imitators, distorted the British scientist's findings by applying them to areas Darwin never dreamed of discussing—human social, economic, and political activities—to justify the fantasies of eternal progress, the dominance of science, the perfectibility of humanity through obedience to the supposedly unchanging laws of society, and the assumption of Anglo-Saxon racial dominance. The Social Darwinists, positivists, and others of their kind followed a simplistic approach to the world based on their comforting belief that humanity is a cog in a machine and that the possibilities of individuals are predetermined by their place in the larger scheme of things.

Auguste Comte. Comte developed the theory of positivism, according to which science is totally objective and value-free.

William Graham Sumner on Socialism

The nineteenth century was the prime age of the "fit." Darwin's scientific theories were applied to, among other things, political theory. William Graham Sumner saw socialism as retrograde.

The origin of socialism, which is the extreme development of the sentimental philosophy, lies in the undisputed facts which I described at the outset. The socialist regards this misery as the fault of society. He thinks that we can organize society as we like and that an organization can be devised in which poverty and misery shall disappear. He goes further even than this. He assumes that men have artificially organized society as it now exists. Hence if anything is disagreeable or hard in the present state of society, it follows, on that view, that the task of organizing society has been imperfectly and badly performed, and that it needs to be done over again. These are the assumptions with which the socialist starts, and many socialists seem also to believe that if they can destroy belief in an Almighty God who is supposed to have made the world such as it is, they will then have overthrown the belief that there is a fixed order in human nature and human life which man can scarcely alter at all, and, if at all, only infinitesimally.

The truth is that the social order is fixed by laws of nature precisely analogous to those of the physical order. The most that man can do is by ignorance and self-conceit to mar the operation of social laws.

From William Graham Sumner, *The Challenge of Facts*, 1914.

The most popular Social Darwinist was the English philosopher Herbert Spencer (1820–1903), who applied Darwin's theories to all aspects of human social and political life. Spencer had a deep influence in both Europe and the United States. As a convenient doctrine to justify the actions and philosophies of those newly arrived at the top of the social and political structure, Social Darwinism dominated Western social thought in the late nineteenth century.

Stressing the role of change and chance in nature, the broadly applied Darwinian theory reinforced the trend away from absolute standards and procedures. The American physicist Charles Sanders Peirce (1839–1914) broke new philosophical ground in this area. In the late 1890s, William James (1842–1910) popularized Peirce's approaches in his philosophy of pragmatism. James stated that "an idea is true so long as to believe it is profitable to our lives." In effect, the pragmatists rejected any concept of truth or reality as an absolute and favored a more flexible, result-oriented approach.

New Identities

The rapid political, social, economic, and intellectual changes that shook Europe and the world led to new ways of defining individuals and groups. Even before Darwin publicized his theory of evolution, pseudoscientists such as Joseph Arthur de Gobineau (1816–1882) laid the foundations of modern racism, justifying the domination of one group over another for "scientific" reasons. Gobineau applied biological theory to politics, regarding nations as organisms. He argued that different races are innately unequal in ability and worth and that the genius of a race depended upon heredity, not external factors. Gobineau stated a widely held belief among Europeans that white peoples alone were capable of cultural creativity and that intermixture with other races would destroy that creativity. Social Darwinist arguments and Gobineau's theories in support of white superiority gave "rational" justifications to blatant bigotry and provided a reassuring sanction for European domination over Asians and Africans.

Supported by the new pseudoscience and the belief that Europeans alone bore the burdens of progress, European nationalism took on a more

William James. In 1875, at Harvard University, James established the first laboratory of experimental psychology in the United States.

blatant and bellicose form. Aggressive nationalism was adhered to almost as a religion; it served as a powerful vehicle for politicians to mobilize their constituents. Nationalistic pressures became especially strong in eastern Europe and the Balkans, where political instability and economic underdevelopment created insecure conditions.

One of the manifestations of the identities was the Anglo-Saxon movement. In Britain and Germany writers and speakers presented the case for the superiority of northern Europeans. They stated that world leadership should naturally reside in London and Berlin because the people living there possessed the proper combination of religion, racial qualities, and culture to dictate the world's future. People as diverse as Kaiser William II and U.S. president Woodrow Wilson were affected by this outlook.

Another manifestation of a regrouping on the basis of new principles came with the so-called pan-cultural movements. Pan-Slavic movements had begun before 1850. These were based either around the Orthodox Slavs' foundation in Moscow or the Catholic Slavs' center at Prague.

Houston Stewart Chamberlain on the Characteristics of the German Race

Houston Stewart Chamberlain had no doubts about the superiority of the Germans. His views found their way into Hitler's beliefs.

Let us attempt a glance into the depths of the soul. What are the specific intellectual and moral characteristics of this Germanic race? Certain anthropologists would fain teach us that all races are equally gifted; we point to history and answer: that is a lie! The races of mankind are markedly different in the nature and also in the extent of their gift, and the Germanic races belong to the most highly gifted group, the group usually termed Aryan. Is this human family united and uniform by bonds of blood? Do these stems really all spring from the same root? I do not know and I do not much care; no affinity binds more closely than elective affinity, and in this sense the Indo-European Aryans certainly form a family. . . .

Physically and mentally the Aryans are pre-eminent among all peoples; for that reason they are by right, as the Stagirite expresses it, the lords of the world. Aristotle puts the matter still more concisely when he says, "Some men are by nature free, others slaves"; this perfectly expresses the moral aspect. For freedom is by no means an abstract thing, to which every human being has fundamentally a claim; a right to freedom must evidently depend upon capacity for it, and this again presupposes physical and intellectual power. One may make the assertion, that even the mere conception of freedom is quite unknown to most men. Do we not see the *homo syriacus* develop just as well and as happily in the position of slave as of master? Do the Chinese not show us another example of the same nature? Do not all historians tell us that the Semites and half-Semites, in spite of their great intelligence, never succeeded in founding a State that lasted, and that because every one always endeavoured to grasp all power for himself, thus showing that their capabilities were limited to despotism and anarchy, the two opposites of freedom?

From Houston Stewart Chamberlain, *Foundations of the Ninteenth Century*, 1900.

In the latter part of the century the Russians would use their Pan-Slavic movement to expand their influence into the Balkans in pursuit of their "destiny" to create and rule a great Slavic empire. The Pan-Germanic League was organized in Berlin in the 1890s to spread the belief in the superiority of the German race and culture.

Anti-Semitism—hatred of the Jews—had been a part of European history since the legalization of Christianity. But the movement attained a new strength and vigor in the last part of the nineteenth century. In Germany, the historian Heinrich von Treitschke (1834–1896) stated that "the Jews are our calamity." In France, anti-Semitism played a significant role in the Dreyfus affair (see p. 664). In eastern Europe, the Jews suffered many injustices, while in Russia many Jews died in organized pogroms. Anti-Semitism became stronger because of the economic dislocation that modernization introduced and of the work of bigoted cranks who turned out pseudo-scientific tracts and forgeries such as the *Protocols of the Elders of Zion*.

In response, a desire for a homeland grew among the Jews. In 1896 Theodor Herzl (1860–1904) came forward with the program of Zionism, which had as its purpose the creation of an independent state within Palestine. The first general congress of Zionists was held in Switzerland in 1896 and a small-scale emigration to Palestine, which had been settled for centuries by Arabs, began. In the first decade of the twentieth century, the election of Karl Leuger (1844–1910), who ran and stayed in power on an anti-Semitic platform, as mayor of Vienna, fore-told the tragic genocide that would occur later in the century. It was in this atmosphere that the young Adolf Hitler spent some of his formative years, reading racist, Social Darwinist, and Pan-Germanic tracts.

Christianity and the Modern Age

Europe's drive to dominate the globe came from a variety of sources. The belief in scientific superiority and the arguments of the pseudo-scientists and racists provided some of the motivation for expansion. Another motivator was the Christian churches, which were themselves experiencing the challenges posed by industrialization and urbanization.

After the Reformation, Christianity endured serious intellectual, political, and social challenges. The Scientific Revolution and the Enlightenment ate away at the authority of the traditional church. Darwin's theories challenged the traditional Christian view of the origins of the world as presented in the Bible. The population increases that resulted from urbanization forced the church to respond to different audiences facing more difficult problems than those of an earlier, simpler age. Yet Christianity endured and adapted.

The Missionary Thrust

During the age of imperialism, European missionaries went forth in their centuries-old function as self-proclaimed messengers of the word of God. Once the European states began competing for land around the globe, the churches often complemented national policy in their religious work. Buttressed by Social Darwinism and the notion of progress, missionaries felt justified in altering the cultures of the peoples with whom they came in contact if that was the price to be paid for eternal salvation.

Changes in the Catholic Church

In 1864 Pope Pius IX (1846–1878), who had become extraordinarily reactionary after having been expelled from Rome in 1848 and in the wake of the Italian unification movement (see p. 635), issued the *Syllabus of Errors*, a document that attacked the critical examination of faith and doctrine. In 1870 he called a general council of the church to proclaim the doctrine of papal infallibility, which states that when speaking *ex cathedra* (from the chair) on issues concerning religion and moral behavior, the pope cannot err.

Pius' successor, Leo XIII (1879–1903) was more flexible and less combative and helped bring the church into the modern age. In his *Rerum novarum* (Concerning new things) issued in 1891, Leo condemned Marxism and upheld capitalism but

This 1895 cartoon satirizes the missionary mania of the age of imperialism. According to the caption, "The Chinaman *must* be converted even if it takes the whole military and naval forces of the two greatest nations of the world [Great Britain and the United States] to do it."

Pope Leo XIII, Rerum Novarum

Pope Leo XIII responded to the radical changes affecting Europe in his encyclical *Rerum Novarum*, issued May 15, 1891. The document addressed the challenges facing Christians and advised them how to respond. See, for example, Leo's advice on unions.

Associations in immense variety and especially unions of workers are now more common than they have ever been. This is not the place to enquire into the origins of most of them, their aims or the methods they employ. There is plenty of evidence to confirm the opinion that many are in the hands of secret leaders and are used for purposes which are inconsistent with both Christian principles and the social good. They do all that they can to ensure that those who will not join them shall not eat. In this state of affairs Christian workers have but two alternatives: they can join these associations and greatly endanger their religion; or they can form their own and, with united strength, free themselves courageously from such injustice and intolerable oppression. That the second alternative must be chosen cannot be doubted by those who have no desire to see men's highest good put into extreme danger. . . .

High praise is due to the many Catholics who have informed themselves, seen what is needed and tried to learn from experience by what honourable means they might be able to lead unpropertied workers to a better standard of living. They have taken up the workers' cause, seeking to raise the incomes of families and individuals, introduce equity into the relations between workers and employers and strengthen among both groups regard for duty and the teaching of the Gospel—teaching which inculcates moderation, forbids excess and safeguards harmony in the state between very differently situated men and organizations. We see eminent men coming together to learn from each other about these things and unite their forces to deal with them as effectively as possible. Others encourage different groups of workers to form useful associations, advise them, give them practical help and enable them to find suitable and well-paid employment. The bishops offer their goodwill and support. . . .

From Leo XIII, *Rerum Novarum*, translated by Joseph Kirwan (London: Catholic Society, 1983).

severely criticized the evils affecting the working classes. By pointing out some of the Christian elements of socialism, Leo placed the church on the side of the workers who were suffering the greatest ills resulting from industrialization. Leo worked to improve relations with Germany, encouraged the passage of social welfare legislation, and supported the formation of Catholic labor unions and political parties.

A New Spirit

Spiritual life in England received a powerful stimulus from the Oxford Movement. At the beginning of the nineteenth century, a core of spiritual activists at Oxford, including the future Cardinal, John Henry Newman (1801–1890), met to defend the church from the various secular and political forces that were besieging it. During the 1830s the group split, some members remaining within the Anglican church, and others—including Newman—joining the Catholic church. During the rest of the century, the Oxford Movement brought new life to the church in England through its missionary work, participation in social concerns, and improvement of the intellectual level of the faith. Similar developments occurred across the continent.

Economic Bases for Imperialism

The nineteenth century's economic growth brought with it demands for more money and better management. Industrialists came to live or die by their efficiency, and efficiency often meant consolidation. Large firms could make more products at a cheaper cost than small firms, because they could raise the money to buy the resources, install the newest technology, and train and employ more workers. Large firms carried more political clout than did small ones and lobbied for state policies and regulations that favored them. Some firms, such as that of Alfred Nobel (1833–1896), the Swedish industrialist and inventor of dynamite, set up branches in many different countries. Others tried to control an entire market in one country as did the Standard Oil firm of John D. Rockefeller (1839–1937) in the United States. Whatever the strategy, the gigantic firm became the dominant industrial force.

With the need for more capital, firms began to sell stock to the middle classes. Joint stock companies were not new, but they had not been favored, because if an enterprise failed the investors were liable for its debts. Britain, followed by other industrial states, adopted statutes—limited liability laws—that protected investors from business failure. As wealth increased more people began to "play" the stock market.

New Structures

Businesses developed new strategies to gain control of discrete segments of the market. One new development was the *trust*, an arrangement in which a body of trustees held a majority of stock in a given industry and can control wages, prices, and merchandising policies of several companies. Another tactic was the *holding company*, in which a corporation was incorporated to gain the same control as with the less formal trust. In Europe these alliances took the form of huge industrial combinations known as *cartels*. The cartel, often secret, controlled prices and markets in fundamentally important goods such as rubber or steel. The ultimate way to dominate an area of business was the *monopoly*, in which one firm gains control of the total economic cycle of a product.

The new generations of industrialists developed more efficient management methods. American engineer Frederick W. Taylor (1856–1912) devised the scientific management system, which recommended breaking down each stage of the industrial process to its most

Assembling magnetos on the assembly line at the Ford Motor Company plant in Highland Park, Michigan. One worker could assemble a magneto in 29 minutes; 29 workers, properly arranged, could assemble one in 5 minutes.

minute segment and studying the efficiency of each step of work to establish the optimum speed of productivity. New methods such as the use of interchangeable parts and the introduction of the assembly line brought productivity to a high level by 1914. The new structures could satisfy the infinite desires of a world market.

The New World Economy

From the fifteenth through the eighteenth centuries, a large part of Europe had expansionist ambitions. Prevailing mercantilist theories encouraged the seeking of colonies and monopolies in overseas trade. A combination of political and economic factors, however, slowed down the imperialistic drive in the half century after 1815. Britain's desire for empire had been diminished after the loss of the thirteen American colonies in 1783, and France had lost nearly all of its overseas possessions by the end of the Napoleonic wars. In addition, the laissez-faire school of economics argued against the possession of colonies.

France reignited the drive for world empire during Louis Napoleon's reign, and the scramble for colonies heated up after 1870. In his six years as British prime minister, Disraeli annexed Fiji and Cyprus, fought a war against the Zulus in southeastern Africa, purchased controlling interest in the Suez canal shares, and proclaimed Queen Victoria empress of India. The other major powers in greater or lesser degree followed Britain's lead and the race to carve up the globe began in earnest. It has been estimated that in 1800 fully half of the world was not known to Europeans. By 1900 more land had been explored and acquired by them than in the previous four centuries. The nations of the small, northwest peninsula of the Eurasian landmass claimed control of 60 percent of the earth's surface.

In 1914 Great Britain with its far-flung empire was the world's richest nation. Even though it imported more goods than it exported, it earned nearly a billion dollars a year from overseas investments, shipping fees, and banking and insurance services. Germany had become the continent's economic giant. Its population had risen from 41 million to 65 million between 1871 and 1910. Close cooperation between government and private industry paid dividends. The state established protectionist tariffs after 1879, supported technical education, and encouraged industrial cartels. France lagged behind Germany in both population and industrial output, but it was still an economic power.

In the fifty years before World War I, international trade rose from $7 billion to $42 billion. European nations were by and large their own best customers, even with the tariff barriers that were erected on the continent after 1879. Europe became the chief supplier of world capital: Britain invested heavily in its empire and the United States, France made huge loans to Russia, and Germany and England extended large loans to the Ottoman Empire. The European economic primacy was felt in the far corners of the world. Soon the Argentinean *gaucho*, the Australian sheep man, and the American cowboy—each a symbol of the *free man* in the mythology of his own country—were cogs in the global economic machine of constantly circulating raw materials and finished goods.

The international economy tied the world to the rhythms of the booms and busts of Europe. Economic historians differ in their interpretations of the frequency and causes of the stages of economic expansion and contraction in the business cycle. Whether one believes in a ten-year, twenty-year, or century-long cycle, the fact remains that the world became increasingly an extension of Europe's economic changes.[2] The depression that lasted from 1873 to 1896 is symbolic of the impact of economic events in Europe on the world. Overall, prices fell by roughly 30 percent in all products. Around the world, suffering was severe, especially in those areas that depended on shipping raw materials to cities or abroad and that had no control over the price their products could demand. But by 1896, there had been a readjustment, and the period to 1914 was generally prosperous.

Political Implications

The internationalization of the economy placed diplomacy and finances into common harness.

In this 1876 cartoon from *Punch,* Queen Victoria exchanges her royal crown for a new imperial crown proclaiming her empress of India.

"NEW CROWNS FOR OLD ONES!"

The developing countries needed money to compete in the new world economic system. The industrialized countries looked on the rest of the world as a supplier of labor and raw materials, a market for finished goods, and a place for capital investments.

For the creditor, the investments abroad broke into three logical groupings. The lenders could purchase the bonds of strong nations—a safe investment but with a low rate of return. They could make loans to underdeveloped countries—a riskier venture but with a much higher rate of return. Finally, the financial powers could put their money into stable countries that needed capital in specialized areas. This would ensure a good return on a safe investment. Within these categories were many variations, all of which held the promise of a handsome payoff, usually in financial and political terms.

For the debtor, however, loans could be helpful or devastating, depending on the circumstances. The United States was able to get needed capital with a minimum infringement on its sovereignty. The opposite extreme was the case of the Ottoman empire, which received its first loan in 1854. Twenty-two years later the Turks were so deeply in debt that they had to put a major portion of their tax base in foreign hands just to pay the interest. Unlike the Americans, the Turks put just 10 percent of the borrowed funds to productive use. Other countries had similar results. Russia by 1914 had a funded debt of 9 billion rubles, half of which was owed to foreigners. Hungary had to use 10 percent of its gross national product to pay to foreign investors to cover loans and interest in the pre-war period.[3] Foreign investments of this type were just one facet of Europe's financial dominance. Economic control implied a profound political impact on the debtor country and represented the most efficient form of imperialism.

The Failed Test: The Eastern Question

One of the key geopolitical questions facing the Europeans was the Eastern Question: What was to be done about the disintegrating Ottoman Empire. At the beginning of the nineteenth century, the Turks had sovereignty over the strategic eastern Mediterranean and North African regions. However, they did not possess the power to rule this broad realm effectively, and parts of the area were virtual power vacuums. The Eastern Question would test whether Europe's political wisdom had kept pace with its increase in material strength.

The Balkans Awaken

By the end of the eighteenth century, Ottoman power had substantially declined in the Balkans, just at a time when the various peoples began to experience the waves of nationalism. In 1799, Sultan Selim III acknowledged the independence of the mountainous nation of Montenegro, after its long and heroic defense of its liberty. Further proof of Ottoman weakness came in 1804 when some renegade Turkish troops in Belgrade went on a rampage, disobeyed the sultan's orders, and forced the Serbian people to defend themselves. This initial act of self-protection blossomed into a rebellion that culminated, after eleven difficult years, with the Serbs gaining an autonomous position under the Turks.

Turkish weakness attracted both Russian and British interests. Russia had made a substantial advance toward the Mediterranean during the reign of Catherine II. By the Treaty of Küchük Kainarji (1774) the Russians gained the rights of navigation in Turkish waters and the right to intervene in favor of Eastern Orthodox Christians in the Ottoman Empire. The British protested these gains, and in 1791 Prime Minister William Pitt the Younger denounced Russia for its supposed ambitions to dismember Turkey. Only the common threat of Napoleon from 1798 to 1815 diverted Great Britain and Russia from their competition in the eastern Mediterranean.

The forces of nationalism in Greece took advantage of the chaotic administration of the Turks in 1821. Unlike the Serbian rebellion, the Greek revolution gained substantial outside support from Philhellenic societies of Great Britain. Even though Metternich hoped the revolt would burn itself out, the Greeks were able to take advantage of intervention by the great powers to gain their independence.

During the Greek revolt, the British feared that Russia would use the Greek independence movement as an excuse for further expansion at Turkish expense. The British intervened skillfully, and the Greeks were able to gain their independence without a major Russian advance toward the Straits. Tsar Nicholas I wanted to weaken Turkey in order to pave the way for Russia to gain control over the Dardanelles and the Bosporous. So much did he want this expansion of his realm that he set aside his obligations to support the European balance of power. Britain became alarmed at this policy, and the upshot was an agreement in 1827 in which Britain, France, and Russia pledged themselves to secure Greek independence. Russia eventually defeated the Turks, and in 1829 the Treaty of Adrianople gave the Greeks the basis for their independence while Serbia received autonomy (see map below left). The Danubian Principalities of Moldavia and Wallachia, the basis of the future state of Romania, became Russian protectorates.

By the 1830s it became apparent that the Turks were to be an object of, rather than a subject in, European diplomacy. The sultan's government had few admirers in Europe, but the European powers agreed—at least for the present—to prop up the decaying Ottoman Empire rather than allow one nation to gain dominance in the strategic area.

In 1832 Mehemet Ali, the virtually independent governor of Egypt, attacked the sultan, easily putting down the forces of the empire. To prevent the establishment of a new and probably stronger government at the Straits, Nicholas I sent an army to protect Constantinople. The Treaty of Unkiar Skelessi (1833) made Turkey a virtual protectorate of Russia.

Britain could not tolerate Russia's advantage, and for the next ten years worked diplomatically to force the tsar to renounce the treaty and sign a general agreement of Turkish independence. This diplomatic game did little to improve the Ottoman Empire's condition. In 1844, while visiting Britain, Nicholas referred to Turkey as a "dying man" and proposed that the British join in a dissection of the body.

The Crimean War

The Crimean War, which lasted from 1853 to 1856, was a major turning point in the course of the Eastern Question. The immediate origins of the war were to be found in a quarrel over the management and protection of the holy places in Palestine. Napoleon III upheld the Roman Catholics' right to perform the housekeeping duties, in a move to gain support from Catholics and the military in France. On the other side, acting under the terms of the treaty signed to Küchük Kainarji in 1774, Nicholas stated that the Orthodox faithful should look after the holy places.

From this obscure argument the Crimean War eventually emerged, as the great powers all intervened in the discussions to protect their interests. The tsarist ambassador to the Turks

THE TREATY OF
ADRIANOPLE 1829

tried to use the dispute to improve Russia's position in the empire while the British told the sultan to stand firm against the Russians. After the Russians occupied the Danubian Principalities in an attempt to show the Turks the seriousness of their demands, the Turks declared war on the Russians in October 1853. By the next summer the French, Sardinians, and British and joined the Turks. Napoleon III saw the war as a chance to enhance his dynasty's reputation, and the Sardinians found an opportunity to gain allies in their drive for Italian unification. Under the impact of anti-tsarist public opinion the British took steps to stop the Russians. The stated aim of all the allies was, of course, the defense of the Sultan.

A combination of the allies' military strength and the tsarist forces' inefficiency stalemated the Russians. Austria, a former close ally of Russia, took advantage of Russia's difficulties to extend Austrian influence into the Balkans.

The Russians sued for peace and the Treaty of Paris (1856) once again attempted to resolve the Eastern Question. The treaty affirmed the integrity of the Ottoman Empire. The Black Sea was to be a neutral body of water, and the Straits were closed to foreign warships. The treaty declared that no power had the right to intervene on behalf of the sultan's Christian subjects. Russian control of the Principalities was ended. The Crimean War momentarily stopped the Russian advance into the Balkans, but the problems posed by the "sick man of Europe" remained. Further, the various Balkans nations became even more inflamed with the desire for self-rule.

The Unanswered Question

In the generation after the Crimean War the problems posed by the disintegrating Ottoman Empire became more severe. To the north, the Russians, who could do little militarily in the Balkans during this period of intense internal reforms, broadcast the message of Pan-Slavic solidarity to their "Orthodox" brothers in the Balkans. The Austrians, appetites whetted by their part in the Crimean War, kept a wary and opportunistic eye on developments in the Balkans. British loans to the Turks cut into the Turkish tax base and led to the destruction of the indigenous Ottoman textile industry. In addition,

with the completion of the Suez Canal in 1869, the eastern Mediterranean came to be even more essential to British interests. Finally, the Germans began to increase their influence in the area after 1871.

Nationalism further inflamed the unresolved Eastern Question. The Bulgarians, who had been under the Turkish yoke since the fourteenth century, started their national revival in the late eighteenth century. By the 1860s they had formed a liberation movement, which was strengthened in 1870 by the founding of the Bulgarian Exarchate, a Bulgarian wing of the Greek Orthodox faith. The Bulgarians took strength from the example of the Romanians, who after centuries of Turkish dominance and a quarter century as a Russian protectorate had gained their independence in 1861, largely as a result of great power influence. Also, during the 1860s the Serbian leader Michael Obrenovich had worked toward a Balkan union against the Turks. Amid this maneuvering and ferment, the Turks were unable to strengthen their rule over areas theoretically under their control.

The crisis came to a head in 1875, when peasants revolted in the district of Bosnia, a Turkish-governed province populated by a religiously diverse group of Slavs. Following this insurrection Serbia and Montenegro declared war on the Turks. In the summer of 1876, the Bulgarians revolted, but the Ottoman forces forcefully put down the rebellion. When highly emotional accounts of the Turkish massacres were published in western Europe, the incident became known as the "Bulgarian horrors" and drew British attention to the Balkans. The Pan-Slav faithful in Moscow and St. Petersburg were naturally thrilled at the exploits of their "little brothers," and money and "volunteers" flowed southward.

The series of nationalistic uprisings in the improperly governed Ottoman provinces had captured the attention of the great powers, and by the end of 1875 the Eastern Question was once again the main focus of international diplomacy. The "sick man of Europe" was still strong enough to devastate the Serbs and Montenegrins in the field. The insurgents were forced to sue for peace, which drew Tsar Alexander II and the Russians into war with Turkey in 1877. After a hard-fought campaign the Russians broke through early in 1878 and were close to achieving their final goal of taking Constantinople, when the sultan sued for peace.

The resulting Treaty of San Stefano in March 1878 recognized the complete independence of Serbia and Romania from the theoretical Ottoman sovereignty and reaffirmed Montenegro's independence. A large Bulgarian state was set up, nominally tributary to Turkey but actually dominated by Russia. The Straits were effectively under Russian control, as the Bulgarian state would have a coast on the Aegean (see map below). The Eastern Question was almost solved.

Britain and Austria, however, correctly perceived a major shift of the balance of power in Russia's favor, and the two of them forced a reconsideration of the San Stefano treaty at the Congress of Berlin in June and July of 1878. Held

under the supervision of Bismarck, the self-styled "honest broker," the congress compelled Russia to agree to a revision of Bulgaria's status. The large state created in March was broken into three parts: the northernmost would be independent, paying tribute to the Turks, while the other two parts would be Turkish controlled. Austria got the right to "occupy and administer" the provinces of Herzegovina and Bosnia (see map below).

The congress turned back the Russian advance, stymied the national independence movement, and did little to impel Turkey to put its house in order. The Austrian gains caused great bitterness among the Serbs and Russians, a mood that added to the tension in the Balkans. The Eastern Question remained unanswered, and the Balkans remained an arena of local

THE TREATY OF SAN STEFANO 1878

▨ Bulgaria as proposed by the Treaty

THE CONGRESS OF BERLIN 1878

▨ Bulgaria as amended by the Congress of Berlin

nationalistic conflicts that would appeal to the imperialistic designs of the great powers, especially the Russians and Austro-Hungarian monarchy.[4]

Conclusion

By 1914 Europe had brought together the material strength, intellectual vitality, and governmental flexibility to dominate the planet. The explosive increase in productivity made possible by industrialization and Europe's massive population growth contributed to the power and personnel to extend economic and political control from the western tip of the Eurasian landmass to the entire world.

In the fields of biology, chemistry, physics, and medicine, European scientists made fundamental discoveries that greatly expanded the frontiers of knowledge. Charles Darwin's work not only upset the understanding of the development of organisms, its popularization had immense, if misdirected social implications. The progress made in economics and science encouraged some Europeans to believe their own superiority and gave them sanction to pursue their destiny. A range of pseudoscientific and racist theories came to be espoused, with terrible consequences.

The Christian faith endured attacks from a number of different quarters during the nineteenth century and made significant changes to respond to new constituents and to play a role in missionary work to the world.

Running like a thread through the century, the Eastern Question, the fate of the disintegrating Ottoman Empire, was transformed from a balance-of-power question to one of small power nationalism and great power expansion. The failure to resolve this question would lead to World War I.

Suggestions for Reading

See Stephen F. Mason, *A History of the Sciences* (Collier, 1962) and Rupert Hall and Marie Boas Hall *A Brief History of Science* (Signet, 1964) for clear and concise surveys of the development of science. The literature on Darwin and his times in voluminous. Darwin's *Origin of Species* and *Voyage of the Beagle* are available in a number of editions. C. C. Gillespie nicely sets the stage for the period in *Genesis and Geology* (Harvard, 1951). G. Himmelfarb's *Darwin and the Darwinian Revolution* (Norton, 1968) and W. Irvine's *Ape, Angels & Victorians: The Story of Darwin, Huxley, & Evolution* (McGraw-Hill, 1955) are excellent studies. R. Hofstadter's *Social Darwinism in American Thought* (Beacon, 1955) is a fascinating study of how a subtle theory can be misapplied. Dubois' *Louis Pasteur: Free Lance of Science* (Little Brown) 1950 is an example of a biography that is sound both as history and literature. J. Bronowski's *The Ascent of Man* (Little, Brown, 1974) is a humane, wise overview of the development of science through the ages.

George F. Mosse provides a valuable overview of intellectual developments during the nineteenth century in *The Culture of Western Europe, the Nineteenth and Twentieth Centuries: An Introduction* (Rand McNally, 1974). Franklin L. Baumer's *Modern European Thought, Continuity and Change in Ideas: 1600–1950* (Macmillan, 1977) is a classic analysis of the development of Western thought and a helpful guide through the nineteenth century.

For background on the factors aiding Europe's expansion abroad, see in addition to suggestions provided in chapter 23; Carl Cipolla, *The Economic History of World Population* (Penguin, 1962); Thomas McKeown, *The Modern Rise of Population* (Academic, 1976); George Lichtheim, *Imperialism* (Praeger, 1971); Heinz Gollwitzer, *Europe in the Age of Imperialism: 1880–1914* (Harcourt Brace Jovanovich, 1979); Roger Price, *The Economic Modernisation of France* (John Wiley, 1975); Sidney Pollard, *European Economic Integration: 1815–1970* (Harcourt, Brace Jovanovich,1974); D. Fieldhouse, *Colonialism: 1870–1945*; (London, 1981); W. J. Mossman, *Theories of Imperialism;* (London, 1981); Alan Hodgart, *The Economics of European Imperialism* (Norton, 1978); G. H. Nadel and P. Curtis, eds., *Imperialism and Colonialism* (Macmillan, 1965).

M. S. Anderson's *The Eastern Question, 1774–1923* (St. Martin's, 1966) is the best treatment of the Balkans dilemma. For the nationalities conflicts in the region see Barbara Jelavich, *History of the Balkans*, I (Cambridge, 1983).

Notes

1. C. Darwin, "The Origin of Species," in *Introduction to Contemporary Civilization in the West*, II (New York: Columbia Univ. Press, 1955), pp. 453–454.
2. David S. Landes, *The Unbound Prometheus: Technological Change and Industrial Development in Western Europe from 1750 to the Present* (Cambridge: Cambridge Univ. Pres, 1969), p. 233.
3. Sidney Pollard, *European Economic Integration: 1815–1970* (New York: Harcourt Brace Jovanovich, 1974), pp. 74–78.
4. See M. S. Anderson, *The Eastern Question, 1774–1923* (New York: St. Martin's Press, 1966), *passim*.

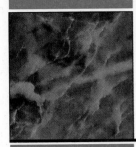

Chapter 27

Europe Transplanted

The British Dominions, the United States, and Latin America

The greatest population movement in history took place between 1500 and 1914, when millions of Europeans crossed the oceans and made new homes for themselves (see map below). At the same time, the slave trade brought vast numbers of Africans to the Americas. These immigrants, whether voluntary or forced, brought with them their languages, religions, cultures, political institutions, and laws.

No matter where they settled—the Americas, South Africa, Australia, and New Zealand—the Europeans faced the same challenges of unexplored lands, racial diversity, isolation, and the search for new identities. The newly ascendant

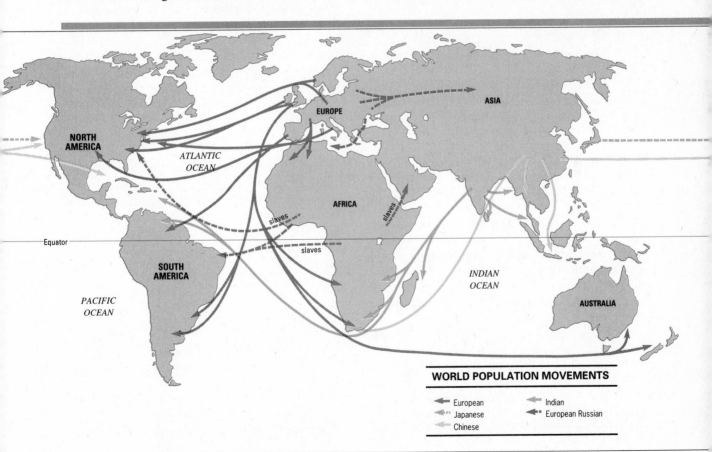

WORLD POPULATION MOVEMENTS

- European
- Japanese
- Chinese
- Indian
- European Russian

middle classes with their generally liberal politics dominated, usually at the expense of the indigenous population or the African slaves.

Although the challenges were the same, the results were unique to each region. Canada, Australia, New Zealand, and the Union of South Africa illustrate the transplantation of British culture to the far corners of the globe. The United States developed the political stability and strong economy that allowed it to grow and prosper, though not without the tragedies of the Civil War, the oppression of its black population, and the devastation of native American culture. Latin America faced fundamental challenges of racial and social diversity, economic exploitation, and political instability.

Common Denominators

In various ways, each of the new lands reflected nineteenth-century movements that had originated in western Europe—nationalism, democracy, and imperialism. In addition, they had problems and opportunities which sprang from conditions specific to their environments. One was the assimilation of the tremendous tide of immigrants entering the new lands. But before the settlers and slaves came, vast spaces had to be explored, paths to the interior mapped, and natural resources located.

Exploration

In what is now Canada, Alexander Mackenzie in 1789 traveled to the Great Slave Lake, then down the river that now bears his name to the shores of the Arctic. Four years later he crossed the Rocky Mountains to the Pacific and thereby became the first European to cross North America at its greatest width.

In the United States, Meriwether Lewis and William Clark started from St. Louis in the winter of 1803–1804, blazed a trail through the unknown Northwest, and reached the Pacific two years later. For a half century the process of exploration and mapping continued, reaching its climax in John Frémont's expeditions to Oregon and California.

The most famous figure in the exploration of South America was the German naturalist Alexander von Humboldt, who from 1799 to 1804 explored Mexico, Cuba, and South America. He investigated the valley of the Orinoco, crossed the Andes, and studied the sources of the Amazon.

The continent of Australia was not crossed from north to south until the middle of the nineteenth century. Between 1860 and 1862 John McDouall Stuart made three attempts before he successfully completed the journey from Adelaide to Van Diemen's Gulf. The penetration of the interior of South Africa differed from explorations in the other new lands. It was achieved by the gradual expansion of white settlement in such movements as the Great Trek rather than by exploratory expeditions.

Immigration

The poor and landless people of Europe settled the vast and often fertile lands found by the explorers. The increase in European population from 200 million to 460 million during the nineteenth century provided the pool of 40 million immigrants who crossed the oceans. By 1914, the number of people of European background living abroad totaled 200 million—a figure almost equal to Europe's population in 1815.

For some 350 years this movement from Europe was accompanied by an equally significant forced migration from West Africa to the Americas. The number transported in the slave trade ran into the millions, and many died from ill treatment at the time of capture and during the forty-day voyage across the Atlantic. This trade cost Africa perhaps 15 million people, not including the Arab slave trade from the East African coast.

Black Africans in the New Lands

In general, the liberal and egalitarian trends in western Europe took root in the new lands. However, the millions of Africans seized and forcibly transplanted to the Americas had little chance to benefit from those ideals.

The slave trade in Latin America began shortly after 1502. Because many native Indians died

A Slave's Memoir

Olaudah Equiano captured the misery of transported slaves in his *Travels*.

One day, when all our people were gone out to their works as usual and only I and my dear sister were left to mind the house, two men and a woman got over our walls, and in a moment seized us both, and without giving us time to cry out or make resistance they stopped our mouths and ran off with us into the nearest wood. Here they tied our hands and continued to carry us as far as they could till night came on, when we reached a small house where the robbers halted for refreshment and spent the night. . . .

The first object which saluted my eyes when I arrived on the coast was the sea, and a slave ship which was then riding at anchor and waiting for its cargo. These filled me with astonishment, which was soon converted into terror when I was carried on board. I was immediately handled and tossed up to see if I were sound by some of the crew, and I was now persuaded that I had gotten into a world of bad spirits and that they were going to kill me. Their complexions too differing so much from ours, their long hair and the language they spoke (which was very different from any I had ever heard) united to confirm me in this belief. Indeed such were the horrors of my views and fears at the moment that, if ten thousand worlds had been my own, I would have freely parted with them all to have exchanged my condition with that of the meanest slave in my own country. When I looked round the ship too and saw a large furnace or copper boiling and a multitude of black people of every description chained together, every one of their countenances expressing dejection and sorrow, I no longer doubted my fate; and quite overpowered with horror and anguish, I fell motionless on the deck and fainted. When I recovered a little I found some black people about me, who I believed were some of those who had brought me on board and had been receiving their pay; they talked to me in order to cheer me, but all in vain. I asked them if we were not to be eaten by those white men with horrible looks, red faces, and loose hair. They told me I was not, and one of the crew brought me a small portion of spirituous liquor in a wine glass, but being afraid of him I would not take it out of his hand. . . .

The stench of the hold while we were on the coast was so intolerably loathsome that it was dangerous to remain there for any time, and some of us had been permitted to stay on the deck for the fresh air; but now that the whole ship's cargo were confined together it became absolutely pestilential. The closeness of the place and the heat of the climate, added to the number in the ship, which was so crowded that each had scarcely room to run himself, almost suffocated us. This produced copious perspirations, so that the air soon became unfit for respiration from a variety of loathsome smells, and brought on a sickness among the slaves, of which many died, thus falling victims to the improvident avarice, as I may call it, of their purchasers. This wretched situation was again aggravated by the galling of the chains, now become insupportable, and the filth of the necessary tubs, into which the children often fell and were almost suffocated. The shrieks of the women and the groans of the dying rendered the whole a scene of horror almost inconceivable. Happily perhaps for myself I was soon reduced so low here that it was thought necessary to keep me almost always on deck, and from my extreme youth I was not put in fetters. . . .

At last we came in sight of the island of Barbados, at which the whites on board gave a great shout and made many signs of joy to us.

From Paul Edwards, ed., *Equiano's Travels: His Autobiography, The Interesting Narrative of the Life of Olaudah Equiano or Gustavus Vassa the African* (London: Heinemann Educational Books, 1967).

from European diseases such as smallpox and measles, the local population could not fill the mounting demand for labor on the plantations. To meet that demand, the influx of black slaves increased geometrically. The first slaves imported into Brazil arrived in 1538. By 1600 they formed the basis of the economy there, along the Peruvian coast, in Mexico's hot lands, in Santo Domingo, in Cuba, and in the mines of Colombia. By 1800 the population of Haiti was predominantly black or mulatto, and the African element was substantial in Brazil and Cuba. There were smaller, though still significant, black populations in the Dominican Republic, Panama, Venezuela, and Colombia.

A century after Africans were brought to Latin America, they appeared in the English colonies to the north. The first blacks landed in Jamestown in 1619, but their status was uncertain for some fifty years. Between 1640 and 1660 there is evidence of slavery, and after the latter date the slave system was defined by law in several of the colonies. White indentured servants, at first an important part of the work force, were soon replaced by African slaves, who provided a lifetime of work to the plantation owner. In 1790 when the white population was just over 3 million, there were some 750,000 blacks in the United States.

During the American Revolution, serious questions arose about the morality of slavery. Some people saw an embarrassing contradiction between human bondage and the ideals of the Declaration of Independence. This antislavery sentiment temporarily weakened as fear grew over a bloody slave insurrection in Santo Domingo, unrest among American slaves, and the unsettling economic and social consequences of the French Revolution. Slave rebellions in the early 1800s shocked many Americans.

The Industrial Revolution played a large role in harnessing slavery to the economy of the southern states. English textile mills required an increased supply of cotton. New technology and new lands made the plantation system more profitable, creating an additional demand for slaves even as their importation ended in 1808.

Race Problems in the New Lands

The imposition of European hegemony over native inhabitants in the far corners of the globe

This 1856 engraving shows slaves pressing cotton on a Louisiana plantation. Slaves often labored 14 hours a day and even as many as 18 hours during harvest time.

COTTON PRESSING IN LOUISIANA

Slaves rose up against the French in Saint Domingue in 1791. Napoleon sent an army to restore slavery in 1799, but many of the French soldiers died of yellow fever, and the rebels defeated the decimated French army in 1803.

and the slave trade created tragic racial conflicts. It is difficult to gain an accurate estimate of the number of Indians in North America, but it is generally held that before European settlement there were around 200,000 in Canada and 850,000 in the United States. Since the arrival of white settlers, the number of Indians in the two North American areas has been reduced by approximately half, largely through disease and extermination. While in modern time attempts have been made to help native Americans make a place for themselves in urban society, these efforts have generally been inadequate. Even though in the past two centuries Canada has compiled a much more humane record dealing with native Americans than the United States, Indians remain the most neglected and isolated minority in North America.

The aborigines of Australia and Tasmania—numbering possibly 300,000 at the time of the arrival of the Europeans—were decimated by the diseases and liquors brought by the white settlers. The native inhabitants could not adjust to the new ways of life brought about by the disappearance of their hunting grounds. At times they were treated brutally: in some places they were rounded up in gangs and shot; sometimes the Europeans encouraged drunkenness among the natives, then gave them clubs to fight each other

for the entertainment of the "civilized" spectators. The natives of Tasmania are now extinct, and the aborigines of Australia are a declining race.

In New Zealand the native Maoris were better able to stand up to the whites. After serious wars in the 1860s peace was finally secured and the Maoris slowly accommodated themselves to the new world created by the whites. Since 1900 the Maoris have shared the same political rights and privileges as the white settlers and have obtained the benefits of advanced education. The Maoris now constitute about 9 percent of the population and their numbers are increasing.

In two areas colonized by Europeans, Latin America and South Africa, the indigenous peoples greatly outnumbered the white settlers. Some authorities, for example, estimate that the population of Latin America in pre-Columbian days was at least 25 million. While a large percentage of these people died following the initial

This 1816 pictograph was meant to demonstrate to Australian aborigines the evenhandedness of British justice.

This family picture of a mestizo father, a Spanish mother, and their daughter, known as a castiza, was part of a racial chart of Mexican peoples.

European impact because of disease, war, and famine, in the long run their numbers substantially increased. There was much racial mixing between the Indians and the Europeans, giving rise to the *mestizo*. This mixed strain together with the Indians outnumbered the white population. In the early twentieth century population there were estimated to be 20 million Indian, 30 million *mestizos*, 26 million black and mulatto, and 34 million white. Only in Argentina, Chile, and a few smaller states such as Costa Rica, Cuba, and Uruguay have European stocks overwhelmed the Indians.

The thousand years of contact between the Spanish and Portuguese with the dark-skinned Moorish people and their early African explorations helped prevent the development of the virulent form of racism found in North America. There was also a difference in the status of the slave in North and South America. In the north the slave was regarded as a piece of property, with no legal or moral rights. In the south, because of the traditions of Roman law and the Catholic church, slaves had a legal personality and moral standing.

Even though slave status was generally considered to be perpetual, gaining freedom was not as difficult in Latin America as in the north. By 1860 free blacks outnumbered slaves 2 to 1 in Brazil while slaves outnumbered free blacks 8 to 1 in the United States. Finally, there has been greater racial mixing in Latin America. The greatest meld of races—red, white, and black—in the history of the world has taken place there. This intermingling has gone a long way to ease racial tensions.[1]

In South Africa the indigenous people were not exterminated, but they were denied the opportunity to share in European civilization. The fierce fighting between the European frontier people (mainly the Dutch) and the Africans caused constant misunderstanding and fear. Despite many political and economic disabilities, in the nineteenth century the South African natives showed a substantial increase in numbers. By 1904 the population breakdown of the roughly 8 million people showed 21.6 percent European, 67.4 percent African, 2.4 percent Asiatic, and 8.6 percent "coloured." Unlike the situation in Latin America, the European minority resolutely opposed any mixing with the nonwhites and enforced unyielding segregation—*apartheid*.

The Search for a New Nationality

The transplanted Europeans generally focused their energies on domestic matters and left world affairs to the European states. Those under the British flag generally accepted British leadership in world affairs and depended on London's fleet for protection. The United States devoted considerable energy to exploiting its vast natural resources and Americanizing the millions of immigrants who flocked to its shores. Latin America was politically unstable but rich in natural resources. The region managed to avoid the cruder imperialistic partitions and outright annexations so evident in Africa, China, and Southeast Asia. This lack of total exploitation owed more to luck rather than to the virtue of the outside powers. The economic interests of the United States—and to some extent of Britain—coincided with the preservation of the status quo in Latin Ameria.

Among all the transplanted Europeans, the United States found the quest for independence the easiest. Its power, size, resources, and heritage of freedom and the rule of law contributed to a distinctive and recognizable national ideal that survived the threat of the Civil War. The search for national unity has not been as successful in Canada, given the split between the closely knit French Canadian minority and the majority English-speaking population.

Nationalism has burned brightly in each of the Latin American nations, sometimes at the expense of political stability. The eight major administrative divisions in the late colonial era have fragmented into nineteen states—a process frequently accompanied by insurrection, rebellion, and war.

Australia and New Zealand have found the search for a new nationality difficult. Remote from Europe, inhabitants of these islands have clung to the traditions and life of their ancestors, even to the point that the New Zealanders claim to be more British than the British. More difficult is the situation in South Africa where the white majority are the Boers rather than the British. These Afrikaners have developed a distinctive, unbending culture based on rigid Calvinism and the Dutch tongue. The dislike of the British segment may have lessened recently because of a common fear of black domination and resentment of the outside world for its criticism of *apartheid*.

<hr />

The British Dominions

The British Dominions became self-governing without breaking their political ties to Great Britain. With the exception of South Africa, these new nations were predominantly British in stock, language, culture, and governmental traditions. In the case of Canada, however, a strong French Canadian minority in Quebec, inherited from the original French regime, persisted and preserved its French heritage. In South Africa, following a confused history of rivalry and war between the British and Dutch settlers, a shaky union was achieved. There were no complications of rival Europeans in Australia and New Zealand, which were settled by the British in the beginning and did not have to adjust to an influx

of other Europeans. Both Australia and Canada attained political unity by merging a number of colonies into a single government.

South Africa

The first European contact in the area later known as the Union of South Africa, located at the southern tip of Africa, occurred in 1487 when Bartholomew Diaz reached the Cape of Good Hope. Ten years later Vasco da Gama rounded the Cape on his way to the Indies. Two centuries later, large fleets of Dutch ships made their way around Africa to the Indies to trade for spices and oriental wares. The cape became a strategic place to get fresh water and replenish supplies.

In 1651 the Dutch established a settlement at the Cape of Good Hope, named Cape Town, which grew slowly. As the Dutch settlers pushed inland, they came into conflict with the Bantu-speaking Africans, who strongly resisted white expansion. The Dutch period of South African history came to an end in 1814 when the Dutch ceded the colony to Great Britain.

Friction between the British and the Boers, or Dutch burghers, quickly developed over the treatment of the native peoples. The Dutch had many slaves and resented the attitudes of the missionaries, who continually accused the Dutch of abusing the natives. Britain's emancipation of all slaves in the empire in 1833 exacerbated ill feeling.

Two years later 12,000 Boers undertook an epic journey in their ox-drawn wagons to a new country where they could pursue their way of life without interference. This Great Trek was a folk movement comparable to the covered wagon epic of the American West.[2] Finally on the high plateau, or *veld*, the Boers established two little republics, the Orange Free State and the Transvaal. The British, in the meantime, extended their settlement along the eastern coast north of the Cape and founded the colony of Natal (see map, p. 698).

The Great Trek did little to resolve the difficulties of the Boers. In the mid-nineteenth century there was much fighting with the Africans, who resisted the incursions of both Boers and British. In 1852 the British government made treaties with the Boers, acknowledging the independence of the Orange Free State and the Transvaal but

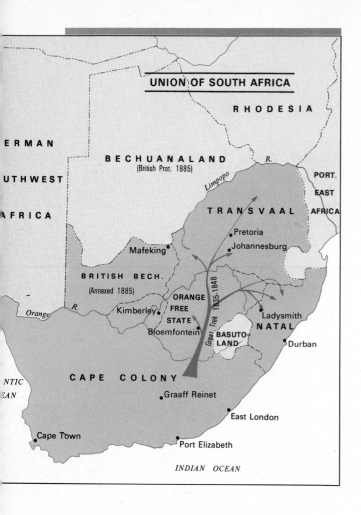

UNION OF SOUTH AFRICA

RHODESIA

GERMAN
SOUTHWEST
AFRICA

BECHUANALAND
(British Prot. 1885)

Limpopo R.

PORT.
EAST
AFRICA

TRANSVAAL

Pretoria
Johannesburg

Mafeking

BRITISH BECH.
(Annexed 1885)

Orange R.

Kimberley

ORANGE
FREE
STATE

Bloemfontein

BASUTO-
LAND

Great Trek 1835-1848

Ladysmith

NATAL

Durban

CAPE COLONY

Graaff Reinet

ATLANTIC
OCEAN

Cape Town

East London

Port Elizabeth

INDIAN OCEAN

British imperial interests. Born in 1853, he had a frail constitution and as a young man emigrated to South Africa to improve his health. He became fabulously wealthy in the diamond fields, the leading figure in the DeBeers diamond syndicate and the owner of many goldmining properties in the Transvaal. Rhodes was determined to thwart Kruger by uniting a self-governing South Africa within the British Empire.

To forestall Kruger's plans, Rhodes persuaded Britain to annex territory on the Transvaal's eastern and western borders. He prevented Boer expansion to the north by gaining extensive settlement and mining right in the high and fertile plateau through which flowed the Zambezi River. In 1890 the town of Salisbury was founded, becoming the capital of the region named Rhodesia.

Meanwhile, the *Uitlanders* began to plot an insurrection. At the close of 1895, a group of Rhodesian mounted police invaded the Transvaal, but they were quickly forced to surrender

Cecil Rhodes. He once declared that his lifelong dream was to "bring the whole civilized world under British rule, to make the Anglo-Saxon race into an empire."

retaining a shadowy right to have a voice in the foreign affairs of the two republics.

The Boer War. The discovery of diamonds in 1868 on the borders of the Cape and of gold in 1885 in the Transvaal attracted thousands of Englishmen and people of other nations to the mines. The president of the Transvaal, Paul Kruger, was determined that these newcomers would not gain control. He was passionately devoted to the Boer way of life, which was simple, mainly rural, and uncomplicated. To curb the growing power of the *Uitlanders* (outlanders), Kruger began to impose heavy taxes on them, while the Boers paid practically nothing. English was banned in the courts and public schools. It was almost impossible for the *Uitlanders* to become naturalized citizens of the Transvaal.

Kruger's main adversary was Cecil Rhodes, a man of driving ambition both for himself and for

Sidney Low on Cecil Rhodes

During his time, Cecil Rhodes stood as the foremost European imperialist in Africa. The journalist Sidney Low captured Rhodes' philosophical essence.

Whatever inconsistency there may have been in his actions, his opinions, so far as I could perceive, did not vary. In fact, he repeated himself a good deal, having a kind of apostolic fervour in expatiating on the broad simple tenets of the Rhodesian religion. His cardinal doctrines I should say were these: First, that insular England was quite insufficient to maintain, or even to protect, itself without the assistance of the Anglo-Saxon peoples beyond the seas of Europe. Secondly, that the first and greatest aim of British statesmanship should be to find new areas of settlement, and new markets for the products that would, in due course, be penalised in the territories and dependencies of all our rivals by discriminating tariffs. Thirdly, that the largest tracts of unoccupied or undeveloped lands remaining on the globe were in Africa, and therefore that the most strenuous efforts should be made to keep open a great part of that continent to British commerce and colonisation. Fourthly, that as the key to the African position lay in the various Anglo-Dutch States and provinces, it was imperative to convert the whole region into a united, self-governing, federation, exempt from meddlesome interference by the home authorities, but loyal to the Empire, and welcoming British enterprise and progress. Fifthly, that the world was made for the service of man, and more particularly of civilised, white, European men, who were most capable of utilising the crude resources of nature for the promotion of wealth and prosperity. And, finally, that the British Constitution was an absurd anachronism, and that it should be remodelled on the lines of the American Union, with federal self-governing Colonies as the constituent States. . . .

From Sidney Low, *Contemporary Recollections,*" in *The Nineteenth Century and After,* 1902.

---

to a force of Boer commandos. This incident alienated the Dutch population in the Cape, pushed the Orange Free State into an alliance with the Transvaal, and strengthened Kruger's policies.

The South African crisis now moved from the area of covert *Uitlander* plots to British diplomacy. Britain did not want totally independent Boer states. British statesmen also feared that a hostile Transvaal, with its immense mining wealth and consequent economic power, would be able to dominate all South Africa. From 1896 to the spring of 1899 continuous efforts were made to reconcile Boer and British differences but without success. Britain began to send troops, and the Transvaal and the Orange Free State prepared for war. Hostilities began in the fall of 1899.

The world was amazed at the war that followed. The Boers were crack shots and expert horsemen. Knowing every inch of ground on which they fought, they frequently outmaneuvered the British troops. But the tide turned in 1900 when the British inflicted several disastrous defeats on the Boers.

The Union of South Africa. After the Boers surrendered in 1902, the British treated them magnanimously. They gave them loans to rebuild burned farmhouses and buy cattle, and more significantly, they extended the right of self-government to the Transvaal in 1906 and to the Orange Free State two years later. The Liberal government in Great Britain permitted the Boer and English states to unite and form the Union of South Africa in 1909. Only seven years after the war, Boer and Briton joined hands to create a new self-governing dominion. The first prime minister of the Union was Louis Botha (1863–1919), who had been a Boer general in the war. Botha's primary purpose was to create neither an English nor a Boer nationality but a blend of the two in a new South African patriotism.

Australia

The discovery of Australia dates back to the seventeenth century, when Dutch explorers sighted its shores. Captain Cook's South Seas voyage in 1769, however, paved the way for British settlement. In 1788 Britain transported a group of convicts to Australia and settled them at Sydney. From the parent colony of Sydney, later called New South Wales, five other settlements were founded.

Although a majority of the first Europeans in Australia were prisoners, most of them were political prisoners and debtors, rather than hardened criminals. After seven years of servitude many were liberated and as "emancipists" became citizens. Quite early in the ninteenth century, many free settlers also came to Australia. They began to protest the dumping of convicts in their new home, and Britain took the first steps to end the practice in 1840. By 1850 the Australian colonies were enjoying a liberal form of self-government.

The Australian colonies grew slowly during the first half of the nineteenth century. Sheep raising became the basis of the economy. The discovery of gold in 1851 quickened the tempo of development, but agriculture continued to be the mainstay of Australia's economy. Railway mileage was expanded, and large investments of foreign capital helped the young nation to develop its resources. In 1850 the population of the country was about 400,000; a decade later it had nearly doubled. In the decade before 1914 the population increased from just under 4 million to 5 million people.

In 1901 the six Australian colonies formed a federal union known as the Commonwealth of Australia, which bears many resemblances to the American system of government. The legislature is composed of a House of Representatives and a Senate. Each state elects six senators, while the lower house is made up of members elected by each state in accordance with its population. In the Commonwealth government the chief executive, the prime minister, is responsible to the legislature, and thus does not prossess the fixed term guaranteed the American president.

New Zealand

About a thousand miles from the Australian mainland is a group of islands, two of which are of particular importance. These lonely projections of British influence in the South Pacific constitute the self-governing Dominion of New Zealand. The total population of this country, which has an area five-sixths the size of Great Britain, is just over 3.3 million. The earliest white

Because it was considered too far from England to be attractive to free settlers, Australia was first used as a penal colony for English convicts. Although many of the convicts were sentenced to deportation for relatively minor offenses, they often suffered great cruelty and hardships in the prison camps. Here, English convicts plow an Australian field while the guard cracks the whip over their heads.

settlers were desperate convicts who had escaped from penal settlements in Australia. The activity of other colonizers forced the British government to assume protection of the islands in 1840, and British agents signed a treaty guaranteeing certain rights, especially land rights, to the Maoris.

New Zealand gradually became a rich pastoral, farming, and fruit-raising country. The chief export, then as now, was wool. Later the development of refrigeration enabled large quantities of meat and dairy products to be shipped to foreign markets, especially to Great Britain.

Both New Zealand and Australia have been seen as sociologial laboratories because of their pioneering activities in democratic government and social welfare legislation. As early as 1855, the state of Victoria in Australia introduced the secret ballot in elections. The "Australian ballot" was later adopted in Great Britain, the United States, and other parts of the world. Woman suffrage was introduced in New Zealand in 1893 and in Australia nine years later. In New Zealand a program of "land for the people" was implemented through the imposition of heavy taxes on large tracts of land held by absentee landlords. New Zealand also led the world in the adoption of noncontributory old-age pensions in 1878 and the establishment of a national infant welfare system in 1907. Before 1914 Australia had passed similar measures.

Canada

From 1534, when Jacques Cartier sailed up the Saint Lawrence River and claimed the area for France, until 1763, Canada was part of the French empire. Unlike the English colonies in the New World, the French colony of Canada was rigidly supervised by Paris. The home government supervised all trade activities, and the Catholic church monopolized education. Few Protestants were allowed to settle in New France. The French king granted huge tracts of land to nobles, who in turn parceled out their estates to peasant farmers. This introduction of a version of European feudalism seriously hampered development in Canada. It limited expansion by denying free land to pioneers, and it also subjected the population to restrictive control by royal officials, priests, and nobles.

Canada became caught up in the worldwide French-British competition. In addition to Britain's interest in its Atlantic seaboard colonies, its fishermen frequently landed at Newfoundland. In 1670 the Company of Gentlemen Adventurers of England Trading into Hudson's Bay was chartered to carry on fur trading with the Indians. When war broke out in Europe between France and Britain, their colonies in the New World also went to war. Britain's ultimate victory was anticipated in the Treaty of Utrecht (1713) in which France gave up Acadia (later known as Nova Scotia), surrendered claims to Newfoundland, and recognized the Hudson's Bay Company territory as English.

The last of the four colonial wars ended in a complete victory for Britain. In 1763, by the Treaty of Paris, the British gained all of Canada. London tried to ensure the loyalty of the French Canadians by issuing a royal proclamation guaranteeing the inhabitants' political rights and their freedom to worship as Roman Catholics. These guarantees were strengthened in 1774 when the British government passed the Quebec Act, called the "Magna Carta of the French Canadian race." This act reconfirmed the position of the Catholic church and perpetuated French laws and customs. However, there was no provision for a representative assembly, such as existed in English-speaking colonies. At that time the French lacked both the interest and experience in self-government.

Canada's Formative Stage. The period from 1763 to 1867 is known as the formative stage of Canada. A number of developments took place during this period; the growth of the English-speaking population, the defeat of an attempted conquest by the United States, the grant of local self-government, and finally the confederation of Canada into a dominion.

The major source of growth of the English-speaking population was the American Revolution. Although the rebellious colonists tried to conquer Canada, the Canadians remained loyal to Britain, largely because of the liberal provisions of the Quebec Act, and the invasion failed. Those inhabitants of the thirteen colonies not in favor of separation from Great Britain suffered at the hands of the victorious patriots, and a large number of them went to Canada. The

The Loyalist encampment at Johnston, a settlement on the banks of the St. Lawrence River in Canada, founded on June 6, 1784.

immigrants, known as United Empire Loyalists, settled in Nova Scotia, along the Saint Lawrence River, and north of the Great Lakes.

The newcomers resented the absence of political representation in their new home and pushed for a measure of self-government. Numerous struggles arose between the French Canadians and the newly arrived Loyalists. To meet this situation the British in 1791 divided British North America into two separate provinces called Upper and Lower Canada and granted each of them a representative assembly. The quarrel between the English- and French-speaking populations has continued to the present day.

Open rebellion in 1837 was put down militarily, and in response, the British government sent a special commissioner, Lord Durham (1792–1840), to study the Canadian situation and make recommendations. A statesman with vision, Durham realized that a much larger degree of self-government had to be granted if the home country wished to keep the loyalty of its colonies. He recommended that certain matters of imperial concern, such as foreign relations, should be directed from London, but that Canada alone should control its own domestic affairs. By the mid-nineteenth century London granted self-government to Canada. Unlike the thirteen colonies that severed their connection with the parent country by revolution, Canada achieved virtual independence peacefully and remained loyal to Britain.

Fear of the United States, the need for a common tariff policy, and a concerted effort to develop natural resources led Canadians into confederation. A plan of union, the British North American Act, was drawn up, approved by the British government, and passed by the Parliament in London in 1867. This act united Canada—until then divided into the provinces of Quebec and Ontario, Nova Scotia, and New Brunswick—into a federal union of four provinces. The new government had some similarities to the political organization of the United States, but it adopted the British cabinet system, with its principle of ministerial responsibility. As a symbol of its connection with Great Britain, provision was made for a governor-general who was to act as the British monarch's person representative to Canada.

Modern Canada. The new nation encountered many problems from the first. Its vast size caused communications problems, which became even more acute in 1869 when the dominion purchased the territories of the Hudson's Bay Company extending from present-day Ontario to the Pacific coast, south to the Columbia River (see map, p. 703). In 1871 the new colony of British

Columbia joined the dominion on the promise of early construction of a transcontinental railroad to link the west coast with eastern Canada.

Another disturbing problem was the lack of good relations with the United States. After the Civil War, Irish patriots in the United States, seeking revenge against the British for their treatment of Ireland, launched armed incursions over the border. However, in 1871 the major differences between the two countries were ironed out in the Treaty of Washington, a landmark in the use of arbitration.

The country developed rapidly under the leadership of the dominion's first prime minister, Sir John A. Macdonald (1815–1891), who served from 1867 to 1873 and again from 1878 to 1891. Canadians developed their country through encouraging new industry, putting a railroad across the country in 1885, and attracting immigrants. Sir Wilfrid Laurier (1841–1919), who served as prime minister from 1896 to 1911, continued Macdonald's work. Between 1897 and 1912, Canada received 2,250,000 new citizens, bringing the total population to over 7 million. Internal restructuring created new provinces out of the former Hudson's Bay Company holdings, so that in 1914 the dominion consisted of nine provinces. At the same time, the country had to deal with the consequences of its rapid growth: labor discontent, corruption, and agrarian unrest. Canada was becoming a mature nation, with all of the accompanying problems of depressions, maldistribution of wealth, and the need for governmental restraint of business.

A more long-lasting challenge has been the bicultural nature of the country. In 1761, the

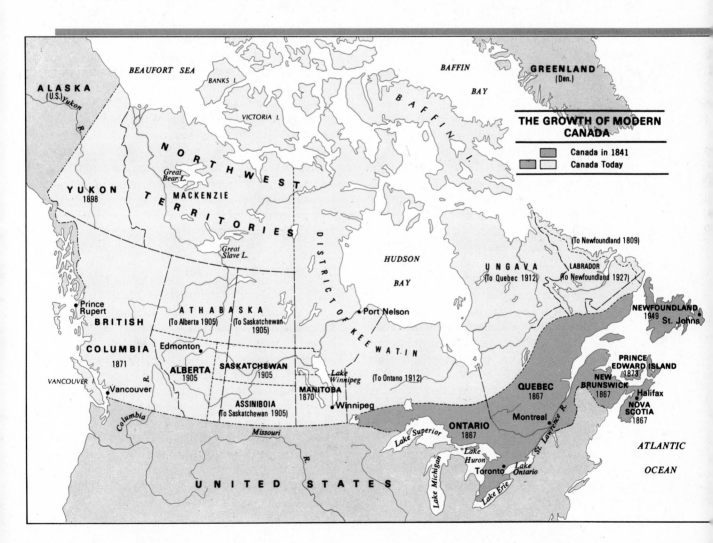

THE GROWTH OF MODERN CANADA

Canada in 1841
Canada Today

entire country was French, but a momentous change began with the American Revolution, when English-speaking American Loyalists wishing to keep their British allegiance fled to Canada. In 1761 there were only 65,000 people in New France; by 1815 the population of all the British North American colonies had increased to 600,000, of whom only 250,000 were French. Between 1815 and 1850 a second wave of immigrants from Britain brought the entire population to 2,400,000, of whom fewer than one-third were French. During the nineteenth century, and indeed down to the present, the population of French origin has remained between 28 and 31 percent of the total.

From the first arrival of significant numbers of British to the latter part of the twentieth century, the relations between the French and English speakers have been strained. Lord Durham saw this clearly in 1837 when he wrote "I found two nations warring in the bosom of a single state; I found a struggle not of principles but of races." Durham singled out the most persistent and disturbing problem facing Canada.

This cultural conflict is based on the French resentment of the British victory two centuries ago and the British pride in that accomplishment. There was also a clash in the field of religion. New France was highly conservative, ruled by an authoritarian regime. When this political authority was removed, the Catholic church in Quebec became the main defender and citadel of French Catholic culture. The English-speaking Canadians, however, tended to be antagonistic to the church's role. Further complicating relations was the fact that the French portion remained largely agricultural with a high rate of illiteracy. The British were more urban and technologically educated, and consequently the English-speaking part became richer and dominant. Although the federal constitution sought to create a bilingual society and a dual school system, the French continued to be bitter over the progressive erosion of this guaranteed equality in the western provinces, where no appreciable French population developed. The English-speaking Canadians assumed a pose of superiority and ridiculed French culture, while making little effort to learn the French language.

At the end of the nineteenth century, while Canada was a united federation in political structure, a common Canadianism had not been achieved. The French had no intention of being absorbed by the culture of the majority. At the end of the twentieth century how to create a single nationality comprised of two separate but offically equal cultures remained Canada's major problem.

The United States

The revolutionary movements in Europe during the nineteenth century fought aristocratic domination or foreign rule—or both. The nineteenth-century struggles in the United States were not quite the same. Instead, there were two major related problems. One was the annexation, settlement, and development of the continent; the other was slavery. Free land and unfree people were the sources of the many political confrontations that culminated in the Civil War, the greatest struggle of nineteenth-century America.

At the conclusion of its successful revolution in 1783, the United States was not a democracy. At the time of the ratification of the Constitution only one male in seven had the vote. Religious requirements and property qualifications ensured that only a small elite participated in government. These restrictions allowed patricians from established families in the south and men of wealth and substance in the north to control the country for nearly half a century.

Democratic Influences

The influence of the western frontier helped make America more democratic. Even before the Constitution was ratified, thousands of pioneers crossed the Appalachian Mountains into the new "western country." In the west, land was to be had for the asking, social caste did not exist, one person was as good as another. Vigor, courage, self-reliance, and competence counted, not birth or wealth. Throughout the nineteenth century the west was the source of new and liberal movements that challenged the conservative ideas prevalent in the east.

Until the War of 1812, democracy grew slowly. In 1791 Vermont had been admitted as a manhood suffrage state, and the following year

Armed members of the White League guard the ballot box to prevent newly enfranchised black citizens from depositing their ballots.

man, by virtue of being an American citizen, could hold any office in the land. Governments widened educational opportunities by enlarging the public school system. With increased access to learning, class barriers became less important. The gaining and keeping of political power came more and more to be tied to satisfying the needs of the people who voted.

Simultaneous with the growth of democracy came the territorial expansion of the country. The Louisiana territory, purchased from France for about $15 million in 1803, doubled the size of the United States (see map, p. 706). In 1844, Americans influenced by "manifest destiny," the belief that their domination of the continent was God's will, demanded "All of Oregon or none." The claim led to a boundary dispute with Great Britain over land between the Columbia River and 54′ 40″ north latitude. In 1846 the two countries accepted a boundary at the 49th parallel, and the Oregon territory was settled. The annexation of Texas in 1845 was followed by war with Mexico in 1846. In the peace agreement signed two years later Mexico ceded California, all title to Texas, and the land between California and Texas to the United States. As a result of these acquisitions, by 1860 the area of the United States had increased by two-thirds over what it had been in 1840.

The addition of the new territories forced the issue of whether slavery should be allowed in those areas. Parallelling developments in Great Britain, abolitionists in the United States, particularly New England, vigorously condemned slavery. Henry Clay's Missouri Compromise of 1820 permitted slavery in Missouri but forbade it in the rest of the Louisiana Purchase. This settlement satisfied both sides for only a short time. The antislavery forces grew more insistent. In the senatorial campaigns of 1858, candidate Abraham Lincoln declared:

A house divided against itself cannot stand. I believe this government cannot endure permanently half slave and half free. I do not expect the Union to be dissolved—I do not expect the house to fall—but I do expect it will cease to be divided. It will become all one thing, or all the other.[3]

Slavery was an important issue; it served as a focus for the differences and tensions separating the North from the South. However, a more

Kentucky followed suit; but Tennessee, Ohio, and Louisiana entered the Union with property and tax qualifications for the vote. After 1817 no new state entered the Union with restrictions on male suffrage except for slaves. Most appointive offices became elective, and requirements for holding office were liberalized.

Andrew Jackson changed the tone and emphasis of American politics. In 1828 he was elected to the presidency following a campaign that featured the slogan "down with the aristocrats." He was the first president produced by the west; the first since George Washington not to have a college education; and the first to have been born in poverty. He owed his election to no congressional clique, but to the will of the people, who idolized "Old Hickory" as their spokesman and leader.

The triumph of the democratic principle in the 1830s set the direction for political development. With Jackson's election came the idea that any

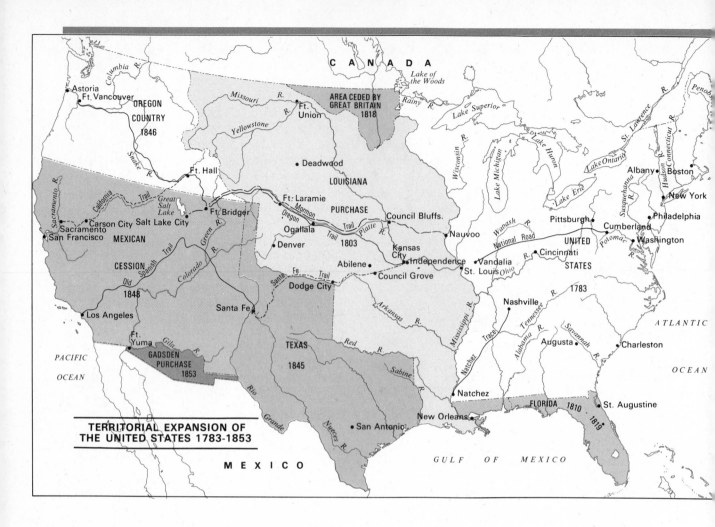

TERRITORIAL EXPANSION OF THE UNITED STATES 1783-1853

fundamental cause of conflict was that, in a sense, the two sections had become separate societies. The former was industrial, urban, and democratic; the latter was mainly agricultural, rural, and dominated by a planter aristocracy. The South strongly opposed the North's desire for higher tariffs, government aid for new railroads, and generous terms for land settlement in the West. These fundamental differences brought North and South to war. Slavery served as a moral irritant.

The Civil War and Its Results

Soon after Abraham Lincoln was inaugurated as president, the southern states seceded from the Union and formed the Confederate States of America. The first shot of the Civil War was fired at Fort Sumter, South Carolina, in

1861, initiating the bloodiest war experienced by any western nation to that time. Four agonizing years of conflict, in which more than one-half million men died, ended when General Robert E. Lee surrendered to General Ulysses S. Grant at Appomattox Courthouse in Virginia in April 1865. A few days later, the nation was stunned by assassination of President Lincoln, who had just begun his second term.

With the final collapse of the Confederacy before the overwhelming superiority of the Union in manpower, industrial resources, and wealth, the Civil War became the grand epic of American history in its heroism, romance, and tragedy. The victorious North used military occupation to try to force the south to extend voting and property rights to the former slaves. Eventually, this so-called Reconstruction period (1865–1877) was ended by a tacit agreement between the northern industrial and the southern white leaders that enabled the latter to regain political control and to deprive blacks of their newly won rights. Southerners invoked Social Darwinist arguments to justify their actions in denying full "blessings of freedom" to the former slaves.

Southern politicians deprived blacks of their voting rights by enacting state laws or employing devices such as poll taxes, literacy tests, property qualifications, and physical threats. Racial segregation in schools, restaurants, parks, and hotels was effectively applied. Laws prohibiting interracial marriage were enacted, and blacks were generally excluded from unions. Between 1885 and 1918, more than 2500 blacks were lynched in the United States. As second-class citizens, freed but landless, the former slaves essentially formed a sharecropping class,

George Washington Carver. As director of agricultural research at Tuskegee Institute, he derived many new products from southern crops.

American artist Henry Ossawa Tanner demonstrated remarkable talent to create a strong and memorable mood, as is evident in *The Banjo Lesson* (1893).

mired in poverty and deprived of equal educational opportunity.[4]

It took more than a century after the Civil War for black Americans to gain a politically equal footing. Despite all of the obstacles they encountered in the half century after the Emancipation Proclamation, by 1914 black Americans made some substantial achievements: the creation of a professional class estimated at 47,000; a 70 percent literacy rate; ownership of 550,000 homes, 40,000 businesses, and savings of some $700 million. Black churches, banks, and insurance companies evoled into substantial institutions. In addition black individuals made major contributions to a number of different fields: Henry Ossawa Tanner (1859–1937) was recognized as a distinguished painter; George Washington Carver (1865–1943) made substantial contributions in the field of agricultural chemistry; and W. E. B. DuBois (1868–1963), a social scientist of national stature, began the first effective black political protest early in the century.

If the causes and consequences of the American Civil War are complex, the all-important result was simple. It settled the issue of whether the United States was an indivisible sovereign nation or a collection of sovereign states. The sacrifice of hundreds of thousands of lives preserved the Union, but the inhuman treatment of blacks remained.

Development, Abuse, and Reform

The North's victory was a boost for industrialization as well as a result of it—and the economic revolution in the United States that followed was more significant than the conflict itself. Railroads were built across broad prairies and the first transcontinental line, the Union Pacific, was completed in 1869.

Settlers swarmed west. Between 1850 and 1880 the number of cities with a population of 50,000 or more doubled. The number of men emloyed in industry increased 50 percent. In 1865 there were 35,000 miles of railroads in the country. By 1900 the trackage was estimated to be about 200,000—more than in all of Europe. In 1860 a little more than a billion dollars was invested in manufacturing; by 1900 this figure had risen to 12 billion. The value of manufactured products increased proportionately. In 1870 the total production of iron and steel in the United States was far below that of France and Britain. Twenty years later the United States had outstripped them and was producing about one-third of the world's iron and steel.

In the age of rapid industrialism and materialistic expansion, many who pursued profits lost sight of ethical principles both in business and government. In five years, between 1865 and 1870, the notorious Tweed Ring cost the city of New York at least $100 million. Ruthless financiers, such as Jay Gould and Jim Fisk, tampered with the basic financial stability of the nation. The administration of President Ulysses Grant was tainted by scandals and frauds. A new rich class failed to appreciate its responsibilities to society. Corruption was a blatant feature of the new order.

Railroad companies distributed elaborately illustrated brochures and broadsides to lure people to the West, where they would settle on land owned by the railroad.

For roughly a century the gospel for the new nation of America had been rugged individualism. As in Europe, governmental interference in business was unwelcome because of the strong belief that individuals should be free to follow their own inclinations, run their own businesses, and enjoy the profits of their labors. In an expanding nation where land, jobs, and opportunity beckoned, there was little to indicate that the system would not work indefinitely. By 1880, however, the end of the frontier was in sight. Free land of good quality was scarce, and the frontier could no longer serve as a safety valve to release the economic and social pressures of an expanding population.

Between 1850 and 1900 the United States became the most powerful state in the western hemisphere, increased its national wealth from $7 billion to $88 billion, established an excellent system of public education, and fostered the spread of civil liberties. But there were many disturbing factors in the picture. Unemployment, child labor, and industrial accidents were common in the rapidly growing cities. Slums grew and served as breeding places for disease and crime. Strikes, often accompanied by violence, brought to a head the tension between labor and capital.

In response, the wide-ranging Progressive reform movement developed between 1890 to 1914. This movement was rooted partly in the agrarian protests against big business sparked by the Populists of the Midwest and South. The Progressives effectively mobilized the middle classes to work to eliminate sweatshops, the exploitation of labor, and the abuse of natural resources.

The success of the Progressive movement was reflected in the constitutions of the new states admitted to the Union and in their introduction of the direct primary, the initiative and referendum, and the direct election of senators. All these measures tended to give the common people more effective control of the government. After the enactment of the Interstate Commerce Act in 1887, which had introduced federal regulation over railroads, a steady expansion of governmental regulation of industry began.

As president of the United States from 1901 to 1909, Theodore Roosevelt launched an aggressive campaign to break up the trusts, conserve natural resources, and regulate railroads, food, and drugs. In 1913 President Woodrow Wilson started a militant campaign of reform called the "New Freedom." His administration reduced the tariff because it was too much the instrument of special economic privilege, enacted banking reform with the Federal Reserve Act of 1913, and regulated businesses in the public interest through the Clayton Antitrust Act and the establishment of the Federal Trade Commission, both in 1914.

In 1914 the United States was the richest, most populous, and most influential nation in the West. The country's first census, taken in 1790, counted a population of just under 4 million; by 1910 the number was 99 million. During the nineteenth century more than 25 million immigrants had made their way to America. Since the days of George Washington, the national wealth had increased at least a hundredfold. Once the producer of raw materials only, the United States by 1914 was the world's greatest industrial power, producing more steel than Britain and Germany combined. A single company—United States Steel—was capitalized for $1.460 billion, a sum greater than the total estimated wealth of the country in 1790.

The United States and the World

From the first, U. S. foreign policy pursued three goals: national security, trade, and the

THE BOSSES OF THE SENATE

This cartoon, "The Bosses of the Senate," appeared in *Puck* in 1889, shortly before the Senate began debate on the Sherman Antitrust Bill. Public uproar over the proliferation of gigantic trusts eventually led to passage of the Antitrust Act in 1890.

spread of democracy. During its first quarter-century, The United States fought a brief naval war with France, became embroiled with Britain in the War of 1812, and sent two expeditions to the Mediterranean to deal with the Barbary pirates. These complications notwithstanding, Americans spent the next century developing their country. Thomas Jefferson summarized the country's foreign policy with these words: "Peace, commerce, and honest friendship with all nations—entangling alliances with none."[5]

Early in the 1820s the policy of noninvolvement was seriously challenged when conservative members of the Quadruple Alliance offered to help the Spanish king regain control of Latin America. Both Britain and the United States viewed this possibility with alarm. George Canning, the British foreign secretary, suggested that his government and the United States make a joint declaration warning against European intervention in South America. U. S. President James Monroe seriously considered the invitation, but decided against it.

Instead Monroe offered a unilateral doctrine in his message to Congress in December 1823. He warned the European powers against any attempt to impose their system in the Western Hemisphere and also declared that the United States had no intention of interfering in European affairs. In 1823 the United States could "have its cake and eat it too." The shield of the British fleet stood behind the Monroe Doctrine, with or without a formal alliance between Washington and London, and the United States avoided the complications and dangers inherent in European intervention.

It was sometimes difficult to reconcile the desire for isolation with the country's stated love of freedom—for example, much sympathy was expressed for the Greeks as they fought against Turkish tyranny in the 1820s, but there was little active support. When the country established new foreign contacts, it went across the Pacific. In 1844 the United States made its first treaty with China, opening certain ports to American trade and securing the rights of American merchants and sailors to be tried in American tribunals in China. In 1853 Commodore Matthew Perry visited Japan, and by his show of force, persuaded the Japanese to open some of their harbors to American ships. By 1854 the United

A LITTLE MONROE DOCTORING MIGHT BE GOOD FOR HIM.

American cartoonist Thomas Nast satirized British imperialism with this cartoon; the caption reads, "A Little Monroe Doctoring Might Be Good For Him."

States was considering the annexation of the Hawaiian Islands, and in 1867 it purchased Alaska from Russia for the amazingly low price of $7.2 million.

Emperor Napoleon III tested the Monroe Doctrine during the Civil War by sending over Maximilian to establish the Mexican empire (see ch. 24). While the war raged, U. S. protests did little to sway the French. But after 1865, the 900,000 veterans backing up the protests plus the actions of the Mexican patriots forced Napoleon to withdraw his military and financial support. In 1867 a Mexican firing squad executed Maximilian.

Foreign affairs were virtually forgotten for the next generation, and one New York newspaper recommended the abolition of the foreign service. However, as productivity increased, the United States was forced to seek new outlets for its goods, especially now that the frontier had disappeared. Foreign trade increased from $393 million in 1870 to more than $1.333 billion in 1900. Investments abroad in the same period went from virtually nothing to $500 million. At the same time American missionary activity greatly expanded in Africa, the Middle East, and Asia. Like their European counterparts, many American leaders were influenced by Darwinism, especially when it was applied to foreign affairs. The slogan "survival of the fittest" had its followers in the U. S. Congress as well as in the British Parliament, French Chamber of Deputies, and German Reichstag. In order to be truly great, many argued, the United States must expand and assume a vital role in world politics. This argument was instrumental in the United States, acquisition of a global empire.

Roosevelt the Activist

The United States began building a modern navy in 1883, and by 1890 the buildup had accelerated greatly. Care was taken not to alarm the country, however, and the new ships were officially known as "seagoing coastline battleships," a handy nautical contradiction. When this naval program was initiated, the U. S. Navy ranked twelfth among the powers; by 1900 it had advanced to third place.

The growing international stature of the United States received startling confirmation in the border dispute between Britain and Venezuela in 1895. When Britain delayed before agreeing to submit the issue to arbitration, the State Department of the United States took the initiative and drafted a blunt note to London. The note warned the British that grave consequences would follow their refusal to accept arbitration. The State Department noted U. S. dominance in the western hemisphere and boasted that America's "infinite resources combined with its isolated position render it master of the situation and practically invulnerable against any or all other powers." Britain was preoccupied with the Boers in South Africa, the Germans on the continent, and the French in the Sudan and thus could not argue too strenuously against the message. The British agreed to resolve the dispute through arbitration.

There were signs of the new dynamism in American foreign policy in Asia as well. In 1899 U. S. Secretary of State John Hay initiated a policy for maintaining equal commercial rights in China for the traders of all nations, and the Open Door Policy in China became a reality. In the melodrama of the Boxer Rebellion (see p. 751), the United States again was a leader rather than a follower.

This heightened activity of the United States is best symbolized by the ideas and actions of Theodore Roosevelt. In his terms as president he was one of the leading figures on the world stage. At the request of the Japanese he assumed the role of peacemaker in the Russo-Japanese War. The peace conference, which met at Portsmouth,

The execution of Maximilian by firing squad in 1867. The protests of the United States against France's violation of the Monroe Doctrine helped convince Napoleon III to withdraw French military support of Maximilian's empire in Mexico. Without this support the empire soon collapsed.

President Theodore Roosevelt visited the Culebra Cut at the Panama Canal in November 1916. Here he is shown sitting on a 95-ton steam shovel.

New Hampshire, in 1905 successfully concluded a treaty, and in 1910 Roosevelt received the Nobel Peace Prize.

Roosevelt was not always a man of peace, however. When he believed the legitimate interests of the United States to be threatened, he did not hesitate to threaten or use force, as could be seen in Panama. In 1901 the British conceded to the United States the exclusive right to control any Isthmian canal that might be dug. For $40 million the United States bought the rights of a private French company that had already begun work on the canal. A lease was negotiated with Colombia, through whose territory the canal would be built, but that country's senate refused to ratify the treaty, claiming the compensation was too small. Roosevelt is reputed to have responded, "I did not intend that any set of bandits should hold up Uncle Sam." The upshot was a revolution, financed with money borrowed

from banker and financier John Pierpont Morgan. Panama, the new republic that seceded from Colombia in 1903, concluded a canal treaty with the United States, and in 1914 the canal was opened. The United States had moved far from its traditional place on the periphery of world affairs.

Latin America

The new nations of Latin America faced a complex of dilemmas that bequeathed a frustrating century of political instability and foreign economic domination. Civil wars, revolutions, and regimes came and went with alarming and costly regularity. Progressive leaders who tried to modernize their countries had to face the opposition of powerful, traditional institutions and massive and complex social problems.

The Creation of the Latin American States

In the first decades of the nineteenth century, the Latin American colonies pursued an irresistible movement for independence (see ch. 23). By 1825, Spanish and Portuguese power was broken in the Western Hemisphere, and nine new political units emerged in Latin America. Mexico, Guatemala, Great Colombia, Peru, Bolivia, Paraguay, Argentina, and Chile were free of Spain, and Brazil had gained its independence from Portugal. Once free of those powers, however, the new nations of Latin America were hampered by European and North American dominance over their economic and political affairs.

For most of the new Latin American nations their first half century was a time of decline and disappointment. The great liberators could not maintain control of the nations they had freed. The liberal, urban Creoles who had begun the independence movements were inexperienced and unable to make the political compromises necessary to govern new countries. They soon lost power to crude military leaders, or *caudillos*, whose armed gangs struggled for power in a confusing series of upheavals. A growing sectionalism accompanied these coups. Mammoth states broke up into tiny republics, which in turn were threatened by localism.

In part, Latin America's problems resulted from the Spanish colonial system that had offered native-born whites little opportunity or responsibility in government. The tradition of autocracy and paternalism was a poor precedent for would-be democratic republics. The emphasis on executive power inspired presidents, generals, landowners, and church officials to wield authority with arrogant disregard for public opinion and representative government.

The colonial economic system, based on raw materials rather than industry, encouraged concentration of land and other forms of wealth in a few hands. The church with its vast properties, monopoly on education and welfare agencies, and command over cultural life complicated the politics of every new nation.

In addition, the new states were cursed by problems associated with the wars of independence. Some of the most productive areas were devastated. Hatred and division remained. Many men who had fought the royalists remained armed, predisposed to a life of violence and pillage and likely to group themselves about the *caudillos*, who promised adventure or profit in revolutions.

The final problem facing the new states was that of racial disunity. In 1825 there were from 15 to 18 million people in the former Spanish empire. About 3 million of them were whites, the wealthiest and most educated population. That figure remained constant until the last third of the century, when immigration from Europe increased drastically. There were about the same number of *mestizos*, who scorned the Indians, but were not accepted by whites. Their numbers steadily increased, as did their ambition. During the nineteenth century at least half of the population in some states was Indian. Deprived of the small protection once offered by the Spanish crown, they either sank into peonage or lived in semi-independence under their tribal rulers. Finally, in Brazil and most of the Caribbean island, blacks were in a large majority. Conflicts of interest quickly developed between these broad racial groups, particularly between the Creoles and the *mestizos*. The pernicious effects of these divisive factors can be seen in the experiences of each nation.

Mexico

Despite its promising beginning in 1821, Mexico suffered a half-century of turmoil. The empire of Iturbide (see p. 603) lasted only a few months, and was replaced by a federal republic. In less than ten years, however, a coup enabled a preposterous military leader name Antonio Lopez de Santa Anna (1795–1876) to become dictator. His notorious rule witnessed the massacre of the defenders of the Alamo in 1836 and the general debasement of Mexico's political life. His conduct of the war with the United States (1846–1848) humiliated Mexico. The overthrow of this corrupt, incompetent *caudillo* in 1855 brought more thoughtful and circumspect men into politics.

The liberals, under the leadership of Benito Juarez (1806–1872) set out to implement a reform program known as the *Reforma*. They planned to establish a more democratic republic, destroy the political and economic force of the church, and include the *mestizos* and Indians in political life. A terrible civil war followed their anticlerical measures; it ended in 1861 with the apparent victory of Juarez, but inability to meet payments on debts owed to foreigners brought an invasion of Mexico by European powers and the establishment of a French puppet regime. By 1867 popular uprisings and pressure from the United States had driven French troops from Mexican soil.

Juarez again set out to institute the *Reforma*, but the poverty of the country hampered progress. After he died, one of his adherents, Porfirio Diaz (1830–1915), took power. Under Diaz, who served as president from 1877 to 1880 and again from 1884 to 1911, Mexican politics stabilized. Foreign capital entered in large amounts. Factories, railroads, mines, trading houses, plantations, and enormous ranches flourished, and Mexico City became one of the most impressive capitals in Latin America.

Diaz's rule, though outwardly conforming to the constitution, was a dictatorship. If there was much encouragement of arts and letters, there was no liberty. The Indians sank lower and lower into peonage or outright slavery. In spite of the anticlerical laws of the Juarez period, the church was quietly permitted to acquire great wealth, and foreign investors exploited Mexico, creating a long-lasting hatred of foreigners.

In 1910 the critics of Diaz found a spokesman in a frail, eccentric man named Francisco Madero (1873–1913) who undertook to lead a revolutionary movement and surprised the world by succeeding. Madero was murdered in 1913, and Mexico endured another period of turmoil during which the country was controlled mainly by self-styled local rulers. Still, a determined group was able to organize a revolutionary party and to bring about the only genuine social revolution that Latin America experienced until the First World War.

Argentina

Until the 1970s, Argentina was probably the most advanced Spanish-speaking country in the world. It attained this position in a period of sudden growth that followed a half century of sluggishness. Its beginning as a free nation was promising. Soon, however, the bustling port city of Buenos Aires, whose energetic population sought to encourage European capital and commerce, found itself overawed by the *caudillos*, the great ranchers of the interior, and their retainers, the *guachos*—colorful, nomadic, cowboys and bandits whose way of life has been romanticized in literature and folklore. The *caudillos* intimidated the supporters of constitutional government in Buenos Aires, and until midcentury, Argentina was not a republic, but rather a *gaucho* paradise, isolated and ruled by men who wanted to keep European influences out.

In 1852 a combination of progressive elements overthrew the *gaucho* leader. Commerce with Europe was revived and within ten years Argentina had become a united republic of admirable stability. The constitution was usually observed and individual rights were respected to a high degree. Immigrants poured in, and soon the population of Argentina became the most European of the New World republics, for it contained few Indians or blacks.

Foreign capital, especially British, brought about amazing developments; port facilities, railroads, light industry, and urban conveniences were among the most advanced in the world. Buenos Aires became by far the largest and most beautiful city in Latin America, despite its location on a monotonous, flat plain beside a muddy estuary.

The flat plain, or pampas, is perhaps the richest land in the world for grass and wheat, and livestock have been multiplying there for centuries. The introduction of refrigerated ships around 1880 made it feasible to transport enormous quantities of fresh beef to Britain in exchange for capital and finished goods. About 1900 wheat joined beef as a major Argentine export. This intimate commercial relationship with Britain, which lasted until after World War II, affected nearly every aspect of Argentine life.

Nevertheless, although elite society was dominated by leaders who were pro-British in business and pro-French in culture, a true Argentine nationalism was developing. Along with the growth of this powerful sentiment came demands for more democracy and a wider distribution of wealth.

Brazil

For many years this former Portuguese colony escaped the turbulence and disorders that befell its Spanish-speaking neighbors, probably because it had achieved independence without years of warfare and military dominance and because it enjoyed the continuity and legitimacy afforded by a respected monarchy. The first emperor, Pedro I (1822–1831), promulgated a constitution in 1824, and the accession to the throne of Pedro II in 1840 initiated a period of political liberty and economic and cultural progress that lasted throughout his fifty-year reign.

Immigrants were attracted to this peaceful land, and foreign investments were heavy, but without the massive exploitation that Mexico experienced under Diaz. Economic growth tended to favor the southeastern part of the country at the expense of the great sugar plantations in the tropical north. The abolition of slavery in 1888 hurt the sugar lords economically, and they rose up against the emperor. Joining them were army officers, who resented the civilian nature of Pedro's regime, and a small number of ideological republicans. In 1889 the aging emperor was forced to abdicate.

For nearly ten years the new federal republic of Brazil underwent civil wars and military upheavals, much like those experienced by other Latin American countries. Finally, the republic

Francisco Madero, The Plan of San Luis Potosí

The Mexican revolutionary movement received its most eloquent definition in the plan of San Luis Potosí, written by Francisco Madero from his exile in San Antonio, Texas.

Peoples, in their constant efforts for the triumph of the ideal of liberty and justice, are forced, at precise historical moments, to make their greatest sacrifices.

Our beloved country has reached one of those moments. A force of tyranny which we Mexicans were not accustomed to suffer after we won our independence oppresses us in such a manner that it has become intolerable. In exchange for that tyranny we are offered peace, but peace full of shame for the Mexican nation. . . .

It may almost be said that martial law constantly exists in Mexico; the administration of justice, instead of imparting protection to the weak, merely serves to legalize the plunderings committed by the strong; the judges instead of being the representatives of justice, are the agents of the executive, whose interests they faithfully serve; the chambers of the union have no other will than that of the dictator; the governors of the States are designated by him and they in their turn designate and impose in like manner the municipal authorities.

From this it results that the whole administrative, judicial, and legislative machinery obeys a single will, the caprice of General Porfirio Díaz, who during his long administration has shown that the principal motive that guides him is to maintain himself in power and at any cost. . . .

For this reason the Mexican people have protested against the illegality of the last election and, desiring to use successively all the recourses offered by the laws of the Republic, in due form asked for the nullification of the election by the Chamber of Deputies, notwithstanding they recognized no legal origin in said body and knew beforehand that, as its members were not the representatives of the people, they would carry out the will of General Díaz, to whom exclusively they owe their investiture.

In such a state of affairs the people, who are the only sovereign, also protested energetically against the election in imposing manifestations in different parts of the Republic; and if the latter were not general throughout the national territory, it was due to the terrible pressure exercised by the Government, which always quenches in blood any democratic manifestation, as happened in Puebla, Vera Cruz, Tlaxcala, and in other places.

But this violent and illegal system can no longer subsist.

I have very well realized that if the people have designated me as their candidate for the Presidency it is not because they have had an opportunity to discover in me the qualities of a statesman or of a ruler, but the virility of the patriot determined to sacrifice himself, if need be, to obtain liberty and to help the people free themselves from the odious tyranny that oppresses them. . . .

Therefore, and in echo of the national will, I declare the late election illegal and, the Republic being accordingly without rulers, provisionally assume the Presidency of the Republic until the people designate their rulers pursuant to the law. In order to attain this end, it is necessary to eject from power the audacious usurpers whose only title of legality involves a scandalous and immoral fraud.

From United States Congress, Senate Subcommittee on Foreign Relations, *Revolutions in Mexico*, 62nd Congress, 2nd Session (Washington, D.C.; Government Printing Office, 1913).

was stabilized with the army in control, and Brazil resumed its progressive course. Foreign capital continued to enter, and immigration from Europe remained heavy. By 1914 Brazil was generally stable and prosperous, with a growing tradition of responsible government.

Other Latin American Nations

Political turmoil, geographical handicaps, and racial disunity all played a part in the development of the other new nations in Latin America. Bolivia, named so hopefully for the Liberator Simon Bolívar, underwent countless revolutions. Peru's course was almost as futile. The state of Great Colombia dissolved by 1830, and its successors—Colombia, Venezuela, and Ecuador—were plagued by instability and civil wars. Paraguay endured a series of dictatorships and Uruguay, created in 1828 as a buffer between Argentina and Brazil, long suffered from interventions by those two countries.

An exception to the prevailing pattern of political chaos was the steady growth of the republic of Chile. in 1830 Chile came under the control of a conservative oligarchy. Although this regime proved to be generally enlightened, the country was kept under tight control for a century and was ruled for the benefit of the large landlords and big business.

Central America narrowly escaped becoming part of Mexico in 1822. After a fifteen-year effort to create a Central American confederation, Guatemala, San Salvador, Honduras, Nicaragua, and Costa Rica asserted their independence. Except for Costa Rica, where whites comprised the bulk of the population, racial disunity delayed the development of national feeling. In the Caribbean the Dominican Republic, after decades of submission to more populous but equally underdeveloped Haiti, maintained a precarious independence.

Foreign Dominance

The Industrial Revolution came into full stride just after the Latin American republics were born. The great industries of western Europe and the United States demanded more and more raw materials and new markets in which to sell finished products. Capital accumulated, and investors eagerly sought opportunities to place their money where they could obtain high rates of interest. This drive for markets, raw materials, and outlets for surplus capital led to classic examples of economic imperialism.

The continual disorder and the lack of strong governments in Latin America gave businesses the opportunity to obtain rich concessions and float huge loans. Many of the Latin American government leaders, brought to power through revolution and interested only in personal gain, often resorted to the vicious practice of selling concessions to foreign corporations for ready cash. Political bosses bartered away the economic heritage of their lands, for Latin America was rich in minerals, oil, and other important resources. Foreign investors sometimes acted in good faith, providing capital at a reasonable rate of interest to Latin American regimes which, it became apparent, had no intention of fulfilling the contract. On other occasions unscrupulous capitalists took full advantage of officials in ignorant or helpless governments.

Injured foreign investors usually appealed to their government to intercede in their behalf, and an unending stream of diplomatic correspondence over debt claims was begun. The United States, Great Britain, Germany, France, Italy, Spain—the chief investor states—would not permit their citizens to be mistreated in their ventures into foreign investments.

In 1902–1903 a dispute between Venezuela and a coalition formed by Germany, Great Britain, and Italy provoked the three European powers into blockading the Latin American country and even firing on some of the coastal fortifications to remind the Venezuelan dictator of his obligations to some of their nationals. U. S. President Theodore Roosevelt at first stood by, watching Venezuela take its punishment. Then he became suspicious of German motives and began to match threat with threat, forcing the Europeans to back down and place the issue into international arbitration.

In 1904 Roosevelt issued the Roosevelt Corollary to the Monroe Doctrine, an addition that was a frank statement that chronic wrongdoing on the part of Latin American governments might force the United States to exercise an international police power. Picturesquely described as the policy of speaking softly but carrying a big stick, the Roosevelt pronouncement launched the era of the Big Stick. The United States established a customs receivership in the Dominican Republic and exercised similar control in Nicaragua and Haiti. The Roosevelt Corollary expanded the Monroe Doctrine from its original purpose of keeping out European political interference in Latin America to enlarging the commercial interests of the United States.

In 1898 the United States had gone to war with Spain over the way the Spaniards ruled Cuba: the mistreatment of the Cubans also affected American commercial interests. Victory in the brief, dramatic, and well-publicized Spanish-American War brought the United States recognition as a world power and a conglomeration of islands in the Pacific Ocean as well as in the Caribbean. The United States annexed Puerto Rico and placed the Philippines, halfway around the world, under American rule. Sensitive to accusations of imperialism in Cuba, the U. S. government offered Cuba an imperfect, closely tutored independence in which the Cubans were obliged by law to acknowledge the right of the United States to intervene for the "preservation of Cuban independence" and the "maintenance of a government adequate for the protection of life,

President William McKinley on Imperialism

Even the Americans joined the imperialistic race. Unlike the Europeans, who propounded intellectually sophisticated rationalizations, the Americans moved for different, often celestial, reasons. McKinley noted:

I have been criticized a good deal about the Philippines, but I don't deserve it. The truth is, I didn't want the Philippines, and when they came to us, as a gift from the gods, I did not know what to do with them. When the Spanish war broke out, Dewey was at Hongkong, and I ordered him to go to Manila, and he had to; because, if defeated, he had no place to refit on that side of the globe, and if the Dons were victorious they would likely cross the Pacific and ravage our Oregon and California coasts. And so he had to destroy the Spanish fleet, and did it. But that was as far as I thought then. When next I realized that the Philippines had dropped into our lap, I confess that I did not know what to do with them. I sought counsel from all sides—Democrats as well as Republicans—but got little help. I thought first we would take only Manila; then Luzon; then other islands, perhaps all. I walked the floor of the White House night after night until midnight; and I am not ashamed to tell you, gentlemen, that I went down on my knees and prayed Almighty God for light and guidance more than one night.

And one night late it came to me this way—I don't know how it was, but it came:

(1) That we could not give them back to Spain—that would be cowardly and dishonorable; (2) that we could not turn them over to France or Germany—that would be bad business and discreditable; (3) that we could not leave them to themselves—they were unfit for self-government—and they would soon have anarchy and misrule over there worse than Spain's was; and (4) that there was nothing left for us to do but to take them all, and to educate the Filipinos, and uplift and civilize and Christianize them, and, by God's grace, do the very best we could by them, as our fellowmen for whom Christ also died. And then I went to bed, and went to sleep, and slept soundly, and next morning I sent for the chief engineer of the War Department (our map-maker), and told him to put the Philippines on the map of the United States (pointing to a large map on the wall of his office); "and there they are, and there they will stay while I am president!"

From G. A. Malcolm and M. M. Kalw, *Philippine Government* (Boston, 1932).

A Critic of Imperialism

Francisco Garcia Calderón saw not only the great powers' political impact but also the debilitating cultural problems.

Interventions have become more frequent with the expansion of frontiers. The United States have recently intervened in the territory of Acre, there to found a republic of rubber gatherers; at Panama, there to develop a province and construct a canal: in Cuba, under cover of the Platt Amendment, to maintain order in the interior; in Santo Domingo, to support the civilising revolution and overthrow the tyrants; in Venezuela, and in Central America, to enforce upon these nations, torn by intestine disorders, the political and financial tutelage of the imperial democracy. In Guatemala and Honduras the loans concluded with the monarchs of North American finance have reduced the people to a new slavery. Supervision of the customs and the dispatch of pacificatory squadrons to defend the interests of the Anglo-Saxon have enforced peace and tranquility: such are the means employed. The New York American announces that Mr. Pierpont Morgan proposes to encompass the finances of Latin America by a vast network of Yankee banks. Chicago merchants and Wall Street financiers created the Meat Trust in the Argentine. The United States offer millions for the purpose of converting into Yankee loans the moneys raised in London during the last century by the Latin American States; they wish to obtain a monopoly of credit. It has even been announced, although the news hardly appears probable, that a North American syndicate wished to buy enormous belts of land in Guatemala, where the English tongue is the obligatory language. The fortification of the Panama Canal, and the possible acquisition of the Galapagos Island in the Pacifiic, are fresh manifestations of imperialistic progress. . . .

Warnings, advice, distrust, invasion of capital, plans of financial hegemony all these justify the anxiety of the southern peoples. . . . Neither irony nor grace nor scepticism, gifts of the old civilizations, can make way against the plebeian brutality, the excessive optimism, the violent individualism of the [North American] people.

All these things contribute to the triumph of mediocrity; the multitude of primary schools, the vices of utilitarianism, the cult of the average citizen, the transatlantic M. Homais, and the tyranny of opinion noted by Tocqueville; and in this vulgarity, which is devoid of traditions and has no leading aristocracy, a return to the primitive type of the redskin, which has already been noted by close observers, is threatening the proud democracy. From the excessive tensions of wills, from the elementary state of culture, from the perpetual unrest of life, from the harshness of the industrial struggle, anarchy and violence will be born in the future. In a hundred years men will seek in vain for the "American soul," the "genius of America," elsewhere than in the undisciplined force or the violence which ignores moral laws. . . .

Essential points of difference separate the two Americas. Differences of language and therefore of spirit; the difference between Spanish Catholicism and multiform Protestantism of the Anglo-Saxons; between the Yankee individualism and the omnipotence of the State natural to the nations of the South. In their origin, as in their race, we find fundamental antagonism; the evolution of the North is slow and obedient to the lessons of time, to the influences of custom; the history of the southern peoples is full of revolutions, rich with dreams of an unattainable perfection.

From Francisco Garcia Calderón, *Latin America: Its Rise and Progress* (London: T. F. Unwin, 1913).

Nearly one-quarter of the invasion force that sailed for Cuba was made up of black troops. This illustration of the Battle of Quasimas near Santiago, Cuba, June 24, 1898, shows the 9th and 10th Colored Cavalry supporting the Rough Riders in the battle against the Spanish. Black soldiers also helped the Rough Riders take San Juan Hill.

property, and individual liberty." These and other restrictions on Cuban independence were embodied in the Platt Amendment (1901) to the new Cuban constitution. Thus the United States established its first American protectorate. Panama soon became another protectorate of the United States. Generally both American business and the local population profited.

Roosevelt oversaw the introduction of what has been called Dollar Diplomacy—the coordinated activites of American foreign investors and the U. S. State Department to obtain and protect concessions for the investors. From 1890 this policy won concessions for Americans in Latin American products such as sugar, bananas, and oil from more than a dozen Latin American republics.

In the face of such activities, the pious assertions of those espousing the Pan-American philosophy—that the nations of the western hemisphere were bound by common geography and democratic political ideals—gained little acceptance. The "Colossus of the North," as the Latin American nations referred to the United States clearly acted in its own self-interest. Sarcastic observers referred to the Pan-American Union, founded in 1889, as "the Colonial Division of the Department of State." By 1914 Latin America's relations with the rest of the world were neither healthy nor comforting. After a century of independence, Latin America still lingered on the margins of international life. Left to shift for itself in the face of a future shaded by U.S. imperialism, Latin America saw only a hard road ahead in its relations with the outside world.

Conclusion

From the seventeenth through the nineteenth centuries the greatest human migration from the smallest continent, Europe, had taken place. This migration surpassed in scope such momentous human wanderings of the past as those of the Indo-Europeans into India and southern Europe and the incursions of the Germanic tribes into the Roman Empire. Transoceanic in character, this mass movement originated in Europe, which during this period, forged ahead of the rest of the world in industry, technology and science, wealth, and military power.

This dispersal of Europeans has been treated mainly in the history of the British Dominions, the United States, and Latin America. However, equally affected were the African peoples, shipped by the million in a vicious slave trade to develop the vast natural resources of the new lands. They contributed substantially to the cultures and economies of their new societies, especially in Latin America and the United States, but paid an incredible cost—especially in the United States.

The United States with its profound varieties of development, despite a common European heritage, was by far the most important of the new lands of the nineteenth century. The frontier and slavery both influenced the formation of a distinctive society, and the latter bequeathed to the country the most intractable of its twentieth century domestic problems. The Civil War had more "revolutionary" consequences—socially, economially, and politically—than any other event occurring in the new lands.

Suggestions for Reading

R. W. Logan, *The Negro in the United States* (Anvil, 1954). *. . . The Nadir, 1877–1901.* traces the plight of blacks in post-reconstruction America. See also C. Vann Woodward, *The Strange Career of Jim Crow* (Oxford, 1974); J. Forbes Munroe, *Africa and the International Economy* (London, 1976). and E. D. Genovese, *Roll Jordan, Roll: The world the Slaves Made* (Random House, 1976). See H. E. Driver, *Indians of North America* (Chicago, 1969) for an overview of the Native Americans' contact with and overwhelming by the whites and Basil Davidson, *Black Mother: The Years of the African Slave Trade* (Little, Brown, 1961).

A. R. M. Lower's *Colony to Nation: a History of Canada*, (Toronto, 1946) a history of Canada from the British conquest to 1850. For two important aspects of Canadian history see Bruce Hutchinson, *The Struggle for the Border* (Longman, 1955), and D. M. L. Faar, *The Colonial Office and Canada* (Toronto, 1948). See L. Lipson, *Politics of Equality*, (Chicago, 1948). For provocative studies of history and society, see O. H. K. Spate, *Australia* (Praeger, 1968) and Douglas Pike, *Australia* (Cambridge, 1969). See M. Wilson and L. Thompson, eds., *The Oxford History of South Africa* (1969). Also recommended is E. Roux, *Time Longer than Rope, A History of the Blackman's Struggle for Freedom in South Africa* (Wisconsin, 1964).

For a brief and stimulating survey of the first half of U. S. history, see M. Cunliffe, *The Nation Takes Shape: 1789–1837* (Univ. of Chicago, 1959), Also recommended is A. M. Schlesinger's classic *The Age of Jackson* (Mentor, 1945). Paul H. Buck's *The Road to Reunion 1865–1900* is a good survey of the consequences of the Civil War (Little, Brown, 1937), A good chance to read great literature and fine biography is Carl Sandburg's three-volume biography of Lincoln. (Many editions)

A critique of the American scene that has become a classic is Alexis de Tocqueville's *Democracy in America* (Mentor). George E. Mowry skillfully characterized *The Era of Theodore Roosevelt* (Torchbook, 1958). See also Arthur S. Link, *Woodrow Wilson and the Progressive Era* (Torchbooks, 1963).

Some useful studies of Latin America in the nineteeth and early twentieth centuries are Miron Burgin, *The Economic Aspects of Argentinian Federalism, 1820–1852* (Harvard, 1946); J. R. Scobie, *Revolution on the Pampas: A Social History of Argentine Wheat* (Texas, 1964); R. L. Gilmore, *Caudillism and Militarism in Venezuela 1810–1910* (Ohio Univ., 1964); T. L. Karnes, *The Failure of Union: Central America 1824–1960* (Univ. of North Carolina, 1961); and M. C. Meyer and W. L. Sherman, *The Course of Mexican History* (Oxford, 1979). See also D. Bushnell and N. Macauley, *The Emergence of Latin America in the Nineteenth Century,* (Oxford, 1988)

Notes

1. Hubert Herring, *History of Latin America* (New York: Alfred A. Knopf, 1956), p. 97.
2. Alfred L. Burt, *The British Empire and Commonwealth* (Boston: D. C. Heath, 1956), p. 286.
3. C. Van Doren, ed., *The Literary Works of Abraham Lincoln* (New York: Limited Editions Club, 1941), p. 65.
4. S. E. Morison, *The Oxford History of the American People* (London: Oxford Univ. Press, 1965), p. 793.
5. Quoted in F. R. Dulles, *America's Rise to World Power* (New York: Harper & Row, 1955), p. 4.

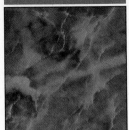

Chapter 28

The Middle East and Africa, 1800–1914

In the eigthteenth and nineteenth centuries, Europeans steadily advanced into the Middle East and Africa. Europe's economic, technological, and military superiority overwhelmed the diverse civilizations and made them targets in the competition for empire.

The Islamic world retained its religious strength in the face of the European onslaught, but the disintegration of the Ottoman Empire brought about massive change. In Central Asia, the Persians and Afghans were caught up in the great power rivalry between the British and the Russians. In Africa the diversity of tribes made a unified political response to the Europeans impossible. By the beginning of the nineteenth century the Africans had begun a slow and painful process of adapting to the industrialized world.

The Middle East

In 1800 the Islamic world stretched from the Atlantic Ocean to the Pacific, in a broad band that reached across North Africa, the Middle East, Central Asia, and down to Indonesia. The Islamic religion retained its original vigor, and the Islamic world followed similar religious and cultural forms. This came from a way of life based on the Koran emphasizing daily prayers, fasting, and pilgrimages to Mecca. By the late nineteenth century, more than 175 million Muslims performed daily religious duties. Whatever their race or nationality, Muslims shared the same sacred language, law, morality, social structure, and institutions. Every year the number of believers traveling to Mecca grew. It is estimated that by 1900 more than 50,000 Indians and 20,000 Malays were making the trip each year.

The Islamic world mirrored the great diversity of peoples, environments, and external pressures that affected the faithful from Ceuta in Morocco to Djakarta in Indonesia. Even in religious matters, doctrinal differences split devout Muslims into rival sects, and these differences were as devastating as those afflicting Christianity.

Fragmentation made the Islamic world vulnerable, especially before the material strength of the industrialized Western world. The diverse populations with the Islamic world, including Arabs, Indians, Berbers, and Egyptians, had little in common except in matters of religion, culture, and language. The absence of political unity made the region militarily vulnerable.

An equally serious problem was economic weakness. Consisting principally of deserts and arid lands, the Islamic world clung to outdated agricultural techniques long abandoned by the West. Islam's prohibition of usury hampered the growth of modern capitalist institutions (banks, for example) and the evolution of a middle class. Despite the fact that Muslims occupied such strategic locations as areas around the Bosporus and the Dardanelles, the Suez, the overland route to India, and the Persian Gulf region, the Islamic world suffered from a poor communications and transportation system.

During the nineteenth century, the Ottoman Empire, Persia, and Afghanistan could not build an adequate political or economic base from which to defend themselves against Britain or Russia. The modern state structure—with its professional bureaucrats, broadly based nationalism and patriotism, ideologies, mass literacy, and civil law structure—did not exist in the Islamic world.

To a large degree the major occupations of nineteenth-century western Europe—research scientist, party politician, state functionary, technologist, and industrial worker—and the social flexibility for men and women were not present among the Muslim nations either. Instead, the function of warrior remained primary, and political life fluctuated between the despotic and the nonchalant. Corruption, social decay, lack of education and literacy also blocked effective government. In short, the Middle Eastern states could not effectively mobilize their resources or move their citizens. The Europeans moved in to take advantage of the Islamic world's vulnerability.[1]

The Disintegrating Ottoman Empire

Even though the Ottoman Empire had been in a state of decline since the end of the seventeenth century, two hundred years later it was still the largest and most prestigious realm in the Islamic world (see map below). The Sultan ruled territory extending from North Africa to the Indian Ocean. But the sultan's control over forty million people living there was often weak and sporadic.

The lines of power and communication to the empire's far corners were not dependable. The farther one went from Constantinople the less secure was Turkish control. At its inception in the sixteenth century the Ottoman administration had been a picture of effectiveness. In the next two centuries it declined as the merit basis for administration came to be replaced by bribery and favoritism. The armed forces, once the most feared in all Europe, also weakened and they came to be as much a threat to the sultan as to foreign enemies.

More than most, the Ottoman state was based on war, and to ensure its stability the Turks needed the momentum of continuous victory. However, their very success as fighters doomed them. They had pushed the Ottoman control to its extreme limits of the Atlas and Caucasus mountains. Short-range wars of conquest were no longer possible, and the warrior class became complacent. In addition, by the late seventeenth century the Europeans had become stronger and for the first time were able to defeat the Turks. Europe profited from the Scientific Revolution,

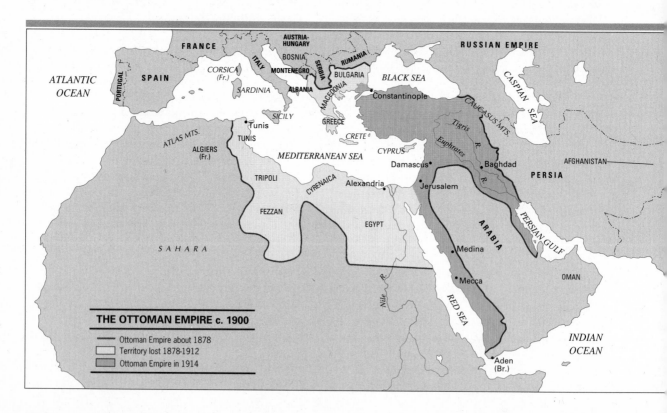

THE OTTOMAN EMPIRE c. 1900
— Ottoman Empire about 1878
☐ Territory lost 1878-1912
▨ Ottoman Empire in 1914

Enlightenment, and industrialization. The Ottoman Empire chose not to pursue these developments, nor did it look to take advantage of the forces of nationalism and patriotism to mobilize its diverse populations. As the western states improved their positions, the Turks could not change to keep up.[2]

Discontent with the Turks' rule resulted in revolts in the 1630s (the Druse), the 1740s (the Wahhabi), and 1769 (the revolt led by Ali Bey Al-Kabir). Instead of addressing the causes of these major rebellions, the Turks rededicated themselves to the defense of their foundation of life and law—Islam.[3] In the nineteenth century this was not a sufficiently flexible basis for competition in the international arena.

From the 1790s on, there were attempts made to reform the Turkish system. The Koran was the foundation for Islam, and although it was the most important basis for a Muslim's daily existence, it did not contain all of the answers to the questions of technological change. Firearms and artillery had been accepted from the infidel for centuries because they could be used in defense of the faith. The clock and the printing press, two symbols of Western advance, were not allowed. Bernard Lewis tells us that no printing was allowed in Istanbul in either Turkish or Arabic until 1729, and then the publication of books was sporadic until the end of the century.

After the 1780s, foreign influences were increasingly felt in the Ottoman empire: military advisers and diplomats entered more and more and the sultans began establishing permanent diplomatic posts in Europe. As is the case with developing states today, the military in the empire came to be the most advanced element in society. The training it received in modern technology necessitated the learning of foreign languages and political theory. A whole new group emerged, trained to look beyond the Koran for their information, and even their inspiration.[4]

The power of tradition and the faith made the drive for reform a hesitant one at best. Those who went too fast, such as Sultan Selim III (1789–1807) were overthrown. Later in the nineteenth century, sultans concerned with becoming more competitive with the Europeans were hampered in their reform attempts by the administrative chaos of the empire. Reforms rarely had reached further than a day's ride from Istanbul.

Eugène Delacroix, *Massacre of Chios* (1824). European liberals and romantics like Delacroix supported the Greeks in their struggle for independence from the Turks, who were seen as cruel oppressors.

Perhaps sensing the weakening at the center and taking advantage of the changes brought by the Napoleonic era, the peoples of the Balkans began to work for independence. The Montenegrins, who never acknowledged Ottoman domination, received recognition of their independent status in 1799. In response to a breakdown of Ottoman administration, the Serbs rose in revolt in 1804, followed by the Greeks in 1821, Romania in the 1850s, and Bulgaria in the 1870s. Russia continued to pressure the Turks while the other powers intruded more and more on the sultan's affairs. Vassals in Albania, Egypt, and Macedonia rebelled. Particularly serious was Mehmet Ali's challenge in the 1820s and '30s when he took Crete and Syria. Not only did he threaten Istanbul, he pushed his gains to the Persian Gulf and Indian Ocean. By the 1840s a combination of the great powers pushed him back to Egypt, where he remained as a viceroy.

The empire's weakness was especially exposed in the prelude to the Crimean War when Russia and France squabbled over the holy places of Christianity. Istanbul served merely as an arena in which Europe's diplomats debated the Turks' fate. Even though the Turks emerged from the turmoil with their great power status guaranteed, it was apparent to all that the empire was kept alive only because the Europeans could think of no other alternative for the strategic state. In 1860 France gained the right to intervene in Syria. In 1874 the Ottoman financial structure collapsed under the pressure of huge foreign loans, just at the time of renewed uprisings in the Balkans.

Young Turks

In 1876 Midhat Pasha, a dedicated reformer and provincial Governor, unveiled a plan for a new, western-style political structure in the Ottoman empire. Under his scheme the empire was declared to be a unitary state with the guarantees of free press, freedom of conscience, equality under the law, and equal taxation. In addition, he proposed the creation of an Ottoman citizenship, a step away from the traditional theocratic basis of power. The plan was proclaimed in Istanbul in December 1876 and Midhat Pasha became grand vizir. Unfortunately for the empire, Abdul Hamid II—the new sultan who came to the throne soon after—destroyed the reform plans, dismissed Midhat Pasha as grand vizir, and suspended the parliament.

By the spring of 1877, Abdul Hamid was trying to rule as his predecessors four centuries earlier had—absolutely. Spies spread throughout the country to track down liberals and other opponents. Censorship was applied and those who had worked for reforms disappeared mysteriously or were forced into exile. At a time when he needed unity and change to preserve his crumbling holdings, Abdul Hamid chose to split up potential opponents and destroy them. The sultan's basic problem was not the reform movement, but the reactionary nature of his policies.

The sultan faced severe challenges on all fronts. Throughout his realm nationalist movements threatened his rule. The European powers continued their economic and political pressures on his holdings: France annexed Tunis in 1881, Britain occupied Egypt in 1882, and

Abdul Hamid II. Widespread discontent with his oppressive rule lent strength to the reform movement of the Young Turks, who ultimately deposed the sultan in 1909.

in 1900 Italy reached for Tripoli. Remaining under Turkish rule were the Arabs of the Middle East, primarily Muslim in religion, with significant Christian minorities in some areas. They were beginning to be affected by the same nationalistic spirit that had spread through nineteenth-century Europe. They joined the Balkans nations in pushing for concessions from the weak Ottoman structure. By the beginning of the twentieth century, opposition to the sultan's tyranny and misrule was widespread among his many subjects.

A nucleus of opposition formed among a group of exciled reformers who had been educated in western European universities. In 1902 these opponents—the Young Turks—and other national groups oppressed by the sultan met in Paris to form a united opposition to Abdul Hamid. They advocated a modernized, western state with a professional police force, a sound economic policy, and substantial social reforms. They adopted the European clock and recommended broad-ranging educational opportunities and revised dress codes to bring women out of seclusion.

At the same time a number of young army officers joined the Young Turks, giving the movement the military power and coordination it needed for a successful rebellion. In 1908 the Young Turks told the sultan to put the 1876 constitution into effect or else face an armed uprising. Abdul Hamid saw the weakness of his position and agreed to the demands. But after gaining their initial goals, the revolutionaries split deeply over the question of the status of non-Turks in the new regime. Some of the Young Turks wanted to grant full political rights to the minorities, while others advocated severe restrictions. The new parliament that came into existence after the restoration immediately bogged down over the rights of subject nationalities. Encouraged by the division within the parliament, the sultan attempted a counterrevolution to regain power. When he turned against the Young Turks—who by this time had gained substantial popular support—he was overthrown in 1909.

Arabs in Syria, Lebanon, and the vast Arabian peninsula were not happy with the new regime. Along with the Albanians in the Balkans, they were repelled by the Young Turks' program of Turkish supremacy and their policy of centralization, which would obviously leave no hopes for Arab home rule. When World War I broke out in 1914, the British, once an Allied victory was assured, had little difficulty in turning the Arab nations against the Turkish sultan.

Other parts of the empire fell away during and after the Young Turk revolt. Between 1908 and 1913, Austria-Hungary annexed Bosnia and Herzegovina, Greece annexed Crete, and Italy—in the course of a short but difficult war—seized Tripoli and Cyrenaica. Finally, in 1912 and 1913, the Balkan nations fought two wars, which resulted in the partitioning of Macedonia. The once mighty Ottoman empire was finally destroyed.

The "Great Game"

The area between the Caspian Sea and the Persian Gulf served as the focus of conflict between Britain and Russia during the nineteenth century. The attention of these two major powers could not have been welcomed by the two nations caught in the crossfire, Persia and Afghanistan (see map, p. 726).

Persia (now Iran), one of the more strategically located areas of the Islamic world, contained many different peoples (Turks, Arabs, Persians, Kurds, Jews, and Armenians) and religions (Islam, Zoroastrianism, Judaism, and Armenian Christianity). Ruling over this crossroads area was the Kajar Dynasty, which had to deal with the Russians to the north and the British to the south.

Afghanistan, which lay to the east of Persia, controlled the Khyber Pass, the most direct land

Young Turks march in triumph after their successful coup and overthrow of the despot Abdul Hamid II and his reactionary government.

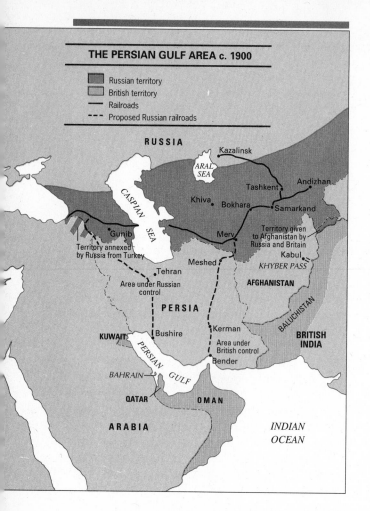

THE PERSIAN GULF AREA c. 1900

- ▓ Russian territory
- ░ British territory
- — Railroads
- --- Proposed Russian railroads

RUSSIA

Kazalinsk

ARAL SEA

Tashkent · Andizhan

Khiva · Bokhara · Samarkand

CASPIAN SEA

Gunib

Territory annexed by Russia from Turkey

Merv

Territory given to Afghanistan by Russia and Britain

Tehran

Meshed

Kabul

KHYBER PASS

Area under Russian control

AFGHANISTAN

PERSIA

KUWAIT

Bushire

Kerman

Area under British control

Bender

BALUCHISTAN

BRITISH INDIA

BAHRAIN

PERSIAN GULF

QATAR

OMAN

ARABIA

INDIAN OCEAN

route from Russia to British-controlled India. The mountainous country had been divided previously between the Mongols and Persians. By the nineteenth century the shah in Kabul, Afghanistan's capital city, ruled over the tribal confederations that roamed the country.

Russia had begun its advance toward the region in the middle of the sixteenth century. From that time to the present, the Russians have had a deep and abiding interest in the Islamic world to the south. Russia had several motives in pursuing control of this region: it needed a warm-water port, a direct trade route to India, and a defensive buffer zone between European Russia and Asia. Throughout the eighteenth and nineteenth centuries the Russians extended their control across the Black Sea, the Caucasus, and into central Asia to the frontiers of Persia and Afghanistan. Their advance drew the worried attention of the British.

Britain wanted to maintain control of the sea lanes of the eastern Mediterranean, and after 1869 it sought sole access to the Suez Canal. European power politics in the 1840s, 1850s, and 1870s had helped the British thwart the Russian drive to control the Straits, Constantinople, and the eastern Mediterranean. But Russia's expansion across the Urals threatened the British from another flank—through central Asia. British foreign policy in the nineteenth

This 1885 cartoon from *Punch* shows the British lion and the Indian tiger watching apprehensively as the Russian bear attacks the Afghan wolf.

A contemporary Russian drawing of a construction train on the Trans-Caspian Railway. Completion of this railway allowed Russia to transport and supply troops to central Asia and extend its economic influence in that area.

century focused equally on defense of India's land frontiers to the north and protection of the Suez Canal, Red Sea, and the Persian Gulf.

During the first half of the century, Persia and Afghanistan were caught up in armed conflicts with the Russians and the British. The Persians, defeated in two wars by the Russians, lost large amounts of territory and had to pay substantial indemnities. In an attempt to gain control of the Khyber Pass, the British fought the Afghans from 1839 to 1842. In the first part of the conflict a 3,000-man British force was massacred. Later, British troops from India took control of the region. Britain's advances were gained by a strong army and controlled by a well-trained colonial government. Persia and Afghanistan weakened as the two major European forces extended their power from north and south.

While the British consolidated their hold on India, Russia expanded toward the southeast. Many indigenous peoples, such as the Mongols, Afghans, Turkomans, and Tatars, came within Russia's sphere of influence. Their cities—Samarkand, Tashkent, and Bokhara—became tsarist administrative centers.

Russia's advance was won not only by its army, but also by the construction of the Trans-Caspian Railway which, at its completion in 1888, reached 1064 miles into the heart of Asia. The Orenburg-Tashkent railway, completed in 1905, stretched 1185 miles farther. Both lines vastly increased Russia's ability to maintain military pressure on and economic superiority over the area. Inspired by the feats of both the army and the engineers, some Russian imperialists

dreamed of conquering Afghanistan and penetrating India itself. The central Asian thrust was part of the "Great Game" between Britain and Russia—Russian pressure against India was designed primarily as a counter against Britain in other areas.[5]

At the end of the nineteenth century Afghanistan and Tibet continued to be serious areas of tension. Effective British pressure blocked Russia's design on Afghanistan and a British military expedition to Lhasa in 1904 countered Russian influence in Tibet. Persia, however, remained a more difficult problem.

The Persian Dilemma

Britain made economic inroads into Persia during the nineteenth century, gaining control of most of the area's mineral wealth and banking operations. The British completed a telegraph line from London to Persia in 1870, symbolizing the direct tie between Britain and that far-off land.

During the last part of the century, the Persians attempted a program of westernization, complete with a new capital at Tehran. They made major investments to establish hospitals, a school system, as well as an army. But all of this cost money, which the Persians borrowed from the British and the Russians. The great powers, in their turn, gained control of a large part of the country's economy.

The British may have blocked the Russians in other areas, but Persia remained an area of competition. The Royal Navy, based at Aden, was charged with keeping communications routes open from India to the Suez and with protecting the entry to the Red Sea. Along the Arabian coast the British gained control, through treaties with a number of friendly, minuscule sheikdoms such as Muscat, Oman, Bahrain, and Kuwait. The maintenance of this sphere of influence effectively blocked German and French efforts to gain footholds along the Persian Gulf.

Germany had tried unsuccessfully to build a terminus on the Persian Gulf for its projected Berlin-to-Baghdad railroad. In 1903 the British foreign secretary issued what has been called a British Monroe Doctrine over the area: "I say it without hesitation, we should regard the establishment of a naval base or a fortified port in the Persian Gulf by any other power as a very grave menace to British interests, and we should certainly resist it by all means at our disposal."[6]

Although Britain had discouraged German attempts to build a railroad to Persia, there was still the possibility that the Russian Trans-Caucasian Railway might be extended south through Persia to the warm waters of the Persian Gulf. In this event the tsar's government might not only profit commercially but might also build a naval base that would threaten the British sea route to India.

Persia was in no position to resist Russian pressure. Its government was corrupt and inefficient, and Russia took advantage of its weakness. By the beginning of the twentieth century parts of northern Persia were in the control of the Russians. Tsarist forces trained the Persian army, put up telegraph lines, established a postal system, and developed trade. Some Persian workers crossed into Russia to work in the Caucasus oil fields. The Russian ministry of finance even set up a bank—The Discount and Loan Bank of Persia—with branches in many parts of the nation. This bank loaned the Persian government 60 million rubles and provided 120 million rubles to Persian merchants to enable them to buy Russian goods.

The British government had no desire to see Russia gain power along the Persian Gulf. To counter this threat to the British-Indian lifeline, the British set up the Imperial Bank of Persia in southeastern Persia. At the same they gained a profitable tobacco monopoly.

Persian patriotic reformers carried out a successful revolution in 1906. The established a parliament and initiated reforms, aided by American advisers. This development, plus the changing diplomatic situation in western Europe brought on by the increase in tensions with the Germans brought the two competitors—Britain and Russia—together in 1907 to sign an agreement to end their rivalry in central Asia.

By the terms of the Anglo-Russian entente, Russia agreed to deal with the sovereign of Afghanistan only through the British government. Great Britain agreed to refrain from occupying or annexing Afghanistan so long as it fulfilled its treaty obligations. Persia became an Anglo-Russian holding, split up into three zones: the northern part was a Russian sphere of influence, the middle section was a neutral zone, and the southern portion was under British control.

The partnership was, however, only a marriage of convenience brought on by larger pressures in Europe. Russia continued intervening in Persian domestic politics, throwing its support to the shah, who was willing to do its bidding. Though upset by the Russians' activities, the British chose not to alienate them because they needed to build an alliance to counter Germany. Britain needed Russia's help and abided by the compromise arrangement in Persia.

The nineteenth-century extension of European state power over the Middle East reflected each great power's views of its own trade and defense needs. But the colonial powers ignored the desires, goals, and legitimate demands of the indigenous population.

North Africa

At the beginning of the nineteenth century, the Ottoman empire controlled—albeit tenuously—all of the African coast along the Mediterranean, with the exception of Morocco. The weakening of Turkish power, however, made the area virtually self-governing or subject to foreign pressures. By 1914 all of North Africa from Casablanca to Cairo had come under direct European control.

Egypt

Europe had long been fascinated by Egypt, and Napoleon's invasion of that country had increased interest in both its historic sights and its economic potential. As the Turkish control weakened in the first quarter of the century, Mehmet Ali came to be the dominant figure in the country. He was able to increase his authority in the theoretically Turkish-controlled land and carry out economic and agricultural changes. By the 1830s he had expanded his power (see p. 723) to the point where the great powers had to step in to save the Turks from his forces.

The dynamism of Mehmet Ali, however, did not touch the life of the Egyptian *fellah* (peasant), who lived amid poverty, disease, and ignorance. Most Egyptians continued to depend on the narrow green strip along the Nile River for survival, just as they had for thousands of years. Mehmet Ali's successes did not bring Egypt prosperity.

In the 1850s the government had to borrow a substantial amount of money from Great Britain to provide basic services. Dependence on foreign finance increased as the Egyptians tried to build railroads, schools, and factories to improve their economy. One of the foremost projects undertaken was that of the Suez Canal, built in cooperation with the French from 1859 to 1869. The more the Egyptians built, the more their debts increased. By 1875 financial difficulties forced Ismail, ruler of Egypt, to sell his block of 175,000 shares in the Suez Canal. The stock was snapped up by Disraeli, the astute prime minister of Great Britain. This maneuver gave Britain virtual control of this essential water link between Europe and the East.

When Ismail tried to repudiate his debts in 1879, Great Britain and France took over financial control of Egypt. The British and French forced Ismail to abdicate in favor of his son. The Egyptian ruling classes and officer corps did not relish foreign control, and violence broke out in 1881 and 1882. The worst outbreak came at Alexandria, where many Europeans lost their lives during rioting. The British, acting unilaterally, then routed the Egyptians at Tell el-Kebir. After that, the British took responsibility for the running of the country.

To reorganize Egyptian finances, eliminate corruption from the administration, and improve the all-important (for the British) cotton industry, Sir Evelyn Baring, later Lord Cromer, was

British troops rest near the pyramids after the British bombardment and occupation of Alexandria, Egypt, in 1882.

The Earl of Cromer on Egypt

The Earl of Cromer looked back after his career in Egypt and claimed the following benefits of European domination.

No one can fully realise the extent of the change which has come over Egypt since the British occupation took place unless he is in some degree familiar with the system under with the country was governed in the days of Ismail Pasha. The contrast between now and then is, indeed, remarkable. A new spirit has been instilled into the population of Egypt. Even the peasant has learnt to scan his rights. Even the Pasha has learnt that others besides himself have rights which must be respected. The courbash may hang on the walls of the Moudirieh, but the Moudir no longer dares to employ it on the backs of the fellaheen. For all practical purposes, it may be said that the hateful corvée system has disappeared. Slavery has virtually ceased to exist. The halcyon days of the adventurer and the usurer are past. Fiscal burthens have been greatly relieved. Everywhere law reigns supreme. Justice is no longer bought and sold. Nature, instead of being spurned and neglected, has been wooed to bestow her gifts on mankind. She has responded to the appeal. The waters of the Nile are now utilised in an intelligent manner. Means of locomotion have been improved and extended. The soldier has acquired some pride in the uniform which he wears. He has fought as he never fought before. The sick man can be nursed in a well-managed hospital. The lunatic is no longer treated like a wild beast. The punishment awarded to the worst criminal is no longer barbarous. Lastly, the schoolmaster is abroad, with results which are as yet uncertain, but which cannot fail to be important.

All these things have been accomplished by the small body of Englishmen who, in various capacities, and with but little direct support or assistance from their Government or its representative, have of late years devoted their energies to the work of Egyptian regeneration. They have had many obstacles to encounter. Internationalism and Pashadom have stood in the path at every turn. But these forces, though they could retard, have failed to arrest the progress of the British reformer. The opposition which he has had to encounter, albeit very embarrassing, merely acted on his system as a healthy tonic. An eminent French literary critic has said that the end of a book should recall its commencement to the mind of the reader. Acting on this principle, I may remind those who have perused these pages that I began this work by stating that, although possibly counterparts to all the abuses which existed, and which to some extent still exist in Egypt, may be found in other countries, the conditions under which the work of Egyptian reform has been undertaken were very peculiar. The special difficulties which have resulted from those conditions have but served to bring out in strong relief one of the main characteristics of the Anglo-Saxon race. Other nations might have equally well conceived the reforms which were necessary. It required the singular political adaptability of Englishmen to execute them. A country and a nation have been partially regenerated, in spite of a perverse system of government which might well have seemed to render regeneration almost impossible.

From Earl of Cromer, *Modern Egypt*, vol. 2 (New York: Macmillan, 1908).

sent to Egypt to oversee the country's affairs from 1883 to 1907. He overhauled the system of government, curbed the use of forced labor, and carried out substantial public works projects. Some authorities have maintained that the best record of British imperialism is to be found in Egypt. European technology, governmental expertise, and financial practices aided the country's development. Despite this, in the first years of the twentieth century, Egyptians were voicing a growing demand for self-government.

Other States of North Africa

In Tripoli, Tunis, Algeria, and Morocco, the Europeans also made steady inroads during the nineteenth century. These four areas lacked the fertile green belt along a river such as Egypt possessed along the Nile. They also lacked both the economic basis and political leaders to attempt such grandiose projects as those pursued by the Egyptians. By the end of the century the rest of the north coast of Africa came under the control of the Italians and the French.

The area around Tripoli had gained its independence from the Turks in the first part of the eighteenth century. For the rest of the century the area served as a base for Mediterranean pirates. In 1835 it once again came under Turkish control where it remained until the Italians focused their attention on the area at the end of the century. The Italians declared war on the Turks, after having gained the consent of the great powers, and after a more difficult campaign than they had expected, Italy forced the Turks to cede the area to them in 1912.

The Ottomans had taken control of Tunis in 1575 and held on to it until the French established a protectorate there in 1881. As in the case with Tripoli, the power of the local government was weak, and the coastline harbored pirates and thieves. As had been the case in Egypt, the Tunisian government became indebted financially to European lenders, even before the French took over. After 1881 most of the country's wealth went abroad, and most of the population lived in desperate poverty.

Algeria's coastline also served as a base for piracy from the sixteenth to the nineteenth century. In the 1820s the French complained forcefully of the pirates' activities along the French coast. When in 1827 the Algerian ruler insulted the French consul in public by hitting him with a flyswatter, France used the incident as a suitable pretext to enter the country. Paris sent down a large army to occupy Algeria, but it took seventeen years to put down the fierce Berber tribesmen. Algeria was then incorporated as an integral part of the French state.

From the 1840s to the end of the century French interests also dominated in Morocco, the first country to experience overseas expansion

Seventeen years of intermittent military clashes followed France's invasion of Algeria in 1830 until the country was finally subjugated and integrated into the French state in 1847.

"Dr. Livingstone, I presume." When the famous Scottish missionary and explorer David Livingstone vanished in the interior of Africa after three decades of travel on that continent, the *New York Herald* commissioned Henry Stanley to locate him.

by Europe. But European states contested the area until 1911, and the Moroccan question increased tensions between Germany and France up to the beginning of World War I.

In general, the North African countries west of Egypt lacked the vigorous leadership, strong economies, and unified populations needed to stand off the European advances. Geographical obstacles were perhaps the major issue, as a nomadic population had to search continuously for the scarce means of existence.

Sub-Sahara Africa

Until the nineteenth century the great continent of Africa, many times the size of Europe, was virtually unknown to most Europeans. Still less was known about the 150 million people living there. But this state of affairs changed rapidly thanks to the intrepid investigations of some European explorers. The most successful representative of this group was David Livingstone (1813–1873), a Scottish missionary who crossed the vast barren wastes and jungles from the Cape of Good Hope to Lake Tanganyika. He began his explorations in 1853 and discovered Victoria Falls and the Zambezi River for the Europeans. After his death in 1873, his work in the

interior was carried on by Henry M. Stanley (1841–1904), the British explorer and journalist who had located Livingstone in 1871 and had with classic British understatement greeted him, "Dr. Livingstone, I presume."

The Europeans Arrive

African tribes and nations were too disunited to mount an effective resistance to the Europeans. The comparative ease with which the whites took and divided the continent may give the impression that there were few effective leaders among the Africans. There were many, especially among the Bantu people of southeastern Africa. Toward the end of the eighteenth century they made contact with the white civilization that spread from the Cape. After 1820, as black populations increased and room for expansion lessened, 2 million people became engulfed in a vast, bloody terror. In this fiery crucible, newly emerging black rulers forged many scattered clans into a few powerful states. The mightiest of these strong men was Shaka, king of the Zulus.

Born in 1787, an illegitimate son of a minor chief, Shaka spent a miserable childhood as an outcast among his mother's relatives. As a youth he became a warrior in the army of Dingiswayo, a powerful chief, who had learned some military tactics from the English and traded with the

Portuguese. In his first battle Shaka distinguished himself and was promoted to captain. Shaka soon became supreme commander, succeeded his father as chief, and later supreme commander of northern Natal. By 1824 he governed 250,000 people along the coast between the Pongola and Umzimbubu rivers.

Shaka was a complex and magnetic personality. He dabbled in magic and witchcraft as well as capricious statecraft. He was customarily attended by executioners who were casually ordered to dispose of those who displeased him. He also was responsible for incidents of mass murder. Yet Zulu traditions have always portrayed him as a folk hero, one who cared for his soldiers and his people and who could cover eighty miles a day and dance all night. Whites who encountered him were appalled by his cruelty and amazed by his dignity, honesty, and intelligence.

CHAKA KING OF THE ZOOLUS.

London. Published by E Churton, 26 Holles St.

Shaka, Zulu chief and military and political leader, holds the traditional Zulu assagai, or spear.

Zulu warriors under Cetshwayo, Shaka's nephew and king of the Zulus from 1873 to 1879, attacked and destroyed the British garrison at Isandlwana in 1879.

Shaka's power attracted hundreds of isolated clans into his nation. Shaka revolutionized the Zulu army by introducing the "stabbing spear," using mass, disciplined infantry tactics, and perfecting the regimental organization begun under Dingiswayo. He tried to transform the ancient pattern of his society, based on kinship, into a territorial state under one absolute ruler, whose subchiefs lost most of their power. He was well on the way to leading his people beyond family and clan loyalty to national consciousness when he was assassinated in 1828. His empire successfully resisted expanding white civilization for half a century after his death, and his legacy lived on to enable his successors to wage the most successful wars ever fought by blacks against Europeans. In 1879 the Zulus under King Cetshwayo defeated a British force, killing 700 soldiers, 130 colonists, and hundreds of their African allies, at Isandlwana.

However, there were neither enough Shakas nor Zulus after 1870. In that year the Europeans controlled only 10 percent of the continent. The two most important foreign holdings were French-administered Algeria and the Cape Colony, governed by Great Britain. Most of the other European holdings were mere coastal ports along West Africa. There were also strong political forces in Africa. In present-day Nigeria there was the Muslim Fulani Empire, created by Usman dan Fodio (1754–1817). In Ethiopia, Theodore II and Menelik II built a united state.

After 1870 the tempo of European intervention in Africa increased rapidly. One of the first European leaders to act was King Leopold II of Belgium. In 1876 he organized the International Africa Association and brought the explorer Stanley into his service. The association, composed of scientists and explorers from all nations, ostensibly was intended to serve humanitarian purposes. But the crafty king had other motives. As an agent of the association, Stanley went to the Congo where he made treaties with several African chiefs and, by 1882, obtained over 900,000 square miles of territory.[7]

Britain's occupation of Egypt and the Belgian acquisition of the Congo moved Bismarck in 1884 to call a conference of major European powers to discuss potential problems of unregulated African colonization. The assembly, meeting in Berlin, paid lip service to humanitarianism by condemning the slave trade, prohibiting the sale of liquor and firearms in certain areas, and expressing concern for proper religious instruction for the Africans. Then the participants moved to matters that they considered to be much more important.

They set down the rules of competition by which the great powers were to be guided in their search for colonies. They agreed that the area along the Congo River was to be administered by Leopold of Belgium, but that it was to be a neutral territory with free trade and navigation. No nation was to stake out claims in Africa without first notifying the other powers of its intention. No territory could be claimed unless it was effectively occupied, and all disputes were to be settled by arbitration.

In spite of these declarations, the competitors often ignored the rules. On several occasions, war was barely avoided. The humanitarian rules were generally ignored. The methods Europeans used to acquire lands continued in many cases to involve the deception of the Africans. European colonists got huge land grants by giving uneducated chiefs treaties they could not read and

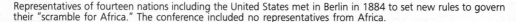

Representatives of fourteen nations including the United States met in Berlin in 1884 to set new rules to govern their "scramble for Africa." The conference included no representatives from Africa.

Lord Lugard Justifies European Imperialism in Africa

Lord Lugard gave as effective a rationale for European imperialism in Africa as one can find. His argument is a model of elevated self-serving.

The "Scramble for Africa" by the nations of Europe—an incident without parallel in the history of the world—was due to the growing commercial rivalry, which brought home to civilised nations the vital necessity of securing the only remaining fields for industrial enterprise and expansion. It is well, then, to realise that it is for our *advantage*—and not alone at the dictates of duty—that we have undertaken responsibilities in East Africa. It is in order to foster the growth of the trade of this country, and to find an outlet for our manufactures and our surplus energy, that our far-seeing statesmen and our commercial men advocate colonial expansion . . . .

There are some who say we have no *right* in Africa at all, that "it belongs to the natives." I hold that our right is the necessity that is upon us to provide for our ever-growing population—either by opening new fields for emigration, or by providing work and employment which the development of over-sea extension entails—and to stimulate trade by finding new markets, since we know what misery trade depression brings at home.

While thus serving our own interests as a nation, we may, by selecting men of the right stamp for the control of new territories, bring at the same time many advantages to Africa. Nor do we deprive the natives of their birthright of freedom, to place them under a foreign yoke. It has ever been the key-note of British colonial method to rule through and by the natives, and it is this method, in contrast to the arbitrary and uncompromising rule of Germany, France, Portugal, and Spain, which has been the secret of our success as a colonising nation, and has made us welcomed by tribes and peoples in Africa, who ever rose in revolt against the other nations named. In Africa, moreover, there is among the people a natural inclination to submit to a higher authority. That intense detestation of control which animates our Teutonic races does not exist among the tribes of Africa, and if there is any authority that we replace, it is the authority of the Slavers and Arabs, or the intolerable tyranny of the "dominant tribe." . . .

From Captain F. D. Lugard, *The Rise of Our East African Empire*, vol. I (London: William Blackwood and Sons, 1893).

whose contents they were not permitted to understand. In return, the natives were rewarded with bottles of gin, red handkerchiefs, and fancy dress costumes. The comparison between the European treaty methods and those of the Americans in the negotiations with the Indians is all too apparent.

The ethical and cultural differences between the Africans and the Europeans were especially vast regarding the subject of land ownership. Since in many cases native customs reserved ownership of the land to tribes, allowing individuals only the use of it, chiefs granted land to European settlers with no idea that they were disposing of more than its temporary use. When the settlers later claimed ownership of the land, the natives were indignant, feeling that the tribe had been robbed of land, contrary to tribal law.

The Division of Africa

By 1914 European imperialists divided Africa among themselves, with two exceptions. Only Liberia and Ethiopia remained independent (see map, p. 736).

Shortly after the Berlin conference, King Leopold organized his African territories into the African Free State, subject to his control alone. He began to exploit the colony's economic resources by granting concessions to private companies, reserving for his own administration an extensive rubber-producing area ten times as

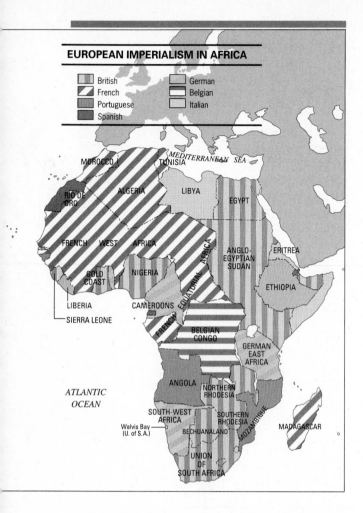

EUROPEAN IMPERIALISM IN AFRICA

British
French
Portuguese
Spanish
German
Belgian
Italian

MEDITERRANEAN SEA
MOROCCO
TUNISIA
RIO DE ORO
ALGERIA
LIBYA
EGYPT
FRENCH WEST AFRICA
GOLD COAST
NIGERIA
LIBERIA
SIERRA LEONE
CAMEROONS
FRENCH EQUATORIAL AFRICA
ANGLO-EGYPTIAN SUDAN
ERITREA
ETHIOPIA
BELGIAN CONGO
GERMAN EAST AFRICA
ATLANTIC OCEAN
ANGOLA
NORTHERN RHODESIA
SOUTH-WEST AFRICA
Walvis Bay (U. of S.A.)
BECHUANALAND
SOUTHERN RHODESIA
MOZAMBIQUE
MADAGASCAR
UNION OF SOUTH AFRICA

mission to eastern Africa. Peters succeeded in obtaining treaties from local chiefs giving him control of 60,000 square miles. The next year, Bismarck proclaimed the region to be German East Africa.

The British had been laying claims to the region directly north of Peters' concessions. Contradictory German and British claims were settled amicably in 1886 and 1890. After the agreements, which included the British concession of the strategic Helgoland Island in the North Sea, the British held Uganda along the shores of Lake Victoria, British East Africa (later known as Kenya), the rich spice island of Zanzibar, and the area of Nyasaland. Germany's claim to its protectorate in East Africa (later called Tanganyika, now Tanzania) was recognized by the British.

Meanwhile, by 1884 the British had gained control over a stretch of African coast fronting on the Gulf of Aden. This protectorate (British Somaliland) was of great strategic value since it guarded the lower approach to the Suez Canal. Equally important were the headwaters of the Nile, situated in the area known later as the Anglo-Egyptian Sudan. In 1898 the British gained control of this area. Among the British acquisitions on the west coast of Africa, the most important were the territories around the mouth of the Niger, stretching back toward the Sudan. These British possessions included Gambia, Sierra Leone, the Gold Coast, and Nigeria.

During this same period British influence in southern Africa had expanded northward from Cape Colony to German East Africa. The main force behind this drive came from the capitalist Cecil Rhodes, who dreamed of an uninterrupted corridor of British territory from the Cape of Good Hope to Cairo (see p. 698).

If overpopulation, lack of trade, and widespread poverty had been the most compelling reasons for gaining colonies, Italy should have obtained the most extensive areas in Africa. But Italy emerged from the scramble for colonies with very little territory. The Italians gained a piece of the Red Sea coast and a slice of barren and desolate land on the Indian Ocean. But these areas were of little value without the rich plateau of Abyssinia (Ethiopia) in the hinterland. An attempt to take the ancient empire in 1896 ended in the humiliating destruction of a 20,000-man Italian army.

large as Belgium. A system of forced labor was introduced, and soon stories of filthy work camps, horrible whippings, and other atrocities leaked out of the "Free State," which was undergoing the process of "civilization" as the Belgians referred to it. In the face of a rising tide of international outrage, Leopold was forced to turn the "Free State" over to the Belgian government in 1908. The conditions of the colony, renamed the Belgian Congo, improved under the direct administration of the government.

In the 1880s Germany acquired three colonies on the west coast of Africa: German Southwest Africa, Togoland, and Cameroons. They made their most important gains, however, on the east coast of the continent. German penetration there was largely the work of one man, Carl Peters, a student of British colonization methods. In 1884 he and three other colonial enthusiasts, disguised as British workers, set out on a secret

THE RHODES COLOSSUS
STRIDING FROM CAPE TOWN TO CAIRO.

An 1892 cartoon from *Punch* captures the dream of empire builder Cecil Rhodes for British domination of Africa from "Cape to Cairo."

Building on Louis Napoleon's ambitions, France continued in 1884 developing a colonial program by acquiring a large section of equatorial Africa along the right bank of the Congo River. From trading posts along the west coast of the continent, France pushed into the interior and obtained most of the basins of the Senegal and Niger rivers. Expeditions from France's north African holdings penetrated the Sahara. Although France did not succeed in getting to the Nile, by 1900 it controlled the largest empire in Africa, one which stretched eastward from the Atlantic to the western Sudan and soutward to the Congo River. The French also took control of the large island of Madagascar in the south Indian Ocean. They completed their colonial gains in 1911—over German protests—by making Morocco a French protectorate.

Costs and Benefits

Africa's wealth surpassed the hopes of the most avid imperialist. By the first decade of this century the continent was the world's greatest producer of gold and diamonds. Rich resources of tin, phosphates, and copper had also been discovered. Africa supplied large amounts of rubber, coffee, and cotton. European imperialists gained not only huge territories and vast reserves of raw materials; they also gained the labor of millions of Africans.

The Africans who came under European domination had to make severe adjustments. The impact of European imperialism was profound and widespread. European imperialists divided Africa by drawing lines on a map with total disregard for traditional political and social structures. For the first time, many villagers were forced to pay money taxes to a distant central authority. In most cases, Africans had lived within a small tribal area of law and political affiliation. With the advent of imperial rule, dozens of formerly distinct—and often antagonistic—tribes were

An Ethiopian painting of the Battle of Adowa in 1896 in which the army of Emperor Menelik II defeated the invading Italians. At the top of the painting, Saint George intercedes for the Ethiopians.

brought together, as in the case of Nigeria, into one colony. In other cases of imperialism, large tribes were split into two or three European colonial segments. Colonies were not usually unified nations, a fact that would have bloody consequences as they became independent after World War II.

The colonization process in Africa, undertaken by a dynamic, self-confident, and technologically advanced civilization, severely disrupted cultures that had been isolated from the mainstream of world affairs. Kinship and family ties were weakened when villagers sought jobs in distant towns and mines. In some areas as many as 50 percent of the young males sought employment in order to pay the new hut taxes or to buy cheap but enticing European wares.

Their mothers, wives, and sisters left behind received a double shock. They had to carry on the increased work load and maintain the family unit single-handedly, with an enormous increase in their hours per week of labor to feed their families. However, they also saw their roles diminished as European notions of the "woman's place" displaced them from their traditional positions of social influence. In the new export markets, men monopolized the raising of cash crops, cutting women out of economic opportunities. Undoubtedly, wages from absent husbands did help raise standards of living, but the effect on family ties and tribal loyalties was destructive.

The old ways of life were most disrupted in colonies that attracted European settlement, such as Kenya and Southern Rhodesia. In such areas, Africans were confined to "native reserves" or to segregated areas in the towns. On occasion large tracts of land were allocated exclusively for European use. It was in these plural societies that racial tensions most rapidly developed.

For a half century after the scramble for colonies began, the incidence of social change was uneven. In some remote areas, Africans may never have seen white persons, let alone worked for them. But tribal life was gradually transformed by the introduction of new forms of land tenure, enforcement of alien systems of law, and the growth of the money economy. In an attempt to imitate the technologically and militarily superior Europeans, many Africans tried to adopt the ways of their new rulers. As a result, some

of them became "detribalized" and often bewildered, as they were also alienated from much of their traditional culture but unable to understand fully and be part of the new. Although the transformation of Africa was probably inevitable at some point, it was unfortunate that this revolutionary change occurred so quickly, and at the hands of intruders, whose motives were so selfish. Much too frequently the imperialists disparaged all African culture, dismissing the Africans as barbarous and uncivilized.

Colonialism may have been an abrupt and rude awakening to the new day of the industrialized world, but it did bring several benefits. The arrival of Europeans introduced more peace between the tribes by imposing more efficient law enforcement methods. The international slave trade ended. The Europeans brought in material and technological advances, such as telegraph and telephone communications, railroads, improved harbors, and improved medical standards. European organizational and educational techniques were introduced in the form of better administrative systems, widespread schools, and a money economy. All of these things may have been necessary to enable Africa to enter the modern age, but they came at a very high price.

Conclusion

By 1914 the European states had established their primacy over the Middle East and Africa. There was no doubting the nature and extent of Europe's material and technological dominance over southwest Asia and Africa. While thousands of Persians crossed into Russia to work in tsarist oil fields, thousands more Africans worked in European-owned mines. Both groups were begrudgingly witnesses to Europe's economic strength. While financiers in London, Berlin, and Paris skimmed the profits off the top of their newly controlled areas, European officials and diplomats dictated policy for most of the region.

Even before 1914, however, the forces that would eventually remove European dominance in the next half century were at work. These forces gained strength from European ideals. All of the apologists in Europe who spoke of carrying the "white man's burden" or of spreading "civilization" to the "lesser peoples" had a major blind spot in their world view. They confused technological and material strength with cultural strength. There could, of course, be no doubting the European material superiority over the Middle East and Africa. There was no military, economic, or technological arena in which the non-Europeans could claim superiority by 1914. Yet the identities of the peoples caught under European dominance did not disappear. Rather, under the influence of the European ideologies and political structures that accompanied the diplomats and industrialists, their identities became more sharply defined.

The rapid expansion of European primacy over the Middle East and Africa failed to establish firm roots. Europeanization remained a surface phenomenon, affecting mainly the material aspects of life. Islam retained its strength and the African peoples the essence of their identities. The contact of both areas with European state systems was immediately tragic, but not fatal. Armed with the technological, intellectual, and political lessons they learned from the Europeans, the Middle East and Africa could hope, someday, to compete on an equal basis.

Suggestions for Reading

R. H. Davison, *Turkey* (Prentice-Hall, 1968) is a brief, well-written survey. Bernard Lewis provides excellent analyses in *The Emergence of Modern Turkey*, 2nd ed. (Oxford, 1968). William Miller, *The Ottoman Empire and Its Successors, 1801–1927* (Octagon, 1966) and L. S. Stavrianos, *The Balkans Since 1453* (Holt, Rinehart & Winston, 1961) provide thorough treatment of the multi-ethnic challenge facing the Turks. P. Coles, *The Ottoman Impact on Europe* (Harcourt Brace Jovanovich, 1968) is a wise survey.

Kenneth Ingham, *A History of East Africa* (Longman, 1962) and J. D. Fage, *An Introduction to the History of West Africa* (Cambridge, 1969) are useful studies, as is J. B. Webster and A. A. Boahen, *History of West Africa* (Praeger, 1967). See also R. Hallett, *Africa to 1975* (Michigan, 1974); J. D. Fage, *History of West Africa*, (Cambridge, 1969). Ronald Robinson and J. Gallagher, *Africa and the Victorians* (St. Martin's, 1969); and Peter Duignan and L. H. Gann, eds., *Colonialism in Africa* (Cambridge, 1969) which contains perceptive essays on the motivations for imperialism. The nature of Britain's imperial mission in Africa is shown in the lives of three men: F. Gross, *Rhodes of Africa* (Praeger, 1957); Lord Elton, *Gordon of Khartoum* (Knopf, 1955); and M. Perham, *Lugard, The Years of Adventure* (Archon, 1968).

Notes

1. Robert Schnerb, "Le XIXe Siècle: L'Apogée de L'Expansion Européene (1815–1914)," *Histoire Générale des Civilisations*, VI (Paris: Presses Universitaires de France, 1955), pp. 347–352.
2. L. S. Stavrianos, *The Balkans Since 1453* (New York: Holt, Rinehart & Winston, 1961), pp. 135–136.
3. Bernard Lewis, *The Emergence of Modern Turkey* (Oxford: Oxford Univ. Press, 1968), pp. 1–17.
4. Ibid., pp. 41–64.
5. Peter Fleming, *Bayonets to Lhasa* (New York: Harper & Row, 1961), p. 21.
6. Quoted in N. D. Harris, *Europe and the East* (Boston, Houghton Mifflin, 1926), p. 285.
7. L. H. Gann and P. Duignan, *Burden of Empire* (New York: Praeger, 1967), p. 286.

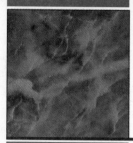

Chapter 29

South and East Asia, 1815–1914

The large countries of south and east Asia—India, China, and Japan—and their smaller neighbors faced decisive challenges from the western powers in the nineteenth century. Only Japan possessed the adaptability to meet the Europeans on their own terms before 1914. As for the rest, their religious, cultural, and political characteristics combined with technological and economic underdevelopment doomed their efforts to resist the western advance. Mughul rule was extremely weak in the Indian subcontinent; the Indochinese peninsula and the islands of the Pacific and Indian oceans had long been subjected to European influence; and China with its unbending sense of superiority refused to recognize a changing world.

All of south and east Asia shared similar geographic problems and challenges. The area contained many regions of densely populated territory that made large-scale agriculture impossible. The people, on the whole, lived in villages, with the exception of a few large cities. In nineteenth-century India, for example, roughly 80 percent of the people lived in communities of less than 2000 inhabitants. The area was and still is vulnerable to natural disasters such as tidal waves, earthquakes, and occasional droughts. These conditions produced a population suffering poor living conditions, high infant mortality rates, endemic diseases, and a lack of adequate nutrition.

India to 1914

Dual Control Under the British

The decline of Mughul power (see chapter 22) proved to be a great opportunity for the British and French, who through the late seventeenth and most of the eighteenth centuries competed for dominance in India. They fought through their trading companies and agents who sought local allies. India, like North America, was part of the world struggle for empire between the two European powers. The British victory over Bengal in the battle of Plassey (1757) ushered in the British phase of Indian history. Britain's naval supremacy and the superior discipline of its European-led armies enabled Britain to defeat France in 1760. French influence in India soon disappeared.

The traders became rulers, assuming the dual roles of businessmen and representatives of a sovereign state. Anarchy spread until 1818 when the British East India Company stepped in to become the subcontinents's police force. Some local rulers accepted the company's rule but others who resisted lost their land. The subcontinent was divided into two sections. British India was ruled directly by London, while in Indian India the local dynasties ruled under British supervision. The British Parliament, concerned that a profit-seeking company controlled the lives of millions of people, enacted legislation in 1773 and 1784 that gave it power to control company policies and appoint the governor-general, the highest company official in India.

The system of dual control lasted until 1858 and brought several benefits to the peninsula, especially to women. The practice of *suttee* in which widows burned themselves on the funeral pyres of their deceased husbands was prohibited. The company worked against the practice of killing female infants. Further, steps were taken to end the seclusion of women from society. A secret police force broke up the brutal system

This drawing by a British officer of a Bengal regiment shows a British magistrate settling a court case in 1853, during the period of dual control when the British East India Company and the British government shared authority over India.

of banditry and murder called *thuggee* (hence our word *thug*). In addition the British introduced a multilevel educational system.

Rebellion and Reform

In the spring of 1857 a serious rebellion interrupted the flow of liberal reforms. Indian troops who formed the bulk of the company's armed forces, called *sepoys*, started the uprising when they complained that a new cartridge issued to them was smeared with the fat of cows and pigs. This outraged both the Hindus, for whom the cow was a sacred animal, and the Muslims, who considered the pig unclean. Fortunately for the British, many areas remained loyal or at least calm. But in the affected areas there was fierce fighting and many lives were lost.

The Sepoy rebellion marked the final collapse of the Mughuls. The mutineers had proclaimed as their leader the last of the Mughul emperors permitted to maintain a court at Delhi. After the British put down the revolt, they exiled him to Burma. The rebellion also put an end to the system of dual control under which the British government and the East India Company shared authority. Parliament removed the company's political role, and after 258 years, the East India Company ended its rule.

Under the new system, the governor-general gained additional duties and a new title—viceroy. The viceroy was responsible to the secretary of state for India in the British cabinet. In the subcontinent, the British maintained direct control of most of the high positions in government, while Indians were trained to carry out administrative responsibilities in the provincial and subordinate systems. London reorganized the courts and law codes, along with the army and public services. English became the administrative language of the country. Only on rare occasions could native civil officials rise to higher positions in the bureaucracy.

India was governed by and for the British, who viewed themselves as the only people able to rule. By 1900, there was still 90 percent illiteracy

The storming of the Kashmir Gate at Delhi during the Sepoy Rebellion of 1857.

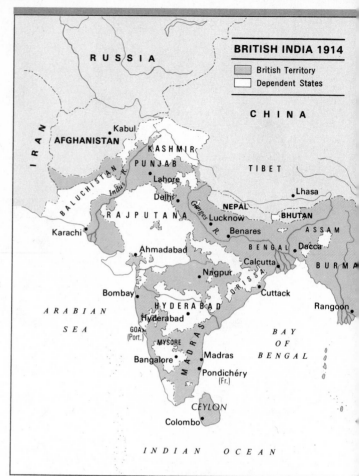

among native men and 99 percent for the women. Few schools existed at the village level to remedy that situation. The masses of the rural poor paid for the government through taxes on beverages and salt. India provided rich resources and vast markets for the British. In return the British introduced improved health standards, better water systems, and political stability.

The English language and British railroads introduced more unity to the country than it had ever known. But the imperial rulers took advantage of the subcontinent's diversity of religions, castes, and principalities (over 700 separate political units) to rule by a policy of divide and conquer. The British justified their political policies and economic dominance over India by pointing out that they were improving the lives of nearly one-fifth of the human race—almost 300 million people. This rationale could not remove the fact that the contrasts between the European and Asiatic ways of life in cities like Bombay, Delhi, and Calcutta were as great as the difference between night and day.

Resentment against British rule led to the rapid growth of the Indian nationalist movement. In 1885, with the help of several Englishmen who had Indian political ambitions, the Indian National Congress was formed. The British educational system, although it touched only a minority of the people, served as one of the most potent forces behind the new movement, as the

Indians embraced many of the liberal causes popular in England. Especially strong was the drive for women's equality and freedom, away from their traditional position of dependence, in which the only position and power women had was in relation to men.

As Indians learned the history of the rise of self-government in England, their desire for political freedom in their own land grew. The system of British control prevented Indians from rising above a certain level. At the same time, newly educated Indian youths, for social and cultural reasons, disdained manual labor. The result was a pool of thousands of frustrated and unemployed educated Indian youths who turned angrily against the government.

The British responded to the spread of violence with a major shift in policy between 1907 and 1909. They allowed the various provincial legislatures to elect Indian majorities, and an

Indian was seated in the executive council of the governor-general. The central government's legislature, however, remained under British control (see map, p. 742). These concessions satisfied moderates, for the time being, but did not appease the more radical protestors. In the twentieth century the spirit of nationalism would become even more insistent.

Southeast Asia to 1914

Southeast Asia includes the lands wedged between India and China and the multitude of islands in the Indian and Pacific oceans (see map below). It is a complex, diverse area whose fragmentation rendered it unable to resist the entry of the Europeans, which had begun in the sixteenth century.

European Incursions

Throughout the area European investors established a plantation economy to develop the coffee, tea, pepper, and other products demanded by the world market. Europeans discovered and exploited important mineral deposits. The Europeans attempted to introduce law and order for the purpose of limiting the chronic civil war and banditry that plagued the area. As was the case in India, the impact of European ways of life, especially western education, created a new generation of nationalists. In the Dutch East Indies, French Indochina, and the Philippines, young intellectuals aspired to complete independence for themselves and their countries.

In the eighteenth and nineteenth centuries Great Britain gained control of Ceylon, Malaya, and Burma. The first colony, taken from the Dutch in 1796, became one of the most valuable British holdings, producing such prized commodities as tea, rubber, lead, and sapphires. The Malayan peninsula, with the important island of Singapore, provided a vantage point from which Britain could dominate the seas surrounding southern Asia and export valuable supplies of tin and rubber. The British conquered Burma in three wars between 1823 and 1885 and annexed it to India.

France returned to the southeastern Asian area in the nineteenth century. French commercial and religious interests were established as

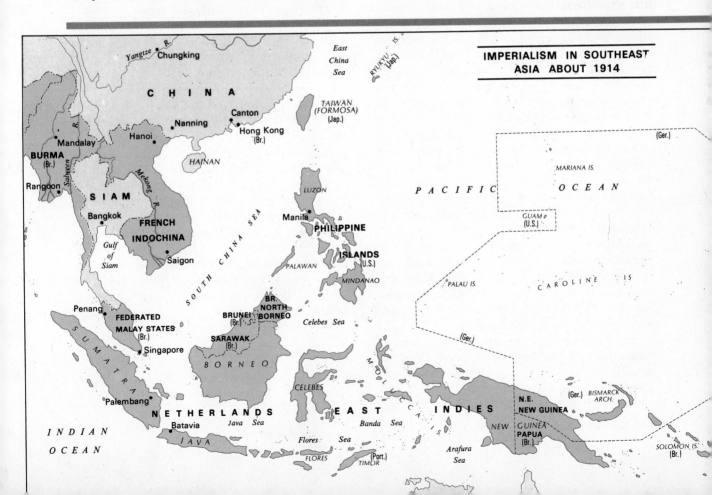

IMPERIALISM IN SOUTHEAST ASIA ABOUT 1914

In 1859, on the pretext of preserving Catholicism in Indochina, a French and Spanish expeditionary force stormed and captured the fortress of Saigon.

early as the seventeenth century, but British power in the Indian Ocean prevented France from stabilizing its position at that time. Not until the mid-nineteenth century did France increase its presence in Indochina. Anti-Christian persecutions in the area in 1856 and the fear that Catholicism would be eliminated if France did not go to its aid moved the French to join the British against China and Vietnam.

France took Saigon in 1860 and from that base expanded its influence and power through treaties, exploration, and outright annexation. The French took Hanoi in 1882, governed Cochin China as a direct colony, and held Annam (central Vietnam), Tonkin, and Cambodia as protectorates in one degree or another. Laos too was soon brought under French "protection." By the beginning of the twentieth century France had created an empire in Indochina nearly 50 percent larger than the parent country. Only Siam (Thailand) managed to hold off the French advance and keep its independence.

Late in the sixteenth century the Dutch had taken most of the East Indies from the Portuguese, and in 1602 the Dutch East India Company was organized to exploit the resources of the Spice Islands. In 1798 the company's holdings were transferred to the Dutch crown. For some time the spice trade had been declining, and early in the nineteenth century the Dutch set about raising new products.

In the 1830s the so-called culture system was introduced, under which one-fifth of all native land was set aside to raise crops for the government. One-fifth of all the natives' time was also required to work the lands. As a result, the production of sugar, tobacco, coffee, tea, and other products increased tremendously. In the long run, the culture system gave the islands a prosperous system of raising crops, but it also often deprived the natives of sufficient land for their own use. Conditions for the natives improved in 1900 when the Dutch abandoned the culture system. Less favorable for the local population was the Dutch neglect of higher education and the failure to prepare them for eventual self-government.

American Imperialism

While the Europeans were pursuing their interests in the far east, a new imperial power was emerging in the Pacific—the United States. In 1867 the Americans occupied the Midway Islands and purchased Alaska from the Russians. The next step was in the Hawaiian Islands.

During the nineteenth century, Americans and Europeans had developed large sugar plantations on the mid-Pacific islands. The United States poured capital into them and by 1881 the U.S. secretary of state referred to the islands as part of the "American system." To ensure United States' control, a revolt in 1893, engineered with the assistance of the Marines, deposed the Hawaiian queen and set up a republic. Five years later the islands were annexed by a joint declaration of both houses of Congress.

The United States' successful war against Spain in 1898 (see chapter 27) affected both Cuba and the Philippines. In May of that year Admiral George Dewey destroyed the Spanish fleet at Manila and the first American soldiers began operations in the Philippines. In the treaty of December 1898 Spain ceded the Phillippines, Guam, and Puerto Rico to the United States. One year

Filipino guerrilla fighters at an outpost. When the United States refused to support Filipino claims of independence, fighting broke out between the Americans and the Filipino insurgents and lasted for three years.

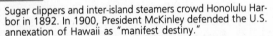

Sugar clippers and inter-island steamers crowd Honolulu Harbor in 1892. In 1900, President McKinley defended the U.S. annexation of Hawaii as "manifest destiny."

later the Americans occupied the small Pacific outpost of Wake island.

Some of the liberal Filipino patriots who had rebelled against the Spanish in 1896 had assisted the Americans, but they had no wish to exchange one master for another. When it became evident that they would not quickly gain self-rule, fighting broke out. The hostilities that began in 1899 lasted for three years. The ironic spectacle of American forces being used in a second conquest of the Philippines brought about a strong revulsion against imperialism in many quarters of the United States. A New York newspaper addressed Rudyard Kipling, an apologist for imperialism, in this way:

> We've taken up the white man's burden
> Of ebony and brown:
>
> Now will you kindly tell us, Rudyard,
> How we may put it down.[1]

American colonial administration in the Philippines proved to be liberal and well-intentioned for the most part. In 1913 the legislature became dominantly native, although final authority in the most important matters was still reserved to the U.S. Congress. The Philippine tariff was shaped to favor American trade, and large amounts of capital from the United States were invested in the islands. Increased educational facilities produced an increasingly strong desire for independence among many Filipinos. In their eyes, American government in the Philippines, no matter how efficient or humanitarian, was no substitute for self-government.

There could be no doubt that by 1900 the United States sat astride the Pacific basin as did no other power. The consequences of this Pacific imperial posture were to become a major and costly constituent of American life in the twentieth century. A massive conflict with Japan, another in Korea, and the tragic war in Vietnam lay in the future. Whether such involvement was essential for American basic interests was to become a crucial and painful question.

The Central Kingdom

At the end of the 1800s China's four million square miles held 450 million people, up from 200 million a century earlier. The ruling dynasty was the Ch'ing, established by Manchus from Manchuria, who in 1644 had superseded the Ming. These descendants of the Tatars appreciated Chinese civilization and adopted a conciliatory attitude toward their subjects. They refused, however, to allow intermarriage with the Chinese, for they realized that only their blood difference kept them from being assimilated and conquered. By and large, however, the Manchus gradually became Chinese in their attitudes and habits.

The Manchu emperors were remarkably successful. The reign of Ch'ien-lung (1736–1795) was a time of great expansion. The Manchus gained Turkestan, Burma, and Tibet. By the end of the eighteenth century Manchu power extended even into Nepal, and the territory under the Ch'ing control was as extensive as under any previous dynasty.

The Perils of Superiority

The prevailing attitude of superiority to the cultures of all other peoples was an obstacle to China's leaders. They regarded with contempt rather than admiration advances in other parts of the world. Evidence of China's problems could be found in the eighteenth-century revolts in Formosa, Kansu, Hunan, Kueichou, and Shantung. All of them were suppressed, but clearly China was not functioning effectively.

In the first part of the nineteenth century, China continued to act imperiously toward foreigners. Merchants from western Europe came to China in increasing numbers, pursuing their trade in the face of great difficulties. Trade restrictions confined the foreign merchants to Canton and the Portuguese colony of Macao. In Canton, the Chinese controlled both trade and taxes. In spite of these obstacles, the foreigners made enough profit to compensate for their being treated as inferiors by the Chinese government.[2]

China knew that the foreigners needed Asian products more than the Chinese required European goods. In addition, the Manchus would neither recognize nor receive diplomatic representatives of foreign powers. In 1793 the imperial court responded to the British request for a permanent trade representative in Peking in this manner:

The Canton waterfront in a 19th-century painting. Canton was the first Chinese port regularly visited by European traders. The Portuguese arrived in 1511, followed by the British in the 17th century, and the French and the Dutch in the 18th.

... to send one of your nationals to stay at the Celestial Court to take care of your country's trade with China ... is not in harmony with the state system of our dynasty and will definitely not be permitted ... there is nothing we lack, as your principal envoy and others have themselves observed. We have never set such store on strange or ingenious objects, nor do we have need of any more of your country's manufactures.[3]

The Western Response

The foreigners were especially irritated by the high customs duties the Chinese forced them to pay and by the attempts of Chinese authorities to stop the growing import trade in opium. The drug had long been used to stop diarrhea, but in the seventeenth and eighteenth century people in all classes began to use it recreationally. Most opium came from Turkey or India, and in 1800 its import was forbidden by the imperial government. Despite this restriction, the opium trade continued to flourish. Privately owned vessels of many countries, including the United States, made huge profits from the growing number of Chinese addicts. The government in Peking noted that the foreigners seemed intent on dragging down the Chinese through the encouragement of opium addiction.

In the meantime, the empire faced other problems. The army became corrupt and the tax farmers defrauded the people. The central bureaucracy declined in efficiency, and the generally weak emperors were unable to meet the challenges of the time. The balance of trade turned against the Chinese in the 1830s, and the British decided to force the issue of increased trade rights. The point of conflict was the opium trade. By the late 1830s more than 30,000 chests, each of which held about 150 pounds of the extract, were being brought in annually by the

The stacking room at an opium factory in Patna, India. Opium smuggling upset the balance of trade and destroyed China's economy.

Lin Tse-hsu on the Opium Trade

Lin Tse-hsu saw that the opium trade, which gave Europe such huge profits, undermined his country. He asked Queen Victoria to put a stop to the trade.

After a long period of commerical intercourse, there appear among the crowd of barbarians both good persons and bad, unevenly. Consequently there are those who smuggle opium to seduce the Chinese people and so cause the spread of the poison to all provinces. Such persons who only care to profit themselves, and disregard their harm to others, are not tolerated by the laws of heaven and are unanimously hated by human beings. His Majesty the Emperor, upon hearing of this, is in a towering rage. He has especially sent me, his commissioner, to come to Kwangtung, and together with the governor-general and governor jointly to investigate and settle this matter.

All those people in China who sell opium or smoke opium should receive the death penalty. If we trace the crime of those barbarians who through the years have been selling opium, then the deep harm they have wrought and the great profit they have usurped should fundamentally justify their execution according to law. We take into consideration, howver, the fact that the various barbarians have still known how to repent their crimes and return to their allegiance to us by taking the 20,183 chests of opium from their storeships and petitioning us, through their consular officer [superintendent of trade], Elliot, to receive it. It has been entirely destroyed and this has been faithfully reported to the Throne in several memorials by this commissioner and his colleagues.

Fortunately we have received a specially extended favor from His Majesty the Emperor, who considers that for those who voluntarily surrender there are still some circumstances to palliate their crime, and so for the time being he has magnanimously excused them from punishment. But as for those who again violate the opium prohibition, it is difficult for the law to pardon them repeatedly. Having established new regulations, we presume that the ruler of your honorable country, who takes delight in our culture and whose disposition is inclined towards us, must be able to instruct the various barbarians to observe the law with care. It is only necessary to explain to them the advantages and disadvantages and then they will know that the legal code of the Celestial Court must be absolutely obeyed with awe.

We find that your country is sixty or seventy thousand *li* [three *li* make one mile] from China. Yet there are barbarian ships that strive to come here for trade for the purpose of making a great profit. The wealth of China is used to profit the barbarians. That is to say, the great profit made by barbarians is all taken from the rightful share of China. By what right do they then in return use the poisonous drug to injure the Chinese people? Even though the barbarians may not necessarily intend to do us harm, yet in coveting profit to an extreme, they have no regard for injuring others. Let us ask, where is your conscience? I have heard that the smoking of opium is very strictly forbidden by your country; that is because the harm caused by opium is clearly understood. Since it is not permitted to do harm to your own country, then even less should you let it be passed on to the harm of other countries—how much less to China!

From Lin Tse-hsu, Letter to Queen Victoria, 1839.

various foreign powers. Some authorities assert that the trade in opium alone reversed China's formerly favorable balance of trade. In the spring of 1839 Chinese authorities at Canton confiscated and burned the opium. In response, the British occupied positions around Canton.

In the war that followed, the Chinese could not match the technological and tactical superiority of the British forces. In 1842 China agreed to the provisions of the Treaty of Nanking. Hong Kong was ceded to Great Britain, and other ports, including Canton, were opened to British residence and trade. It would be a mistake to view the conflict between the two countries simply as a matter of drug control; it was instead the acting out of deep cultural conflicts between east and west.[4]

The French and Americans approached the Chinese after the Nanking Treaty's provisions became known, and in 1844 gained the same trading rights as the British. The advantages granted the three nations by the Chinese set a precedent that would dominate China's relations with the world for the next century. The "most favored nation" treatment came to be extended so far that China's right to rule in its own territory was limited. This began the period referred to by the Chinese as the time of unequal treaties—a time of unprecedented degradation for China. The humiliation the Central Kingdom suffered is still remembered and strongly affects important aspects of its foreign policy. Meanwhile, the opium trade continued to thrive.

The British and French again defeated China in a second opium war in 1856. By the terms of the Treaty of Tientsin (1858) the Chinese opened new ports to trading and allowed foreigners with passports to travel in the interior. Christians gained the right to spread their faith and hold property, thus opening up another means of western penetration. The United States and Russia gained the same privileges in separate treaties.

The Manchu empire appeared to be well on the way to total physical dismemberment and economic collapse. Three provisions of these treaties caused long-lasting bitterness among the Chinese: extraterritoriality, customs regulations, and the right to station foreign warships in Chinese waters. Extraterritoriality meant that in a dispute with the Chinese, westerners had the right to be tried in their own country's consular court. Europeans argued that Chinese concepts of justice were more rigid and harsh than those in the west. But the Chinese viewed extraterritoriality as not only humiliating to China's sovereignty, but also discriminatory in favor of western nations. The other two provisions greatly weakened China's fiscal and military structure. After 1860 China was a helpless giant.

China's Response

The Chinese competition with the westerners had been carried on in military and economic terms. But the basic conflict was in the realm of civilization and values. The Chinese could note the obvious—that the Europeans possessed technological and military superiority. The question they faced was how to adapt the strength of Europe to the core of Chinese civilization. In Chinese terms, this was the t'i-yung concept. T'i means "substance" and yung means use. Under this concept, China should make use of western advances in order to become able to compete effectively with the west.

Combining the two elements presented the severe problem of gaining a proper balance. Those who wanted to keep the old culture opposed those who wanted to modernize the country. In 1860 the T'ung ch'ih Restoration movement attempted to strengthen the Manchus. Serious attempts were made to preserve Chinese culture while trying to make use of western technology. If these attempts at adaptation could have been carried out in a time of peace, perhaps the Chinese could have adjusted but China did not enjoy the luxury of tranquility. The concessions to the "foreign devils" resulted in a great loss of prestige for the Manchus.

More dangerous for the Manchus than the west was the spate of revolts in the north, west, and south of the country. The most tragic was the Taiping rebellion that lasted from 1850 to 1864. The uprising, fought to attain the Heavenly Kingdom of Great Peace (T'ai-p'ing t'ien-kuo) stemmed from widespread discontent with the social and economic conditions of Manchu rule and the perception of the lack of authority in Peking. The revolt began near Canton and centered on the plans f Hung Hsiu-ch'uan, a person who was driven to desperation by consistently failing the lowest examination to gain entry into the civil service. After contact with American missionaries and some reading of Christian tracts, he came to identify himself as a son of God, Jesus' little brother. His task was to bring salvation to China. He accumulated followers, especially from the poor, and prepared to fight. He and his forces controlled the southern part of China for ten years from Nanking, and he set out to create a new society, totally detached from the traditional Chinese fabric. Hung struck out at vice, Confucianism, private property, and the landlords. By taking on all that was established in China, he ensured his defeat. The Taiping rebellion was one of the most costly movements in history. It was felt in seventeen of China's eighteen provinces. Estimates of the number of deaths range between 20 and 30 million.[5]

After the external buffeting from the west and the internal uprising, the Manchu dynasty limped along for another half century, led by a conservative coalition of Manchu and Chinese officials who advised the empress dowager, Tzu-hsi, who served from 1861 until her death in 1908. Known first as Orchid, then as Yehonala, then as the Yi Concubine, then as Tzu-hsi, and finally as the Old Buddha, she followed the most direct path for a bright and ambitious Manchu female—she entered court circles as a concubine. After receiving the traditional training in court, she honed her political skills. She understood the intricate ceremonial life and mastered the intrigue of palace politics. When the senior concubine failed to give birth to a healthy heir to the throne, Tzu-hsi bore the emperor a strong and healthy child.

Her position as mother of the heir-apparent opened the door to power, and during the reigns of the next three emperors she was a dominant power, either as co-regent or regent. She built a network of powerful allies and informers that helped her to crush internal revolts and restore a measure of prestige to China during a brief period of tranquility from 1870 to 1895. She and her circle were so removed from the world that she used funds earmarked for the navy to rebuild her summer house, in honor of her sixtieth birthday. At a time when the Japanese were rapidly modernizing and foreign powers introduced

Tzu-hsi, the Empress Dowager or Old Buddha. The Boxer Rebellion near the end of her reign indicated the degree to which the central government had lost power in China.

many forms of their technology in their factories, railroads, and communications, China held to the policies based on tradition and custom.

Carving Up China

During the first wars against the Europeans, the Chinese began the process of ceding territory and spheres of influence to foreigners. By 1860, as a result of the Treaty of Peking, Russia gained the entire area north of the Amur River and founded the strategic city of Vladivostok. In 1885 France took Indochina and Britain seized Burma. In 1887 Macao was ceded to Portugal. China was too weak to resist these encroachments on its borders. But the crowning blow came not from the western nations, but from Japan—a land the Chinese had long regarded with amused contempt.

Trouble had long brewed between China and Japan, especially over the control of Formosa and Korea. War broke out in 1894 in a dispute over China's claims on Korea. The brief Sino-Japanese struggle resulted in a humiliating defeat for China. By the treaty of Shimonoseki (1895), China was forced to recognize the independence of Korea and hand over the rich Liaotung peninsula and Formosa to Japan (see map below).

The Chinese defeat was the signal for the renewal of aggressive actions by western powers, who forced Japan to return the strategic Liaotung peninsula to China. Shortly thereafter, the European powers made their demands of China. Germany demanded a ninety-nine-year lease to Kiaochow Bay and was also given exclusive mining and railroad rights throughout Shantung province. Russia obtained a twenty-five-year lease to Dairen and Port Arthur and gained the right to build a railroad across Manchuria, thereby achieving complete domination of that vast territory. In 1898 Britain obtained the lease of Weihaiwei, a naval base, and France leased Kwangchowan in southern China.

The United States, acting not from any high-minded desires but rather from the fear that American business was being excluded from China, brought a halt—or at least a hesitation to the

The imperialist contenders line up for the race to acquire territory in China in this 19th-century cartoon entitled "The China Cup Race."

process of dismemberment. In 1899 Secretary of State John Hay asked the major powers to agree to a policy of equal trading privileges. In 1900 several powers did so, and the Open Door policy was born.

The humiliation of the defeat by Japan had incensed the younger Chinese intellectuals who agitated for liberation from foreign dominance. Led by enlightened and concerned patriots such as K'ang yu-wei, the liberals proposed a wide-ranging series of economic, social, political, and educational reforms, and the young emperor, Tzu-hsi's nephew, approved them. What followed came to be known as the "hundred days of reform."

Tzu-hsi and her advisers encouraged antiforeign sentiment and opposed the patriots' attempts to bring about basic democratic reforms on a Confucianist basis. The reform attempts threatened the interests of the Tzu-hsi's supporters, and she came out of retirement in 1898, imprisoned her nephew, and revoked all of the proposed reforms.

After the suppression of the reform movement, a group of secret societies united in an organization known as the Righteous Harmony Fists, whose members were called Boxers by the westerners. At first they were strongly anti-Manchu, but by 1899 the chief object of their hatred had become the foreign nations who were stripping China of land and power. The Boxers started a campaign to rid China of all "foreign devils." Many Europeans were killed and the legations at Peking were besieged. In August 1900

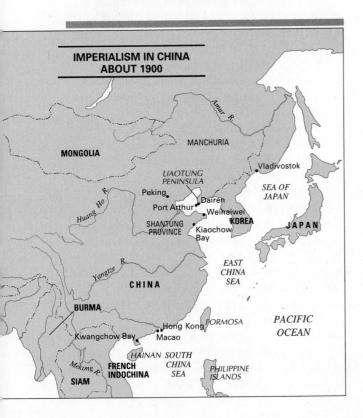

IMPERIALISM IN CHINA
ABOUT 1900

MONGOLIA

MANCHURIA

Amur R.

Vladivostok

LIAOTUNG
PENINSULA

Peking

Port Arthur   Dairen
              Weihaiwei
SHANTUNG   Kiaochow
PROVINCE   Bay

Huang Ho R.

SEA OF
JAPAN

KOREA

JAPAN

EAST
CHINA
SEA

Yangtze R.

CHINA

BURMA

Hong Kong   FORMOSA
Macao

Kwangchow Bay

Mekong R.

HAINAN   SOUTH
FRENCH   CHINA
INDOCHINA SEA

SIAM

PACIFIC
OCEAN

PHILIPPINE
ISLANDS

The Benefits of Imperialism

Imperialism provided a previously unattainable standard of living for Europeans, as a letter from Miss Eden proves.

I wish you could see my passage sometimes. The other day when I set off to pay George a visit I could not help thinking how strange it would have seemed at home. It was a rainy day, so all the servants were at home. The two tailors were sitting in one window, making a new gown for me, and Rosina by them chopping up her betel-nut; at the opposite window were my two Dacca embroiderers working at a large frame, and the sentry, in an ecstasy of admiration mounting guard over them. There was the bearer standing upright, in a sweet sleep, pulling away at my punkah. My own five servants were sitting in a circle, with an English spelling-book, which they were learning by heart; and my jemadar, who, out of compliment to me, has taken to draw, was sketching a bird. Chance's (Miss Eden's dog) servant was waiting at the end of the passage for his "little excellency" to go out walking, and a Chinese was waiting with some rolls of satin that he had brought to show.

From *The Sahibs*, ed. Hilton Brown (London: Willam Hodge & Company Limited, 1948).

---

an international army forced its way to Peking and released the prisoners. China was forced to apologize for the murder of foreign officials and pay a large indemnity.

By this time, even the Old Buddha acknowledged the need for change. After 1901 she sanctioned reforms in the state examination system, education, and governmental structure, and economic life; she even approved of the drive to end the binding of girls' feet—all to no avail.

Only a decade after the conclusion of the Boxer rebellion, a revolution broke out all over China, and in 1912 the Republic of China was proclaimed with Sun Yat-Sen as president. The revolutionary Chinese leaders knew that there had to be radically different approaches taken in China to allow it to survive and compete. As one official wrote in the 1890s:

Western nations rely on intelligence and energy to compete with one another. To come abreast of them China should plan to promote commerce and open mines; unless we change, the westerners will be rich and we poor. We should excel in technology and the manufacture of machinery; unless we change, they will be skillful and we clumsy.... Unless we change, the westerners will cooperate with each other and we shall stand isolated; they will be strong and we shall be weak.[6]

The Japanese Alternative

Western powers gained effective control of India, southeast Asia, and China by the end of the nineteenth century. Japan, however, responded in an alert and united manner, successfully adapting elements of strength from the west to the core of its own structures and ways of life.

At the beginning of the eighteenth century Japna was ruled from Edo (now Tokyo), the largest city in the country, by the head of the Tokugawa clan, whose leaders had declared themselves *shogun* since 1603. As the military dictator with a retinue of feudal lords and warriors, the *shogun* kept the country united and at peace. The Tokugawa strengthened the feudal framework of unity and stability that helped give Japan the basis for a successful response to the European challenge.

The Japanese emperor, in residence at Kyoto, served as a figurehead with no real function other than as a symbol around which the nation could rally. The Tokugawa ruled the country through their feudal lords, the *daimyo*. These officials in turn governed their regions with the aid of the *samurai*, the soldiers who also acted as administrators and governed and taxed the peasants.

Below the peasants on the social scale were the artisans and merchants who lived in the cities, a reflection of the fact that the Tokugawa saw agriculture as the foundation of politics and society.

The stratified society may well have ensured the power of the Tokugawa, but over a period of two centuries it was tested by peasant uprisings in the countryside and discontent in the cities. The peasant rebellions could be put down by force. But in the cities in the late eighteenth and early nineteenth centuries there was remarkable economic growth accompanied by rapid urbanization. New social and political forces posed difficulties for the Tokugawa structure. The spread of education and the increase in wealth helped spur the growth of the new urban classes drawn from young, aggressive merchants and intellectuals. The lower end of the social scale became wealthier than many of the *samurai*. These social forces could not be dealt with so easily by the Tokugawa governmental structure.

By the nineteenth century the shogunate lost much of its force and authority. The once-efficient government had become lax, especially in the realm of tax collection. Changing conditions in the cities and the flow of western information from the open port of Nagasaki worked to undermine the traditional system.

The Western Advance

Both European and American merchants and diplomats tried to open relations with Japan during the first part of the nineteenth century, but by 1850 foreign traders and missionaries still found their ability to move throughout the country greatly limited. Within the country the question of how and when to open up to the west was discussed. European inventions such as the daguerreotype and new manufacturing techniques had already made their appearance, but in response to Japanese policy towards foreigners would not be defined until 1853. On July 7 of that year the United States under the command of Commander Matthew Perry sailed into Edo Bay.

Perry, commanding a force of two steam frigates and two sloops-of-war, had been sent by the American government to convince the Japanese that a treaty opening trade relations between the two countries would be of mutual interest. He had been instructed to be tactful and to use force only if necessary. After delivering

Westerners and Japanese gather at the Foreign Merchants' Building in Yokohama, a major trading port.

Commodore Perry meeting the imperial commissioners at Yokohama. In 1854 Perry secured a treaty in which Japan agreed to permit foreign vessels to obtain provisions within Japanese territory and to allow U.S. ships to anchor in the ports at Shimoda and Hakodate.

a letter from the U.S. president, he remained in port ten days. When he departed, he told the authorities in Edo that he would return in a year for an answer. He actually came back eight months later, in February 1854. The Americans returned with more ships and before the deadline because they feared that the French or the Russians might gain concessions sooner from the Japanese.

The *shogun*, after a period of intense debate within his country, agreed to Perry's requests. The Treaty of Kanagawa, the first formal agreement between Japan and a western nation, was signed. By its terms, shipwrecked sailors were to be well treated and two ports were to be opened for provisioning ships and a limited amount of trade. European traders soon obtained similar privileges, plus the right of extraterritoriality.

The entry of the west placed a severe strain on the already weakened Japanese political structure. Antiforeign sentiment grew, even as many Japanese recognized that accommodation with the west was bound to come. The western representatives in Japan were caught in the middle, and there were a number of attacks against them. By 1867, after a time of strife and confusion, Japan reached the point of revolution. European and American fleets had illustrated their military superiority in 1863 and 1864 by bombarding Kagoshima and Shimonoseki, and thereby convinced some of the antiforeign elements

of the hopelessness of their position. In 1867 the system of dual government, with the emperor at Kyoto and the shogun at Edo, was abandoned. The capital was moved from Kyoto to Edo, which was renamed Tokyo (eastern capital).

The Meiji Restoration

The next generation of Japanese accomplished what no other non-western leaders were able to do—they adapted the Europeans' strengths to their own situation and successfully competed against the west. The new leaders who oversaw the ending of the dual power system were young and most were of *samurai* origin. They understood the nature of western power and the threat it posed to their country. They proposed as Japan's best defense the forming of a "rich country and strong military," based on western technology and institutions adapted to their country's needs. The young emperor, whose rule was known as the *Meiji* (enlightened government), reigned from 1868 to 1912. During that time Japan became a dynamic, modern power the west had to recognize as an equal.

Centuries earlier the Japanese had gained a great deal from China. Now they set out to learn from the west the lessons of how to construct an industrialized, bureaucratized state. For the next generation, the results of those lessons would be applied in a broad variety of areas. The voluntary abolition of feudal rights accompanied and facilitated the restoration of the emperor's supreme authority. In 1871 the end of the feudal system was officially announced, although it was far from actual fact. At the same time the government established a new territorial division and reformed the education and mail systems.

In 1882 a commission went out to study the world's various governmental systems in order to write a new constitution for Japan. The committee members were particularly impressed by Bismarck's German system, and the new constitution proclaimed in 1889 gave the premier a postion analogous to that held by the chancellor in Germany. Under the new system the cabinet was responsible to the emperor alone. Only the army and the navy could appoint their respective ministers. Since no statesman could form a cabinet without a war minister, and the army could overthrow any cabinet by simply withdrawing its

During the Meiji period, Japan undertook a successful program of industrialization, as is evident in this 1905 photo of a Japanese silk-weaving factory.

This 1905 photo illustrates the coming together of traditional and modern Japan. Farmers pull their carts through the streets while, above them, workers install electric power lines.

minister, ultimate control of policies rested with military interests. The constitution provided for a Diet, which wielded financial influence through its refusal power over unpopular budgets in peacetime. Under the new system the emperor, who held sovereign power, was considered "sacred and inviolable."

The Japanese adapted the lessons they learned from the west in other areas. In 1876 national conscription went into effect, and a modern military machine was created. German and French advisers trained army officers while naval officers received their instructions from the British. The government initiated the founding of banks, factories, and business concerns. Later, when they became successful, these establishments were turned over to private ownership and management. Japan also changed to the modern calendar, symbolizing its entry into the modern age.

Although the Japanese went to the west to find the best ways to modernize their country, they themselves, and not foreigners, made the major changes. The railways, telegraphs, lighthouses, and dockyards may have been constructed by foreigners and the warships may have been made in Britain, but the authorities in Tokyo kept their control.

Ito Hirobumi on the New Japanese Constitution

The Japanese were the only non-Europeans to adopt, choose, and use European concepts successfully for their own purpose. Ito Hirobumi's thoughts on drafting the new Japanese constitution represent one instance of how this system worked.

It was in the month of March, 1882, that His Majesty ordered me to work out a draft of a constitution to be submitted to his approval. No time was to be lost, so I started on the 15th of the same month for an extended journey to different constitutional countries to make as thorough a study as possible of the actual workings of different systems of constitutional government, of their various provisions, as well as of theories and opinions actually entertained by influential persons on the actual stage itself of constitutional life. . . . I sojourned about a year and a half in Europe, and having gathered the necessary materials, in so far as it was possible in so short a space of time, I returned home in September, 1883. Immediately after my return I set to work to draw up the Constitution . . . .

It was evident from the outset that mere imitation of foreign models would not suffice, for there were historical peculiarities of our country which had to be taken into consideration. For example, the Crown was, with us, an institution far more deeply rooted in the national sentiment and in our history than in other countries. It was indeed the very essence of a once theocratic State, so that in formulating the restrictions on its prerogatives in the new Constitution, we had to take care to safeguard the future realness or vitality of these prerogatives, and not to let the institution degenerate into an ornamental crowning piece of the edifice. At the same time, it was also evident that any form of constitutional régime was impossible without full and extended protection of honor, liberty, property, and personal security of citizens, entailing necessarily many important restrictions on the powers of the Crown. . . .

Another difficulty equally grave had to be taken into consideration. We were just then in an age of transition. The opinions prevail ing in the country were extremely heterogeneous, and often diametrically opposed to each other. We had survivors of former generations who were still full of theocratic ideas, and who believed that any attempt to restrict an imperial prerogative amounted to something like high treason. On the other hand there was a large and powerful body of the younger generation educated at the time when the Manchester theory was in vogue, and who in consequence were ultra-radical in their ideas of freedom. Members of the bureaucracy were prone to lend willing ears to the German doctrinaires of the reactionary period, while, on the other hand, the educated politicians among the people having not yet tasted the bitter significance of administrative responsibility, were liable to be more influenced by the dazzling words and lucid theories of Montesquieu, Rousseau, and other similar French writers. A work entitled *History of Civilization*, by Buckle, which denounced every form of government as an unnecessary evil, became the great favorite of students of all the higher schools, including the Imperial University. On the other hand, these same students would not have dared to expound the theories of Buckle before their own conservative fathers. At that time we had not yet arrived at the stage of distinguishing clearly between political opposition on the one hand, and treason to the established order of things on the other. The virtues necessary for the smooth working of any constitution, such as love of freedom of speech, love of publicity of proceedings, the spirit of tolerance for opinions opposed to one's own, etc., had yet to be learned by long experience.

From Rusaku Tsunoda et al., eds., *Sources of Japanese Tradition* (New York: Columbia University Press, 1958), pp. 673– 676. © 1958, Columbia University Press. Reprinted by permission of Columbia University Press.

Japan's Success

On the surface the Japanese government was liberal and parliamentary. In reality it was ultraconservative, giving the emperor and the cabinet dominant power. Though Japan was the first Asian nation to achieve a high degree of literacy, education remained the tool of the government, and one of its chief functions was to produce docile servants of the state. The press was subjected to wide control and censorship. The army was used as a means of instilling conscripts with unquestioning loyalty and obedience to the emperor. In army barracks young soldiers learned that the noblest fate was death on the battlefield. Unlike the Chinese, who revered the scholar most of all, the Japanese admired the soldier—warfare was the supreme vocation.

The Japanese were ready to seize the new methods and ideas of the west to serve their own military ends. It should not be forgotten, however, that ultimately it was through a display of military power that the west forced home the notion of its own superiority on Asia.

In adopting many of the aspects of the western state system—universal conscription, professional bureaucracy, mass literacy, state ideology— some Japanese institutions were forced to change. The *samurai*, who had formerly made their living as warriors or by serving their feudal lords, had to change their life styles. Many of them made the transition to the new system effortlessly. The conservative *samurai* were upset when the government passed a law in 1876 that diminished their financial advantages and also forbade the carrying of swords in public. Civil war broke out in some districts, and the government's forces put down the stubborn *samurai* and their armies.

The oligarchy that carried out the revolution through which Japan passed was able to keep a fair amount of control. They brought all of the people into the new system in one form or another. They could accomplish such a major revolution with a minimum of turmoil because all the changes were done within the traditional reverence for the emperor.

Through Shintoism, virtually the state religion, the restoration leaders devised the ultimate political and religious ideology. In Shinto the emperor, directly descended from the Sun Goddess, can demand unlimited loyalty to himself. He expresses the gods' will. As a former president of the privy council, Baron Hozumi, wrote:

> The Emperor holds the sovereign power, not as his own inherent right, but as an inheritance from his Divine Ancestor. The government is, therefore, theocratical. The Emperor rules over his country as the supreme head of the vast family of the Japanese nation. The government is, therefore patriarchal. The Emperor exercises the sovereign power according to the Constitution, which is based on the most advanced principles of modern constitutionalism. The government is, therefore, constitutional. In other words, the fundamental principle of the Japanese government is theocratic-patriarchal-constitutionalism.[7]

This cartoon, "A Dangerous Venture," pictures the Russo-Japanese War as a contest between a small but clever acrobat and a large but stupid bear. The acrobat, representing Japan, lures the Russian bear onto a fragile bamboo pole stretched over a chasm.

The process of industrialization coincided with this fundamental social and political revolution. In its rapid economic growth, Japan faced the same problems of demographic and urban growth the west faced. Social and cultural discontent naturally followed from such a rapid transformation. But the ideological and political structure constructed in the Meiji restoration was enough to hold the country together while at the same time repelling the Europeans and the Americans.

In the eyes of western diplomats, Japanese prestige had begun to increase soon after the conclusion of the Sino-Japanese war of 1894–1895. In 1902 Japan scored a diplomatic triumph in allying itself with Great Britain, an alliance viewed by both nations as a deterrent to Russian expansion. When a year later the Russians rebuffed Japanese attempts to negotiate a sphere-of-influence agreement over Korea and Manchuria, the Tokyo government attacked Port Arthur and bottled up Russia's fleet, without a formal declaration of war. The quick series of Japanese victories that followed forced the Russians to agree to the Treaty of Portsmouth in September 1905. Japan gained half the island of Sakhalin, the leaseholds on the Liaotung peninsula and Port Arthur, and various Russian railway and mining rights in southern Manchuria. Japan's paramount position in Korea was also conceded, paving the way for its annexation of that nation in 1910.

Japan's victory in the war with Russia in 1904–1905 astounded the world. Japan had successfully met the challenge of European primacy and was now accepted as a first-class power in its own right.

Conclusion

In the Indian subcontinent, southeast Asia, China, and Japan there were a variety of reactions to the European advance during the eighteenth and nineteenth centuries. In India the Mughul Dynasty was unable to control the myriad of peoples and religions over which it ruled, and the resulting instability furnished a convenient pretext for the ultimate imposition of British control. Only Siam (Thailand) maintained its independence in southeast Asia, and that only because the French and British wanted a buffer state between their holdings in the region. China suffered a distressing decline in the nineteenth century from its position as Central Kingdom to a helpless giant split into spheres of influence. Japan alone was able to adapt and successfully compete with the western nations.

Japan had a number of advantages, compared to its neighbors. The Confucian base of Japanese culture promoted a rational consideration of western technological and intellectual advantages that might be useful. It also emphasized hard work, self-sacrifice, loyalty, and the role of the family. Japan's island location helped it resist direct foreign rule. Its leadership was in the hands of a group of aggressive young officials who embraced the theories and practices of a modern economy. The Japanese brought back from the west the best and most useful elements of a modern economy and applied them to their cultural and social base. The speed with which they accomplished this transformation, barely forty years after the fall of the *shogun*, is an impressive indication of the strength of Japanese society.

The Japanese defeat of the Russians in 1905 did not alter any basic power relationships. Yet it was the first step in a new direction. The nineteenth century, by and large, saw the west expand its holdings over colonies worldwide, building on sheer technological and economic superiority. At the same time the foreigners' successes did not fundamentally change the cultural basis of the native peoples. The Japanese showed one example the non-western world could follow, by adapting the strong technology of the west to its own strong culture. They paved the way for other countries during the course of the twentieth century who would find their own paths to reassert their self-rule, after they too had mastered some of the western tools.

Suggestions for Reading

For valuable insights into British rule and its consequences see M. Edwards, *British India* (Taplinger, 1968) and S. Gopal, *British Policy in India* (Cambridge, 1965).

P. Speare provides a good short history in *The Oxford History of Modern India: 1740–1795* (Oxford, 1979). Two good studies of British imperial rule are P. Woodruff, *The Men Who Ruled India*, 2 vols. (St. Martins, 1954) and J. Morris, *Pax Britannica* (Harcourt, Brace, Jovanovich, 1980).

Li Chien-nung, *The Political History of China* (Van Nostrand, 1956), is a fine history of nineteenth-century China. For a good discussion of the transition China faced, see A. Feuerwerker, ed., *Modern China* (Prentice-Hall, 1964). Another useful study of China is Immanuel Hsu, *The Rise of Modern China* (Oxford, 1975). A key study on China's greatest rebellion is Franz Michael, *The Taiping Rebellion* (Univ. of Washington, 1972). P. W. Fay's *The Opium War, 1840–1842* (Norton, 1976) is a fine study. For views on the stresses of the late imperial period, see D. H. Bays, *China Enters the Twentieth Century . . .* (Michigan, 1978).

W. B. Beasley, *The Modern History of Japan* (Holt, Rinehart, Winston, 1973) is a useful overview. For an investigation into the early contacts between Europe and Asia see George B. Sansom, *The Western World and Japan* (Knopf, 1974) and *Japan: A Short Cultural History* (Stanford, 1952). Thomas Haber, *The Revolutionary Origins of Modern Japan* (Stanford, 1981) and G. M. Beckmann, *The Modernization of China and Japan* (Harper & Row, 1962) are essential to an understanding of the Meiji programs.

The Americans' entry into the Pacific is outlined in F. R. Dulles, *America's Rise to World Power* (Harper & Row, 1955). Recommended surveys of Southeast Asia are D. G. E. Hall, *A History of Southeast Asia* (St. Martin's, 1968); and H. J. Benda and J. A. Larkin, *The World of Southeast Asia* (Harper & Row, 1967).

Notes

1. Quoted in T. A. Bailey, *The American Pageant* (Lexington: D. C. Heath, 1956), p. 630.
2. K. S. Latourette, *A Short History of the Far East* (New York: Macmillan, 1947), p. 184.
3. Quoted in F. H. Michael and G. E. Taylor, *The Far East in the Modern World* (New York: Holt, Rinehart & Winston, 1956), p. 122.
4. Li-Chien-nung, *The Political History of China, 1840–1928*, trans. by Sau-yu Teng and J. Ingalls (Princeton: D. Van Nostrand Co., 1956), p. 29.
5. Michael and Taylor, *The Far East in the Modern World*, p. 183.
6. Quoted in Ch'u Chai and Winberg Chai, *The Changing Society of China* (New York: Mentor Books, 1962), p. 189.
7. Michael and Taylor, *The Far East in the Modern World*, pp. 253–256.

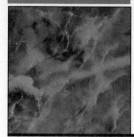

Chapter 30

Tragic War and Futile Peace: World War I

In 1914 Europeans had many reasons to be optimistic about the future. The growth produced by the previous three generations was supported by a sturdy belief in progress. Business and labor leaders had avoided the explosive class conflicts that Marx had forecast. Statesmen made serious efforts toward international cooperation.

There were, however, danger signs for the continent. Revolutionaries around the globe challenged Europe's stability. Within Europe the competitive energies generated by the states came to be harnessed in two conflicting alliance systems. The nagging Eastern Question eventually dragged the alliances into war.

In the four years of bloodshed that began in 1914, over 13 million Europeans died. Europe lost a generation of the best and bravest of its sons. The world economy lost what little equilibrium remained. Four empires—the German, the Austro-Hungarian, the Russian, and the Ottoman—either disappeared or were in the process of disappearing. In Russia Lenin gained power largely due to the impact of the war on the tsarist empire. In Germany Adolf Hitler took advantage of postwar conditions to make a bid for power. Europe's golden age was brought to an end by a combination of tragic forces: militarism, rival alliances, economic imperialism, secret diplomacy, and narrow, bellicose nationalism.

Forces of Progress and Signs of Danger

At the beginning of the twentieth century, Europe was Christian, Caucasian, capitalist, in-dustrialized; and it dominated the world. Europeans shared the same vibrant Western tradition; the rulers of the various European states were all related to one another. With all that the Europeans had in common, there was little reason to expect the outbreak of the First World War.

International Cooperation

Europeans devised new ways to organize international communication, defuse conflicts, and maintain peace. As early as 1865 a meeting was held in Paris to coordinate the use of telegraph lines and to establish a unified rate structure. The International Telegraph Union made up of twenty nations was formed. Ten years later a Universal Postal Union was set up to handle the world's mail. To protect the rights of authors, an agreement was drawn up in 1886 for an international copyright union.

International cooperation could be found in a number of other areas. In 1896 Baron de Coubertin revived the ancient Greek Olympic games. The organized world peace movement gained a foothold and increased influence throughout the nineteenth century. The Christian-based British Society for the Promotion of Permanent and Universal Peace was formed in 1816. Thirty years later workers for peace began the League for Universal Brotherhood in the United States.

Scholars and statesmen worked to strengthen international law, the rules of warfare, and the use of arbitration. A significant example of this was the opening of the Hague Conference in 1899. The Russian foreign minister invited the great powers to the Dutch city to discuss arms reductions. Although no progress was made on disarmament, the conference did reform the rules of war by improving the treatment of prisoners, outlawing the use of poisonous gas, and defining the conditions of a state of war. An international court of arbitration, the Hague Tribunal, was established. A list of jurists from which nations could select judges was drawn up. Appearance before the court was voluntary, as was acceptance of its decisions. The effectiveness of arbitration as a means to solve problems could be seen the ten years before the war. Various powers signed 162 arbitration treaties that pledged the signatories to arbitrate disagreements such as boundary disputes and conflicts over fishing rights.

Alfred Nobel, the Swedish manufacturer of dynamite, personified the contradictions of the age. This international producer of explosives established a Peace prize two weeks before his death in November 1896. The first prizes were awarded in 1901. Andrew Carnegie, the steel maker, founded the Carnegie Endowment for International Peace and built a peace palace at the Hague to be used for international conferences. Ironically, the building was finished just weeks before the outbreak of the First World War.

All of these developments encouraged believers in progress to see a peaceful future. They pointed out that wars during the nineteenth century were generally local and short. They believed that if war should break out in the future, the murderous new technology would ensure that it would not be lengthy or costly. Some Social Darwinists asserted that humanity might well evolve from the stage of fighting wars altogether. These optimists conveniently ignored the brutal, lengthy, and costly American Civil war, in many ways the first modern war.

Social Compromises

In 1848, it had looked as though Marx's predictions in the *Communist Manifesto* about the inevitability of class conflict, the destruction of capitalism and the *bourgeoisie*, and revolution might come true. But capitalism proved to be stronger and more flexible and labor unions more effective than Marx had predicted. Europe industrialized so successfully that a communist revolution, contrary to Marx's forecast, had never occurred in an industrialized country.

In the late nineteenth century, Europe moved toward the modern welfare-state concept. Some governments provided unemployment insurance, old-age pensions, and accident compensation. Because these social programs were often paid for out of tax revenues, some states, such as Britain, introduced the graduated income tax, by which individuals paid an amount relative to their earnings. The gulf between the rich and the poor did not disappear—the poor got less poor as the rich got richer. It has been estimated that "real wages" of workers (calculated as the amount of goods their take-home pay could actually buy) went up 50 percent between 1870 and 1900.

Business managers began to work more closely with the better organized unions. Bosses realized that a contented and healthy work force would be more productive. At the same time they knew that the unions could inflict damaging, costly strikes. In addition, business adapted to the constantly changing conditions to guard

The futility of disarmament agreements is the subject of this British cartoon in which heavily armed Germany, France, Russia, and Great Britain politely invite one another into the Hague "Temple of Disarmament."

itself against government regulation of its activities, such as was occurring in the United States.

Workers also tried to make business decisions more democratic and products less expensive by establishing cooperatives. Capital was secured by selling stock, goods were sold at prevailing prices, and profits were distributed annually in proportion to the amount of goods each consumer had purchased. By 1913 at least half of the British population was buying some of its purchases from cooperatives.

Mass education also contributed to the reduction of social tensions before 1914. As the common people were granted suffrage, it became apparent that they needed at least the basics of education to vote intelligently. As a result of the education bill passed in 1870, school attendance in Great Britain jumped from 1 to 4 million in ten years. Similar acts were passed in France, Germany, the Low Countries (Holland and Belgium), and Scandinavia. By 1914 southern and eastern Europe pursued a similar course to educate all of their people.

By 1900 international and domestic conflicts were well on their way to being defused. Political and business leaders learned that it was in their own best interest to guarantee a decent standard of living. This relative tranquility, along with the progress in international cooperation, justified much of the optimism held by many Europeans before 1914.

Portents of Change

As strong as the case for optimism might have been, observant critics could point to several signs of danger. The United States was beginning to overtake Europe economically. The Japanese victory over Russia in 1904–1905 suggested that the tide of western domination might be turning. Non-Europeans could master the west's skills and apply them to their own culture for their own ends.

Independence and revolutionary movements erupted around the globe. In South Africa, Mohandas K. Gandhi (1869–1948) developed his strategy of passive resistance that would later lead to liberation in India. The Chinese revolutionary movement was under way by 1914, laying the foundation for the return of the world's most populous nation to major power status by mid-century. In Vienna, Adolf Hitler was formulating his racial philosophy that would have such tragic results in the 1930s and 1940s. In Mexico the forces that carried out the successful revolutionary movement gained strength. In Africa, led by Ethiopia, forces that would culminate in the expulsion of the Europeans began to grow. In Russia, Lenin formed a cadre and developed a plan to bring about revolution.

In France, a new form of radicalism took root. It opposed the gradual improvement of relations between labor and capitalism and refused to

This cartoon portrays international power politics as a deadly billiard game in which the players use rifles and swords as cue sticks to strike the cannonballs. Bombs are stacked beneath the table, which is covered with a map of Europe. The snake-haired figure at center is identified as Diplomacy.

The U.S.S. *New Jersey* leads the Great White Fleet of 16 warships in a show of American naval strength. The fleet sailed world sea lanes from 1907 to 1909.

abandon the use of violence. Starting in Paris in the 1890s, the syndicalists argued that labor leaders were becoming capitalist tools. The syndicalists' goal was to overthrow the bourgeois state and replace it with a society consisting of "cells," each one representing an industrial union. Although they lacked disciplined leadership and a rigorous program of action, they were a disruptive and potentially dangerous element of society.

State Competition

Europe's greatest danger came not from critics or the occasional radical group, but from competition among the great powers. Europe's militarism, rival alliances, secret diplomacy, imperialism, and nationalism were the underlying, long-range causes of the First World War. These elements had long been present on the European scene, but at the turn of the century they were made even more explosive by the ambitions and policies of Germany.

At the beginning of the twentieth century, European politics remained much the same as it had in the previous three centuries—a competition among states. The main difference in 1900 was that there were some twenty-five independent political units instead of about five hundred. The laws were the same as those

established at Westphalia in 1648. The states recognized no authority above themselves and followed international law only when it suited their interests. They were ready to take advantage of a neighbor's weakness and threaten war if the prize to be won was substantial enough. War, whether the threat or the reality, remained the prime instrument of national policy. This "extension of politics" was frequently used whenever peaceful methods did not work.

Military force was the ultimate arbiter in international affairs. By the end of the 1870s, five of the six major powers had introduced compulsory military training. Although the British had not done so, they were in the process of expanding their fleet. By the first decade of this century the great powers had nearly 4.5 million men in the military and spent annually more than $2 billion on arms. The weapons industry became an important part of the European economy.

Economic rivalry and tariff restrictions heightened the competitions between states. In the new mercantilism, states acted as aggressive champions for their own businesses. In some cases economic rivalry led to fighting: Japanese designs on the Asian mainland caused war with China in 1894; Great Britain fought the Boer War in South Africa from 1899 to 1902; Japan and Russia fought over Manchuria in 1904–1905; and Italy took Tripoli from Turkey in 1912.

Friedrich von Bernhardi Summarizes Germany's Intentions

Friedrich von Bernhardi stated German dreams and frustrations a full two years before the outbreak of World War I.

Duties of the greatest importance for the whole advance of human civilization have thus been transmitted to the German nation, as heir of a great and glorious past. It is faced with problems of no less significance in the sphere of its international relations. These problems are of special importance, since they affect most deeply the intellectual development, and on their solution depends the position of Germany in the world.

The German people has always been incapable of great acts for the common interest except under the irresistible pressure of external conditions, as in the rising of 1813, or under the leadership of powerful personalities, who knew how to arouse the enthusiasm of the masses, to stir the German spirit to its depths, to vivify the idea of nationality, and force conflicting aspirations into concentration and union.

We must therefore take care that such men are assured the possibility of acting with a confident and free hand in order to accomplish great ends through and for our people.

Within these limits, it is in harmony with the national German character to allow personality to have a free course for the fullest development of all individual forces and capacities, of all spiritual, scientific, and artistic aims. "Every extension of the activities of the State is beneficial and wise, if it arouses, promotes, and purifies the independence of

free and reasoning men; it is evil when it kills and stunts the independence of free men." This independence of the individual, within the limits marked out by the interests of the State, forms the necessary complement of the wide expansion of the central power, and assures an ample scope to a liberal development of all our social conditions.

We must rouse in our people the unanimous wish for power in this sense, together with the determination to sacrifice on the altar of patriotism, not only life and property, but also private views and preferences in the interests of the common welfare. Then alone shall we discharge our great duties of the future, grow into a World Power, and stamp a great part of humanity with the impress of the German spirit. If, on the contrary, we persist in that dissipation of energy which now marks our political life, there is imminent fear that in the great contest of the nations, which we must inevitably face, we shall be dishonourably beaten; that days of disaster await us in the future, and that once again, as in the days of our former degradation, the poet's lament will be heard:

O Germany, the oaks still stand,
But thou art fallen, glorious land!
                                    Körner

From Freidrich von Bernhardi, *Germany and the Next War,* translated by Allen H. Powles (New York: Longmans, Green, and Co., 1914).

Nationalism was the greatest force fueling the rise in tensions on the continent. As used by Europe's politicians, the spirit of nationalism took on narrow, blatant, and warlike qualities to unite the populations of Europe behind the policies of their leaders. Among both ruling groups and state minorities, nationalism became a new religion and an essential tool of power politics.

The greatest danger to peace came in the nationalistic ambitions of the Balkan nations. Proud of their new freedom, they were determined to extend it to their compatriots still under the Turks or Austrians. Serbia in particular was ready to liberate the other Slavs. However, there was no reason that this local problem should have plunged the Europe into war.

In this atmosphere of international anarchy, most states did not feel strong enough to rely solely on their own resources for defense. Nations whose interests ran along parallel lines joined together. In response, nations outside an alliance formed unions to match their competitors. The creation of the two major rival alliances—the Triple Alliance (Germany, Austria-Hungrary, and Italy) and the Triple Entente (Britain, France, and Russia)—was the key fact in European diplomacy before 1914. However the alliances brought no assured peace. Rather, they increased the possibility of major war, because it was impossible now to localize a problem such as that of the Balkan Slavs.

Closely tied to the system of alliances was the practice of secret diplomacy. Some diplomats threatened, intimidated, and jockeyed for power. The traditional activities of spies with their secret reports and unscrupulous methods poisoned the atmosphere even further. The increase in tension overwhelmed the efforts of decent and honorable statesmen to keep peace.

Diplomatic Failure

From 1870 to 1890 the German chancellor Otto von Bismarck dominated European diplomacy. He built a foreign policy devoted to the diplomatic isolation of France by depriving it of potential allies. He reasoned that the French would try to take revenge on Germany and regain Alsace and Lorraine, but he knew they could do little without aid from the Austrians or Russians. In 1873 Bismarck made an alliance, known as the Three Emperors' League *(Dreikaiserbund)*, with Russia and Austria-Hungary.

The System of Shifting Alliances

The conflicts between the Austrians and Russians in the Balkans soon put a strain on the League, and at the Congress of Berlin (1878) Bismarck was forced to choose between the conflicting claims of Vienna and St. Petersburg. He chose to support Austria-Hungary for a number of reasons, including fear of alienating Great Britain if he backed the Russians. In addition, he felt that he could probably dominate Austria

more easily than Russia. This momentous shift paved the way for a new arrangement. In 1879 Bismarck negotiated the Dual Alliance with the Austro-Hungarian monarchy; in 1882 a new partner—Italy—joined the group, now called the Triple Alliance.

The choice of Austria over Russia did not mean that Bismarck abandoned his ties with the tsars. In 1881 the Three Emperor's League was renewed. Rivalries between the Dual Monarchy and Russia in the Balkans put an effective end to the arrangement, and the *Dreikaiserbund* collapsed for good in 1887. Bismarck negotiated a separate agreement with Russia called the Reinsurance Treaty, in which both sides pledged neutrality—except if Germany attacked France or Russia attacked Austria—and support of the status quo.

Under Bismarck's shrewd hand, Germany kept diplomatic control for twenty years. Bismarck chose his goals carefully and understood the states with which he worked. He made every effort to avoid challenging Britain's interests and to continue isolating France. As a result, Germany was not surrounded by enemies. The chancellor kept from alienating Russia while maintaining his ties with Austria.

In the 1890s, however, the rash actions of the new kaiser, William II, destroyed Germany's favorable position. He dismissed Bismarck in 1890, took foreign policy in his own hands, and frittered away the diplomatic advantages the chancellor had built up. France had been attempting to escape from its isolation for some time, and through its loans had begun to make important inroads into Russia, even before Bismarck retired. When the kaiser allowed the Reinsurance Treaty to lapse, the Russians sought new allies. By 1894 France got what it had wanted for twenty years—a strong ally. The Triple Alliance of Germany, Italy, and Austria-Hungary was now confronted by the Dual Alliance of Russia and France. Germany's worst fears had come to pass as it was now encircled by enemies.

Britain Ends Its Isolation

At the end of the nineteenth century Britain found itself involved in bitter rivalries with Russia—both in the Balkans and in the Middle East—and with France in Africa. During the Boer

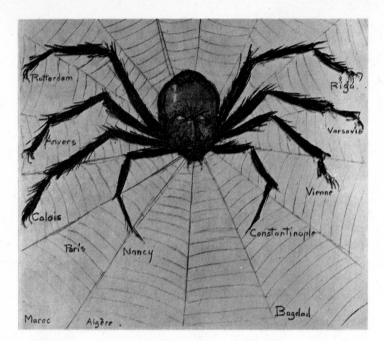

Rotterdam
Riga
Anvers
Varsovie
Vienne
Caldis
Constantinople
Paris
Nancy
Maroc
Algère
Bagdad

War, all of the great powers in Europe were anti-British. However, the supremacy of the British fleet helped discourage intervention. As the new century began, London became concerned that its policy of splendid isolation might need to be abandoned. In these circumstances, the most normal place for Britain to turn would be to Germany.

On the surface, nothing seemed more natural than that these two dominant European powers should adjust their national interests to avoid conflict. From the 1880s to 1901 both sides made several approaches to investigate an "understanding" between the major sea power, Britain, and the strongest land power, Germany. Tradition and dynastic relations spoke in favor of a closer tie between the two. By 1900, Berlin and London may have competed in economic and imperialistic terms, but they were far from any major strife in any either area.

The two countries could not, however, come together in an alliance. Even though important figures on both sides could see the advantages of an alliance, strong forces worked against this development. German and British interests did not match sufficiently to permit equal gain from an alliance. The kaiser's numerous bellicose statements and clumsy actions—such as his meddling in British colonial affairs with his telegram to South African President Paul Kruger in 1896—offended many British leaders. Germany's expanding influence in the Middle East and the Balkans worried the British as did Germany's tremendous economic progress.

Most threatening for London was Germany's plan to build a fleet that would compete with Britain's. In 1900, Germany initiated a huge naval program providing for, within a twenty-year timetable, a fleet strong enough to keep Britain from interfering with German international goals. The British knew that the German program was aimed directly at them. For the island nation, the supremacy of the Royal Navy was a life-or-death matter. Since food and raw materials had to come by sea, it was crucial that the navy be able to protect British shipping.

Challenged by Germany, Britain looked elsewhere for allies. In 1904 officials from London and Paris began to settle their outstanding differences and proclaimed the *Entente Cordiale* ("friendly understanding") setting aside a tradition of hostility going back to the fourteenth century. The *Entente*, and an alliance with Japan in 1902, ended Britain's policy of diplomatic isolation and brought it into the combination that would be pitted against Germany's Triple Alliance. In 1907 London settled its problems with Russia, thereby establishing the Triple Entente.

The British made no definite military commitments in the agreements with France and Russia. Theoretically they retained freedom of action, but they were now part of the alliance system.

The Moroccan Crises

In the decade before the First World War Europe experienced a series of crises on its peripheries, none of which vitally threatened the great powers' survival. However, because of the alliance systems, these incidents increased tensions and brought Europe ever closer to war.

The first serious test came in 1905 over Morocco (see map below). France sought control of this territory in order to establish a continuous line of dependencies from the Atlantic across the

North African coast to Tunisia. Carefully timing their moves, the Germans arranged for the kaiser to visit the Moroccan port of Tangier, where he declared that all powers must respect the independence of the country. The French were forced to give up their immediate plans for taking over Morocco and agree to Germany's suggestion that an international conference be called at Algeciras (1906) to discuss the matter.

At this meeting the Germans hoped for a split between the British and French. This did not occur. On the contrary, all but one of the nations in attendance—even Italy—supported France rather than Germany. Only Austria-Hungary remained on the kaiser's side. The conference agreed that Morocco should still enjoy its sovereignty, but that France and Spain should be given certain rights to police the area.

DIPLOMATIC CRISES 1905-1914

In 1911 a second Moroccan crisis escalated tensions. When France sent an army into the disputed territory, ostensibly to maintain order, Germany responded by sending the gunboat *Panther* to the Moroccan port of Agadir. Great Britain came out with a blunt warning that all of its power was at the disposal of France in this affair. A diplomatic bargain was finally struck in which France got a free hand in Morocco and Germany gained a small area in Equatorial Africa. The two rival alliance systems managed to avoid war over Morocco. Feelings were soothed when the imperial powers compensated each other with pieces of the African landscape.

The Balkan Crises

The two rival alliances came to blows over the Balkans, where the interests of Austria-Hungary and Russia directly collided. In that complex area, the forces of local nationalism drew the great powers into a military showdown.

Austria and Russia had long kept a wary eye on each other's policies in southeastern Europe. During the nineteenth century each country had had an obsessive interest in the Balkan holdings of the Ottoman Empire. Neither side could afford for the other to gain too great an advantage in the area. Throughout the last part of the nineteenth century the two had occasionally disagreed over issues involving Macedonia, railroads, and boundary revisions. In 1908 a crisis erupted that threatened to draw Europe into war. The issue that increased hostility was the Dual Monarchy's annexation of Bosnia and Herzegovina.

The Austro-Hungarian monarchy had administered the two areas since the 1878 Congress of Berlin, so the annexation actually changed very little. But the Slavs perceived the annexation as humiliating to them and their "protector," Russia. The fact that the Russians, through an ill-considered plan, had initiated the train of events that led to the annexation made the whole affair doubly frustrating for the Slavs.

A tsarist diplomat Count Izvolskii had initiated discussions whereby the Russians would approve the annexation in return for increased Black Sea rights for the Russians. Bosnia and Herzegovina were annexed, but the Russians

THE BOILING POINT.

In this *Punch* cartoon, European leaders are barely able to keep the lid on the boiling kettle of Balkan crises.

never got their part of the bargain. Serbia was outraged by the incorporation of more Slavs into the Habsburg domain and expected its Slavic, Orthodox protector, Russia, to do something about it. The Russians had been badly bruised in their war with Japan and the Revolution of 1905. Aside from making threatening noises, they could do little, especially in the face of Germany's support for Austria-Hungary.

Austro-Hungarian interests in the Balkans were primarily concerned with defense and keeping Serbia under control. The Dual Monarchy was experiencing serious domestic strains as the multinational empire limped along under the terms of the renegotiated *Ausgleich*. Austro-Hungarian pretensions to great power status increasingly outdistanced its ability to play that role.

Germany's motives in the Balkans were largely strategic in the long term and diplomatic in the short term. The Germans envisioned a Berlin-based political and economic zone stretching from the Baltic Sea to the Persian Gulf. Berlin could not afford to alienate its Austrian ally through lukewarm support.

After 1908 tensions remained high in the Balkans. The Austrians looked to increase their advantage, knowing they had the full support of Germany. Serbia searched for revenge, while Russia found itself backed into a corner. The Russians in the future would be forced to act strongly and encourage aggressive policies on the part of their Balkan allies or lose forever their position of prestige. The 1908 crisis changed relatively few of the major features of the competition for influence in the Balkans, except to limit further the major powers' options.

In 1912 Serbia and its neighbors, especially Greece and Bulgaria, formed an alliance with the objective of expelling Turkey from Europe. The First Balkan War began later in the year and came to a quick end with the defeat of the Turks. Each of the Balkan allies had its own particular goals in mind in fighting the Ottomans. When the great powers stepped in to maintain the balance, problems arose.

Serbia had fought for a seaport and thought it had gained one with the defeat of the Turks. However, the Italians and Austrians blocked Serbia's access to the Adriatic by overseeing the creation of Albania in the Treaty of London of 1913. Denied their goals, the Serbs turned on their former ally, the Bulgarians, and demanded a part of their spoils from the first war. Bulgaria refused and, emboldened by its successes in the first war, attacked its former allies, starting the Second Balkan War. The Serbs were in turn joined by the Romanians and the Turks. The Bulgarians were no match for the rest of the Balkans and signed a peace which turned over most of the territory that they had earlier gained. The Turks retained only a precarious toehold in Europe, the small pocket from Adrianople to Constantinople (see maps, p. 771).

Had the great powers found a way to place a fence around the Balkans and allow the squabbling nations to fight their miniwars in isolation, then the two Balkan wars of 1912 and 1913 would have had little significance. As it was, however, they added to the prevailing state of tension. The two competing alliances effectively tied their policies to the narrow constraints of the Balkans. In effect, the tail wagged the dog, as the alliances reacted to every flareup in the turbulent peninsula.

By the end of 1913 no permanent solution had been found to the Balkan problems. Austria was more fearful than ever of Serbia's expansionist desires. Serbian ambitions had grown larger since its territory had doubled as a result of the recent wars. The Serbian prime inister declared: "The first round is won: now we must prepare the second against Austria." Russia's dreams of Balkan grandeur had not been blocked but only interrupted. The rest of Europe lay divided.

Assassination at Sarajevo

The spark that set off World War I was struck on June 28, 1914 with the assassination of the heir to the Austrian throne, Archduke Francis Ferdinand. The archduke and his wife were visiting the Bosnian town of Sarajevo which his realm had recently annexed. While they were driving through the narrow streets in their huge touring car, a nineteen-year-old Bosnian student named Gavrilo Princip, one of seven youthful terrorists along the route, shot them.

Princip had been inspired by propaganda advocating the creation of a greater Serbia and assisted by Serbian officers serving in a secret organization. The direct participation of the Serbian government was not proved; even so, the Belgrade authorities were likely to have been involved, at least indirectly.

The legal details of the case were lost in Vienna's rush to put an end to the problem of Serbia. Count Leopold von Berchtold, the foreign minister, believed that the assassination in Bosnia justified crushing the anti-Austrian propaganda and terrorism coming from the Serbs. The kaiser felt that everything possible must be done to prevent Germany's only reliable ally from being weakened, and so he assured the Austrians of his full support. Berchtold received a blank check from Germany. Vienna wanted a quick, local Austro-Serbian war, and Germany favored quick action to forestall Russian intervention.

On July 23 the Austro-Hungarian foreign ministry presented an ultimatum to the Serbs.

Expecting the list of demands to be turned down, Berchtold demanded unconditional acceptance within forty-eight hours. On July 25 the Austro-Hungarian government announced that Serbia's reply, which was conciliatory, was not satisfactory. The Austrian authorities immediately mobilized their armed forces.

The Alliances' Inevitable War

The Germans, having second thoughts, urged their ally to negotiate with Russia, which was anxiously following developments. Russia realized that if the Austrians succeeded in humbling the Serbs, Russia's position in the Balkans would suffer irreparably. The French, in the meantime, assured the Russians of their full cooperation and urged full support for Serbia. The British unsuccessfully advised negotiation.

Europe had reached a point of no return: the Austrians had committed themselves to the task of removing a serious opponent, and the Russians could not permit this removal to happen. Neither side would back down, and each had allies ready to come to its aid. Fearful that Serbia would escape from his clutches, Berchtold succeeded on July 27—thanks in part to deception—

in convincing the Habsburg emperor that war was the only way out. On the following day the Austro-Hungarian empire declared war against Serbia.

As the possibilities of a general European war loomed, Berlin sent several frantic telegrams to Vienna. The German ambassador was instructed to tell Berchtold that "as an ally we must refuse to be drawn into a world conflagration because Austria does not respect our advice."[1] Had the Germans spoken to their ally in such tones a month earlier, war might have been avoided. But Austria's belligerence moved the Russians to act. The tsar ordered mobilization on July 30.

Germany was caught in a dilemma that Bismarck would never have allowed. Surrounded by potential enemies, the Germans had to move decisively or face defeat. The Russian mobilization threatened them, because in the event of war on the eastern front, there would also be war on the western front. The best plan to Berlin, one that had been worked out since 1905, seemed to be to launch a lightning attack against France—which could mobilize faster that Russia—crush France, and then return to meet Russia, which would be slower to mobilize. To allow Russian

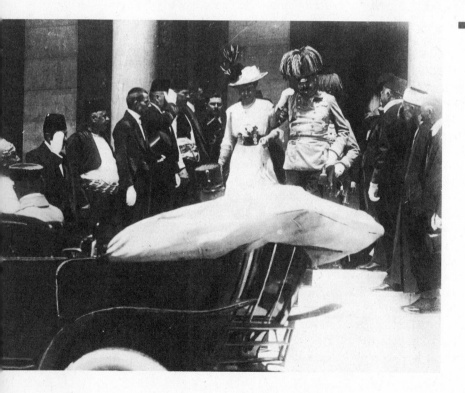

Archduke Francis Ferdinand and his wife Sophie leave the Senate House in Sarajevo on June 28, 1914. Five minutes after this photograph was taken, Serbian terrorist Gavrilo Princip assassinated them both, helping to touch off World War I.

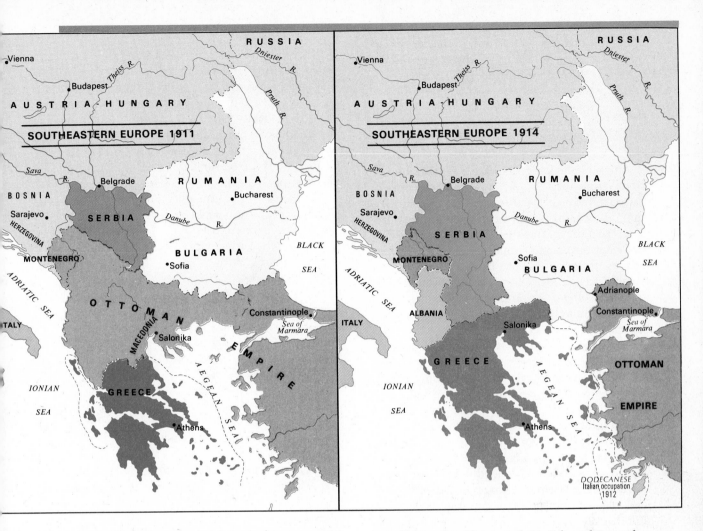

mobilization to proceed without action would jeopardize this plan. In the wake of the crisis, the Germans set into effect their long-planned strategy to gain European dominance.

On July 31 Germany sent ultimata to Russia and France, demanding cessation of mobilization from the former and a pledge of neutrality from the latter. Failing to receive satisfactory replies, Germany declared war on Russia on August 1 and on France two days later. On August 2, the German ambassador in Brussels delivered an ultimatum to the Belgian government announcing his country's intention to send troops through Belgium, in violation of the 1839 Neutrality Treaty. The Belgian cabinet refused to grant permission and appealed to the Triple Entente for help.

A majority of the British cabinet did not want war, but with the news of the German ultimatum

to Belgium, the tide turned. Sir Edward Grey, the British foreign secretary, sent an ultimatum to Germany demanding that Belgian neutrality be respected. Germany refused, and on August 4, Great Britain declared war.

Because Germany and Austria-Hungary were not waging a defensive war, Italy declined to carry out its obligations under the Triple Alliance and for a time remained neutral. In the latter part of August, Japan joined the allies. Turkey, fearing Russia, threw in its lot with the Central Powers.

In the last days of peace, diplomats tried desperately to avert general war. Through confusion, fear, and loss of sleep, the nervous strain among them was almost unbearable. Many broke down and wept when it became apparent they had failed. Grey himself noted in his autobiography that one evening, just before the outbreak of the war, he watched the streetlights being lit from his office window and remarked: "The lamps are going out all over Europe; we shall not see them lit again in our lifetime."[2]

World War I

Although the terrible struggle that racked the world from 1914 to 1918 was fought mainly in Europe, it is rightly called the First World War. In the sixteenth and seventeenth centuries European powers had competed across the globe; however, never had so many fighters and such enormous resources been brought together in a single conflict. Altogether twenty-seven nations became belligerents, ranging the globe from Japan to Canada and from Argentina to South Africa to Australia. The Central Powers—German, Austria-Hungary, Bulgaria, and Turkey—mobilized 21 million men. The Allies eventually called 40 million men to arms, including 12 million Russians (see map, p. 773). The two sides were more equally matched than the numbers would indicate, however. Since the Russian divisions were often poorly equipped and ineffectively used, the Allies' apparent advantage was not so great as numbers would indicate. In addition, in the German army the Central Powers boasted superb generalship and discipline. Another advantage was that the Central Powers fought from a central position and were able to transfer troops quickly and efficiently to various fronts.

The Allies had the advantages of greater resources of finance and raw materials. Britain maintained its naval dominance and could draw on its empire for support. In addition, because Germany was effectively blockaded, the United States, even though officially neutral for most of the war, served as a major source of supplies for the Allies.

The warring nations went into battle in a confident mood. Each side was sure of its strength and felt it had prepared carefully. Each nation's propaganda machine delivered reassuring messages of guaranteed victory. All expected that the war would soon be over, concluded in a few decisive battles. It was generally believed that the war would be over by Christmas.

The First Two Years of War

All of the general staffs had been refining their war plans for years. The Germans knew that Allied naval supremacy would cut them off from needed sources abroad. They realized that they were potentially surrounded and that they should strike a quick knockout blow to end the war. Following the plan devised by Chief of the General Staff Alfred von Schlieffen, the Germans aimed to push the Belgians aside and drive rapidly south into France. The plan then called for the German forces to wheel west of Paris, outflank the French forces, and drive them toward Alsace-Lorraine, where they would be met by another German army. Within six weeks, the French would be destroyed, caught between the western hammer and the eastern anvil. Meanwhile, a small German force would be holding the presumably slow-moving Russians on the eastern front, awaiting the arrival via the excellent German rail system of the victorious western forces. The plan nearly worked.

The Germans marched according to the plan until they got so close to Paris that they could see the top of the Eiffel Tower. They were hurled back by a bold French offensive through a gap that opened between their armies in the First Battle of the Marne, fought between September 5 and 12. With the assistance of a small British

The Queen's Lancers pass a detachment of French mounted troops during the advance from the Marne to the Aisne in September 1914. This Aisne Valley was the site of four major battles of World War I.

WORLD WAR I

	Triple Entente
	Central Powers
	Allies of Triple Entente
	Neutral nations
→	Allied thrust
→	Central Powers' thrust
	Battles:
×	Allied victory
⊗	Central Powers' victory

expeditionary force and Parisian taxi drivers providing transportation, the French then marched north in a race with the Germans to reach and control the vital ports along the English Channel. After much desperate fighting, the enemies established battle positions that stabilized, creating the "western front." This solid line of opposing trenches, which stretched from the Channel to near Nancy, was the scene for a grisly new war of attrition.

The other part of the German scheme that did not go according to plan was the unexpected speed with which the Russians mobilized. They penetrated deeply into East Prussia and overran the Austrian province of Galicia. However, confused leadership resulted in two catastrophic Russian defeats in East Prussia, and Germany never again faced a serious threat on its eastern frontier.

By the end of 1914 all sides knew that they were trapped in a new type of war, one of

Soldiers manning a Vickers machine gun at the Somme in July 1916 wear gas masks as protection against phosgene. The new technology of World War I included increased use of the machine gun and poison gas.

horrible consequences. Single battles claimed hundreds of thousands of lives, and the toll during the first few months of the conflict ran as high as one and one-half million dead and wounded.

In 1915 the British attempted a major campaign to force open the Dardanelles, closed by Turkey when it joined the Central Powers. This plan, attributed to Winston Churchill, then first lord of the admiralty, was designed to open up the sea route to Russia, which was badly in need of war supplies, and to take the pressure off the western front. After heroic and costly attacks, Allied Australian and New Zealand troops, known as Anzacs, were forced to withdraw from their landing positions on the Gallipoli peninsula in European Turkey.

Another major Allied setback in 1915 was the defeat of the Russian forces in Poland. More than 1,200,000 Russians were killed and wounded, and the Germans took nearly 900,000 prisoners. Although Russia somehow remained in the war, fighting well against the Dual Monarchy, it was no longer a concern for the Germans. These defeats generated rising criticism against the tsar's government, and Russian morale deteriorated.

Serbia was the next Allied victim. In September 1915, Bulgaria, still aching from its defeat in the Second Balkan War, entered the war on the side of the Central Powers. Surrounded by enemies, Serbia was helpless, and resistance was quickly crushed. The Austrians had finally gained their goal of the previous summer, but in the context of the continental tragedy, this achievement no longer seemed significant.

The Allies' only bright spot in 1915 was Italy's entry into their ranks. Italy had remained neutral in August 1914 when it had defected from the Triple Alliance, of which it had been at best a token member. Italy joined the Allies following promises made in a secret treaty in London promising the Italians huge concessions of territory once victory had been attained.

Stalemate

The Allies' strategy on the western front was to restrict attacks in France to intermittent nibbling, thus saving manpower and at the same time concentrating on their naval blockade. Denied badly needed imports, it was assumed, the German war effort would be seriously weakened. Countering this tactic, the German high command launched a massive offensive against the strategic fortress of Verdun in the spring of 1916. This forced the Allies to throw hundreds of thousands of men into battle. The slaughter brought

The Battle of Verdun

The initial euphoria accompanying World War I soon dissolved in the face of disasters such as the Battle of Verdun.

There are slopes on Hill 304 where the level of the ground is raised several meters by mounds of German corpses. Sometimes it happens that the third German wave uses the dead of the second wave as ramparts and shelters. It was behind ramparts of the dead left by the first five attacks, on May 24th, that we saw the Boches take shelter while they organized their next rush.

We make prisoners among these dead during our counterattacks. They are men who have received no hurt, but have been knocked down by the falling of the human wall of their killed and wounded neighbors. They say very little. They are for the most part dazed with fear and alcohol, and it is several days before they recover.

From Charles F. Horne, ed., *Source Records of the Great War*, vol. 4 (New York: National Alumni, 1923).

Unlike previous wars, World War I became a war of position and defense rather than one of movement and territorial conquest. Soldiers on both sides dug trenches, piled sandbags, and stretched barbed wire to protect their positions.

on by massed artillery and infantry charges between the trenches was horrible. The total loss of wounded and dead from this battle came to some 700,000 men.

To ease the pressure against Verdun, the British army began an offensive along the Somme River along the western front. The attackers' losses were catastrophic: 60 percent of the officers and 40 percent of the men became casualties the first day of the battle. Despite these awesome figures—which included the British firing 2 million shells at the first battle of the Somme—the attacks continued for three months without any substantial gains. Total German losses at the Somme were about 450,000, while the British and French lost about 600,000 men.

The only major naval engagement of the war, the Battle of Jutland (May 31–June 1, 1916), reaffirmed British control of the seas. The Germans maneuvered brilliantly and took risks. They could afford to gamble, because defeat would in no way worsen their existing position. The British fleet, on the other hand, had to act cautiously and absorbed greater losses. However the Germans retreated to their base and remained there for the rest of the war.[3]

On the eastern front in 1916 the Russians continued their generally successful campaigns against the Austro-Hungarian forces. But the Germans were always there to save their allies from destruction. Romania, impressed by the Russian victories, finally joined the Allies and launched an attack on the Hungarians. After an initial success, the Romanians were soon knocked out of the war by a joint German-Bulgarian invasion.

Total War and the Home Front

At the close of 1916, after more than two years of fighting, neither side was close to victory. Instead, the war had turned into a dreary contest of stamina, a far cry from the glories promised by the propaganda of 1914. War was no longer fought between armies, it was fought between states and every component within the state participated.[4]

On the home front, rationing was instituted to ensure sufficient supplies for soldiers at the front. As men went off to fight, women took over their jobs in the workplace. Intensive propaganda campaigns encouraged civilians to buy more bonds and make more weapons. Nations unleashed a barrage of propaganda inciting total hatred of the enemy, belief in the righteousness of the cause, and unquestioned support for the war effort.

Civil liberties suffered, and in some cases distinguished citizens were thrown into prison for opposing the war effort. In Britain, for example, the philosopher and mathematician Bertrand Russell was imprisoned for a short time for his pacifist views. Governments took over control of their national economies, gambling everything on a victory in which the loser would pay all the expenses incurred in the war. The various states outlawed strikes and rigidly controlled currencies and foreign trade.

At the beginning of the war, all was flag-waving and enthusiasm. The international socialist movement, whose policy it was to promote international proletarian unity, fell victim to the

Traditional warfare mixed with new technology in World War I; here, French cavalry officers watch a scout fighter plane.

Battle of the Somme

The "glories of war" were exposed for what they were—pain and suffering. These diary extracts show what war was like.

Diary of Private Tom Easton

A beautiful summer morning, though we'd had a bit of rain earlier. The skylarks were just singing away. Then the grand mine went up, it shook the earth for nearly a minute, and we had to wait for the fallout. The whistles blew and we stepped off one yard apart going straight forward. We were under orders not to stop or look or help the wounded. Carry on if you're fit, it was. . . .

Men began to fall one by one. . . . One officer said we were OK, all the machine-guns were firing over our heads. This was so until we passed our own front line and started to cross No Man's Land. Then trench machine-guns began the slaughter from the La Boiselle salient [German positions]. Men fell on every side screaming. Those who were un-wounded dare not attend to them, we must press on regardless. Hundreds lay on the German barbed wire which was not all destroyed and their bodies formed a bridge for others to pass over and into the German front line.

There were few Germans, mainly in machine-gun posts. These were bombed out, and there were fewer still of us, but we con-solidated the lines we had taken by preparing firing positions on the rear of the trenches gained, and fighting went on all morning and gradually died down as men and munitions on both sides became exhausted.

When we got to the German trenches we'd lost all our officers. They were all dead, there was no question of wounded. About 25 of us made it there. . . .

. . . Yes, as we made our way over the lat-ter stages of the charge, men dropped all around like ninepins. Apart from machine-guns, the German artillery was also very ac-tive, great sheets of earth rose up before one. Every man had to fend for himself as we still had to face the Germans in their trenches when we got there.

I kept shouting for my MOTHER to guide me, strange as it may seem. Mother help me. Not the Virgin Mother but my own maternal Mother, for I was then only 20 years of age.

Diary of Captain Reginald Leetham

I got to my position and looked over the top. The first thing I saw in the space of a tennis court in front of me was the bodies of 100 dead or severely wounded men lying there in our own wire. . . .

The dead were stretched out on one side [of the trench] one on top of the other six high. . . . To do one's duty was continually climbing over corpses in every position. . . . Of the hundred of corpses I saw I only saw one pretty one—a handsome boy called Schnyder of the Berkshires who lay on our firestep shot through the heart. There he lay with a sandbag over his face: I uncovered it as I knew he was an officer. I wish his Mother could have seen him—one of the few whose faces had not been mutilated.

Diary of Subaltern Edward G. D. Liveing

There was the freshness and splendor of a summer morning over everything. . . .

A hare jumped up and rushed towards me through the dry yellowish grass, its eyes bulg-ing with fear. . . .

Suddenly I cursed. I had been scalded in the left hip. A shell, I thought, had blown up in a water logged crump hole and sprayed me with boiling water. Letting go of my rifle, I dropped forward full length on the ground. My hip began to smart unpleasantly, and I felt a curious warmth stealing down my left leg. I thought it was the boiling water that had scalded me. Certainly my breeches looked as if they were saturated with water. I did not know they were saturated with blood.

From Michael Kernan. "Day of Slaughter on the Somme," *The Washington Post,* June 27, 1976, pp. C1, C5, passim. Reprinted by permission.

As the men marched off to war, women left their homes to work in munitions plants. Here, women workers operate cranes in a British shell-filling factory.

rabid patriotism that infected the continent. Workers of one country were encouraged to go out and kill workers of the enemy country in the name of the state. There was much idealism, sense of sacrifice, and love of country. At first there was no understanding of the horror, death, and disaster that comes with modern, industrialized war. British poet Rupert Brooke caught the spirit in his poem "The Soldier":

> If I should die, think only this of me:
> That there's some corner of a foreign field
> That is forever England. There shall be
> In that rich earth a richer dust concealed;
> A dust whom England bore, shaped, made aware,
> Gave, once, her flowers to love, her ways to roam,
> A body of England's breathing English air,
> Washed by the rivers, blest by suns of home.[5]

But this early idealism, this romantic conception of death in battle, gradually changed to one of war weariness and total futility. This growing

mood is best seen in the poetry of the young British officer and poet Wilfrid Owen, himself a victim on the western front:

> What passing-bells for those who die as cattle?
> Only the monstrous anger of the guns....
> No mockeries for them; no prayers nor bells,
> Nor any voice of mourning save the choirs,—
> The shrill, demented choirs of wailing shells;
> And bugles calling for them from sad shires.[6]

By the end of 1916 a deep yearning for peace dominated Europe. Sensing this mood, leaders on both sides put forth peace feelers. But these half-hearted overtures achieved nothing. Propaganda was used effectively to continue the war and support for it. The populations of the warring states were made to believe that their crusade was somehow divinely inspired. In reality, the Dual Monarchy and France fought for survival; Russia, German, and Italy all fought to

The face of a battle-weary corporal in the Argonne Forest reflects the disillusionment of many who set out to fight what they believed would be a short-lived, "glorious war."

Wilfrid Owen, "Dulce et Decorum Est"

Leading antiwar poet Wilfrid Owen, who was killed in action in 1918, expressed the bitterness of the war's victims.

Bent double, like old beggars under
sacks, Knock-kneed, coughing like
hags, we cursed through sludge,
Till on the haunting flares we turned our
backs
And towards our distant rest began to trudge.
Men marched asleep. Many had lost their
boots
But limped on, blood-shod. All went lame; all
blind;
Drunk with fatigue; deaf even to the hoots
Of tired, outstripped Five-Nines that dropped
behind.

Gas! Gas! Quick, boys!—an Ecstasy of
fumbling,
Fitting the clumsy helmets just in time;
But someone still was yelling out and
stumbling
And flound'ring like a man in fire or lime . . .
Dim, through the misty panes and thick green
light,
As under a green sea, I saw him drowning.

In all my dreams, before my helpless sight,
He plunges at me, guttering, choking,
drowning.

If in some smothering dreams you too could
pace
Behind the wagon that we flung him in,
And watch the white eyes writhing in his
face,
His hanging face, like a devil's sick of sin;
If you could hear, at every jolt, the blood
Come gargling from the froth-corrupted
lungs,
Obscene as cancer, bitter as the cud
Of vile, incurable sores on innocent tongues,—
My friend, you would not tell with such high
zest
To children ardent for some desperate glory,
The old Lie: Dulce et decorum est
Pro patria mori.

improve their respective positions in Europe; while Britain fought for Belgium and a renewed balance of power on the continent.

Allied Fatigue and American Entry

In 1917 British and French military strength reached its highest point, only to fall precipitously. Allied commanders were hopeful that the long-planned breakthrough might be accomplished, but a large-scale French attack was beaten back, with huge losses. Some French regiments mutinied rather than return to the inferno of "no-man's land" between the trenches. The British sacrificed hundreds of thousands of men without any decisive results in several massive offensives into German machine guns. The Allies also launched unsuccessful campaigns in Italy. Aided by the Germans, the Austrians smashed the Italian front at the battle of Caporetto (1917), an event vividly described by Ernest Hemingway in *A Farewell to Arms.* Italian resistance finally hardened, and collapse was barely averted.

The growing effectiveness of the German submarine menace deepened Allied frustration. By 1917 Allied shipping losses had reached dangerous proportions. In three months 470 British ships fell victim to torpedoes. Britain had no more than six weeks' supply of food on hand, and the supply situation became critical for the Allies. As it turned out, the very weapon that seemed to doom their cause, the submarine, was the source of the Allies' salvation: Germany's decision to use unrestricted submarine warfare brought the United States openly into the war.

The Americans had declared their neutrality in 1914 when President Woodrow Wilson announced that the American people "must be impartial in thought as well as in action." The events of the next two years showed that this would not be the case. American sentiment was overwhelmingly with the Allies from the first. France's help to the colonies in the American Revolution was warmly recalled. Britain and America were closely tied by language, literature, and democratic institutions. Because Britain cut off communications between Germany and the United States, British propaganda and management of the war news dominated public opinion. Another factor predisposing the United States to the Allied cause was Germany's violation of international law in the invasion of Belgium. This buttressed the widely-held view created by the kaiser's saber-rattling speeches that the Germans were undemocratic, unpredictable, and unstable.

These attitudes were reinforced by the fact that the United States had made a substantial investment in the Allied war effort. As the war progressed it became apparent that the British blockade would permit American trade to be carried on only with the Allies. Before long, American factories and farmers were producing weapons and food solely for Great Britain and France. Industry expanded and began to enjoy a prosperity dependent on continued Allied purchases. Between 1914 and 1916 American exports to the Allies quadrupled. Allied bonds totaling about $1.5 billion were sold in the United States in 1915 and 1916. It was quite apparent to the Germans that there was little neutrality on the economic front in the United States.

The immediate cause of the U.S. entry into the war on the Allied side was the German submarine campaign. Blockaded by the British, Germany decided to retaliate by halting all shipping to the Allies. Its submarine campaign began in February 1915, and one of the first victims was the luxury liner *Lusitania*, torpedoed with the loss of more than a thousand lives, including one hundred Americans. This tragedy aroused public opinion in the United States. In the fall of 1916 Wilson, campaigning with the slogan "he kept us out of war," was reelected to the presidency. Discovery of German plots to involve Mexico in the war against the United States and more

submarine sinkings finally drove Wilson to ask Congress to declare war against Germany on April 6, 1917.

Submarine warfare and a wide range of other causes brought the president to the point of entering the war. Once in the conflict, however, he was intent on making the American sacrifice one "to make the world safe for democracy." Wilson's lofty principles caused a great surge of idealism among Americans.

Germany's Last Drive

The United States mobilized its tremendous resources of men and materiel more rapidly than the Germans had believed possible when they made their calculated risk to increase submarine warfare. Nonetheless the Central Powers moved to try to gain a decisive victory before U.S. aid could help the Allies.

The fruitless offensives of 1917 had bled the British army white, and the French had barely recovered from their mutinies. The eastern front collapsed with the February/March revolution in Russia. Eight months later, Lenin and the Bolsheviks took power in Russia and began to negotiate for peace. By the Treaty of Brest-Litovsk early in 1918, Russia made peace with Germany, giving up 1,300,000 square miles of territory and 62 million people.[7]

Freed from the necessity of fighting on the east, the Germans unleashed a series of major offensives against the west in the spring of 1918. During one of these attacks, a brigade of American marines symbolized the importance of U.S. support when they stopped a German charge at Chateau-Thierry. The Germans made a final effort to knock out the French in July 1918. It was called the *Friedensturm*, the peace offensive. The Germans made substantial gains, but did not score the decisive breakthrough. By this time the German momentum was slowing down, and more than a million American "doughboys" had landed in France. The final German offensive was thrown back after a slight advance.

With the aid of U.S. troops, Marshal Ferdinand Foch, the supreme Allied commander, began a counterattack. The badly beaten and continually harassed German troops fell back in rapid retreat. By the end of October, German

German assault troops attack the French in the Montdidier-Noyon area in June 1918. The Germans tried to force the Allies to sue for peace before Allied reinforcements arrived from the United States.

forces had been driven out of France and Allied armies were advancing into Belgium. The war of fixed positions separated by "no man's land" was over. The Allies had smashed the trench defenses and were now in open country.

Already on October 1 the German high command urged the kaiser to sue for peace, and three days later the German chancellor sent a note to President Wilson seeking an end to hostilities. Wilson responded that peace was not possible as long as Germany was ruled by an autocratic regime. The German chancellor tried to keep the monarchy by instituting certain liberal reforms, but it was too late. Revolution broke out in may parts of Germany. The kaiser abdicated and a republic was proclaimed.

While Germany was staggering under the continual pounding of Foch's armies, the German allies were suffering even greater misfortunes. Bulgaria surrendered on September 30 and Turkey a month later. Austria stopped its fighting with Italy on November 3. Nine days later the Habsburg empire collapsed when Emperor Charles I fled Vienna to seek sanctuary in Switzerland.

At five o'clock on the morning of November 11, 1918, in a dining car in the Compiegne Forest, the German delegates signed the peace terms presented by Marshal Foch. At eleven o'clock the same day hostilities were halted. Everywhere except in Germany, the news was received with an outburst of joy. The world was once more at peace, confronted now with the task of binding up its wounds and removing the scars of combat. Delegates from the Allied nations were soon to meet in Paris, where the peace conference was to be held.

The Allied Peace Settlement

In November 1918 the Allies stood triumphant, after the costliest war in history. But the Germans could also feel well pleased in 1918. They had fought well, avoided being overrun, and escaped being occupied by the Allies. They could acknowledge they had lost the war but hoped that U.S. President Wilson could help them. In February 1918 Wilson had stated that "there shall be no annexations, no contributions, no punitive damages," and on July 4 he affirmed that every question must be settled "upon the basis of the free acceptance of that settlement by the people immediately concerned."[8] As events transpired, the losers were refused seats at the peace conference and were the recipients of a dictated settlement.

Idealism and Realities

The destructive nature of World War I made a fair peace settlement impossible. The war had been fought on a winner-take-all basis, and now it was time for the Central Powers to pay. At the peace conference, the winning side was dominated by a French realist, a British politician, and an American idealist. The French representative was the aged French Premier Georges Clemenceau, representing Britain was the British Prime Minister David Lloyd George, and the U.S. representative was President Woodrow Wilson. The three were joined by the Italian Prime Minister Vittorio Orlando, who attended to make sure his country gained adequate compensation for its large sacrifices. These four men made most of the key decisions, even though most of the interested nations and factions in the world were represented in Paris, except for the Soviet Union.

Clemenceau had played a colorful and important role in French politics for half a century. He had fought continuously for his political beliefs, opposing corruption, racism, and antidemocratic forces. He wanted to ensure French security in the future by pursuing restitution, reparations, and guarantees. Precise programs, not idealistic statements, would protect France.

The two English-speaking members of the big three represented the extremes in dealing with the Germans. Lloyd George had been reelected in December on a program of "squeezing the German lemon until the pips are squeaked." He wanted to destroy Berlin's naval, commercial, and colonial position and to ensure his own political future at home. In January 1918 U.S. President Wilson had issued to Congress the Fourteen Points describing his plan for peace. Wilson wanted to break the world out of its tradition of armed anarchy and establish a framework for peace that would favor America's traditions of democracy and trade. At the peace conference he communicated his beliefs with a coldness and an imperiousness that masked his shy and sensitive nature and offended his colleagues.

The World War had not been a "war to end all wars" or a "war to make the world safe for democracy," as Wilson had portrayed it. The United States had hardly been neutral in its loans and shipments of supplies to the Allies before 1917. In fact, during the war, the financial and political center of balance for the world had crossed the ocean. The Americans made a rather abrupt shift from debtor to creditor status. The United States had entered the war late and had profited from it, and Wilson could afford to wear a rather more idealistic mantle.

The Europeans had paid for the war with the blood of their young and the coin of their realms.[9] The Allies now looked forward to a healthy return on their investment. The extent of that harvest had long been mapped out in secret treaties, copies of which the Bolsheviks released for the world to see.

Open Covenants, Secret Treaties

Wilson wanted to use his Fourteen Points as the base for a lasting peace. He wanted to place morality and justice ahead of power and revenge as considerations in international affairs. The first five points were general in nature and guaranteed: "open covenants openly arrived at," freedom of the seas in war and peace alike, removal of all economic barriers and establishment of an equality of trade among all nations, reductions in national armaments, and readjustment of all colonial claims, giving the interests of the population concerned equal weight with the claim of the government whose title was to be determined. The next eight points dealt with specific issues involving the evacuation and

John Maynard Keynes on Clemenceau

John Maynard Keynes caught the spirit of the peacemakers at Versailles in his work, *The Economic Consequences of the Peace*. His portrait of Clemenceau is especially revealing.

He felt about France what Pericles felt of Athens—unique value in her, nothing else mattering; but his theory of politics was Bismarck's. He had one illusion—France; and one disillusion—mankind, including Frenchmen, and his colleagues not least. His principles for the peace can be expressed simply. In the first place, he was a foremost believer in the view of German psychology that the German understands and can understand nothing but intimidation, that he is without generosity or remorse in negotiation, that there is no advantage he will not take of you, and no extent to which he will not demean himself for profit, that he is without honor, pride, or mercy. Therefore you must never negotiate with a German or conciliate him; you must dictate to him. On no other terms will he respect you, or will you prevent him from cheating you. But it is doubtful how far he thought these characteristics peculiar to Germany, or whether his candid view of some other nations was fundamentally different. His philosophy had, therefore, no place for "sentimentality" in international relations. Nations are real things, of whom you love one and feel for the rest indifference—or hatred. The glory of the nation you love is a desirable end,—but generally to be obtained at your neighbor's expense. The politics of power are inevitable, and there is nothing very new to learn about this war or the end it was fought for; England had destroyed, as in each preceding century, a trade rival; a mighty chapter had been closed in the secular struggle between the glories of Germany and of France. Prudence required some measure of lip service to the "ideals" of foolish Americans and hypocritial Englishmen; but it would be stupid to believe that there is much room in the world, as it really is, for such affairs as the League of Nations, or any sense in the principle of self-determination except as an ingenious formula for rearranging the balance of power in one's own interest.

From John Maynard Keynes, *The Economic Consequences of the Peace* (New York: Harcourt Brace Jovanovich, 1920).

restoration of Allied territory, self-determination for minority nationalities, and the redrawing of European boundaries along national lines.

The fourteenth point contained the germ of the League of Nations—a general association of all nations, whose purpose was to guarantee political independence and territorial integrity to great and small states alike. When Wilson arrived in Europe, the crowds on the streets and the victorious and the defeated nations alike greeted him as a messiah. His program had received great publicity, and its general, optimistic nature had earned him great praise.

The victorious Allies came to Paris to gain the concrete rewards promised them in the various secret treaties. Under these pacts, which would not come to public knowledge until the beginning of 1919, the Allies had promised the Italians concessions that would turn the Adriatic into an Italian sea, the Russians the right to take over the Straits and Constantinople, the Romanians the right to take over large amounts of Austro-Hungarian territory, and the Japanese the right to keep the German territory of Kiaochow in China. In addition, the British and French divided what was formerly Ottoman-controlled Iraq and Syria into their respective spheres of influence. An international administrative organization would govern Palestine. In 1917 Great Britain pledged its support of "the establishment in Palestine of a national home for the Jewish people."

Wilson refused to consider these agreements, which many of the victors regarded as IOUs now

The "Big Four" at the Versailles Peace Conference were, left to right, British prime minister Lloyd George, Italian prime minister Vittorio Orlando, French premier Georges Clemenceau, and President Woodrow Wilson of the United States. Representatives from Germany were excluded from the negotiating tables. The Big Four became the Big Three when Orlando withdrew abruptly because the conference refused to grant Italy all it demanded.

due to be paid in return for their role in the war; but the contracting parties in the treaties would not easily set aside their deals to satisfy Wilson's ideals. Even before formal talks—negotiations that would be unprecedented in their complexity—began, the Allies were split. Lloyd George and Clemenceau discovered early that Wilson had his price, and that was the League of Nations. They played on his desire for this organization to water down most of the thirteen other points. They were also aware that Wilson's party had suffered a crushing defeat in the 1918 elections and that strong factions in the United States were drumming up opposition to his program.

The League of Nations

When the diplomats began their first full meetings, the first issue was the formation of the League of Nations. Wilson insisted that the first work of the conference must be to provide for a league of nations as part of the peace treaty. After much negotiation, the covenant was approved by the full conference in April 1919. In order to gain support for the League, however, Wilson had to compromise on other matters. His Fourteen Points were partially repudiated, but he believed that an imperfect treaty incorporating the League was better than a perfect one without it.

The Covenant of the League of Nations specified its aims "to guarantee international cooperation and to achieve international peace and security." To achieve this goal, Article X, the key section of the document, provided that

> The Members of the League undertake to respect and preserve against external aggression the territorial integrity and existing political independence of all Members of the League. In case of any such aggression or in case of any threat or danger of such aggression, the Council shall advise upon the means by which this obligation shall be fulfilled.[10]

The League of Nations was the first systematic and thorough attempt to create an organization designed to prevent war and promote peace. It was a valiant effort to curb the abuses of the state system while maintaining the individual sovereignty of each member of the community of nations.

The League's main organs were the Council, the Assembly, and the Secretariat. Dominated by the great powers, the Council was the most important body. It dealt with most of the emergencies arising in international affairs. The Assembly served as a platform from which all League members could express their views. It could make recommendations to the Council on specific issues, but all important decisions required the unanimous consent of its members, and every nation in the Assembly had one vote.

The Secretariat, which had fifteen departments, represented the bureaucracy of the League. Numbering about 700, the personnel of the Secretariat constituted the first example in history of an international civil service whose loyalty was pledged to no single nation but to the interests of the world community. All treaties made by members of the League had to be registered with the Secretariat. It handled routine administrative matters relating to such League concerns as disarmament, health problems, the administration of former German colonies, and the protection of oppressed minorities.

Two other important bodies created by the Covenant of the League were the Permanent Court of International Justice and the International Labor Organization (ILO). The first was commonly referred to as the World Court. Its main purpose was to "interpret any disputed point in international law and determine when treaty obligations had been violated." It could also give advisory opinions to the Council or Assembly when asked for them. By 1937 forty-one nations had agreed to place before the World Court most basic international disputes to which they were a party. The ILO was established to "secure and maintain fair and humane conditions of labor for men, women, and children." The organization consisted of three divisions: a general conference, a governing body, and the International Labor Office.

Redrawing German Boundaries

After establishing the League, the diplomats got down to the business of dealing with Germany. France reclaimed Alsace-Lorraine, and plebiscites gave part of the former German empire to Denmark and Belgium (see map, p. 787). The French wanted to build a buffer state made up of former German territory west of the Rhine to be dominated by France. The Americans and the British proposed a compromise to Clemenceau which he accepted. The territory in question would be occupied by Allied troops for a period of from five to fifteen years, and a zone extending 50 kilometers east of the Rhine was to be demilitarized.

In addition, the French claimed the Saar basin, a rich coal area. Although they did not take outright control of the area—it reverted to the League administration—they did gain ownership of the mines, in compensation for the destruction of their own installations in northern France. It was agreed that after fifteen years a plebiscite would be held in the area. Finally Wilson and Lloyd George agreed that the United States and Great Britain by treaty would guarantee France against aggression.

To the east, the conference created the Polish Corridor, which separated East Prussia from the rest of Germany, in order to give the newly created state of Poland access to the sea. This creation raised grave problems, as it included territory in which there were not only Polish majorities but also large numbers of Germans. The land in question had been taken from Poland by Prussia in the eighteenth century. A section of Silesia was also ceded to Poland, but Danzig, a German city, was placed under Leage jurisdiction. All in all, Germany lost 25,000 square miles inhabited by 6 million people, a fact seized upon by German nationalist leaders in the 1920s.

The Mandate System and Reparations

A curious mixture of idealism and revenge determined the allocation of the German colonies and certain territories belonging to Turkey. Because outright annexation would look too much like unvarnished imperialism, it was suggested that the colonies be turned over to the League,

When Wilson arrived in Europe in December 1918, cheering crowds hailed him as the "peacemaker from America." This photograph is from the parade in Paris.

which in turn would give them to certain of its members to administer. The colonies were to be known as mandates, and precautions were taken to ensure that they would be administered for the well-being and development of the inhabitants. Once a year the mandatory powers were to present a detailed account of their administration of the territories of the League. The mandate system was a step forward in colonial administration, but Germany nevertheless was deprived of all colonies, with the excuse that it could not rule them justly or efficiently.

As the Treaty of Versailles took shape, the central concept was that Germany had been responsible for the war. Article 231 of the treaty stated explicitly:

The Allied and Associated Governments affirm and Germany accepts the responsibility of Germany and her allies for causing all the loss and damage to which the Allied and Associated Governments and their nationals have been subjected as a consequence of the war imposed upon them by the aggression of Germany and her Allies.[11]

Britain and France demanded that Germany pay the total cost of the war, including pensions. The United States protested this demand, and eventually a compromise emerged in which, with the exception of Belgium, Germany had to pay only war damages, including those suffered by civilians, and the cost of pensions. These payments, called reparations (implying repair) were exacted on the ground that Germany should bear the responsibility for the war.

Although the Allies agreed that Germany should pay reparations, they could not agree on how much should be paid. Some demands ran as high as $200 billion. Finally, it was decided that a committee should fix the amount; in the meantime Germany was to begin making payments. By the time the committee report appeared in May 1921, the payments totaled nearly $2 billion. The final bill came to $32.5 billion, to be paid off by Germany by 1963.

The Allies required Germany, as part of "in kind" reparations payments, to hand over most of its merchant fleet, construct one million tons of new shipping for the Allies, and deliver vast amounts of coal, equipment, and machinery to them. The conference permitted Germany a standing army of only 100,000 men, a greatly reduced fleet, and no military aircraft. Munitions plants were also to be closely supervised.

The treaty also called for the kaiser to be tried for a "supreme offense against international morality and the sanctity of treaties," thus setting a precedent for the Nuremberg tribunals after World War II. Nothing came of this demand, however, as the kaiser remained in his Dutch haven.

THE PEACE SETTLEMENT IN EUROPE

- Newly Created States
- Ceded Territories

Dictated Treaties

Before coming to Paris in April 1919 to receive the Treaty of Versailles, the German delegation was given no official information about its terms. Even though the German foreign minister denied that "Germany and its people . . . were alone guilty . . . ,"[12] he had no alternative but to sign. The continued blockade created great hardships in Germany, and the Allies threatened an invasion if the Germans did not accept the peace. The treaty was signed on June 28, the fifth anniversary of the assassination of the Archduke Francis Ferdinand, in the Hall of Mirrors at Versailles, the same room where the German empire had been proclaimed. As one American wrote, "The affair was elaborately staged and made as humiliating to the enemy as it well could be."[13]

The Allies imposed equally harsh treaties on Germany's supporters. The Treaty of St. Germain (1919) with Austria recognized the nationalist movements of the Czechs, Poles, and South Slavs. These groups had already formed states and reduced the remnants of the former Dual Monarchy into the separate states of Austria and Hungary. Austria became a landlocked country of 32,000 square miles and 6 million people. It was forbidden to seek *Anschluss*—union with Germany. Italy acquired sections of Austria, South Tyrol, Trentino (with its 250,000 Austrian Germans), and the northeastern coast of the Adriatic, with its large numbers of Slavs.

To complete their control of the Adriatic, the Italians wanted a slice of the Dalmatian coast and the port of Fiume. Fiume, however, was the natural port for the newly created state of Yugoslavia, and it had not been promised to the Italians in 1915. Wilson declared the Italian claim to be a contradiction of the principle of self-determination, and the ensuing controversy almost wrecked the peace conference. The issue was not settled until 1920, when Italy renounced its claim to Dalmatia and Fiume became an independent state. Four years later it was ceded to Italy.

By the Treaty of Sèvres (1920), the Ottoman empire was placed on the operating table of power politics and divided among Greece, Britain, and France. An upheaval in August 1920 in Constantinople led to the emergence of the

This German cartoon, "The Mask Falls," expresses German reaction to the terms of the Treaty of Versailles, which held Germany and its allies totally responsible for the war and demanded huge reparations.

Nationalists under Mustapha Kemal, who refused to accept the treaty. Not until July 1923 did Turkey's postwar status become clear in the milder Treaty of Lausanne, which guaranteed Turkish control of Anatolia.

Hungary (Treaty of Trianon, 1920) and Bulgaria (Treaty of Neuilly, 1919) did not fare as well as Turkey in dealing with the Allies. The Hungarians lost territory to Czechoslovakia, Yugoslavia, and Romania. Bulgaria lost access to the Aegean Sea and territory populated by nearly one million people, had to pay a huge indemnity, and underwent demilitarization.

Those eastern European states that profited from the settlements proved to be useful allies for France in the first fifteen years of the interwar period. Those that suffered were easy prey for the Nazis in the 1930s.

Evaluating the Peacemakers

The treaties ending the First World War have received heavy criticism from diplomatic historians, especially when compared with the work of the Congress of Vienna. The peace that emerged brought only weariness, new disagreements, and inflation.

There was a complete disregard of Russia. Lenin's government, in it weak position, indicated a willingness to deal with the west on the issue of prewar debts and border conflicts, if the west would extend financial aid and withdraw its expeditionary forces. The anti-Bolshevik forces in Paris did not take the offer seriously.[14] By missing this opportunity the Allies, in the view of a major American observer, took a course that had tremendous consequences for "the long-term future of both the Russian and the American people and indeed of mankind generally."[15]

Many commentators have laid the genesis of the Second World War just one generation later at the feet of the Paris peacemakers. The opportunism of Orlando and the chauvinism and revenge-seeking nature of both Clemenceau and Lloyd George appear short-sighted. Other critics point that the United States' reversion to isolationism doomed the work of the conference. Furthermore, never were there any broad plans for European economic recovery.

Considering the difficult conditions under which it was negotiated, the peace settlement was as good as could be expected. The delegates were the prisoners of their own constituents, who had themselves been heavily influenced by wartime propaganda. In addition, the diplomats had to deal with the nationalistic pressures and territorial conflicts of the newly formed eastern European nations. Given the costs of the war and the hopes for the peace, it is not surprising that the treaties left a legacy of disappointment for those who won and bitterness for those who lost. Symbolic of the obstacles faced by the statesmen was the fact that while they worked to return order, the globe reeled under the blows of a Spanish influenza outbreak that, when the costs were added up, was shown to have killed twice

as many as had died in the war. The influenza outbreak was both a tragic conclusion to the war years and a sign for the future.

Conclusion

For more than four years, the science, wealth, and power of Europe had been concentrated on the business of destruction. Germany's rapid economic growth, military buildup, ambitious foreign policy, and inability to control its Austro-Hungarian ally helped bring the normally competitive European economic arena to a crisis in the summer of 1914. By violating Belgian neutrality and declaring war on Russia and France, Germany stood clearly as the aggressor in the First World War, a fact for which it was severely punished in the Treaty of Versailles.

When the victorious Allies gathered at Paris in 1919 to settle the peace, they did not have the luxury of time, distance, and power the leaders at the Congress of Vienna had enjoyed in 1815. The 1919 peacemakers had endured the most destructive war in history. In this total war, psychological methods were used to motivate all the people of each of the states to hate the enemy, during and after the war. In these conditions, the treaty settled at Versailles produced a mere break in the hostilities. Some observers have referred to the period from 1914 to 1945 as the "New Thirty Years' War."

With all that the Europeans shared, World War I was a conflict that need never have been fought. The Europeans threw away the advantages they had gained since 1815 and set in motion a series of disasters from which they did not recover until the second half of the twentieth century.

Suggestions for Reading

The standard account on the causes of the war is F. Fischer, *Germany's Aims in the First World War* (Norton, 1968). Classic views on the war are to be found in W. L. Langer, *European Alliances and Alignments, 1871–1890* (Vintage, 1931) and the *Diplomacy of Imperialism, 1890–1902* (Knopf, 1935) and S. B. Fay, *The Origins of the World War* (Macmillan, 1928). Bernadotte Schmidt, *Triple Alliance and*

Triple Entente (Fertig, Holt, 1934) is a good introduction. See also R. Albrecht-Carrié, *A Diplomatic History of Europe Since the Congress of Vienna* (Harper, 1973). A good overview of the war's origins is L. Lafore's *The Long Fuse: An Interpretation of the Origins of World War I* (Lippincott, 1971).

Specific topics are dealt with by Oron J. Hale, *The Great Illusion, 1900–1914* (Torchbooks, 1971); V. Dedijere, *The Road to Sarajevo* (Simon & Schuster, 1966); Colin Simpson, *The Lusitania* (Harper, 1976); A. Moorehead, *Gallipoli: Account of the 1915 Campaign* (Harper, 1956); A. Horne, *The Price of Glory: Verdun 1916* (St. Martin's, 1979); E. Coffman, *The War to End all Wars: The American Military Experience in World War I* (Oxford, 1968); G. Ritter, *The Schlieffen Plan* (Praeger, 1958); G. Feldman, *Army Industry, and Labor in Germany, 1914–1918* (Princeton, 1966).

Alexander Solzhenitsyn's *August 1914* (Bantam, 1974) is a fine piece of literature describing Russia's entry into the war. Barbara Tuchman's *The Guns of August* (many eds.) (Dell) is a fine history that is beautifully written. Paul Fassell brutally portrays the nature and impact of the war in *The Great War and Modern Memory* (Oxford, 1977).

See A. S. Link, *Wilson the Diplomatist* (Hopkins, 1957) regarding the U.S. president's participation at Paris. Charles L. Mee, Jr., captures the aura of Paris during the negotiations in *The End of Order, Versailles, 1919* (Dutton, 1980). Harold Nicolson's beautifully written *Peacemaking, 1919* (Houghton Mifflin, 1939) is a fine firsthand account, as is J. M. Keynes, *The Economic Consequences of the Peace* (Macmillan, 1924).

Notes

1. Quoted by C. J. H. Hayes, *A Political and Cultural History of Modern Europe*, II (New York: The Macmillan Co., 1939), p. 572.
2. Viscount Grey of Fallodon, *Twenty-Five Years*, II (New York: Frederick A. Stokes Co., 1925), p. 20.
3. *The New Cambridge Modern History*, 2nd ed., XII (Cambridge: Cambridge Univ. Press, 1968), p. 191.
4. Quoted in F. P. Chambers, *The War Behind the War, 1914–1918* (New York: Harcourt Brace Jovanovich) p. 473.
5. "The Soldier," *The Collected Poems of Rupert Brooke* (Canada: Dodd, Mead, & Co., 1915).
6. Wilfred Owen, "Anthem for a Doomed Youth," *Collected Poems* (Chatto & Windus, Ltd., 1946).
7. D. W. Treadgold, *Twentieth Century Russia* (Chicago: Rand McNally & Co., 1959), p. 154.
8. Quoted in L. M. Hacker and B. B. Kendrick, *The United States Since 1865* (New York: F. S. Crofts and Co., 1939), p. 520.
9. A. J. Ryder, *Twentieth Century Germany: From Bismarck to Brandt* (New York: Columbia Univ. Press, 1973), pp. 132–141.
10. Quoted in F. P. Walters, *A History of the League of Nations*, I (London: Oxford Univ. Press, 1952), p. 48.
11. Quoted in R. J. Sontag, *European Diplomatic History, 1871–1932* (New York: Century Co., 1933), p. 275.
12. Quoted in E. Achorn, *European Civilization and Politics Since 1815* (New York: Harcourt Brace Jovanovich, 1938), p. 470.
13. Quoted in Sontag, *European Diplomatic History, 1871–1932*, p. 392.
14. Louis Fischer, *The Soviets in World Affairs* (New York: Vintage Books, 1960), p. 116.
15. George F. Kennan, *The Decision to Intervene* (Princeton: Princeton Univ. Press, 1958), p. 471.

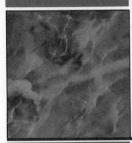

Chapter 31

The Eclipse of the Democracies

Economic Crises and Political Retreat, 1918–1939

World War I, the war that was to make the world "safe for democracy," left a legacy of physical damage, economic disruption, and doubt that endangered the hard-won liberal victories of the nineteenth century. The twenty years between the first and second global wars was a perilous time for democracy (see map, p. 792). The horrible costs of the war made the victory a hollow one for the European victors, and after the initial taste for revenge had been satisfied, revulsion for war became widespread. The economic dislocation caused by inflation and depression sapped the strength of the middle classes, the traditional supporters of democracy. The certainty and belief in progress that had helped fuel Europe's dominance in the nineteenth century was replaced by doubt and cynicism.[1]

Economic Disasters

One of the most serious problems facing the survivors of World War I was the confused and desperate situation of the European economy. Much of the direct and indirect cost of the war had been covered by borrowing, and now the bills had come due in a world unable to pay them. The lasting results of the war touched many areas. The conflict altered world trading patterns, reduced shipping, and weakened Europe's former economic dominance. The various peace treaties multiplied the number of European boundaries, which soon became obstacles to the flow of goods, especially in the successor states of the Habsburg monarchy and in Poland.

The Costs of the War

It is impossible to give a true accounting of the costs of any war, because there is no way to calculate the contributions that might have been made by those killed in battle. From 2 to 3 million Russians died, and more perished in the civil war. Among the other major participants, almost 2 million Germans, over 1.5 million French, close to a million English, a half-million Italians, 1.2 million from Austria-Hungary, and 325,000 from Turkey died in battle. These figures do not count the wounded whose lives may have been shortened as a result of their injuries. Put another way, the young paid the highest price; it is estimated that Germany and France each lost over 15 percent of its young men.

Estimates of the financial drain of the war range between $250 billion and $300 billion, figuring the dollar at its early 1920s level. These figures do not bring home the depth of the war's impact on trade, shipping, and monetary stability. Belgium, for example, lost over 300,000 houses and thousands of factories, and 15,000 square miles of northeastern France were in ruins.

There is no balance sheet or set of figures to measure the psychological expense of the conflict. How does one calculate the cost of taking 75 million men who were mobilized away from their jobs and their homes? How can the mental carnage inflicted on the participants be measured?

Political institutions felt the effects of the war in different ways. The German, Habsburg, Russian, and Ottoman empires crumbled and disappeared from the historical stage. Replacing them

**EUROPEAN DEMOCRACIES
1920-1940**

Democracies in 1920
Remaining democracies in 1940

being able to deal with the Germans, blocking further profits, but by 1919 Europeans owed the United States more than $10 billion. This tremendous debt posed what economists call a transfer problem. The international obligations could be paid only by the actual transfer of gold or by the sale of goods.

To complicate the picture, Allied powers in Europe had also lent each other funds, with the British acting as the chief banker, lending more than £1.7 billion. When their credit dried up, they turned to the United States for financial help. Even though Britain owed huge sums to U.S. financiers, it remained a net creditor of $4 billion because of its own European debtors. France, on the other hand, stood as a net debtor of $3.5 billion. In addition to war debts, the French government suffered greatly when the Bolsheviks renounced the tsarist debt of some 12 billion francs—one quarter of France's foreign holdings.

Some of the Allies argued that the inter-Allied debts were political, that all of them had, in effect, been poured into a common pool for victory. These people wondered how France's

were uncertain republics or dictatorships. Those colonial empires that remained were weakened and indigenous nationalist movements made substantial progress. Rail and communications lines had to be reconfigured to reflect the interests of newly created states.

The roots of the economic problems that plagued Europe after the war—agricultural overproduction, bureaucratic regulations, and protectionism—could be seen before 1914. Compounding these factors were the traditional challenges encountered in shifting from a wartime to a peacetime economy—especially that of demobilizing millions of soldiers and bringing them back into the labor market.

The Debt Problem

A radical change had taken place during the war in Europe's economic relationship with the United States. In 1914 the United States had been a debtor nation, mostly to Europe, for the amount of $3.75 billion. The war totally reversed this situation. The United States lent billions of dollars and sold tons of supplies to the Allies. British blockades kept the United States from

A British cartoonist's view of the debt and reparation problems following World War I. Germany's inability to pay reparations meant that the Allies were unable to pay their inter-Allied war debts.

PASSING THE BUCK.

contribution in the lives of its young men could be figured into the equation in terms of francs, dollars, or pounds. They proposed that, with victory, all debts should be cancelled. The United States, which had gone to Paris with a conciliatory spirit toward Germany in the treaty negotiations, changed its tune when dollars and cents were involved. This attitude was best expressed in a remark attributed to Calvin Coolidge, who expected full repayment, when he said: "They hired the money, didn't they?"[2] Beneath the extremes of these positions was understandable motives of getting out of paying a huge debt. The German side resorted to financial mismanagement. In the first three years after the war, the German government, in a policy of deliberate inflation, spent much more than its income. This policy was masked by "floating debts . . . in other words, by the printing press."[3]

The situation became so serious in the summer of 1922 that Great Britain proposed that it collect no more from its debtors—Allied and German alike—than the United States collected from Britain itself. Such statesmanship was prompted by the fact that London had gained what it wanted from the peace settlement: Germany's navy was destroyed; Germany's merchant ships were transferred as reparations; Germany's empire was gone. No more could be squeezed out. Britain saw that Germany would not be able to meet its reparations payments, and without them, the payments of the inter-Allied debts, especially debts owed to the United States, would be extremely difficult, if not impossible, to make.

Although the United States insisted that there was no connection between the inter-Allied debts and German reparations, negotiations were carried on, and debt payment plans were set up with thirteen nations. No reductions were made in principal, but in every case the interest rate was radically decreased. The total amount owed came to more than $22 billion.

Germany's debt problem was complicated by the additional problem of reparations. Although reparations constituted a drain of major proportions on the German economy, they were far more significant as a political factor.

The German government's calculated inflationary policies contributed far more to the economic disaster that occurred in 1923 than did reparations. Between May and September 1921 the value of the German mark fell some 80 percent. A year and a half later, after Germany defaulted on some payments, French troops, supported by Belgian and Italian contingents, marched into the rich industrial district of the Ruhr, undeterred by American and British objections. This shortsighted French move contributed nothing to the solution of Europe's problems and indeed played into the hands of radical German politicians.

Encouraged by the Berlin government, German workers defied the French army and went on strike, many ending up in jail. The French toyed for a while with the idea of establishing a separate state in the Rhineland to act as a buffer between Germany and France. Chaotic conditions in the Ruhr encouraged the catastrophic

In January 1923, after Germany defaulted on reparations payments, French and Belgian troops occupied the Ruhr district to collect reparations in kind, mainly coal. The German workers responded by calling a general strike, and the occupation accomplished nothing, except to exacerbate Europe's already catastrophic economic problems. Here, French soldiers guard a German locomotive during the Ruhr district strike.

inflation of the German currency to make up for the loss of exports and to support the striking workers. The French, in return, gained very little benefit from the occupation.

Inflation and Stabilization

All European nations encountered a rocky path as they attempted to gain equilibrium after the war. Britain had minimal price increases and returned to prewar levels within two years after the signing of the Versailles treaty. On the continent, price and monetary stability came less easily. Only Czechoslovakia seemed to have its economic affairs well in hand.

France did not stabilize its currency until 1926, when the franc was worth fifty to the dollar (as contrasted to five to the dollar in 1914). In Austria prices rose to 14,000 times their prewar level until stability of sorts came in 1922. Hungary's prices went to 23,000 times prewar level, but this increase is dwarfed by Poland's (2.5 million times prewar level) and Russia's (4 billion times prewar level).

But Germany served as the laboratory of the horrible impact of inflation on society. Germany's prices went up a trillion times (a thousand billion) what they were in 1914. The German mark had been worth four to the dollar in prewar times. At its weakest point in November 1923, after the French occupation of the Ruhr, the German mark reached the exchange rate of 4.2 trillion to the dollar. During the worst part of the inflation, the Reichsbank had 150 firms using 2000 presses running day and night to print Reichnotes. To get out of their dilemma, the Germans made an effective transition to a more stable currency by simply forgetting the old one.[4]

The millions of middle-class Germans, small property owners who would be the hoped-for base of the new Weimar Republic, found themselves caught in the wage-price squeeze. Prices for the necessities of life rose far faster than did income or savings. As mothers wheeled baby carriages full of money to bakeries to buy bread, fathers watched a lifetime of savings dwindle to insignificance. Pensioners on fixed incomes suffered doubly under this crisis. The bourgeoisie, the historical basis for liberal politics throughout Europe, suffered blows more devastating than those of war, for inflation stole

Inflation in Germany during the 1920s grew so drastic that the German mark became nearly worthless. It was cheaper, for example, to burn the marks for fuel than to use them to purchase kindling.

not only the value of their labor, but the worth of their savings and insurance.

Where the middle classes and liberal traditions were strong, democracy could weather the storm. But in central Europe, especially in Germany where the inflation was the worst, the cause of future totalitarianism received an immense boost. Alan Bullock, a biographer of Adolf Hitler, has written that "the result of inflation was to undermine the foundations of German society in a way which neither the war nor the revolution of 1918, nor the Treaty of Versailles had ever done."[5]

Temporary Improvements

After 1923 the liberal application of U.S. funds brought some calm to the economic storm. Business was more difficult to conduct because protectionism became more and more the dominant

Alex de Jonge on Inflation in Weimar Germany

Alex de Jonge captured the truly devastating impact of inflation in Weimar Germany.

Hyperinflation created social chaos on an extraordinary scale. As soon as one was paid, one rushed off to the shops and bought absolutely anything in exchange for paper about to become worthless. If a woman had the misfortune to have a husband working away from home and sending money through the post, the money was virtually without value by the time it arrived. Workers were paid once, then twice, then five times a week with an ever-depreciating currency. By November 1923 real wages were down 25 percent compared with 1913, and envelopes were not big enough to accommodate all the stamps needed to mail them; the excess stamps were stuck to separate sheets affixed to the letter. Normal commercial transactions became virtually impossible. One luckless author received a sizable advance on a work only to find that within a week it was just enough to pay the postage on the manuscript. By late 1923 it was not unusual to find 100,000 mark notes in the gutter, tossed there by contemptuous beggars at a time when $50 could buy a row of houses in Berlin's smartest street.

A Berlin couple who were about to celebrate their golden wedding received an official letter advising them that the mayor, in accordance with Prussian custom, would call and present them with a donation of money.

Next morning the mayor, accompanied by several aldermen in picturesque robes, arrived at the aged couple's house, and solemnly handed over in the name of the Prussian State 1,000,000,000,000 marks or one half-penny.

From Alex de Jonge, *The Weimar Chronicle, Prelude to Hitler* (New York: New American Library, 1978).

---

trait of international trade. *Autarky*, the goal of gaining total economic self-sufficiency and freedom from reliance on any other nation increasingly became the unstated policy of many governments.

Nonetheless, production soon reached 1913 levels, currencies began to stabilize by mid-decade, and the French finally recalled their troops from the Ruhr. Most significantly, in September 1924 a commission under the leadership of U.S. banker Charles Dawes formulated a more liberal reparations policy in order to get the entire repayment cycle back into motion. Dawes' plan, replaced in 1929 by the Young plan (named for its principal formulator, U.S. businessman Owen Young), reduced installments and extended them over a longer period. A loan of $200 million, mostly from the United States, was floated to aid German recovery. The Berlin government resumed payments to the Allies, and the Allies paid their debt installments to the United States—which in effect received its own money back again.

Prosperity of a sort returned to Europe. As long as the circular flow of cash from the United States to Germany to the Allies to the United States continued, the international monetary system functioned. The moment the cycle broke down, the world economy headed for the rocks of depression. One economic historian has written:

In 1924–31 Germany drew some one thousand million pounds from abroad and the irony was that Germany, in fact, received far more in loans, including loans to enable her to pay interest on earlier loans than she paid out in reparations, thus gaining in the circular flow and re-equipping her industries and her public utilities with American funds in the processes in the 1920s before repudiating her debts in the 1930s.[6]

The system broke down in 1928 and 1929 when U.S. and British creditors needed their capital for investments in their own countries. Extensions on loans, readily granted a year earlier, were refused. Even before the U.S. stock market crash on October 29, 1929, disaster was on the horizon.

Few people in America could admit such a possibility during the decade, however. The United States had become the commercial center of the world, and its policies were central to the world's financial health. The United States still had an internal market in the 1920s with a seemingly inexhaustible appetite for new products such as radios, refrigerators, electrical appliances, and automobiles. This expansion, based on consumer goods and supported by a seemingly limitless supply of natural resources, gave the impression of solid and endless growth.

Tragically, the contradictions of the postwar economic structure were making themselves felt. The cornerstones of pre-1914 prosperity—multilateral trade, the gold standard, interchangeable currencies—were crumbling. The policies of autarky, with their high tariff barriers to protect home products against foreign competition, worked against international economic health. Ironically, the United States led the way toward higher tariffs, and other nations quickly retaliated. American foreign trade seriously declined, and the volume of world trade decreased.

There were other danger signals. Europe suffered a population decline. There were 22 million fewer people in the 1920s in the western part of the continent than had been expected.[7] The decrease in internal markets affected trade, as did the higher external barriers. Around the globe, the agricultural sector suffered from declining prices during the 1920s. At the same time that farmers received less for their products, they had to pay more to live—a condition that afflicted peasants in Europe and Asia and farmers and ranchers in the United States.

In the hopes of reaching an expanding market, many food raisers around the world borrowed money to expand production at the beginning of the decade. Many farmers went bankrupt as they could not keep up with payments on their debts. The food surplus benefitted consumers, but across the world agricultural interests suffered. Tariff barriers prevented foodstuffs from circulating to the countries where hunger existed. By the end of the decade, people in the Orient were starving, while wheat farmers in Whitman County, Washington, dumped their grain into the Snake River and coffee growers in Brazil saw their product burned to fuel steam locomotives. The countryside preceded the cities into the economic tragedy.[8]

The Great Crash

Because of America's central position in the world economy, any development, positive or negative, on Wall Street reverberated across the globe. The United States, with roughly 3 percent of the world's population, produced 46 percent of the globe's industrial output. The country was ill-equipped to use its new-found power. Its financial life in the 1920s was dominated by the activities of daring and sometimes unscrupulous speculators who made the arena of high finance a precarious and exciting world of its own. This world, however, was not dominated by businessmen pursuing long-term stability. Their blind rush for profit led to America's crash, which in turn sparked a world disaster.[9]

Even before the stock market crash, Wall Street had been showing signs of distress such as capital shortfalls, overly large inventories, and agricultural bankruptcies. But nothing prepared financiers for the disaster that struck on October 29, 1929—Black Thursday. By noon, Wall Street was caught in a momentum of chaotic fear. The initial hemorrhage of stock values stopped by the end of the trading session, but the damage was done.

John Kenneth Galbraith has written: "On the whole, the great stock market crash can be much more readily explained than the depression that followed it."[10] Overspeculation, loose controls, dishonest investors, and a loss of confidence in the "ever-upward" market trend can be identified as causes for the crash. Further causes can be traced to the inequitable distribution of wealth, with the farmers and workers left out—while the top 3 percent grew incredibly rich and irresponsible. Industrial overexpansion was fueled by speculators buying stock on the margin, with insufficient cash backing for the investments. In addition, the government's hands-off policies permitted massive abuses to take place unchecked.

The international impact of the crash can be explained by the involvement of investors and

Anxious crowds throng the street in front of the New York Stock Exchange during the crash of October 1929 that touched off a worldwide economic depression.

bankers from a number of countries in the U.S. market, the interdependent world economic structure, the peculiar Allied debt and reparations structure, the growing agricultural crisis, and the inadequate banking systems of the world.

Some economic historians believe that the cycle of highs and lows hit a particularly vicious low point in 1929. Crashes had occurred before, but never with such widespread repercussions over such a long period of time. In the United States, stock prices declined one-third overall within a few weeks, wiping out fortunes, shattering confidence in business, and destroying consumer demand. The disaster spread worldwide as American interests demanded payment on foreign loans and imports decreased. The Kredit-Anstalt of Vienna did not have enough money to fill demands for funds from French

banks and failed in 1931. This set in motion a domino-like banking crisis throughout Europe. Forecasts by Washington politicians and New York financiers that the worst was over and that the world economy was fundamentally sound after a "technical readjustment" convinced nobody. There would be no easy recovery.

The World Depression

By 1932 the value of industrial shares had fallen close to 60 percent on the New York and Berlin markets. Unemployment doubled in Germany, and 25 percent of the labor force was out of work in the United States. In nation after nations, industry declined, prices fell, banks collapsed, and economies stagnated. In the western democracies the depression contributed even more to the feelings of uneasiness that had

Nationwide bankruptcy forced Germany to close all its banks in 1931. The smiling faces of the guards surrounding the crowd belie the grim economic reality that resulted in the bank closures.

existed since 1918. In other countries, the tendency to seek authoritarian solutions became even more pronounced. Throughout the world people suffered from lowered standards of living, unemployment, hunger, and fear of the future.

The middle classes on the continent, which had suffered from inflation during the 1920s, became caught in a whiplash effect during the depression. Adherence to old liberal principles collapsed in the face of economic insecurity, and state control of the economies increased. Governments raised tariffs to restrict imports and used command economies, an expedient usually reserved for wartime. As conditions deteriorated, fear caused most governments to look no farther than their own boundaries. Under the competing systems of autarky, each nation tried to increase exports and decrease imports.

After almost a century of free trade, modified by a comparative few protective duties levied during and after World War I, Great Britain finally enacted a high tariff in 1932 with provisions to protect members of its empire. In the United States the Hawley-Smoot Act of 1930 increased the value added duty to 50 percent on a wide variety of agricultural and manufactured imports.

Another technique to increase exports at the expense of others was to depreciate a nation's currency—reduce the value of its money. When Japan depreciated the yen, for example, U.S. dollar or British pound could buy more Japanese goods. In effect, lowering the yen reduced the price of Japanese exports. In most cases, however, devaluation brought only a temporary trade advantage. Other nations could play the same game, as the United States did in 1934 when it reduced the amount of gold backing for the dollar by 40 percent, thus going off the gold standard.

The debt problem that grew out of the war worsened during the depression. In 1931, U.S. president Herbert Hoover gained a one-year moratorium on all intergovernmental debts. The next year at the Lausanne Conference, German reparations payments were practically canceled in the hope that the United States would make corresponding concessions in reducing war debts. The Americans, for a variety of domestic financial and political reasons, refused to concede that there was a logical connection between reparations and war debts. As the depression deepened, the debtors could not continue their payments. France refused outright in 1932; Germany after 1933 completely stopped paying reparations; Britain and four other nations made token payments for a time and then stopped entirely in 1934. Only Finland continued to meet its schedule of payments.

Individual families had as many, or more, problems in paying their bills as did the governments of the world. Factories closed down and laid off their workers. Harvests rotted in the fields as the price of wheat fell to its lowest figure in 300 years. The lives of the cacao grower in the African Gold Coast, the coffee grower in Brazil, and the plantation worker in the Dutch East Indies were as affected as those of the factory worker in Pittsburgh, Lille, or Frankfurt.

The 1929 crash occurred in an economic framework still suffering from the dislocations of World War I. It began a downturn in the world economy that would not end until the world armed for another global conflict. Whether the depression ended because of World War II or whether the world would have eventually come out of the low part of the cycle is a question that will always be debated. The weaknesses in American stock market operations were by and large addressed in a series of reforms.

From the major banks to the soup lines in villages, the depression had profound implications for politics. The combination of inflation and depression threatened representative government. Unemployed and starving masses were tempted to turn to dictators who promised jobs and bread. The hardships of economic stability, even in those countries where the democratic tradition was strongest, led to a massive increase in state participation in the daily life of the individual.

Politics in the European Democracies

During the interwar period, the belief in the genius of big business and free-market capitalism received a death blow in most quarters, as business itself had to turn more and more to the powers of the state to survive. After 1918 parliamentary government, the basis of all that the liberals of the nineteenth century had wanted, came under attack everywhere.

For the most part, only in the Scandinavian countries—Norway, Sweden, and Denmark—did representative government operate smoothly throughout the interwar period. Economic prosperity was the general rule here throughout the 1920s, and during the depression these countries suffered comparatively less than did Britain, France, or the United States. Switzerland,

Germans line up for bread and soup during the Great Depression. Similar scenes were common in many other countries, including the United States.

Friedrich A. Hayek

Friedrich A. Hayek deftly portrayed the malaise affecting liberal Europe in the interwar period. His judgement is deeply controversial.

The crucial point of which our people are still so little aware is, however, not merely the magnitude of the changes which have taken place during the last generation but the fact that they mean a complete change in the direction of the evolution of our ideas and social order. For at least twenty-five years before the specter of totalitarianism became a real threat, we had progressively been moving away from the basic ideas on which Western civilization has been built. That this movement on which we have entered with such high hopes and ambitions should have brought us face to face with the totalitarian horror has come as a profound shock to this generation, which still refuses to connect the two facts. Yet this development merely confirms the warnings of the fathers of the liberal philosophy which we still profess. We have progressively abandoned that freedom in economic affairs without which personal and political freedom has never existed in the past. Although we had been warned by some of the greatest political thinkers of the nineteenth century, by De Tocqueville and Lord Acton, that socialism means slavery, we have steadily moved in the direction of socialism. And now that we have seen a new form of slavery arise before our eyes, we have so completely forgotten the warning that it scarcely occurs to us that the two things may be connected.

From Friedrich A. Hayek, *The Road to Serfdom* (Chicago: University of Chicago Press, 1944).

---

the Netherlands, and Belgium also maintained relatively high standards of living and kept their governments on the democratic road. But in the twenty years after peace came to Europe, Britain, France, and most of the other democracies exhibited lethargy and short-sightedness in the face of crisis.

Britain, 1919–1939

The 1920s was not a tranquil decade for Great Britain. The country endured a number of social and political crises that were tied to the bitter labor disputes and unemployment that disrupted the nation. Neither Liberals nor Conservatives could do little to alter the flow of events immediately after the war. From 1919 to 1922 David Lloyd George led a coalition, but it broke apart, leading to the division and decline of the Liberals. From May 1923 to January 1924 Stanley Baldwin led an unsuccessful Conservative government.

Ramsay MacDonald formed the first Labour government and became the first socialist prime minister. For ten months he and his party pursued a program to introduce socialism slowly and within the democratic framework. His move to recognize the Soviet Union was controversial. When the London *Times* published the so-called Zinoviev letter, a document in which the Communist Third International supposedly laid out the program for revolution in Britain, the public backlash defeated the Labour government in the October 1924 elections.

For the next five years the Conservatives under Baldwin held power. After renouncing the treaties the Labour cabinet had made with Russia, the Conservatives set out on a generally unsuccessful and stormy tenure. Britain returned its currency to the gold standard in 1925, a policy that led indirectly to an increase in labor unrest. The government struggled through a coal strike and a general strike in which more than 2.5 million of the nation's more than 6 million workers walked out. Baldwin reduced taxes on business, but this did little to remedy the deflationary effect of a return to the gold standard.

In May 1929 Labour under MacDonald won another victory. Once again the Labourites

The democratic genre art of the 1830s in the United States expressed the romantic adventure of the rapidly expanding frontier of Jacksonian America. George Caleb Bingham (1811–79) graphically portrayed lively images of frontier life in his paintings of riverboatmen, local politicians, and domestic scenes. *The Jolly Flatboatmen* (c. 1848) is one of a series of paintings of the same subject.

Leader of the expressionists, Henri Matisse emphasized the arrangement of simple, rhythmic forms and vivid areas of color. *Roumanian Blouse* (1940), left, is a late work. The experience of European imperialism affected all aspects of African life, including art. In the car below, an early twentienth-century work from the Congo, a Belgian magnate reclines in the back seat while the African chauffer drives.

Although Pablo Picasso is considered a founder of cubism, the range of his works extends over most of the significant trends in twentieth-century art. With its clearly defined shapes and boldly curved outlines, *Girl Before a Mirror* (1932) is an example of what has been described as curvilinear cubism.

The most famous surrealist painter is Salvador Dali (b. 1904), who sought to express the subjective world of dreams through disturbing and bizarre images like those in *The Persistence of Memory* (1931), below. The paintings of Marc Chagall (1887–1985), a forerunner of surrealism, also have a dreamlike quality, but the images are light and whimsical, as in *Birthday* (1915–23), right.

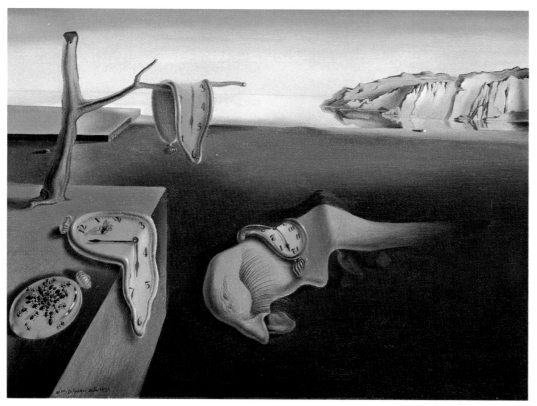

A master of twentieth-century art who, like Picasso, transcends any one movement or style is Paul Klee (1879–1940). *Senecio* (1922) combines elements of primitive art, cubism, surrealism, and children's drawings. In Klee's works, it is not only the subject, color, and spaces that give meaning to the picture; it is also the process of creation through which these elements are placed on the canvas that contributes to the total impression.

The American Alexander Calder (1898–1976) pioneered in the construction of kinetic, or mobile, sculptures in which physical motion is an essential part of the piece. Calder's mobiles are constructions of sheet metal and wire hinged together and so delicately balanced that the slightest breath of air sets the pieces in graceful motion. One of the largest hanging mobiles, *Lobster Trap and Fish Tail* (1939), is more than 8½ feet high and over 9½ feet in diameter.

Portfolio Eight

The great American architect of the twentieth century, Frank Lloyd Wright adapted the structure, materials, and plan of a building to its natural setting so that the land and the building become a unified whole. In the Kaufman House, *Falling Water,* at Bear Run, Pa. (1936), the overhanging concrete slabs blend harmoniously with the rocky ledges, while the interior of the house is a continuous flow of interrelated and interpenetrating areas.

Uninfluenced by twentieth-century trends in art, Edward Hopper (1882–1967) pursued his own course, using bold patterns of light, shadow, and color to convey the loneliness and isolation of modern urban life. The absence of distracting details and the geometric arrangement of strong verticals and horizontals contribute to the mood of haunting loneliness of the *Automat* (1927), in which a solitary woman sits in a deserted cafeteria, brooding over a cup of coffee.

A campaign poster for the British general election of 1931 urges voters to support the new national coalition government rather than the labour party with its failed socialist program.

WHAT HAVE THE SOCIALISTS DONE FOR ME?

NOTICE

Factory Closed

Vote for the **NATIONAL GOVERNMENT**

resumed relations with the Soviet Union and attempted their measured socialist program. The effects of the depression, however, condemned MacDonald and his government to failure. In two years, exports and imports declined 35 percent and close to 3 million unemployed people roamed the streets. Labour could do little to address the basic causes of the disaster; in fact, no single party could. When MacDonald's government fell in 1931, it was replaced by a national coalition government which was dominated primarily by the Conservatives.

The coalition government initiated a recovery program featuring a balanced budget, limited social spending, and encouragement of private enterprise. By 1933, a substantial measure of prosperity had been regained, and productivity increased by 23 percent over that of 1929.

To achieve this comeback, some of what remained of laissez-faire policy was discarded. The

During the general strike of 1926 in England, armored cars equipped with machine guns patrolled London to suppress riots.

government regulated the currency, levied high tariffs, gave farmers subsidies, and imposed a heavy burden of taxation. The taxes went to expanded educational and health facilities, better accident and unemployment insurance, and more adequate pensions as a prelude to post World War II legislation that attempted to ensure security from "the cradle to the grave." As for the rich, they had a large portion of their income taxed away, and what might be left at death was decimated by inheritance taxes. It was ruefully declared that the rich could hardly afford to live, much less to die.

During the twenty years between the wars, with the decline of the Liberals, there was an absence of forward-looking programs by the political parties. The parties seemed unable to measure up to the demands of a difficult new age. To many people, unemployed and maintained on a government pittance, the interwar period was aptly symbolized by a popular play of the time, *Love on the Dole*.

Interwar France

France suffered the most of any of the democracies from World War I; loss of lives as a proportion of the population and direct property damage were enormous. More than two

out of every ten young Frenchmen died. Years later, the nation, which had not experienced as rapid a population growth in the nineteenth century as other European states, still felt the war's heavy losses.

Victory did not address any of France's basic political problems. The French labored under much the same political stalemate and social stagnation after 1918 as it had before 1914. The economic impact of the war and the social disruptions that occurred during and after the conflict exacerbated these conditions. A dangerous inflation that threatened the franc plagued the country and undermined the rather shallow prosperity. The multiparty system hampered the parliamentary system of the Third Republic, and the brief tenure of governments formed from shaky coalitions. The exhausted country lacked vitality and a sense of national purpose after gaining revenge against the Germans.

After 1919, the British wished to withdraw from Europe to look after their imperial interests, and the United States withdrew into isolationism. Working from a dispirited domestic base, France had to bear the burden of overseeing international affairs on the continent. Overall, with the exception of the counterproductive occupation of the Ruhr, the French carried their duties well in the 1920s. In the next decade, however, France retreated into the so-called Maginot mentality, after the construction of the Maginot Line, a supposedly impenetrable line of fortresses to the east.

The depression struck France later than other countries, but in some ways the damage was greater. French leadership was no more astute than those of the other democracies before and during the depression. France managed to maintain a false prosperity from the 1920s for a while, partially because of its large gold holdings, but by the early 1930s it suffered much the same fate as the other countries. Tourism dried up, contributing to the already rising unemployment rate and budget deficits. In the face of these problems, the French carried the additional financial burden of rearming to face the renewed German threat.

Ministry after ministry took power, then collapsed a few months later. Citizens became impatient with the government, especially when the press exposed corruption in high places. One of the more shocking scandals was that surrounding the schemes of Alexander Stavisky, a rogue who had bribed officials and cheated French investors out of some 600 million francs. When the ministry in power in December 1933 refused to authorize an investigation after Stavisky's assumed suicide, thousands of angry citizens took to the streets of Paris in protest. In February 1934, mobs tried to storm the Chamber of Deputies.

The outcome of this affair was a new government, the National Union, a rightist coalition that endured strikes and avoided civil war for the next two years. France was becalmed. The leftists were unable to reorganize their forces quickly to gain control, and the rightists failed to deal with either domestic or foreign problems. In the spring of 1936 the leftist Popular Front took power.

This coalition, under the leadership of Léon Blum (1872–1950), won a national election and set in motion a program to bring socialist reforms to France's struggling economy. Blum's government tried to reduce the domination of the traditional ruling elite over the finances of the country on the one hand, and on the other work with the communists to block the growing fascist influences. The cooperation with the communists caused serious problems, including the usual one of how to work with the Moscow-dominated party without being captured by it. Many French voters refused to support the Popular Front from fear that it might commit France to fight against Germany for the benefit of the Soviet Union.

In foreign affairs the Popular Front worked closely with Great Britain and supported the

A Popular Front demonstration in Paris against the Nationalists in Spain who were seeking to overthrow the Spanish Republic. Despite this show of support for the Spanish Republicans, Blum's Popular Front government remained officially neutral during the Spanish Civil War.

work of the League of Nations. It also attempted to appease Germany, though it remained hostile to Italy. During the Spanish civil war (1936–1939), Blum's government, along with the British, declared neutrality in the face of fascist aggression, out of fear of a potential civil war.

In this atmosphere of social, economic, and international turmoil, Blum was unable to govern successfully. Further, an epidemic of sit-down strikes involving some 300,000 workers embarrassed the government. Gradually, laws introducing a forty-hour work week, higher wages, collective bargaining, and paid vacations were enacted to satisfy many of labor's demands. In addition, the government extended its control over the Bank of France and instituted a public works program. Blum navigated as best he could, favoring the worker against monopoly and big business while avoiding the totalitarian extremes of fascism and communism. After only a year in office, however, he was forced to resign. The unfavorable trade balance, huge public debt, and unbalanced budget brought down the Popular Front government. France swung back to the right with a government that ended the forty-hour week and put down strikes.

The National Union and the Popular Front mirrored the widening split between the upper and lower classes. The workers believed that the Popular Front's reforms had been sabotaged and that a France ruled by a wealthy clique deserved little or no allegiance. On the other hand, some business owners and financiers were horrified at the prospect of communism and openly admired Hitler's fascism. Soviet and German propagandists subtly encouraged the widening of the gulf.

While the French quarreled and France's economic strength declined, Germany—regimented and feverishly working—outstripped France in the manufacture of armaments. There were no leaders to bring France together, and the ingredients for the easy and tragic fall of the country in the spring of 1940 were in place.

Eastern Europe

With the exception of Finland and Czechoslovakia, democratic governments fared poorly in eastern Europe in the interwar period. By 1939, most of the states retained only the false front of parliamentary forms. Real power was exercised by varying combinations of secret police, official censors, armed forces, and corrupt politicians.

Most of these countries had an unhappy legacy of oppression by powerful neighbors, minority problems, economic weakness, and backward peasant societies. Poland, the Baltic States, Finland, Czechoslovakia, Yugoslavia, and Albania had not existed as states before 1913. Hungary, Bulgaria, and Austria had been on the losing side in World War I and paid dearly for that alliance in the treaties ending the war. Romania, which had been among the victors, gained large amounts of land and also a number of non-Romanian minorities.

For the first decade after the war, the small countries of eastern Europe had the opportunity to develop without undue external influence or interference. However, the exclusivist, aggressive, perhaps paranoid nationalism that dominated each nation thwarted any possibility of regional cooperation. The peace treaties had settled few of the problems plaguing the area and instead constructed a series of arbitrary political boundaries that brought far more conflict than accord. The countries in the region all sought autarkist solutions to their economic problems by erecting huge tariff barriers, which only served to emphasize the states' weaknesses.

Czechoslovakia With its combination of a strong middle class, accumulation of capital, technology base, and high literacy rate, Czechoslovakia possessed the greatest possibility among the eastern European states for successful democratic government. Four hundred years of Austrian domination had not crushed Czech national spirit. After the collapse of the Dual Monarchy in November 1918, the Czechs joined with the Slovaks, who had been under Hungarian domination for a thousand years, to establish a republic.

The new state possessed a literate and well-trained citizenry and a solid economic base and managed to avoid the roller coaster ride of inflation in the immediate postwar period. The country was an island of prosperity, boasting solid financial institutions, advanced industry,

In 1918, Czechs turned out to welcome back from exile Edvard Beneš, who was named foreign minister of the new Czech republic.

and a small-farm-based agricultural sector. As in the other eastern European successor states, there were serious minority problems. But of all the new states Czechoslovakia extended the most liberal policies toward minorities. By the time of the depression, Czechoslovakia showed every indication of growing into a mature democratic country. The depression, however, heavily affected the country's export trade and hit especially hard in the textile industry, which was centered in the German-populated Sudetenland. By 1935 the economic blows had made the area ripe for Nazi agitation and infiltration.

Poland Aside from Czechoslovakia, Poland had the best chance of the successor states to form a democratic government. The Poles, however, had to overcome several problems: a border conflict with the Soviet Union, the dilemma of the Polish Corridor to Danzig, minority issues, and the fact that Poland had been

partitioned for over a century. When the country was reunited after the war, the Poles chose to imitate the constitutional system of the French Third Republic. The multiplicity of parties, a weak executive, and the resultant succession of governments led to a political paralysis until 1926 when Marshal Josef Pilsudski (1867–1935) led a military revolt against the Warsaw government. For the next nine years Pilsudski imposed his generally positive, benevolent rule on the country. After his death in 1935, a group of colonels ruled Poland, and they permitted the formtion of several proto-fascist organizations. By the time the Poles turned back toward a more liberal government in 1938, it was too late. For three years, they had played up to the Nazis and now they stood isolated before Hitler's advance.

The Baltic and Balkan States Problems of geography plagued the Balkan states of Latvia, Lithuania, and Estonia, which came into existence in 1918. The democratic governments of these countries endured much political and economic strife before they eventually gave way to dictatorial forms of government to defend themselves against the Nazis.

Yugoslavia, Albania, and Greece were buffeted by the ambitions of Italian imperialism, economic upheaval, and political corruption. Disintegration seemed a real possibility for Yugoslavia in the 1920s, but the conglomerate state stubbornly attempted to hold together the six major ethnic groups within its boundaries. King Alexander established himself as dictator in 1929 and ruled until 1934, when he was assassinated by Croatian separatists. Thereafter, the rising Nazi state drew parts of economically depressed Yugoslavia into its orbit, deeply splitting the country. By the end of the 1930s, both Greece and Albania were ruled by dictators.

Romania gained greatly from the First World War, doubling its area and its population. Although the state had great economic potential, the government was unable to impose a stable rule during the interwar period. Severe problems with minorities and peasants and foreign control of the economy foiled the attempts of moderate politicians to rule, so by the 1930s fascist groups wielded a large amount of influence. In 1938 King Carol tried unsuccessfully to counter the pro-Nazi forces in Romania. Two years later the country lost one-third of its territory and population to the Bulgarians, Russians, and Hungarians, and Carol fled to Spain.

The Iberian Peninsula

During the interwar period, economic problems, aristocratic privilege, and peasant misery worked against successful democratic or parliamentary government in the Iberian peninsula. After the end of World War I, Portugal endured ten years of political indecision until Oliveira Salazar (1889–1970), a professor of economics, became minister of finance in 1928. After helping straighten out some of the country's financial problems, Salazar became Portugal's premier and virtual dictator. He maintained Portugal's close ties with Britain while lending assistance to right-wing elements in Spain.

None of the political parties could deal adequately with Spain's problems in the 1920s.

Revolts and strikes plagued the country until 1931, when the king abdicated and left the country. At the end of the year, a new liberal constitution was adopted, and a republic was proclaimed. The new constitution was extremely liberal, but it had the support of neither the left nor the right. Mob violence and the threat of military coups continually harassed the republic. By 1936 the peasants and workers were beginning to take matters into their own hands, while the military pursued its own political ends. In July, the army made its move and attacked the republican government. Even without Generalissimo Francisco Franco (see p. 881), there would have been a civil war in Spain. It would have come from the country's purely indigenous social antagonisms.[11]

Democracy Overseas

The United States emerged from World War I as the strongest country in the world. But while other states looked to Washington to play its proper role in the world, the U.S. government turned inward, away from the international scene. Americans shelved Wilson's wartime idealism, ignored the League of Nations, and returned to isolationism.

The United States in the 1920s

During the 1920s, three Republican presidents, Warren G. Harding, Calvin Coolidge, and Herbert Hoover, profited from the well-being of the country and presided over a generally carefree time. Although refusing to join the League of Nations, the United States did participate in the Washington Naval Conference in 1921–1922 to limit the race in warship construction, the Dawes and Young plans for economic stabilization (see p. 795), and the Kellogg-Briand pact (1928) to outlaw war.

Harding's domestic policies were marked by protectionist economics, probusiness legislation, and scandal. After Harding died suddenly in 1923, the widespread corruption of his administration was exposed. His vice-president, Coolidge, easily weathered the storm and after his 1924 election advocated high tariffs, tax

Throngs of unemployed line up in front of New York City's Municipal Lodging House for Sunday dinner in 1930.

reduction, and a hands-off policy on federal regulation of business. Only nagging problems in the agricultural sphere detracted from the dazzling prosperity and honest government that marked his administration.

In the 1928 elections, Herbert Hoover, a successful mining engineer who had directed Belgian relief during the war, been present at the Versailles negotiations, and overseen the Russian relief plan in the early 1920s, overwhelmed the governor of New York, Alfred E. Smith—the first Catholic to be nominated for president. When he took office in 1929, Hoover had the support of a Republican Congress and a nation enjoying unbounded industrial prosperity. It would be his incredibly bad luck to have to deal with, and be given the blame for, the worst depression the United States has ever experienced.

The United States in the Depression

By 1932 Americans felt the tragic blows of the depression—25 percent unemployment, 30,000 business failures, numerous bank collapses, and a huge number of foreclosed mortgages. Hoover tried unprecedented measures to prop up faltering businesses with government money, devise new strategies to deal with the farm problem, and build confidence among the shaken citizenry. He failed to shift the tide of the depression. Indeed, some observers note that the only force that brought an end to the crisis was the arrival of the Second World War.

In the 1932 elections, Franklin D. Roosevelt, only the third Democrat elected to the presidency since 1860, overwhelmed Hoover by assembling a coalition of labor, intellectuals, minorities, and farmers—a coalition the Democratic party

President Hoover's inability to solve the problems of the Great Depression helped Franklin D. Roosevelt win a landslide victory in the 1932 presidential election. Roosevelt is shown here at a political parade in Indianapolis, Indiana.

could count on for nearly a half century. The country had reached a crisis point by the time Roosevelt was inaugurated in 1933 and quick action had to be taken in the face of a wave of bank closings.

Under Roosevelt's leadership the New Deal, a sweeping, pragmatic, often hit-or-miss program, was developed to cope with the emergency. The New Deal's three objectives were relief, recovery, and reform. Millions of dollars flowed from the federal treasury to feed the hungry, create jobs for the unemployed through public works, and provide for the sick and elderly through such reforms as the Social Security Act. In addition, Roosevelt's administration substantially reformed the banking and stock systems, greatly increased the rights of labor unions, invested in massive public power and conservation projects, and supported families who were in danger of losing their homes or who simply needed homes.

The Democrats' programs created much controversy among those who believed that they went too far toward creating a socialistic government and those who believed that they did not go far enough toward attacking the depression. Hated or loved, Roosevelt was in control, and the strength and leadership he provided were unparalleled in the interwar democracies.

Interwar Latin America

The huge wartime demand for Latin American products resulted in an economic boom which, with a minor contraction, continued on into the 1920s. However, the area's crucial weakness remained—its economic dependence on only a few products. Among Latin America's twenty republics, Brazil based its prosperity on coffee, Cuba depended on sugar, Venezuela on oil, Bolivia on tin, Mexico on oil and silver, Argentina on wheat and meat, and the various Central American countries on bananas.

Another problem was that of land distribution. On many large estates, conditions resembled medieval serfdom. Because the Catholic church was a great landowner, certain churchmen combined with the landed interests to oppose land reforms.

During the 1920s, Mexico spearheaded the movement for social reform in Latin America. A series of governments, each claiming to be faithful to the spirit of the 1910 revolt, sought to gain more control over the vast oil properties run by foreign investors. The government solved the agrarian problem at the expense of the large landowners. These changes were accompanied by a wave of anticlericalism. Under these attacks, the Catholic church lost much property, saw many churches destroyed, and had to work through an underground priesthood for a time.

Mexico exerted a strong influence over other Latin American countries. Between 1919 and 1929 seven nations adopted new, liberal constitutions. In addition, there were growing demands for better economic and social opportunities, a breakdown of the barriers that divided the few extremely rich from the many abysmally poor, and improvement in health, education, and the status of women. Above all there was an increasing desire for more stable conditions.

Because of their dependence on raw material exports, the Latin American countries suffered a serious economic crisis during the depression. Largely as a result of the disaster, six South American countries had revolutions in 1930.

During the 1930s the "colossus of the north," the United States, attempted to improve its relations with Latin America and to stimulate trade. The Good Neighbor Policy, originated in Hoover's administration and begun in 1933, asserted that "no state has the right to intervene in the internal or external affairs of another." Less pious, but more effective, was the $560 million worth of inter-American trade that the new policy encouraged.

Rivalries among industrialized nations for the Latin American market became very intense during the 1930s. Nazi Germany concluded many barter agreements with Latin American customers and at the same time penetrated the countries politically by organizing German immigrants into pro-Nazi groups, supporting fascist politicians, and developing powerful propaganda networks. When war came, however, most of Latin America lined up with the democracies.

The British Empire

Demands for home rule grew during the interwar period in the British Empire, especially in

José Ortega y Gasset on the Rise of the Masses

José Ortega y Gasset captured the fear of the tyranny of the majority in his *Revolt of the Masses*.

There is one fact which, whether for good or ill, is of utmost importance in the public life of Europe at the present moment. This fact is the accession of the masses to complete social power. As the masses, by definition, neither should nor can direct their own personal existence, and still less rule society in general, this fact means that actually Europe is suffering from the greatest crisis that can afflict peoples, nations, and civilisation. Such a crisis has occurred more than once in history. Its characteristics and its consequences are well known. So also its name. It is called the rebellion of the masses. . . .

There exist, then, in society, operations, activities, and functions of the most diverse order, which are of their very nature special, and which consequently cannot be properly carried out without special gifts. For example: certain pleasures of an artistic and refined character, or again the the functions of government and of political judgment in public affairs. Previously these special activities were exercised by qualified minorities, or at least by those who claimed such qualification. The mass asserted no right to intervene in them; they realised that if they wished to intervene they would necessarily have to acquire those special qualities and cease being mere mass. They recognised their place in a healthy dynamic social system. . . .

The characteristic of the hour is that the commonplace mind: knowing itself to be commonplace, has the assurance to proclaim the rights of the commonplace and to impose them wherever it will. As they say in the United States: "to be different is to be indecent." The mass crushes beneath it everything that is different, everything that is excellent, individual, qualified and select. Anybody who is not like everybody, who does not think like everybody, runs the risk of being eliminated. And it is clear, of course, that this "everybody" is not "everybody." "Everybody" was normally the complex unity of the the mass and the divergent, specialised minorities. Nowadays, "everybody" is the mass alone. Here we have the formidable fact of our times, described without any concealment of the brutality of its features.

From José Ortega y Gasset, *The Revolt of the Masses*. Reprinted by permission of W. W. Norton & Co., Inc. (New York, 1932), pp. 11, 16, 18.

India, Ceylon, Burma, and Egypt. An ominous trend was the growing antagonism between the Arab inhabitants of mandated Palestine and the Jewish Zionist immigrants. Yet, these issues would not come to a crisis until after the Second World War.

Happier developments could be seen in the attainment of home rule by the Irish Free State (the southern part of Ireland) in 1921 and Britain's recognition in the Statute of Westminster (1931) of a new national status for the dominions (Canada, Australia, New Zealand, and South Africa). Collectively, the four states were then known as the British Commonwealth of Nations and would be held together henceforth only by loyalty to the crown and by common language, legal principles, traditions, and economic interests. Democratic traditions in the dominions did not succumb to the pressures of the depression, even though they were painfully susceptible to the effects of the world slump.

The Western Tradition in Transition

In the first two decades of the twentieth century, science made great strides, and such figures as Max Planck, Albert Einstein, Ivan

Pavlov, and Sigmund Freud, enlarged understanding of the universe and the individual. Even before the war, which had dealt a death blow to the nineteenth-century legacy of optimism, these physicists and psychologists pointed out that the old foundations and beliefs on which the European world rested had to be rethought. They and others like them opened new scientific vistas, and after 1918 their work began to have a much wider impact.

In the interwar period, artists too served as observant witnesses and penetrating critics of the difficult age in which they lived. After 1918, questioning of the accepted values and traditions of Western civilization increased.

Science and Society

As we saw in chapter 26, the British physicist Ernest Rutherford advanced the theory in 1911 that each atom has a central particle, or nucleus, which is positively charged. This did away with the belief that the atom was indivisible. On the continent, even greater discoveries were being made.

Max Planck (1858–1947), studied radiant heat, which comes from the sun and is identical in nature with light. He found that the energy emitted from a vibrating electron proceeds not in a steady wave—as traditionally believed—but discontinuously in the form of calculable "energy packages." To such a package, Planck gave the name *quantum*, hence the term *quantum theory*. This jolt to traditional physics was to prove invaluable in the rapidly growing study of atomic physics.

The scientific giant of the first half of the twentieth century, Albert Einstein (1879–1955), supported Planck's findings. In 1905 Einstein contended that light is propagated through space in the form of particles, which he called photons. Moreover, the energy contained in any particle of matter, such as the photon, is equal to the mass of that body multiplied by the square of the velocity of light (approximately 186,300 miles per second). This theory, expressed in the equation $E=mc^2$ provided the answer to many mysteries of physics. For example, questions such as how radioactive substances such as radium and uranium are able to eject particles at enormous velocities and to go on doing so for millions of years

could be examined in a new light. The magnitude of energy contained in the nuclei of atoms could be revealed. Above all, $E=mc^2$ showed that mass and energy are equatable.

That same year, Einstein formulated his special theory of relativity, which called for a radically new approach to explain the concepts of time, space, and velocity. For example, he maintained that time and distance are interrelated and that the mass of a body increases with its velocity. Again, he showed that mass and energy are equatable by $E=mc^2$.

In 1915 Einstein proposed his general theory, in which he incorporated gravitation into relativity. He showed that gravitation is identical to acceleration and that light rays would be deflected in passing through a gravitational field—a prediction confirmed by observation of an eclipse in 1919 and by various experiments carried out in the American space programs in the 1960s and 1970s. The theory of relativity has been subsequently confirmed in other ways as well. The interconversion of mass and energy was dramatically demonstrated in the atomic bomb, which obtains its energy by the annihilation of part of the matter of which it is composed.

Einstein's theories upset the Newtonian views of the universe. Einstein's universe is not Newton's three-dimensional figure of length, breadth, and thickness. It is, instead, a four-dimensional space-time continuum in which time itself varies with velocity. Such a cosmic model calls for the use of non-Euclidean geometry. Einstein's theory changed scientists' attitude toward the structure and mechanics of the universe. On a broader scale, his relativistic implications have penetrated philosophical, moral, and esthetic concepts of the twentieth century.

Planck and Einstein investigated the infinite extent of the external universe, with a massive impact on the state of knowledge. At the same time, the equally infinite extent of that universe known as the mind also began to be studied in greater depth than ever before.

The Russian scientist Ivan Pavlov (1849–1936) gave the study of psychology a new impetus. In 1900 he carried out a series of experiments in which food was given to a dog at the same time that a bell was rung. After a time, the dog identified the sound of the bell with food. Henceforth, the sound of the bell alone conditioned the dog to salivate, just as if food had been presented. Pavlov demonstrated the influence of physical stimuli on an involuntary process.

The psychology of "conditioned reflexes," based on Pavlov's work, achieved a wide popularity, especially in the United States, as the basis for behaviorism, which considered the human as analogous to a machine responding mechanically to stimuli. Behaviorism stressed experimentation and observational techniques and did much to create relatively valid intelligence and aptitude tests. It also served to strengthen the materialist philosophies of the period.

Probably the most famous and controversial name associated with psychology is that of Sigmund Freud (1856–1939). Placing far greater stress than any predecessor on the role of the unconscious, Freud pioneered the theory and methods of psychoanalysis. This theory is based

Sigmund Freud. Freud's theory of psychoanalysis gave people a new way of understanding and interpreting human behavior and new methods for treating mental disorders.

on the idea that human beings are born with unconscious drives that from the very beginning seek some sort of outlet or expression. Young children often express their drives in ways that violate social conventions for proper behavior. Parents typically forbid these behaviors and punish children for performing them. As a result, many innate drives are repressed, that is, pushed out of conscious awareness. Repressed drives, however, continue to demand some kind of expression. Freud believed that many repressed drives were sublimated, that is, channeled into some kind of tolerated or even highly praised behavior.

Freud was particularly interested in psychological disorders, and he treated emotional disturbances by encouraging patients to bring back to the surface deeply repressed drives and memories. By making patients aware of their unconscious feelings, Freud hoped that patients would understand themselves better and be able to respond more effectively to the problems they faced. Freud used the techniques of free association and dream interpretation to explore how unconscious feelings might be related to patients' symptoms. He believed that many of his patients' symptoms resulted from repressed sexual and aggressive drives. Freud's theories not only have had tremendous influence in the science of psychology, they have also had a profound impact on our culture as a whole.

The Testimony of Artists

Even before the war, many of Europe's writers, and artists, and musicians had begun to question the generally held faith in European progress. The barbarism and tragedy of the war and its aftermath merely confirmed their perceptions. A whole generation of artists and thinkers cast doubts on their society and the worth of individuals caught in civilization's web. The war had shown to many the fallacies of the old order. Some artists sought release in drugs, oriental religions, or bohemian lifestyles. Other found comfort in ideas drawn from Einstein's relativity theory, which held that nothing was "fixed" in the universe, or in Freud's notions of the overwhelming power of the unconscious.

Franz Kafka (1883–1924) perhaps best captured the nightmarish world of the twentieth century. In works such as *Metamorphosis* and *The Trial*, he portrayed a ritualistic society in which a well-organized insanity prevails. Rational, well-meaning individuals run a constant maze from which there is no exit, only more structures. Many sensitive artists and writers cast serious doubt on the Renaissance notion that "man is the measure of all things." The western world had gone very far off course, and the best that could be hoped for was survival.

Historians worked under the profound influence of Oswald Spengler's *Decline of the West.* The book, finished one year before the defeat of the Central Powers, was more widely quoted than read. In it, the German historian traced the life span of cultures—from birth through maturity to death—and identified the symptoms of the west's demise. Other writers expressed a similar fascination with the death of their civilization, but perhaps more significant was that people in the west knew Spengler's name, just as earlier they had known the names of Freud, Einstein, and Darwin and their general messages.

Since before 1914, a number of composers had been rebelling strongly against lyrical romanticism and engaged in striking experimentation. Breaking with the "major-minor" system of tonality, which had been the musical tradition since the Renaissance, some of them used several different keys simultaneously, a device known as polytonality. Outstanding among such composers was Igor Stravinsky (1882–1971). He was less concerned with melody than with achieving effects by means of polytonality, dissonant harmonies, and percussive rhythms. Other composers, such as Arnold Schoenberg (1874–1951), experimented with atonality, the absence of any fixed key. Schoenberg developed the twelve-tone system, an approach in which compositions depart from all tonality and harmonic progressions, while at the same time stressing extreme dissonances. Stravinsky's and Schoenberg's music may strike the first-time listener as harsh and unpleasant, yet it must be acknowledged that these experiments with polytonality and atonality had validity for a time in which the old absolute values were crumbling, a time of clashing dissonance.

Young artists all over the world took up abstract, nonrepresentational painting. During the interwar period (1881–1973) Pablo Picasso modified his cubist style and became a public figure

Franz Kafka. In his visionary, psychological, and metaphorical fiction, Kafka expressed the anxiety and alienation of 20th-century Western society.

through paintings such as *Guernica,* a mural that vividly depicts the destruction of a small town in Spain by fascist air forces during that country's civil war. Henri Matisse (1869–1954) continued to exercise a major influence on young painters through his abstract works. Less significant, but a useful example of artistic response to the times was the Dada schools, which viewed World War I as proof that rationality did not exist, and that therefore, neither did artistic standards. Salvador Dali (1904–1989) perhaps indicated his convictions about the artistic establishment and the society it represented when he gave a lecture on art while wearing a diver's helmet.[12]

A more lasting movement that came out of the 1920s was surrealism. The proponents of this approach saw the subconscious mind as the vehicle that could free people from the shackles of modern society and lead them to total creative freedom. They felt an affinity with "primitive art" and its close associations with magical and mythological themes. They exalted the irrational, the violent and the absurd in human experience. French writer André Breton (1896–1966) wrote a manifesto of surrealism in 1924, but the movement had its greatest impact in the visual arts, in the works of such artists as Dali, Georgio de Chirico (1888–1978) and René Magritte (1898–1967).

Sculpture and Architecture

These two most substantial forms of art went through radical changes during the generation before and after the war. Auguste Rodin (1840–1917) has been called the father of modern sculpture. The realistic honesty and vitality of his work made him the object of stormy controversy during his career. He shared the impressionist painters' dislike of finality in art and preferred to let the viewers' imagination play on his work. Rodin's technique of "rough" finish can best be seen in his bronze works, which feature a glittering surface of light and shadow and convey a feeling of immediacy and incompleteness that emphasizes their spontaneous character.

While Rodin was making major contributions in sculpture, architects in Europe were taking advantage of new materials and technologies developed through industrialization to make major improvements in construction. With new resources and methods, architects were able to span greater distances and enclose greater areas than had hitherto been possible.

The Great Chicago fire of 1871 may have leveled much of the city, but it had the beneficial effect of permitting new building on a large scale. A new form of structure emerged—the steel-skeleton skyscraper, which enabled builders to erect much taller structures. Before, high buildings had required immensely thick masonry walls or buttresses. Now a metal frame allowed the weight of the structure to be distributed on an entirely different principle. Also, the metal frame permitted a far more extensive use of glass than ever before.

Outstanding among the pioneers in this new approach was American architect Louis Sullivan (1856–1924), who did most of his important work in Chicago. Like others, Sullivan saw the value of the skyscraper in providing a large amount of useful space on a small plot of expensive land.

He rejected all attempts to disguise the skeleton of the skyscraper behind a false front and boldly proclaimed it by a clean sweep of line. Sullivan's influence on function had a far-reaching influence.

In Europe, the French engineer Alexandre Gustave Eiffel (1832–1923) planned and erected a 984-foot tower for the Paris International Exposition in 1889. Delicately formed from an iron framework, the tower rests on four masonry piers on a base 330 feet square.

In the decade prior to World War I, an "international" style of architecture, which broke sharply with tradition, developed in Germany. This style, which stressed the use of different techniques from the machine age, was particularly well suited to early twentieth-century industrialization. In 1914 one of the outstanding leaders of this movement, Walter Gropius (1888–1969) designed an exhibition hall in Cologne that emphasized horizontal lines, used glass, exposed staircases, and did not hide its

Louis Sullivan, Carson Pirie Scott & Co. Building, Chicago (1899–1904). Sullivan influenced the development of the skyscraper, the dominant architectural form of the 20th century.

functionalism. Even at the end of the twentieth century this hall is still regarded as contemporary. Proponents of this new movement in architecture established a highly influential school of functional art and architecture, the *Bauhaus*, in 1918.

One of Louis Sullivan's pupils, Frank Lloyd Wright (1869–1959), originated revolutionary designs for houses. One feature of Wright's structures was the interweaving of interiors and exteriors through the use of terraces and cantilevered roofs. He felt that a building should look appropriate on its site; it should "grow out of the land." His "prairie houses," with their long, low lines, were designed to blend in with the flat land of the Midwest. Much of what is today taken for granted in domestic architecture stems directly from Wright's experiments at the beginning of the century.

Mass Culture

While the creative geniuses of high culture responded in their own ways to the era, purveyors of mass culture made amazing strides to please and entertain a widening audience. Movies became the most popular, most universal art form of the twentieth century. Movie newsreels brought home to millions the immediacy of the rise of Adolf Hitler, the drama of Franklin D. Roosevelt, or the home run power of Babe Ruth.

From the theaters of Main Street, U.S.A., to the private projection rooms of the Kremlin, artists such as Charlie Chaplin became universal favorites. Chaplin's favorite character, the Little Tramp, was an archetypal figure that communicated across all cultures. The tramp's struggle for food and shelter was universal, as was his appeal for freedom and dignity. Despite the odds, he always struggled against the forces of inhumanity, whether the soulless mechanization of the assembly line, as brilliantly shown in *Modern Times* (1935) or jackboot tyranny, as in *The Great Dictator* (1940) where the ranting "Furore" is ironically juxtaposed with the little Jewish barber who pleads for decency and predicts that "so long as men die, liberty will never perish."

Technology touched the common people in many ways and vastly expanded mass culture. Henry Ford's Model T made cars widely accessible and opened up the world to those who cared to drive. In cities, virtually every home had electricity, which powered bright lights, refrigeration, and other conveniences. Radio brought music, drama, and news into millions of living rooms. Politicians quickly learned the usefulness of the new medium; Stanley Baldwin in Britain, Franklin D. Roosevelt in the United States, and Adolf Hitler in Germany became masters at projecting their personalities and their ideas over the airwaves. The three great networks in the United States and organizations such as the British Broadcasting Corporation (BBC) in Europe got their start during these years.

The combination of increased leisure time, greater mobility, and improved communications led to the development of the modern "star" system in sports and entertainment. As times became more difficult and while front-page news was grim, Americans, Germans, and French citizens could find some diversion in reading about their boxers—Jack Dempsey, Max Schmeling, and Georges Carpentier. In the United States golfers and baseball stars became better known and better paid than presidents.

Through radio and phonograph records the mass audience discovered jazz, formerly the special preserve of black musicians and their audiences. Louis Armstrong and his trumpet and Paul Whiteman and his band became known worldwide. At the same time, Rosa Ponselle, Arturo Toscanini, and other figures from the opera and concert world became celebrities known to millions more than could ever have seen them perform in person.

Mass culture, with its movie stars, athletic heroes, and musical favorites, provided a diversion for many, even if it drew criticism from the élite. While intellectuals struggled to comprehend and express the changes occurring around them, mass culture provided release and relief from the stresses of the interwar period.

Conclusion

The democracies won World War I, and they dictated the peace at Paris, but the peace did not bring them the fruits of victory they so ardently desired. In the west, the vanguard of progress since the Middle Ages had been the middle classes. This group, originally small property owners, pursued private enterprise in an urban setting and favored an economy based on minimal governmental interference and free markets. After the war, the economic disasters of inflation and the depression strongly attacked the middle classes' economic strength and weakened the democracies.

Other basic institutions and assumptions also came under attack. The total mobilization for victory during the war laid the foundations for increased state dominance over society. By the end of the 1930s, Bismarck's welfare state had been copied in almost every country in the west. The family's innate obligation to care for its own people soon passed to the society and the state. Whether in the identification card of the French citizen or the social security number of the United States, every adult came to find a tentacle of the state reaching out to him or her to insure, support, and protect, while at the same time taxing and restricting.

Suggestions for Reading

E. H. Carr, *The Twenty Years' Crisis* (Torchbooks, 1964) and A. J. P. Taylor, *From Sarajevo to Potsdam* (Brace Jovanovich, 1966) give compelling and eloquent coverage of the malaise of the democracies in the interwar period. The problems of peacemaking and the aftermath of Versailles are discussed by J. M. Keynes, *The Economic Consequences of the Peace* (Macmillan, 1921) and F. P. Walters, *A History of the League of Nations* (Oxford, 1952). Harold Nicolson's thoughtful *Peacemaking* (Houghton Mifflin, 1939) is an essential introduction to the era.

The economic situation is well treated in David Landes, *The Unbound Prometheus* (Cambridge, 1969) and Sidney Pollard, *European Economic Integration, 1815–1870* (Harcourt Brace Jovanovich, 1974). See Fritz Ringer, ed., *The German Inflation of 1923* (Oxford, 1969) and Gustav Stolper, *et al.*, *The German Economy 1870 to the Present* (Harcourt Brace Jovanovich, 1967) for the view from Berlin.

J. K. Galbraith's *The Great Crash 1929* (Houghton Mifflin, 1965) is wise and beautifully written. The global perspective of the thirties is found in C. P. Kindelberger, *The World in Depression* (California, 1975). C. Maier surveys the social and political consequences of the difficult interwar period in *Recasting Bourgeois Europe* (Princeton, 1975).

Two first-rate biographies of interwar British leaders are David Marquand, *Ramsay MacDonald* (Jonathan Cape, 1977) and Keith Midlemas, *Baldwin, A Biography* (Macmillan, 1970). J. Stevenson and C. Cook provide a good survey of British life between the wars in *Social Conditions in Britain Between the Wars* (Penguin, 1977). For France, John T. Marcus, *French Socialism in the Crisis Years, 1933–1936* (Praeger, 1963) and Peter Larmour, *The French Radical Party in the 1830s* (Stanford, 1964).

Notes

1. E. H. Carr, *The Twenty Years' Crisis* (New York: Harper & Row, 1964), p. 224.
2. T. Harry Williams, Richard N. Current, and Frank Friedel, *A History of the United States Since 1865* (New York: Alfred A. Knopf, 1960), p. 426.
3. A. J. Ryder, *Twentieth Century Germany: From Bismarck to Brandt* (New York: Columbia Univ. Press, 1973), p. 216.
4. David S. Landes, *The Unbound Prometheus* (Cambridge: Cambridge Univ. Press, 1969), pp. 361–362. Gustav Stolper, Karl Hauser, and Knut Borchardt, *The German Economy: 1870 to the Present*, trans. Toni Stolper (New York: Harcourt Brace Jovanovich, 1967), p. 83.
5. Alan Bullock, *Hitler, A Study in Tyranny* (New York: Torchbooks, 1964), p. 91.
6. Sidney Pollard, *European Economic Integration, 1815–1970* (New York: Harcourt Brace Jovanovich, 1974), p. 138.
7. Landes, *The Unbound Prometheus*, p. 365.
8. Pollard, *European Economic Integration, 1815–1970*, pp. 140–142.
9. William R. Keylor, *The Twentieth Century World* (Oxford: Oxford Univ. Press, 1984), p. 133.
10. John Kenneth Galbraith, *The Great Crash 1929* (Boston: Houghton Mifflin Co., 1961), p. 173.
11. Brian Crozier, *Franco* (London: Eyre & Spottiswoode, 1967), p. 13.
12. A. J. P. Taylor, *From Sarajevo to Potsdam* (New York: Harcourt Brace Jovanovich, 1965), p. 116.

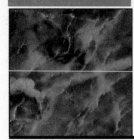

Chapter 32

The Quest for Total Power

The USSR, Italy, and Germany

World War I and its aftershocks prepared the way for authoritarian rule in Europe. By 1939, dictators ruled Russia, Italy, and Germany. Using modern technology, they tried to form a new kind of state, described as *totalitarian* by Benito Mussolini in 1925.

Totalitarian regimes, such as those led by Josef Stalin and Adolf Hitler, are at an opposite pole from democratic governments, which respect laws, representative assemblies, and civil and human rights. Totalitarianism exalts the leader of the state, who uses the law and society for personal ends. It invades and controls all areas of an individual's life, using propaganda to manipulate the masses. It orchestrates elections to achieve the "democratic fiction" of popular support. When totalitarian rule is perfected, society is atomized so there is no obstacle between the might of the leader and the individual.[1]

The costs of war and the incompetence of dual power destroyed the Provisional Government in Russia. The disappointments of the peace and unsettled economic conditions undermined the Italian government and the German Weimar Republic. Even before the war and the economic upheaval, the political soil in these countries had not been conducive to the development of liberal government. The postwar conditions combined with the exhaustion of the democracies led to the authoritarian alternative.

The Russian Revolution, 1917–1939

The Russians who survived World War I, revolution, civil war, and the 1930s endured one of the cruelest epochs in history. In passing from the rule of the inept tsar Nicholas II to the tyrannical Josef Stalin, they experienced the transformation of every aspect of their lives.

The enormous costs of the war set the stage for the revolution.[2] Nicholas and his subjects entered the war in a buoyant and patriotic mood.[3] It took only two months to dampen the initial optimism and to expose the army's weakness and the government's corruption. By the middle of 1915 the drastic losses (more than 2 million in that year alone) and food and fuel shortages lowered morale. Strikes increased among the factory workers during 1916, and the peasants, whose sons were dying in large numbers and whose desire for land reform were being ignored, became discontented.

The tsar and his government did little. Nicholas came more under the influence of his wife, Alexandra. She, in turn, had fallen under the control of the outrageous "holy man" Rasputin, the man who professed to be able to stop the bleeding of the tsar's hemophiliac son. Rasputin scandalized Petrograd by his influence over Alexandra and by his well-known seductions—he believed that "great sins made possible great repentances"[4] and in pursuit of that goal became one of history's notable sexual athletes.

When Nicholas took the symbolic act of assuming command of his armies in the field—a move that did nothing to help the Russian forces—Alexandra and Rasputin seized the opportunity to increase their power. The two capriciously dismissed capable generals and officials, making the government and army even less efficient. In December 1916 a group of Russian nobles tried to kill Rasputin by luring him to an

Tsar Nicholas and Tsarina Alexandra surrounded by their daughters (left to right) Marya, Tatiana, Olga, and Anastasia. The young tsarovitch sits below his parents. Nicholas and his entire family were executed by the Bolsheviks in July 1918.

apartment and poisoning him. When the massive amounts of poison had no effect, they shot him and then threw him into the Neva River. According to the autopsy, he finally died by drowning.

Alexandra's and Rasputin's roles in the capital reflected the sad state of the tsarist government in 1917. Under the pressure of war, the Russian economic and political bases dissolved. The tsarina and her associate did not cause the outbreak of the revolution. Rather, "the complex revolutionary situation of 1917 was the accumulated deposit of Russian history, detonated by the explosion of war."[5]

The February/March Revolutions of 1917

While politicians, ideologists, and generals acted out their parts in the drama, a spontaneous event from below sparked the 1917 Russian revolution. In the first part of March (late February in the Julian calendar in use in Russia at the time, all dates will be given in the new style), a strike broke out in a Petrograd (known in the west as St. Petersburg and in modern times as Leningrad) factory. By March 8 sympathy strikes had virtually paralyzed the city. At the same time, a bread shortage occurred, which brought more people into the streets. Scattered fighting broke out between the strikers and protesters on one side and the police on the other.

The tsar ordered the strikers back to work and dismissed the Duma (parliament) on March 11. These orders touched off the revolutionary crisis. The Duma refused to go home and the strikers held mass meetings in defiance of the government. The next day the army and police openly sided with the workers.

Three events occurred between March 12 and March 15 that marked the end of the old regime. On March 12 the Duma declared the formation of a provisional committee (renamed the Provisional Government on March 15) to serve as a caretaker administration until a constituent assembly could be elected to write a constitution for the future Russian republic. On the same day Marxist socialists in Petrograd formed the Soviet (council) of Workers' Deputies (renamed three days later the Soviet of Workers' and Soldiers' Deputies). Nicholas abdicated on March 15 to his brother Michael, who turned down the throne the next day in favor of the Provisional Government. After more than three centuries in power, the Romanov dynasty ceased to rule.

For the next six months, Russia proceeded under a system Leon Trotsky, the great Marxist theoretician and revolutionary, described as dual power—the Provisional Government and the Soviet. The moderates and liberals in the Provisional Government quickly produced a program of civil rights and liberties that gave Russia a

The Program of the Provisional Government

The freedom enjoyed by Russia from March to November 1917 was the most ever experienced in that country. A major reason for the freedom was the program of the Provisional Government.

Citizens, the Provisional Executive Committee of the members of the Duma, with the aid and support of the garrison of the capital and its inhabitants, has triumphed over the dark forces of the Old Regime to such an extent as to enable it to organize a more stable executive power.

The cabinet will be guided in its actions by the following principles:

1. An immediate general amnesty for all political and religious offenses, including terrorist acts, military revolts, agrarian offenses, etc.
2. Freedom of speech and press; freedom to form labor unions and to strike. These political liberties should be extended to the army in so far as war conditions permit.
3. The abolition of all social, religious and national restrictions.
4. Immediate preparation for the calling of a Constituent Assembly, elected by universal and secret vote, which shall determine the form of government and draw up the Constitution for the country.
5. In place of the police, to organize a national militia with elective officers, and subject to the local self-governing body.
6. Elections to be carried out on the basis of universal, direct, equal, and secret suffrage.
7. The troops that have taken part in the revolutionary movement shall not be disarmed or removed from Petrograd.
8. On duty and in war service, strict military discipline should be maintained, but when off duty, soldiers should have the same public rights as are enjoyed by other citizens.

The Provisional Government wishes to add that it has no intention of taking advantage of the existence of war conditions to delay the realization of the above-mentioned measures of reform.

President of the Duma, M. Rodzianko
President of the Council of Ministers,
   Prince Lvov
Ministers Miliukov, Nekrasov, Manuilov,
   Konovalov, Tereschenko, Vl. Lvov,
   Shingarev, Kerenski.

March 16, 1917.

From *Documents of Russian History, 1914–1917*, ed. F. A. Golder, tr. E. Aronsberg (New York: Appleton-Century-Crofts, Inc. 1927).

---

springtime of freedom in 1917 the likes of which the country had never known before and would not experience again for seventy years. From the first, however, the Provisional Government was hampered by its temporary nature: it refused to take permanent action on major issues until the constitutent assembly, elected by all Russians, could convene.

The Soviet was dominated by the Menshevik wing of the Russian Social Democratic party. The Mensheviks believed, in accord with Marx' teachings, that a liberal, bourgeois revolution had to run its course. Even though they had greater popular support than the Provisional Government, they refused to take power until what they deemed to be the historically proper moment as defined by Marx's theories. After the fall of the tsar, power passed to those who could not rule or would not rule.

From the first, the dual power system functioned in a contradictory and ineffective way. On March 14 the Soviet issued its first law, Order No. 1, which placed the running of the army on a democratic basis, through a committee structure. Soldiers were to obey only those orders that agreed with the official position of the Soviet, which wanted peace. At the same time, the Provisional Government insisted on carrying out the war, in hopes of gaining the Bosporous, Constantinople, and the Dardanelles.

As the months wore on, the position of moderates in both parts of the system weakened, and all the parties involved became discredited. The Provisional Government put off calling the constituent assembly and thereby deferred any possibility of finding solutions to the problems facing Russia. It continued to pursue the war to "honor its commitments" and to gain the prizes promised in the secret treaties. The Mensheviks refused to take control, reasoning that the liberal, bourgeois phase of history had not run its course in Russia.[6] The masses who suffered from economic hardships or fought and died on the front lines could find little consolation in either branch of dual power.

By July, the liberals and moderates had given up the reins of power. Alexander Kerensky (1881–1970), who was further to the left and who had been the only real revolutionary in the original cabinet, became the head of the Provisional Government. He was in an impossible situation. Leftists accused Provisional Government of heartlessly pursuing the war, while rightists condemned it for tolerating too may leftists. In the meantime the Soviet extended its organization throughout Russia by setting up local affiliates. Through the summer, however, the Soviets lacked the forceful leadership to take control of the country.

Lenin's Opportunity, October/November 1917

In 1917 Lenin returned to Russia from exile in Switzerland, (see ch. 25), intent on giving the revolution the leadership it lacked. He had spelled out his tactics and ideas in the previous decade, and his disciples in Russia, the Bolsheviks, had built up a core of supporters in the factories and the army. As late as December 1916 he had stated that the revolution would not occur within his lifetime. Four months later, working through Swiss contacts and with German assistance, he returned to Russia. The Germans gave him transportation and financial support in the hope that he would cause widespread chaos that would force Russia to withdraw from the war.

From the moment he stepped off the train at the Finland station on the evening of April 16,

Lenin speaks to a crowd in Petrograd. The city was renamed Leningrad in 1924, but in 1991 residents voted to restore the original name of the city, St. Petersburg.

Lenin tried to control the revolution. He proposed immediately stopping the war against Germany and starting one against "social oppressors." He called for giving all power to the Soviets and nationalizing all land. He also pushed for calling all Social Democrats, of whatever persuasion, communists. Lenin badly misjudged his audience, and the Mensheviks and Social Revolutionaries rejected his program.

During the summer and fall of 1917 the Provisional Government and the Soviet continued their misgovernment. Kerenski tried to rule through a series of coalitions in which the political balance continually shifted to the left. By the middle of July, after a moderately successful offensive against the Austrians, soldiers began to desert in large numbers rather than face a useless death. The Russian front, along with the army, disintegrated. In the capital, the Mensheviks continued their refusal to take power through the Soviet: the historical time was not right.[7] As if to match the ineptness of dual power, the Bolsheviks made an ill-conceived attempt to take power. The move backfired, and Lenin was forced to flee in disguise to Finland.

After surviving the Bolshevik crisis, Kerensky faced a new threat from the right when General Lavr Kornilov tried to "help" the government by sending his troops to the capital. Kerensky and the Soviet interpreted this action as a right-wing counterrevolutionary move and mobilized to head it off. Kornilov's ill-advised manuever failed and, ironically, he weakened the people he wanted to help.

Between March and October 1917, the force of the revolution ground to bits all of Russia's structures and parties, from monarchist to Menshevik. The economic system fell apart as the rhythms of planting and commerce were disrupted by the uproar. To the people caught in this chaos, the moderates' political dreams, the Mensheviks' revolutionary timing, and the Bolshevik's schemes for the seizure of power were all totally irrelevant.

The actual revolution took place far away from the politicians and "great men." The army withered away as mass desertions and the execution of officers became commonplace. In the countryside the peasants began carrying out land reform on their own, expelling landowners and killing those who would not leave. In the cities, workers began to take over factories. The Russian empire broke apart from internal conflicts, the continued pressure of war, and the rising spirits of the nationalities who had been oppressed for centuries.

Only the Bolsheviks seemed to have an answer to Russia's crisis; even their slogans, such as "Peace, Land, and Bread," reflected what was already happening. Furthermore, they had the discipline and adaptability to take advantage of events. The Mensheviks clung to brittle intellectual formulas, while the Provisional Government continued to dream of Russian control of the Bosporous and Constantinople. Lenin and his colleagues took advantage of the Kornilov debacle and the failure of dual power to form their own revolution.

By October 1917 the Bolsheviks had discarded their slogan of "All Power to the Soviets." Frankly, Lenin, the unchallenged Bolshevik leader, no longer needed these local organizations. After much hesitation, he decided to move on November 6 (October 24 in the Russian calendar). The Bolshevik Military Revolutionary Committee led by Leon Trotsky, and supported by the communist-dominated crew of the battleship *Aurora*, took control of the communications and police centers in Petrograd. With the exception of sporadic fighting around the Winter Palace, Trotsky's military forces had little trouble. They arrested those members of the Provisional Government who could be found. Kerensky escaped from the capital in a car flying the U.S. flag.

Lenin suddenly found himself leading a party of over 200,000 people (an increase from 23,600 in February), which claimed control of a state of more than 170 million people. It was not his

Soldiers gathered in Petrograd's Admiralty Square in April 1917 and held banners reading (from left): "Long Wave the Democratic Republic," "Land and Freedom," and "Let Us Reject the Old World."

The Bolshevik attack on the Winter Palace in Petrograd, November 1917. The next day Lenin announced that the Bolsheviks had taken power.

individual genius or his plans but rather his discipline and opportunism that enabled him to gain power. He endured the mistakes of April and July to take power. He did not make the revolution, but he did pick up the pieces and profit from the changes brought about by the breakdown of the tsarist government under the pressure of war.

Power, Allied Intervention, Civil War

The Bolsheviks assumed power over a war-weakened, revolution-ravaged state that was in terrible condition. Lenin's takeover split the Soviet itself when the Mensheviks and the Social Revolutionaries refused to participate. Lenin had a bare majority at the Soviet's first postrevolutionary meeting. In the free elections held in December to form a constituent assembly, the Bolsheviks received just one fourth of the votes.

Yet such details as democratic representation did not stop Lenin. He proceeded to rule Russia. The Bolsheviks immediately put through decrees to declare peace and settle the land question. In the meantime, his cadres imposed their control over Moscow and the other cities in the country.

Lenin then began to lay the foundations for the single-party dictatorship that characterized Russia until 1989. When the constituent assembly convened in Petrograd on January 18, 1918 and proved that it would not be a tool for Lenin, the Bolsheviks closed it down at bayonet point the next day. By dissolving the constituent assemble, Lenin crushed all remnants of the briefly flowering democracy. This indecisive step sealed the fate of the Mensheviks and most other opposition leftist parties. Not for seventy-one years would there be contested elections, open criticism of the central power, and the possibility of a potential democratic opposition.

Lenin faced the need to make peace with Germany by concluding, after two months of negotiations, the Treaty of Brest-Litovsk. This agreement (see pg. 780) drastically reduced the territory under Russian control and made the centers of government much more exposed to attack. In reality, Lenin sacrificed territory over which he had no control and took his country out of a war it could not fight.

In the late spring the revolutionary government came under attack from the White forces and the Allies. The Whites, a powerful but fragmented group of anti-Bolsheviks began a civil war that would claim as many casualties in its three years as the country had lost in World War I. The Allied Powers sent several expeditionary armies to Russia for the stated purpose of controlling material they had sent the former tsarist army. In reality, they helped the Whites. The Allies, still at war with Germany, feared that the Bolsheviks were in a conspiracy with the Germans, especially after the terms of the Brest-Litovsk treaty became known. They also hoped that if Lenin could be overthrown, the Whites might reopen fighting against the Central Powers. By the fall of 1918, the Bolsheviks were besieged.

From its new capital at Moscow, the Red (Bolshevik) government took all means to defend the revolution. Lenin's forces reimposed the death penalty (it had been abolished by the Provisional Government) and unleased a ghastly reign of terror. The Red Army and the Cheka (secret police) systematically destroyed the enemies of the revolution as well as those who were only lukewarm in their support of the new regime. Prison camps and repressive terror harsher than any since Ivan IV dominated life in the Russian state. In July 1918, the former tsar and his family, under house arrest since the outbreak of the revolution, were herded into the cellar of the house in which they were being held and executed.

After the Central Powers surrendered in November 1918, Allied intervention in Russia ceased, and the Bolsheviks concentrated their energies against the Whites. Trotsky turned the Red Army into a disciplined, centralized force. The disorganized and dispersed White opposition, whose units ranged from Siberia to the Caucasus to Europe, could not match the Red forces. Taking advantage of their shorter supply lines, ideological unity, and dislike of Allied intervention, the Bolsheviks put an end to White resistance by 1920. The Whites were united on few issues besides their hatred of the Bolsheviks. After their defeat, nearly a million of them scattered across the globe, eternal émigrés grieving the loss of their country and their dreams.

Theory, Reality, and the State

Lenin had no hesitation about revising Marx' doctrines to fit Russian conditions. He had long opposed all democratic parliamentary procedures, especially the concept of an officially recognized opposition party. He advocated instead a revolutionary "dictatorship of the proletariat" under Bolshevik leadership. The new order would rule in accord with "democratic centralism," in which the vanguard party would anticipate the best interests of the masses and rule for them.

Lenin altered certain aspects of the Marxist concept of the historical process.[8] He accepted the view that the proletarian-socialist revolution must be preceded by a bourgeois-democratic revolution. He interpreted the March 1917 events as the first democratic revolution and his own coup d'état in November as the second, or proletarian-socialist, revolution. This approach drastically shortened the historical process by which the bourgeois stage was to run its course. Lenin justified dissolving the constituent assembly on the grounds that a higher form of democratic principle had now been achieved, making the constituent assembly superfluous. The November revolution had vested all power

This photograph of Lenin with Josef Stalin was taken in 1922, shortly after Stalin had been appointed general secretary of the Central Committee of the Communist Party.

in the Russian republic in the people themselves, as expressed in their revolutionary committees, or soviets.

Many orthodox Marxists believed that the state would "wither away" once the dictatorship of the proletariat had eliminated the bourgeoisie. Once in power, however, Lenin found that he had to create a far stronger, more efficient state to govern Russia. The Bolsheviks, as the ultimate democratic centralists, ruled with an iron hand and prepared the way for the totalitarianism of Josef Stalin.

The state acted in many spheres. In policies reminiscent of Robespierre's tenure during the French Revolution, the new government attacked the church, changed the calendar (adopting the Gregorian and rejecting the Julian system), and simplified the alphabet. The Cheka enforced ideological unity with a level of terror that set a standard for later Soviet secret police organizations. The individual came to be ground down by the all-encompassing power of the state.

In the first six years after Lenin seized power, there were three major developments relating to the Communist party, the name adopted by the Bolsheviks in 1918. First, all other parties were suppressed. Second, the function of the party itself was changed from that of carrying out the revolution to that of governing the country.[9] Third, within the party itself, a small elite group, the Politburo, consolidated power in its hands. The first Politburo included Lenin, Trotsky, Stalin, Zinoviev, Kamenev, Bubnov, and Sokolnikov. The second major organ of the party was the Secretariat for the Central Committee which oversaw the implementation of policy into practice.

The state, itself, came to be known as the Russian Socialist Federated Soviet Republic (RSFSR). As the Moscow-based communist government extended its authority after the civil war, the jurisdiction of the RSFSR grew. In 1922, the Union of Soviet Socialist Republics (USSR) was formed consisting of the four constituent socialist republics: the RSFSR, the Ukraine, White Russia (Belorussia), and Transcaucasia.

The communists had established the first constitution for their government in 1918, but events and growth soon led to the need for a new one, which was adopted in 1924. It set up a system based on a succession of soviets in villages, factories, and cities. This pyramid of soviets in each constituent republic culminated in the All-Union Congress of Soviets at the apex of the federal government. But, while it appeared that the congress exercised sovereign power, this body was actually governed by the Communist party, which was controlled in turn by the Politburo.

So great did the authority of the Communist party become over the formation and administration of policy that before Lenin's death in early 1924 it could be said without exaggeration that party and state were one. Consequently, whoever controlled the party controlled the state, and in the new Soviet state the key person would be Josef Stalin.

War Communism and the NEP

Lenin's ability as a politician can be seen in his flexibility between 1917 and 1924. From 1918 to 1921 he tried to apply undiluted Marxist principles to eliminate private ownership of land, nationalize banks, railways, and shipping, and restrict the money economy. This policy, known as war communism, was widely unpopular. The peasants who had just attained their centuries-long goal of controlling their own land did not like the prospects of collectivization and the surrender of their surplus grain to the state. Many workers did not want to be forced to work in factories. Former managers showed little enthusiasm for running enterprises for the state's benefit.

In the early months of 1920 the new government faced its most dangerous crisis to date. Six years of war and civil strife had left Russia exhausted. Industrial production was 13 percent of what it had been 1914. Crop failures, poor management, and transportation breakdowns contributed to the disaster. Famine brought more than 20 million people to the brink of starvation. The government was forced to ask for help, and organizations such as Herbert Hoover's American aid project helped Russia through the crisis, but not before about 5 million people died.[10]

Internal chaos plus controversy with Poland over disputed borders further plagued Lenin's government. From 1918–1921 other areas of the former Russian empire—Finland, Estonia, Latvia, Lithuania, and Bessarabia—chose to go their own way. In February 1921 sailors at Kronstadt, formerly supporters of the regime, rebelled against the Bolsheviks and were massacred by the Red Army. Lenin said that the revolt "illuminated reality like a flash of lightning,"[11] and chose to make an ideological retreat.

War Communism was a total failure. Lenin decided that it was necessary to take "one step backwards in order to go two steps forward." He explained that Russia had tried to do too much too soon in attempting to change everything at once. He also noted that there had not been a firestorm of complementary communist revolutions sweeping the globe. The outbreaks in Germany and Hungary had been brutally squashed. Russia stood alone. Compromise was necessary to survive, and besides altering his diplomatic front abroad, he recommended a return to certain practices of capitalism, the so-called new Economic Policy, or NEP.

This retreat from War Communism lasted from 1921 to 1928 and allowed the Russian state to get on its feet. Peasants were relieved from the wholesale appropriation of grain. After paying a fixed tax, they were permitted to sell their surplus produce in the open market. Private management could once again run firms and factories employing less than twenty employees. Workers in state industries received a graduated wage scale. Foreign commerce and technology were actively sought. These compromises proved to be highly beneficial, and the Soviet economy revived.

Ideological purists criticized the policy and pointed out that the kulaks, as those ambitious peasants who accumulated property were called, and private businesses profited greatly. Lenin's concessions and compromises gave the communists time to regroup and recover, and the Russian people gained much-needed breathing space. Lenin emphasized the absolute necessity for the party to "control the commanding heights of the economy." The state continued to manage banking, transportation, heavy industry, and public utilities.

The NEP was Lenin's last major contribution. In broken health since he survived an assassin's bullet in 1918, he worked as much as he was able until his death in January 1924. In his fifty-four years Lenin deeply changed the world's history. He bequeathed to the globe its first Marxist state and provided the base from which his variant of Marxism could spread. He changed the tone and tactics of Marxism, stripping it of much that was humane and tolerant. His defenders argue that such steps were needed to apply a theory intended for industrialized society to an agrarian state. His critics argue that his methods and ideas were merely the reflection of his own ego. His tomb in Moscow's Red Square in which his embalmed body was placed on display became a Mecca for thousands of followers to come to pay homage to the creator of the Soviet state. Ironically, this secular, atheistic man who led a spartan existence was made by Stalin into a cult figure at the center of a new religion.

Trotsky vs. Stalin

A weakness of all dictatorships is that there is no well-defined mechanism to pass power from one leader to the next. Lenin was the one person in the party who possessed unchallenged authority and whose decrees were binding. After his death, Leon Trotsky and Joseph Stalin, rivals with conflicting policies and personalities, fought for power.

Leon Trotsky (1879–1940), born Lev Davidovich Bronstein, was a star in the political arena. He was a magnificent, charismatic orator, and energetic and magnetic leader in all areas, and a first-rate intellectual and theoretician. He turned to Marxism as a teenager and, like Lenin, had been exiled to Siberia for his revolutionary activities. He participated in the major events of Russian Social Democracy. Trotsky was a member of the *Iskra* group, had been present in London in 1903 for the Bolshevik-Menshevik split (see p. 666), played a key role in the 1905 Russian revolution, and was an essential figure in the 1917 revolutions and the Civil War. He had an ego and arrogance that contrasted with the shrewd and cunning nature of his less colorful, but more calculating rival.

Joseph Stalin (1879–1953), born in Georgia as Joseph Vissarionovich Dzhugashvili, labored for the revolution in obscurity. Where Trotsky was a star, Stalin worked behind the scenes. Trotsky was a crowd-pleasing orator; Stalin, when he spoke in his second language, Russian—Georgian was his first—was not an inspiring speaker. Admitted to a seminary to be trained for the priesthood, the young Stalin was later expelled for radical opinions. In the years before the revolutions, Stalin served the Bolsheviks by robbery to gain funds for the party's organization and propaganda activities. In all ways he faithfully supported Lenin, unlike Trotsky, who had not been a uniformly obedient disciple. Stalin was exiled a number of times east of the Urals before he returned to Petrograd in 1917 to play an active role in the events of that year. He knew his own strengths and weaknesses. He also formed his opinion of Trotsky rather early on, characterizing him in 1907 as being "beautifully useless."[12]

After the 1917 revolutions Stalin did a lot of the less glamorous organizational work of the party, along with being responsible for dealing with the various nationalities. While others in the Politburo dealt with ideological questions or fought the civil war, Stalin built up his own network of associates and gained control of the bureaucracy. In 1922, *Pravda*, the official party newspaper, carried a brief announcement that the Central Committee had confirmed Stalin as general secretary of the secretariat, a position that became the most powerful in the Soviet Union.

After Lenin's death, Stalin moved to construct a new secular religion for the Soviet Union. Leninism—complete with the renaming of Petrograd to Leningrad—formed in 1924, remained powerful for more than sixty years. The mark of faith came to be unquestioning loyalty to Lenin. Stalin became Lenin's St. Peter, even though Lenin had criticized both Trotsky and him in his so-called last will and testament, which, although written in 1922, was not widely published until the 1950s.[13]

In the competition with Trotsky, Stalin won because he was the better organizer and the more skillful manipulator of people. Staying in the background, the modest "helper," Stalin played the game of divide and conquer as members of the Politburo fought among themselves. By 1926 party members realized that Stalin had consolidated his position and had the full support of the party apparatus. By the end of that year, Trotsky and other opponents were removed from the Politburo. By 1929, Stalin was referred to as the "Lenin of today." Stalin's supporters occupied the key posts in both government and party, and he became the chairman of the Politburo. By 1940 he had eliminated all of the old Bolsheviks, including Trotsky, who was exiled and finally struck down by an assassin's ice axe in Mexico, on Stalin's orders.

More than just an opportunist or a superbureaucrat, Stalin too had ideological views on the future of the country. Trotsky and others had believed along with Lenin that the USSR could not survive indefinitely as a socialist island in a capitalist ocean. It was the duty, they held, of Russian communists to push for revolution elsewhere. Stalin, less a theorist than a political realist, viewed the idea of a world revolution as premature. He correctly noted that Marxism had made little headway outside the USSR, despite the existence of what, from the Marxist standpoint, were advantageous conditions for revolution in Germany and Italy. Stalin called for a new policy—"building up socialism in a single state." (Lenin had once hinted at that alternative in 1921.) He put an end to the NEP, and began taking "two steps forward"—with results that were both brutal and far-reaching.

Economics and Totalitarianism

Russia had begun industrialization at a late date, and from the 1890s on was continuously aware of its backwardness. The drastic impact of the war and civil war destroyed much of the progress that had been made, and by the late 1920s Stalin was deeply concerned with the country's economic weakness. He ordered a radical overhaul of the entire country and society to make fifty years progress in ten.

The NEP was scrapped in 1928 and Stalin imposed a series of five-year plans calling for heavy industrialization and collectivization of agriculture. Long working hours and a six-day week were instituted in the attempt to revolutionize Russia's economic structure. For the first time in history, a government truly controlled all significant economic activity through a central planning apparatus.

In the struggle to achieve its goals, the USSR went through what one scholar has called the "totalitarian breakthrough," in which there was "an all-out effort to destroy the basic institutions of the old order and to construct at least the framework of the new."[14] To drive the entire population along, Stalin strengthened his secret police so they could force the nation through what would be a decade of convulsive internal struggle. By 1939 Stalin had consolidated his personal dictatorship, at the cost of between 10 and 20 million lives.

War on the Peasants

Stalin wanted to transform the peasants into a rural proletariat, raising food on state and collective farms, not on their own plots. He had little doctrinal help from Marx, who had not considered that the revolution he forecast could take place in a peasant-dominated society. Marx left little guidance about what to do with the peasants, beyond mention of collectivized agriculture. He had assumed that capitalism would convert peasants into day laborers before the socialist revolution took place. Hence farming would continue, except now the state would own the farms.

Lenin's War Communism programs had failed, yet Stalin went back to them as he drew up his guidelines to transform agriculture. The major problem he faced was to convince the peasants to surrender their private lands, which they had finally got in 1917, to the state and collective farms.

Under Stalin's program, the state farms (*sovkhoz*) would be owned outright by the government, which would pay the workers' wages. The collective farms (*kolkhoz*) would be created from land taken from the *kulaks*—that hazily defined group of farmers who owned implements or employed others—and from the peasants who would voluntarily accept the government's decree to merge their own holdings. The *kolkhoz* members would work the land under the management of a board of directors. At the end of the year, the farm's net earnings would be totaled in cash and in kind, and the members would be paid on the basis of the amount and skill of their labor.

The theoretical advantages of large-scale mechanized farming over small-scale peasant agriculture were obvious. In addition, the government intended the reforms to permit the more efficient political education of the peasants. Further, the new programs would liquidate the *kulaks*, successful capitalist farmers who owned more property than their neighbors and who represented a disturbing element on the socialist landscape.

In actual practice, Stalin's collectivization program was a disaster. The vast majority of the peasants disagreed violently with Stalin's program. They did not want to give up their land. When the peasants did not flock to the government's banners, Stalin ordered harsher methods. When the class war between the poor peasants and the *kulaks* did not take place, he sent the secret police and the army to the villages. The transition to collectivization was carried out under some of the most barbarous and brutal measures ever enacted by a government against its own people.

In the butchery that followed, millions of people, especially in the Ukraine, died either from direct attack or starvation or in work camps. By a decree of February 1930, the state forced about one million *kulaks* off their land and took their possessions. Many peasants opposed these measures and slaughtered their herds and destroyed their crops rather than hand them over to the state. The number of horses in 1933 fell to below 50 percent of the 1928 number and there were 40 percent fewer cattle and half as many sheep and goats.[15]

In some sections the peasants rebelled en masse, and thousands were executed by firing squads. Villages that failed to capitulate were surrounded by army units which opened fire with machine guns. Official policy resulted in dislocation, destruction of animals and crops, and famine that claimed millions of lives. After nine years of war on the peasants, 90 percent of the land and 100 million peasants were in the collective and state farms.

Stalin's plan for economic revitalization of Russia called for collectivization of agriculture and heavy industrial development. The introduction of new machinery, like tractors, was intended to increase agricultural output and at the same time allow the state to remove agricultural laborers from the land and put them to work in factories.

Stalin and State Terror

Stalin's totalitarianism brought the development of state terror to unparalleled heights.
Nadezhda Mandelstam defined the nature of the terror.

When I used to read about the French Revolution as a child, I often wondered whether it was possible to survive during a reign of terror. I now know beyond doubt that it is impossible. Anybody who breathes the air of terror is doomed, even if nominally he manages to save his life. Everybody is a victim—not only those who die, but also all the killers, ideologists, accomplices and sycophants who close their eyes and wash their hands—even if they are secretly consumed with remorse at night. Every section of the population has been through the terrible sickness caused by terror, and none has so far recovered, or become fit again for normal civic life. It is an illness that is passed on to the next generation, so that the sons pay for the sins of the fathers and perhaps only the grandchildren begin to get over it—or at least it takes on a different form with them. . . .

The principles and aims of mass terror have nothing in common with ordinary police work or with security. The only purpose of terror is intimidation. To plunge the whole country into a state of chronic fear, the number of victims must be raised to astronomical levels, and on every floor of every building there must always be several apartments from which the tenants have suddenly been taken away. The remaining inhabitants will be model citizens for the rest of their lives—this will be true for every street and every city through which the broom has swept. The only essential thing for those who rule by terror is not to overlook the new generations growing up without faith in their elders, and to keep on repeating the process in systematic fashion. Stalin ruled for a long time and saw to it that the waves of terror recurred from time to time, always on an even greater scale than before. But the champions of terror invariably leave one thing out of account—namely, that they can't kill everyone, and among their cowed, half-demented subjects there are always witnesses who survive to tell the tale. . . .

Excerpted from *Hope Against Hope: A Memoir* by Nadezhda Mandelstam, pp. 297–298, 304–305, 316–317, 369–371. Translated from the Russian by Max Hayward with introduction by Clarence Brown. Copyright © 1970 Atheneum Publishers. English translation copyright © 1970 Atheneum Publishers. Introduction copyright © 1970 Atheneum Publishers. Reprinted with the permission of Atheneum Publishers and Collins Publishers.

At the time, the atrocities accompanying Stalin's programs were largely overlooked or unknown in the west. Not until World War II was a casualty figure given, and then only casually when Stalin mentioned to British Prime Minister Winston Churchill a loss of life totalling around 10 million people. Only now are Soviet authorities telling the story of the massive suffering inflicted on the Soviet peasantry.[16]

The Five-Year Plans

Stalin introduced the system of central planning in 1928. He and his advisers assumed that by centralizing all aspects of the allocation of resources and removing market forces from the economy they could ensure a swift buildup of capital goods and heavy industries. The five-year plans, which began in 1929, restricted the manufacture of consumer goods and abolished capitalism in the forms permitted under the NEP. Citizens were allowed to own certain types of private property, houses, furniture, clothes, and personal effects. They could not own property that could be used to make profits by hiring workers. The state was to be the only employer.

The first five-year plan called for a 250 percent increase in overall industrial productivity. The state and police turned their entire effort to this goal. Even in the chaos that occurred—when buildings were erected for no machines and machines were shipped to where there were no buildings—growth did take place.

Whether the statistics the party cited to prove that the plan had been achieved in four- and one-half years were accurate—and they have been vigorously challenged—Soviet industry and society were totally transformed. The costs were disastrous, but Stalin portrayed Russia as being in a form of war with the world, and without strength, he pointed out, Russia would be crushed.

The second five-year plan began in 1933 and sought to resolve some of the mistakes of the first. The government placed greater emphasis on improving the quality of industrial products and on making more consumer goods. The third plan, begun in 1938, emphasized national defense. State strategies called for industrial plants to be shifted east of the Urals, and efforts were made to develop new sources of oil and other important commodities. Gigantism was the key, as the world's largest tractor factory was built in Chelyabinsk, the greatest power station in Dnepropetrovsk, and the largest automobile plant in Gorki.

The plans achieved remarkable results. In 1932 Soviet authorities claimed an increase in industrial output of 334 percent over 1914; 1937 output was 180 percent over 1932. But the high volume of production was often tied to mediocre quality, and the achievements were gained only with an enormous cost in human life and suffering. At first the burdensome cost of importing heavy machinery, tools, equipment, and finished steel from abroad forced a subsistence scale of living on the people. These purchases were paid for by the sale of food and raw material in the world's markets at a time when the prices for such goods had drastically fallen.

In the rush to industrialize, basic aspects of Marxism were set aside. The dictatorship *of* the proletariat increasingly became the dictatorship *over* the proletariat. Another ideological casualty was the basic concept of economic egalitarianism. In 1931 Stalin declared that equality of wages was "alien and detrimental to Soviet production" and a "petit-bourgeois deviation." So much propaganda was used to implant this twist that the masses came to accept the doctrine of inequality of wages as a fundamental communist principle. Piecework in industry became more prevalent, and bonuses and incentives were used to speed up production. It is ironic that capitalist practices were used to stimulate the growth of the communist economy. Stalin and Russia had deviated far from the Marxist maxim of "from

Economic activity in Stalinist Russia was carefully regulated by Stalin's five-year plans. Here, workers operate an oil rig.

This scene from a purge trial in Moscow in 1930 shows one of the eight defendants, all accused of treason, giving testimony. All eight were convicted; five were accorded the death penalty, the other three were given ten-year sentences.

each according to his ability, to each according to his need." Until the 1950s centralized planning enabled Russia to build a powerful industrial base and survive Hitler's assault. However, in the past four decades, as the Soviet economy has had to become more flexible, the system has proven to be counterproductive.

The Great Purges

During the 1930s Stalin consolidated his hold over the communist party and created the political system that would last until the ascent to power of Mikhail Gorbachev. Stalin established an all-powerful, personal totalitarian rule by doing away with all of his rivals, real and potential, in the purges. He also took the opportunity to remove all scientific, cultural, and educational figures who did not fit in with his plans for the future. By the end of the decade, Russians marched to Stalin's tune, or they did not march.[17]

The long arm of the secret police gathered in thousands of Soviet citizens to face the kangaroo court and the firing squad. All six original members of the 1920 Politburo who survived Lenin were purged by Stalin. Old Bolsheviks who had been loyal comrades of Lenin, high officers of the Red Army, directors of industry, and rank-and-file party members were liquidated. Millions more were sent to forced labor camps. It has been estimated that between 5 and 6 percent of the population spent time in the pretrial prisons of the secret police.

Party discipline prevented party members from turning against Stalin, who controlled the party. The world watched a series of show trials in which loyal communists confessed to an amazing array of charges, generally tied after 1934 to the assassination—probably at Stalin's orders—of Sergei Kirov, Leningrad party chief and one of Stalin's chief aides. Western journalists reported news of the trials to the world, while the drugged, tortured, and intimidated defendants confessed to crimes they had not committed. A large portion of the leadership of the USSR was destroyed. By 1939, 70 percent of the members of the central committee elected in

1934 had been purged. In the armed forces officer corps, the purges claimed 3 of 5 army marshals, 14 of 16 army commanders, 8 of 8 admirals, 60 of 67 corps commanders, 136 of 199 divisional commanders, 221 of 397 brigade commanders, and roughly one-half of the remaining officer corps, or some 35,000 men.[18] In a sense, the purges culminated in Mexico with Trotsky's assassination in 1940.

The lessons of the purges were chilling and effective. The way to succeed, to survive, was to be a dependable member of the apparatus—an *apparatchik*.

Changes in Soviet Society

In the twenty years after 1917, all aspects of Soviet society came under the purview of the party. The atomization of society, a prime characteristic of totalitarian government, did not permit such secret and trustful groups as the family to exist at ease. The party dealt in contradictory terms with various aspects of social life, but by and large the government worked to weaken the importance of the family. Initially after the revolution, divorces required no court proceedings, abortions were legalized, women were encouraged to take jobs outside the home, and communist nurseries were set up to care for children while their mothers worked. Pressure on the family continued under Stalin, but in different ways. Children were encouraged to report to the authorities "antirevolutionary" statements made by their parents.

The party did work to upgrade medical care, improve the treatment of the nationalities—at least initially—and extend educational opportunities. But even here political goals outweighed humanitarian objectives. Education existed primarily to indoctrinate pupils with communist precepts and values. Religious persecution was widespread. The church lost most of its power in education, and religious training was prohibited, except in the home.

The constitution of 1936 declared, "All power in the USSR belongs to the workers of town and country as represented by the Soviet of workers' deputies." Ironically, this document did not mention the Soviet Union's official ideology of Marxism-Leninism and referred only once to the communist party. On the surface, the 1936 constitution affirmed many basic rights, such as free speech, secret ballot, and universal suffrage, but it was mere window-dressing with no relationship to reality. Secret ballots meant little in a one-party state, and the parliament of the people, the Supreme Soviet, had no power. The Communist party, with a membership of less than 1.5 percent of the total population, dictated the life of each individual.

In the first decade after the revolution, intellectuals and artists experienced much more freedom than they would in the 1930s. The party emphasized the tenets of social realism but permitted some innovation. The Bolsheviks initially tolerated and even encouraged writers of independent leanings. Even though a large number of artists and writers fled the country after the revolution, others, including the poet Alexander Blok (1880–1921) and Vladimir Mayakovsky (1893–1930), remained and continued to write. During the NEP, Russia's cultural life bloomed in many areas, especially the cinema as can be seen in the works of the great director Sergei Eisenstein (1898–1948). In music, composers Sergei Prokofiev (1891–1953) and Dmitri Shostakovich (1906–1975) contributed works that added to the world's musical treasury.

Once Stalin gained control, he dictated that all art, science, and thought should serve the party's program and philosophy. Artists and thinkers were to become, in Stalin's words, "engineers of the mind." Art for art's sake was counterrevolutionary. Socialist realism in its narrowest sense was to be pursued. History became a means to prove the correctness of Stalin's policies.

Under Stalin's totalitarian rule, critics and censors tightened their control over artists and scholars. Artists and intellectuals found it safer to investigate, write, and perform according to the party line. Literary hacks and propagandists gained official favor, churning out what western critics referred to as "tractor novels."

Italy and Mussolini

After entering the war on the Allied side in 1915, Italy entered the peace negotiations with great expectations. The Italians had joined the

Allies with the understanding that with victory they would gain a part of Albania, Trieste, Dalmatia, Trentino, and some territory in Asia Minor. They came away from Versailles with minor gains, not nearly enough to justify the deaths of 700,000 of their youth.

Postwar Italy suffered social and economic damage similar to that of the other combatants. Inflation—the lira fell to one-third of its prewar value—and disrupted trade patterns hampered recovery. These ailments exacerbated the domestic crises the country had been struggling with before the war.[19] There were not enough jobs for the returning soldiers, and unemployed veterans were ripe targets for the growing extremist parties. In some cities residents refused to pay their rent in protest over poor living conditions.

Benito Mussolini, shown here speaking to a crowd in 1934, promised that a strong state could cure Italy's postwar ills, strengthen its economy, and rebuild national pride.

In the countryside, peasants took land from landlords. Everywhere food was in short supply.

In the four years after the armistice, five premiers came and went, either because of their own incompetence or because of the insolubility of the problems they faced. The situation favored the appearance of "a man on a white horse," a dictator. Such a man was a blacksmith's son named Mussolini, who bore the Christian name of Benito, in honor of the Mexican revolutionary hero Benito Juarez.

Benito Mussolini (1883–1945) grew up in and around left-wing political circles. Although he became editor of the influential socialist newspaper *Avanti* ("*Forward*") in 1912, he was far from consistent in his views and early on demonstrated his opportunism and pragmatism. When a majority of the Italian Socialist party called for neutrality in World War I, Mussolini came out for intervention. Party officials removed *Avanti* from his control and expelled him from the party. He then proceeded to put out his own paper, *Il Popolo d'Italia* ("*The People of Italy*"), in which he continued to call for Italian entry into the war on the Allied side.

To carry out his interventionist campaign, Mussolini organized formerly leftist groups into bands called *fasci*, a named derived from the Latin *fasces*, the bundle of rods bound around an axe, which was the symbol of authority in ancient Rome. When Italy entered the war, Mussolini volunteered for the army, saw active service at the front, and suffered a wound. When he returned to civilian life, he reorganized the *fasci* into the *fasci di combattimento* ("fighting groups") to attract war veterans and try to gain control of Italy.

The Path to Power

In the 1919 elections, the freest until 1946, the Socialists capitalized on the mass unemployment and hardship to become the strongest party. But the party lacked effective leadership and failed to take advantage of its position.

The extreme right-wing groups did not elect a single candidate to the Chamber of Deputies, but they pursued power in other ways. The fiery writer and nationalist leader, Gabriele D'Annunzio (1863–1938), had occupied the disputed city of Fiume with his corps of followers, in direct

Mussolini on Fascism

Benito Mussolini laid out his definition of fascism in the *Enciclopedia Italiana* in 1932.

He noted that fascism like every sound political conception . . . is both practice and thought; action in which a doctrine is immanent, and a doctrine which, arising out of a given system of historical forces, remains embedded in them and works there from within. . . .

The nation as the State is an ethical reality which exists and lives in so far as it develops. To arrest its development is to kill it. Therefore the State is not only the authority which governs and gives the form of laws and the value of spiritual life to the wills of individuals, but it is also a power that makes its will felt abroad, making it known and respected, in other words, demonstrating the fact of its universality in all the necessary directions of its development. It is consequently organized and expansion, at least virtually. Thus it can be likened to the human will which knows no limits to its development and realizes itself in testing its own limitlessness.

The Fascist State, the highest and most powerful form of personality, is a force, but a spiritual force, which takes over all the forms of the moral and intellectual life of man. It cannot therefore confine itself simply to the functions of order and supervision as Liberalism desired. It is not simply a mechanism which limits the sphere of the supposed liberties of the individual. It is the form, the inner standard and the discipline of the whole person; it saturates the will as well as the intelligence. Its principle, the central inspiration of the human personality living in the civil community, pierces into the depths and makes its home in the heart of the man of action as well as of the thinker, of the artist as well as of the scientist: it is the soul of the soul.

Fascism, in short, is not only the giver of laws and the founder of institutions, but the educator and promoter of spiritual life. It wants to remake, not the forms of human life, but its content, man, character, faith. And to this end it requires discipline and authority that can enter into the spirits of men and there govern unopposed. Its sign, therefore, is the Lictors' rods, the symbol of unity, of strength and justice.

---

violation of the directives of the Paris peace conference. This defiance of international authority appealed to the fascist movement. D'Annunzio provided lessons for the observant Mussolini, who copied many of the writer's methods and programs.[20]

The fascists gained the backing of landowning and industrial groups, who feared the victory of Marxist socialism in Italy. Mussolini's toughs beat up opponents, broke strikes, and disrupted opposition meetings in 1919 and 1920 while the government did nothing. Despite these activities, the extreme right-wing politicians still failed to dominate the 1921 elections. Only thirty-five fascists, Mussolini among them, gained seats in the Chamber of Deputies while the liberal and democratic parties gained a plurality. Failing to succeed through the existing system, Mussolini established the National Fascist party in November.

The Liberal-Democratic government of 1922 proved to be as ineffective as its predecessors, and the socialists continued to bicker among themselves. Mussolini's party however, attracted thousands of disaffected middle-class people, cynical and opportunistic intellectuals, and workers. Frustration with the central government's incompetence, not fear of the left, fueled the fascist rise. One historian has noted," . . . it was not on political ideas that fascism thrived, but on the yearning for action and the opportunities it provided for satisfying this yearning."[21]

In August 1922 the trade unions called a general strike to protest the rise of fascism. Mussolini's forces smashed their efforts. In October, after a huge rally in Naples, 50,000 fascists swarmed into Rome and soon thereafter king Victor Emmanuel III invited Mussolini to form a new government. During the next month Mussolini constructed a cabinet composed of his party members and nationalists and gained dictatorial powers to bring stability to the country. The fascists remained a distinct minority in Italy, but by gaining control of the central government they could place their members and allies in positions of power. The October "March on Rome" ushered in Mussolini's twenty-year reign.

Building the Fascist State

Mussolini followed no strict ideology as he consolidated his dictatorial rule. He threw out all the democratic procedures of the postwar years and dissolved rival political parties. He and his colleagues ruthlessly crushed free expression and banished critics of their government to prison settlements off Italy's southern coast. They censored the press and set-up tribunals for the defense of the state (not the citizens). Although he retained the shell of the old system, Mussolini established a totally new state.

Mussolini controlled all real power through the Fascist Grand Council, whose members occupied the government's ministerial posts. At one

The Fascists, dressed in their characteristic black shirts, began their march on Rome in October 1922. On October 29, the king telegraphed Mussolini in Milan to ask him to form a new government. The next day Mussolini arrived in triumph in Rome.

One of the most ominous acts of Mussolini's fascist regime was the burning of books and other literature considered "subversive."

time, Mussolini himself held no fewer than eight offices. All this activity and centralization of power provided a striking contrast to the lethargy of the four years immediately after the war. Encouraged by the popular support for his regime, Mussolini passed a series of laws in 1925 and 1926 in which the Italian cities lost their freely elected self-governments, and all units of local and provincial government were welded into a unified structure controlled from Rome.

Once he centralized Italian political life, Mussolini pursued the development of his ideology in a pragmatic manner. As one scholar noted, "If he had any principle or prejudice it was against the capitalists, the Church, and the monarchy; all of his life he abused the bourgeoisie."[22] But he would learn to work with all of those elements in his flexible pursuit of power. He once stated in an interview, "I am all for motion."[23] Movement, not consistency and science, marked his ideology.

Early in the 1920s Mussolini, a former atheist, began to tie the church into the structure of his new society. In 1928 he negotiated the Lateran Treaty with church representatives in order to settle the longstanding controversy between Rome and the Vatican. The new pact required compulsory religious instruction and recognized Catholicism as the state religion. Vatican City, a new state of 108 acres located within Rome itslef, was declared to be fully sovereign and independent. In addition the state promised the Vatican $91 million. Mussolini gained a measure of approval from devout Italians and the Vatican's support for his fascist government.

Mussolini's economic system, which has come to be known as state capitalism, aimed to abolish class conflict through cooperation between labor and capital, by state force if necessary. In communist theory, labor is the basis of society. In fascism, labor and capital are both instruments of the state. The fascists constructed a corporate state, in which the country was divided into syndicates, or corporations: thirteen at first, later twenty-two. Initially six of these came from labor and an equal number represented capital or management. The thirteenth group was established for the professions. Under state supervision, these bodies were to deal with labor disputes, guarantee adequate wage scales,
control prices, and supervise working conditions. After 1926 strikes by workers and lockouts by employers were prohibited.

The pragmatic Mussolini believed that private enterprise was the "most efficient method" of production. "The state intervenes in economic production only when private enterprise fails or is insufficient or when the political interests of the state are involved."[24] Mussolini liked to claim that his structure embodied a classless economic system that stood as one of fascism's greatest contributions to political theory.

Reflecting the practice of the time, the Italians sought economic self-sufficiency, especially in the areas of food supply, power resources, and foreign trade. Wheat production and hydroelectric generating capacity both increased, but the drive for self-sufficiency was carried to an extreme and unprofitable degree. The state, in its quest for economic independence, launched many projects to provide for a home supply of products that could be obtained much more cheaply from other nations.

State and Struggle

Mussolini's ideology built in a haphazard way on the cult of the leader, or "great man." The Italian dictator asserted that "life for the Fascist is a continuous, ceaseless fight . . . ," and "struggle is at the origin of all things."[25] Aside from statements of this type and his economic theories, it is difficult to determine exactly what Mussolini intended fascism to be, beyond being nationalistic, anti-communist, anti-democratic, expansionist, and statist. The lack of a theoretical base for his programs and policies did not concern Mussolini. He simply believed that his corporate state offered a solution to the basic social questions of the twentieth century.[26]

In his speeches, Mussolini referred constantly to the legacy of the Roman empire. He encouraged a high birth rate, but noted that individuals were significant only in so far as they were part of the state. Children were indoctrinated "to believe, to obey, and to fight."

Beneath the talk of struggle and the trappings of grandeur was the reality of Italy. Mussolini was no Stalin or Hitler, and his fascism was a far milder form of totalitarianism than that seen in the USSR or Nazi Germany. The Italian people simply defused many of the potentially atrocious elements of fascist rule. There was no class destruction or genocide in Italy.[27] The Italians, who had endured control by Goths, Normans, French, and Austrians before unification, were survivors.

As in the case of the other dictatorships, Mussolini's programs had some worthwhile features such as slum clearance, rural modernization, and campaigns against illiteracy and malaria. The trains *did* run on time, as Mussolini boasted, and the omnipresent Mafia was temporarily dispersed, with many of its more notable figures fleeing to the United States. But these positive achievements were more than outweighed by the ruinous drives into Ethiopia (see p. 879), excessive military spending, and special benefits to large landowners and industrialists. In 1930 real wages remained low in comparison to the rest of industrialized Europe.

The depression hit Italy later than other countries, but it lasted longer and its effects were devastating to Mussolini's economy. The 33 percent increase in gross national product over that of 1914 was soon wiped out and the old problems of inadequate natural resources, unfavorable balance of trade, and expanding population made the country vulnerable to economic disaster. In 1933 the number of unemployed reached one million and the public debt soared to an alarming level.

Despite a reorganization of the nation in 1934 into twenty-two government controlled corporations, a massive public works program, and agricultural reforms, Italy continued to suffer. In the 1930s Italy's fate and future came to be closely tied to that of Germany.

The German Tragedy

In the first week of Novemver 1918, revolutions broke out all over Germany. Sailors stationed at Kiel rebelled; leftists in Munich revolted. The kaiser fled to Holland after the authority of his government crumbled. On November 9 the chancellor transferred his power to Friedrich Ebert, the leader of the majority party, the Social Democrats, and the new leader announced the establishment of a republic.

Violence spread quickly. The Spartacists, led by Karl Liebknecht and Rosa Luxemburg, who formed the German Communist party at the end of 1918, wanted a complete social and political revolution. Ebert's Social Democrats favored a democratic system in which the property rights would be maintained. At the beginning of 1919 the radical and moderate socialists clashed violently. Experiments in revolutionary government in Bavaria and Berlin horrified traditionalists and even the Social Democrats. In the spring a coalition of forces ranging from moderate

Military training began early in Mussolini's fascist state. There were youth organizations for every age group over the age of four.

Rosa Luxemburg. A radical Marxist and one of the leaders of the Spartacist insurrection in Germany, she was arrested and murdered while being taken to prison.

socialists to right-wing bands of unemployed veterans crushed the leftists and murdered Liebknecht and Luxemburg.

By the end of the year, Germany had weathered the threat of a leftist revolution. Meanwhile, the moderate parties triumphed in elections to select a constitutional convention, with the Social Democrats winning the most votes. The constitution they wrote at Weimar, adopted in mid-1919, created some of the problems that would plague the new government.

The liberal document provided for a president, a chancellor who was responsible to the Reichstag, and national referenda. In addition, the constitution guaranteed the rights of labor, personal liberty, and compulsory education for everyone up to the age of eighteen. Once the new system was put into operation, its weaknesses were readily apparent. The multitude of parties permitted by the constitution condemned the

government to function solely by shaky coalitions that often broke apart and forced the president to rule by emergency decree—thus bypassing legal constitutional procedures.

Failure of the Weimar Republic

The Weimar Republic faced overwhelming obstacles. First, the new republic had to live with the stigma of having accepted the Versailles treaty, with its infamous war guilt clause. The defeatist image, combined with opposition from both right- and left-wing extremists, plagued the Weimar moderates. The myth of betrayal in accepting the Versailles treaty helped Field Marshal Paul von Hindenburg, a stalwart Prussian and war hero, win election to the presidency in 1925. In 1927 he formally renounced the theory of war guilt, a politically popular move but one with little effect on the obligation to pay reparations. Although these payments did not noticeably affect the standard of living after 1925, they continued to be a visible sign of defeat— especially insofar as the money used to pay the victorious Allies had to come from foreign loans.[28]

The Weimar government ruled during an economically chaotic period. The government caused inflation, wiped out savings, and destroyed much of the middle classes' confidence, shaking the resolve of the group on whom the fate of the republic rested. Even after 1923, when the economy took a turn for the better, perceptive observers noted that the new prosperity rested on shaky foundations.

During the five years before the depression, Germany rebuilt its industrial plant with the most up-to-date equipment and techniques available to become the second-ranking industrial nation in the world. Rebuilding, however, was financed largely with foreign loans, including some $800 million from the United States.[29] In fact, the Germans borrowed almost twice as much money as they paid out. When the short-term loans came due, the economic bubble burst.

In addition to these economic difficulties, other problems plagued the Weimar government. Many people in Germany still idealized the authoritarian Prussian state. The German General Staff and its numerous and powerful supporters were not placed under effective civilian control. Disregarding the Versailles restrictions on military growth, Germany, in cooperation with the Soviet Union, the other European outcast, increased its armed forces in the 1920s. Probably more dangerous to the Weimar republic's existence was that group of individuals described by Peter Gay as the *Vernunftrepublikaner*, "rational republicans from intellectual choice rather than passionate conviction." These intellectuals, politicians, and businessmen who should have been the strength of Weimar, "learned to live with the Republic . . . but they

George Grosz, *The Pillars of Society*. The satirical painting captures the artist's contempt for militarism, capitalism, the complacent bourgeoisie, and the corrupt society of the Weimar Republic.

never learned to love it and never believed in its future."[30]

The insecurity of the middle classes was the factor most responsible for the failure of the Weimar republic. After the war and inflation, what professionals, white-collar workers, and skilled tradespeople feared most was being dragged down to the level of the masses. Right-wing orators played on such fears and warned that the Weimar republic could not stop the growth of communism. After 1929, the insecurity and discontent of the middle classes crystallized around their children, who blamed their parents for the catastrophe of 1918 and the humiliations that followed. German youth, many of them unemployed after 1929, repudiated the Weimar republic and sought a new savior for their country and themselves. In their rise to power, the Nazis skillfully exploited the fears and hopes of German middle-class youth.

Adolf Hitler

The man who was to "save the fatherland" came from outside its borders. Adolf Hitler (1889–1945) was born in Austria, the son of minor customs official in the Austro-Hungarian monarchy. A mediocre student and something of a loner during his school days, he went to Vienna in 1908 hoping to become an architect or artist. When he failed to gain acceptance to the art institute, his hopes of pursuing a career in art came to an early end.

In the cosmopolitan capital of Vienna, surrounded by a rich diversity of nationalities and religions, Hitler, always the loner, formed his political philosophy. He avidly read pamphlets written by racists who advocated the leader concept and variations of social Darwinism. Hajo Holborn has written that it was on the basis of such "popular and often cranky and murky writings that Hitler formed his original racist and anti-Semitic ideas . . . [He] derived his ideology from few sources, all of them of a rather low type."[31] Anti-Semitism was a popular political platform, and the city's mayor openly espoused it. Hitler also dabbled in Pan-Germanism and Marxian socialism. The swirl of ideas and theories percolated in the brain of the impoverished young man and furnished him with the motivations and ambitions that drove him forward.

A year before World War I, Hitler moved to Munich where he earned a meager living by selling his drawings. When the conflict erupted in 1914 he joined a German regiment and was sent to France where he fought well and bravely.[32] At the time of the armistice in 1918 he was in a hospital recovering from being blinded in a gas attack. He later said that news of Germany's defeat caused him to turn his face to the wall and weep bitterly.

Following his recovery, Hitler returned to Munich where he was hired by city authorities to act as a special agent to investigate extremists. In the line of duty he checked on a small organization called the German Workers' party. Hitler became attracted to the group's fervently nationalistic doctrine and agreed with their anti-democratic, anti-communist, and anti-Semitic beliefs. He joined the party and soon dominated it.

In 1920, the party took the name National Socialist German Workers' Party, and the words National Socialists (*Nationalsozialistiche*) became abbreviated to Nazi. That same year the party founded a newspaper to spread its views, formed a paramilitary organization from out-of-work veterans—the Storm Troops (SA), and adopted a symbol—the swastika set on a red background. The swastika has been used by many cultures to express the unending cycle of life. The red background symbolized the community of German blood.

More important than the party or its symbol was Hitler, who became widely known for his remarkable powers as a speaker. His ability to arouse and move mass audiences drew large crowds in Munich. Even those who hated all that he stood for were fascinated by his performances. In the early days he would hire a number of beer halls for his adherents and speed from one to the next delivering his emotion-filled message. He called for land reform, the nationalization of trusts, the abolition of all unearned incomes, expansion to include all German-speaking peoples in Europe, and the cancellation of the Versailles treaty. The points of his arguments were less important than the way he delivered them. As the ultimate demagogue he could package his concepts to fit whatever audience he addressed, and his popularity soared.

In November 1923, at the depth of Germany's crisis, Hitler staged his *Putsch*, or revolt, in Munich. Poorly planned and premature, the attempt failed. Hitler was sent to prison after his arrest and there, in comparatively luxurious conditions, he dictated his statement of principles in *Mein Kampf* (*My Struggle*). This work, far from a literary masterpiece, was both an autobiography and a long-winded exposition of Nazi philosophy and objectives.

In *Mein Kampf* Hitler wrote that history is fashioned by great races, of which the Aryan is the finest. The noblest Aryans, according to Hitler, are the Germans, who should rule the world. He charged that the Jews are the archcriminals of all time, that democracy is decadent, and communism is criminal. He stated that expansion into the Soviet Ukraine and the destruction of France are rightful courses for the Germans, who will use war and force, the proper instruments of the "strong," to achieve their goals.

The book, which was initially dismissed as the ravings of a wild man, was widely read in the 1930s. Its sales made Hitler a wealthy man.

Hitler's Chance

Hitler's first attempt to take advantage of economic disaster failed, but he would not fail the second time. After 1930 the *Führer* ("leader") took advantage of the desperate conditions resulting from closed banks, 6 million unemployed, and people roaming the streets for food. Night after night police and military police battled mobs of rioting communists and Nazis. The depression was "the last ingredient in a complicated witches' brew" that led to Hitler's takeover.[33]

The depression brought on the collapse of the moderates' position in the Weimar goverment. In the 1930 elections the Nazis increased their number of seats in the Reichstag from 12 to 107. As conditions grew worse, the hungry and frightened as well as rich and powerful turned to Hitler. The latter groups feared the communists and saw the *Führer* as a useful shield against a proletarian revolution.

As the Nazi movement grew in popularity, Hitler's brilliant propaganda chief, Joseph Goebbels, used every communications device available to convert the masses to Nazism. He staged huge spectacles all over Germany in which thousands of Storm Troopers and the audiences themselves all became supporting players to the "star" of the

drama, Adolf Hitler. Such controlled hysteria was more important than the message Hitler continued to repeat.

In March 1932 presidential elections, Hitler lost to Hindenburg. However, after a strong showing by the Nazis in the July Reichstag elections, Hindenburg asked Hitler to join a coalition government. The *Führer* refused, demanding instead the equivalent of dictatorial power. The stalemate led to the dissolution of the Reichstag in September, and for the next two months the government limped along, until a second general election was held. This costly campaign nearly emptied the Nazis' treasury. It was also politically costly in that they lost some of their seats in the Reichstag.

Some observers believed that the Nazis had passed the crest of their power. At this critical point, however, a clique of aristocratic nationalists and powerful industrialists, fearing a leftist revolution, offered Hitler the chancellorship. In January 1933 a mixed cabinet was created with Hitler at the head. Because he did not have a clear majority in the Reichstag, Hitler called another general election for March 5.

The Nazis used all the muscle at their disposal during this campaign. They monopolized the radio broadcasts and the press and their Storm Troopers bullied and beat the voters. Many Germans became disgusted with the strong-arm methods, and the tide definitely swung against the Nazis. Hitler needed a dramatic incident to gain a clear majority in the election.

On the evening of February 27, a fire gutted the Reichstag building. The blaze had been set by a twenty-four-year-old Dutchman, Marinus van der Lubbe, as a statement against capitalism. Apparently acting alone, van de Lubbe gave the Nazis the issue they needed to mobilize their support. Goebbels propaganda machine went into action to blame the fire on the international communist movement. Uncharacteristically, the propaganda minister overplayed the story, and most of the outside world came to believe that the Nazis themselves had set the fire.[34]

Hitler may not have made much profit from the incident internationally, but he did use it to win the election. The Nazis captured 44 percent of the deputies which, with the 8 percent controlled by the Nationalist party, gave them a bare

The Nazis attributed the burning of the Reichstag building to the Communists and used the incident to mobilize support for Hitler.

majority. Quickly, Hitler's forces put through the Enabling Act, which gave the *Führer* the right to rule by decree for the next four years.

Every aspect of the Weimar government was overturned, legally. The Nazis crushed all opposition parties and put aside the Weimar constitution, a document that was never formally abolished. Germany for the first time became national, not a federal, state. When Hindenburg died in 1934, Hitler became both chancellor and president. As if to put the world on notice that a renewed German force was rising in central Europe, he withdrew Germany from the League of Nations in 1933. Two years later, he introduced conscription, in defiance of the Versailles treaty.

Hitler proclaimed his regime to be the Third Reich, succeeding the First Reich of Otto the Great, which had lasted from 962 until 1806 and Bismarck's Second Reich, which lasted from 1871 to 1918. Hitler quickly introduced aspects of his Nazi variant of fascism, which was much more pernicious than Mussolini's. Hitler's ideology united the diverse German peoples and

expressed resentment against the rapid industrialization that had cut many of the people away from their traditional values. But it was primarily the racist elements of Aryan supremacy and hatred of the Jews that set Nazism apart.

War on the Jews

An essential part of the Nazi ideology was an absolute hatred of the Jews, an element of society the Nazi's considered unfit to continue in the new world. After crushing all opposition, real and potential, Hitler began to destroy the Jews. When he took power, he ruled over 500,000 Jews and 66 million Germans. Since 1880 the number of Jews in the population had been declining and would continue to do so through assimilation.[35] Hitler, however, proclaimed that Jews were everywhere and pledged to destroy the Jewish plot to gain control of the world. He based his policy on his own contempt for the Jews, not on the demographic reality.

All Jewish officials in the government lost their jobs, Jews were forbidden to pursue their business and industrial activities, and Jewish businesses were boycotted. Non-Jews snatched up at bargain prices valuable properties formerly owned by Jews. Non-Jewish doctors and

The banners proclaim the Nazis' message to Jews: "The Jews Are Our Ruin." "The Jews Are Our Disaster."

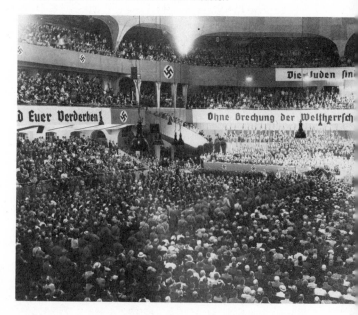

lawyers profited when Jewish professionals were forced from their practices. Hitler gained solid supporters among the business and professional classes as he pursued his racist policies.[36] Germans willingly believed that the Jews deserved their fate as the price they had to pay for the Versailles treaty, for the harmful aspects of capitalism, and for internationalism.

Half-hearted international protests failed to limit the anti-Semitic policies. Hitler had many fervent supporters both inside and outside Germany.

The Nazis built concentration camps immediately, but it was some time before they turned into death camps. In the meantime, the immediate pressures of government policies pushed many Jews into committing suicide. It has been estimated that in 1933 alone, 19,000 German citizens killed themselves and 16,000 more died from unexplained causes.

In 1935 the so-called Nuremberg laws came into force. Aryans and non-Aryans were forbid-

Nazi propaganda against the Jews was everywhere. This beer coaster reads, "Who buys from Jews is a traitor."

On *Kristallnacht,* thousands of shops owned by Jews were vandalized. Synagogues were set afire, valuables were confiscated, and many Jews were killed or sent to concentration camps.

den to marry. Jews (defined as any person of one-fourth or more Jewish blood) lost their citizenship, and anti-Semitic signs were posted in all public places. (During the 1936 Berlin Olympic games, these notices were taken down in order not to upset visitors.) Increasingly, there was public mention of the "inferior blood" of the Jews. As the state came to need more and more money for armaments, the Jews would be made to pay. This enterprise reached a climax on the evening of November 9, 1938, "the *Kristallnacht* or night of broken glass . . . [when] above the loss of life and heavy property damage, a fine of a billion marks was imposed on the Jewish community in retaliation for the murder of a German diplomat in Paris."[37]

Attacked, deprived of their citizenship and economic opportunities, barred from public service, the Jews of Germany, most of whom considered themselves to be good German citizens, bore the barbaric blows with remarkable resilience. Some, including a number of Germany's best scientific minds, were able to flee the country—a loss that may well have doomed Hitler's war effort. Most stayed. They, and the outside world which showed little concern, did not realize that Hitler's true goal was the "final solution," which would lead to the deaths of at least

6 million Jews throughout central and eastern Europe and the Soviet Union and 3 million others not "lucky" enough to be Aryan.

Nazi Propaganda and Education

Hitler and Goebbels controlled all of the media in the totalitarian Third Reich. A Reich culture cabinet was set up to instill a single pattern of thought in literature, the press, broadcasting, drama, music, art, and the cinema. Forbidden books, including works of some of Germany's most distinguished writers, were seized and destroyed in huge bonfires. The cultural vitality of the Weimar Republic, represented by the likes of Thomas Mann, Erich Maria Remarque, Kurt Weill, and Bertolt Brecht, was replaced by the sterile social realism of the third Reich.

The state used mass popular education, integrated with the German Youth Movement, to drill and regiment boys and girls to be good Nazis. Boys learned above all else to be ready to fight and die for their *Führer*. The girls were prepared for their ultimate task, bearing and rearing the many babies to be needed by the Third Reich.

German universities, once renowned for their academic freedom, became agencies for propagating the racial myths of Nazism and for carrying out far-fetched experiments in human genetic engineering on selected concentration camp inmates. Only good Nazis could go to universities, and professors who did not cooperate with the regime were fired. As Jacob Bronowski wrote, "When Hitler arrived in 1933 the tradition of scholarship in Germany was destroyed, almost overnight."[38]

Religion became entrapped in the totalitarian mechanism. Since Nazism elevated the state above all else, a movement was started to subordinated religion to the Hitler regime. The organized churches originally backed the Nazis warmly, until it became apparent that they were to serve the larger aim of the Aryan cause. The Protestant churches suffered under the Nazi attempt to make them an arm of the state, and several dissident ministers were imprisoned. By

Nazi persecution of Jews sometimes included humiliation. Here, a Nazi officer stops a Jewish businessman and orders him to sweep the gutter.

The Nazi message to women proclaimed that "German girls must be strong, to bear more children for the armies, for death in the victorious battles of the Fatherland."

the end of the decade, the Catholic church too came under constant and subtle attack.

Economic Policies

As in Italy, fascism in Germany revolved around a form of state capitalism. In theory and practice, Nazism retained capitalism and private property. The state, however, rigidly controlled both business and labor. The Nazis dissolved labor unions and enrolled workers and employers in a new organization, the Labor Front. As in Mussolini's corporate state, the right of the workers to strike or of management to call a lockout was denied. The Nazis took compulsory dues from the workers' wages to support Nazi organizations. As a sop, the state set up the "Strength Through Joy" movement, which provided sports events, musical festivals, plays, movies, and vacations at low cost.

The Nazis' ultimate goal was self-sufficiency—autarky, which they would try to reach through complete state control of the economy. They assumed, as did the Fascists in Italy, that only the state could ensure the social harmony needed to attain the maximum productive potential for the state's benefit.

The government tried to solve the nation's very serious economic problems by confiscating valuable Jewish property, laying a huge tax load on the middle class, and increasing the national debt by a third to provide work for the unemployed. To create jobs, the first four-year plan, established in 1933, undertook an extensive program of public works and rearmament. The unemployed were put to work on public projects (especially noteworthy was the system of superhighways, the *Autobahnen*), in munitions factories, and in the army.

Overlapping the first program, the second four-year plan was initiated in 1936. The objective of this plan was to set up an autarkist state. In pursuit of self-sufficiency, substitute commodities—frequently inferior in quality and more costly than similar goods available on the world market—were produced by German laboratories, factories, and mills. The gross national product increased by 68 percent by 1938, but the standard of living did not rise to meet the improved economic growth rate. As of the beginning of World War II, the industrial plant still produced insufficient munitions, even after Germany's appropriation of the Czech Skoda works. Germany's war economy did not hit its stride until 1942.[39]

Conclusion

The Soviet Union, Italy, and Germany each had separate and distinct cultural, social, and political roots which gave unique qualities to the authoritarian governments that developed in them. However, each of the states shared similar circumstances. Each faced economic upheavals, had weak traditions of middle-class dominance and liberal rule, and ambitious individuals ready to take command. In the absence of dynamic democratic forces in the world, these circumstances produced the interwar government structures of the totalitarian states.

To be sure, the communists and the fascists differed in theory: the fascists used capitalism while the communists opposed it; fascism emphasized nationalism while communism preached internationalism; fascism had a weak dogmatic basis while communism was based on Marx's scientific socialism; fascism made use of religion while communism attacked it. But by 1939 the common interests of the totalitarian states, whether fascist or communist, were much more important than theoretical differences. Although they may have been philosophically separate, in their impact on the individual, the totalitarian states were remarkably similar.

In the face of economic chaos and hardship, communism promised a society of well-being and peace, in which each person could work at full potential. In the face of governments marked either by weakness or a desperate pragmatism, the certainty and effectiveness of the fascists was especially attractive.

The ultimate figure symbolizing totalitarian rule was Adolf Hitler. How an advanced "civilized" nation such as Germany could have thrown itself willingly under Hitler's control is one of history's great questions. Other nations had stronger authoritarian traditions, greater economic problems, and more extreme psychological strain. Some observers maintain that there could have been no Third Reich without this unparalleled demagogue, that in fact the reason why Germany erupted as it did is due solely to the happenstance of his personality mixing with the disruptive elements of the postwar world.

Suggestions for Reading

Attempts to analyze the new forms of government in the twentieth century have occupied H. Arendt in *The Origins of Totalitarianism* (Brace Jovanovich, 1968); E. Weber in *Varieties of Fascism* (Anvil, 1973), and C. J. Friedrich and Z. K. Brzezinski in *Totalitarianism, Dictatorship and Autocracy* (Praeger, 1966). Novelist A. Koestler has perhaps best captured the essence of the diminution of the individual in *Darkness at Noon* (Signet, 1961).

Michael Florinsky's analysis of the forces destroying the tsarist regime, *The End of the Russian Empire* (Collier, 1961) is still useful. Alexander Solzhenitsyn beautifully sketches the shifting moods of Russia on the entry into the war in *August 1914* (Bantam, 1974). The best overall survey of Russian history in this century is Donald W. Treadgold, *Twentieth Century Russia* (Houghton Mifflin, 1981) Alec Nove, *The Soviet Economic System* (Allen & Unwin, 1977) is an essential study.

B. Wolfe's classic *Three Who Made a Revolution* (Delta, 1974) is a fine study of Lenin, Trotsky, and Stalin. Adam Ulam's *The Bolsheviks* (Macmillan, 1964) gives a clear discussion of the party's development, while S. Cohen in *Bukharin and the Bolshevik Revolution* (Random House, 1974) provides another perspective. J. L. H. Keep dissects the multifaceted and complex actions of the various elements in Petrograd in *The Russian Revolution: A Study in Mass Mobilization* (Norton, 1977). R. Daniels in *Red October* (Scribner, 1969) gives scholarly depth to the journalistic enthusiasm of John Reed in *Ten Days That Shook the World* (Vintage, 1960).

The most detailed analysis of the Russian revolutions and their aftermath is the multivolumed work of E. H. Carr, *The Russian Revolution* (Pelican, 1966). A discussion of the revolutionary aftermath in the outlying areas is in R. Pipes, *The Formation of the Soviet Union* (Atheneum, 1968). The Civil War is nicely outlined in J. F. N. Bradley's *Civil War in Russia 1917–1920* (Batsford, 1975). George F. Kennan has written the best analysis of Western relations with the young Soviet regime in *Decision to Intervene* (Princeton, 1958) and *Russia and the West Under Lenin and Stalin* (Mentor, 1961). Louis Fischer's *The Soviets in World Affairs* (Vintage, 1960) is a thorough discussion of east-west relations in the 1920s.

Isaac Deutscher has written sharply drawn biographies of *Stalin* (Vintage, 1961) and *Trotsky*, 3 vols. (Vintage, 1965). Placed in the context of A. Rabinowitch's *The Bolsheviks Come to Power* (Norton, 1978), Deutscher's two works provide a compelling description of the generation after 1917. Robert C. Tucker has compiled the most complete set of analyses of the influence of this century's most powerful man in *Stalinism* (Norton, 1977). Important social changes that occurred in the Soviet Union are discussed in H.

Geiger, *The Family in Soviet Russia* (Harvard, 1968). The relationship between the Marxist ideals and the peasantry is discussed in David Mitrany, *Marx Against the Peasant* (Collier, 1961). Stalin's purges are thoroughly analyzed in Robert Conquest, *The Great Terror* (Penguin, 1971). Conquest details the campaign against the peasantry in *Harvest of Sorrow* (Oxford, 1986) and the prison camp system in *Kolyma, the Arctic Death Camps* (Viking, 1978). The most passionate description of the labor camps is Alexander Solzhenitsyn's *The Gulag Archipelago*, 3 vols. (Harper, 1973). R. Medvedev approaches the same subject from another perspective in *Let History Judge* (Random House, 1973). The response of some western intellectuals to events in the Soviet Union is covered in David Caute, *The Fellow Travelers* (MacMillan, 1973).

Events in Italy have been concisely and clearly detailed by C. Seton-Watson in *Italy from Liberalism to Fascism: 1870–1925* (Methuen, 1967). A collection of Musolini's ideas has been compiled in Benito Mussolini, *Fascism: Doctrine and Institution* (Fertig, 1968). A clear and concise study of Italy under Mussolini is Elizabeth Wiskemann, *Fascism in Italy: Its Development and Influence* (St. Martin's, 1969). A more detailed discussion of the Fascist advance can be found in A. Lyttelton, *The Seizure of Power: Fascism in Italy 1919–1929* (Scribner, 1973).

Weimar Germany's brief time in the sun can be studied in A. J. Ryder, *Twentieth Century Germany: From Bismarck to Brandt* (Columbia, 1973) and Erich Eyck, *History of the Weimar Republic*, 2 vols. (Atheneum, 1962). Peter Gay's *Weimar Culture* (Torchbooks, 1968) and *Freud, Jews, and Other Germans* (Oxford, 1979) are penetrating studies of a turbulent time. Fritz Stern, *The Politics of Cultural Despair* (California, 1974) and G. Mosse, *The Crisis of German Ideology* (Grosset and Dunlap, 1964) are essential to understand the mental underpinnings supporting the rise of Hitler. A. Dorpalen, *Hindenburg and the Weimar Republic* (Princeton, 1964) is fine study of the dilemma faced by liberals in the 1920s. J. P. Nettl, *Rosa Luxemburg*, 2 vols. (Oxford, 1966) is a fine study of the socialists' dilemma in Germany.

Alan Bullock, *Hitler: A Study in Tyranny* (Torchbooks, 1964) remains the best biography. John Toland, *Adolf Hitler* (Ballantine Books, 1977) is more readable. William S. Allen, *Nazi Seizure of Power: The Experience of a Single Town 1930–1935* (New Viewpoints, 1969) makes Hitler's takeover more comprehensible. A. Schweitzer, *Big Business and the Third Reich* (Indiana, 1977) details the collaboration between capitalism and fascism. A Beyerchen, *Scientists under Hitler* (Yale, 1977) shows institutional responses to the Führer. K. D. Bracher gives a good structural analysis of fascism in operation in *The German Dictatorship* (Praeger, 1970). D. Schoenbaum discusses the social effects of the Nazi in *Hitler's Social Revolution: Class and Status in Nazi Germany* (Anchor, 1967).

Notes

1. Leonard Schapiro, "Totalitarianism," *Survey*, Autumn, 1969.
2. Michael T. Florinsky, *The End of the Russian Empire* (New York: Collier Books, 1961), pp. 246–248

3. Novelist Alexander Solzhenitsyn captures the mood in chapter 7 of *August 1914,* trans. Michael Glenny (New York: Bantam Books, 1974).

4. Sir Bernard Pares, "Rasputin and the Empress, Authors of the Russian Collapse," *Foreign Affairs,* VI, no. 1 (October 1927), p. 140.

5. *The New Cambridge Modern History,* XII, (Cambridge: Cambridge University Press, 1960), p. 9.

6. Donald W. Treadgold, *Twentieth-Century Russia* (Chicago: Rand McNally & Co., 1959), p. 127.

7. Treadgold, *Twentieth-Century Russia,* p. 133.

8. Alfred G. Meyer, *Leninism* (New York: Frederick A. Praeger, 1957), p. 276

9. Zbigniew Brzezinski, "The Nature of the Soviet System," in Donald W. Treadgold, ed., *The Development of the USSR* (Seattle: University of Washington Press, 1964), p. 6.

10. J. N. Westwood, *Endurance and Endeavour: Russian History 1812–1986,* 3rd ed. (Oxford: Oxford University Press, 1987), p. 278.

11. Westwood, *Endurance and Endeavor,* p. 276.

12. Isaac Deutscher, *Stalin: A Political Biography,* (New York: Vintage Books, 1961), p. 91.

13. Harry Schwartz, "The Lenin Cult and Its Uses," in *Lenin and Leninism,* ed., Bernard Eissenstat, (Lexington, Mass.: Lexington Books, 1971), p. 238.

14. Brzezinski, "The Nature of the Soviet System," pp. 6–8.

15. See Robert Conquest, *The Harvest of Sorrow: Soviet Collectivization and the Terror-Famine,* (New York: Oxford University Press, 1986).

16. Winston S. Churchill, *The Second World War: The Hinge of Fate,* IV, (New York: Bantam Books, 1962), pp. 434–435.

17. Robert Conquest, *The Great Terror,* (New York: Macmillan Co., 1973), pp. 450–475.

18. Conquest, *The Great Terror,* p. 485.

19. Christopher Seton-Watson, *Italy from Liberalism to Fascism: 1870–1925,* (London: Methuen & Co., 1967), p. 503.

20. Elizabeth Wiskemann, *Fascism in Italy: Its Development and Influence* (New York: St. Martin's Press, 1969), pp. 6–10.

21. Seton-Watson, *Italy from Liberalism to Fascism,* p. 518.

22. Wiskemann, *Fascism in Italy,* p. 12.

23. Benito Mussolini, *Fascism: Doctrine and Institutions,* (New York: Howard Fertig, 1968), p. 38.

24. Wiskemann, *Fascism in Italy,* p. 23.

25. Mussolini, *Fascism,* pp. 35–38.

26. Wiskemann, *Fascism in Italy,* p. 35.

27. Seton-Watson, *Italy from Liberalism to Fascism,* pp. 702–703.

28. Hajo Holborn, *Germany and Europe: Historical Essays* (New York: Anchor Books, 1971), p. 173.

29. A. J. Ryder, *Twentieth-Century Germany: From Bismarck to Brandt* (New York: Columbia University Press, 1973), pp. 245–246.

30. Peter Gay, *Weimar Culture,* (New York: Torchbooks, 1968), p. 23.

31. Holborn, *Germany and Europe,* pp. 221–224.

32. John Toland, *Adolf Hitler* (New York: Ballantine Books, 1977), pp. 79–97.

33. David S. Landes, *The Unbound Prometheus* (Cambridge: Cambridge University Press, 1969), p. 398.

34. Toland, *Adolf Hitler,* p. 406.

35. Karl A. Schleunes, *The Twisted Road to Auschwitz: Nazi Policy toward German Jews: 1933–1939,* (Urbana: University of Illinois Press, 1970), pp. 37–38.

36. Landes, *The Unbound Prometheus,* pp. 416–417

37. Ryder, *Twentieth-Century Germany,* p. 348.

38. J. Bronowski, *The Ascent of Man* (Boston: Little, Brown and Co., 1973), p. 367.

39. Landes, *The Unbound Prometheus,* pp. 400, 406, 413.

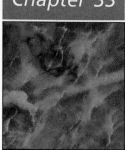

Chapter 33

Asia and Africa in the Interwar World

Fifty years of aggressive expansion by the West had spread a veneer of Europeanization on its holdings. At the same time, the imperialists also exported Western social and political ideas to their colonies. The explosive concepts of nationalism and self-rule, tied to Western science and technology, revitalized the societies of Asia and Africa.

World War I and its aftershocks strengthened independence movements in Africa and Asia. Nationalist campaigns, present in embryonic form in most of the colonies before the war, grew rapidly in virtually all of the European possessions and mandates.

Japan emerged as a world power, but by the late 1920s the impact of the depression and a population crisis threatened its weakly rooted democratic institutions. China endured revolution and civil strife as the areas of Southeast Asia pursued independence. India's independence movement strengthened under the leadership of Mohandas Gandhi. Across the Islamic world and Africa, indigenous peoples emerged from under the shadow of European domination, which was in full retreat by the end of the 1930s.

Japan

Japan's victory over Russia in the 1904–1905 Russo-Japanese War served notice of the success of Japan's Meiji era reforms. In two generations, the island nation had changed from a static, mostly agricultural nation into a modern, highly industrialized state. There were, however, serious problems. The rapidly increasing population strained the nation's limited size and resources.

In the government, liberal statesmen tried to strengthen democratic practices in a hostile social and political setting. Ten years after World War I, population and economic pressures combined with a revival of militarism to launch the Japanese toward war and dictatorship.

The Asian Great Power

Japan's expansionist goals in China remained remarkably consistent after the Meiji restoration. In 1914 the Japanese ordered the Germans to remove their warships from the Far East and to surrender Kiaochow territory in China to Japan. When the Germans refused to reply to this order, Japan declared war on Germany and seized the territory without consulting China. In 1915, Japan presented China with the Twenty-one Demands, a document whose frank statement of Japan's aims on the Asian continent startled the world.

The Chinese government, weakened by a half century of decline and revolution, could do little but give in to the first sixteen demands, reserving the final five for further consideration. By leaking news of the demands to the press, the Chinese attracted the attention of the United States. Washington kept China from falling totally under Japan's domination. Nevertheless, the Chinese had no choice but to recognize Japan's authority in Shantung province and extend Japanese land and rail concessions in southern Manchuria. In 1917 the Allies secretly agreed to support Japanese claims against China, in return for Japan's respecting the Open Door policy.

Japan's sphere of economic dominance expanded during the 1920s in Shantung, Manchuria, and south Mongolia: It also occupied the

Kita Ikki's Plan for Japan

While liberal Europe struggled with the burdens of victory, Japan experimented with a variety of governmental approaches. A radical social and economic concept was enunciated by Kita Ikki, who was executed in 1937.

Suspension of the Constitution: In order to establish a firm base for national reorganization, the Emperor, with the aid of the entire Japanese nation and by invoking his imperial prerogatives, shall suspend the Constitution for a period of three years, dissolve the two houses of the Diet, and place the entire country under martial law.

The true significance of the Emperor: We must make clear the fundamental principle that the Emperor is the sole representative of the people and the pillar of the state. . . .

Abolition of the peerage system: By abolishing the peerage system, we shall be able to remove the feudal aristocracy which constitutes a barrier between the Emperor and the people. In this way the spirit of the Meiji Restoration shall be proclaimed. . . .

The members of the Deliberative Council shall consist of men distinguished in various fields of activities, elected by each other or appointed by the Emperor.

Limitation on private property: No Japanese family shall possess property in excess of one million yen. A similar limitation shall apply to Japanese citizens holding property overseas. No one shall be permitted to make a gift of property to those related by blood or to others, or to transfer his property by other means with the intent of circumventing this limitation.

Nationalization of excess amount over limitation on private property: Any amount which exceeds the limitation on private property shall revert to the state without compensation. No one shall be permitted to resort to the protection of present laws in order to avoid remitting such excess amount. Anyone who violates these provisions shall be deemed a person thinking lightly of the example set by the Emperor and endangering the basis of national reorganization. As such, during the time martial law is in effect, he shall be charged with the crimes of endangering the person of the Emperor and engaging in internal revolt and shall be punished by death.

Limitation on private landholding: No Japanese family shall hold land in excess of 100,000 yen in current market value. . . .

. . . Lands held in excess of the limitation on private landholding shall revert to the state. . . .

Distribution of profits to workers: One half of the net profits of private industries shall be distributed to workers employed in such industries. . . .

Continuation of the conscript system: The state, having rights to existence and development among the nations of the world, shall maintain the present conscript system in perpetuity. . . .

Positive right to start war: In addition to the right to self-defense, the state shall have the right to start a war on behalf of other nations and races unjustly oppressed by a third power. (As a matter of real concern today, the state shall have the right to start a war to aid the independence of India and preservation of China's integrity.)

As a result of its own development, the state shall also have the right to start a war against those nations who occupy large colonies illegally and ignore the heavenly way of the co-existence of all humanity. (As a matter of real concern today, the state shall have the right to start a war against those nations which occupy Australia and Far Eastern Siberia for the purpose of acquiring them.)

From David John Lu, *Sources of Japanese History*, vol. 2 (New York: McGraw-Hill, 1974), pp. 131–136. Reprinted by permission.

former German islands north of the equator (see map below). The Washington Conference of 1921 acknowledged the Japanese navy as the third most powerful in the world. The signatories (United States, Great Britain, France, Italy, Japan, Belgium, Netherlands, Portugal, and China) of the Nine-Power Treaty, signed in Washington in 1922, agreed to respect the independence, sovereignty, territoriality, and administrative integrity of China and to respect the Open Door policy.

The United States and Britain, however, were alarmed by the growth of Japanese power. By 1931, Japanese investments in China were second only to those of Great Britain, constituting around 35 percent of all foreign investment in China. That same year, responding to population pressures and resource needs, the Japanese disregarded international treaties and opinions and invaded China.

Authoritarian Victory

From 1889 to 1918 an aristocratic oligarchy of elder statesmen called the *Genro* controlled the Japanese government. By the 1920s most of the patriarchs had passed away and the field of politics was open to new blood. Hara Takashi, the first commoner to hold the post of prime minister, was elected to the office in 1918.

Over the next twelve years, Japan seemed to be moving toward the establishment of a democratic, parliamentary government under its new political leaders. However, the liberals faced serious obstacles. There was no widespread tradition of democratic or parliamentary practices in Japan. Japanese society had concentrated wealth and power in the hands of a few families, while the traditional culture encouraged a militaristic system of values. The secret societies and the cult of Shintoism favored authoritarianism over liberalism.

Despite these obstacles, liberals in the Japanese parliament, the Diet, showed great promise and courage as they tried to lead the nation away from militant nationalism. They pressed for reforms at home while criticizing the imperialistic intervention of the Japanese army in Siberia during the Russian Civil War. Although the democratic cause suffered a serious setback in 1921 with the assassination of Prime Minister Hara, the liberals continued their work. Passage of the Universal Manhood Suffrage Bill in 1925 strengthened the liberal base. By 1930, after a reactionary interlude, Prime Minister Hamaguchi Yuko established the most liberal government Japan had ever had.

As was the case in Europe, as long as the economy remained strong, the liberals did well. In the 1920s the Japanese built thousands of factories that turned out products that enabled Japan to claim a major share of the world textile market and to flood the world with mass-produced, cheap, low-quality goods. Japanese industrialists were quick to adopt modern machine techniques and slow to raise wages A few giant concerns working together controlled the greater part of the country's wealth.

Prosperity—and by implication the liberals' position—rested on fragile foundations. Japan lacked natural resources, and its population grew at a rapid rate. In 1920 there were more than 55 million inhabitants. Eleven years later there were 65 million people, crowded into a land area smaller than the state of California. By 1932 the average annual population increase was

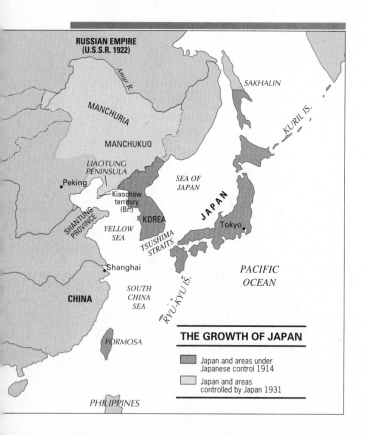

THE GROWTH OF JAPAN

Japan and areas under Japanese control 1914

Japan and areas controlled by Japan 1931

Japan's invasion of Manchuria in September 1931 violated a number of treaties, covenants, agreements, and promises that were made after World War I in the hope of creating a world-wide and lasting peace.

1 million. The Japanese economy had to create 250,000 jobs yearly and find the food to feed the growing population. Up to 1930 Japan paid its way by expanding its exports. But between 1929 and 1931, the effects of the great depression cut export trade in half. Unemployment soared, leading to wage cuts and strikes. As in Germany on the eve of Adolf Hitler's rise to power, frustration became widespread among the younger generation.

In response to the economic crisis, Prime Minister Hamaguchi adopted measured fiscal reforms and a moderate foreign policy. The first approach failed to satisfy the workers and the second approach offended the militarists. Hamaguchi was shot in November 1930 and died the following spring. The assassin's bullets dealt a blow to Japanese liberalism which was not overcome until after World War II.

A new group of ultranationalistic and militaristic leaders came to power, ruling not through a charismatic leader as in Germany and Italy but through a military clique. The members of the clique, who had nothing but contempt for democracy and peaceful policies, terrorized the civilian members of the government, plotted to shelve parliamentary government, and planned to use force on the mainland of China. Their goals were to gain resources for the economy, living space for the population, markets for Japanese goods, and cultural domination throughout Asia. They referred to their program as a "beneficial mission" and called it the "New Order in Asia." The military clique took its first step with the invasion of Manchuria in 1931, setting off the sequence of aggression that would lead to World War II (see ch. 34).

China: Revolution and Republic

During the nineteenth century China endured one of the darkest periods in its four thousand years. The old Confucianist, imperial government failed as China lost territory, suffered under the imposition of extraterritoriality, and witnessed its customs and tariffs come under foreign control. The 1898 reform movement and the Boxer Uprising of 1899–1900 were, in effect, two attempts to remove the Manchu dynasty. Thereafter, there were two approaches to change: the constitutionalist attempt to set up representative government and the revolutionary program to overthrow the dynasty.

Sun Yat-sen and Revolution

Sun Yat-sen (1867–1925) proved to be the key figure in the transition from the old to the new China. The son of a tenant farmer born near Canton, he received a western education in Hawaii. He converted to Christianity and in 1892 earned a diploma in medicine in Hong Kong. Soon, he became a leader in the Chinese nationalist movement, directing his energies toward the overthrow of the Manchus and the formation of a republic. For his activities, he was forced into exile in 1895 and thereafter traveled widely throughout the world seeking political and financial aid from Chinese living abroad. During that

Statesman and revolutionary leader Sun Yat-sen, the organizer of the *Kuomintang,* is known as the father of modern China.

period he organized the movement that eventually became the *Kuomintang,* or Nationalist party.[1]

In 1911 a revolt broke out in China over a foreign loan to finance railways. The outbreak spread like wildfire throughout the country. Yuan Shih-kai (1859–1916), an outstanding north Chinese military leader with modern ideas, persuaded the imperial clan that the Manchu dynasty was doomed. In 1912 the child emperor abdicated, and Yuan was asked to form a republican government. Although a few months earlier a revolutionary assembly in Nanking had elected Sun president of the new republic, he stepped aside in the interest of national unity and the Nanking assembly elected Yuan.

During the next fifteen years China went through a period quite similar to the dynastic interregnums that had punctuated its previous history. Trouble broke out in 1913 when Yuan negotiated a large loan with bankers from Britain, France, Germany, and Russia that gave these powers substantial influence in the government of the republic. Resentment over this agreement led to a new rebellion, backed by Sun. Yuan still had control of the army and put down the revolt, forcing Sun to flee to Japan until 1917. Overestimating his strength, Yuan dismissed parliament and proclaimed the restoration of the monarchy with himself as emperor. This act sparked another rebellion, and this time Yuan's prestige evaporated. In June 1916 the now discredited dictator died.

China then entered a period of political anarchy. Warlords heading armies based on local power centers marched across the country seeking control of Peking. Possession of the city apparently was seen as conferring legitimacy on its occupier. For a time, China was divided between two would-be governments, one in the north at Peking and the other in the south at Canton. The southern force was composed largely of those who had engineered the revolution of 1911–1912. The Canton government elected Sun president in 1921, and he remained there until his death in 1925, unable to unify the country.

Sun's genius was in making revolution, not in governing. His social ideology, however, provided some key elements for twentieth-century Chinese political theory. Sun's *The Three Principles of the People,* developed from a series of

lectures, became the political manual of the *Kuomintang*. The three principles are: nationalism, the liberation of China from foreign domination and the creation of a Chinese nation-state; democracy, "government by the people and for the people"; and livelihood, economic security for all the people.

In 1923, after failing to obtain from the West aid to overthrow the Peking government, Sun turned to the Soviet Union for advice and assistance. A military and political advisory group arrived, led by Michael Borodin. Under Borodin's guidance, the *Kuomintang* adopted many of the planks of the program subscribed to by the Soviet Communist Party as well as the party's organizational structure.

Chiang Kai-shek "Unites" China

Sun's successor as leader of the *Kuomintang* was Chiang Kai-shek (1886–1975), the son of a minor landlord. Chiang studied at a military academy in Japan before becoming caught up with Sun's vision for a new China. He returned home to take an active part in the revolution. His obvious abilities and loyalty attracted Sun's attention, and in 1923 he was sent to Russia for a brief period of training. Before establishing himself as leader of the *Kuomintang*, he formed a united force and began to drive northward in 1926. Chiang's group encountered little

opposition, and by the early spring of the following year they reached the Yangtze valley. However, dissension broke out between the radical and the conservative elements of the *Kuomintang*, and Chiang crushed the communists in his ranks when he occupied Shanghai. He went on to create a moderate government at Nanking, and before the end of 1927, public opinion had swung behind his regime.

Chiang continued to purge the leftist elements. The end of the *Kuomintang* alliance with the communists was written in blood, when a proletarian uprising in Canton was crushed, with the loss of 5,000 lives. The Soviet advisers returned to Moscow and many radicals, including the widow of Sun Yat-sen, were driven into exile. The Chinese communists fled to the hills and mountains of China.

The 1927 split of the *Kuomintang* is a major event in modern Chinese history. Not only were Marxist radicals ousted, but many moderate liberals also began to be eliminated. Chiang built his strength on the urban professional, banking, and merchant classes. His government depended for financial support on the foreign bankers of Shanghai. The regime took on a conservative, urban character, far removed from the huge mass of the Chinese people, the peasantry in the countryside.

With his government established at Nanking, Chiang, his armies, and his warlord allies again

more colloquial written language, while scholars labored for the adoption of Mandarin (a standardized version of the Peking dialect, used in government affairs) so that people from all parts of China could speak together. Social customs changed and western dress and folkways appeared. Large cities installed telephones, electric lights, modern water systems, and movie palaces. Much of the import of western conveniences was paid for by the foreign entrepreneurs who controlled most of Chinese industry. Despite all the changes, civil war, a weak currency, inadequate transportation, and grinding poverty kept China an underdeveloped nation.

A fervent patriot, Chiang unfortunately had little appreciation for the social and economic problems of his nation. The people were still tyrannized by bandits while famine in the northwest of the country claimed the lives of millions. Instead of responding to the plight of his nation, Chiang, a Christian whose faith incorporated much from Confucian principles, pursued the moral regeneration of his people through a combination of his religion and his culture–the New Life Movement which he established in the mid-1930s. He would have done better to appreciate the intellectual changes taking place and the social and economic hopes of the peasants.

The New Culture Movement and Chinese Communism

A Chinese intellectual revolution began at Peking University during World War I and spread from there to students all over the country.[2] The first influential voice for this intellectual group was the magazine *New Youth*. This journal transmitted the ideas of students who had returned from universities in the United States and Europe on subjects ranging from western science to liberalism to socialism. These students wanted to establish a new order and a new set of values to replace much of the old Confucian tradition.

The students became disillusioned with the west after the Versailles peace treaty, which gave Chinese Shantung to Japan. A violent student demonstration on May 4, 1919, featured virulent anti-western sentiment. A new ideological orientation began in the New Culture Movement. Study groups were formed, especially at Peking university where professors and students began

moved north and occupied Peking. China once again appeared to be united, but it was a unity more in appearance than in fact (see map above). While large areas of the country had been conquered by Chiang's forces, other regions came under the *Kuomintang* by agreement between Chiang and local warlords. In theory the warlords were subordinate to Chiang, but they maintained power in their spheres of influence.

Chinese foreign relations improved during the 1920s. The Nine-Power Treaty guaranteed China's territorial integrity, and China was a member of the League of Nations. The government regained the right to set its own tariffs in 1929, when ten foreign powers gave up or lost the right of extraterritoriality. Partially in response to the development foreign trade was seven times as great in 1929 as in 1894. In addition, while the liberals were in power in Japan, Tokyo was relatively conciliatory toward China.

Chiang engineered substantial changes in Chinese urban life. More Chinese received education. Linguists championed the use of a new,

to read Marx and Lenin and to apply their thoughts to China. Lenin's analysis of and attack on imperialism struck a responsive chord.

With some guidance from Russian Comintern agents, the First Congress of the Chinese Communist Party was held in July 1921. A young student at Peking University named Mao Tse-tung was a delegate. About the same time, Chinese worker-students in France established the Young China Communist party in Paris. One of its leaders was Chou En-lai, later premier of Chinese People's Republic.

Mao Tse-tung (1893–1976) was born in Hunan province, a traditional center of Chinese revolutionary activity.[3] In 1918 he went to Peking University where he worked as library assistant under Li Ta-chao, the founder of an important Marxist study group and one of the founders of the Chinese Communist Party. Mao began to

Mao Tse-tung has been called the "Stalin" of Chinese communism.

emerge as a distinctive leader with a new program for revolution when he wrote a report for the Communist party in 1927 about the peasant movement in Hunan. In that document Mao expressed his belief that the revolution must base itself on peasant uprisings, a view that was condemned by the Central Committee of the Chinese Communist party, which closely adhered to the Russian policy of basing the revolution on the urban proletariat.

Mao led a Hunanese peasant uprising that became known as the Autumn Harvest Uprising. It was crushed, and in May 1928 Mao and other Communist leaders joined forces in the border region of Hunan and Kiangsi provinces. Acutely conscious of peasant needs, Mao organized the peasants in his region into a Chinese "soviet." Other Communist leaders did the same in other regions, and in 1931 delegates from the various local soviets in China met and proclaimed the birth of the Chinese Soviet Republic. Even though Chiang Kai-shek destroyed the Shanghai apparatus of the Communist party, Mao and his colleagues could still claim control of regions containing 9 million people.

Mao's success as a Communist leader stemmed from his observation that it was the Chinese peasant, not the urban worker, who could be made the agent of the revolution. In pursuit of this objective, Mao encouraged the establishment of farmers' cooperatives and equitable tax systems. He also redistributed land in the areas he controlled. Mao's achievements worried Chiang, who between 1931 and 1934 launched five military campaigns against the Communists—the last one using one million men and a German military staff. To avoid annihilation, the communists made their famous Long March 2000 miles to the northwest. Only a remnant of the original force reached Yenan, in Shensi province, where in 1935 a new Communist stronghold was set up.

Nationalism in Southeast Asia

The drive for independence became stronger in Southeast Asia between the two world wars. Taking advantage of the war-weakened colonialists, local leaders adapted the ideologies of the day—whether Wilson's "self-determination of peoples" or socialism, or a combination of the two—to their campaigns for freedom. The example of Japan's rise to the status of a great power showed that the west had no monopoly on technology and organization.

Populations grew dramatically in Southeast Asia during the interwar period. From 1930 to 1960 the number of people in Siam, Malaya, and the Philippines increased more than 100 percent; in Indonesia, Burma, and Indochina the number increased more than 50 percent. Population pressures naturally contributed to unrest.

Certain economic trends also characterized most of the region. The imperialist powers continued to exploit their colonies, ignoring the democratic rhetoric they had mouthed during the First World War. Europe's draining of the area's resources coupled with an irregular world market which crashed in 1929 led to increased hardship in much of the region. The Chinese played an increasingly important role as merchants and middlemen in the local economies. In Burma, Indians played the same role. European and Chinese capital investment encouraged a rapid growth in exports of minerals and forest products. In Siam, Indochina, and a few other countries rice production grew more rapidly than population, and as a result the economies became based on rice exports.

Throughout the area the élite became assimilated to European culture as more and more young people went to the "parent countries" to be educated. The masses, however, were barely touched by this process. The result was a growing cultural and social divide between the local leadership and the people at large. With the exception of the United States in the Philippines and Great Britain in Burma and Ceylon, none of the imperialist powers undertook to prepare their colonies for eventual self-government, as they had no intention of letting them go.

Indochina

French rule in Indochina was in some ways the least enlightened of all the colonial regimes in Southeast Asia. In 1941, for example, the colonial government had the highest proportion of Europeans in its service of any in the region—some 5100 French officials to 27,000 Indochinese.[4] Four fifths of the population was illiterate, and of the more than 21 million people, only about 500,000 children received any higher education. French rule was characterized by political oppression, severe economic exploitation, and a rigid and stagnant traditional culture.

Revolution seemed the answer to Vietnam's problems. During World War I over 100,000 Vietnamese laborers and soldiers were sent to France, where many of them came in contact with liberal and radical thinking, which they then brought home. The Vietnam Nationalist party, patterned organizationally and intellectually on the Chinese *Kuomintang*, was officially outlawed, and by the late 1920s resorted to terrorism as the only form of political expression open to it.

Communism rapidly became the major revolutionary ideology in the French colony. In 1920 a young Vietnamese calling himself Nguyen Ai Quoc ("Nguyen, the Patriot"), and later known to

Ho Chi Minh found in Communist ideology a road to his ultimate goal: the liberation of his native Vietnam.

the world as Ho Chi Minh (1890–1969), participated actively in the formation of the communist party in France. In 1930 he organized in Hong Kong what eventually became the Vietnamese (later Indochinese) Communist party. Communist ideas and organization spread throughout Vietnam in the 1930s while the colonial government answered Vietnamese uprisings against French oppression with strong repressive measures. As a result, when World War II began, the communist party was the major vehicle for the expression of Vietnamese nationalism.

The Philippines

The United States established its form of government in the Philippines on July 4, 1901, under William H. Taft as civil governor of the area. President McKinley declared that the primary aim was to prepare the Filipinos for self-government. The first elections were held in 1907 and by 1913 Filipinos dominated both houses of the legislature, while an American remained as governor-general. By 1935, when the Philippine Commonwealth was inaugurated with a new constitution and the promise of independence within ten years, the islands had developed a complex governmental structure and a sophisticated political life.

Economic developments, however, constricted Philippine independence at the same time that the islands were being prepared for self-rule. Before the outbreak of World War II, four-fifths of Philippine exports went to the United States and three-fifths of its imports came from America. Like most underdeveloped economies, the export trade was dominated by a very few products: hemp, sugar, coconuts, and tobacco. Independence, with its accompanying imposition of tariffs would have been economically difficult. The United States had prevented the development of a colonial-type plantation economy by forbidding non-Filipinos to own plantation lands, but native landlordism was rampant, and the oppressed peasants launched a brief uprising in the mid-1930s.

Dutch East Indies

Unlike other western imperial powers which loosened their controls over their colonies, either through domestic weakness or planned decolonization, the Dutch increased their control in the East Indies. Stretched over 3100 miles of water, the numerous islands of Indonesia were integrated into a communications and political system by the Dutch. At the same time, the strict limits put on the power and advancement of native élites led to bitterness and resentment. Dutch imperialism strengthened Indonesian self-consciousness and nationalism.

A communist party, organized in 1920, attempted unsuccessful uprisings in Java and Sumatra in late 1926 and early 1927. Police repression increased. In 1930 the Dutch attempted to crush the Nationalist party and arrested one of its leaders, Achmed Sukarno (1901–1970), the man who after World War II became the first president of independent Indonesia. The Dutch banned all discussions of any subject that might involve the concept of national independence. Even the name Indonesia was censored from official publications.

Siam/Thailand

In the interwar period, Siam, which changed its name to Thailand in 1939, continued to modernize. Educational improvements, economic growth, and increased political sophistication contrasted sharply, however, with the political and administrative domination of the country by the rather extensive royal family. In 1932 a French-trained law professor led a bloodless coup d'état, and a new constitution was promulgated with the agreement of the king, turning him into a reigning, not ruling, monarch. Since then the country has been ruled by an alliance of army and oligarchy.

Burma and Malaya

The Burmese independence movement modeled itself on the tactics practiced by the Indian National Congress, but Buddhism provided the focus for organizational activity. A Young Men's Buddhist Association, formed in 1906, organized a General Council of Burmese Associations in 1921. The General Council brought nationalism to the village level.

British promises to promote Indian self-government created a similar demand in Burma, and in 1937 Burma was administratively split off from India. A parliamentary sytem was begun with a Burmese prime minister under a British governor who held responsibility for foreign relations, defense, and finance.

No strong nationalist movement developed in Malaya, perhaps because the large ethnic groups living there distrusted one another more than they felt the need to make common cause against the British. The Malays feared Chinese ethnic domination; eventually, the Chinese came to outnumber the Malays themselves. The Chinese were primarily interested in commerce and in developments in China. The Indians, for the most part workers on plantations and in mines, were loyal to India as their homeland.

India: The Drive for Independence

Before 1914, many observers had predicted that in the event of war, Great Britain would find India a serious liability. When hostilities began, however, nearly all anti-British activity against Britain in India ceased.

Gradual Steps Toward Self-Rule

By 1917 Indian nationalists expected immediate compensation for their loyalty in terms of more self-government. The British, however, pursued a policy stressing gradual development of self-government within the British Empire. To this end, in 1918, a British commission was sent to India to study the question of self-government within the British Empire. To this end, in 1918, a British commission was sent to India to study the question of self-government and recommended a new constitution. The Government of India Act provided for a system of double government in the provinces by which certain powers were reserved to the British while the provincial legislatures were granted other, generally lesser, powers.

To Indian nationalists, this act represented only a small step toward self-rule. Their frustrations led to the outbreak of a struggle with the British in 1919. In an ill-advised move the British passed the Rowlatt Act (1919), which allowed the police and other officials extraordinary powers in searching out subversive activity. Although the act was never enforced, it was deeply resented as a symbol of repression.

Disgruntled and disheartened by the Government of India Act and the violence that followed, many nationalists demanded sweeping changes. Britain, however, lacked a comprehensive plan to grant independence, and a large segment of British public opinion strongly opposed any threat to the breakup of the empire, such as Indian independence.

Gandhi and Civil Disobedience

The foremost nationalist leader in India was Mohandas K. Gandhi (1869–1948). Born of middle-class parents, Gandhi had been sent to London to study law; later he went to South Africa, where he built up a lucrative practice. During these years his standard of values changed completely. The new Gandhi repudiated wealth, practiced ascetic self-denial, condemned violence, and believed firmly that true happiness could be achieved only by service to others.

Gandhi began his career as a reformer and champion of his people in South Africa. The Indians there were subject to numerous legal restrictions which hampered their freedom of movement, prevented them from buying property, and imposed added taxes on them. Disdaining the use of violence, Gandhi believed that a just cause will triumph if its supporters attempt to convince those in power of injustices by practicing "civil disobedience." With Gandhi as their leader, the Indians in South Africa carried out various protests, including hunger strikes. They refused to work, held mass demonstrations, and marched into areas where their presence was forbidden by law. By the use of such passive resistance, or noncooperation, Gandhi forced the government to remove some restrictions.

When he returned to his native land shortly after the outbreak of World War I, Gandhi was welcomed as a hero. During the war he cooperated with the British government, but the disappointing concessions in the new constitution and the Rowlatt Act led him to announce his determination to force the British to give India self-rule.

Mohandas Gandhi used the weapons of nonviolent protest and noncooperation in his struggle to win independence for India. An immensely popular and beloved leader, Gandhi was given the title Mahatma, or "Great Soul," by the people.

Gandhi introduced his campaign in 1919. A mass strike was declared in which all work was to cease and the population was to pray and fast. Contrary to Gandhi's plan, however, riots took place. After Europeans were killed soldiers came in to restore order. Although the British forbade public gatherings, a large body of unarmed Indians assembled at Amritsar. British troops broke up the meeting, killing hundreds.

This incident put a temporary end to all hope of cooperation between Indians and Britons. Many British colonials supported the bloody suppression of the Amritsar demonstrators. Arrested in 1922, Gandhi seemed to welcome being placed on trial; he assured the British magistrate that the only alternative to permitting him to continue his opposition was to imprison him. Sentenced to six years imprisonment, Gandhi suffered a temporary eclipse.

Road to Reform

A promising road to conciliation opened in 1930 when a series of round-table conferences was arranged in London. A new scheme of government was hammered out, providing for a federal union, which would bring the British provinces and the states of the princes into a central government. In the provinces the double government system was displaced by full autonomy, while in the federal government all powers were transferred to the Indians except defense and foreign affairs, which remained in the control of the British viceroy. From 1937, when this new Government of India Act came into operation, until 1939 the scheme of self-government worked smoothly. The possibility of federation, however, faded when the native princes refused to enter the central government.

The new system of government failed to satisfy the demands of the Indian nationalists, who continued to push for complete independence through demonstrations and articles in the popular press. The chief element in the independence movement was the powerful Indian National Congress, which had become the organ of the militant nationalists. The membership of several million was predominantly Hindu but also included many Muslims and members of other religious groups. Soon after the First World War, the congress had come under the leadership of Gandhi, whose personal following among the people was the chief source of the party's tremendous influence.

Gandhi transformed the congress, which had been primarily a middle-class organization, into a mass movement that included the peasants. Gandhi had other goals besides freeing India. He sought to end all drinking, raise the status of women, remove the stigma attached to the untouchables, and bring about cooperation between Hindus and Muslims. Permeating all of Gandhi's ideas and actions was his belief in nonviolence; he was convinced that injustices could be destroyed only through the forces of love, unselfishness, and patience.

In the 1930s Gandhi shared his leadership with Jawaharlal Nehru (1889–1964), who came from a Brahmin family of ancient lineage. In his youth Nehru had all of the advantages of wealth:

Jawaharlal Nehru, along with Gandhi a leader of Indian nationalism, served as prime minister of independent India.

English tutors, enrollment in the English public schools of Harrow and later Trinity College, Cambridge, where he obtained his B.A. in 1910. Two years later he was admitted to the bar. On his return to India, he showed little interest in the law and gradually became completely absorbed in his country's fight for freedom.

A devoted friend and disciple of Gandhi, Nehru could not agree with the older leader's mystical rejection of much of the modern world. At heart, Nehru was a rationalist, an agnostic, an ardent believer in science and a foe of all supernaturalism. Above all, he was a blend of the cultures of both East and West, perhaps with the latter predominating. As he himself said: "I have become a queer mixture of the East and the West, out of place everywhere, at home nowhere. Perhaps my thoughts and approach to life are more akin to what is called Western than Eastern, but India calls me."[5]

The Hindu-Muslim Clash

India is the classic example of a fragmented society. The major division in India was between the Hindus and Muslims, who were poles apart in culture and values. As Britain's imperial control over India began to show signs of ending, hostility between the two communities surfaced. Many Muslims believed that with independence they would become a powerless minority. Thus the conflict was a struggle for political survival.

In the early 1930s the Muslim League, a political party, began to challenge the claim of the Indian National Congress to represent all of India. The leader of the Muslim League, Muhammad Ali Jinnah (1876–1948), originally a member of the congress and once dubbed by Indian nationalists the "ambassador of Hindu-Muslim unity," had become alienated by what he considered the Hindu domination of the congress and its claim to be the sole agent of Indian nationalism.

The Muslim League began to advance the "two-nation" theory, and in 1933 a group of Muslim students at Cambridge Uniersity circulated a pamphlet for the establishment of a new state to be known as Pakistan. This leaflet was the opening act of a bloody drama. In 1939 the Muslim League emphatically denounced any scheme of self-government of India that would mean majority Hindu rule.[6]

Changes in the Muslim World

The Ottoman empire clung to a shaky dominance over the Muslim world of the Middle East and North Africa at the beginning of the nineteenth century. With the exception of Morocco, North Africa was nominally ruled by the Turkish sultan. By the end of the century, however, Europeans dominated North Africa, while the Middle East discontentedly remained under the sultan. World War I and its aftershocks fundamentally changed this situation.

The Arab Revolt

In 1913 an Arab Congress meeting in Paris demanded home rule and equality with the Turks in the Ottoman Empire. Because the Middle East was so important to Britain, the London government followed the Arab movement with great interest, especially after Turkey joined the Central Powers in the war. In the latter half of 1915, the British High Commissioner in Cairo carried on an extensive correspondence with Sherif Husein of Mecca (Husein ibn-Ali, 1856–1931), guardian of Islam's holy places. The British told Husein that in the event of an Arab revolt against the Turks, Great Britain would recognize Arab independence except in those regions of coastal Syria that were not wholly Arab—presumably excluding Palestine—and in those places that might be claimed by France.

In addition to the British alliance with the Arab nationalist movement, the desert warrior Abdul ibn-Saud (1880–1953), sultan of Nejd in south-central Arabia, agreed to adopt a policy of benevolent neutrality towards Britain. The wooing of the Arabs blocked the Turkish attempt to rouse the Muslim Middle East by preaching *jihad*, or holy war, against the British.

The Arab revolt began in late 1916. Husein raised the standard of rebellion in Hejaz, proclaimed independence from the Turks, and captured Mecca. In the fighting that followed, the Arab forces were commanded by the third son of Sherif Husein, Emir Faisal (1885–1933), who was assisted by a charismatic English officer, Colonel T. E. Lawrence (1888–1935), later known as Lawrence of Arabia.

Faisal al Husein cooperated with T. E. Lawrence in the campaign which captured Jerusalem and Damascus from the Ottomans in 1917 and 1918.

Under Lawrence, the Arabs played a decisive role in the last battle against the main Turkish forces in September 1918. When World War I ended, Syria was occupied by the victorious Allied forces; a small French force was located along the coast of Lebanon; emir Faisal and his Arab forces were in the interior, grouped around Damascus; and the British controlled Palestine.

A Flawed Peace

With Turkey defeated, the Arab leaders sought the independence they thought the British had promised in their correspondence with Husein. When the peace conference met in Paris, it became painfully clear that the problem of political settlement in the Middle East was a jumble of conflicting promises and rivalries.

A number of important commitments had been made during World War I, beginning with Britain's pledge to Sherif Husein in 1915. Britain, France, and Russia signed the secret Sykes-Picot Agreement in 1916. Under this pact, Syria and

Iraq were divided into four zones with London and Paris each controlling two and Russia gained parts of Asiatic Turkey. Palestine was to be placed under an international administration. The most important commitment bearing on the postwar history of the Middle East was Britain's declaration to the Jewish Zionist organization in 1917.

Jewish hopes to create a national home in Palestine grew rapidly after 1900. In 1903 a sympathetic British government had offered Theodore Herzl, the creator of the Zionist idea of a Jewish state, land in East Africa for a Jewish settlement. This proposal, however, had not been accepted. Following Herzl's death in 1904, the leadership of the Zionist movement had been assumed by Dr. Chaim Weizmann (1874–1952), a Russian Jew who had become a British subject. An intimate intellectual friendship developed between Weizmann and the English statesman Arthur James Balfour (1848–1930), who came to support the Zionist program. Balfour held a deep admiration for Jewish religious and cultural contributions. He believed that "Christian religion and civilization owed to Judaism a great debt and [one] shamefully repaid."[7]

During the course of World War I, the British government, strongly influenced by Balfour, then foreign secretary, became convinced that its support of a Zionist program in Palestine would not only be a humanitarian gesture but would also serve British imperial interests in the Middle East. Thus in November 1917 Britain issued the Balfour Declaration:

> His Majesty's Government views with favour the establishment in Palestine of a national home for the Jewish people, and will use their best endeavors to facilitate the achievements of that object, it being clearly understood that nothing shall be done which may prejudice the civil and religious rights of existing non-Jewish communities in Palestine or the rights and political status enjoyed by Jews in any other country.

Zionists were disappointed that the declaration did not unequivocally state that Palestine should be *the* national home for the Jewish people. In 1918 Great Britain made several declarations recognizing Palestinian national aspirations, and an Anglo-French pronouncement pledged the establishment of national governments "deriving their authority from the initiative and free choice of the indigenous populations."

At the Paris Peace Conference Emir Faisal, aided by Lawrence, pleaded the cause of Arab independence, but in vain. Faisal was still ruler in Damascus, and in March 1920, while the statesmen in Paris argued, a congress of Syrian leaders met and resolved that he should be king of a united Syria, including Palestine and Lebanon. But in April the San Remo Conference decided to turn over all Arab territories formerly in the Ottoman empire to the Allied powers to be administered as mandates. Syria and Lebanon were mandated to France; Iraq and Palestine to Britain (see map below).

Mandated Areas

The Arabs saw the mandate system as a poor substitute for independence and a flimsy disguise for imperialism. The great powers were caught up in their web of conflicting aims and promises. Apologists for Britain and France pointed out that Britain made promises to France during the war because the British could hardly deny the requests of their most important

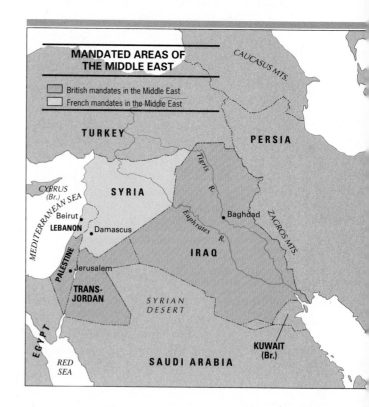

Memorandum of the General Syrian Congress

World War I and its destruction of the old empires paved the way for the rise of Arab nationalism. The memorandum of the General Syrian Congress sounded themes that would be heard throughout the twentieth century.

We the undersigned members of the General Syrian Congress, meeting in Damascus on Wednesday, July 2nd, 1919, made up of representatives from the three Zones, viz., The Southern, Eastern, and Western, provided with credentials and authorizations by the inhabitants of our various districts, Moslems, Christians, and Jews, have agreed upon the following statement of the desires of the people of the country who have elected us. . . .

1. We ask absolutely complete political independence for Syria. . . .
2. We ask that the Government of this Syrian country should be a democratic civil constitutional Monarchy on broad decentralization principles, safeguarding the rights of minorities, and that the King be the Emir Feisal, who carried on a glorious struggle in the cause of our liberation and merited our full confidence and entire reliance.
3. Considering the fact that the Arabs inhabiting the Syrian area are not naturally less gifted than other more advanced races and that they are by no means less developed than the Bulgarians, Serbians, Greeks, and Roumanians at the beginning of their independence, we protest against Article 22 of the Covenant of the League of Nations, placing us among the nations in their middle stage of development which stand in need of a mandatory power.
4. In the event of the rejection of the Peace Conference of this just protest for certain considerations that we may not understand, we, relying on the declarations of President Wilson that his object in waging war was to put an end to the ambition of conquest and colonization, can only regard the mandate mentioned in the Covenant of the League of Nations as equivalent to the rendering of economical and technical assistance that does not prejudice our complete independence. And desiring that our country should not fall a prey to colonization and believing that the American Nation is farthest from any thought of colonization and has no political ambition in our country, we will seek the technical and economic assistance from the United States of America, provided that such assistance does not exceed 20 years.
5. In the event of America not finding herself in a position to accept our desire for assistance, we will seek this assistance from Great Britain, also provided that such does not prejudice our complete independence and unity of our country and that the duration of such assistance does not exceed that mentioned in the previous article.
6. We do not acknowledge any right claimed by the French Government in any part whatever of our Syrian country and refuse that she should assist us or have a hand in our country under any circumstances and in any place.
7. We oppose the pretensions of the Zionists to create a Jewish commonwealth in the southern part of Syria, known as Palestine, and oppose Zionist migration to any part of our country; for we do not acknowledge their title but consider them a grave peril to our people from the national, economical, and political points of view. Our Jewish compatriots shall enjoy our common rights and assume the common responsibilities.

From *Foreign Relations of the United States: Paris Peace Conference,* vol. 12 (Washington, D.C.: Government Printing Office, 1919), pp. 780–781.

ally, which had close missionary and educational ties to Syria. In 1915 Britain made its ambiguous pledge to Husein because of its desperate need for Arab friendship. In the Balfour Declaration, Britain acted according to short-range interests—to swing the support of the world's Jewish community to the Allied cause and to maintain communications in the Middle East.

It should be kept in mind that British statesmen sincerely believed that a Jewish national home could be reconciled with Palestinian interests. They had no idea of the massive influx of Jewish immigration that would come in the 1930s. The fact remains, however, that the Allied statesmen during the war and at the peace conference were profoundly unaware of the intensity of Arab nationalism.

Against strong Arab opposition, France took control of both Syria and neighboring Lebanon, which it separated into two mandates. Its regime harshly suppressed political liberties but did construct new roads, public buildings, and irrigation works. The Lebanese situation was especially complex. While its population was predominantly Arab, it was divided by many religious groups. Among the Christians there were ten different sects, the Maronites being the largest. There were also various Muslim groups, including the ultra-orthodox Druze. Rivalries between these faiths plagued the life and politics of the country.

In Iraq, Arab rebellion immediately confronted British mandatory rule, and the British moved rapidly to try to satisfy Iraqi nationalism. In 1920 Faisal was recognized as king, with Britain retaining control of the finances and military control of the new state. Ten years later Iraq gained its full independence. By these concessions, Britain avoided the conflict that France experienced with Arab nationalism in Syria and Lebanon.

Arab-Jewish Conflict

Between the two world wars, Palestine was the most complex area in the Middle East. Britain tried to protect its imperial interests and at the same time reconcile them with Zionist and Palestinian nationalism. Almost as soon as the mandate was set up, the Palestinians rioted.

In 1919 the population of Palestine was estimated to be 700,000, of which 568,000 were Palestinians. Of the remaining about 58,000 were Jews and 74,000 were others, mainly Christians. Recognizing the concerns of the Arabs, the British sought to define the Balfour Declaration more precisely. While not repudiating Palestine as a national home for the Jews, the British government declared that it "would never impose upon them [the Palestinians] a policy which that people had reason to think was contrary to their religious, their political, and their economic interests."[8]

Such pronouncements and the fact that Jewish immigration was not large made possible a period of peace and progress from 1922 to 1929. As the Zionists reclaimed land, set up collective farms, harnessed the Jordan River for power, and established many new factories, a veritable economic revolution took place. Unfortunately, this brought little benefit to the Palestinian majority. Tel-Aviv grew into a thriving modern city, an excellent university was founded at Jerusalem, and Palestine became the center of a Hebrew renaissance.

The era of peace ended in 1929 when serious disorders broke out, mainly Palestinian attacks on Jews. Violence continued in the early 1930s as the Nazi persecution of the Jews brought about a steep rise in immigration to Palestine and threatened the Palestinians' predominant position in the area. In 1937 a British commission of inquiry recommended a tripartite division: Palestine would be divided into two independent states, one controlled by the Palestinians and one by the Jews, with Britain holding a third portion, a small mandated area containing Jerusalem and Bethlehem. This recommendation satisfied no one and was not accepted.

Throughout the 1930s the "Palestine question" provoked heated discussion in many parts of the world. Zionists argued that Jews had a historic right to the Holy Land, their original home. They stated that Palestine had been promised to them in the Balfour Declaration and that promise had been legalized by the League of Nations. They also pointed out that Jewish colonization constituted a democratic and progressive influence in the Middle East and Palestinian hostility was mainly the work of a few wealthy *effendis*, since the mass of Palestinians were profiting from the wealth being brought into the area.

The Palestinians responded that Palestine had been their country for more than a thousand years and declared that the Balfour Declaration did not bind them because they had not been consulted in its formulation. They further insisted that much of Zionist economic development was not healthy because it depended on subsidization by huge amounts of outside capital. Finally, they asked how any people could be expected to stand idly by and watch an alien immigrant group be transformed from a minority into a majority.

With the threat of war looming in 1939, Britain sought desperately to strengthen its position in the Middle East by attempts to regain Arab goodwill. A white paper was issued declaring that it was Britain's aim to have as an ally an independent Palestine, to be established at the end of ten years, with guarantees for both Palestinian and Jewish populations. During this ten-year period land sales were to be restricted. After the admission of 50,000 Jews, with the possibility of another 25,000 refugees from Nazi Germany, no more immigration would take place without the consent of the Palestinians. War between the two groups erupted in 1938, but the greater conflict of World War II shelved the quarrel in Palestine. The controversy would break out again with dire consequences.[9]

Saudi Arabia, Iran, and North Africa

The defeat of Turkey in 1918 left several rival states contending for supremacy in the Arabian peninsula. Following some hostilities, ibn-Saud welded all tribal groups into the new kingdom of Saudi Arabia. The discovery of vast oil reserves gave it enormous wealth.

Persia (or Iran as it came to be known in the 1920s), a land Muslim in religion, but not Arabic in culture, came under the rule of Riza Shah Pahlavi (1878–1944) following World War I. The new shah rapidly followed the path of modernization, especially in the military and in industry, and pursued an independent path. Iran became caught up in the events surrounding World War II, and in August 1941 Riza Shah Pahlavi was forced out by the British and Russians and replaced by his more cooperative son, Mohamed Riza Pahlavi (1919–1980).

While the Muslims in the Asian part of the Islamic band of countries struggled for the right of self-determination, a parallel development was taking place in North Africa. After three

Riza Shah Pahlavi. As shah of Iran from 1925 to 1941, he modernized the country by strengthening its infrastructure.

years of disorder in Egypt, the British government announced that Egypt would no longer be a protectorate of Britain. It was to be a sovereign state. However, Britain remained responsible for defense of the country, protection of foreign interests, and the Suez Canal, an essential link in the British Empire's communcations. Egypt grudgingly accepted this declaration, made its sultan a king, and proclaimed a constitution in 1923. Anglo-Egyptian relations remained unsettled, however, until 1936 when common fear of Mussolini's Italy brought the two nations together in a defense treaty.

In North Africa, the economy prospered and living standards advanced under French colonial rule. Algeria had become politically integrated with France, long before World War I. Tunisia had prospered under French rule and had maintained its native ruler, the bey, In the French Moroccan protectorate, the native sultan had been retained. Nevertheless, the storm signals of bitter nationalism appeared in North Africa, particularly in Morocco. A fundamental split existed between the privileged French Christian minority and the overwhelming Muslim majority.[10]

Mustafa Kemal and the New Turkey

Forty years before the war, the Young Turks had sought to establish a modern secular state. In 1908 they began to implement their dreams. However, defeat in the war and the Arab revolt convinced some Turkish patriots that only the most drastic measures, such as the massacre of more than 700,000 Armenians in 1915, could save their country. In addition, they bitterly rejected the Treaty of Sèvres (1920). It was bad enough to lose their empire, but it was much worse to see their homeland—namely Anatolia—partitioned and the city of Smyrna (Izmir) invaded by the Greeks.

As president of the Turkish republic from its beginning until his death in 1938, Mustafa Kemal instituted many civil and cultural reforms. In 1934 he was given the name Atatürk ("father of Turks").

The patriots rallied around the military hero Mustafa Kemal (1880–1938), who had a brilliant record against the British imperial forces at Gallipoli in World War I. An important figure in the Young Turks movement, Kemal was a born leader, thoroughly western in outlook and education. After the defeat of Turkey, he had been sent by the sultan to demobilize the Turkish troops in Asia Minor. Disregarding instructions, he reorganized the troops and successfully defied the Allies. A new government was set up in Ankara and Kemal was selected as president and commander in chief. The National Pact, a declaration of principles supported by Kemal, galvanized Turkish patriotism. This document upheld self-determination for all peoples, including the Turks, and proclaimed the abolition of the special rights previously enjoyed by foreigners in Turkey.

In 1921 Kemal's armies blocked Greek designs on Turkish land. The following year, the sultanate was abolished and a republic was established. The Allies agreed to a revision of the Treaty of Sèvres, and the Treaty of Lausanne, signed in 1923, returned to Turkey some Aegean islands and territory adjoining Constantinople (Istanbul). The Turkish heartland, Anatolia, remained intact, and no reparations were demanded.

The new constitution was democratic in form, but in reality, Kemal was a dictator who tolerated no interference with his plans. In the new Turkey there was little of the cult of the superior race and no concentration camps or purges. There was just the rule of a single individual in a situation where rough, efficient power was seen to be superior to that of the more lengthy processes of parliamentary rule. Kemal saw his dictatorial rule as a necessary state in raising his people to that level of education and social well-being that democratic government and parliamentary rule requires. Under his rule the old institutions and customs of a backward state were transformed or replaced within a few years.

Africa: From Colonialism to Nationalism

After 1890 the Europeans organized and consolidated their colonial possessions in sub-Saharan Africa. They mapped previously unknown areas, defined boundaries, and set up railroads and communications systems. The improvement of indigenous products such as rubber and palm oil, the introduction of new cash crops such as cotton and cocoa, and the importation of better breeds of cattle enriched the African economies. The colonialists placed forestry on a scientific basis, opened diamond, gold, and tin mines, and rapidly increased trade throughout Africa. European settlement also increased, especially in the highland areas.

The Europeans exported their systems of bureaucracy and tried to stamp out intertribal warfare, cannibalism, and dangerous secret societies. They opened educational facilities, primarily through the churches, and began the laborious task of transcribing the native tongues so that they could become written languages. The colonial governments introduced clinics, hospitals, and sanitation campaigns to improve public health. Meanwhile, agricultural and veterinary officers taught the Africans methods of fighting erosion, securing better seed, using fertilizers, and managing their herds more efficiently.

In the two decades following World War I European culture and technology spread throughout Africa, affecting all parts of the continent in varying degrees. While in some isolated bush areas tribes lived in Neolithic isolation, in the new cities, many Africans led lives almost wholly European, at least in externals. Under colonial rule, Africans had to obey the laws and regulations of white administrators as well as those of their tribal councils and chiefs. To pay for better roads, public buildings, health and agricultural departments, taxes now had to be paid in cash, forcing many Africans to seek employment outside of their tribal areas in the towns, mines, menial domestic or governmental service, or on plantations. Habits of living changed, new styles of dress were adopted, and new farming methods designed to produce cash crops were introduced. The desire to buy imported goods grew.

Contacts with European modes of life rapidly undermined old faiths, customs, tribal loyalties, and social institutions—a process known as detribalization. The Africans belonged neither to their old tribal world nor to the white world. No longer bound by tribal laws, they were uneasy about the courts and the law of the Europeans.

While accepting Christian doctrine, they retained their belief in the powers of tribal deities. No matter what the benefits of imperial rule might be, it was paternal at its best and exploitative at its worst. Perhaps it was necessary and perhaps desirable that Africa be brought into the mainstream of the modern world, but it was a profoundly disruptive experience.

Colonial Rule

While colonial systems of administration varied, few Africans were allowed to participate in the important aspects of colonial government. In British and French colonies, a modicum of training in self-government was available to a small minority. In British Nigeria, one of the most advanced colonies in terms of potilical participation, the Legislative Council of forty-six members in 1922 included ten Africans, four of whom were elected. These were the first elected Africans in the legislatures of British tropical Africa.

The colonial policies of Portugal and Belgium between 1914 and 1939 differed from those of Britain and France in important ways.[11] Belgium had virtually no colonial policy in the Congo, a territory more than three time the size of Texas with vast mineral wealth. Belgian officials ran a day-to-day, efficient economic system with little thought of ultimate objectives. Race relations were relatively harmonious, and the color bar was generally mild. The main emphasis was placed on the material improvement of the Africans and the development of valuable exports. Excellent medical services were provided together with the best system of elementary education in tropical Africa. There was, however, little secondary training, and university education was nonexistent. White settlement was not encouraged and the few thousand nonofficials who worked in the Congo were denied any voice in its political affairs. During the two decades after 1919, Belgium prided itself on the success of this paternal rule. It had created a population of artisans, mechanics, medical assistants, and clerks devoid of any dangerous thoughts of self-government.

The territories of Angola and Mozambique were constitutionally part of Portugal, so any ideas of separation and self-determination were unthinkable. The most backward in Africa, these territories stagnated in part because of Portugal's poverty and an exploitative administration. In early years, the territories were poorly staffed and badly governed. Their officials were described as "spending their time collecting taxes and mistresses."[12]

In theory, Portugal's objective was to develop an integrated society. Once Africans became assimilated, they would become Portuguese citizens with full voting rights. To become assimilated, they had to become Christian (Roman Catholic), practice monogamy, and learn to speak and write Portuguese. Above all, they had to learn "the dignity of labor." While this colonial system often referred to its "civilizing mission" in Africa, reality and practice fell far short. In Mozambique, for example, out of a population of 6 million, only some 5000 had become legally assimilated. The white population grew slowly, in the 1930s numbering only about 30,000 in Angola and some 18,000 in Mozambique. Many of the immigrants were poor and untrained, and a goodly number "went native"—ending up in African bush villages. The most admirable feature

was the absence of any color bar. The most deplorable aspect of Portuguese colonial rule was its extensive use of forced labor, frequently accompanied by cruel punishments, for the benefit of private business.

Mandate Administration

As a result of growing liberal sentiments and opposition to imperialism, all territories conquered by the Allies in World War I were declared to be mandates. Article XXII of the League of Nations Covenant stated that the "well-being and development" of backward colonial lands was a "sacred trust of civilization." In essence, the mandate system was a compromise between annexation of the spoils of war by the victors (although the mandatory powers were never accorded any sovereign rights over the mandates) and establishment of an international trusteeship. Parts of the Cameroons, Togoland, and German East Africa (Tanganyika) were to be administered by Great Britain. The remaining portions of the Cameroons and Togoland became French-administered mandates. Belgium

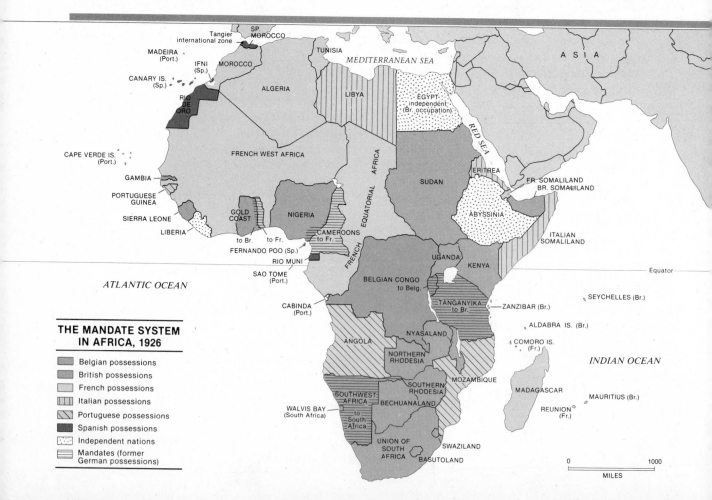

THE MANDATE SYSTEM IN AFRICA, 1926

After World War I, a new wave of liberal thinking and the League of Nations mandate system produced new efforts to improve the standard of living (by European standards) for Africans by building hospitals, libraries, and schools. The schools, like that shown here in the Congo, were run by Europeans and taught European, rather than African, history and culture.

received the mandate of Ruanda-Urundi (also a part of German East Africa), while the former German colony of Southwest Africa was allotted to the Union of South Africa (see map at left).

The Permanent Mandates Commission inspected the annual reports the mandatory governments submitted. While the commission had no effective power to improve unsatisfactory conditions in a mandate, it could place the matter before the eyes of the world. On numerous occasions the mandatory powers accepted the criticisms and heeded the suggestions and criticisms of the commission.

Judgments of the mandate system, a radically new concept in colonial administration, have differed widely. To many critics, international supervision was a unique invasion of national sovereignty. To others, the Permanent Mandate Commission did not have enough power, especially the right to send its own observers into the mandated areas.

"New Britains" Kenya and Rhodesia

Few Europeans lived in the French and British colonies of West Africa, and even they did not think of themselves as permanent settlers. Most returned home for retirement to escape the inhospitable climate. Such was not the case in British East and Central Africa, however, where Kenya and Rhodesia experienced the last thrust of European colonialism.

In the rich gold mines of South Africa, whites held relatively high-paying, skilled jobs while native workers received miserable wages for the grueling tasks they performed, like drilling veins in the cramped tunnels of the mines.

Although located on the equator, Kenya's highland area, which ranges from 6000 to 9000 feet above sea level, has a cool and bracing climate. With the British government's encouragement, the first settlers arrived in 1903, securing rich farmland in the interior. They attempted to make Kenya a white country, although the majority of the population was African. That was the goal of Lord Delamere, the leader of the white settlers, who wrote:

> In East Africa, England has possessed herself of a miniature new dominion, a little New Zealand tucked away between deserts and tropics and lakes, where yet another cutting from the British parent stock could be planted and would grow and flourish.[13]

Nairobi, the capital, became a modern city. New methods of agriculture and stock raising were introduced, which were later to form the basis of prosperity for a new black African nation. White settlement lagged, however, and by 1939 there were only 18,000 Europeans as compared with 3 million Africans. The rapid development of black nationalism in the 1930s made it obvious that Kenya would ultimately obtain self-government, not for the white settlers, but for the Africans.

To the south, in central Africa, another attempt to establish a British outpost was in the making. With the support of Cecil Rhodes, white immigrants began entering the region known as Rhodesia in the 1890's. The country had rich mineral and agricultural resources, and its white population increased more rapidly than in Kenya. Britain granted self-government to the area in 1923, subject to British retention of certain powers relating to the rights of the African majority.

By 1931 the population of Rhodesia consisted of 50,000 whites and 1 million Africans. The European community, whose numbers were growing slowly, controlled the country's best land and resources as well as its government. As the country developed economically and race relations remained calm, Europeans in the late 1930s were optimistic about their dominant role. The stormy days of the 1970s, with their militant rise of African nationalism, lay ahead.

White Exploitation in the Union of South Africa

South Africa was the most explosive area in the interwar period. Here African discontent was the deepest and the breakdown of traditional ways of life was the most widespread. Within the white population, the Dutch (called Boers) were rivals of the British settlers. Since 1902 when Britain defeated the two Boer republics, there had been tension between victors and vanquished.

United in 1909, the country had become a self-governing dominion in the British Commonwealth. But this union did not bring cooperation between the two dominant white groups, beyond enshrining segregation in law in a series of enactments between 1910 and 1913. In 1914 one Boer faction staged an unsuccessful rebellion against South Africa's participation in "England's war." Partnership between Boers and Britons continued to be strained into the 1930s. Even though the Boers gained official recognition of their language, Afrikaans (developed mainly from seventeenth-century Dutch), they continued to insist on their own flag and national anthem. Constantly they discussed secession from the Commonwealth.

Although the rift between Britons and Boers was serious, even more dangerous was the increasing numerical gap between all Europeans on the one hand and the native population on the other. After World War I, the Europeans began to eye the statistics nervously. There were 5.5 million Africans in the Union and 1.8 million whites—just under 50 percent of them of British stock. In addition, there were 200,000 Asians and 600,000 "coloured." Fearful of being overwhelmed by sheer numbers, many whites became convinced that the blacks had to be kept separate from the European community socially and politically and that all political control must remain in the hands of the Europeans.

Segregation and the color bar continued to spread rapidly in the 1920s and 1930s. Africans were restricted to their tribal reserves. Only those who obtained special permission could work on farms owned by Europeans or in the cities, and in urban areas they were obliged to live in squalid, segregated "locations." If found without their passes and identity cards, they were subject to arrest and fine or imprisonment. Native labor unions were discouraged and strikes forbidden. In addition, governmental regulations of the white labor unions excluded Africans from certain skilled trades.

Uneducated Europeans, the so-called poor whites, found it hard to make a living, competing, as they did, with the black majority which would work for pathetically low wages for limited jobs. To support the "poor whites" the white government passed laws allocating to them certain jobs with inflated wages on the railroads and in city services. Special subsidies, drawn from taxes on the entire population, paid for these jobs. This discriminatory practice resulted in huge wage disparities, the average wage for Europeans being just under four dollars a *day*,

while that for the African was just over three dollars a *week*. Africans were also excluded from politics. They could not vote or hold office in any influential elective body or parliament outside their own tribal reserves.

The pressures of increasing population in the reserves forced Africans to seek their livelihood outside. By 1936 more than 1 million Africans worked in white urban areas; another 2 million worked on European farms. About 3.5 million remained on the tribal reserves, which were neglected or impoverished. African unrest manifested itself in the increasing crime rate in the cities, in the formation of underground organizations, and in efforts to work for political rights. In the back alleys and cellars of Johannesburg and other cities, young Africans ran mimeograph machines, turning out handbills and papers advertising their grievances.

In spite of the political and social unrest, the country experienced substantial economic progress, as did much of sub-Saharan Africa, where by the early 1930s outside investments totaled nearly $5 billion. In South Africa agricultural production soared, together with mining products such as gold and diamonds. Africans, however, had little share in this economic progress.

Pan-Africanism and African Nationalism

All over Africa, opposition to imperialism grew throughout the war years. The fact that Europeans were killing one another on the battlefields did much to weaken white prestige. At the Paris Peace Conference, Wilson's ideology with its message of self-determination found a ready response among African intellectuals. Black leaders in the United States demanded greater recognition of rights for blacks, especially in Africa, and argued that the peace conference should help form an internationalized, free Africa. Dr. W. E. B. Du Bois (1868–1963), one of the organizers of the National Association for the Advancement of Colored People (NAACP) and editor of the influential newspaper *Crisis*, proposed the nucleus for a state of some 20 million people, guided by an international organization.

In 1919 Du Bois and other black leaders from the United States traveled to Paris to present

W. E. B. Du Bois shown here (standing at far right) in the editorial offices of the *Crisis,* was the pioneer advocate of the Pan-African movement.

their ideas in person to the delegates at the peace conference. While there, Du Bois was instrumental in convening a Pan-African Congress with representatives from fifteen countries. The gathering urged that the former German colonies be placed under an international agency, rather than under the rule of one of the victorious colonial powers, such as Britain.

Complementing the sentiments expressed at the Pan-African Congress were the ideals of black nationalism. In a convention held in New York in 1920, the members issued the Declaration of Rights of the Negro Peoples of the World. This document protested race discrimination in the United States and the "inhuman, unchristian, and uncivilized treatment" of Africans in the colonial empires. Frustrated by the patronizing attitudes of Christian missionaries, many Africans founded their own churches, based on the doctrine of the "fatherhood of God and the brotherhood of man regardless of color or creed."[14]

Africans in most colonies formed nationalist groups, but they were largely ineffectual. The most important center for nationalist aspirations was in London, where a group of Nigerian students organized. African rights groups existed in South Africa, but the white government there was already perfecting its method of police repression that were to be so effective throughout the twentieth century.

Closely connected with Pan-Africanism and black nationalism was the movement among black intellectuals to recover and rediscover the African past. Relatively little was known about the religious systems, tribal organization, and agriculture of sub-Saharan Africa. Students of social anthropology, a new branch of the social sciences, took field trips to Africa as the interest in African life and culture spread among anthropologists, missionaries, and learned societies. New discoveries made it clear that Africa's comparative backwardness was due in large part to disease and isolation. The International Institute of African Languages and Cultures was organized in 1926. It was claimed with some justification that this project opened up a new era of international cooperation in the service of Africa. New departments in African studies were set up in various universities, and a small number of Africanists began to be trained in the United States.

Perhaps the most significant consequence of colonialism was the emergence of a small nucleus of African intellectuals, who took advantage of scattered educational opportunities and rare chances for study abroad, mainly in Britain, France, and the United States. The most prominent among this group of indigenous African leaders included Jomo Kenyatta (c. 1894–1978) of Kenya, Leopold Sedar Senghor (b. 1906) of Senegal, Kwame Nkrumah (1909–1972) of the Gold Coast (Ghana), and Benjamin Azikwe from Nigeria. It was largely from their ranks that the future leaders of independent Africa were recruited.[15]

Conclusion

Between the two world wars, imperialism went on the defensive before the rise of nationalism in the non-Western world. In the opening decades of the twentieth century, Japan made amazing progress in industrialization and attempted to introduce a democratic system of government. By 1919 the island nation had become one of the world's leading powers. Its spectacular rise to power was accompanied by serious demographic and resource problems that endangered the weakly rooted democratic forces.

Although China was not, strictly speaking, part of the colonial world, in many ways this vast land was under the indirect influence of the great powers. Chinese Nationalists, under the leadership of Sun Yat-sen, overthrew the Manchu Dynasty and established a republic. After years of confusion and conflict among rival factions, Chiang Kai-shek consolidated power in the Kuomintang regime. A nascent Chinese Communist movement, under Mao Tse-tung, survived efforts of the Chinese Nationalists to destroy it.

The strongest nationalist movement was that in India, under the leadership of Mohandas Gandhi. He preached a message of nonviolence and civil disobedience to force Britain to grant a substantial measure of self-government to the Indians. In the lands formerly controlled by the Ottomans, Arab nationalists bitterly contested European control in the mandated areas. Outbreaks of violence occurred in Palestine, where the Arabs resented the British attempt to set up a national home for the Jews.

In Africa, black nationalists sought to replace colonial rule with self-government and to bring about the cultural resurgence of a people whose way of life was slowly disintegrating in the face of western imperialism. The Pan-African movement did not affect the masses of the people in most areas; only in the troubled multiracial society of South Africa was there widespread unrest among Africans.

Suggestions for Reading

P. Welty, *The Asians: Their Heritage and Their Destiny* (Lippincott, 1973). A thorough coverage of Japan is E. O. Reischauer, *Japan: The Story of a Nation* (Knopf, 1974) and Takashi Fuktake, *The Japanese Social Structure: Its Evolution in the Modern Century* (Univ. of Tokyo, 1982). For a detailed description of how the military extremists undermined parliamentary government in Japan, see Richard Storry, *The Double Patriots: A Story of Japanese Nationalism* (Greenwood, 1973). Economic pressures in internal Japan are discussed in James Morley, Ed, *Dilemmas of Growth in Prewar Japan* (Princeton, 1971).

J. K. Fairbank and K. C. Liu, *The Cambridge History of China*, XII, "Republican China 1912–1949," (Cambridge, 1983) is the essential starting point for pre-Mao China. For a solid analysis of the four decades of revolution in China see Lucien Bianco, *Origins of the Chinese Revolution* (Stanford, 1971). See also Edward Friedman's study on Sun Yat-sen, *Backward Toward Revolution* (California, 1974). Stuart Schram, ed. *Mao Tse-Tung Unrehearsed* (London Penguin, 1974) is a good selection of the Chairman's thoughts. D. G. E. Hall, *A History of Southeast Asia*, (St. Martin's, 1968) and H. J. Berda and J. A. Larkin, *The World of Southeast Asia* (Harper and Row, 1967) provide good general coverage of the area.

For invaluable studies of the architects of Indian nationalism see K. Kripalani, *Gandhi: A Life* (Verry, 1968); E.

Thomson, *Rabindranath Tagore* (Greenwood, 1975) and M. C. Rau, *Jawaharlal Nehru* (Interculture, 1975). See also B. R. Nanda, *Gokhale, Gandhi, and the Nehrus: Studies in Indian Nationalism* (St. Martin's, 1975). T. W. Wallbank, *India in the New Era* (Scott, Foresman) is a useful and authoritative survey.

See S. N. Fisher, *The Middle East: A History* (Knopf, 1968) for a comprehensive outline of forces and events. A short history of the Jewish people is Abba Eban, *My Country* (Random House, 1972). See also B. Halpern, *The Idea of the Jewish State* (Harvard, 1969). An analysis of Arab changes is presented in M. Halpern, *The Politics of Social Charge in the Middle East and North Africa* (Princeton, 1967). On the impact of westernization in Turkey see Bernard Lewis, *The Emergence of Modern Turkey* (Oxford, 1968). See also studies by S. H. Longrigg: *Syria and Lebanon under French Mandate* (Octagon, 1972) and *Iraq, 1900 to 1950* (Verry, 1972)

An astute observer surveying Africa as it was before World War II is John Hatch, *Africa Emergent* (Regnery, 1974). See also C. G. Segre, *Fourth Shore: The Italian Colonization of Libya* (Univ. of Chicago, 1975); Michael Crowder, *West Africa Under Colonial Rule* (Northwestern, 1968); and W. Cartey and M. Kilson, eds., *The Africa Reader* I, *Colonial Africa* (Vintage, 1970). Robin Mallett gives a solid survey in *Africa Since 1875* (Michigan, 1974).

Notes

1. Harold Z. Scheffrin, *Sun Yat-sen and the Origins of The Chinese Revolution* (Berkeley: University of California Press, 1968).

2. Michael Gasster, *Chinese Intellectuals and the Revolution of 1911* (Seattle: University of Washington Press, 1969).

3. Stuart Schram, *Mao Tse-tung* (Baltimore: Penguin Books, 1967).

4. E. O. Reischauer, J. K. Fairbank, and A. M. Craig, *East Asia: The Modern Transformation* (Boston: Houghton Mifflin, 1965).

5. J. Nehru, *Toward Freedom* (New York: John Day, 1942), p. 353.

6. T. Walter Wallbank, *The Partition of India: Causes and Responsibilities* (Boston: D. C. Heath, 1966).

7. Blanche E. C. Dugdale, *Arthur James Balfour* (G. P. Putnam's Sons, 1937), p. 325.

8. Quoted in Hans Kohn, *Nationalism and Imperialism in the Hither East* (G. Routledge and Sons, 1932), pp. 132–133.

9. Walter Laqueur, *A History of Zionism* (New York: Holt, Rinehart, and Winston, 1972).

10. Edward Behr, *The Algerian Problem* (London: Hodder and Stoughton, 1961), pp. 13–54.

11. Raymond L. Buell, *The Native Problem in Africa*, 2 vols. (New York: Macmillan Co., 1928), a pioneer and classic study.

12. Robin Hallett, *Africa since Eighteen Seventy-five* (Ann Arbor: University of Michigan, 1974) p. 51.

13. T. Walter Wallbank, "British East Africa—A Case Study in Modern Imperialism," *World Affairs Interpreter*, Autumn 1983, p. 293.

14. Robert I. Rotberg, *A Political History of Tropical Africa* (New York: Harcourt Brace Jovanovich, 1965), p. 341.

15. Ronald Segal, *Political Africa: A Who's Who of Personalities and Parties* (New York: Praeger, 1961).

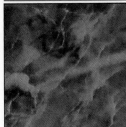

Chapter 34

Troubled Peace and World War II, 1920–1945

I n the first decade after World War I, statesmen with global vision made serious attempts to control conflict through international organizations and treaties limiting arms and outlawing war. In the 1930s, however, the competition among states resumed its traditionally violent course. Ambitious dictators in Asia, Africa, and Europe made war, while representatives from the democracies tried to reason with them.

From 1939 to 1945 the Second World War, with its new and horrible technologies, ravaged the globe. Large bombers took the war to civilians hundreds of miles behind what used to be known as the front lines. Hitler made use of industrial technology to try to destroy an entire people. Only a massive counterattack by the Allied powers, capped by the use of the atomic bomb in Japan, brought an end to the fighting.

The Troubled Calm: The 1920s

The aftershocks of the First World War totally dominated the interwar period. The horror, expense, and exhaustion of the tragedy dominated the losers and winners alike. The better part of a young generation had died. Political leadership fell either to the old who had gained authority before 1914 or to the untried young. It was in this uncertain environment that the League of Nations began its work.

The League of Nations

The League's record from 1919 to 1929 was one neither of dismal failure nor of complete triumph.

Such threats to peace as disputes between Sweden and Finland and between Britain and Turkey were resolved. When a state defied the League, however, as in the case of Italy's quarrel with Greece over Corfu, the organization could do nothing. The refusal of the United States, the world's strongest democracy, to join weakened the League's peacekeeping possibilities.[1]

Through no fault of the League's, little progress was made in the field of disarmament. On one occasion, perhaps because of its relative weakness, Russia proposed complete disarmament. The British delegates, among others, were suspicious of Russia's sincerity in wanting to surround the world in a "loving embrace."[2] The member-states' firmly rooted feelings of mutual distrust and fear of losing sovereignty hurt the League's ability to keep the peace.

However, the League had a distinguished list of accomplishments in other areas. It supervised the exchange and repatriation of prisoners of war and saved thousands of refugees from starvation. It helped Austria, Bulgaria, and Hungary to secure badly needed loans. The League also provided valuable service in administering the region of the Saar Basin and the Free City of Danzig. It investigated the existence of slavery in certain parts of the world, sought to control traffic in dangerous drugs, and stood ready to offer assistance when disasters brought suffering and destruction to the globe.

In the intellectual and cultural realm the League published books and periodicals dealing with national and international problems of all kinds and from its own radio station broadcast important information, particularly in the field of health. Unfortunately, the League's excellent

The Senate's refusal to ratify the Treaty of Versailles meant that the United States would not join the League of Nations.

armistice the French wanted to impose maximum financial penalties on the Germans. In 1923, assisted by the Belgians, they occupied the Ruhr region in a move that had immense short- and long-range implications. Some historians have seen in this act the first step toward World War II because it hardened the German desire for revenge. Even though the Dawes Plan (see p. 795) eased the situation, the French attitude divided the former Allies and provided ammunition to the German ultranationalists.

The rift between the French and Germans was papered over in Locarno, Switzerland, in 1925. In the Locarno Pact, Germany, Great Britain, France, and Italy agreed to guarantee the existing frontiers along the Rhine, to establish a demilitarized zone 50 kilometers deep along the east bank of the Rhine, and to refrain from attacking one another. The problems along France's eastern frontier would be dealt with by international guarantee (although the British dominions stated their disagreement) and U.S. money. Germany received, and accepted, an invitation to join the League of Nations, a symbolic act that seemed to indicate its return to the international community. Still, the Locarno Pact

record in these areas has been obscured by its failure to maintain a lasting peace.

France Seeks Security

Because the United States chose to play a limited role in international affairs and Great Britain returned to its traditional focus on the empire and Commonwealth, France assumed the leadership of postwar Europe. In 1919 the French pursued a very simple, but difficult, foreign policy goal—absolute security. Since the Napoleonic heights a century earlier, the French had seen their power and authority diminish while German economic and military strength had increased. Twice in fifty years Germany had invaded France with terrible results. The obsession with security could be easily understood.

France spent much of the postwar decade trying to guarantee its own safety by keeping Germany weak. In the first five years after the

The artist of this hopeful cartoon pictured the 1925 Locarno Pact as the agreement that would put an end to a thousand years of war and bloodshed.

addessed only the western frontier of Germany and left unresolved the controversial issues of the territories of the newly formed and contentious nations of eastern Europe. Another well-meaning but ultimately ineffectual agreement was the Kellogg-Briand Pact (1928), developed by U.S. Secretary of State Frank Kellogg and French Foreign Minister Aristide Briand. This pact, which was eventually signed by sixty-two nations, outlawed war as an instrument of national policy, but omitted provisions to enforce the agreement.

The Paris government had little faith in the Covenant of the League of Nations as a guarantee of France's survival. The French, instead, depended more and more on their own diplomats. They tried to construct a wall of allies along Germany's eastern frontier that would simultaneously surround the Germans and isolate the Soviet Union. While Germany was weak and dependent on western loans, France could stand as the strongest diplomatic power on the continent. But even in the 1920's, France lacked the strength to serve as the leader of Europe. When Germany and Italy began to flex their muscles in the 1930s, France—even with British help—faced fascist aggression from a position of weakness.

Soviet and German Cooperation

The Soviet Union and Germany, the two diplomatic outcasts of the 1920s, quickly forged a working relationship that was useful to both of them. The USSR had isolated itself by signing the Treaty of Brest-Litovsk, nationalizing foreign property, and repudiating foreign debts as well as by its communist ideology. Probably the greatest barrier was the ideological one, as expressed through the activities of the Third Communist International, or Comintern. That body, organized in 1919, was dedicated to the overthrow of capitalism throughout the world.

In the 1920s the Comintern spread communist propaganda, established communist parties throughout the world, and infiltrated labor unions and other working class groups. Even after Lenin had given up hope for an immediate world revolution and started to normalize relations with the west, the Comintern encouraged radicals who had broken off from moderate socialist groups to organize Communist parties. Communists of all countries became members of the Comintern, meeting in congresses held in Moscow and setting up committees to coordinate their activities. Communist parties were different from other national political groups because they owed their allegiance to an international organization rather than to the nations in which they resided.

By 1922 the Soviet Union was pursuing a two-pronged foreign policy—one through the Communist parties to further the spread of communism, as in China, where the communists were active until defeated by Chiang-Kai-shek,

U.S. secretary of state Frank Kellogg signs the Kellogg-Briand Pact, which renounced war as an instrument of national policy. The agreement included no provisions for enforcement of this noble sentiment and thus was powerless to prevent war or punish aggressors.

and the other through normal international channels for traditional economic and diplomatic goals, generally in Europe.

From the time Lenin left Switzerland to return to Petrograd the Soviet Union enjoyed a mutually advantageous relationship with Germany. At the beginning of the 1920s the two nations carried on secret agreements allowing for joint military training enterprises. Their first major open diplomatic contact came at Rapallo, Italy, in 1922, where they renounced the concept of reparations. In the Rapallo pact, the Germans and Russians agreed to cooperate in a number of areas. Germany was extremely bitter about the treatment it had received at Versailles; the Soviets had faced Allied intervention during the civil war. It naturally followed that a main feature of the foreign policies of both countries would be either to ignore the Versailles settlement or to escape from its consequences. Both countries shared a common interest to dominate Poland, against whom the USSR had fought at the beginning of the decade.

Although, as Lenin perceptively noted, Russia wanted revolution while Germany sought revenge, the two nations cooperated closely until 1934. Then after a five-year gap they cooperated again in the Nazi-Soviet nonaggression pact.

The Weimar government under Gustav Stresemann wanted to rearm but was forbidden to do so by the Versailles treaty. Stresemann backed the cooperation between his government and the Soviet Union to build up both Russian and German military might. Berlin supplied technical aid while German pilots and specialists went on maneuver in Russia. Even after the proclamation of the so-called spirit of Locarno, the two nations worked with each other. In 1926 the Rapallo pact was renewed for another five years.[3]

The Epoch of the Aggressors

The world found little peace or stability after the First World War. Economic and social discontent, buttressed by widespread disillusionment with the peace treaties, posed grave problems for the victorious Allies. Almost as weak as the defeated powers, the Allies had to take on the responsibility for maintaining the peace. The awful toll taken by World War I convinced the democracies that never again should humanity have to endure such a tragedy. From the point of view of the new aggressors, however, this attitude reflected weakness and cowardice—and opportunity.

Japan Invades Manchuria

The first challenge to the fragile peace occurred in September 1931 when Japan moved into the traditional Chinese buffer zone of Manchuria. In occupying this region, Tokyo pursued centuries-old goals made more urgent by present-day pressures of resource scarcity and overpopulation. The Japanese invasion of Manchuria was the first step on the road to World War II.

Unable to cope with the invader, the Chinese appealed to the League of Nations, which appointed a committee of inquiry in 1933. The committee's report condemned the aggression, but at the same time tried not to provoke Japan. The outcome was that the League neither put an end to the aggression nor kept Japan as a member—two years later Tokyo withdrew from the organization.

The 1920s "Locarno spirit" of international conciliation and hope for peace ended with the aggressive acts of the 1930s, including Japan's invasion of Manchuria in 1931. The photo below shows Japanese soldiers in a street in Peking in 1937.

Erich Maria Remarque, The Road Back

Erich Maria Remarque, who wrote so eloquently of the horrors of war in *All Quiet on the Western Front*, compellingly expressed the despair and frustration of German veterans in *The Road Back*. He captures the mood that helped Hitler gain power.

Demonstrations in the streets have been called for this afternoon. Prices have been soaring everywhere for months past, and the poverty is greater even than it was during the war. Wages are insufficient to buy the bare necessities of life, and even though one may have the money it is often impossible to buy anything with it. But ever more and more gin palaces and dance halls go up, and ever more and more blatant is the profiteering and swindling.

Scattered groups of workers on strike march through the streets. Now and again there is a disturbance. A rumour is going about that troops have been concentrated at the barracks. But there is no sign of it as yet.

Here and there one hears cries and counter-cries. Somebody is haranguing at a street corner. Then suddenly everywhere is silence.

A procession of men in the faded uniforms of the front-line trenches is moving slowly toward us.

It was formed up by sections, marching in fours. Big white placards are carried before: *Where is the Fatherland's gratitude?—The War Cripples are starving. . . .*

It was no good to go on assuming that a common basis for all the different groups and classes in Germany could be found. The break between them became daily wider and more irreparable. The plebiscite of the Right "against the Young Plan and the war-guilt lie" proved just as unsuccessful as those arranged in former years by the Left, but the poison of the defamatory agitation remained in the body of the community, and we watched its effects with anxiety.

In my own family the political antagonism was growing past endurance. In October Fritz had finished his apprenticeship in an old-established export house, at the precise moment when the firm went bankrupt—a minor incident compared with such events as the breakdown of the Frankfurt General Insurance Company and the Civil Servants' Bank or the enforced reorganization and amalgamation of the Deutsche Bank and the Disconto-Gesellschaft, which all happened in the course of the year and dangerously damaged the whole economic life of Germany. Yet for my brother the bankruptcy of his firm overshadowed all other happenings, since it meant that he lost his job. His three years' training was in vain—there was not a single export firm which was not forced to dismiss as many of its employees as possible. . . .

"Yes, that's just it—millions! If it isn't my fault, whose fault is it? I tell you—your friends, the French, the English, the Americans, all those damnable nations who inflict on us one dishonorable penalty after the other—they are to blame for all this. Before the war the whole world bought German goods. My firm exported to Africa, to the German colonies. Hundreds of thousands we turned over every year. But they have robbed us of our colonies, of all our foreign markets. They have stolen the coalmines in the Saar and in Upper Silesia, they squeeze millions of marks out of our bleeding country. We'll never rise again unless we free ourselves by another war."

"Don't be foolish, Fritz. Things are bad in the whole world."

"I don't care about the world, I care only about Germany, which you and your pacifists have delivered into the hands of our enemies. I despise you, you are not worthy to call yourself a German."

From *The Road Back* by Erich Maria Remarque. "Der Weg Zurück." Copyright © 1931 by Ullstein, A. G.: Copyright renewed 1958 by Erich Maria Remarque.

Japan's war with China began with the invasion of Manchuria in 1931, escalated with the spread to Peking and Shanghai in 1937, and continued until 1945, even though there was never any formal declaration of hostility. Between 1937 and 1945, more than 20 million Chinese died—many of them civilians killed in bombing attacks. The photo here is one of the attack on Chucheng in 1939.

When the Chinese resorted to an effective nationwide boycott of Japanese goods, the invaders attacked Shanghai in 1932 and began to push deeper into northern China. To slow down the invasion and give themselves a chance in the inevitable struggle, the Chinese agreed to a truce in May 1933 that recognized Tokyo's conquests in Manchuria and northern China.

Despite virtual civil war between Chiang Kai-shek's nationalist forces and the communist movement led by Mao Tse-tung, China strengthened its position in the face of the Japanese threat. Following Soviet directions, Mao stated that the first objective of all China should be wholehearted resistance against foreign imperialists. A united front between Chiang and Mao was difficult, but in December 1936–January 1937 the communists and nationalists put aside their conflicts, proclaimed a truce, and established a united front against the Japanese. Neither of the parties in the front trusted the other, but both feared the Japanese more.

In 1937 the Japanese, with no official declaration of hostility, renewed their advance and began what would be an eight-year period of war. Tokyo's forces advanced rapidly up the Yangtze River to Nanking where they committed atrocities, captured Peking, and proclaimed the "New Order" in eastern Asia. The New Order's objectives were to destroy Chiang Kai-shek's regime, expel western interests from east Asia, and establish a self-sufficient economic bloc to include Japan, Manchuria, and China.

The outbreak of war in Europe in 1939 gave Japan a golden opportunity to expand the New Order in China and into the Asian colonies of the western powers. The Japanese took the island of Hainan in 1939 and after the fall of France in June 1940, built naval and air bases in Indochina. From there they put pressure on the Dutch East Indies and the British outposts at Hong Kong and Singapore.

None of the three great powers that might have halted the Japanese advance in the 1930s did anything. Britain was in the depths of an economic crisis. France was suffering from political and economic paralysis. The United States was totally absorbed in fighting the depression.

Italy Attacks Ethiopia

While Japan pursued old goals in new ways, Italy set out to claim a prize it had failed to take in 1896—Ethiopia, the only important independent native state left in Africa. Late in 1934 fighting broke out between the Ethiopians and the Italians, and in the following year, Mussolini's forces invaded the country.

Emperor Haile Selassie made a dramatic appearance before the League to appeal for help. The League tried to arrange for arbitration. Unconvinced by the shameless Italian argument that Ethiopia, not Italy, was the aggressor, the League voted to prohibit shipment of certain goods to Italy and to deny it credit. But the effect of the sanctions was minor because oil—without which no modern army can fight—was not included in the list of prohibited articles. France and Britain gave only lukewarm support to the sanctions because they did not want to alienate Italy. The United States, which had not joined the League, and Germany, which had left it by that time, largely ignored the prohibitions. Only outraged public opinion, moved by newspaper photographs showing barefooted Ethiopians fighting the modern Italian army drove the governments to even the pretense of action.

Using bombs, mustard gas, and tanks the Italians advanced swiftly into Ethiopia and crushed Haile Selassie's valiant but poorly armed soldiers. Meanwhile, the German reoccupation of the Rhineland in March helped shift international attention away from the conflict in Africa. The whole, sorry story ended in July 1936 when sanctions were removed. Haile Selassie, an emperor without a country, went to live in Britain, the first of several royal exiles who would be forced from their countries in the next decade.

The Rhineland and the Axis

Soon after taking power, Hitler carried out the revisions the Germans wanted in the Versailles treaty. He also won his country's support by seeking revenge against the Allies. As George F. Kennan noted at the time, "The man is acting in the best traditions of German nationalism, and his conception of his own mission is perhaps clearer that that of his predecessors because it is uncomplicated by any sense of responsiblility to European culture as a whole."[4] During his first two years in power Hitler paid lip service to peace while increasing the tempo of rearmament. In March 1935 he negated the disarmament clauses of the Versailles treaty, and a year later reoccupied the Rhineland.

The move, which Hitler described as producing the most nerve-wracking moments of his life, sent German troops marching boldly into the Rhineland in defiance of the Versailles treaty and the Locarno agreements. The Germans could not have resisted had the British and French moved in response. London did nothing and Paris mobilized 150,000 troops behind the Maginot line—but did no more. Hitler later confessed that had the French advanced against him, "We would

Veteran Ethiopian soldiers and young boys barely into their teens march together to the front to battle the Italians who had invaded Ethiopia in 1935.

General Francisco Franco addresses a crowd shortly after he announced establishment of Spain's rebel Nationalist government in October 1936. The Spanish Civil War, which pitted the Loyalist defenders of the Spanish Republic against the rebel fascist Nationalists, served as a bloody and tragic prelude to World War II.

have had to withdraw with our tails between our legs, for the military resources at our disposal would have been totally inadequate for even a moderate resistance."[5]

The League's weak response to the Japanese invasion of China and the Italian attack on Ethiopia combined with the feeble British and French reaction to German reoccupation of the Rhineland encouraged the aggressors and served as the prelude to the forming of the Axis alliance. Until Hitler gained power, Germany had been without close allies. After the Ethiopian crisis and the League sanctions, Italy and Germany began to work more closely together. In 1936 they formalized the friendship in the Rome-Berlin Axis, and one year later, Mussolini followed Hitler's lead by withdrawing from the League of Nations.

Japan, the third major member of the Axis joined forces with Germany in 1936 in the Anti-Comintern pact. A year later, Italy also joined in that agreement, which effectively ringed the Soviet Union. Relations between Moscow and Berlin had cooled after 1934, and the Soviet Union now became the object of anti-Communist rhetoric. Many right-wing leaders in the west hoped that the "Red menace" would be taken care of by the *Führer* and his allies.

All in all, 1936 was a banner year for Hitler. He had gained allies, pleased his own people by remilitarizing the Rhineland, learned the weakness of the democratic powers and the League, and gained international prestige from his successful staging of the Olympic games. Finally, he found a successful device to distract potential opponents' attention in the Spanish Civil War.

The Spanish Tragedy

By 1936 the Spanish republic was disintegrating. It had brought neither prosperity nor stability to Spain. Reactionary forces had tried to gain control of the government while left-wing groups had resorted to terrorism. The liberal approach had failed, and in the summer of 1936 the army revolted against the legal government in Madrid.

General Francisco Franco (1892–1975) commanded the insurgents, who included in their ranks most of the regular army troops. Mussolini strongly backed Franco, and the rightist forces expected a quick victory. However, many groups stood by the republic, and they put up a strong resistance against the insurgents, stopping them at the outskirts of Madrid.

By the end of 1936 each side had gained the backing of a complicated alliance of forces. Franco had the support of the Italians, who sent large numbers of planes, troops, and weapons, and the Germans, who tested their latest military technology against the republicans. The republic gained the support of the Soviet Union, which sent arms, "advisers," and other supplies and large numbers of disorganized but idealistic anti-fascist fighters, including a number from Britain and the United States.

The insurgents capitalized on the Soviet support for the republic, and Franco pronounced his cause to be strictly an anti-communist crusade—a cunning oversimplification that would not have any validity except "for a few months (in 1938) the communists were in firm control of a remnant of republican Spain," until Stalin decided to pull out his support.[6] While Spain bled, suffering more than 700,000 deaths, outside forces took advantage of the tragic situation for their own selfish purposes.

The democratic powers—Great Britain, France, and the United States—attempted to stay officially out of the conflict. Britain did not want to risk a continental war. France suffered from internal divisions that made its leaders fear that their country, too, might have a civil war. The United States declared its official neutrality. Instead of permitting arms to be sent to the recognized, legally constituted republican government which had the right under international law to purchase weapons for self-defense, Great Britain

After the fall of Barcelona in 1939, which marked the end of the Spanish Republic, thousands of Spanish refugees streamed to the French frontier to escape the fascists.

and France set up a nonintervention system by which the nations of Europe agreed not to send arms to either side. This arrangement, meant to limit the scope of the conflict, was adhered to only by the democracies. The various dictators continued to send their support to their respective sides.

Madrid fell in March 1939, and the Spanish republic was no more. Franco, at the head of the new state, gained absolute power, which he held until his death. The Spanish civil war was a national catastrophe that left permanent scars on a proud and gallant people.

Appeasement and Weakness

In 1937, Neville Chamberlain (1869–1940) became prime minister of Great Britain. Years before he took office, the British had tried to build a detente with the Germans backed by "an efficient bomber air force." Chamberlain tried a new strategy: a defense policy based on a fighter air force and centered solely on protecting Britain. He wanted to make "more positive overtures to Germany to appease her grievances and reach a settlement on the basis not of fear by deterrence but of mutual interests and separate spheres of influence." Chamberlain's name came to symbolize the policy of appeasement, "the policy of meeting German demands and grievances without asking firm reciprocal advantages; asking instead only for future 'mutual understandings.'"[7]

Chamberlain took the direction of foreign policy on his own shoulders in his attempt to explore every possibility for reaching an understanding with the dictators. He dedicated himself to an effort to ease international tensions despite snubs from those he wished to placate and warnings from his military and foreign policy advisers. He

Hitler accomplished his goal of *Anschluss*, or union of Germany and Austria, in March 1938. Cheering Nazi supporters greeted Hitler's triumphant march into Vienna.

based his policy on the most humane of motives—peace—and on the most civilized of assumptions—that Hitler could be reasonable and fair minded. By showing good faith—by withdrawing from any possibility of being able to wage war on the continent—Chamberlain froze himself into a position of having to avoid war at any cost.[8] His policies were strongly supported in Great Britain and throughout most of the British Commonwealth.

France had shown that it would not move militarily without British backing, and under Chamberlain the entente with France was put on the back burner, a development that hurt French resolve. The democratic world became uneasily aware of its growing weakness in comparison with the dictators. As the European balance of power shifted, the small states began to draw away from the impotent League of Nations.

The Axis' prestige blossomed. Some nations tried to make deals with Germany and Italy, while others, including the Scandinavian countries and Holland, withdrew into the shelter of neutrality and "innocent isolation." In eastern Europe semi-fascist regimes came to be the order of the day, as the states in that unhappy region, with the exception of Czechoslovakia, lined up to get in Germany's good graces. In 1934 Poland had signed a nonaggression pact with Germany. Belgium gave up its alliance with France. In eastern Europe, only Czechoslovakia remained loyal to Paris.

Hitler became increasingly aware of the opportunity presented by Britain's "peace at any price" policy and the decline of the French alliance system. On November 5, 1937 in a meeting at the Reich Chancellery in Berlin that lasted for more than four hours, Hitler laid out his plans and ideas for the future. According to the notes of the meeting taken by Colonel Hossbach, the *Führer* gave a statement that was to be regarded "in the event of his death, as his last will and testament."

"The aim of German policy," Hitler noted, "was to make secure and to preserve the racial community and to enlarge it. It was therefore a question of space. . . . Germany's future was wholly conditional upon the need for space." The answer to that question was "force" which was to be applied in the next six years, because after 1943

German technological and military superiority would be lost. Hossbach noted that "the *Führer* believed that almost certainly Britain, and probably France as well, had already tacitly written off the Czechs."[9]

Historians still debate the importance of the Chancellery meeting. Hitler's message was not favorably received by the military staff present, for they knew full well that Germany was in no shape to fight. Yet the significance of the message can be found in the wholesale changes in personnel Hitler introduced at the end of 1937 and in the contrast it affords to the views of Chamberlain. The prime minister wanted peace at any price. The *Führer* wanted space at any price.

Toward Austria and the Sudetenland

When Hitler announced the military reoccupation of the Rhineland in the spring of 1936 he stated, "We have no territorial demands to make in Europe." He lied. By 1938, with the German army growing in strength and the air force becoming a powerful unit, the *Führer* began to implement one of his foreign policy goals—placing the German-speaking peoples under one Reich. The first step on that path was to unite Austria and Germany in the *Anschluss* (literally, a joining).

In 1934 the Nazis had badly bungled an attempt to annex Austria. Two years later, softening up operations began again, and by 1938 intense pressure had been levied against Austrian chancellor Kurt von Schuschnigg to cooperate with Berlin. After a stormy meeting with Hitler in February, Schuschnigg restated his country's desire to be independent, although concessions would be made to Germany. He called for a plebiscite in March to prove his point. Outraged at this independent action, Hitler ordered Schuschnigg to resign and to cancel the vote. Both actions were taken, but Hitler sent his forces into Austria anyway.

By March 13, 1938 a new chancellor, approved by Hitler, announced the union of Austria and Germany. After a month in which all opposition was silenced, Hitler held his own plebiscite and gained a majority of 99.75 percent in favor of union. The democratic powers did not intervene

The Hossbach Memorandum

Two years before the outbreak of World War II, Adolf Hitler recapitulated his goals in a secret meeting. Colonel Friedrich Hossbach took down Hitler's comments.

The aim of German policy was to make secure and to preserve the racial community and to enlarge it. It was therefore a question of space.

The German racial community comprised over 85 million people and, because of their number and the narrow limits of habitable space in Europe, constituted a tightly packed racial core such as was not to be met in any other country and such as implied the right to a greater living space than in the case of other peoples. . . .

Germany's future was therefore wholly conditional upon the solving of the need for space, and such a solution could be sought, of course, only for a foreseeable period of about one to three generations. . . .

The question for Germany ran: where could she achieve the greatest gain at the lowest cost. . . .

Case 1: Period 1943–1945

After this date only a change for the worse, from our point of view, could be expected.

The equipment of the army, navy, and Luftwaffe, as well as the formation of the officer corps, was nearly completed. Equipment and armament were modern; in further delay there lay the danger of their obsolescence. In particular, the secrecy of "special weapons" could not be preserved forever. The recruiting of reserves was limited to current age groups; further drafts from older untrained age groups were no longer available.

Our relative strength would decrease in relation to the rearmament which would by then have been carried out by the rest of the world. If we did not act by 1943–45, any year could, in consequence of a lack of reserves, produce the food crisis, to cope with which the necessary foreign exchange was not available, and this must be regarded as a "waning point of the regime." Besides, the world was

expecting our attack and was increasing its counter-measures from year to year. It was while the rest of the world was still preparing its defenses that we were obliged to take the offensive. . . .

Case 2

If internal strife in France should develop into such a domestic crisis as to absorb the French Army completely and render it incapable of use for war against Germany, then the time for action against the Czechs had come.

Case 3

If France is so embroiled by a war with another state that she cannot "proceed" against Germany.

For the improvement of our politico-military position our first objective, in the event of our being embroiled in war, must be to overthrow Czechoslovakia and Austria simultaneously in order to remove the threat to our flank in any possible operation against the West. In a conflict with France it was hardly to be regarded as likely that the Czechs would declare war on us on the very same day as France. The desire to join in the war would, however, increase among the Czechs in proportion to any weakening on our part and then her participation could clearly take the form of an attack toward Silesia, toward the north or toward the west. . . .

The Fuehrer saw case 3 coming definitely nearer; it might emerge from the present tensions in the Mediterranean, and he was resolved to take advantage of it whenever it happened, even as early as 1938.

From *Auswartiges Amt: Documents on German Foreign Policy*, Series D (Washington, D.C.: Government Printing Office, 1949), vol. 1. pp. 29–49, passim.

At the Munich Conference in September 1938, British prime minister Neville Chamberlain (left) and French premier Edouard Daladier (next to him) capitulated to Hitler's demands regarding Czechoslovakia. Italian dictator Benito Mussolini stands to the right of Hitler.

to help Austria. "Indeed, Neville Henderson (the British ambassador to Berlin) had indicated only too clearly that Britain would welcome alteration in Austria's status, if it were done peaceably."[10]

Following his success in Austria, Hitler moved on to his next objective, the annexation of the Sudetenland. This area along the western border of Czechoslovakia was populated mainly by German textile workers who had suffered economically during the depression. The Sudetenland was also the site of the extremely well-fortified Czech defenses. In September 1938 the *Führer* bluntly informed Chamberlain that he was determined to gain self-determination for the Sudeten Germans. He charged, falsely, that the Czechs had mistreated the German minorities. In fact, among the eastern European states Czechoslovakia had the best record in dealing with minority nationalities. But in this affair, Great Britain and France consistently overlooked both the record of the Prague government and the Czech statesmen themselves.

Chamberlain persuaded French premier Edouard Daladier that the sacrifice of Czechoslovakia would save the peace. When the French joined the British to press the Czechs to accept the Nazi demands, the Prague government had little choice but to agree. Chamberlain informed Hitler of the Czech willingness to compromise, only to find that the German demands had increased considerably. Angered by the *Führer's* duplicity, Chamberlain refused to accept the new terms, which included Czech evacuation of some areas and the cession of large amounts of material and agricultural goods.

Munich and Democratic Betrayal

The crisis over Czechoslovakia would be the last major international issue decided only by European powers.[11] Symbolically it would be viewed as a failure that would affect diplomatic decisions for generations to come. On September 28, 1938, Chamberlain received a note from Hitler inviting him to attend a conference at

THE PARTITION OF CZECHOSLOVAKIA

— Czechoslovakia boundary 1937

ESTONIA

LITHUANIA

EAST PRUSSIA

Elbe R.

Oder R.

Vistula R. • Warsaw

POLAND

G E R M A N Y

To Germany Oct. 1938

ORE MTS.

SUDETENLAND

Teschen To Poland Oct. 1938

BOHEMIAN FOREST

• Prague

• Krakow

PROTECTORATE OF BOHEMIA-MORAVIA

SLOVAKIA

CARPATHIAN MTS.

Danube R.

Munich•

• Vienna

To Hungary Nov. 1938

CARPATHO-UKRAINE

ALPS

AUSTRIA To Germany Mar. 1938

• Budapest

HUNGARY

ROMANIA

ITALY

Po R.

YUGOSLAVIA

Danube R.

Munich. The following day, Chamberlain flew to Germany to meet with Hitler, Mussolini, and Daladier at Nazi headquarters. They worked for thirteen hours on the details of the surrender of the Sudetenland. No Czech representative was present, nor were the Russians—outspoken allies of the Czechs—consulted.

The conference accepted all of Hitler's demands and, in addition, rewarded Poland and Hungary with slices of unfortunate Czechoslovakia (see map above). The tragedy for the Czechs brought relief for millions of Europeans, half-crazed with fear of war. But thoughtful individuals pondered whether this settlement would be followed by another crisis. Winston Churchill, who was then in political eclipse in Britain, solemnly warned: "And do not suppose that this is the end. This is only the beginning of the reckoning."[12]

The mounting fears of French and British statesmen were confirmed in 1939. Deprived of its military perimeter, the Czech government stood unprotected against the Nazi pressure that came in March. Hitler summoned Czech president Emil Hacha to Berlin. Subjected to all kinds of threats during an all-night session, Hacha finally capitulated and signed a document placing his country under the "protection" of Germany. His signature was a mere formality, however, for German troops were already crossing the Czech frontier. Not to be outdone, Mussolini took Albania the following month. The two dictators then celebrated by signing a military alliance, the so-called Pact of Steel.

In response to the taking of Czechoslovakia and violation of the Munich pledges, Britain ended its appeasement policy and for the first time in its history authorized a peacetime draft. In Paris, Daladier gained special emergency powers to push forward national defense.

In the United States, isolationism reigned supreme. Between 1935 and 1937, in response to feelings of revulsion stemming from World War I, the U.S. Congress passed neutrality acts that made it unlawful for any nation at war to obtain munitions from the United States. At the same time, in response to events in Ethiopia, Spain, and along the Rhine, President Franklin D. Roosevelt and the State Department worked quietly to alert the American people to the dangers of the world situation. In October 1937 Roosevelt pointed out that "the peace, the freedom, and the security of 90 percent of the population of the world is being jeopardized by the remaining 10 percent who are threatening a breakdown of all international order and law." The president's call, in this so-called quarantine speech, for "positive endeavors to preserve peace brought forth a hostile reaction from the press and public."[13] Two years later Roosevelt told political leaders that the Germans and Italians could win the next war. His warnings went unheeded, as a significant portion of the American public hoped that the Nazis could do away with the communists in Russia.

The Nazi-Soviet Pact

The final step on the road to World War II was Germany's attack on Poland. The treaty of Versailles had turned over West Prussia to Poland as a Polish corridor to the sea. While 90 percent of the corridor's population was Polish, the Baltic city of Danzig—a free city under a League of

Nations high commissioner—was nearly all German. Late in March 1939 Hitler proposed to Poland that Danzig be ceded to Germany and that the Nazis be allowed to occupy the narrow strip of land connecting Germany with East Prussia. Chamberlain, with French concurrence, warned the Nazis that "in the event of any action that clearly threatens Polish independence," the British, "[will] at once lend the Polish government all support in their power." This was an essentially symbolic gesture, as Poland's geography made any useful western aid impossible.

In the months that followed the Allied warnings, France and Britain competed with Germany for an alliance with Russia. Stalin had closely observed the actions of the democratic powers since Hitler's rise to power. He was aware of the hope expressed in some western conservative circles that Hitler might effectively put an end to the Soviet regime. Further, he pledged to stay out of a war between "imperialists." He had to make a closely reasoned choice between the two sets of suitors competing for Soviet partnership.

Chamberlain and Daladier had ignored Moscow at Munich, and generally British relations with the communists were quite cool. Now, with the Polish question of paramount importance, the French and British approaches struck Stalin as being opportunistic. In May, Vyacheslav Molotov became the Soviet foreign minister. While Molotov negotiated publicly with the British and French, who sent negotiators not empowered to make agreements, he was also in secret contact with the highest levels of the Third Reich.

For centuries, Germany and Russia had shared a common concern with the fate of Poland. They had been able to reach agreement at Poland's expense in the eighteenth and nineteenth centuries. From late 1938 on, Moscow and Berlin pondered yet another division of the country. Negotiations between the two proceeded intensely from June through August 1939. While top-ranking German and Soviet diplomats flew between the two capitals, the lower-ranking mission sent to Moscow by Britain traveled leisurely by boat.

By 1939 Stalin had to choose wisely between the western democracies with their spotty record of defending their friends and Nazi Germany which could offer him concrete advantages in eastern Europe. On August 21, to the world's great amazement, the Soviet Union and Germany signed a nonaggression pact.

In retrospect, it is not at all surprising that Stalin chose to work with the Nazis. Through this agreement, Stalin gave Hitler a free hand in Poland and the assurance of not having to fight a two-front war. After the British and French guarantees to the Poles in March, Hitler knew that his attack on Poland would precipitate a general European war. The *Führer* had prepared plans that called for the invasion to begin in August 1939, and with the nonaggression pact, Hitler could attack without fear of Moscow's intervention. Furthermore, he did not believe that Britain and France would dare oppose him.

The nonaggression pact gave Russia time to build up its strength while the imperialists weakened themselves in war. In addition, through secret agreements, Russia would gain Finland, Estonia, Latvia, eastern Poland, and Bessarabia. Germany would get everything to the west including Lithuania. In addition, the Nazis got guarantees of valuable raw materials and grain from the Soviets. Ideological differences could be set aside for such a mutually profitable pact.

World War II

When Nazi forces crossed the Polish border early on the morning of September 1, 1939, they started World War II, the conflict that killed more people more efficiently than any previous war. In all areas, the latest scientific and technological advances were placed in the service of war. New techniques and attitudes revolutionized the field of intelligence. Scientists made major advances in both codemaking and codebreaking. Intelligence gathering no longer depended on the old cloak-and-dagger stealing of messages and secrets. Now high altitude aerial reconnaissance aircraft, radar, the first computers, and radio intercepts allowed enemies to find out each others' plans. Among the major advances on the Allied side were the breaking of the Japanese code and the discovery of the German code mechanism. Less than a decade before the war an American statesman had noted that "gentlemen do not read other gentlemens' mail."

In the new style of warfare, information meant victory, and the cultured assumptions of an earlier age had to be discarded.

A New Way of War

Tactics and weaponry changed greatly between the two world wars. Tanks and planes had been used in World War I, but the concept of the *Blitzkrieg*, massive mobile mechanized movements and saturation bombings behind the lines, made the weapons far more lethal. The trench warfare of the First World War and the concept of fixed, fortified positions such as the Maginot line proved to be useless.

Mobility was the key—even more so that superior numbers of men and weapons. Better communications, provided by improved radio systems, increased mobility. To strike quickly, in great force, and then to exploit the advantage proved to be the main characteristics of the German successes in 1939 and 1940. The Germans broke through enemy lines by using a large number of tanks, followed by the infantry. Rarely, since Napoleon, had speed and concentrated force been used so effectively.

Complementing increased mobility on the ground was the expanded use of air power, which could spread devastating firepower across continents. The new forms of war, however, sparked the inventive genius of the scientists as each technological advance elicited a response—long-range German bombers brought the need for improved radar; improved propeller-driven

The new technology of World War II meant that fighting took place in the air as well as on the sea and on the ground.

A German motorized detachment rides through a Polish town badly damaged by *Luftwaffe* bombs. Poland was unable to withstand Hitler's *Blitzkrieg* of a combined air and ground attack and fell to the Germans within a month.

aircraft set off the development of jet-powered airplanes. No matter how sophisticated the aerial technology became, however, the war proved that, with the exception of nuclear weapons, air power alone could not bring an enemy to its knees.

Other innovations appeared during the wars — paratroopers, advanced landing crafts, flying bombs such as the V-1, rockets such as the V-2 used by the Germans. Aircraft carriers and amphibious forces played an important part in the war in the Pacific. The Japanese used carriers in their attack on Pearl Harbor and the Americans used amphibious forces in "island hopping" across the Pacific.

As in World War I, however, military success lay in the ability of the states to mobilize their populations and resources. During World War II, states came to control all aspects of life. But the final, deciding factor was the ability of the individual soldier, following the directions of such brilliant commanders as Rommel or Eisenhower, to apply all of these resources.

In the end, all of these factors were overwhelmed by the ultimate scientific and technological accomplishment, the atomic bomb. Ironically, although created to protect state interests, this ultimate weapon could destroy civilization.[14]

Blitzkrieg and Sitzkrieg

After staging an "incident" on the morning of September 1, 1939, Nazi troops crossed the Polish frontier without a declaration of war. At the same time the *Luftwaffe* began to bomb Polish cities. On the morning of September 3 Chamberlain sent an ultimatum to Germany demanding that the invasion be halted. The time limit was given as 11 A.M. the same day. At 11:15 Chamberlain announced on a radio broadcast that Britain was now at war. France also soon declared war. After twenty-one years, Europe was once again immersed in war.

The world now had the chance to see the awesome speed and power of Nazi arms. The Polish forces collapsed, crushed between the German advance from the west and, two weeks later, the Russian invasion from the east. By the end of the month, after a brave but hopeless resistance, the Poles once again saw their country partitioned between the Germans and the Russians.

Britain and France did not try to breach Germany's western defensive line — the Siegfried line along the Rhine. With their blockade and mastery of the seas, they hoped to defeat Hitler by attrition. During the winter of 1939–1940 there was little fighting along the Franco-German frontier. The lull in action came to be referred to as the phony war, or *Sitzkrieg*.

Russia took advantage of the lull to attack Finland in November. This campaign revealed to Moscow's embarrassment the Finns' toughness and the Soviet Union's military unpreparedness in the wake of the purges. After an unexpectedly difficult four-month-long campaign, the immense Soviet Union forced tiny Finland to cede substantial amounts of territory.

Forced to retreat by onrushing German tank units and nearly continuous bombing, British, French, and Belgian soldiers wait on the beaches of Dunkirk to be taken across the English Channel to England.

"Blood, Toil, Tears, and Sweat"

In the spring of 1940 the Nazi high command launched its attack on western Europe. In its scope, complexity, and accomplishments it would be one of the most successful military campaigns ever carried out. In April, Nazi forces invaded Norway and Denmark. The Norwegians fought back fiercely for three weeks before being vanquished, while Denmark was taken in even less time. In the second week of May the German armies overran neutral Holland, Belgium, and Luxemburg. The next week they went into northern France and to the English Channel. In the process they trapped an Anglo-French army of nearly 400,000 on the beach at Dunkirk.

The reversals in Norway and the Low Countries and the military crisis in France led to Chamberlain's resignation. Winston Churchill (1874–1965) became prime minister of Great Britain. Churchill had uneven success in both his political and military careers. In the 1930s his warnings against Hitler and Mussolini had been largely ignored. He was viewed as a "might-have-been; a potentially great man flawed by flashiness, irresponsibility, unreliability, and inconsistency."[15] Yet in 1940, at the age of sixty-six, Churchill offered qualities of leadership equal to the nation's peril. For the next five years he was the voice and symbol of a defiant and indomitable Britain.

Faced with the prospect of the destruction of the British army at Dunkirk, Churchill refused to be publicly dismayed. Appearing before Parliament as the new prime minister he announced, "I have nothing to offer but blood, toil, tears, and sweat." He prepared his people for a long and desperate conflict, knowing full well that only the Channel, a thin screen of fighter aircraft, and an untried device called radar protected Britain. Churchill's example inspired his people. Hitler had found his match in the area of charismatic leadership.

Hitler hesitated to squash the forces trapped at Dunkirk, thereby allowing time for hundreds of small craft protected by the Royal Air Force to evacuate 335,000 soldiers across the Channel, including more than 100,000 French troops. At first, military leaders had hoped to save 30,000 of the trapped men; now they had eleven times that number. An army had been saved, even though it had lost all of its heavy equipment.

After Dunkirk, the fall of France was inevitable. Eager to be in on the kill, Mussolini declared war on France on June 10. Designated as an open city by the French to spare it destruction, Paris fell on June 14. As the German advance continued, the members of the French government who wanted to continue resistance were voted down. Marshal Philippe Pétain (1856–1951), the eighty-four-year-old hero of Verdun in the First World War, became premier. He immediately asked Hitler for an armistice, and in the same dining car in which the French had imposed armistice terms on the Germans in 1918, the Nazis and French on June 22, 1940 signed another peace agreement. The Germans had gained revenge for their shame in 1918.

France was split into two zones, occupied and unoccupied (see map below). In unoccupied France, Pétain's government at Vichy was supposedly free from interference, but in reality it became a puppet of the Nazis. The Third Republic, created in 1871 from the debris of defeat suffered at Germany's hands, now came to an end because of a new blow from the same country.

A remarkable patriot, Brigadier-General Charles de Gaulle (1890–1970), fled to London and organized the Free French Government, which adopted as its symbol the red cross of Lorraine, flown by Joan of Arc in her fight to liberate France five centuries earlier. De Gaulle worked to keep alive the idea of France as a great power and continued to aid the Allied cause in his sometimes quixotic way throughout the war.

Only Britain remained in opposition to Hitler, and the odds against the British seemed overwhelming. The Nazis planned a cross-Channel assault, while in Buckingham Palace, the Queen, the present Queen mother, took pistol lessons saying, "I shall not go down like the others."[16] Britain possessed an army that left its best equipment at Dunkirk, radar, and fast fighter aircraft flown by brave pilots. Churchill had his eloquence to inspire his people:

> We shall go on to the end.... we shall defend our island, whatever the cost may be, we shall fight on the beaches, we shall fight on the landing grounds, we shall fight in the fields and in the streets, we shall fight in the hills; we shall never surrender....[17]

The Germans sent an average of 200 bombers over London every night for nearly two months in the summer and fall of 1940. They suffered heavy losses to the Royal Air Force which profited from a combination of superior aircraft, pilots, radar sightings, and visual detection. Yet, all through the fall and winter of 1940–1941 Britain continued to be racked by terrible raids. Night bombing destroyed block after block of British cities. Evacuating their children and old people to the north, going to work by day and sleeping in air raid shelters and underground stations at night, Britain's people stood firm—proof that bombing civilians would not break their will.

THE DIVISION OF FRANCE

German-occupied France
Unoccupied Vichy France

ENGLISH CHANNEL
NETHERLANDS
BELGIUM
GERMANY
LUXEMBOURG
Seine R.
Paris
Rhine R.
Loire R.
BAY OF BISCAY
FRANCE
SWITZERLAND
Vichy
ITALY
Garonne R.
Rhône R.
CORSICA
SPAIN
MEDITERRANEAN SEA

Mastery of Europe

During the fall and winter of 1940–1941 Hitler strengthened his position in the Balkans, but not without some difficulty. By March 1941 Hungary, Bulgaria, and Romania joined the Axis. Hitler had to control the Hungarians and Bulgarians, who were pursuing ancient ambitions for Romanian land. In the process Romania lost a third of its population and territory to its two neighbors. The Romanians emerged, however, as helpful allies for the Germans.

Mussolini, eager to gain some glory for his forces, invaded neutral Greece in October 1940. This thrust proved to be a costly failure when in December, the Greeks successfully counterattacked. The Italians met other defeats in North Africa and Ethiopia, which the British recaptured.

Partially in an attempt to pull Mussolini out of a humiliating position, the Germans in the first four months of 1941 overran Yugoslavia and Greece. Two months of intense aerial and infantry attacks were needed to defeat the Yugoslavs and Greeks, forcing Hitler to spend considerable amounts of men and resources. But, by the end of that time, the *Führer* had secured his right flank prior to his invasion of Russia.

The results of these forays into the Balkans may have been positive for the Axis in the short run. But by going into the Balkans, Hitler delayed his attack on Russia by six to eight weeks. This delay plus inadequate intelligence and bad planning may have cost him victory on the Russian front. In addition, the Germans and the Italians controlled only the major cities of Yugoslavia. Large bands of resistance fighters and partisans, among them communist forces led by Joseph Tito, roamed the area. Hitler had to leave behind German troops formerly committed to the Russian invasion and replace them with lesser Bulgarian and Hungarian forces.[18]

By the spring of 1941 nearly all of Europe had come under German control (see map at right). Only Portugal, Switzerland, Sweden, Ireland, and Turkey remained neutral. While ostensibly neutral, Spain under Franco was pro-Nazi. Britain, though still dangerous, could do little to interfere on the continent. The United States became more disturbed over the Nazi successes, but not enough to take action.

The Nazi air attacks on London in the Battle of Britain caused widespread devastation but failed to bring the city to a halt or destroy the morale of its people.

War with Russia

Hitler and Stalin had signed the nonaggression pact for their own specific, short-term advantages. From the first there was tension and mistrust between the two, and neither side had any illusions about a long-lasting friendship. Stalin had hoped for a much more difficult war in the west among the "imperialists" and had not expected that Hitler would so quickly be the master of Europe.

As early as July 1940 Hitler resolved to attack Russia in an operation code name Barbarossa. In the fall of the year he decided not to invade Britain, but instead to pursue his original goal of obtaining living space. During 1941 British and American intelligence experts told Stalin of

THE CREST OF AXIS POWER

Allies and areas they controlled
Axis nations
Area occupied by the Axis
Vichy France
Neutral nations

Battles: Allied victory × Axis victory ⊗
Thrusts: →(allied) →(axis)

ARCTIC OCEAN

ATLANTIC OCEAN

WHITE SEA

• Murmansk

• Arkhangelsk

N. Dvina R.

Narvik •

FAEROE IS.
(Den.)

SHETLAND IS.
(Br.)

ORKNEY IS.
Scapa Flow

NORTH SEA

Trondheim
Apr. 1940

N O R W A Y

S W E D E N

GULF OF BOTHNIA

F I N L A N D

Lake Onega

Lake Ladoga

S O V I E T

• Kazan

Bergen •

Oslo •

Goteborg

Helsinki •

Stockholm •

Tallinn •

• Leningrad

• Gorki

• Moscow

Saratov

Volga R.

• Glasgow
GREAT

IRELAND
Dublin •

• Liverpool
BRITAIN

Birmingham •
Air battle for Britain
July–Oct. 1940

London •

Southampton
May–June 1940

DENMARK
Apr. 1940

Copenhagen •

BALTIC SEA

ESTONIA

Pskov •

LATVIA

Riga •

LITHUANIA

Kaunas •

Danzig •

U N I O N

• Smolensk

• Voronezh

Dvina R.

Minsk •

Don R.

NETHERLANDS
May 1940

Hamburg •

Elbe R.

Hanover •

Berlin •

Warsaw •

Germany invaded Poland
Sept. 1, 1939

P O L A N D

Kiev •

Dnieper R.

• Kharkov

• Rostov

BELGIUM
1940

Dunkirk
May–June 1940

Cologne •

Dresden •

G E R M A N Y

Krakow •

Lvov •

Dniester R.

Sea of Azov

La Havre •

Lux.

Frankfurt •

Prague •

CZECHOSLOVAKIA
Mar. 1939

Paris •

Rhine R.

Nantes •

Loire R.

F R A N C E

Munich •

Vienna •

Budapest •

HUNGARY
Oct. 1940

R U M A N I A
Nov. 1940

Odessa •

• Sevastopol

Bordeaux •

Vichy •

SWITZERLAND

AUSTRIA
Mar. 1938

Lyons •

Milan •

Venice •

Trieste •

Y U G O S L A V I A
Apr. 1941

Bucharest •

Danube

BLACK SEA

• Trabzon

VICHY
FRANCE

Genoa •

Belgrade •

BULGARIA
Mar. 1941

Sofia •

Marseilles •

CORSICA

I T A L Y

ADRIATIC SEA

Istanbul •

Ankara •

Kizil R.

T U R K E Y

SPAIN

Madrid •

Barcelona •

BALEARIC IS.

SARDINIA

Rome •

Naples •

ALBANIA
Apr. 1939

Salonika •

GREECE
Apr. 1941

Athens •

AEGEAN SEA

Smyrna •

CYPRUS
(Br.)

Adana •

• Aleppo

S Y R I A

Valencia •

TYRRHENIAN SEA

IONIAN SEA

Beirut •

Damascus •

Oran •

Algiers •

Bône •

Tunis •

Palermo •

SICILY

MALTA
(Br.)

M E D I T E R R A N E A N   S E A

CRETE

Jerusalem •
PALESTINE

TRANSJORDAN

ALGERIA

TUNISIA

Tripoli •

Bengasi •

Alexandria •

Cairo •

Suez Canal

SAUDI
ARABIA

L I B Y A

E G Y P T

Nile R.

RED SEA

German troops at the Kharkov front in Russia pass a burning farmhouse. The same factors that had halted Napoleon and his army more than a hundred years earlier—bitter cold and inadequate protection against it—helped stop the German advance. Russia paid a heavy price for stopping the Germans, losing nearly 10 percent of its population in the war.

Hitler's intentions to attack, but the Soviet dictator clung to his obligations under the non-aggression pact. Even while the Nazis were invading Russia in June 1941, shipments of Soviet grain were headed to Germany.

Operation Barbarossa required far more effort and resources than were expended later against the British and Americans in North Africa. Along a battlefront 1800 miles long, 9 million men became locked in struggle. At the outset, the Nazi panzer units were unstoppable, as they killed or captured enormous numbers of Russian troops. In October Hitler's army neared the center of Moscow (a monument today between the city's Sheremetevo Airport and the Kremlin marks the farthest advance of the German army). A month earlier, the Nazis had besieged Leningrad, beginning a two-year struggle in which over one million civilians died. Russia appeared to be on the verge of collapse.

When winter came earlier, and more severely, than usual, the Nazi offensive broke down. Weapons froze, troops were inadequately clothed, and heavy snows blocked the roads. The German attack halted and in the spring of 1942 the Russian army recovered some territory. One reason the Russians could bounce back was the success of the five-year plans in relocating industry behind the Urals. Another reason was the sheer bravery and tenacity of the Soviet people. Also, the United States and Britain had begun sending lend-lease supplies to Russia.

The United States Enters the War

Following the collapse of France and during the Battle of Britain, the American people had begun to comprehend the implications of an Axis victory. After Dunkirk, the United States sent arms to Britain, set forth on a rearmament program, and introduced the peacetime draft. The Lend-Lease Act of 1941 empowered the president to make arms available to any country whose defense was thought to be vital to the U.S. national interest. Despite ideological differences, America sent more than $11 billion worth of munitions to Russia.

To define the moral purpose and principles of the struggle, Roosevelt and Churchill drafted the Atlantic Charter in August 1941. Meeting "somewhere in the Atlantic," the two pledged that "after the final destruction of Nazi tyranny," they hoped to see a peace in which "men in all the lands may live out their lives in freedom from fear and want." If the United States had not yet declared itself at war in the fall of 1941, it was certainly not neutral.

One event on December 7, 1941, brought the full energies of the American people into the war against the dictators—the Japanese attack on Pearl Harbor. Even though Hitler was seen as the most important enemy, it was Japan's expansionist policy that brought the United States into the war.

Confronted with Tokyo's ambitions for the New Order in Asia and widely published accounts of Japanese atrocities, the United States had failed to renew trade treaties, frozen Japanese funds, and refused to sell Japan war materiel. Despite these measures Japan decided to continue its expansion. In October 1941 General Hideki Tojo (1884–1948), a militarist, became premier of Japan. On Sunday, December 7, while special "peace" envoys from Tokyo were negotiating in Washington, ostensibly to restore harmony in Japanese-American relations, Japanese planes launched from aircraft carriers attacked the American bases at Pearl Harbor, Hawaii. The stunningly successful attack wiped out many American aircraft on the ground and crippled one-half of the United States Pacific fleet.

On the following day the United States declared war on Japan, as did Britain. The British dominions, the refugee governments of Europe, and many Latin American nations soon followed the Americans and British. Four days later, Germany declared war on the United States. On January 2, 1942, the twenty-six nations that stood against Germany, Italy, and Japan solemnly pledged themselves to uphold the principles of the Atlantic Charter and declared themselves united for the duration of the war.

The Apogee of the Axis

After Pearl Harbor, Japanese power expanded over the Pacific and into Southeast Asia. Tokyo conquered Hong Kong, Singapore, the Dutch East Indies, Malaya, Burma, and Indochina. The Philippines fell when an American force surrendered at Bataan. The Chinese, however, from their remote inland fortress capital of Chungking, still managed to hold off the Japanese (see map, p. 896).

The summer of 1942 was an agonizing period for the nations allied against the Axis. A new German offensive pushed deeper into Russia, threatening the important city of Stalingrad. The forces

A Navy launch rescues a sailor from the blazing U.S.S. *West Virginia* during the Japanese attack on Pearl Harbor. The attack on Pearl Harbor brought the United States formally into the war.

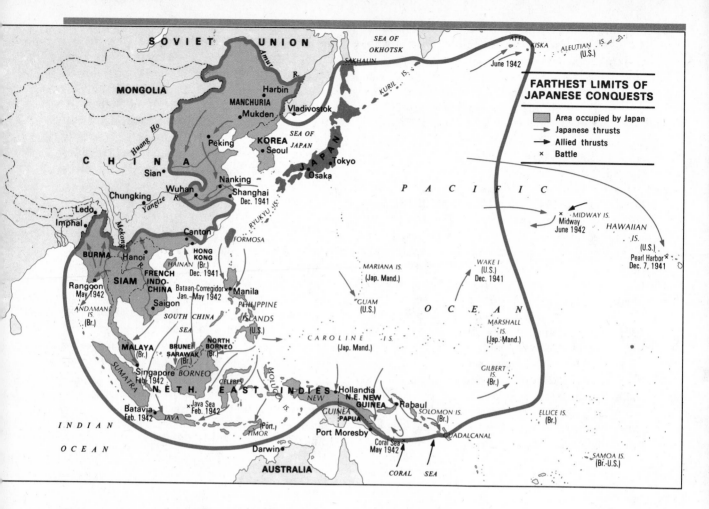

FARTHEST LIMITS OF JAPANESE CONQUESTS

Area occupied by Japan
→ Japanese thrusts
➤ Allied thrusts
× Battle

of the gifted German general Rommel menaced Egypt and inflicted a decisive defeat on the British army in Libya. All over the globe the Axis powers were in the ascendancy. But their advantage was to be short-lived.

Further Japanese expansion in the Pacific was halted by two major American naval victories, the Coral Sea in May and Midway in June. In the first the Americans sank more than 100,000 tons of Japanese shipping and stopped the Japanese advance toward Australia. In the second the Americans turned back the advance toward Hawaii by devastating the Japanese carrier force. In both cases the American forces benefited by having broken the Japanese code and intercepting key messages. After these spectacular victories, U.S. marines began the tortuous rooting out of the Japanese at Guadalcanal and driving them back, island by island. In November 1942 British and American troops landed in

The British victory over Axis troops at El Alamein, Egypt, in 1942 helped turn the tide of the war in favor of the Allies.

North Africa and the British defeated Axis troops at El Alamein in Egypt. By May 1943 all Axis troops in North Africa had been destroyed or captured.

In July 1943 the Allied forces invaded and captured Sicily. On the twenty-fifth of that month, the whole edifice of Italian fascism collapsed, as Mussolini was stripped of his office and held captive. (He was rescued by Nazi agents in September.) In the meantime, the Allies began their slow and bitter advance up the Italian boot. The new Italian government signed an armistice in September 1943, months before Rome was taken in June 1944. German resistance in northern Italy continued until the end of the war.

The Russian Turning Point

As important as the victories in the Pacific, North Africa, and Italy were, the decisive campaign took place in Russia. Hitler threw the bulk of his men and resources against the Soviet troops in the hope of knocking them out of the war and of gaining badly needed resources and food supplies. Hitler's strategy and operations along the Russian front were one mistake after another.

The Nazis lost a great opportunity to further the disintegration of the Soviet Union in 1941, because they treated the peoples they encountered as *Untermenschen*, or subhumans. Often the Nazis, far from encountering resistance, would be treated as liberators by the villages they entered and given the traditional gifts of bread and salt. Often peasants dissolved the unpopular collective farms in the hope that private ownership would be restored. The separatist Ukrainians looked forward to German support for reinstituting their state. The Nazi occupation negated all of these potential advantages. The Nazis carried their mobile killing operations of genocide with them, conscripted Slavs for slave labor in Germany, and generally mistreated the population in areas that they occupied.

Hitler's campaign gave Stalin the opportunity to wrap himself in the flag of Russian patriotism. He replaced the ideological standards with those of nationalism and orthodoxy. He even went so far as to announce the end of the Comintern in 1943, an act more symbolic than real. For the first and perhaps the only time, the communist party and the Soviet people were truly united in a joint enterprise.

The long (September 14, 1942–February 2, 1943) and bloody battle between the Germans and the Russians was focused on the strategic, industrial city of Stalingrad on the Volga River. Hitler had fanatically sought to take the city, which under the constant pounding of artillery had little of importance left in it. His generals advised him to stop the attempt and retreat to a more defensible line. Hitler refused, and the German Sixth Army of 270,000 men was surrounded and finally captured in February 1943. A German soldier trapped at Stalingrad wrote in a letter:

> Around me everything is collapsing, a whole army is dying, day and night are on fire, and four men busy themselves with daily reports on temperatures and cloud ceilings. I don't know much about war. No human being has died by my hand. I haven't even fired live ammunition from my pistol. But I know this much: the other side would never show such a lack of understanding for its men.[19]

Along the long front 500,000 German and affiliated troops were killed or taken prisoner. By the autumn of 1943 an army of 2.5 million Germans faced a Soviet force of 5.5 million.

The initiative had definitely passed to the Allies in the European theater. The Germans lost their air dominance and the American industrial machine was cranking up to full production. By the beginning of 1944 the Germans were being pushed out of the Soviet Union, and in August Soviet troops accepted the surrender of Romania. Bulgaria was next to be "liberated" by the Soviet Union, while the Allies continued doggedly fighting their way north in Italy. But whereas the western Allies were—in their fashion—fighting the war to its military end, Stalin placed the postwar political objectives in the forefront of his advance into Europe.

An example of the Soviet use of military tactics to gain political goals could be seen in the action around Warsaw in August–September 1944, when the Red Army deferred the capture of the Polish capital to allow the Nazis to destroy potential opponents. The Polish resistance, which was centered in Warsaw and in contact with the exile government in London, had noted the arrival of Soviet forces in Warsaw's eastern suburbs. When the Nazis prepared to evacuate the city, the resistance rose up to claim control of the capital. As these were non-communist Poles, Stalin's forces refused to advance to the city, choosing instead to withdraw back across the Vistula.

During the next five months, the Soviets refused to permit the British and the Americans, who wanted to airdrop supplies to the resistance, to land and refuel in the Ukraine. Because the flight to Warsaw from London was too far to make in a round trip, the Allies could not supply the resistance. The Nazis stopped their retreat, returned to Warsaw, and totally destroyed the resistance. Russian forces then advanced and took the capital in January. Poland was now deprived of many of its potential postwar, non-communist leaders. When the Soviets advanced, they brought with them their own properly prepared Polish forces, both military and political, to control the country.[20]

Axis Collapse

Following months of intense planning and days of difficult decision making, the Allies on June 6, 1944 launched a vast armada of ships that landed half a million men on the beaches of Normandy. The Allied armies broke through the German defenses and liberated Paris at the end of August and Brussels at beginning of September. The combined forces wheeled toward Germany. After fending off a major German offensive in the Battle of the Bulge in December, the Allies were ready to march on Germany.

It took four more months for the Allies from the west and the Russians from the east to crush the Third Reich. By May 1, the Battle of Berlin had reached a decisive point, and the Russians were about to take the city. Unlike in the First World War, German civilians suffered greatly in the Second. The Allies gained total command of the skies and for every ton of bombs that fell on English cities, more than 300 tons fell on German settlements.

With victory in sight, Stalin, Roosevelt, and Churchill met at Yalta in the Crimea in February 1945 to discuss the peace arrangements. They agreed the Soviet Union should have a preponderant influence in eastern Europe, decided that Germany should be divided into four occupation zones, discussed the makeup and functioning of the United Nations, and confirmed that Russia

Supplies and reinforcements for the D-Day (June 6, 1944) invasion of Normandy pour onto the beach to be loaded onto trucks and funneled inland.

Churchill, Roosevelt, and Stalin at the Yalta Conference. The discussions at the conference, especially those concerning the establishment of new governments in liberated countries, exposed the mounting tensions that would divide the Allies after the war.

would enter the war against Japan after the defeat of Germany, which they did—two days after the atomic bomb was dropped on Hiroshima. Yalta was the high point of the alliance. After this conference, relations between the western powers and the Soviets rapidly deteriorated.

The European Axis leaders did not live to see defeat. Mussolini was seized by anti-fascist partisan fighters and shot to death, and his mutilated body, and that of his mistress, was hung by the heels in a public square in Milan on April 28, 1945. Hitler committed suicide two days later. His body and that of his mistress, Eva Braun, whom he had just married, were soaked in gasoline and set afire.

President Roosevelt also did not live to see the end of the war. He died suddenly on April 12, 1945, less than a month before the German armies capitulated. The final surrender in Europe took place in Berlin on May 8, 1945, named by the newly installed president, Harry Truman, as V-E Day, Victory in Europe Day.

The Unspeakable Holocaust

As the Allied armies liberated Europe and marched through Germany and Poland they came on sites that testified to the depths to which human beings can sink—the Nazi death camps.

Nazi Propaganda Minister Joseph Goebbels wrote in his diary on March 14, 1945 that "it's necessary to exterminate these Jews like rats, once and for all. . . . In Germany, thank God, we've taken care of that. I hope the world will follow this example."[21]

He was only too accurate in his assessment: Germany had "already taken care of that." In Belsen, Buchenwald, Dachau, Auschwitz, and other permanent camps and in mobile killing operations that moved with the armies, Hitler's forces sought to "purify the German race" and to "remove the lesser breeds as a source of biological infection." Working under the efficient efforts of the Gestapo, led by Chief Heinrich Himmler, and with the aid of hardworking Deputy Chief Reinhard Heydrich, the Nazis set out to gain the "final solution" of the Jewish question.

Although preparations had been under way for ten years, the completed plan for the final solution came in 1942. More than 3 million men, women, and children were put to death at Auschwitz, where more than 2000 people at a time could be gassed in half an hour; the operation could be repeated four times a day. The able-bodied worked until they could work no more, and then they were gassed. Millions more died from starvation, on diets that averaged from 600 to 700 calories a day. Torture, medical experimentation, and executions all claimed a large toll. The victims' eyeglasses were collected, their hair shaved off, their gold fillings were removed, and their bodies were either burned or buried.

Thus the captured Jews and assorted *Untermenschen* served a "biological necessity" by being destroyed and made an economic contribution on the way. The Nazis did not act alone, as they were aided by anti-Semitic citizens in Poland, Romania, France, Hungary, and the Soviet Union. Few of the more than 3 million Polish Jews survived the war, and similar devastation occurred among the Romanian Jewry.

With the exception of a few human beasts, all of this was done with bureaucratic efficiency, coldness, discipline, and professionalism. Himmler believed that his new variety of knights must make "this people disappear from the face of the earth." Had this been done in a fit of insanity and madness by savages, it perhaps could be comprehended. But that it was done by educated bureaucrats and responsible officials from a civilized nation made the act all the more chilling and incredible.

Between 1939 and 1945 the Jewish population in Nazi-occupied Europe decreased from 9,739,200 to 3,505,800. Six million were killed directly in Nazi gas chambers or in executions. In addition, another 6 million people—Slavs, Gypsies, and others—also fell victim to direct Nazi slaughter.[22]

The Atomic Bomb

While the Allied armies finished off the Germans, the Americans from the summer of 1943 advanced toward Japan, capturing on the way the islands of Tarawa, Kwajalein, and Saipan

The Nazi Death Camps

Henry Friedlander gave a dispassionate description of the functioning of the Nazi death camps.

The largest killing operation took place in Auschwitz, a regular concentration camp. There Auschwitz Commandant Rudolf Hoess improved the method used by Christian Wirth, substituting crystalized prussic acid—known by the trade name Zyklon B—for carbon monoxide. In September, 1941, an experimental gassing, killing about 250 ill prisoners and about 600 Russian POWs, proved the value of Zyklon B. In January, 1942, systematic killing operations, using Zyklon B, commenced with the arrival of Jewish transports from Upper Silesia. These were soon followed without interruption by transports of Jews from all occupied countries of Europe.

The Auschwitz killing center was the most modern of its kind. The SS built the camp at Birkenau, also known as Auschwitz II. There, they murdered their victims in newly constructed gas chambers, and burned their bodies in crematoria constructed for this purpose. A postwar court described the killing process:

Prussic acid fumes developed as soon as Zyklon B pellets seeped through the opening into the gas chamber and came into contact with the air. Within a few minutes, these fumes agonizingly asphyxiated the human beings in the gas chamber. During these minutes horrible scenes took place. The people who now realized that they were to die an agonizing death screamed and raged and beat their fists against the locked doors and against the walls. Since the gas spread from the floor of the gas chamber upward, small and weak people were the first to die. The others, in their death agony, climbed on top of the dead bodies on the floor, in order to get a little more air before they too painfully choked to death.

From Henry Friedlander, "The Nazi Camps," in *Genocide: Critical Issues of the Holocaust,* ed. Alex Grobman and David Landes (Los Angeles: The Simon Wiesenthal Center, 1983), 222–231.

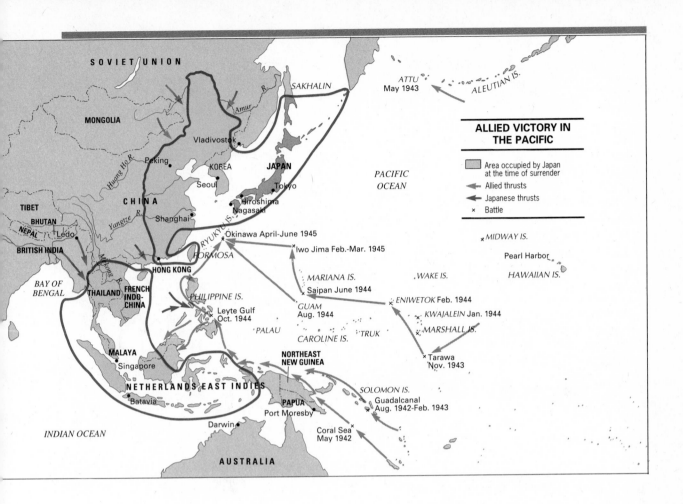

Map: **ALLIED VICTORY IN THE PACIFIC**

Legend:
- Area occupied by Japan at the time of surrender
- Allied thrusts
- Japanese thrusts
- × Battle

Map labels: SOVIET UNION, MONGOLIA, Vladivostok, Peking, KOREA, Seoul, JAPAN, Tokyo, Hiroshima, Nagasaki, Shanghai, CHINA, TIBET, BHUTAN, NEPAL, Ledo, BRITISH INDIA, BAY OF BENGAL, THAILAND, FRENCH INDO-CHINA, HONG KONG, FORMOSA, RYUKYU IS., Okinawa April–June 1945, Iwo Jima Feb.–Mar. 1945, PHILIPPINE IS., Leyte Gulf Oct. 1944, MARIANA IS., Saipan June 1944, GUAM Aug. 1944, PALAU, CAROLINE IS., TRUK, MALAYA, Singapore, NETHERLANDS EAST INDIES, Batavia, NORTHEAST NEW GUINEA, PAPUA, Port Moresby, Darwin, INDIAN OCEAN, AUSTRALIA, SAKHALIN, ATTU May 1943, ALEUTIAN IS., PACIFIC OCEAN, MIDWAY IS., Pearl Harbor, WAKE IS., HAWAIIAN IS., ENIWETOK Feb. 1944, KWAJALEIN Jan. 1944, MARSHALL IS., Tarawa Nov. 1943, SOLOMON IS., Guadalcanal Aug. 1942–Feb. 1943, Coral Sea May 1942

after bloody struggles on sandy beaches. In October 1944, with their victory in the battle of Leyte Gulf, the greatest naval engagement in history, the Allies ended the threat of the Japanese fleet.

The final phase of the war against Japan began to unfold. The Allies took Iwo Jima and Okinawa, only a few hundred miles from Japan. From these bases waves of American bombers rained destruction on Japanese cities. In the China-Burma-India theater, the Chinese with U.S. aid, made inroads on areas previously captured by Japan (see map above).

But the decisive developments took place across the Pacific in New Mexico, where by 1945 U.S. scientists, with the help of scientists who had fled central Europe to escape Hitler, invented a new and terrible weapon—the atomic bomb. Based on figures from the island-hopping campaigns, the projected casualty rate for the taking of the main island of Japan ran into the hundreds of thousands. When the Japanese refused to surrender, an American bomber on August 6 dropped the atomic bomb on the city of Hiroshima. As the mushroom-shaped cloud rose over the city, only charred ruins were left behind. An expanse of approximately three square miles, 60 percent of the city, was pulverized. The Japanese government estimated the bomb killed 60,000 people, wounded 100,000, and left 200,000 homeless. Three days later, a second bomb was dropped on the city of Nagasaki, with similar results.

The Japanese finally sued for peace. The surrender ceremony took place aboard the battleship *Missouri* on September 2, 1945, almost six years to the day after Hitler plunged the world into the Second World War.

The Bombing of Hiroshima

Nuclear weapons totally changed the nature and possibilities of warfare. The U.S. Strategic Bombing Survey gave a detached version of what happened at Hiroshima.

At about 0815 there was a blinding flash. Some described it as brighter than the sun, others likened it to a magnesium flash. Following the flash there was a blast of heat and wind. The large majority of people within 3,000 feet of ground zero were killed immediately. Within a radius of about 7,000 feet almost every Japanese house collapsed. Beyond this range and up to 15,000–20,000 feet many of them collapsed and others received serious structural damage. Persons in the open were burned on exposed surfaces, and within 3,000–5,000 feet many were burned to death while others received severe burns through their clothes. In many instances clothing burst into spontaneous flame and had to be beaten out. Thousands of people were pinned beneath collapsed buildings or injured by flying debris. Flying glass particularly produced many non-lethal injuries and the distances at which they occurred are discussed in the following chapter, but the foregoing presentation was necessary for one to appreciate the state of the population immediately after the bomb exploded.

Shortly after the blast fires began to spring up over the city. Those who were able made a mass exodus from the city into the outlying hills. There was no organized activity. The people appeared stunned by the catastrophe and rushed about as jungle animals suddenly released from a cage. Some few apparently attempted to help others from the wreckage, particularly members of their family or friends. Others assisted those who were unable to walk alone. However, many of the injured were left trapped beneath collapsed buildings as people fled by them in the streets. Pandemonium reigned as the uninjured and slightly injured fled the city in fearful panic.

From "The Effects of Atomic Bombs on Health and Medical Services in Hiroshima and Nagasaki," in *The United States Strategic Bombing Survey* (Washington, 1948).

Conclusion

When the war was finally over, the living counted the dead. The Germans lost 4.2 million military and civilian dead, while the western Allies lost 1.5 million. The Soviet Union suffered the greatest losses: close to 25 million citizens. Yugoslavia had the greatest per capita casualty rate—one in every ten. In Asia, the census for 1950 showed a loss of some 55 million people, even after a five-year period of recuperation.[23] A meaningful financial accounting for the six years of bloodshed is not possible.

The world went through this carnage to put an end to German, Italian, and Japanese aggression, which came frighteningly close to succeeding in its goal of world dominance. Unlike the First World War, which has spawned many historiographical controversies concerning its causes, there is no doubt that the key figure in the Second World War was Adolph Hitler. He was the essential link, the man whose policies and ideas welded together the dictators.

Unlike the Japanese and the Italians, whose global influence was limited by either geographical or internal problems, Hitler could build on Germany's industrial might and central location to forge a force for world conquest. Historians vary sharply on his goals and motivations. Some see him as a politician playing the traditional game of European power politics in a most skillful way while others view him as a single-minded fanatic pursuing the plans for conquest laid out in *Mein Kampf*. Between these two extremes are the scholars who believe that the *Führer* had deeply thought out, long-term goals but pursued them haphazardly, as opportunities presented themselves.

Hitler struck the spark that set off the worldwide conflagration. Aiding and abetting his ambitions was the obsessive desire of the democracies for peace. By 1939, the lesson had been learned that appeasement does not guarantee peace, and that it does not take two equally belligerent sides to make a war.

Suggestions for Reading

Two helpful introductions to the 1919–1945 period are Laurence Lafore, *The End of Glory* (Lippincott, 1970) and Joachim Remak, *The Origins of the Second World War* (Prentice-Hall, 1976).

The diplomacy leading up to and conducted during the war has received extensive study. Hans Gatzke, ed., *European Diplomacy between the Two Wars, 1919–1939* (Quadrangle, 1972) gives definition to some of the major problems involved in this period. His *Stressemann and the Rearmament of Germany* (Norton, 1969) emphasizes an interwar continuity. Jon Jacobson discusses a pivotal four years in *Locarno Diplomacy: Germany and the West 1925–1929* (Princeton, 1972). Gerhard Weinhard gives a penetrating analysis in *The Foreign Policy of Hitler's Germany: Diplomatic Revolution in Europe 1933–1936* (Chicago, 1970). Equally essential is Weinhard's follow-up study, *The Foreign Policy of Hitler's Germany . . . 1937–1939* (Chicago, 1980). Still one of the best studies of Soviet foreign policy is George Kennan's *Russia and the West Under Lenin and Stalin* (Mentor, 1961). W. L. Langer and S. E. Gleason discuss important aspects of U.S. foreign policy in *The Challenge to Isolation* (Harper, 1952). Herbert Feis' *Churchill, Roosevelt, Stalin* (Princeton, 1967) is a classic. René Albrecht-Carrié traces France's travail in *France, Europe, and the Two World Wars* (Harper, 1961). George Kennan's *Memoirs*, vol. I (Bantam, 1969) offers perceptive contemporary observations. Other fine studies on interwar affairs are Etienne Mantoux, *The Carthaginian Peace* (Ayer, 1978) and Sally Marks, *International Relations in Europe: 1918–1939* (St. Martin's, 1976). Robert Young's *In Command of France: French Foreign Policy and Military Planning, 1933–1940* (Harvard, 1978) gives needed perspective on France's dilemma.

One of the most discussed aspects of the interwar period is appeasement and the Munich Conference. Keith Middlemas, *The Strategy of Appeasement* (Quadrangle, 1972) gives a balanced survey of this very controversial issue. Francis L. Loewenheim, ed., *Peace or Appeasement* (Houghton Mifflin, 1965) provides a selection of documents, including the Hossbach Memorandum. Keith Eubank's study, *Munich* (Oklahoma, 1963) is a good summary.

The Spanish Civil War has also received much scholarly attention. John Coverdale discusses one aspect of the conflict in *Italian Intervention in the Spanish Civil War* (Princeton, 1975). Gabriel Jackson, *The Spanish Republic and the Civil War 1931–1939* (Princeton, 1965); Stanley G. Payne, *Spanish Revolution* (Norton, 1970); and Hugh Thomas, *The Spanish Civil War* (Harper & Row, 1977) are all first-rate studies. George Orwell, *Homage to Catalonia* (Harcourt) remains an invaluable contemporary description of that tragedy.

The war from the German perspective has to take into consideration the Führer himself, and Robert G. Waite's *The Psychopathic God: Adolf Hitler* (Mentor, 1983) offers fascinating insights into his personality. Harold C. Deutsch's *Hitler and His Germans: The Crisis of January–June 1938* (Minnesota, 1974) provides good insights into German planning and policies. David Irving's *Hitler's War* is a first-rate survey (Viking, 1977). Albert Speer gives an insider's point of view in *Inside the Third Reich* (Macmillan, 1970). Alexander Dallin's *German Rule in Russia 1941–1945* (St. Martin's, 1957) discusses occupation policies and problems. Albert Seaton's *The Russo-German War 1941–1945* (Praeger, 1970) is especially strong in its analysis of Soviet strategy.

The diplomacy surrounding Poland is well covered in Anna Cienciala, *Poland the the Western Powers 1938–1939* (Toronto, 1968). John A. Armstrong, *Soviet Partisans in World War II* (Wisconsin, 1964) is a deft analysis of a subtle theater of action. George Bruce gives thorough coverage of the 1944 Polish tragedies in *Warsaw Uprising 1 August 2 October* (Hart-Davis, 1972). Harrison Salisbury, *The Nine Hundred Days: The Siege of Leningrad* (Harper, 1975) is a heartbreaking story of heroism. The tragic story of repatriated Soviet citizens is told in Nikolai Tolstoy, *Victims of Yalta* (Hodder & Stoughton, 1978).

Three good books on the Pacific theater are Christopher Thorne, *Allies of a Kind: The United States, Britain, and the War Against Japan* (Oxford, 1978); Gordon W. Prange, *At Dawn We Slept: The Untold Story of Pearl Harbor* (McGraw-Hill, 1981); and Yoshiburo Ienaga, *The Pacific War, 1937–1945* (Pantheon, 1978), which views the war from Japan's perspective.

Other aspects of the war are covered in Anthony Adamthwaite, *France and the Coming of the Second World War 1936–1939* (Frank Cass, 1977); Maurice Cowling, *The Impact of Hitler: British Politics and British Foreign Policy 1933–1940* (Chicago, 1977); Henri Michel, *The Shadow War, European Resistance 1939–1945* (Harper, 1972); Leila J. Rupp, *Mobilizing Women for War, 1939–1945* (Princeton, 1977); Len Deighton, *Fighter: The True Story of the Battle of Britain* (Johnathan Cape, 1977). Three books dealing with intelligence activities are F. W. Winterbotham, *The Ultra Secret* (Dell, 1979); William Stevenson, *A Man Called Intrepid* (Ballantine, 1976); and R. V. Jones, *The Wizard War: British Scientific Intelligence 1939–1945* (Coward, McCann, 1978).

The Nazis' genocide policies have been analyzed by Raul Hilberg, *The Destruction of the European Jews* (Quadrangle, 1961); Karl A. Schleunes, *The Twisted Road to Auschwitz: Nazi Policy Toward German Jews 1933–1939* (Illinois, 1970); and Lucy S. Dawidowicz, ed., *A Holocaust Reader* (Behrman House, 1976). See also Dawidowicz's *The War Against the Jews: 1933–1945* (Bantam, 1976).

Just about all major participants who survived the war—on all sides—have produced memoirs. The classics among them are Churchill's *The Second World War*, 6 vols. (Bantam) and Charles De Gaulle, *Mémoires* (Plon).

Notes

1. Harold Nicolson, *Peacemaking 1919* (New York: Harcourt Brace, 1933), p. 207.
2. Quoted in A. G. Mazour, *Russia Past and Present* (New York: Van Nostrand Reinhold Co., 1951), p. 576.
3. A. J. Ryder, *Twentieth-Century Germany: From Bismarck to Brandt* (New York: Columbia Univ. Press, 1973), pp. 220–226.
4. George F. Kennan, *Memoirs* (New York: Bantam Books, 1969), p. 122.
5. John Toland, *Adolf Hitler* (New York: Ballantine Books, 1977), pp. 522–529.
6. Donald W. Treadgold, *Twentieth Century Russia* (Chicago: Rand McNally & Co., 1959), pp. 324–325.
7. Keith Middlemas, *The Strategy of Appeasement* (Chicago: Quadrangle Books, 1972), pp. 1–8.
8. Middlemas, *The Strategy of Appeasement*, pp. 410–412.
9. The minutes of the conference in the Reich Chancellery, as extracted and quoted in Francis L. Loewenheim, *Peace or Appeasement* (Boston: Houghton Mifflin, 1965), pp. 2–4.
10. Middlemas, *The Strategy of Appeasement*, p. 177.
11. Laurence Lafore, *The End of Glory* (Philadelphia and New York: J. B. Lippincott, 1970), p. 226.
12. W. S. Churchill, *Blood, Sweat, and Tears* (New York: G. P. Putnam's Sons, 1941), p. 66.
13. F. D. Roosevelt, "Address at Chicago, October 5, 1937," in *The Literature of the United States*, II, W. Blair, T. Hornberger, and R. Stewart, eds. (Chicago: Scott, Foresman, 1955), pp. 831–832.
14. Maurice Crouzet, "L'Epoque Contemporaine," *Histoire Générale des Civilisations*, VII (Paris: Presses Universitaires de France, 1957), pp. 303–349. F. W. Winterbotham, *The Ultra Secret* (New York: Harper & Row, 1974), pp. 1–55. William Stephenson, *A Man Called Intrepid* (New York: Ballantine Books, 1976), *passim*.
15. S. E. Ayling, *Portraits of Power* (New York: Barnes & Noble, 1963), p. 159.
16. Nigel Nicolson, ed., *Harold Nicolson, The War Years 1939–1945, Volume II of Diaries and Letters* (New York: Atheneum, 1967), p. 100.
17. Churchill, *Blood, Sweat, and Tears*, p. 297.
18. Albert Seaton, *The Russo-German War 1941–1945* (New York: Praeger, 1970), pp. 37–38.
19. *Last Letters From Stalingrad*, translated by Franz Schneider and Charles Gullas (New York: Signet Books, 1965), p. 20.
20. Seaton, *The Russo-German War*, pp. 453–456.
21. Quoted in John Vinocur, "Goebbels, in Published 1945 Diary Blames Goring for Nazis' Collapse," *New York Times*, January 3, 1978.
22. See Raul Hilberg, *The Destruction of the European Jews* (Chicago: Quadrangle Books, 1961), *passim*, and Crouzet, "L'Epoque Contemporaine," pp. 358–359.
23. Simon Kuznets, *Postwar Economic Growth: Four Lectures* (Cambridge, MA: Harvard Univ. Press, 1964), pp. 72–76, as cited in David Landes, *The Unbound Prometheus* (Cambridge: Cambridge Univ. Press, 1969), p. 487.

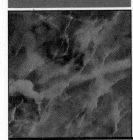

Chapter 35

The Bipolar "North," 1945–1991

Soviet and American Spheres

The Cold War—the 44 years of great power tension after World War II—did not see a formal state of war between the U.S. and USSR. However, "proxy wars" fought by the clients of each superpower and conflicts occurring in the wake of decolonization killed millions in Asia, Africa, and Latin America. Ironically, Europe, caught in the stalemate between the United States and the Soviet Union enjoyed its longest time of peace in recorded history.

Washington and Moscow led their allies through the postwar decades with a mixture of aggressiveness and wisdom. From the first, the west's economic and social structures were more productive than those of the eastern bloc. Yet through a massive effort, the Soviet Union achieved military parity with the west by the mid-1970s. By the last decade of the twentieth century, economic exhaustion brought an end to the Cold War. Increased cooperation characterized the relations between Moscow and Washington, as both looked to a new era in which they would try to keep their dominant roles in the world.

The Elusive Peace

After World War II, many of the living had reason to envy the dead. Fire bombs and nuclear weapons depopulated and spread radiation to parts of Japan. One-fourth of Germany's cities were in rubble as were much of Italy and central Europe. The war claimed 10 percent of Yugoslavia's population. In China, after 15 years of fighting, the survivors faced hunger, disease, civil war, and revolution. Twenty-five million people died in the Soviet Union, and the country lost one-third of its national wealth. Although casualty rates in Britain and France were lower than in World War I, both countries paid dearly in lives and in the ruin that took one-fourth of their national wealth. The allied countries such as the United States—which suffered 389,000 casualties—Canada, Australia, and New Zealand suffered no material damage but paid a heavy price in combat dead.

Postwar Problems

Postwar Europe faced two immediate problems: the fate of collaborators and millions of Nazi labor slaves. In countries that had been occupied by the Nazis, resistance groups began to take vigilante justice against those who had worked with the Germans. Across Europe they executed thousands of collaborators. In France alone 800 were sent to their deaths. After the war, courts sentenced thousands more to prison terms. Eight million foreign labor slaves who had been used by the Nazis remained to be dealt with. By the end of 1945, five million of them had been sent home, including many Soviet citizens who were forced to return. Some of them chose suicide rather than return to Stalin's rule.

In Germany, following the Yalta agreement, the Allies established four occupation zones—French, British, American, and Russian (see map, p. 906). They divided the capital, Berlin, located in the Soviet sector, into four parts. The Russians promised free access from the western zones to Berlin. The Allies then began to carry out a selective process of denazification. Some former Nazis

After World War II, the bombed-out cities of Europe seemed almost beyond hope. In 1947 Churchill described the Continent as "a rubble heap, a charnel house, a breeding ground of pestilence and hate."

were sent to prison while thousands received the benefits of large-scale declarations of amnesty. Many ex-Nazis were employed by the scientific and intelligence services of the Allies.

The most important denazification act came at the 1945–1946 trials of war criminals held at Nuremburg. An international panel of jurists conducted the proceedings and condemned 12 leading Nazis to be hanged and sent seven to prison for crimes against humanity. The panel acquitted three high officials. Critics condemned the trials as an act of vengeance, "a political act by the victors against the vanquished." The prosecution stated, however, the Nazi crimes were so terrible that "civilization cannot tolerate their being ignored because it cannot survive their being repeated."[1]

By the end of 1945, the growing tension between the Soviet Union and the United States made it impossible to construct a peace settlement. At the Potsdam Conference in the summer of 1945 a council of ministers was set up to draft peace treaties. After two years of difficult negotiations treaties were signed with Italy, Romania, Bulgaria, Hungary, and Finland. In 1951, an accord between the western powers and the Japanese reestablished Japan as a sovereign state. Austria's position remained uncertain until 1955 when a peace treaty was signed and occupation forces withdrawn. The western allies and the Soviets were completely at odds over the German peace settlement. Not until the signing of the Helsinki Accords in 1975 was a status quo for Europe acknowledged, and that agreement did not have the force of a binding legal treaty. Finally, in the summer of 1990 the diplomatic issues spawned by World War II were put to rest in a series of treaties signed by all European parties.

The United Nations

On only one issue, the establishment of an international peacekeeping organization, could the powers agree after the war. Great Britain and the United States laid the foundations for the United Nations in 1941 when they proposed "the establishment of a wider and permanent system of

THE DIVISION OF GERMANY

general security" so "that men in all lands may live out their lives in freedom from fear and want." Subsequent meetings at Moscow and Yalta led representatives of fifty governments meeting at San Francisco from April to June 1945 to draft the Charter of the United Nations.

To pursue its goals of peace and an improved standard of living for the world, the UN would work through six organizations: the Security Council, to maintain peace and order; the General Assembly, to function as a form of town meeting of the world; the Economic and Social Council, to improve living standards and extend human rights; the Trusteeship Council, to advance the interests of the colonial peoples; the International Court of Justice, to resolve disputes between nations; and the Secretariat, headed by the secretary-general, to serve the needs of other organizations. Much of the responsibility for improving the economic and social conditions of the world's people was entrusted to a dozen specialized agencies, such as the International Labor Organization, the Food and Agricultural and the World Health Organizations, and the UN Educational, Scientific, and Cultural Organization.

The greatest controversy at San Francisco arose over the right of veto in the Security Council. The smaller countries held that it was unjust for the big powers to be able to block the wishes of the majority. But the Big Five—the United States, the Soviet Union, China, France, and Great Britain—affirmed that singly and collectively they had special interests and responsibilities in maintaining world peace and security. The UN Charter, therefore, provided that the Security Council should consist of 11 members, five permanent members representing the great powers and six elected by the General Assembly for a term of two years. These numbers would be increased as the membership of the UN grew. On purely procedural matters a majority of seven votes was sufficient; on matters of substance, all permanent members had to agree.

The UN proved to be more effective than the League of Nations. The UN, like the League, lacks the sovereign power of its member states. However, as was shown in the Korean conflict in the 1950s and in the Gulf War in 1991 it has become more wide-reaching in its impact. In 1946 it had 51 members. At the beginning of the 1990s membership stood at more than 160. Over the years the UN's usefulness has repeatedly been demonstrated despite the difficulties of the Cold War, the strains of massive decolonization, and four Arab-Israeli wars—not to mention an interminable series of smaller crises. As was the case with the League, the UN cannot coerce the

Nations put their hope in a new international organization, the United Nations, to rebuild the shattered world and preserve the peace. Here, U.S. senator Arthur Vandenberg signs the charter of the United Nations on June 16, 1945, as other members of the U.S. delegation wait for their turns. U.S. president Harry Truman and Secretary of State Edward Stettinius, Jr., watch from Vandenberg's right.

great powers when any of them decide a major national interest is involved.

The Cold War

The Cold War between Washington and Moscow dominated the world in the half century after World War II. When it began the United States held the advantage in nuclear weapons and world trade; when it ended each power had equal military power and dissimilar, but serious, economic crises. From 1945 to 1953 the struggle was centered in Europe. In the wake of decolonization the conflict shifted to Asia, Latin America, the Middle East, and Africa.

The Soviets and Americans have differed in their views on economics, politics, social organization, religion, and the role of the individual since 1917. The Nazi threat produced a temporary unity, but by 1943 Soviet frustration with the slowness of its allies to open the second front, discontent with being shut out of participation in the Italian campaign, and unhappiness with the amount of U.S. financial assistance increased tension. The western allies were suspicious of Soviet secrecy. London and Washington gave detailed data on strategy and weapons to Moscow, but got little information from the Soviets. Over $12 billion dollars in Lend-Lease aid was sent to the Soviet Union, but its extent and value were not publicly acknowledged for four decades in the Soviet Union.[2]

After the February 1945 Yalta Conference it soon became clear that Stalin had his view of the composition of postwar eastern Europe and Roosevelt and Churchill had theirs. As early as April 1, 1945, Roosevelt sent a telegram to Stalin protesting the violation of Yalta pledges. A month later Churchill sent a long message of protest to Stalin in which he concluded:

> There is not much comfort in looking into a future where you and the countries you dominate . . . are all on one side, and those who rally to the English speaking nations . . . are on the other . . . their quarrel would tear the world to pieces.[3]

From 1945 to 1948 Stalin expanded his control over the region carefully, working through coalition governments. He had a number of advantages. Most of the local élites had either been killed during the war or were condemned for collaborating with the Nazis. The communist parties, most of whom were underground during the interwar period, had gained public support by leading the resistance to the Nazis after June 1941. Further, the Red Army remained in place to intimidate eastern Europe.

The communists occupied the most powerful positions in the coalition governments; opposition parties gained largely symbolic posts. The communists soon used intimidation and outright force. The Czechs remained free longer than the other eastern European states. In the 1946 elections the communists had received only 38 percent of the vote, and they were losing support. In the spring of 1948 the Soviets forced Czechoslovakia to submit to communist control. By the end of 1948, when the Americans had totally withdrawn from Europe, the governments in Warsaw, East Berlin, Prague, Budapest, Bucharest, Sofia, and Tirana operated as satellites orbiting the political center of Moscow.

Stalin used the Soviet bloc as a four-hundred-mile-deep buffer against capitalist invasion and as a source to help the USSR rebuild. He blocked any political, economic, or cultural contact with the west. Once his allies gained control, he ordered a purge of the local parties, based on those in the Soviet Union in the 1930s. The main target for the purge was the national communists, those who were seen as being more loyal to their own nation than to Moscow or Stalin. Overall, the purge removed one in every four party members. Many of those eliminated had been loyal communists since the beginning of the century.

Meanwhile, in the three years after 1945, the four-power agreement on the governing of Germany soon broke apart. In the fall of 1946, Britain and America merged their zones into one economic unit, which came to be known as Bizonia. The French joined the union in 1948. Germany was now split into two parts, one administered by the western allies and the other by the Russians, and would remain divided until the line between the two powers—dubbed the Iron Curtain by Churchill—disappeared in 1990.

The Marshall Plan and Containment

The Soviets did not return their armies to a peacetime status after 1945. They and their allies challenged the west in Greece, Turkey, and Iran. Britain was too weak to play its former role in the region. The Americans, as they would subsequently do throughout the globe, filled the gap left by the British and French. President Harry Truman responded to Soviet pressure by announcing that the United States would support any country threatened by communist aggression. Soon after proclamation of the Truman Doctrine in 1947, the United States sent economic and military aid to Greece and Turkey, a move traditionally held to mark the American entry into the Cold War.

The United States' wartime goodwill toward the Soviet Union turned quickly to paranoid fear of international communism. The Americans, comfortable with their nuclear monopoly, had looked forward to a postwar peaceful world. They were angered by Soviet actions in the United Nations, Eastern Europe, China, and the growth of communist parties in western Europe. Conservatives attacked the Yalta agreement as a "sellout" and launched a new "Red Scare" campaign. A French observer noted the rapid change in attitude by pointing out that "a whole nation, optimistic and naive, placed its trust in a comrade in arms."[4] Now that comrade was the enemy.

The American diplomat, George F. Kennan, explained that the correct stance to take toward Stalin's policies was one of containment. In an article entitled "The Sources of Soviet Conduct," written under the byline of "Mr. X" in the July 1947 issue of *Foreign Affairs*, Keenan proposed a "realistic understanding of the profound and deep-rooted difference between the United States and the Soviet Union" and the exercise of "a long-term, patient but firm and vigilant containment

The Truman Doctrine

Once the Americans recovered from their post-1945 euphoria, President Truman spelled out his response to perceived Soviet aggression.

The peoples of a number of countries of the world have recently had totalitarian regimes forced upon them against their will. The Government of the United States has made frequent protests against coercion and intimidation, in violation of the Yalta agreement, in Poland, Rumania, and Bulgaria. I must also state that in a number of other countries there have been similar developments.

At the present moment in world history nearly every nation must choose between alternative ways of life. The choice is too often not a free one.

One way of life is based upon the will of the majority, and is distinguished by free institutions, representative government, free elections, guaranties of individual liberty, freedom of speech and religion, and freedom from political oppression.

The second way of life is based upon the will of a minority forcibly imposed upon the majority. It relies upon terror and oppression, a controlled press and radio, fixed elections, and the suppression of personal freedoms.

I believe that it must be the policy of the United States to support free peoples who are resisting attempted subjugation by armed minorities or by outside pressures.

I believe that we must assist free peoples to work out their own destinies in their own way.

I believe that our help should be primarily through economic and financial aid, which is essential to economic stability and orderly political processes.

From U.S. Congress *Congressional Record*, 80th Congress, 1st Session (Washington, D.C.: U.S. Government Printing Office, 1947), vol. 93, p. 1981; and U.S. Congress, Senate Committee on Foreign Relations, *A Decade of American Foreign Policy: Basic Documents. 1941–1949* (Washington, D.C.: U.S. Government Printing Office, 1950), pp. 1270–1271.

of Russian expansive tendencies."[5] This advice shaped U.S. policy throughout Europe.

The policy of containment was first used in Yugoslavia where a split between Joseph Broz Tito (1891–1980) and Stalin marked the first breach in the Soviet advance. The Yugoslavs initiated the ideological break known as national communism. Supported financially by the west, the Yugoslavs were able to survive Stalin's attacks.

The broad economic and political arms of containment came into play. Secretary of State George C. Marshall proposed a plan of economic aid to help Europe to solve its postwar financial problems. Western European nations eagerly accepted the Marshall Plan while the Soviet Union rejected American aid for itself and the bloc. Congress authorized the plan, known as the European Recovery Program, and within four years the industrial output of the recipients climbed to 64 percent over 1947 levels and 41 percent over prewar levels. The European Recovery Act stabilized conditions in western Europe and prevented the communists from taking advantage of postwar problems.

Rival Systems

In July 1948, after opposing a western series of currency and economic reforms, the Soviets blocked all land and water transport to Berlin from the west. For the next ten months the allies supplied West Berlin by air. They made over 277,000 flights to bring 2.3 million tons of food and other vital materials to the besieged city. Rather than risk war over the city and the use of American nuclear weapons, the Russians removed their blockade in May 1949. In the same month the Federal Republic of Germany, made up of the three western allied zones came into existence. Almost immediately, the Soviet Union established the German Democratic Republic in East Germany. Germany would remain divided for the next 41 years.

In the spring of 1949 Washington established the North Atlantic Treaty Organization (NATO), an alliance for mutual assistance. The initial members were Great Britain, France, Belgium, Luxembourg, the Netherlands, Norway, Denmark, Portugal, Italy, Iceland, the United States, and Canada. Greece and Turkey joined in 1952, followed by West Germany in 1955. In 1955 also the Soviets created the Warsaw Pact, which formalized the existing unified military command in Soviet-dominated eastern Europe, (see map at right). Warsaw Pact members included, in addition to the Soviet Union, Albania, Bulgaria, Romania, Czechoslovakia, Hungary, Poland, and East Germany. The alliance lasted until 1991.

The tension between the rival systems finally snapped in Korea. After Japan's surrender, Korea had been divided at the 38th parallel into

To try to force the Western powers out of Berlin, in July 1948 the Russians imposed a blockade on the city. In response, the allies organized an airlift to fly in supplies to the city and its beleaguered citizens. In May 1949, the Soviets lifted the blockade.

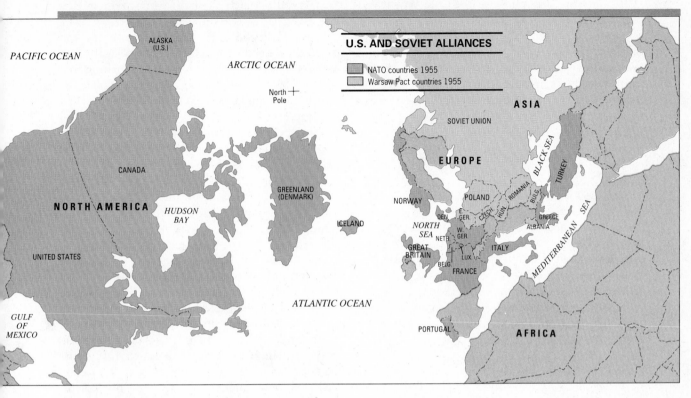

U.S. AND SOVIET ALLIANCES

NATO countries 1955

Warsaw Pact countries 1955

American and Soviet zones of occupation. When the occupying troops left, they were replaced by two hostile forces, each claiming jurisdiction over the entire country. On June 25, 1950 North Korean troops crossed the 38th parallel into South Korea. Washington immediately called for a special meeting of the UN Security Council, whose members demanded a cease fire and withdrawal of the invaders. The Soviet delegate was boycotting the Council at the time and was not present to veto the action.

When North Korea ignored the UN's demand, the Security Council sent troops to help the South Korean government. Three years of costly fighting followed, in what the UN termed a "police action." UN forces led by the United States, which suffered over 140,000 casualties, repelled the invaders, who were supported by the USSR and the Chinese Peoples' Republic. An armistice was signed in July 1953, after Stalin's death in March and the U.S. threat to use nuclear weapons against China.[6] The border between the two parts of the country was established near the 38th parallel, and South Korea's independence was maintained. The peninsula remained a crisis point for the next 40 years.

The Cold War erupted into heated fighting in Korea in 1950, when North Korean troops crossed the border into South Korea in an attempt to force reunification of the country. The United States, with UN backing, rushed to South Korea's defense. Here, a U.S. soldier surveys the smoldering ruins of a village north of Chunchon, South Korea, near the 38th parallel.

By 1953 the first phase of the Cold War was over. Both the Soviet Union and the United States possessed terrifying arsenals of nuclear weapons, both competed in all aspects of the Cold War, and both constantly probed for weaknesses in the other's defenses. Varied forms of controlled conflict characterized the next four decades of relations between Moscow and Washington.

The Soviet Union in the Postwar Era

Stalin rewarded the Soviet people for their sacrifices in World War II with a return to the iron repression of the 1930s. In the city of Leningrad, which had lost one million people, streets had been renamed in honor of the war dead. Stalin's party ripped down these spontaneous tributes and restored the old, officially approved names.

Postwar Stalinism

Despite the immense destruction it had suffered the USSR emerged after the war as one of the world's two superpowers. Stalin took seriously his role to build communism and pursue world revolution. He used the secret police to rid Soviet society of any Western contamination. To achieve military equality with the United States, he launched the fourth Five-Year Plan in 1946 pushing growth in heavy industry and military goods. To increase Soviet output, he imposed double shifts on many workers.

Huge new factories producing an estimated 80 percent of industrial output sprang up east of a line from Leningrad to Moscow to Stalingrad (now Volgograd). The state lured workers to the new sites with salary increases and other benefits, but much of the need for workers was filled by mass deportation of people to labor camps. Those whose loyalty to Stalin was in the least suspect were sent to a network of camps spread from Siberia to central Asia to the Arctic region. "The economic demand for cheap labour [dictated] the supply of the guilty."[7] Thousands died in the camps from overwork, inadequate food, and the bitter cold.

To rebuild the devastated farming regions Stalin returned to his collectivization policies. Smaller farms became parts of larger units, and the ultimate goal remained to make peasants into members of the rural proletariat, working in a kind of food factory. After 1950 the effort was stepped up, but at the cost of discontent and low productivity.

The dictator continued to place his supporters in all important offices, combining "the supreme command of the party with the supreme administration of the state."[8] He made entry into the party more difficult and purged those people who had slipped in during the war. The party became a haven for the managerial elite rather than the ideologically pure. The 1946 Supreme Soviet elections illustrated Stalin's total control. The voters were given only one choice for each office. Officials reported that 99.7 percent of the citizens voted; of this total fewer than 1 percent crossed out the name of a candidate.

In the early 1950s Stalin lashed out more ruthlessly and unpredictably than ever before, as he came to suspect everyone. His half-million strong security police squashed any sign of dissent, criticism, or free expression. He ordered genocidal attacks on entire peoples such as the Crimean Tatars. The purges went beyond the functions of "élite self-renewal." Stalin removed and later executed the director of national economic planning. There were indications that Stalin was preparing a major purge in January 1953. The police announced that a "doctors' plot" had been uncovered and charged a group of physicians serving high military and governmental officials with planning to undermine their patients' health. Seven of the nine accused were Jewish, and in some quarters it was feared that an anti-Zionist purge was in the making. The purge did not occur because on March 5, 1953, Stalin died after a painful illness.

Thus passed one of the most powerful men in world history. He had taken Lenin's revolution and preserved it in Russia while exporting it to the world. In a quarter-century he remade his society, withstood Hitler's strongest attacks, and emerged from the Second World War as leader of one of the two superpowers. He built the Soviet economic and political systems that lasted until 1987 and cultivated a group of bureaucratic

The first major movement in painting to develop after World War II was abstract expressionism, sometimes called action painting because the activity of painting seems as important as the finished product. One of the leaders of abstract expressionism is Willem de Kooning (b. 1904), whose best-known works are his woman paintings, a series of female nudes, such as *Woman IV* (1952–53), executed in broad, violent brush strokes on large canvases.

The act of painting is as important as color-field painting as it is in abstract expressionism, although the technique is quite different. Morris Louis (1912–1962), for example, applied extremely thin acrylic paint to absorbent, unstretched canvas, allowing the paint to sink in and stain the fabric rather than lie on top of the surface. The technique produces shapes of rich, although subdued, colors and soft, fuzzy edges. A characteristic example is *Point of Tranquillity* (1959–1960).

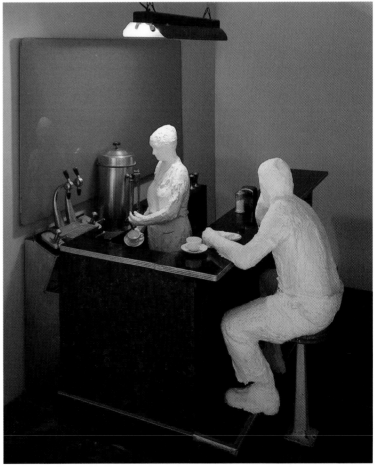

Pop art, a movement of the 1960s, emphasizes the materialism of contemporary industrialized culture by focusing on the realistic presentation of commonplace items of popular culture, such as soup cans, comic strips, and drugstores. Andy Warhol (b. 1931) uses images of advertising in his paintings, producing facsimiles of familiar products, such as *Campbell's Soup* (1965). Roy Lichtenstein (b. 1923) is noted for his use of comic-strip techniques, flat surfaces, hard edges, and bright colors. In *Stepping Out* (1978), upper right, the female companion of the dapper young man is reminiscent of surrealist images of the 1920s. The most famous pop art sculptor is George Segal (b. 1924), who frequently uses white plaster casts of the human figure set in realistic environments. His works, such as *The Diner* (1964–66), lower right, with their mood of loneliness, have been compared to Edward Hopper's paintings.

The realistic portrayal of real objects and images reaches an extreme in photo, or super, realism, in which images are first photographed, then translated into meticulously realistic paintings. The result is a painting of a photograph, executed in a completely detached, impersonal, and objective manner. The devotion to detail and complete accuracy characteristic of photo realism are evident in the works of Richard Estes (b. 1936), such as *Drugstore* (1970).

Stalin's chief supporters surround his bier at his funeral, March 6, 1953. Left to right, they are Vyacheslav Molotov, Kliment Voroshilov, Lavrenti Beria, Georgi Malenkov, Nikolai Bulganin, Nikita Khrushchev, Lazar Kaganovich, and Anastas Mikoyan. Khrushchev was the victor in the power struggle to succeed Stalin.

survivors—*apparatchiki*—who ran the country until the advent of Mikhail Gorbachev. In doing all of this, he killed at least twice as many people as Hitler.

Khrushchev's Contribution

A committee made up of Lavrenti Beria (secret police), Georgi Malenkov (chief Stalin aid), and Vyacheslav Molotov (foreign affairs) succeeded Stalin. The new rulers issued orders urging the people to guard against enemies and prevent "any kind of disorder and panic." They placed Stalin's embalmed body in the tomb next to Lenin and then relaxed his policies. They dropped the doctors' plot charges, eased censorship, reduced terror, and released many from prison and the labor camps. Within three years, the initial triumvirate had disappeared, elbowed aside by the Ukranian Nikita Sergeyevich Khrushchev (1894–1971).

Khruschchev was a self-made man who rose by his wits and ability. Born of peasant parents, he was a shepherd at seven and later a miner and factory worker. He joined the communist party and quickly rose through its ranks. Like so many of his colleagues, he came to power in the 1930s by taking the jobs of people killed by Stalin and ascended to the Politburo by 1939. By July 1953 he was the first secretary of the party; by 1955 he led the country. Educated Russians viewed Khrushchev as uncultured and uncouth. He delighted in shocking people by his blunt and frequently profane remarks. His crude behavior disguised a subtle, supple, and penetrating mind, which got rapidly to the center of a problem.

One of Khrushchev's main goals was to reform agriculture. He proposed increasing incentives for the peasants and enlarging the area under production in Soviet Siberia and central Asia—the virgin lands. Between 1953 and 1958 production rose by 50 percent. Thereafter farming in the

Khrushchev and Soviet foreign minister Andrei Gromyko pound the table to register their approval of the proceedings at a meeting of the UN General Assembly in 1960.

virgin lands proved to be economically wasteful and this, combined with other setbacks, ultimately undermined his position.

Khrushchev's greatest contribution was to begin the de-Stalinization campaign. In February 1956 at the Twentieth Party Congress he gave a speech entitled the "Crimes of the Stalin Era." He attacked his former patron as a bloodthirsty tyrant and revealed many of the cruelties of the purges and the mistakes of World War II. He carefully heaped full responsibility on the dead dictator for the excesses of the past twenty-five years, removing the blame from the *apparatchiki* such as himself who Stalin placed in power. Khrushchev blamed Stalin's crimes on the dictator's "cult of the personality." The speech hit like a bombshell and shocked every aspect of Soviet life from foreign policy to art and literature. In 1961 Stalin's body was removed from the Lenin mausoleum and placed in a grave by the Kremlin wall. His name disappeared from streets and cities; the "hero city" of Stalingrad was renamed Volgograd. Yet, the governing structure Stalin had built was carefully preserved, and his protégés remained in place until Gorbachev came to power in 1985.

Khrushchev's speech echoed throughout the communist world, helping to spark uprisings in Poland and Hungary and to widen the gulf between China and the Soviet Union. After 1956 Chinese-Soviet relations soured drastically and by 1960 Khrushchev had pulled all Soviet technicians and assistance out of China. During the next decade, the split grew still wider as Mao proclaimed himself to be Khrushchev's equal in ideological affairs.

Khrushchev survived an attempt to oust him from power in the summer of 1957, and from then until 1962, he dominated both Soviet and international affairs. During his rule, the standard of living in Russia gradually improved. Soviet scientists made remarkable strides, launching the first earth satellite, Sputnik, in the fall of 1957, and building a powerful fleet of intercontinental ballistic missiles. Khrushchev also relaxed, until 1959, the tensions of the Cold War and pursued "peaceful coexistence."

From 1959 to 1962 Khrushchev pursued aggressive policies in Asia, Africa, and Latin America. After drawing the world to the brink of catastrophe in the Cuban missile crisis in October 1962, he pulled back from the final step that would have resulted in nuclear war.

Khrushchev's blunders in Cuba and failures in agricultural policies led finally to his removal from power. While on vacation in October 1964 he received news from his colleagues that he had been "released from state duties" and that he had to return to Moscow. The fallen leader became a pensioned "un-person" under a mild form of house arrest in a comfortable compound outside of Moscow. He remained largely isolated from the public, writing his memoirs until his death in 1971.

The Last of Stalin's Protégés

After Khrushchev's "retirement" Leonid Brezhnev (1906–1982) and Aleksei Kosygin (1904–1980) strengthened the rule by Stalin's aging proteges. For the first ten years the two men split power: Brezhnev acted as General Secretary and Kosygin as premier, overseeing sporadic reform attempts. Brezhnev became president of the country under terms of the 1977 constitution.

Politics remained based on Stalin's foundations, as modified by Khrushchev. The central planners continued to emphasize industrial growth and slowly increase the supply of consumer goods. In foreign policy, the new team pursued peaceful coexistence at the same time that they greatly strengthened the Soviet armed forces. Brezhnev worked closely with military leaders to ensure that they had everything needed to gain equality with the United States in missiles, air, land, and sea forces. During the eighteen years of his rule, the Soviet Union built a powerful, global navy to support its foreign policies.

While the USSR gained military parity with the west, its civilian economy ground to a halt. The longstanding agricultural crisis grew worse. The Soviets spent huge amounts to import grain from abroad to cope with food shortages at home. Especially maddening to the Soviet leaders was the extraordinary amount of crops that rotted in the fields or en route to market. Private plots worked by peasants after hours for their own profit, which accounted for only 3 percent of sown land, provided 30 percent of all the table food in the Soviet Union.

The party leaders struggled to deal with low per capita output, poor quality, technological

Nikita Khrushchev, Address to the Twentieth Party Congress

After a quarter-century of Stalinist rule, the USSR badly needed a policy change. Khrushchev justified the change on the basis that Stalin had departed from Leninist norms and pursued the "cult of the personalities."

When we analyze the practice of Stalin in regard to the direction of the party and of the country, when we pause to consider everything which Stalin perpetrated, we must be convinced that Lenin's fears were justified. The negative characteristics of Stalin, which, in Lenin's time, were only incipient, transformed themselves during the last years into a grave abuse of power by Stalin, which caused untold harm to our party.

We have to consider seriously and analyze correctly this matter in order that we may preclude any possibility of a repetition in any form whatever of what took place during the life of Stalin, who absolutely did not tolerate collegiality in leadership and in work, and who practiced brutal violence, not only toward everything which opposed him, but also toward that which seemed to his capricious and despotic character, contrary to his concepts.

Stalin acted not through persuasion, explanation, and patient cooperation with people, but by imposing his concepts and demanding absolute submission to his opinion. Whoever opposed this concept or trend to prove his viewpoint, and the correctness of his position—was doomed to removal from the leading collective and to subsequent moral and physical annihilation. This was expecially true during the period following the 17th party congress, when many prominent party leaders and rank-and-file party workers, honest and dedicated to the cause of communism, fell victim to Stalin's despotism. . . .

. . . Lenin's traits—patient work with people; stubborn and painstaking education of them; the ability to induce people to follow him without using compulsion, but rather through the ideological influence on them of the whole collective—were entirely foreign to Stalin. He (Stalin) discarded the Leninist method of convincing and educating; he abandoned the method of ideological struggle for that of administrative violence, mass repressions, and terror. He acted on an increasingly larger scale and more stubbornly through punitive organs, at the same time often violating all existing norms of morality and of Soviet laws. . . .

During Lenin's life party congresses were convened regularly; always when a radical turn in the development of the party and the country took place Lenin considered it absolutely necessary that the party discuss at length all the basic matters pertaining to internal and foreign policy and to questions bearing on the development of party and government. . . .

Were our party's holy Leninist principles observed after the death of Vladimir Ilyich?

Whereas during the first few years after Lenin's death party congresses and central committee plenums took place more or less regularly; later, when Stalin began increasingly to abuse his power, these principles were brutally violated. This was expecially evident during the last 15 years of his life. Was it a normal situation when 13 years elapsed between the 18th and 19th party congresses, years during which our party and our country had experienced so many important events? These events demanded categorically that the party should have passed resolutions pertaining to the country's defense during the patriotic war and to peacetime construction after the war. Even after the end of the war a congress was not convened for over 7 years. . . .

In practice Stalin ignored the norms of party life and trampled on the Leninist principle of collective party leadership. . . .

From U.S. Congress, *Congressional Record*, 84th Congress, 2nd Session, 1956, CII, pp. 9389–9403, passim.

backwardness, transport breakdowns, and widespread corruption. Over the next twenty years, despite numerous reform attempts, the Soviet economy stagnated. The military sector absorbed most economic and technological improvements. Living standards slowly improved, but at a terrific cost. The Soviet Union exacerbated its economic problems by allowing political and ideological considerations to take precedence over productive efficiency.[9]

Until 1985 the Soviet Union plodded along under an aging, often ill, leadership. Brezhnev was succeeded by Yuri Andropov (1914–1984), a railway worker's son who worked his way up the ranks to become Soviet ambassador to Hungary from 1954 to 1957. After putting down the 1956 revolution in Hungary, Andropov returned to Moscow to take a number of increasingly important party and political jobs. In 1967 he became chief of the KGB, the organization which combined the powers and responsibilities of the U.S. FBI and CIA but without the legal restraints affecting those two groups. He remained in that post for the next fifteen years. He entered the Politburo in 1973 and seven months before Brezhnev's death Andropov became the secretary of the Central Committee. He rose to the top position in the Soviet Union the day after Brezhnev's death.

Andropov's jobs put him at the crossroads of all information. He knew the rotten condition of the USSR's infrastructure. He brought a large number of people from the provinces to work in high party positions in Moscow and set out immediately to increase output, fight corruption, and strengthen the military. He started campaigns to fight alcoholism and cheating and fired people who did not perform up to his standards. However, his own health problems caught up with him, and from the summer of 1983 until his announced death in February, 1984, Andropov was out of public view.

The last of the Stalin protégés was Konstantin Chernenko (1911–1985), who succeeded Andropov to the posts of first secretary and president. Chernenko had ridden Brezhnev's coattails since the 1950s but had been soundly defeated by Andropov for the top job in 1982. His age and poor health signified that he would be a transition figure between the old guard and a new generation. The strain of leadership almost immediately broke Chernenko's fragile health, and even before his death in March 1985, wholesale changes were taking place in the highest levels of the Soviet government.

The Gorbachev Revolution

Mikhail Gorbachev, representing a new college-educated generation of Soviet leaders, moved rapidly to take power, implementing a platform based on *glasnost* (openness) and *perestroika* (restructuring) to try to bring new life to the Soviet system. *Glasnost* was Gorbachev's way to motivate the Soviet people to be more creative and work harder. *Perestroika* attempted to remove the structural blocks to modernization. These two themes launched the final act in the de-Stalinization campaign begun by Khrushchev in 1956.

Gorbachev tried to mobilize the support of the cultural and scientific elite by encouraging them to participate in political life. As examples of the policy, he brought physicist Andrei Sakharov back from internal exile and permitted publication of the works of exiled author Aleksandr Solzhenitsyn. For the first time the party acknowledged mistakes, such as the Chernobyl nuclear disaster in April 1986. Past tragedies— especially from the 1930s—that had long been common knowledge were now openly discussed. Gorbachev permitted unprecedented criticism of party and political leaders by the press and television. He sponsored broad reforms in Soviet society, imposing the strongest anti-alcoholism campaign in history, making the force of the drive felt at the highest levels.

One of *glasnost's* unexpected results was a revival of separatist movements in the various Soviet republics. People in Estonia, Lithuania, Latvia, Armenia, Azerbaijan, the Ukraine, Moldavia, Kazakhstan, and Georgia declared the supremacy of their laws, institutions, and programs over those of the central government and claimed ownership of resources found within their borders.

Gorbachev originally sought to use *perestroika* to fine-tune the traditional central planning apparatus and party and state procedures, but the total failure of the Stalinist system has demanded a much more wide-ranging program. By 1990 the depth and severity of the Soviet

The coming to power of Soviet premier Mikhail Gorbachev and the election of U.S. president George Bush ushered in a new era of cooperation between rival superpowers the Soviet Union and the United States. In a White House ceremony on June 1, 1990, Gorbachev and Bush signed a series of accords between their two governments.

Union's problems drove Gorbachev to attempt to impose a market economy, reduce the role of the "vanguard party," and alter the governmental structure. The broader scope of *perestroika* has sought foreign capital, markets, and technology in order to make the USSR competitive. Gorbachev has had to rebuild most aspects of the Soviet economic structure, such as its banking system.

In politics until the summer of 1991, Gorbachev was the undisputed master of the party and the state, putting down rivals with great skill and using public opinion and free elections to neutralize opponents, while building a new power base. After being named president in October 1988, he set out to reform that most secret and powerful of all Soviet institutions, the KGB, urging its new leaders to imitate the structure of the U.S. CIA.

Until 1989 the Supreme Soviet was a carefully preselected, rubber-stamp body. Real power was concentrated in the Council of Ministers, headed by a prime minister. But after the elections of March and April 1989, in which many powerful officials were voted down, the Congress of People's Deputies replaced the old Supreme Soviet. The Congress is to be reelected every five years and meet annually. From its ranks comes the new Supreme Soviet. Unlike the old Supreme Soviet which never saw a no vote, the Congress and the new Supreme Soviet have proven to be outspoken and controversial bodies, even with the guaranteed positions for communist leaders.

The communist party posed a special problem for Gorbachev, a dedicated Leninist. He criticised the cumbersome and unresponsive functioning of the organization with its theoretical capstone, the Party Congress, which typically met once every five years and elected the 450-strong (300 voting, 150 nonvoting) Central Committee. The Committee, in turn, typically met at least once every six months to consider policies and elect the highest party body, the Politburo, with its 12 voting and 8 nonvoting members. From his post as General Secretary, he could see that the party and its special commissions would not attack the basic problems of the country.

The party had become corrupt and reactionary, concerned more with its privileges than its responsibilities. It was so inflexible that Gorbachev had to diminish its role after the July 1990 party congress. Thereafter, no major political figure sat on the Politburo, with the exception of the Soviet president. The party became subordinate to the state, losing its leading role. Millions gave up their party memberships after 1989, many of them going to work in city and republic governments where there was greater opportunity.

Gorbachev tried to deal with the USSR's systemic problems by firing large numbers of government, industry, military, and party officials, replacing them with younger, more aggressive people who could better implement his program. Unfortunately, he faced challenges that demanded more than just a change in personnel, and the longer he pursued his program, the smaller his constituency became. Nagging economic problems and resistance from the *apparatchiki* and party functionaries blocked Gorbachev's plans for reforms and forced him to make continual adjustments in order to hold power. In September, he abandoned a bold plan to bring a market economy to the Soviet Union within 500 days, dashing the hopes of progressives. For the next ten months his former liberal advisers and supporters either resigned or were dismissed from their positions.

As economic and social conditions deteriorated, Gorbachev increased concessions to party and bureaucratic hardliners, buying time to hold power and pursue his foreign policy objectives. In the spring hundreds of thousands of people marched in the streets of Moscow protesting the hardliners and Gorbachev's attempts to molify them. In the Baltic Republics, Georgia, the Ukraine, and Moldavia, separatist pressures increased. The economic system continued to decline, and standards of living plummeted along with productivity.

Although the revolution became mired in crisis domestically, it remained at high tide in the foreign policy arena. The Soviet president continued the policies begun in 1985. He had already renounced the Brezhnev doctrine permitting Soviet armed intervention into Socialist states. By doing so he allowed the Soviet bloc and its Warsaw Pact military strength to disintegrate, thereby opening the way for the revolutionary events of 1989 in Eastern Europe. He pulled Soviet troops out of Afghanistan in 1989 and worked to bring peace to several hot spots in Africa, including Angola. Most remarkably, he chose not to obstruct the reunification of Germany. He joined in the UN resolutions condemning Iraq's takeover of Kuwait in 1990 and cooperated in the alliance's military defeat of Saddam Hussein's forces in 1991. In July 1991 he initialed the Strategic Arms Reduction Treaty, continuing a process of working closely with U.S. presidents Ronald Reagan and George Bush at summits in Geneva, Iceland, Washington, Malta, and Moscow. The START treaty, which is yet to be ratified, took the disarmament campaign a major step ahead of the Intermediate Range Nuclear Forces agreeement signed in December 1987 (see ch. 37). Long running talks to reduce conventional forces in Europe began to produce results.

Domestic problems grew more severe during the summer of 1991. Agriculture faced an estimated grain shortfall of 77 million metric tons in the 1991 harvest, assuming the crop could even be brought in from the field. The tailspin in which the economy found itself continued to intensify. Economists who had predicted an 11 percent decline in Soviet GNP for 1991 were revising those figures to forecast an even greater decline. Boris N. Yeltsin, who had been popularly elected president of the Russian Republic in the spring, became an increasingly powerful figure as rudimentary public opinion polls gave Gorbachev a 7 percent approval rating.

In response to these crises, Gorbachev and Soviet Republic officials negotiated the Union Treaty that was to reallocate both authority and resources in the Soviet Union between the USSR government and the various republics. To be signed on August 20, it would have sharply reduced the authority of both the central power of the Soviet Union and the party.

In the face of this, an eight-man State Emergency Committee made up of leaders of the KGB, the military, the interior department, and other offices of the central government—all appointed by Gorbachev—launched an attempt to take power on August 19 while Gorbachev (like Khrushchev before him) was on vacation in the Crimea. Gorbachev's vice president announced that his leader was ill and that a state of emergency was to be imposed for six months.

The attempted coup was immediately denounced by Yeltsin, who barricaded himself inside the offices of the Russian parliament building in Moscow and instructed all army and KGB units not to obey the coup leaders' orders. The next day, 50,000 people turned out in Moscow to face down tanks sent by the central government. Larger groups mobilized in Leningrad and Kishinev. Several units of KGB and army forces refused to obey the central command's orders, and the coup began to unravel. By August 21, the crisis was over, and Yeltsin had emerged as the man of the hour.

When Gorbachev returned, he immediately attempted to resume power and to follow his old Leninist convictions. He soon found that he,

On August 19, 1991, president of the Russian Republic Boris Yeltsin stands atop an armored carrier in Moscow to read a statement urging people to resist the attempted hardline coup.

compared to Yeltsin, had little standing, especially after Gorbachev reiterated his belief that the party was the proper vehicle to carry out reform. Even as the coup leaders languished under arrest—or committed suicide—Gorbachev continued to defend the party. Finally, six days after the attempted coup, the reality of the situation became clear; Gorbachev resigned as leader of the Soviet Communist party and recommended dissolution of the Central Committee. Yeltsin claimed control of party archives and KGB records, and across the Soviet Union in a vast revolution the party—after 74 years of almost total power—was cut off from all its vanguard roles in running the country. In addition, the party had to surrender its wealth and property to the parliaments of the various republics. Gorbachev remained as president of the Soviet Union, at least until popular elections could be held.

But the future of the Soviet Union itself was in doubt. The Baltic republics of Lithuania, Latvia, and Estonia gained diplomatic recognition; and the Ukraine, Moldavia, Bielo-Russia, and Georgia declared independence. The Soviet Union as constituted before August 19, 1991, would not remain. Whether a loose economic federation or a series of squabbling successor states would emerge was a question debated both within and without the Soviet Union. The communist party of the Soviet Union and the Soviet Union itself faced possible extinction. Gorbachev had lost much of his political authority.

Where Peter the Great had overwhelmed his opposition with sheer power, and Stalin had sent his secret police, Gorbachev used *glasnost* and limited force to respond to his growing number of opponents. Ironically, it was the very people he chose who brought him down, and his defense of the party and the concepts he embraced that kept him down. His greatest gift to the Soviet people was that through *glasnost*, he had removed fear, and in the third week of August, people acted with great bravery. But the overwhelming problems of a nonfunctional infrastructure remained.

Eastern Europe

Eastern Germany

Since 1945 eastern Europe has reflected the changes that have taken place in the USSR. No place was this more evident than in East Germany from 1945 to 1991. Following the organization of the eastern zone of Germany into the German Democratic Republic, communist authorities broke up large private farms and expanded heavy industry. Thousands of discontented East Germans fled each week to West Germany through Berlin. In June 1953, severe food shortages coupled with new decrees establishing longer working hours touched off a workers' revolt, which was quickly put down. The westward flow of refugees continued, however, until 1961, when the Berlin Wall was constructed, in direct violation of the Four Power agreements.

The wall stopped the exodus of people, and East Germany stabilized. For the next 28 years the country had the highest density of armed men per square mile in the Soviet bloc and the communist world's highest economic growth rate. The country's athletes and businesses did well in world competition, and slowly and subtly under Erich Honecker and a new generation of *apparatchiki*, the German Democratic Republic improved relations with West Germany.

Gorbachev's program of liberalization threatened Honecker and his colleagues. After 1987 East German authorities stopped the circulation of Soviet periodicals that carried stories considered to be too liberal. At the same time, analysts noted the slowing economic growth rate of East Germany and the fact that the standard of living in West Germany was far higher. Old facilities, old managers, and old ideas eroded the economy of East Germany.

In September 1989, East Germans looking for a better life again fled in the thousands to the west, this time through Hungary and Czechoslovakia. This exodus, followed by Gorbachev's visit to Berlin in October, helped precipitate a crisis bringing hundreds of thousands of protestors to the streets of Berlin. Honecker was removed in October and on November 9 the Berlin Wall was opened. Once that symbolic act took place, both East and West Germans began to call for a unified Germany. Press exposés revealed the corruption and scandals among the communist élite. In the East German elections of March 1990 pro-western parties won an overwhelming triumph. By October 1990 Germany was reunited, with the first free all-German elections since Hitler took power.[10] Berlin was once again the capital of all Germany. Once the thrill of reunification had passed, Germans faced the difficult task of making the two parts of their country into one efficient unit.

In a scene that has come to symbolize the end of the Cold War, people dance atop the Berlin Wall, November 10, 1989.

Poland

In Poland, as in Yugoslavia, communism acquired a national character after a slow, subtle struggle that broke open in the fall of 1956 — following Khrushchev's "Crimes of the Stalin Era" speech. Polish leader Wladyslaw Gomulka set out on a difficult path to satisfy both Moscow and Warsaw — Soviet power and Polish nationalism. Gomulka governed skillfully through the 1960s until 1970, when he fell victim to the pressures caused by economic discontent on one hand and an increasingly corrupt party structure on the other.

Demonstrations and strikes broke out around the country and some, such as those at the Baltic port city Gdansk, were bloodily repressed. Gomulka was replaced by Edward Gierek, who throughout the 1970s walked the same narrow line as Gomulka between satisfying Moscow and Poland. Gierek borrowed extensively from the west and made several ill-advised economic decisions. By 1980 Poland was laboring to pay the interest on a foreign debt of $28 billion, and in the summer of 1980 the delicate compromise created by Gomulka and Gierek fell apart in a series of strikes caused by increases in food prices.

A nationwide labor movement came into being, *Solidarnosc*, or Solidarity. By October, around 10 million Poles from all segments of society had joined this movement, which stood for reform, equality, and workers' rights. In many ways, Solidarity's programs were protests against the Leninist concept of the party. It was Solidarity's proletarian base that made it so appealing to the world and so threatening to the other Marxist-Leninist leaders of the Soviet bloc.

At first the Polish government tried to work with the labor leaders, and Gierek made a symbolic purge of some of his less important associates. In September 1980 Gierek fell from power and in October Solidarity gained legal status — the first recognized union in a Soviet-dominated country. For the next ten months Solidarity pursued its goals. Workers won some concessions: a forty-hour, five-day work week and increased power in decision making in factories and offices.

Poland's economic problems did not disappear. Foreign debt increased. The currency, the

In Warsaw in 1965 Polish communist leader Gomulka (wearing glasses) stands between Soviet Communist party chief Leonid Brezhnev and Soviet premier Alexei Kosygin, viewing a medal representing a pledge of friendship, assistance, and cooperation between Poland and the Soviet Union.

zloty, inflated into meaninglessness with the pay increases and by the fall of 1981 the barter system was well on the way to replacing currency. Solidarity programs became increasingly radical. Conflict with the government, now headed by General Wojciech Jaruzelski, appeared inevitable. Solidarity's leader, Lech Walesa — an out-of-work electrician who had been fired for earlier attempts to organize a trade union in Gdansk — showed an instinctive genius for dealing effectively with every element of the Polish spectrum and the Soviet Union. He attempted to maintain a moderate position.

When Walesa's backers pushed him to call for a national vote to establish a noncommunist government, the Jaruzelski government responded with force, partially to maintain itself, partially to avoid Soviet intervention. Jaruzelski declared martial law and security forces rounded up Solidarity leaders. Outward shows of protest were squelched within two weeks.

Through the 1980s, communist party morale dipped as membership fell 20 percent. Although

Under the dynamic leadership of Lech Walesa, Solidarity, the Polish workers' union, grew into a nationwide social movement. In this photo from 1981, Solidarity members carry Walesa on their shoulders to celebrate a Polish Supreme Court decision upholding the workers' right to stage protest strikes throughout Poland.

In July Jaruzelski was elected president, though only with the minimum of votes, and Solidarity adviser Tadeusz Mazowiecki confirmed as prime minister. The party gave up its dominance, holding only four seats in the new cabinet. In January 1990, Poland decided to adopt a market economy. Even with substantial western financial support, the country faced rising unemployment and recession. The strains produced by this difficult step tested even the Solidarity movement, which split into two wings: that led by Mazowiecki and that led by Lech Walesa, who eventually emerged to be the Polish president.

Czechoslovakia

After the fall of the democratic government in 1948, the Czechoslovak communist party, the most Stalinist of the European parties, imposed harsh control for twenty years. However, in the spring of 1968, the country's liberal traditions came into the open. Under the influence of Marxist moderates, a new form of communism—"socialism with a human face"—was put into effect by the Slovak leader Alexander Dubček. As in Yugoslavia under Tito, the Czechoslovaks chose not to rebel against Moscow, but rather to adapt communism to their own conditions, but in August 1968 the Soviet Union and four Soviet bloc allies invaded Prague with more than 500,000 troops. Within 20 hours, the liberal regime, which advocated policies strikingly similar to those to be supported by Gorbachev twenty years later, was overthrown. The Soviets captured Dubček and took him to Moscow to confront Brezhnev.

The Soviets took their action against Czechoslovakia under the so-called Brezhnev Doctrine, under which communist states were obliged to aid their fraternal colleagues against "aggression," even when the fraternal colleague does not ask for aid, in order to safeguard the communal gains of the socialist movement. The Soviet-led forces crushed the Czechoslovak reforms to "protect the progress of socialism." Like that of East Germany, the Czech economy by the late 1980s was hampered by outmoded technology, timid leadership, and obsession with discredited ideology. The country suffered greatly from polluted

banned, Solidarity retained the genuine affection of the Poles and the support of the Roman Catholic Church, headed by Pope John Paul II, the former Polish Cardinal Wojtyla. To the embarrassment of the Polish state, Lech Walesa received the Nobel Peace prize in 1983. The economic situation deteriorated as inflation rates increased, the standard of living plummeted, and foreign debt soared to $40 billion. The party could not solve the problems it faced and in desperation, turned to Solidarity—which had been outlawed for eight years—in 1989. The June 1989 elections resulted in an overwhelming victory for the union, and in July it took its place in the Polish parliament, the *Sejm*, as the first opposition party to win free elections in eastern Europe since 1948. Solidarity won 99 out of 100 seats in the upper house and 161 seats (35 percent) in the lower house—all that was allotted to it in a preparatory round table.

On December 29, 1989, Czech playwright Vaclav Havel flashes the victory sign to thousands of Czechs after his election as president of Czechoslovakia.

repairing the effects of two generations of communist rule. By 1991 serious political and Slovak separatist demands were threatening progress of Czechoslovakia, now called the Czech and Slovak Federated Republic.

Hungary

After the Stalin purges, the Hungarian communist party became increasingly inept, until October 1956 when discontent with Soviet dominance erupted into revolution. For a week, a popular government existed, and Russian troops withdrew from Budapest. When the new government announced its intentions to leave the Warsaw Pact and be neutral, Soviet forces returned and crushed the rebellion. More than 200,000 refugees fled to the west.

Over the next thirty years, Janos Kadar (1912–1989) oversaw an initial bloody repression of the revolution and the execution of Imre Nagy, while he led a subtle pursuit of a Hungarian

In the 1956 Hungarian revolution, angry crowds burn Soviet propaganda—including photographs of Lenin—to protest Soviet domination of Hungary. Moscow responded by sending in tanks and troops to crush the uprising.

air and acid rain, and the population suffered under a declining standard of living.

The wave of change from Moscow caught the Czech party out of place. Dissidents who in January 1989 had been thrown in jail for human rights protests, including president-to-be, writer Vaclav Havel, found themselves running the country by December. Events in East Germany precipitated the events in Prague in October, 1989, when a pro-democracy meeting by over 10,000 demonstrators was savagely broken up. Similar protests in November met similar results. Still the Czechoslovaks were not deterred. In the "Velvet Revolution" of November 1989 200,000 demonstrators demanded free elections and the resignation of the communist leaders. Alexander Dubček came out of internal exile, and in December Valclav Havel became president, a result confirmed in the June 1990 elections. As in the other Eastern European states, however, the high spirits of the 1989 revolution were soon replaced by the sober realities of

variant of communism. In the process, the Hungarians gained a higher standard of living than the Soviets, an active intellectual life, and a range of economic reforms. In the mid-1980s, however, the Hungarian economic system, which encouraged more private initiative and decentralization, experienced difficulties. Hungary's foreign debt increased and inflation rose. Gorbachev encouraged the Hungarians to pursue their reforms, sometimes at the discomfort of Kadar, who was gently moved from power in 1987.

In 1989 the Hungarians dismantled the barriers, fences, and mine fields between themselves and the Austrians. Hungary imposed the first income tax and value added tax in eastern Europe, allowed 100 percent foreign ownership of Hungarian firms, opened a stock market, and set up institutions to teach western management methods to Hungarian businessmen.

By March 1990 Hungary had installed a multiparty system and was holding free elections, which led to the election of a right-of-center government led by Joszef Antall and the overwhelming repudiation of the communists. The coming years may be difficult for Hungary, as the country makes the transition from a centrally planned to a market-oriented economy.

The Balkans

Bulgaria proved to be a loyal ally of Moscow after 1945, and its standard of living has greatly improved. The Bulgarian economy averaged a growth rate of close to 3 percent a year and became increasingly diversified. Todor Zhivkov skillfully followed the Soviet lead and showed flexibility in responding to the early Gorbachev programs, especially the agricultural reforms. Until the autumn of 1989 the party appeared to be conservative and nationalist, as shown in its campaign against the country's Turkish minority (nearly 8 percent of the population) to deprive them of their heritage.

The wave of freedom hit Bulgaria at the end of 1989. Zhivkov was ousted in a party-led coup and replaced by Peter Mladenov. It seemed in the free elections in May 1990 that Mladenov and his allies would be the only party group to make the transition and maintain power in east Europe. But even he was thrown out in July when his role as orchestrator of the Zhivkov Palace coup was noticed, and the non-communist philosopher Zhelyu Zhelev became president.

Since the 1960s Romania under Nicolae Ceaucescu was the most independent of the Warsaw Pact countries in foreign policy. Domestically, the country labored under one of the most hardline and corrupt regimes in the bloc, whose economic policies of self-sufficiency plunged the standard of living to unprecedented depths. Ceaucescu achieved his goal to become free of the foreign debts by the summer of 1989, but at a cruel cost in human suffering.

Ceaucescu, accused by critics of desiring to achieve "socialism in one family," developed the "cult of the personality" to new heights. While imposing severe economic hardship on the nation, he built grandiose monuments to himself. Protected by his omnipresent secret police, the *Securitatea,* he seemed to be totally secure. But the 1989 wave of democracy spread even to Romania, which was the only country to experience widespread violence during that revolutionary year. Ceaucescu was captured and on Christmas day he and his wife were executed, thus bringing an end to their dreadful regime.

The Romanian pattern of political corruption continued, and Ion Iliescu manipulated the elections of May 1990 to keep power. The National Salvation Front made shameless use, later in the summer, of miners and ex-*Securitatea* officials to terrorize its critics. An uneasy equilibrium was attained, but little progress has been made to heal the devastating wounds inflicted by the Ceaucescu regime.

Albania under Enver Hoxha (d. 1985) worked closely with the Soviet Union until 1956. After Khrushchev's denunciation of Stalin, the country switched its allegiance to the Chinese until 1978. For the next decade Albania the poorest, most backward country in Europe, went its own way. Slowly, the Albanians entered into trade, diplomatic, and sporting relations with other nations. Even Albania felt the pressure of change in the summer of 1990, when people desperate to escape the country flooded foreign embassies. In early 1991 some 40,000 Albanians fled to Italy and Greece. Democratic elections were held in March in this last of the Stalinist states to enter the post-Cold War world. But even here, the Albanians marched to their own tune as the Communists carried two-thirds of the vote. However,

Marshal Tito, shown here delivering a speech while on an election campaign in Dalmatia, successfully pursued a policy of nonalignment with the Soviet Union and with the West.

as economic conditions worsened, the country suffered under increasing instability.

Yugoslavia

One of Stalin's major failures after 1945 was in his dealings with Marshal Josef Broz Tito of Yugoslavia. Tito had been a loyal communist and a good Stalinist in the 1930s. During the war he was an effective resistance leader, surviving attacks from Germans, Italians, and various right-wing factions in Yugoslavia. He had been in close contact with the western allies and after the war began to receive substantial assistance from them. Tito led the liberation of Yugoslavia from the Nazis and kept the country out of Moscow's orbit.

Stalin noted Tito's independence and from 1946 on sought measures to oppose him. Ethnically divided Yugoslavia overcame its internal divisions and a 10 percent casualty rate during the war to unite behind Tito. The Yugoslav leader's national backing, geographical distance from the Soviet Union, and support from the west enabled him to stand firm against increasing Soviet meddling in his country.

Tito became the first national communist— that is, a firm believer in Marxism who sought to apply the ideology within the context of his nation's objective conditions. This position placed him directly against Stalin, who believed that communists the world over must work for the greater glory and support of the Soviet Union. Tito believed that the setting in which ideology was found had to be taken into consideration, pointing out that Lenin had to adapt Marxist doctrine to conditions in Russia. Stalin insisted that Moscow's orders and examples must be slavishly followed. In 1948 Tito and Yugoslavia were expelled from the Soviet bloc. Successfully withstanding Stalin's pressures, including assassination attempts, Tito emerged as a key figure in the development of world communism.

Since 1948 the six republics containing ten ethnic groups that form Yugoslavia have survived the pressures of national diversity, the political stresses of the bipolar world, and serious economic difficulties. Many observers doubted that the country could survive Tito's death in 1980. However, Yugoslavia has remained tenuously united under its unique annually rotating head of state system despite an inflation rate of 80 percent and a 30 percent decline in the standard of living. The serious ethnic strife among Serbs and Croats and Albanians remains and continues to threaten the unity of the multinational state. Armed conflict broke out in the summer of 1991, as the Slovenes and Croats sought to break away from the Serbian-dominated coalition.

Life and Politics in the United States

The United States emerged from World War II with its landscape unscathed and its economy the most powerful in the world. This wealth enabled the United States over the next thirty years to assume vast global responsibilities, such as those mandated by the Marshall Plan, and to expand public services to improve health and education, provide unemployment, medical, and social security insurance, build housing, and launch anti-pollution campaigns. Until 1981 both Democratic and Republican administrations based their policies firmly on the legacy of Franklin D. Roosevelt's New Deal. Those who opposed the Roosevelt legacy suffered decisive defeats.

In addition to his foreign policy accomplishments after 1945, Harry Truman, who served as president from 1945 to 1953, continued to crusade for the rights of the "common man" and against the "fat cats" as he extended the New Deal. Republican Dwight David Eisenhower, the former supreme commander of Allied forces in Europe, was twice elected to the presidency with overwhelming victories. He continued, with somewhat less enthusiasm, to oversee the growth of federal programs. Eisenhower's successor, John F. Kennedy, was elected president in 1961 and promised a "New Frontier" spirit for America. While working actively for programs to aid the poor and minorities, he was unable to deal effectively with Congress. He captured the nation's idealism, especially with the Peace Corps, but his assassination in November 1963 cut short his presidency.

Johnson's Triumphs and Defeats

Kennedy's vice-president, Lyndon B. Johnson picked up the burden of the slain chief executive and completed a series of major domestic reforms. Johnson could claim credit for the Civil Rights Act of 1964, the war on poverty, Medicare, important environmental legislation, and the creation of the Department of Housing and Urban Development. However, major problems such as environmental pollution, decay of the urban "inner cores," and minority discontent—the crisis of rising expectations—remained unsolved.

Dr. Martin Luther King, Jr. (at left in front row) leads marchers on the historic trek from Selma to Montgomery, Alabama, to protest voting discrimination against blacks.

In foreign affairs, the increasingly unpopular Vietnam conflict plagued Johnson's presidency. The war alone cost upward of $30 billion annually, and that plus the expensive domestic programs fueled the inflation of the 1970s. Congress was slow to provide the massive funds needed to improve conditions for minorities and the inner cities and at the same time carry on the Vietnam war. In response, a powerful protest movement developed and many average Americans found themselves in deep and serious opposition to their government's policies. The political turmoil led in 1968 to the assassination of civil rights leader Dr. Martin Luther King, Jr. and of Senator Robert F. Kennedy, brother of the former president, who was close to gaining the Democratic presidential nomination before being shot in Los Angeles.

The Nixon Administration

The fragmentation of the liberal opposition led to the 1968 election by a razor-thin margin of Richard M. Nixon, Eisenhower's vice-president who had himself been narrowly defeated by John F. Kennedy in 1960. Nixon, re-elected by a landslide in 1972, shifted toward a more conservative philosophy of government. To fight inflation, caused in part by the costs of the Vietnam war and social programs, the administration imposed a wage-price freeze from August to November 1971 and wage-price controls from November 1971 to January 1973. These measures helped reduce the rate of inflation from 5 to about 3 percent. But when the administration returned to a free-market policy by the end of April 1974, prices began to rise. An oil embargo imposed by Arab nations opposed to American support of Israel contributed to the rise in inflation rates to 12 percent and a 6 percent unemployment rate.

The Nixon administration concentrated on foreign affairs during this time, especially those relating to ending the war in Vietnam, keeping peace in the Middle East, opening relations with China, and maintaining detente with the Soviet Union. In each area Nixon and his chief advisor, Henry Kissinger, compiled a substantial record of success. However, this record was overshadowed by the taint of scandal.

Nixon's vice-president, Spiro Agnew, resigned his office under the weight of charges of bribery, extortion, and kickbacks dating from his time as governor of Maryland. President Nixon himself resigned from office in the wake of the Watergate affairs. Men connected with the president's 1972 reelection campaign were arrested and charged with the break-in at the Democratic campaign headquarters. Nixon withheld information concerning these activities from a special prosecutor, a grand jury, and the public on the grounds of presidential confidentiality. After lengthy televised hearings and the conviction of his closest associates, Nixon lost the confidence of most of the nation. In May 1974 the Judiciary Committee of the House of Representatives began impeachment proceedings and in July the committee voted to recommend an impeachment trial in the Senate. Repudiated and disgraced, Nixon resigned in August. His appointed successor, Gerald R. Ford, who had also been appointed to the office of vice-president on Agnew's resignation, granted Nixon a full pardon.

The Carter Presidency

Economic problems, including high inflation, high unemployment, and a falling dollar, continued to plague the nation. In 1976 Ford ran against the relatively unknown Jimmy Carter, former governor of Georgia. Carter campaigned on promises to restore trust in government, extend social programs, and improve economic conditions. Carter won the close election, becoming

His attempt to cover up his personal involvement in the Watergate scandal brought President Richard Nixon into conflict with Congress. The House Judiciary Committee voted three articles of impeachment against Nixon, charging him with obstruction of justice, abuse of power, and contempt of Congress. On August 9, 1974, Nixon resigned the presidency.

Henry Kissinger, White House Years

Henry Kissinger, who served as Secretary of State under Presidents Nixon and Ford, advocated a balance-of-power approach to foreign relations and a policy of détente with the Soviet Union.

In my view, Vietnam was not the cause of our difficulties but a symptom. We were in a period of painful adjustment to a profound transformation of global politics; we were being forced to come to grips with the tension between our history and our new necessities. For two centuries America's participation in the world seemed to oscillate between overinvolvement and withdrawal, between expecting too much of our power and being ashamed of it, between optimistic exuberance and frustration with the ambiguities of an imperfect world. I was convinced that the deepest cause of our national unease was the realization—as yet dimly perceived—that we were becoming like other nations in the need to recognize that our power, while vast, had limits. Our resources were no longer infinite in relation to our problems; instead we had to set priorities, both intellectual and material. In the Fifties and Sixties we had attempted ultimate solutions to specific problems; now our challenge was to shape a world and an American role to which we were permanently committed, which could no longer be sustained by the illusion that our exertions had a terminal point. . . .

But in our deliberations at the Pierre Hotel the President-elect and I distilled a number of basic principles that were to characterize our approach to US-Soviet relations as long as we were in office:

The principle of concreteness. We would insist that any negotiations between the United States and the Soviet Union deal with specific causes of tensions rather than general atmospherics. Summit meetings, if they were to be meaningful, had to be well prepared and reflect negotiations that had already made major progress in diplomatic channels. We would take seriously the ideological commitment of Soviet leaders; we would not delude ourselves about the incompatible interests between our two countries in many areas. We would not pretend that good personal relations or sentimental rhetoric would end the tensions of the postwar period. But we were prepared to explore areas of common concern and to make precise agreements based on strict reciprocity.

The principle of restraint. Reasonable relations between the superpowers could not survive the constant attempt to pursue unilateral advantages and exploit areas of crisis. We were determined to resist Soviet adventures; at the same time we were prepared to negotiate about a genuine easing of tensions. We would not hold still for a détente designed to lull potential victims; we were prepared for a détente based on mutual restraint. We would pursue a carrot-and-stick approach, ready to impose penalties for adventurism, willing to expand relations in the context of responsible behavior.

The principle of linkage. We insisted that progress in superpower relations, to be real, had to be made on a broad front. Events in different parts of the world, in our view, were related to each other; even more so, Soviet conduct in different parts of the world. We proceeded from the premise that to separate issues into distinct compartments would encourage the Soviet leaders to believe that they could use cooperation in one area as a safety valve while striving for unilateral advantages elsewhere. . . .

We would have to learn to reconcile ourselves to imperfect choices, partial fulfillment, the unsatisfying tasks of balance and maneuver, given confidence by our moral values but recognizing that they could be achieved only in stages and over a long period of time.

It was a hard lesson to convey to a people who rarely read about the balance of power without seeing the adjective "outdated" precede it.

the first president from the Deep South since the civil war.

Carter inherited the same problems as his predecessors and incurred some new ones. To deal with the crisis in the Middle East he brought together at the presidential retreat of Camp David the leaders of Egypt and Israel. He continued to pursue limitations on nuclear arms, but for many his greatest accomplishment was that he made human rights considerations an operative part of American foreign policy. Domestically Carter attempted to enact an extremely ambitious program of social and economic benefits while maintaining sufficient military strength. Not surprisingly, spending increased despite the goal of a balanced budget.

Rising fuel prices and declining per capita output exacerbated economic difficulties. American helplessness and frustration grew when Iranian militants captured fifty-three hostages during a takeover of the U.S. embassy in Teheran. The combination of economic problems, the foreign policy crisis surrounding the Soviet invasion of Afghanistan, and the hostage dilemma led to Carter's defeat in November 1980 by former actor and Governor of California Ronald Reagan. Cruelly for Carter, the hostages were released just as Reagan took the oath of office in January 1981, after 444 days of captivity.

Ronald Reagan

Reagan won the presidency with an overwhelming victory, and he promised to set about reversing a half century of increasing federal involvement in American life by making drastic cuts in federal programs. This was part of his "New Federalism" program to reduce the budget, which went along with his program to make a 25 percent nominal cut in individual tax rates and a huge reduction in taxes paid by businesses. The administration planned, at the same time, substantially to increase military spending. The assumption underlying the policy was that the budget cuts and tax cuts would simultaneously cure inflation and bring about economic growth. However, the tax cuts were not matched by reduced federal spending, as the percentage of gross national product spent by government increased during Reagan's first term. The federal deficit had soared to unprecedented heights by

the time he left office. Inflation rates fell significantly, although interest rates remained high.

The economic problems posed little obstacle to Reagan in the 1984 election, in which he took 49 states. Not even his most bitter critic could deny the effect of his will and personality on the office of president. Observers looked back to Franklin D. Roosevelt to find Reagan's equal as a communicator and master of the legislative process. Reagan won major tax and budget victories in the Democrat-controlled House of Representatives and gained backing in the Senate for such controversial diplomatic initiatives as the sale of sophisticated equipment to Saudi Arabia and the INF treaty (see ch. 37). He survived an assassination attempt in March 1981, and this, plus his considerable charm, gave him an aura of authority and respect—despite a sometimes shocking lack of mastery of the details of his own programs—that no president since Eisenhower had enjoyed.

Reagan faced a number of foreign policy challenges in the rapidly changing period of the latter part of the Cold War. He sent contingents of Marines to Lebanon in 1982 to act as part of an international peacekeeping force in that fragmented country. A bombing in October 1983 killed 241 of the Marines. This atrocity forced Reagan to withdraw U.S. troops from the area. Relations with Israel cooled when Israeli forces bombed an Iraqi nuclear facility, annexed the Golan heights, and invaded Lebanon. The aggressive policies of Libyan leader Muammar el-Kadaffi led to conflicts with the United States, which included U.S. air attacks on Libya in the spring of 1986. In another controversial move, Reagan sent U.S. naval forces to the Persian Gulf when the Iran-Iraq war threatened to disrupt international oil shipments.

Festering social and economic problems in Latin America erupted into revolutionary movements in El Salvador and Nicaragua. The Reagan administration sent in military advisers and millions of dollars to support those factions it considered to be democratic. When Congress withdrew support for efforts to support the Contra rebels against the Sandinista government of Nicaragua, officials in the Reagan administration conspired to carry out illegal maneuvers to gain financial support, including the shipping of weapons to supposed moderates in Iran. The

"Iran-Contra" controversy cast a pall over the last two years of the Reagan administration and led to felony convictions of high-ranking Reagan aides.

George Bush

The Republicans maintained their hold on the White House with the election of George Bush in 1988. Bush's first two years were marked by increasing fiscal problems, resulting from the budget deficit, productivity declines, balance of trade problems, and a domestic economy suffering from the excesses of the deregulated Reagan years—the failure of many Savings and Loan institutions and the fear of recession sparked by the rise in oil prices. However, Bush built on the improving relationship with the Soviet Union, and worked closely with allies and opponents alike to maintain stability during the massive changes in Eastern Europe and the Soviet Union during 1989. Makeshift solutions to the deficit crisis and other pressing domestic problems harmed the president's standing in the polls, until the Persian Gulf crisis of 1990–1991. Deftly working through the United Nations and mobilizing a broad coalition, Bush effectively stymied the Iraq government diplomatically and then sent U.S. troops to lead the UN coalition forces

General Norman Schwarzkopf, commander of the U.S.-led military victory over Iraq in 1991, and President Bush pose for photographers in the White House Rose Garden, April 23, 1991.

in a powerful bombing campaign against Iraq. A one hundred-hour ground offensive ultimately drove Saddam Hussein's Iraqi forces out of Kuwait. Even though Bush's popularity soared to unprecedented heights, the nagging economic problems plaguing the country remained unsolved.

The Western European Powers

Great Britain emerged from World War II at the height of its prestige in the twentieth century, but the glow of victory and the glory earned by its sacrifices served only to conceal Britain's dismal condition. The country was in a state of near-bankruptcy. As a result of the war, its investments had drastically declined and huge bills had been run up for the support of British armies overseas. In addition, the increase in welfare benefits drained the economy.

After 1945 the London government could not reinstate the delicately balanced formula under which Britain had paid for the massive imports of food and raw material through exports and income from foreign investments, banking, and insurance. The British people, who had paid dearly to defeat the Axis powers, did not produce the necessary export surplus to restore Britain's wealth. Over the next forty years they would watch their vanquished enemies become wealthy while they struggled with aging industrial facilities and extremely costly welfare programs.

Conservative Rule in Great Britain

Since 1945 the Conservatives have dominated politics, with interludes of Labour rule. The Conservatives oppose nationalization of industry, encourage private enterprise, and favor a reduced social welfare program. Labour supports nationalization of industry and a thoroughgoing welfare state. Neither party has been able to find a wholesale cure for the serious ailments afflicting the country.

After the wartime coalition government of Conservatives and Labour, the country held its first peacetime regular election in July 1945, and to the amazement of many, Labourite Clement Attlee defeated Churchill. Attlee was a low-key, hardworking, honest politician who came from a comfortable middle-class background. In foreign affairs the Labour government continued to work closely with the United States, while in domestic policy it set out to improve basic living standards while converting back to a peacetime economic base. Within two years most major industrial and financial functions had been nationalized. In Britain's "mixed economy," 80 percent remained employed by private enterprise. The Labour party suffered, as it would for the next forty years, from factionalism between its left wing, which was inclined to be anti-American and pro-Russian, and the mainstream. Weakened by this split, Labour lost the general election in 1951, and the Conservatives began a thirteen-year dominance.

Churchill returned as prime minister until 1955, when he resigned and was succeeded by Anthony Eden. Eden resigned in January 1957 following the Suez crisis, and Harold Macmillan took the party's leadership until July 1963. During the 1950s economic conditions slowly improved until 1959, when they rapidly deteriorated. Britain went deeply in the red in its balance of payments. By the end of 1960 the economic outlook was grim. The next year the government applied for membership in the European Economic Community (EEC), more popularly known as the Common Market, in the belief that a closer trading association with the continent would reverse the terrible economic condition. The issue of membership in the EEC split both the Conservative and Labour parties. Further, during the negotiations with the EEC, French president Charles de Gaulle moved successfully to block British membership.

The long period of Conservative rule ended in 1964 with the election of a small Labour majority headed by Harold Wilson, who had previously been the youngest cabinet minister in 150 years. Under his leadership Labour made important advances in education, slum clearance, and housing. But the old economic problems remained to plague the government. In 1967 Wilson was forced to devalue the pound. Labour's lackluster performance in the late 1960s led to a Conservative victory in the 1970 election under the leadership of Edward Heath. Heath's only significant achievement was bringing his country into the Common Market. Labor unrest in

Shortly after being named president of the new French Fifth Republic in 1958, Charles de Gaulle (left) met with West German Chancellor Konrad Adenauer. The two European leaders issued a joint communique in which they agreed to defend "with vigor the maintenance of the status of Berlin."

1973 and the Arab oil embargo dealt a crippling blow to the British economy, and Heath's bland leadership could not save his party from defeat in the 1974 elections. Labour returned once again, led by Wilson, who commanded a narrow majority. Continued industrial unrest, declining production, and alarming inflation led to major changes.

In 1975 Wilson resigned, to be succeeded by James Callaghan, a pragmatic moderate. He warned that "we are still not earning the standard of living we are enjoying. We are only keeping up our standards by borrowing, and this cannot go on indefinitely." During 1976, Britain had to borrow $5.3 billion from ten other countries. Massive cuts were proposed for social services and the armed forces. Many unions denounced this action, but it seemed imperative to all responsible leaders. Callaghan's inability to deal with what one authority called "the most serious challenge in [Britain's] recent history as a liberal democracy"[11] led to yet another change in the spring of 1979.

Margaret Thatcher led her Conservative forces to victory by proposing radical changes in Britain's economic and social programs.

Thatcher's success in carrying out her programs gave her overwhelming victories in 1983 and again in 1987. She demanded—and received—sacrifices from her own people, a more favorable treatment from the Common Market, and firm backing from the United States. She built a solid political base against a disorganized Labour opposition. From there she proceeded to change the nature of the Conservative party and to attempt to reform British society, until she was removed by her party in 1990 and replaced by John Major.

Slow economic growth and unemployment have been constant problems since 1945. Britain continues to try to find the difficult balance between making an industrial comeback without seriously sacrificing the extensive welfare services. Another serious dilemma is the stark contrast between the rich southeastern part of the country and the permanently depressed areas of the Midlands, Scotland, and Wales. The Irish problem remained, with violent incidents occurring almost daily in Northern Ireland. Racial problems generated by English resentment over the influx of "coloured" peoples from the Commonwealth defy solution.

France: Grandeur and Reality

While most of France agreed to do the "rational" thing and capitulate to the Nazis in June 1940, Charles de Gaulle urged the government to move to North Africa and continue the struggle. During the war he personified France as a great power, rather than a humiliated Nazi victim. In a famous broadcast to the French people from his exile in London de Gaulle declared:

Whatever happens, the flame of French resistance must not and shall not die. . . . Must we abandon all hope? Is our defeat final and irremediable? To those questions I answer—No![12]

After the liberation of Paris in August 1944, de Gaulle was proclaimed provisional president and for fourteen months was a virtual dictator by consent. Elections held in October 1945 confirmed that the people wanted a new constitution. Sharp differences, however, developed between de Gaulle and members of the government. The general resigned in January 1946, occupying himself with the writing of his memoirs.

In the fall of that year, the Fourth Republic was established. Unfortunately, the old confusing patterns of the Third Republic were repeated. Too many parties and too much bickering precluded any significant action. The Fourth Republic had a mixed record during its dozen years of existence.

The Fourth Republic collapsed over the issue of Algeria. Revolt against the French colonial government there began in 1954 and for the next eight years drained French resources. The French population in Algeria, more than a million, insisted that Algeria be kept French. Army leaders supported them. Plots to overthrow the government in Paris were started. Faced with the prospects of a civil war, the ineffectual French government, which had been referred to as a "regime of mediocrity and chloroform," resigned in 1958, naming de Gaulle as president. His new government was granted full power for six months.

De Gaulle had been awaiting his nation's "call" in his country home. Eager to reenter the political arena, he returned to Paris and oversaw the drafting of a new constitution, this for the Fifth French Republic. The new code was overwhelmingly approved by referendum in September 1958. De Gaulle was named president for seven years and proceeded to make this office the most important in the government. In both the Third and Fourth Republics the legislature had been dominant, but now the president and his cabinet were the supreme power. During a crisis the executive could assume nearly total power. De Gaulle once commented, "The assemblies debate, the ministers govern, the constituent council thinks, the president of the Republic decides."

De Gaulle ended the Algerian war and shrugged off assassination plots and armed revolts. Then he set forth on his foremost objective—to make France a great power, to give it grandeur. He noted in his *Memoirs* that "France cannot be France without greatness." For the next seven years he worked to make France the dominant power in Europe, a third force free from domination by either the United States or the Soviet Union. To this end he persisted in making France an independent nuclear power. In 1966 he withdrew French military forces from active participation in NATO, although France remained a consultative member of the alliance.

Above all, de Gaulle was opposed to membership in any supranational agency. For this reason, while he tolerated the Common Market, he blocked any attempts to transform it into a political union. Even though he wielded great influence internationally, at home his position weakened.

A serious upheaval of university students and workers' strikes in 1968 further diminished de Gaulle's authority. A national referendum had been called to reorganize the government on a regional basis. De Gaulle unnecessarily made it a vote of confidence. When the referendum failed, he resigned his office and retired to his country estate, where he died eighteen months later.

His successor was Georges Pompidou, an able administrator who gave evidence of vision in his leadership. When Pompidou died prematurely in 1974, the country elected Valéry Giscard d'Estaing as president. A resistance hero and brilliant student, he had entered government service and became a high-ranking civil servant by the age of twenty-six. The new president initiated a series of important reforms relating to urban growth, real estate, and divorce. He also favored a voting age of eighteen.

Despite the generally high level of leadership in France, the country was also afflicted by the international economic difficulties relating to the energy crisis and American financial problems since 1973. Problems of inflation and housing shortages helped the rise to power of the communist and socialist parties, whose active participation in the wartime resistance had increased their popularity. There was a real possibility that a combined political program by the two parties might lead to a Marxist domination of the government. The March 1978 election, however, proved the alliance to be a weak one. Nevertheless the strength of the left was evident and continued to grow in the face of economic problems and discontent with Giscard's personal rule. In May 1981, Socialist leader François Mitterand was elected president, and twenty years of right-of-center government came to an end.

In June the Socialist party gained a majority in the National Assembly, and Mitterand set out to reverse two centuries of French tradition by decentralizing the governmental apparatus installed by Napoleon. In addition, he pursued a program to nationalize some of France's largest business and banking enterprises. Mitterand's "honeymoon" did not last long, as the parties to his right began to practice stalling tactics in the Assembly to block his programs. The communists, on the other hand, who had lost badly in the 1981 elections, received four relatively insignificant seats in the Cabinet, in return for which they promised cooperation with the new government.

Mitterand has had to deal with the economic problems of slow industrial growth, inflation, and unemployment, and he found these to be as resistant to solution as did Giscard. By the end of 1985 the economy began to improve. The president lost his majority in elections in March 1986 but regained it in 1988. Since then he has continued his policy of close cooperation with the United States and moderate domestic government.

West Germany: Recovery to Reunification

The most dramatic postwar European transformation has been that of West Germany. Recovering from the death, disaster, and destruction of World War II, the Bonn government accomplished political and economic miracles. When the Soviet bloc disintegrated in 1989, the Bonn government moved rapidly to extend economic aid and work for reunification. By October 1990, unification had been accomplished, justifying the dreams of postwar Germany's most important leader, Konrad Adenauer, who led his country from the status of despised outcast to that of valued western ally.

Adenauer was born in 1876 and entered politics in 1906 as a member of the city council of Cologne. In 1917 he became mayor of the city, holding office until 1933, when the Nazis dismissed him. During Hitler's regime he was imprisoned twice, but lived mostly in retirement at home, cultivating his rose garden. After 1945 he entered German national politics, becoming leader of the new Christian Democratic party. With the approval of the allied occupation authorities, German representatives drafted a constitution for the German Federal Republic, which was ratified in 1949. Adenauer, at the age of seventy-three, became chancellor of West Germany.

In the new democratic government, the presidency was made weak, while the real executive, the chancellor, was given specific authority to determine "the fundamental policies of the government." The chancellor was responsible to the Bundestag, a popularly elected legislative body. One of the weaknesses of the Weimar Republic had been the existence of many small parties, leading to unstable multiparty coalitions. In the new government, no party was recognized that did not win at least 5 percent of the total election votes.

Adenauer assumed power when Germany was still an outcast and its economy was in ruins. His one driving obsession was to get his people to work. Taking advantage of the tensions of the Cold War, he succeeded admirably. Under the force of his autocratic and sometimes domineering leadership, the Germans rebuilt their destroyed cities and factories using some $3 billion in Marshall Plan assistance. As early as 1955 West German national production exceeded prewar figures, with only 53 percent of former German territory. Providing the initial economic guidance for this recovery was Adenauer's minister of economics Dr. Ludwig Erhard, a professional economist and a firm believer in laissez-faire economics. Germany's economic growth was accompanied by little inflation, practically no unemployment, and few labor problems.

Adenauer's achievements in foreign affairs were as remarkable as his leadership in domestic affairs. The German Federal Republic gained full sovereignty in 1955. At that same time, West Germany was admitted into the NATO alliance. Adenauer decided to align closely with the west and cultivated close ties with the United States. In 1963 he signed a treaty of friendship with France, ending a century-long period of hostility. Adenauer expressed his attitude toward foreign affairs when he said "Today I regard myself primarily as a European and only in second place as a German." It was natural that he brought his nation into Europe's new institutions: the European Coal and Steel Community and the Common Market. Adenauer's great frustration in foreign affairs was his failure to achieve the reunification of West and East Germany.

In 1963, after fourteen years in office, Adenauer retired and was succeeded by Ludwig Erhard as chancellor, who was in turn succeeded by Kurt Kiesinger. The big change in German politics occurred in 1969 with the victory of the Social Democratic party. This moderate, nondoctrinaire socialist party was led by Willy Brandt, who became chancellor. A foe of the Nazis, Brandt had fled to Norway where he became a member of the resistance after Hitler's conquest. After the war he returned to Germany and became prominent in the Social Democratic party. In 1957 he became mayor of West Berlin, then in 1966 foreign minister in Bonn. Brandt was very active in setting West Germany's foreign policy. He was instrumental in getting Britain into the Common Market, he tried to improve relations with eastern Europe and the Soviet Union through *Ostpolitik*, a policy of cooperation with Warsaw Pact nations. In journeys to both Moscow and Warsaw in 1970 he negotiated a treaty with the USSR renouncing the use of force and an agreement with Poland recognizing its western border along the Oder and Neisse rivers. A treaty was also signed with East Germany for improving contacts and reducing tensions. These negotiations and others paved the way for the entry of the two Germanies into the United Nations.

Brandt's concentration on foreign affairs led to the appearance of neglect of domestic issues such as inflation and rising unemployment. Important segments of German public opinion attacked him on the policy of *Ostpolitik*. Finally a spy scandal rocked the government, and Brandt resigned in the spring of 1974. Helmut Schmidt, who succeeded him, paid closer attention to domestic affairs.

Under Schmidt's leadership Germany continued its strong economic growth in the wake of the oil embargo. German workers did not suffer the unemployment problems of other countries because of the practice of firing and sending home foreign workers when job cutbacks were needed. Germany's economy in the 1980s was not immune to issues such as foreign trade fluctuations and oil imports. Still, Schmidt, as head of the most powerful western European nation had the prestige and record to ensure his victory in the 1980 elections.

In the late 1970s Schmidt had asked the United States to counter the Soviet placement of SS-20 intermediate range missiles by placing intermediate range ballistic missiles in Europe, thereby setting off controversial debate that did not end until 1983. Schmidt faced both the disapproval of antinuclear demonstrators who did not want the missiles and the displeasure of conservatives in his country and the United States over German economic ties with the Soviet Union. In the autumn of 1982 political power passed again to the Christian Democratic Party, now led by Helmut Kohl.

For the rest of the decade Kohl's party proved to be a staunch supporter of the United States, in particular of its program to place U.S. intermediate range missiles in Europe. In the face of strident Soviet protests, Kohl guided a bill through the West German parliament in November 1983 to deploy the missiles. After that success, and a strong victory in 1987, Kohl—despite the reputation of being a plodding politician—came to play a strong role in European affairs and in relations with the Soviet Union. In the course of his tenure, Kohl changed with the times to deal with environmental issues brought forcefully to the public forum by the Green party. He masterfully took advantage of the breakdown of the German Democratic Republic in 1989 to claim the issue of reunification for himself and his party. By the end of 1990, Kohl had confounded those who had contempt for his intellect and those who thought him politically naive.

Italy: Political Instability, Economic Growth

Following the end of Mussolini's regime, Italy voted by a narrow margin to end the monarchy. A new constitution, adopted in 1947 provided for a premier and a ministry responsible to the legislature. The Christian Democratic party—strongly Catholic, pro-western, and anti-Communist—was the leading middle-of-the-road group. Its spokesman and leader was Alcide de Gasperi, whose ministry governed the country from 1947 to 1953. Like Adenauer, de Gasperi was a strong adherent of democracy and supported European unity. Italy joined NATO in 1949 and became a member of the Common Market in 1957.

Within little more than a decade the Italian economy changed from predominantly agricultural to industrial. For a time, in the late 1950s and early 1960s, industry advanced faster in Italy than in any other part of Europe. In 1960 the output of manufacturing tripled pre-1939 levels, and in 1961 steel production was more than one million tons. By the end of the 1980s Italy ranked among the world's leaders in high-tech industry, fashion, design, and banking. Most economic development occurred in northern Italy around the thriving cities of Turin, Milan, and Bologna.

Southern Italy has not progressed as rapidly. Too many people, too few schools, inadequate roads, landlordism, and inefficient, fragmented farms worked by poor peasants are among the problems besetting the area. The government has offered help in the form of subsidies, tax concessions, and programs for flood control and better highways, but southern Italy remains a challenge and an urgent problem.

While the Italian economy was a source of optimism, politics was another story. After de Gasperi's retirement in 1953, politics became increasingly characterized by a series of cabinet crises, shaky coalitions, and government turnovers. By 1990 there had been forty-nine governments since the end of World War II.

Corruption and inefficiency were widespread in the Christian Democratic-dominated system. In the 1970s labor unrest, unemployment, and inflation posed problems that politicians could not deal with, even in coalitions in which the Communist party joined with other factions. For a while terrorism dominated political life. In 1978 the anarchist Red Brigade kidnapped one of Italy's most prominent public figures, former premier Aldo Moro, and assassinated him nearly two months later, leaving his body in a car parked equidistant between the Christian Democratic and Communist Party headquarters in Rome. Terrorists spread chaos among business and political leaders. During the 1980s the government, dominated by Bettino Craxi and Ciriaco de Mita, improved conditions. The terrorist networks were broken and law enforcement agencies attacked the Mafia organization in southern Italy and Sicily.

Portugal, Spain, and Greece

In the western and eastern peninsulas of Europe, politics since 1945 has been marked by dictatorships and radicalism, but parliamentary forces have clung tenaciously to power. Portugal, Spain, and Greece have all experienced severe economic problems and traditions of instability.

Portugal was an incredibly corrupt monarchy until 1910. The country then became a republic, but its record of internal turmoil continued. Between 1910 and 1930 there were twenty-one uprisings and forty-three cabinets. Toward the end of that period the army ousted the politicians and took control of the government. In 1932 the generals called on Antonio de Oliveira Salazar to run the country. This former economics professor, a fervent and austere Catholic, shunned social life and was content to live on a very small salary. He devoted all of his time to running an authoritarian government. The press was censored and education—in a country in which two-thirds of the population was illiterate—was neglected. Some economic improvement did take place, but the people, who were frozen out of politics, remained poor. In 1955 a five-year program to stimulate the economy was launched, but its gains were cancelled by an increase in population and by huge financial drain of the national budget resulting from colonial wars in Portugal's African holdings.

Salazar retired in 1968 because of ill health, and six years later a group of junior army officers overthrew the government. Serious divisions appeared between the moderate liberal factions and the communists. In the summer of 1976, however, elections confirmed the victory of the moderate socialists. A new constitution was enacted, establishing a democratic system. The government faced difficult economic problems. Six hundred thousand refugees from Portuguese Africa had to be absorbed, adding to the high unemployment and runaway inflation. After the 1974 revolution workers had seized many businesses, large farms, and hotels. In most instances, private ownership had to be restored under efficient management. During the 1980s political and economic stability returned to the country, led in the latter part of the decade by Mario Soares, ruling through a socialist coalition. Compared with the rest of Europe, Portugal remained poor, with over 10 percent inflation and only 80 percent literacy, but in terms of the Iberian peninsula, much progress had been made.

In the four decades after the Second World War, Spain passed from the Franco dictatorship to a rapidly industrializing, modern European state. Franco ruled over an almost ruined country after taking control in 1939. Many of Spain's most talented and productive people had fled, and 700,000 people had died in the civil war. So horrible was the conflict and so great the losses, that Franco gained a grudging toleration from the majority of the exhausted population. Those who did not cooperate faced his secret police.

Cold War tensions eased Spain's reentry into the community of nations in the 1950s. The United States resumed diplomatic relations and Spain became a member of the UN in 1955. The following year the Pact of Madrid provided naval and air bases for the Americans, in return for which Spain received more than $2 billion a year in aid. In the 1960s and 1970s the widespread poverty and backwardness that had long characterized Spain began to diminish. Inspired by the Portuguese revolution of 1974, workers and students began to demonstrate and show their unrest. In the summer of 1975 Franco died. He had named Prince Juan Carlos as his successor, thereby indicating his wish that the monarchy be restored.

The young king was crowned in November 1975, and in his speech of acceptance he promised to represent all Spaniards, recognizing that the people were asking for "profound improvements." In 1976, the reformed government announced amnesty for political prisoners, freedom of assembly, and more rights for labor unions. An orderly general election took place in the spring of 1977. Post-Franco Spain began its parliamentary-monarchy phase with impressive stability. Underneath, deep ideological divisions remained, which decreased over time. The major crisis came in February 1981 when radical elements of the army invaded the parliament building to attempt a coup. It immediately became apparent that there was no support for the coup either in the military or among the public at large, and the attempt was brushed aside.

In May 1982 Spain joined NATO—still a controversial decision—and, later that year, elected the Socialist party led by Felipe Gonzales to run the country. Gonzales brought Spain into the Common Market and worked hard to diversify the country's economy. He strengthened his

Spanish prime minister Felipe Gonzales signs the treaty admitting Spain and Portugal to membership in the European Common Market in June 1985.

position in the 1986 elections and by 1990 was governing a country attractive to investors in high-tech industries. Spain looked forward to hosting the 1992 Olympic games.

Greece, since its modern creation in 1821, has rarely enjoyed political stability. From that year until 1945 there were fifteen different types of government with 176 premiers who obviously averaged less than one year in office. Inefficiency in government, economic backwardness, and political crises have continued to plague Greece since 1945. In the Greek civil war (1946–1949) pro-western forces, who controlled only the major cities, turned back a powerful communist surge for power and re-established the monarchy. Greek politicians ignored the complex economic issues affecting the peasants, preferring instead to attempt to regain control of various islands and territories controlled by Greeks in the long-distant past. In the spring of 1967 a group of army colonels seized power. A dictatorship was established which jailed many political figures and harshly punished any criticism of its rule. Many Greeks fled into exile. The military junta made a serious miscalculation in 1974 when it connived to increase Greek authority on

Cypress, a move that led to a Turkish invasion of the island. This mistake led to the junta's downfall.

Thereafter the Greeks created a republic, complete with a new constitution. They applied for membership into the Common Market in 1975, and were admitted in 1981. In its application, the government stated that its desire to join the European Community was "based on our earnest desire to consolidate democracy in Greece within the broader democratic institutions of the European Community to which Greece belongs." Since that time, Greek leaders have maintained their democratic traditions. In November 1981 the Socialist party led by Andreas Papandreou gained power and held it through 1989, gaining increased support in 1985. Papandreou ran on pledges to evict U.S. forces from Greek bases and to move Greek foreign policy away from western orientation. Yet the Greeks remained active participants in NATO and the Common Market. Like Portugal Greece is, by European standards, a poor country with a stagnant economy and an inflation rate of over 20 percent. In the 1989 elections, these factors plus scandals surrounding Papandreou's personal life led to the defeat of the Socialists and the forming of an unlikely coalition made up of the Communist and Conservative parties.

Conclusion

In the first decade after the war, Europe stood caught and divided between the superpowers of the United States and the Soviet Union. Only the most optimistic person would have believed that a tragic war between the two would *not* break out. But by the last decade of the twentieth century, the Cold War had ended, and the allies of Washington and Moscow looked ahead to a more independent and prosperous existence.

The Soviet Union and the United States both underwent profound social and economic changes in the postwar period. Suffering the losses from World War II and the effects of an unproductive economic system, the USSR faced a severe crisis. The United States, blessed with a productive industrial system, successfully weathered its economic difficulties.

The eastern European states paid the price for Soviet reconstruction and domination. Only East Germany showed any ability to compete economically during the postwar period, and that country had lost its edge in the 1980s. The Marxist-Leninist system, especially in its Stalinist variant, was widely acknowledged to have failed, and the transition to new systems promised to be difficult. The western European states had absorbed the changes more easily, but not without pain. A new age of dominance for the western European states loomed on the horizon in 1992.

Suggestions for Reading

Lynn E. Davis, *The Cold War Begins* (Princeton, 1974) is a thorough accounting of the origins of the conflict. Various points of view on American-Soviet relations can be found in Walter La Feber, *America, Russia, and the Cold War* (Wiley, 1976); P. Hammond, *Cold War and Détente: The American Foreign Policy Process Since 1945* (Harcourt Brace Jovanich, 1975); and L. Wittner, *Cold War America: From Hiroshima to Watergate* (Praeger, 1974). Other studies of note on the Cold War are J. C. Donovan, *The Cold Warriors: A Policy Making Elite* (Heath, 1974) and H. S. Dinerstein, *Soviet Foreign Policy Since the Missile Crisis* (Johns Hopkins, 1976). Adam Ulam gives a good survey of Moscow's policies in *Expansion and Coexistence: Soviet Foreign Policy 1917–1973* (Holt, 1974) A penetrating study of the major figures in U.S. foreign policy formation is *The Wise Men* by W. Isaacson and E. Thomas (Touchstone, 1988). Robbin F. Laird and Erik P. Hoffman, eds., *Soviet Foreign Policy in a Changing World* (Aldine, 1986) is a solid collection of articles on the dilemmas facing the Soviets. Peter Zwick, *Soviet Foreign Relations: Process and Policy* (Prentice Hall, 1990) spells out the factors shaping Moscow's policies. The Committee on Foreign Affairs analysis of *Soviet Diplomacy and Negotiating Behavior—1979–1988: New Tests for U. S. Diplomacy* (Government Printing Office, 1988) gives good insights into Washington's understanding of Soviet diplomacy.

The Soviet world at the beginning of the 1990s still labored under the impact of Stalin's policies and accomplishments. R. C. Tucker, ed., presents the panorama of his life and policies in *Stalinism: Essays in Historical Interpretation* (Norton, 1977). M. Djilas, *Conversations with Stalin* (Harcourt Brace Jovanovich, 1962) gives a vivid, first-hand account of Stalin's personality. Khrushchev's tenure is competently covered in E. Crankshaw, *Khrushchev, a Career* (Viking, 1966) and in Khrushchev's own words in *Khrushchev Remembers* (Ballantine, 1976). Hedrick Smith, *The New Russians* (Random House, 1990) is an outstanding update of his classic introduction to the "way things really work." Martin McCauley, ed., presents an all-encompassing study of Khrushchev's time in power in *Khrushchev and Khrushchevism* (MacMillan, 1987).

Impressionistic and important is Roy Medvedev's *Khrushchev* (Doubleday, 1983). Elizabeth Valkenier discusses the problems of overextension in *The Soviet Union and the Third World: An Economic Bind* (Praeger, 1983). The Brezhnev years are examined by Archie Brown and Michael Kaser, eds., in *The Soviet Union Since the Fall of Khrushchev* (Free Press, 1976). Gail Lapidus examines the difficult lot of women in *Women, Work and Family in the Soviet Union* (M. E. Sharpe, 1982). Frederick Starr's splendid *Red and Hot: The Fate of Jazz in the Soviet Union, 1917–1980* (Oxford, 1983) gives a unique insight into cultural vitality in the "totalitarian" Soviet Union. A work anticipating the current crisis of the USSR is Paul Dibb, *The Soviet Union: The Incomplete Super Power* (Illinois, 1986). Martin Ebon gives essential background to the key figure in Soviet political change in the *The Andropov File . . .* (McGraw-Hill, 1983). Marshall Goldman's perceptive *Gorbachev's Challenge: Economic Reform in the Age of High Technology* (Norton, 1987) anticipates the Soviet crisis in the 1990s. A good primer on the "Balance of Terror" is Ray Perkins Jr. *The ABCs of the Soviet-American Nuclear Arms Race* (Brooks/Cole, 1991).

Eastern European developments through the 1960s can be studied in the surveys by Hugh Seton-Watson, *The East European Revolution* (Praeger, 1961), Ivan Volgyes, *Politics in Eastern Europe* (Dorsey, 1986), and Z. Brzezinski, *The Soviet Bloc: Unity and Conflict* (Harvard, 1971). F. Fejto, *History of the People's Democracies* (Pelican, 1973) is a solid survey of post-1945 Eastern Europe. Dennis Rusinow, *The Yugoslav Experiment, 1948–1974* (London, 1977) and Dusko Doder, *The Yugoslavs* (New York, 1976) give two views of the multinational state to the mid-1970s. Jorg K. Hoensch *A History of Modern Hungary: 1867–1986* (Longman, 1988) is an objective survey. The Czech crisis of 1968—and after—is well covered in G. Golan, *Reform Rule in Czechoslovakia* (Cambridge, 1971). Norman Davies, *Heart of Europe: A Short History of Poland* (Oxford, 1987) gives the best short survey of recent events in that country in chapters 1 and 7.

Post-1945 events in the United States are discussed in Jim Heath, *Decade of Disillusionment: The Kennedy-Johnson Years* (Indiana, 1984). Allen J. Matusow, *The Unraveling of America: A History of Liberalism in the 1960s* (Harper, 1984) traces the political results of that shocking decade. At the end of the 1980s, Joseph S. Nye, Jr., wrote a magisterial analysis of the changing nature of the United States's role in *Bound to Lead: The Changing Nature of American Power* (Basic Books, 1989). Most of the postwar presidents have produced their memoirs. Probably the best and most enjoyable are Truman's *Memoirs* (Doubleday, 1955–1956). See also Lyndon B. Johnson, *The Vantage Point*, (Holt, Rinehart and Winston, 1971) and Dwight D. Eisenhower, *The White House Years* (Doubleday, 1963). See also, Doris Kearns, *Lyndon Johnson and the American Dream* (Harper/Row, 1976).

The resurgence of Western Europe is dealt with in J. Robert Wegs, *Europe Since 1945* (St. Martins, 1991). See also Neil McInnes, *The Communist Parties of Western Europe* (Oxford, 1979) and T. Geiger, *The Fortunes of the West: The Future of the Atlantic Nations* (Indiana, 1973). Good accounts of the various western European countries are: David McKie and Chris Cook, eds., *The Decade of Disillusionment: Britain in the 1960s* (St. Martin's, 1973); C. J. A. Bartlett, *A History of Postwar Britain* (Longman, 1977);

John Darby, *Conflict in Northern Ireland* (Barnes and Noble, 1976); and George Dangerfield, *The Damnable Question* (Little, Brown, 1976). See also P. A. Allum, *Italy: Republic Without Government* (Norton, 1974) and Roy C. Macridis, *French Politics in Transition* (Winthrop, 1975). Max Gallo, *Spain under Franco* (Dutton, 1974) and Paul Preston, ed., *Spain in Crisis* (Barnes and Noble, 1976) study the evolution of that country under Franco. Neil Bruce, *Portugal: The Last Empire* (Halstad, 1975) presents the background of the 1974 revolution.

Notes

1. Max Radin, "Justice at Nuremberg," *Foreign Affairs*, April 1946, p. 371.
2. A useful guide to the historiography of the Cold War can be found in J. L. Black, *Origins, Evolution, and Nature of the Cold War: An Annotated Bibliographic Guide* (Santa Barbara, CA: ABC-Clio, 1986).
3. Winston Churchill, *Triumph and Tragedy* (Boston: Houghton Mifflin, 1953), p. 497.
4. Raymond Aron, "The Foundations of the Cold War," in *The Twentieth Century*, Norman F. Cantor and Michael S. Werthman, eds., (New York: Thomas Y. Crowell, 1967), p. 157.
5. David Rees, *The Age of Containment* (New York: St. Martin's Press, 1967), p. 23.
6. Joseph L. Nogee and John Spanier, *Peace Impossible—War Unlikely, The Cold War Between the United States and the Soviet Union* (Glenview: Scott, Foresman/Little, Brown, 1988), p. 67.
7. J. P. Nettl, *The Soviet Achievement* (New York: Harcourt Brace Jovanovich, 1967), p. 198.
8. Leonard Schapiro, *The Communist Party of the Soviet Union* (London: Methuen, 1963), pp. 534–535.
9. Alec Nove, *The Soviet Economic System* (London: George Allen & Unwin, 1977), p. 320.
10. Ferdinand Protzman, "East Germany Losing its Edge," *The New York Times*, May 15, 1989, D-1.
11. Michael R. Hodges, "Britain Tomorrow: Business as Usual," *Current History*, March 1975, p. 138.
12. Charles de Gaulle, *The Call to Honor* (New York: Viking Press, 1955), p. 33.

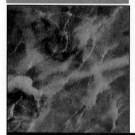

Chapter 36

The Emerging "South" Since 1945

After 1945 the old European empires disappeared, replaced by over 80 new countries. These new states, primarily located to the south of the European powers, were born into a difficult environment, buffeted by the Cold War and economic upheavals. As of the last decade of the millennium, the "South" contained most of the world's expanding population and grim challenges.

In east Asia, Japan recovered from its postwar devastation to become a center of world finance. China participated in Cold War episodes from Korea to Vietnam and fought its own ideological battles before entering a period of rapid modernization after 1978. Indochina's fate was bound up in a series of bloody, devastating proxy wars.

In the rest of Asia and in Africa, nations freed themselves from the yoke of European dominance, but independence unleashed powerful ethnic and religious antagonisms, most of which remain unresolved. Great power intervention in the Middle East and in Africa exacerbated an already difficult situation and led to increased bloodshed.

More than Cold War tensions, economic upheavals have affected the Latin American states. The region's accumulation of massive debts and its dependence on the export of oil or agricultural products left it at the mercy of the North Atlantic powers. This economic domination provided a rich opportunity for revolutionaries in Cuba and Nicaragua who profited from the obvious exploitation of the population.

At the end of the twentieth century, Japan, South Korea, Hong Kong, and Singapore competed effectively in the world arena. Other countries, such as Brazil, India, China, and Zimbabwe, showed signs of potential strength. However, the vast majority of the nations of the "South" remain trapped by the cruel forces of poverty and overpopulation.

Japan: Conquered Nation to World Power

On August 28, 1945, nineteen days after the atomic bomb was dropped at Nagasaki, an advance party of 150 Americans, the lead group of a substantial army of occupation, landed on Japan. Supreme Commander General Douglas MacArthur soon arrived to preside over Japan's transition from one military authority to another.

Postwar Japan

The terms of armistice took all territory outside the four main islands away from Japan and imposed complete demilitarization on the Japanese. Key wartime military leaders were placed on trial, and General Tojo, along with six colleagues, was executed. Other militarist governmental and business leaders were blocked from postwar activities. For a while, industries were dismantled for reparations, but this practice was soon stopped.

In return, the allies gave aid to rebuild the shattered economy, while insisting on democratic institutions in the government and society. The new education system was based on the American pattern of decentralized public schools, with textbooks rewritten to delete militant nationalism. A land reform policy intended to reduce

Frantz Fanon, The Wretched of the Earth

Frantz Fanon noted the growing inequality between northern and southern parts of the globe—the industrialized and the nonindustrialized worlds.

The colonial world is a world cut in two. The dividing line, the frontiers are shown by barracks and police stations. In the colonies it is the policeman and the soldier who are the official, instituted go-betweens, the spokesmen of the settler and his rule of oppression. . . .

It is obvious here that the agents of government speak the language of pure force. The intermediary does not lighten the oppression, nor seek to hide the domination; he shows them up and puts them into practice with the clear conscience of an upholder of the peace; yet he is the bringer of violence into the home and into the mind of the native. . . .

The settlers' town is a strongly-built town, all made of stone and steel. It is a brightly-lit town; the streets are covered with asphalt, and the garbage-cans swallow all the leavings, unseen, unknown and hardly thought about. The settler's feet are never visible, except perhaps in the sea; but there you're never close enough to see them. His feet are protected by strong shoes although the streets of his town are clean and even, with no holes or stones. The settler's town is a well-fed town, an easy-going town; its belly is always full of good things. The settler's town is a town of white people, of foreigners.

The town belonging to the colonised people, or at least the native town, the negro village, the medina, the reservation, is a place of ill fame, peopled by men of evil repute. They are born there, it matters little where or how; they die there, it matters not where, nor how. It is a world without spaciousness; men live there on top of each other, and their huts are built one on top of the other. The native town is a hungry town, starved of bread, of meat, of shoes, of coal, of light. The native town is a crouching village, a town on its knees, a town wallowing in the mire. It is a town of niggers and dirty arabs. The look that the native turns on the settler's town is a look of lust, a look of envy; it expresses his dreams of possession—all manner of possession: to sit at the settler's table, to sleep in the settler's bed, with his wife if possible. The colonised man is an envious man. And this the settler knows very well; when their glances meet he ascertains bitterly, always on the defensive "They want to take our place." It is true, for there is no native who does not dream at least once a day of setting himself up in the settler's place.

This world divided into compartments, this world cut in two is inhabited by two different species. The originality of the colonial context is that economic reality, inequality and the immense difference of ways of life never come to mask the human realities. When you examine at close quarters the colonial context, it is evident that what parcels out the world is to begin with the fact of belonging to or not belonging to a given race, a given species. . . .

It is not enough for the settler to delimit physically, that is to say with the help of the army and the police force, the place of the native. As if to show the totalitarian character of colonial exploitation the settler paints the native as a sort of quintessence of evil. Native society is not simply described as a society lacking in values. It is not enough for the colonist to affirm that those values have disappeared from, or still better never existed in, the colonial world. The native is declared insensible to ethics; he represents not only the absence of values, but also the negation of values. . . .

The Church in the colonies is the white people's Church, the foreigner's Church. She does not call the native to God's ways but to the ways of the white man, of the master, of the oppressor. And as we know, in this matter many are called but few chosen.

From Frantz Fanon, *The Wretched of the Earth*, trans. by Constance Farrington. Copyright © 1963 by Presence Africaine. Used by permission of Grove Weidenfeld.

tenancy and absentee landlordism was introduced. Unions gained the right of collective bargaining, and their membership grew rapidly. American authorities tried with limited success to reduce the great concentration of wealth in the hands of monopolistic industries, the *zaibatsu.*

A new constitution, drafted in consultation with the occupation government, came into effect in May 1947. It set up a democratic, two-house parliamentary-cabinet system in which the majority party selected the prime minister. Sovereignty rested in the people; the emperor, forced to renounce his divinity, was referred to as "the symbol of state." No limitations were placed on voting because of income or sex. War was renounced as a sovereign right and "land, sea, and air forces, as well as other war potential will never be maintained."

As a result of the Cold War in Europe and the communist invasion of South Korea in 1950–1957, Japan became the United States' principal ally in the Pacific. Despite Soviet opposition and without the participation of the USSR, a peace treaty was signed in 1951 and went into effect the next year, giving Japan full sovereignty. A security pact between Japan and the United States allowed Americans to station troops in Japan.

Political and Social Change

Since 1945 conservatives have consistently, with the exception of two brief periods, controlled the Japanese government. In 1955 two conservative parties merged to form the Liberal Democratic party, which was friendly to the west, favored modest rearmament, and backed the alliance with the United States. Based on professional civil servants and business interests, it was sufficiently strong to endure periodic charges of corruption. The Socialist party, the major opposition, demanded nationalization of industry, opposed the 1947 security pact, and favored neutrality in foreign affairs. The small Communist party was vocal but weak.

The new system was flexible enough to absorb the radical transformation Japan has experienced in the past half century. Rapid urbanization posed the greatest challenges. Rural areas lost population while city populations—and consequent environmental problems—skyrocketed. With more than 11 million people, Tokyo became the largest urban area in the world. Three great concentrations of industry and population clustered around Tokyo, Osaka, and Nagoya occupy only 1 percent of the country's land area but contain over one-fourth of the country's population.

Two reflections of modern Japan. The influence of both the West and the media is reflected in the large group of Japanese teens dressed as Elvis impersonators. The presence of women at the welcoming ceremony for new railway employees reflects a 1985 equal opportunity law.

In the cities traditional values and attitudes have changed. Parental authority and family ties weakened as young married couples, forsaking the traditional three-generation household, set up their own homes. The stresses and strains of urbanization were reflected in student riots and in the appearance, for the first time in Japanese history, of juvenile delinquency. Western influence—seen in fashions, television, sports, and beauty contests and heard in rock music— clashed with the traditional culture.

Perhaps the greatest changes are those affecting women. Before World War II there was little opportunity for Japanese women outside the family. After 1945 they gained the right to own property, sue for divorce, and pursue educational opportunities. By the end of the 1980s, women constituted nearly 50 percent of the nation's work force, and more than 30 percent of women high school graduates attended post-secondary institutions.

Economic Dominance

Japan faced serious obstacles in its path to economic development. It had to import much of the food for its growing population (123 million by 1990) and most of the raw materials for its industries. The Korean war gave Japan an initial boost, as the American troops made large purchases. In 1950 the gross national product (GNP) was $10 billion; by 1973, it had risen to $300 billion. The 1973 oil embargo and subsequent price increases of more than 400 percent by all of the OPEC (Organization of Petroleum Exporting Countries) producers severely affected Japan. Inflation skyrocketed, economic growth plunged, and for a while the balance of trade was negative.

Japan's business managers made the necessary adjustments for recovery. By the end of the 1970s the Japanese built half the world's tonnage in shipping and had become the world's biggest producer of motorcycles, bicycles, transistor radios, and sewing machines. The Japanese soon outpaced the United States in automobile production and drove the American domestic television industry virtually out of business. By the 1990s, the Japanese boasted one of the world's strongest economies. Japan's per capita GNP was nearly $22,000—compared to the U.S. per capita

GNP of $19,800. After the October 1987 stock market slide, Tokyo became the world financial center, dominating banking.

In the late 1980s the Japanese began to watch uneasily as South Korea, Taiwan, Hong Kong, and Singapore using the Japanese formula of a strong and disciplined work force and efficient use of new technology, became effective competitors in the world market. South Korea especially launched a direct challenge to Japan in high-technology and automotive markets.

Chinese Revolutions

Between 1927 and 1937 Chiang Kai-shek's Nationalist Chinese (Kuomintang) government initiated useful reforms in the cities which, had it not been for Japanese aggression in China, might have expanded to include the rest of the country. Unfortunately for Chiang, the Nationalists after 1937 lost many of their strongest supporters and most of their prosperous area to Japanese control. By the end of World War II, after eight years of combat, the Chinese Nationalist government of Chiang Kai-shek was a defeated and worn-out regime. In contrast, the communists came out of the war with great popularity, control of an area with 90 million people, and a disciplined and loyal army of 500,000.

Civil War in China

Following the victory over Japan, U.S. troops, cooperating with Chinese Nationalist forces, recaptured land taken by the Japanese. The Americans helped move Chinese troops to strategic areas such as Manchuria. At the same time, the Soviet Union reclaimed areas formerly controlled by the tsars. During this time Chiang tried unsuccessfully to negotiate a settlement with Mao Zedong (Mao Tse-tung). In October 1945 heavy fighting broke out between the Chinese Nationalist and Communist forces.

For the next three years the United States tried to end the conflict. In December 1945 President Truman defined American policy toward China: The United States regarded the Nationalist regime as the legal government of China, but since it was a one-party system, it was necessary that full opportunity be given to other groups to participate in a representative government. To that end, Truman urged an end to the fighting.

General George C. Marshall, U.S. army chief of staff, went to China to implement Truman's policy and to act as friendly mediator. Marshall, newly appointed as American secretary of state, returned home in January 1947, his mission a failure. In his final report, he blasted extremists on both sides for failing to make peace.

The Communist Victory

Chiang's army—poorly equipped, miserably paid, and suffering low morale—began to disintegrate. The communists captured city after city, frequently facing only token resistance. Economic problems added to Chiang's military dilemma. The Nationalists had been unable to rebuild the economy after 1945, and inflation soared: the U.S. dollar came to be worth 93,000 Chinese dollars on the black market. Serious riots broke out, and thousands of workers went on strike in Shanghai.

By the end of 1947 the Nationalist forces went into retreat. In 1948 the Nationalist presence in

Celebrating the first anniversary of Mao's government in 1950, Chinese workers, carrying giant placards of their leader, march through the streets of Peking.

Manchuria collapsed. The complete defeat of Chiang's armies occurred in 1949 when the "People's Liberation Army" captured the major cities in China. Mao proclaimed the establishment of his government on October 1, 1949, and by the middle of 1950 Mao ruled all of mainland China. Chiang's Nationalists sought refuge on Formosa (see map at right).

Mao and his forces imposed a tightly centralized administration extending to Manchuria, Inner Mongolia, and Chinese Turkestan. In 1950 his armies moved into Tibet. The Peking government continued to seek to regain the traditional holdings of the "Central Kingdom," especially those lands gained by Russia during the nineteenth century. Such a policy caused serious problems not only for the Soviet Union but also for Vietnam, Burma, and India.

Mao's policy attracted a large following, calling as it did for a mild program of reform, including the confiscation of large farms, state control of large businesses, protection of small private concerns, rapid industrialization under state control, and increased benefits to labor such as social insurance. The government that eventually appeared, however, was far more fierce and totalitarian.

Right-wing Americans, influenced by the demagoguery of Senator Joseph McCarthy, charged that liberals and "fellow travelers" (those who espoused social aims similar to the communists') lost China.[1] U.S. American military aid to China during World War II totaled $845 million; from 1945 to 1949 it came to slightly more than $2 billion. It is extremely doubtful whether additional American military aid poured into China would have changed the final outcome of the civil war. The bulk of the Nationalist forces had lost the will to fight. Large quantities of American arms sent to Chiang's army were turned over to the communists by apathetic Nationalist leaders.

Mao's Government

After 1949, Mao used his version of Marxism to change the whole order of society from its traditional patterns. Tolerating no opposition, he concentrated all power in the communist party, which was led by the People's Central Committee. This group held all major civil and military

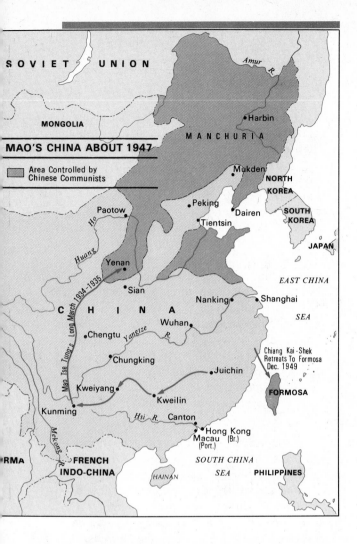

SOVIET UNION

MONGOLIA

MANCHURIA

MAO'S CHINA ABOUT 1947

Area Controlled by
Chinese Communists

Amur R.

Harbin

Mukden

NORTH
KOREA

Peking

Dairen

SOUTH
KOREA

Paotow

Tientsin

JAPAN

Yenan

Huang Ho

EAST CHINA

Sian

Nanking

Shanghai

CHINA

SEA

Wuhan

Yangtze R.

Chengtu

Long March 1934-1935

Chungking

Juichin

Chiang Kai-Shek
Retreats To Formosa
Dec. 1949

Mao Tse Tung's

Kweiyang

FORMOSA

Kweilin

Kunming

Hsi R.

Canton

Mekong

Hong Kong (Br.)
Macau
(Port.)

RMA

FRENCH
INDO-CHINA

HAINAN

SOUTH CHINA
SEA

PHILIPPINES

in theory, all labor, farm equipment, and land were pooled.

In 1953 a Soviet-style Five-Year Plan for economic development in industry was begun. The Chinese made impressive advances in heavy industry, and the success of the first plan led to the second Five-Year Plan, the so-called Great Leap Forward. The Chinese built on their own experience, rejecting parts of the Soviet model. They launched the Great Leap Forward with a huge propaganda campaign and galvanized millions of urban and rural workers into a frezied effort to increase tremendously the production of steel, electricity, and coal. Thousands of small, backyard furnaces sprang up to produce steel. The Chinese boldly predicted that they would surpass British industrial capacity in fifteen years.

In the countryside Mao installed the People's Communes. The state created some 26,000 of these units, each averaging 5000 households, or about 25,000 people. The heads of the communes collected taxes and ran schools, child-care centers, dormitories, communal kitchens, and even cemeteries in this massive attempt at social experimentation. Mao tried to convert peasants into a rural proletariat paid in wages. All land, dwellings, and livestock reverted to the effective ownership of the communes until the late 1970s. During the two decades in which the People's Communes functioned, they helped produce improvements in medical care and literacy.

The Great Leap Forward ultimately proved to be disastrous for China. Central planners erred in allocating resources and capital, and farm production fell. The steel and iron produced in the backyard furnaces turned out to be unusable. At the same time the Great Leap was failing, the Soviet Union withdrew its technological and financial support. From 1959 to 1961 Chinese industry lacked essential raw materials and millions of people went without adequate food. Between 1960 and 1962 the combination of bad weather and chaos bequeathed by the failure of the Great Leap Forward resulted in malnutrition and the premature death of between 16 and 30 million people.

Faced with this crisis, the government radically changed its economic policy. In the communes social experimentation and centralized control were relaxed. Working conditions were

positions. The day-to-day work of the central committee fell to a smaller politburo, headed by Mao, the chairman of the republic.

The new government brought both inflation and corruption under control, and then began to apply the Soviet model of the 1930s to China. As more than 70 percent of farmland was owned by 10 percent of the rich landlords, the government proceeded to confiscate large holdings and redistribute them, temporarily, to landless peasants. Late in 1953 the party stripped the large landowners and even prosperous peasants of their holdings, executing an estimated 2 to 4 percent (from 2 to 5 million) of them in the process. The party then established huge farm collectives. Within three years, nearly all peasants had become members of rural collectives in which, although individual land ownership was retained

Mao Tse-tung on Communism in China

Mao Tse-tung adapted Marxism to China. After paying tribute to the Soviet Union in 1949, he stated his goals for the future.

Communists the world over are wiser than the bourgeoisie, they understand the laws governing the existence and development of things, they understand dialectics and they can see farther. The bourgeoisie does not welcome this truth because it does not want to be overthrown.

As everyone knows, our Party passed through these twenty-eight years not in peace but amid hardships, for we had to fight enemies, both foreign and domestic, both inside and outside the Party. We thank Marx, Engels, Lenin and Stalin for giving us a weapon. This weapon is not a machine-gun, but Marxism-Leninism. . . .

The Russians made the October Revolution and created the world's first socialist state. Under the leadership of Lenin and Stalin, the revolutionary energy of the great proletariat and labouring people of Russia, hitherto latent and unseen by foreigners, suddenly erupted like a volcano, and the Chinese and all mankind began to see the Russians in a new light. Then, and only then, did the Chinese enter an entirely new era in their thinking and their life. They found Marxism-Leninism, the universally applicable truth, and the face of China began to change. . . .

There are bourgeois republics in foreign lands, but China cannot have a bourgeois republic because she is a country suffering under imperialist oppression. The only way is through a people's republic led by the working class. . . .

Twenty-four years have passed since Sun Yat-sen's death, and the Chinese revolution, led by the Communist Party of China, has made tremendous advances both in theory and practice and has radically changed the face of China. Up to now the principal and fundamental experience the Chinese people have gained is twofold:

1. Internally, arouse the masses of the people. That is, unite the working class, the peasantry, the urban petty bourgeoisie and the national bourgeoisie, form a domestic united front under the leadership of the working class, and advance from this to the establishment of a state which is a people's democratic dictatorship under the leadership of the working class and based on the alliance of workers and peasants.
2. Externally, unite in a common struggle with those nations of the world which treat us as equals and unite with the peoples of all countries. That is, ally ourselves with the Soviet Union, with the People's Democracies and with the proletariat and the broad masses of the people in all other countries, and form an international united front.

To sum up our experience and concentrate it into one point, it is: the people's democratic dictatorship under the leadership of the working class (through the Communist Party) and based upon the alliance of workers and peasants. This dictatorship must unite as one with the international revolutionary forces. This is our formula, our principal experience, our main programme. . . .

The Communist Party of the Soviet Union is our best teacher and we must learn from it. The situation both at home and abroad is in our favor, we can rely fully on the weapon of the people's democratic dictatorship, unite the people throughout the country, the reactionaries excepted, and advance steadily to our goal.

From Mao Tse-tung, Speech "In Commemoration of the 28th Anniversary of the Communist Party of China, June 30, 1949," in *Selected Works*, vol. 5 (New York: International Publishers, n.d.), pp. 411–423.

improved and private plots in which peasants were allowed to keep or sell the crops and animals they raised were used as incentives to increase agricultural production. Between 1961 and 1964 industry also recovered, and the discovery of petroleum provided new energy sources. China made advances in light industry, especially in consumer goods and cotton production. Signs of technological progress included the detonation of a nuclear device in 1964 and a hydrogen bomb in 1967.

The Cultural Revolution and After

By the early 1960s an ideological schism widened between Mao and some of his longtime comrades. The moderates advocated gradual social change and economic development; the radicals sought to carry on immediately with the drastic restructuring of Chinese society. Mao believed, or so it seemed, that many in the party had lost their revolutionary zeal. He advocated a continuous revolution in which the masses should be kept in motion lest the revolution die.

In this photograph from the Cultural Revolution, members of the Red Guard display for public shame several Chinese students, wearing dunce caps, and denounce them as leaders of "antirevolutionary" groups.

In the mid-1960s Mao mobilized the Red Guards, a radical student militia. They attacked the moderates and forced Maoist orthodoxy on party members and populace alike. In all areas, from surgery to nuclear physics and beyond, Mao's words were law. Application of the wisdom of Chairman Mao, as contained in the little red book, *The Thoughts of Chairman Mao*, was to lead to miraculous achievements. Placing political purity above economic growth, the Red Guards hampered production and research. Their rallies and demonstrations disrupted the entire educational system.

The effects of this "Cultural Revolution" were dire. By 1967 industrial production had plummeted and basic education and research had ceased; some areas of the country were approaching anarchy. Into this void stepped the People's Liberation Army (PLA), which was the most important element in Chinese politics until 1985. The PLA brought the Red Guards under control, restored order, and put an end to the excesses of the Cultural Revolution.

Mao's long-time associate, Premier Chou Enlai (1898–1976) restored the country's industrial productivity. The return to political stability was more difficult, but Chou managed to hold the country together while rival factions intrigued for power. Chou removed China from the diplomatic isolation in which it had resided since 1958. He responded to a diplomatic initiative made by the Nixon administration in 1971 and moved closer to the United States, motivated perhaps by the armed border clashes with the USSR that occurred along the Amur River. In addition, China sought to develop its industrial capacity through the use of foreign technology and to bring in foreign currency through an expanded banking system based in the British crown colony of Hong Kong and the development of a tourist industry.

China Since 1976

After Chou's—and Mao's—death in 1976, the jockeying for control continued with varying intensity. Leading the more militant faction, the so-called Gang of Four, was Mao's widow, Jiang Xing (Chiang Ching), who was overthrown, disgraced, and brought to a televised show trial in

1980. Her demise paved the way for the advent of a more moderate, pragmatic group of officials led by Deng Xiaoping (Teng Hsiao-Ping).

Deng was a political survivor, whose roots in the party went back to the 1920s. He survived political exile and the cultural revolution to introduce his variant of reform Marxism in which the party kept control of the "commanding heights" of the economy. Aided by his liberal chief lieutenants, Hu Yaobang and Zhao Ziyang, Deng introduced a pragmatic series of economic reforms.

The first major move to introduce a more market-oriented economy came in the countryside in 1978. The party allowed greater personal profit for the peasants, and this resulted in a vast increase in productivity. China had a grain surplus in six of the next seven years. With more food in the cities, and a contented peasantry, Deng in 1985 encouraged the introduction of the free market economy in the cities, with the goal of gaining similar economic gains there. To foster the rapid transformation of the underdeveloped country, Deng permitted the entry of Western experts and technology. Western, especially American, influence grew in the cities in China during the 1980s, along with foreign trade and the influx of foreigners.

The government continued to keep the cost of medicine low and supplemented wages with accident insurance, medical coverge, day-care centers, and maternity benefits. The standard of living in China improved, but the removal of price controls on food and other staple items led to inflation. Even with economic progress, the standard of living in China remained far below the standards in industrialized countries.

The educational system changed drastically under the communists. In the 1930s only 20 percent of the people had been literate. By the end of the 1980s, the figure had risen to 75 percent. Across China, a crash program of schooling was initiated, and "spare-time" schools with work/study programs for those unable to attend school full-time were established. Thousands of Chinese students emigrated abroad to study, including some 40,000 who went to the United States.

Deng Xiaoping had worked for the economic liberalization of his country but had not sponsored similar reform on the political front. The students in 1987 were the first to express

In May 1989, Chinese students in Peking's Tiananmen Square rally around the 33-foot replica of the Statue of Liberty, which they had dubbed "The Goddess of Democracy."

discontent with inflation and corruption in China. In the spring of 1989, students across China demonstrated in honor of the liberal politician Hu Yaobang, who had died in March. The demonstrators went on to criticize the government of Deng Xiaopeng. The protest reached a climax in May and June when thousands of demonstrators calling for democracy occupied the ceremonial center of modern China, Tiananmen Square in Peking.

The party split over how to deal with the protestors and their supporters, sometimes numbering a million strong. Zhao advocated accommodation but Li Peng called for a crackdown. While the debate went on within the party, the students erected a tall replica of the Statue of Liberty to symbolize their demands for democracy and an end to corruption. By the end of May the students had won the enthusiastic support of the workers and citizens of Peking, Shanghai, and Chengdu. Finally, in June the party had decided what to do about the protestors. The People's Liberation Army, using tanks and machine guns, cleared the Square and the surrounding area of the student demonstrators. Over 3000 people were killed in the massacre.

By 1990, it was apparent that China would not retreat into another period of diplomatic isolation. Deng Xiaoping had integrated his country too firmly into the world economy for that. Chinese leaders worked skillfully to maintain their commercial relations and to regain two traditionally Chinese areas to help their struggling economy.

The leaders in Peking had already worked out an agreement with the British in which the rich crown colony of Hong Kong would come under Chinese authority in 1997. Peking saw a major potential source of economic strength across the Straits of Formosa in Taiwan, where Chiang and the remnant of his forces had fled in 1949. For the next quarter century, the United States recognized the Taipei government as the legitimate government of China. By 1989 Taiwan's GNP had reached $100 billion, and its 23 million people had an average annual per capita income of close

to $5000. Mainland China, in contrast, had a GNP of $440 billion, and a per capita income of $360 for its 1.15 billion people.

Southeast Asia

One of the first indications that the whole structure of imperialism would quickly collapse came in the late 1940s when Indonesian nationalists demanded a complete break with the Netherlands. An ugly war ensued, and finally in 1948, through UN mediation, the Dutch East Indies became the nation of Indonesia. The biggest and potentially richest nation in Southeast Asia (see map below), Indonesia has enjoyed little tranquillity since it gained independence. The state is 88 percent Muslim but encompasses a mixture of many cultures in its 3000 islands, ranging from Stone Age people to urban professionals and intellectuals. Complicating the situation is

Indonesian students demonstrate in front of the parliament building in Djakarta to protest parliament's violations of the constitution and agitate for President Sukarno's expulsion.

the prominence of the Chinese minority, which dominates. There have been anti-Chinese riots and plots in various islands against the central government in Java.

For the first fifteen years after independence, Indonesia experienced declining exports, inflation, and food shortages. Its population increased while its economy declined. The main responsibility for this situation belonged to Indonesia's flamboyant president Achmed Sukarno (1901–1970). He contracted huge Russian loans for arms, fought a costly guerrilla campaign against Malaysia, confiscated foreign businesses, and wasted money on expensive, flashy enterprises.

Muslim students in Indonesia triggered the events that led to Sukarno's downfall. At the beginning of 1966 they launched attacks on Indonesians they believed to have communist connections. An estimated 300,000 to 500,000 were killed. The army's chief of staff, General T. N. J. Suharto became effective head of state, and in March 1967 became president officially.

Suharto brought stability to the country and initially installed a more west-leaning government. In return he got substantial American aid. In the next twenty-five years Suharto's essentially military regime faced serious problems. In 1971 and again in 1974 there were serious racial outbursts during which thousands of students went on rampages, looting and damaging Chinese shops and homes. During the 1970s some

30,000 political dissidents were imprisoned, while rampant corruption dominated government, the civil service, and business. Enormous wealth remained concentrated in the hands of a very few individuals.

Created out of former British holdings, the Federation of Malaysia was admitted into the British Commonwealth in 1957. In 1963 it became independent and immediately faced Sukarno-sponsored guerrilla attacks. As in Indonesia, a major problem in Malaysia is the country's racial mix and the resulting hostilities. The majority of the population is Malay, but the Chinese hold the majority of the wealth, and what they do not control is largely owned by the small Indian minority. In the late 1960s and early 1970s Malays attacked the other two groups.

One of the richest areas in Southeast Asia after the war was Singapore, a city-state roughly three times the size of Washington, DC. Singapore withdrew from the Federation of Malaysia in August 1965 and after that was dominated by the People's Action Party, run by Lee Kuan Yew. Taking advantage of its superb location at the Straits of Malacca, Singapore became one of the richest places in the world. At the end of the 1980s its 2.5 million people generated a GNP of more than $29 billion. What Lee Kuan Yew did not provide in terms of unfettered civil rights, he more than made up for in the efficiency and stability of his rule.

Vietnam: The Postwar French Phase

After World War II France was forced to grant a measure of autonomy to Cambodia and Laos, its former colonial possessions in Southeast Asia. The status of Vietnam posed a greater problem. In 1945 a nationalist and pro-communist movement led by Ho Chi Minh had established the independent Republic of Vietnam, usually referred to as the Vietminh regime.

Negotiations between the Vietminh and the French led nowhere, and war broke out in December 1946. The cruel and violent struggle, anti-colonial as well as ideological, lasted for nearly eight years. In May 1950 the United States began sending substantial financial and military support to the French. The end came dramatically in 1954 when the French, despite U.S. assistance, surrendered their isolated outpost at Dien Bien Phu, along with 10,000 troops.

In a conference at Geneva later that year a truce line was established at the 17th parallel, to be regarded as a temporary boundary pending nationwide elections (see map below). These elections were never held, and instead a new group proclaimed the Republic of South Vietnam, based in Saigon, south of the truce line. Meanwhile, the division between the Vietminh regime in Hanoi and the Saigon government increased. Along with the movement of hundreds of thousands of Roman Catholic Vietnamese refugees from the north came a powerful infiltration of communist military personnel and materiel from Hanoi.

The United States shipped large numbers of men and weapons to Saigon in an attempt to create a South Vietnamese state capable of holding its own against the Vietminh and their allies in South Vietnam. The military activity on both sides violated the Geneva agreements, but it could be argued that since none of the governments had signed them, they simply were not binding. Washington sponsored the establishment of the Southeast Asia Treaty Organization (SEATO) to stop the spread of communism into Cambodia, Laos, and South Vietnam.

Increasing American Involvement

At first the Americans gave full support to Ngo Dinh Diem, the leading figure of the non-communist south. He rejected Ho Chi Minh's requests to hold elections throughout all Vietnam under the Geneva agreements because he feared that his government would lose. He also refused to carry out comprehensive land reforms desired by Washington, choosing instead to rely for support on the landlord and the urban middle classes.

At the same time, the communists, thwarted in their aim to unite north and south by an election, began guerrilla operations against Diem's government. This so-called Second Vietnamese War began in 1957. Many peasants, disillusioned by Diem's failure to carry out land reform, tacitly or actively supported the communist guerrilla effort. In December, the National Liberation Front (NLF)—popularly known as the Viet Cong—was established in the south and gained full support from Hanoi.

Diem, in the face of a rising crisis, became even more autocratic and less inclined to make reforms, perhaps reflecting Washington's shift in policy from Eisenhower emphasis on "nation-building" to the Kennedy strategy of "counter-insurgency." The NLF threatened to take over the

THE VIETNAM WAR

| x | Major battles |
| ▲ | Major U.S. air bases |

0 — 100 — 200
MILES

Map labels:
Railroads to China bombed 1972
U.S. air raids 1966–1968, 1972
Dien Bien Phu 1954
Hanoi
Haiphong
CHINA
Gulf of Tonkin
x Gulf of Tonkin incident 1964
LAOS
Vientiane
Mekong R.
NORTH VIETNAM
DEMILITARIZED ZONE (DMZ)
17th Parallel
Hue
x Tet offensive 1968
Invasion of Laos 1971
My Lai massacre 1968
THAILAND
Ho Chi Minh Trail
SOUTH VIETNAM
CAMBODIA
Invasion of Cambodia 1970
Phnom Penh
Cam Ranh Bay
Gulf of Thailand
▲x Saigon
Tet offensive 1968
Fall of Saigon 1975
Mekong Delta
SOUTH CHINA SEA

A marine helicopter drops off U.S. troops in Vietnam in 1965. In 1963, there were 16,000 U.S. combat forces in Vietnam; five years later, the number had increased to 500,000. More than 57,000 Americans were killed in action in Vietnam, making the Vietnam conflict the United States' fourth deadliest war—after the Civil War and World Wars I and II.

entire government by force, and a coup and Diem's assassination did little to improve the situation. Following a series of short-lived, essentially military governments, Nguyen van Thieu became president of South Vietnam in 1967.

In 1960 there were only 800 U.S. military advisers in the country. Four years later, this figure had risen to 23,000. In August 1964 Washington accused North Vietnam of attacking United States destroyers in the Gulf of Tonkin. Following President Johnson's request, Congress adopted—by a Senate vote of 88–2 and a House vote of 416–0—a joint resolution approving "all necessary measures . . . to prevent further aggression" and authorized the president to assist South Vietnam in its defense, using military force if required.

Thereafter, the war in all of its aspects became increasingly Americanized, and by 1968 there were more than 500,000 U.S. troops in the country. In 1965 the United States started an intensive air campaign against North Vietnam. The aerial campaign failed to intimidate the North Vietnamese and became a subject of bitter controversy in the United States.

Pulling Out

By 1968 many Americans had begun to question the U.S. role in Vietnam. Their doubts were sharpened in the early spring of 1968 when the Viet Cong launched the Tet offensive against the Saigon forces and the Americans. Widely covered by television and print journalists, the offensive turned into a military disaster for the NLF and Hanoi, but the images of death and destruction communicated a notion of helplessness to the American people. The U.S. military victory became a political defeat for President Johnson.

As the number of Americans killed in Vietnam grew, the antiwar movement spread from a few score campus radicals to include moderate politicians, suburbanites, and mainstream clergy. The financial costs of the war were enormous, helping fuel an inflation that continued through the 1970s. The political cost for Lyndon Johnson was equally high, forcing him to step down after one term.

During the final months of Johnson's administration peace talks began in Paris with all interested parties represented. The Nixon administration continued the talks through three years of frustrating negotiations until, in January 1973, the Paris accord was signed. It provided for a cease-fire, the withdrawal of U.S. troops, and the release of all prisoners of war.

Pending elections to be arranged later, Nguyen van Thieu's South Vietnamese government was to remain in power. An international commission was to be established to investigate cease-fire violations. The Paris Accord contained no provision for the withdrawal of North

Vietnamese forces. Once the Americans withdrew, the North Vietnamese continued their advance, and the commission was predictably ineffectual. In early 1975, the Hanoi forces, soon to be the fifth strongest military in the world, began a massive offensive. Deprived of U.S. support, the southern forces fell apart once the northern frontiers were overrun. Saigon, now named Ho Chi Minh City, was captured in late April. Many South Vietnamese fled their homeland and some 140,000 gained sanctuary in the United States.

For the United States the legacy of the Vietnam conflict was 58,000 killed, a financial outlay of at least $146 billion, a society bitterly split, and a host of veterans who were rebuked or ignored. It took ten years for the United States to come to terms with the war. The legacy for Vietnam was a twenty-year delay in the Vietminh takeover and incalculable human and material losses. The country has barely begun to recover economically.

Indochina after 1975

The United States had expanded the fighting into neutral Cambodia in the spring of 1970, invading it with the goal of cutting North Vietnamese supply lines and driving the Hanoi army from its sanctuaries there. Following the North

After the United States withdrew its troops from Vietnam in 1973, many South Vietnamese fled the country. Above, thousands of refugees crowd the U.S. embassy in Saigon. Below left, a mother and her children struggle across a river to escape aerial bombardment of their village.

Vietnamese victory in 1975, communists took control of Cambodia and Laos. The ruthless and brutal Khmer Rouge regime created a reign of terror in Cambodia, which was renamed Kampuchea. In Phnom Penh, the capital, nearly all the inhabitants—more than 2 million people—were driven into the countryside, regardless of age or infirmity. People in other cities suffered the same fate; many died from sickness or starvation. A new social system of farm units with labor brigades and communal kitchens was set up. The slightest sign of disobedience resulted in death.

The leader of the Chinese-supported Khmer Rouge regime was Pol Pot. His followers murdered thousands of innocent peasants along with "anyone who had been associated with the cities, with foreigners, or with intellectual, business, or technical activities."[2] The regime's goal seems to have been a self-sufficient agricultural society in which most people would have food and shelter but no pay. It is estimated that between 1975 and 1980 between 2 and 3 million Cambodians have died, "shot, beaten to death, starved, brutalized. Few people in modern times have been subjugated to such barbarism."[3] The Pol Pot regime was overthrown when Vietnamese armies invaded the country. The Cambodians now suffered the ravages of war in addition to continued, indiscriminate killings and massacres.

While China supported Pol Pot, the Soviet Union supported the Vietnamese invaders and a Cambodian faction opposed to Pol Pot. Early in 1979 Chinese armies invaded Vietnam, destroying several of its northern towns, but failed to draw Vietnamese armies out of Cambodia. After this brief sortie, the Chinese forces withdrew, and the world gained an appreciation of the military strength of the Vietnamese regime.

Although the situation in Laos was not so chaotic, yet there also the Vietnamese regime imposed some regimentation and abuse of the Laotians, some of whom were sent to "reeducation camps." Many professional people fled the country, and soon the lack of food and deplorable health conditions made Laos' standard of living nearly the lowest in the world.

Since the 1980s, much of Indochina has been a confused mass of fleeing refugees. Unwilling to accept North Vietnamese rule, thousands took to the sea in rickety boats. Many Chinese living in Vietnam were mistreated by the new regime and retreated across the border to China. Great numbers of refugees fled from Laos and Cambodia to Thailand, Malaysia, Indonesia, and Hong Kong. In addition, thousands of "boat people" have drowned at sea in their leaky craft, been attacked by pirates in the South China Sea, or died of thirst and starvation when refused permission to land.

The Subcontinent of India

In the Indian subcontinent, the western thrust of the Japanese armies induced the British government to make substantial concessions to Indian Nationalists leaders. In 1942 Britain offered India independence within or without the British Commonwealth following the war. Tragically, during and immediately after the war, antagonism between the Muslim and Hindu populations in India became acute. Britain,

represented by Lord Mountbatten, eased tensions by persuading both groups that partition of the country was inevitable. Thus, with the coming of independence in 1947, the fragile economic and geographical unity of the subcontinent was shattered (see map below).

Pakistan was an artificial creation, separated by about 1000 miles of intervening Indian territory. India itself is not a single nation but consists of numerous racial, linguistic, and cultural groups. "Nowhere do so many linguistically differentiated peoples, all of them so self-aware, all numbered in millions and tens of millions, confront each other within a single national body politic."[4] Once the British left, there was no longer an external force to bind together the ancient and conflicting cultural and regional loyalties.

The immediate aftermath of the partition was a rash of bloody riots between Hindus and Muslims. One of the victims of this violence was

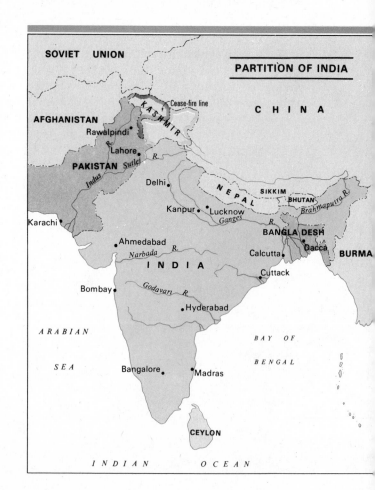

Mahatma Gandhi, who because of his tolerance toward Muslims, was assassinated by a Hindu.

India: The Largest Democracy

In the long list of newly independent states after 1945, few have retained genuine liberal regimes. Until 1975, the only outstanding example was India, the world's largest democratically governed state.

After independence, India's parliament functioned with little friction. This success was due to Jawaharlal Nehru (1889–1964), the country's first prime minister and an ardent devotee of democratic government. Nehru sought to maintain close relations with both the Soviet Union and China, often to the discomfort of the United States. However, a border conflict that led to major military action between India and China in the first part of the 1960s drained India's economic growth.

After Nehru's death his daughter, Indira Gandhi (1917–1984), was elected prime minister in 1966. Her popularity reached a peak with the defeat of Pakistan in the 1971 war that led to the creation of the country of Bangladesh. Within two years, however, India's mildly socialist economy was battered by serious crop failures, food riots, strikes, and student unrest. In June 1975 Gandhi announced a state of emergency and assumed dictatorial powers. She jailed 10,000 of her critics, imposed a rigid press censorship, and suspended fundamental civil rights.

With all opposition muzzled, the people were exhorted to "work more and talk less." After a year, the new order claimed numerous gains, advances in productivity, a drop in inflation, curbs in the black market, and stepped-up birth control measures to alleviate India's population pressures. Although Gandhi declared that her drastic measures were only temporary, some critics observed that she was trying to move "from dictatorship to dynasty." Early in 1977, there was some relaxation of authoritarianism.

In that same year, the government released many political prisoners and announced that national elections would be held. In the elections Gandhi lost her seat in parliament and resigned her post as prime minister. A new government, led by aged politicians, tried with little success to solve India's problems. Caste tensions were on

Indira Gandhi was elected prime minister of India in 1966 and served until 1977, when she was defeated and imprisoned briefly for abuses while in power. Reelected in 1980, she held office until she was assassinated in 1984.

the rise, there was widespread violence, strikes increased, and student demonstrations closed universities. In addition, all the old economic problems remained. More than half of the population was illiterate and lived below the poverty level.

Disenchanted with the incompetent rule of bickering politicians, the Indian voters brought Gandhi back to power in the 1980 elections. She promised the country strong leadership, but with no more "excesses." For the next four years she pursued a neutral course, reflecting the geopolitical position in which India found itself. India's alliance with Russia served as a defensive shield against both Pakistan and China. The Soviet invasion of Afghanistan raised some disturbing questions, but Gandhi refrained from criticizing the action.

In October 1984 Gandhi was assassinated by Sikh bodyguards who were connected to the Sikh separatist movement. She was succeeded by her son Rajiv Gandhi, a former pilot and political novice who soon showed a surprising degree of confidence and competence in governing the world's largest democracy, containing over 800 million citizens. Continuing his mother's basic policies, he consolidated his political position. Still, the country's widespread poverty and vast diversity—especially the continuing Sikh separatist movement and the longstanding Kashmir border dispute with Pakistan posed great challenges that Rajiv Gandhi could not overcome. He was defeated in elections at the end of 1989 and was replaced by V. P. Singh of the National Front party, who similarly could not find solutions to India's overwhelming problems. The world's largest democracy balanced tenuously between sectarian fragmentation and unity in the elections of 1991, when Rajiv Gandhi was assassinated in May.

Pakistan

After its creation in 1947, Pakistan was plagued by feuds between its eastern and western wings. Shortly after independence the prime minister was assassinated, a number of short-lived governments followed, accompanied by intermittent rioting and states of emergency.

In 1958 General Mohammad Ayub Khan (1907–1974) gained power. His regime gave Pakistan reasonable stability and some relief from corrupt politicians. Under his tutelage, the country made economic progress. Ten years later, however, pent-up dissatisfaction against corruption in the government led to a new military dictatorship under General Yahya Khan. In the interim, regionalism continued to be a major problem. While Pakistan's population was predominantly Muslim, its two main provinces differed widely in race, economic interest, and language—not to mention the geographical separation. East Pakistan complained continually of being exploited by more prosperous West Pakistan, and these complaints escalated into riots and threats of secession.

In 1971 the Pakistani government sent troops into the eastern region and began a reign of terror. The influx of refugees into India created an intolerable burden, and in December the Indian army invaded East Pakistan, defeating the central government's forces. India encouraged the region to break away, and in 1972 East Pakistan became the new state of Bangladesh. Bangladesh, covering an area not much larger than the state of Arkansas, was an instantaneous economic disaster with twice the population density of Japan and nothing approaching the Japanese economic productivity. The Bangladesh population in 1990 was 121 million, while the per capita GNP was a mere $155.

A civilian government was reestablished in Pakistan, led by Zulkifar Ali Bhutto (1928–1979), who governed under a democratic constitution. Throughout the decade, Pakistan's economic problems persisted, along with its domestic instability. Bhutto, overthrown in 1977 by General Mohammad Zia al Haq, was executed in 1979. The new military dictator, who faced widespread opposition, invoked martial law and postponed elections indefinitely. Like his predecessors, he had to contend with both Indian hostility and potential Soviet intervention. Pakistan retained

Bengali guerrilla soldiers at Dacca, the site where Pakistani forces surrendered to Indian and rebel troops in 1971.

its traditional alignment with China, while India kept close ties with Moscow.

In 1979, events in Iran and Afghanistan posed particular threats to Pakistan. Thirty-six Islamic foreign ministers meeting in Pakistan condemned the Soviet aggression against the Afghan people. In 1981, however, a substantial American aid agreement was negotiated, providing for $3.2 billion in arms over a period of six years. Pakistan, thereafter, served as the American support base for the Afghan resistance.

In 1988 Zia al Haq was assassinated and succeeded by Bhutto's daughter Benazir, the first woman elected to govern a Muslim nation. She lasted twenty months, until, under pressure from the army she was dismissed under accusations of incompetence and corruption.

The Middle East

Decolonization in the Middle East began with British recognition of the independence of Jordan in 1946 and the end of the British mandate in Palestine in 1948. In the meantime, the arrival of European Jews seeking refuge in the area after the war, Zionist terrorist activities, and great power political pressure led to the creation of the state of Israel in May 1948. This touched off a bitter conflict between the new state and the Arab world that was intensified by the perennial statelessness of the more than million Palestinian Arab refugees represented by the Palestine Liberation Organization. Complicating this volatile situation were the Islamic fundamentalist revival, Iraqi aggression, and the overall great power competition between the Soviet Union and the United States.

At the end of World War II, Arab leaders joined forces to form the Arab League. Set up to advance common Arab interests and, in part, to counter Israel, it was used to further the pan-Arab ambitions of Egypt, a republic since 1953. The dominant figure in the Arab world was Colonel Abdul Gamel Nasser (1918–1970), leader of the Egyptian military junta, which had overthrown King Farouk in 1952. From his base in Cairo Nasser offered guidance and assistance to liberation movements in Sudan, Tunisia, Morocco, and Algeria.

Prime Minister Benazir Bhutto of Pakistan, the first woman elected to govern a Muslim nation.

The Arab-Israeli Conflict

Conscious of their hostile surroundings, the Israelis took steps to become militarily, economically, and politically strong. The success of their efforts became quite evident in 1956 when, as allies of the British and French, they overwhelmed the Egyptians in a war for control of the Suez Canal. International pressure applied by the United States, the USSR, and the United Nations forced the Israelis to withdraw from their territorial gains.

The conclusion of this crisis brought only a temporary reprieve from hostilities. In the next decade the issues of oil, Palestinian rights, the existence of the state of Israel, and free access to the Suez Canal monopolized the attention of foreign offices within the region, as well as in Moscow and Washington. As it became apparent that there were no simple solutions to the Middle Eastern problems, the Arabs sought to solve them in 1967 by mobilizing their forces. They requested the withdrawal of the UN peacekeeping forces and blockaded the Gulf of Aqaba, Israel's access to the Red Sea. War broke out on June 5. Within seventy-two hours an Israeli blitzkrieg completely overwhelmed and humiliated the combined Arab forces. When a cease-fire was arranged five days later, Israel occupied the Sinai peninsula, including the east bank of the Suez Canal, old Jerusalem, and border areas inside Syria commanding tactically important heights. This was no lasting solution to the conflict, however, and in 1973 the threat of war reappeared.

As in 1967, the opening of this chapter of hostility was preceded by a period of rising tension, characterized by attacks by Arab guerrillas and regular army detachments into Lebanon. The Soviet Union was a major supplier of arms and technicians to the Arabs. The United States committed itself to the existence of Israel, investing billions of dollars a year in foreign aid in the 1980s. Realizing the danger of a Russo-American confrontation in the Middle East should a new round of war explode, Britain, France, the United States, and the USSR explored ways to bring the contending parties to agreement.

The issues discussed were to the possibility of some return of captured Arab territory, the internationalization of Jerusalem, and a solution to the refugee problem. The Israelis, however, insisted on the Arabs' unequivocal recognition of Israel as a sovereign state with the right to exist. Acceptance of a cease-fire in the summer of 1970 gave some hope for a settlement, but the situation deteriorated a few months later when Israel charged Egypt with cease-fire violations and Nasser suddenly died.

On October 6, 1973 war broke out again when the Egyptians and Syrians launched a coordinated attack on Israel. For the first few days the Arabs held the initiative, but Israeli forces counterattacked, crossing the Suez Canal into Egypt and driving to within twenty-five miles of Damascus, the capital of Syria. In some of the most concentrated armored combat since World War II 1800 tanks and 200 aircraft were destroyed.

During the fighting, the United States organized a large airlift of arms to Israel, and the Russians responded with troop movements. Soviet and American leaders averted a possible showdown through consultations, and the danger passed when the UN arranged a cease-fire. In January 1974 Egypt and Israel signed a final pact, providing for mutual troop withdrawals, the occupation of the east bank of the canal by Egypt, a UN buffer zone, and the return

of prisoners. Fighting continued between Israel and Syria in the strategic Golan Heights area. U.S. Secretary of State Henry Kissinger led the efforts for a cease-fire on that front in May 1974. This agreement provided for the return by Israel of some captured Syrian territory, a UN zone, and the return of prisoners.

The 1973 war and its spin-offs were costly for the world. Israel spent $5 billion and suffered 5000 casualties, plus an ever-increasing rate of inflation since that time generated by war expenses. Arab casualties were more than five times the Israeli losses. But where the Israelis came to a sober realization of their population and financial limitations, the Arabs came out of the second war with improved morale. After the 1967 war, Arab radicals, especially those in the Popular Front for the Liberation of Palestine, pushed the oil-producing countries to use the "oil weapon"—cutting or drastically reducing the export of petroleum—against Israel and its allies. Such a policy was following after the 1973 war, and this spread devastation throughout the economy of the industrial world.

Egyptian-Israeli Détente

In September 1975 Egypt and Israel reached a second pact in which additional territory in the Sinai peninsula was returned to Egypt and both sides agreed not to resort to force. The United States agreed to provide up to 200 civilian technicians to maintain a precautionary warning system between the two sides. Washington also committed additional arms and financial aid to Israel.

In late November 1977 President Anwar Sadat (1918–1981) initiated a dramatic shift in regional affairs when he flew to Jerusalem to conduct peace talks with Israeli leaders. He had already shown his ability to make controversial decisions in 1972 when he ordered the 18,000-member corps of Soviet military and technical advisers out of his country. Sadat faced serious problems at home brought on by a faltering economy and a rapidly increasing population. These problems had led to serious riots, sparked by runaway inflation. He understood his country's compelling need for peace and recovery.

Sadat, born of a peasant family, had excelled in school and entered the Royal Military

Academy. He had worked with other officers to rid Egypt of British domination and in the coup to expel King Farouk. He was a loyal follower of Abdul Nasser, and succeeded him as president in 1970. He showed his mettle in fighting off attempts Israel in 1973. Nothing he did was more courageous than making the trip to Jerusalem in 1977.

The United States strongly supported Sadat's venture and U.S. President Jimmy Carter invited Sadat to meet Israeli Prime Minister Menachem Begin, at Camp David in September 1978. After intense negotiations, the three leaders produced a framework for a permanent peace treaty. Israel agreed to return all the Sinai to Egypt, but no definite agreement was reached on the status of the west bank, where the one million displaced Palestinian Arabs lived. It was agreed, however, that negotiations should begin to set up an elected self-governing authority of Palestinians and also to end the Israeli military government. Following this step, there would be a transitional period of five years during which negotiations would take place on the final status of the west bank, an issue that remained in conflict at the end of the 1980s. Sadat and Begin received the Nobel Peace Prize in 1978.

The formal peace treaty signed in March 1979 ended the state of war between Egypt and Israel and began the process of returning all of the Sinai to Egypt. It also opened the Suez canal to Israeli ships. In 1980 the two nations opened their borders to each other, exchanged ambassadors, and began air service between the countries.

The Iranian Revolution

Iran, which had served as an area of competition between the British and the Russians since the nineteenth century, became a bone of contention between the United States and the Soviet Union after World War II. As a result of an agreement between the British and the Russians in 1941, Shah Mohammad Reza Pahlavi (1919–1980) gained the Iranian throne. After the war he asked foreign troops to withdraw from this country, but following the slow return of the Soviet army to its borders, aggressive activities of the Iranian communist party (Tudeh), and an assassination attempt on the Shah's life, Iran firmly tied itself to the west.

In 1953, Iranian premier Mohammad Mosaddeq advocated nationalization of Iran's oil fields and a comparatively radical tax program, and forced the Shah to flee the country. Mosaddeq was overthrown in 1954 in a CIA-supported military coup, and the Shah was restored to power. For the next twenty-five years, Iran rested firmly within the orbit of the United States, a valuable source of oil and an independent military force in a vitally strategic region.

Israeli Prime Minister Menachem Begin embraces U.S. president Jimmy Carter as Egyptian president Anwar Sadat looks on and applauds. Carter invited Begin and Sadat to a summit meeting at Camp David in September 1978 to work out a peace agreement between Israel and Egypt.

The Shah attempted a rapid modernization of his country, but the so-called White Revolution threatened the integrity of the Iranian cultural fabric. The presence of over 100,000 foreigners, including 47,000 Americans, alienated orthodox Muslim forces, who perceived the Shah as attacking the Muslim political and economic base. Opposition to the Shah's rule spread widely, from militant communists to Shi'ite clergy to discontented nationalities. In addition, inflation alienated some of the business classes and the laborers.

In the face of this growing opposition, the Shah began a reign of terror. After seven years, the storm broke in January 1978 when large numbers of students demonstrated against the absolute monarchy. Many were killed and wounded by the Shah's troops. Strikes and demonstrations paralyzed the country. The army and secret police proved helpless in the face of the national revolt. In January 1979 the Shah fled the country, seeking asylum first in the United States, then Panama, and finally in Egypt, where he died in 1980.

The diffuse and widespread revolution found its focus in the aged Ayatollah Ruhollah Khomeini, a Shi'ite holy man who had been in exile since 1963. From Iraq and then from Paris he had carried on an incessant propaganda effort against the "godless and materialistic" rule of the Shah. Khomeini was intensely opposed to western culture and once in power set to work to purge Iran of its "wickedness." Western music on radio and television was banned, as were "provocative" bathing suits, liquor, and a broad range of other items. The Ayatollah stamped out secular western political forms and instituted instead a theocratic state based on the Koran.

The Ayatollah viewed the United States as the "Great Satan" and encouraged Iranians to express anti-American sentiments. In November 1979 a mob of young Iranians stormed and seized the U.S. embassy and took fifty-three hostages, whom they held for over a year. Finally, the financial drain of the war with Iraq—begun when Iraqi leader Saddam Hussein attacked Iranian airfields and oil refineries in September 1980—forced the Iranians to release the hostages in return for the United States' release of Iranian assets frozen in response to the hostage taking.

The Iran-Iraq war lasted for the rest of the decade until an armistice—caused by exhaustion—in 1989. It had been a war of attrition in which both sides suffered enormous losses. The Iranians employed all of their resources including twelve- and thirteen-year-old children in human wave attacks against the well-ensconced but smaller Iraqi army. The Iraqis on their side violated the accepted rules of combat by using chemical weapons and poison gas.

The Soviet Invasion of Afghanistan

Armed coups and assassinations characterized the postwar political history of Afghanistan. Since 1945 the Soviet Union has extended its influence in the area, capping its overtures in 1978 with a "friendship treaty" between Kabul and Moscow. Postwar leaders have sought to introduce changes based either on Western or Marxist models such as nationalization and land redistribution, but they have encountered fierce

Iranian workers in Teheran, Iran, demonstrate their support for the Ayatollah Khomeini and for the Iranian students who seized and held hostage 53 Americans in the Ayatollah's name.

resistance. The strongly conservative Muslim tribes oppose modernization in almost any form, and civil war broke out in the late 1970s.

By 1979 it appeared that President Amin's government, which received support from the USSR, would be toppled by the rebellion. Earlier the Soviets had sent in 5000 military and civilian advisers to assist Amin and they could not now tolerate loss of their client state. In late December, thousands of Soviet troops crossed the border, captured the airport, and stormed the presidential palace in Kabul. They killed Amin and installed Babrak Karmal in his place. Karmal announced that Soviet troops had been invited in to save Afghanistan from imperialist plots fomented by the United States. Few nations accepted this fabrication. But, coming as it did during the U.S. dilemma with Iran, the invasion gave the USSR the opportunity to dominate this strategic region with little risk of armed opposition.

In the next year the USSR gained control of Afghan cities, while an assortment of tribal guerrilla forces roamed the countryside, but the Soviet advance sputtered during the 1980s. The Afghan resistance, supported by the United States, stalemated the Soviets and their puppets. The one advantage the USSR had in the battlefield, air power, was negated by the Afghans' use of U. S.-supplied Stinger anti-aircraft missile. As the decade wore on, Afghanistan became for the Soviet Union what Vietnam had been for the United States in the 1960s and 1970s—a costly, divisive conflict. The cost to the Afghan people was immense. Millions were uprooted, villages were destroyed, and many areas were littered with booby traps and mines. Finally, in the spring of 1989, the Soviet Union withdrew its forces from Afghanistan. The civil war continued, and to the surprise of many, the government did not collapse before a disjointed rebel offensive.

Toward a New Balance

Since the 1980s the four key elements in the Middle East have come to be Egypt, Israel, the United States, and Iraq. In 1990, an event occurred which cut across the traditional antipathies and its resolution gave a small opening for U.S. and Soviet diplomats to try to nudge the region onto a new path.

During the first part of the 1980s Egypt remained an outcast among Arab countries because of its détente with Israel. In October 1981, a small group of Islamic militants assassinated Sadat while he was reviewing a military parade. Shortly before his death, he had ordered a crackdown on the Muslim brotherhood, which opposed his reconciliation with Israel and Egypt's increasingly secular nature.

Sadat's successor, Hosni Mubarak, pledged continued support of Sadat's commitments and welcomed the support and friendship of the United States. During the 1980s Mubarak improved Egypt's relations with other moderate Arab states as he struggled with his country's overwhelming economic problems brought on by a mushrooming population along the Nile Valley and Delta. Mubarak solidified his position and maintained Sadat's foreign policies.

Huge outlays for defense drove Israel's inflation rate to average over 50 percent in the last part of the 1980s. The Israelis came to depend more and more on aid from the United States, whose annual announced subsidies exceeded $4 billion a year. Adding to Israel's concern was a shift in American public opinion as extreme Arab provocations in the Intifada—Palestinian active and passive resistance to Israeli policies—drew harsh Israeli police responses, which on American television almost uniformly cast them in a bad light.

While committed to Israel's security, the United States, especially in the administration of President George Bush, increased its interests in aiding friendly Arab states who opposed what they saw as Israeli aggression. This was particularly the case with Saudi Arabia, the main supplier of American oil imports. It was this concern that led the United States to sell the Saudis large quantities of sophisticated weapons and to send the U.S. Navy to keep the Persian Gulf oil shipment lanes open during the latter stages of the Iran-Iraq war.

Iraq, a country with immense oil and agricultural potential, had squandered much of its wealth on military strength. Under Saddam Hussein, the Iraqis had developed extensive capabilities in chemical and bacteriological warfare. Their nuclear facilities, destroyed by the Israelis in 1980, were rebuilt. Iraq had launched a war against Iranian airfields and oil refineries in

September 1980, and in the succeeding nine years, more than a million people died in fighting that saw the use of poison gas and chemical weapons. In August 1990, 100,000 Iraqi troops invaded and overran the oil-rich sheikdom of Kuwait in one day. This aggressive act, plus the implied threat to Saudi Arabia of Saddam Hussein's one million-man army produced an immediate response. The fear that Iraq, if it took the Saudi oil fields, would control one-third of the global oil reserves—moved the UN Security Council to impose a series of strict sanctions on Baghdad.

For the next six months the United Nations, led by a coalition assembled by U.S. President George Bush, increased the diplomatic pressure on Saddam Hussein by increasing sanctions and embargoes on his country. Hussein received the support of the Palestinians, and the young throughout much of the Arab world, and Jordan.

When sanctions and embargoes failed to move Iraq to withdraw from Kuwait, the American-led 26 nation coalition (including Egypt, Saudi Arabia, Syria, Turkey, France, Italy and United Kingdom) began heavy bombardment of Iraq beginning in January 1991. A month later, the allies launched a land offensive that in 100 hours evicted Iraq from Kuwait and left the coalition in possession of one-fifth of Iraq.

The successful smashing of Iraq's forces by the coalition opened the possibility that the Middle East might be able to break out of its entrenched and unchanging hostilities. Fervent diplomatic activity throughout the major capitals of the world prepared the way for conferences that could bring a lasting peace to the region.

A Tragic Stage

Few areas better illustrate the tragedy of the Middle East during the past half century than Beirut. Once the most beautiful and civilized city in the Middle East, a center for prosperity and a crossroads of cultures and religions, by 1991 Beirut had finally recovered from the tragic stage on which all of the competing factions of the Middle East waged virtually continuous warfare.

The problems were rooted in a number of causes. The Palestine Liberation Organization (PLO) led by Yasir Arafat from its headquarters in Lebanon stepped up demands for Israeli withdrawal from the west bank of the Jordan River and the Gaza Strip, both captured by Israel during the 1967 war. The PLO wanted an independent Palestinian state and in pursuit of that launched terrorist raids from its bases in southern Lebanon and encouraged riots to harass Israeli authorities. In response, beginning in 1978, Israel made repeated incursions during the next decade into Lebanese territory strike back at the PLO bases.

Civil war adds to Lebanon's dire situation. This small and racially mixed nation—its area is slightly less than that of Connecticut—is divided between Christian and Muslim factions. Before the influx of the Palestinians, the Christians held a slight majority, and the various factions maintained a delicately adjusted political balance. The influx of Palestinians in 1975 shattered that balance. The Christians—at first supported by the Syrians—and the Muslims with their Palestinian allies fought until the October 1976 cease-fire. The cost was 25,000 dead, thousands more wounded, and sections of the city gutted. The country's once flourishing economy was at a standstill.

A symbolic episode occurred in the summer of 1981 when PLO forces fired rockets into Israel, which responded with massive air attacks on Palestinian strongholds in Beirut. Hundreds of civilians were killed. In the summer of 1982 the

The allied coalition launched its war to drive Iraq out of Kuwait with a huge-scale air attack. Smoke pours out of the Defense Ministry in Baghdad, after its bombing by allied forces.

Israelis invaded Beirut, surrounding Muslim-held west Beirut. The PLO evacuated Beirut in September, under the direction of a French, Italian, and United States multinational contingent. After the multinational force departed, the newly elected president, the Phalange Christian Bashir Gemayel and 26 of his colleagues were killed by a bomb. In apparent response, Christian militiamen, allies of the Israelis, massacred hundreds of Palestinian men, women and children in two refugee camps.

In the succeeding decade the skeletal outlines of bombed buildings, shadowy videotapes of hostages, and pictures of young and old darting through streets to avoid gunfire have given the world an image of the total futility of violence. Beirut's tough citizens remained, hopeful that, perhaps finally, an equilibrium could once again be found in the Middle East.

Africa

In Africa, the European powers approached decolonization in a variety of ways. The British devised programs to provide financial and technical aid to prepare their colonies for independence within the Commonwealth. France also gave loans and grants, but the French wanted a political and economic structure dominated by Paris. Belgium showed no understanding of the need to prepare the Congo for the future and continued its paternalistic approach. Portugal had neither the resources nor the will to prepare its colonies for the future.

In the first decade after World War II, however, it was apparent that independence would come to Africa faster than anyone had anticipated. While on a visit to British Africa in 1960, Prime Minister Harold Macmillan declared:

The wind of change is blowing through this continent, and whether we like it or not, this growth of national consciousness is a political fact and our national policies must take account of it.[5]

Africans rightly think of 1960 as their year. Eighteen new nations emerged, the most important being Nigeria and the Congo.

The Challenges of State-Making

France had enacted various reforms to keep its African territories as autonomous republics within a French community. (Guinea, however, had elected to become completely independent in 1958.) This compromise did not satisfy African hopes. In 1960 all thirteen African republics within the French community proclaimed their independence. While the dream of a great French imperial structure had ended, France did retain a unique status in its former colonies. Its culture persisted in Africa, and France maintained its financial and technical dominance.

In 1945 there had been four independent African nations; by the end of the 1980s over fifty sovereign states could be identified. But independence did not bring a golden age. The optimism that accompanied the gaining of sovereign status did not last. State-building in the late twentieth century was a difficult process.

Each of the new states had to bear the heavy costs of creating a trained corps of bureaucrats, diplomats, and soldiers. All of the new states worked to build stable democratic governments led by just and strong executives. They wanted to work through responsible and freely elected legislatures and enjoy the benefits of incorruptible courts. But all of them, especially Kenya, which had emerged from revolutionary struggle, faced serious challenges.

The most pressing problem was how to build and maintain national unity among distinct and sometimes antagonistic religious, cultural, and ethnic groups. In most cases, the new African states were not the product of a long historical process such as took place in Europe where small feudal principalities were hammered into homogeneous nation-states. Most African boundaries were arbitrary creations of the imperialists and had little relationship to the people who lived there. Nigeria, for example, the result of British arms and the imagination of British geographers, encompassed many diverse and hostile ethnic and tribal segments. Throughout sub-Saharan Africa, tribal fragmentation worked against the development of nationalism.

These difficulties plus the economic problems—some produced by unwise investments in prestige-enhancing but economically wasteful enterprises—made the attainment of stable democratic governments difficult. Between 1960 and 1967 twenty-seven newly independent states experienced forceful takeovers. In four months in 1967 there were four military coups. In 1980 a dozen revolts took place, five of which successfully toppled the governments in power. Imitating some communist states, many of the leaders—including moderates such as Daniel Arap Moi of Kenya—discarded the two-party system in favor of a single party government, while insisting that their political systems were essentially democratic. In fact, in some countries, the one-party states did provide stability and progress. But this was not always the case; for example in Uganda under General Idi Amin from 1971 to 1979 thousands of people were killed and the country's economy went to ruin as the capricious and uneducated general pursued a quirky and unpredictable rule.

North Africa

France's two protectorates in North Africa, Tunisia and Morocco, gained independence in a relatively peaceful way in 1956. In sharp contrast stands the transfer of autonomy to Algeria. France had invested millions of dollars in the development of this territory, and by 1960 French immigrants constituted about one-tenth of the population. The French dominated Algeria's industry, agriculture, and government, while the Muslim majority remained hopelessly poor.

Although Algeria was an integral part of France and sent representatives to Paris, resentment against foreign control grew among the non-French majority. Following a mounting campaign of violence, revolution broke out in 1958. After four years of savage conflict, whose repercussions brought down the French Fourth Republic, Charles de Gaulle paved the way for Algeria's independence in 1962. Seventy percent of the Europeans left the scarred and battered country, emigrating to France. Well over 200,000 people had been killed and the number of seriously wounded was even higher.

Since its independence, Algeria has played an important diplomatic role in the world, serving as a crossroads in the Arab world. The economy has become more diversified, with important sectors in petroleum and agricultural exports. By 1990 Algeria's per capita gross national product reached $2400.

Libya made the transition from Italian colony to independent nation with help from the United Nations. The military led by Colonel Mu'ammar el-Kaddafi took power from the monarchy in 1969 and eight years later the country became known as the Socialist People's Libyan Arab Jamahiriya. Since that time the quixotic leader has pursued, generally unsuccessfully, military adventures against Egypt (1977), Uganda (1979), and Chad (1980). He has also supported international terrorism, drawing the anger of the United States which on three occasions in the 1980s shot down attacking Libyan jets in the Mediterranean and bombed Tripoli once. Revenues from the country's rich oil fields help finance Qaddafi's ventures and contribute to a per capita GNP of more than $5600 for the roughly 4 million Libyans.

Middle Africa

Ghana was the first nation south of the Sahara to gain independence. In 1957 Kwame Nkrumah, its prime minister, was the idol of African nationalists, and his newly freed nation was the symbol of liberalism and democracy in Africa. But almost immediately, Nkrumah began to muzzle the press and imprison the opposition. He quickly developed into an outright dictator while at the same time embarking on ruinous economic policies such as showy projects and a large military establishment. Nkrumah's controlled press called him the Great Redeemer and His Messianic Majesty, while his economy slid downhill under the impact of incompetence and corruption.

In 1966 a group of army officers seized control of the government. Anxious to speed economic recovery and to restore some semblance of political freedom, the army leaders permitted the return to parliamentary institutions in 1969. Ghana thus became the first African country to return to multiparty government after being a one-party state. During the 1970s another military junta carried off a coup, but by the end of the decade, civilian rule returned again. In 1981 the military under Flight Lieutenant Jerry Rawlings once again took control, and remained in control throughout the 1980s.

Jomo Kenyatta (center), flanked by his wife Njina and Chief Justice Sir John Ainley, is sworn in as president of the newly independent Republic of Kenya, December 12, 1964.

In contrast, the independent nation of Kenya gained stability and a sound economy under the sole political party, the Kenya African National Union, founded by the statesman Jomo Kenyatta. The state was able to mediate between the Kikuyu and Luo tribes and make its capital at Nairobi into a showplace for the continent. Kenya's history is not uniformly positive, however, as in 1972 Kenyatta expelled the East Indians, who had dominated trade.

Events were not so fortunate in the Belgian Congo (Zaire), a huge dependency as large as western Europe but lacking any ethnic or economic unity. In 1959 the Belgians, in the face of general unrest and serious rioting, promised independence. When self-government came the next year, civil war broke out among some of the seventy major groups. At the request of the Congolese government, UN forces intervened to restore order, which they did by 1964. By the mid-1970s a new regime under (Joseph) Mobutu Sese Seko succeeded in establishing the central government's uneasy authority over the tribal groups. The large, resource-rich country suffered from ineffective rule and terrible poverty among the general population. By the end of the 1980s the per capita GNP was only $172.

When it gained independence in 1960, Nigeria offered the most promise of the new African states of a prosperous and stable future. It had several thousand well-trained civil servants,

more than 500 doctors, an equal number of lawyers, and a substantial body of engineers and other professionals. It made rapid progress toward modernization, endowed as it was with a variety of important natural resources, especially oil. Unlike the Belgian Congo, it had some forty years of training in self-government. Its constitution was the result of a decade of constitutional experiments and discussion with British officials.

Nigeria, however, was similar to the Congo in its tribal and ethnic complexity. It had more than 200 tribes and a dozen important languages. Yet it appeared to have the forces of unity to overcome any fragmenting tendencies in its state structure. Nigeria was held up to be democracy's best hope in Africa; unfortunately this hope was not realized.

Between 1962 and 1966 a series of crises—disputed elections, corruption, and crime waves—threatened to tear the new nation apart. After witnessing these events, the Ibo tribal region proclaimed its independence as the state of Biafra. The Hausa and Yoruba encircled the Ibo, and crowded them into a small area without sufficient food or supplies. Thousands, especially children, died of starvation. In 1970 the Ibo surrendered and reconciled with the other tribes.

After thirteen years of military rule, civilian government was restored in 1979, along with a new constitution patterned after that of the

United States. Designed to prevent a return of the ethnic-regional feuds that had wrecked the first republic, the new constitution created a federal system providing for the allocation of powers between a central and nineteen state governments. However, Nigeria returned to military rule in 1983 and all political parties were banned, and it has thus remained.

The Eastern Horn of Africa, consisting of the Somali Republic and Ethiopia, became geopolitically significant after 1945 because of its proximity to the sea lanes of the Red Sea and the Persian Gulf. The British liberated Ethiopia from the Italians in 1941, and permitted Emperor Haile Selassie to return. While not an unenlightened ruler, he was unable to adapt to postwar conditions.

The crisis that led to his expulsion began with a famine in 1973 that killed 100,000 people. Strikes, student unrest, scandal among the royal family, and mismanagement all combined to bring success to the coup attempt that removed Haile Selassie. The new rulers were bitterly divided among moderates and radicals, and following two years of quarrels, the radicals gained control. Their governing council immediately set to work to abolish the country's traditional feudal system, transforming Ethiopia into a socialist state with a one-party system of a Stalinist type: collective farms, censorship, government control of all productive property, imprisonment, and mass execution of at least 10,000 opponents.

The council then turned to the problems in the Ethiopian provinces of Ogaden, adjacent to Somalia, and Eritrea on the Red Sea. Somalia took possession of Ogaden in 1977 but the next year the Ethiopians signed a treaty with the Soviet Union that gave them $1 billion in aid, 17,000 Cuban troops, and modern weapons. The Ethiopians launched a counter offensive and pushed the Somalis back. In the late 1970s the Ethiopians turned their attention on the Eritrean rebels and were able to expel them from some of their urban strongholds.

Overwhelming all of the political and diplomatic maneuvering was the series of massive famines that rocked the area during the 1980s. The government of Mengistu Haile-Mariam who ruled until May, 1991 either through intent or incompetence allowed thousands of Ethiopians to die, despite the massive outpour of aid from such diverse groups as churches, charitable organizations, and rock musicians.

Southern Africa

Many significant events rocked the southern part of the continent. In 1974 the revolt of the Portuguese army in Lisbon ended nearly half a century of dictatorial rule. The military junta concluded thirteen years of costly revolt by black nationalists in Portugal's African territories—Angola, Mozambique, and Guinea-Bissau. The last two gained independence with little difficulty. Freedom for Angola was complicated by the presence of a half a million European inhabitants. Following the granting of independence in 1975, bloody strife between three rival nationalist groups broke out. Fighting continued until 1989 among the groups, which drew support from Cuba, the Soviet Union, and South Africa.

Zimbabwe, formerly Rhodesia, shares a common border with Mozambique. In the first part of the 1960s this colony contained some 250,000 whites and more than 5 million Africans. In 1963 the white minority-controlled colony declared its

independence from Great Britain, which had insisted that such action could not be agreed to without the prior grant of full political rights to the African majority. Despite a crippling trade embargo imposed by Britain and economic sanctions levied by the United Nations, Rhodesia refused to compromise. In 1970 the final ties with Britain were severed when the former colony assumed the status of a republic.

During the 1970s violence increased as forces crossed over Mozambique and Zambia, while South African troops joined local forces in search-and-destroy missions against the guerrillas. By the end of the decade, the 250,000 Europeans voted to accept black-majority rule. Black factions led by Robert Mugabe boycotted the elections held in April 1979, and new elections were held in 1980. Mugabe, a Marxist, won and ruled Zimbabwe through the decade.

The country recovered quickly from the conflicts of the 1970s that left 25,000 dead and many more wounded and produced massive unemployment and food shortages. Mugabe proved to be a skilled leader, keeping the white infrastructure in place, and producing a per capita GNP of $540 by 1986. Tourism picked up and economic obstacles began to disappear. The de facto one-party state appeared to be one of the more stable and progressive on the continent.

Conditions in South Africa remained tense in the post-1945 period. With its booming cities, rapidly growing industries, and rich mining enterprises, South Africa was a thoroughly modern state, except for its racial policies. The Republic of South Africa, with a population was 70 percent black, 18 percent European, and the remainder "coloured," had to deal with the rising discontent of the African majority and with the censure of its racial policies of apartheid by the world community.

The South African government tried a program of territorial segregation, setting up ten distinct and partially self-governing African states known as Bantustans, which were aided by substantial economic grants (see map at left). First to be established was Transkei, with its Bantu population of 3.5 million people. This program did not satisfy the African populations, and strikes and political protests against apartheid continued through the 1980s. The government continued the program, granting partial independence to Transkei in 1976 and establishing two additional Bantustans three years later. The fact remains that the Homelands are generally poor and underdeveloped, forcing a constant exodus of blacks to find employment in white urban areas. Those who cannot find work and housing and meet other requirements are classed as illegal immigrants and shipped back to their Homelands.

In 1978, Prime Minister P. W. Botha, who retained that position until 1989, declared that the country "must adapt or die." Advocating a new program of race relations, he urged a lessening of race discrimination in the areas of loans and mortgage opportunities, jobs, working conditions, and wage disparities. In 1980 a new plan of government was announced. A President's Council was to be created, consisting of a white-nominated majority, coloured and East Indian members, and one Chinese representative. This body was to advise on constitutional proposals. Symbolically, this was the first time some political representation was given to non-Europeans. The plan denied Africans any such rights except in their tribal Homeland.

Botha oversaw some relaxation of apartheid: races began to mix freely in public places, areas reserved for whites only were reduced, and new black unions were legalized. Ultra-right wingers forced the prime minister to pull back. In effect apartheid remained intact. Meanwhile, the frustrations of the non-Europeans increased, fueled by the gain of independence in Angola and Zimbabwe. Militancy increased. When a new constitution was adopted in 1983, providing for a strong executive presidency and a three-part parliamentary body—whites, coloured, and Asians—blacks remained unrepresented and without rights except in their tribal "homelands." Only the white part of the parliament had any power.

F. W. DeKlerk, who replaced Botha in September 1989, moved to try to defuse the seemingly inevitable bloodshed between the races. In the face of death threats launched by extreme right-wing, proto-Nazi white parties, he opened negotiations with the African National Congress. He made the symbolically important step of releasing ANC founder and symbolic leader of many South African blacks, Nelson Mandela, from almost three decades of imprisonment and

In May 1990, South African president DeKlerk and deputy president of the African National Congress Nelson Mandela pose for photographers before beginning talks to end racial strife in South Africa.

began serious negotiations to pave the way for a multi-racial political structure. In response, the ANC suspended its twenty-nine-year declaration of war against the South African government.

DeKlerk's white opponents accused him of capitulation. Realistic observers noted that by the year 2000, whites will number a bare 13 percent of the population. South African industry will depend largely on black labor and expertise. Apartheid will be an unworkable anomaly in a black, hostile continent, a situation brought increasingly to world attention in 1985 and 1986 when the scale of violence steadily increased. Without wide-ranging reforms, the long-term prospects look bleak. At best the South African government will find itself increasingly isolated in the world community, and at worst a bloody civil war will result.

Another controversial area is Namibia. A German colony until 1919, the area was known as Southwest Africa and administered as a mandate under the supervision of the League of Nations. Following World War II, South Africa refused to transfer its jurisdiction to the United Nations, which formally ended South Africa's mandate in 1966. South Africa held on to control this huge area—half the size of Alaska—which is inhabited by a million blacks and one hundred thousand whites. Namibia contained valuable mineral deposits, but more importantly to South Africa, it served as a buffer against potentially unfriendly black nations to the north. While South Africa reached an agreement with a coalition of blacks and whites for a form of self-rule, it refused to recognize the militant Southwest African Peoples' Organization (SWAPO), which was based in Angola and supplied by the Soviets. In the early 1980s a UN-sponsored plan for an election was blocked by the South Africans, who sent troops in to attack the guerrillas, killing hundreds and also killing Soviet advisers. At the end of the 1980s, the Namibia crisis was being negotiated once again.

Latin America: Reform or Revolt

After the war, Latin America shared many of the problems experienced by the developing countries of the non-European world. Formerly competitive economies such as those of Argentina, Mexico, and Brazil have fallen far behind rapidly advancing areas such as South Korea, Taiwan, and Singapore. Whether in countries of primarily European stock (Argentina, Uruguay, and Chile); dualistic Indian-Spanish societies (Peru, Bolivia, Ecuador, and Mexico); melting pot societies such as Brazil and Venezuela; or single crop economies such as those of Central America, Latin America faced serious problems at the end of the century.

The Perils of the Postwar Era

The period since 1945 witnessed much political instability and social unrest in the region. For example, the only countries with continuously elected governments after 1950 have been those dominated by a single major party. Between 1950 and 1966 fourteen governments were forcefully overthrown and dictatorial rule was imposed on more than half of the Latin American population. The political instability and the seeds of social upheaval spring from appalling socioeconomic disparities. Despite the region's great natural resources, the average citizen of Latin America is young and poor. Shanty towns on the edges of large cities house thousands amid filth, disease, hunger, and crime. Life expectancy for Latin American males is around 55 years—fifteen years less than in North America. Agricultural productivity is inefficient and low. The population increases by about 3 percent yearly. By 1990 the region's population topped 500 million, most in cities. Educational and health services are insufficient and literacy rates remain low.

Since 1948 the countries south of the Rio Grande have been aligned with the United States in the Organization of American States (OAS). Dominated by the United States, the OAS has sought to prevent communists from acquiring control in Latin American countries by well-meaning, if incomplete, social and economic aid. After 1959, when Fidel Castro rapidly transformed Cuba into a communist country, his attempts to export his revolution have been countered by an OAS boycott.

In Castro's Cuba, educational and health standards rose appreciably, as did living conditions among the peasants who comprised the great majority of the population. The professional and middle classes, however, suffered losses in both living standards and personal liberties and many hundreds of thousands fled to the United States. Cuba exported sugar to other communist countries in exchange for major economic subsidies from the Soviet Union. In 1975 sixteen members of the OAS voted to end the embargo and the United States intimated a desire for détente. This last possibility was made remote with the intervention of thousands of Cuban troops and advisers in Angola and other African countries.

By the end of the 1980s global political changes isolated Castro. Cuba's role overseas ended with peace talks in Africa. The Soviet Union could no longer afford the luxury of propping up Castro's failing economy. His version of Marxism-Leninism was shared only in North Korea and Albania.

Castro's rule in Cuba sharpened the United States' interest in the area south of its border. After the failure of the American invasion attempt at the Bay of Pigs in 1961, President John F. Kennedy initiated, with Latin American cooperation, the Alliance for Progress. The United States pledged $20 billion, to be matched by the other members of the alliance. After twenty years, the Alliance had done little to change basic

conditions. Oligarchic rule, paternalism, and incompetence hindered economic and political reform. By the end of the 1980s, the major Latin American countries such as Brazil and Mexico were deeply in debt, unable to pay even the interest on foreign loans. Rapidly increasing inflation also hampered economic growth. In Brazil there was substantial indication that a large percentage of the foreign loans were not being invested in needed industrialization and regional integration, but were instead being funneled to Swiss banks by top-ranking bureaucrats.

The Yankee Factor

A key element in Latin America is the relationship between the United States and its neighbors. American economic involvement in Latin America has remained massive. American companies continue to employ about 2 million people, pay 25 percent of the region's taxes and produce one-third of its exports. Softening the imperialist presence are the activities of humanitarian efforts from the Rockefeller foundation and churches, and federal programs of educational, agricultural, and social improvements.

At the same time, the U.S. Central Intelligence Agency (CIA) used large sums to support the opponents of President Salvador Allende of Chile. An avowed pro-Soviet Marxist, Allende had been elected to power. In his hasty efforts to nationalize industry, both domestic and foreign-owned, and to redistribute land holdings, he had antagonized many of his own people. Allende's regime came to a bloody end in a 1973 coup. Military leaders ousted the president, who died—perhaps by his own hand—during the fighting. The new repressive regime, under General Auguste Pinochet, imposed a harsh rule and acted aggressively to curb all opposition, which had been growing since the early 1980s. Pinochet stepped down in 1990 and was replaced by the moderate Patricio Aylwin.

One long-standing source of discord between the United States and Latin America was removed in 1978 when the United Senate approved the treaty that returned the Panama Canal Zone to the Republic of Panama, while safeguarding American interests in the area. This agreement, negotiated over a period of fourteen years under four American presidents, was a sign to some that the United States was eager to improve its relations with its neighbors. The American military invasion of Panama in December 1989, however, indicated that there were some excesses the United States would not tolerate. Allegations that Panamanian President Manuel Noriega cooperated in drug running and overturned democratic elections moved U.S. President Bush to order the preemptive strike to oust Noriega.

In the last decade the countries of Latin America dealt differently with the economic, social, and political challenges they faced. Many remained under military rule. Others, such as Nicaragua, carried out successful socialist revolutions, but faced the powerful overt and covert opposition of the United States, the economic effects of which drastically lowered the country's standard of living. Democratic elections in the spring of 1990 led to the defeat of the Sandinista party in Nicaragua, but economic and social problems remained to plague the new government. Tiny El Salvador struggled through a bloody civil war, in which death squads from both right and left brought terror to the countryside. Brazil made tentative economic progress before a series of poor policy decisions darkened that country's future. Out-of-control inflation destroyed Argentina's economy but Presidents Alfonsin and Salinas were able to restore normal democratic politics in the country. Mexico was stable under a single-party domination but faced a population rate that outstripped its economic progress. Colombia found its basic sovereignty undermined by drug lords, both foreign and domestic.

In the Caribbean, the British successfully ushered in independence in the West Indies—Jamaica, Tobago, Trinidad, and Barbados—but unrest continued in Haiti. President for Life Jean Claude Duvalier, "Baby Doc," was forced out of office and fled the country in February 1986. The Caribbean island of Grenada fell to a leftist government, before President Reagan sent the Marines to the island to overthrow the regime in 1983.

With the end of the Cold War, the United States began to take a longer-term, more economically focussed view of Latin America. Enhanced perceptions of stability moved Washington to policies that may well prove to be mutually beneficial to North and South.

Conclusion

The last half century has seen the emergence of the "south" as the major theater of action for the next century. This area, with the exception of Japan, Singapore, Hong Kong, Taiwan, and South Korea, has also been known as the "Third World," the "underdeveloped world," or the "less-developed world." It contains the fastest growing populations, the most essential resources, and the most politically explosive situations.

The countries range from the richest to the poorest. All of them have been affected by decolonization, the Cold War and its conclusion, and the technological revolution. All of them were brought into the modern age by forceful contact with the Europeans, but in the next century they will have to choose their own paths. All face major economic and demographic crises that are expressed in political instability. The North—the developed world—could find no comprehensive response to the needs of the South. The search for solution to the region's problems will form the opening chapter of the third millennium.

Suggestions for Reading

Edwin O. Reischauer, *Japan: The Story of a Nation* (Knopf, 1974) is the best general coverage. See also Reischauer's *The Japanese* (Harvard, 1977). K. Kawai, *Japan's American Interlude* (Chicago, 1960) discusses occupation policies and their impact. R. P. Dore traces one major problem in *Land Reform in Japan* (California, 1958). John K. Fairbank et al. discuss the challenges of change in *East Asia: Tradition and Transformation* (Boston, 1973).

Stuart Schram, *Mao Tse-tung* (Penguin, 1966) is good for the formative stages of the leader's life. R. H. Soloman, *Mao's Revolution and the Chinese Political Culture* (California, 1971) ties political change to social transformation. Edward F. Rice gives a good summation of Mao's theories in *Mao's Way* (California, 1975). Roderick Mac Farquar, *Origins of the Cultural Revolution* (Oxford, 1983) is first rate. Changes in the countryside are considered in Jan Myrdal, *Report from a Chinese Village* (Signet, 1969) discusses political change from a rural perspective. Thomas Raski gives an overall view of economic moderization in *China's Transition to Industrialism* (Michigan, 1980). See also I. K. Y. Hsu, *China Without Mao: The Search for the New Order* (Oxford, 1982).

For studies of Southeast Asia see Michael Leifer, *The Foreign Relations of the New States* (Longman, 1979); R. N. Kearney, *Politics and Modernization in South and*

Southeast Asia (Halstead, 1974); Robert Shaplan, *A Turning Wheel: The Long Revolution in Asia* (Random House, 1979). On Indonesia, see W. T. Neill, *Twentieth Century Indonesia* (Columbia, 1973) and A. M. Taylor, *Indonesian Independence and the United Nations* (Greenwood, 1975).

On the Vietnam War, see Stanley Kavnow, *Vietnam: A History* (Penguin, 1984). Thomas Powers, *The War at Home* (Grossman, 1973) and Paul Kattenberg, *The Vietnamese Trauma in American Foreign Policy* (Transaction, 1980) deal with the anti-Vietnam war movement. For personal assessments see J. Buttinger, *Vietnam: The Unforgettable Tragedy* (Horizon, 1976); A. M. Schlesinger, Jr., *The Bitter Heritage: Vietnam and American Democracy* (Premier, 1972); and F. Fitzgerald, *Fire in the Lake* (Vintage, 1973). Also, George C. Herring, *America's Longest War: The United States and Vietnam, 1950–1975* (Wiley, 1979).

Some valuable surveys of modern India include W. Norman Brown, *The United States and India, Pakistan, and Bangladesh* (Harvard, 1972) and Stanley Wolpert, *A New History of India* (Oxford, 1982). A solid biography of Indira Gandhi is Z. Masani, *Indira Gandhi* (Crowell, 1976). An informative guide to Indian politics is Richard L. Park and Bruce Bueno de Mesquita, *India's Political System* (Prentice Hall, 1979).

The Middle East's complexity is dealt with in M. Halpern, *The Politics of Social Change in the Middle East and North Africa* (Princeton, 1967) and W. R. Polk, *The Elusive Peace: The Middle East in the Twentieth Century* (St. Martin's, 1980). T. C. Bose gives a basic history of the international rivalry over the area since 1945 in *The Superpowers and the Middle East* (Asia, 1972). On the Arab point of view see W. R. Polk, *The United States and the Arab World* (Harvard, 1975). Two insightful books on Iran are R. K. Ramazani, *The Persian Gulf: Iran's Role* (Virginia, 1972) and Sepehr Zabih, *Iran's Revolutionary Upheaval* (Alchemy Books, 1979). David Pryce-Jones writes of the Arab victims in *The Face of Defeat: Palestinian Refugees and Guerrillas* (Holt Rinehart, Winston, 1973). Soviet participation in the area is spelled out in Jon D. Glassman, *Arms for Arabs: The Soviet Union and War in the Middle East* (Johns Hopkins, 1976). Two phases of Arab-Israeli war are studied in R. and W. Churchill, *The Six Day War* (Houghton Mifflin, 1967) and Chaim Herzog, *The War of Atonement, October 1973* (Little, Brown, 1975). See also H. M. Sachar, *A History of Israel* (Knopf, 1976) and W. Laqueur, *A History of Zionism* (MacMillan, 1968).

The difficulties of transition from white-dominated to black-dominated African states can be seen in the collection gathered on the former Rhodesia in George M. Daniels, ed., *Drums of War* (Third Press, 1974). See also Henry Wiseman and A. M. Taylor, *Rhodesia to Zimbabwe: The Politics of Transition* (Pergamon, 1981). A study of Ethiopia on the eve of Haile Selassie's fall is Patrick Gilkes, *The Dying Lion* (St. Martin's, 1975). Leonard Thompson and Jeffrey Butler, *Change in Contemporary South Africa* (California, 1975) is a superior collection of interpretive essays. L. H. Gann and Peter Duignan, *Africa South of the Sahara: The Challenge to Western Security* (Stanford, 1981) details this region's strategic importance to the West. See also Gwendolyn Carter and Patrick O'Meara, *Southern Africa: The Continuing Crisis* (Indiana, 1979). A solid collection of essays dealing with the global economic response to South Africa's racial policies is Robert E. Edgar, ed., *Sanctioning Apartheid* (Africa World Press). John Seiler's *Southern Africa Since the Portuguese Coup* (Westview, 1980) discusses some of the most contentious regions of the continent. For a fine overall view of politics since independence, see Basil Davidson, *Let Freedom Come: Africa in Modern History* (Little, Brown, 1978).

The following works help illuminate the complex developments in Latin America: Julio Cotler and Richard Fagen, eds., *Latin America and the United States: The Changing Political Realities* (Stanford, 1974); R. J. Shafer, *A History of Latin America* (Heath, 1978); Irwin Isenburg, ed., *South America: Problems and Prospects* (Wilson, 1975). See also R. E. Poppino, *Brazil: The Land and the People* (Oxford, 1973) and J. N. Goodsell, *Fidel Castro's Personal Revolution in Cuba* (Knopf, 1973).

Notes

1. Richard Rovere, *Senator McCarthy* (London: Methuen, 1959), p. 24.
2. Sheldon W. Simon, "Cambodia: Barbarism in a Small State Under Siege," *Current History*, December 1978, p. 197.
3. Robert A. Scalapino, "Asia at the End of the 1970s," *Foreign Affairs*, 1980, no. 3, p. 720.
4. Selig Harrison, *India: The Most Dangerous Decade* (Princeton, N.J.: Princeton Univ. Press, 1960), p. 4.
5. From Prime Minister Harold Macmillan's speech, 3 February 1960. *Vital Speeches*, 1 March 1960.

Chapter 37

Toward the Third Millennium: Integration and Diversity

I n the last half century scientific and technological advances have made the globe an ever more compact sphere. Common problems such as the nuclear threat, environmental crises, economic upheavals, and the population explosion have forced leaders to cooperate more closely.

While common interests and problems have brought leaders to work together, the world has maintained and extended its rich diversity. The dynamic and often tragic nature of the twentieth century has produced a variety of cultural and social responses. Television, radio, cinema, shared styles and music, and safe and easy travel broke down walls that formerly isolated nations one from the other. Far from producing a homogenized culture, however, greater understanding has refined nations' definitions and sharpened the diversity of the world's peoples.

Nuclear War or Survival?

By 1953, the United States and the Soviet Union had concluded the first phase of the Cold War. With the death of Stalin in March of that year, the USSR endured a three-year period of transition, and its foreign policy shifted from military probing to a more sophisticated approach. When Khrushchev gained control in 1956, he imposed his point of view that nuclear war would be suicidal for all concerned. He returned to the Leninist doctrine of peaceful coexistence and renounced the idea that war between the socialist and capitalist worlds was inevitable.

Varieties of Peaceful Coexistence

Peaceful coexistence ushered in temporarily better relations between Washington and Moscow and led to a summit meeting in Geneva in 1955 and Khrushchev's 1959 visit to the United States. Tensions increased in other parts of the globe, however. In Asia, Latin America, Africa, and the Middle East the rival systems competed to gain the support of the nonaligned nations. Two technological triumphs in 1957 escalated the tension between the United States and the USSR: Soviet scientists put the first artificial satellite into orbit and began producing intercontinental ballistic missiles (ICBMs). These achievements gave the Soviet Union the ability to deliver a nuclear weapon to U.S. territory in 25 minutes.

These developments made Cold War competition even more dangerous. Berlin, which had long been a thorn in the Soviet side, became the focal point of competition between the two major powers. West Berlin had become a showplace of freedom and affluence, compared with East Berlin and its drab surroundings and repressive police control. Thousands of the technical and intellectual élite from the east escaped to the west through Berlin. The Soviets, presumably seeking to bring the whole metropolis under communist control, demanded the withdrawal of all western forces and recognition of Berlin as a "free city." The allies refused to give in to this demand, strengthened in their resolve, partially at least, by the substantial advances in U.S. rocket power.

A series of events from 1960 to 1962 brought the superpowers closer to the brink of nuclear war. A summit convened in Paris in 1960 broke up angrily, the situation exacerbated by the shooting down of an American U-2 reconnaissance plane over the Soviet Union. In that same year, Khrushchev, speaking at the UN, demanded the resignation of Secretary-general Dag Hammarskjold, who, he believed, opposed the Soviet-backed force in the Congolese civil war. In 1961, with John F. Kennedy, a young and inexperienced president in office, Moscow stepped up its pressures around the world. The Soviets again demanded the withdrawal of allied forces from West Berlin. Once again the west refused to back down. In response, the USSR-backed East Germans erected a wall between the two halves of the city, thereby blocking the escape route formerly used by thousands. In Laos and Vietnam, tensions also increased. To a generation of leaders in the United States, students of the lessons of "appeasement" and the success of containment, it seemed evident that force had to be met by force.

In October 1962 the world came as close as it ever has to full-scale nuclear war. Three years earlier, Fidel Castro had wrested power from the right-wing Batista dictatorship in Cuba and had begun to transform the island into a communist state. During the early months of his administration in 1961, Kennedy had approved a previously developed plan to send an expedition of Cuban exiles to try to overthrow Castro. In a badly botched operation, the force was decisively defeated at the Bay of Pigs. The following year, the Soviet Union began to install missile sites in Cuba.

To the United States, these missiles represented a dangerous threat to the Cold War balance of power. Kennedy ordered what was, in effect, a naval blockade around Cuba and demanded that Moscow withdraw the offensive weapons. After a few days of "eyeball-to-eyeball" crisis in which one incident might possibly have triggered direct military action between the United States and the Soviet Union, Khrushchev ordered the missiles removed after having received assurance that the United States would respect Cuba's territory.

Creative Diplomacy

After 1962, the Soviet Union and the United States did not approach the brink of nuclear conflict, even though Moscow made significant advances in its military position vis-à-vis the United States. Close consultation between the two capitals, even during intense competition, helped avoid danger. The "hot line" in its increasingly sophisticated forms kept the Kremlin and the White House in minute-by-minute contact and helped avoid direct confrontations in Vietnam and the Middle East.

The Cuban crisis underscored the urgency of reducing the peril of nuclear war and ushered in a three-decade-long process of tortuous and complex negotiations. An immediate result was a limited nuclear test ban treaty negotiated in 1963 and signed on August 5 of that year by Great Britain, the Soviet Union, and the United States. The treaty outlawed the testing of nuclear devices in outer space, the atmosphere, or under water. Although France, China, and India—all of which became nuclear powers—refused to sign, over 100 other states did.

U.S. secretary of state Dean Rusk, Soviet foreign minister Andrei Gromyko, and Lord Home of Great Britain sign the nuclear test ban treaty of 1963. The treaty outlawed nuclear testing in the atmosphere, but it did not ban underground testing nor did it include provisions for on-site inspection. Still, the treaty was an important step forward on international agreement to halt the proliferation of nuclear weapons.

U.S. president Richard Nixon clinks glasses with presidential advisor Henry Kissinger to celebrate the signing of SALT I (the Strategic Arms Limitations Treaty) in May 1972.

This agreement was followed by the Latin American Nuclear-Free Zone Treaty (1968) and treaties and conventions dealing with the nonproliferation of nuclear weapons (1970, expanded 1978), a treaty to reduce the risk of nuclear war (1971), an updating of the "hot line" (1971), a convention dealing with biological weapons (1975), and other agreements dealing with the threat of catastrophic war. In addition, the Mutual Balanced Force Reduction talks between NATO and the Warsaw Pact to limit conventional forces in central Europe, which dragged on for over a decade, entered a new and vital phase in 1990.

The two most important treaties were the Strategic Arms Limitation Talks (SALT I and SALT II). In these negotiations the two superpowers acknowledged, in effect, an equivalence in kill power that led to the capacity for "mutual assured destruction" (MAD). After two years of complicated talks, SALT I was signed by President Richard M. Nixon in Moscow in 1972. SALT I limited the number of ICBMs that each side could deploy for five years and restricted the construction of antiballistic missile systems to two sites, to maintain MAD. Technological advances soon made the limits of SALT I obsolete, as both sides developed the ability to deploy multiple independently targeted reentry vehicles (MIRVs), which vastly expanded the kill power of each ballistic missile.

At a meeting in Vladivostok in November 1974, U.S. president Gerald Ford and Soviet general secretary Leonid Brezhnev established guidelines to deal with the addition of MIRVs, that led to the SALT II agreement. Even though considerations such as the Soviet invasion of Afghanistan and domestic politics in each country precluded the formal adoption of SALT II, the attempt to maintain parity continued. Each side charged the other at times with violating the agreement, which was eventually signed by President Jimmy Carter and Brezhnev in Vienna in 1979. Through the 1980s Moscow and Washington both adhered to the general framework, while maneuvering for strategic superiority.

The arms control talks were complex, difficult, and subject to frustration, as neither side could permit the other to gain an advantage. While the negotiations continued, so too did full-scale weapons research and espionage. In the first half of the 1980s, the Soviet Union upset the balance of force in Europe by placing SS-20 missiles in the Soviet bloc nations of Eastern Europe. The Americans responded by deploying Pershing II and ground-launched cruise missiles, a strategic necessity given NATO's military inferiority in conventional forces.

Both sides returned to yet another summit (the eighth in twenty-five years) in November 1985 in Geneva. President Ronald Reagan met with General Secretary Mikhail Gorbachev to discuss arms control issues as well as a range of other mutual concerns. The two nations agreed to further consultations, but in the interim both argued forcefully over Soviet violations of the 1972 SALT I agreement and the U.S. Strategic Defense Initiative (SDI), a space-deployed system employing the most advanced technologies against nuclear missiles. American negotiators asserted that SDI was an attempt to change the nature of arms control negotiations from assured destruction to assured defense. The Soviets saw SDI as a technological quantum leap that would upset the weapons parity between the two powers. Domestic opposition and Soviet flexibility defused the SDI issue to allow the two powers to sign the Intermediate Nuclear Forces agreement in Washington in 1987. The INF accord set up the destruction of all intermediate and shorter range missiles within three years.[1] Further, the treaty would be monitored by on-site verification, with Soviet and U.S. experts confirming the fulfillment of the treaty's provision.

At the end of the decade, new talks on strategic long-range weapons were resumed, as were negotiations to shut down plutonium production plants. Conventional force talks in Central Europe made more progress in two months than in ten years. Clearly, the combination of economic pressures, especially serious for the Soviet Union, and mutual interest brought the superpowers into close accord to control weapons that could destroy the planet. The need to survive and prosper brought the superpowers together on the nuclear weapons issue. The end of the Cold War removed the nightmare of bipolar nuclear annihilation from the world, as could be seen in the signing of the Strategic Arms Reduction Treaty (START) in July 1991. Even though it is not yet ratified, it makes the first step to cutting down the large stockpiles of nuclear warheads on both sides. However, nuclear proliferation continued, and analysts estimated that by the mid-1990s twenty countries would have the ability to build and deliver nuclear bombs. In addition, terrible new chemical and biological weapons threatened humanity. Perversely, some commentators had begun to look upon the period of the Cold War with some nostalgia, as a time when there was some dependable order.

Trade and Economics

Even before the defeat of the Axis in World War II, the Allies made plans to avoid the horrendous economic chaos that had followed World War I. Forty-four nations met in July 1944 at the New Hampshire resort town of Bretton Woods to put the peacetime world economy on a solid footing. Recalling the protectionist lesson of the 1930s, the financial leaders devised plans to ensure a free flow of international trade and capital.

Plans for a Global Economy

The Bretton Woods conference created the International Monetary Fund (IMF) to restore the money system that had collapsed in previous decades when countries abandoned the gold standard and embraced protectionist devices such as currency devaluations that seriously harmed world trade.

It established as system of fixed exchange rates, founded on the dollar, which could be easily

Soviet general secretary Mikhail Gorbachev and U.S. president Ronald Reagan met at a summit in Geneva, Switzerland, in November 1985. The two leaders announced several agreements on scientific and cultural issues but failed to come to terms on an arms control treaty.

exchanged for gold ($35.00 an ounce). The IMF was based on a foundation of currencies paid in by the member states that served as a world savings account from which a member could take money to handle debt payments without having to resort to the disruptive tactics of manipulating exchange rates or devaluation. The standard for the exchange rates among the various currencies was that in existence as of the first day of the Bretton Woods conference. Member countries could not change their currency's values without approval of the IMF. Although the system faced some problems based on the weaknesses of many of the member states' economies after the war, the Bretton Woods agreement set up a generation of monetary stability that allowed businesses to carry on their affairs with confidence.

Another economic development indicating the integration of the world was the establishment in 1947 of the General Agreement on Tariffs and Trade (GATT), under U.S. leadership. Again, having absorbed the lessons of the protectionist and autarchic 1930s, the allies put together an international institution to set up rules for business worldwide that would give nations the confidence to break down old barriers that blocked free trade. GATT operated through a series of meetings between nations to remove protectionist restrictions. The assurance a nation received for entering the GATT framework was the most-favored-nation-clause, which guaranteed that any trade advantage worked out on a nation-to-nation agreement would be automatically shared by all members of GATT. Over the next quarter century, thanks to the Bretton Woods agreement and GATT, world trade grew at a phenomenal annual rate of 7 percent—adjusted for inflation.

President Nixon's decision in 1971 to end the policy of the dollar's convertibility into gold dealt a fatal blow to the Bretton Woods framework. Yet the development of international organizations such as the International Bank for Reconstruction and Development—part of the Bretton Woods structure, established in 1956—the Organization for Economic Cooperation and Development, and many more organizations, helped to keep the international economy on track.

Ideological warfare between Moscow and Washington prevented the chance for the economic integration of Europe offered by the Marshall Plan. While the individual economies of the west prospered with the aid received through the plan, the economies of the Soviet bloc stagnated. By the 1980s, the economic gap between the two sides forced Moscow and its allies in the Council for Mutual Economic Assistance (COMECON) to seek admission to the IMF and GATT. In the postwar period it became evident that the global political economy was the most important factor in world relations. Nations such as the Soviet Union that allowed ideological considerations to determine economic policy did so with disastrous results.

After 1945 the world experienced incredible economic growth and change. Multinational firms, headquartered in one country but with operations throughout the world, spread rapidly. The United States lost its financial dominance as it faced competition from the European Common Market, Japan, and the "four tigers"—South Korea, Taiwan, Hong Kong, and Singapore. New technologies and cheaper labor overseas produced high-quality items that cost less than U.S. manufactured goods. Competition was especially severe in the high-tech and automobile markets. The resulting foreign trade deficits increased the desire for protectionist legislation in the 1980s. Many congressional members argued that EEC and Japanese trade restrictions and subsidies hampered U.S. agricultural and technological exports while American markets remained relatively open to foreign imports. The GATT mechanism was pushed to the breaking point. In 1989 the United States invoked Section 301 of the Trade Act of 1974 to levy sanctions against India, Brazil, and Japan for unfair trade practices.

The oil embargo of the 1970s imposed by the Organization of Petroleum Exporting Countries (see p. 981) dealt a serious blow to international stability, but even worse was the debt crisis of the 1980s. Banks in the United States, Europe, and Japan made substantial loans to eastern Europe, Latin America, and Africa—whose total debt by the end of the decade topped $1.3 trillion. Brazil had close to $100 billion in debt, Mexico close to $90 billion. To ensure their survival, nations such as Brazil, Hungary, and Poland allowed World Bank personnel to impose regulations on domestic economic policy in return for loans, an unprecedented sacrifice of national sovereignty to an international body. Nonetheless, nonpayment by the debtor nations threatened to topple the world's banking structure. The crisis pressed the International Monetary Fund to the limit. Debts continued to be rescheduled, but the largest debtors showed an ever-declining ability to pay.[2]

The world recession of 1978 to 1985 had different effects on different parts of the globe. Unemployment soared across the world, especially in the lesser developed countries, which were also plagued with soaring population. In the United States the recession contributed to the huge trade deficits and federal budget deficits. The United States was the first nation to recover from the recession, largely at the expense of generating a huge internal debt and borrowing heavily from foreigners. A creditor since 1917, the United States now became a debtor nation.

The Common Market and 1992

The most significant development in postwar Europe was the progress toward economic integration. The desire for cooperation came from the lessons learned during World War II, taught by visionaries such as the French statesmen Jean Monnet and Robert Schumann. In 1950 Monnet and Schumann put forth a program to create the European Coal and Steel Community to coordinate the supply of those two essential industrial commodities in West Germany, France, Italy, Belgium, the Netherlands, and Luxembourg. Five years later, the European Atomic Energy Community was created.

The same six nations that participated in these supranational organizations in 1957 established the European Economic Community, colloquially known as the Common Market. The organization's goal was to build "the foundations of an enduring the closer union between European peoples." To that end it reduced tariffs among its members and created a great free trade union that became the fastest growing area in the western free world.

From its headquarters in Brussels, a staff of some 3000 experts administered the affairs of the EEC. In the 1950s the income of its members

---

Jean Monnet on European Unity

Jean Monnet was a pioneer in building the foundations for a unified Europe. He expressed his hopes in a future—to be attained in 1992—in a 1953 speech.

Mr. President, Ladies and Gentlemen, on behalf of my colleagues of the High Authority and myself, I wish to say how very pleased we are to have this meeting to-day with the members of the Common Assembly and the members of the Consultative Assembly. The co-operation between the Council of Europe and the European Coal and Steel Community has now definitely entered a concrete phase. . . .

In respect of coal and steel, the community has set up a huge European market of more than 150 million consumers, *i.e.* equal in number to the population of the United States of America. Under the terms of the Treaty, customs duties and quota restrictions have been abolished between Germany, Belgium, France, Italy, Luxembourg and the Netherlands; the principal discriminations in respect of transport have been done away with. . . . the road along which the six countries of the Community have set out is the right road, but we must continue to seek even more zealously ways and means of achieving a more complete understanding with the other countries of Europe. When they have seen and understood, as we have done, what this new and living Europe means for them, they will, one of these day, I hope, themselves join in.

From the *Joint Meeting of the Members of the Consultative Assembly of the Council of Europe and of the Members of the Common Assembly of the European Community of Coal and Steel. Official Report of the Debate,* Strasbourg, 22 June 1953.

One indicator of a global economy in the 1980s and 1990s was the growth of multinational firms with operations throughout the world. Here, hundreds of Soviet citizens crowd around the first McDonald's in Russia, which opened in Moscow on January 31, 1990.

doubled. While the U.S. economy grew at a rate of 3.8 percent, that of France expanded 7.1 percent, Italy by 8.4 percent, and West Germany by 9.6 percent. During the rest of the decade trade nearly doubled among EEC members. As their factories and power plants hummed with activity, their work force was augmented by more than 10.5 million workers who migrated, many with their families, from southern Europe.

Lagging far behind these advances, Britain became a member of the Common Market in 1973; Ireland and Denmark also joined in that year. The admission of Spain and Portugal in 1986 brought the number to twelve. While the member nations jealously guarded their sovereignty, they made substantial strides toward total economic integration. Various advances have been made toward adopting a common passport, setting a basic work week and holiday policy for all workers and equalizing welfare benefits.

By the end of 1992 Europe will be a single market similar to that created by the 1707 Act of Union between England and Scotland, the Constitution of the United States, and the north German *Zollverein* of the first part of the nineteenth century. Reaching the goal of "Europe 1992" has not been easy. Serious controversies over agricultural policy, banking policies, and

tax differences had to be overcome. The European leaders worked hard to reassure the rest of the world that their twelve-nation market would not be protectionist, while they went about putting together the 300 directives that would form the laws for the commercial union. The program of the twelve nations involved the opening up of their union's boundaries so that there would be no restriction to stop the movement of goods and people and the establishment of the "social dimension" to define the "rights or ordinary people in the great market and to help the poorer among them . . . ." There was also a drive toward economic and monetary union including a single European currency and central bank. Economic union also included single standards on electricity, pressures, safety, and health.

Many obstacles, some born of a thousand years of nationalism, remain. The issues of a state's favoring its own industries in the purchase of supplies and equipment, protection of particular industries by sovereign states, and the value-added tax are unresolved. Japan and the United States feared they would by excluded from future economic possibilities and yet were excited by the promises of the largest market in the world. Members of the European Free Trade

Association—Finland, Austria, Iceland, Sweden, Switzerland, and Norway—were left to determine their relationship to the powerful group of twelve, as they approached 1992.[3]

The Soviet Bloc

After 1945, Moscow's consolidation of its power gave it control over an area that extended from Berlin to the Bering Straits and from the North Pole to the Black Sea and the Amur River. Soviet leaders imposed a centralized, Stalinist control over hundreds of millions of people in a way never before seen. By the end of the 1980s Moscow found itself caught between the forces of nationalism and Russian centralism, between inflation and Soviet economic demands, and between rising feelings of liberal democracy and a declining interest in Marxism.

Nowhere were the bloc's problems more effectively portrayed than in the dilemmas faced by COMECON. The Soviet Union set up COMECON in 1949 as a response to the Marshall Plan and other Western projects to promote economic growth. In its first decade, COMECON served Soviet postwar recovery needs, as Moscow worked a reverse system of mercantilism on the region: exporting raw materials at high prices, buying back finished goods at low cost. Eastern Europe suffered greatly under this system, as could be seen in the sharp contrast between West and East Berlin. In the 1960s and 1970s the Soviet bloc states primarily the Soviet Union, German Democratic Republic, Poland, Czechoslovakia, Hungary, Romania, and Bulgaria) began to profit from buying cheap energy supplies from the Soviet Union, in return for which they sent goods they could not market in the west, and their standards of living began to improve, along with their economic growth rates.

Soviet premier Yuri Andropov wanted to turn COMECON into a functioning and competitive trade bloc, but severe structural problems hampered the system's efficiency. The restrictive bilateral nature of the relationship between Moscow and its allies prohibited, for example, Prague and Budapest working directly to achieve production or trade—COMECON countries had far more barriers than the Common Market in 1967. The nonconvertibility of each country's currency meant that each bloc country's currency could be spent only within that country. The stagnant nature of each regime's central planning apparatus fostered an industrial plant that produced inferior goods wastefully. Central planning dictated the prices of resources and commodities, usually with no relation to their actual value. Shackled with these problems, COMECON could not compete with the Common Market.

Aggravating the situation for the Eastern Europeans was the fact that as world energy prices fell in the latter part of the 1980s, they were trapped into paying premium prices for Soviet oil and gas. Several eastern European states, including Poland, Hungary, and Romania, borrowed heavily from the west and invested the proceeds unwisely. Romania escaped the foreign debt problem only by slashing the standard of living for its people. Poland and Hungary in 1989 appealed openly to the United States for help. The COMECON plan announced in the mid-1980s to equal the west technologically by the year 2000 appeared to be little more than feeble rhetoric.

There was no doubt that the Soviet Union and eastern Europe had made great progress in recovering from the devastation of World War II. In basic industry, metals, chemicals, and armaments, the Soviets sometimes led the world. They trained more engineers, scientists, and technicians than any country in the world. Their nuclear arsenal and space explorations were testimony to their accomplishments. However, in other areas—computers, robotics, biogenetic engineering, superconductivity to name a few—the west far outpaced the Soviet Union. Western tourists visiting Moscow at the end of the 1980s were amazed to see clerks in major stores using abacuses to figure the cost of purchases.

As energy prices declined, the Soviet Union— the leading oil producer in the world, exporting 3 billion barrels a day for 60 percent of its hard currency earnings—saw its earnings cut by over 60 percent when oil dipped to $10 a barrel. By the end of the decade the price had gone back to $20, but the problems remained. The Soviets and their allies invested heavily in industrial espionage in the hope of gaining high-tech parity with the west.

Premier Mikhail Gorbachev launched a frontal attack on the Soviet Union's economic problems through his programs of *glasnost* and *perestroika*. Gorbachev attacked the Stalinist central planning system with its layers of bureaucracy and managerial ethic built around satisfying the plan and not on solving problems. His economists spoke of letting market forces set prices. The philosophy that justified the Marxist-Leninist system was rejected, at least in its economic components. Universities in eastern Europe dropped not only the compulsory study of Russian but also the works of Karl Marx, expecially *Das Kapital*. Westerners were amazed to hear communist officials in the Soviet bloc speaking the rhetoric of American neoconservatives, or nineteenth-century liberals. Leading spokesmen, up to and including Gorbachev, spoke of the fact that the welfare and happiness of the individual would be best served by economic individualism, the free operation of the marketplace, with the role of government severely reduced.

Merit and productivity were goals to be pursued, objectives that were anathema to the *apparatchiki*, who felt seriously threatened by Gorbachev's reforms. From the time of Stalin on, life was good for the managerial élite. They enjoyed the best apartments, summer houses, automobiles, access to the best schools, doctors, and hospitals, and the right to shop at special shops featuring foreign goods. The *apparatchiki* lived well while the workers had no right to strike and had to have permission to change jobs. For workers, housing and food were in short supply. Workers often had to wait in long lines to get what little was available, which frequently was of poor quality. In the countryside, life for the peasants was, if anything, worse. Despite Gorbachev's efforts, alcoholism remained a serious problem, as did the "unofficial" economy—an estimated 30 percent of the GNP—through which people could circumvent the system through bribes, corruption, and cheating.[4]

But the system endured because, even for the most oppressed, things were better than they had been. *Glasnost* and *perestroika* disturbed many traditionalists, but they gave the young some hope that conditions might improve. The nations of the Soviet bloc worked hard to join the market economies, and COMECON leaders tried frantic changes such as dealing with one another only in hard currency and decentralizing all aspects of the organizations' activities. By the beginning of the 1900s, critics pointed out that Gorbachev had to achieve rapid improvements in the face of figures that the infant mortality rate in the Soviet Union had fallen beneath that of the Barbados and that the average life span for a

The shift to a market economy could create hardships for Soviet citizens. Here, shoppers at the Kirovsky supermarket in the large industrial city of Sverdlovsk wait in line for food. Shoppers in the top line are waiting for meat; those in the bottom line are waiting for butter.

Soviet man had fallen more than five years in the past twenty. The general population was becoming increasingly aware of the relatively backward conditions.

The Nonindustrialized World

The newly independent states came into existence buffeted by the Cold War and the rapid economic and technological changes that dominated the past five decades. Their status ranged from the potentially wealthy, such as Indonesia and Nigeria to the miniscule and weak, such as the Republic of the Maldive Islands, with an area of 115 square miles and a population of 100,000. The new nations had to walk the thin line of gaining aid from the great powers while avoiding being dominated by them. The use of business managers, technicians, and capital from abroad made the less-developed countries (LDC) especially sensitive to the dangers of neocolonialism.

The LDCs tried to cooperate with one another in various conferences and regional associations. The first such effort, the Asian Relations Conference, held in New Delhi in 1947, pledged support for all national movements against colonial rule and explored the basic problems of Asian peoples. A more prominent meeting was the Afro-Asian conference at Bandung in 1955 attended by twenty-nine countries representing more than half the population of the world. In the Middle East the new states established the Arab League in 1945, with a permanent secretariat in Cairo. Africa witnessed the establishment of various regional organizations, the most prominent being the Organization of African Unity created at Addis Ababa in 1963. However, not until 1973 were the LDCs able to organize effectively to make their cause heard in the industrialized world.

In October of that year the Organization of Petroleum Exporting Countries (OPEC), a cartel that until that time had cooperated sporadically in setting a standard price for oil, drastically hurt the industrial world. Angered by U.S. support of Israel, ten Arab nations began cutting their oil production by 5 percent each month. Saudi Arabia cut production 10 percent and then banned all oil exports to the United States. Libya, Algeria, and Abu Dhabi joined the embargo that was eventually also applied to the Netherlands,

Industrialization and manufacturing have stimulated economic growth throughout the world. Here, Thai women assemble circuit boards at an electronics plant in Bangkok.

Portugal, Rhodesia, and South Africa. The United States, which imported only 11 percent of its oil supplies from the Arabs, was not as badly affected as Japan and the western Europeans, which imported 82 and 72 percent respectively of their oil from the Middle East (see map, p. 982). By March 1974 when the embargo was lifted, Arab oil production was 15 percent lower than in October.

The embargo caused economic and diplomatic dislocations throughout the world. It especially strained relations between Washington and its European allies who had refused to cooperate in the U.S. effort to supply arms to Israel. It also caused a number of nations friendly to Israel to change their policies in favor of the Arabs. However, in the next decade the west developed methods of oil conservation, while the united OPEC front fell apart, as could be seen in the Iraqi invasion of Kuwait and the U.S.-Saudi Arabian-Egyptian response in 1990.

By the end of the 1980s a few former LDCs, the so-called newly industrializing countries (NIC) mastered new technologies, gained sufficient capital, and developed domestic stability to become competitive with the traditional industrialized countries. In the 1980s South Korea, for example, was a major player in the high-tech world economy. Indonesia, Thailand, and India showed indications of putting together the necessary resources and capital to join the productive circle. Most of the other LDCs fell behind the developed world, however, and countries such as

Brazil, Mexico, and Argentina for which the future had once seemed promising, paid dearly for poor economic choices. These countries continued to run a tragic race between population explosion and financial collapse.

Less than 8 percent of the world's population lived in areas where the per capita GNP exceeded $3000. Two-thirds of the world's population lived in areas classified as underdeveloped, producing less than one-sixth of the world's income. Some observers feared that three consecutive crop failures in the grain-exporting nations could bring famine to one-third of the world's people. This widespread backwardness was due to dependence on a single export crop, the dominance of a peasant subsistence economy, lack of capital, lack of education, rising fuel prices, and inflation.

Women's Struggle for Economic Equality

In 1989 Switzerland extended the franchise to women, the last of the western nations to allow women the right to vote. This struggle still goes on throughout the nonindustrialized countries. Throughout the developed world women gained legal and political equality at varying rates, although progress once gained, was neither continuous nor consistent, as could be seen in the failure to pass the Equal Rights Amendment in the United States.

Even in countries where women had gained citizenship rights, they remained subject to wage and job discrimination and to commercial exploitation as sex objects. In the United States the National Organization of Women (NOW) and a number of other organizations worked to mobilize support to achieve economic equality and to gain adequate child care centers, legalization of abortion, and tax deductions by working parents for child-care expenses.

At the beginning of the 1990s the United States labor force was more than one-half female. However, the average woman earned only about 65 percent as much as the average man for comparable work. New patterns in work, marriage, and family had profound implications for

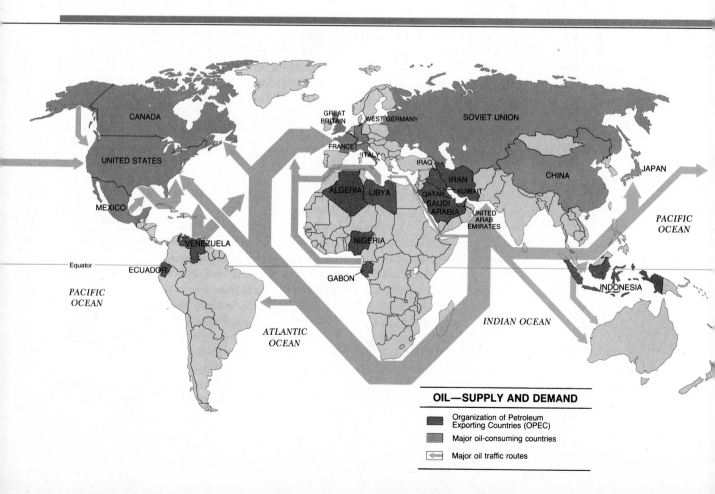

OIL—SUPPLY AND DEMAND

- Organization of Petroleum Exporting Countries (OPEC)
- Major oil-consuming countries
- Major oil traffic routes

The Feminist Movement

A profound, far-reaching postwar movement was the struggle undertaken to improve the status of women. Simone de Beauvoir compared women's status to that of other oppressed groups.

The parallel drawn . . . between women and the proletariat is valid in that neither ever formed a minority or a separate collective unit of mankind. And instead of a single historical event it is in both cases a historical development that explains their status as a class and accounts for the membership of *particular individuals* in that class. But proletarians have not always existed, whereas there have always been women. They are women in virtue of their anatomy and physiology. Throughout history they have always been subordinated to men, and hence their dependency is not the result of a historical event or a social change—it was not something that *occurred*.

From Simone de Beauvoir, *The Second Sex*, trans. H. M. Parshley (New York: Alfred A. Knopf, 1952).

society. Throughout the industrialized world birthrates declined, as much a result of women's new aspirations as of the availability of birth-control pills.

Precedent-making events occurred, despite the slow pace of progress. Britain became the first European country to elect a woman as head of its government with the election of Margaret Thatcher as prime minister in 1979. Norway followed suit in 1981. In 1988 Pakistan became the first Muslim country to elect a woman as head of its government and in 1991 Edith Cresson became Prime Minister of France. In the United States Sandra Day O'Connor became the first woman Supreme Court justice and in 1984 Geraldine Ferraro was the first woman to run for the office of vice-president. In societies throughout the world, women are gaining access to significant public responsibility, but they continue to suffer economic inequality.

One highly industrialized country where progress toward women's equality particularly lagged was Japan. Throughout the 1980s the cult of motherhood maintained its strength in Japan. What was most demanded of a Japanese woman was that once married, she deferred to her husband's career. Above all, the mother was to be devoted and self-sacrificing, an image widely reinforced by the media.

By contrast, since 1949 China made a fairly sustained attempt to change the deeply ingrained Confucian attitudes toward the roles of women. According to an old maxim, "As the Emperor should have a father's love for his people, so a father should have a sovereign's power over the family." With urbanization and the change away from a system of production centered in the household toward larger units of production the way was open for a concerted push for equal rights for women. The state passed laws changing patterns of inheritance and control over children, allowing young men and women to choose

The first woman to head a major British party (the Conservative party) and the first woman to be prime minister of Great Britain, Margaret Thatcher held that post for eleven-and-a-half years.

Women's Rights

This statement on women's rights was issued July 7, 1969, by Redstockings, a feminist organization.

I. After centuries of individual and preliminary political struggle, women are uniting to achieve their final liberation from male supremacy. Redstockings is dedicated to building their unity and winning our freedom.

II. Women are an oppressed class. Our oppression is total, affecting every facet of our lives. We are exploited as sex objects, breeders, domestic servants, and cheap labor. We are considered inferior beings, whose only purpose is to enhance men's lives. Our humanity is denied. Our prescribed behavior is enforced by the threat of physical violence.

Because we have lived so intimately with our oppressors, in isolation from each other, we have been kept from seeing our personal suffering as a political condition. This creates the illusion that a woman's relationship with her man is a matter of interplay between two unique personalities, and can be worked out individually. In reality, every such relationship is a *class* relationship, and the conflicts between individual men and women are *political* conflicts that can only be solved collectively.

III. We identify the agents of our oppression as men. Male supremacy is the oldest, most basic form of domination. All other forms of exploitation and oppression (racism, capitalism, imperialism, and the like) are extensions of male supremacy: men dominate women, a few men dominate the rest. All power structures throughout history have been male-dominated and male-oriented. Men have controlled all political, economic, and cultural institutions and backed up this control with physical force. They have used their power to keep women in an inferior position. *All men* receive economic, sexual, and psychological benefits from male supremacy. *All men* have oppressed women.

IV. Attempts have been made to shift the burden of responsibility from men to institutions or to women themselves. We condemn these arguments as evasions. Institutions alone do not oppress; they are merely tools of the oppressor. . . . .

We also reject the idea that women consent to or are to blame for their own oppression. Women's submission is not the result of brainwashing, stupidity, or mental illness but of continual, daily pressure from men. We do not need to change ourselves, but to change men. . . .

V. We regard our personal experience, and our feelings about that experience, as the basis for an analysis of our common situation. We cannot rely on existing ideologies as they are all products of male supremacist culture. We question every generalization and accept none that are not confirmed by our experience. . . .

The first requirement for raising class consciousness is honesty, in private and in public, with ourselves and other women.

VI. We identify with all women. We define our best interest as that of the poorest, most brutally exploited woman.

We repudiate all economic, racial, educational, or status privileges that divide us from other women. We are determined to recognize and eliminate any prejudices we may hold against other women.

We are committed to achieving internal democracy. We will do whatever is necessary to ensure that every woman in our movement has an equal chance to participate, assume responsibility, and develop her political potential.

VII. We call on all our sisters to unite with us in struggle.

We call on all men to give up their male privileges and support women's liberation in the interests of our humanity and their own.

In fighting for our liberation we will always take the side of women against their oppressors. We will not ask what is "revolutionary" or "reformist," only what is good for women.

The time for individual skirmishes has passed. This time we are going all the way.

Chief Justice Warren Burger administers the oath of office to Sandra Day O'Connor, the first woman named to sit on the U.S. Supreme Court, in September 1981.

their own marriage partners and giving women equal access as men to economic and political processes. Despite these advances, women lagged far behind in income and access to important offices in China.

In the years following the Russian revolution Lenin's government passed a series of laws establishing the formal equality of women with men in civic, political, economic, and family life in the USSR. During the 1920s and 1930s women played a major role in the economic reforms and Five-Year Plans. After World War II, they had to fill the gaps left by the war dead and entered all phases of the Soviet work force. Into the 1980s women constituted more than half of the labor force, including fields such as medicine—three-quarters of all Soviet physicians were women—and science and technology, where there was a larger percentage of women employed than in the west.

In the Soviet Union, as in the United States, women generally earned less than men for doing the same work. In any field of endeavor, the higher the level of authority, power, and prestige, the lower the percentage of women. The pattern of the Soviet economy and the nature of Soviet society forced an extra burden on private households and thus on women, who waited in long lines to do their shopping, performed most household tasks, and bore most of the responsibility for the rearing of children.

In most of Africa the bulk of agricultural labor was done by women, and it was common for African women to have to support a large number of children and older relatives. In Egypt about 80 percent of women were poor peasants who worked long hours in the fields and at home. They worked within the Arab-Islamic tradition that required female subordination in all areas. Even with a subordinate status, women played key roles in national liberation movements throughout Africa and the Arab countries.

Much remained to be done. In the 1980s close to three-fourths of women in Africa and the Arab countries were illiterate. Throughout wide areas of the African continent the ritual sexual mutilation of girls and young women—female circumcision to enhance the husband's sexual pleasure—was common. This physically and psychologically damaging practice drew the attention of the World Health Organization, which began a tentative discussion on ways to deal with the problem.

The word *machismo* continued to express the aggressive masculinity that played a key role in Latin cultures. Traditionally, women were totally subordinated to their husbands. In the latter part of the century, more women entered the job market, but with little improvement in their general status. In rural areas the role of women continued to be one of unceasing hard work with little opportunity for improvement. Some countries, such as Colombia, introduced reforms that promoted equal partnership in marriage. Cuba encouraged women to join the work force, providing them with child care facilities and paid maternity leaves. The Cuban family code made husbands and wives equally responsible for housework and rearing children. But even in Cuba, centuries-old attitudes did not change overnight.

Shared Concerns: Poverty, Famine, Racism, and the Environment

By the 1990s it appeared that the gap between the developed and the less-developed portions of the globe would continue to widen. However, nations such as Japan expressed increasing concern and in the summer of 1989 backed their concern with a $42 billion dollar program to help the LDCs. The major industrial powers worked through the 1980s to bring debt relief, reschedule loan repayments, provide technological assistance, and open markets to products from LDCs. The realization spread that as the world's population increased to 5.8 billion—increasingly poor and young—that the status quo could not be perpetuated. Competition continued, but with an eye to the common good that had not been present in an earlier age.

Another problem drawing the concern of the world was the severe and continuing food shortage throughout the 1980s in sub-Saharan Africa. This tragedy was brought on by a drought that lasted several years, wars and internal conflict, political instability, and rapid urbanization. Well-intentioned governments deepened the crisis by adhering to policies that favored industry or agriculture or by failing to diversify food production. Other governments used food supply as a weapon against political foes in civil wars. Several times nations crossed ideological barriers to join together in unprecedented shows of generosity to aid the victims of famine.

South Africa presented a special problem with its soundly condemned policy of apartheid. Outside of the Soviet Union, South Africa held the greatest supply of special metals, essential for the high-tech warfare of the era. South Africa's resources, as well as its location on the Cape, led

In the "Live Aid" concerts of July 1985, pop and rock stars from all over the world played to over 160,000 fans in London and Philadelphia. Broadcast by satellite to all corners of the globe, the concerts raised millions of dollars for African famine relief.

certain U.S. administrations to soften their opposition to the segregationist government, whose policies perpetuated black poverty. Ironically, Americans who advocated the withdrawal of U.S. investments in South Africa to punish the government unintentionally withdrew a major source of leverage for increased black rights that American firms represented.

Another general concern shared by the world's financial and political leaders was that of pollution and environmental deterioration. The UN Conference on the Human Environment held in Stockholm in 1972 produced no serious negotiations but did sound the call that environmental problems knew no national boundaries. This led to the creation of the UN Environmental Program (UNEP) based in Nairobi, Kenya, which unfortunately failed to live up to its expectations because of inadequate funding and jurisdictional disputes. However, in the 1970s and 1980s a series of conventions relating to the environment were signed, including agreements dealing with pollution from ships, prevention of marine pollution from land-based sources, transboundary air pollution, conservation of migratory species, protection of the Mediterranean Sea from land-based pollution, various regional pollution agreements, and in 1987 the convention for the protection of the ozone layer.

The international media brought to the world's attention serious accidents such as the 1986 fire in a Swiss chemical plant that poured 30 tons of toxic substances into the Rhine River, oil spills in France and Alaska, and the nuclear reactor disaster at Chernobyl in the Soviet Union in 1986. This concern and activity barely affected the rate at which modern industry and technology produced by-products that destroyed the environment and the equivalent pace of the destruction of the planet's forests.[5]

New Revolutions in Science and Technology

Technology and science and their by-products can affect any economic system or ideology. They cut across all political boundaries and ideological camps. The radioactive fallout from the

American tests in the Pacific poisoned entire coral reefs and islands just as surely as the radioactive discharge from the nuclear accident at Chernobyl poisoned the reindeer herds in Lapland. The technological dilemma of the modern age was best symbolized by the promises and perils of using atomic energy.

Energy Needs in the Atomic Age

The efficiency and productivity of societies depend largely on their access to and use of energy. Paleolithic people used their own muscles along with fire to get things done. Neolithic societies domesticated animals, while still later civilizations harnessed wind and water. Not until the eighteenth century was steam power effectively used and in the nineteenth century appeared the means to generate electricity and use the energy in petroleum. All of these sources, from muscle power to electricity, were limited and largely inefficient.

A technological revolution transformed society, making ever greater energy demands. The atom appeared to be a useful source. Before World War I, physicists studied the structure of the atom and the nature of its energy. They determined that the atom has a positively charged nucleus around which negatively charged electrons revolve. Einstein's relativity theory suggested that the nucleus must contain enormous energy. For example, a pound of coal, if converted entirely into energy, would release as much energy as the burning of 1.3 million tons of coal. But the atoms of radioactive elements such as radium and uranium disintegrated at their own speed, and physicists did not know how to speed up this process in order to release enough energy capable of being harnessed.

In the interwar years, however, the situation changed. In 1919 Ernest Rutherford was able to transmute one element into another by bombarding its nucleus with positively charged particles. The discovery in 1932 of the neutron in the nucleus enabled Enrico Fermi and his associates to produce nuclear reactions, but as in Rutherford's case, more energy had to be expended than was in turn released from the bombarded nuclei.

Just as a fire could continue to burn only because the combustion of each portion of fuel raised adjoining portions to the temperature of combustion, so an atomic "chain reaction" was required to split atoms in a way that produces more neutrons, which might then hit other atoms and cause them in turn to split and emit neutrons and so on. In January 1939, eight months before the outbreak of World War II, two German physicists found that the splitting of a uranium atom caused its nucleus to produce barium and also to emit large amounts of energy. Subsequent studies in the United States and elsewhere confirmed that the neutrons released during such fission made a chain reaction possible. Thus was born the atomic age, and the possibility of energy virtually without limits to fuel the future.

Just as in Greek mythology, when Prometheus paid a heavy price to acquire fire for humanity, so the atomic age ushered in both the promise of infinite energy and the peril of human self-destruction. The peril was evident in the fission bombs that pulverized Hiroshima and Nagasaki in 1945. The destructive power of these weapons was soon dwarfed by that of thermonuclear weapons using the principle of hydrogen fusion which is triggered by splitting uranium atoms, generating helium, and the resulting liberated energy creates enormous force: hundreds of times more powerful than fission weapons. These weapons could be sent to any point on the earth's surface by ICBMs, each of which could carry eight hydrogen bombs.

The promise could be seen by the use of the atom to generate energy cheaply and efficiently. Unfortunately atomic energy carried with it serious environmental hazards. Potentially lethal accidents occurred in numerous atomic installations. Another problem was the cost of providing suitable storage containers for radioactive waste and of maintaining them indefinitely. The use of atomic energy became a serious political issue throughout the world. In 1976 a Swedish government was toppled because of its plan to increase the use of nuclear power. The accident at Three Mile Island in Pennsylvania brought nuclear issues to the forefront, making them a major part of environmental protests. The massive nuclear accident at Chernobyl in the Soviet Union spread radioactivity across Europe.

The search for an efficient and safe energy source continues. Coal power creates serious problems in air pollution and acid rain. Oil supplies are finite. Solar energy is attractive but difficult to harness. Wind power has been explored and used in limited areas. Geothermal stations are used for energy supplies in New Zealand and Iceland. A number of alternate sources of power are available, awaiting research and development. The advent of superconductivity that promised virtually friction-free transmission of energy offers unprecedented possibilities, but much research is still required.

Biology and Biochemistry

As in the technological field, there has been an exciting revolution within the life sciences. By the second decade of the twentieth century, the concept that chance variations in organisms alone accounted for evolution had been replaced by an understanding of the ordered systems of genes and chromosomes. In the 1920s and 1930s scientists isolated enzymes. These comprised essential amino acids, of which proteins are built, and they directed the chemistry of the cell.

The average human body contained about a million billion cells, each of which had a complete copy of a fundamental genetic material known as DNA (deoxyribonucleic acid). In 1953 James D. Watson and Francis H. C. Crick revealed a model of the structure of the DNA molecule. It was built like a spiral staircase, in a double helix, and had four building blocks—small molecules called nucleotides. These four components were the same for all plants and animals. However, they were thematically programmed, so that their sequence along the double spiral not only made every species unique but in turn distinguished each member of that species.

> It is as though, in every room of a gigantic building, there was a book-case containing the architect's plans for the entire building. The "book-case" in a cell is called the nucleus. The architect's plans run to 46 volumes in man—the number is different in other species. The volumes are called chromosomes.[6]

Since DNA is a fundamental genetic material, analysis of its structures provided far-reaching insights into the processes of heredity and might lead to the possibility of shaping the future of numerous species, including our own.

This capability posed profound social and ethical issues. The ability to determine gender led to improvements in animal breeding and made food production more profitable. If "genetic engineering" could be employed to eradicate undesirable traits in our existing hereditary makeup, what should be the criteria for determining what was "undesirable," and who should make the determination?

Biological and biochemical advances have proved invaluable in medical research and treatment. During the interwar years, various new synthetic drugs based on sulfanilamide successfully treated diseases due to streptococcus and pneumococcus infections. There was similar success in developing bacterial products derived from molds. In 1928 Alexander Fleming discovered that a genus of fungus known as *penicillium* was toxic to staphylococcus. From his discovery came the development of the first antibiotic, penicillin, which with related drugs has proven the most effective means of treating certain types of pneumonia, syphilis, gonorrhea, and other infections. The result of such medical advances and improved diet lengthened life spans across the globe and contributed to a massive population increase.

Science and Technology

In the first phase of industrialization, which began in Britain in the latter part of the eighteenth century, machine power replaced animal and human power; productivity was thereby greatly increased. The early technical innovations were made by practical people with immediate problems to solve, rather than by scientists or teams of researchers. Later this situation changed. Increasingly science came to be involved in the production process. This development began in Germany in the last decades of the nineteenth century and has sometimes been called the scientific revolution in industry.

At the beginning of the century, the "scientific management" movement was applied to the industrial process to bring about profound changes not only in what society produced but in the nature of the work itself. Complex jobs were broken into a series of elementary steps, each performed by a different person according to a predetermined routine. This system enabled the rate of production to be increased, even by less-skilled workers hired at less cost, as can be seen in factory methods used to produce television sets, computers, and pocket calculators.

Since 1945 the organized application of science to industry has reached unprecedented levels. Scientific discoveries in laboratories rapidly reached the production lines in high-tech goods. Through the processes of mass production and distribution an incredible range of products were made available to a world market. Thus, while the post-1945 era marked a new stage in industry, it also was the latest chapter in the scientific revolution that began more than a century ago.

The potential for automation in industry was vastly enhanced by the development of the silicon chip. This was a complex miniature electric circuit etched onto a tiny wafer of silicon crystal. One type of chip, the microprocessor, is the "brain" of a computer. Besides being able to carry out computing functions in a very small space—no larger than a thumbnail—it was much cheaper than earlier technology and more reliable.

Microtechnology has markedly affected corporate structure and organization. Communications systems have become more sophisticated, inventories can be more effectively monitored, and financial operations have been simplified. Some manufacturers introduced robotic machines to their assembly lines. Everywhere industry was being organized by means of a systems approach that subdivided and then coordinated all activities to increase efficiency and productivity. Countries that adapted the new processes at the end of the century competed. Others, such as the Soviet Union, fell farther and farther behind.

The Worldwide Implications of Technology

Industrialization began in the west, where advanced economies exploited their indigenous resources and also imported raw materials from the rest of the world, thereby creating a global capitalist economy. By the end of the century all parts of the world were industrializing. There were petrochemical complexes in the Middle East, automated steel mills in India, computer factories in Brazil, and hydroelectric installations in Africa, All of Asia experienced techno logical transformation.

A vast network of highways, pipelines, railways, shipping and air lanes, fiber optic cables and communications satellites united the world. All of these served the needs of multinational firms and publicly owned enterprises. Technology in turn transformed agriculture and diet. Food canning and refrigeration, together with the bulk transport of grains, permitted the shipment of perishable goods to all parts of the world. Food production was increased by plant genetics, new managerial methods, and large-scale agribusinesses—with machines steadily reducing the number of workers doing menial labor.

As fewer people were required in agriculture, millions migrated from the countryside to the towns on every continent. In 1900 there were fourteen cities with a population of one million or more, six of them in Europe and three in Asia. By the 1980s there were more than seventy metropolitan areas with populations of over two million. Thirty of these were in Asia and nine in Latin America. It is projected that by the year 2000 there will be more than sixty cities with over 5 million people.

The impact of economic and technological change has integrated the human experience the world has become westernized. Although non-Western societies, in India, Mexico, and sub-Saharan Africa, for example, fought to rediscover and adapt their native cultures, there could be little doubt that every continent was marching to the drummer of the developed world.

Cultural Diversity

Throughout much of the nineteenth century, Europe enjoyed relative stability. People believed both in their ability to conquer their environment and in a concept of progress that was inevitable and unending. All this was shattered by a war intercontinental in scope and unprecedented in carnage. After 1918 there was widespread disillusionment with the old order; the world had not been made "safe for democracy." Social upheaval, economic depression, disillusionment, and experimentation marked the interwar years, which ended with the most distructive conflict in history, culminating with annihilation of Hiroshima and Nagasaki. Since 1945, the mushroom-shaped clouds of the atomic bomb have cast their shadow over the globe. Yet these atomic explosions were merely the first in a series of "explosions" that rocked the postwar world. We speak of the population explosion, the information explosion, and the urban explosion. World War II marked the end of the era of European hegemony and set the world on a new course: one of the global interaction of peoples, governments, economies, and resources.

European Transitions

Although the 1920s in the west have often been portrayed as an era of gaiety and triviality, the real picture was not quite so rosy. The prewar liberal complacency about the direction of society was shattered by the experiences of 1914–1918. Youths who had been promised that the war would save the world for democracy emerged from the trenches to become—if they were not already—bitterly disillusioned. The war did nothing to correct the inequalities of wealth and power in society, and labor unrest flared in numerous places.

This sense of disillusion was reflected in the arts. Writers clung to scientific notions such as the uncertainty theory of German physicist Werner Heisenberg (1901–1976) that nothing was "fixed" in the universe. Freud and the psychoanalytic psychologists were cited as authorities that society was little more than thinly veneered savagery, while behavioral psychology was seen to offer "proof" that the individual was little more than a set of conditioned reflexes. Perhaps the Anglo-American poet T. S. Eliot (1888–1965) captured the mood best in *The Waste Land* (1922). This long poem expressed weariness with the ugliness and sterility of industrialized civilization. It captured the skepticism and negation pervading the intellectual world in Britain and the United States.

A number of psychological studies appeared during the interwar period. English novelist D. H. Lawrence (1885–1930) emphasized the absolute significance of the sexual drive in such works as *Women in Love* (1920) and *Lady Chatterly's Lover* (1928). In the multivolumed *Remembrance of Things Past*, French writer Marcel Proust (1871–1922) explored psychological time,

human relationships, and his own perceptions and mental processes. A writer who employed the stream of consciousness method was Irish writer James Joyce (1882–1941), who underscored the complexity and disorder of contemporary civilization in *Ulysses* (1922), a report on the experiences of a group of people during a single day in Dublin.

Truly vibrant, although only for a tragically short time, was cultural life in Weimar Germany. Disillusionment with old values along with new perspectives revealed by science and technology was evident in the painting of the expressionists. They employed distortion and clashing colors to break free from surface appearances and attempt to penetrate to the "essence" of their subjects. Wassily Kandinsky (1866–1944) devoted his talents to abstract art, allowing viewers to derive their own interpretation and significance from the artist's arrangement of colors and forms.

In his major work, *The Magic Mountain* (1924) novelist Thomas Mann (1875–1955) presented a realistic story of life in a tuberculosis sanitarium in the Alps that was also a symbolic evocation of European civilization on the eve of the war. In portraying the struggle between the promise of life and the lure of death, Mann was describing a conflict that occupied the spirit of many Germans. Playwright Bertolt Brecht (1898–1956), who with composer Kurt Weill (1900–1950) created *The Threepenny Opera* (1928), called for a theatre of political criticism and social protest. In his writings, Rainer Maria Rilke (1875–1926) used striking images and metaphorical language to create a universe in which life, death, and all things were celebrated as elements of a single organic whole.

The functionalism that became an internationally accepted style of architectural design in the interwar years had its most influential center in Germany's Bauhaus school. The school's staff included architect Ludwig Mies van der Rohe (1886–1969) and artist Paul Klee (1879–1940), as well as Kandinsky. Teachers and students worked together in programs aimed at joining artistic expression and industry in order to reconcile contemporary humanity with its technologically altered environment. From architecture to pottery, from typography to home furnishings, the Bauhaus design for living

Wassily Kandinsky, *In the Black Square* (1923). Kandinsky attempted to free painting from what he saw as the limitations of representational art.

reflected the belief that art and function should be synthesized. After Hitler closed down the school in 1933, many of its prominent members fled to other countries to carry on their work and to spread the Bauhaus philosophy.

Following the liveliness of Weimar German was the grotesqueness of Nazi culture. One of the roots of the Third Reich's beliefs came from the German Monist League. This group was hostile to the alienating and debilitating aspect of urban civilization and, instead, praised the virtues of rural life and called for a Germany rooted in strong peasant communities. This longing for roots and tradition was characteristic of the related folkism movement. Young people, in particular, were seeking an organic philosophy of life that emphasized a love of nature and an idealization of the German past. Such thinking opposed mechanical civilization in favor of *Kultur*, which meant a type of society joining the German people in an intimate union with the forces of nature. Houston Stewart Chamberlain (1855–1927), a leading racist ideologist who had considerable influence on Hitler, claimed that

the difference between *Kultur* and civilization could be summed up in the difference between the peasant and the factory worker: the peasant daily and subconsciously learned truth and living from nature while the worker lived in an essentially artificial urban environment. Nazi Minister for Propaganda Joseph Goebbels shared this point of view as he defined socialism. "We want socialism as the doctrine of the community. We want socialism as the ancient German idea of destiny."[7]

In this fuzzy philosophy there was no place for the sophistication of modern art and music or the critical role of the writer. Modern art, like the work of the Bauhaus artists, was condemned, as were cultural ideas of the "folkish" groups, which Hitler criticized as obsolete and backward. For the Nazis film, art, and writing were to exult Germans and Germany. A notable example was the film *The Triumph of the Will* by Leni Reifenstahl. The *Kultur* concept that was central to the Nazi world view was destroyed with Hitler in the Berlin bunker in 1945.

Characteristic of the literary works of postwar Germany were the novels of Günter Grass, such as the *Tin Drum*, which offered a dwarf's eye view of the events of the 1930s and 1940s. In his novel *1984*, published in 1949, George Orwell (1903–1950) created a society completely totalitarian in structure, methods, and values in which technology was employed to enslave people and destroy humanistic values. In *The Technological Society* (1954) Jacques Ellul painted a bleak picture of a world dominated by an "aristocracy of technicians," in which moral values were subordinated to the requirements of "technique," and human beings became mere appendages of technical processes.

One of the most widely read writers of the postwar period was the novelist, essayist, and dramatist Albert Camus (1913–1960). Camus, a liberal intellectual from French Algeria, combined a belief in the absurdity of human existence with the concept of self-esteem and a certain joy in living. This attitude was explicit in *The Myth of Sisyphus* (1942) in which he likened the human lot to that of the ancient Greek figure of Sisyphus, sentenced by the gods to push a rock to the top of a mountain, only to have it roll back down, and to have to repeat this task forever. Camus saw Sisyphus as not only accepting this task with dignity but finding satisfaction in his work. During the period of the Cold War and the struggles against colonialism Camus found himself caught between the dictates of his philosophy of rebellion and his allegiance to western cultures and values.

A more radical political position was adopted by Jean-Paul Sartre (1905–1980) in his existentialist philosophy. His belief that human beings are "condemned to be free" was expounded in *Being and Nothingness* (1943) and reflected in his plays and stories. After the war Sartre increasingly recognized the constraints and responsibilities imposed on individual freedom by social forces—a move evident in his three *Roads to Freedom* novels. Sartre became one of the leading advocates of *littérature engagée* (committed literature), which claimed that since all writing is bound up with social life, writers should be conscious of this fact and strive to help their readers understand the problems of society. In his massive philosophical work, *Critique of Dialectical Reason,* Sartre attempted to integrate existential insights into the situation of the individual with the historical perspective of Marxism. After the Soviet invasion of Czechoslovakia in 1968, Sartre, along with a number of other French Marxist adopted an increasingly critical tone toward communism.

The United States

Many of his fellow citizens shared the belief of Henry Luce, the co-founder of *Time* magazine, that the twentieth century was the American century. By the end of the century it was apparent that at least in the areas of life-style Luce was right. American popular culture, style, and attitudes had spread throughout the world.

The young country was thrust into world responsibilities in World War I, tried to avoid them in the interwar period, and became the "arsenal of democracy" during World War II. From the end of the war until the assassination of John F. Kennedy, the country basked in a period of innocence and power. Thereafter, the divisiveness of the Vietnam war and the upheavals of the civil rights and sexual revolutions shook the country to its foundations.

America's writers served as compelling witnesses for the century. Sinclair Lewis (1885–

1951) satirized the materialism and shallowness he saw in American life in a series of novels such as *Elmer Gantry.* Other Americans expatriated themselves to Paris. F. Scott Fitzgerald (1896–1940) is associated with the term *jazz age* and in his novels such as *The Great Gatsby* (1925) examined problems of wealth and violence on the American scene. Another expatriate, Ernest Hemingway (1899–1961), rocketed to fame with vivid stories glorifying manliness and action for its own sake. In the crisis-ridden 1930s Hemingway turned to the theme of the destructive impact of modern warfare, for example, in *For Whom the Bell Tolls* (1940). The depression spurred writers to social consciousness. William Faulkner (1897–1962) dealt with the poverty and ignorance of some parts of the U.S. south in such works as *The Sound and the Fury* (1929), while the plight of the "Okies" who trekked to California in search of survival was recounted by John

In his life F. Scott Fitzgerald embodied the "jazz age" that he described and criticized in his fiction.

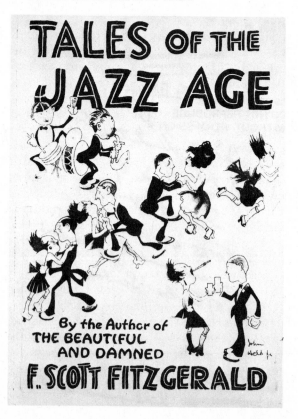

Our vision of the Great Depression owes much to the photographs of Dorothea Lange. Her 1937 photograph of this "Skid Row" scene on Howard Street in San Francisco captures the hopelessness of the urban unemployed during the 1930s.

Steinbeck (1902–1968) in his powerful novel *The Grapes of Wrath* (1939).

The revolt against traditional ways of thinking became especially apparent in the photographic arts. Still photography and motion pictures, whose basic principles had been developed in the nineteenth century, became major vehicles of expression following World War I. True photoreportage began in the mid-1920s when improved equipment and technical facilities enabled fleeting expressions and movements to be caught under varying light conditions. The movies became the most popular and universal art form of the century. While most movies were made and watched for entertainment, the medium lent itself to the visual depiction of relationships and issues in contemporary society. The best films, such as those of Charlie Chaplin (1899–1977), combined entertainment and social commentary.

As books and mass-circulation magazines replaced art exhibits as showcases for talented photographers, they helped spur a preoccupation with everyday people and situations. During the depression, Dorothea Lange (1895–1965) and other photographers working for federal agencies, notably the Farm Security Administration, employed their art as a powerful weapon to awaken Americans to the plight of their fellow citizens.

The depression also stimulated a new interest in folk songs of all kinds: regional, social, humorous, sad, but together projecting the vitality of a society determined to get on top of its problems. Perhaps the most significant interwar development in western popular music was jazz, an American form that originated with black musicians in New Orleans and in time spread over the continent and into Europe. Jazz musicians made use of both western and African cultural contributions, drawing on brass-band marches, French and Spanish songs and dances, and the spirituals and work songs of American blacks.

In the period from 1945 until the early 1960s J. D. Salinger (b. 1919) spoke to the "silent generation" of students in novels such as *Catcher in the Rye* (1951). Lawrence Ferlinghetti, Jack Kerouac, and Allen Ginsburg typified the writers of the "beat" generation of the 1950s. The film industry suffered the attacks of Senator Joseph McCarthy and his followers, who accused numerous actors, writers, and directors of being Communists and "blacklisted" them to prevent them from working. One of America's major contributions from this period was rock 'n roll. White musicians such as Elvis Presley, Jerry Lee Lewis,

Superstars of rock 'n roll in the 1950s and 1960s included Elvis Presley, "the King" (left), and the Beatles (right). Some members of the older generation cited the antics and lyrics of these rock performers as evidence of the decline of the younger generation.

and Buddy Holly took the work of black musicians and, adding their own interpretations, sang to a larger audience. Widely derided at the time by proponents of "high culture," rock n' roll in its various manifestations became popular throughout the world, inspiring such British groups as the Beatles and the Who in the 1960s.

Vietnam, the civil rights movement, and the sexual revolution set the 1960s and 1970s in vivid contrast to the rather more complacent 1950s. After the assassination of President John F. Kennedy, a number of factors came together to shake the foundations of American life: the large number of young people—the "baby boom"—the unprecedented amount of wealth they possessed, the impact of television's coverage of events, as well as the compelling nature of the issues themselves. Students and other young people challenged the right of those in power to rule. Demonstrations sometimes met with violence from authorities, such as the incident in 1970 at Kent State University in Ohio when National Guardsmen fired on and killed four students. Two students were killed in a similar incident a week later at Jackson State University in Mississippi.

Popular music provided one of the major means of communications during this turbulent period. The folk music revival of the 1960s went hand in hand with the civil rights and antiwar movements, where no rally was complete without its inspirational songs. In rock music the simple and somewhat naive themes of the music of the 1950s gave way to protests of rock musicians like Jimi Hendrix and Janis Joplin. Mindless disco music dominated for a while during the mid-1970s, as the idealism, selflessness, and fascination with abstractions that characterized an earlier generation were replaced with a desire for economic well-being, business success, and a thoroughgoing materialism.

The Soviet Union: Experiment and Debate

After the civil war and War Communism, the Soviet Union in the 1920s entered a vigorous debate over the kind of culture that should be encouraged for the Soviet masses. Should a specifically "proletarian" culture be arranged, or were "bourgeois" forms to be tolerated? Lenin himself, before his death in 1924, sided with those who advocated considerable freedom of expression in cultural fields and argued that there was much in prerevolutionary art and literature that could benefit the masses. "Culture" was not something that could be imposed from the top, but had to develop through the participation of everyone.

The early 1920s saw an explosion of creative endeavor in all fields of life. Some writers, including Maxim Gorky (1868–1936) and the poet Vladimir Mayakovsky (1893–1930) aligned their works specifically with the revolution. Others were less politically oriented, seeing in the revolution the opportunity for individual liberation and personal expression. The "constructivist" artists were interested in practical design and sought to integrate art with many aspects of everyday life. Soviet theater flourished under influential directors such as Vsevolod Meyerhold (1874–1940), while Sergei Eisenstein (1898–1948) and others produced notable documentary films.

The period of experimentation did not survive the 1920s, however. With the desperate and painful rush to industrialize that began once Stalin was firmly in power, restrictions were imposed in many areas. Experimental art and literature were discouraged, and things became difficult for those who did not conform. Yevgeny Zamyatin (1884–1937), who anticipated Orwell with his novel *We* (1920), felt it necessary to go into exile to pursue his literary career. Distinguished historians such as M. I. Pokrovsky found themselves trapped by Stalin's directive to shape their findings to agree with the "party line." Even scientists and linguists were forced to adhere to a predetermined order.

After 1945 the Soviet government strengthened the wall around its extended frontiers and attempted to isolate its citizens from contamination from the west by preventing outside books, periodicals, and radio signals from reaching the Soviet Union. The party took all these measures to aid the formation of the "new Soviet man." So that this superior individual could attain the necessary qualities, it was essential to control every aspect of life, expecially education.

As in the 1930s, Stalin continued to exercise harsh restrictions on both artists and intellectuals. The war had given a brief opportunity for the creation of spontaneous patriotic works. Afterwards, controls were even more firmly imposed. Stalin's word and tastes dominated both the arts and sciences, and the censors did their work thoroughly. In 1946 they launched an attack on artists and writers whose works did not

Through the masterful use of montage (the way a director arranges shots in order to assault the emotions of the viewer), Sergei Eisenstein created films of astounding impact. In this scene from *Potemkin* (1925), a horrified mother defies the tsarist troops who have killed her child.

sufficiently support the Soviet system. Distinguished composers such as Dmitri Shostakovich (1906–1975), Sergei Prokofiev (1891–1953), and Aram Khachatarian (1903–1978) felt the party's lash. Writers were controlled by an agency called *Glavlit* whose permission and approval were essential for any author or artist to publish, speak, or exhibit in any of the media. At the back of books and journals, the most important number was not that of the copies printed, but that noting the censors' approval. Artists who failed to meet the censors' standards were simply cut off from access to the public through the official media and also from contact with the Union of Soviet Writers. The automobiles, special stores, summer houses, preferred apartments, and other economic privileges that came with membership in the union were denied recalcitrant writers.

With Stalin's death, controls were relaxed and western readers gained the opportunity to read the works of Boris Pasternak (1890–1960) Alexander Solzhenitsyn (b. 1918), and Yevgeny Yevtushenko (b. 1933). Pasternak's *Doctor Zhivago* (1957) did not find favor with Soviet authorities, who refused Pasternak permission to accept his Nobel prize for literature. Solzhenitsyn, who had been imprisoned in the labor camp system of the Soviet Union, had been permitted to publish his book *One Day in the Life of Ivan Denisovich* by Khrushchev. Solzhenitsyn's later works, *Cancer Ward, August 1914*, and the *Gulag Archipelago*, did not bring him official favor, and he was exiled from the USSR in 1974. During the Brezhnev years Yevgeny Yevtushenko gave impassioned public readings of his work, expecially poems criticizing Stalin's regime. Other, more popular figures, such as Bulat Okudzhava, used satirical and antiwar songs to reach their audience.

Until Gorbachev came to power, many Soviet writers published their works in the underground

Charged with treason because of his dissident activities and writings critical of the Soviet Union, Alexander Solzhenitsyn was expelled from Russia before his case came to trial. The treason charges were officially dropped in 1991.

press, the *samizdat* (literally "self-publishing"). After 1985, under the tenets of *glasnost*, artists in the Soviet Union enjoyed the most creative freedom since 1917. Filmmakers led the way in producing works closely detailing the abuses of Stalin's era and the disappointments of contemporary society. Pasternak, Solzhenitsyn, and Zamyatin all were published. Solzhenitsyn, who had won the Nobel prize for literature in 1970, was readmitted to the Union of Soviet Writers in 1989. Plays and novels hidden on closet shelves for twenty years were produced and published. The Soviet Union, in the midst of its economic problems, experienced a cultural renaissance in the Gorbachev years.

China: Which Road Forward?

Classical Chinese culture was centered in the cities and was the preserve of a small sophisticated and literate ruling class. At the end of the First World War such scholars as Chen Tu-hsiu (1879–1942) and Hu Shih (1891–1962) broke with classical traditions, substituting vernacular for literary Chinese in their writings. They stressed the relation of contemporary thought to the life of the average Chinese, in contrast to the stereotyped and stilted subject matter of traditionalism. Vernacular literature spread rapidly during the interwar years and acquired a strongly social character. Lu Hsun (Lu Xun) (1881–1936), a writer much admired in China, used satire to expose social evils in the 1920s and 1930s and also translated many foreign works into Chinese.

In 1966 Mao Zedong and the more radical among the Chinese leadership, disenchanted with the Soviet model for building socialism, initiated the Cultural Revolution. The aim of the radicals, many of them students and young workers, was to reestablish the ideals of egalitarianism and encourage participation in political and cultural life among the masses. In particular, the objective was to break down the "three major differences" that they held to be retarding progress toward a just social order: between town and country, between worker and peasant, and between mental and manual labor. Even bureaucrats and intellectuals were now expected to engage in periodic stints of manual labor.

During the Cultural Revolution, the radical line was to "put politics in command" in all areas

A scene from "Red Detachment of Women" performed by the Peking Ballet. The ballet, which dates from China's Cultural Revolution era, tells the story of an early Communist uprising against the Nationalist government when it was still in power.

of life, whether in the factory or on the stage. Literary culture, which stresses individual creativity, was de-emphasized in favor of cooperative and visual art forms. Such operas as *Taking Tiger Mountain by Strategy* and such ballets as *Red Detachment of Women* were used to get political messages across to mass audiences. Artistic expression was stifled and the Chinese turned their backs on almost all foreign culture.

After Mao's death in 1976, a less dogmatic attitude to the arts began to emerge. Among the signs of this change was the reappearance of the traditional Peking Opera, which, with its acrobatics and dazzling costumes, provides one of the most entertaining spectacles in world theatre.

India's Cultural Revival

The centuries of British rule in India influenced both Indian institutions and values. The Indian intelligentsia was schooled in English educational forms and immersed in English literature and prepared itself for the professions and civil service, which in turn were English in structure and largely in content. Yet decades before independence, a cultural renaissance began.

While a number of European scholars, such as Max Müller (1823–1900) were studying the intellectual treasures of the ancient Indian classics, some outstanding Indian philosophers, including Swami Vivekenanda (1863–1902) and Sri Aurobindo (1872–1950) began not only to reinterpret the Vedanta and other classical schools of thought but to place their teachings in a new

relationship with western tradition as well. In addition, Indian culture produced a world-famous literary figure Rabindranath Tagore (1861–1914), a poet, author, painter, and dramatist. Steeped in India's literary and philosophical traditions, Tagore described the *Vedas*—the ancient Sanskrit collection of hymns, epic poems, and ritual formulas—as "the poetic testament of a people's collective reaction to the wonder and awe of existence." In his own works he sought in return to interpret afresh the contents of the *Vedas* and *Upanishads*, employing both English and Bengali as literary media.

Although primarily a nationalist leader and politician, Jawaharlal Nehru also encouraged the Indian cultural revival by his own rediscovery of the subcontinent's varied past. Nor was this national renaissance simply backward looking: by embodying the cultural heritage and ethos in twentieth-century forms of expression, it made Indian thought and art relevant to contemporary times and problems. In this connection, India developed one of the largest and most dynamic film industries in the world, and the government employed this art form for purposes of entertainment and education alike.

African Expression

Over the past century Africa absorbed the blows of colonialism and faced the challenges of developing new states. In his epic work *The Wretched of the Earth* (1961), Frantz Fanon (1925–1961) analyzed the psychological damage that resulted to the African peoples from the colonial experience and continued western dominance. According to Fanon, the colonizing force defined out of existence any reality in which black people could be accepted—by themselves or by others—as human beings with creative potential. Blacks were powerless because their experience had no validity in that realm, which both they and others accepted as "reality." Fanon took issue with the African cultural revolution epitomized in the *Négritude* movement, which rejected western history and culture and sought to describe a uniquely African culture and personality. *Négritude*, argued Fanon, was a reaction to the European challenge rather than a positive action to gain a true identity for blacks.

At the beginning of the 1960s a number of African leaders proclaimed socialism as the path their newly independent countries should take, because it was claimed that precolonial societies of sub-Saharan Africa exhibited a form of preindustrial socialism. What resulted was a socialism that could be described as African, but it was too broad and diverse to be described as a single ideology. Governments is Guinea, Mali, and Mozambique represented a more self-consciously revolutionary form of socialism, whereas Senegal's socialism had a more utopian character. No matter what the character of socialism, all variants rejected the view that African socialism must reflect socialist developments in other parts of the world. Julius Nyerere of Tanzania noted that "The differences between . . . societies will reflect both the manner of their development and their historical tradition."[8]

Latin America's Self-Discovery

For nearly 175 years, the countries of Latin America were politically independent, but only during the present century has their quest for cultural independence and a recognizable self-identity assumed major proportions. As a result, much Latin American art possessed a cultural character different from that of either Iberia or North America. In Brazil, which has a large black population, there was the growth of a black art style as well as the emergence of *Indianismo*, with its rediscovery of pre-Columbian America.

The National Museum of Anthropology in Mexico City was a monument to this search, as were the vivid frescoes of several brilliant Mexican painters, including Jose Clemente Orozco (1883–1949) and Diego Rivera (1886–1957).

The period since 1945 saw a flowering of Latin American literature, much of it rooted in the social and historical context of that part of the world. For example, in the works of Miguel Angel Asturias of Guatemala the special world view of the Mayan Indians is a central concern. In several of his other novels, he concerned himself with the plight of his compatriots under the yoke of local despots and foreign exploiters.

The Chilean poet and Nobel prize winner Pablo Neruda (1904–1973) expressed both his social commitment and an intense feeling for his landscape and history of Latin America. On the other hand, the surreal fantasies of Argentina's Jorge Luis Borges (b. 1899) could not be considered peculiarly Latin American, although they influenced the style of other regional writers. In *One Hundred Years of Solitude*, a tale that embodies much of the Latin American experience, Gabriel Garcia-Marques (b. 1928) of Colombia wove together fantasy and history in an epic tale about successive generations of a small-town family.

Conclusion

The postwar period witnessed the development of a number of concerns that brought the leaders of the world together: nuclear weapons, trade and economic policies, the environment, women's rights, and innovations in energy and technology. As the century came to an end, substantial international progress had been made in each area, although in none of the areas was there anything approaching a complete solution. Nuclear proliferation still concerned the globe even if the superpowers were on the path to arranging accords; the debt issue and the increasing gap between the developed and less-developed nations posed problems for the future; pollution problems frustrated nations' best efforts; women still suffered seriously from economic and other forms of discrimination; and technological innovations that increased efficiency also produced a jarring disruption of old patterns.

Throughout this century of war and upheaval, the artists and writers of the different regions of the world responded to changes in diverse ways. European artists and writers reflected the exhaustion of two world wars and the Cold War. America's mass culture tended to reflect society, not try to profoundly change it, as was the case in the Soviet Union. Chinese artists tried to turn the western influences to their own best advantages, while in India artists returned to their cultural roots. Africans struggled to gain some means to define their present and forecast their future, and in Latin America, the rich cultural heritage dominated contemporary creative expression.

Suggestions for Reading

For pioneering works of environmental concern see Barbara Ward and René Dubos, *Only One Earth: The Care and Maintenance of a Small Planet* (Penguin, 1973) and Barbara Ward, *The Home of Man* (Norton, 1976). On the profound transformation of women's roles in this century see Simone de Beauvoir, *The Second Sex* (Vintage, 1974) and Betty Friedan, *The Feminine Mystique* (Dell, 1977). For a worldwide survey see Kathleen Newland, *The Sisterhood of Man* (Norton, 1979). For poverty and north-south relations see Robert L. Rothstein, *The Weak in the World of the Strong* (Columbia, 1977) and Richard Critchfield, *Villages* (Anchor/Doubleday, 1981).

Christopher Lasch takes a provocative look at contemporary American society in *The Culture of Narcissism* (Norton, 1979). For lively accounts of two decades in American society, see Frederick Lewis Allen, *Only Yesterday: An Informal History of the 1920's* (Harper & Row, 1964) and Eric F. Goldman, *The Crucial Decade—and after: America, 1945–1960* (Vintage Books, 1960). A vivid portrait of the intellectual, artistic, and social life of France from the 1930s to the early 1970s can be found in three of the volumes of Simone de Beauvoir's autobiography: *The Prime of Life* (Penguin, 1965), *Force of Circumstance* (Penguin, 1968), and *All Said and Done* (Penguin, 1977). The problems of individual alienation within a German context, as depicted in the literature of Rilke, are analyzed in Erich Heller, *The Disinherited Mind: Essays in Modern German Literature and Thought* (Harcourt Brace Jovanovich, 1975) an Peter Gay, *Weimar Culture* (Torch-

books, 1970). Russian cultural trends [...] Nettl, *The Soviet Achievement* ([...] Jovanovich) and Hedrick Smith, *The Russi[...]* gle, 1976). V. S. Naipul examines a peo[...] preoccupation in *India: A Wounded Civilization* ([...] 1978). Contemporary trends in life and culture in C[...] are analyzed in the Committee of Concerned Asian Scholars, *China! Inside the People's Republic* (Bantam). Developments in Africa have been vividly portrayed in three novels. Chinua Achebe, *Things Fall Apart* (Fawcett, 1959), described as a "classic of modern African literature," dramatizes traditional Ibo life, the pre-Christian tribal life, and shows how the old ways were broken up by colonialism at the turn of the century. In *A Bend in the River* (Penguin, 1980), V. S. Naipul describes the problems of a postcolonial Africa that is losing touch with its past. Nadine Gordimer in *Burger's Daughter* (Viking, 1979) depicts contemporary South Africa and the lives of individuals caught in its maelstrom of historical and racial forces.

The relation of art to a society is explored in historical perspective by Ernst Fischer in *The Necessity of Art* (Penguin, 1978). For trends in painting and architecture, see Alan Bowness, *Modern European Art* (Thames and Hudson, 1980); E. H. Gombrich, *The Story of Art*, 12th ed. (Phaidon, 1974); and H. W. Janson, *History of Art*, 2nd ed. (Prentice-Hall, 1979), Part 4, "The Modern World." Directions in music are dealt with briefly in A. Einstein, *A Short History of Music* (Vintage) and Arthur Jacobs, *A Short History of Western Music* (Pelican, 1976)—see chapters 17–20 for twentieth-century developments.

Notes

1. Alvin Z. Rubinstein, *Soviet Foreign Policy Since World War II*, 3rd ed. (Glenview, IL: Scott, Foresman, 1989), p. 266.
2. For a cogent discussion of international economics and politics see Walter S. Jones, *The Logic of International Relations* (Glenview, IL: Scott, Foresman, 1988), chapters 12–14.
3. Nicholas Colchester, "Europe's Internal Market, A Survey," *The Economist*, 8–14 July 1989, after p. 48, insert, pp. 1–52.
4. Hedrick Smith, *The Russians* (New York: Ballantine Books, 1977), chapters 2, 3, 4, 9.
5. Seyom Brown, *New Forces, Old Forces, and the Future of World Politics*, (Glenview, IL: Scott, Foresman, 1988), pp. 278–281.
6. Richard Dawkins, *The Selfish Gene*, (Oxford: Oxford Univ. Press, 1976), p. 23.
7. Joseph Goebbels, from a 1926 speech, "Lenin or Hitler?" quoted in Z. A. Zeman, *Nazi Propaganda* (London: Oxford Univ. Press, 1973), p. 206.
8. Julius Nyerere, *Freedom and Socialism* (Dar es Salaam: Oxford Univ. Press, 1968), p. 3.

*T*ime present and time past
Are both present in time future . . .
Time past and time future
What might have been and what has been
Point to one end, which is always time present.
    T. S. Eliot, "Burnt Norton" (Four Quartets)

Here one of the twentieth century's greatest poets wrestles with that mysterious dimension, time, which some have defined as a "flow" of distinguishable events. *Civilization Past & Present* has narrated the past-to-present flow of global events; but events can also be assessed in terms of a future which has yet to occur. In what way, if any, does that future "point" to our present situation?

The human species seems unique in that we can conceive of time in three phases: where and what we have been, where and what we are now, and where and what we might be tomorrow and beyond. To survive, corporations and governments alike have to be able to think ahead. This process is called *planning*, which, of course, is another way of speaking about "time future." Anyone familiar with systems concepts will understand the term *feedback*. In order to heat a room, for example, a furnace transforms an input of oil into an output of heat, which then raises the room's temperature to the desired level (say 72 degrees) set on the thermostat. When the level is reached, the thermostat will feed back that information to the furnace, which then discontinues its input of fuel. This simple example shows how the future environment we desire can set in motion activities affecting present behavior.

Nobel laureate Denis Gabor has stated that although we cannot prophesy the future, we can help invent it. Science and technology have already initiated actions of such potency that we must plan as intelligently and creatively as possible for the coming century if our global society is to endure and prosper. Casey Stengel, with his inimitable logic, put the matter succinctly: "If you don't know where you're going, you'll wind up somewhere else." So where do we want to go?

The Gulf War

On August 2, 1990, less than a year after the demolition of the Berlin Wall had marked the end of the Cold War between the superpowers, Iraqi troops poured across the border into Kuwait. A week later Iraq formally annexed Kuwait. Worldwide condemnation resulted in the UN Security Council enacting economic and other sanctions against Saddam Hussein's regime. In January 1991, Operation Desert Storm was launched by a coalition of governments, spearheaded by more than half a million U.S. air, sea, and land forces, to liberate Kuwait. Unrelenting high tech aerial bombing of Iraq, followed by a swift and overwhelming ground attack, settled the outcome within a month.

The Persian Gulf War would have long-range consequences, but its immediate effects were obvious. U.S. president George Bush spoke for a large majority of Americans in claiming that the victory had ended the "Vietnam syndrome" and restored the country's "credibility" in world affairs. The credibility of the United Nations was also restored, at least as that body exists as a useful mechanism for legitimizing collective security measures (but which it was never mandated to supervise). The economic consequences were bound to be momentous. Kuwait's infrastructure and oil fields had been devastated while Iraq, already impoverished after years of warfare with Iran, had now to repair vast wreckage in Basra and Baghdad and restore its own shattered oil industry to working order. Moreover, it could have to pay billions of dollars in reparations to Kuwait.

The social consequences were no less devasting. Many thousands in the region had been displaced, wounded, or killed. Only time will tell how many civilians had been permanently traumatized by the incessant bombings or how deeply humiliation and resentment runs in the Arab world. The political destabilization of the Middle East could make this area of the world more volatile than ever. Like nature itself, geopolitics abhors a vacuum. All in all, the war raised serious questions about Iraq's future as a country, to say nothing about a festering problem which the Gulf War had done nothing to resolve: Israeli-Palestinian relations and the occupation of the West Bank.

Conceivably, the most terrible immediate consequence of Desert Storm was the damage inflicted upon the region's environment. The largest oil spill in history covered vast regions of the Gulf, endangering species, fisheries, and coastal settlements. Hundreds of oil wells were set on fire, so that during the many months before the fires were extinguished, huge clouds of smoke poisoned the atmosphere of the region and beyond.

Ironically, the Gulf War occurred in the very region where (as we saw in chapter 1) the first civilization arose. During the conflict, archaeologists requested Washington to do everything possible to preserve priceless historical artifacts, but some destruction was inevitable. Their concerns raise a somber question: After 5000 years, how far has society progressed? We humans are still warring with one another and destroying the environment to an extent inconceivable to the men and women who built Ur with its ziggurat, crowned by a sanctuary or "high place." Have we demonstrated yet again a fixation to enlist science and technology to be ever more destructive in the "killing fields," or in this case, a "desert storm"?

North and South: Mutually Vulnerable

Our study of global civilization attests abundantly that societies everywhere have interacted and enriched one another. We can recall how the great riverine civilizations of North Africa

A Saudi Arabian government official examines a dead oil-coated cormorant. The massive oil slick that resulted from the war in the Persian Gulf is expected to devastate the Gulf's wildlife for years.

and Asia created mathematics, atronomy, irrigation systems, and a host of scientific discoveries and inventions which in time found their way to Europe. Europeans, utilizing inventions from China — printing, gunpowder, and the compass — embarked upon oceanic exploration and political expansion. From the resulting colonial empires came a cornucopia of raw resources which, with the advent of the Industrial Revolution, enabled the developed countries of the North to establish a global economy and to control the underdeveloped societies of the South.

Prosperous and complacent, the North's peoples have thought that they could insulate themselves from the South's poverty and problems; but such complacency is dangerously false because of developments that make the two segments of global society mutually vulnerable. We encounter this vulnerability in four areas.

1. Environmental. Scientists warn about the increasing pollution and heating of the earth's atmosphere, as well as the teratogenic consequences of weakening the ozone layer in the stratosphere. The burning of tropical forests in the South, notably in Brazil, and of fossil fuels, primarily in the North, might lead to a global temperature increase by one degree or more in 20 years. Such a trend, unless checked, will shift weather and rainfall patterns, global agriculture, and even raise sea levels (which could have disastrous consequences for, say, Florida and Bangladesh). The situation in the next century could become even more serious if China and India, whose combined population in A.D. 2000 will be double that of the North, continue to employ current technologies to increase energy production.

2. Economic. The economic gap between the North and South is huge. Some 70 percent of world income is produced and consumed by 15 percent of the world's population. Whereas the per capita annual income of developed market economies averges $14,500, in the 41 least developed countries the yearly average is under $300.[1] In Latin America, living standards are lower than they were in the 1970s, while those in Africa have fallen to the 1960s level. Each year in the South, 14 million children die before their fifth birthday, and another 150 million under five

This photograph of a shanty town slum in Brazil reveals the devastating poverty of the nonindustrial South. Scenes like this are common throughout Latin America.

are malnourished. The UN Economic Commission for Africa has described the 1980s as a "lost decade."

Much of the South's foreign exchange comes from the export of commodities — sugar, rubber, coffee, tea, cocoa — whose prices are controlled by the North's commodity exchanges, whereas manufactured goods come from the North at prices which it sets. For years developing countries have tried to work through the UN to make the global economy operate more equitably, and to this end call for a new international economic order. But without success. Meanwhile, in an effort to modernize and develop their economies, countries in the South have borrowed from the North well in excess of a trillion dollars. Although they receive considerable development assistance, this aid is less than the interest they have to pay on their loans. In 1988, interest amounted to $43 billion more than the amount of aid received: a situation described as "a perverse, unsustainable transfer of wealth from poor to rich."

But this imbalanced, inequitable relationship in the global economy has rendered the North vulnerable as well. Many developing economies are unable to pay back foreign loans, as U.S. and other banks have discovered. Take the case of Colombia. In 1989, the volume of its coffee exports increased by 14 percent, yet the country earned $192 million less because of falling prices (which were controlled elsewhere). Facing poverty conditions, many farmers in Colombia and other parts of the South shifted to raising illegal products—marijuana, cocaine, heroin—for which users in the North pay a high and ultimately tragic price.

3. *Demographic.* We face the following situation: the rich countries get richer, the poor countries get children—and lots of them. After millions of years of high birth and death rates, genus *Homo* reached the 1.7 billion mark in 1900. Half a century later, the figure rose to 2.5 billion, while after another 37 years there were 5 billion. Growth at this rate represents a net increase of some 9000 persons per hour, or 100 million a year for at least another 35 years. As of A.D. 2000, when it reaches 6.25 billion, global population will have almost quadrupled in one century, only to increase by billions more in the next. By A.D. 2000, too, more than three-fourths of the world's peoples will be in developing countries.

This population explosion is accompanied by yet another major phenomenon: the world is rapidly urbanizing. In 1960, only 3 of the world's 10 largest cities were in the South; in the year 2000, the South will have 45 of the 60 largest cities, 18 of them with more than 10 million inhabitants each. More than half—51.2 percent—of the world's population will be urban. And in the South, 35 percent will be under age 14. Lacking economic opportunity, all too many now find themselves abandoned, uneducated, and alienated from any societal norms. As many as a billion people may be living at or below "absolute poverty," which the United Nations defines as having caloric intake insufficient to supply energy to perform a day's work. Wretchedly poor people turn upon themselves and deplete their environment. More and more they seek relief by migrating, thereby placing immense pressures upon neighboring countries. As the South's population continues to expand, the North's rich countries will in turn be confronted by increasing pressures to relax immigration restrictions drastically, thereby risking new domestic tensions or conflicts.

4. *Political.* All of these problems exacerbate political instability in the South. But as the Gulf War proved, they can also draw the North into international political and military operations. Moreover, the industrialized countries have contributed to that instability. For example, the five permanent members of the UN Security Council which authorized force against Iraq had previously sold or transferred to that country and its neighbors hundreds of billions of dollars of sophisticated weapons, which those countries neither needed nor could afford. In a highly competitive international arms industry, the developing nations have been encouraged to forgo building their infrastructures, such as roads, schools, and irrigation systems, in favor of purchasing jet fighters, tanks, armored vehicles, and the gadgetry for operating them.

For millennia nations have armed in the attempt to be secure. But security is now taking on a new dimension. So long as people do not have equitable access to such necessities as food, health, education, and economic opportunity, no society can feel secure—as the apartheid regime in South Africa attests. This lack of equity is largely responsible for the South's political instability; and unless corrected, social turbulence could become an increasingly infectious phenomenon that will be immune to traditional, simplistic reliance on armed force.

The North and its political institutions are also being challenged. America's success in the Gulf War did nothing to address major problems at home: unemployment, homelessness, inner city crime, the drug crisis, polluted lakes and toxic waste dumps, and mounting governmental debt. All too often, minorities in the North feel that their governments treat them inequitably. In the United States, democratic institutions have existed for more than two centuries. Perhaps we need to take stock of their present health and effectiveness, as demonstrated, for example, by our presidential elections.

In 13 elections held between 1840 and 1900, 76.6 percent of entitled American voters went to the polls. Yet in our last 9 elections, the average percentage had fallen to 56.7. On three occasions in the nineteenth century, the turnout was above 80 percent; in two elections in this country, it was below 50 percent. In 1988, a bare half—50.2 percent—of voters exercised their right of ballot, with President Bush obtaining 54 percent of the votes cast. This means that while winning a large electoral vote, Bush had actually been endorsed by only 27.1 percent—scarcely more than a quarter—of all Americans entitled to vote.

This raises disturbing questions. Why has the percentage of voters exercising their ballot fallen so dramatically? Is the fall in voter participation due to apathy? Disillusionment? To a belief that one's vote does not count because "you can't change the system"? Can anything be done to reverse this trend? A feature of *Civilization Past & Present* throughout its many editions has been its continued interest in the genesis and prospects of democracy. We saw how Greek citizens participated directly in making political decisions, while Americans have made an invaluable contribution to representative government. can our democratic model be improved to make it as effective as its creators had envisaged?

"A New World Order": What It Might Involve

For over four decades following World War II, people everywhere had to live under the shadow of a nuclear holocaust while two superpowers were locked in a Cold War. But this ended with the demolition of the Berlin Wall, the collapse of Communist regimes in Eastern Europe, and desperate efforts by President Gorbachev and other Soviet leaders to restructure an overcentralized political structure and collapsing economy to prevent the fragmentation of the Soviet Union. A critical juncture in global affairs had been reached in the early 1990s. Would traditional international rivalries and power struggles continue to plague humanity, or had this crux presented a unique "window of opportunity," described by President Bush as "a new world order"? What might be required to bring about this novel dispensation?

1. Environmental Action. Our plant has been increasingly plundered and degraded throughout this century. In the late 1980s we heard warnings about global warming, accompanied by dire predictions of melting ice caps and ozone depletion.

Burned-out jungle vegetation in Jaru, Brazil. Among the disastrous effects of destruction of tropical rain forests, which absorb much of earth's carbon dioxide and produce much of its oxygen, are great climatic changes and the demise of thousands of species, some of which will be extinct before they are ever known.

Children display their environmental awareness and concern on Earth Day, April 21, 1990. Standing on the steps of the Museum of Natural History in New York, children hold a mile-long banner decorated with the handprints of children from across the country who have promised to honor the earth.

Satellites revealed for the first time the monumental scale of manmade fires destroying vast tracts of rainforest in the Amazon basin. These fires have created unprecedented amounts of carbon dioxide, a heat-trapping gas which warms the planet's atmosphere; they are wiping out the richest and most diverse region of natural life anywhere, together with a pharmaceutical treasury of incalculable value. These tragic events affect the future not just of Brazil but of every continent.[2] If we are to save our planet, concerted international remedial action is required—and there is no time to lose.

We need to begin by getting our priorities straight. We must acknowledge that while critical ecological problems may start in a given country, they do not respect national boundaries. Consequently, no government can logically claim that it has no responsibility to the world community for how its activities affect the environment. Further, as we saw in chapter 1 of *Civilization Past & Present*, our planet came into existence billions of years ago, while the biosphere with its multitude of faunal and floral species existed millions of years before genus *Homo* evolved. And the biosphere can continue to exist without us—arguably, it might be better off! But the converse does not hold: we cannot exist without the biosphere of which we are an integral part. In the final analysis, humankind's survival depends upon giving first priority to the continued well-being of our planet and its ecosystems. This means adopting a new attitude toward the environment. As far back as 1864, a remarkable American conservationist, George Perkins Marsh, warned that only a strong commitment to conserving the forest and other natural resources could save the nation from destroying its environmental endowment. "Man has too long forgotten that the earth was given to him for usufruct alone"—that is, to enjoy the benefits of someone else's property—"not for consumption, far less for profligate waste."[3]

The environment is not ours to destroy in the name of economic development, mistakenly called "progress." Instead, our role must be that of stewardship in order to preserve and enhance it for all species and future generations. An international conference on the global environment to be held in Brazil in 1992 will analyze ecological and related problems in depth, and set forth a strategy of action to save the planet's ecosystems. On the implementation of its recommendations could hinge humankind's survival.

2. Social and Economic Action. If global warming is the most critical environmental issue confronting us in the next century, the global population explosion might well be the most vexatious social problem. By 2025, the world's resources will have to support an estimated 8.2 billion people. But whereas the industrialized countries will have approached or reached zero growth, for a total of 1.4 billion, the Third World of the less-developed nations will have almost doubled its population to 6.8 billion.[4] In other words, the South will be then have almost five times as many people as the North. There can be no quick fix for getting the planet's population under control. In industrialized countries, rising incomes, urbanization, and improved education and social status for women have contributed to the decline in the birth rates. Developing countries will have to initiate mass programs aimed at health care, family planning, and eradicating urban slums and shanty towns.

Social instability and violence are bound to continue until the South's proliferating masses acquire new economic opportunities to allow escape from conditions of malnutrition, disease, ignorance, and ubiquitous poverty. That reality poses a fundamental challenge which *Our Common Future* (the report of the World Commission on Environment and Development) sums up in its term *sustainable development*. This means "development that meets the needs of the present without compromising the ability of future generations to meet their own needs."[5] It makes clear that societal development can only be based upon a viable global environment, which our excessive exploitation has been putting ever more at risk. *Our Common Future* remains committed to the concept of continued economic growth. However, environmental sustainability requires the industrialized nations to use less resource materials and become more energy efficient. The global economy must also ensure that developing countries grow fast enough to outpace their internal problems and so continue economic growth and diversification. At best, the planet's physical resources and its environment will be enormously taxed if such global development is to be possible. In the words of the report: "We do not pretend that the process is easy or straightforward. Painful choices have to be made. Thus, in the final analysis, sustainable development must rest on political will."[6]

3. Political Action. The Cold War reflected the realities of a division of political and military power within a bipolar world. The end of the cold War and the outcome of the Gulf War appeared to have created a unipolar world. But is this assessment accurate? Some international analysis suggests that the victor emerging from the end of the Cold War is Japan. While the United States devoted huge amounts of technological resources to producing stealth bombers and Patriot missiles, Japan concentrated on robotics and automobiles, in the process becoming the dominant player in the global economic game. Meanwhile, the consolidation of the European Community in 1992 will create a powerful economic and political rival to North America.

As we saw in chapter 17, the Thirty Years' War ended with the creation of the modern nation-state system. This system recognized the sovereignty of individual states, giving to each an unrestricted right to act as it wished within its own borders, and free to pursue its interests abroad. *Independence*, with all its patriotic and nationalistic trappings, is the key concept of this system. But over the past hundred years, commerce, migration, tourism, science, technology, communications, and of course environmental problems have increasingly transcended national boundaries. Today as never before, the key word to express the reality of our world is *interdependence*.

The volatile situation which resulted in the Gulf War raises a critical question: how can independent states pursuing national interests ensure security for an interdependent world? Involved is the issue of arms control. The world's annual arms bill amounts to about $1 trillion, yet in this century reliance on weapons has resulted in two global wars as well as conflicts in Korea, Vietnam, the Gulf, and scores of other hot spots. Surely we need effective arms control, restraints on the world trade in weapons, and regional security arrangements which can be enforced.

Given the instability of the current era, marked by long-standing national rivalries, intense ethnic and religious turmoil, poverty and deep economic inequities, and population pressures, no one nation, or even a coalition of a few nations, can assume the role of global policeman. The United Nations, which the United States took the lead in creating but for two decades largely ignored, will have to be given a stronger role in securing international peace. The permanent membership of the Security Council should be expanded to include, say, Japan and Germany, as well as large Third World countries such as India and Brazil. Its peacekeeping machinery can be further strengthened, with units deployed in dangerous areas, where possible anticipating a crisis. The UN charter has always possessed a strong enforcement capacity, largely ignored during the Cold War. The Charter envisaged the gradual conversion of the existing military setup into a worldwide system of collective security, and the Council's Military Staff Committee could be instructed to study how this conversion might best be brought about. "Such a system would be a giant step forward from the belated and improvised efforts to which the United Nations has so far been limited. . . . Governments, if they want the United Nations to be respected and taken seriously, will also have to respect its decisions, and make decisions that can if necessary be enforced. Such changes in attitude would be the best practical test of a commitment to a 'new world order.'"[7]

The Continuing Relevance of History

In a widely publicized article, "The End of History," Francis Fukuyama argues that "What we may be witnessing is not just the end of the Cold War, or the passing of a particular period of postwar history, but the end of history as such: that is, the end point of mankind's ideological evolution and the universalization of Western liberal democracy as the final form of human government."[8] Fukuyama's central thesis is that history, which he defines as the record of human conflict, is determined by ideas—by "ideology," which provides a framework for choice and action, with each historical epoch developing its own internal contradictions and conflicts; but this process is ending because Western democracy has produced a socioeconomic and political system that contains no irresolvable internal contradictions. Since we have reached a point where "theoretical truth is absolute, and could not be improved upon," the need for new ideologies ends, and consequently history as defined by Fukuyama ends.

We reject such a reading of the historical record, and therefore the author's thesis. Far from one ideology triumphing over all others, the world remains a hodgepodge of conflicting beliefs.

Moreover, we regard history as much more than the conflict of ideas; it is also the record of human accomplishments among all our diverse cultures and societies, and humanity's endless challenge to live in harmony with its planetary environment. Finally, Fukuyama has failed to understand that the most basic characteristic of Western democracy is its own contradictions. It is precisely because democracy derives from the point of view that absolute truths are unreachable that it is necessary to consult majorities on a continuing basis over what they consider to be right.

The Gulf War demonstrated dramatically a unique interplay of human and impersonal forces: the megalomania of Saddam Hussein; the critical importance of oil to industrialized, energy-hungry economies; long-standing religious bitterness; and geopolitical rivalries in the Middle East. History is neither at an end, nor is it irrelevant. Its practitioners have meticulously documented the forces responsible for destabilizing the Middle East, which for decades was a powder keg waiting to explode. Despite history's proved relevance, governments failed to profit from its portents and take appropriate preventive measures in time. To paraphrase George Santayana, our failure to learn from past mistakes resulted in our repeating their tragic consequences.

History's role can be likened to Janus, the two-faced Roman god. History enables us to view the past as past and, in turn, to visualize the past and present as prologue. Past and present conjoin to alert us to the need not only to engage in new forms of planning for the turbulent years ahead but also to rethink our traditional social goals and value systems. The historical evolution of humanity is open-ended. Far from being immutable, humanity's beliefs and goals are continuously undergoing change. The historical record provides us with what we shall continue to require: as long and accurate a perspective as possible from our global experience, in order to safeguard our planetary inheritance and improve the quality of life for humans everywhere.

This edition of *Civilization Past & Present* has appeared in 1992, the 500th anniversary of Columbus' discovery of the New World. That event had incalculable consequences—societal, biological, and environmental—for global history.

It meant the expansion of European colonization and Christianity into the Western Hemisphere; it also meant the destruction of many indigenous societies and cultures as a result of imperialism and exposure to Old World diseases to which the native inhabitants had no immunity. The environment of the New World was permanently altered. Hundreds of millions of acres of forest were destroyed by trans-Atlantic settlers who brought with them new species of plants and animals in their desire to recreate the ecological conditions they had known in Europe. These hemispheric developments exemplify the vast changes which have occurred in the past half millennium, the most momentous epoch in all the hundreds of thousands of years in which our species has inhabited the earth.

The year 1992 also marks the anniversary of fifty years of existence for *Civilization Past & Present*. The half century immediately past has been the most dynamic and dramatic era in the past 500 years. Far more people have lived during these fifty years than in any previous half century. More physical resources have been consumed, and more damage has been inflicted upon the earth's environment than ever before. But also more inventions and scientific breakthroughs have occurred. So we move toward the twenty-first century with a dual heritage: unprecedented perils, and unprecedented promises. What will happen? To repeat Gabor's thought: the future is ours to invent.

Viewed from this perspective, our epilogue becomes a prologue to a new state of human experience and societal attainment. Our Paleolithic ancestors lived in a largely undifferentiated planet. Their descendants have spiraled through stages of ever-increasing complexity until we inhabit today a single but highly differentiated and interrelated planet. One species as ever, yet occupying innumerable ecological and cultural niches within a shared global ecosystem. It is true that, as Winston Churchill suggested, history often seems to be "one damn thing after another." But it is also the story of one achievement after another. And now a new chapter in our irreversible history is being written. We began this epilogue by quoting from Eliot's *Four Quartets*. Let us cite it again: "In our ending is our beginning."

Notes

1. Ivan L. Head, President, International Development Research Centre, "A World Turned Outside Down," Agricultural Institute of Canada, 1991, pp. 1–30.
2. See *World Resources, 1990–1991: A Guide to the Global Environment*, A Report by the World Resources Institute, Oxford University Press, 1991. See also Pearce Wright, *Environmental Damage and Climatic Change*, Ditchley Foundation Report Number D88/4, 1988.
3. George Perkins Marsh, *Man and Nature*, 1864.
4. United Nations, Department of International Economic and Social Affairs, *World Population Prospects Estimates* (New York: United Nations, 1986).
5. World Commission on Environment and Development, *Our Common Future* ("Brundtland Report") (Oxford: University Press, 1987).
6. Ibid., p. 9.
7. Brian Urquhart, former Undersecretary General of the United Nations, "Learning from the Gulf," *The New York Review of Books*, March 7, 1991, pp. 34–37.
8. Francis Fukuyama, "The End of History?" *The National Interest;* see *The Toronto Globe and Mail*, December 1 and 28, 1989.

Chronological Tables

Credits

Index

Reference Maps

	Near East and Egypt	India and China
	Neolithic revolution c. 7000 Sumerian city-states emerge c. 3500	
3000 B.C.	Menes unites Egypt c. 3100 Old Sumerian period c. 2800–2370 Old Kingdom in Egypt c. 2700–2200 Akkadian Empire c. 2370–2150 Neo-Sumerian period c. 2113–2006 Middle Kingdom in Egypt c. 2050–1800	Indus valley civilization c. 2500–1500—capitals at Mohenjo-Daro and Harappa
2000 B.C.	Hittites enter Asia Minor c. 2000 Hammurabi rules lower Mesopotamia 1760 Hittites sack Babylon 1595 New Kingdom or Empire in Egypt c. 1570–1090	
1500 B.C.	Thutmose III c. 1490–1436—the "Napoleon of Egypt" Hittite Empire c. 1450–1200 Akhenaton c. 1369–1353 Era of small states 1200–700 Phoenician and Aramean traders; the alphabet Period of Decadence in Egypt c. 1090–332	Invasion of India by Aryans from Black and Caspian seas c. 1500 Early Vedic Age c. 1500–1000—beginning of three pillars of Indian society: autonomous village, caste system, joint family. *Vedas*—oldest Sanskrit literature Shang Dynasty 1700–1122—China's first civilization Chou Dynasty 1122–221—China's "classical age"—Mandate of Heaven promulgated
1000 B.C.	United Hebrew kingdom 1020–922: Saul, David, Solomon Divided Hebrew kingdom: Israel 922–721; Judah 922–586 The great Hebrew prophets 750–550 Assyrian Empire 745–612 Lydians and Medes Chaldean Empire 604–539: Nebuchadnezzar Zoroaster, early sixth century Persian Empire 550–330: Cyrus; Darius 522–486 End of the Babylonian Exile of the Jews 538	Later Vedic Age in India c. 1000–500—caste system becomes more complex: priest, warrior, merchant, serf, "untouchable" *Upanishads* 800–600—foundation of Hinduism
500 B.C.		Gautama Buddha 563?–483—founder of Buddhism Confucius 551–479—most famous and influential Chinese philosopher Chinese poetry collected in *Shih Ching*, or *Book of Odes* Two greatest Indian epics composed: the *Mahabharata* (including the *Bhagavad-Gita*) and the *Ramayama*
400 B.C.	Conquests of Alexander the Great 334–331	Lao-tzu and Taoism—aim: intuitive approach to life: *Tao te Ching* Mencius c. 372–289 links theory of Mandate of Heaven to democratic concept of the will of the people in government Alexander the Great crosses Indus valley 326 Chandragupta Maurya founds Mauryan Dynasty in India 322–c. 185
300 B.C.	Death of Alexander 323; Ptolemy seizes Egypt; Seleucus rules Asia	Ashoka 273–232—"the first great royal patron of Buddhism" Period of Warring States in China—Ch'in defeat Chou 221 China reunited under First Emperor, Shih Huang-ti 221–210 Han Dynasty of China 202 B.C.–A.D. 220
200 B.C.	Maccabean revolt wins independence for Judea 142	Tamil kingdoms—Hindu states, chief trading area with the West Mauryan Empire falls 185; Bactrian rule extends to India and Punjab; Graeco-Bactrian kingdom created Han Emperor Wu Ti 141–187
100 B.C.	Dead Sea Scrolls Pompey annexes Syria and Palestine 63 Herod the Great, king of Judea 37–4 Jesus Christ c. 4 B.C.–A.D. 30 Paul d. c. 65	Kushan Empire in India first century B.C.–A.D. 220 Kanishka, Kushan ruler c. 78–128, sponsors *Mahayana* ("Great Vehicle") school of Buddhism spreads north and east; *Hinayana* ("Lesser Vehicle") Buddhism spreads south and east
A.D. 100	Jews revolt from Rome 66–70—end of the ancient Hebrew state	

Greece	Rome	
		3000 B.C.
Aegean civilization c. 2000–1200 Achaean Greeks invade Peloponnesus c. 2000 Zenith of Minoan culture 1700–1450	Indo-Europeans invade Italian peninsula 2000–1000; Latins settle in lower Tiber valley (Latium)	**2000** B.C.
Mycenaean Age 1450–1200 Dorian invasion c. 1200		**1500** B.C.
	Etruscans settle on Italy's west coast	
Greek Dark Ages c. 1150–750 and Homeric Age		**1000** B.C.
	Carthage founded in North Africa by Phoenicians c. 800 Rome founded 753 Greeks colonize southern Italy and Sicily Etruscans conquer Rome c. 600 Roman Republic established 509	
Hellenic Age c. 750–338 Age of Oligarchy c. 750–500: Hesiod; colonization Athens—growth of democracy: Solon 594, Pisistratus 560, Cleisthenes 508 Sparta—militaristic totalitarian state, Spartan League	Plebeians vs. patricians 509–287—tribunes and *Concilium Plebis*	
Persian Wars 490–479: Marathon, Thermopylae Delian League 478 and Athenian imperialism Athens' Golden Age under Pericles 461–429 Peloponnesian War 431–404—Athens vs. Sparta	Laws of the Twelve Tables c. 450	**500** B.C.
Philip II of Macedonia conquers Greece 338 Hellenic culture: Thales, Pythagoras, Democritus, Hippocrates, Socrates, Plato, Aristotle, Herodotus, Thucydides, Sappho, Aeschylus, Sophocles, Euripides, Aristophanes, Phidias, Praxiteles Alexander the Great conquers Persia 331 Hellenistic Age 323–31—Ptolemaic Egypt, Seleucid Asia, Macedonia; Greek federal leagues	Roman expansion in Italy 338–270: Latins, Etruscans, Samnites, Greeks	**400** B.C.
Hellenistic culture: Epicurus, Zeno, Eratosthenes, Aristarchus, Euclid, Archimedes, Hipparchus, Polybius, Theocritus	Roman expansion in western Mediterranean 270–146—Punic wars: Hannibal	**300** B.C.
	Roman expansion in eastern Mediterranean 200–133—wars with Macedonia and the Seleucids; Macedon and Greece annexed 146; first Roman province in Asia 133 Reform movement of the Gracchi 133–121	**200** B.C.
	Marius vs. Sulla 88–82: dictatorship of Sulla 82–79 Pompey vs. Caesar 49–46: dictatorship of Julius Caesar 46–44 Antony vs. Octavian 32–30 Augustus' reconstruction—the Principate 30 B.C.–A.D. 180	**100** B.C.
	Golden Age of literature: Cicero, Catullus, Lucretius, Virgil, Horace	**A.D. 100**

	Europe	
100 B.C.		
A.D. 1		
100	End of the *Pax Romana* 180–285—civil war, economic decline, invasions Reconstruction by Diocletian 285–305—the Dominate	
300	Constantine 306–337—Edict of Milan 313, Council of Nicaea 325, founding of Constantinople 330 Ulfilas d. 383, missionary to Goths	Theodosius divides Roman Empire 395 Battle of Adrianople 378—German invasions begin
400	Alaric sacks Rome 410 Attila crosses the Rhine—battle near Troyes 451 Pope Leo the Great 440–461	Odovacar deposes last Western emperor 476 Clovis 481–511 unites Franks and rules Gaul
500	Theodoric 493–526 rules Italy; Cassiodorus and Boethius St. Benedict establishes Benedictine Order 529	Lombards invade Italy 568 Merovingian decline sixth–seventh centuries
600	Pope Gregory the Great 590–604 Isidore of Seville d. 636—the *Etymologies*	
700	Charles Martel 714–741 rules the Franks; defeats Muslims at Tours 732 The Venerable Bede d. 735 St. Boniface d. 755, "apostle to the Germans" Pepin the Short 741–768 ends rule of Merovingian kings; Donation of Pepin to pope Charlemagne 768–814 revives Roman Empire in the West 800; fosters Carolingian Renaissance	
800	Treaty of Verdun divides Carolingian Empire into West Frankland, East Frankland, and Lorraine 843 Magyar, Muslim, and Viking invasions terrorize Europe ninth–tenth centuries Alfred the Great 871–899 establishes strong Anglo-Saxon kingdom in England Kievan Russia emerges	
900	Feudalism well established in France c. 900 Henry I, the Fowler 919–936, founds Saxon Dynasty in Germany Otto I, the Great 936–973—alliance of crown and church; routs Magyars at battle of Lechfeld 955; crowned emperor by pope 962 Ethelred the Unready 978–1016—power of English government lags; invasion by Canute, Viking king Hugh Capet 987 founds Capetian Dynasty in France	

1000	Peace and Truce of God eleventh century
	Normans arrive in Italy 1016
	Yaroslav the Wise 1019–1054—peak of Kievan Russia;
	  Byzantine influences in art and literature
	Salian House succeeds Saxon kings in Germany 1024
	College of Cardinals formed to elect pope 1059
	Pope Gregory VII 1073–1085 supports Cluniac religious
	  reform; Investiture struggle
		Norman Conquest of England 1066
		Fall of Bari to Normans 1071—last Byzantine
		  stronghold in Italy
		Reconquista gains Toledo from Muslims 1085
		First Crusade—Jerusalem captured; Latin kingdom of
		  Jerusalem established 1099

1100	Renaissance of twelfth century; revival of trade and
	  towns
	Welf-Hohenstaufen rivalry 1106–1152 wrecks structure
	  for strong German state
	Louis the Fat 1108—first strong Capetian ruler in France
	Concordat of Worms 1122
	Second Crusade 1147
	Frederick Barbarossa 1152–1190 centralizes feudal
	  monarchy; struggle with popes and Lombard League
		Henry II 1154–1189 reforms English judicial system;
		  Thomas à Becket
		St. Dominic 1170–1221; St. Francis of Assisi 1182?–1226
		Philip II Augustus 1180–1223 extends royal power
		Third Crusade, "Crusade of Kings," 1189
		Frederick II 1194–1250—end of medieval German
		  Empire

1200	Pope Innocent III 1198–1216—zenith of medieval papacy Fourth Crusade 1202–1204—crusaders sack Constantinople King John of England signs Magna Carta 1215 St. Thomas Aquinas 1225?–1274 reconciles faith and reason in *Summa Theologica;* zenith of scholasticism Louis IX 1226–1270 brings dignity to French crown Edward I 1272–1307—rise of Parliament in England; power of nobility curtailed Philip IV, the Fair 1285–1314, centralizes French Government; humiliates Pope Boniface VIII Acre, last Christian stronghold in Holy Land, conquered by Muslims 1291	
1300	Dante d. 1321 Hundred Years' War between France and England 1337–1453	
1400	Chaucer d. 1400	

Near East and Byzantine Empire	Far East	
	Rule by Yamato clan in Japan	**100 B.C.**
	Kanishka ruler in India c. 78–128	**A.D. 1**
Christian missionaries	Expansion of Indian culture into Southeast Asia begins Fall of Han Dynasty in China 220	**100**
Eastern church Fathers: Clement of Alexandria Council of Nicaea 325—Nicene Creed Constantine established New Rome (Constantinople) 330	Buddhism gains popularity in China third century Chandra Gupta I founds Gupta Dynasty in India 320 Chandra Gupta II c. 380–c. 413—zenith of Gupta power	**300**
	Kalidasa c. 400–455, India's greatest poet and dramatist of Gupta age: *Shakuntala*	**400**
Justinian 527–565—reconquests; *Corpus Juris Civilis;* Hagia Sophia	Buddhism enters Japan sixth century Sui Dynasty in China 589–618	**500**
Muhammad 570–632—the Hijra 622 Heraclius 610–641—regains Syria, Palestine, Egypt	Harsha 606–647 rules northern India T'ang Dynasty founded 618	**600**
Umayyad Dynasty 661–750—expands in North Africa, Tur- kestan, Indus valley, Spain; defeated by Franks at Tours 732 Leo III 717–741 repulses Muslims 718; administrative and military reforms	T'ang poets: Li Po and Tu Fu Japanese imperial court established at Nara 710 New Japanese imperial court at Heian-kyo (Kyoto) 794 Heian period in Japan 794–1185	**700**
Abbasid Dynasty 750–1258—end of Arab predominance; Cyril and Methodius—missionaries to the Slavs	*Diamond Sutra* printed 868	**800**
Golden age of Muslim learning 900–1100—advances in medicine, mathematics, literature, philosophy, architec- ture, decorative arts; al-Razi, Avicenna, Alhazen, al- Khwarizmi, Omar Khayyám, Averroës, ibn-Khaldun	T'ang Dynasty falls 906 Expansion of Indian culture into Southern Asia ends tenth century Sung Dynasty founded in China 960	**900**
Basil II 976–1025 defeats Bulgars Final separation of the churches 1054 Seljuk Turks seize Persia and Iraq, conquer Bagdad 1055 Battle of Manzikert 1071—loss of Asia Minor to Seljuks	Vietnam achieves independence from China Wang An-shih 1021–1086, Chinese Socialist reformer Muslims invade India; Turks and Afghans annex Punjab 1022	**1000**
Kingdom of Jerusalem 1099–1291 and crusader states Saladin regains Jerusalem 1187	Angkor Wat built c. 1100 China divided between empires of Sung (south) and Chin (north) 1127 Yoritomo 1147–1199 rules Japan as shogun from Kamakura 1185 Temujin 1162–1227 unites Mongols; recognized as "Genghis Khan" 1206	**1100**
Fourth Crusade 1202–1204—Constantinople sacked Latin Empire 1204–1261 Fall of Abbasid Dynasty—Baghdad conquered by Mongols under Hulagu Khan 1258 *Michael Palaeologus regains Constantinople 1261*	Peak of Khmer Empire in Southeast Asia Delhi Sultanate established 1206; Indian culture divided into Hindu and Muslim Mongols conquer China, portions of Middle East and Southeast Asia 1241–1279; *Pax Tatarica* Kublai Khan 1260–1294 proclaims himself founder of Yuan Dynasty of China Marco Polo arrives at Kublai Khan's court c. 1275 Japan stops Mongol invasion 1281	**1200**
Ottoman Turks invade Europe 1356 Constantinople falls to Ottoman Turks 1453	Ashikaga shogunate replaces Kamakura 1336 Ming Dynasty established in China 1368	**1300**
		1400

	Europe
100 900	
1000	
1100	
1200	Mongols conquer Kiev 1240 Transitional period in Italian art c. 1250–c. 1400; Giotto d. 1336 Pope Boniface VIII 1294–1303 feuds with Philip IV
1300	Avignon papacy 1305–1377; Babylonian Captivity of the church Hundred Years' War 1337–1453 Black Death 1348 Golden Bull 1356 Classical revival, Humanism; Petrarch, Boccaccio Great Schism 1378–1417 John Wycliffe d. 1384 Grand Prince of Moscow defeats Mongols at Kulikovo 1380
1400	*Quattrocento* of Italian Renaissance; early Renaissance masters in Italy—Brunelleschi, Ghiberti, Donatello, Masaccio, Mantegana, Botticelli, Verrocchio Council of Constance 1414 Medici family rules Florence 1434–1494 Commercial Revolution 1450–1650 Gutenberg uses movable type to print Bible 1454 Wars of the Roses 1455–1485 Louis XI (the "universal spider") of France 1461–1483 Ivan III, the Great, of Russia 1462–1505 Ferdinand and Isabella begin joint rule in Spain 1479 Henry VII 1485–1509 founds Tudor Dynasty in England *Reconquista* ends with conquest of Granada 1492; unification of Spain completed Maximilian I 1493–1519, Holy Roman Emperor Italian wars 1494–1513 begin
1500	Northern Renaissance sixteenth century—Erasmus, More, Rabelais, von Hutten, Montaigne, van Eyck, Dürer, Holbein, Brueghel, Bosch High Renaissance in Italy c. 1500–1530—Bramante, Michelangelo, da Vinci, Raphael, Giorgione, Titian, Castiglione, Cellini Henry VIII of England 1509–1547; founds Anglican church 1534 Luther nails ninety-five theses 1517; excommunicated, declared heretic at Diet of Worms 1521 Charles V elected Holy Roman emperor 1519 Suleiman rules Turks 1520–1566 Machiavelli, *The Prince* 1532 Loyola establishes Jesuit order 1534 John Calvin publishes *Institutes of the Christian Religion* 1536 Council of Trent 1545–1563 Ivan IV, the Terrible, of Russia 1547–1584
1550	Mary Tudor reinstates Catholicism in England 1553–1558 Peace of Augsburg 1555 Philip II of Spain 1556–1598 Elizabeth I of England 1558–1603 Massacre of St. Bartholomew's Eve 1572 Shakespeare 1564–1616 Battle of Lepanto 1571 Dutch United Provinces declare independence 1581 Time of Trouble in Russia 1584–1613 Spanish Armada 1588 Henry IV 1589–1610 founds Bourbon Dynasty in France Edict of Nantes 1598
1600	James I 1603–1625 founds Stuart Dynasty in England Bank of Amsterdam founded 1609 Michael Romanov founds Romanov Dynasty in Russia 1613 Thirty Years' War 1618–1648—Peace of Westphalia 1648

Asia	Americas and Africa	
	Classical Period of Mesoamerican civilization 150–900	**100**
	Postclassical period of Mesoamerican civilization 900–1492	**900**
	Peak of development in Ghana	**1000**
	Incas settle Cuzco valley in Andes eleventh century	
		1100
	Fall of Ghana state 1203	**1200**
	Zenith of Great Zimbabwe 1250–1450	
	Peak of Swahili civilization 1200–1500	
	Aztec confederacy in Mexico fourteenth century	**1300**
	Reign of Mansa Musa of Mali 1312–1337	
Chinese naval expeditions to India, Near East, Africa fifteenth century		**1400**
Early Ming policy encourages foreign trade	Portuguese navigate West African coast	
Muslim commercial center at Malacca founded 1400	Atlantic slave trade begins fifteenth century	
	Reign of Montezuma I 1440–1468 of Aztec Empire	
	Reign of Zara Yakob of Ethiopia 1434–1468	
	Songhai Empire in the African Sudan c. 1468–1590	
	Zenith of Inca Empire 1438–1532	
	Arrival of Portuguese in Benin c. 1440	
	Diaz rounds Cape of Good Hope 1488	
	Columbus discovers New World 1492	
	Bull of Demarcation 1493; Treaty of Tordesillas 1494	
	North America claimed by Cabot for England 1497–1498	
	Da Gama reaches India 1498	
	Cabral sights east coast of Brazil	
Portuguese trade monopoly in Far East sixteenth century	Balboa sights Pacific Ocean 1513	**1500**
Malacca falls to Portuguese 1511	Cortés arrives in Mexico 1519; Aztec Empire falls 1521	
Peak of Ottoman power under Suleiman the Magnificent 1520–1566	Magellan rounds South America 1520	
	Pizarro reaches Peru 1531, conquers Incas	
Babur (the Tiger) defeats Delhi sultanate and Rajput Confederacy 1525–1527; founds Mughul Empire in India	Cartier explores St. Lawrence River for France 1534	
Waning of Ming power and effectiveness		
Portuguese traders in Japan		
Momoyama period in Japanese art		
Akbar 1556–1605 expands Mughul Empire; promotes religious tolerance	Bartolomé de las Casas 1474–1566 argues for Indian rights	**1550**
Portuguese granted right to trade with Chinese at Macao 1557	Saint Augustine, first colony in North America, founded 1565	
Spanish use Philippines as trading stop c. 1565	Coronado, de Sota explore North America	
Abbas the Great of Persia 1587–1629	Reignot Mai Idris Alooma of Kanem-Bornu 1580–1617	
Christian missionaries in Japan		
Hideyoshi 1536–1598 makes war against China and Korea, persecutes Christians in Japan		
Dutch East India Company formed 1602	Jamestown founded 1607; Champlain founds Quebec 1608	**1600**
English East India Company chartered 1609	Henry Hudson establishes Dutch claims in North America	
Tokugawa shogunate in Japan begins 1603		
Foundations for Dutch East Indies laid by Coen 1618	Plymouth founded 1620	
Shah Jahan 1628–1658; height of Mughul Empire in India	Dutch West India Company supplants Portuguese in West Africa, takes over Atlantic slave trade 1630	
Japan expels all Europeans 1637	Montreal established 1642	
Dutch expel Portuguese from Moluccas 1641, establish trade monopoly in Indonesia	Dutch settlement at Cape Town 1651	
Manchus establish Ch'ing Dynasty 1644	La Salle claims Louisiana for France 1683	

	Politics	Science and Technology, Thought and Art	
1500		Revolution in astronomy—Copernicus, *Concerning the Revolutions of Heavenly Spheres*, 1543; Brahe, Kepler, Galileo; heliocentric theory	**1500**
1600	James I 1603–1625 and Charles I 1625–1649 of England antagonize Parliament; Petition of Right 1628 Richelieu becomes real power behind French throne 1624–1642 Frederick William, the Great Elector 1640–1688, makes Brandenburg the most important Protestant state in Germany English Civil War 1642–1648; Charles I executed 1649; Oliver Cromwell takes control of government Louis XIV 1643–1715 transforms French state into absolute monarchy Colbert develops French mercantilist system—Colbertism; de Louvois revolutionizes French army House of Orange controls political regime in Holland c. 1640	William Gilbert describes magnetic force 1600 Bacon champions inductive method of philosophic inquiry; *Novum Organum*, 1620 Descartes proposes deductive method of philosophic inquiry; *Discource on Method*, 1627 Robert Boyle, father of modern chemistry, conceives crude atomic theory Neoclassical dramatists in France—Corneille, Racine, Molière Inventions of seventeenth century—telescope, microscope, thermometer, pendulum clock, micrometer, barometer, air pump Baroque style in art—Rubens, Velázquez, Vermeer, Hals, Rembrandt, Bernini; opera originates in Italy William Harvey describes human circulatory system	**1600**
1650	Restoration of Stuart monarchy in England 1660; Charles II 1660–1685 and James II 1685–1688 attempt to establish absolutist rule in England Leopold I 1657–1705 strengthens Austrian monarchy Peter the Great 1682–1725, absolutist tsar of Russia, attempts to Westernize realm Louis XIV revokes Edict of Nantes 1685 Glorious Revolution 1688 overthrows James II; William of Orange invited to rule England; William and Mary become joint sovereigns of England Aurangzeb 1658–1707 extends Mughul Empire over entire Indian subcontinent 1690	Hobbes of England (*Leviathan*, 1651) and Bossuet of France (*Politics Drawn from Scripture*) defend absolutism Scientific societies founded: Royal Society of London 1662; French Academy of Science 1664 Spinoza publicizes pantheistic philosophy (*Ethics*, 1663) Newton expounds theory of gravitation (Principia, 1687) Locke (*Essay Concerning Human Understanding*, 1690) advances doctrine of popular sovereignty as argument against absolutism; spreads ideas of Enlightenment	**1650**
1700	War of the Spanish Succession 1701–1713; Treaty of Utrecht 1713 Great Northern War 1709–1721; Charles XII of Sweden defeated by Peter the Great and allies Frederick William I of Prussia 1713–1740 creates powerful Prussian state George I 1714–1727 initiates Hanoverian Dynasty in England Robert Walpole becomes first prime minister of England 1721–1742 War of Jenkins' Ear 1739–1745; Peace of Aix-la-Chapelle 1745 Persian invaders sack Delhi 1739 Frederick II, the Great 1740–1786, makes Prussia important power in European politics	"Age of Reason" (eighteenth century); rococo style in art—Watteau, Boucher, Fragonard, Gainsborough, Reynolds Novel appears: Defoe (*Robinson Crusoe*, 1719); Swift (*Gulliver's Travels*, 1726); Richardson (*Pamela*, 1740–1741); Fielding (*Tom Jones*, 1749) Pope, foremost neoclassical English poet (*An Essay on Man*, 1733) Nonconformists in art: Hogarth (*The Rake's Progress*, 1735); Goya (*The Disasters of War*, 1810) Tull, Townshend, Bakewell develop improvements in agriculture Industrial Revolution begins in Britain Inventions revolutionize textile industry: flying shuttle, 1733; spinning jenny, 1764; water frame, 1769; spinning mule, 1779; power loom, 1785; cotton gin, 1793 Further experiments with electricity: Leyden Jar 1745; Franklin's experiment with kite 1752 Intellectual assault on absolutism led by *philosophes* Montesquieu (*The Spirit of Laws*, 1748), Rousseau (*Social Contract*, 1762)	**1700**

	Politics	Science and Technology, Thought and Art	
1750	Diplomatic revolution aligns Austria, Russia, France against England and Prussia Seven Years' War (in America, the French and Indian War) 1756–1763; Peace of Paris 1763 Catherine the Great 1762–1796 makes Russia a major European power George III of England 1770–1782 secures control of Parliament Poland partitioned in three stages among Russia, Prussia, and Austria 1772–1795 American Revolution 1775–1783; Declaration of Independence 1776 American Articles of Confederation 1781; Constitutional Convention 1787; U.S. Constitution adopted 1789; Washington first president of U.S. Pitt the Younger becomes prime minister 1783; restores cabinet government First phase of French Revolution 1789–1791; storming of Bastille; Declaration of the Rights of Man Second phase of French Revolution; Jacobin movement; Marat, Danton, Robespierre Louis XVI executed 1793; Reign of Terror begins under Robespierre 1793; Robespierre executed 1794; Directory governs France 1795–1799 Napoleon establishes Consulate 1799	Reaction on the Continent against baroque and rococo styles of architecture manifested in neoclassical style c. 1750 Formalism in music: Handel, Bach, Mozart, Haydn Voltaire, prince of *philosophes*, publishes *Candide* 1759; Diderot spreads doctrines of rationalism and Deism, edits *Encyclopédie* Great works of social science: Rousseau (*Emile*, 1762); Beccaria (*Essay on Crimes and Punishment*, 1764); Gibbon (*Decline and Fall of the Roman Empire*, 1776–1788); Condorcet (*Progress of the Human Mind*, 1794) Modern canal building in Britain begins 1759 Priestly isolates ammonia; discovers oxygen 1774; produces carbon monoxide gas 1799 Adam Smith (*An Inquiry into the Nature and Causes of the Wealth of Nations*, 1776) defends laissez-faire economics Lavoisier formulates law of the conservation of matter Kant (*Critique of Pure Reason*, 1781) sets forth doctrine of philosophic idealism James Watt's steam engine put to commercial use 1785 Hutton's *Theory of the Earth*, 1795, pioneer work in geology	**1750**
1800	Napoleon proclaims himself emperor 1804; is defeated by British at Trafalgar; defeats Prussia 1805–1806; invasion of Russia fails 1812 British and allies defeat Napoleon at Leipzig 1813; Napoleon exiled to Elba 1814; returns to France and is defeated by Britain and Prussia at Waterloo; exiled to St. Helena 1815 Revolutions in Latin America—Miranda fails in attempt to establish independence of Venezuela; Simon Bolívar, José de San Martin win independence for Spanish colonies in South America; Augustin de Iturbide proclaims independence of Mexico; Pedro crowned emperor of independent Brazil 1822 Congress of Vienna 1814–1815; Metternich, Talleyrand, Alexander I, Lord Castlereagh; Quadruple Alliance formed—Austria, Prussia, Russia, Britain Louis XVIII of France establishes constitutional monarchy 1814–1824 Workers' rebellions in Britain 1816, 1819 Quintuple Alliance 1818—Austria, Russia, Prussia, Britain, France Carlsbad Decrees temporarily discourge German nationalist youth movement 1819	Romantic movement in art: preromantic writers—Rousseau, Schiller, Goethe Conservatives advocate return to old order—de Maistre, Karamzin, Donoso-Cortés Romantic writers: Wordsworth, Coleridge, Shelley, Byron, Keats, Scott Liberals: Bentham advocates utilitarianism; Mill, early proponent of welfare state Romantic painters: Delacroix, Constable, Turner Romanticism in music: Beethoven, Brahms, Tschaikovsky, Chopin, operas by Wagner and Verdi Romantic nationalist writers: Hugo, Pushkin, Hegel Michelet, Macauley, Bancroft write national histories McAdam develops new method of road construction 1815 Industrial Revolution spreads to Continent 1815–1870 Utopian socialists Saint-Simon, Fourier, Owen propose cooperative societies early 1800s	**1800**

	Politics	Science and Technology, Thought and Art	
1820	Revolutions in Spain and Italy 1820–1821 Greeks rise against Turkish rule 1821–1827; Greek independence attained at Treaty of Andrianople 1829 Charles x, exponent of divine right, ascends French throne 1824 Tsar Nicholas I crushes Decembrist Revolt 1825; imposes reactionary repressive system Catholic Emancipation Act in Britain 1829	Philhellenic movement in Britain 1820s	1820
1830	Revolutions of 1830: July Revolution in Paris enthrones Louis Philippe; Belgians throw off Dutch rule; unsuccessful revolt in Poland Mazzini initiates Italian *Risorgimento* c. 1830 Whigs end reactionary Tory rule in Britain 1830; Reform Bill 1832; slavery abolished 1833 Treaty of Unikar Skelessi 1833 makes Turkey protectorate of Russia Victoria ascends British throne 1837 Chartist movement for reform in Britain fails 1839, 1842, 1848	Gothic revival in architecture c. 1830 Lyell's *Principles of Geology* 1830–1833 Faraday's electric dynamo 1831 *Zollverein* stimulates industry in German states	1830
1840	Famine devastates Ireland 1845 Corn Laws repealed 1846 Revolutions of 1848: France, Germany, Italy, Austria France—Second Republic, "June Days" insurrection crushed, Louis Napoleon becomes president Germany—Frederick William IV of Prussia grants constitutional government, Frankfort Assembly fails to establish new union Italy—revolution put down by Austria Austria—nationalist revolutions fail	First Law of thermodynamics stated 1847 Marx and Engels publish *Communist Manifesto* 1848 Victorian writers, poets: Thackeray, Tennyson, Browning Proudhon found anarchism Comte initiates science of sociology	1840
1850	Olmutz conference restores German Confederation, sets up Austria as major German power 1850 Cavour becomes prime minister of Italy 1852 Louis Napoleon proclaims himself Emperor Napoleon III 1852 Russia invades Turkey 1853; Crimean War 1854–1856; Russians defeated at Sevastopol; Treaty of Paris 1856 stops Russian advance in Ottoman Empire Italy united under Cavour; Austro-Italian War 1859; first Italian parliament 1861; Rome capital of united Italy 1871 Tsar Alexander II issues Emancipation Proclamation 1861; introduces reforms 1864–1874	Realist mvoement in literature: Balzac, Flaubert, Baudelaire, Dickens, Tolstoy, Dostoevski, Hardy, James, Clemens Social criticism: Arnold, Carlyle, Ruskin Realism in painting: Courbet, Daumier Bessemer improves smelting, refining of iron ore 1850s Great Exhibition, Crystal Palace, London 1851 Darwin publishes *Origin of Species* 1859 Lister introduces antiseptic surgical practices c. 1860 First International fails; anarchists under Bakunin oppose Marxist majority 1864–1873	1850
1860	Bismarck appointed Prussian prime minister 1862; advocates policy of *Realpolitik* Policy of repression reimposed by Alexander II 1863 Germany unified under Bismarck; Prussia defeats Denmark 1864, Austria 1866; wins Franco-Prussian War 1870–1871 *Ausgleich* establishes Dual Monarchy of Austria-Hungary 1867 Gladstone and Disraeli alternate as British prime minister 1867–1880; Reform Bill of 1867 extends vote; Gladstone's Glorious Ministry 1868–1874	International Telegraph Union formed 1865 Mendel explains laws of heredity 1866 Marx' scientific socialism expounded in *Das Kapital* 1867–1894 French impressionist painters: Monet, Degas, Renoir; sculptor: Rodin Spencer applies Darwin's theory to social, political, economic activities; Social Darwinism	1860

Politics	Science and Technology, Thought and Art
1870 Third Republic proclaimed in France 1870 German Second Reich proclaimed: William of Prussia emperor of united Germany Revolutionary Paris Commune suppressed 1871 Bismarck begins *Kulturkampf* 1872; forms Three Emperors' League with Russia and Austria-Hungary 1873; Triple Alliance with Austria and Italy 1882 Social Democratic party formed in Germany 1875; demands social legislation; wins popular support Turkey crushes Bosnian, Bulgarian revolts; defeats Serbia, Montenegro 1875 Russia defeats Turkey 1877–1878; Treaty of San Stefano 1878 Abdul Hamid II attempts to impose absolute rule over Ottoman Empire 1877 Congress of Berlin 1878	Mendeleev classifies all known elements in periodic table 1869 **1870** Suez Canal 1869 Darwin publishes *Descent of Man* 1871 Clerk-Maxwell advances electromagnetic theory of light 1873 Universal Postal Union set up 1875 Weismann distinguishes somatic and germ cells
1880 Alexander II assassinated 1881; Alexander III revives system of repression; attempts policy of Russification 1881–1884 Three Emperors' League collapses 1887; Bismarck negotiates Reinsurance Treaty with Russia 1887 Spirit of internationalism and peace—annual Universal Peace Congresses begin 1889; Hague Conference 1899 establishes Hague Tribunal	Railroads link major markets in Britain, U.S. 1880 **1880** Naturalism in literature: Zola (*Nana*, 1880) Pasteur and Koch prove germ theory of disease 1881 Fabian Society organized in Britain 1883 Postimpressionist painters: Cézanne, van Gogh Realist dramatists: Ibsen, Chekhov, Shaw Symbolist movement: Mallarmé, Verlaine Hertz proves existence of electromagnetic waves 1886 Second International founded 1889; attracts socialists from many countries Pope Leo XIII endorses Christian democracy (*Rerum Novarum*, 1891)
1890 Emperor William II dismisses Bismarck 1890; allows Reinsurance Treaty to lapse; France forms Dual Alliance with Russia 1894 Dreyfus case 1894–1906 Nicholas II becomes tsar of Russia 1894 Herzl introduces Zionism; first Zionist congress meets 1897	Freud pioneers psychoanalytic theory 1890s **1890** Syndicalists emerge in France 1890s Gobineau advances theory of "scientific racism" First moving picture performance, Paris 1895 X rays discovered 1895 Baron de Coubertin revives Olympic games 1896 Electron theory formulated c. 1897 Pierre and Marie Curie discover radium 1898
1900 Labour party formed in Britain 1900: advocates social legislation Britain forms alliance with Japan 1902; proclaims Entente Cordiale with France 1904; establishes Triple Entente with Russia and France 1907 Social Democrats divide into moderate Mensheviks and radical Bolsheviks undere Lenin 1903; massacre of Bloody Sunday 1905; October Manifesto calls national Duma 1905 Anticlerical movement in France severs ties between church and state 1904–1905 Diplomatic crises (Morocco, Balkans) 1905–1914 Young Turks rebel 1908 Parliament Bill of 1911 curtails power of House of Lords Archduke Francis Ferdinand of Austria assassinated 1914; World War I begins	James develops philosophy of pragmatism from Darwinian theory **1900** Planck formulates quantum theory 1900 Pavlov advances study of conditioned reflexes 1900 First Nobel Prizes awarded 1901 Music: Richard Strauss (post-Wagnerian); Debussy (impressionism); Stravinski (polytonality); Schönberg (twelve-tone system) Architecture: Sullivan, Wright, Gropius, steel-skeleton skyscraper Expressionist (Matisse) and cubist (Picasso) movements in painting Trans-Siberian Railroad reaches Pacific 1903 Einstein proposes special theory of relativity 1905; general theory 1915 Ford's Model T 1909 Rutherford's theory of positively charged atomic nucleus 1911

	United States and Latin America	British Dominions
1750	American Revolution 1775–1783 U.S. Constitution adopted 1789	Peace of Paris 1763; Canada becomes British possession Canada's formative period 1763–1867; Quebec Act 1774 guarantees French custom and Catholicism in Canada; division into Upper and Lower Canada 1791 Sydney, first English colony in Australia, established 1788
1800	Westward expansion of U.S. 1800–1860; Louisiana Purchase 1803; annexation of Texas 1845 War of 1812—U.S. vs. Britain and Canada 1812–1814 Missouri Compromise establishes boundaries of slave territory in U.S. 1820 Brazil achieves independence 1822 Monroe Doctrine 1823 Andrew Jackson president 1829–1837 New nations of Latin America—Bolivia, Peru, Columbia, Venezuela, Ecuador, Paraguay, Uruguay—experience revolutions, insurrections, dictatorships Chile controlled by conservative oligarchy 1830 Central American states—Guatemala, San Salvador, Honduras, Nicaragua, Costa Rica—assert independence c. 1840 Pedro II brings political liberty and economic and cultural progress to Brazil 1840–1899 U.S. signs first treaty with China 1844 U.S.-Mexican War 1846–1848; Mexico cedes California, Texas, territory in Southwest to U.S.	British government assumes protection of New Zealand, 1840
1850	Rapid industrial expansion in U.S. 1850–1880 Perry visits Japan 1853 Mexican dictator Santa Anna overthrown 1855; Juarez institutes anticlerical *Reforma*; civil war ensues U.S. Civil War 1861–1865; Union preserved, slavery abolished Argentina becomes united republic 1862 Napoleon III invades Mexico, establishes brief empire under Maximilian 1863–1867 Reconstruction period in U.S. 1865–1877 U.S. occupies Midway Islands 1867 U.S. buys Alaska from Russia 1867	Australian colonies achieve near self-government c.1850; secret ballot in Australia 1855 Province of Canada form federal union under British North America Act; Canada becomes Confederation 1867
1870	Porfirio Díaz, dictator, brings order without liberty to Mexico 1877–1880, 1884–1911 U.S. Interstate Commerce Act 1887 initiates expansion of government regulation of industry Slavery ends in Brazil 1888 First Pan-American Conference 1889 Ten years of civil war in Brazil 1889–1899 follows abdication of Pedro II Progressive movement in U.S. initiates economic reform c. 1890–1914 "Dollar diplomacy"—U.S. exercises indirect controls in Latin America to protect investments 1890–1920s Spanish-American War 1898; U.S. gains Philippines, Guam, Puerto Rico; Cuba becomes protectorate 1901 U.S. annexes Hawaii 1898	Treaty of Washington 1871; Canada and U.S. arbitrate major differences Woman suffrage introduced in New Zealand 1893
1900	Open Door Policy in China declared 1900 U.S. emerges as most powerful nation in Western Hemisphere c. 1900 Theodore Roosevelt 1901–1909 follows policy of trustbusting, conservation of resources, extended government regulation of railroads, foods, drugs	Commonwealth of Australia formed 1901

Asia	Africa	
Battle of Plassey 1757 begins domination of India by British East India Company and Britain; Parliament takes control of East India Company 1773; appoints its highest official, governor general of India 1784 English acquire Ceylon from Dutch 1796 Dutch government takes over East Indies; abolishes Dutch East India Company 1798		
	Britain acquires Cape Colony from France 1806 French army occupies Algeria 1830 Boer Great Trek 1836; Boers establish Orange Free State and the Transvaal	**1800**
China wars with Britain over opium and Western exploitation 1839–1842; Treaty of Nanking 1842; Hong Kong ceded to Britain, new ports opened to trade		
Taiping rebellion—revolt against the Manchu 1850–1864; Manchu Empress Tsu-hsi establishes national stability and furthers Chinese hatred of West 1861–1908 Japan opens first ports to West after Perry's visit 1854 British crush Indian mutiny 1857; relieve British East India Company of political responsibilities 1858 Russia penetrates land of the Caucasus, Turkestan c. 1860–1870 Meiji period in Japan 1868–1912; emperor made supreme authority; Japan modernized	Britain makes treaties with Boers acknowledging their independence 1852, 1854 Livingstone begins explorations in Central Africa 1853 Algeria incorporated into French state 1857 Increased friction between Britons and Boers 1860–1870 Suez Canal completed 1869	**1850**
Russia pushes south to Afghanistan and India c. 1870–1880 Indian National Congress formed 1885 Burma conquered by British c. 1885; Burma annexed to India French gain control over Indochina c. 1885 Macao ceded to Portugal 1887 New constitution promulgated in Japan 1889 Japan defeats China in Sino-Japanese War 1894–1895 Filipinos rebel against American forces 1899–1902	Europe's golden age of imperialism 1870–1914 Belgium—Leopold II acquires Congo region 1876–1882; Leopold forced to turn over Congo Free State to Belgian government 1908 France—Egypt under joint financial control of Britain and France 1879; French obtain Tunisia 1881; Morocco made a French protectorate 1912 Britain gains practical control of Suez Canal 1875; joint control of Egypt by Britain and France 1879; Lord Cromer assumes administration in Egypt 1883–1907; Somaliland is taken 1884; protectorate over Bechuanaland declared 1885; area developed for Britain by Rhodes' British South Africa Company named Rhodesia 1890; Anglo-Egyptian Sudan conquered 1898; Gambia, Sierre Leone, Gold Coast, Nigeria gained through Royal Niger Company 1900 Germany acquires Togoland, Cameroons, German East Africa, German Southwest Africa 1800s; British and Germans settle dispute over territories in East Africa 1886, 1890 Italy fails in attempted capture of Abyssinia (Ethiopia) 1896 Zulu war with British in South Africa 1879 Gold discovered in Transvaal 1885 Boer War 1899–1902; British defeat Dutch	**1870**
Anglo-Russian entente; Persia put under dual control of Britain and Russia 1907 Japan annexes Korea 1910; accepted as first-class power	Boers and Britons join states and form Union of South Africa 1909 Italy wrests Tripoli from Turks 1912	**1900**

International Politics	Western Democracies
1914 World War I—Germans invade Belgium, France, Poland 1914; Italy joins Allies 1915; Allies' Somme offensive 1916; Italian front smashed at Caporetto, U.S. enters war 1917; Russia signs Treaty of Brest Litovsk with Germany, armistice signed 1918 Wilson presents Fourteen Points 1918 Paris Peace Conference; League of Nations established 1919; Treaty of Versailles signed with Germany, Treaty of St.-Germain with Austria, Treaty of Neuilly with Bulgaria 1919; Treaty of Sèvres with Ottoman Empire, Treaty of Trianon with Hungary 1920 Little Entente (Czechoslovakia, Rumania, Yugoslavia) formed 1920–1921 Washington Conference—limited naval disarmament 1921–1922 Nine-Power Treaty—signatories agree to respect sovereignty of China 1922 Russia negotiates Treaty of Rapallo with Germany 1922 Mussolini defies League of Nations in Corfu incident 1923 France invades German Ruhr 1923–1924 Dawes Plan eases German reparations. France evacuates Ruhr 1924 Locarno Pact 1925 Kellogg-Briand Pact renounces war 1928	U.S. rejects membership in League of Nations 1919 Irish Free State created in southern Ireland 1921 Conservative Republican era in U.S. politics—Harding 1921–1923; Coolidge 1923–1929; Hoover 1929–1933 U.S. Hawley-Smoot (1930) Tariff Act levies high tariffs, jeopardizes war-debt payments, reparations MacDonald, Britain's first Labour prime minister 1924; Conservatives in power 1924–1929; general strike 1926
1929 Young Plan scales down reparations payments 1930 Mussolini conquers Ethiopia 1936 Rome-Berlin Axis formed, Japan and Germany form Anti-Comintern Pact 1936; Italy joins Pact 1937 Spanish civil war 1936–1939 Hitler engineers coup in Austria 1938 Surrender of Sudetenland to Germany at Munich 1938; Hitler seizes Czechoslovakia, Mussolini seizes Albania 1939	Stock market crash in U.S. leads to world depression 1929 Labour party regains power in Britain 1929–1931 Revolutions in six South American nations 1930 Spain becomes republic 1931 Statute of Westminster creates constitution for British Commonwealth of Nations (Canada, Australia, New Zealand, South Africa) 1931 U.S. inaugurates Good Neighbor Policy with Latin America 1933 Franklin D. Roosevelt becomes president of U.S. 1933; inaugurates New Deal Leftist Popular Front gains power in France 1936 Conservatives regain control in France 1937 Neville Chamberlain, advocate of appeasement, becomes prime minister of Britain 1937
1939 Russia, Germany sign nonaggression pact 1939 World War II—Germany invades Poland; France, Britain declare war 1939; *Sitzkrieg*; Russia defeats Finland 1939–1940; Hitler seizes Denmark, Norway, Low Countries, France 1940; Battle of Britain; Italian invasion of Greece and Africa fails; Hitler seizes Hungary, Balkans 1940–1941; Germany attacks Russia; Atlantic Charter signed; Pearl Harbor attack brings U.S. into war 1941; Japanese victories in Pacific 1941–1942; battles of Midway and Coral Sea; Rommel victorious in Libya 1942; Soviets seize offensive in Russia; Axis surrender in Africa; Italy invaded; Teheran Conference 1943; Allies launch second front; battle of Leyte 1944; Yalta agreements; Germany surrenders; A-bomb dropped on Japan	Churchill becomes prime minister of Britain 1940 U.S. passes Lend-Lease Act 1941
1945 Japanese surrender 1945	

Rise of Totalitarianism	Asia and Africa	
Russian Revolution—Duma names provisional government, tsar abdicates, Bolsheviks under Lenin seize government 1917; Bolsheviks destroy White Russian resistance 1918–1920	Japan presents Twenty-one Demands to China 1915 Arabs revolt against Ottoman rule 1916–1918 Balfour Declaration 1917	**1914**
Period of war communism 1918–1921 German revolution 1918; Weimar Republic set up 1919 Third Communist International (Comintern) formed 1919	Mustafa Kemal Pasha of Turkey defies Allies 1918–1922 Government of India Act of 1919, Rowlatt Act passed, Gandhi begins campaign for independence 1919	
NEP—Lenin restores some capitalistic practices 1921–1928 Mussolini establishes National Fascist party 1921; seizes Italian government in march on Rome 1922; divides Italian economy into government-controlled syndicates Union of Soviet Socialist Republics established 1922 Hitler stages unsuccessful *Putsch* in Munich 1923; begins *Mein Kampf* 1925	French repress Arab nationalism in Morocco, Tunisia, Algeria, Syria, Lebanon 1919–1939 San Remo Conference—Allies overrule Arab nationalism, create mandates from Arab territories 1920 Communist party 1920, Indonesian Nationalist part 1927 oppose Dutch rule in East Indies Sun Yat-sen controls Canton government in China 1921–1925 Riza Shah Pahlavi seizes Iran government 1921–1925 British grant constitution to Burma 1922	
Election of Hindenburg as president underlines rising German ultranationalism 1925	Egypt becomes sovereign, with British restrictions 1923 Republic of Turkey set up, Teaty of Lausanne signed 1923 Ibn-Saud gains control of Arabian peninsula 1924–1925 Universal Manhood Suffrage Bill passed in Japan 1925 Chiang Kai-shek purges Communists 1927; conquers Peking, unites China 1928	
Dictatorships formed in Lithuania 1926; Yugoslavia 1929 Trotsky loses bid for power to Stalin 1927 Stalin purges rivals 1928–1931, 1934–1938 Stalin inaugurates first Five-Year Plan 1928 Mussolini negotiates Lateran Treaty with Catholic church 1928; Vatican City declared sovereign independent state	Hamaguchi's ministry peak of liberalism in Japan 1929; Hamaguchi assassinated, liberal setback 1930 Iraq gains full independence from Britain 1930 Round-table conferences in India 1930–1932 Arab violence in British mandate of Palestine 1930s Italian Fascists cement rule in Libya 1930s Segregation, unrest grow in Union of South Africa 1930s Communists oppose French rule in Indochina 1930s British grant progressive constitution to Ceylon 1931	**1929**
Russia begins second Five-Year Plan 1933 Hitler becomes dictator of Germany, proclaims Third Reich; Germany withdraws from League of Nations 1933; first Four-Year Plan established 1933, second 1936 Nuremberg laws enacted 1935 Germany reoccupies Rhineland 1936	Japan invades Manchuria 1931 Chinese Communists proclaim Chinese Soviet Republic 1931; Chiang launches campaigns against Communists 1931–1934 Ibn-Saud's holdings renamed Saudi Arabia 1932 Japan attacks Shanghai 1932 Japan withdraws from League of Nations 1933 Chinese-Japanese truce 1933 recognizes Japanese conquests in Manchuria, northern China	
Italy withdraws from League of Nations 1937 Russia initiates third Five-Year Plan 1938	Commonwealth of Philippines formed 1935 Government of India Act of 1935 goes into effect in British India 1937–1939; rejected by native princes 1939 British grant Burma restricted home rule 1937 War breaks out again between Japan and China 1937; Japan proclaims New Order in Asia 1938	
Fascist dictator Franco gains power, ends republic after Spanish civil war 1939		**1939**
	Tojo becomes premier of Japan 1941	
		1945

International Politics	**Asia and Africa**
1945 Yalta Conference (Roosevelt, Churchill, Stalin) February 1945; Cold War begins Surrender of Nazi Germany May 1945 UN Charter signed June 1945 Hiroshima bombed August 1945 Surrender of Japan August 1945 Germany divided into four zones October 1946 Truman Doctrine enunciated March 1947 Berlin blockade and airlift June 1948–September 1949 Korean War begins 1950 Korean armistice signed at Panmunjon July 1953 French defeated at Dien Bien Phu May 1954; Vietnam divided July 1954	Civil war in China 1946–1949 Independence of India and Pakistan August 1947 Mahatma Gandhi assassinated January 1948 State of Israel established May 1948 Republic of Korea proclaimed August 1948 Communist victory in China; People's Republic of China established September 1949 Indonesia becomes independent December 1949 Mau Mau rebellion in Kenya 1952 Egypt declared a republic June 1953 Nassar becomes premier of Egypt February 1954 Beginning of nationalist revolt in Algeria 1954 Laos, Cambodia, Vietnam become independent states 1954 Suez crisis July 1956 Israelis invade Sinai peninsula October 1956 Beginning of decolonization in sub-Saharan Africa 1957 First conference of independent African states April 1958
1960 Big Four Paris summit meeting collapses May 1960 UN Security Council authorizes peacekeeping forces in Congo February 1961 Increasing U.S. involvement in Vietnam 1961 Berlin Wall constructed August 1961 U.S., Britain, USSR sign nuclear test ban treaty August 1963 U.S. begins bombing North Vietnam February 1965 Arab-Israeli Six-Day War June 5–10, 1967 Suez Canal closed 1967–1973 UN accepts nuclear nonproliferation treaty June 1968 U.S. bombing of North Vietnam ends October 1968	Many African states become independent; civil war in Belgian Congo 1960 Sino-Soviet dispute begins 1960 South Africa becomes independent republic 1961 Sino-Indian war 1962 Algeria becomes independent 1962 Communist China explodes its first atomic bomb October 1964 Indo-Pakistan war 1965 Military takeover in Indonesia 1965 Rhodesia declares its independence from Britain November 1965 Indira Gandhi becomes prime minister of India January 1966 Cultural Revolution in China 1966 Civil war in Nigeria; secession of Biafra 1967–1970
1970 U.S. detente with China, USSR 1971 People's Republic of China admitted to UN December 1971 SALT I treaty May 1972 Paris Accord ends U.S. fighting in Vietnam January 1973 U.S. troops withdraw from Vietnam 1973 Suez Canal reopened 1973 Arab oil embargo October 1973–April 1974 U.S., USSR sign five-year nuclear test treaty May 1976 UN orders arms embargo against South Africa November 1977 Camp David Accords between Sadat of Egypt and Begin of Israel September 1978 U.S., People's Republic of China establish full diplomatic relations January 1979 Egypt, Israel sign peace treaty March 1979 U.S. embassy seized, U.S. hostages taken in Iran November 1979	Rhodesia becomes republic March 1970 Nasser dies; Sadat becomes premier of Egypt September–October 1970 Bangladesh declares independence from Pakistan March 1971 Communist takeover of Vietnam, Laos, Cambodia April 1975 Fall of Shah of Iran; Ayatollah Khomeini takes over government January–February 1979 Vietnam invades Cambodia, expelling Khmer Rouge government 1979 South Korean president Park Chung Lee assassinated October 1979
1980 U.S. hostages freed by Iran January 1981 Argentina invades Falkland Islands April 1982 U.S., USSR open SALT talks June 1982 Britain reclaims Falkland Islands June 1982 U.S. President Reagan, USSR General Secretary Gorbachev meet at Geneva summit conference November 1985 U.S. bombs Libya 1986 U.S., USSR sign INF treaty providing for elimination of intermediate-range land-based nuclear weapons 1987 Berlin Wall opened November 1989	Zimbabwe wins independence April 1980 Shah of Iran dies July 1980 Iran-Iraq war breaks out September 1980 Mao's widow, nine others found guilty of counterrevolutionary crimes December 1980 Egyptian president Sadat assassinated; succeeded by Mubarak October 1981 Israel invades Lebanon June 1982 Massacre of Palestinian refugees in Beirut September 1982 Libya invades Chad August 1983 Famine in Ethiopia 1984 Indira Gandi assassinated October 1984 Civil unrest in South Africa 1985 Corazon Aquino replaces Marcos as Philippines president February 1986 South Africa declares national state of emergency in response to racial tensions June 1986 Palestinian uprising (*intifada*) against Israeli-occupied territories 1988 Ceasefire in Iran-Iraq war 1988 Emperor Hirohito of Japan dies; succeeded by son Akihito 1989 Ayatollah Khomeini dies 1989 Student demonstrators massacred at Tiananmen Square in China May–June 1989
1990 Germany reunited 1990 Multi-party elections throughout Eastern Europe 1990	Namibia becomes independent 1990 Nelson Mandela released from prison in South Africa 1990 Iraq invades Kuwait; announces annexation of Kuwait August 1990 Operation "Desert Storm" in Persian Gulf January– February 1991

Western Democracies	Soviet Bloc Nations	
New constitution establishes French Fourth Republic October 1946 Greek civil war 1947–1949 European Recovery Plan (Marshall Plan) introduced June 1947 Organization of American States (OAS) established 1948 Formation of NATO alliance April 1959 German Federal Republic (West Germany) established May 1949 Turkey and Greece join NATO September 1951 West Germany admitted to NATO May 1955 Creation of European Economic Community (Common Market) March 1957 Fifth Republic in France; de Gaulle becomes premier of France June 1958 Cuban Revolution 1959	Communist coup in Czechoslovakia February 1968 Communist takeover in Hungary 1968 Tito defects from Soviet bloc; Yugoslavia expelled from Cominform June 1968 German Democratic Republic (East Germany) formed May 1949 Explosion of first Soviet atomic bomb announced September 1949 USSR, People's Republic of China sign 30-year alliance February 1950 Stalin dies March 1953 USSR, Eastern European satellites sign Warsaw Pact May 1955 Revolution in Hungary crushed by Soviet army October–November 1956 USSR launches Sputnik; Space Age begins October 1957 Khrushchev becomes Soviet premier March 1958	**1945**
Cuban missile crisis October 1962 France vetoes British entry to Common Market January 1963 West German chancellor Adenauer resigns October 1963 U.S. President Kennedy assassinated November 1963 France announces withdrawal of French troops from NATO March 1966 De Gaulle resigns April 1969 Pompidou elected premier of France June 1969 U.S. astronauts land on moon July 1969 Willy Brandt elected chancellor of West Germany October 1969	Sino-Soviet rift splits Communist world 1963 Khrushchev ousted; replaced by Brezhnev and Kosygin October 1964 Soviet invasion of Czechoslovakia August 1968	**1960**
Britain, Ireland, Denmark join Common Market (EEC) 1973 Major recession in U.S. 1973 Brandt resigns; Schmidt becomes West German chancellor May 1974 Nixon resigns as U.S. president August 1974 Franco dies; succeeded by Juan Carlos I; end of dictatorship in Spain November 1975 Democratic elections in Spain 1977 Margaret Thatcher becomes British prime minister May 1979 Civil war in Nicaragua; Somoza overthrown 1979	Brezhnev named Soviet chief of state June 1977 USSR invades Afghanistan December 1979	**1970**
Mitterand elected president of France May 1981 Greece joins Common Market (EEC) 1981 Kohl elected West German chancellor October 1982 U.S., six Caribbean nations invade Grenada October 1983 Democracy restored in Brazil, Uruguay 1985 U.S. space shuttle Challenger explodes on takeoff January 1986 Soares sworn in as Portugal's first civilian president in 60 years March 1986 Spain and Portugal join Common Market (EEC) 1986 U.S. invades Panama December 1989	Tito dies May 1980 Independent Polish trade union Solidarity created October 1980 Brezhnev dies; succeeded by Andropov November 1982 Andropov dies; succeeded by Chernenko February 1984 Chernenko dies; Gorbachev comes to power in USSR March 1985 Nuclear reactor disaster at Chernobyl in USSR April–May 1986 Gorbachev announces policies of *glasnost* and *perestroika* 1988 Communist regimes in East Germany, Czechoslovakia, Bulgaria, Romania fall 1988 USSR withdraws troops from Afghanistan 1989 Spread of nationalism in USSR; Lithuania declares independence 1989	**1980**
Democratic elections in Nicaragua end Sandinista rule	Nationalist uprisings in Armenia and Azerbaijan result in communal massacres	**1990**

Color Photographs

Cover The British Library

Portfolio Five following p. 464
1 (t) Courtesy of the Freer Gallery of Art, Smithsonian Institution, Washington, D. C. (45.9) (b) W. H. Purnell/Shostal/SuperStock
2 (t) The Cleveland Museum of Art, Bequest of John L. Severance (b) Tokyo National Museum
3 (both) Lee Boltin
4 Lee Boltin

Portfolio Six following p. 528
1 Dulwich Picture Gallery/Bridgeman/Art Resource, NY
2 Sir Joshua Reynolds, *Lady Elizabeth Delme and Her Children.* National Gallery of Art, Washington, Andrew W. Mellon Collection
3 The Metropolitan Museum of Art, Wolfe Fund, 1931. Catharine Lorillard Wolfe Collection (31.45)
4 Carle/Shostal/SuperStock

Portfolio Seven following p. 656
1 Jim Howard/Alpha/FPG
2 (t) The Metropolitan Museum of Art, Bequest of Mary Stillman Harkness, 1950 (50.145.8) (b) Scala/Art Resource, NY
3 The Metropolitan Museum of Art, Gift of Harry Payne Bingham, 1940 (40.175)
4 Claude Monet, *Water Lilies,* 1906, oil on canvas, 87.6 × 92.7 cm, Mr. and Mrs. Martin A. Ryerson Collection, 1933.1157. © 1992 The Art Institute of Chicago. All Rights Reserved.
5 (tl) Mary Cassatt, *The Bath,* 1891/92, oil on canvas, 39½ × 26″, Robert A. Waller Fund, 1910.2. ©1992 The Art Institute of Chicago. All Rights Reserved. (tr) Pierre Auguste Renoir, *Two Sisters (On the Terrace),* 1881, oil on canvas, 100.5 × 81 cm, Mr. and Mrs. Lewis Larned Coburn Memorial Collection, 1933.455. © 1992 The Art Institute of Chicago. All Rights Reserved. (b) The Metropolitan Museum of Art, Bequest of Mrs. H. O. Havemeyer, 1929. The H. O. Havemeyer Collection (29.100.128)
6 Philadelphia Museum of Art, George W. Elkins Collection
7 Vincent van Gogh, *The Starry Night,* (1889). Oil on canvas, 29 × 36¼″. Collection, The Museum of Modern Art, New York. Acquired through the Lillie P. Bliss Bequest
8 Cliché des Musées Nationaux, Paris

Portfolio Eight following p. 800
1 The Saint Louis Art Museum, Museum purchase
2 (t) Art Resource, NY (b) Werner Forman Archive
3 Pablo Picasso, *Girl Before a Mirror,* 1932. Oil on canvas, 64 × 51¼″. Collection, The Museum of Modern Art, New York. Gift of Mrs. Simon Guggenheim

4 (t) Copyright 1992 ARS, N.Y./ADAGP (b) Salvador Dali, *The Persistence of Memory,* 1931. Oil on canvas, 9½ × 13″. Collection, The Museum of Modern Art, New York. Given anonymously
5 Kunstmuseum, Basel. © COSMOPRESS, Geneva/VAGA, New York
6 Alexander Calder, *Lobster Trap and Fish Tail* (1939). Hanging mobile: painted steel wire and sheet aluminum, about 8′ 6″ high × 9′ 6″ diameter. Collection, The Museum of Modern Art, New York. Commissioned by the Advisory Committee for the stairwell of the Museum
7 Michael Fedison
8 Des Moines Art Center, James D. Edmundson Fund, 1958

Portfolio Nine following p. 912
1 The Nelson-Atkins Museum of Art, Kansas City, Missouri. Gift of William Inge, 56–128
2 Hirshhorn Museum and Sculpture Garden, Smithsonian Institution
3 (tl) Andy Warhol, *Campbell's Soup,* (1965). Oil silkscreened on canvas, 36⅛ × 24″. Collection, The Museum of Modern Art, New York. Philip Johnson Fund (tr) © Roy Lichtenstein. The Metropolitan Museum of Art, Purchase, Lila Acheson Wallace Gift, Arthur Hoppock Hearn Fund, Arthur Lejwa Fund in honor of Jean Arp, the Bernhill Fund, Joseph H. Hazen Foundation, Inc., Samuel I. Newhouse Foundation, Inc., Walter Bareiss, Marie Bannon Mchnery, Louise Smith and Stephen C. Swid Gifts, 1980 (1980.420) (b) Collection Walker Art Center, Minneapolis, Gift of the T. B. Walker Foundation, 1966
4 Richard Estes, *Drugstore,* 1970, oil on canvas, 152.4 × 112.7 cm, Restricted gift of Edgar Kaufmann, 1970.1100. © 1992 The Art Institute of Chicago. All Rights Reserved.

Black and White Photographs

451 Brian Seed/Tony Stone Worldwide
457 Reproduced by courtesy of the Trustees of the British Museum
459 Reproduced by courtesy of the Trustees, The National Gallery, London
464 Reproduced by courtesy of the Trustees, The National Gallery, London
477 From J. Lagniet, *Recueil de Proverbes,* 1657–63
479 Cliché des Musées Nationaux, Paris
481 The Metropolitan Museum of Art, Gift of the Wildenstein Foundation, Inc., 1951 (51.34)
484 Rijksmuseum, Amsterdam
498 Photo-Verlag Gundermann
499 Giraudon/Art Resource, NY
507 The Metropolitan Museum of Art, Harris Brisbane Dick Fund, 1932 (32.35(124))
508 The Bettmann Archive
509 Alinari/Art Resource, NY
517 Courtesy of Hillwood Museum, Washington, D. C.
519 Austrian National Library, Vienna
524 Universitätsbibliothek, Basel

792 Historical Pictures Service, Chicago
793 UPI/Bettmann
794 UPI/Bettmann
797 New York Daily News Photo
798 UPI/Bettmann
799 UPI/Bettmann
801 (t) *Illustrated London News*, October 17, 1931 (b) AP/Wide World
802 AP/Wide World
803 David Seymour/Magnum
805 UPI/Bettmann
807 (t) UPI/Bettmann (b) The Franklin D. Roosevelt Library
811 Brown Brothers
812 Courtesy Schocken Books
813 Chicago Architectural Photo Co.
817 UPI/Bettmann
819 UPI/Bettmann
821 UPI/Bettmann
822 Sovfoto
826 Sovfoto
828 UPI/Bettmann
829 UPI/Bettmann
831 AP/Wide World
833 (both) UPI/Bettmann
835 UPI/Bettmann
836 UPI/Bettmann
837 Staatliche Museen Preussischer Kulturbesitz, Nationalgalerie, Berlin
838 Popperfoto
840 (t) UPI/Bettmann (b) AP/Wide World
841 (t) Wiener Library, London (b) Ullstein Bilderdienst
842 (l) U.S. Information Agency/National Archives (r) Pressefoto: E. Thaler, Berlin
849 Jerry Doyle, *Philadelphia Daily News*, 1931
851 Culver Pictures
853 UPI/Bettmann
854 UPI/Bettmann
857 Margaret Bourke-White, *Life* Magazine, © Time Warner Inc.
858 AP/Wide World
859 The Hulton Picture Company
863 The Hulton Picture Company
864 The Hulton Picture Company
867 Brown Brothers
868 AP/Wide World
870 NAACP
874 (t) Reprinted by permission: Triburn Media Services (b) William A. Ireland, *The Columbus Dispatch*
875 UPI/Bettmann
876 UPI/Bettmann
878 UPI/Bettmann
879 UPI/Bettmann
880 U.S. Information Agency/National Archives
881 UPI/Bettmann
882 Austrian National Library, Vienna
885 AP/Wide World
888 Photo by Kerlee/U.S. Navy/National Archives
889 UPI/Bettmann
890 Imperial War Museum, London
892 British Information Services, New York
894 AP/Wide World

895 AP/Wide World
896 Imperial War Museum, London
898 U.S. Coast Guard
899 The Franklin D. Roosevelt Library
906 Otto Hagel
907 United Nations
910 Consulate General of Germany
911 U.S. Army
913 (t) Sovfoto (b) AP/Wide World
917 AP/Wide World
919 AP/Wide World
920 AP/Wide World
921 AP/Wide World
922 UPI/Bettmann
923 (t) AP/Wide World (b) UPI/Bettmann
925 UPI/Bettmann
926 UPI/Bettmann
927 Alex Webb/Magnum
930 AP/Wide World
931 AP/Wide World
937 Contifoto/Sygma
942 (l) Nik Wheeler/Black Star (r) Asahi Shimbun Photo
944 Sovfoto/Eastfoto
947 AP/Wide World
948 AP/Wide World
950 UPI/Bettmann
952 Larry Burrows, *Life* Magazine, © Time Warner Inc.
953 (t) Nik Wheeler/Black Star (b) UPI/Bettmann
955 AP/Wide World
956 AP/Wide World
957 AP/Wide World
959 UPI/Bettmann
960 AP/Wide World
962 Reuters/Bettmann
965 UPI/Bettmann
968 AP/Wide World
973 UPI/Bettmann
974 UPI/Bettman
975 Pete Souza/The White House
978 AP/Wide World
980 Bill Swersey/NYT Pictures
981 Robert Nickelsberg/Gamma-Liaison
983 Peter Jordan/Gamma-Liaison
985 Michael Evans/The White House
986 Syndication International/Photo Trends
991 Wassily Kandinsky, *In the Black Square*, 1928. Collection, Solomon R. Guggenheim Museum, New York. Photo: Robert E. Mates
992 Jacket illustration by John Held, Jr. of F. Scott Fitzgerald's *Tales of the Jazz Age* is reproduced by permission of Charles Scribner's Sons
993 Dorothea Lange for FSA/Library of Congress
994 (l) Bob Verlin/Monkmeyer Press (r) AP/Wide World
995 The Museum of Modern Art/Film Stills Archive
996 Vyto Starinskas/Sygma
997 John Dominis/*Time* Magazine
E2 AP/Wide World
E3 Ken Heyman
E5 AP/Wide World
E6 AP/Wide World

Index

Suggested pronunciations for difficult or unusual words are respelled according to the table below. The local pronunciation of many foreign words are too unusual for persons untrained in linguistics, and pronunciations given here are those commonly acceptable in unaffected, educated American speech.

a	hat, cap	j	jam, enjoy	u	cup, son
ā	age, face	k	kind, seek	u̇	put, book
ã	care, air	l	land, coal	ü	rule, move
ä	father, far	m	me, am	ū	use, music
		n	no, in		
b	bad, rob	ng	long, bring	v	very, save
ch	child, much			w	will, woman
d	did, red	o	hot, rock	y	you, yet
		ō	open, go	z	zero, breeze
e	let, best	ô	order, all	zh	measure, seizure
ē	equal, see	oi	oil, toy		
ėr	term, learn	ou	out, now		
				ə	represents:
f	fat, if	p	pet, cup	a	in about
g	go, bag	r	run, try	e	in taken
h	he, how	s	say, yes	i	in pencil
		sh	she, rush	o	in lemon
i	it, pin	t	tell, it	u	in circus
ī	ice, five	th	thin, both		
		TH	then, smooth		

Foreign Sounds

Y as in French *lune*. Pronounce ē with the lips rounded as for English ü in *rule*.

Œ as in French *deux*. Pronounce ā with the lips rounded as for ō.

N as in French *bon*. The N is not pronounced, but shows that the vowel before it is nasal.

H as in German *ach*. Pronounce *k* without closing the breath passage.

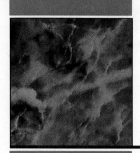

The Reference Maps

History accounts for human activities in time, and maps depict them in space. Therefore, to understand humanity's experiences, knowledge of the planetary environment is essential. These reference maps show key areas at significant periods; they include basic physical features that affect human attempts to control the environment and their fellow beings.

Map 1: The Ancient Near East and Greece   In the area displayed, we can trace the progressive expansion of human environmental control resulting from the invention of new tools and social institutions. The transition from food collecting to farming occurred in well-watered sites bordering the Syrian, Arabian, and Iranian deserts — such as at Jarmo in uplands to the east of the Tigris. The breakthrough from Neolithic barbarism to civilization, that is, to societies sufficiently complex to permit the emergence of urban centers, occurred in two important river basins, the Tigris-Euphrates and the Nile — linked by a Fertile Crescent with minimal natural obstacles to impede the movement of peoples and goods.

Employing primitive craft, Neolithic seafarers hugged the Mediterranean coasts and slowly pushed westward — as attested by Neolithic sites in Cyprus, Rhodes, and Crete. Improvements in maritime technology permitted the emergence of a splendid Aegean civilization centering at Knossos in Crete, Pylos on the Greek mainland, and Troy in northwest Asia Minor. Civilization's center of gravity shifted progressively northward across the eastern basin of the Mediterranean, culminating in Hellas with its sea-oriented city-states: Corinth; Thebes; and, above all, Athens. Continued advances in maritime technology enabled the Greeks to master the eastern Mediterranean and Black seas and to establish colonies,

while the Phoenicians carried their mercantile ventures from their port cities of Tyre and Sidon along the North African coast. What the Tigris-Euphrates had been to the Babylonians and the Nile to the Egyptians, the Mediterranean became to the Greeks, the Phoenicians, and eventually to the Romans — the "middle of the earth."

Map 2: The Roman Empire, c. A.D. 117   This map underscores the importance of physical features in the creation of the Roman world-state. From its east-west maritime axis, the Roman *imperium* stretched into the hinterland, which was linked by rivers and roads to strategically located ports that provided transshipment to other parts of the Empire.

The expansion of the Roman world began with the conquest of the Italian peninsula and Great Greece (including Sicily). The Punic Wars opened up the entire western basin of the Mediterranean, while subsequent intrusion into the eastern basin extended Roman dominion over the Hellenistic world. During the first century B.C., Rome consolidated its control in Asia Minor; conquered transalpine Gaul; and annexed Egypt, Numidia, and Cyrenaica. The territorial domain was rounded out later by the acquisition of Mauretania, Dacia, Armenia, and Mesopotamia.

In this map, we see the Roman world at its broadest expanse, encompassing almost 100 million people and linked by the greatest communications network then devised. However, the world-state soon entered its time of troubles, attended by declines in population, administrative efficiency, and military power. The Empire then found itself overextended and had to reduce its territorial perimeter. Armenia, Mesopotamia, and Dacia were abandoned, and eventually the Roman legions were recalled from Britain.

In the fourth century, the once majestic Roman Empire was polarized into two unequal segments. The western section, administered from Rome, had the weaker but spatially larger area; the eastern section, controlled from New Rome (Constantinople, formerly Byzantium), had a larger population, a more compact territory, and a stronger economy. When the two segments, each centering on one of the major basins of the Mediterranean, were split asunder by barbarian invasions, the classical world gave way to the medieval world.

Map 3: The Ancient East Here we encounter the homelands of two major fluvial civilizations (societies originating in river basins) centering on the Indus-Gangetic and the Huang Ho (Yellow River) drainage basins. The remarkable longevity of Indian and Chinese societies owes much to physical factors that inhibited alien intrusion. The Indian triangle was protected by the Indian Ocean and the Himalayas, although invasion was possible through the western passes; as for China, the obstacles posed by the Pacific Ocean, the forbidding Taklamakan and Gobi deserts, and a series of mountain ranges effectively limited entrance into the Huang Ho valley.

The map also shows the boundaries of three empires: the Han in China, the Mauryan in India, and the Parthian in western Asia. Note that these empires were contemporary with the Roman world-state at its zenith. After centuries of feudal fragmentation, China was reunited, and under Shih Huang-ti (the First Emperor), the Great Wall was rebuilt and lengthened to keep the nomadic tribes in the north and west from pillaging the sedentary farmers in the south. The centuries marked by the Han Dynasty were stable and prosperous. So too were the centuries of Mauryan rule in India. Under Ashoka, a single administration extended from the Himalayas across the Narbada River and included the Deccan—leaving only the southernmost part of the subcontinent outside its rule. Meanwhile, to the northwest lay Bactria, where Hellenistic and Indian culture interfused, producing the Gandharan art found in Taxila.

This is the era, too, when the western and eastern segments of the Eurasian land mass were in commercial and cultural contact. Ships plied the Indian Ocean, taking advantage of the recently discovered monsoon mechanism, and a tenuous but profitable overland Silk Route stretched from Ch'ang-an to Kashgar and Samarkand and across Parthian lands to Ecbatana, Ctesiphon, and Seleucia.

Map 4: Medieval France, Spain, and the British Isles, 1328 We can perceive here the emerging outlines of the national state system in western Europe. For example, in 1328 Edward II had to recognize Scotland officially as independent, while across the Channel, the extinction of the Capetian line set the stage for a protracted struggle over the succession to the French throne. Known as the Hundred Years' War (1337–1453), it was marked by the loss of large English holdings obtained in Plantagenet days. Meanwhile, ambitious French kings enlarged their domain from the Ile de France around Paris southward to the Mediterranean and then sought to expand their territory eastward at the expense of the feudal-fragmented Holy Roman Empire. The Iberian peninsula was also fragmented, but here the Christian kingdoms were girding to clear the peninsula of the Moors in Granada.

Noteworthy for their economic importance during this era were the Low Countries, where the textile industry enriched such towns as Bruges, Lille, Ghent, Ypres, and Cambrai; Champagne in northeastern France, where the most famous medieval fairs in all Europe were held; and southern France, with its thriving commercial centers at Narbonne and Marseille.

Whereas in the classical era urban centers predominated on the coasts, in medieval Europe a large number of river-oriented towns were founded or acquired increasing importance. Roads were poor, and river transport was both economical and efficient. The Thames, Meuse, Seine, Loire, Rhone, Garonne, Tagus, Guadalquivir, and Po rivers were being constantly utilized, while the Rhine and the Danube—important as political and military boundaries in Roman times—were vital waterways throughout the medieval period.

Map 5: Europe, 1648 The year 1648 is a crucial one for it marks the end of the Thirty Years' War, which started as a religious conflict and concluded with the victory of the national state, which acknowledged no authority higher than its own sovereignty and interests. The map indicates the further territorial consolidation of the national state system (as compared with Map 4). Thus Scotland and England are now one political entity; the Iberian peninsula is demarcated as Spain and Portugal (although neither is any longer a first-class power); France has acquired bishoprics in Lorraine and a foothold in Alsace. The map also shows the emergence of Switzerland, the three Scandinavian countries, Poland, and Russia.

Germany and Italy remain territorially fragmented and politically unstable, as the Holy Roman Empire has vanished in everything but name and pretensions. The situation in the flat north European plain remains fluid as the boundaries of Brandenburg, Poland, and Russia are always shifting, reflecting the fluctuating balance of power in those states. Meanwhile, despite their defeat at Lepanto in 1571, the Ottoman Turks continue to threaten central Europe.

Map 6: Africa, A.D. 700–1500 The historical development and cultural evolution of Africa owe much to two physical features of the continent—the Sahara Desert and the Great Rift Valley. The valley runs from the Jordan Valley in Palestine to the Red Sea, through Ethiopia to form the basin containing Uganda and Lake Victoria, and southward through western Tanzania and Lake Tanganyika to Lake Nyasa. The Sahara cuts off northern Africa from the rest of the continent. Northwest Africa is largely oriented to the Mediterranean and to Europe; northeast Africa has long been linked with southwest Asia and the Arabian peninsula. Sub-Saharan Africa is drained by the Niger, Congo, Zambezi, and Limpopo rivers. In this huge region, the Sudanese savanna lands, equatorial rain forest, and steppes and deserts of southern Africa succeed one another from north to south. The map depicts the major cultures of the area and the various empires that flourished during the millenium under review, as well as trade routes across the Sahara, over which caravans carried Islamic proselytizers, ivory, slaves, and the wares of the marketplace and mind alike.

Map 7: European Empires, c. 1700 With the age of exploration, western Europeans set out for the unmapped portions of the globe, spreading their religion, cultures, and languages into new territories. In the wake of the explorer came the missionary, merchant, and musketeer so that in time

Europeans controlled most, or all, of the land surface of every other continent. The age of exploration both intensified and territorially expanded European national rivalries.

European states bordering the Atlantic attempted to explore and colonize lands in the New World in latitudes roughly comparable to their own. Thus, the Danes proceeded nortwestward to Iceland and Greenland, the English and French competed for lands north of the Gulf of Mexico, and Spain and Portugal staked their respective claims in more southerly latitudes. Following Portuguese initiative, other Europeans sought out—and fought over—islands, coastal strips, and spheres of interest on the African and Indian coasts and in the archipelagoes of Southeast Asia.

On the map, we can see clearly the contrasting depths of European penetration of the New and Old Worlds. In the Americas, Europeans encountered either Stone Age Amerinds or pre-Columbian civilizations incapable of assimilating, much less fighting off, the newcomers. Consequently, the European acquisition of North and South America—and later of Australia—was complete. In contrast, in sub-Saharan Africa as well as South and East Asia, the Europeans were invariably outnumbered. Hence, although they managed to establish trading settlements along the coast and eventually acquire political ascendancy in most of these regions, they did not succeed in replacing the indigenous culture patterns.

Map 8: Europe, August 1939 As a result of the defeat of the Central Powers in World War I, Germany was shorn of its overseas colonies, while in Europe it lost Alsace-Lorraine, half of Schleswig, three western districts to Belgium, the Polish Corridor, and a zone in the Rhineland, which was demilitarized. The Austrian Empire was dismembered: the nationalist movements of the Czechs, Poles, and Slavs achieved formal territorial recognition; the remnant of the Empire was converted into the separate states of Austria and Hungary; and further Austrian territories were awarded to Italy. The Ottoman Empire was also dissected: Greece obtained nearly all of European Turkey, Syria was mandated to France, and Palestine and Iraq went to Great Britain. After the Bolshevik Revolution, Russia lost much of its western territory, resulting in the establishment of Finland, Estonia, Latvia, and Lithuania, as well as the major portion of reconstituted Poland, while Bessarabia was ceded to Rumania.

In the interwar years, as the map shows, national appetites were whetted to gain new territory or reannex lost possessions. Under Hitler, Nazi Germany reoccupied the Rhineland in 1936, seized Austria and occupied Sudetenland in 1938, and the following year seized other Czech territory in addition to Memel. In 1939, too, Hungary annexed part of Slovakia, while Mussolini's Italy defeated and annexed Albania. The stage was also set for Russia to reannex territory lost after the Bolshevik Revolution.

Map 9: Africa, 1914 Africa possesses three major cultural environments, each with unique historical developments. Northeast Africa, partly cut off from the rest of the continent by the Sahara, has long been linked with southwest Asia. Africa east of the Great Rift Valley is oriented toward the Indian Ocean, toward the Arab trader, and since the last century, toward the European who has farmed the plateaus of Kenya, Uganda, and Tanzania. The lands in the southern section of the Great Rift Valley constitute a huge area drained by the Niger, Congo, Zambezi, and Limpopo rivers. In these lands occurred Europe's great scramble for empire in the nineteenth century. By 1914 all Africa had been partitioned among European powers except for Liberia (founded by ex-slaves from the United States) and Abyssinia, which successfully resisted Italian attempts at conquest in 1896.

Map 10: Africa Profound political and territorial changes have occurred in Africa since 1914 — undoubtedly the most spectacular to be found in any continent during the past half century. From being a vast collection of colonial holdings, Africa has emerged as an agglomeration of national states, virtually all having minimal political stability or economic viability. During the interwar years, some major changes took place on the political landscape. German Togoland and the Cameroons were mandated to Great Britain and France; German East Africa was divided into two mandates: Ruanda-Urundi (Belgium) and Tanganyika (Great Britain); and German Southwest Africa was mandated to South Africa. Egypt became an independent kingdom but Italy's possessions in East Africa were enlarged by the conquest of Abyssinia. Since World War II, however, a spectacular alteration has occurred. The entire continent has passed into indigenous political control, with the exception of South Africa where domination by the white minority, of European descent, remains entrenched.

Map 11: USSR and Asia Dominating Eurasia, the greatest land mass on earth, is the enormous area of the Soviet Union (more than 8 million square miles), extending along a west-east axis for nearly 5000 miles. European Russia, largely a continuation of the north European plain, is drained by the Dvina, Dnieper, Don, and Volga rivers, the last three flowing southward. East of the Urals, virtually all rivers flow north to the Arctic, except the Amur, which in its eastward journey also serves as a border with China. Soviet Asia is separated from middle- and low-latitude Asia by steppes, deserts, and mountains.

Russian eastward expansion reached the Pacific by 1649. In the next two centuries, the Russians penetrated east of the Caspian into what is now the Kazakh, Uzbek, and Turkmen Soviet Socialist Republics. In the process, they collided with the Chinese in Sinkiang, Mongolia, and Manchuria. These border regions today constitute areas of tension and jockeying between the two major Communist powers.

China has continued to develop south of the Great Wall and Gobi Desert and east and north of such massive mountain ranges as the Tien Shan, Pamirs, and Himalayas. Indian society occupies the subcontinent below the Himalyas and influences the culture patterns of neighboring lands to the east and south. Southeast Asia has long been subject to recurrent cultural and military intrusions. Its highly indented coastline and physical terrain have contributed to a fragmentation of cultures and languages. Offshore in East and Southeast Asia are three archipelagoes: Japan, the most highly industrialized and prosperous of non-Western countries; the Philippines; and Indonesia.

Map 12: Latin America Latin America was first colonized by southern Europeans, notably the Spaniards and Portuguese. Exploiting the mountain ranges that run the length of Central and South America for their precious metals, the Spaniards increased their holdings until the close of the eighteenth century. They created several vice-royalties: New Spain, including Mexico and

Central America; Peru, at first embracing all of Spanish South America; New Granada, in what is now Colombia and Venezuela; and La Plata, which subsequently became Bolivia, Paraguay, Uruguay, and Argentina. Brazil, discovered by the Portuguese Cabral in 1500, was made a vice-royalty in 1714.

In half a century (1776–1826) of colonial revolutions in the New World, Spanish and Portuguese America became independent (except for Cuba and Puerto Rico, which remained Spanish until 1898).

The tropical regions of Latin America — including Mexico; Central America; and the lands drained by the Magdalena, Orinoco, and Amazon rivers — have predominantly Amerind populations. In contrast, temperate South America, comprising southern Brazil, Uruguay, Argentina, and Chile, finds Europeans in the majority.

Map 13: The Middle East This region — segmented by deserts and seas but with the latter providing interconnecting routes of travel — has long permitted maximal movement of peoples, goods, and ideas in all directions. In this area, which is unique for the convergence of three continents, we find the birthplace of "civilization" and of three major religions, as well as a continuous succession of dynasties and empires. For centuries, Islamic political authority and cultural vitality were bound with the fortunes of the Ottoman Empire. When the Empire fell to the European powers, the Muslim people of the region were in turn subordinated in status and made to feel inferior. The twentieth century, however, has witnessed a resurgence of Islamic culture and political strength — attended by the creation of numerous independent states, including Morocco, Algeria, Libya, Egypt, Sudan, Syria, Lebanon, Jordan, Iraq, and Pakistan. This resurgence has capitalized on the strategic value of the region in the geopolitical programs of the superpowers, as well as on its massive oil resources.

The region has also been in a state of continuous tension and intermittent conflict since the end of World War II because of Arab-Israeli animosities. When the British mandate of Palestine was terminated in 1948, the area proclaimed itself the new state of Israel — a step sanctioned by the United Nations as well as by both the United States and the Soviet Union. But the Arab states remained opposed to any such recognition, and several campaigns were mounted in an effort to regain Palestine for the Muslim Arabs. Arab-Israeli hostilities erupted into war in 1967 and 1973. An Israeli victory resulted in occupation of the west bank of the Jordan River; the Sinai peninsula and the east bank of the Suez Canal have since been returned to Egypt. The Middle East in the 1980s is still the scence of violent and bloody conflicts. A revolution in Iran was followed by war between Iran and Iraq that continues with no apparent end in sight. Various factions in Lebanon are waging civil war. In addition, throughout the region, terrorist activities threaten both natives and visitors.

Map 14: Europe Compare this map with Map 8 to obtain a clearer picture of territorial changes resulting from the outcome of World War II. As after World War I, defeated Germany and its allies lost territory, and the Soviet Union emerged as the greatest single territorial beneficiary.

In 1945, Germany was stripped of East Prussia, while its eastern boundary was set at the Oder-Neisse rivers — the farthest line west achieved by the Slavs since the twelfth century. Moreover, postwar Germany was both ideologically and territorially split — its western segment associated in military and economic pacts with the Western world and its eastern section integrated in the Communist world and a member of the Warsaw Pact. Defeated Italy lost its overseas colonies and Albania.

The Soviet Union expanded westward, annexing part of Finland; all of Estonia, Latvia, and Lithuania; and the eastern portion of Poland, shifting that country's center of gravity westward at the expense of Germany. Stalinist policies and power created a series of "people's democracies" from the Baltic to the Black seas, resulting in the iron curtain. Yet, the region was to prove far from monolithic. Shortly after the war, Tito declared Yugoslavia an independent Communist state.

Tiny Albania was later to ally itself with China in the great split within the Communist world. In the 1980s, Soviet leader Mikhail Gorbachev introduced the new policies of *glasnost* (openness) and *perestroika* (restructuring) to encourage a freer economy. By the late 1980s, the Communist regimes in many Eastern European states had fallen, free multiparty elections had taken place, and democratic parties had come to power. All barriers between East and West Germany had been removed, and Germany was once more a unified state.

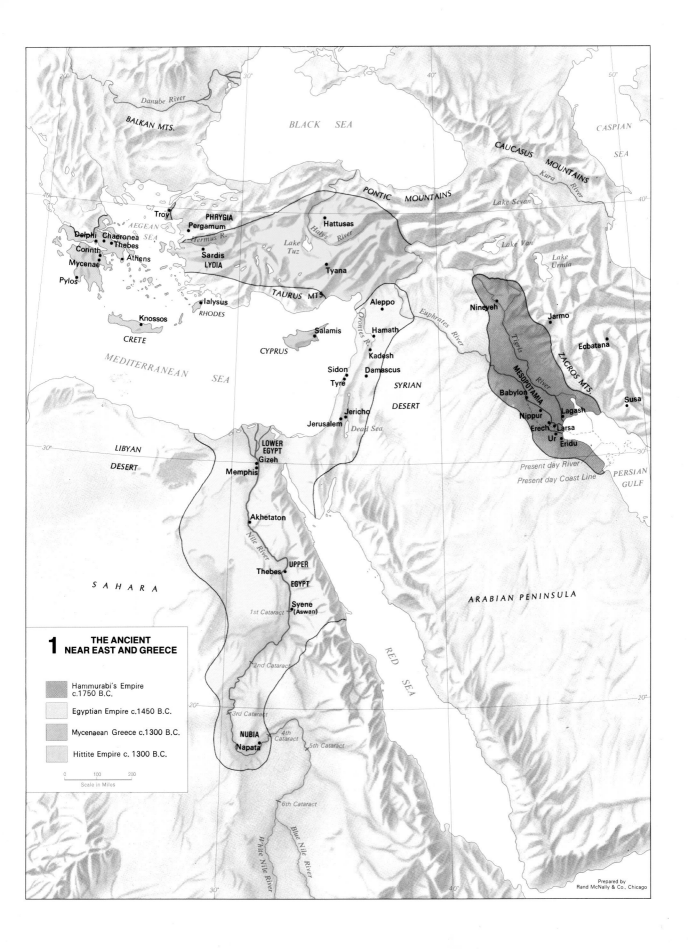

THE ANCIENT
NEAR EAST AND GREECE

Hammurabi's Empire
c.1750 B.C.

Egyptian Empire c.1450 B.C.

Mycenaean Greece c.1300 B.C.

Hittite Empire c. 1300 B.C.

0   100   200
Scale in Miles

Prepared by
Rand McNally & Co., Chicago

ATLANTIC

OCEAN

IRELAND

IRISH
SEA

NORTH

SEA

BALTIC

Antoninus' Wall
(C. 140 A.D.)

Hadrian's Wall
(C. 122 A.D.)

York

Chester • PENNINES • Lincoln

BRITAIN

Colchester

Bath • • London
Thames R.

ENGLISH CHANNEL

GERMANIA

Elbe

Oder R.

SUDETES

Cologne

Rhine River

BELGICA

Paris •

Seine River

Meuse R.

Mainz

Loire River

Saône R.

Danube

BAY OF
BISCAY

Bordeaux •

Garonne R.

GAUL

CENTRAL
MASSIF

Lyons •

Rhône River

ALPS

CISALPINE GAUL

Po River

Genoa • Ravenna

CANTABRIAN MTS.

Douro River

Segovia •

PYRENEES

Ebro River

Marseilles •

Pisa •

Salonae

APENNINES

ADRIATIC SEA

Tagus River

SPAIN

Toledo •

Saguntum •

CORSICA

ITALY

Rome •

Guadiana River

SIERRA MORENA
Cordova •

Valencia •

SARDINIA

Naples • • Pompeii

Guadalquivir R.

Cádiz •

SIERRA NEVADA

New
Carthage

BALEARIC
ISLANDS

MEDITERRANEAN

TYRRHENIAN
SEA

Strait of Gibraltar

Tangier • Pillars of Hercules

MADEIRA
ISLANDS

MAURETANIA

MOUNTAINS

Moulouya R.

ATLAS

Chélif R.

Medjerda R.

Utica •

Carthage •

Messina •

SICILY

Syracuse •

MALTA

CANARY
ISLANDS

Chott
Djerid

NUMIDIA

Oea • Leptis
Magna

GRAND ERG OCCIDENTAL

GRAND ERG ORIENTAL

2 THE ROMAN EMPIRE
C. A.D. 117

0   100   200   300

Scale in Miles

AHAGGAR

MOUNTAINS

SAHARA

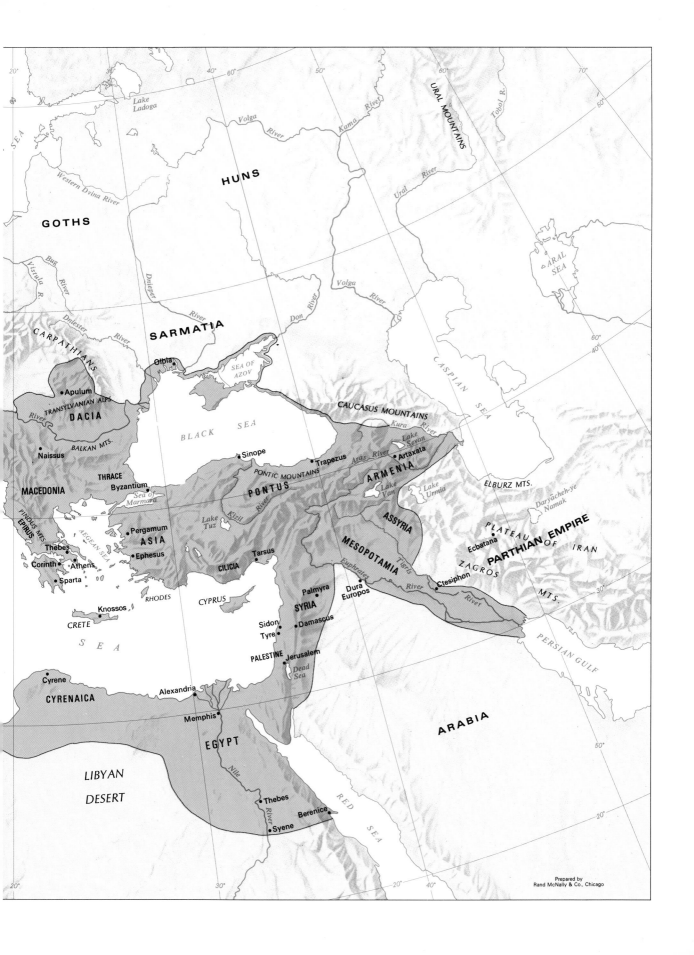

GOTHS

HUNS

SARMATIA

SEA

Lake Ladoga

Western Dvina River

Volga River

Kama River

URAL MOUNTAINS

Tobol R.

Ural River

Bug River

Vistula R.

Dnieper River

Volga River

Don River

ARAL SEA

CARPATHIANS

Dniester River

Apulum

TRANSYLVANIAN ALPS

DACIA

River

BALKAN MTS.

Naissus

THRACE

MACEDONIA

Byzantium

Olbia

SEA OF AZOV

BLACK SEA

Sinope

PONTIC MOUNTAINS

Trapezus

CAUCASUS MOUNTAINS

Kura River

Lake Sevan

Aras River

Artaxata

ARMENIA

Lake Van

Lake Urmia

CASPIAN SEA

ELBURZ MTS.

Daryācheh-ye Namak

PONTUS

Sea of Marmara

Kizil River

ASSYRIA

PLATEAU

PARTHIAN EMPIRE

OF IRAN

PINDUS MTS.

EPIRUS

AEGEAN SEA

Pergamum

ASIA

Lake Tuz

Ephesus

Thebes

Corinth

Athens

Sparta

Tarsus

CILICIA

MESOPOTAMIA

Euphrates River

Tigris River

ZAGROS

Ecbatana

Ctesiphon

MTS.

RHODES

CYPRUS

Palmyra

Dura Europos

SYRIA

Sidon

Damascus

Tyre

Knossos

CRETE

SEA

PALESTINE

Jerusalem

Dead Sea

PERSIAN GULF

Cyrene

CYRENAICA

Alexandria

Memphis

ARABIA

EGYPT

Nile River

LIBYAN

DESERT

Thebes

Berenice

Syene

RED SEA

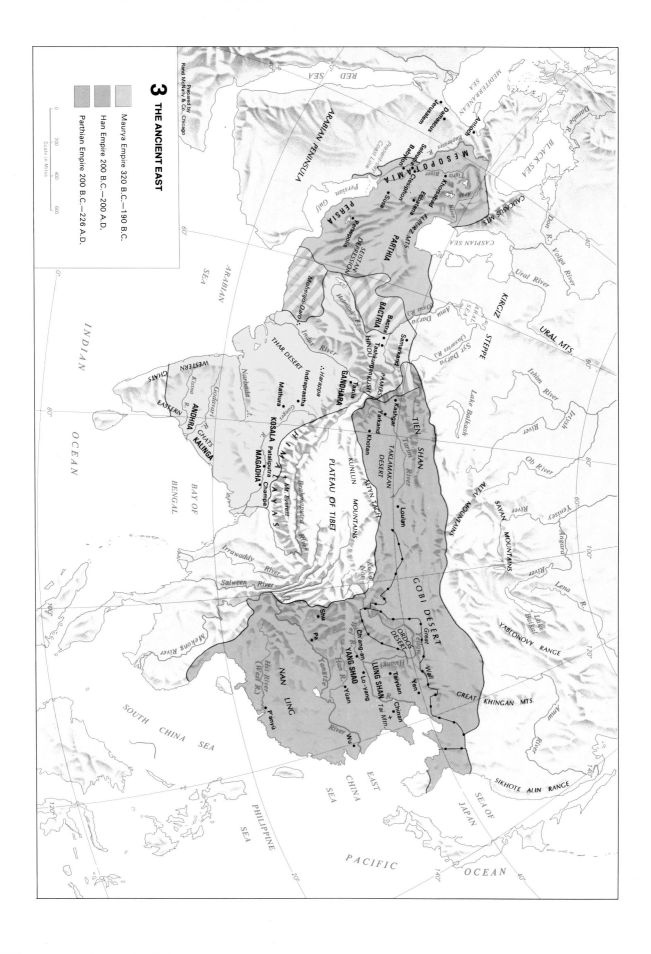

3 THE ANCIENT EAST

Maurya Empire 320 B.C.—190 B.C.

Han Empire 200 B.C.—200 A.D.

Parthian Empire 200 B.C.—226 A.D.

Scale in Miles

0   200   400   600

MEDITERRANEAN SEA

Danube

BLACK SEA

Damascus

Jerusalem

Antioch

CAUCASUS MTS.

Don R.

Volga River

CASPIAN SEA

Ural River

URAL MTS.

RED SEA

ARABIAN PENINSULA

Present Coast Line
Seleucia
Babylon
Ctesiphon
Euphrates River
MESOPOTAMIA
Nineveh
Ecbatana
Tigris River
ELBURZ MTS.
PERSIA
Susa
PARTHIA
Persepolis
SEISTAN DEPRESSION

KIRGIZ STEPPE

ARAL SEA

Ishim River

Irtish River

Syr Darya (Jaxartes R.)

Amu Darya (Oxus R.)

BACTRIA
Bactra
Samarkand

HINDU KUSH
Tashkurgan
PAMIRS
Kashgar
Yarkand
Khotan

TIEN SHAN

Lake Balkash

Ob River

ALTAI MOUNTAINS

SAYAN MOUNTAINS

Yenisey River

Angara River

TAKLAMAKAN DESERT
Tarim River
ALTYN TAGH
KUNLUN MOUNTAINS
Loulan
Koko Nor

Lena R.

Lake Baikal

YABLONOVY RANGE

GOBI DESERT

Great Wall

GREAT KHINGAN MTS.

Amur River

PERSIAN GULF

ARABIAN SEA

Mohenjo-Daro
Indus River
THAR DESERT
GANDHARA
Taxila
Harappa
Indraprastha
Mathura
Ganges
KOSALA
Pataliputra
MAGADHA
Champa
Brahmaputra River

Narbada
Krishna
Godavari
WESTERN GHATS
EASTERN GHATS
ANDHRA
KALINGA

HIMALAYAS
Mt. Everest

PLATEAU OF TIBET

NAN LING

Snu
Pa

Hsi River (West R.)
P'anyu

Mekong River

Salween River

Irrawaddy River

Yangtze
Han R.
Wei R.
Ch'ang-an
YANG SHAO
(Sian)
Lo-yang
Yuan
LUNG SHAN
Tai Min.
Chinan
Taiyuan
Yen
Yellow (Huang) River
ORDOS DESERT

Wu River

SIKHOTE ALIN RANGE

INDIAN OCEAN

BAY OF BENGAL

SOUTH CHINA SEA

PHILIPPINE SEA

EAST CHINA SEA

SEA OF JAPAN

PACIFIC OCEAN

0°   60°   80°   100°   120°   140°

20°   40°   60°

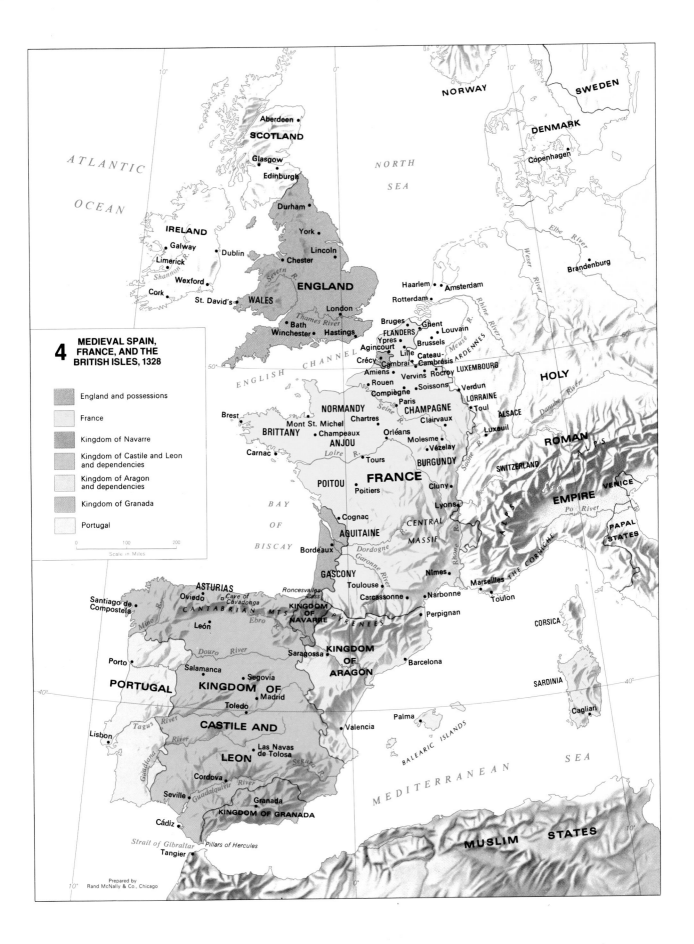

NORWAY

SWEDEN

DENMARK

Copenhagen

ATLANTIC

OCEAN

NORTH

SEA

SCOTLAND

Aberdeen

Glasgow

Edinburgh

Durham

IRELAND

York

Galway

Dublin

Lincoln

Limerick

Chester

Wexford

ENGLAND

Cork

St. David's

WALES

London

Bath

Winchester

Hastings

Elbe River

Brandenburg

Weser River

Haarlem

Amsterdam

Rotterdam

Rhine River

Bruges

Ghent

FLANDERS

Louvain

Ypres

Brussels

Agincourt

Lille

Cateau-

LUXEMBOURG

Crécy

Cambrai

Cambrésis

Rocroy

ENGLISH CHANNEL

Amiens

Vervins

Soissons

Verdun

HOLY

Rouen

LORRAINE

Compiègne

Paris

Toul

ALSACE

NORMANDY

Chartres

CHAMPAGNE

Luxeuil

Brest

Mont St. Michel

Seine

Clairvaux

Danube River

ROMAN

BRITTANY

Champeaux

ANJOU

Orléans

Molesme

SWITZERLAND

Carnac

Loire R.

Tours

Vézelay

ALPS

VENICE

BURGUNDY

FRANCE

EMPIRE

Po River

POITOU

Cluny

Poitiers

Lyons

PAPAL

BAY

CENTRAL

STATES

OF

Cognac

MASSIF

BISCAY

AQUITAINE

Dordogne

Bordeaux

Garonne River

Rhône R.

GASCONY

Nîmes

Toulouse

Marseilles

THE CORNICHE

CORSICA

Carcassonne

Narbonne

Toulon

ASTURIAS

Roncesvalles

Perpignan

Santiago de

Oviedo

Cave of

Pass

Compostela

Covadonga

CANTABRIAN MTS.

KINGDOM

PYRENEES

León

Ebro

OF NAVARRE

SARDINIA

Douro

River

Saragossa

KINGDOM

Barcelona

Cagliari

Porto

Mino

OF

Salamanca

ARAGON

Segovia

KINGDOM OF

Madrid

PORTUGAL

Toledo

Palma

Valencia

Lisbon

CASTILE AND

Tagus

River

Las Navas

BALEARIC ISLANDS

de Tolosa

LEON

Segura R.

MEDITERRANEAN

SEA

Cordova

Guadalquivir

River

Seville

Granada

Cádiz

KINGDOM OF GRANADA

Strait of Gibraltar

Pillars of Hercules

MUSLIM

STATES

Tangier

Prepared by
Rand McNally & Co., Chicago

4 MEDIEVAL SPAIN,
FRANCE, AND THE
BRITISH ISLES, 1328

England and possessions

France

Kingdom of Navarre

Kingdom of Castile and Leon
and dependencies

Kingdom of Aragon
and dependencies

Kingdom of Granada

Portugal

0   100   200
Scale in Miles

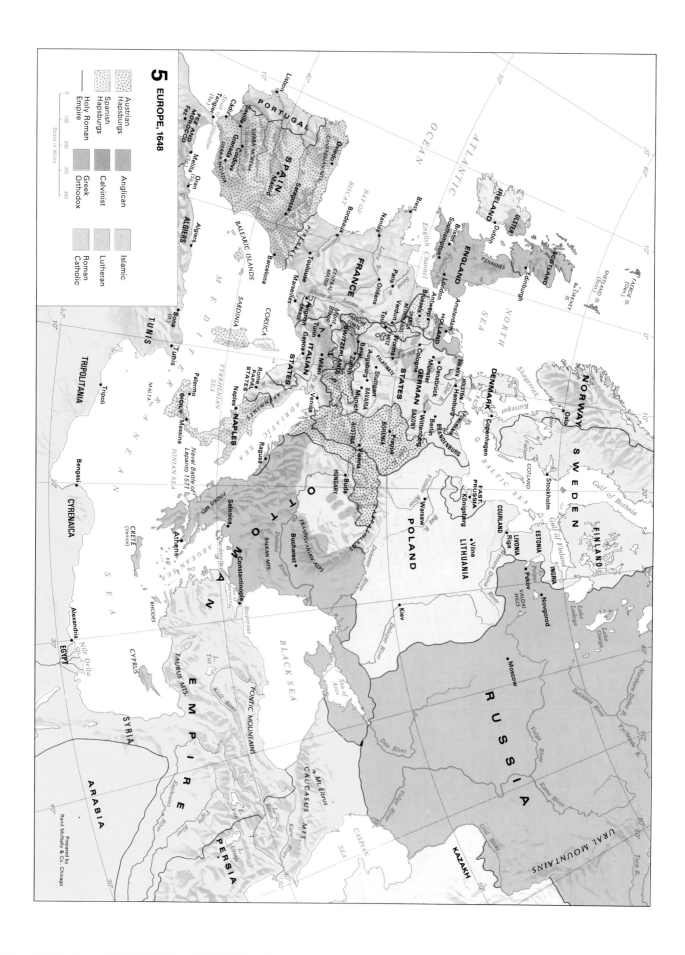

5 EUROPE, 1648

Austrian Hapsburgs

Spanish Hapsburgs

Holy Roman Empire

Scale in Miles
0   100   200   300   400

Austrian Hapsburgs	Anglican
Spanish Hapsburgs	Calvinist
	Greek Orthodox

	Islamic
	Lutheran
	Roman Catholic

Prepared by
Rand McNally & Co., Chicago

ATLANTIC OCEAN

NORTH SEA

BALTIC SEA

MEDITERRANEAN SEA

TYRRHENIAN SEA

ADRIATIC SEA

IONIAN SEA

AEGEAN SEA

BLACK SEA

CASPIAN SEA

BAY OF BISCAY

PORTUGAL

SPAIN

FRANCE

ENGLAND

IRELAND

SCOTLAND

NORWAY

SWEDEN

DENMARK

FINLAND

POLAND

LITHUANIA

RUSSIA

HUNGARY

GERMAN STATES

ITALIAN STATES

PAPAL STATES

NAPLES

SICILY

SARDINIA

CORSICA

SWITZERLAND

HOLLAND

SPANISH NETHERLANDS

BAVARIA

BOHEMIA

SAXONY

BRANDENBURG

AUSTRIA

EAST PRUSSIA

COURLAND

LIVONIA

ESTONIA

INGRIA

TRANSYLVANIA

OTTOMAN EMPIRE

TUNIS

ALGIERS

TRIPOLITANIA

CYRENAICA

EGYPT

SYRIA

ARABIA

PERSIA

KAZAKH

FEZ AND MOROCCO

CRETE (Venice)

CYPRUS

RHODES

MALTA

BALEARIC ISLANDS

Lisbon
Madrid
Seville
Córdoba
Granada
Cádiz
Oviedo
Saragossa
Barcelona
Toulouse
Marseilles
Bordeaux
Nantes
Brest
Paris
Orléans
Avignon
Montpellier
Turin
Genoa
Milan
Venice
Rome
Naples
Palermo
Messina
Ragusa
Athens
Salonica
Constantinople
Bucharest
Buda
Warsaw
Königsberg
Vilna
Riga
Pskov
Novgorod
Moscow
Kiev
Stockholm
Oslo
Copenhagen
Hamburg
Bremen
Amsterdam
Brussels
Antwerp
London
Southampton
Bristol
Dublin
Edinburgh
Cologne
Münster
Osnabrück
Berlin
Wittenberg
Dresden
Prague
Vienna
Munich
Augsburg
Stuttgart
Basel
Zürich
Worms
Metz
Verdun
Toul
Algiers
Bona
Tunis
Tripoli
Bengasi
Alexandria
Oran
Melilla
Tangier

Naval Battle of Lepanto 1571

URAL MOUNTAINS
CAUCASUS MTS.
BALKAN MTS.
PINDUS MTS.
TAURUS MTS.
PONTIC MOUNTAINS
SIERRA MORENA
SIERRA NEVADA
CANTABRIAN MTS.
PYRENEES
CENTRAL MASSIF
TRANSYLVANIAN ALPS
PENNINES
VALDAI HILLS

Loire R.
Seine R.
Rhône R.
Saône R.
Ebro R.
Danube River
Don River
Volga River
Dnieper River
Dniester River
Ural River
Kama River
Vistula River
Oder R.
Rhine R.
Elbe R.
Euphrates River
Tigris River
Nile Delta

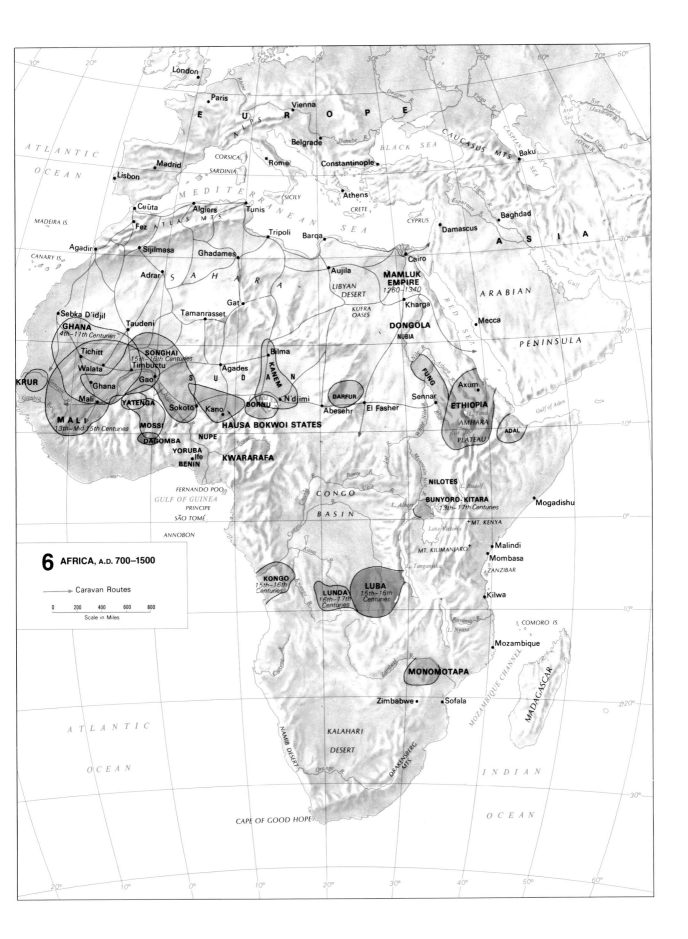

ATLANTIC OCEAN

London
Paris
Vienna
EUROPE
Belgrade
BLACK SEA
CAUCASUS MTS.
Baku
CASPIAN SEA
ALPS
Danube R.
Constantinople
Rome
MADRID
CORSICA
SARDINIA
SICILY
Athens
CRETE
CYPRUS
Damascus
Baghdad
ASIA
Lisbon
Madrid
MADEIRA IS.
Ceūta
Algiers
Tunis
ATLAS MTS.
Fez
Tripoli
Barqa
Cairo
MEDITERRANEAN SEA
Agadir
Sijilmasa
Ghadames
MAMLUK EMPIRE 1260–1340
Damascus
ARABIAN
CANARY IS.
Adrar
SAHARA
Aujila
LIBYAN DESERT
Kharga
Mecca
PENINSULA
RED SEA
Sebka D'idjil
GHANA 4th–11th Centuries
Taudeni
Gat
Tamanrasset
KUFRA OASES
DONGOLA
NUBIA
Tichitt
SONGHAI 15th–16th Centuries
Bilma
Walata
Timbuctu
Agades
KANEM
FUNG
Axum
KRUR
Ghana
Gao
N
DARFUR
Sennar
ETHIOPIA
Gulf of Aden
Mali
YATENGA
Sokoto
Kano
BORNU
N'djimi
Abeshr
El Fasher
AMHARA PLATEAU
L. Tana
ADAL
MALI 13th–Mid 15th Centuries
MOSSI
DAGOMBA
NUPE
HAUSA BOKWOI STATES
YORUBA
Ife
BENIN
KWARARAFA
NILOTES
L. Rudolf
Mogadishu
FERNANDO POO
GULF OF GUINEA
PRINCIPE
SÃO TOMÉ
CONGO BASIN
L. Albert
BUNYORO-KITARA 13th–17th Centuries
MT. KENYA
ANNOBON
Lake Victoria
MT. KILIMANJARO
Malindi
Mombasa
ZANZIBAR
KONGO 15th–16th Centuries
LUNDA 16th–17th Centuries
LUBA 15th–16th Centuries
L. Tanganyika
Kilwa
L. Nyasa
COMORO IS.
Mozambique
MONOMOTAPA
Zimbabwe
Sofala
MOZAMBIQUE CHANNEL
MADAGASCAR
KALAHARI DESERT
NAMIB DESERT
Orange R.
DRAKENSBERG MTS.
INDIAN OCEAN
ATLANTIC OCEAN
CAPE OF GOOD HOPE

6 AFRICA, A.D. 700–1500

→ Caravan Routes

0   200   400   600   800
Scale in Miles

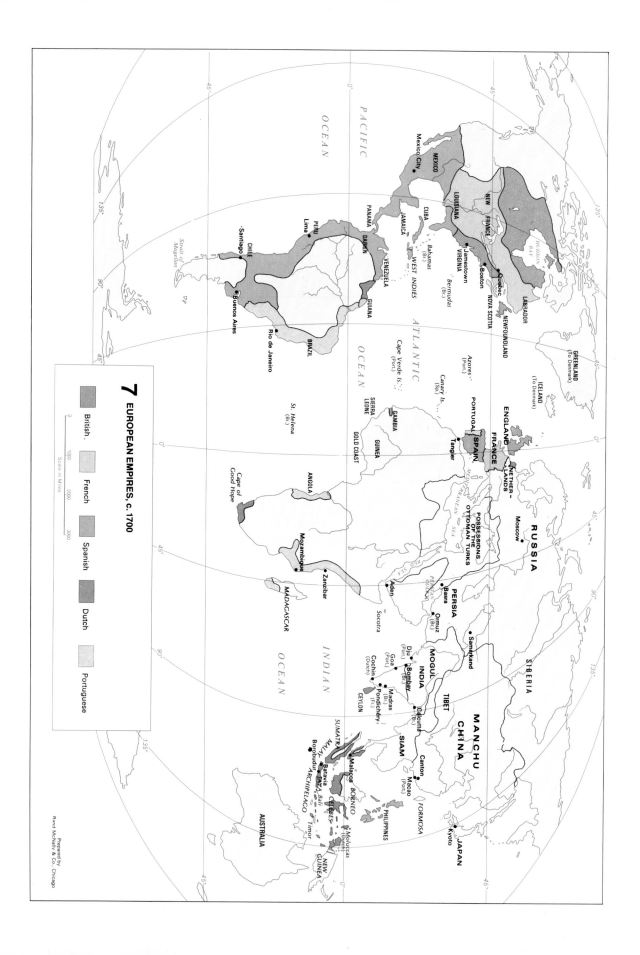

7 EUROPEAN EMPIRES, c. 1700

British,   French   Spanish   Dutch   Portuguese

Scale in Miles

0   1000   2000   3000

Prepared by
Rand McNally & Co., Chicago

PACIFIC OCEAN

MEXICO
Mexico City

PANAMA
CUBA
JAMAICA
WEST INDIES
Bahamas (Br.)
Bermudas (Br.)

NEW FRANCE
LOUISIANA
VIRGINIA
Jamestown
Boston
Quebec
NOVA SCOTIA
NEWFOUNDLAND
LABRADOR
HUDSON BAY

PERU
Lima
Santiago
CHILE
Buenos Aires
VENEZUELA
GUIANA
BRAZIL
Rio de Janeiro

Strait of Magellan

ATLANTIC OCEAN

Cape Verde Is. (Port.)
Canary Is. (Sp.)
Azores (Port.)

St. Helena (Br.)

SIERRA LEONE
GAMBIA
GUINEA
GOLD COAST

Cape of Good Hope

GREENLAND (To Denmark)
ICELAND (To Denmark)

PORTUGAL SPAIN
ENGLAND
FRANCE
NETHER-LANDS

MEDITERRANEAN SEA

POSSESSIONS OF THE OTTOMAN TURKS

RUSSIA
Moscow

SIBERIA

PERSIA
Basra
Ormuz (Br.)
Samarkand

MOGUL
INDIA
Diu (Port.)
Goa (Port.)
Bombay (Br.)
Cochin (Dutch)
Madras (Br.)
Pondichéry (Fr.)
CEYLON
Calcutta (Br.)

TIBET

MANCHU CHINA

SIAM
Canton
Macao (Port.)
FORMOSA

JAPAN
Kyoto

INDIAN OCEAN

Aden
RED SEA
PERSIAN GULF

ANGOLA
Mozambique
Zanzibar
MADAGASCAR
Socotra

Tangier

SUMATRA
MALAYA
Malacca
BORNEO
Batavia
JAVA Bali
CELEBES
ARCHIPELAGO
Borobudur
Moluccas (Dutch)
Timor
PHILIPPINES
NEW GUINEA

AUSTRALIA

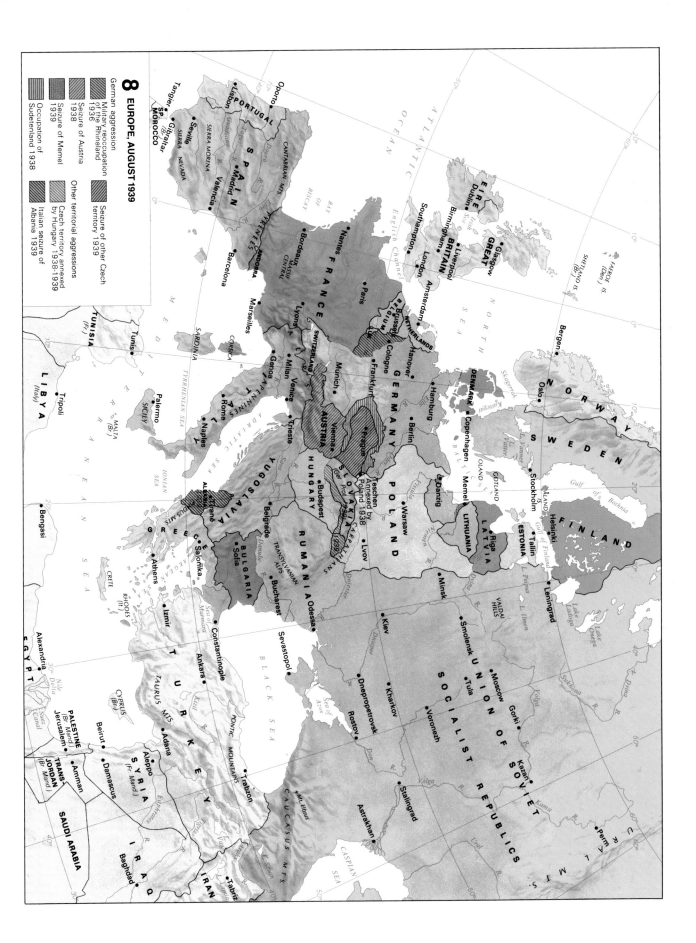

8 EUROPE, AUGUST 1939

German aggression

Military reoccupation
of the Rhineland
1936

Seizure of Austria
1938

Seizure of Memel
1939

Occupation of
Sudetenland 1938

Seizure of other Czech
territory 1939

Other territorial aggressions

Czech territory annexed
by Hungary 1938–1939

Italian seizure of
Albania 1939

FAEROE IS.
(Den.)

SHETLAND IS.
(Br.)

ATLANTIC OCEAN

NORTH SEA

NORWAY

SWEDEN

FINLAND

Bergen
Oslo
Stockholm
Helsinki
Leningrad
Lake Ladoga
Lake Onega

ÅLAND IS.
GOTLAND
Gulf of Bothnia
Gulf of Finland

EIRE
Dublin
GREAT BRITAIN
Glasgow
Liverpool
Birmingham
London
Southampton

Irish Sea
English Channel

NETHERLANDS
Amsterdam
BELGIUM
Brussels
Hanover
Cologne
Frankfurt
Hamburg

DENMARK
Copenhagen

BALTIC SEA
Danzig
Memel

ESTONIA
Tallin
L. Peipus
LATVIA
Riga
LITHUANIA

UNION OF SOVIET SOCIALIST REPUBLICS

Minsk
Smolensk
Moscow
Gorki
Kazan
Tula
Voronezh
Kiev
Kharkov
Dnepropetrovsk
Rostov
Stalingrad
Astrakhan
Perm
Mt. Elbus

VALDAI HILLS
URAL MTS.
CAUCASUS MTS.
CASPIAN SEA
Volga R.
Don R.
Ural R.
Kama R.
Sukhona R.
N. Dvina R.

PORTUGAL
Oporto
Lisbon

SPAIN
Seville
Madrid
Valencia
Barcelona

SP. MOROCCO
Tangier
Gibraltar (Br.)

ANDORRA

FRANCE
Nantes
Paris
Bordeaux
Lyons
Marseilles

GERMANY
Berlin
Munich

POLAND
Warsaw
Lvov
Teschen Annexed by Poland 1938

SWITZERLAND
AUSTRIA
Vienna
Prague
SLOVAKIA (Ger. Prot.)
HUNGARY
Budapest

CARPATHIANS

RUMANIA
Bucharest
Odessa

YUGOSLAVIA
Belgrade

BULGARIA
Sofia

ALBANIA
Tiranë

GREECE
Athens
Salonika

ITALY
Genoa
Milan
Venice
Trieste
Rome
Naples

CORSICA
SARDINIA
SICILY
Palermo
MALTA (Br.)

TUNISIA (Fr.)
Tunis

LIBYA (Italy)
Tripoli
Bengasi

MEDITERRANEAN SEA
TYRRHENIAN SEA
ADRIATIC SEA
IONIAN SEA
AEGEAN SEA
CRETE
RHODES (It.)

BLACK SEA
Sevastopol
Sea of Azov
Constantinople
Izmir
Ankara
Trabzon

TURKEY
Sea of Marmara
PONTIC MOUNTAINS
TAURUS MTS.
CYPRUS (Br.)

SYRIA (Fr. Mand.)
Aleppo
Damascus
Beirut
Adana

PALESTINE (Br. Mand.)
Jerusalem
TRANS JORDAN (Br. Mand.)
Amman

SAUDI ARABIA

IRAQ
Baghdad

IRAN
Tabriz

EGYPT
Alexandria
Nile Delta
Suez Canal

BAY OF BISCAY
CANTABRIAN MTS.
PYRENEES
SIERRA MORENA
SIERRA NEVADA
MASSIF CENTRAL
ALPS
APENNINES
PINDUS MTS.
TRANSYLVANIAN ALPS

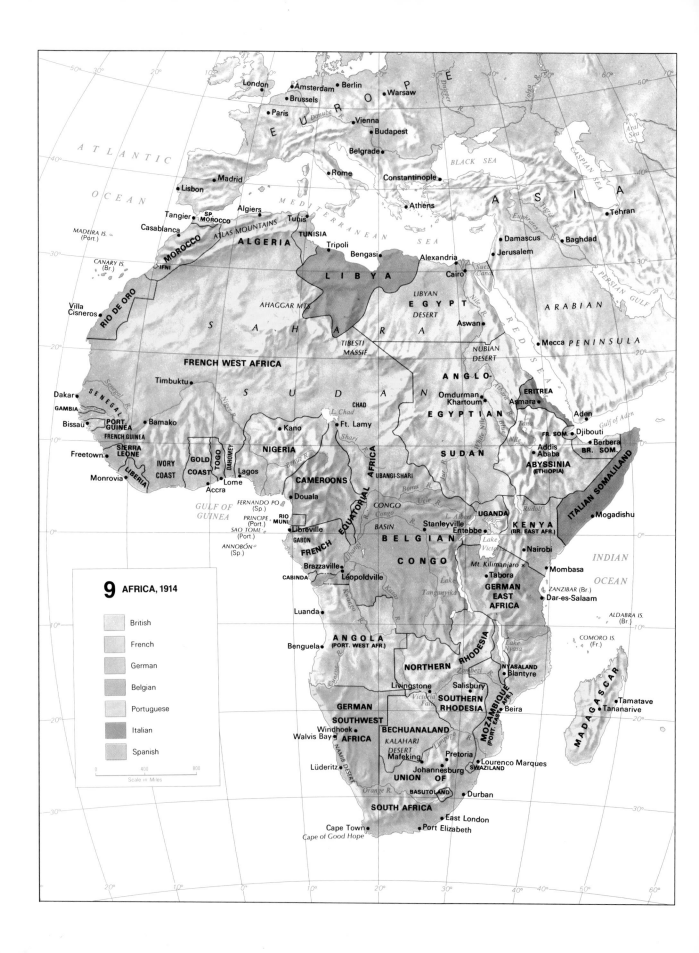

9 AFRICA, 1914

British
French
German
Belgian
Portuguese
Italian
Spanish

Scale in Miles
0   400   800

ATLANTIC OCEAN

EUROPE

London
Amsterdam • Berlin
Brussels
• Warsaw
Paris
• Vienna
• Budapest
Belgrade
• Rome
BLACK SEA
Constantinople
Madrid
• Athens
Lisbon
Tangier • Algiers
SP. MOROCCO
Casablanca
MADEIRA IS. (Port.)
MEDITERRANEAN SEA
Damascus • Baghdad
Jerusalem
Tehran
ASIA
ATLAS MOUNTAINS • Tunis
MOROCCO TUNISIA
IFNI • Tripoli
Bengasi
Alexandria
Cairo
Suez Canal
ARABIAN
ALGERIA
LIBYA
CANARY IS. (Br.)
RIO DE ORO
Villa Cisneros

S A H A R A
AHAGGAR MTS.
LIBYAN
EGYPT
DESERT
Aswan
RED SEA
Mecca PENINSULA
PERSIAN GULF

TIBESTI MASSIF
NUBIAN DESERT
FRENCH WEST AFRICA
Dakar
SENEGAL
Timbuktu
SUDAN
ANGLO-
Omdurman
Khartoum
ERITREA
Asmara
Aden
Gulf of Aden
GAMBIA
PORT. GUINEA
Bissau
FRENCH GUINEA
Bamako
Kano
L. Chad
CHAD
Ft. Lamy
Shari
EGYPTIAN
FR. SOM. Djibouti
Berbera
BR. SOM.
SIERRA LEONE
Freetown
NIGERIA
Benue R.
UBANGI-SHARI
SUDAN
Addis Ababa
ABYSSINIA (ETHIOPIA)
ITALIAN SOMALILAND
Monrovia
LIBERIA
IVORY COAST
GOLD COAST
TOGO
DAHOMEY
Lagos
Lome
Accra
CAMEROONS
Douala
FERNANDO PO (Sp.)
GULF OF GUINEA
PRINCIPE (Port.)
RIO MUNI
SAO TOME (Port.)
ANNOBÓN (Sp.)
Libreville
GABON
FRENCH EQUATORIAL AFRICA
CONGO
Congo
Uele R.
L. Albert
UGANDA
Stanleyville
Entebbe
KENYA (BR. EAST AFR.)
L. Rudolf
Mogadishu
CONGO BASIN
BELGIAN
Lake Victoria
Nairobi
INDIAN OCEAN
Brazzaville
Léopoldville
CABINDA
CONGO
Mt. Kilimanjaro ×
Mombasa
ZANZIBAR (Br.)
GERMAN EAST AFRICA
Tabora
Dar-es-Salaam
Luanda
Lake Tanganyika
ALDABRA IS. (Br.)
COMORO IS. (Fr.)
Benguela
ANGOLA (PORT. WEST AFR.)
NORTHERN RHODESIA
RHODESIA
Lake Nyasa
NYASALAND
Blantyre
Livingstone
Salisbury
Victoria Falls
SOUTHERN RHODESIA
Zambezi
MOZAMBIQUE (PORT. EAST AFR.)
Beira
MADAGASCAR
Tamatave
Tananarive
GERMAN SOUTHWEST AFRICA
BECHUANALAND
Windhoek
Walvis Bay
KALAHARI DESERT
Mafeking
Pretoria
Lourenço Marques
SWAZILAND
Lüderitz
NAMIB DESERT
Johannesburg
Limpopo
UNION OF
BASUTOLAND
Durban
Orange R.
SOUTH AFRICA
East London
Cape Town
Port Elizabeth
Cape of Good Hope

Danube
Dnieper
Volga
CASPIAN SEA
Aral Sea
Euphrates R.
Tigris R.
Nile
Blue Nile
White Nile
Tana
Niger R.
Senegal R.
Kwango
Kasai
Ubangi R.
Bomu R.

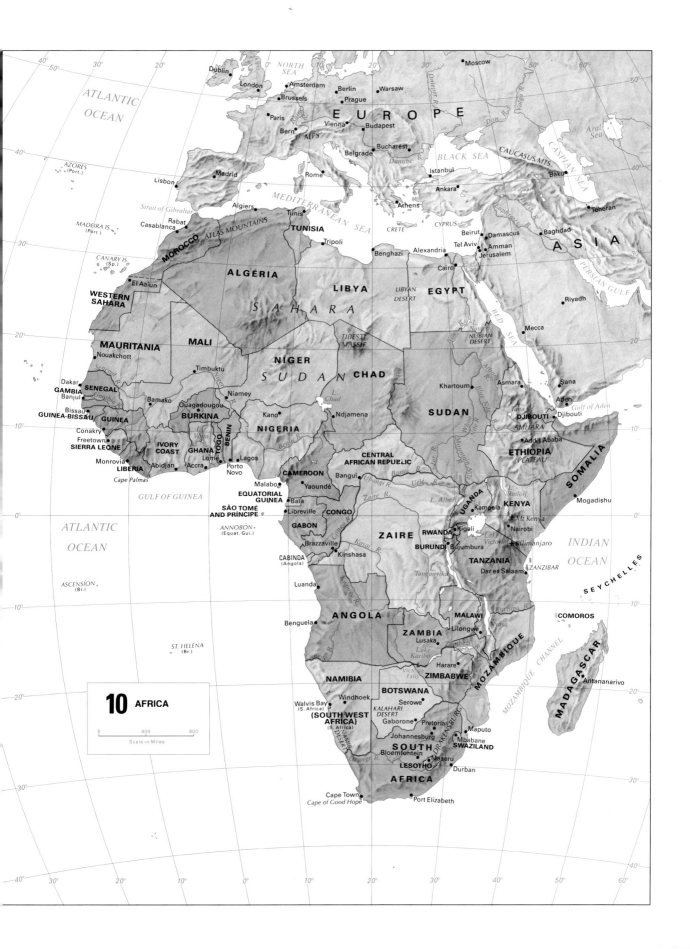

ATLANTIC OCEAN

NORTH SEA

Dublin
London
Amsterdam
Brussels
Berlin
Warsaw
Prague
Paris
EUROPE
Moscow
Vienna
Budapest
Bern
ALPS
Belgrade
Bucharest
Danube R.
BLACK SEA
CAUCASUS MTS.
Volga R.
CASPIAN SEA
Aral Sea
Baku

AZORES
(Port.)
Lisbon
Madrid
Rome
Istanbul
Ankara
Athens
CRETE
CYPRUS
Beirut
Damascus
Tel Aviv
Jerusalem
Amman
Baghdad
ASIA
Teheran

MADEIRA IS.
(Port.)
Strait of Gibraltar
Rabat
Casablanca
Algiers
MEDITERRANEAN SEA
Tunis
TUNISIA
Tripoli
Benghazi
Alexandria
Cairo
Suez Can.
PERSIAN GULF
Riyadh

MOROCCO
ATLAS MOUNTAINS

CANARY IS.
(Sp.)
El Aaiun
WESTERN SAHARA

ALGERIA
SAHARA
LIBYA
LIBYAN DESERT
EGYPT
RED SEA
NUBIAN DESERT
Mecca

MAURITANIA
Nouakchott
MALI
NIGER
TIDESTI MASSIF
Nasser
CHAD
Khartoum
Asmara
Sana
Aden
Gulf of Aden

Dakar
SENEGAL
GAMBIA
Banjul
Timbuktu
SUDAN
L. Chad
Ndjamena
SUDAN
Blue Nile
DJIBOUTI
Djibouti
AMHARA

Bissau
GUINEA-BISSAU
GUINEA
Bamako
Niamey
Kano
NIGERIA
Benue R.
Addis Ababa
ETHIOPIA
PLATEAU
SOMALIA

Conakry
Freetown
SIERRA LEONE
Ouagadougou
BURKINA
BENIN
TOGO
Lagos
Porto Novo
CAMEROON
Yaoundé
CENTRAL AFRICAN REPUBLIC
Bangui
Ubangi R.
Uele R.
KENYA

Monrovia
LIBERIA
IVORY COAST
GHANA
Volta
Abidjan
Accra
Lomé
Cape Palmas
EQUATORIAL GUINEA
Malabo
Bata
Libreville
CONGO
Zaire R.
L. Albert
UGANDA
Kampala
Mt Kenya
Nairobi

GULF OF GUINEA
SÃO TOMÉ AND PRÍNCIPE
ANNOBÓN
(Equat. Gui.)
GABON
Brazzaville
Kinshasa
ZAIRE
RWANDA
Kigali
BURUNDI
Bujumbura
Lake Victoria
Kilimanjaro
INDIAN OCEAN
SEYCHELLES

ATLANTIC OCEAN
CABINDA
(Angola)
Kasai R.
Mogadishu
Rudolf
TANZANIA
Dar es Salaam
ZANZIBAR

ASCENSION
(Br.)
Luanda
Tanganyika

ST. HELENA
(Br.)
ANGOLA
Benguela
MALAWI
Lilongwe
COMOROS
Ruvuma R.
Nasa

ZAMBIA
Lusaka
Zambezi R.
Lake Kariba
Victoria Falls
Harare
ZIMBABWE
MOZAMBIQUE
MOZAMBIQUE CHANNEL
MADAGASCAR
Antananarivo

NAMIBIA
BOTSWANA
Serowe
Windhoek
Walvis Bay
(S. Africa)
KALAHARI DESERT

10 AFRICA
0   400   800
Scale in Miles

SOUTH WEST AFRICA
(S. Africa)
NAMIB DESERT
Gaborone
Pretoria
Johannesburg
Maputo
Mbabane
SWAZILAND
Bloemfontein
Maseru
LESOTHO
Durban
SOUTH AFRICA
Orange R.

Cape Town
Cape of Good Hope
Port Elizabeth

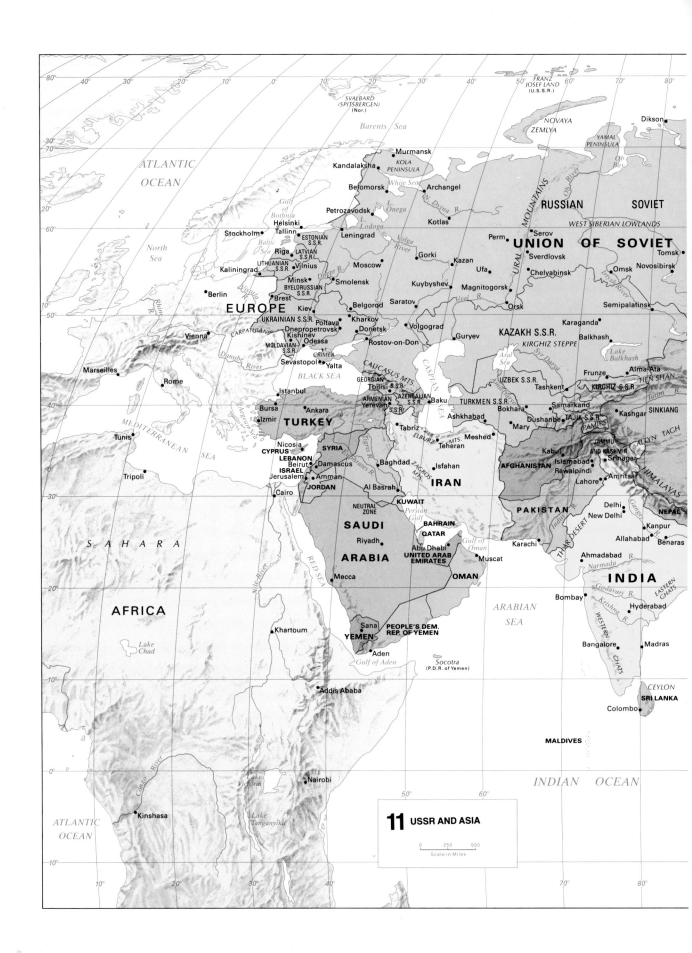

ATLANTIC
OCEAN

Barents Sea

SVALBARD
(SPITSBERGEN)
(Nor.)

FRANZ
JOSEF LAND
(U.S.S.R.)

NOVAYA
ZEMLYA

YAMAL
PENINSULA

Dikson

Murmansk
Kandalaksha
KOLA
PENINSULA

Ob
Bay

Belomorsk   *White Sea*   Archangel

RUSSIAN   SOVIET

Petrozavodsk
L.
Onega

N. Dvina R.

Kotlas

WEST SIBERIAN LOWLANDS

Helsinki
Gulf
of
Bothnia

L.
Ladoga

Perm   Serov

Stockholm   Tallinn   Leningrad
ESTONIAN
S.S.R.

Volga
River

Gorki

Kazan

Sverdlovsk

Tomsk

UNION   OF   SOVIET

Baltic
Sea

Riga
LATVIAN
S.S.R.

Moscow

Ufa

Chelyabinsk

Omsk   Novosibirsk

Kaliningrad
LITHUANIAN
S.S.R.

Vilnius

Kuybyshev

Magnitogorsk

Berlin

Minsk
BYELORUSSIAN
S.S.R.

Brest

Smolensk

Saratov

Orsk

Semipalatinsk

EUROPE

Kiev

Belgorod

Volgograd

Karaganda

KAZAKH S.S.R.

Balkhash

Vienna

UKRAINIAN S.S.R.   Poltava
Dnepropetrovsk
Kishinev
MOLDAVIAN
S.S.R.
Odessa

Kharkov
Donetsk

Rostov-on-Don

Guryev

KIRGHIZ STEPPE

Lake
Balkhash

CARPATHIANS

Danube
River

Sevastopol
CRIMEA
Yalta

BLACK SEA

CAUCASUS MTS.

Aral
Sea

Syr Darya

Frunze   Alma-Ata

Rhine

Marseilles

Vistula R.

Istanbul

GEORGIAN
S.S.R.
Tbilisi

AZERBAIJAN
S.S.R.

CASPIAN

UZBEK S.S.R.

Tashkent

KIRGHIZ S.S.R.

TIEN SHAN

Rome

Bursa
Izmir

Ankara

ARMENIAN
S.S.R.
Yerevan

Baku

TURKMEN S.S.R.

Bokhara

Samarkand

Kashgar   SINKIANG

Tarim R.

MEDITERRANEAN

Aegean Sea

TURKEY

Tabriz

ELBURZ
MTS.

Ashkhabad

Mary

Dushanbe
TAJIK S.S.R.

PAMIRS

ALTYN TAGH

Tunis

Nicosia
CYPRUS
LEBANON

Beirut
Damascus
SYRIA

Tigris R.

Teheran

Meshed

Kabul
JAMMU
AND KASHMIR

HIMALAYAS

SEA

Tripoli

ISRAEL
Jerusalem
Amman
JORDAN

Euphrates R.

Baghdad

Isfahan

ZAGROS MTS.

IRAN

AFGHANISTAN

Islamabad
Rawalpindi

Srinagar

Amritsar

Cairo

Al Basrah

KUWAIT

Lahore

Delhi

NEPAL

SAHARA

NEUTRAL
ZONE

SAUDI

Riyadh

Persian
Gulf

BAHRAIN
QATAR

PAKISTAN

THAR DESERT

Indus R.

New Delhi

Kanpur

INDIA

Karachi

Allahabad

Benaras

RED SEA

Nile River

ARABIA

Mecca

Abu Dhabi
UNITED ARAB
EMIRATES

Gulf of
Oman

Muscat

OMAN

Ahmadabad
Narmada R.

Godavari R.

AFRICA

Lake
Chad

Khartoum

Bombay

Hyderabad

ARABIAN
SEA

Krishna R.

EASTERN
GHATS

Sana
YEMEN

Aden

PEOPLE'S DEM.
REP. OF YEMEN

Gulf of Aden

Socotra
(P.D.R. of Yemen)

WESTERN GHATS

Bangalore

Madras

CEYLON

SRI LANKA

Colombo

MALDIVES

Addis Ababa

Congo River

Lake
Victoria

Nairobi

INDIAN   OCEAN

ATLANTIC
OCEAN

Kinshasa

Lake
Tanganyika

11 USSR AND ASIA

0   250   500
Scale in Miles

GULF OF CALIFORNIA

Great Salt Lake

ROCKY MOUNTAINS

Colorado R.

Missouri River

Mississippi R.

Chicago
New York
Washington
Denver
St. Louis

UNITED STATES

Dallas

SIERRA MADRE OCCIDENTAL

Conchos R.

SIERRA MADRE ORIENTAL

Rio Grande

New Orleans

ATLANTIC

OCEAN

Bermuda Is.
(Br.)

Laredo
Monterrey
Tampico
Guadalajara
Mexico City
Veracruz

M E X I C O

Bolsas R.

Acapulco
Oaxaca

Mérida
Uxmal
Chichén Itzá

GULF OF MEXICO

Miami

BAHAMAS

Havana

CUBA

Kingston
JAMAICA

WEST INDIES

CARIBBEAN SEA

DOMINICAN REPUBLIC
Port-au-Prince
HAITI
Santo Domingo

ST. CHRISTOPHER AND NEVIS
ANTIGUA AND BARBUDA
PUERTO RICO (U.S.)
Guadeloupe (Fr.)
DOMINICA
Martinique (Fr.)
ST. LUCIA
BARBADOS
ST. VINCENT AND THE GRENADINES
GRENADA
TRINIDAD AND TOBAGO
Port of Spain

BELIZE
Belize City
Belmopan
GUATEMALA
Guatemala
EL SALVADOR
San Salvador
HONDURAS
Tegucigalpa
NICARAGUA
Managua
COSTA RICA
San José
PANAMA
Colón
Panama

Barranquilla
Caracas
VENEZUELA

Lake Maracaibo
Orinoco R.

Georgetown
GUYANA
SURINAME
Paramaribo
FRENCH GUIANA
Cayenne

GUIANA HIGHLANDS

Bogotá
COLOMBIA
Buenaventura

Quito
ECUADOR
Guayaquil

GALÁPAGOS IS. (Ec.)

Iquitos
Marañón R.

Río Negro

Japurá R.

Manaus

Belém

PERU

Lima

Amazon River

Purús R.

Madeira River

Tapajós R.

Xingu River

Tocantins River

Recife

ANDES MTS.

Lake Titicaca

Arequipa
La Paz
BOLIVIA
Sucre

Guaporé R.

Mamoré R.

BRAZIL

PLATEAU OF MATO GROSSO

BRAZILIAN HIGHLANDS

São Francisco R.

Rio Grande R.

Brasília

Belo Horizonte

Salvador

PACIFIC

OCEAN

Antofagasta

ATACAMA DESERT

GRAN CHACO

PARAGUAY
Asunción

Pilcomayo R.

Paraná River

São Paulo
Santos
Rio de Janeiro

Iguassú Falls

Tucumán

Salado R.

C H I L E

Mt. Aconcagua
Valparaiso
Santiago
Mendoza

Córdoba

Santa Fé
Rosario

URUGUAY
Montevideo

Uruguay R.

Río de la Plata

ATLANTIC

OCEAN

Buenos Aires

Colorado R.

PAMPA

A R G E N T I N A

Bahía Blanca

Valdivia

P A T A G O N I A

Punta Arenas

TIERRA DEL FUEGO

Cape Horn

FALKLAND IS.
(ISLAS MALVINAS)
(Br.)

SOUTH GEORGIA
(Br.)

Drake Passage

SOUTH ORKNEY IS.
(Br.)

ANTARCTICA

12 **LATIN AMERICA**

Map information based upon data available March 1981

0   400   800

Scale in Miles

Prepared by
Rand McNally & Co., Chicago

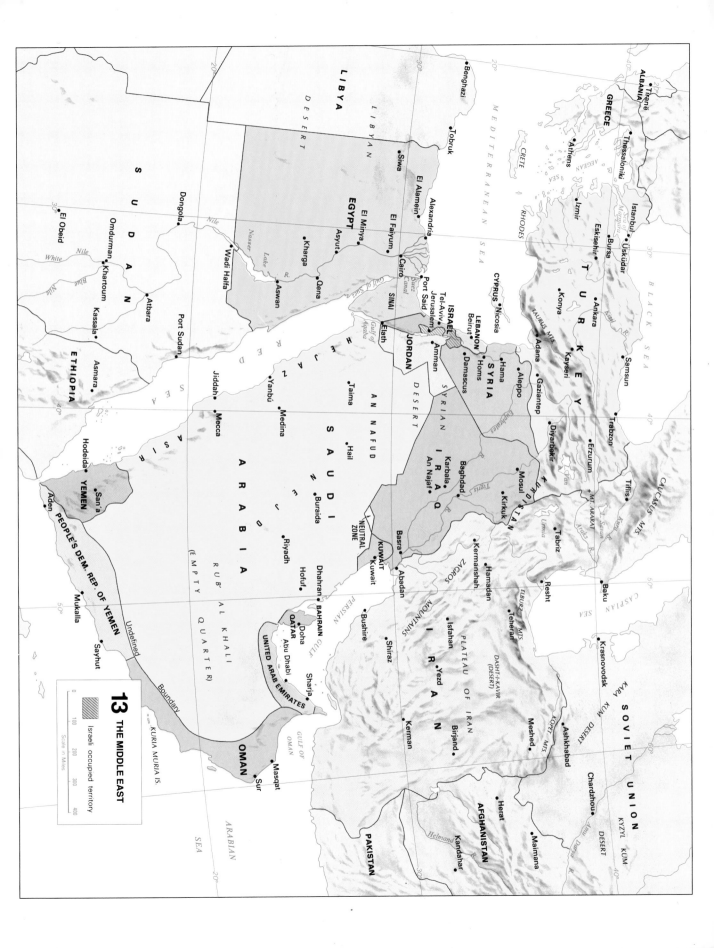

13 THE MIDDLE EAST

Israeli occupied territory

Scale in Miles
0   100   200   300   400

GREECE

Tiranë
ALBANIA
Thessaloniki
Athens
Izmir
Eskisehir
Bursa
Üsküdar
Istanbul

T U R K E Y

Ankara
Konya
Kayseri
Adana
Gaziantep
Diyarbekir
Erzurum
Trabzon
Samsun

B L A C K   S E A

Tiflis
MT. ARARAT
CAUCASUS MTS.
Baku
CASPIAN SEA
Krasnovodsk
Ashkhabad
Chardzhou

S O V I E T   U N I O N

KARA KUM DESERT
KYZYL KUM DESERT

M E D I T E R R A N E A N   S E A

CRETE
RHODES
AEGEAN SEA

CYPRUS
Nicosia
Beirut
LEBANON
Damascus
Homs
Hama
Aleppo
SYRIA

S Y R I A N   D E S E R T

Mosul
Kirkuk
KURDISTAN
Tabriz
Urmia
Resht
Teheran
Hamadan
Kermanshah

I R A Q

Baghdad
Karbala
An Najaf
Basra
Abadan
NEUTRAL ZONE
KUWAIT
Kuwait

I R A N

PLATEAU OF IRAN
DASHT-I-KAVIR (DESERT)
Istahan
Yezd
Birjand
Kerman
Shiraz
Bushire
Meshed

ELBURZ MTS.
ZAGROS MOUNTAINS

KOPET MTS.

AFGHANISTAN
Herat
Maimana
Kandahar
Helmand

ISRAEL
Tel-Aviv
Jerusalem
Amman
JORDAN
Elath
Gulf of Aqaba

SINAI
Suez Canal
Port Said
Cairo
Gulf of Suez

LIBYA

L I B Y A N   D E S E R T

Benghazi
Tobruk
Siwa
El Alamein
Alexandria

EGYPT

El Faiyum
El Minya
Asyut
Kharga
Qena
Aswan
Wadi Halfa
Lake Nasser
Nile R.
Nile

S U D A N

Dongola
El Obeid
Omdurman
Khartoum
Atbara
Kassala
Port Sudan
White Nile
Blue Nile

ETHIOPIA
Asmara

R E D   S E A

Jiddah
Mecca
Medina
Yanbu
Taima
Hail

S A U D I   A R A B I A

H E J A Z
A S I R
A N   N A F U D

N E J D
R U B '   A L   K H A L I
(E M P T Y   Q U A R T E R)

Buraida
Riyadh
Hofuf
Dhahran
BAHRAIN
QATAR
Doha
Abu Dhabi
Sharja
UNITED ARAB EMIRATES
PERSIAN GULF
GULF OF OMAN

OMAN
Masqat
Sur

YEMEN
San'a
Hodeida
Aden
PEOPLE'S DEM. REP. OF YEMEN
Mukalla
Sayhut

Undefined Boundary
KURIA MURIA IS.

ARABIAN SEA

PAKISTAN

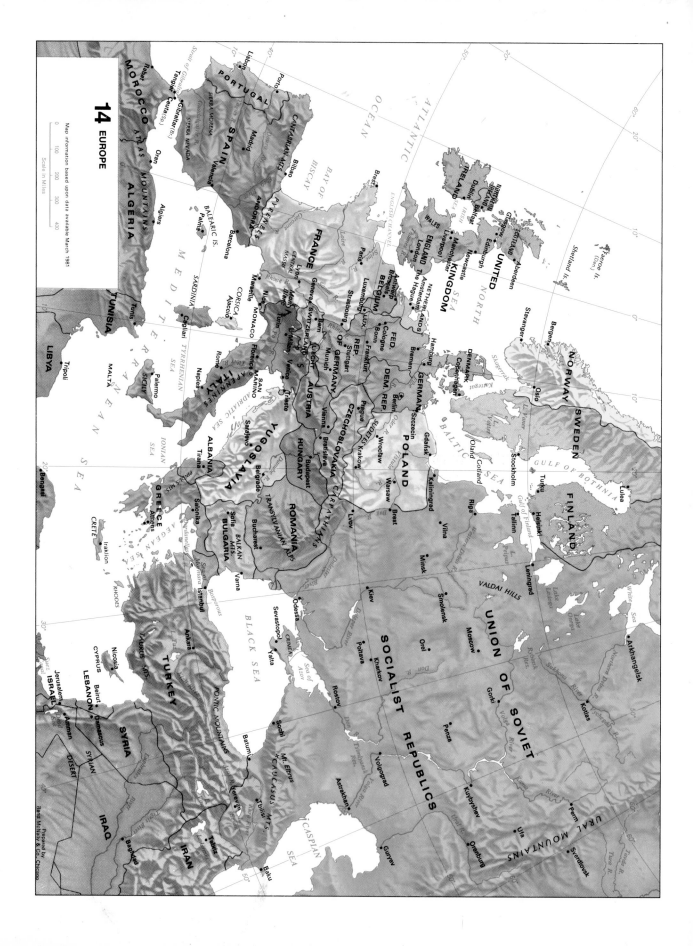

Map information based upon data available March 1981

Scale in Miles

0   100   200   300   400

Prepared by
Rand McNally & Co., Chicago